Costa Rica

Carolina A Miranda, Paige R Penland

Contents

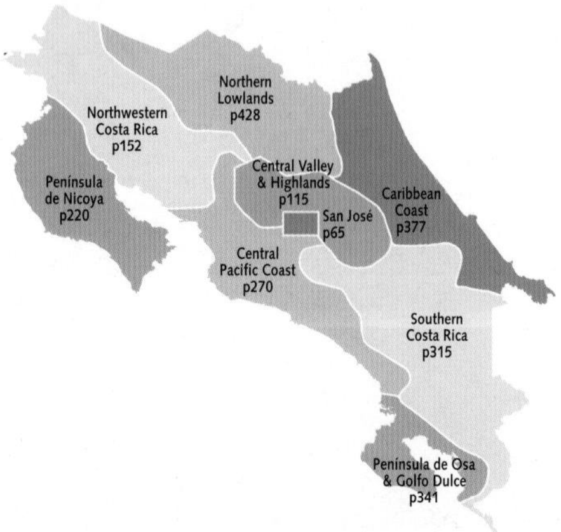

Northern Lowlands p428
Northwestern Costa Rica p152
Península de Nicoya p220
Central Valley & Highlands p115
San José p65
Caribbean Coast p377
Central Pacific Coast p270
Southern Costa Rica p315
Península de Osa & Golfo Dulce p341

Destination: Costa Rica

Surfer dudes, bird nerds, hiking fiends, mountain trekkers, back-to-the-land fans, beach bums and party animals have all found something in common in Costa Rica. The waves are prime, the natural beauty staggering, the pace of life slow, the beer plentiful and the locals friendly. A stronghold of peace in a region torn by strife, this tiny nation attracts a stream of more than a million eager visitors annually.

The country stands apart from its Central American neighbors on various points. The first is that it has no army. Armed forces were abolished after the 1948 civil war, and Costa Rica has avoided the despotic dictatorships, military coups and internal turmoil that have plagued other countries in the region.

The country is also unique globally for its enlightened approach to conservation. More than 27% of the country is protected in one form or another, and more than 14% is within its national park system. Lush jungles are home to playful monkeys, languid sloths, crocodiles, countless lizards, poison-dart frogs and a mind-boggling assortment of exotic birds, insects and butterflies. Endangered sea turtles nest on both coasts and cloud forests protect elusive birds and jungle cats.

Thrill seekers can fly through the forests on zip lines, peer into boiling volcanoes, surf oversized waves, scuba dive with dolphins and whales and come face-to-face with poisonous snakes – all in the course of a normal day. Then again, if you have some serious chilling to do, you can always lounge in a hammock and enjoy the pure life, or *pura vida* – a national expression that sums up the desire to live the best, most hassle-free existence.

ALFREDO MAIQUEZ

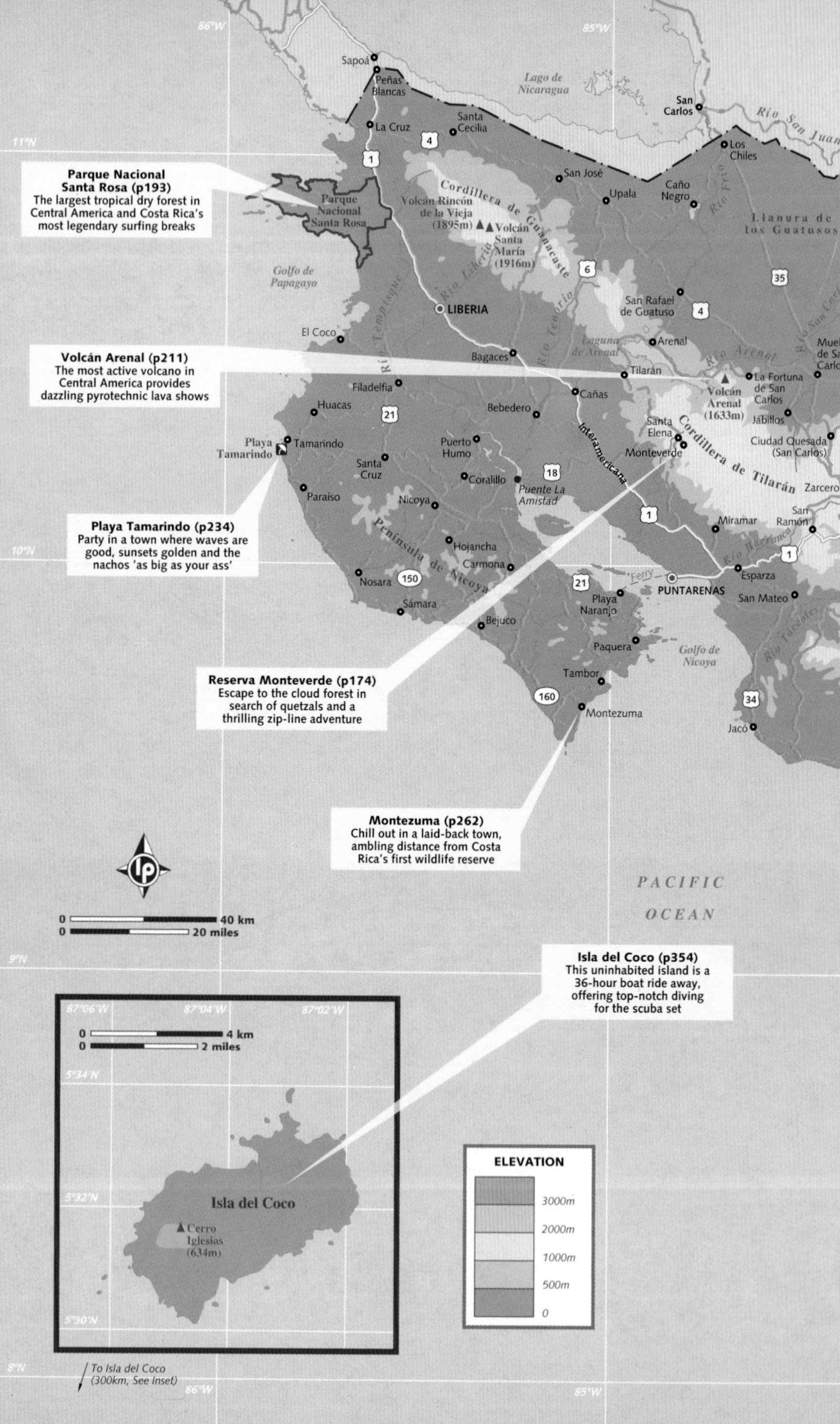

Parque Nacional Santa Rosa (p193)
The largest tropical dry forest in Central America and Costa Rica's most legendary surfing breaks
Volcán Arenal (p211)
The most active volcano in Central America provides dazzling pyrotechnic lava shows
Playa Tamarindo (p234)
Party in a town where waves are good, sunsets golden and the nachos 'as big as your ass'
Reserva Monteverde (p174)
Escape to the cloud forest in search of quetzals and a thrilling zip-line adventure
Montezuma (p262)
Chill out in a laid-back town, ambling distance from Costa Rica's first wildlife reserve
Isla del Coco (p354)
This uninhabited island is a 36-hour boat ride away, offering top-notch diving for the scuba set
Lago de Nicaragua
Río San Juan
Cordillera de Guanacaste
Llanura de los Guatusos
Golfo de Papagayo
Cordillera de Tilarán
Península de Nicoya
Golfo de Nicoya
PACIFIC OCEAN
LIBERIA
PUNTARENAS
Volcán Rincón de la Vieja (1895m)
Volcán Santa María (1916m)
Volcán Arenal (1633m)
Isla del Coco
Cerro Iglesias (634m)
ELEVATION
3000m
2000m
1000m
500m
0
0 40 km
0 20 miles
0 4 km
0 2 miles
To Isla del Coco (300km, See Inset)

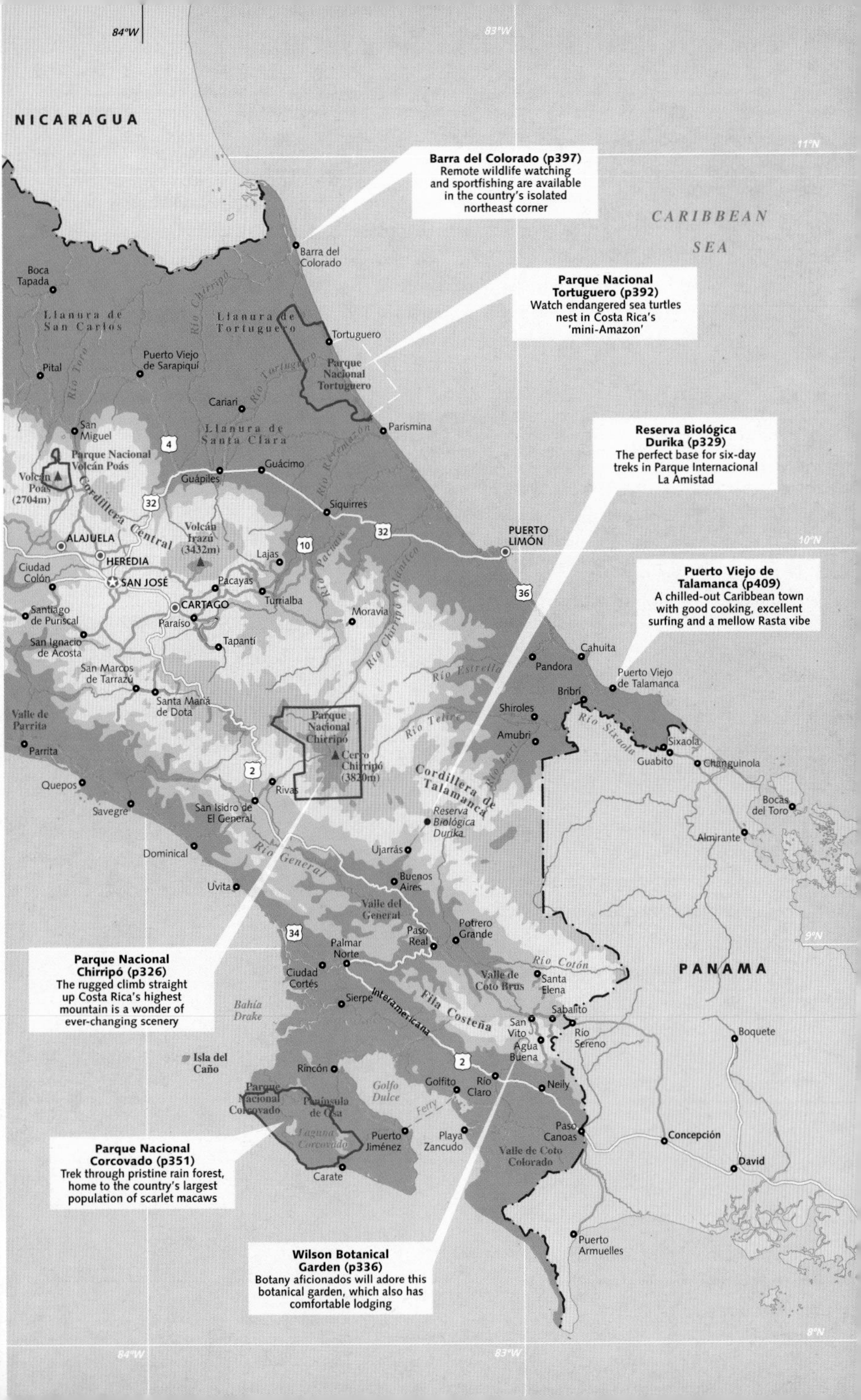

84°W
83°W
11°N
10°N
9°N
8°N
NICARAGUA
CARIBBEAN SEA
PANAMA
Barra del Colorado (p397)
Remote wildlife watching and sportfishing are available in the country's isolated northeast corner
Parque Nacional Tortuguero (p392)
Watch endangered sea turtles nest in Costa Rica's 'mini-Amazon'
Reserva Biológica Durika (p329)
The perfect base for six-day treks in Parque Internacional La Amistad
Puerto Viejo de Talamanca (p409)
A chilled-out Caribbean town with good cooking, excellent surfing and a mellow Rasta vibe
Parque Nacional Chirripó (p326)
The rugged climb straight up Costa Rica's highest mountain is a wonder of ever-changing scenery
Parque Nacional Corcovado (p351)
Trek through pristine rain forest, home to the country's largest population of scarlet macaws
Wilson Botanical Garden (p336)
Botany aficionados will adore this botanical garden, which also has comfortable lodging
Barra del Colorado
Boca Tapada
Llanura de San Carlos
Llanura de Tortuguero
Río Chirripó
Tortuguero
Parque Nacional Tortuguero
Pital
Río Toro
Puerto Viejo de Sarapiquí
Río Tortuguero
Cariari
San Miguel
Parismina
Llanura de Santa Clara
Parque Nacional Volcán Poás
Volcán Poás (2704m)
Río Reventazón
Guápiles
Guácimo
Cordillera Central
Siquirres
Volcán Irazú (3432m)
PUERTO LIMÓN
ALAJUELA
HEREDIA
Lajas
Río Pacuare
Río Chirripó Atlántico
Ciudad Colón
SAN JOSÉ
Pacayas
Turrialba
CARTAGO
Santiago de Puriscal
Paraíso
Moravia
San Ignacio de Acosta
Tapantí
Cahuita
Pandora
Río Estrella
San Marcos de Tarrazú
Puerto Viejo de Talamanca
Bribrí
Santa María de Dota
Shiroles
Río Sixaola
Valle de Parrita
Parque Nacional Chirripó
Río Telire
Amubri
Parrita
Cerro Chirripó (3820m)
Sixaola
Guabito
Changuinola
Quepos
Rivas
Cordillera de Talamanca
Río Lari
Savegre
San Isidro de El General
Bocas del Toro
Reserva Biológica Durika
Almirante
Dominical
Ujarrás
Río General
Uvita
Buenos Aires
Valle del General
Potrero Grande
Paso Real
Palmar Norte
Río Cotón
Ciudad Cortés
Valle de Coto Brus
Santa Elena
Bahía Drake
Sierpe
Interamericana
Fila Costeña
Sabalito
San Vito
Río Sereno
Agua Buena
Boquete
Isla del Caño
Rincón
Golfito
Río Claro
Neily
Parque Nacional Corcovado
Península de Osa
Golfo Dulce
Ferry
Laguna Corcovado
Puerto Jiménez
Playa Zancudo
Paso Canoas
Concepción
Valle de Coto Colorado
Carate
David
Puerto Armuelles

National Parks & Reserves

Without a doubt, Costa Rica's top draw is its glorious and numerous national parks and reserves, covering an infinite number of diverse habitats and offering activities aplenty. In addition to the parks described below, you can trek up the flanks of **Cerro Chirripó** (p326), admire the dense flocks of birds in **Caño Negro** (p435), go caving in **Barra Honda** (p247), saunter around the beaches of popular **Manuel Antonio** (p303) or the tropical dry forest of **Santa Rosa** (p193) and revel in the stillness of the rarely visited **Parque Internacional La Amistad** (p337), which continues into Panama.

LUKE HUNTER

Hike along the palm-fringed coast at Parque Nacional Corcovado (p351)

LUKE HUNTER

Admire the tumultuous Volcán Arenal (p211) in Parque Nacional Volcán Arenal

Stop for a break alongside Río Colorado in Parque Nacional Rincón de la Vieja (p190)

LUKE HUNTE

Wildlife Watching

Why watch *National Geographic* specials when you can live them? Pictured here are a few animals you can observe. Also there's leatherback turtles, which lay eggs on **Playa Grande** (p233) and near the dense jungles of **Tortuguero** (p392). Keep your ears open for the deep croon of howler monkeys near **Cabo Blanco** (p269) and listen for the plaintive chirp of the toucan in **Río Nuevo** (p355). Catch glimpses of the quetzal in the cloud forests of **Monteverde** (p174) and admire whales off the coast of **Bahía Drake** (p345).

ALFREDO MAIQUEZ

Do as the brown-throated three-toed sloth *(Bradypus variegatus)* does in Parque Nacional Cahuita (p408) and take it easy

RALPH LEE HOPKINS

Spot scarlett macaws *(Ara macao)* at Parque Nacional Corcovado (p351)

Maybe, just maybe, catch a glimpse of a jaguar *(Panthera onca)* in Parque Internacional La Amistad (p337)

TOM BOYDEN

Water World

For those who aren't afraid to get a little wet, there is a vast array of activities. Surfers will dig the powerful swells at **Witch's Rock** (p194) in Parque Nacional Santa Rosa, the general feistiness of the **Salsa Brava** (p412) and the long left hander at **Pavones** (p374). Rafters can chase an adrenaline rush by roaring down the Central Valley rivers including **Río Reventazón** (p149), while windsurfers can take on **Laguna de Arenal** (p218). Snorkelers will appreciate the reefs around **Manzanillo** (p423) and **Isla del Caño** (p351), while divers will be dazzled by the sea life of the **northern Península de Nicoya** (p225) and the remote **Isla del Coco** (p354).

BRENT WINEBRENNER

Surf the fine waves at Playa Tamarindo (p234)

Kayak to the beach at Isla del Caño (p351)

LEE FOSTER

Pump the adrenaline on Río Pacuare (p151)

MARK NEWMAN

Getting Started

Costa Rica can easily accommodate the impulsive adventurer who wants to just get up and go, as well as the more methodical visitor who prefers their itinerary neatly sketched out. For budget types, transport around the country is plentiful, and local buses can carry you to just about every nook and cranny there is to see. Boats will pick up where many buses leave off.

For the more discriminating or time-pressed, the strong network of tourist transport, from minivans with air-con to regular domestic flights and charters, is easily reserved ahead of time. Lodging is abundant and it's quite easy to casually arrive in a town and find a place to stay. The exceptions to this rule are the weeks between Christmas and New Year's Day and before and during Semana Santa (the week preceding Easter Sunday), when transport is packed – if not shut down – and the hotels are bursting with locals, all enjoying a well-deserved vacation. It is also a good idea to book your accommodations before you arrive at your destination during the school vacation in January and February.

All budgets can be accommodated, from the backpacker looking for basic meals and lodging, to the luxury-loving sophisticate who wants first-rate resorts loaded with every service imaginable. Do note that because Costa Rica has a high standard of living, prices here tend to be a good deal higher than those of other Central and Latin American nations.

See the Directory for more information on climate (p452) and festivals (p455).

WHEN TO GO

Traditionally the best time to visit Costa Rica has been the high season (or dry season), the period from December through April which locals refer to as *verano* (summer). Costa Rican school children are off from December to February and, during this time, beach towns are busy and often full on weekends and holidays. Lodgings during Semana Santa are usually booked months ahead.

In May the rainy season begins – or *invierno* (winter), as it's known locally. (The tourism ministry has come up with the more attractive denomination of 'green season'.) The early months of the rainy season are

DON'T LEAVE HOME WITHOUT...

- Checking the latest visa situation (p461) and government travel advisories (p453)
- Insect repellent containing DEET (p481); and if you're planning large-scale jungle adventures (or staying in budget lodging), a mosquito net
- Pepto-Bismol or an anti-diarrheal, in case you get a bad dose of the trots (p480)
- Sunblock so that you don't get cooked by the tropical sun (p481)
- Clothes that you don't mind getting absolutely filthy or wet
- A pair of river sandals or reef-walkers and sturdy jungle boots (p52)
- A windproof jacket and warm layers for highland hiking
- A towel, for hotels that don't have them
- Miscellaneous necessities: an umbrella, binoculars, a pocket flashlight (torch), padlock, matches, pocket knife
- Your sense of adventure

actually a wonderful time to travel to Costa Rica if you prefer to avoid the tourist bustle – and you'll find that lodging is slightly cheaper. During this time, however, rivers start to swell and dirt roads get muddy, making travel challenging. Some more remote roads may not be accessible to public transportation, so always ask locally before setting out. Bring your umbrella and a little patience and you'll be fine.

Because of the number of North American and European tourists, some Costa Rican towns experience a mini-high season in June and July, during the northern summer holidays. Expect to pay high-season prices in some towns at this time.

For surfers the travel seasons vary slightly. For the most part, the Pacific coast begins to see increased swells and bigger, faster waves during the rainy season, starting in late June and peaking in the worst rainy months of September and October. The Caribbean side, however, has better waves from November through May. Some breaks are consistent year-round.

LP INDEX

Liter of gas (petrol) US$0.65

Liter of bottled water US$0.75

Bottle of Imperial beer US$1.25

Pipa fría (cold coconut water) US$0.50

Souvenir T-shirt US$8

HOW MUCH?

SkyTrek zip line adventure in Monteverde US$40

Admission to Parque Nacional Manuel Antonio US$7

A bus from San José to Puerto Viejo de Talamanca US$5.50

Taxi from the international airport into central San José US$12

Two hours of surfing lessons in Tamarindo US$30

COSTS & MONEY

Travel costs are significantly higher here than in most Central American countries, but are generally cheaper than in the USA or Europe (though not always so). And if you're arriving from inexpensive Central American nations such as Nicaragua, get ready to bust that wallet wide open. Prices in Costa Rica are frequently listed in US dollars, especially at upmarket hotels and restaurants, where you can expect to pay international prices. (Hey, somebody's got to pay for all that infrastructure!)

Some of the more popular tourist areas (Monteverde, Jacó, Manuel Antonio and many of the beaches on the Península de Nicoya) are more expensive than the rest of the country and prices are, by and large, higher in the dry season (December to April). Wildlife, nature and most types of tours are charged in US dollars.

Shoestring travelers can survive on about US$35 a day, covering just the basics of food, lodging and public transportation. The cheapest hotels start at about US$5 per person for a bed, four walls and shared bathrooms. Better rooms with private bathrooms start at roughly US$10 per person, depending on the area. It is possible to eat cheaply at the many *sodas* (lunch counters), where you can fill up on tasty casados (set meals) for about US$2 to US$3.

Mid-range travelers can expect a good selection of lodging and eating options. Hotels in this category offer a very good value, and double rooms come with comfortable beds, private bathrooms, hot water (most of the time) and even breakfast, for US$30 to US$80 per night. Many hotels in this price range also have shared or private kitchenettes, which allows travelers the opportunity to cook. (This is a great option for families.) A variety of restaurants cater to mid-range travelers, offering entrees (often as filling as a main meal) that range in price from US$5 to US$10.

Top-end visitors can find a good selection of restaurants and hotels in the touristy towns and within some of the major resorts. Luxurious beachside lodges and boutique hotels can cost anywhere from US$100 to US$400 a night – and up – and offer meals that begin at US$20.

TRAVEL LITERATURE

Peter Ford's *Around the Edge* is the story of the author's travels along the Caribbean coast from Belize to Panama, on foot and by boat. In Lonely Planet's *Green Dreams: Travels in Central America* by Stephen Benz, the author astutely analyzes and questions the impact visitors are having on a region and its people.

TOP TENS

COOLEST ANIMALS

Go hog-wild over nature's creatures; read more on what to look for on p41.

- **Morpho** (p41) Butterflies don't get any more spectacular
- **Sloth** (p45) Lethargic tree-huggers of the neotropics
- **Leafcutter ant** Diligent formations of them scurry along the ground in Hacienda Barú (p306)
- **Toucan** (p44) See a flock in the lowland forests
- **Squirrel monkey** (p47) A threatened species that's still swinging around Manuel Antonio (p303)
- **Manatee** (p45) Canoeing quietly through Tortuguero (p392) is the best way to see them
- **Leatherback turtle** (p45) Playa Grande attracts nesters (p234)
- **Quetzal** (p43) Spot the most legendary of birds near San Gerardo de Dota (p317)
- **Fer-de-lance** (p41) Snakes with poison that'll kill 10 men; watch your toes at lower elevations
- **Jaguar** (p48) Good luck seeing one, but it's worth a try in La Amistad (p337)

BEST PLACES FOR SUNSETS

Abundant nature + peaceful surroundings + great views = No more worries.

- The mountaintop hostel on Cerro Chirripó (p328)
- Sitting on the Banana Company Dock in Golfito (p363)
- Watching Volcán Arenal from La Fortuna (p200)
- On a sunset sail from Playa del Coco (p223)
- Bar La Culebra in Tortuguero (p397)
- El Avión in Manuel Antonio (p300)
- Overlooking Escazú and the Central Valley from Tiquicia restaurant (p111)
- Listening to reggae next to the beach in Puerto Viejo de Talamanca (p418)
- Margarita Sunset Bar at Casa Corcovado Jungle Lodge (p351) near Bahía Drake
- On the twilight hike at Finca Ecológica (p164) in Monteverde

WORST ROADS

It is a badge of honor for travelers to boast about the disastrous roads they've survived in Costa Rica. A list of the most bragworthy:

- **Oldie, but goodie** The road from Tilarán to Monteverde (p173)
- **The punisher** Puerto Jiménez to Río Nuevo (p355)
- **Dude, where's the transmission?** Bumping and grinding to the waves at Playa Naranjo (p194)
- **A river runs through it** Crossing the Río Ora between Playa Carrillo and Islita (p256)
- **You call this a road?** Golfito to Pavones (p373)
- **Bone-cruncher** Buenos Aires to Durika reserve (p329)
- **Car-nivore** The stretch between Tamarindo and Avellana gobbles up vehicles like candy (p241)
- **Road less traveled** Rocks, gravel and 45° inclines – another day in the Escaleras area (p309)
- **Death of me** Blind curves on sheer cliffs near Cerro de la Muerte (p320)
- **Lake defect** The lakeside axle-destroyer from Arenal to Tronadora (p213)

Traveler's Tales Central America, edited by Larry Habegger and Natanya Pearlman, is a collection of striking travel essays on the region from renowned writers such as Paul Theroux and Tim Cahill. *The Old Patagonian Express: By Train Through the Americas*, by Paul Theroux, details the author's journey by train from a suburb of Boston all the way to Patagonia. Sadly, many of the train routes he took are no longer in operation, but it's still a great book.

So Far from God: A Journey to Central America, by Patrick Marnham, was the winner of the 1985 Thomas Cook Travel Book Award. It's an insightful and often amusing account of a leisurely meander from Texas down to Mexico City and on into Central America.

Through the Volcanoes: A Central American Journey, by Jeremy Paxman, is the story of a journey through the region in the early 1980s. Though not specifically about Costa Rica, bird-watchers will enjoy *Birders: Birds of Tribe* by Mark Cocker, a true celebration of the bird enthusiast's determination to endure hours of boredom and terrible weather – all to catch a glimpse of some rare and spectacular avian species.

Incidents of Travel in Central America, Chiapas and Yucatan, in two volumes (1969 and later reprints of the original 1841 edition), is available in paperback at some bookstores in the region, among other places.

INTERNET RESOURCES

Costa Rica Link (www.1costaricalink.com) An online directory that provides a great deal of information on transport, hotels, activities and more.

Costa Rica Map (www.costaricamap.com) Nicely organized website with maps and travel information on each region.

Guías Costa Rica (www.guiascostarica.com) Links that connect you with everything you'd ever need to know – from entertainment to health to government websites.

Lanic (www.lanic.utexas.edu/la/ca/cr/) An exceptional collection of links to sites of many Costa Rican organizations (mostly in Spanish), from the University of Texas.

Lonely Planet (www.lonelyplanet.com) Provides summaries on traveling to most places on Earth, including the all-important Thorn Tree bulletin board, where you can ask questions of travelers who've been to Costa Rica recently; the site's subwwway section links you to useful travel resources elsewhere on the Web.

Itineraries

CLASSIC ROUTES

SURF & TURF

Eight Days / San José to Playa Tamarindo

This popular route takes travelers by bubbling volcanoes, steamy hot springs and tranquil cloud forest before hitting the beach.

From San José head north to **La Fortuna** (p200) on the eastern folds of Cordillera de Tilarán, where you hike through thick forest on the flanks of **Volcán Arenal** (p211), followed by a good soak in the hot springs. Then hop on the jeep-boat-jeep service across Laguna de Arenal to **Monteverde** (p157) and search for the elusive quetzal at **Reserva Biológica Bosque Nuboso Monteverde** (p174). End your stay with a zip-line canopy tour.

Then, make the arduous road trip to **Tilarán** (p217) and through **Cañas** (p179) and over the new **Puente La Amistad** (p248). In **Guaitil** (p243) make a pit stop for some pre-Columbian–style ceramics before landing in **Santa Cruz** (p243) to enjoy the cowboy atmosphere and tasty local cooking.

After this it's off to the pretty surf of **Playa Tamarindo** (p234), where travelers can loll by the beach, or pursue water- and land-based frolics. Nature buffs will not want to miss seeing nesting leatherback turtles in **Parque Nacional Marino Las Baulas** (p234). Then it's back to San José.

This 605km loop could take over three weeks if you study Spanish or volunteer in Monteverde, make a stop for world-class windsurfing in Laguna de Arenal, celebrate Guanacaste day in Santa Cruz, or explore the beaches south of Tamarindo.

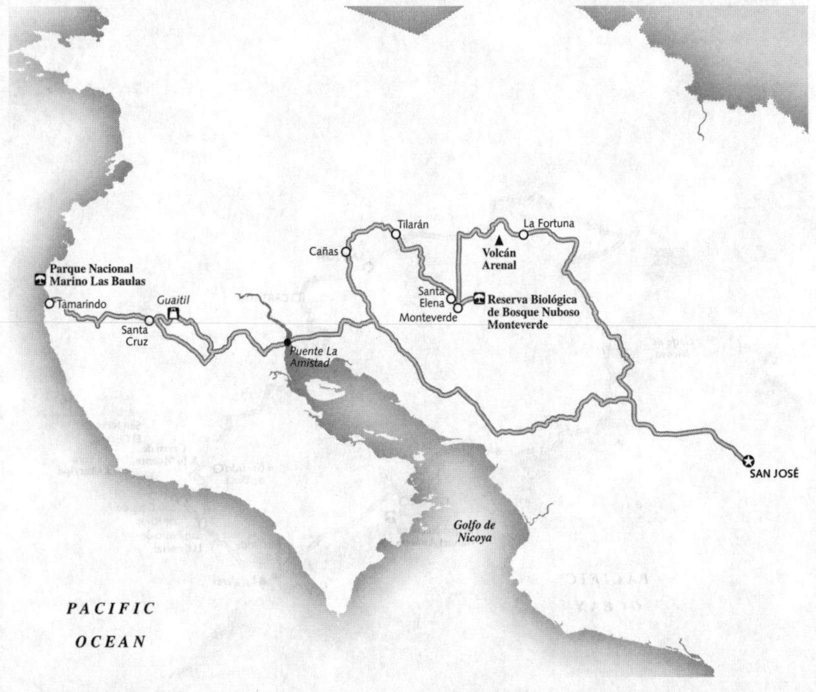

PEAK TO BEACH

12 Days / San José to Manuel Antonio

A 675km loop leads from San José inland to San Isidro and then on to the Pacific coast at Dominical and up the coast, so there's no need to backtrack. Add another week if you decide to use Dominical as a base for exploring the wonders of the southern coast.

From the highest summit down to tropical beaches, this itinerary takes you high and low and through everything in between.

Start by heading south on the Interamericana out of San José, through **Cartago** (p138) and up the steep winding hills for quetzal-watching near **San Gerardo de Dota** (p319). Continue past the looming **Cerro de la Muerte** (p320) and straight down the mountain to the pleasant agricultural city of **San Isidro de El General** (p321). From here, ride the winding dirt road northeast to **San Gerardo de Rivas** (p324) and prepare for the two-day climb up Costa Rica's highest peak, **Cerro Chirripó** (p326). Linger around the summit for incredible day hikes before making your way back down.

Return through San Isidro down to **Dominical** (p307) and enjoy a laid-back vibe and powerful surf. If you're addicted to Pacific sunsets, stay in **Escaleras** (p309) for staggering views. Continue on north to **Hacienda Barú** (p306), where you can clamber on a canopy platform and sloth-spot in the trees. Head further up the coast to the port of **Quepos** (p290) before dipping south and landing in the country's most popular national park, **Manuel Antonio** (p303). Wind your trip down with top-of-the-line lodging options, relaxing hikes and pretty, white-sand beaches where you can soak up the rays. San José is 3½ hours away by car.

ROADS LESS TRAVELED

ADVENTURE ON THE RÍO SAN JUAN

Eight Days / Puerto Viejo de Sarapiquí to Tortuguero

Travel exclusively by boat in some of Costa Rica's (and Nicaragua's) most remote regions near the sparsely populated northern Caribbean Coast.

Begin the journey in **Puerto Viejo de Sarapiquí** (p442), where you can take a day or two to wander through banana plantations, spot wildlife and mingle with busy scientists at the **Estación Biológica La Selva** (p445). Leave terra firma and grab the morning boat up the Río Sarapiquí to **Trinidad** (p443), on the south bank of the Río San Juan. Stay on a working ranch, ride horses and go birding before setting out, again by boat, on the **Río San Juan** (p444), with your eye to the Caribbean coast.

This river (Nicaraguan territory) offers an incredible ride, which will take you through a combination of ranches, forest, wildlife and old war zones (from when Contras inhabited the area), and through the remote **Refugio Nacional de Vida Silvestre Barra del Colorado** (p397) and its loose assortment of lodges, where travelers can go sportfishing, bird-watching and looking for crocs. Afterwards, continue to the more touristed town of **Tortuguero** (p394), where you can watch green sea and leatherback turtles nest on the beaches, and canoe through the infinite canals of **Parque Nacional Tortuguero** (p392), Costa Rica's mini-Amazon. Then head to San José via water taxi and bus through **Cariari** (p381) and **Guápiles** (p379).

This trip is only 175km, and could be done in five days if the tides, weather and the various independent boatmen you'll need all work out. But if you're going to the trouble (and expense), get your captain to take it slow and you'll see more wildlife and incredible scenery than you ever imagined.

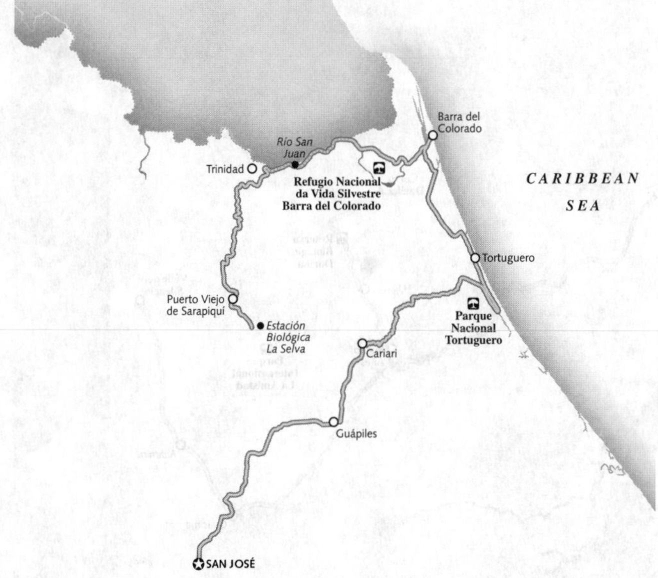

EXPLORING THE TALAMANCAS

Two Weeks / San Isidro to Parque Internacional La Amistad

It's 210km straight up and down mountains in the isolated Cordillera de Talamanca, one of the most remote areas in the country and home to various indigenous communities, unspoiled wildlife and incredible vistas. Stay and work as a volunteer in the Durika reserve if you wish.

Delve into the mountainous area that remains Costa Rica's most unexplored. You can do either hike below separately (for a shorter trip) or bundle them into one if you've got plenty of time.

Gear up in **San Isidro de El General** (p321) before heading southeast through pineapple plantations to the small agricultural town of **Buenos Aires** (p328). Arrangements can be made here for transport via dirt road to the wonderfully remote **Reserva Biológica Durika** (p329), where you can visit **Finca Anael** (p329), a self-sustaining community nestled in the Cordillera de Talamanca. From this point, undertake the six-day round-trip hike-and-climb of **Cerro Durika** (3280m), situated inside the Parque Internacional La Amistad. Visits to the neighboring indigenous community of **Ujarrás** (p329) are also available.

If you haven't had your fill of nature yet, then continue on south from Buenos Aires along the road that lies on the Fila Costeña to the town of Guácimo. Continue inland to Altamira, after which you'll reach the park headquarters for **Parque Internacional La Amistad** (p337). From here you can make the 20km guided trek through **Valle del Silencio**, one of the most isolated and remote areas in all of Costa Rica, ending up at a small refuge at the base of the **Cerro Kamuk**. From here, make the return trip through Altamira and back to the rowdy roads near the Interamericana.

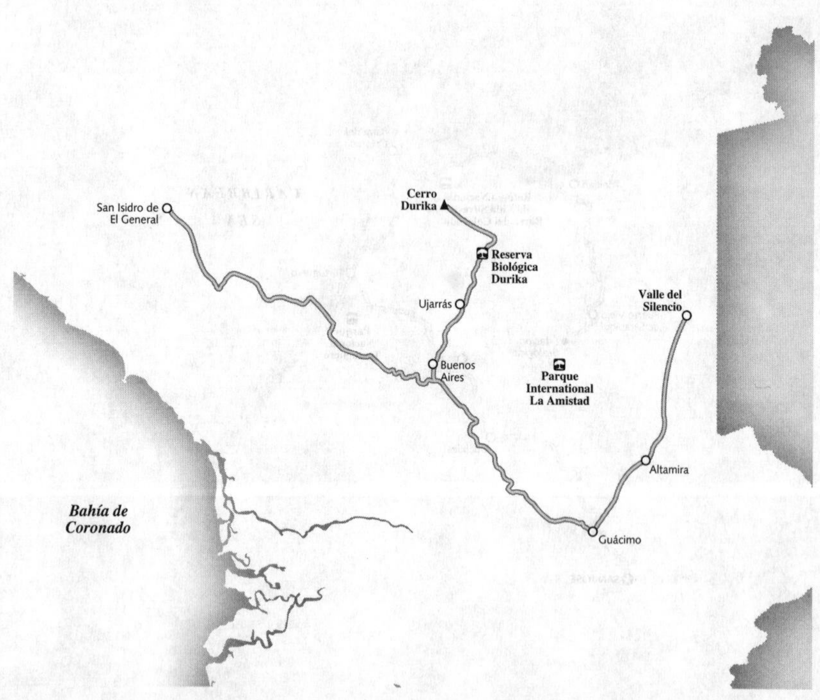

TAILORED TRIPS

SURFING COSTA RICA

As long as you like

Costa Rican shores have been attracting surfers since *Endless Summer II* profiled some of the country's most appealing breaks.

Playa Tamarindo (p234) serves as a good base for several tasty surfing sites. Start with a boat trip to the granddaddies of all surf breaks, **Witch's Rock** and **Ollie's Point** (both p194). Then hit the isolated beaches at **Playas Avellana** and **Negra** (p241), whose famous waves were featured in the movie. Down the coast **Playa Nosara** (p248) is cooking all year long, and from there it's just a hop, skip and long jump to the oh-so-trendy **Mal País** and **Santa Teresa** (both p267).

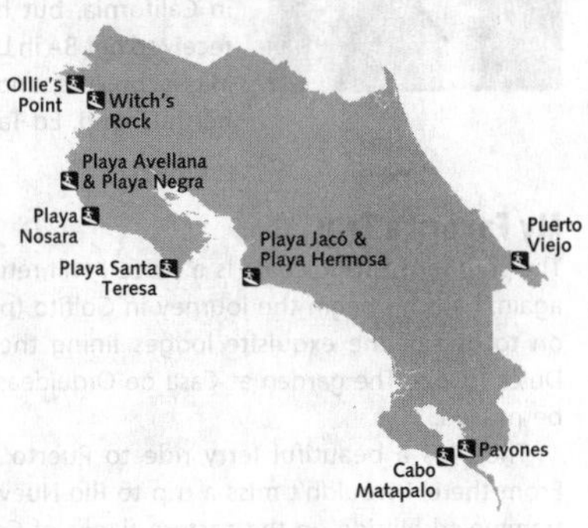

The next big stop is **Jacó** (p281) and **Playa Hermosa** (p289) on the central Pacific coast, offering consistent waves, but keep moving south for good reef breaks at **Dominical** (p307). Afterwards, hightail it way south for **Cabo Matapalo** (p360) before skipping back to the mainland for one of the continent's longest left-hand breaks at **Pavones** (p374).

And don't forget the Caribbean. The famous Salsa Brava at **Puerto Viejo de Talamanca** (p412) is crashing all dry season long.

RAFTING SAFARI

10 Days

Experience the country's world-class rivers while soaking in the sight of pristine rain forests and wildlife on a 10-day safari.

From San José head east to the **Río Pacuare** (p151) for two days of enchanted Class IV white water. Move on to the nearby Pascua section of the **Río Reventazón** (p149) for 24km of heart-pumping Class IV+. Then try southern Costa Rica for three days of high-volume Class III-IV on the steep and scenic **Río General** (pp54-5), spilling from the country's highest peak, Cerro Chirripó. Travel west to the central Pacific coast and spend a day of gentler rafting, taking in the beach-fringed rain forest of **Parque Nacional Manuel Antonio** (p303), home to more than 350 species of bird. After, suit-up for a quick half-day down the challenging **Río Naranjo**, close by. Cap it all off with two days on the largely unexplored **Río Savegre**, putting in on the remote, Class IV+ upper **Río División**, the main tributary of the Savegre. The next day will have you continuing downstream to the bridge take-out on the Costanera, the Pacific coastal highway leading north to San José.

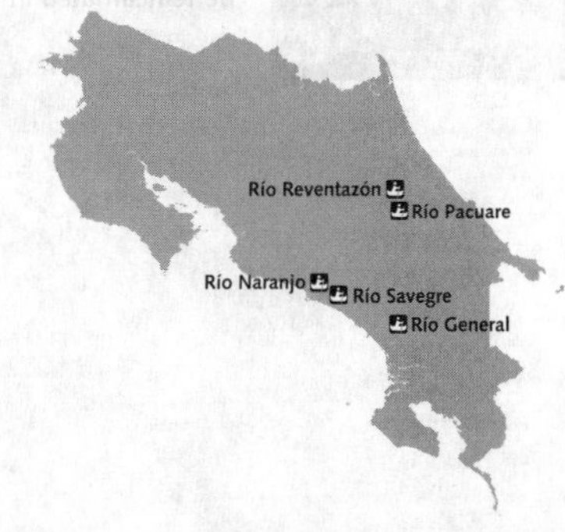

The Authors

CAROLINA A MIRANDA

Coordinating Author, San José, Península de Nicoya, Central Pacific Coast, Southern Costa Rica, Península de Osa & Golfo Dulce

During her trips to Costa Rica, Carolina has become obsessed with everything Tico (especially *gallo pinto*). She spent months tooling in school buses, cars and boats for this book, in addition to the companion *Central America on a shoestring*. Born of Chilean and Peruvian parents, Carolina grew up primarily in California, but has lived for spells in Chile, Iran and South Africa. She received her BA in Latin American Studies from Smith College, Northampton, Massachusetts, and currently works as a reporter for *Time*. She lives with her husband, Ed Tahaney, in New York City.

My Favorite Trip

The southern Pacific coast is a place I will return to again and again. I always begin the journey in Golfito (p362), continuing on to one of the exquisite lodges lining the northern Golfo Dulce (p362). The garden at Casa de Orquídeas (p369) is not to be missed.

Then it's a beautiful ferry ride to Puerto Jiménez (p356). From there, I wouldn't miss a trip to Río Nuevo (p355), an untrammeled hillside on the eastern flanks of Corcovado (p351). From Jiménez, there's the sweaty trek through Corcovado, ending up in Bahía Drake (p345), one of the most beautiful areas in the country.

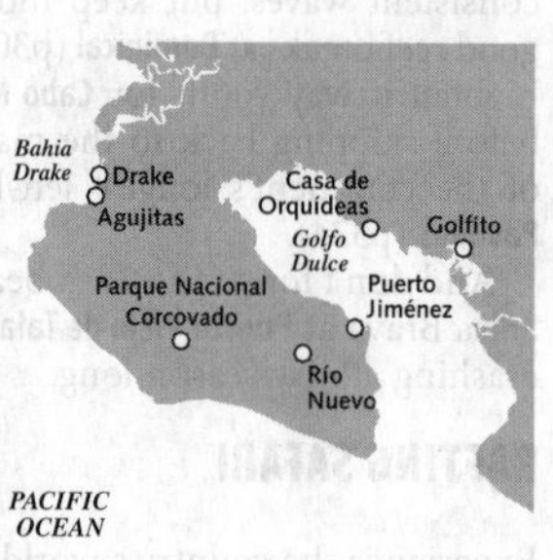

PAIGE R PENLAND

Central Valley & Highlands, Northwestern Costa Rica, Caribbean Coast, Northern Lowlands

Paige is a freelance writer who specializes in automotive, science and travel writing. Though she's covered destinations from Alaska to Florida for Lonely Planet, this was her first business trip outside her native USA. All that she saw from the roads and waterways of beautiful Costa Rica only reaffirmed her first impression: maybe, if you're a very good person in this life, you'll be reincarnated in Costa Rica. And that's a thought worth recycling for.

CONTRIBUTING AUTHORS

Bridget Crocker wrote the Water Sports boxed text (pp54-5). Raised on the banks of the Snake River in Jackson Hole, Wyoming, she has navigated wilderness white-water rivers in Costa Rica, Zambia, Ethi-opia, Peru, Chile, the Philippines and the USA. A professional river- and sea-kayaking guide, Bridget writes water-based narratives for magazines and is currently working on a collection of river tales from her home in Ventura, California.

Dr David Goldberg wrote the Health chapter (p476). He completed his training in internal medicine and infectious diseases at Columbia-Presbyterian Medical Center in New York City, where he has also served as voluntary faculty. At present he is an infectious diseases specialist in Scarsdale, New York, and the editor-in-chief of the website MDTravelHealth.com.

David Lukas wrote the Environment chapter (p34) and Wildlife Guide (p41). He is an avid student of natural history who has traveled widely to study tropical ecosystems, including Borneo and the Amazon. He has also spent several years leading natural history tours to all corners of Costa Rica, Belize and Guatemala. Now working as a professional naturalist and writer, David has contributed Environment and Geology chapters to Lonely Planet's *Yosemite National Park, Grand Canyon National Park* and *Banff, Jasper & Glacier National Parks*.

Snapshot

With their country's high standard of living, Costa Ricans lead a more comfortable existence than do other Central Americans. Nonetheless, the country faces numerous pressing issues.

The most significant of these is debt. Impressive social services, such as free health care, have left the country with staggering public arrears. Costa Rica's internal and external debt is experiencing booming double-digit growth – not the kind of economic indicators anyone's bragging about. The administration spends nearly a quarter of its budget on foreign-debt payments, leaving little for programs such as education or environmental regulation.

FAST FACTS

Population: 4.1 million

Life expectancy at birth: 76 years (US: 74 years)

Adult literacy: 96% (US: 97%)

Female adult literacy: 96% (US: 97%)

Population living below the poverty line: 21% (US: 13%)

Fertility rate: 2.4 (US: 2.1)

Infant mortality per 1000 live births: 11 (US: 7)

Annual carbon dioxide emissions per person (metric tons): 1.2 (US: 19.9)

Annual coffee consumption per person: 4.1kg (US: 4kg)

Passenger cars per 1000 people: 82.2 (US: 477.8)

The government also finds itself in the midst of dealing with fallout from the Central American Free Trade Agreement (Cafta) recently negotiated with other Latin American countries and the US. While the agreement hasn't been ratified on either side, small-business owners are already worried about competing with mass-produced US imports. The deal also requires the opening up of the state-owned telecommunications and insurance monopolies to foreign competition, an act that has some local experts concerned that the cost of public services will go up. Foreign critics say that Cafta fails to implement internationally recognized labor standards and the environmental impact is, as yet, undetermined. Whether or not Cafta will become a reality remains to be seen. The government swears up and down that the public just needs to wait for the benefits to pour in, but if the plan does as little for Costa Rica as the North American free-trade deal has done for Mexico, it could be a long wait.

In the meantime, tourism remains one of Costa Rica's top sources of foreign income. The influx of relatively wealthy travelers spending US dollars has kept the local standard of living high, even as the nation's two other most profitable sectors have cooled (coffee and microchip processing). However, much of the money made from the tourist trade goes to Europeans and Americans who have landed in the country in droves to set up hotels. As a result, costs have skyrocketed and many Ticos (Costa Ricans) have been priced out of their own towns. Authorities are therefore beginning to clamp down on foreign tourists who overstay their visas or don't follow proper residency procedures.

Furthermore, the number of visitors and hotels is putting a real stress on the environment – the very thing that people come to enjoy. Costa Rica has avoided developing Cancun-style megaresorts, but the result has been hundreds of smaller, poorly regulated hotels that aren't always ecologically responsible. (Not that the big ones are always good either; see the boxed text, p261). The government passes laws to protect the environment, but with little money available for enforcement, they often go unheeded. Communities are also contending with other side effects of the tourist boom, such as child prostitution and drug addiction.

Thankfully, the nonprofit sector has stepped up to the plate. Conservationist, educational and cultural organizations have helped protect the environment, preserve local culture and continue to provide support to the needy. For travelers, these organizations offer a great opportunity to lend a hand – see p462 for more details.

History

PRE-COLUMBIAN PERIOD

On September 18, 1502, when Christopher Columbus docked his boat offshore what is now Puerto Limón, there were roughly 19 indigenous chiefdoms with an estimated 400,000 inhabitants in the area that is now Costa Rica. Lacking written languages, these civilizations (and the Spanish colonizers) left little record of that life, and Costa Rica is bereft of the grand pyramids and temples that dot Mexico, Guatemala and Honduras.

What is significant about the region is that it represented a vital link – or bridge – between Mesoamerican cultures to the north and Andean ones to the south (dating all the way back to the early presence of humans on the continent.) When the Spanish arrived, inhabitants of the area practiced religious rites associated with Aztec and Maya cultures, but also chewed coca leaves, evidence of contact with Inca and Aymara civilizations.

Despite the dearth of historical sources, tidbits about pre-Columbian culture surface now and again. The leading archaeological site is at Guayabo (p148) in the Central Valley, just 85km east of San José. Archaeologists here have uncovered stone streets, aqueducts, causeways and a few gold and stone artifacts. It is unclear what the purpose of these constructions was, but experts presume that it served as a ceremonial center and was thought to have been inhabited from about 1000 BC to AD 1400.

But archaeological finds aren't limited to the Central Valley. In southern Costa Rica, archaeologists are still scratching their heads over the dozens of astonishing, perfectly carved granite spheres whose purpose remains entirely unknown. Artfully carved by pre-Columbian cultures in the Diquis Valley from about AD 800, some spheres are no bigger than a grapefruit, while others are more than two meters tall. You can see them at the Museo Nacional in San José (p77) and strewn around Palmar (p330). There are even a few at Isla del Caño (p351), off the coast of the Península de Osa.

On the northern Pacific coast, the Greater Nicoya area (consisting of Costa Rica's Península de Nicoya and reaching north along the Pacific coast into Nicaragua) continues to be the focus of study. In this area, workers have found a wealth of ceramics, stonework, and jade, which has provided excellent insight into the pre-Columbian peoples who lived here.

A good place to get an overview of what does exist is at the Museo de Jade (p73) and Museo de Oro Precolombino (p76) in San José, where you can view numerous artifacts, primarily jewelry and items intended for personal use. The latter museum has a collection of more than 2000 incredible pieces on display, though little is known about the cultures that produced them.

DID YOU KNOW?

Today, the few remaining indigenous groups are often known by the name of their last chief, as recorded by Spanish chroniclers.

The most comprehensive and complete book on Costa Rican history and culture is *The Ticos: Culture and Social Change in Costa Rica*, by Mavis, Richard and Karen Biesanz. A must-read for anyone interested in the country!

CONQUEST & COLONIZATION

Columbus would spend only 17 days anchored in Costa Rica on his fourth and final voyage, but the impact of his arrival would be felt for centuries. His 'discovery' of the New World would lead to the eventual decimation of indigenous civilizations throughout the Americas and the establishment of a European-influenced Creole culture that has remained dominant in Latin American politics and society for more than 500 years.

TIMELINE

1000 BC	AD 800
Construction and habitation of Guayabo begins	Production of granite spheres in Diquis region begins

In 1506 King Ferdinand of Spain appointed Diego de Nicuesa governor of the region and sent him to colonize it. About half of the initial Spanish expedition died and the rest returned home. The Spaniards would ultimately succeed in colonizing the region, but it would not be easy. They were hampered by the jungle, tropical diseases and the small bands of Indians who used guerrilla tactics to fight them off. One Indian was Garabito (see the boxed text, p23).

Other expeditions followed. The most successful, from the Spaniards' point of view, was a 1522 journey to the Golfo de Nicoya area led by Spanish Captain Gil González Dávila. This was a bloodthirsty affair, with large numbers of the indigenous inhabitants killed or tortured for all sorts of reasons, primarily for their gold. Despite the brutal tactics, González was unable to form a permanent colony and many members of the expedition died of hunger and disease. González returned to Spain with a hoard of gold, claiming that he had converted thousands of Indians to Catholicism.

DID YOU KNOW?

You can buy works similar to those produced by pre-Columbian cultures from their descendants in Guaitil (p243).

Although the area became known as *la costa rica*, it had limited mineral wealth and the Spaniards devoted themselves, instead, to plundering the more affluent indigenous urban centers to the north and south. For the first 60 years after Nicuesa was given the orders to colonize, Costa Rica was the region's neglected stepchild.

It wasn't until 1561 that a significant effort was made on behalf of the Spanish crown to establish a lasting presence. By 1564 Juan Vásquez de Coronado had founded the first permanent settlement inland at Cartago and the fertile volcanic soil would allow the colony to flourish. (This was an unusual move for the Spanish as they generally preferred to settle coastal areas first, but the Caribbean had proved problematic because of disease and Vásquez and his men sought cooler climes.)

In the meantime, the indigenous population had been decimated. Initially there had been pockets of Indian resistance, but the small and fractured tribes were unable to stop the growing onslaught of Spanish *conquistadores* (conquerors) and their deadly European diseases. Any natives that managed to survive were quickly turned into slaves or sought refuge in the highlands.

The amount of gold Gil González Dávila 'discovered' in the Nicoya area led him to baptise the area *la costa rica* (the rich coast).

For the next 150 years, the colony remained a backwater of the captaincy of Guatemala. Cartago proved to be different from other Spanish colonies in more ways than one. There were few Indians around to use as labor or intermarry with, providing little opportunity to establish the grand civilizations that the Spanish had envisioned. Furthermore, its isolation from important trading routes meant it lay distant from any significant access to wealth – though it also meant that it sat out the raging battles that weighed down other colonial administrations. There just wasn't much to fight over. It was under these circumstances that Costa Rica emerged as a nation of subsistence farmers. While slavery and distinctions of class certainly existed, it was nowhere near the social stratification that divided other colonial centers – providing limited opportunity for political unrest.

Not that the colony was without setbacks. Much of Cartago was destroyed in an eruption of Volcán Irazú (p140) in 1723, but the survivors rebuilt the town and throughout the 18th century, the colony managed

1400
Guayabo abandoned for unknown reasons

1502
Christopher Columbus docks his boat at Puerto Limón during his fourth and final voyage

GARABITO

The area that is now encompassed by Parque Nacional Carara (p278) was once home to one of Costa Rica's legendary indigenous heroes, a local cacique named Garabito. He controlled a land area that extended from Carara north along the Golfo de Nicoya and into the Central Valley. He and his subjects fiercely resisted Spanish colonial rule.

In 1560, under orders from the Guatemalan high court, two Spaniards were ordered to capture the chieftain, but Garabito's intimate knowledge of the terrain gave him the upper hand and he successfully eluded capture. The Spaniards then settled on capturing his wife, Biriteka. After they imprisoned her, Garabito convinced one of his men to dress up as a chieftain and allow himself to be captured. While the Spaniards were celebrating their catch, Garabito snuck into their camp and liberated his wife. (No word on what happened to the other guy...)

Unfortunately, disease would accomplish what the Spaniards could not – and the chief and many of his subjects would perish with the many plagues that accompanied Spanish settlement. Today, the county where Carara lies is named after the famous Garabito.

to grow. Settlements were established throughout the central highlands, including Heredia in 1706, San José (1737) and Alajuela (1782). But despite this expansion, it remained one of the poorest outposts in the empire.

BIRTH OF A NATION

Its political distance from the crown meant that there were few Costa Ricans incensed enough to lay down their lives for self-determination. Most inhabitants, in fact, were surprised to learn on September 15, 1821, that Guatemala had declared independence for all of Central America. Mexico, Guatemala and Nicaragua then all scrambled to dominate Costa Rica politically – even though there wasn't much to control. It was a loose federation of provinces that had agreed not to disagree about gaining independence. (Some historians joke that even then, avoiding conflict was ingrained in the national character.) In 1823 Costa Rica joined the Central American Federation and in 1824 the province of Guanacaste-Nicoya was voluntarily annexed from Nicaragua. Most of the modern borders were established.

The first elected head of state, Juan Mora Fernández (1824–33), provided an impetus for development by offering rewards to whomever built roads or ports. In the meantime coffee, which had been introduced from Cuba in 1808, was beginning to take off as an important and lucrative crop. Braulio Carrillo, chief of state from 1835 to 1842, would foment coffee production. The rest of the 19th century saw a steady growth in coffee exports that would transform Costa Rica into the most prosperous nation in Central America. A wealthy entrepreneurial class was born and in 1849 a coffee grower, Juan Rafael Mora, became president and governed for 10 years.

DID YOU KNOW?

San José became the seat of government in 1823 after skirmishes, which the residents of Cartago lost.

Mora's presidency is remembered most for economic and cultural growth in addition to a bizarre military incident that has earned a place in every local child's history books. In June, 1855, an American renegade military adventurer named William Walker arrived in Nicaragua with his band of followers. Their intention was to conquer Central America and convert the area into slaving territory and then use slaves to build a canal through

1522

Captain Gil González Dávila refers to the Nicoya peninsula area as *la costa rica* (the rich coast)

1564

First permanent colonial settlement established in Cartago by Juan Vásquez de Coronado

Nicaragua to join the Atlantic and Pacific. He defeated the Nicaraguans and marched south, entering Costa Rica more or less unopposed, reaching a hacienda at Santa Rosa (now a national park, see p193).

Then, as now, Costa Rica had no army, so Mora organized 9000 civilians to gather their arms and head off Walker in February of 1856. In a decisive battle at Santa Rosa, the Costa Ricans defeated the pesky Walker, who retreated to Rivas, Nicaragua. The victors gave chase and Walker and his men took refuge inside a wood fort. A drummer boy from Alajuela named Juan Santamaría torched the building, forcing Walker to flee. Santamaría was killed in this action, and has since been sanctified as one of Costa Rica's greatest heroes. (You can see the statue built in honor of this battle in the Parque Nacional in San José, p77.)

DID YOU KNOW?

The land in Santa Rosa where William Walker was defeated in 1856 would later be owned by Nicaraguan dictator Anastasio Somoza in the 1950s. These were expropriated in 1978 when the Costa Rican government severed diplomatic relations with Nicaragua.

Walker survived the incident, but inadvertently had united disparate Costa Ricans behind a common national cause. Having not learned his lesson the first time around, he made several other unsuccessful invasion attempts before facing a Honduran firing squad in 1860. In the meantime, President Mora's cronyism and a burgeoning cholera epidemic (that he and his men reportedly brought back with them) would become his undoing. He was deposed in 1859, led a failed coup in 1860 and was executed in the same year as Walker.

THE ROOTS OF DEMOCRACY

The next three decades were characterized by violence, rigged elections decided only by the rich and powerful, and continuous power struggles between the church, state and *cafetaleros* (coffee barons). In 1869 a free and compulsory elementary education was established, though it had little benefit for families in more remote areas that did not have nearby schools. In 1889 the first democratic elections were held, though, not surprisingly, neither women nor blacks were allowed to vote.

BANANAS IS MY BUSINESS *Paige R Penland*

When 23-year-old American railroad scion Minor Keith was contracted in 1871 to connect Puerto Limón to San José by rail (see p384), he underestimated its cost: just the first 40km sent some 5000 men to their graves, including his two brothers. To cut expenses, Keith planted bananas along the tracks to feed his workforce, mostly made up of US convicts, Chinese indentured servants and Jamaican slaves; free folks just wouldn't risk the mortality rate.

Once built, coffee alone couldn't pay the railway's bills. Keith decided in desperation to fill his empty railcars with conveniently located bananas, which he sent to the USA for a trial run. They were a hit, and by 1900 Keith's banana holdings extended from Colombia to Guatemala, he was married to future President León Cortés Castro's daughter, and was arguably the most powerful man in Central America.

After Keith formed United Fruit in 1909, there was no more argument.

United Fruit did more than just transform Costa Rica's economy and culture – it would also come to shape the history of the rest of the continent. Also known as 'El Pulpo' (the octopus), this massive multinational had its tentacles in dealings throughout Latin America; from building the Tropical Radio Telegraph Company, Central America's first communications network, to lobbying for the 1954 CIA-led coup of democratically elected Guatemalan president Jacobo Arbenz.

And, to think, it all started with a few pieces of fruit in Costa Rica.

1737
San José founded

1821
Costa Rica gains independence from Spain

Democracy has been a steady (if sometimes tenuous) hallmark of Costa Rican politics ever since. One lapse occurred in 1917 when Minister of War Federico Tinoco overthrew the democratically elected president and formed a dictatorship. Resistance from his own people and the US government soon put an end to his regime. The following year, Tinoco fled to Europe.

In 1940, Rafael Angel Calderón Guardia became president and introduced minimum-wage laws, an eight-hour work day and provided the right to organize. To garner support for the new edicts, he constructed an odd alliance between the Communist party and the Catholic church, forming a group of Christian Socialists. The reforms he introduced were supported by workers, the poor and the growing middle class, but antagonized landowners, businessmen, conservatives and intellectuals. Fiscal mismanagement and corruption amplified this discontent. In the 1944 elections, Calderón was succeeded by Teodoro Picardo, a supporter of Calderón's policies, but the conservatives claimed the elections were a fraud.

For details on the role of Minor Keith and United Fruit in lobbying for a CIA-led coup in Guatemala, pick up a copy of the highly readable *Bitter Fruit*, by Stephen Schlesinger and Stephen Kinzer.

In 1948 Calderón again ran for the presidency, but was beaten by Otilio Ulate. However, unwilling to concede defeat, Calderón fraudulently claimed victory, claiming that some of the ballots had been destroyed. The tense situation escalated into civil war, with the opposing forces led by José (Don Pepe) Figueres Ferrer. After weeks of warfare and more than 2000 deaths, Figueres emerged as the winner. He led an interim government for 18 months, and in 1949 handed the presidency over to Ulate.

DID YOU KNOW?

In the 1940s children learned to read with a text that stated, 'Coffee is good for me. I drink coffee every morning.'

That year marked the formation of the modern Costa Rican constitution. Women and blacks received the vote and presidents were not allowed to run for successive terms. In addition, a neutral electoral tribunal was established to guarantee free and fair elections, and voting was made mandatory for all citizens over the age of 18. (The latter law is not legally enforced, though Costa Rica retains a higher voter turnout than most Western countries.) Most importantly, the country abolished the armed forces – something that has made a long-lasting impact on this peaceful nation. Since then, no administration has come into power by force.

Although Costa Rica has countless political parties, Figueres' Partido de Liberación Nacional (PLN; National Liberation Party) has been a dominant player in national politics since 1949. Figueres himself remained popular and was returned to two more terms in office: in 1953 and the other in 1970. (He died in 1990.)

Currently, the PLN's most notable leader remains Oscar Arias Sánchez, who served as president from 1986 to 1990 and famously prevented the US from using Costa Rica as a base to launch Contra guerrillas into Nicaragua. Arias' predecessor, Luis Alberto Monge, had allowed the Contras (and the CIA) to treat the country as a military base for all of its operations into Costa Rica's northern neighbor. Arias overturned this decision on the grounds that it violated Costa Rican neutrality and his subsequent work on framing the accords that ended the war in Nicaragua and instability in other parts of the region would earn him a Nobel Peace Prize in 1987.

1856

Costa Rica defeats American filibuster William Walker in the battle of Santa Rosa

1889

First democratic elections held (blacks and women not allowed to vote)

Several recent elections have gone to the Partido de Unidad Social Cristiana (PUSC; Social Christian Unity Party), the heirs to Calderón's 1940s alliance. And in fact, Calderón's son, Rafael Ángel Calderón Fournier, was elected president in 1990, succeeding Arias. It seems that every political heir should have his moment, because his term in office was followed by the election of Pepe Figueres' son, Jose María Figueres, a PLN candidate. Figueres' presidency was unpopular, marked by price hikes, tax increases and strikes by teachers and other groups. Clearly, the history of politics in Costa Rica is strongly influenced by a handful of families, as shown by the father-son associations that have dominated the presidency. In fact, 75% of the 44 presidents of Costa Rica prior to 1970 were descended from just three original colonizers.

The leading daily newspaper *La Nación* keeps a trove of historic photographs dating back to the 19th century on its website. View them at www.nacion.com/ln_ee/ESPECIALES/visual/.

The presidency went back to the PUSC in 1998, when Miguel Ángel Rodríguez was elected. But in a continuing trend that shows that Costa Ricans are beginning to tire of two-party dominance, Rodríguez squeaked into the presidency with a slim lead of 2.5%. His term was not marked by major changes. Increases in tourism, high-tech products, and the traditional coffee and banana exports buoyed the president's attempts to fix the economy during the first two years of his administration, but he then proceeded to ignite mass protests and work stoppages when he attempted to privatize the state-owned power and telecommunications agencies. He was forced to back down from his wish to over quadruple the presidential annual salary. The economic downturn in the high-tech and agricultural sectors after 2000 resulted in a faltering economy.

Costa Rica's parks didn't just happen. Pick up *The Quetzal and the Macaw: The Story of Costa Rica's National Parks,* by David Rains Wallace, for the full contentious history that pitted the government against communities against environmental activists.

THE 21ST CENTURY

Another PUSC representative took the presidency in 2002 – and again, it was a by a hair. Psychiatrist and television commentator Abel Pacheco won the election after submitting to a run-off vote – the first since the 1948 civil war. But it is clear that the public is frustrated with the status quo. This election, held in April of 2002, had the highest voter abstention rate ever, with almost 40% of Costa Ricans not voting.

Pacheco began his term favorably enough. He had promised to eliminate the public debt within four years and launched a conservationist platform that banned any new oil drilling and mining. He also proposed a series of constitutional amendments that would guarantee every citizen the fundamental right to a healthy environment. In 2003, however, Pacheco's mandate had shriveled. A campaign finance scandal – in which he was alleged to have illegally accepted foreign donations – clouded his presidency, leading some opponents to demand his resignation. He managed to weather the storm, but not without a political price. At the time of writing, the Costa Rican legislature was attempting to pass a campaign-finance reform law.

Pacheco seems to have recovered enough political will from the scandal to negotiate a controversial free trade agreement with the United States. The Central America Free Trade Agreement (Cafta) has yet to be approved by the Costa Rican legislature or the US congress, but the full political force of the agreement will likely not be felt until it is put to the vote. The pact calls for the opening up of state monopolies (telecommunications and insurance) to foreign competition – a similar

1940
Rafael Angel Calderón Guardia elected president; minimum-wage laws and eight-hour day introduced

1948
Six-week civil war leaves 2000 dead; army abolished and a new constitution established; women and blacks granted the vote

proposal sent Costa Ricans into protest-mode when President Rodríguez tried it in the late 1990s. It is unclear whether this agreement will pass – on either side.

The next presidential election, in 2006, promises to be an interesting one for the country. In March, 2004, Oscar Arias announced his intention to run for the presidency under the banner of the PLN. Though out of the presidential limelight since 1990, the 63-year-old candidate has remained active in party politics and is one of the most popular political figures in all of Costa Rica. At the time of writing, it is still too early to tell what his chances will be.

1987

Oscar Arias Sánchez wins the Nobel Prize for his work on the Central American peace accords

2002

First run-off vote required for a presidential election since 1948 signaling unrest with the two major parties

The Culture

THE NATIONAL PSYCHE

Costa Ricans take pride in defining themselves by what they are not. In comparison with their Central American neighbors, they aren't poor, they aren't illiterate and they aren't beleaguered by political tumult. It's a curious line-up of negatives that somehow add up to one big positive.

Ticos (Costa Ricans) are very proud of their country, from its ecological jewels, high standard of living and education rate to, above all, the fact that it has flourished without an army for the past 50-plus years. They view their country as an oasis of calm in a land that has been continuously degraded by warfare. The Nobel Prize that Oscar Arias received for his work on the Central American peace accords is a point of pride and confirms the general feeling that they are somehow different from a grosser, more violent world. Peace is priceless.

DID YOU KNOW?

The Space Propulsion Lab at NASA is run by a Tico. Renowned astronaut Franklin Chang-Díaz is designing an engine that will someday get humans to Mars. He is revered in Costa Rica and even has a beetle named after him, *Phanaeus changdiazi*.

And to maintain it, Ticos will avoid conflict at all costs, no matter how trifling the topic. People will say 'yes' even if they mean 'no', and 'maybe' often replaces 'I don't know.' This is a habit that can flummox foreigners, who try to figure out if anyone really means what they say. Tough negotiating is not a strong suit.

Ticos are well-mannered to a fault and will do everything they can to *quedar bien* (leave a good impression). Conversations start with a cordial *buenos días* or *buenas tardes* and friendly inquiries about your well-being before delving into business. Bullying and yelling will get you nowhere, but a smile and a friendly greeting will always succeed.

Ticos are cautious and rarely get passionately involved in a debate or fight. Disputes tend to be settled amicably through careful negotiation and compromise, rather than a winner-takes-all mentality. Ticos do not respond well to boastfulness or arrogance. And while the stereotype of Costa Rican friendliness is largely true, it's also just as true that they wouldn't tell you if they didn't like you because, well, it'd be rude.

LIFESTYLE

A lack of war, strong exports and stronger tourism have meant that Costa Rica enjoys the highest standard of living in Central America. Primary education is free and compulsory for all school-aged children and, though it is overburdened, a nationwide system provides free health care.

DID YOU KNOW?

The expression *matando la culebra* (meaning 'to be idle', literally 'killing the snake') originates with peons from banana plantations. When foremen would ask what they'd been doing, the response was, '*¡Matando la culebra!*'

Even though 23% of the populace lives below the poverty line, beggars are few and you won't see the packs of ragged street kids that seem to roam around other Latin American capitals. In the poorer lowland areas, *campesinos* (peasants) and *indígenas* (Indians) often live in windowless houses made of *caña brava*, a local cane. Big-city areas such as San José have hastily constructed shanty towns where many of the urban poor dwell, but certainly not on the scale of countries such as Peru.

But for the most part, Costa Ricans tend to live fairly comfortably. The home of an average Tico is a one-story construction made of concrete blocks, wood or a combination of both. By the early 1990s more than 93% of all dwellings had running water and a little under one-third were connected to a sewer system. In city areas some of the more affluent homes will be surrounded by a wall capped with barbed wire or broken glass to keep out thieves. Smaller units will have windows covered in heavy wrought-iron grills or a conspicuously placed guard dog.

Life expectancy exceeds that of the US by two years and most Costa Ricans are more likely to die of heart disease or cancer than the childhood diseases that tend to claim lives in many developing nations. In 1920 one in every four babies died in its first year of life; almost 80 years later that statistic had declined to just one in 85. Various public health programs and the preponderance of clean water and well-managed sewer systems account for these positive statistics.

Family remains the nucleus of social and cultural life in Costa Rica. When people get together it tends to be with family, and groups of the same clan will often live near each other in clusters. Federal law supports this type of unity: spouses are legally responsible for supporting each other, their children and immediate family members requiring assistance (eg a disabled sibling).

Generally speaking, most families have the requisite 2.4 children and, for the most part, Costa Rican youths spend ample time on middle-class worries such as dating, music, belly-baring fashions and *fútbol* (soccer).

Modernization is continually affecting family ways. Society is increasingly geographically mobile and the Tico that was born in Puntarenas might end up managing a lodge on the Península de Osa. And, with the advent of better paved roads, cell (mobile) phones, electrification and the presence of 50,000 North American expats, change will continue to come at a steady pace for the Tico family unit.

DID YOU KNOW?

The movie *1492*, about the arrival of Christopher Columbus in the Americas, was filmed in Costa Rica.

POPULATION

Costa Ricans call themselves Ticos (men and groups of men and women) or Ticas (females). Two-thirds of the nation's almost four million people live in the Meseta Central (Central Valley), and almost one-third is under the age of 15.

Most inhabitants are *mestizo*, a mix of Spanish with Indian and/or black roots (though most Ticos consider themselves white). Indigenous Costa Ricans make up only 1% of the population; tribes include the Bribrí, Boruca and Guaymí.

Less than 3% of the population is black, much of it concentrated on the Caribbean coast. This population speaks English, Spanish and a Creole dialect and traces its ancestry to Jamaican immigrants who were brought to build railroads in the 19th century. Chinese immigrants (1%) arrived in Costa Rica through similar methods, though there have been regular, more voluntary waves of immigration since then.

In recent years North American and European immigration has greatly increased and it is estimated that roughly 50,000 North American expats live in the country.

A winning oral history of the black communities on the Caribbean Coast is covered in Paula Palmer's *What Happen*. It can be difficult to find because it's out of print, but used copies pop up on www.amazon.com and www.half.com.

MULTICULTURALISM

The mix of mainstream *mestizo* society with blacks, Asians, Indians and North Americans provides the country with an interesting fusion of culture and cuisine. And while the image of the welcoming Tico is largely true, there are still problems with prejudice.

For the black population, this has been a reality for more than a century. About 75% of the country's black population resides on the Caribbean coast, and this area has been historically marginalized and deprived of services by a succession of governments (black Costa Ricans were not allowed in the Central Valley until after 1948). In addition, some Ticos have the attitude that black Costa Ricans aren't truly Costa Rican. Despite this, good manners prevail and black travelers can feel comfortable traveling around the entire country. Asian Ticos and the small Jewish population

DEALING WITH NORTH AMERICAN IMMIGRATION

Costa Rica is currently grappling with identity issues raised by the influx of North American (and some European) settlers. Many Ticos are starting to feel that they are being discriminated against in their own country. It is not hard to see why. The best beaches – and 80% of all coastal property – are owned by foreigners. Signs are in English, prices are in dollars and many top-end places are managed exclusively by foreigners, with locals serving primarily as maids and gardeners.

During my research for this book, I encountered countless numbers of foreign hotel-owners who would announce that every aspect of their business was foreign-operated, with the implication that this was somehow better. 'No Ticos,' one hotel manager on the Pacific coast told me proudly. Yet another confided in me, 'These Latin Americans don't like to work.'

This is certainly not the case with the majority of North American immigrants, most of whom are very accepting. But it is a delicate problem. Foreigners affiliated with the tourist trade attract tourist dollars and it's those dollars that keep the wheels of the economy well greased. Hence, most people are reluctant to do or say too much about this. But the country is reaching a saturation point in tourism – and there's no telling how long Ticos will tolerate being marginalized in their own country.

On a similar note, some travelers have complained that Costa Rica is somehow a 'less authentic' destination because of the large numbers of North Americans. The country is certainly in a state of cultural evolution. But it is worthwhile to recognize the contributions immigrants have made – regardless of their race, creed or origin. Some of these European and North American immigrants have been key in organizing, supporting and financing some of the nation's major conservation and environmental efforts. It was two immigrants from Scandinavia who helped found the country's first national park, the Reserva Natural Absoluta Cabo Blanco (p269).

Immigration is part of history and part of society. But hopefully some North American immigrants will give just as much as they take.

have frequently been the subject of immature jokes, though Jewish and Asian travelers alike can expect to be treated well. It is Nicaraguans that are currently the butt of some of society's worst prejudice. Many nationals like to blame Nicas (a diminutive term for Nicaraguans) for an increase in violent crime; though no proof of this claim exists.

Indigenous populations remain largely invisible to many Costa Ricans – and to foreigners as well. While many Indians lead Westernized, inherently Tico lives, others inhabit the country's reserves. Many of these actively discourage visits by outside visitors. (Note that one translation of Indian is *indio*, which is an insulting term; *indígena* is the preferred term, meaning 'indigenous.')

SPORTS

Get player statistics, game schedules and find out everything you ever needed to know about La Sele, the Costa Rican national soccer team (in Spanish), at www.fedefutbol.com.

The national sport is, you guessed it, *futból* (soccer). Every town has a soccer field which usually serves as the most conspicuous landmark. On it you'll find any number of neighborhood aficionados heatedly playing.

The *selección nacional* (national selection) team – known affectionately as La Sele – has its every move deconstructed by legions of rabid Tico fans. Their most memorable achievements have been reaching the quarterfinals at the 1990 World Cup in Italy, qualifying for the Japan/Korea games in 2002 and making the quarterfinals of the Copa America in 2004. Women's soccer is picking up steam as well and there is now a female national team. The regular season is from August to May.

Surfing, though limited among Ticos, is growing in popularity. Costa Rica annually hosts numerous national and international competitions that are widely covered by local media. Bullfighting is also popular, particularly in the Guanacaste region. (The bull isn't killed in the Costa Rican version of the sport, which is really a ceremonial opportunity to watch a drunk cowboy run around with a bull.) The popular Latin American sport of cockfighting is illegal.

MEDIA

While Costa Rica certainly enjoys more press freedom than most Latin American countries, do not expect a great deal of probity from its media organizations. The outlets are limited and coverage tends to be cautious, largely due to conservative media laws.

In 2002 the country still had a *desacato* – insult law – on its books. This is common in most Latin American countries and allows public figures to sue journalists if their honor has been 'damaged' by the media. This is a criminal offense and journalists could spend two months to two years in jail for 'insulting' a public official. The law had only been applied once in Costa Rica – to *La Nación* columnist Bosco Valverde in 1994, convicted for calling three judges 'stubborn' – and has since been repealed.

'journalists could spend two months to two years in jail for 'insulting' a public official'

However, other laws prevent journalists from doing an effective job. A 2003 poll in *La Nación* showed that 96% of journalists felt the system was in dire need of reform. Libel and slander laws put the burden of proof on reporters and they are frequently required to reveal their sources in court. While the government doesn't have an exceedingly heavy hand with the press, journalists will regularly find themselves facing a judge when reporting on sensitive issues (especially corruption).

Moreover, the 2001 assassination of radio journalist Parmenio Medina has given reporters another reason not to dig deep. Medina was the host of a popular investigative program called *La Patada* (The Kick). Shortly before broadcasting a series on financial irregularities at a now-defunct Catholic radio station, he was shot to death outside his home in Heredia. At the time of writing, several men, including a priest, had been held on charges of orchestrating his death, though no one had yet been charged with his murder.

RELIGION

More than 75% of Ticos are Catholic (at least in principle). And while many show a healthy reverence for the Virgin Mary, they rarely profess blind faith to the dictates coming from Rome – apparently 'pure life' doesn't require being excessively penitent. Most people tend to go to church for the sacraments (baptism, first communion, confirmation, marriage and death) and the holidays.

Religious processions on holy days are generally less fervent and colorful than those found in Latin American countries such as Guatemala or Peru. (Though the procession for the patron virgin, La Virgen de Los Ángeles, held annually on August 2 does draw penitents who walk from all over Central America to Cartago to show devotion. For details, see p138.) Semana Santa (the week before Easter) is a national holiday: everything (even buses) stops operating at lunchtime on Maundy Thursday and doesn't start up again until the afternoon of Holy Saturday.

When New Flowers Bloomed: Short Stories by Women Writers from Costa Rica & Panama, edited by Enrique Jaramillo Levi, is a worthwhile read.

Roughly 14% of Costa Ricans are evangelical Christians. The black community on the Caribbean is largely Protestant and there are small Jewish populations in San José and Jacó. There are a sprinkling of Middle Easterners and Asians who practice Islam and Buddhism, respectively.

WOMEN IN COSTA RICA

Women are traditionally respected in Costa Rica (Mother's Day is a national holiday), and since 1974 the Costa Rican family code has stipulated that husband and wife have equal duties and rights. In addition, women can draw up contracts, assume loans and inherit property; sexual harassment and sex discrimination are against the law. But only recently have women made gains in the workplace, with growing roles in political, legal, scientific and medical fields.

In 1993 Margarita Penon (Oscar Arias Sánchez's wife) ran as a presidential candidate and in 1998 both vice presidents (Costa Rica has two) were women: Astrid Fischel and Elizabeth Odio. In early 2004 a group of female legislators were attempting to get a historic domestic-violence law approved by congress. This would include stiff incarceration penalties for husbands who kill or beat their wives.

Despite some advances, machismo is not a thing of the past. Anti-discrimination laws are rarely enforced and women are generally lower paid and have a harder time being considered for high-level jobs. They also have a tougher time getting loans, even though their repayment record is better than men's. In the countryside many women maintain traditional roles: raising children, cooking, and running the home.

ARTS

Costa Rica is famous more for its natural beauty and tropical ecology than for its culture. There is little indigenous cultural influence in the nation's arts, and cultural activities of any kind tend to be centered on Western-style entertainment. And because the country was so poor until the middle of the 19th century, cultural and artistic activities have only really developed since then.

San José is not only the political capital, but the artistic one as well and it is here that you will find the lion's share of the nation's museums, in addition to a lively theater and gallery scene. This is also the spot for musical entertainment and you'll be able to catch a regularly rotating lineup of domestic and international rock, folk and hip-hop artists. On the Península de Nicoya, marimba performances are popular in the interior and on the Caribbean Coast, local music is infused with plenty of reggae flavor. The one group that has made a significant name for themselves at a regional level are the salsa group Los Brillanticos, who once shared the stage with Cuban legend Celia Cruz during a tour stop she made in San José.

DID YOU KNOW?

A *bomba* is a funny (usually ribald) verse stated during a musical interlude. These are popular in marimba performances in Santa Cruz, Guanacaste (p243).

Literature

Few writers or novelists are available in translation and, unfortunately, much of what is written on Costa Rica and available in English (fiction or otherwise) is written almost exclusively by foreigners.

One writer of note is Carmen Naranjo (1930–), one of the few contemporary Costa Rican writers who has risen to international acclaim. She is a novelist, poet and short-story writer who also served as ambassador to India in the 1970s and, a few years later, as Minister of Culture. In 1996 she was awarded the prestigious Gabriela Mistral medal from the Chilean government. Her works have been translated into several languages, and her collection of short stories *There Never Was a Once Upon a Time* is widely available in English. Two of her stories can also be found in *Costa Rica: A Traveler's Literary Companion*.

Another noteworthy author is Tatiana Lobo (1939–), who was actually born in Chile but has lived in Costa Rica since 1967 and whose many books are set here. She received the noteworthy Premio Sor Juana Inés de la Cruz for Latin American women novelists for her novel *Asalto al Paraíso* (Assault on Paradise).

Costa Rica: A Traveler's Literary Companion, edited by Barbara Ras, is a fine collection of 26 short stories by modern Costa Rican writers, offering a valuable glimpse of society from Ticos themselves.

One of the most significant contributions to Costa Rican literature has been by internationally renowned memoirist José León Sánchez (1930–). A Huetar Indian from the border of Costa Rica with Nicaragua, he was convicted for stealing from the famous Basílica de Nuestra Señora de Los Ángeles in Cartago (p138) and sentenced to serve his term at Isla San Lucas (p259), one of Latin America's most notorious jails. Illiterate when he was incarcerated, Sánchez taught himself how to read and write, and clandestinely authored one of the continent's most poignant memoirs: *La isla de los hombres solos* (called *God Was Looking the Other Way* in the translated version). He ultimately served 20 years of his 45-year-sentence and went on to produce 14 other novels and serve in a variety of high-level public appointments.

For a searing and engaging fictional story set during the first days of Cartago, don't miss *Assault on Paradise* by award-winning Chilean/Tica author Tatiana Lobo.

Theater

Theater is one of the favorite cultural activities in Costa Rica, and San José is the center of a thriving acting community. Plays are produced mainly in Spanish, but the Little Theater Group stages English-language performances (p95).

The most famous theater in the country is the Teatro Nacional in San José (p95).The story goes that a noted European opera company was on a Latin American tour but declined to perform in Costa Rica for lack of a suitable hall. Immediately, the coffee elite put a special cultural tax on coffee exports for the construction of a world-class theater. The Teatro Nacional is now the premier venue for plays, opera, performances by the national symphony orchestra, ballet, poetry readings and other cultural events. It also is an architectural work in its own right and a landmark in any city tour of San José.

Visual Arts

Costa Rican painters have yet to hit the big time internationally, but the country is host to a small but burgeoning visual arts scene that serves as an informal center for contemporary artists from all over Central America. Many art galleries are geared toward tourists and specialize in 'tropical art' (for lack of an official description): brightly-colored, whimsical folk paintings depicting flora and fauna and evocative of the work of French artist Henri Rousseau.

See a stunning and comprehensive visual database on Central American contemporary art at the website for the Museo de Arte y Diseño Contemporáneo at www.madc.ac.cr/.

Other artists incorporate an infinite variety of contemporary themes in various media, from painting and sculpture to video and site-specific installations. The Museo de Arte y Diseño Contemporáneo (p73) is the top place to see this type of work and its permanent collection is a great primer. Numerous galleries in nearby Barrio Amón offer good opportunities to see (and buy) works, and in Manuel Antonio the Hotel Si Como No (p295) has a worthwhile gallery.

Environment David Lukas

THE LAND

Despite its tiny size, Costa Rica is an extremely varied country. At 51,100 sq km, it is slightly smaller than the state of West Virginia in the USA and slightly larger than Switzerland, yet it encompasses one of the world's most diverse natural landscapes. Divided neatly by a series of volcanic mountain chains that run the length of the country from Nicaragua to Panama, Costa Rica hosts markedly different climates on its Pacific and Caribbean sides. These in turn support entirely separate assemblages of plants and animals.

Costa Rica Natural History, edited by Daniel H Janzen, is the classic reference for anyone seeking detailed information on topics ranging from climate and geology, to agriculture, to native flora and fauna.

At a length of 1254km, the Pacific coastline is infinitely varied as it twists and turns around gulfs, peninsulas, and many small coves. Rugged, rocky headlands alternating with classic white- and black-sand beaches and palm trees make this a tropical paradise along some stretches. Strong tidal action creates an excellent habitat for waterbirds as well as visually dramatic crashing surf (an excellent habitat for surfers). Inland, the landscapes of the Pacific lowlands are equally dynamic, ranging from dry deciduous forests and open cattle country in the north to lush and magnificent tropical rain forests in the south.

Monotonous in comparison, the Caribbean coastline runs a straight 212km along a low flat plain that is strongly inundated with brackish lagoons and waterlogged forests. A lack of strong tides allows plants to grow right over the water's edge along inland sloughs, creating a wall of green vegetation. Broad, humid plains that scarcely rise above sea level and murky waters characterize much of this coastal region, though agriculture is now widespread on all upland areas.

DID YOU KNOW?

Parque Nacional Tapantí is one of the wettest national parks. If you visit be prepared to get wet because the area averages 7000mm of rainfall a year.

Running down the center of the country, the mountainous spine of Costa Rica is a land of active volcanoes, clear, tumbling streams, and chilled peaks clad in impenetrable cloud forests. These mountain ranges generally follow a northwest to southeast line, with the highest and most dramatic peaks near the Panamanian border (culminating at the 3820m-high Cerro Chirripó). The difficulties of traveling through and farming on these steep slopes have until recently saved much of this area from development and made it a haven for wildlife.

In the midst of the highlands lies the Meseta Central – or Central Valley – which is surrounded by mountains (the Cordillera Central to the north and east and the Cordillera de Talamanca to the south). It is this fertile central plain, between about 1000m and 1500m above sea level, that contains four of Costa Rica's five-largest cities and more than half of the country's population.

BOSQUE ETERNO DE LOS NIÑOS

One of Costa Rica's most touching conservation stories is the creation of the first international children's rain forest in 1987. Starting as a spontaneous outpouring of hope by nine-year-old students in Sweden who sold homemade cards and donated their allowances to save the rain forest, this effort grew into a groundswell of support from schoolchildren in more than 40 nations. Now totaling more than 56,800 acres (23,000 hectares), the Children's Eternal Forest also runs a Children's Nature Center and research station that welcomes visitors and children from all over the world. No matter your age, you can always learn more about this project and make contributions to the **Monteverde Conservation League** (☎ 645 5104; www.acmonteverde.com).

Like most of Central America, Costa Rica's geological history can be traced to the impact of the Cocos Plate moving northeast and crashing into the Caribbean Plate at a rate of about 10cm every year – quite fast by geological standards. The point of impact is called a 'subduction zone,' and this is where the Cocos Plate forces the edge of the Caribbean Plate to break up and become uplifted. It is not a smooth process, and hence Central America is an area prone to earthquakes and volcanic activity (see p453).

This process began when most of Costa Rica was underwater and has been going on for about five million years. Costa Rica itself is about three million years old, with the exception of the Península de Nicoya, which is many millions of years older. Most of the mountain ranges in Costa Rica are volcanic; the exception is the massive Cordillera de Talamanca in the south, the largest range in Costa Rica. This is a granite batholith of intruded igneous rock that formed under great pressure below the surface of the earth and was uplifted.

DID YOU KNOW?

On a clear day, half of Costa Rica can be seen from the summit of Cerro Chirripó.

WILDLIFE

Nowhere else in the world are so many types of habitats squeezed into such a tiny area. The range of habitats in Costa Rica, a consequence of its unique geography, creates an incredibly rich diversity of flora and fauna – in fact no other country on the planet has such variety. Measured in terms of number of species per 10,000 sq km Costa Rica tops the list of countries at 615 species, compared to a wildlife-rich country such as Rwanda that has 596, or to the comparatively impoverished USA with its 104 species. This simple fact alone (not to mention the ease of travel and friendly residents!) makes Costa Rica the premier destination for nature lovers from all over the world.

Along with its diverse geography, the large number of species in Costa Rica is also due to the relatively recent appearance of the country. Roughly three million years ago Costa Rica rose from the ocean and formed a land bridge between North and South America, and as species from these two vast biological provinces started to mingle and mix, the number of species was essentially 'doubled.'

DID YOU KNOW?

The seven species of poison-dart frog in Costa Rica are beautiful to look at but have exceedingly toxic skin secretions that cause paralysis and death.

Animals

Though tropical in nature – with a substantial number of tropical animals such as poison-arrow frogs and spider monkeys – Costa Rica is also the winter home for more than 200 species of migrating birds that arrive from as far away as Alaska and Australia. So don't be surprised to see one of your familiar backyard birds here feeding alongside trogons and toucans. For more details on individual animals and insects, see the Wildlife Guide, p41.

With more than 850 species recorded in Costa Rica (comparable to what's found in much larger areas such as North America, Australia or Europe), it's understandable that birds are one of the primary attractions for naturalists. You could stay for months at a stretch and you'll still have barely scratched the surface in terms of seeing all these species. Birds in Costa Rica come in every imaginable color, from strawberry-red scarlet macaws to the iridescent jewels called violet sabrewings (a type of hummingbird). Because many birds in Costa Rica have restricted ranges, you are guaranteed of finding completely different species almost everywhere you travel.

DID YOU KNOW?

Sloths move so slowly that they may take several days to move the distance a monkey can travel in seconds.

Though visitors will almost certainly see one of Costa Rica's four monkey or two sloth species, there are an additional 260 animal species awaiting the patient observer. Night walks with a naturalist guide are an excellent bet for finding amazing creatures such as the four-eyed opossum

> **WHALE WATCHING IN COSTA RICA**
>
> Growing in popularity are a number are special tours and opportunities to experience coastal and marine wildlife. The whale-watching industry alone has grown from three operators in 1997 to more than 36 today, and concern is mounting that this might be too much disturbance for these gentle creatures. In a survey conducted by the Cetacean Society International, 17 of the operators refused to cooperate by answering survey questions, and all of the tour companies investigated made mistakes ranging from harassing animals, to not carrying lifejackets and having motor problems. Only one company had knowledgeable guides that could provide 'reasonable natural history information.'

and silky anteater while a lucky few might spot the elusive tapir, or have a jaguarundi cross their path.

No season is a bad season for exploring Costa Rica's natural environment, though most visitors arrive during the peak dry season when trails are less muddy and more accessible. An added bonus of visiting between December and February is that many of the wintering migrant birds are still hanging around. A trip after the peak season may mean fewer birds, but it is a stupendous time to see dried forests transform into vibrant greens and it's the time when resident birds begin their nesting season.

ENDANGERED SPECIES

As expected in a country that has both unique habitats and widespread cutting of its forests, there are numerous species whose populations are declining or in danger of extinction. Even the legendary resplendent quetzal – the bird at the top of every naturalist's must-see list – teeters precariously as its home forests are felled at an alarming rate. The same can be said of the leatherback and hawksbill sea turtles that emerge from the sea at night to lay their eggs on beaches trampled all day by eager bathers. Visitors are encouraged to learn more about these vulnerable animals and contribute toward organizations working to save them.

Plants

Les D Beletsky's *Costa Rica: The EcoTraveller's Wildlife Guide* provides a handy overview of the area's flora and fauna.

The floral biodiversity is also high – well over 10,000 species of vascular plants have been described in Costa Rica, and more are being added to the list every year. Orchids alone account for about 1300 species, the most famous of which is the March-blooming *Cattleya skinneri* (*guaria morada* in Spanish), Costa Rica's national flower (see the boxed text opposite).

Experiencing a tropical forest for the first time can be a bit of a surprise for visitors from North America or Europe, where temperate forests tend to have little variety. Such regions are either dominated by conifers, or have endless tracts of oaks, beech, and birch. Tropical forests, on the other hand, have a staggering number of species – in Costa Rica, for example, almost 2000 tree species have been recorded. If you stand in one spot and look around, you'll see scores of different species of plants, and if you walk several hundred meters you're likely to find even more.

The National Biodiversity Institute is a clearinghouse of information on both biodiversity and efforts to conserve it. It's at www.inbio.ac.cr.

The diversity of habitats created as these many species mix is a wonder to behold –one day you may find yourself canoeing in a muggy mangrove swamp, and the next day squinting through bone-chilling fog to see orchids in a montane cloud forest. If at all possible, it is worth planning your trip with the goal of seeing some of Costa Rica's most distinctive plant communities, including a few of the following examples.

Classic rain-forest habitats are well represented in parks of the southwest corner of Costa Rica or in mid-elevation portions of the central mountains.

GUARIA GOING, GOING...GONE? *Carolina A Miranda*

Of the more than 1300 species of orchid found in Costa Rica, it is the *Cattleya skinneri* (*guaria morada* in Spanish) that has special resonance in Costa Rica. Though it is found in many parts of Central America, it is here that the flower truly flourishes and the beautiful, fuschia-colored bloom has come to be known as the country's national flower. As a result, many a Tico (Costa Rican) home, at one time or another, has been decorated with this lovely and delicate plant.

That seems to be the problem.

A report issued in early 2004 shows that the *guaria morada* is in danger of becoming extinct in the next 25 years if indiscriminate harvesting continues. The study, issued by a local environmental organization, has had the aim of drawing attention to this growing problem. (They got it!)

Various environmental organizations have banded together to press the government to help control harvesting of the plant in the wild – and a US orchid association has gotten involved as well. Hopefully, it won't be too late.

Here you will find towering trees that completely block out the sky, long looping vines, and many overlapping layers of vegetation. Many large trees may show buttresses, a feature of tropical trees whereby they grow winglike ribs extending out from the base of their trunks for added structural support. If you are lucky you will find magnificent examples of the ceiba (silk cotton tree), including a gigantic 70m elder in Parque Nacional Corcovado.

Along brackish stretches of both coasts, mangrove swamps are a world onto themselves. Growing stilt-like out of muddy tidal flats, five species of trees crowd together so densely that no boat and few animals can penetrate. Striking in their adaptations for dealing with salt, mangrove trees thrive where no other land plant dares tread. Though often thought of as a mosquito-filled nuisance, mangrove swamps play some extremely important roles. Not only do they buffer coastlines from the erosive power of waves, they also have very high levels of productivity because they trap so much nutrient-rich sediment, and serve as spawning and nursery areas for many species of fish and invertebrates.

If wildlife is your thing bring along Lonely Planet's *Watching Wildlife in Central America*, by Luke Hunter and David Andrew.

Most famous of all, and a highlight for many visitors, are the fabulous cloud forests of Monteverde reserve (p174) with fog-drenched trees so thickly coated in mosses, ferns, bromeliads, and orchids that you can hardly discern their true shapes. Cloud forests, however, are widespread at high elevations throughout Costa Rica (such as the Cerro de la Muerte area, p320) and any of them would be worth visiting. Be forewarned, however, that in these habitats the term 'rainy season' has little meaning because it's always dripping wet from the fog!

For a complete change of pace try exploring the unique drier forests along the northwest coast. During the dry season many trees drop their leaves, creating carpets of crackling, sun-drenched leaves and a sense of openness that is largely absent in other Costa Rican habitats. The large trees here, such as Costa Rica's national tree, the guanacaste, have broad, umbrella-like canopies, while spiny shrubs and vines or cacti dominate the understory. At times, large numbers of trees erupt into spectacular displays of flowers, and at the beginning of the rainy season everything transforms with a wonderful flush of new green leaves.

Consult *Costa Rica's National Parks and Preserves: A Visitor's Guide*, by Joseph Franke, for detailed trail and travel information on the country's parks.

NATIONAL PARKS

The national park system began in the 1960s, and now there are about 26 national parks, comprising about 11% of the country. In addition, there are scores of wildlife refuges, biological and forest reserves, monuments, and other protected areas in Costa Rica; therefore the Costa Rican authorities

NATIONAL PARKS & PROTECTED AREAS
0 100 km
0 60 miles
86°W
85°W
84°W
83°W
11°N
10°N
9°N
8°N
NICARAGUA
CARIBBEAN
SEA
PACIFIC
OCEAN
PANAMA
Barra del Colorado
Liberia
Tortuguero
Santa Cruz
Nicoya
Garza
Puntarenas
Alajuela
Heredia
Puerto Limón
SAN JOSÉ
Cartago
Golfo de Nicoya
Jacó
Quepos
San Isidro de El General
Palmar Norte
Bahía de Coronado
Golfito
Puerto Jiménez
87°06'W
87°03'W
5°33'N
5°30'N
Isla del Coco
68
0 6 km
0 4 miles
To Isla del Coco (300km, see inset)
1 Refugio Nacional de Vida Silvestre Bahía Junquillal
2 Parque Nacional Guanacaste
3 Parque Nacional Santa Rosa
4 Estación Experimental Horizontes
5 Parque Nacional Rincón de la Vieja
6 Refugio Nacional de Vida Silvestre Caño Negro
7 Parque Nacional Volcán Tenorio
8 Reserva Indígena Guatuso
9 Refugio Nacional de Vida Silvestre Barra del Colorado
10 Parque Nacional Tortuguero
11 Parque National Marino Las Baulas de Guanacaste
12 Reserva Biológica Lomas de Barbudal
13 Parque Nacional Volcán Arenal
14 Estación Biológica La Selva
15 Refugio Nacional de Vida Silvestre Ostional
16 Reserva Indígena Matambú
17 Parque Nacional Barra Honda
18 Parque Nacional Palo Verde
19 Reserva Biológica Isla de los Pájaros
20 Reserva Biológica Bosque Nuboso Monteverde
21 Refugio Silvestre de Peñas Blancas
22 Parque Nacional Juan Castro Blanco
23 Parque Nacional Volcán Poás
24 Parque Nacional Braulio Carrillo
25 Reserva Natural Absoluta Cabo Blanco
26 Refugio Nacional de Vida Silvestre Curú
27 Reserva Biológica Isla Guayabo
28 Reserva Biológica Islas Negritos
29 Parque Nacional Carara
30 Reserva Indígena Quitirrisí
31 Reserva Indígena Zapatón
32 Parque Nacional Volcán Irazú
33 Parque Nacional Volcán Turrialba
34 Monumento Nacional Guayabo
35 Reserva Indígena Barbilla
36 Parque Nacional Barbilla
37 Reserva Indígena Alto y Bajo Chirripó
38 Parque Nacional Tapantí-Macizo Cerro de la Muerte
39 Parque Nacional Manuel Antonio
40 Parque Nacional Chirripó
41 Reserva Indígena Telire
42 Reserva Indígena Tayní
43 Reserva Biológica Hitoy-Cerere
44 Reserva Indígena Talamanca-Cabécar
45 Reserva Indígena Talamanca Bribri
46 Parque Nacional Cahuita
47 Reserva Indígena Cocles/KéköLdi
48 Refugio Nacional de Vida Silvestre Gandoca-Manzanillo
49 Parque Nacional Marino Ballena
50 Parque Internacional La Amistad
51 Reserva Indígena Ujarrás
52 Reserva Indígena Salitre
53 Reserva Indígena Cabagra
54 Reserva Indígena Térraba
55 Reserva Indígena Boruca
56 Reserva Indígena Curré
57 Parque Nacional Chirripó
58 Zona Protectora Las Tablas
59 Reserva Biológica Isla del Caño
60 Humedal Nacional Térraba-Sierpe
61 Reserva Indígena Guaymí Coto Brus
62 Parque Nacional Corcovado
63 Reserva Indígena Guaymí de Osa
64 Parque Nacional Corcovado (Piedras Blancas Sector)
65 Refugio Nacional de Vida Silvestre Golfito
66 Reserva Indigena Abrojo-Montezuma
67 Reserva Indígena Conte Burica
68 Parque Nacional Isla del Coco

enjoy their claim that more than 25% of the country has been set aside for conservation. In addition, there are various buffer zones, such as indigenous reservations, that boost the total area of 'protected' land to about 27%. These buffer zones still allow farming, logging, and other exploitation, however, so the environment within them is not totally protected.

What this means for the traveler is that, in addition to the national-park system, there are hundreds of small, privately owned lodges, reserves, and haciendas that have been set up to protect the land, and many of these are well worth visiting.

Although the national-park system appears wonderful on paper, a report from the national conservation body (Sinac; Sistema Nacional de Areas de Conservación) amplifies the fact that many of the parks are, in fact, paper tigers. The government doesn't exactly own the parks – almost half of the areas are in private ownership – and there isn't a budget to buy these lands. Technically, the private lands are protected from development, but many landowners are finding loopholes in the restrictions and selling or developing their properties.

Sinac (☎ 192, 283 8004; www.sinac.go.cr) is a branch of the oddly paired environmental and energy ministry (Minae; Ministerio del Ambiente y Energía). The agency has developed a project to link geographically close groups of national parks and reserves, private reserves, and national forests into 11 conservation areas that cover the country. The system will have two major effects. First, larger areas of wildlife habitats will be protected in blocks (so-called megaparks), allowing greater numbers of species and individual plants and animals to exist. Second, the administration of the national parks will be delegated to regional offices, allowing a more individualized management approach for each area. Each conservation area has regional and subregional offices delegated to provide effective education, enforcement, research, and management, although some regional offices play what appear to be only obscure bureaucratic roles.

Sinac provides admission and other information from 7am to 5pm weekdays. For specific parks, call the numbers given in the regional chapters.

Most of the national parks have been created in order to protect the different habitats and wildlife of Costa Rica. A few parks are designed to preserve other valued areas, such as the country's best pre-Columbian ruins at Monumento Nacional Guayabo (p148); an important cave system at Parque Nacional Barra Honda (p247); and a series of geologically active and inactive volcanoes in several parks and reserves.

Most national parks can be entered without permits, though a few parks limit the number they admit on a daily basis and others require advance reservations for accommodations within the park's boundaries (Chirripó,

Red Costarricense de Reservas Naturales Privadas maintains a listing of many private reserves and their activities. See www.costaricareservas.org.

DID YOU KNOW?

The fabulous limestone caves of Parque Nacional Barra Honda were formed in the remains of ancient coral reefs that were subsequently uplifted out of the ocean.

WORLD HERITAGE SITES IN COSTA RICA

Out of Costa Rica's many outstanding natural sites, two have been highlighted for special protection as Unesco World Heritage sites. Parque Nacional Isla del Coco, located 550km off the Pacific coast of Costa Rica, is important as the only island in the eastern Pacific with a tropical rain forest, and it is famous as one of the best places in the world to view large pelagic species such as sharks, rays, tuna and dolphins. Area de Conservación Guanacaste (encompassing four national parks and reserves in the northwest corner of the country) is recognized as the best remaining example of dry forest habitat left in Central America and Mexico, but even more importantly this area protects a complete transect from marine ecosystem to high altitude cloud forest – a biological corridor – where animals can migrate with the seasons.

DID YOU KNOW?

Costa Rica's most famous insect, the morpho butterfly, hides cryptically on bark then, when disturbed, explodes into flight with a glittering flash of blue.

Corcovado, La Amistad). The entrance fee to most parks is US$6 to US$8 per day for foreigners, plus an additional US$2 for overnight camping where it is permitted. Some of the more isolated parks may charge higher rates.

Many national parks are in remote areas and are rarely visited – they also suffer from a lack of rangers and protection. Others are extremely – and deservedly – popular for their world-class scenic and natural beauty, as well as their wildlife. In the idyllic Parque Nacional Manuel Antonio, a tiny park on the Pacific coast, the number of visitors reached 1000 per day in the high season as annual visits rocketed from about 36,000 visitors in 1982 to more than 150,000 by 1991. This number of visitors threatened to ruin the diminutive area by driving away the wildlife, polluting the beaches, and replacing wilderness with hotel development. In response, park visitors have since been limited to 600 people a day, and the park is closed on Mondays to allow it a brief respite from the onslaught.

DID YOU KNOW?

More than 30% of Costa Rica's forests have been cut to raise low-grade beef that goes into American fast-food hamburgers, TV dinners, and pet food.

Costa Rica has a world-famous reputation for the excellence and far-sightedness of its national-park system – but lack of funds, concentrated visitor use, and sometimes fuzzy leadership have shown that there are problems in paradise. A further complication is that the Costa Rican government changes every four years, and this can mean a lack of cohesive, standard-operation plans.

With Costa Rican parks contributing significantly to both national and local economies through the huge influx of tourist monies, there is little question that the country's healthy ecosystems are important to most citizens. In general, national support for land preservation remains high because it provides income and jobs to so many people. An added benefit is that the parks provide important opportunities for scientific investigation. Most adversely affected are agricultural enterprises that rely on the regular clearing of rain forest to open up new plots.

POPULAR PROTECTED AREAS

Popular protected area	Features	Activities	Best time to visit	Page
Parque Nacional Corcovado	vast remote rain forest: giant trees, jaguar, scarlet macaw, tapir	exploring off the beaten path, wildlife watching	anytime, though trails bad in rainy season	p351
Parque Nacional Manuel Antonio	beautiful accessible beaches: mangrove swamp, diverse marine life, eroded rocks	beach walking, exploring	avoid peak season if possible	p303
Parque Nacional Santa Rosa	unique dry forest: guanacaste (Costa Rica's national tree), monkey, peccary, coati	wildlife watching, hiking for spectacular flowering trees	dry season (Jan-Mar)	p193
Parque Nacional Tortuguero	wild Caribbean coast: sea turtle, sloth, manatee, crocodile, river otter	beach walking, canoeing, turtle watching	best during turtle egg-laying season (Feb-Nov)	p392
Reserva Biológica Bosque Nuboso Monteverde	world-famous cloud forest: resplendent quetzal, epiphyte, orchid, three-wattled bellbird	bird-watching, wildlife viewing	avoid peak season if possible	p174
Reserva Natural Absoluta Cabo Blanco	scenic remote beaches, seabirds, marine life, three species of monkey	beach walking, bird-watching	anytime	p269

(Continued on page 49)

Wildlife Guide

David Lukas

Costa Rica has some of the most diverse wildlife in the world, and it's the reason many people travel here. From stunning, colorful birds to fleeting glimpses of rare mammals, it is a land of surprises and enchantment. Included in this guide are a tiny fraction of the common or 'target' species that you could see in Costa Rica. Wildlife enthusiasts are encouraged to bring along one of the many excellent wildlife guides (listed throughout the Environment chapter, p34), for suggestions.

INSECTS

More than 35,000 species of insects have been recorded in Costa Rica, but thousands remain undiscovered. Butterflies and moths are so abundant that Costa Rica claims 10% of the world's butterfly species. Over 3000 species have been recorded in Parque Nacional Santa Rosa alone.

The distinctive **morpho** butterfly (right), with its electric-blue upper wings, lazily flaps and glides along tropical rivers and through openings in the forests across Costa Rica. When it lands, though, the wings close and only the mottled brown underwings become visible, an instantaneous change from outrageous display to modest camouflage.

One dazzling Costa Rican butterfly is the morpho *(Morpho amathonte)*, which has a 15cm wingspan.

PHOTO BY TOM BOYDEN

AMPHIBIANS

The 160 species of amphibians include the tiny and colorful **poison-dart frogs** (right), in the family of Dendrobatidae. Some are bright red with black legs, others are red with blue legs, and still others are bright green with black markings. Several species have skin glands exuding toxins that can cause paralysis and death in many animals, including humans. Dendrobatids, which are widespread in tropical areas, have been used by forest Indians for a poison to dip the tips of their hunting arrows.

The toxins of a poison-dart frog *(Dendrobates auratus)* are potent when introduced into the bloodstream (as with arrows or through a cut), so touching them is not advisable.

PHOTO BY ALFREDO MAIQUEZ

REPTILES

Over half of the 220-plus species of reptiles in Costa Rica are snakes. Though much talked about, snakes are rarely seen. But keep an eye out for the **fer-de-lance** (right) and the **bushmaster**, two deadly poisonous snakes. Both have broadly triangular heads and are widespread at lower elevations. The fer-de-lance, which can be anything from olive to brown or black in color, has a pattern of X's and triangles on its back, while the bushmaster is usually tan-colored with dark diamond-shaped blotches.

Although the notoriety of the fer-de-lance *(Bothrops asper)* is exaggerated, it is fast moving and will readily bite if annoyed.

PHOTO BY TOM BOYDEN

Nicknamed Jesus Christ lizards, basilisk lizards *(Basilisk plumifroms)* can literally run across water when disturbed.
PHOTO BY TOM BOYDEN

Of the country's lizards, the most frequently seen are the abundant **ameiva lizards**, which have a white stripe running down their backs. Also common are bright-green **basilisk lizards** (left), noted for the huge crests running the length of their heads, bodies and tails, which gives them the appearance of small dinosaurs almost a meter in length. They are common along watercourses in lowland areas. Also seen in the same areas is the stocky **green iguana**, which is regularly seen draping its 2m-long body across a branch over water.

The long forked tail of the magnificent frigatebird *(Fregata magnificens)* gives it the nickname *tijerata* or 'scissor tail.'
PHOTO BY RALPH LEE HOPKINS

BIRDS

The wealth of Costa Rica's world-famous avifauna is one of the top reasons visitors choose to travel here. The country hosts more bird species (approximately 850) than do huge areas such as Europe, North America or Australia. The sheer numbers and variety is somewhat baffling and overwhelming, and in patches of healthy rain forest, the din of countless birds all calling at once will leave a lasting impression on even the most hardened travelers.

In addition to diverse forest birds, Costa Rica also hosts a spectacular assortment of seabirds, including the **magnificent frigatebird** (middle). This distinctive black bird, with an inflatable red throat pouch, is large, elegant and streamlined. It makes an acrobatic living by aerial piracy, often harassing smaller birds into dropping or regurgitating their catch and then swooping to catch their stolen meal in midair. Frigatebirds are found along both coasts but are more common along the Pacific.

The **brown pelican** is unmistakable with its large size and huge pouched bill. Pelicans are often seen in squadron-like formation, flapping and gliding in unison. They are found on both coasts but are more common on the Pacific. A pelican feeds by shallow plunge-diving and scooping up fish and water in its distensible pouch, then draining the water through the bill.

Larger species of herons include the **boat-billed heron**, a stocky, mostly gray bird with a black cap and crest and distinctively large and wide bill. The **yellow-crowned night-heron** (photo opposite p385) is quite common in coastal areas and has an unmistakable black-and-white head with a yellow crown. Despite its name, it's mainly active by day.

The roseate spoonbill *(Ajaia ajaja)* is the only large pink bird in Costa Rica.
PHOTO BY LUKE HUNTER

The descriptively named **roseate spoonbill** (left) is most often seen in the Palo Verde (p184) and Caño Negro (p435) areas. It has a white head and a distinctive spoon-shaped bill. Unlike most birds, which feed by sight, spoonbills, ibises and many storks feed by touch. The spoonbill swings its open bill back and forth,

Left to right:

Scarlet macaw *(Ara macao)* pairs mate for life (as is generally true of all parrots).

PHOTO BY TOM BOYDEN

The violet sabrewing *(Campylopterus hemileucurus)* is often seen in Monteverde reserve.

PHOTO BY TOM BOYDEN

submerged underwater, while stirring up the bottom with its feet, until it feels a small fish, frog or crustacean and then snaps the bill shut.

Vultures are often seen hovering ominously in the sky, searching for carrion. The largest vulture in Costa Rica is the **king vulture**, which is easily identified by its off-white body and legs, black primary wing feathers and tail, and a wattled head colored black with various shades of orange-yellow. It's most frequently seen in Corcovado, though it lives almost countrywide in small numbers.

A favorite waterbird for many visitors is the **northern jacana**, which has extremely long, thin toes that enable it to walk on top of aquatic plants, earning it the nickname 'lily-trotter.' It is common on many lowland lakes and waterways. At first glance its brown body, black head, yellow bill and frontal shield seem rather nondescript, but when disturbed the bird stretches its wings to reveal startling yellow flight feathers.

Of the 16 species of parrots recorded in Costa Rica, none are as spectacular as the **scarlet macaw** (above left) – unmistakable for its size (84cm long), bright red body, blue-and-yellow wings, long red tail and white face. Macaws are often seen flying overhead, in pairs or small flocks, calling raucously to one another. Recorded as common in 1900, they have suffered devastating reductions in numbers due to deforestation and poaching for the pet trade. Now it is rare to see these birds outside of Carara (p278) and Corcovado (p351).

Over 50 species of hummingbirds have been recorded and their delicate beauty is matched only by their extravagant names. Largest is the **violet sabrewing** (above right), which has a striking violet head and body, with dark green wings. It is found in mid-elevations. Upwards of 20 species have been seen at local feeders, including such jewels as the **purple-throated mountain-gem** and **crowned woodnymph**.

The most famous of Costa Rica's 10 species of trogons is undoubtedly the **resplendent quetzal** (pronounced 'ket-SAL'; right), easily the most dazzling and culturally important bird of Central America. It had

The male quetzal *(Pharomachrus mocinno)* tries to impress the duller-colored female by almost vertical display flights during which the long tail coverts flutter sensuously.

PHOTO BY RALPH LEE HOPKINS

Left to right:

If you don't see a keel-billed toucan *(Ramphastos sulfuratus)* in the wild, you're sure to see plenty on posters, T-shirts and signs.

PHOTO BY TOM BOYDEN

Small flocks of collared aracaris *(Pteroglossus torquatus)* are common in forests.

PHOTO BY TOM BOYDEN

great ceremonial significance to the Aztecs and the Mayas and is now the national bird and symbol of Guatemala. It is extremely difficult to keep in captivity, where it usually dies quickly, which is perhaps why it became a symbol of liberty to Central Americans during the colonial period. The male lives up to its name with glittering green plumage set off by a crimson belly, and white tail feathers contrasting with bright-green tail coverts that stream over 60cm beyond the bird's body. The head feathers stick out in a spiky green helmet through which the yellow bill peeks coyly. A glimpse of this bird is the highlight of many birders' trip. The quetzal is fairly common from 1300m to 3000m in forested or partially forested areas. Locals usually know where to find one; good places to look are in Monteverde reserve (p174) and the Cerro de la Muerte area (p320). The March to June breeding season is the easiest time to see the birds. At other times they are less active and quite wary, as are all the trogons.

Toucans are classic rain forest birds and six species are found in lowland forests throughout Costa Rica. Huge bills and flamboyant plumage make species such as the **chestnut-mandibled toucan** and **keel-billed toucan** (top left) hard to miss. The chestnut-mandibled toucan is mainly black with a yellow face and chest and red under the tail, and has a bicolored bill – yellow above and chestnut below. The keel-billed toucan is similarly plumaged but the bill is multicolored. But with toucans, even smaller species such as the **collared aracari** (top right) are notable.

About half of Costa Rica's birds are passerines, a sprawling category that includes warblers, sparrows, finches and many other types of birds. Nearly limited to the tropics, however, are tanagers and cotingas. One of the country's most common birds is the **blue-gray tanager** (below), a resident of open, humid areas up to 2300m. The male **scarlet-rumped tanager** is jet black with a bright-scarlet rump and lower back, a flashy and unmistakable combination.

The male **red-headed barbet** is striking with its bright red head and chest, yellow bill, green back, and yellow belly. It forages in trees at mid-elevations. The **white-fronted nunbird** is an upright-perching black bird of the Caribbean lowlands. It's immediately identified by its red bill with white feathers at the base.

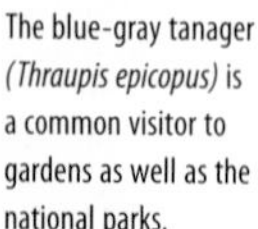

The blue-gray tanager *(Thraupis epicopus)* is a common visitor to gardens as well as the national parks.

PHOTO BY RALPH LEE HOPKINS

Cotingas are even more dramatic and include two species that are pure white and two that are a sparkling blue color. One of the strangest cotingas is the **three-wattled bellbird**, a highlight for visitors to Monteverde reserve because of their penetrating metallic *bonk!* and eerie whistling calls (not to mention the male's odd appearance).

MARINE ANIMALS

Long famous are the giant sea turtles of Costa Rica, impetus for the establishment of Tortuguero and several other coastal national parks. With a shell up to 1.6m long, the massive 360kg **leatherback turtle** (right) is a stunning creature. The smaller **olive ridleys** are legendary for their remarkable synchronized nesting, when tens of thousands of females emerge from the sea on the same night. All sea turtles are highly endangered and the conservation efforts on their behalf are some of the most important projects in Costa Rica.

The annual nocturnal pilgrimages of sea turtles, including the leatherback *(Dermochelys coriacea)*, to lay eggs on secluded beaches rank as one of Costa Rica's foremost wildlife spectacles.

PHOTO BY TIM ROCK

Sightings of pods of more than 1000 dolphins at a time are not uncommon. The spotted dolphin *(Stenella attenuatal)* is featured here.

PHOTO BY RALPH LEE HOPKINS

In a few of the rivers, estuaries and coastal areas (especially around Tortuguero) you may glimpse the endangered **West Indian manatee**, a large marine mammal (up to 4m long and weighing 600kg, though usually smaller), which feeds on aquatic vegetation. There are no seals or sea lions in Costa Rica, so a manatee is easy to recognize.

Because Costa Rica has one of the most biologically diverse marine ecosystems in the world, there is an astounding variety of marine mammals found here. Migrating whales arrive from both the Northern and Southern Hemispheres. The deepwater upwellings that make these waters so productive are constant year-round, creating ideal viewing conditions at any season. **Humpback whales** may be seen almost every month – perhaps the only place in the world where this is possible – while the **common dolphin**, **bottle-nosed dolphin** and **spotted dolphin** (middle) are year-round residents. Seeing over a dozen other species of dolphins and whales is possible, including **orca**, **blue** and **sperm whales**, and several species of poorly known **beaked whales**. All of these animals are best seen on guided boat tours along both coasts.

LAND MAMMALS

Five species of sloths are found in the neotropics, and the two species widespread in Costa Rica are the **brown-throated three-toed sloth** (see p7) and **Hoffman's two-toed sloth** (right). The diurnal three-toed sloth is often sighted, whereas the nocturnal two-toed sloth is less often seen. Both are 50cm to 75cm in length with stumpy tails. Sloths hang motionless from branches or slowly progress upside down along a branch toward leaves, which are their primary food.

Sloths, including Hoffman's two-toed sloth *(Choloepus didactylus)*, are related to anteaters, though they have a few rudimentary teeth.

PHOTO BY JOHN HAY

Anteaters lack teeth and use a long, sticky tongue to slurp up ants

Building up the number of spider monkeys *(Ateles geoffroyi)* is slow because reproductive rates are low, and females only give birth once every two to four years.

PHOTO BY RALPH LEE HOPKINS

Howler monkeys *(Alouatta pigra)* maintain their territorial boundaries by the male's defiant calls.

PHOTO BY LUKE HUNTER

and termites. There are three species of anteaters in Costa Rica including the **giant anteater**, which reaches almost 2m in length and has an amazing tongue that protrudes an astonishing 60cm up to 150 times a minute!

Two species of armadillo inhabit Costa Rica. The best known is the **nine-banded armadillo**. Despite its name, there can be from seven to 10 bands. These armadillos grow up to 1m long, of which about one-third is tail. Mainly nocturnal, they have a diet of mainly insects, and some fruit, fungi and carrion.

Costa Rica has four monkey species, all members of the family Cebidae. These are the tropical mammals most likely to be seen and enjoyed by travelers, and in some places you can see all four at the same location. The **Central American spider monkey** (top) is named for its long and thin legs, arms and tail, which enables it to pursue an arboreal existence in forests throughout Costa Rica. Spider monkeys swing from arm to arm through the canopy and can hang supported just by their prehensile tail while using their long limbs to pick fruit. They rarely descend to the ground, and require large tracts of unbroken forest. Logging, hunting (their flesh is eaten) and other disturbances have made them endangered.

The loud vocalizations of a male **mantled howler monkey** (middle) an carry for over 1km even in dense rain forest. Variously described as grunting, roaring or howling, this crescendo of noise is one of the most characteristic and memorable of all rain forest sounds. Inhabiting wet lowland forests, howlers live in small groups. These stocky blackish monkeys with coiled prehensile tails reside high in the canopy so they can be hard to spot.

The small and inquisitive white-faced **capuchin** (below) is the easiest to observe in the wild. Unlike the squirrel monkey, it has a prehensile

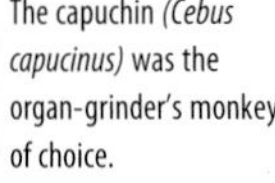

The capuchin *(Cebus capucinus)* was the organ-grinder's monkey of choice.

PHOTO BY RALPH LEE HOPKINS

Left to right:

Although they feed on the ground, white-nosed coatis *(Nasua narica)* are agile climbers and sleep and copulate in trees.

PHOTO BY LUKE HUNTER

Kinkajous *(Potos flavus)*, often called honey bears, have tails that can support them as they hang from a branch.

PHOTO BY TOM BOYDEN

tail that is typically carried with the tip coiled. Capuchins occasionally descend to the ground where foods such as corn and even oysters are part of their diet. Their meticulous foraging and prying into leaves, litter and bark makes them enjoyable to watch.

The diminutive **Central American squirrel monkey** (photo opposite p177) persists only in isolated areas of the south Pacific coastal rain forests, including Manuel Antonio and Corcovado national parks, where it travels in small to medium-size groups during the day, squealing or chirping noisily and leaping and crashing through vegetation in search of insects and fruit in the middle and lower levels of lowland forests.

The **white-nosed coati** (above left) is the most frequently seen member of the raccoon family. It is brownish and longer, but slimmer and lighter, than a raccoon. Its most distinctive features are a long, mobile, upturned whitish snout with which it snuffles around on the forest floor looking for insects, fruit and small animals; and a long, faintly ringed tail held straight up in the air when foraging. Coatis are found countrywide in all types of forest up to 3000m.

Lacking the facial markings and ringed tail of its cousins, the cuddly **kinkajou** (above right) is a raccoon relative found in lowland forests. It is an attractive reddish-brown color and is hunted both for food and the pet trade. Nocturnal and mainly arboreal, it jumps from tree to tree searching for fruits (especially figs), which comprise most of its diet.

The **southern river otter** (below right) lives in and by fast-moving lowland rivers, but is infrequently seen. It is a rich brown color with whitish undersides and has the streamlined shape of an aquatic weasel. The similarly shaped **tayra** is more easily spotted; it is blackish brown, with a tan head, and is territorial and arboreal. It is over 1m long (the tail is about 40cm) and is found in forests up to 2000m.

Distinctive for its color is the large weasel called the **grison**. Its body, tail and the crown of its head are light gray and the legs, chest and lower face are black. A white band across the forehead, ears and sides of the neck gives the head a black/white/gray tricolor. The tail is shorter than that of most weasels. It is found in the lowland rain forests but is uncommon.

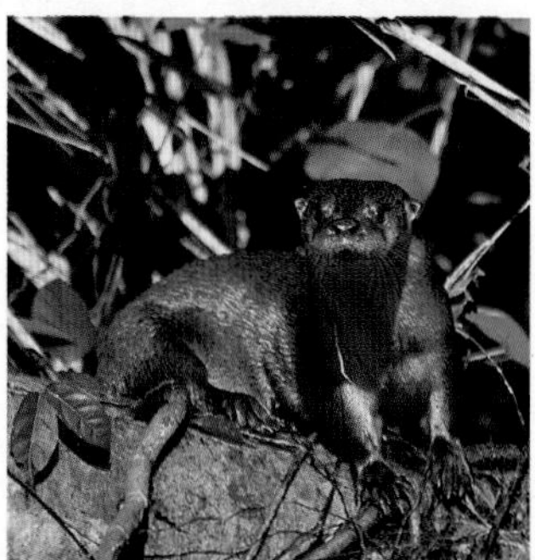

The play sessions of the river otter *(Lutra longicaudis)* are a delight to the viewer.

PHOTO BY LUKE HUNTER

Jaguars *(Panthera onca)* are the largest Central American carnivore (males occasionally reach more than 150kg).
PHOTO BY TOM BOYDEN

It is every wildlife-watcher's dream to see a **jaguar** (above) in the wild. However, these big cats are extremely rare and well camouflaged, so the chance of seeing one is remote. Jaguars have large territories and you may see their prints or droppings in large lowland parks with extensive forest such as Corcovado. Occasionally you may hear them roaring – a sound more like a series of deep coughs. There's no mistaking this 2m-long yellow cat with black spots in rosettes and a whitish belly. Good luck seeing one.

Other Costa Rican felids include the spotted **ocelot**, a little more than 1m in length with a short tail. Though it is the most common of the Costa Rican cats, it is shy and rarely seen. It adapts well to a variety of terrain, wet and dry, forested and open, and has been recorded in most of the larger national parks.

Known as javelinas in the USA, the widespread **collared peccary** (middle) lives in a wide variety of habitats. An adult is about 80cm long, weighs around 20kg, and has coarse gray hair with a light collar. The larger **white-lipped peccary** is darker and lacks the collar but has a whitish area on the lower chin. Peccaries are noisy and rather aggressive with audible tooth gnashing and clicking – rather frightening if you hear 300 animals at once!

Corcovado rangers warn visitors to be prepared to climb a tree if they are charged by a herd of collared peccaries *(Dicotyles tajacu)*, though this rarely happens.
PHOTO BY LUKE HUNTER

Some large rodents are among the most commonly seen rain-forest mammals, including the **Central American agouti** and the **paca** (left). The agouti is diurnal and terrestrial and found in forests up to 2000m. It looks like an oversize cross between a rabbit and a squirrel, with a very small tail and short ears. The closely related paca looks similar, except it has white stripy marks on its sides and is twice the size of an agouti. It is common but nocturnal.

The paca *(Agouti paca)* can remain underwater for some minutes, a behavior that has helped them survive hunting.
PHOTO BY TOM BOYDEN

(Continued from page 40)

ENVIRONMENTAL ISSUES

Despite Costa Rica's national-park system, the major problem facing the nation's environment is deforestation. Costa Rica's natural vegetation was originally almost all forest, but most of this has been cleared, mainly for pasture or agriculture. It is estimated that only 5% of the lands outside of parks and reserves remains forested, while only 1% of the dry forests of northwestern Costa Rica are left.

Few organizations are as involved in building sustainable rain forest–based economies as the Rainforest Alliance. See their website for special initiatives in Costa Rica: www.rainforest-alliance.org.

The World Resources Institute recently calculated that Costa Rican forests were still being cleared at the rate of almost 4% a year, making it one of the world's most rapidly disappearing forests. Tree plantations are being developed, however, and the availability of commercially grown timber (hopefully) means there may be less pressure to log the natural forests. Nevertheless, deforestation continues at a high rate and even within national parks some of the more remote areas have been logged illegally because there is not enough money to hire guards to enforce the law.

Apart from the direct loss of tropical forests and the plants and animals that depend on them, deforestation has led directly or indirectly to other severe environmental problems. The first and greatest issue is soil erosion. Forests protect the soil beneath them from the ravages of tropical rainstorms, and after deforestation much of the topsoil is washed away, lowering the productivity of the land and silting up watersheds. Some deforested lands are planted with Costa Rica's main agricultural product, bananas, the production of which entails the use of pesticides and blue plastic bags to protect the fruit. Both the pesticides and the plastic bags end up polluting the environment (see the boxed text, p440, for information on how this has affected humans as well).

Deforestation and related logging activities also create inroads into formerly inaccessible regions, leading to an influx of humans. One

TRAVELING RESPONSIBLY

The impact you have on other people's as well as your own experience while traveling are both functions of being responsible and having respect for another country's environment. Common sense and awareness are your best guides, but other considerations include:

- **Shopping Responsibly** Avoid purchasing animal products, no matter how cute. Despite the assurances of the salesperson, there is virtually no way to guarantee that they were collected in an ecologically sensible or legal manner. This includes turtle shells, feathers, skins, skulls, coral, shells, and almost anything made of wood.
- **Waste Disposal** Don't litter. Patronize hotels that have recycling programs. Travel with tour operators who provide and use waste receptacles aboard buses and boats and who dispose of trash properly. Carry out anything you take onto trails or into parks, because most parks are too underfunded and understaffed to collect trash regularly.
- **Wildlife** Don't disturb animals or damage plants. Stay on trails. Observe wildlife from a distance with binoculars. Follow the instructions of trained naturalist guides, and don't request that guides disturb animals so you can have a better look.
- **Education** Learn about wildlife and local conservation, environmental, and cultural issues before your trip and during your visit. Ask questions and listen to what locals have to say.
- **Sustainability** Avoid conservation areas saturated by travelers unless you absolutely need to. Support tourism companies and environmental groups that promote conservation initiatives and long-term management plans.

THE PRICE OF ECOTOURISM

Costa Rica has so much to offer the wildlife enthusiast that it is no small wonder that ecotourism is growing in the country. More than 70% of foreign travelers visit one or more nature destinations, and half of these visitors come specifically to see Costa Rica's wildlife.

Such has been its popularity that, from the late 1980s to the mid-1990s, the annual number of visitors has doubled, and now almost a million foreign tourists visit every year. Tourism revenues recently surpassed those of the banana and coffee industries, and prices for the traveler have risen in tandem. At first, the growth in tourism took the nation by surprise – there was no overall development plan and growth was poorly controlled. Some people wanted to cash in on the short term with little thought for the future. Unfortunately, this attitude has changed little even as pressure has grown to regulate the industry more closely.

Traditionally, tourism in Costa Rica has been on a small and intimate scale. The great majority of the country's hotels are small (fewer than 50 rooms), staffed with friendly local people that work closely with tourists, to the benefit of both. This intimacy and friendliness has been a hallmark of a visit to Costa Rica, but this is changing.

The financial bonanza generated by the tourism boom means that new operations are starting up all the time – many are good, some are not. The big word in Costa Rica is 'ecotourism' and everyone wants to jump on the green bandwagon. There are 'ecological' car-rental agencies and 'ecological' menus in restaurants. People want tourists, they want the money that tourists carry, but unfortunately there's little infrastructure to take care that these very tourists don't wreck the environment or have a role in despoiling any more wilderness.

Taking advantage of Costa Rica's 'green' image, some developers are promoting mass tourism and are building large hotels with accompanying environmental problems (for more on this see the boxed text on p261, and the Papagayo Project on p228). Apart from the immediate impacts, such as cutting down vegetation, diverting or damming rivers, and driving away

consequence, especially in national parks where wildlife is concentrated, is unrestrained poaching. This problem has become so serious in Parque Nacional Corcovado that there's been recent discussion about temporarily closing the park so that guards can take a stand against the poachers.

The world-famous Organization for Tropical Studies runs three field stations and offers numerous classes for students seriously interested in tropical ecology. See www.ots.ac.cr.

The other great environmental issue facing Costa Rica comes from the country being loved to death, directly through the passage of one million foreign tourists every year, and indirectly through the development of extensive infrastructure to support this influx (see the boxed text above). Every year, more resort hotels and lodges pop up, most notably on formerly pristine beaches or in the middle of intact rain forest. These necessitate additional support systems, including roads and countless vehicle trips, and much of this activity appears to be unregulated and largely unmonitored. For instance, there is growing concern that many hotels and lodges are simply dumping wastewater into the ocean or nearby creeks rather than following expensive procedures for treating it. With an official estimate that only 4% of the country's wastewater is treated and with thousands of unregulated hotels in operation there's a good bet that even some of the fanciest 'ecolodges' aren't taking care of their wastes.

Other times, lodges keep wild animals under the guise that they are running a rescue center. This, undoubtedly, serves as a draw for tourists who are enchanted with many a hotel operator's claim that they are 'saving' these animals from grave dangers. Unfortunately, this has created a black market for supplying wildlife that is already under threat. Permits from Minae are required to keep wild animals, and visitors can ask hotel operators to see this paperwork (many will claim to have it but will likely be unable to actually produce it).

wildlife, there are secondary impacts such as erosion, lack of adequate waste-treatment facilities for huge hotels in areas away from sewage lines, and the building of socially, environmentally, and economically inadequate 'shanty towns' to house the maids, waiters, cooks, janitors, and many other employees needed.

Another problem is that many developers are foreigners – they say that they are giving the local people jobs, but locals don't want to spend their lives being waiters and maids while watching the big money go out of the country. We recommend staying in smaller hotels that have a positive attitude about the environment and are more beneficial to the locals, rather than the large, foreign-owned mass-tourism destinations.

Amidst all this, the government tourist board (ICT; Instituto Costarricense de Turismo) has launched mass-marketing campaigns all over the world, touting 'Costa Rica: No Artificial Ingredients,' yet hasn't followed up with the kind of infrastructure necessary to preserve those ingredients (nor does it lobby for them). Many people feel a certain degree of frustration with the ICT for selling Costa Rica as a green paradise but doing little to help preserve it. For example, the organization recently spent millions of dollars to host a massive Pavarotti concert at a time when the yearly annual budget for Parque Nacional Tortuguero is a few thousand dollars.

The big question is whether future tourism developments should continue to focus on the traditional small-hotel, ecotourism approach, or turn to mass tourism, with planeloads of visitors accommodated in 'megaresorts' such as the ones in Cancún, Mexico. From the top levels of government on down, the debate has been fierce. Local and international tour operators and travel agents, journalists, developers, airline operators, hotel owners, writers, environmentalists, and politicians have all been vocal in their support of either ecotourism or mass tourism. Many believe that the country is too small to handle both forms of tourism properly. It remains to be seen which faction will win out – or if both can co-exist peacefully together.

It is worth noting, however, that many private lodges and reserves are also doing some of the best conservation work in the country, and it's incredibly inspiring to run across homespun efforts to protect Costa Rica's environment spearheaded by hardworking families or small organizations tucked away in some forgotten corner of the country. These include projects to boost rural economies by raising butterflies or native flowers, efforts by villagers to document their local biodiversity, or amazingly resourceful campaigns to raise funds to purchase endangered lands. The Refugio Nacional de Vida Silvestre Curú (p260), Tiskita Lodge (p375) and Rara Avis (p446) are but a few examples. Costa Rica is full of wonderful tales about folks who are extremely passionate and generous in their efforts to protect the planet's resources.

Adventure Travel

If you want it, Costa Rica's got it. The extraordinary array of national parks, reserves and other scenery provides an incredible stage for the adventure traveler in search of everything from mountain-biking excursions to multiday jungle treks to running some of the best white water in Central America. Seafaring types will appreciate the good surfing and diving opportunities that abound on both of Costa Rica's coasts.

The Big Book of Adventure Travel, by James C Simmons, is a worthwhile investment for anyone interested in the subject; it covers the entire planet, but numerous itineraries in Costa Rica are featured.

While Costa Rica is the place for a good adrenaline rush, travelers should be aware that there is a small but ever-present risk of injury or death in any adventure-tourism activity. Numerous tourism-related deaths in the early '00s led the government to pass sweeping laws in an attempt to regulate the industry. In 2003 Costa Rica became the first country in Latin America to pass a universal set of safety standards to which all adventure-tour operators need comply. Unfortunately, compliance is dependent on enforcement, which in Costa Rica always tends to be weak. The good will is there, but the money for checking up isn't.

By and large, most of these activities are safe, but be careful and choose adventure-tour operators who come well recommended and have a good safety track record. Do your homework and then enjoy!

HIKING & TREKKING

There is no shortage of hiking opportunities around Costa Rica, from day hikes in the countless private reserves to more extended trips in some of the national parks.

A reward for walking to Naranjo beach is the famous surf at Peña Bruja – Witch's Rock.

Especially notable for day hikes are the fumaroles and tropical dry forest in Parque Nacional Rincón de la Vieja (p190), the sloth-spotting and pretty beaches of Parque Nacional Cahuita (p408) and the cloud forest reserves of Santa Elena (p177) and Monteverde (p174).

For those who want multiday adventures, the (minimum) two-day hike through Parque Nacional Corcovado (p351) is nothing less than incredible. This last remaining stand of coastal Pacific rain forest is packed with macaws, monkeys and peccaries and offers totally rugged adventure. (This hike is recommended for people in very good physical condition.)

Historic Parque Nacional Santa Rosa (p193) offers opportunities to hike and camp in tropical dry forest. Easily accessible from the Interamericana, travelers here may spot peccaries, coatis and tapirs concentrated at watering holes during the dry season. Longer trips can be made through the park and to the pristine beaches of Nancite and Naranjo.

Mountaineers will enjoy the ruddy (and steep and arduous) hike through the *páramo* (highland shrub forests and grasslands) up Cerro Chirripó (p326) – the highest mountain in Costa Rica. And for the trekker

TO TAKE OR NOT TO TAKE HIKING BOOTS

With its ample supply of mud, streams and army ants, hiking through Costa Rica's parks can be quite an adventure – particularly for your shoes. The jungles have claimed many pairs of US$200 hiking boots. So do as the locals and invest in galoshes (rubber boots), especially for the rainy season. (If you're larger than a size 44 – men's 10 in the USA – consider buying them abroad.) A good pair will cost you about US$6 at any Costa Rican shoe or farm-supply store. Rubber boots are indestructible, protect you from snakes and ticks, provide excellent traction and can be easily hosed off at the end of the day. And of course there's the US$194 saving.

that appreciates complete solitude in absolute wilderness, there's Parque Internacional La Amistad (p337). This heavily forested and rarely traversed park offers some of the most breathtaking scenery in the country.

Many local companies offer guided hikes in different parts of Costa Rica (see p474). For general advice on hiking and trekking, see p450.

Trail Source (www.trailsource.com) provides information on hiking in Costa Rica. It also has info on horse riding and mountain biking. A monthly fee applies.

MOUNTAIN BIKING

Some cyclists claim that the steep, narrow, winding and potholed roads and aggressive Costa Rican drivers add up to a generally poor cycling experience. This may be true of the main roads, but there are numerous less-trafficked roads that offer plenty of adventure – from winding and scenic mountain paths with sweeping views to rugged trails that take riders through streams and by volcanoes.

Local outfitters can organize trips. Aventuras Naturales (p474) has one- and two-day bike tours. Costa Rica Expeditions (p474) organizes multisport trips that include cycling, rafting and kayaking. These tours provide bikes as part of the deal.

Tour companies from the USA also arrange guided cycling trips, which usually combine highland and beach riding. Serendipity Adventures and Backroads (p474) both offer multiday biking adventures. You must bring all your own gear (including your bike); because of the poor condition of the roads, it's mountain bikes only.

DID YOU KNOW?

Michael Crichton's book *Jurassic Park* is set in Costa Rica. In it, he refers to Ticos as 'Ticans.'

DIVING

There's good news...and there's bad news. The good news is that Costa Rica offers body-temperature water with few humans and abundant marine life. The bad news is that the visibility is low because of silt and plankton. If you are looking for turquoise waters and plenty of hard coral, head for Belize. However, if you're looking for fine opportunities to see massive schools of fish as well as larger marine animals such as turtles, sharks, dolphins and whales, then you have arrived.

Some of the best areas for diving are off the northern part of the Península de Nicoya at Playas del Coco, Ocotal and Hermosa (p225), where you can expect to see manta rays, sharks and dozens of species of fish, all in large numbers. Dive shops in the area provide gear, boats and guides, and offer courses.

Another top dive center is in the waters off Bahía Drake (p346). Several of the hotels organize excursions to Isla del Caño (p351) and other sites offering the opportunity to put yourself in the path of giant schools of barracuda, grouper, manta ray, Moorish idol and puffer fish.

The mack daddy of dive sites is Isla del Coco (p354), 500km to the southwest of the Costa Rican mainland. There you can expect to find 18 species of coral reef, 57 types of crustacean, three species of dolphin and innumerable other types of marine life. It's a 36-hour ocean journey to get there and it's for intermediate and advanced divers only. In addition, the island does not allow camping and does not provide accommodations, so you'll be spending a lot of quality time on your boat.

For practical information see p449. Tour companies appear on p474.

RAFTING & KAYAKING

Rivers tumbling from the central mountains down to the coast afford fantastic white-water rafting opportunities. The wildest months are from June through October though rafting can be done year-round. More leisurely kayaking, either on rivers or the sea, is also available, with the backdrop of rain forests, viewing wildlife and listening to the sound of

The Rivers of Costa Rica, a kayaking and rafting guide by Michael W Mayfield, is just the ticket for river runners.

WATER SPORTS *Bridget Crocker*

River Rafting & Kayaking

A paddler's paradise, white-water boaters the globe over flock to Costa Rica's incredible world-renowned rivers. From Class II to Class V, magical white-water experiences for both families and seasoned river enthusiasts are easily accessible. Since the mid-1980s, white-water rafting and kayaking have been major contributors to the country's ecotourism-based economy, and Costa Rica has become one of the most developed paddling centers in Latin America. Many local tour operators offer half-day to multiday river excursions, providing bus transportation to and from the river, state-of-the-art equipment (rafts, kayaks, helmets, paddles), bilingual guides, lodging and food, all starting at around US$65 per person. Several outfitters offer river-kayaking rentals and tours, and many boaters choose to run multiple rivers as part of a package deal (see the Rafting Safari itinerary, p17).

Thousands of travelers go river running in Costa Rica each year, and the vast majority enjoy a memorable, safe trip. However, wild rivers are powerful and uncontrollable by nature, and white-water river running is a risky and potentially dangerous undertaking. River-running companies are not bound by safety regulations in Costa Rica so be sure to choose an outfitter with bilingual guides certified in swift-water rescue and emergency medical training. Of the companies in San José/Turrialba, Ríos Tropicales, Costa Rica Expeditions and Aventuras Naturales (p475) are well established and provide the most training for their guides. In the Manuel Antonio area (p475), H2O Adventures and Amigo Tico Complete Adventure Tours employ well-trained local guides and also work with international guides who often bring knowledge of the latest developments in river-rescue and first-aid practices used elsewhere in the world.

The country's most popular rivers are the Pacuare and Reventazón, both located on the Caribbean side near the town of Turrialba (p144). Home to toucans, herons, monkeys and sloths, the Río Pacuare is often flooded during the rainy season (June to October) due to erosion from rampant deforestation upstream, and is best run during the dry season (November to early April). Considered one of the world's top 10 white-water runs, the Pacuare is currently threatened by a hydroelectric project (see p150), which, if implemented, would greatly diminish ecotourism in the area and impact on lands vital to the Cabecar and Awari indigenous groups.

The Río Reventazón Class V Peralta section was destroyed by a hydroelectric dam built in the late 1990s for energy to export to neighboring countries. The remaining white water and fragile wilderness of these two extraordinary rivers desperately need protection from future hydroelectric projects. Contact **Fundación Ríos Tropicales** (www.riostropicales.com) for more information.

Several rivers near the thriving tourist mecca of Manuel Antonio (p300) on the central Pacific coast offer great white water and wildlife viewing year-round. The Río Naranjo boasts an experts-only Class V upper section known as the Labyrinth (depending on flows, which is best run from

birdlife the main attractions. For more details on these activities see the boxed text above.

SURFING

Surfers should pick up a copy of Mike Parise's *Surfer's Guide to Costa Rica* and log on to the *Costa Rica Surf Report* (www.crsurf.com) for everything you need to know before your trip.

Point and beach breaks, lefts and rights, reefs and river mouths, warm water and year-round waves make Costa Rica a favorite surfing destination. Greg Gordon of *Costa Rica Surf Report* says that the country has a lot to offer – inexpensive hotels and a wide variety of breaks, with most of them in decent range of a local clinic (in case you get hurt). Some beaches may be difficult to get to but are uncrowded, and even the accessible ones tend to be much more sparsely populated than the beaches of California or Sydney. See the surfer's map on p56 for an idea of what's around.

Waves are big (though not Hawaii-big) and the many reef breaks offer hollow and fast rides. And basically there is a wave, somewhere, waiting to be surfed at any time of the year. For the most part, the Pacific coast has

December to early March), with the more forgiving Class III-IV Villa Nueva section downstream. The neighboring Class III-IV+ Río Savegre, plunging from its source near 3820m Cerro Chirripó in the Cordillera de Talamanca, offers continuous, world-class white water, and is touted as one of the cleanest rivers in Central America. A family favorite, the nearby Class II+ Río Parrita has excellent bird-watching and frequent wildlife sightings in a luscious, tropical-wilderness setting.

Near San Isidro de El General, the free-flowing Río General is long enough for a three- to four-day excursion. Dropping 9.5m/km with flows up to 283-cubic-meters/second, the General dishes up more than 100 Class III-IV rapids in the first 64km alone. Beautiful waterfalls cascade into the river and tropical birds, monkeys and iguanas (along with leishmaniasis-carrying sand fleas) frequent the shores. The lower section of the General is known for its great kayak-surfing rapids.

Details on river trips and outfitters are given in the regional chapters of this book.

Sea Kayaking

With 1228km of coastline, two gulfs and plentiful mangrove estuaries, Costa Rica is an ideal destination for sea kayaking. Several outfitters offer guided coastal or estuary tours with trained bilingual naturalists, as well as renting out equipment for self-guided excursions. Sea kayaking is a great way for beginning or expert paddlers to comfortably access remote areas and catch rare glimpses of birds and wildlife.

On the Pacific side, the Península de Nicoya's Refugio Nacional de Vida Silvestre Curú (p260) offers stunning paddling along palm-lined beaches, rock arch formations and estuaries teeming with birds and colorful crabs. Outfitter Ríos Tropicales' private camp at Playa Quesera (about 3km across the bay from the registration building at Curú) is the ideal spot for post-paddling stargazing and relaxing.

On the central Pacific coast, Isla Damas (p283) and the nearby Parque Nacional Manuel Antonio (p303) are equally as riveting. The delicate mangrove ecosystem of Isla Damas is home to a wealth of wildlife including boa constrictors, white-faced monkeys, crocodiles and shore birds best described by the naturalist guides of Amigo Tico Complete Adventure Tours (p475). Following the tide out to the Pacific Ocean, it's not far to Parque Nacional Manuel Antonio and the nearby tiny Islas Gemelas and Olinga, where nesting shore birds may be spotted. You can rent kayaks or sign up for a guided tour with H20 Adventures (p475).

Heading over to the Caribbean side, Parque Nacional Tortuguero (p392), a 192-sq-km coastal park, is well known for its amazing biodiversity and is the Caribbean's most important breeding ground for the green sea turtle. Paddling the network of lagoons and canals provides unlimited opportunities for solitude and wildlife sightings (monkeys, sloths, anteaters, kinkajous, peccaries, tapirs and manatees).

bigger swells and better waves during the latter part of the rainy season, but the Caribbean gets cooking from November to May.

Gordon, who has been surfing in Costa Rica since the mid-90s, says that the top five surf destinations in the country are:

Playa Hermosa (p289) Very consistent.
Playa Grande (p233) Likewise.
Pavones (p374) A long left hand.
Witches Rock/Ollie's Point (p194) Legendary.
Salsa Brava (p413) Not for beginners.

Other popular spots include Dominical (p307) and the breaks at Playas Negra (p241), Avellana (p241) and Junquillal (p242). The powerful waves at Santa Teresa (p267) attract a steady following as well. Near Pavones, on the Península de Osa, you'll find good and steady waves at the beaches of Matapalo (p360).

DID YOU KNOW?

The surf destination known as Ollie's Point is named after US Colonel Oliver North. Situated near the break is an old airstrip that was used by US airplanes to smuggle goods to the Nicaraguan Contras in the 1980s.

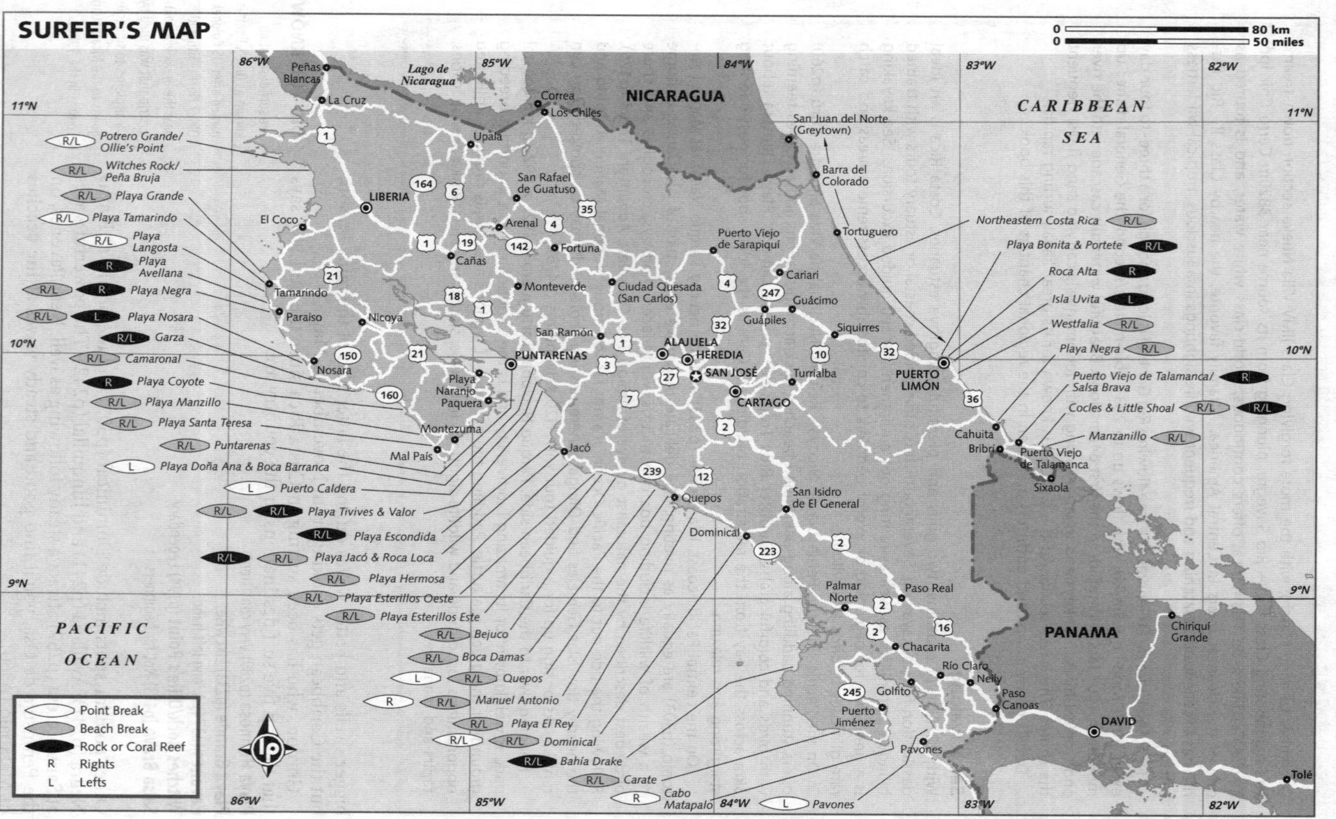
SURFER'S MAP
0 80 km
0 50 miles
CARIBBEAN SEA
PACIFIC OCEAN
NICARAGUA
PANAMA
Lago de Nicaragua
11°N
10°N
9°N
86°W
85°W
84°W
83°W
82°W
Point Break
Beach Break
Rock or Coral Reef
R Rights
L Lefts
R/L Potrero Grande/ Ollie's Point
R/L Witches Rock/ Peña Bruja
R/L Playa Grande
R/L Playa Tamarindo
R/L Playa Langosta
R Playa Avellana
R/L R Playa Negra
R/L L Playa Nosara
R/L Garza
R/L Camaronal
R Playa Coyote
R/L Playa Manzillo
R/L Playa Santa Teresa
R/L Puntarenas
L Playa Doña Ana & Boca Barranca
L Puerto Caldera
R/L R/L Playa Tivives & Valor
R/L Playa Escondida
R/L R/L Playa Jacó & Roca Loca
R/L Playa Hermosa
R/L Playa Esterillos Oeste
R/L Playa Esterillos Este
R/L Bejuco
R/L Boca Damas
L R/L Quepos
R R/L Manuel Antonio
R/L Playa El Rey
R/L R/L Dominical
R/L Bahía Drake
R/L Carate
R Cabo Matapalo
L Pavones
Northeastern Costa Rica R/L
Playa Bonita & Portete R/L
Roca Alta R
Isla Uvita L
Westfalia R/L
Playa Negra R/L
Puerto Viejo de Talamanca/ Salsa Brava R
Cocles & Little Shoal R/L R/L
Manzanillo R/L
Peñas Blancas
La Cruz
Correa
Los Chiles
Upala
San Rafael de Guatuso
LIBERIA
El Coco
Arenal
Fortuna
Cañas
Tamarindo
Paraíso
Nicoya
Monteverde
Ciudad Quesada (San Carlos)
Puerto Viejo de Sarapiquí
San Juan del Norte (Greytown)
Barra del Colorado
Tortuguero
Cariari
Guácimo
Guápiles
Siquirres
San Ramón
ALAJUELA
HEREDIA
SAN JOSÉ
CARTAGO
Turrialba
PUNTARENAS
Nosara
Playa Naranjo
Paquera
Montezuma
Mal País
Jacó
Quepos
Dominical
San Isidro de El General
PUERTO LIMÓN
Cahuita
Bribri
Puerto Viejo de Talamanca
Sixaola
Palmar Norte
Paso Real
Chacarita
Río Claro
Neily
Golfito
Paso Canoas
Puerto Jiménez
Pavones
DAVID
Chiriquí Grande
Tolé
1
164
6
35
4
19
142
21
18
150
160
3
27
7
32
247
10
36
2
239
12
223
16
245

For the uninitiated, there are dozens of surf camps in all of the Costa Rican surf communities that can get you riding in no time. For more practical information turn to the Directory (p451), and for surfing tours check out p475.

WATERFALL RAPPELING

With its many pretty waterfalls, it just had to be a matter of time before someone in Costa Rica decided it'd be a good idea to rappel down one of them. (Great fun for rock-climbing types who like to get wet.) This is a nascent sport, but will likely grow in popularity as adventure travel in Costa Rica continues to grow.

The main destination for waterfall rappeling is the area around Puerto Jiménez (p356) and Cabo Matapalo (p360) on the Península de Osa. Everyday Adventures (p356) specializes in the sport, but most of the lodges in the Jiménez area can book you on tours. In the Monteverde area, Desafío Adventure Company (p166) also offers these types of adventures. In the Central Valley, try Jungla Expeditions in Turrialba (p145).

Food & Drink

From sushi to *sangría*, this little country has it all. Typical hearty local cooking – *cocina típica* – is available far and wide and at every price range. Thatched country kitchens can be found all over, with local women ladling out basic home-cooked specials. But you can get your Tico (Costa Rican) fare upscale and with a nouveau twist in trendier, more touristed areas.

Entradas: Journeys in Latin American Cuisine by Joan Chatfield-Taylor has some of Costa Rica's most popular recipes – and many others.

The high level of immigration from the USA to Costa Rica assures a wide selection of just about anything you might want to munch on: Italian, Spanish, Chinese, Japanese, French, Mexican, American and even Greek. You can even have a Big Mac Attack.

STAPLES & SPECIALTIES

Costa Rican food, for the most part, is very basic. Some might even call it bland and uninteresting. The complex and varied dishes concocted in Mexico and Guatemala just didn't make it past the border over here. The diet consists largely of rice and beans – and beans and rice – and any combination thereof.

Macadamia de Costa Rica (www.macadamiacr.com) has dozens of recipes using macadamia nuts – from macadamia coconut sundaes to nutty salmon.

Breakfast is usually *gallo pinto*, a stir-fry of rice and beans served with eggs, cheese or *natilla* (sour cream). This is generally cheap (US$2) and filling and sometimes can be downright tasty. If you'll be spending the whole day surfing or hiking you'll have energy to spare! Many hotels will provide what they refer to as a 'tropical breakfast' – usually bread along with a selection of fresh fruits. American-style breakfasts are available in most eateries.

Most restaurants offer a set meal at lunch and dinner called a *casado* which is cheap and filling. It usually includes meat, beans, rice and cabbage salad – and for good measure one or two more carbohydrates, including potatoes or pasta.

Breakfast and lunch is often served with bread or toast, though some places will offer fresh tortillas (most popular in Guanacaste), made from a thickly ground corn.

Food is not heavily spiced, unless you're having traditional Caribbean-style cuisine. The vast majority of Ticos have a distinct aversion to hot sauce, though most local restaurants will lay out a spicy *curtido* (a pickle of hot peppers and vegetables) or little bottles of Tabasco-style sauce for the diehards. Another popular condiment is *salsa lizano*, the Tico version of Worcestershire sauce.

TRAVEL YOUR TASTE BUDS

Perhaps the tastiest local cuisine is found on the Caribbean side. Spicy coconut milk stews *(rondón)*, garlic potatoes, well-seasoned fish and chicken dishes are all lip-smackingly good. Also, don't miss the savory 'rice and beans' (in English), red beans and rice cooked in coconut milk.

In the Guanacaste region, keep your eye out for *chan*, the black seeds of the chan plant, soaked and served in *agua dulce* (sugar-cane water) or with tamarind juice. It's space-age looking and rather slimy, but the locals swear that nothing will refresh you more.

In palm-producing regions, expect to find *palmitos* (hearts of palm) in just about everything: salad dishes, stews and even lasagna. In Guanacaste, the locals produce a palm wine (only available in the dry season) called *vino coyol*. You think *guaro* (local firewater made from sugar cane) is intense? Try this stuff. It's not usually available in bars, so keep your eyes peeled for signs offering it outside private homes and *pulperías* (corner grocery store).

At Christmas, and other times, some restaurants will serve *tamales*, banana leaves packed with a cornmeal and meat filling and then steamed.

The most popular foreign foods in Costa Rica are Chinese and Italian. Nearly every town has a Chinese place, and even if it doesn't, the menu will likely include *arroz cantonés* (fried rice). Pizza parlors and Italian restaurants of varying quality abound, though the locally produced pizza can sometimes be heavily loaded (read: cheese bomb).

If an establishment doesn't exactly impress you with its cleanliness, then it might be advisable not to eat fruits, vegetables or salads there. If they are improperly washed, you could be sending your stomach a little bacteria surprise. See more on this in the Health chapter (p480).

DRINKS

Non-alcoholic Drinks

Coffee is probably the most popular beverage in the country and wherever you go, someone is likely to offer you a *cafecito*. Traditionally, it is served strong and mixed with hot milk to taste, also known as *café con leche*. Most drinkers get *café negro*, and for those who want a little milk, you can ask for *leche al lado* (milk on the side). Many trendier places serve cappuccinos and espressos. The milk is pasteurized and safe to drink.

The usual brands of soft drinks are available, although many people prefer *batidos* – fresh fruit drinks (like smoothies) made either *al agua* (with water) or *con leche* (with milk). The array can be mind-boggling, and includes mango, papaya, *piña* (pineapple), *sandía* (watermelon), *melón* (cantaloupe), *mora* (blackberry), *zanahoria* (carrot), *cebada* (barley) or *tamarindo* (made from the fruit of the tamarind tree). If you are wary about the condition of the drinking water, ask that your *batido* be made with *agua enbotellada* (bottled water) and *sin hielo* (without ice.)

A bottled, though far less tasty alternative, is a local fruit beverage called 'Tropical'. It's sold in many stores and restaurants and the most common flavors are *mora*, *piña*, *cas* (a tart local fruit) and *frutas mixtas*. Just shake vigorously before drinking or the powder-like substance at the bottom will remain intact.

Pipas are green coconuts that have a hole macheted into the top of them and a straw for drinking the 'milk' – a very refreshing and filling drink.

Agua dulce is sugar-cane water, or in many cases boiled water mixed with brown sugar. *Horchata*, found mostly in the countryside, is a sweet drink made from cornmeal and flavored with cinnamon.

'Coffee is probably the most popular beverage in the country and wherever you go, someone is likely to offer you a *cafecito*.'

Alcoholic Drinks

The most popular alcoholic drink is beer and there are several local brands. Imperial is perhaps the most popular and recognizable (T-shirts emblazoned with their eagle-crest logo are available everywhere), followed by Pilsen, which is also known for its saucy calendars featuring *las chicas Pilsen* (the Pilsen girls). Both beers are comparable to Corona from Mexico. Bavaria produces a lager and Bavaria Negro, a full-bodied dark beer, but the brand isn't as easy to find as the first two.

Most of these beers contain 4% or 4.5% alcohol. Rock Ice, with 4.7% alcohol content, has a slightly more bitter taste. Domestic beer costs about US$0.75 in the cheapest places, but will generally run about US$1.50 per bottle or US$3 in fancier tourist lodges. Other beers are imported and expensive.

After beer, the poison of choice is *guaro*, which is a colorless alcohol distilled from sugar cane and usually consumed by the shot, though you can order it as a sour. It goes down mighty easily, but leaves one hell

DID YOU KNOW?

Coffee was thought to energize workers, so in 1840 the government decreed that all laborers building roads should be provided with one cup of coffee every day.

of memorable hangover. Also inexpensive and worthwhile is local rum, usually drunk as a *cuba libre* (rum and cola). Premixed cans of *cuba libre* are available in stores but it'd be a lie to say the contents didn't taste weirdly like aluminum. The best rum available is Ron Centenario, which is definitely worth the price (US$12 a bottle at a liquor store; US$9 at airport duty-free).

DID YOU KNOW?

No alcohol is served on Election Day or in the three days prior to Easter Sunday.

Local vodkas and gins aren't bad (but they aren't great either), and the whisky is poor. Expensive imported liquors are available, as are domestic liqueurs. One locally made liqueur is Café Rica, which, predictably, is based on coffee and tastes like the better-known Mexican Kahlua.

Most Costa Rican wines are cheap, taste cheap, and will be unkindly remembered the next morning. Imported wines are available but expensive. It's also important to take note how they've been stored: wine that has been sitting around in the tropical heat usually isn't all that good. Chilean brands are your best bet for a palatable wine at an affordable price.

WHERE TO EAT & DRINK

Lunch is usually the main meal of the day and is typically served at around noon. Dinner tends to be a lighter version of lunch and is usually eaten around 7pm.

Pick up the necessary skills to make *gallo pinto* and a good *casado*. The Costa Rican Language Academy in San José (p102) can teach you all you need to know about Tico cooking.

By far the most popular eating establishment in Costa Rica is the *soda*. These are small and informal lunch counters dishing up a few daily *casados* (US$2 to US$3). These are the best places to eat if you are on a budget and they are easily found in any neighborhood as well as the central market – *mercado central* – of any town. The ones inside the *mercado* will usually be the cheapest. Look for the ones that are packed, they're always the best and serve the freshest food. Many *sodas* are only open for breakfast and lunch. Other popular cheapies include the omnipresent fried and rotisserie chicken stands.

A regular *restaurante* will usually be a little higher on the price scale and have slightly more atmosphere. These will frequently have a more formal menu (*carta*) and can serve just about everything – from *comida típica* to American and foreign specialties. Many restaurantes will serve *casados*, while the fancier places will refer to the set lunch as the *almuerzo ejecutivo*.

DID YOU KNOW?

Costa Rican macadamia nuts are frequently marketed as Hawaiian abroad.

In San José and in touristy areas, eg Tamarindo, Manuel Antonio and Jacó, specialty and ethnic restaurants are widely available. Prices at *restaurantes* can range from US$3 for a *casado* to US$40 for lobster in Manuel Antonio. Pizza parlors and Chinese restaurants are usually the cheapest ethnic eats. Pizzas are usually personal size and generally start at US$3. Prices at Chinese restaurants start at US$2 for fried rice; a plate of cashew chicken can run to about US$6, depending on the establishment.

Upmarket restaurants add a 13% tax plus 10% service to the bill, so check the menu to see if the tax is included in the list prices. Sometimes it is and at other times it isn't so don't be surprised when the bill comes.

Pastelerías and *panaderías* sell pastries and bread, respectively, and sometimes a combination of the two. Some also sell sandwiches.

Many bars serve snacks called *bocas*. In the countryside, these were frequently provided free of charge, but this practice is getting harder to find. Most times, *bocas* are snack-sized portions of main meals, including *ceviche* (fish cocktail), *arroz con pollo* (chicken and rice) or *patacones* (thick wedges of fried plantain bananas with bean dip). Order a few *bocas* and you'll have a delicious (and varied) dinner on your hands.

Quick Eats

There is not a vast selection of street snacks to choose from in Costa Rica. For the most part, street vendors sell fresh fruit (sometimes pre-chopped and ready to go), cookies, chips (crisps) and fried plantains. Many *sodas* will have little windows that face the street, and from there dispense *empanadas* (a meat or chicken turnover), tacos (usually a tortilla with meat) or *enchilados* (pastry with spicy meat). Many of these places also offer fried chicken, which has to be one of the most consistently popular foods in all of Costa Rica.

The best ice-cream treat is, by far, the 'Mmmio': vanilla ice cream topped with caramel and nuts and bathed in chocolate – it's mmm-good and available just about everywhere.

VEGETARIANS & VEGANS

If you don't mind rice and beans, Costa Rica is a relatively comfortable place for vegetarians to travel. Most restaurants will make veggie *casados* on request and many are now including them on their menu. They usually include rice and beans, cabbage salad and one or two selections of variously prepared vegetables or legumes.

With the high influx of tourism, there are also many specialty vegetarian restaurants or restaurants with a veggie menu in San José and tourist-centric towns. The Vishnu chain in San José (p91) enjoys a popular local following and has an outlet in Heredia (p133). The many yoga and holistic retreat centers also offer veggie cooking. Also check out:

Finca Anael At Reserva Biológica Durika (p329).
Finca Flor de Paraíso In Cartago (p141).
Luna Lodge In Carate (p361).
Pura Vida In Alajuela (p122).
Samasati Near Puerto Viejo de Talamanca (p417).

GOING BANANAS *Beth Penland*

Despite Costa Rica's cultural diversity, Ticos everywhere agree that no meal is complete without a side dish of *plátanos* (plantains), an oversized, starchy banana that must be cooked before eaten. Ah, but how to cook it? The Spanish side prefers them soft and sweet, like Ileana Castro's heirloom recipe, while Caribbean cooks serve them up as crunchy, savory *patacones*.

Ileana's Plátanos

2 plantains
40ml butter (to fry plantains)
40ml brown sugar

Let plantains ripen until the peel is completely black. Peel and slice them into 3cm pieces. Melt butter (no substitutes!) in skillet and fry plantains until they are brown on each side. Sprinkle each side with a little brown sugar and cook until sugar has caramelized. For variety, melt mozzarella cheese on top.

Patacones

2 green plantains
40ml cup of oil
40ml cup of milk

Peel and slice the plantains into 4cm pieces, fry them in oil until golden brown and remove from pan onto a cutting board. With the broad side of a large knife, smash the plantains until they are about 2cm thick. Dip the smashed pieces in milk and fry them again until they are golden brown. Add salt to taste.

DOS & DON'TS

- When you sit down to eat, it is polite to say *buenos días* or *buenas tardes* to the waitstaff or any people you might be sharing a table with.
- If you're eating with a group of locals, it's polite to say *buen provecho* (bon appetit) at the start of the meal.
- Tipping is not customary at low-end *sodas*, though leaving spare change is always appreciated.
- Mid-range and top-end restaurants frequently include tips in the bill.

Lodges in remote areas that offer all-inclusive meal plans can all accommodate vegetarian diets with advance notice. Be sure to note your preference at the time you make your reservation.

Vegans, macrobiotic and raw-foods-only travelers will have a tougher time as there are fewer outlets accommodating those diets. A couple of places include Shakti in San José (p75) and Pura Vida in Alajuela. If you intend to keep to your diet, it's best to choose a lodging where you can prepare foods yourself. Many towns have health-food stores (*macrobióticas*), but selection varies. Fresh vegetables can be hard to come by in isolated areas and will often be quite expensive.

Are you worried that you'll head back home and dearly miss *salsa lizano* or Tropical drinks? Thankfully www.lapulpe.com sells Costa Rican products and will ship the goods to just about anywhere in the world.

WHINING & DINING

If you're traveling with the tots, you'll find that 'kids' meals' (small portions at small prices) are not normally offered in restaurants, though some fancy lodges do them. However, most local eateries will accommodate two children splitting a meal or can produce child-size portions on request. You can ask for restaurant staff to bring you simple food, rice with chicken or steak cooked on the grill (*a la plancha*).

If you are traveling with an infant, stock up on formula and baby food before heading to remote areas. Avocados are safe, easy to eat and nutritious and they can be served to children as young as six months old. Young children should avoid water and ice in drinks as they are more susceptible to stomach illnesses.

Always carry snacks for long drives in remote areas – sometimes there are no places to stop for a bite.

For other tips on traveling with the tykes, see Children (p452).

DID YOU KNOW?

Many Tico men believe that eating turtle eggs will give them increased sexual prowess. Hopefully Viagra will alleviate the illegal traffic in these eggs.

EAT YOUR WORDS

The thrill of eating; the agony of ordering in a foreign language. This handy guide is set up to help you eat – and order – well. For further guidance with Spanish pronunciation, see p484.

Useful Phrases

Do you have a menu (in English)? — *¿Hay una carta (en Inglés)?*
ai *oo*-na *kar*-ta (en een-*gles*)?

What is there for breakfast/lunch/dinner? — *¿Qué hay para el desayuno/el almuerzo/la cena?*
ke ai pa-ra el de-sa-*yoo*-no/el al-*mwer*-so/la *se*-na?

Is this water purified? — *¿Ésta agua es purificada?*
es-ta *a*-gwa es poo-ree-fee-*ka*-da?

I'm a vegetarian. — *Soy vegetariano/a.*
soy ve-khe-te-*rya*-no/a

I don't eat meat, chicken, fish or eggs. — *No como carne, pollo, pescado o huevos.*
no *ko*-mo *kar*-ne *po*-yo pes-*ka*-do o *we*-vos

I'd like the set lunch. *Quisiera un casado.*
kee-*sye*-ra oon ka-*sa*-do
The bill, please. *La cuenta, por favor.*
la *kwen*-ta por fa-*vor*

Menu Decoder

a la parrilla/plancha – grilled over charcoal/in a pan
almuerzo – lunch
almuerzo ejecutivo – inexpensive set lunch; special of the day (literally 'business lunch')
arreglados – puff pastries stuffed with beef, chicken or cheese
arroz con pollo – a basic dish of rice and chicken
batido – fresh fruit shake made with water or milk
bocas – small savory dishes served in bars
cajeta – a thick caramel fudge
caldo – broth, often meat-based
carne – meat; though frequently refers to beef
casado – a set meal, normally rice, black beans, a small salad, a cooked vegetable and either chicken, fish, meat or cheese
ceviche – seafood marinated with lemon, onion, sweet red peppers and cilantro; can be made with fish, shrimp or conch
chicharrón – pork crackling
chorreada – a pan-fried cornmeal cake served with sour cream
churrasco – grilled steak; frequently a skirt steak
comida/cocina típica – typical Costa Rican fare
cuba libre – rum and cola
dorado – mahi mahi fish
dulce de leche – milk and sugar boiled to make a thick caramel paste often used in pastries
elote – corn on the cob served boiled *(elote cocinado)* or roasted *(elote asado)*
empanadas – turnovers stuffed with chicken, beef or cheese
enchilados – pastries stuffed with potatoes and cheese and sometimes meat
ensalada – salad
filete de pescado – fish filet
flan – a cold caramel custard
frijoles – black beans
gallo pinto – stir-fry of rice and beans, served with eggs, cheese or sour cream
gallos – tortilla sandwiches containing meat, beans or cheese
guaro – local firewater made from sugar cane
hamburguesa – hamburger
huevos fritos/revueltos – fried/scrambled eggs
mariscos – seafood
mazamorra – a pudding made from cornstarch
olla de carne – a hearty soup containing beef, potatoes, corn, squash, plantains and yuca, a type of tuber
patacones – slices of plantain deep-fried like french-fried potatoes; usually served with bean dip
pejibaye – a rather starchy tasting palm fruit also eaten as a salad
pescado al ajo – fish in garlic sauce (frequently butter)
plátano – fried sweet plantain; also applies to uncooked banana
postre – dessert
rice and beans (in English) – rice and red beans cooked in coconut milk, served on the Caribbean side
rondón – thick seafood-based soup blended with coconut milk, found on the Caribbean
taco – a snack or hors d'ouevres
tamales – boiled cornmeal pies usually wrapped in a banana leaf (you don't eat the leaf) and stuffed with chicken or pork
tortillas – either Mexican-style corn pancakes or Spanish omelets

TOP FIVE BEST EATS

- A steaming hot *churro* (doughnut tube) from Manolo's in San José (p91)
- The garlicky potatoes at Miss Edith's restaurant in Cahuita (p407)
- The scrumptious, finger-licking *empanadas* from Cevichera in Sámara – perfect with a cold beer (p254)
- Asian *bocas* at Hotel Plinio in Manuel Antonio (p299)
- Nachos 'as big as your ass' at Witch's Rock Surf Camp in Tamarindo (p239)

Food Glossary

agua (enbotellada)	*a*-gwa (*en*-bot-el-*a*-da)	(bottled) water
arroz	*a*-ros	rice
azúcar	a-*soo*-kar	sugar
bebida	be-*bee*-da	drink, soda
bistek	*bis*-tek	steak
camarones	ka-ma-*ro*-nes	shrimp
cerveza	ser-*ve*-sa	beer
coco	*ko*-ko	coconut
frutas	*froo*-tas	fruit
helado	e-*la*-do	ice cream
jamón	kha-*mon*	ham
jugo	*hoo*-go	juice
lechuga	le-*choo*-ga	lettuce
leche	*le*-che	milk
limón	*lee*-mon	lime or lemon
maíz	mai-*ees*	dried corn or corn meal
mantequilla	man-te-*kee*-ya	butter
manzana	man-*za*-na	apple
margarina	mar-ga-*ree*-na	margarine
mélon	me-*lon*	cantaloupe
mora	mo-*ra*	blackberry
naranja	na-*ran*-kha	orange
natilla	na-*tee*-lya	sour cream
pan	pan	bread
papa/papas fritas	*pa*-pa/*pa*-pas *free*-tas	potato/French fries
pargo rojo	*par*-go *ro*-ho	red snapper
pescado	pes-*ka*-do	fish
piña	*pee*-nya	pineapple
pollo	*po*-lyo	chicken
pimienta	pee-*myen*-ta	pepper (black)
puerco	*pwer*-ko	pork
queso	*ke*-so	cheese
repollo	re-*po*-lyo	cabbage
sal	sal	salt
pastel	pas-*tel*	pastry or cake
verduras	ver-*doo*-ras	vegetables
zanahoria	sa-na-*o*-rya	carrot

San José

CONTENTS

Packed with office towers, shopping malls and fast-food restaurants, men chattering on cell phones and girls in low-rise jeans, San José is more cosmopolitan than other Central American capitals. For most travelers, though, a stopover in San José is regarded as the necessary evil before heading to more virtuous rural landscapes. Traffic is heavy, the streets are congested and the architecture is largely unremarkable. Almost every international flight lands here and nearly every bus makes its way to the crowded stations on the west side of town.

But the city has its charms. World-class restaurants offer gourmet delicacies alongside typical eateries serving traditional Tico treats. Museums, theatres and cinemas dot the cityscape and nightlife – as is to be expected in this region – is vibrant, with packed bars, live music and nightclubs operating every day of the week.

San José was founded in 1737, but little remains of the colonial era. There are few buildings of note, except for the Teatro Nacional (built in the 1890s) and a few Spanish-style structures. But to *josefinos*, as inhabitants of San José are called, their city might not be a thing of beauty, but it is the center of it all.

HIGHLIGHTS

- Enjoying the museum scene – from **contemporary art** (p73) to priceless **jade** (p73)
- Dining out in historic **Barrio Amón** (p89 and p88)
- Pub crawling through the many bars at **Centro Comercial El Pueblo** (p93)
- Munching on a hot *churro* (doughnut tube; p91) while strolling amid the crowds on **Avenida Central** (see opposite)
- Sipping cocktails at any of the eateries with a view in **Escazú** (p111), a pleasant San José 'burb

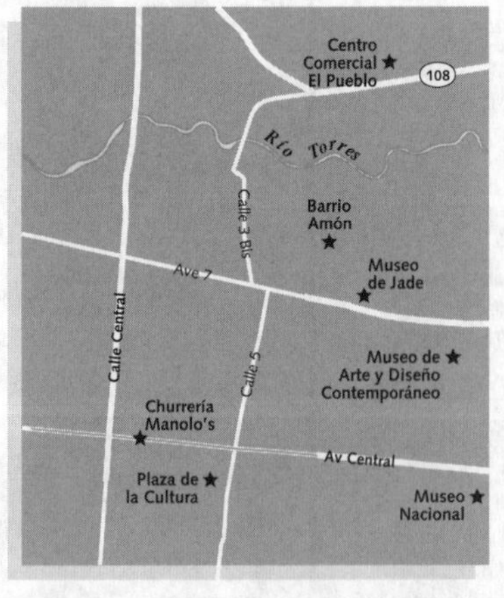

- POPULATION: CITY LIMITS 340,000; GREATER METRO AREA 1 MILLION
- ELEVATION: 1150 M

HISTORY

For much of the colonial period, San José played second fiddle to the bigger and (relatively) more established Cartago, which had been founded back in 1564 and initially served as the provincial capital. Villanueva de la Boca del Monte – as San José was first known – was founded in 1737 after the Catholic Church had issued an edict that forced the populace to settle near churches. (Attendance was down.) The city remained a backwater for decades, though it did experience some growth as a stop in the tobacco trading route. In 1840 the capital was switched here from Cartago.

But even through the time of World War II, San José was hardly a booming metropolis. By the early 1940s, the city had only 70,000 residents as, even then, Costa Rica remained largely agricultural with a widely dispersed population. But as arable land was snatched up and many country folk moved into the cities in search of a better life, the size and population of San José would mushroom well into the 1970s and 1980s – and today, the city is one of the largest and most cosmopolitan in Central America.

GETTING INTO TOWN

Taxis to downtown San José from Juan Santamaría airport will cost about US$12. When leaving the airport terminal, look for the official **Taxi Aeropuerto stand** (☎ 221 6865; www.taxiaeropuerto.com) as you exit the baggage-claim area, and pay the flat rate in advance. The official airport taxis are orange. The ride generally lasts about 20 minutes, but may take over an hour during rush hour.

The cheapest option is the red **Tuasa bus** (US$0.60; up to 45min) running between Alajuela and San José and passing the airport every few minutes from 5am to 11pm. The stop is on the far side of the parking lot outside the terminal. (It's a short walk, even with luggage.) Some taxi drivers will tell you there are no buses; don't believe them. The **Interbus** (☎ 283 5573; www.interbusonline.com) is a good deal and it runs an airport shuttle service that costs US$5 per person. Call ahead to arrange pick-up.

International and domestic buses all arrive at one of the many bus terminals sprinkled around the west and south of downtown San José. The downtown area is perfectly walkable provided you aren't hauling a lot of luggage. If arriving at night, take a taxi to your hotel as most bus terminals are in seedy areas; a cab to any part of downtown costs US$1 to US$2.

ORIENTATION

The city is in the heart of a wide and fertile valley called the *Meseta Central* (Central Valley). San José's center is arranged in a grid with avenidas running east to west and calles running north to south. Avenida Central is the nucleus of the city center and is a pedestrian mall between Calles 6 and 9. It becomes Paseo Colón to the west of Calle 14.

Street addresses are given by the nearest street intersection. Thus the address of the tourist office is Calle 5 between Avenidas Central and 2. Most locals, however, do not use street addresses and instead use landmarks to guide themselves. Learn how to decipher Tico (Costa Rican) directions by turning to the boxed text on p453.

The center has several districts, or *barrios*, which are all loosely defined. The central area is home to innumerable businesses, shops, bus stops and cultural sights. Perhaps the most interesting district to visitors is Barrio Amón, northeast of Avenida 5 and Calle 1, with its concentration of landmark mansions, largely converted into hotels and fine-dining establishments. Just west of the city center is La Sabana, named after the park, and just north of it is the elegant suburb of Rohrmoser. Further west again is the affluent outer suburb of Escazú, which is described on p106. Southeast of the downtown area are the lively student areas of Los Yoses and San Pedro, which are described on p101.

Look for maps at either Lehmann's (p69), Librería Universal (p69), or the tourist center (p72).

INFORMATION

Bookstores

The following bookstores are among the most noteworthy. English-language magazines, newspapers and books are also available in the gift shops of the international airport and several of the top-end hotels.

7th Street Books (Map p74; ☎ 256 8251; Calle 7 btwn Avs Central & 1; 🕑 9am-6pm) An attractive shop with new and used books in English and other languages as

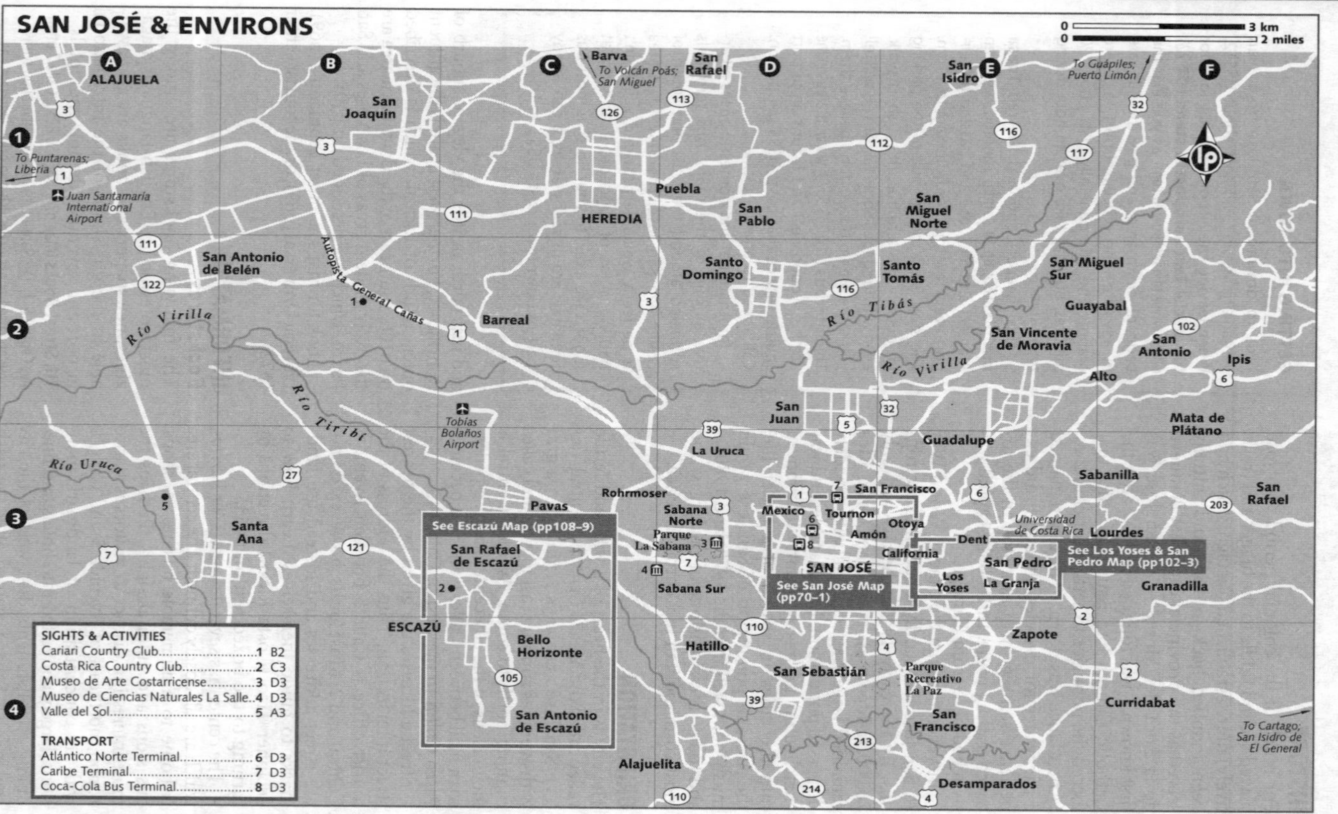
SAN JOSÉ & ENVIRONS
0 3 km
0 2 miles
A
B
C
D
E
F
1
2
3
4
ALAJUELA
To Puntarenas; Liberia
Juan Santamaría International Airport
San Joaquín
Barva
To Volcán Poás; San Miguel
San Rafael
San Isidro
To Guápiles; Puerto Limón
HEREDIA
Puebla
San Pablo
San Miguel Norte
San Antonio de Belén
Autopista General Cañas
Santo Domingo
Santo Tomás
San Miguel Sur
Guayabal
Barreal
Río Virilla
Río Tibás
San Vincente de Moravia
San Antonio
Ipis
Alto
Río Tiribí
Tobías Bolaños Airport
San Juan
Mata de Plátano
Guadalupe
La Uruca
Río Uruca
Sabanilla
Rohrmoser
San Francisco
San Rafael
Pavas
Sabana Norte
Mexico
Tournon
Otoya
Universidad de Costa Rica
Lourdes
Santa Ana
See Escazú Map (pp108–9)
Parque La Sabana
Amón
Dent
San Rafael de Escazú
California
See Los Yoses & San Pedro Map (pp102–3)
SAN JOSÉ
San Pedro
Los Yoses
La Granja
Granadilla
Sabana Sur
See San José Map (pp70–1)
ESCAZÚ
Hatillo
Zapote
Bello Horizonte
San Sebastián
Parque Recreativo La Paz
Curridabat
San Antonio de Escazú
San Francisco
To Cartago; San Isidro de El General
Alajuelita
Desamparados
SIGHTS & ACTIVITIES
Cariari Country Club....1 B2
Costa Rica Country Club....2 C3
Museo de Arte Costarricense....3 D3
Museo de Ciencias Naturales La Salle..4 D3
Valle del Sol....5 A3
TRANSPORT
Atlántico Norte Terminal....6 D3
Caribe Terminal....7 D3
Coca-Cola Bus Terminal....8 D3

well as magazines and newspapers; Ecole Travel (see p78) is also here.

Mora Books (Map p74; ☎ 255 4136, 383 8385; Omni Center, Av 1 btwn Calles 3 & 5) Highly recommended secondhand bookstore has books mainly in English; guidebooks and comic books are a specialty.

Librería Internacional (☎ 290 3331; in front of the Centro Comercial Plaza Mayor, 200m east of Restaurant Fogoncito, Rohrmoser; 🕑 9:30am-7:30pm Mon-Sat, 1-5pm Sun) Large store chain offering new books mostly in Spanish (but some in English) as well as travel and wildlife guides.

Lehmann's (Map p74; ☎ 223 1212; Av Central btwn Calles 1 & 3) It has some books, magazines and newspapers in English, and a selection of topographical and other Costa Rican maps in the upstairs map department.

Librería Francesa (Map p74; ☎ 223 7979; Av 1 btwn Calles 5 & 7) Spanish books and magazines, as well as a selection of French, German and English titles, are sold here.

Librería Universal (Map p74; ☎ 222 2222; Av Central btwn Calles Central & 1) Situated on the 2nd floor of the Universal department store, the shop has road and topographical maps, a few books in English and a small bookstore café.

Libro Azul (Map p74; Av 10 btwn Calles Central & 1; 🕑 8:30am-12:30pm & 1:30-5:30pm Mon-Fri, 9am-noon Sat) A tiny, well-known shop offering secondhand books mostly in Spanish and some in English.

Emergency

Emergencies (☎ 911)
Fire (☎ 118)
Police (☎ 117)
Red Cross (☎ 128)
Traffic Police (☎ 222 9330)

Internet Access

Checking email is easy in San José, where cybercafés are more plentiful than fruit peddlers. For the most part, rates are US$0.75 to US$2 per hour. Be aware that some places charge by the full hour, meaning that if you've been on for 61 minutes, you'll be paying for a full two hours. Many upmarket hotels have Internet access as well. Here are some good options:

CyberCafé searchcostarica.com (Map p74; ☎ 233 3310; Las Arcadas, Av 2 btwn Calles 1 & 3; per hr US$0.75; 🕑 7am-11pm) Also houses Lavandería Las Arcadas (see later), a book exchange and a pizza and fresh-juice bar.

Internet Café Costa Rica (Map p74; cnr Av Central & Calle 4, 4th fl; per hr US$1; 🕑 9am-10pm)

Internet Club (Map p74; Calle 7 btwn Avs Central & 2; per hr US$1.50; 🕑 24hr)

Netopia Cybercafé (Map p74; cnr Av 1 & Calle 11; 1st hr US$1.25, then per hr US$0.75; 🕑 9am-midnight Mon-Sat, 10am-10pm Sun)

1@10 Café Internet (Map pp70-1; ☎ 258 4561; www.1en10.com; per hr US$1; Calle 3 btwn Avs 5 & 7) Also serves as the gay and lesbian information center.

Laundry

Plan on dragging your dirty socks around town since a do-it-yourself laundry service is hard to find in San José. Most *lavanderías* offer only dry-cleaning services. Many hotels and hostels offer laundry service, but beware of top-end places that charge by the piece – this gets pricey. The following places will get your tighty whities right:

Lavandería Las Arcadas (Map p74; Las Arcadas, Av 2 btwn Calles 1 & 3; ☎ 233 3310; 🕑 7am-11pm) The machines are all self-service and cheap; a wash is US$3 and a dry is US$0.75. It's a popular place so you might have to wait.

Lavandería Lavamex (Map p74; ☎ 258 2303; Calle 8 btwn Av Central & 1; 🕑 8am-6pm Mon-Fri, 8am-5pm Sat) The best bet in town: the friendly folks here will wash and dry your clothes within a few hours for US$6 per load; it offers travel information to boot.

Lavandería Sixaola (Map p74; ☎ 221 2111; Av 2 btwn Calles 7 & 9) Charges about US$10 a load for wash/dry/fold and offers same-day service – expensive!

Medical Services

For details of a hospital in Escazú, see p106. Note that both the Bíblica and Católica have pharmacies.

Hospital San Juan de Dios (Map pp70-1; ☎ 257 6282; cnr Paseo Colón & Calle 14) The free public hospital is centrally located, but waits are long.

Clínica Bíblica (Map pp70-1; ☎ 257 5252; www.clinicabiblica.com; Av 14 btwn Calles Central & 1) The top private clinic in the downtown area; doctors speak English, French and German; an emergency room is open 24 hours. Be prepared to pay for medical attention, though costs are generally much cheaper than in the USA or Europe.

Hospital Clínica Católica (☎ 246 3000; www.clinicacatolica.com; Guadalupe) A private clinic located north of downtown.

Money

Any bank will change foreign currency into colones, but US dollars are by far the most accepted currency for exchange, with euros following a distant second. Upmarket hotels have exchange windows for their guests, but commissions can be steep, so check before changing large sums. Exchanging money on the street is not recommended. The following banks are good:

Banco de Costa Rica (Map p74; ☎ 221 8143; www.bancobcr.com; Av 1 btwn Calles 7 & 9; 🕑 8:30am-6pm Mon-Fri)

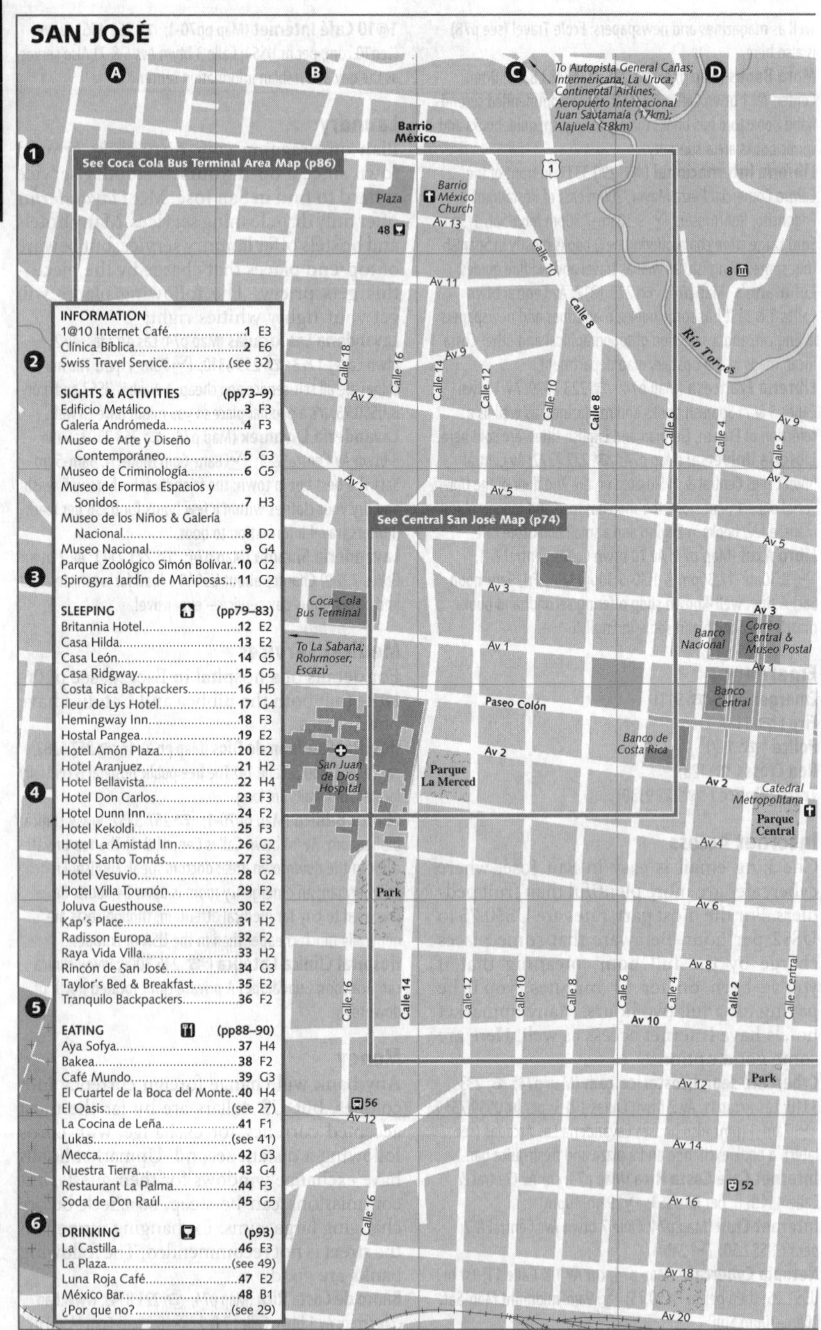
SAN JOSÉ
A
B
C
D
1
2
3
4
5
6
To Autopista General Cañas; Intermericana; La Uruca; Continental Airlines; Aeropuerto Internacional Juan Sautamaía (17km); Alajuela (18km)
Barrio México
See Coca Cola Bus Terminal Area Map (p86)
Plaza
Barrio México Church
48
Av 13
Calle 10
Av 11
Calle 8
8
Río Torres
Av 9
Av 7
Calle 18
Calle 16
Calle 14
Calle 12
Calle 10
Calle 8
Calle 6
Calle 4
Calle 2
Av 9
Av 7
Av 5
Av 5
See Central San José Map (p74)
Av 5
Av 3
Av 3
Coca-Cola Bus Terminal
Banco Nacional
Correo Central & Museo Postal
Av 1
Av 1
To La Sabana; Rohrmoser; Escazú
Paseo Colón
Banco Central
San Juan de Dios Hospital
Av 2
Parque La Merced
Banco de Costa Rica
Av 2
Catedral Metropolitana
Parque Central
Av 4
Park
Av 6
Av 8
Calle 16
Calle 14
Calle 12
Calle 10
Calle 8
Calle 6
Calle 4
Calle 2
Calle Central
Av 10
Park
Av 12
56
Av 12
Av 14
52
Av 16
Calle 16
Av 18
Av 20
INFORMATION
1@10 Internet Café 1 E3
Clínica Bíblica 2 E6
Swiss Travel Service (see 32)
SIGHTS & ACTIVITIES (pp73–9)
Edificio Metálico 3 F3
Galería Andrómeda 4 F3
Museo de Arte y Diseño Contemporáneo 5 G3
Museo de Criminología 6 G5
Museo de Formas Espacios y Sonidos 7 H3
Museo de los Niños & Galería Nacional 8 D2
Museo Nacional 9 G4
Parque Zoológico Simón Bolívar 10 G2
Spirogyra Jardín de Mariposas 11 G2
SLEEPING (pp79–83)
Britannia Hotel 12 E2
Casa Hilda 13 E2
Casa León 14 G5
Casa Ridgway 15 G5
Costa Rica Backpackers 16 H5
Fleur de Lys Hotel 17 G4
Hemingway Inn 18 F3
Hostal Pangea 19 E2
Hotel Amón Plaza 20 E2
Hotel Aranjuez 21 H2
Hotel Bellavista 22 H4
Hotel Don Carlos 23 F3
Hotel Dunn Inn 24 F2
Hotel Kekoldi 25 F3
Hotel La Amistad Inn 26 G2
Hotel Santo Tomás 27 E3
Hotel Vesuvio 28 G2
Hotel Villa Tournón 29 F2
Joluva Guesthouse 30 E2
Kap's Place 31 H2
Radisson Europa 32 F2
Raya Vida Villa 33 H2
Rincón de San José 34 G3
Taylor's Bed & Breakfast 35 E2
Tranquilo Backpackers 36 F2
EATING (pp88–90)
Aya Sofya 37 H4
Bakea 38 F2
Café Mundo 39 G3
El Cuartel de la Boca del Monte 40 H4
El Oasis (see 27)
La Cocina de Leña 41 F1
Lukas (see 41)
Mecca 42 G3
Nuestra Tierra 43 G4
Restaurant La Palma 44 F3
Soda de Don Raúl 45 G5
DRINKING (p93)
La Castilla 46 E3
La Plaza (see 49)
Luna Roja Café 47 E2
México Bar 48 B1
¿Por que no? (see 29)

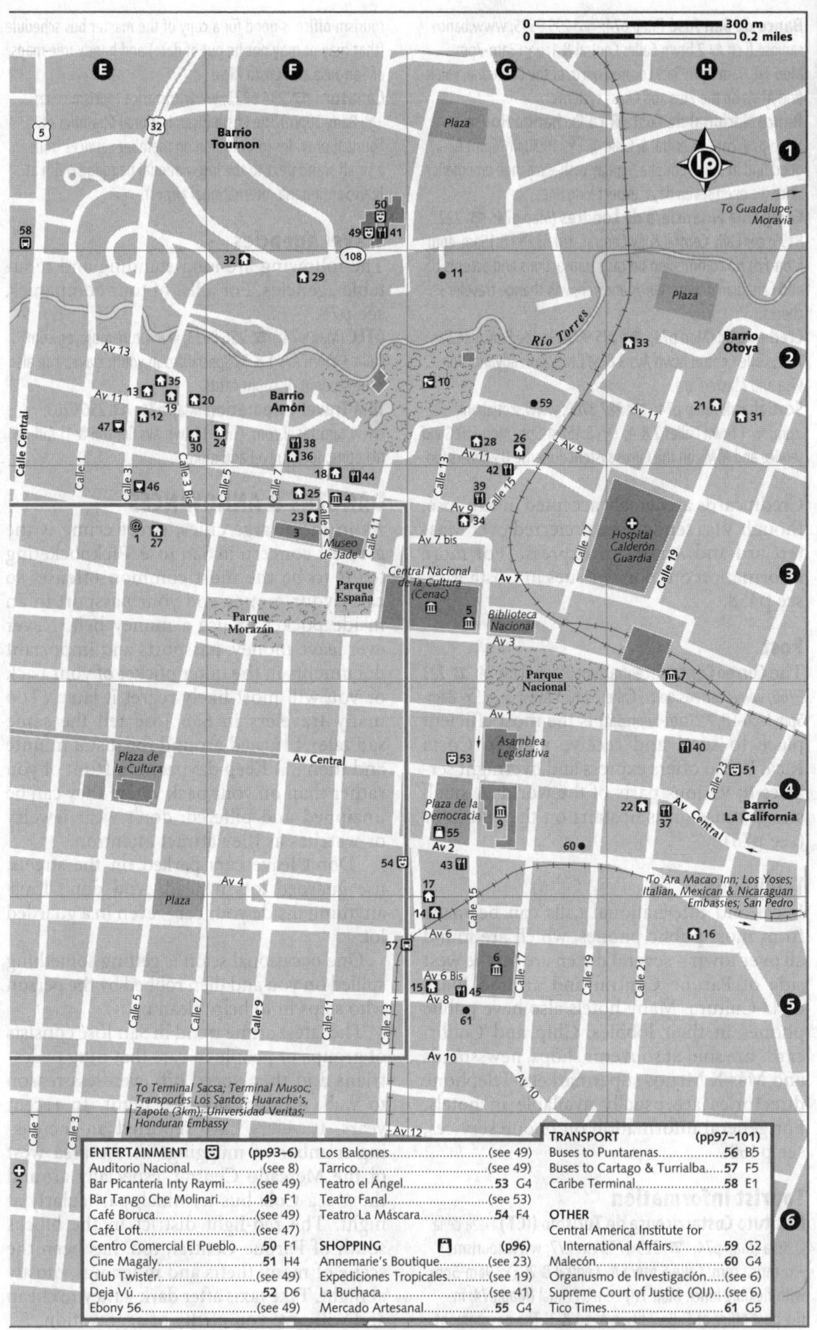
0 300 m
0 0.2 miles
E
F
G
H
1
2
3
4
5
6
Barrio Tournon
Plaza
To Guadalupe; Moravia
Río Torres
Barrio Otoya
Barrio Amón
Av 13
Av 11
Av 9
Av 7 bis
Av 7
Av 3
Av 1
Av Central
Av 2
Av 4
Av 6
Av 6 Bis
Av 8
Av 10
Av 12
Calle Central
Calle 1
Calle 3
Calle 3 Bis
Calle 5
Calle 7
Calle 9
Calle 11
Calle 13
Calle 15
Calle 17
Calle 19
Calle 21
Calle 23
Museo de Jade
Parque España
Central Nacional de la Cultura (Cenac)
Biblioteca Nacional
Hospital Calderón Guardia
Parque Morazán
Parque Nacional
Asamblea Legislativa
Plaza de la Cultura
Plaza de la Democracia
Barrio La California
To Ara Macao Inn; Los Yoses; Italian, Mexican & Nicaraguan Embassies; San Pedro
To Terminal Sacsa; Terminal Musoc; Transportes Los Santos; Huarache's, Zapote (3km); Universidad Veritas; Honduran Embassy
ENTERTAINMENT (pp93–6)
Auditorio Nacional (see 8)
Bar Picantería Inty Raymi (see 49)
Bar Tango Che Molinari 49 F1
Café Boruca (see 49)
Café Loft (see 47)
Centro Comercial El Pueblo 50 F1
Cine Magaly 51 H4
Club Twister (see 49)
Deja Vú 52 D6
Ebony 56 (see 49)
Los Balcones (see 49)
Tarrico (see 49)
Teatro el Ángel 53 G4
Teatro Fanal (see 53)
Teatro La Máscara 54 F4
SHOPPING (p96)
Annemarie's Boutique (see 23)
Expediciones Tropicales (see 19)
La Buchaca (see 41)
Mercado Artesanal 55 G4
TRANSPORT (pp97–101)
Buses to Puntarenas 56 B5
Buses to Cartago & Turrialba 57 F5
Caribe Terminal 58 E1
OTHER
Central America Institute for International Affairs 59 G2
Malecón 60 G4
Organusmo de Investigación (see 6)
Supreme Court of Justice (OIJ) (see 6)
Tico Times 61 G5

Banco de San José (Map p74; ☎ 295 9595; www.bancosanjose.fi.cr; Av 2 btwn Calles Central & 1; 🕑 8am-7pm Mon-Fri, 9am-1pm Sat) Located north of the Cathedral, you'll find ATMs on the Plus and Cirrus systems.
Banco Nacional de Costa Rica Exchange House (Map p74; cnr Av Central & Calle 4; 🕑 10:30am-6pm) A good find in the event of a Sunday cash-exchange emergency since it's open seven days; expect long lines.
Compañía Financiera de Londres (Map p74; ☎ 222 8155; cnr Calle Central & Av Central, 3rd fl; 🕑 8:15am-4pm Mon-Fri) No commission on cash transactions and accepts US and Canadian dollars, euros and yen; will change traveler's checks.
Credomatic (Map p74; ☎ 295 9000; inside Banco de San José; Calle Central btwn Avs 3 & 5) Gives cash advances on Visa and MasterCard.
Scotiabank (Map p74; ☎ 287 8700; www.scotiabank.com; Av 1 btwn Calles 2 & 4; 🕑 8:15am-5pm Mon-Fri) Good service and ATMs on the Cirrus system dispense US dollars too.

Credit cards are widely accepted in San José, though Visa tends to be preferred over MasterCard and American Express. (For more information on money issues in Costa Rica, see p458.

Post

The **Correo Central** (Central Post Office; Map p74; ☎ 223 9766; www.correos.go.cr; Calle 2 btwn Avs 1 & 3; 🕑 8am-5pm Mon-Fri, 7:30am-noon Sat) is the most efficient place to send and receive mail in Costa Rica. It also offers express and overnight services to various parts of the world. A small stamp museum is upstairs on the 2nd floor (see p75).

Telephone

Local and international calls can be made from most public phones, which are found all over town – several dozen are on the west side of Parque Central and around Plaza de la Cultura. Many hotels also have public phones in their lobbies. Chip and Colibrí cards are sold at souvenir shops, newsstands and Más X Menos supermarkets. Telephone directories are usually available in hotels. For general information on phone services, see p460.

Tourist Information

Instituto Costarricense de Turismo (ICT) Plaza de la Cultura (Map p74; ☎ 223 1733 ext 277; www.tourism-costarica.com; Calle 5 btwn Av Central & 2; 🕑 9am-5pm with flexible lunch Mon-Fri) Correo Central (Map p74; in the post office at Calle 2 btwn Avs 1 & 3) The government tourism office is good for a copy of the master bus schedule (that may or may not be out of date) and handy free maps of San José and Costa Rica.
Canatur (☎ 234 6222; www.costarica.tourism.co.cr; 🕑 8am-10pm) The Costa Rican National Chamber of Tourism provides information on member services from a small stand next to the international baggage claim at Juan Santamaría international airport.

Travel Agencies

The following are long-standing and reputable agencies. For a list of tour companies, see p78.
OTEC (Map p74; ☎ 256 0633; www.turismojoven.com; Calle 3 btwn Avs 1 & 3) Specializes in youth travel; can also issue student discount cards.
TAM Travel Corporation (Map p74; ☎ 256 0203; www.tamtravel.com; Calle 1 btwn Avs Central & 1) Airline ticketing, local travel and more.

DANGERS & ANNOYANCES

As in most large cities, street crime is the greatest concern in San José. Pickpocketing tends to be the most common offense, so carry your money and your passport in an inside pocket or use a money belt. Never ever leave money, passports and important documents in the outer pocket of your pack or you will most likely regret it later. (Too many travelers in San José tell the same sad tale: 'I turned around for just a minute and then...'.) Keep daypacks in front of you rather than on your back where they can be unzipped and pilfered; don't wear jewelry or watches as they attract attention.

Don't leave cars parked on the streets; use guarded lots instead. And don't leave anything inside your car – even in a guarded lot.

One occasional scam is getting something spilled on you and then robbed by the person who steps in to help 'clean up'.

The latest crime trend in San José consists of groups of people in cars that mug pedestrians and then speed off; even less reason to walk around alone at night. In recent years, travelers have reported an increasing number of muggings in the area west of the Mercado Central, especially around the Coca-Cola bus terminal, particularly at night. The red-light district in the blocks south of Parque Central, too, has been the scene of many thefts and muggings, mostly at night. Take taxis after dark – they're cheap and will save you plenty of aggravation.

The best way to prevent problems is to first find out (from your hotel or other travelers) about the area you are going to and, especially if bar-hopping at night, to go with a friend. The following neighborhoods are reportedly unsafe at night and dodgy during the day (though few of these are on the travelers' trail): Leon XIII, 15 de Septiembre, Cuba, Cristo Rey, Sagrada Familia, México, Bajo Piuses, Los Cuadros, Torremolinos.

Women traveling alone should take extra precautions. In the past, some women have complained of being harassed by cab drivers at night. Avoid taking unlicensed taxis. (Further information for women travelers is available on p461.)

Men should beware of friendly prostitutes; they are known for their abilities to take more than their customers bargained for – namely their wallets.

Finally, noise and smog are unavoidable components of the San José experience and most central hotels are victim to a considerable amount of street noise, no matter how nice they are. Most importantly, however, take care not to be swallowed up by the pit-sized gutters and potholes.

SIGHTS

The downtown area is fairly small and is best visited on foot as the streets are congested with heavy traffic and parking is difficult. The most pleasant area for walking is Barrio Amón, which is home to many of the city's few surviving *cafetalero* (coffee baron) mansions from the late 19th and early 20th century. Many of them have been restored and are used as hotels, restaurants and offices.

The sights below are listed in counterclockwise fashion around the city, beginning with the contemporary art museum just east of Parque España.

Museo de Arte y Diseño Contemporáneo

The underrated **contemporary art and design museum** (Map pp70-1; ☎ 257 7202; www.madc.ac.cr/; Av 3 btwn Calles 13 & 15; admission US$1; ⏲ 10am-5pm Tue-Sat) is inside the Centro Nacional de la Cultura (Cenac), a city-block-sized arts complex that also features a theater and outdoor sculpture. The museum is housed in the historic National Liquor Factory building that dates back to 1856. Contemporary artists from around the world – including many from Costa Rica – are exhibited here regularly and the installations are well presented and definitely worth a visit. The museum's website is a comprehensive resource on Central American contemporary artists.

Museo de Jade

This is perhaps Costa Rica's most famous **museum** (Map pp70-1; ☎ 287 6034, 223 5800 ext 2527; Edificio INS, Av 7 btwn Calles 9 & 11, 11th fl; adult/child 10 & under US$2/free; ⏲ 8:30am-3:30pm Mon-Fri) and is located in the black glass building for the Instituto Nacional de Seguros (INS). Remodeled in late 2003 and reopened in 2004, the museum houses the world's largest collection of American jade and you'll find hundreds of pieces on display. (Note that 'jade' is written the same in English as in Spanish, but is pronounced 'HA-day' in Spanish.) Many pieces are mounted with a backlight so the exquisite translucent quality of the gemstone can be fully appreciated. There are also archaeological exhibits of ceramics, stonework and gold, arranged by cultural regions. The 11th-floor vantage point offers a good view of the city so bring your camera. And if you're hungry, one reader recommends the employee canteen as a good place for a cheap, tourist-free casado (fixed menu) lunch for US$2.

Galería Andrómeda

If you're wandering around Barrio Amón, this free local **art space** (☎ 223 3529; andromeda@amnet.co.cr; cnr Calle 9 & Av 9), behind the Museo de Jade, is worth a peek to see works by emerging local artists. It also has a selection of literary magazines, all in Spanish.

Zoológico Nacional Simón Bolívar

After seeing animals in the wild all over Costa Rica's national parks, it seems a shame to cage them up purely for viewing purposes. However, the **zoo** (Map pp70-1; ☎ 233 6701, Av 11 btwn Calles 7 & 9; admission US$2; ⏲ 8am-3:30pm Mon-Fri, 9am-4:30pm Sat-Sun) claims that it is more than just an exhibit space and has launched various conservation-awareness initiatives. Here, you can see many of Costa Rica's animals, but, as in many Central and Latin American countries, the cages are too small. The zoo is popular with Tico fam-ilies on weekends and gets very crowded. Go north along Calle 7 and east on Avenida 11 to get there.

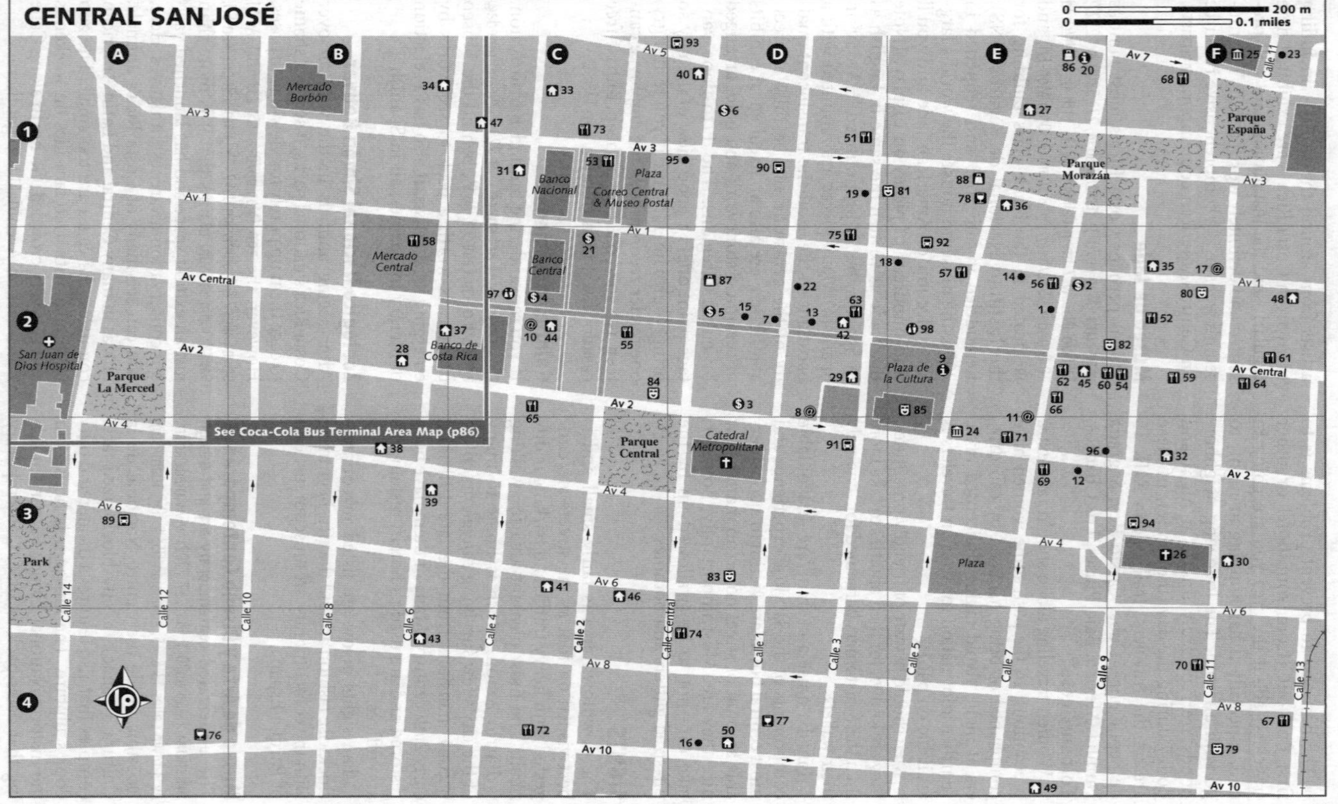
CENTRAL SAN JOSÉ
0 200 m
0 0.1 miles
Mercado Borbón
Mercado Central
Banco de Costa Rica
Banco Central
Banco Nacional
Correo Central & Museo Postal
Plaza
Parque Central
Catedral Metropolitana
Plaza de la Cultura
Parque Morazán
Parque España
Plaza
San Juan de Dios Hospital
Parque La Merced
Park
See Coca-Cola Bus Terminal Area Map (p86)
Av 7
Av 5
Av 3
Av 1
Av Central
Av 2
Av 4
Av 6
Av 8
Av 10
Calle 14
Calle 12
Calle 10
Calle 8
Calle 6
Calle 4
Calle 2
Calle Central
Calle 1
Calle 3
Calle 5
Calle 7
Calle 9
Calle 11
Calle 13

Spirogyra Jardín de Mariposas

This small **butterfly garden** (Map pp70-1; ☎ 222 2937; parcar@racsa.co.cr; 150m east & 150m south of Centro Comercial El Pueblo; adult/student US$6/5; 🕑 8am-4pm) offers ample opportunity to get up close and personal with various breeds of native species of butterfly. There is a small café open during the high season. The garden can be reached on foot (about a 20- to 30-minute walk from downtown), by taxi, or by bus to El Pueblo where there is a sign.

Museo de los Niños & Galería Nacional

The **museum** (Map pp70-1; ☎ 258 4929; www.museocr.com; Calle 4, north of Av 9; admission US$2; 🕑 8am-4:30pm Tue-Fri, 9:30am-5pm Sat-Sun) is not just for kids. This fascinating place resides in an old penitentiary built in 1909 and known locally as 'La Peni'. The children's museum has shows for the tots on science, music, geography and other subjects. Grown-ups, however, will be captivated by the Galería Nacional, a modern exhibit area using old cells as viewing spaces. There is no charge to enter the Galería.

Museo Postal, Telegráfico y Filatélico de Costa Rica

Go postal at the **stamp museum** (Map p74; ☎ 223 6918; Correo Central; Calle 2 btwn Avs 1 & 3; admission free; 🕑 9am-2pm Mon-Fri) with its semi-interesting exhibit of Costa Rican stamps. It's a good way to kill time while your friends are waiting to mail some letters home.

Markets (Mercados)

The **Mercado Central** (Map p74; Avs Central & 1 btwn Calles 6 & 8) is interesting if you've never been to a Latin American market, although it is a little tame compared to the markets of countries such as Perú or Guatemala. Nevertheless, it is crowded and bustling and has a variety of produce and other goods ranging from fresh sausage and spices to T-shirts and knick-knacks for sale (see p96). In addition, some of the cheapest fresh meals in town are served here (see p90). One block away is the similar **Mercado Borbón** (Map p74; cnr Av 3 & Calle 8). The streets surrounding the markets are jam-packed with vendors and pickpockets. Dress down and leave the Rolex at home.

INFORMATION

- 7th Street Books....1 E2
- Banco de Costa Rica....2 E2
- Banco de San José....3 D2
- Banco Nacional de Costa Rica Exchange House....4 C2
- Compañía Financiera de Londrés....5 D2
- Credomatic....6 D1
- Cubana de Aviación....7 D2
- CyberCafé searchcostarica.com....8 D2
- ICT (Tourist Office)....9 E2
- Internet Café Costa Rica....10 C2
- Internet Club....11 E2
- Lavandería Las Arcadas....(see 8)
- Lavandería Sixaola....12 E3
- Lehmann's....13 D2
- Libería Francesa....14 E2
- Librería Universal....15 D2
- Libro Azul....16 D4
- Mora Books....(see 18)
- Netopia Cybercafé....17 F2
- Omni Center....18 E2
- OTEC....19 D1
- Rainforest Aerial Tram Office....20 E1
- Scotiabank....21 C2
- TAM Travel Corporation....22 D2

SIGHTS & ACTIVITIES (pp76–9)

- Casa Amarilla....23 F1
- Galería García Monge....24 E3
- Museo de Jade....25 F1
- Museo de Oro Precolombino y Numismática....(see 9)
- Parroquia Nuestra Señora de la Soledad....26 F3

SLEEPING (pp83–5)

- Aurola Holiday Inn....27 E1
- Gran Hotel Centroamericano....28 B2
- Gran Hotel Costa Rica....29 D2
- Gran Hotel Doña Inés....30 F3
- Hotel ABC....31 C1
- Hotel Avenida Segunda....32 F3
- Hotel Capital....33 C1
- Hotel Compostela....34 B1
- Hotel Del Rey....35 F2
- Hotel Diana's Inn....36 E1
- Hotel Diplomat....37 B2
- Hotel Doral....38 B3
- Hotel El Descanso....39 B3
- Hotel Europa....40 D1
- Hotel Fortuna....41 C3
- Hotel La Gran Vía....42 D2
- Hotel Los Recuerdos....43 B4
- Hotel Plaza....44 C2
- Hotel Presidente....45 E2
- Hotel Príncipe....46 C3
- Hotel Washington....(see 32)
- Nuevo Hotel Central....47 C1
- Pensión de la Cuesta....48 F2
- Tica Linda #1....49 E4
- Tica Linda Anexo....50 D4

EATING (pp90–2)

- Automercado supermarket....51 D1
- Balcón de Europa....52 F2
- Café del Correo....53 C1
- Café Parisienne....(see 29)
- Chelle's....54 F2
- Churrería Manolo's....55 C2
- Del Rey Café....(see 35)
- Faro's Mexican Grill & Bar....56 E2
- La Vasconia....57 E2
- Las Delicias....58 B2
- Manolo's....59 F2
- Mariscar....60 F2
- Más X Menos....61 F2
- News Café....62 E2
- Perimercado....63 D2
- Pops Ice Cream....64 F2
- Pops Ice Cream....65 C2
- Restaurant Fuluso....66 E2
- Restaurant Shakti....67 F4
- Restaurant y Cafetería La Criollita....68 F1
- Restaurante Don Wang....(see 70)
- Restaurante El Pollo Campesino....69 E3
- Restaurante Tin-jo....70 F4
- Ristorante Pizza Metro....71 E3
- Soda Castro....72 C4
- Soda Nini....73 C1
- Vishnu....74 D4
- Vishnu....75 D2

DRINKING (p93)

- Bar Chavelona....76 A4
- La Avispa....77 D4
- Nashville South Bar....78 E1

ENTERTAINMENT (pp93–6)

- Bochinche....79 F4
- Casino Club Colonial....80 F2
- Complejo Salsa 54 y Zadidas....81 E1
- El Túnel de Tiempo....82 F2
- Los Cucharones....83 D3
- Omni....(see 18)
- Teatro Melico Salazar....84 C2
- Teatro Nacional....85 E2

SHOPPING (p96)

- Galería Namú....86 E1
- La Casona....87 D2
- Suraksa....88 E1

TRANSPORT (pp97–101)

- Buses to Escazú....89 A3
- Buses to Guadalupe....90 D1
- Buses to Irazú....91 D3
- Buses to Moravia....92 E2
- Buses to Santo Domingo....93 D1
- Tica Bus (International)....94 F3

OTHER

- Costa Rica Expeditions....95 D1
- Ecole Travel....(see 1)
- Instituto Universal de Idiomas....96 E3
- McDonald's....97 C2
- McDonald's....98 E2

Parque La Sabana

This **park** (Map p68) at the west end of the Paseo Colón is home to both the Museo de Arte Costarricense and the Estadio Nacional (National Stadium), where international and Division-1 soccer matches are played. It is a spacious park, with a lagoon, fountain and a variety of sports facilities (see p78). It's a good place for a daytime stroll or a picnic and offers relief from the congestion of downtown. Don't wander the grounds after dark.

Museo de Arte Costarricense

This sunny **art museum** (Map p68; ☎ 222 7155; musarco@racsa.co.cr; Parque La Sabana; adult/student US$5/3, free on Sun; 🕑 10am-4pm Tue-Sun) is at the west end of Paseo Colón. The museum has a permanent collection of Costa Rican art from the 19th and 20th centuries in a Spanish colonial-style building that housed San José's airport until 1955. Regular rotating exhibits feature works by Tico artists past and present.

Museo de Ciencias Naturales La Salle

The **natural history museum** (Map p68; ☎ 232 1306; in the old Colegio La Salle (high school); admission US$1.50; 🕑 7:30am-4pm Mon-Sat), near the southwest corner of Parque La Sabana, is a small, somewhat dated and dusty collection of mounted animals and butterflies that could be used as a resource for identifying species in the wild. Unless you're fanatical about taxidermy this might not be a priority. For the diehard, there are also exhibits on paleontology and archaeology. A cab to the museum from any part of downtown will usually cost less than US$2. Taxi drivers know it as the Colegio La Salle. A Sabana-Cementario or Sabana-Estadio city bus from Parque Central will take you there for about US$0.25 – ask the driver to let you know when to get off for the museum.

Parque Central

This **park** (Map p74; Avs 2 & 4 btwn Calles Central & 2) is the place to catch a taxi or a local city bus. It's also home to many pickpockets, so watch the wallet. To the east of the square is the modern and refreshingly well maintained **Catedral Metropolitana** (Map p74; Avs 2 & 4 btwn Calles Central & 1). On the north side of Parque Central is **Teatro Melico Salazar** (Map p74; Av 2 btwn Calle Central & 2), which was the sight of the 2002 presidential inauguration and is host to regular fine arts engagements (see p93).

Plaza de la Cultura

The **Plaza de la Cultura** (Map p74; Avs Central & 2 btwn Calles 3 & 5), in the middle of town, is the site of the Teatro Nacional, the Museo de Oro Precolombino and the ICT office. It's not particularly prepossessing but it's a perfect place to people watch.

Museo de Oro Precolombino y Numismática

This three-in-one **museum** (Map p74; ☎ 243 4202; www.museosdelbancocentral.org; Plaza de la Cultura, basement; admission US$5; 🕑 9:15am-4:30pm Tue-Sun) has a glittering collection of pre-Columbian gold and other artifacts. This is one of the better-presented museums in San José, though much smaller than similar collections in Mexico and Peru. A small exhibit details the history of Costa Rican currency and another room houses a temporary display space for local art. The museum is owned by the Banco Central and its architecture brings to mind all the warmth and comfort of a bank vault. Security is tight; all visitors must leave bags at the door.

Teatro Nacional

The **national theater** (Map p74; ☎ 221 1329; Calles 3 & 5 btw Avs Central & 2; admission US$3; 🕑 9am-5pm Mon-Fri, 9am-12:30pm & 1:30-5:30pm Sat) is considered San José's most impressive public building. Built in 1897, the building features a columned neoclassical facade and is flanked by statues of Beethoven and Calderón de la Barca, a 17th-century Spanish dramatist. The lavish lobby and auditorium are lined with paintings depicting various facets of 19th-century life. The most famous is *Alegoría al café y el banano*, an idyllic canvas showing coffee and banana harvests. The painting was produced in Italy and shipped to Costa Rica for installation in the theater and the image was reproduced on the five-colón note (now out of circulation), which you can find in some souvenir shops. It is clear that the painter never witnessed a banana harvest because of the way he portrayed a central man awkwardly grasping a bunch. (Actual banana workers hoist the stem onto their shoulders.)

The marble staircases, gilded ceilings and parquet floors of tropical hardwoods are worth seeing. For information on viewing a performance, see p93. At the time of research, the whole complex was receiving a needed cleaning and renovation. During this process, the theater café will be closed and it is unclear when and if it will reopen.

Belonging to the Teatro is the very worthwhile **Galería García Monge** (cnr Av 2 & Calle 5; admission free), across the street, with exhibits by contemporary artists.

Museo de Criminología

The objective of the **crime museum** (Map pp70-1; ☎ 295 3850; Calle 17 btwn Avs 6 & 8, 2nd fl; admission free; 🕑 7:30am-noon, 1-4pm Mon-Fri), inside the OIJ building (Organismo de Investigación Judicial; Supreme Court of Justice), is the prevention of crime through the presentation of exhibits related to criminal acts. The museum is part gore and part thrill – exhibiting artifacts used in a variety of crimes, including a severed hand and a variety of photographs depicting the country's most notorious offenses. This place will undoubtedly prove to be a delight for young boys everywhere.

Museo Nacional de Costa Rica

Located inside the Bellavista Fortress, the **Museo Nacional** (Map pp70-1; ☎ 257 1433; Calle 17 btwn Avs Central & 2; admission US$0.50; 🕑 8:30am-4:30pm Tue-Sun) will provide you with a good survey of Costa Rican history. You'll find a wide range of pre-Columbian artifacts from ongoing digs at archeological sites such as Guayabo (see p148), as well as numerous colonial objects and plenty of religious art. A natural-history wing has plant and fauna specimens, minerals and fossils. The building once served as the old army headquarters and the walls around the garden are pockmarked by bullets from the 1948 civil war. There is a gift shop.

Museo de Formas, Espacios y Sonidos

This curious **interactive museum** (Map pp70-1; ☎ 222 9462; Av 3 btwn Calles 17 & 23; admission US$1; 🕑 9:30am-3pm Mon-Fri) is geared to small kids or people who like to act like them. Housed in the old San José Atlantic train station, you can clamber on an antique locomotive and traipse through old rail cars. Several small exhibits are dedicated to the senses of sound, touch and sight. Large groups should call ahead to schedule a tour.

Eastern Parks & Plazas

Numerous other green areas dot downtown San José, providing a small respite from the grit of the capital. Note that many of these parks are not safe after dark and many others become centers of prostitution.

One of the nicest plazas in San José is the shady **Parque Nacional** (Map pp70-1; Avs 1 & 3 btwn Calles 15 & 19). In its center, you'll find the dramatic Monumento Nacional, showing the Central American nations driving out the American filibuster William Walker. (See p23 to learn more about this pesky gringo.) Important buildings surrounding the park include the **Biblioteca Nacional** (National Library) to the north, the Cenac complex, which houses the modern art museum (p73) to the northwest and the **Asamblea Legislativa** (Congressional Building) to the south. In the Asamblea's gardens is a statue of national hero Juan Santamaría. (For more on his exploits, turn to p24.)

South of the Asamblea Legislativa is the stark **Plaza de la Democracia** (Map pp70-1; Avs Central & 2 btwn Calles 13 & 15), which is architecturally unremarkable though it does provide decent views of the mountains surrounding San José. On its western flank, you'll find an open-air crafts market that has a good selection of gifts (see p96).

Parque España (Map p74; Avs 3 & 7 btwn, Calles 9 & 11) is surrounded by heavy traffic, but manages to become a riot of birdsong every day at sunset as the local avian types come in to roost. The park is bordered by the black glass INS building to the north, which serves as the home of the Museo de Jade. A block to the west is the **edificio metálico** (Map p74; cnr Av 7 & Calle 9), an interesting two-story yellow-and-blue metal building that was designed in France and prefabricated in Belgium. The pieces were shipped piece by piece from Europe and constructed in San José in the 1890s. It now serves as a school.

To the northeast of Parque España, is the splendid **Casa Amarilla** (Map pp70-1; Av 7 btwn Calles 11 & 13). This beautiful colonial-style building is home to the ministry of foreign affairs and is not open to the public. It's exterior, however, is exquisitely maintained and is worth a look or a photo.

To the southwest, you'll find the slightly run-down **Parque Morazán** (Map p74; Avs 3 & 5 btwn Calles 5 & 9) capped in the center by a concrete gazebo referred to as the Templo de Música – a handy landmark. (Take care when walking through this park at night as it's a booming prostitution center.)

ACTIVITIES

Parque La Sabana (Map p68) has a variety of sporting facilities. There are tennis courts, volleyball, basketball and baseball areas, jogging paths and an Olympic-size swimming pool, but it costs about US$3 to swim and it is open only noon to 2pm. Many Ticos prefer the excursion to the Ojo de Agua springs (in San Antonio de Belén, see p117), where swimming is available all day.

Tennis, gym facilities and a swimming pool are also available at the **Costa Rica Tennis Club** (☎ 232 1266) on the south side of La Sabana for US$10 per person per day. There are 11 indoor and outdoor courts, three pools, a sauna and gym facilities.

You can sign up with a local gym for about US$20 a month. Look under 'Gimnasios' in the yellow pages telephone directory.

Golfers can lose their golf balls at either the **Cariari Country Club** (Map p68; ☎ 293 3211; cariari@racsa.co.cr), the **Costa Rica Country Club** (Map p68; ☎ 228 9333, 208 5000) or **Valle del Sol** (Map p68; ☎ 282 9222, ext 218/219). For details, see p113, and p106, respectively.

Adrenaline junkies can sign up for the daily bungee jumps at the nearby Río Colorado Bridge with **Tropical Bungee** (☎ 248 2212, 383 9724; www.bungee.co.cr; one jump US$60). Transportation from San José hotels is included.

COURSES

There are fine Spanish-language schools in and around San José. The schools listed have been operating since at least 1998 and/or they have received reader recommendations. See San Pedro (p102) for other options. For dance schools, see the boxed text opposite.

Centro Lingüístico Conversa (☎ 221 7649, in the USA 800-367 7726, in the Caribbean 880-354 5036; www.conversa.net; Centro Colón, cnr Calle 38 & Paseo Colón)

Central America Institute for International Affairs (ICAI; ☎ 233 8571; www.educaturs.com; 100m west, 25m north, 25m west from the emergency room entrance of Hospital Calderón Guardia)

Instituto Universal de Idiomas (Map p74; ☎ 223 9662; www.universal-edu.com; Av 2 btwn Calles 7 & 9, 2nd fl)

Universidad Veritas (☎ 283 4747; www.uveritas.ac.cr; Edificio ITAN, Carretera a Zapote, 1km west of Casa Presidencial)

SAN JOSÉ FOR CHILDREN

Most children will probably want to get out of San José as fast as possible in order to sample the adventures of the rain forest, beaches and erupting volcanoes. But if you're spending a day – or two or three – in San José there are a number of activities to keep the tykes busy and/or exhausted.

The **Museo de los Niños** (p75) and the **Museo de Formas, Espacios y Sonidos** (p77) are a hit with young children who just can't keep their hands off the exhibits. Interactive is what they're all about.

Both **Teatro Eugene O'Neill** (p105) and **Teatro Fanal** (p95) have children's theater groups. If your child is learning Spanish, this experience might make a vivid lesson.

Young nature lovers will enjoy getting up close and personal with butterflies at the **Spirogyra Jardín de Mariposas** (p75) or checking out all of the exotic animals over at the **Zoológico Nacional Simón Bolívar** (p73). Also, the **Museo de Criminología** (p77) may be of interest to pre-adolescent boys, who will likely enjoy getting totally grossed out by the somewhat grisly exhibits.

Teens might dig checking each other out at the **Plaza de la Cultura** (p76), which has a number of nearby fast-food outlets. In the suburbs, **Mall San Pedro** (p106) and the **Escazú Multiplaza** (p112) are good for young consumers craving mall action.

To wear them out with a day of outdoor activities, there are always the swimming pools at the **Costa Rica Tennis Club** (see earlier), which are open to the public. For more extensive water-based activities, head northwest of San José for **Ojo de Agua** (p117).

TOURS

Tour companies include:

Calypso Tours (☎ 256 2727; www.calypsotours.com) Does tours to the islands near Bahía Gigante by bus and 70-foot motorized catamaran (see p259 for details).

Ecole Travel (Map p74; ☎ 223 2240; www.ecoletravel.com; Calle 7 btwn Avs Central & 1) Good for budget and mid-priced tours of Costa Rica.

Swiss Travel Service (Map pp70-1; ☎ 221 0944; 250m west of Centro Comercial El Pueblo) Long-time, reputable travel agency for tours all over Costa Rica. There is a branch office at the Radisson Europa.

Tiquicia Travel (☎ 256 9682; www.tiquiciatravel.com; Condominios Pie Montel, La Uruca) A small agency focusing on tours to gay and gay-friendly locales around Costa Rica.

The city is easily navigable by the independent traveler and walking tours aren't necessary if you have a little time on your hands. If you have just a few hours and don't want

DANCE SCHOOLS

If you want to improve your moves on the dance floor, then check out one of the many classes offered in the San José area. These are geared at Ticos, not tourists, but travelers who speak Spanish are welcome. You can learn all types of Latin dancing – salsa, cha-cha, merengue, bolero, tango. Classes cost around US$20 for two hours of group lessons per week. Travelers can also find dance classes by inquiring at many language schools.

- **Academia de Bailes Latinos** (☎ 233 8938; Av Central btwn Calles 25 & 27, next to Pizza Hut in Barrio Escalante)
- **Malecón** (Map pp70-1; ☎ 222 3214; Av 2 btwn Calles 17 & 19)
- **Merecumbé** (☎ 228 6253; Escazú)
- **Kurubandé** (☎ 234 0682; Guadalupe)

to miss the key sights, Swiss Travel Service offers a three-hour tour that covers the San José basics: the Teatro Nacional, Museo Nacional, Asamblea Legislativa, the Cathedral and the Supreme Court building (OIJ). It also includes visits to Parque Nacional and Parque La Sabana and a drive through the residential area of Rohrmoser. Guides are bilingual and the fee is US$26, including transport and museum tickets.

The agency also organizes day trips to any place you might have never thought of going in the San José and Central Valley area.

FESTIVALS & EVENTS

Every even year, San José becomes host to the biannual **Festival de Arte**, a city-wide arts showcase featuring theater, music, dance and film. It is held for two weeks in March. Keep an eye out for information in the daily newspapers. On **Día de San José**, on the 19th of March, San José marks the day for its patron saint with masses in some churches. The day used to be a holiday, but modernization has quickly done away with that.

SLEEPING

Accommodations in San José run the gamut from grim little boxes to sumptuous world-class luxury. Many cheap hotels are found west of Calle Central and near the Coca-Cola bus terminal. Unless you're a die-hard fan of grunge and bustle, this is one of San José's less pleasant neighborhoods. More upscale places reside west of downtown, in La Sabana and Rohrmoser, and others can be found on the east end of town in Barrio Amón. See also the many options in Los Yoses and San Pedro (p103) and Escazú (p106). Both neighborhoods lie just a few minutes ride outside of downtown. Some options near San Antonio de Belén are given on p113.

Reservations are recommended during the high season (December through April) and the two weeks around Christmas and Semana Santa (the week before Easter Sunday). For more general information on hotels in Costa Rica, see p448. High-season prices are listed throughout.

Before reserving with a credit card, please turn to p449 for advice.

North & East of the Centre — Map pp70-1

BUDGET

The author's choice for this price range is Hostal Pangea in Barrio Amón (see the boxed text on p81).

Tranquilo Backpackers (☎ 223 3189, 222 2493, 355 5103; www.tranquilobackpackers.com; Calle 7 btwn Avs 9 & 11; dm US$7, s/d US$11/19; 💻) In Barrio Amón, Tranquilo is one of the newest hostels on the scene and has been recommended by readers. This sunny German-run outpost offers clean and spacious dorm-style rooms, laundry service (US$4.75 per load), communal kitchen, free luggage storage and Internet access and a distinctly mellow vibe. The gleaming and whimsically decorated mosaic tile showers are all shared. A big draw is the free pancake breakfast that the hosts cook up every morning. Hammocks are available in the patio for chilling and a nice verandah overlooks the street.

Casa Ridgway (☎ 222 1400; friends@racsa.co.cr; cnr Calle 15 & Av 6 bis; dm US$10, s/d US$12/24; ⊠) This welcoming guesthouse, on a quiet side street near the Supreme Court building, is run by the adjacent Friends' Peace Center, whose stated mission is to promote understanding of social-justice issues. Rooms are immaculate, the water is hot and the atmosphere is, well, peaceful. A communal kitchen and laundry service (US$5 per load) are available; all bathrooms are shared. A lending library offers an extensive collection of books on Central American politics and society. This isn't the place for party people – there's no smoking, alcohol or drugs allowed and quiet hours are from 10pm to 6am.

Costa Rica Backpackers (☎ 221 6191; www.costarica backpackers.com; Av 6 btwn Calles 21 & 23; dm US$9, d US$20; P 🖳 🏊) This downtown hostel near the Supreme Court building is one of the many budget traveling options vying for customers in the San José area. The hostel has colorful rooms around a garden courtyard along with a game room. Some travelers report that the place could use a few more bathrooms. There is free coffee and tea and laundry service is available (US$5 a load).

Casa Hilda (☎ 221 0037; c1hilda@racsa.co.cr; Av 11 btwn Calles 3 & 3 bis; d incl breakfast US$25-35) The Quesadas will make you feel like a member of the family at this peaceful, peach-colored inn in Barrio Amón. Rooms of different sizes are simple, but all have a bathroom and hot water. Some rooms face a small, pretty garden courtyard with a natural spring. Information on tours and travel to other parts of Costa Rica is provided here.

Hotel Bellavista (☎ 223 0095, in the USA 800-637 0899; wimberly@racsa.co.cr; Av Central btwn Calles 19 & 21; s/d US$23/29) This dark, but clean hotel is much larger than it appears from the outside. Service is good and all rooms have a bathroom and hot water. Prices include breakfast at the attached diner. Some readers have complained of thin walls. Welcome to Central America.

Casa León (☎ 222 9725; Av 6 btwn Calles 13 & 15; dm US$10, s/d US$20/25) This minimally signed, sparkling hotel is right on the bend of the railroad tracks. The hot showers are shared and there is a communal kitchen. The owners are friendly and can provide tourist information.

> **SCAMS**
>
> Many taxi drivers in San José (and other parts of Costa Rica) are commissioned by hotels to bring them customers. In the capital, the hotel scene is so competitive that drivers will say just about anything to steer you to the places they represent. They'll tell you the establishment you've chosen is a notorious drug den, it's closed down, or that, sadly, it's overbooked. (Many owners will tell you wild stories about the horrible condition of the of the rooms at the competition down the street.) Do not believe everything you hear. Tell drivers firmly where it is you would like to go, and if you have doubts about the place you're about to decide to stay at, ask to see a room before paying up.

MID-RANGE

Kap's Place is the author's mid-range choice (see the boxed text opposite).

Hotel Aranjuez (☎ 256 1825; www.hotelaranjuez .com; Calle 19 btwn Avs 11 & 13; s/d US$21/24, d with bathroom US$39-42; P 🖳) This rambling wood hotel consists of several nicely maintained vintage homes strung together with connecting gardens and a lush backyard containing a mango tree. Spotless rooms vary in size and price and the hosts serve a sumptuous daily breakfast buffet in the garden courtyard (included in the rates). There is free Internet and local calls and laundry service is available (US$5 per load). The place is run by a friendly Costa Rican family (English and German are spoken) that enjoys hosting international guests. Be sure to confirm your reservation before arriving.

Taylor's Bed & Breakfast (☎ 257 4333; taylorsinn@ catours.co.cr; Av 13 btwn Calles 3 & 3 bis; d US$46; ⊠ 🖳) A quaint well-maintained brick house in Barrio Amón, it has 10 spotless rooms of varying sizes and styles. Rooms have a phone and hot shower and are set around a pleasant interior courtyard with a fountain where breakfast is served. Laundry service is available (US$7 per load) and there's free email.

Joluva Guesthouse (☎ 223 7961; www.joluva.com; Calle 3 bis btwn Avs 9 & 11; s/d US$35/50; 🖳) This is a small, clean and well-run gay-operated guesthouse in Barrio Amón. Old-fashioned public areas are the most attractive feature and the seven rooms are rather small but well appointed; all have a bathroom and cable TV. Continental breakfast is included in the rates and Internet access (US$1 per hour) and VCR rental are available. The management speaks English, can provide information on the local gay scene and suggest travel arrangements.

Hotel Dunn Inn (☎ 222 3232, 222 3426; www.hotel dunninn.com; cnr Calle 5 & Av 11; s/d US$40/52, ste US$64; P 🖳) This rambling brick-and-wood, 24-room hotel is in an attractive late-19th-century house. The newer rooms at the back feel airier while older quarters are darker. All units come with fan and cable TV and suites have king-size beds. Laundry service

AUTHOR'S CHOICE

Budget

Hostal Pangea (Map pp70-1; ☎ 221 1992; www.hostelpangea.com; Av 11 btwn Calles 3 & 3 bis; dm US$9, d without/with bathroom US$24/28; 💻) If you're going cheap, do it here. Run by a pair of animated Tico twin brothers, this renovated hostel in Barrio Amón has dozens of clean dorm beds, shiny shared bathrooms and a spacious communal kitchen. A light breakfast is served (US$1) and there's free Internet and free phone calls to North America. A living room has cable TV and there's a bean-bag lounge and bar – all within crawling distance of your room. The brothers will be opening up a similar hostel in La Fortuna in 2005.

Mid-range

Kap's Place (Map pp70-1; ☎ 221 1169; www.kapsplace.com; Calle 19 btwn Avs 11 & 13; s US$27-30, d US$35-40, tr US$48-50, apt US$80; 💻) Knowledgeable owner Karla Arias runs a meticulously maintained, colorfully painted guesthouse with 13 cozy rooms of varying sizes and prices. All of them have cable TV, phone and hot shower; there's a shared kitchen and Internet access. Arias speaks English and French and gathers with guests in the sitting area, where free coffee and tea are provided.

Top End

Hotel Grano de Oro (☎ 255 3322; www.hotelgranodeoro.com; Calle 30 btwn Av 2 & 4; s US$94, d standard/superior/deluxe US$99/117/135, ste US$158-280, additional person US$5; P ⊠) This 35-room hotel, west of downtown, is a great choice all around. Housed in an early-20th-century mansion (check out the old photos), the rooms are nothing less than exquisite and the service excellent. Rooms are nonsmoking, have cable TV, phone and are furnished with Victorian-style pieces. There is a top-notch restaurant (p92). Credit cards accepted.

and Internet access (US$2.50 per hour) are available. There is a plant-filled **restaurant** (🕑 7am-8:30pm Mon-Sat, 7:30-11:30am Sun) in the courtyard and the bar stays open late. There is a guarded parking lot (US$4 per night). Visa is accepted.

Hemingway Inn (☎ 257 8630, 221 1804; www.hemingwayinn.com; cnr Calle 9 & Av 9; s/d/tr economy US$37/47/57, standard US$40/50/60; deluxe US$50/57/67; 💻) This inn in Barrio Amón is in a solid-looking 1930s house and is decorated with plenty of photos of the cantankerous author that the inn is named after. Seventeen old-fashioned rooms each bear the name of a different (male) 20th-century writer and offer comfortable beds, ceiling fan, cable TV, clock radio, phone (free calls within Costa Rica) and electric hot shower. Economy rooms are the smallest and darkest, while standard and deluxe rooms get progressively bigger and better as you move upstairs. Laundry service (US$7 per load) is available. All rates include breakfast. Credit cards accepted.

Hotel Vesuvio (☎ 221 8325, 256 1616; www.hotelvesuvio.com; Av 11 btwn Calles 13 & 15; s/d/tr US$45/55/65, d deluxe US$59; P 💻) This family-owned hotel is on a quiet street in Barrio Amón. Twenty smallish, clean and carpeted rooms line a long corridor. All units have cable TV, phone, fan and hot shower. Deluxe rooms have bathrooms with tubs. Hairdryers are provided on request and email service is free for the first 15 minutes. The rooms are nothing to write home about, but the friendliness of the owners makes up for it. Breakfast is included; an onsite **restaurant** (dishes US$4-7) is open daily and serves a variety of Italian specialties at moderate prices.

Hotel La Amistad Inn (☎ 258 0021; cnr Av 11 & Calle 15; centralamerica.com/cr/hotel/amistad.htm; s/d/tr US$43/58/73, s/d deluxe $55/70, apt US$67/82; P ❄) The hotel has 40 rooms of various categories in a secure terracotta-colored building. Larger deluxe rooms are newer and have air-con and minibar; studio apartments have a kitchenette. The hallways don't look like much, but the rooms are sparkling and the owner will change traveler's checks. All units have hot shower, cable TV and safe. There is free luggage storage. Rates include breakfast; credit cards accepted.

Hotel Kekoldi (☎ 248 0804; www.kekoldi.com; Av 9 btwn Calles 5 & 7; s/d/tr US$53/68/83, d master queen US$82)

The Kekoldi is in a fabulously light and airy Art Deco building in Barrio Amón and features spotless, freshly painted rooms. All rooms have hot-water bathroom, phone, cable TV and safe. The 'master queen' room features a garden view, two queen-size beds and a larger bathroom. Note that singles are limited in high season. Luggage storage, laundry service and tour arrangements are available, and English, German and Italian are spoken. This hotel is gay-friendly and popular with younger travelers. It has a sister hotel in Manuel Antonio (p298). Rates include breakfast and credit cards are accepted.

Hotel Don Carlos (☎ 221 6707; www.doncarlos.co.cr; Calle 9 btwn Avs 7 & 9; s/d standard US$64/76, superior US$76/88, child under 12 free; P 💻) A popular hotel, the Don Carlos is in a beautifully remodeled mansion and each of the 33 tile-floored rooms is different but comfortable. All are nicely decorated and have cable TV, phone, lockbox and bathroom with hot shower and hairdryer. Rates include tropical breakfast and a welcome cocktail. There is also free Internet and covered parking, a Jacuzzi and an excellent gift shop (Annemarie's Boutique, see p96). The attractive indoor patio, garden and sundeck have a pre-Columbian theme. There is a restaurant and, occasionally, live marimba music.

Rincón de San José (☎ 221 9702; www.hotelrincondesanjose.com; Av 9 btwn Calle 13 & 15; s/d/tr US$46/58/70; 💻) This charming little hotel in a landmark house in Barrio Amón is beautifully kept and furnished with period-style pieces. The rooms are large and have shiny wood or ceramic-tile floors. Breakfast, included in the rate, is served in an attractive garden courtyard; a small bar is open until 10pm. There is free Internet, laundry service (US$5 per load) and secure parking nearby. Credit cards accepted.

Fleur de Lys Hotel (☎ 257 2621; www.hotelfleurdelys.com; Calle 13 btwn Avs 2 & 6; s/d US$68/78, junior ste US$93) Housed in a beautifully restored 1926 building, this fine hotel features 31 individually decorated rooms, each named after a native flower and all with cable TV, phone, sparkling bathroom and hairdryer. The six junior suites are more spacious and three have a Jacuzzi. Rates include breakfast. Both public areas and private rooms feature Costa Rican art, attractive furnishings and beautifully polished woodwork. There is a good restaurant (see p89).

TOP END

All of the following accept credit cards.

Hotel Villa Tournón (☎ 233 6622; www.hotel-costa-rica.com; s/d standard US$83/89; s/d superior US$96/102; ❄ 🏊) This clean, well-run and modern hotel has 80 well-appointed rooms, all with cable TV and phone. Standard rooms are spacious and superior units more so, the latter feature king-size beds, a minibar, hairdryer and sitting area. The hotel is popular with business travelers who take advantage of the Internet port in every room and the kidney-shaped pool and Jacuzzi in the garden out the back. There is a fitness area and conference center. The hotel has a decent restaurant, the **Rincón Azul** (🕑 6:30am-11pm) and a popular bar called ¿Por que no? (see p93). Cab drivers know the hotel as being 100m east of the *República* newspaper office.

Hotel Santo Tomás (☎ 255 0448; www.hotelsantotomas.com; Av 7 btwn Calles 3 & 5; d standard/superior/deluxe US$75/91/105, additional person US$15; 💻 🏊) This excellent downtown choice features 20 superior and larger deluxe rooms with polished wood floors and 4m-high ceilings in a refurbished early-20th-century landmark mansion that once belonged to the Salazar family of *cafetaleros*. Antique pieces add to the elegance of the public areas and spacious rooms, all of which are set back from the busy street so noise is not an issue. Quarters have hot shower, cable TV, phone and 30 minutes of free Internet a day. English is spoken and a tropical breakfast is included in the rates. There is a garden courtyard with a solar-heated swimming pool, a Jacuzzi and a small gym. Also there is a small, recommended restaurant, the El Oasis (see p89).

Hotel Amón Plaza (☎ 257 0191; www.hotelamonplaza.com; cnr Av 11 & Calle 3 bis; s/d US$128/140, s/d ste from US$193/205, additional person US$20, child under 12 free; P ❄) This freshly renovated hotel has modern carpeted rooms with all the amenities you would expect for the price: phone, clock radio, cable TV, hairdryer, spacious bathroom, a safe and 24-hour room service. The staff speaks English. A pleasant outdoor café serves a tasty all-you-can-eat breakfast buffet (US$8) and a more formal eatery serves pricier dinners.

Raya Vida Villa (☎ 223 4168; www.rayavida.com; off Av 11; s/d US$88/111, additional person US$20; P) This secluded and elegant gleaming, white home is a treasure of a B&B. The bedrooms, dining and sitting areas reflect the owner's interest in art and antiques and visitors can expect to spot original works by Dalí and Toulouse-Lautrec. Stained glass, hardwood floors, a patio with fountain, a fireplace and a small garden make this a charming place to stay. Owner Michael Long can help with reservations at other B&Bs. The four bedrooms have cable TV, and one room's bathroom has a whirlpool tub. Breakfast is included and Michael will accommodate any low-carb dieters. Laundry service (US$15 per load) is available and there is free airport pick-up if you reserve ahead. For the cab driver: the hotel is 100m north of Hospital Calderón Guardia on Calle 17, then 50m west on Avenida 11, then another 50m north.

Britannia Hotel (☎ 223 6667, in the USA 800-263 2618, 888-535 8832; www.hotelbritanniacostarica.com; cnr Calle 3 & Av 11; s/d US$90/104, deluxe US$108/122, ste US$123/136, child under 10 free;) The Britannia is a small but elegant hotel in a renovated 1910 mansion in the heart of Barrio Amón. The attractive rooms are large and come with cable TV, phone and good-sized bathroom. Larger deluxe rooms offer a better value and also have air-con and writing desk. Five junior suites offer a sitting area. Ask for rooms at the back to avoid street noise. There is a good **restaurant** (6am-2pm & 6-10pm), popular with local businessmen, and a bar.

Central San José — Map p74

Noise is a drawback at some of the following places.

BUDGET

Hotel Compostela (☎ 257 1514; Calle 6 btwn Avs 3 & 5; r per person with bathroom US$8) Despite the sketchy neighborhood, this well-maintained hotel is large and clean. Single and double rooms have a private hot-water bathroom, but it's across the corridor; ask for rooms at the back to avoid noise. The owners are friendly.

Hotel El Descanso (☎ 221 9941; jolin_w@hotmail.com; Calle 6 btwn Avs 4 & 6; r per person US$8) This new backpacker outpost is run by the same people who operate the Nuevo Johnson and the Generaleño in the Coca-Cola bus terminal area (see p86). While the entrance looks forbidding, this family-run operation has freshly painted colossal rooms. All have a bathroom, some of which have been remodeled.

Nuevo Hotel Central (☎ 222 3509; Av 3 btwn Calles 4 & 6; s/d US$14/18) The hotel is secure, the staff helpful, the rooms are big and clean, and the 4th floor is nice and quiet. All rooms have a hot shower and, for a bit extra, you can get a TV. Rooms with five beds are also available. Credit cards accepted.

Hotel Capital (☎ 221 8497; Calle 4 btwn Avs 3 & 5; s/d US$16/20) This hotel tends to be frequented by single men and units are clean, though simple and all have a bathroom with hot water and TV. Outside rooms are noisy, but interior rooms are dark.

Hotel ABC (☎ 221 5007; Calle 4 btwn Avs 1 & 3; s/d US$10/15) Basic, though clean, small, simple rooms are up a flight of stairs and all have a bathroom and fan. There is a public lounge area with a TV and phone.

Pensión de la Cuesta (☎ 256 7946; www.suntoursandfun.com/lacuesta; Av 1 btwn Calles 11 & 15; s/d US$23/35, child under 12 free) On a slope, on the eastern edge of the center this pink-and-blue hotel looks as if it was decorated by Ken and Barbie. It is situated on a little hill behind the Asamblea Legislativa in an attractive 1920s wood house. The nine rooms with shared bathroom seem a little small for the price, but the homey living room with cable TV makes up for it. Helpful staff can arrange tours. Continental breakfast is included in the rate and there is free luggage storage. Some rooms can be noisy.

Gran Hotel Centroamericano (☎ 221 3362; Av 2 btwn Calles 6 & 8; s/d/tr/q US$18/23/28/36) The lobby of this hotel popular with Tico travelers is a hive of activity at all times. Rooms here are clean, though rather small, and have electric shower and phone. Some rooms sleep up to six people. Its main attraction is the central location; the management is friendly and laundry service is available. Credit cards are accepted and there is a 10% discount for students with a valid ISIC card.

Hotel Diplomat (☎ 221 8133, 221 8744; Calle 6 btwn Avs Central & 2; s/d US$18/25) Standard, small and clean rooms have private hot showers but they're all looking a little tired. There is a restaurant.

Hotel Avenida Segunda (☎ 222 0260; acebrisa@racsa.co.cr; Av 2 btwn Calles 9 & 11; dm US$8, r per person with bathroom US$12) Accommodations are very basic and consist of bare rooms though bathrooms have hot water. It has a small TV lounge and laundry service (US$4 per load). Be prepared for some noise – this hotel faces serious traffic on Avenida 2.

Hotel Washington (☎ 222 3172; hotelwashington@hotmail.com; Av 2 btwn Calles 9 & 11; per person without/

with bathroom US$6.30/8.80) Similar in atmosphere and facilities to the Avenida Segunda next door. Choose between musty interior rooms and exterior rooms filled with street noise.

Hotel Fortuna (☎ 223 5186; Av 6 btwn Calles 2 & 4; s/d US$22/28) This is a clean, quiet choice that has decent though smallish rooms with good beds, bathroom with hot water, phone, cable TV and fan. The neighborhood is close to the Calle 2 red-light district and is on a rowdy block filled with vegetable vendors.

Hotel Príncipe (☎ 222 7983; Av 6 btwn Calles Central & 2; s/d US$11.30/13.80) The rooms are spartan, but clean and have a bathroom with hot water. If you get a room facing the street, expect to awake to the sounds of produce vendors plying their wares at full volume.

Tica Linda No 1 (Av 10 btwn Calles 7 & 9; dm US$4, r per person US$5) and **Tica Linda Anexo** (☎ 221 3120; ticalindaanexo@hotmail.com; Av 10 btwn Calles Central & 1, next to Libro Azul) Both hotels are basic, cramped and rather noisy, but the friendliness of the owners will make up for any of that – and it is one of the cheapest deals in town. Rates are the same at both hotels, run by the Tico brother and sister team of José Luis and Charo. (José Luis currently doesn't have a phone or email at Tica Linda No 1, so call Charo at the Anexo if you want to make a reservation.) At both, you'll find communal kitchens, dozens of beds in a variety of rooms, hot showers and free luggage storage. In addition, if you're worried about getting into town from the airport on your own, Charo will come to pick you up (by bus or in a taxi depending on your budget).

Hotel Los Recuerdos (☎ 222 7320; Av 8, cnr Calle 6; d weekday/weekend US$17.50/25; ❄) This new hotel is surprisingly nice for a neighborhood that isn't. Clean well-lit hallways lead to tiled rooms in a Spanish-style terracotta building. All rooms have a bathroom and hot water.

MID-RANGE

Hotel Diana's Inn (☎ 223 6542; dianas@racsa.co.cr; cnr Calle 5 & Av 3; s/d US$30/40; ❄) This is an attractive peach clapboard house overlooking Parque Morazán. Rooms are simple and spacious and have air-con, cable TV and phones. The staff is friendly and helpful; one drawback is that all rooms overlook a busy street.

Hotel La Gran Vía (☎ 222 7737, 222 7706; www.granvia.co.cr/gran/via.html; Av Central btwn Calles 1 & 3; s/d US$45/60) This hotel has some attractive rooms with balconies facing the pedestrian mall below and quieter rooms inside. The 32 modern, carpeted units feature direct dial phone, cable TV, refrigerator on request, and either two queen beds or one bed and a desk area. It has a reasonably priced restaurant and breakfast is included from Monday to Saturday December through April. Some rooms may be noisy. Credit cards accepted.

Hotel Plaza (☎ 222 5533, 257 1896; hotplaza@racsa.co.cr; Av Central btwn Calles 2 & 4; s/d/tr US$31/37/48.50) In the heart of downtown, this place has 40 nice, if worn, rooms with cable TV, phone and fan. The central location is convenient, but the variety of musical street acts below may mean early wake-ups. Breakfast is an extra US$5 per day. Credit cards accepted.

Hotel del Bulevar (☎ 257 0022; Calle Central btwn Av Central & 2; s/d/tr/q US$35/42/55/72; ❄) This downtown hotel has a decent 2nd-floor restaurant overlooking the avenue below as well as numerous fairly quiet rooms with wall-to-wall carpeting, air-con, TV and phone. Quarters are simple, but roomy and comfortable. All rates include breakfast.

Hotel Doral (☎ 233 9410; www.hotels.co.cr/doral.html; Av 4 btwn Calles 6 & 8; s/d/tr US$24/35/47) The hotel has 42 spacious and well-kept standard rooms with tiled floors, cable TV, clock radio, phone, safe and hot shower. The staff is friendly, there is free luggage storage and breakfast costs an extra US$3. There is a **restaurant** (🕒 6-10am & noon-2pm & 5-9:30pm). Credit cards accepted.

Gran Hotel Doña Inés (☎ 222 7443, 222 7553; www.donaines.com; Calle 11 btwn Avs 2 & 6; s/d/tr US$40/50/60) In an older house converted into a small hotel, the quaint rooms here are set around a pretty courtyard. Continental breakfast is included in the rate and American-style breakfasts are available for US$3. Most rooms are set off the street, so it's quiet and all rooms come with TV, radio, phone and hot-water bathroom. The staff speaks English, Spanish and Italian and can help with travel arrangements. Credit cards are accepted.

Hotel Europa (☎ 222 1222; www.hoteleuropacr.com; Calle Central btwn Avs 3 & 5; s/d US$58/70; 💻 ❄ 🏊) This central hotel is popular with business travelers for its location. All of the 72 carpeted rooms have air-con, phone, cable TV and hot shower. There is also a business center with Internet access, a pool, casino, tour desk and a pricey restaurant, open 24 hours except Sunday. Credit cards are accepted.

Hotel Del Rey (☎ 257 7800; www.hoteldelrey.com; cnr Av 1 & Calle 9; s/d US$64/80, deluxe US$99/111; P ✖) This shocking-pink, six-story, renovated neoclassical building has 104 rooms and is renowned for the high per-capita density of prostitutes that congregate in its public areas. The place is popular with American sportfishermen who come here to gamble in the 24-hour casino and drink in the rowdy bar. All rooms come with TV, phone, shower, carpeting and air-con. Larger deluxe rooms have king-sized beds. There's a restaurant, the Del Rey Café (p91) and the folks at the tour desk know Costa Rican waters like the backs of their hands. Credit cards accepted. Solo female travelers, stay away – particularly from the Blue Marlin bar.

Gran Hotel Costa Rica (☎ 221 4000; granhcr@racsa.co.cr; Calle 3 btwn Avs Central & 2; s/d standard US$58/76, junior ste US$76/94, ste US$94/111) Dating back to the 1930s as the city's first prominent hotel, the 95 rooms here do have a certain old-world charm. They all have modern necessities such as cable TV, phone and 24-hour room service, but many of them are showing their age. Breakfast is included in the rate. The 24-hour pavement Café Parisienne (see p91), outside the lobby, is very popular. There's also a restaurant and a 24-hour casino. Credit cards accepted.

TOP END

All of the following hotels accept credit cards.

Aurola Holiday Inn (☎ 222 2424, in the USA 800-465 4329; www.aurola-holidayinn.com; cnr Calle 5 & Av 5; d standard US$146, ste junior/standard/presidential US$176/263/527, child under 12 free; P ✖) You'll find this luxurious hotel conveniently situated downtown, right off Parque Morazán. The 18-story tower, with a fancy 17th-floor **restaurant** (6am-11pm) serves as one of San José's most visible landmarks and it has all the amenities you might expect – from cable TV and minibar to an indoor pool and underground parking.

Hotel Presidente (☎ 222 3022, 256 1175; www.hotel-presidente.com; Av Central btwn Calles 7 & 9; s/d/tr US$76/88/105, master ste US$293; ✖) This modern, 96-room hotel is well appointed and has all the right amenities: spacious rooms with air-con and cable TV and direct-dial phones, business center, sauna and a decent restaurant with room service. An American breakfast is included in the rates. The one master suite even has its own outdoor Jacuzzi. The hotel houses the News Café (p91), which is popular with gabby gringos.

> **HOMESTAYS**
>
> A homestay is a good alternative if you'd like an in-depth look into Costa Rican life.
>
> **Bell's Home Hospitality** (☎ 225 4752; www.homestay.thebells.org; s/d/tr incl breakfast US$30/45/50) is a recommended agency that can set up a stay with a local family, most of whom are Ticos. This organization is run by Vernon Bell (a Kansan who has lived in Costa Rica for more than 30 years) and his Tica wife, Marcela. The couple have some 70 homes available, each of which has been personally inspected to maintain their high standards of cleanliness and wholesomeness. All are close to public transportation and readers have sent only positive comments about these places.
>
> The agency can book rooms accommodating one to three guests. Note that there is a US$5 surcharge for one-night-only stays and for private bathrooms. The Bells can also arrange airport transfers (US$15), car rental and other reservations to help with guest itineraries.

Coca-Cola Bus Terminal Area — Map p86

BUDGET

Hotel Cocorí (☎ 233 0081, 233 2188; cnr Calle 16 & Av 3; s/d/tr US$13/17/24) Rooms here all have a hot shower, clean linoleum floor and TV set. The hotel is basic, but appears freshly painted. This is a rough neighborhood at night.

Hotel Musoc (☎ 222 9437; Calle 16 btwn Avs 1 & 3; s/d US$8.50/14.50, s/d/tr with bathroom US$9/16/18) This large building close to the Coca-Cola is nicer inside than it would appear on the outside. The linoleum-tiled rooms are simple and clean and showers are hot, but noise can be a problem with an infinite number of buses passing below its windows. The staff speaks some English and credit cards are accepted.

Hotel Boruca (☎ 223 0016; Calle 14 btwn Avs 1 & 3; s/d US$5/7) The rooms are small cells, the management isn't exactly congenial, but it's cheap, has regular warm water and is convenient for early buses. (Though be prepared to listen to those buses day and night.)

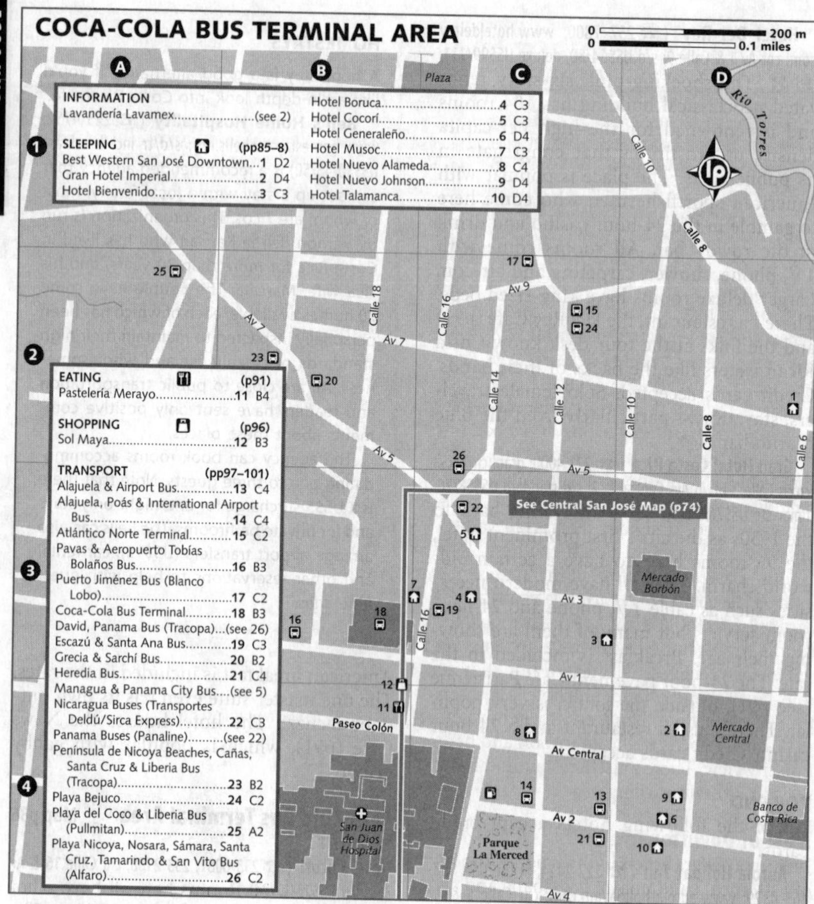

Hotel Bienvenido (☎ 233 2161; Calle 10 btwn Avs 1 & 3; d US$18) The Bienvenido's rooms are shabby but clean and have a semiregular hot shower. The walls are thin, so entertainment is provided by any activities developing in the next room. The street outside is forbidding even during daylight hours; take extra care at night.

Gran Hotel Imperial (☎ 222 8463; granhimp@racsa.co.cr, Calle 8 btwn Avs Central & 1; s/d US$4/8, d with bathroom US$14; 💻) Despite its unwelcoming 1950s office-building facade, this hotel is quite popular with shoestringers and comes recommended. Security is tight and the desk manager doesn't take any funny business from anyone. Rooms consist of dimly lit wood stalls with fairly clean hard beds. Internet access is available and a restaurant serves cheap breakfasts.

Hotel Nuevo Johnson (☎ 223 7633; www.hotelnuevojohnson.com; Calle 8 btwn Avs Central & 2; r per person US$10) Under new management, the place has thankfully received a good scrubbing and repainting. The hallways are dark, but the reasonably sized rooms are clean and have hot showers. It's nothing fancy, but it's cheap and well run. There is a game room with a pool table. The same Tico family runs the hotels Generaleño, El Descanso and Nuevo Alameda.

Hotel Generaleño (☎ 233 3061; jolin_w@hotmail.com; Av 2 btwn Calles 8 & 10; r per person without/with bathroom US$5/7) At the time of research, the 47 basic rooms in this spartan hotel were about to be gussied up with a fresh coat of paint and some needed bathroom renovations. Shared showers are cold, but rooms with private bathroom have hot water.

Hotel Nuevo Alameda (☎ 233 3551; www.hotelnuevoalameda.com; cnr Calle 12 & Av Central; r per person US$12) Slightly more upscale, this hotel has a bathroom and TV in every room and the upstairs units have good views of Plaza de la Merced.

MID-RANGE

Both hotels listed accept credit cards.

Best Western San José Downtown (☎ 255 4766; www.bestwestern.com; cnr Av 7 & Calle 6; s/d/tr US$64/75/87, child under 18 free; P) This chain hotel has a heated indoor pool, tour and car-rental information, guarded parking and a bar and restaurant. Standard-issue rooms have air-con, cable TV, phone and hot water. Rates include continental breakfast, free local calls, coffee and a cocktail hour. This is fair value – but the neighborhood is not the best. Take taxis and ask about safe walking routes.

Hotel Talamanca (☎ 233 5033; hoteltalamanca@racsa.co.cr; Av 2, Calles 8 & 10; d US$40; P) Although the rooms are cramped and lower rooms are quite noisy, they do all have a hot shower, safe, fan, TV and phone. The hotel's best feature is a 9th-floor bar (recently renovated) that usually opens in the afternoon and has a fine city view. There's also a restaurant, room service and safe parking.

West of Downtown

This area covers hotels in the neighborhoods of La Uruca, La Pitahaya, La Sabana and environs. All of these hotels are off-map.

BUDGET

Gaudy's (☎ 258 2937; www.backpacker.co.cr; Av 5 btwn Calles 36 & 38; dm US$7, d with bathroom US$20) Located in a residential area east of Parque La Sabana, this homey hostel is an excellent value. Internet access, free coffee and laundry service (US$5 per load) are available onsite. An outdoor patio has hammocks for lounging and the sitting room has cable TV. One reader described it as 'fantastic.' This hostel is 200m north and 150m east of the Banco de Costa Rica on Paseo Colón.

Galileo Hostel (☎ 221 8831, 248 2094; www.galileohostel.com; cnr Calle 40 & Av 2; dm US$6, d US$16-18) Also located near the park is this recent addition to the San José hostel scene, which has been praised by several readers. There are 32 bunk beds and five private double rooms of various sizes, as well as a communal kitchen, a lounge with cable TV and free Internet, coffee and tea. Laundry service is also available (US$5 per load). In Tico-style directions, this hostel is 100m south of the Banco de Costa Rica in La Sabana.

Kalexma Inn (☎ 232 0115, 290 2624; www.kalexma.com, 50m west, 25m south of John Paul II traffic circle, La Uruca; s/d/tr US$15/25/35, s/d with bathroom US$20/30) The Kalexma is about 5km west of downtown (near a bus stop) in a quiet neighborhood that offers restaurants, a bank and Internet cafés. Rooms are simple, but very clean and three of them have cable TV. Breakfast is included in the rate and Internet is available (US$1 per hour). Water in the bathrooms is hot and the amiable Tica owner is very congenial and speaks English. Credit cards are accepted at a small surcharge.

MID-RANGE

Hotel Cacts (☎ 233 0486, 221 6546, 221 2928; www.hotelcacts.com; Av 3 bis btwn Calles 28 & 30, La Pitahaya; s/d standard US$37/42, deluxe US$47/59) A little out of the way, this small but popular hotel is nice and quiet and the management is helpful and friendly. The whitewashed, tiled rooms are clean and spacious with TV, phone and hot shower; a Tico breakfast included in the price. There's a pool, Jacuzzi, TV lounge, laundry service (US$1 per piece), Internet access (US$4 per hour), rooftop terrace and travel agency. English, German and French are spoken. Directions for taxis: 100m north and 50m west from Pizza Hut on Paseo Colón. Credit cards are accepted.

Hotel Ambassador (☎ 221 8155, 221 8205, 221 8311; www.hotelambassador.co.cr, Paseo Colón btwn Calles 26 & 28; s/d/tr US$47/53/64, master ste US$94/99, additional person US$10, child under 12 free) This modern hotel has 74 rooms, including some top-floor master suites with good views of the city. The rooms are nothing special, but as their website advertises, they have 'all the adequate elements' including cable TV, phone, safe, minibar, air-con and breakfast. There are also wheelchair-accessible rooms. Group discounts are available; credit cards accepted.

TOP END

Hotel Grano de Oro is the author's top-end choice (see the boxed text on p81).

Colours (☎ 296 1880, in the USA 877-932 6652; www.colours.net; Blvd Rohrmoser, northwest cnr of 'El Triangulo'; d US$93-128, ste US$163-174, apt US$221;) This charming gay-run B&B is in the quiet, elegant, residential Rohrmoser district. Bright and spacious rooms of various sizes have cable TV, direct-dial phones and clock radios. The rooms surround a pretty courtyard and there is a garden with a pool, Jacuzzi and sunbathing deck, and a fitness area. Call ahead for directions.

Hotel Occidental Torremolinos (☎ 222 5266, 222 9129; www.occidental-hoteles.com; cnr Calle 40 & Av 5 bis; d US$87, ste US$110; P) Featuring a pool and garden, this clean 84-room hotel is in a quiet neighborhood. Tiled rooms are smallish but very clean and have TV, radio, phone and hairdryer. Guests have one free hour of Internet access a day, after which they are charged US$1.30 an hour. Larger suites feature air-con and terrace. Breakfast is included. There is a restaurant and bar. Credit cards accepted.

Hotel Centro Colón (☎ 257 2580, in the USA 800-228 5151; www.hotelcentrocolon.com; Av 3 btwn Calles 38 & 40; d US$88, d/tr/q superior US$99/111/115; P) This establishment is part of the Quality chain in the USA. The 105 rooms and suites come with air-con, TV, hairdryer, phone and minibar. Bathrooms meet the standards you would expect from this chain (ie fairly high but rather bland). There is a café and room service, a bar and a casino.

Meliá Tryp Corobicí (☎ 232 8122; www.solmelia.com; Calle 42, 200m north of Parque La Sabana; d standard/executive US$140/164, ste US$181; P) The architecture is all *Battlestar Galactica*, but the 213 modern rooms are quite comfortable. The 200 units have air-con, cable TV, phone, minibar and large bathroom with hairdryer. The restaurants, although expensive (see Fuji, p92), serve excellent food and a coffee shop provides 24-hour room service. There's a casino, spa, sauna, pool, massage service and a gym. Check the website for discounts. Credit cards accepted.

EATING

Cosmopolitan San José has a wide variety of restaurants – something to satisfy most tastes and budgets. You'll find everything from Peruvian to Middle Eastern to French and plenty of American chain restaurants. And, of course, there are Tico specialties – in ample supply all over town.

Approximate prices are given as a guide, but anything with shrimp, lobster or crab will be more expensive. Many of the better restaurants in San José get very busy – especially on evenings and weekends – so make a reservation. For general information on eating in Costa Rica see p58.

Eateries in the suburbs of Escazú (p111) and Los Yoses & San Pedro (p104) are listed later in this chapter.

There are many supermarkets that have been marked on various maps, including **Perimercado** (Map p74; Calle 3 btwn Avs Central & 1), **Automercado** (Map p74; Calle 3 btwn Avs 3 & 5) and **Más X Menos** (Map p74; Av Central, east of Calle 11).

North & East of the Centre — Map pp70-1

BUDGET

The Nuestra Tierra (see the boxed text opposite) is the author's choice for this price range.

Soda de don Raúl (Calle 15 btwn Avs 6 bis & 8) Just around the corner from Casa Ridgway, this basic *soda* (small and informal lunch counter) has yummy *gallos pintos* (stir-fry of rice and beans, served with eggs; US$1.50) and abundant lunch specials (US$2.30) that attract a steady stream of suited Ticos from the nearby courts.

El Cuartel de la Boca del Monte (Av 1 btwn Calles 21 & 23; dishes US$5-8; 11:30am-2pm, 6-10pm) This casual restaurant, one block east of the Parque Nacional, also serves as a popular nightclub (see p93). The place definitely has a well-worn feel, with exposed brick walls, trampled wooden floors, cross-beamed ceilings and plenty of iron grillwork. The food is unexciting but filling; meals range from soups and salads to meaty main courses. The cheese empanada appetizers are worth a try (US$2.50).

MID-RANGE

Mecca is the author's mid-range choice (see the boxed text opposite).

La Cocina de Leña (☎ 223 3704, 255 1360; Centro Comercial El Pueblo; dishes US$7-14; 11am-11pm Sun-Thu, 11am-midnight Fri-Sat) One of the best-known places in town, its name means 'the wood stove'. The restaurant has a distinct homey feel (with strings of onions hanging from the rafters), though the prices are hardly 'country kitchen'. Regardless, it's a good Tico-style place and the food is well prepared. The restaurant also has the endearing tradition

THE AUTHOR'S CHOICE

Budget

Nuestra Tierra (Map pp70-1; cnr Av 2 & Calle 15; casados US$3-4; 24hr) Cheap and tasty casados and well-prepared traditional favorites such as *chorreadas* (pan-grilled corn cake served with cheese or sour cream) and tamales, make this a local must-eat. The restaurant is nestled underneath a traditional thatched patio strung with bunches of onions and plantain bananas and the service is friendly.

Mid-range

Mecca (Map pp70-1; ☎ 222 8957; cnr Av 11 & Calle 15; tapas US$2.50-7.50; 11am-3pm & 5-11:30pm Mon-Sat) This brightly painted restaurant features plenty of pleasing art and an eclectic international menu that covers every type of world cuisine. Dozens of tapas-sized portions run the gamut of Asian, Spanish, Mexican, Indian and even Greek. There are also full-sized pasta and seafood dishes. The food is superb and the service excellent.

Top End

Bakea (Map pp70-1; ☎ 248 0303; cnr Av 11 & Calle 7; appetizers US$3-7, dishes US$7-16; noon-midnight Tue-Fri, 7pm-midnight Sat) What a welcome addition to the San José gourmet scene! This new restaurant resides in a beautiful converted vintage home, with numerous intimate dining rooms as well as a pleasant patio. The menu consists of nouveau international dishes – from risotto to steak frites to seafood – all of it world class. Don't miss the scrumptious *desgustación* dessert sampler. Credit cards accepted.

of printing its menu on brown paper bags. Typical dishes include corn soup with pork, black-bean soup, tamales, *gallo pinto* with meat and eggs, stuffed peppers and oxtail served with yucca and plantain. It also serves local desserts and alcoholic concoctions, including *guaro* (local firewater). There's live marimba music on some nights.

Café Mundo (☎ 222 6190; cnr Av 9 & Calle 15; dishes US$6-14; 11am-11pm Mon-Fri, 5pm-12:30am Sat) This mid-priced restaurant is housed in a beautiful old mansion and has a great outdoor terrace that overlooks a lush garden. Diners have a choice of several dining rooms, a garden or the terrace. A nice selection of international dishes include some with a Costa Rican flavor, as well as pizzas (highly recommended by several readers), pastas, meats and large salads. This is a choice place for a drink at the bar, or for dessert and espresso.

Aya Sofya (cnr Av Central & Calle 21; dishes US$5-8; 11:30am-3pm & 6-11pm Mon-Fri, 11:30am-midnight Sat) A homey spot great for authentic Turkish cuisine, Aya Sofya is also good for cheap weekday lunch specials (US$3). The restaurant is a pleasant place for dinner and hosts belly dancing parties twice a month.

Fleur de Lys (☎ 223 1206; Calle 13 btwn Av 2 & 6; dishes US$8-12; 6:30am-9:30pm) This hotel restaurant has a good Swiss-influenced menu that is popular with locals. There is live music on Friday nights and a popular happy hour on Tuesday and Friday evenings from 5pm to 7pm.

Lukas (☎ 233 2309, 233 8145; Centro Comercial El Pueblo; dishes US$7-12; 11am-2am) The Lukas has a good mid-priced selection of standard meat and seafood meals, as well as Italian dishes and sandwiches. It's locally recommended for good steaks at reasonable prices and is a convenient location for carbo-loading before a night of drinking at the surrounding bars. The weekday *almuerzo ejecutivo* (set lunch), from noon to 2pm, is a good deal at US$5.

TOP END

Bakea (see the boxed text above) is the author's choice for this price range.

Restaurant La Palma (☎ 258 4541; Av 9 btwn Calles 9 & 11; dishes US$8-15; 5-11pm Tue-Sun) Just east of the Hemingway Inn, this elegant wood-paneled restaurant has both interior and garden seating and an eclectic menu featuring Peruvian and Italian food. Credit cards accepted.

El Oasis (☎ 255 0448; Av 7 btwn Calles 3 & 5; mains US$9-17; 4-11pm Tue-Sat, 3-11pm Sun) Situated in Hotel Santo Tomás (see p82), this well-reviewed restaurant has an international menu that includes everything from teriyaki to stroganoff to *bourguignon*. There are also some modern Latin American dishes as well as an extensive seafood menu.

Central San José & Coca-Cola Bus Terminal Area

BUDGET

Soda Nini (Map p74; Av 3 btwn Calles 2 & 4; dishes US$1-4; 10:30am-10pm) Packed with local office workers, this bustling joint serves large portions of Tico and Chinese food.

Soda Castro (Map p74; Av 10 btwn Calles 2 & 4; dishes US$2-4) The area outside is frightful, but inside it's so delightful. So it's not in the best neighborhood, but if you happen to be coming through here, Castro is a good place to feed a sweet tooth. The vast hall is an old-fashioned Tico family spot (there's a sign prohibiting public displays of affection) where you can get heaping ice-cream sundaes and banana splits.

Restaurante y Cafetería La Criollita (Map p74; Av 7 btwn Calle 7 & 9; meals US$4-7; 7am-8pm Mon-Sat) A recommended eatery 50m west of INS in Barrio Amón, La Criollita serves full American or Tico breakfasts, with coffee and juice included for about US$4. There are free refills on coffee and the service is fast and friendly. Casados (from 11am to 3pm Monday to Friday) cost about US$4.50 and include soup, salad and a drink along with a small choice of meals including veggie options. These attract huge crowds of in-the-know office workers at lunch time. The restaurant has added a nice bar and garden terrace and is a fine place for a drink. English is spoken.

Faro's Mexican Grill & Bar (Map p74; cnr Calle 7 & Av 1; meals US$3-6; 11am-10:30pm) With its downtown location and a daily happy hour that lasts for three (5pm to 8pm), Faro's has a following among the inhabitants of Hotel Del Rey. The food is vaguely Tex-Mex and it ain't all bad.

La Vasconia (Map p74; cnr Av 1 & Calle 5; casado US$2.50, dishes US$2-6; 7am-midnight) La Vasconia is a cheap, basic but decent place with plenty of atmosphere, a largely Tico clientele and a wide variety of food on the chalkboard menu. Breakfasts are cheap, with a *pinto con huevo* (rice and beans with egg) costing about US$1.50.

Chelle's (Map p74; cnr Av Central & Calle 9; dishes US$3-6; 24hr) This unpretentious spot is centrally located and serves local dishes – none of which are very exciting. Regardless, some Ticos say you haven't really experienced San José until you've had a wee-hours breakfast here after a night of drinking. (And there's even a bar in case you want to keep on going.)

Restaurante El Pollo Campesino (Map p74; Calle 7, btwn Avs 2 & 4; meals US$2-4; 10am-11pm) The chicken from a wood-burning spit will satisfy any post-beer need for munchies at this pleasant place with booth seating and homey atmosphere (though plan on smelling like chicken when you leave). A quarter bird with tortillas or mashed potatoes and a drink is US$2; a whole chicken is less than US$4. There is take-out.

Mariscar (Map p74; Av Central btwn Calles 7 & 9; dishes US$2-4) A cavernous Chinese/Costa Rican restaurant, it is popular for good reason: the food is heaping, fresh and good. The chicken soup can halt any flu in its tracks and the fried rice is a meal in itself. In the evenings, the open-air bar at the back gets cranking with loud music and plenty of young Ticos engaged in rapt conversation.

Restaurant Fuluso (Map p74; Calle 7 btwn Avs Central & 2; meals US$3-7; 11am-11pm) This small, dark restaurant is a cheap choice for spicy Szechwan and Mandarin food, and its popular bar attracts a steady stream of local men with its cheap-beer specials.

EATING VEGGIE IN SAN JOSÉ

Of all the cities in Costa Rica, San José is the best-equipped to offer a better variety to vegetarians. Beyond the obvious veggie havens of Vishnu (opposite) and Shakti (opposite), the city's numerous Chinese restaurants offer plenty of vegetable stir-fries, while in many Italian places you can carbo-load on simple dishes of pasta with tomato or cheese sauces. For the most part, restaurants are very conscientious about the needs of vegetarians, so if you specify that you want it meat-free, most kitchens will be happy to honor it.

While they're not exclusively vegetarian, other good places to eat at are Mecca (p89), Tin-Jo (p92), Don Wang (opposite) and La Criollita (above), all of which have regular vegetarian items featured on their menus. See also Comida Para Sentir (p105).

For more tips on veggie eating in Costa Rica, see the Food & Drink chapter (p58).

Vishnu Avenida 1 (Map p74; Av 1 btwn Calles 1 & 3) Calle Central (Map p74; Calle Central btwn Avs 6 & 8) Veg-heads go nuts at this popular local chain serving bounteous fare at good prices. A US$3 lunch special buys you soup, brown rice, veggies, a fruit drink and dessert. The veggie burger and fruit-drink combo is probably the best item on the menu. Note that some of the fruit salads come with ice cream, so you may end up eating the equivalent of a sundae.

Restaurant Shakti (Map p74; cnr Av 8 & Calle 13; dishes US$3-6) This is a recommended macrobiotic establishment with tasty fare and a rotating lunch combo costing US$3.

One of the cheapest places for a good lunch is at the **Mercado Central** (Map p74; Av Central btwn Calles 6 & 8), where you'll find a variety of restaurants and *sodas* serving casados, tamales, seafood and everything in between. If you happen to be here, stop for dessert at **Las Delicias** (ice cream US$0.75), a San José institution that has been whipping up ice cream for more than a century. Get the tasty homemade cinnamon-spiced vanilla and do as the locals and order *barquillos* (cylindrical sugar cookies) to go with it.

Churrería Manolo's Downtown West (Map p74; Av Central btwn Calles Central & 2; 24hr) Downtown East (Map p74; Av Central btwn Calles 9 & 11; 24hr) A perennial favorite famous for its cream-filled *churros* (doughnut tubes), this place packs in the crowds in search of a sugar rush throughout the day or night. (Though the best time to stop by is at around 5pm, when all the office workers start pouring out of neighboring buildings and the *churros* are delectably hot and fresh.) The Downtown West location has a great 2nd-floor balcony from which you can spy on passersbys on the pedestrian mall below. Casados cost about US$3, while *churros* from the street stand are US$0.40.

Pastelería Merayo (Map p86; Calle 16 btwn Paseo Colón & Av 1) This busy pastry shop is one of the best in town and has a wide variety of cavity-inducing cakes and pastries. The coffee is strong and it's a sweet way to pass the time if waiting for a bus at the Coca-Cola.

People who need their fix of Western-style fast food can find a range of places on or near the pedestrianized section of Avenida Central as well as at other localities in San José. **McDonald's** Plaza de la Cultura Branch (Map p74; Av Central btwn Calles 3 & 5) Banco Central Branch (Map p74; Calle 4 btwn Avs Central & 1) is mentioned here for its clean bathrooms and the handy ATM on the Cirrus system at its Plaza de la Cultura outlet. Ice-cream eaters craving a cone should look for Pops, an ice-cream chain with several locations in San José.

MID-RANGE

Restaurante Don Wang (Map p74; Calle 11 btwn Avs 6 & 8; dishes US$2-12; 8am-3pm & 6-11pm Mon, 8am-11pm Tue-Sat, 8am-10pm Sun) The Don Wang specializes in dim sum as well as an extensive menu of vegetarian and other Chinese dishes.

News Café (Map p74; cnr Av Central & Calle 7; dishes US$4-11; 6am-10pm) On the ground floor of Hotel Presidente, the News is a central, modern coffee shop packed with a primarily North American clientele. The restaurant serves a variety of American-style sandwiches and salads and recommended steaks. There is a selection of foreign newspapers to choose from.

Del Rey Café (Map p74; 24hr) This café is part of Hotel del Rey. It serves huge sandwiches (about US$6) as well as pies, coffee and full meals. Often blues or jazz plays in the background and an all-night guard makes this a safe place to eat in the wee hours, if you don't mind the prostitutes sizing you up.

Balcón de Europa (Map p74; ☎ 221 4841, Calle 9 btwn Avs Central & 1; dishes US$6-10; 11:30am-10pm Sun-Fri) One of San José's most popular eateries, this restaurant has been in the city since 1909 and claims to be one of the oldest in Costa Rica. The menu has a selection of pastas, antipasto and salads – an especially tasty one made from *palmitos* (hearts of palms) keeps visitors coming back.

Restaurante Pizza Metro (Map p74; Av 2 btwn Calles 5 & 7; dishes US$7-12; noon-3pm & 6-10:30pm) It's consistently filled with locals munching on pizza and pastas.

Café de Correo (Map p74; Calle 2 near Av 3; 9am-7pm Mon-Fri, 9am-5pm Sat) Located in the Correo Central, this is an excellent place to read and write letters over a good cup of espresso and a pastry. Both hot and iced drinks are available and there is a small selection of pasta dishes for the hungry.

Café Parisienne (Map p74; Calle 3 btwn Avs Central & 2; dishes US$6-12; 24hr) Part of the upmarket Gran Hotel Costa Rica, this European-style café is the people-watching place if you want to observe the activities in front of the Teatro Nacional. The meals are nothing special, but the waiters will leave you alone if you just order coffee.

TOP END

Restaurante Tin-Jo (Map p74; ☎ 221 7605, 257 3622; Calle 11 btwn Avs 6 & 8; dishes US$8-15; 11:30am-3pm & 5:30-10pm Mon-Thu, 11:30am-3pm & 5:30-11pm Fri-Sat, 11:30am-10pm Sun) This long-standing Pan-Asian restaurant is incredibly popular with locals and travelers alike and has been highly recommended by several readers. Elements of Szechwan, Thai, Indian and Chinese cooking are all featured on the varied menu and there is a selection of vegetarian curries as well. The restaurant is attractive and cozy and the wait-staff is gracious. Reservations are highly recommended – this place gets packed.

West & South of Downtown

All of the following places are off the San José map.

BUDGET

Huarache's (Av 22 btwn Calles 5 & 7; dishes US$2-5; 11am-11pm) This frenetic restaurant makes up for all the bland meals you've had in Costa Rica – and it's worth the walk or taxi ride (350m east of Hospital de la Mujer). Here you'll find fresh honest-to-goodness tacos, quesadillas, guacamole, tortilla soup and hot sauces that'll make you think you've died and gone to Mexico.

Soda Tapia (cnr Av 2 & Calle 42; casados US$3-4; 6am-midnight) If you're out near Parque La Sabana, stop by this locally popular place for sandwiches and set meals – and if you're a sweet tooth, try one of their bounteous sundaes.

MID-RANGE

El Chicote (☎ 232 0936; appetizers US$4-8, mains US$8-15; 11am-3pm & 6-11pm Mon-Fri, 11am-11pm Sat-Sun) Protein-fiends can go wild at this venerable steakhouse on the north side of La Sabana, 400m west of the ICE building. It includes pricier seafood on its menu but the steaks are the best reason to eat here; they are cooked on a grill in the middle of the restaurant and served with black beans and fried banana slices, along with a baked potato. A small pavement patio has seating and the large interior is filled with flowers. You can get to the north side of the Parque La Sabana on the Sabana Estadio bus, which goes out along Paseo Colón.

Arirang (☎ 223 2838; Edificio Centro Colón, Paseo Colón btwn Calles 38 & 40, 2nd fl; dishes US$7-12; 11:30am-3pm & 5:30-10pm Mon-Fri, 11:30am-10pm Sat) The Arirang serves moderately priced Japanese food as well as popular Korean barbecues, which are cooked at your table. Credit cards accepted.

Machu Picchu (☎ 222 7384; Calle 32 btwn Av 1 & 3; meals US$6-11; 11am-3pm & 6-10pm Mon-Sat) This popular Peruvian outpost is 125m north of KFC on Paseo Colón. The menu includes a variety of fish and seafood *ceviches* (marinated raw seafood) for US$3 to US$5 and other well-prepared traditional specialties, including Peru's infamous national cocktail, the pisco sour.

Restaurant/Bar Libanes Lubnán (☎ 257 6071, Paseo Colón btwn Calles 22 & 24; 11am-3pm & 6-11pm Tue-Sat; 11am-4pm Sun) This is the place to go for mid-priced Lebanese food. It serves everything from kebabs to falafel. Credit cards accepted.

TOP END

Fuji (☎ 232 8122, ext 191; Calle 42, 200m north of Parque La Sabana; dishes from US$10; noon-3pm & 6:30-11pm Mon-Sat, noon-10pm Sun) A recommended Japanese restaurant, Fuji is in the Meliá Tryp Corobicí (see p88). Credit cards accepted.

Restaurant y Galería La Bastille (☎ 255 4994; cnr Paseo Colón & Calle 22; dishes US$13-18; 11:30am-2pm & 6:30pm-midnight Mon-Fri; 6pm-midnight Sat) Out along Paseo Colón towards Parque La Sabana, this cheerfully elegant place has excellent French cuisine at relatively low prices. This is one of the area's longest-standing French restaurants and also serves as a colorful art gallery. Traditional specialties include escargot, various meats, a prodigious amount of sauces and one superb garlic soup.

La Piazzetta (☎ 222 7896; Paseo Colón near Calle 40; dishes US$7-18; noon-2:30pm & 6:30-11pm Mon-Fri, 6-11pm Sat) This place has a lengthy mouth-watering menu of creative Italian food served on silver platters. Dishes include pastas, risottos, veal, beef and seafood. There is an extensive wine list and several luscious desserts. It is in front of the Banco de Costa Rica on Paseo Colón. Credit cards accepted.

Grano de Oro (☎ 255 3322; Calle 30 btwn Avs 2 & 4; dinner mains US$20; 6am-10pm) Foremost among small hotel-restaurants is Grano de Oro (see boxed text, p81), which has received good reviews both for its attractive dining area and its well-prepared international food. Dishes include inventive items such as coconut chicken and sea bass in macadamia nut sauce. The restaurant is popular, so reservations are highly recommended – even for weeknights. Guests can have their meals delivered to their rooms at no additional charge. Credit cards accepted.

DRINKING

Beer, *guaro*, margaritas and more. San José has plenty of options to keep you well lubricated at all hours of the day and into the night. And there's something for everyone – from good local hangouts, to trendy lounges to gringo-centric dives. Some bars will offer dancing on some nights as well. (For nightclubs and gay bars, see p94).

El Cuartel de la Boca del Monte (Map pp70-1; ☎ 221 0327; Av 1 btwn Calles 21 & 23) A restaurant by day (see p88), this roomy bar is a major outpost for San José nightlife, young and old. The music is sometimes live, but it's always loud, and the place is elbow-room-only at the back, where there is a small dance floor. In front, the bar is less frenzied but still crowded. Popular Monday night offers live music and free admission for the ladies.

In Barrio Amón, **Luna Roja Café** (Map p74; ☎ 223 2432; Calle 3 btwn Avs 9 & 11) is another option – but leave the khakis and Tevas in your room. This trendy place is all black, all the time. It has a ladies night every Monday and even features the occasional Goth night. It charges a cover (US$2.50) most nights, though Wednesday is free.

Bar Chavelona (Map p74; Av 10 btwn Calles 10 & 12; 24hr) Another all-night place, Bar Chavelona is a historic, 77-year-old bar situated in a somewhat deserted neighborhood south of the town center (so take a taxi). The service is good, the atmosphere pleasant and the locale is frequented by radio and theater workers, giving the place an old-world bohemian feel. If you want good local flavor, this is the best place for it.

Across the street and about 100m west of Centro Comercial El Pueblo, you'll find **¿Por que no?** (☎ 233 6622; open 5:30pm), connected to Hotel Villa Tournón (p82). The popular night here is Friday, when there is usually a band and locals pack it in.

Nashville South Bar (Map p74; Calle 5 btwn Avs 1 & 3) A honky-tonk style bar serves burgers, chili dogs and other fixins to a bar full of tired-looking gringos.

Shakespeare Bar (☎ 257 1288; cnr Av 2 & Calle 28; 3pm-midnight) Considerably classier is this more tranquil spot, which derives its name from its proximity to several small theaters. (This is the place to go before or after a show.) It has a dartboard, piano bar and occasional live music.

México Bar (cnr Av 13 & Calle 16) An interesting and somewhat upscale (for the neighborhood) bar with good *bocas* and mariachi music some nights. It's next to the Barrio México church. This is definitely a good local hangout, devoid of tourists or expats, but the neighborhood leading to it is a poor one, so take a cab.

Chelle's (Map p74; ☎ 221 1369; cnr Av Central & Calle 9; 24hr) This 24-7 downtown bar is a local landmark. It serves meals as well (see p90), though the liquor helps with digestion. Its main attraction is that it's always open.

The Blue Marlin, attached to Hotel Del Rey (see p85), is mentioned here solely because some regard a visit here as a part of the country's wildlife experience. Ageing anglers and lithe young prostitutes are the most common species. Women should either come here with a guide or stay away.

For other options, see Los Yoses & San Pedro (p105) and Escazú (p112).

ENTERTAINMENT

Pick up *La Nación* on Thursday for a complete listing (in Spanish) of the coming week's nightlife and cultural events. The *Tico Times* 'Weekend' section has a calendar of theater, music, museums and events – including events in English. A handy publication to look for is the *Guía de Ciudad*, published by *El Financiero*, a free salmon-colored city guide featuring all the latest events. It is usually available at the tourist office and at better hotels. Visit www.entretenimiento.co.cr for more up-to-date movies, bar and club listings all over the San José area.

Cinemas

Many cinemas show recent Hollywood films with Spanish subtitles and the English soundtrack. Occasionally, films are dubbed over in Spanish *(hablado en español)* rather than subtitled; ask before buying a ticket. Movie tickets cost about US$3. Check the latest listings in *La Nación* or the *Tico Times*.

Larger and more modern multiplexes are located in the suburbs of San Pedro (p105) and Escazú (p112). But, in town, try:

Cine Magaly (☎ 223 0085; Calle 23 btwn Avs Central & 1)
Omni (Map p74; ☎ 221 7903; Calle 3 btwn Avs Central & 1)
Sala Garbo (☎ 222 1034; cnr Av 2 & Calle 28)

Nightclubs

If you've got the urge to get your groove on or listen to a little music, there is no shortage of booming places to go in San José. Places with live music and full-on dance floors will usually charge a cover of US$2 to US$5 depending on the night and the caliber of artist.

See also Los Yoses & San Pedro (p105) for more options in a student area nearby.

Take identification when going to clubs.

North of the zoo in Barrio Tournón is **Centro Comercial El Pueblo** (Map pp70-1; P), which has a variety of places to choose from – and a thick density of human activity on weekends. This is a perfect area for a bar crawl since all of the places are just meters apart. Many of these spots feature live music, mainly on weekends. Nightclubs sometimes charge a cover of US$2 to US$4 depending on whether there is live music. There is even a 24-hour ATH (A Toda Hora) ATM on the Cirrus network by the parking lot. The complex usually gets going at about 9pm and shuts down by 3am. Some of the hot spots here include:

Bar Picantería Inty Raymy Has a Peruvian flavor.

Bar Tango Che Molinari (☎ 226 6904) An intimate Argentine bar featuring live tango for a small cover charge.

Café Boruca A more mellow place featuring folk and acoustic music.

Club Twister (☎ 222 5746) Serious dancers (and partyers) should boogie over here; there's plenty of room for drinking, dancing and general hell-raising. The DJs play a steady mix of contemporary Latin and international music.

Ebony 56 A brand new restaurant and disco that took over where the old Club Infinito – and its many dance floors – left off. It attracts a wide variety of people, but Thursday night is the big party for ladies night.

La Plaza (☎ 233 5516) Across the way from Ebony 56, you'll find it to be a dressier club with a large dance floor.

Los Balcones (☎ 223 3704) A small bar specializing in live socially conscious Latin American folk music known as *nueva trova*. There are regular acoustic musicians and no cover charge.

Tarrico (☎ 222 1003) Has a big bar, a *foosball* table and features live music on a regular basis.

A couple of downtown nightclubs are a bit downscale, attracting more of a working-class crowd. Covers usually run between US$2 and US$5. **El Túnel de Tiempo Disco** (Map p74; Av Central btwn Calles 7 & 9) starts pumping the techno late at night and keeps it going 'til the break of dawn. Another good place to shake it is **Complejo Salsa 54 y Zadidas** (Map p74; Calle 3 btwn Avs 1 & 3), a vast 2nd-story club that is all Latin, all the time, playing a continuous selection of salsa and merengue. Be prepared to cut some serious rug, the local dancers here are expert *salseros*.

Next door to the Luna Roja (see p93), you'll find **Café Loft** (☎ 221 2302; 7pm-2am) which has DJs spinning house, ambient and other types of modern music on a nightly basis. There's a dress code, so be spiffy or you're not getting in.

Gay & Lesbian Venues

San José has a thriving gay and lesbian scene – whether you just want a drink or to get down on the dance floor. Covers are charged on weekends and special nights with prices fluctuating between US$2 and $5. Clubs may close on some nights and may have women- or men-only nights. To get the latest, log on to **Gay Costa Rica** (www.gaycostarica.com) for up-to-the-minute club info in English and Spanish or drop by the **1@10 Café Internet** (Map p74; ☎ 258 4561; www.1en10.com; Calle 3 btwn Avs 5 & 7), which serves as the gay and lesbian information center. See Gay & Lesbian Travelers (p456) for additional information.

La Castilla (Map p74; ☎ 221 0656; Calle 3 btwn Avs 7 & 9) Young professionals from all over San José pack into this intimate spot in Barrio Amón to drink, dance and be merry. During the week, the bar is good for quiet conversation. It is also one of the more consistently popular lesbian destinations in town.

Other popular places are found in the area south of Parque Central. This area has higher-than-typical crime rates, so don't go around alone at night.

Deja Vú (Map p86; ☎ 223 3758; Calle 2 btwn Avs 14 & 16) A massively big city dance club, this place is especially popular with gay men. The club hosts a men's open-bar night on Wednesday and features go-go boys on Saturday.

La Avispa (Map p74; ☎ 223 5343; Calle 1 btwn Avs 8 & 10) Further east, this long-standing black-and-yellow club has been around for over 25 years and has a bar, pool tables and a great dance floor that's been recommended by readers. It is most popular with gay men, though they do host a lesbian night once a month.

Bochinche (Map pp70-1; ☎ 221 0500; Calle 11 btwn Avs 10 & 12) is a more upscale bar that is popular with professional young Ticos out for a night of drinking and flirting.

Los Cucharones (Map p74; ☎ 233 5797; Av 6 btwn Calles Central & 1) This raucous place is frequented by young, working-class men for its over-the-top (and recommended) drag shows.

Sports

International and national football (soccer) games are played in **Estadio Nacional** (☎ 257 6844) in Parque La Sabana. Call ahead for game schedules. For more information on this national passion, turn to p30.

Theater

There are a wide variety of theatrical options in San José, provided you speak Spanish – though there are a few options in English. Local newspapers, including the *Tico Times*, list current shows. The Teatro Nacional is the city's most important theater. Most other theaters are not very large, performances are popular and ticket prices are quite reasonable. This adds up to sold-out performances, so get tickets as early as possible. Theaters rarely have performances on Monday.

Auditorio Nacional (Map pp70-1; ☎ 249 1208; www.museocr.com; in Museo de los Niños) A grand stage for concerts, dance theater and plays – and even the site of the Miss Costa Rica pageant.

Little Theater Group (LTG; ☎ 289 3910) This English-language theater group has been around since the 1950s and presents several plays a year; call to find out when and where the works will be shown.

Teatro Carpa (☎ 234 2866; Av 1 btwn Calles 29 & 33) Known for alternative and outdoor theater, as well as performances by the Little Theater Group.

Teatro de la Aduana (☎ 225 4563; Calle 25 btwn Avs 3 & 5) The National Theater Company performs here.

Teatro el Ángel (Map pp70-1; ☎ 222 8258, Av Central btwn Calles 13 & 15) A comedy venue.

Teatro Fanal (Map pp70-1; ☎ 257 5524; in the Cenac Complex; Av 3 btwn Calles 11 & 15) Adjacent to the contemporary art museum, it puts on a variety of works, including children's theater – all in Spanish.

Teatro La Máscara (Map pp70-1; ☎ 222 4574; Calle 13 btwn Avs 2 & 6) Dance performances as well as alternative theater.

Teatro Laurence Olivier (☎ 223 1960; cnr Calle 28 & Av 2) LTG also performs at this place, a small theater, coffee shop and gallery.

Teatro Melico Salazar (Map pp70-1; ☎ 233 5434; Av 2 btwn Calles Central & 2) The restored 1920s theater named after one of Costa Rica's most notable coffee barons has a variety of performances, including music and dance, as well as drama.

Teatro Nacional (Map pp70-1; ☎ 221 5341; Av 2 btwn Calles 3 & 5) Stages plays, dance, opera, symphony, Latin American music and other major cultural events. The season runs from March to November, although less frequent performances occur during other months. Tickets start as low as US$4. The National Symphony Orchestra (Orquesta Sínfonica Nacional) plays here.

Teatro Sala Vargas Calvo (Map p74; ☎ 222 1875; Av 2 btwn Calles 3 & 5) Known for theater-in-the-round performances.

Other important theaters are **Teatro Eugene O'Neill** (Los Yoses; see p105), **Teatro de la Comedia** (Map pp70-1; ☎ 255 3255; Av Central btwn Calles 13 & 15), **Teatro Moliére** (Map pp70-1; ☎ 223 5420; Calle 13 btwn Avs 2 & 6) and **Teatro Lucho Barahona** (Map p74; ☎ 223 5972; Calle 11 btwn Avs 6 & 8).

GAMBLING TICO-STYLE

The most popular card game is 21, which is similar to Las Vegas–style blackjack but with Tico rules. You get two cards and then ask for another card *(carta)* or stay put with the two you have *(me quedo)*. As in blackjack, the idea is to get as close to 21 points as possible without going over, with face cards counting as 10 points and aces counting as one or 11. If your first three cards are the same number (eg three kings) or a straight flush (eg five, six, seven of the same suit), you have a 'rummy' and are paid double. And if your three-of-a-kind happens to be three sevens (equaling 21), you get an even higher bonus. If you get 21 with two cards or get five cards without breaking 21, there's no double bonus as you get in many international casinos. Splitting pairs is allowed.

Other games played include roulette, where the numbers are drawn from a lottery tumbler rather than spun on a roulette wheel and slot machines.

Casinos

Gamblers will find casinos in several of the larger and more expensive hotels. Most casinos are fairly casual, but in the nicer hotels it is advisable to clean up as there may be a dress code.

Aurola Holiday Inn (Map p74; ☎ 222 2424; cnr Calle 5 & Av 5, 17th fl)

Casino Club Colonial (Map p74; ☎ 258 2807; Av 1 btwn Calles 9 & 11; 24hr)
Casino del Faraón (Map p74; ☎ 222 1222; in Hotel Europa, Calle Central btwn Avs 3 & 5; 3pm-4am)
Gran Hotel Costa Rica (Map p74; ☎ 221 4000; Calle 3 btwn Avs Central & 2)
Hotel del Bulevar (Map p74; ☎ 257 0022; Calle Central btwn Avs Central & 2) Slot machines only.
Hotel Del Rey (Map p74; ☎ 257 7800; cnr Av 1 & Calle 9; 24hr)
Meliá Tryp Corobicí (☎ 232 8122; Calle 42, 200m north of Parque La Sabana; 6pm-2am)
Hotel Centro Colón (☎ 257 2580; Av 3 btwn Calles 38 & 40; 2pm-6am)

SHOPPING

San José offers a good selection of handicraft shopping – and in many cases can offer better deals on some items than popular tourist beach towns will. For general information on shopping in Costa Rica, turn to p459.

The **Mercado Central** (Map p74; Avs Central & 1 btwn Calles 6 & 8) is good for deals on hammocks, T-shirts and a limited selection of handicrafts. It's also a good place to buy fresh coffee beans at a fraction of the price you'll pay in the tourist shops. All of the supermarkets also sell export-quality coffee beans at local prices.

Good handicraft shopping can be done at the outdoor **mercado artesanal** (Map pp70-1; Plaza de la Democracia; Avs Central & 2 btwn Calles 13 & 15) where you can find everything from jewelry made from native seeds to woodwork, cigars, clothing and hammocks.

Galería Namu (Map 70-1; ☎ 256 3412; Av 7 btwn Calles 5 & 7) is described in the boxed text, opposite.

Annemarie's Boutique (Map pp70-1; ☎ 221 6707; www.doncarloshotel.com; Hotel Don Carlos, cnr Calle 9 & Av 9) is a recommended souvenir shop and is not just the usual hotel gift store. Annemarie's has an extensive selection of items from all over Costa Rica and the public is welcome to come in and browse. A limited selection of its items is also available for purchase from abroad through its website.

Sol Maya (Map p86; ☎ 221 0864; Calle 16 btwn Av Central 1; Sun-Fri), a small shop near the Coca-Cola bus terminal, has a worthwhile selection of Guatemalan textiles.

La Casona (Map p74; Calle Central btwn Avs Central & 1; Mon-Sat) is a large complex of many stalls, with a wide selection of items and imports for sale from other Central American countries.

La Buchaca (Map pp70-1; ☎ 223 6773, 253 8790; Centro Comercial El Pueblo; 4-8pm Mon-Sat) is a tiny shop that has well-made jewelry, ceramics and sculptures – all from Costa Rica. Of particular interest are the beautifully executed modern paintings featuring Pre-Columbian motifs from around Central America. Other shops in the complex sell the usual tourist items: T-shirts, woodwork etc.

Suraksa (☎ 222 0129; cnr Calle 5 & Av 3; 9am-6pm Mon-Sat) has a good selection of gold work in pre-Columbian style, tropical wood products and fine ceramicware.

If you're in San José it is absolutely worth the trip to go visit Biesanz Woodworks in Escazú (p112). And if you have the time and the inclination you can also find wide selections of well-priced items in the suburb of Moravia (p138), about 8km northeast of downtown, or by taking a day trip to the village of Sarchí (p126), where Costa Rica's colorful oxcarts and many leather goods are produced.

INDIGENOUS ART *John Thompson*

Galería Namu (Map pp70-1; ☎ 256 3412; www.galerianamu.com; Av 7 btwn Calles 5 & 7; 9:30am-6:30pm Mon-Sat, 9:30am-1:30pm Sun), which was selected as an official site for the annual Costa Rican Arts Festival in San José, has done an admirable job of bringing together artwork and crafts from Costa Rica's small but diverse population of indigenous tribes. If you want a quick education about indigenous culture in the country, this is a good place to start.

Owner Aisling French regularly visits artists in remote villages around the country and can provide background information on the various traditions represented. Boruca ceremonial masks, Guaymí dolls and dresses, Bribrí dugout canoes, Chorotega ceramics, Huetar carvings and mats and Guatuso blankets are all among the works that can be found at the gallery.

There is also some work by contemporary urban artists, including art produced by Central American street children through a nonprofit program.

English is spoken. In the rainy season it is closed on Sunday, and shop hours may vary.

GETTING THERE & AWAY

San José is the hub of all transportation around the country. Unfortunately, the transport system is rather bewildering to the first-time visitor. Most people get around the country by bus, but there is no central bus terminal. Instead, there are dozens of bus stops and terminals scattered around the city, all serving different destinations. Efforts have been made to consolidate bus services and the use of the Atlántico Norte, Caribe and Musoc terminals have definitely helped the situation.

Air

There are two airports serving San José. For information on getting to them, turn to p99.

Aeropuerto Internacional Juan Santamaría (☎ 437 2626; near Alajuela) handles international traffic from its sparkling new terminal and Sansa domestic flights from the diminutive blue building to the right of the main terminal. **Sansa** (☎ 221 9414; www.flysansa.com; cnr Av 5 & Calle 42, La Sabana) also has an office in town.

Aeropuerto Tobías Bolaños (☎ 232 2820; Pavas) is for domestic flights by NatureAir and is also home to the **NatureAir office** (☎ 220 3054; www.natureair.com). Any travel agent can book and confirm flights on Sansa and NatureAir. It is not necessary to travel to their offices to do so.

INTERNATIONAL AIRLINES

International carriers that have offices in San José are listed here. Airlines serving Costa Rica directly are marked with an asterisk; they also have desks at the airport. For websites of airlines serving Costa Rica see p463.

Air France (☎ 280 0069; 100m east & 10m north from Pops, Curridabat)
Alitalia (☎ 295 6820; cnr Calle 24 & Paseo Colón)
American Airlines* (☎ 257 1266; Av 5 bis btwn Calles 40 & 42, La Sabana)
British Airways (☎ 257 6912; Barrio Otoya)
Continental* (☎ 296 4911; next to Hotel Barceló, La Uruca)
COPA* (☎ 222 6640; cnr Calle 1 & Av 5)
Cubana de Aviación* (Map p74; ☎ 221 7625, 221 5881; Edificio Lux, cnr Av Central & Calle 1, 5th fl)
Delta* (☎ 256 7909, press 5 for reservations; Paseo Colón, 100m east & 50m south of Toyota)
Grupo TACA* (☎ 296 0909; cnr Calle 42 & Av 5; across from Datsun dealership)
Iberia* (☎ 257 8266; Paseo Colón, cnr Calle 40, 2nd fl)
Japan Air Lines (☎ 257 4646, 257 4023; Calle 42 btwn Avs 2 & 4, La Sabana)
KLM* (☎ 220 4111; Sabana Sur)
LTU (☎ 234 9292; Barrio Dent)
Mexicana* (☎ 295 6969; Torre Mercedes Benz on Paseo Colón, 3rd fl)
SAM/Avianca* (☎ 233 3066; Edificio Centro Colón, Paseo Colón btwn Calles 38 & 40)
United Airlines* (☎ 220 4844; Oficentro Ejecutivo, La Sabana)
Varig (☎ 290 5222; 150m south of Channel 7, west of Parque La Sabana)

CHARTER AIRCRAFT

Sansa and NatureAir both offer charter flights out of San José as do a number of aerotaxi companies. Most charters are small (three- to five-passenger) aircraft and can fly to any of the many airstrips around Costa Rica. Each listing below includes the San José airport that the company operates out of.

Aero Bell (☎ 290 0000; aerobell@racsa.co.cr; Tobías Bolaños)
Aviones Taxi Aéreo SA (☎ 441 1626; Juan Santamaría)
Helicópteros Turísticos Tropical (☎ 220 3940; Tobías Bolaños)
Pitts Aviation (☎ 296 3600; Tobías Bolaños)
Viajes Especial Aéreos SA (Veasa; ☎ 232 1010, 232 8043; Tobías Bolaños)

Bus

The **Coca-Cola terminal** (Map p86; Coca-Cola; Av 1 btwn Calles 16 & 18) is a well-known landmark in San José and an infinite number of buses leave from a four-block radius around it. Several other terminals serve specific regions. Just northeast of the Coca-Cola, the **Terminal Atlántico Norte** (Map p86; cnr Av 9 & Calle 12) serves northern destinations such as Monteverde, La Fortuna and Sarapiquí. The **Gran Terminal del Caribe** (Map pp70-1; Caribe Terminal; Calle Central, north of Av 13) serves the Caribbean coast. On the south end of town, **Terminal Musoc** (Av 22 btwn Calles Central & 1) caters for San Isidro.

Many of the bus companies, though, have no more than a bus stop (in this case pay the driver directly); some have a tiny office with a window on the street; some operate out of a terminal. Be aware that bus schedules change regularly. Pick up the useful but not always correct master bus schedule at the ICT office (p72) or look for the helpful *Hop on the Bus*, an up-to-date brochure published by Exintur; the brochure has locations of bus terminals and covers major destinations.

Buses are crowded on Friday evening and Saturday morning, even more so during Christmas and Easter. Thefts are common in the area around the Coca-Cola terminal, so stay alert – especially at night.

INTERNATIONAL BUSES FROM SAN JOSÉ

Take a copy of your passport when buying tickets to international destinations. For more on border crossings, see the boxed text on p466.

Changuinola/Bocas del Toro, Panama (Map p86; Panaline; cnr Calle 16 & Av 3) US$10; eight hours; departs at 10am.

David, Panama (Map p86; Tracopa; Calle 14 btwn Avs 3 & 5) US$9; nine hours; 7:30am.

Guatemala City (Map p74; Tica Bus; cnr Calle 9 & Av 4) US$39; 60 hours; 6am & 7:30am.

Managua, Nicaragua US$10-11.50; nine hours; Nica Bus (Map p86; Caribe Terminal) departs at 5:30am & 9am; Transportes Deldu/Sirca Express (Map p86; Calle 16 btwn Avs 3 & 5) departs 4:30am; Tica Bus (Map p74; cnr Calle 9 & Av 4) departs 6am & 7:30am; Trans Nica (Calle 22 btwn Avs 3 & 5) departs 4:30am, 5:30am & 9am.

Panama City US$23/40 for Tica/Panaline; 15 hours; Tica Bus (Map p74; cnr Calle 9 & Av 4) departs 10pm; Panaline (Map p86; cnr Calle 16 & Av 3) departs 1pm.

San Salvador, El Salvador (Map p74; Tica Bus; cnr Calle 9 & Av 4) US$30.50; 48 hours; 6am & 7:30am.

Tegucigalpa, Honduras (Map p74; Tica Bus; cnr Calle 9 & Av 4) US$27; 48 hours; 6am & 7:30am.

DOMESTIC BUSES FROM SAN JOSÉ

For destinations within Costa Rica, consult the following.

To the Central Valley

Alajuela (Map p86; Tuasa; Av 2 btwn Calles 12 & 14) US$0.60; 40 minutes; departs every 15 minutes from 4:45am to 11pm.

Cartago US$0.50; 40 minutes; Sacsa (Calle 5 btwn Avs 18 & 20) departs every five minutes; Transtusa (Map p000; Calle 13 btwn Avs 6 & 8) departs hourly from 8am to 8pm.

Grecia, for connection to Sarchí (Map p86; Av 5 btwn Calles 18 & 20) US$0.40; one hour; departs every 30 minutes from 5:30am to 10pm.

Heredia (Map p86; Av 2 btwn Calles 10 & 12) US$0.50; 20 minutes; departs every 20 to 30 minutes from 4:40am to 11pm.

Sarchí (Map p86; Av 5 btwn Calles 18 & 20) US$0.50; 1½ hours; departs 12:15pm, 5:30pm & 6pm.

Turrialba (Map pp70-1; Calle 13 btwn Avs 6 & 8) US$1.80; 1¾ hours; departs hourly 8am to 8pm.

Volcán Irazú (Map p74; Av 2 btwn Calles 1 & 3) US$4.50; departs 8am on weekends only.

Volcán Poás (Map p86; Tuasa; Av 2 between Calles 12 and 14) US$4, five hours; departs 8:30am.

To Northwestern Costa Rica

Cañas US$2.50-2.75; 3¼ hours; Tralapa (Map p86; Av 7 btwn Calles 20 & 22) departs hourly; Transportes Cañas (Map p86; Calle 16 btwn Avs 1 & 3) departs 8:30am, 10:20am, 12:20pm, 1:20pm, 2:30pm & 4:45pm.

Ciudad Quesada (San Carlos) (Map p86; Autotransportes San Carlos; Atlántico Norte terminal) US$2.25, 2½ hours; departs hourly 5am to 7pm.

La Fortuna (Map p86; Atlántico Norte terminal) US$3, 4½ hours; departs 6:15am, 8:40am & 11:30am.

Liberia US$4; four hours; Pullmitan (Map p86; Calle 24 btwn Avs 5 & 7) departs hourly from 6am to 7pm; Tralapa (Map p000; Av 7 btwn Calles 20 & 22) departs 3:25pm.

Monteverde/Santa Elena (Map p86; Trans Monteverde; Atlántico Norte terminal) US$4.25, 4½ hours; departs 6:30am & 2:30pm. (This bus fills up very quickly – book ahead.)

Peñas Blancas, the Nicaragua Border Crossing (Map p86; Transportes Deldú; Calle 16 btwn Avs 3 & 5) US$5.50; 4½ hours; departs 5am, 7am, 7:45am, 10:30am, 1:20pm & 4:10pm weekdays, every 15 minutes from 3am to 4pm weekends.

Tilarán (Map p86; Autotransportes Tilarán; Atlántico Norte terminal) US$3; four hours; departs 7:30am, 9:30am, 12:45pm, 3:45pm & 6:30pm.

To Península de Nicoya

Nicoya (Map p86; Empresas Alfaro; Calle 16 btwn Avs 3 & 5) US$5.25; five hours; departs 6:30am, 8am, 10am, 1:30pm, 2pm, 3pm & 5pm.

Playa Bejuco (Map p86; Empresas Arza; Calle 12 btwn Avs 7 & 9) US$5.75; 5½ hours; 6am & 3:30pm.

Playa del Coco (Map p86; Pullmitan; Calle 24 btwn Avs 5 & 7) US$5.25; five hours; 8am, 2pm & 4pm.

Playa Flamingo, via Brasilito (Map p86; Tralapa; Av 7 btwn Calles 20 & 22) US$5.50; six hours; 8am, 10:30am & 3pm.

Playa Junquillal (Map p86; Tralapa; Av 7 btwn Calles 20 & 22) US$8; six hours; 2pm.

Playa Nosara (Map p86; Empresas Alfaro; Calle 16 btwn Avs 3 & 5) US$5.50; seven hours; 12:30pm.

Playa Sámara (Map p86; Empresas Alfaro; Calle 16 btwn Avs 3 & 5) US$5; five hours; 5:30am.

Playa Panamá & Playa Hermosa (Map p86; Tralapa; Av 7 btwn Calles 20 & 22) US$5; five hours; 3:25pm.

Playa Tamarindo (Map p86; Empresas Alfaro; Calle 16 btwn Avs 3 & 5) US$5.50; five hours; 11am.

Santa Cruz, via Tempisque bridge US$5.25; 4¼ hours; Tralapa (Map p86; Av 7 btwn Calles 20 & 22) departs 7am, 9am, 10am, 10:30am, noon, 1pm, 2pm, 4pm & 6pm; Empresas Alfaro (Map p86; Calle 16 btwn Avs 3 & 5) departs 6:30am, 8am, 10am, 1:30pm, 3pm & 5pm.

To the Central Pacific Coast

Dominical (Map p86; Transportes Morales; Coca-Cola) US$4.50; 6½ hours; departs 7am, 8am, 1:30pm & 4pm.
Jacó (Map p86; Transportes Jacó; Coca-Cola) US$2.50; three hours; 7:30am, 10:30am, 1pm, 3:30pm & 6pm.
Puntarenas (Map pp70-1; Empresarios Unidos; cnr Av 12 & Calle 16) US$2.75; 2¼ hours; many buses from 6am to 7pm.
Quepos/Manuel Antonio (Map p86; Transportes Morales; Coca-Cola) US$4.25; four hours; 6am, noon & 6pm.
Uvita, via Dominical (Map p86; Transportes Morales; Coca-Cola) US$4.75; seven hours; 6am & 3pm.

To Southern Costa Rica & Península de Osa

Ciudad Neily (Map p86; Tracopa; Calle 14 btwn Avs 3 & 5) US$7, seven hours; departs 5am, 10am, 1pm, 4:30pm & 6pm.
Golfito (Map p86; Tracopa; Calle 14 btwn Avs 3 & 5) US$5.75, eight hours; 7am & 3pm.
Palmar Norte (Map p86; Tracopa; Calle 14 btwn Avs 3 & 5) US$4.50; five hours; 5am & 6pm.
Paso Canoas, the Panama Border Crossing (Map p86; Tracopa; Calle 14 btwn Avs 3 & 5) US$7.50; 7¼ hours; 5am, 7:30am, 11am, 1pm, 4:30pm & 6pm.
Puerto Jiménez (Map pp70-1; Blanco Lobo; Calle 12 btwn Avs 9 & 11) US$6.25; eight hours; noon.
San Isidro de El General (Transportes Musoc; cnr Calle Central & Av 22) US$3.75; three hours; 5:30am, 7:30am, 10:30am, 11:30am, 2:30pm, 4:30pm, 5pm & 5:30pm.
Santa María de Dota (Map pp70-1; Transportes Los Santos; Av 16 btwn Calles 19 & 21) US$2.75; 2½ hours; 7:15am, 9am, 11:30am, 12:30pm, 3pm, 5pm and 7:30pm.
San Vito (Map p86; Empresa Alfaro; Calle 16 btwn Av 3 & 5) US$5.25; seven hours; 5:45am, 8:15am, 11:30am & 2:45pm.

To the Caribbean Coast

All of the following buses depart from the Caribe terminal (Map pp70-1):
Cahuita (Autotransportes Mepe) US$5; 3¾ hours; departs 6am, 10am, 1:30pm & 3:30pm.
Cariari, for transfer to Tortuguero (Empresarios Guapileños) US$2; 2¼ hours; 6:30am, 9am, 10:30am, 1pm, 3pm, 4:30pm, 6pm & 7pm; for detailed information on transfer to Tortuguero, see p397.
Guápiles (Empresarios Guapileños) US$1.50; 1¼ hours; departs hourly from 6:30am to 7pm.
Puerto Limón (Autotransportes Caribeños) US$3.25; three hours; departs every 30 minutes from 5:30am to 7pm.
Puerto Viejo de Talamanca (Autotransportes Mepe) US$5.50; 4¼ hours; 6am, 10am, 1:30pm & 3:30pm.
Siquirres (Líneas Nuevo Atlántico) US$2; 1¾ hours; 6:30am, 8am, 9am, 9:30am, 10am, 11am, noon, 1pm, 2pm, 3pm, 4pm, 5pm & 6pm.
Sixaola, the Panama Border Crossing (Autotransportes Mepe) US$7; five hours; 6am, 10am, 1:30pm & 3:30pm.

To the Northern Lowlands

Ciudad Quesada (San Carlos) See under To Northwestern Costa Rica, see p98.
Los Chiles, the Nicaragua Border Crossing (Map p86; Atlántico Norte terminal) US$3.75; five hours; departs 5:30am & 3:30pm.
Puerto Viejo de Sarapiquí (Map pp70-1; Autotransportes Sarapiquí; Caribe Terminal) US$2.30; 1½ hours; 6:30am, 8am, 10am, 11:30am, 1:30pm, 2:30pm, 3:30pm, 4:30pm, 5:30pm & 6pm.
Rara Avis (Map p86; Atlántico Norte terminal) US$4; four hours; 7am.
Upala (Map p86; Transportes de Upala; Atlántico Norte terminal) US$5.50; four hours; departs 10:15am, 3pm & 5:15pm.

TOURIST BUSES

Grayline's Fantasy Bus (☎ 220 2126; www.graylinecostarica.com) and **Interbus** (☎ 283 5573; www.interbusonline.com) shuttle passengers from all over San José to a long and growing list of popular tourist destinations around Costa Rica. They're more expensive than the standard bus service, but they will get you there faster. See p470 for more information.

GETTING AROUND

Downtown San José is very busy and relatively small. The narrow streets, heavy traffic and complicated one-way system often mean that it is quicker to walk than to take the bus. The same applies to driving: if you rent a car, don't drive downtown – it's a nightmare! If you're in a hurry to get somewhere that is more than 1km away, take a taxi.

To/From the Airports

TO AEROPUERTO INTERNACIONAL JUAN SANTAMARÍA

You can reserve a pick-up with **Taxi Aeropuerto** (☎ 221 6865; www.taxiaeropuerto.com), which charges a flat rate of US$12 from most parts of San José. You can also take a street taxi, but the rates may vary wildly. It should cost roughly US$12 to US$15, but this will depend largely on traffic conditions (see p67). A cheaper option is the red **Tuasa bus** (map p86; cnr Calle 10 & Av 2; US$0.60) bound for Alajuela. Be sure to tell the driver that you are getting off at the airport when you board (*Voy al aeropuerto, por favor*). **Interbus** (☎ 283 5573; www.interbusonline.com) runs an airport shuttle service that will pick you up at your hotel for US$5 – a good value.

TO AEROPUERTO TOBÍAS BOLAÑOS

Buses to Tobías Bolaños depart every 30 minutes from Avenida 1, 150m west of the Coca-Cola terminal. A taxi to the airport from downtown costs about US$3.

Bus

Local buses are useful to get you into the suburbs and surrounding villages, or to the airport. They leave regularly from particular bus stops downtown – though all of them will pick up passengers on the way. Most buses run between 5am and 10pm and cost US$0.25 to US$0.50.

Buses from Parque La Sabana head into town on Paseo Colón, then go over to Avenida 2 at the San Juan de Dios hospital. They then go three different ways through town before eventually heading back to La Sabana. Buses are marked Sabana-Estadio, Sabana-Cementario, or Cementario-Estadio. These buses are a good bet for a cheap city tour. Buses going east to Los Yoses and San Pedro go back and forth along Avenida 2 and then switch over to Avenida Central at Calle 29. (These buses are easily identifiable because many of them have a big sign that says 'Mall San Pedro' on the front window.) These buses start at the corner of Avenida 2 and Calle 7, near Restaurante El Pollo Campesino.

Buses to the following outlying suburbs and towns begin from bus stops at the indicated blocks. Some places have more than one stop – only the main ones are listed here. If you need buses to other suburbs, inquire at the tourist office (p72.)

Escazú Calle 16 (Map p86; Calle 16 btwn Avs 1 & 3) Avenida 6 (Map p74; Av 6 btwn Calles 12 & 14)
Guadalupe (Map p74; Av 3 btwn Calles Central & 1)
Moravia (Map p74; Av 3 btwn Calles 3 & 5)
Pavas (Map p86; cnr Av 1 & Calle 18)
Santa Ana (Map p86; Calle 16 btwn Avs 1 & 3)
Santo Domingo (Map p74; Av 5 btw Calles Central & 2)

Car

It is not advisable to rent a car just to drive around San José. The traffic is heavy, the streets narrow and the meter-deep curb-side gutters make parking a nerve-wracking experience. In addition, car break-ins are frequent and leaving a car – even in a guarded lot – might result in a smashed window and stolen belongings. (Never ever leave anything in a rental car.) If you are remaining in San José hire the plentiful taxis – available at all hours – instead.

If you are renting a car to travel throughout Costa Rica, you will not be short of choices: there are more than 50 car-rental agencies in and around San José and the travel desks at travel agencies and upmarket hotels can all arrange rentals of various types of vehicles. *Naturally Costa Rica*, a magazine published by the ICT and Canatur (available at many hotels and the ICT office) has an extensive list of car-rental companies in the area. You can also check the local yellow pages (under Alquiler de Automóviles) for a complete listing. See p470 for general information on rental agencies.

Note that there is a surcharge of about US$25 for renting cars from rental agencies at Juan Santamaría airport. Save yourself the expense by renting in town.

Motorcycle

Given the narrow roads, deep gutters and homicidal bus drivers, riding a motorcycle in San José is recommended only for those who are not in complete need of their appendages. But, for the foolhardy – and careful – road warrior, renting a bike is an option. Rental bikes are usually small (185cc to 350cc) and rates start at about US$50 per day for a 350cc motorcycle and skyrockets from there. (Plan on paying US$200 a day for a Harley.) These are a couple of agencies worth trying in San José.

Wild Rider (☎ 258 4604; www.wild-rider.com; in Hotel Ritmo del Caribe, cnr Paseo Colón & Calle 32) Prices start at US$230 per week for a Yamaha TT-R 250 or a Suzuki DR-350; rates include insurance, taxes, maps and helmets. It will do on- and off-road guided tours as well. Wild Rider also has a handful of used 4WD cars that can be rented at significantly cheaper weekly rates than the big agencies.

Harley Davidson Rentals (see p106) in Escazú rents Harleys.

Taxi

Red taxis can be hailed on the street day or night or you can have your hotel call one for you. You can also hire taxis at any of the taxi stands at the Parque Nacional, Parque Central and near the Teatro Nacional. The most difficult time to flag down a taxi is when it's raining.

Marías (meters) are supposedly used, but some drivers will pretend they are broken and try to charge you more – especially if you're a tourist who doesn't speak Spanish. (Not using a meter is illegal.) Make sure the *maría* is operating when you get in or negotiate the fare up front. Within San José fares are US$0.60 for the first kilometer and US$0.30 for each additional one. Short rides downtown cost about US$1. A cab to Escazú from downtown will cost about US$4, while a ride to Los Yoses or San Pedro will cost less than US$2. There's a 20% surcharge after 10pm that may not appear on the *maría*.

You can hire a taxi and driver for half a day or longer if you want to do some touring around the area, but rates vary wildly depending on the destination and the condition of the roads. For a short trip on reasonably good roads, plan on spending at least US$7.50 an hour for a sedan and significantly more for a 4WD sport utility vehicle or minivan. You can also negotiate a flat fee.

AROUND SAN JOSÉ

As the city centre has expanded, some of San José's suburbs have been caught up in the tourist trade as well, offering plenty of comfy hotels, good eateries and comparatively safer neighborhoods to hang out during the evenings. If you're going to be in San José for more than a night or don't mind the short commutes to one of the more scenic 'burbs, then it's definitely worth staying in the 'burbs. You'll enjoy cleaner air, quieter hotels and a better atmosphere all round.

LOS YOSES & SAN PEDRO

About 2km east of central downtown, on San José's eastern border, lie the well-to-do residential zones of Los Yoses and San Pedro. The two neighborhoods are intersected by a rotunda, where Avenida Central meets the road to Zapote in a roundabout that bus drivers love to careen through at full throttle. (Pedestrians beware.) On the west side of the rotunda is Los Yoses, with the Fuente de la Hispanidad (a large fountain) and the Mall San Pedro, both serving as area landmarks. To the east of this bustling roadway lies San Pedro, anchored by a small plaza and the Iglesia de San Pedro (San Pedro church).

In the north of San Pedro is the Universidad de Costa Rica (the national university), which sits on a tree-lined campus a few blocks north of Avenida Central. Because of the high ratio of students and other academic types, the neighborhood is brimming with interesting – and crowded – bars, restaurants and clubs and serves as a nightlife destination, particularly for the under-30s. It's a great area to stroll around in the evenings and much safer than downtown.

Information

Most streets in Los Yoses and San Pedro are unnamed and locals rely almost entirely on the landmark method to orient themselves. (See the boxed text on p453 for more on this.) Two major area landmarks are the old ICE building *(el antiguo ICE)* in Los Yoses and the old Banco Popular building *(el antiguo Banco Popular)* in San Pedro.

The neighborhood abounds with Internet cafés, so there's no problem logging on. **Net Café** (☎ 234 8200; Calle 3, north of Av Central; per hr US$1; 🕙 7am-10pm) is a good place to check email, as is **Internet Café Costa Rica** (☎ 224 7295; 75m west of the old Banco Popular; per hr US$0.60; 🕙 24hr) around the corner. In Barrio Dent, **Librería Internacional** (☎ 253 9553; 300m west of Taco Bell, behind San Pedro Mall; 🕙 9:30am-7:30pm Mon-Sat, 1-5pm Sun) has new books mostly in Spanish (but some in English) as well as travel and wildlife guides.

Wash the skivvies at **Burbujas** (☎ 224 9822; 50m west & 25m south of Más X Menos, San Pedro; 🕙 8am-6pm Mon-Fri, 8:30am-4:30pm Sat) or **Lava-más** (☎ 225 1645; 100m west of the old ICE building, next to Spoon coffee shop, Los Yoses; 🕙 9am-5pm Mon-Fri, 9am-3pm Sat). Both laundries offer self-service machines and a wash-and-dry will cost about US$5.

The **Scotiabank** in San Pedro (☎ 280 0604; Av Central btwn Calles 5 & 7) changes cash and has a 24-hour ATM on the Cirrus network.

Pick up a copy of the student weekly, *Semana Universitaria*, for a comprehensive source of local events.

Sights & Activities

The **Museo de Insectos** (☎ 207 5318, 207 5647; admission US$1; 🕙 1-5pm Mon-Fri), also known as the Museo de Entomología, has a fine collection of insects curated by the Facultad de Agronomía at the Universidad de Costa Rica

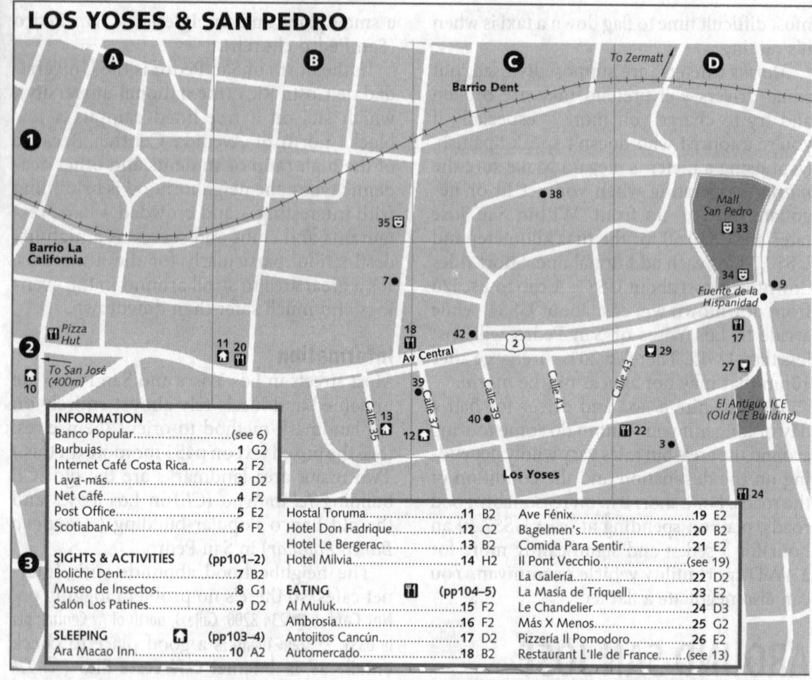

and housed (incongruously) in the basement of the music building (Facultad de Artes Musicales) on campus. It is claimed that this is the only insect museum of its size in Central America. The collection is certainly extensive and provides a good opportunity to view a vast assortment of exotic – and downright alarming – creepy crawlies. The museum is signposted from San Pedro church, or you can ask for directions. Ring the bell to gain admission if the door isn't open.

If you're interested in knocking down some pins, one block south of the North American-Costa Rican Cultural Center you'll find **Boliche Dent** (☎ 234 2777, cnr Av Central & Calle 23, Los Yoses) where you can bowl for US$7 per hour. Just east of the rotunda in San Pedro, you can strap on the roller skates and hang out with what seems like every last teenager in San José at **Salón Los Patines** (☎ 224 6821), the local roller rink.

Courses

There are a number of places where you can learn Spanish. Some also offer dance classes and organize volunteer placements.

Academia Latinoamericana de Español (☎ 224 9917; www.alespanish.com; Av 8 btwn Calles 31 & 33, San Pedro)

Amerispan Unlimited (☎ in the USA 215-751 1100, in the USA & Canada 800-879 6640, www.amerispan.com)

Costa Rican Language Academy (☎ 280 1685, in the USA 866-230 6361; www.learn-spanish.com; from the Subaru dealership, go 300m north and 50m west) This organization also offers cooking, Latin dance lessons and can provide you with enrollment information for a variety of volunteer programs.

Forester Instituto Internacional (☎ 225 3155, 225 1649, 225 0135; www.fores.com; 75m south of the Automercado, Los Yoses) The institute can also arrange cultural excursions and offers free Internet access and Latin dance classes.

Instituto Británico (☎ 225 0256; www.institutobritanico.co.cr; 75m south of the Subaru dealership in Los Yoses)

Institute for Central American Development Studies (Icads; ☎ 225 0508; www.icadscr.com; off the main road to Curridabat) This school also offers extra lectures and activities focused on environmental and regional socio-political issues. It can also help place you in local volunteer positions.

Instituto Latinoamericano de Idiomas (Ilisa; ☎ 280 0700, in the USA 800-454 7248; www.ilisa.com; 100m east, 400m south, 50m east from the San Pedro church) Though pricey, this San Pedro school is a bit different: classes are

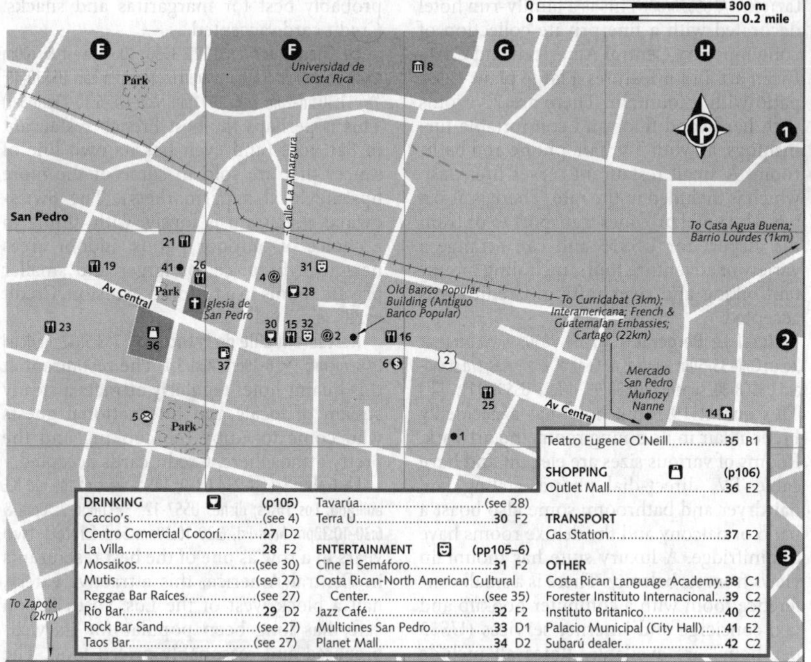

customized for professionals, primarily for businesspeople and include curriculums such as 'Spanish for CEOs' and less exclusive management titles. Cultural outings and cooking classes are part of the deal.

Intensa (☎ 281 1818, in the USA & Canada 866-277 1352; www.intensa.com; Calle 33 btwn Avs 1 & 3, San Pedro)

Sleeping

Hostal Toruma (☎ 234 8186; www.hicr.org; Av Central btwn Calles 29 & 31, Los Yoses; HI members per person US$11, nonmembers US$15; Ⓟ) Accommodations at Toruma consist of sex-segregated dorms with bunk beds featuring railway-compartment-like shutters. The building is a spacious and brightly painted old mansion that sits above Avenida Central and backpackers congregate for cheap meals at the cafeteria and watch cable TV in the lounge. Prices include breakfast. Though it's a little pricey for a hostel, this is a popular place and it books up in advance. Make reservations to be sure of a bed. You can also make reservations here for other HI-affiliated hostels in Costa Rica.

Ara Macao Inn (☎ 233 2742; www.hotels.co.cr/aramacao.html; Calle 27 btwn Avs Central & 2; s/d/tr US$40/50/60, s/d apt US$45/55) This is a nice place in a quiet area about four blocks east of the Museo Nacional (tell cab drivers it's 50m south of the Pizza Hut in Barrio California). Its eight rooms all have bathroom, fan, clock radio and cable TV. Apartments have a kitchenette. The staff is bilingual and friendly and there is a pleasant outdoor courtyard for dining and barbecuing. Continental breakfast and laundry services are included. Credit cards accepted.

Hotel Milvia (☎ 225 4543; www.hotelmilvia.com; San Pedro; s/d/tr incl breakfast US$69/81/88; 💻) This beautiful, small hotel once served as the home of Ricardo Fernández Peralta, an artillery colonel who fought in Costa Rica's 1948 civil war. It was restored to its original grandeur by his grandson and is now under new ownership. Each spacious room combines just the right touch of modern and antique and has a bathroom with hot water. An upstairs terrace provides incredible views. Credit cards accepted. For cab drivers: it's 100m north and 200m east of Mercado San Pedro Muñoz y Nanne.

Hotel Don Fadrique (☎ 225 8166, 224 7583; www.hoteldonfadrique.com; cnr Calle 37 & Av 8, 2nd entrance to

Los Yoses; s/d US$70/82) This is a family-run hotel decorated with a fine private collection of contemporary Central American and Costa Rican art and it features a large plant-filled patio with a fountain. There are 20 rooms with hardwood floor and comfortable furnishings, all with TV, fan, phone and bathroom. A small restaurant serves breakfast, which is included in the rate. There is also a bar. The hotel provides transport to or from the airport for US$15 and can arrange a variety of adventure tours, including mountain biking and river rafting. Credit cards accepted.

Hotel Le Bergerac (☎ 234 7850; www.bergerac.co.cr; Calle 35, 50m south of Av Central, Los Yoses; s/d standard US$68/80, superior US$88/99, deluxe US$99/111; 💻) This quaint 19-room hotel has a decidedly French flair in its dining room and artwork. Rooms of various sizes are elegant and have cable TV, direct-dial phone, ceiling fan, hairdryer and bathroom; some also boast a patio or balcony and the deluxe rooms have a minifridge. A luxury suite has mountain views from its balcony. There is a small conference room with a computer hookup and fax; concierge and Internet services (US$3 per hour) are available. Rates all include breakfast. Credit cards accepted. The French restaurant is excellent (see opposite).

Casa Agua Buena (☎ 234 2411; www.aguabuena.org/casabuena/index.html; Barrio Lourdes east of San Pedro; r per night US$12-15, r per week US$60-80) For long-term stays, this group-house arrangement is a great choice and is very popular with international students. Two simple peach-colored homes with rooms of various sizes sit side-by-side on a quiet dead-end street. Houses are equipped with a common kitchen, washing machine (use of the machine is included in the rates), a lounge with cable TV and phone. Some rooms share bathrooms, while others have private ones – all with hot water. The Casa is gay-friendly.

Eating

Antojitos Cancún (☎ 225 9525; 50m west of the Fuente de Hispanidad, Los Yoses; dishes US$3-13; 🕑 11:30am-12:30am) Although this place has several locally popular locations, the best known is this one in Los Yoses. The food is inexpensive, though not terribly authentic (the staff call it 'Mexi-tico'). Choices range from a couple of tacos to a full-blown plate of beef *fajitas*, with seafood dishes as well. It's probably best for margaritas and snacks. Credit cards accepted.

Le Chandelier (☎ 225 3980; 100m west & 100m south of the old ICE building, Los Yoses; meals US$10-40; 🕑 11:30am-2pm & 6:30-11pm Mon-Fri, 6:30-11pm Sat) This is perhaps the best French restaurant in San José (and even has its own line of sauces that are sold in some of the more upscale local supermarkets). The Swiss-owned restaurant is lovely, with dining in a choice of outdoor patios, indoor areas next to a fireplace, or larger and smaller private rooms in a restored mansion. Credit cards accepted.

Restaurant L'Ile de France (☎ 283 5812; in Hotel Le Bergerac; 🕑 6-10pm Mon-Sat) The restaurant at this quaint hotel regularly attracts a steady stream of locals and international guests who come to enjoy the cooking and the pretty atmosphere. Credit cards accepted.

La Galería (☎ 234 0850; 125m west of the old ICE building, Los Yoses; dishes US$7-12; 🕑 noon-2:30pm & 6:30-10:30pm Mon-Fri, 6:30-10:30pm Sat) Listed two years in a row as one of the best restaurants in Central America, this attractive eatery, half a block west of the Los Yoses Spoon café, has long been popular for its well-prepared and reasonably priced food. The cuisine shows strong German influence, serving specialties such as *schpaetzel* and strudel. Credit cards accepted.

Zermatt (☎ 222 0604; Av 11 & Calle 23, Barrio Dent; dishes US$6-20; 🕑 noon-2pm & 6-10:45pm) A fancy place for a wide variety of sweet and savory fondues (US$26 to US$38 for two people) and other gourmet Swiss delights, this pleasant place is 100m north and 25m east of the Santa Teresita church in Barrio Dent.

Ave Fénix (180m west of San Pedro church; meals US$3-10) This is a well-known local favorite that has served Szechwan meals for over three decades.

Il Pont Vecchio (☎ 283 1810; 150m east of Fuente de Hispanidad & 10m north, San Pedro; dishes US$6-15; 🕑 noon-2:30pm & 6-10:30pm Mon-Sat) Next door, this elegant Italian place vies for the 'best of' in the greater San José area and has been recognized as one of the top restaurants in Central America. Chef Antonio D'Alaimo, who once worked in New York City, makes all of his own fresh pastas and imports many of his ingredients directly from Italy. Credit cards accepted.

La Masía de Triquell (☎ 296 3528; Edificio Casa España, Sabana Norte; 100m east & 180m north of the old

ICE, San Pedro; dishes US$10-20; 11:30am-2pm & 6:45-10:30pm Mon-Sat) The service is excellent and the surroundings superlative at this refined and long-standing Spanish establishment. The chef specializes in Catalan cuisine and there is a selection of paellas; the dishes are expensive, but more than worth the splurge. Credit cards accepted.

Pizzería Il Pomodoro (60m north of San Pedro church; pizzas US$4-8) Students like to grab a pizza at this lively and informal place near the Universidad de Costa Rica that is open seven days a week. Locals claim it's the best pizza in town.

Up the street, you'll find the fine veggie venue, **Comida Para Sentir** (daily specials US$4.30), serving whole grain pastas, meat-less meals and mean cappuccinos to a packed house.

Al Muluk (Calle 3, north of Av Central; dishes US$3-7) This popular new Lebanese restaurant has delectable falafel (US$2.80) in addition to a wide variety of traditional Lebanese dishes. Daily specials are US$4.30.

Ambrosia (☎ 253 8012; Centro Comercial de la Calle Real, opposite Banco Popular, San Pedro; dishes US$8-14; 11:30am-10:30pm Mon-Sat, 11:30am-4pm Sun) The Ambrosia has an unconventional and indefinable European-influenced menu, covering pastas, crepes, salads, chicken, seafood and beef.

Bagelmen's (Av Central & Calle 33, Los Yoses) This outpost of the popular bagel chain is just up the street from Hostal Toruma and serves decent bagels (US$0.50) and sandwiches (US$3 to US$5). It's usually very crowded, though it has a drive-thru.

The **Automercado** (Av Central btwn Calles 39 & 41, Los Yoses) and the **Más X Menos** (Av Central, San Pedro) are large, modern supermarkets that offer plenty of options for self-caterers.

Drinking

Río Bar (Av Central & Calle 39, Los Yoses) Just west of the fountain, this popular bar has live bands on some nights and a pyrotechnic house drink called the cucaracha. There are two-for-one drink specials on Monday night.

Further east in Los Yoses and just south of Los Antojitos Cancún, you'll find the nightlife hub of **Centro Comercial Cocorí** (south of Av Central). Most of the places here get started after 9pm and run late ('til the last customer leaves). And basically, if you want it, they've got it. Rock Bar Sand is the regular watering hole for local rockers, as is Mutis out front. Around the back, Reggae Bar Raíces draws in the Rasta crowd, while Taos Bar, next door, is slightly mellower, but still gets packed.

In San Pedro, Calle 3, to the north of Avenida Central is also known as Calle La Amargura (Street of Sorrow). It should be called Calle de la Cruda (Street of Hangovers) because it has perhaps the highest concentration of bars of any single street in town, many of which are packed with customers even during daylight hours. Terra U, Mosaikos, Caccio's and Tavarúa are raucous, beer-soaked places packed with a steady stream of rowdy young customers. A more relaxed (and slightly grown-up) place is La Villa, in a distinctive wood house with a candlelit back patio that is much larger than it appears from outside. There is live music some weekends.

See Nightclubs below, for other options.

Entertainment

Cinemas are plentiful in the neighborhood. **Multicines San Pedro** (☎ 283 5715/6; top level of Mall San Pedro; admission US$4.25) has 10 screens showing the latest Hollywood flicks. Better yet, head to **Cine El Semáforo** (☎ 253 9126; www.cineselsemaforo.com; beside train tracks, east of Calle 3; admission US$3; 11am-8pm), a hip little theater showing Spanish and Latin American movie classics every day. (It's Spanish only, so it's great if you want to come to practice.)

If live theater is your bag, there are a couple of choices in the area. **Teatro Eugene O'Neill** (☎ 207 7554; www.cccncr.com; cnr Av Central & Calle 37, Los Yoses) has performances sponsored by the Centro Cultural Costarricense Norteamericano (Costa Rican-North American Cultural Center). On the east side of the Universidad de Costa Rica campus is the **Teatro Bellas Artes** (☎ 207 4327) which offers a wide variety of programming, including works produced by the fine-arts department at the university.

NIGHTCLUBS

See also Drinking previous, and options in San José on p94.

Jazz Café (☎ 253 8933; 50m west of old Banco Popular; 6pm-2am) is the destination in San Pedro for live music, with a different band every night. Cover charges vary, depending on the prominence of the musical act featured, but usually fluctuate between US$4 and US$6 for local groups.

For a full-blown dance party, hit **Planet Mall** (☎ 280 4693; 🕑 8pm-2:30am Thu-Sat), one of San José's most expensive nightclubs. The enormous, warehouse-sized disco has a couple of levels, several bars and is situated on the 4th and 5th stories of Mall San Pedro where you can admire the twinkling lights of San José from its oversized windows. Covers here can fluctuate depending on who is spinning or performing, but can easily creep up to US$10 on any given night.

Shopping

Both **Mall San Pedro** (☎ 283 7516; northwest of Fuente de la Hispanidad) and the **Outlet Mall** (Av Central, east of the road to Zapote) offer ample opportunities for mall rats looking to shop 'til they drop.

Getting There & Away

From San José, take any bus marked 'Mall San Pedro.' A taxi ride from downtown will cost US$1.50 to US$2.

ESCAZÚ

Situated just 7km west of downtown San José via the Autopista Próspero Fernández, this affluent suburb is spread out on a hillside overlooking San José and Heredia in the distance. The area is really comprised of the three adjoining neighborhoods of San Rafael de Escazú, Escazú Centro and San Antonio de Escazún – the latter is at the highest point on the hillside.

Packed with gringo expats, the area of San Rafael is one part Costa Rica, one part USA – and is dotted with strip malls, nice homes, nicer cars and restaurants that print their menus largely in English. (The US Ambassador lives in this area in a very secure-looking white-walled compound.) Escazú Centro thankfully retains a more unhurried Tico ambience, with its narrow streets and numerous shops and *sodas*. And the area around San Antonio remains almost entirely residential though it does house a handful of hotels that offer spectacular views of the valley.

Information

A branch of the bookshop **Libreria Internacional** (☎ 201 8320; 🕑 10am-8pm Mon-Sat, 10am-7pm Sun) can be found in Multiplaza Escazú. To check email, stop in at **Escazú Internet** (Centro Comercial Plaza Escazú, ground fl; per hr US$0.50; 🕑 8:30am-10pm Mon-Sat, 9am-9pm Sun) in Escazú Centro.

For medical care – emergency or otherwise, visit **Hospital CIMA** (☎ 208 1000; www.hospitalsanjose.net; 500m west of the Próspero Fernández toll booth). This is in the area of Guachipelín, on the west side of Escazú and is one of the most modern hospitals in the greater San José metropolitan area. It is affiliated with Baylor University Medical Center in the USA and has been recommended.

Banco Nacional de Costa Rica (cnr Calle 2 & Av 2; 🕑 8:30am-3:45pm), on the main plaza in Escazú Centro, can change money and traveler's checks and it even has a drive-thru window. In San Rafael there is a **Scotiabank** (Carretera JF Kennedy) with a Cirrus ATM. On the northwestern end you'll find a similar 24-hour ATM at **Banex** (Centro Comercial Guachipelín, Carretera JF Kennedy).

Activities & Events

You can arrange motorcycle tours or rent bikes at **Harley Davidson Rentals** (☎ 289 5552; www.mariaalexandra.com), which has an office inside the Apartotel María Alexandra (p110). Riders have to be more than 25 years of age and have a valid motorcycle driving license. Rates start at US$195 per bike per day and include helmet, goggles and unlimited mileage (insurance and tax not included). The agency can deliver bikes to other destinations at an extra charge.

Reputable **Swiss Travel Service** (☎ 282 4898; www.swisstravelcr.com; Autopista Próspero Fernández, 300m west of Cruce de Piedeades de Santa Ana) offers tours all over Costa Rica.

Those who want to practice their golf swing can head to the **Costa Rica Country Club** (☎ 228 9333, 208 5000; www.costaricacountryclub.com), which has a nine-hole course. There are also tennis courts and a pool. In Santa Ana, west of Escazú, is **Valle del Sol** (☎ 282 9222, ext 218/219; www.vallesol.com), inside a community of the same name, which has a new 18-hole (7000 yard, par 72) public course. Greens fees are US$7 and golf carts another US$20.

On the second Sunday of March Escazú celebrates **Día del Boyero**, which is a celebration in honor of oxcart drivers. Dozens of *boyeros* from all over the country decorate the traditional, brightly-painted carts and form a colorful (if slow) parade.

Sleeping

Escazú has a variety of accommodations – all in the mid-range to top-end categories. Street addresses aren't given here – refer to the map or call the hotel for directions (which are invariably unwieldy and complicated).

B&BS

Escazú is dotted with a fine selection of B&Bs that all offer a homey alternative to chain hotels. All of the establishments below include breakfast in the rates.

Posada El Quijote (☎ 289 8401; www.quijote.co.cr; s/d/tr standard US$64/76/99, superior US$76/88/111, deluxe US$88/99/123, apt per month US$1160; P ⊠ ❄) This *posada* definitely rates as one of the top B&Bs in the San José area. Nestled on a hillside, the hotel has magnificent views of the Central Valley and its rooms and public areas are all sumptuously decorated. Standard units are bright and spacious, with cable TV, phone and modern bathroom. Larger superior rooms have a small patio and deluxe units have views and private terrace. Two studio apartments have private entrances. Credit cards are accepted.

Park Place B&B (☎ 228 9200; Interlink 358, PO Box 025635, Miami, FL 33102; s/d US$40/45; P) Retired dentist Barry Needman runs this small and friendly place, situated in an attractive whitewashed alpine-style house. (There's no sign out the front, so look for the high eaves.) Four immaculate guest bedrooms share two bathrooms, kitchen privileges and a roomy lounge with cable TV – and are a good value. Barry cooks a heaping American-style breakfast for his guests and he can also hook you up with tours run by locals. Weekly and monthly rates are available. Buses to San José stop just outside several times an hour.

Villa Escazú (☎ 289 7971; www.hotels.co.cr/vescazu.html; s/d/tr US$40/60/75; P) A Swiss chalet-type building is surrounded by terraced gardens and fruit trees and is patrolled by a very friendly pooch named Felíz. The verandah is good for watching birds and eating the full gourmet breakfast. Six pretty wood rooms share three bathrooms and all feature wood paneling, bookshelf, sofa and artwork. A sitting room with a fireplace invites you to relax in this tranquil getaway. There is also a studio apartment with a small kitchen, cable TV and good-size tiled bathroom (US$250 per week) – an excellent deal. English is spoken.

Costa Verde Inn (☎ 228 4080; www.costaverdeinn.com; s/d/tr US$47/64/76, apt US$88; P 🏊) This is an attractive and friendly country inn with a hot tub, lighted tennis court, pool, sundeck, barbecue area and fireplace. Rooms all have fan, king-size bed, cable TV and hot shower; three studio loft-style apartments have a balcony, high ceilings and a kitchen. Room number eight has a pretty stone shower. A Tico breakfast is served on an outdoor terrace. Low-season and weekly rates are available; credit cards accepted. This hotel has a sister lodge in Manuel Antonio (p298).

Casa María (☎ 228 0190; www.costarica.org; d US$53-76, tr US$81-104, apt per night/month US$105/1111; P 🏊) Casa María is a seven-room hotel situated in a '70s-style ranch house. Room rates vary greatly depending on room size and whether or not they share a bathroom; all showers have hot water. The common areas are covered in trippy murals – and the whole place looks like it could use an update. There is a pool and a few banana trees in the ample backyard. Lunch and dinner are provided on request. Maps, books and travel information are available.

Casa de las Tías (☎ 289 5517; www.hotels.co.cr/casatias.html; Calle León; s/d US$63/76, junior ste US$90; P ⊠) In a quiet area of San Rafael, this brightly painted Cape Cod–style house with a yellow picket fence is decorated with art and crafts from all over Latin America. Four genteel, nicely decorated rooms and one junior suite have ceiling fan and bathroom with hot water. Breakfast is served in the lovely garden and the congenial owners speak English, Spanish, French and Hebrew. Smoking is not allowed indoors and no child under 12 is admitted. Airport pickup (US$15 to US$22) is available with an advanced reservation.

Posada del Bosque (☎ 228 1164; posada@amerisol.com; d US$69; P ⊠ 🏊) This country inn is set in pleasant gardens. The helpful Tico owners enjoy chatting in English with their international guests and will cook for you on request. There are eight rooms with private bathrooms in this nonsmoking inn. There is a fireplace, laundry service and a barbecue area. A swimming pool, tennis court and horseback-riding trails are nearby. Airport pickup is available for an extra charge.

HOTELS & APARTOTELS

Mid-range

Pine Tree Inn (☎ 289 7405; www.hotelpinetree.com; Av 23, northwest of Av L Cortés; s/d/tr US$50/74/75; P 🏊) Beyond the María Alexandra, you'll find this inn, which looks like a 1950s motel on the outside, but is very pleasant inside. Fifteen

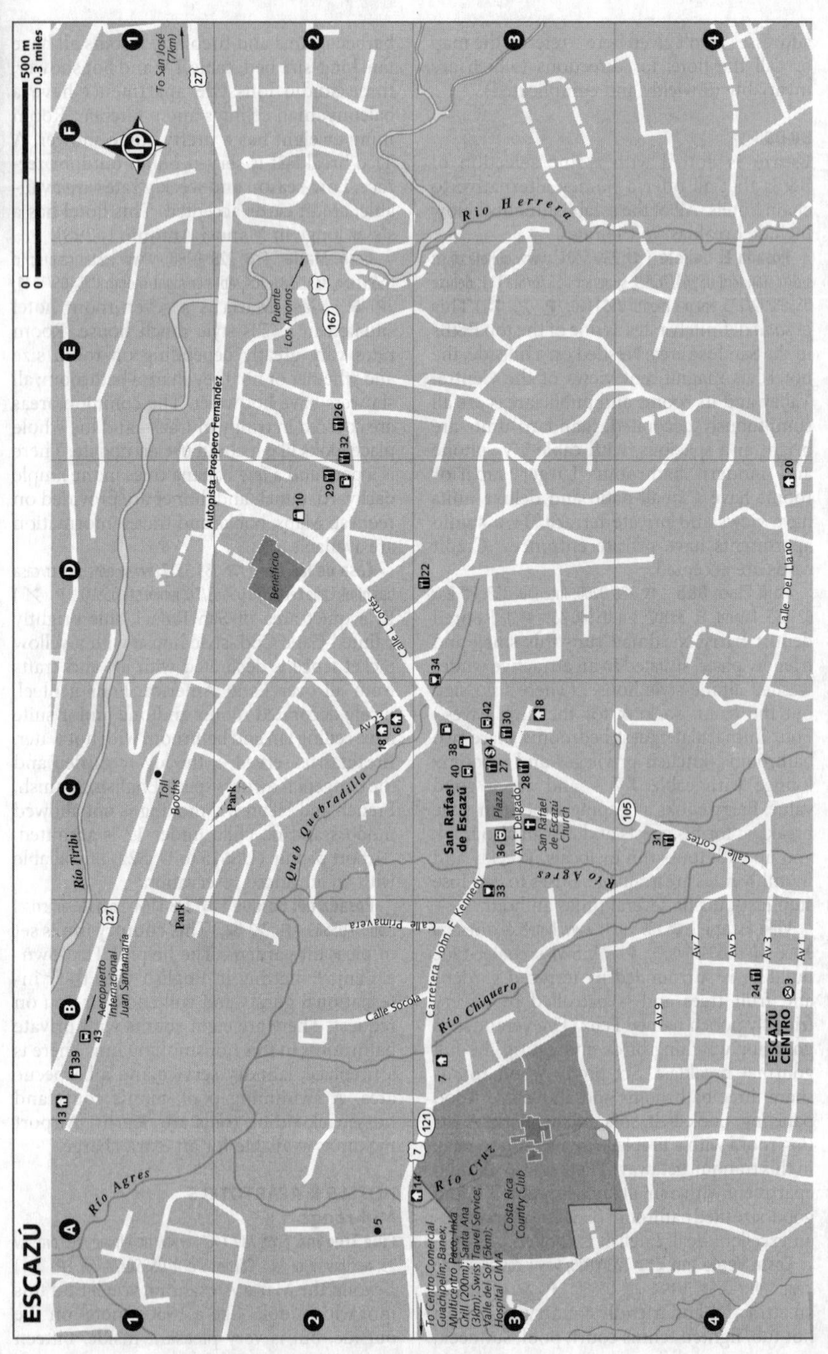
ESCAZÚ
500 m
0.3 miles
To San José (7km)
Autopista Prospero Fernandez
Puente Los Anonos
Río Herrera
Beneficio
Calle L Cortes
Calle Del Llano
San Rafael de Escazú
Plaza
Av F Delgado
San Rafael de Escazú Church
Río Agres
Calle Primavera
Carretera John F Kennedy
Calle Socola
Río Chiquero
Queb Quebradilla
Park
Toll Booths
Río Tiribi
Aeropuerto Internacional Juan Santamaría
Av 23
Av 9
Av 7
Av 5
Av 3
Av 1
ESCAZÚ CENTRO
Río Cruz
Costa Rica Country Club
To Centro Comercial Guachipelín; Banex; Multicentro Paco; Inka Grill (200m); Santa Ana (3km); Swiss Travel Service; Valle del Sol (5km); Hospital CIMA

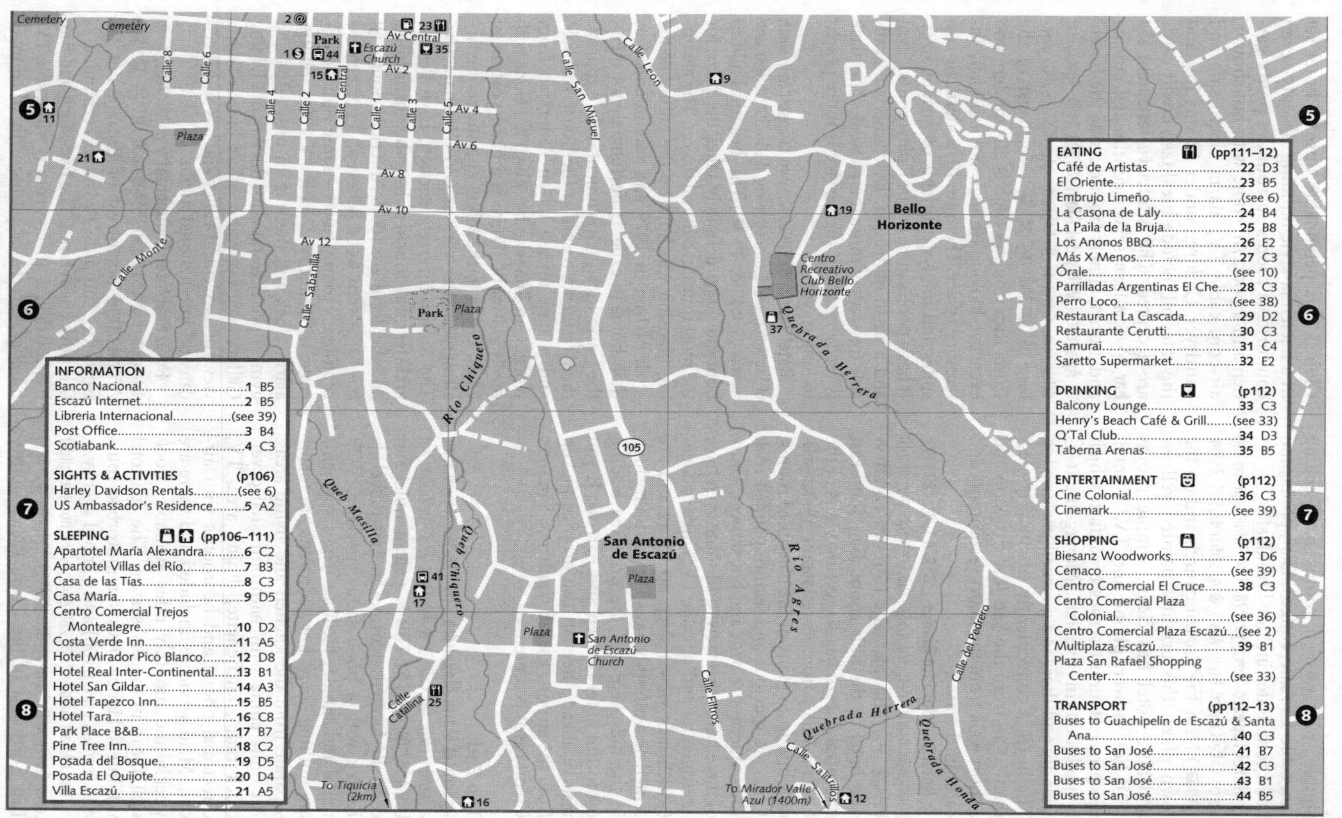
INFORMATION
Banco Nacional.....1 B5
Escazú Internet.....2 B5
Libreria Internacional.....(see 39)
Post Office.....3 B4
Scotiabank.....4 C3
SIGHTS & ACTIVITIES (p106)
Harley Davidson Rentals.....(see 6)
US Ambassador's Residence.....5 A2
SLEEPING (pp106–111)
Apartotel María Alexandra.....6 C2
Apartotel Villas del Río.....7 B3
Casa de las Tías.....8 C3
Casa María.....9 D5
Centro Comercial Trejos Montealegre.....10 D2
Costa Verde Inn.....11 A5
Hotel Mirador Pico Blanco.....12 D8
Hotel Real Inter-Continental.....13 B1
Hotel San Gildar.....14 A3
Hotel Tapezco Inn.....15 B5
Hotel Tara.....16 C8
Park Place B&B.....17 B7
Pine Tree Inn.....18 C2
Posada del Bosque.....19 D5
Posada El Quijote.....20 D4
Villa Escazú.....21 A5
EATING (pp111–12)
Café de Artistas.....22 D3
El Oriente.....23 B5
Embrujo Limeño.....(see 6)
La Casona de Laly.....24 B4
La Paila de la Bruja.....25 B8
Los Anonos BBQ.....26 E2
Más X Menos.....27 C3
Órale.....(see 10)
Parrilladas Argentinas El Che.....28 C3
Perro Loco.....(see 38)
Restaurant La Cascada.....29 D2
Restaurante Cerutti.....30 C3
Samurai.....31 C4
Saretto Supermarket.....32 E2
DRINKING (p112)
Balcony Lounge.....33 C3
Henry's Beach Café & Grill.....(see 33)
Q'Tal Club.....34 D3
Taberna Arenas.....35 B5
ENTERTAINMENT (p112)
Cine Colonial.....36 C3
Cinemark.....(see 39)
SHOPPING (p112)
Biesanz Woodworks.....37 D6
Cemaco.....(see 39)
Centro Comercial El Cruce.....38 C3
Centro Comercial Plaza Colonial.....(see 36)
Centro Comercial Plaza Escazú.....(see 2)
Multiplaza Escazú.....39 B1
Plaza San Rafael Shopping Center.....(see 33)
TRANSPORT (pp112–13)
Buses to Guachipelín de Escazú & Santa Ana.....40 C3
Buses to San José.....41 B7
Buses to San José.....42 C3
Buses to San José.....43 B1
Buses to San José.....44 B5
Cemetery
Park
Escazú Church
Av Central
Av 2
Av 4
Av 6
Av 8
Av 10
Av 12
Calle 8
Calle 6
Calle 4
Calle 2
Calle Central
Calle 1
Calle 3
Calle 5
Calle Leon
Calle San Miguel
Calle Monte
Calle Sabanilla
Plaza
Río Chiquero
Queb Masilla
Queb Chiquero
Bello Horizonte
Centro Recreativo Club Bello Horizonte
Quebrada Herrera
San Antonio de Escazú
San Antonio de Escazú Church
Río Agres
Calle Filtros
Calle del Pedrero
Calle Catalina
Calle Salitrillos
Quebrada Honda
To Tiquicia (2km)
To Mirador Valle Azul (1400m)

simple, whitewashed rooms have ceiling fan, cable TV, safe, coffee maker, phone and bathroom. Rates include breakfast.

Hotel Tapezco Inn (☎ 228 1084; info@tapezco-inn.co.cr; Calle Central btwn Avs 2 & 4; s/d/tr US$41/53/64; P) Near the Escazú church and on the town plaza, this brightly painted yellow-and-blue hotel has clean, simple rooms with hot shower, phone and TV. A small upstairs restaurant serves breakfast, which is included in the fee. Management is friendly and there is a guarded parking lot. The hotel is conveniently situated: it's less than 100m from the San José bus stop and a short walk from the many restaurants and cafés in the area.

Hotel Mirador Pico Blanco (☎ 228 1908, 289 6197; pblanco@costarica.net; s/d US$47/65, cottage per month US$400; P) This pleasant 15-room countryside hotel in the hills about 3km southeast of central Escazú has staggering views of the Central Valley from its **restaurant** (7am-midnight) and from many of the balconied rooms. Units are spacious and feature painted rock walls, queen-size beds and hot shower. Many of these have great views and some even have a refrigerator and/or cable TV. Three cottages (which lack views) sleep up to six and are rented on a monthly basis. You're pretty high in the hills here and the driveway leading up to the hotel is steep and narrow. If you reserve ahead, the staff can arrange pickup from the airport, Escazú Centro or San José. Credit cards accepted.

Top End

Apartotel María Alexandra (☎ 228 1507; www.mariaalexandra.com; cnr Calle 3 & Av 23; 1-/2-/3-bedroom apt US$84/95/104; P) This is a clean, quiet and centrally located apartotel in San Rafael de Escazú with a pool, sauna, parking, VCR rental and laundry facilities. The apartments are nothing fancy, but bedrooms are totally separate from the kitchen and living areas. All units come with bathroom, hairdryer, clock radio, kitchenette, dining area, TV, direct-dial phone and bedrooms with air-con. Maid service is included and there are weekly and monthly rates available. Book well ahead in the dry season. The apartotel is home to Harley Davidson motorbike tours and rentals (see p106) and a travel agency.

Hotel San Gildar (☎ 289 8843; www.hotelsangildar.com; Carretera JF Kennedy; d/tr US$114/132; P) Just northwest of the Costa Rica Country Club is this personable upscale hotel set in a hacienda-style building. Twenty-seven comfortable rooms surround a pretty garden and a pool. All come with hot shower, air-con, cable TV, alarm clock, safe and hairdryer. Children under 12 stay free and the rates all include breakfast; credit cards are accepted. The attractive **restaurant and bar** (6am-10pm) serves continental cuisine and attracts diners from outside the hotel.

Apartotel Villas del Río (☎ 208 2400; www.villasdelrio.com; Carretera JF Kennedy; ste US$125-200, penthouse US$200-300; P) Northeast of the Costa Rica Country Club is this modern and exclusive-looking (though not especially interesting) place. There are 40 modern, air-con suites and mini-apartments of various sizes. It has a pool, sauna, Jacuzzi, playground, gym and a small minisuper. Discounts are available for stays of more than a week. The place is really nice, but the service is more geared to long stays.

Hotel Tara (☎ 228 6992; www.tararesort.com; south of San Antonio de Escazú cemetery; d US$130, ste standard/superior US$160/195; P) This beautiful hilltop boutique hotel definitely takes the prize for the most unusual cultural fusion. The gleaming mansion was built by the family of the Shah of Iran in 1979 and was intended as their home in exile. Unfortunately for them, the Costa Rican government didn't approve their residency visas, so the house was sold and is now owned by an American from North Carolina who has given it a *Gone with the Wind* motif. There is a giant portrait of Clark Gable in the lobby and the rooms are all named after various GWTW characters. The rooms, bizarrely enough, have Persian architectural touches, but the furnishings and the decor are 100% American South. (It has to be seen to be believed.) Fourteen exceptionally roomy suites – some with views – come with hairdryer, cable TV, robes, phone, alarm clock and there is an onsite spa and gym. A pretty restaurant, the Atlanta Dining Gallery (see opposite) offers breath-taking views of the Central Valley and has an American and international menu.

Hotel Real Inter-Continental (☎ 289 7000; www.interconti.com; r US$250, ste US$400-1000; P) About 2km northwest of Escazú, not far from the Autopista Próspero Fernández, is this posh chain hotel. The five-story building has 260 deluxe air-con rooms with cable TV, minibar, direct-dial phone with voice mail, clock radio and hairdryer. It also houses a pool, spa, gym, three restaurants, two bars, a convention and business center, concierge service including babysitting and a small gift shop. All rooms have DSL lines for laptop modems. More expensive suites are available. The country's largest shopping mall, the Multiplaza (see p112), is across the street.

Eating

Inka Grill (☎ 289 5117; Multicentro Paco Escazú; dishes US$5-13; 🕑 11:30am-11:30pm) This beautifully decorated Peruvian restaurant in the area of Guachipelín serves a wide selection of well-prepared specialties. You'll find it all here, from *chupe de camarones* (shrimp soup) to *aji de gallina* (spicy chicken). Also delicious is the *papa rellena* (stuffed potatoes) appetizer, which is almost the size of a full meal. The spice level has been toned down for the milder Tico palate, but you can ask for their scalding homemade hot sauce on the side. Reservations are recommended for dinner.

Tiquicia (☎ 289 5839; 🕑 5pm-midnight Tue-Fri, 1pm-2am Sat, 11am-6pm Sun) For Costa Rican food, this is a little upmarket price-wise, but the rustic setting and spectacular views through the large windows are worth it. There is sometimes live local music. In addition, the roads were recently paved all the way to the restaurant, which is about 5km south of central Escazú, so it is now possible to get there in a regular car; the road is well signed. Call ahead as the hours can be erratic.

La Paila de la Bruja (dishes US$2-5; 🕑 4pm-midnight Mon-Thu, noon-midnight Fri-Sun) This country-style place in San Antonio de Escazú is a popular local institution serving traditional Tico specialties from a terraced restaurant with good views and several country-style outdoor brick ovens. There are marimba players on some weekend evenings.

Mirador Valle Azul (☎ 254 6281; 700m south & 700m west from Hotel Mirador Pico Blanco; dishes US$10; 🕑 4pm-midnight Mon-Sat) A tough steep drive takes you to the aptly named Mirador Valle Azul, from where the views of the San José valley are breathtaking – so get there before sunset. The food is pretty good, too, with a wide selection of the usual pastas, meats and seafood, accompanied by live music on Saturday and Sunday.

Atlanta Dining Gallery (dishes US$9-13; 🕑 6am-10pm) This elegant restaurant is part of Hotel Tara (see earlier). The menu is continental, offering upscale meat-and-potato meals as well as pastas. The attraction here is the view – and the somewhat unusual setting.

La Casona de Laly (cnr Av 3 & Calle Central; dishes US$1-5; 🕑 11am-12:30am) In Escazú Centro, this popular local hang-out is a small, typical restaurant that sells traditional Tico food and snacks. It is also a great place to get a beer in the evening.

El Oriente (cnr Av Central & Calle L Cortés; 🕑 7am-2pm weekdays) This Argentinean-run lunch counter is great for a cheap, quick and tasty bite. Señora Maria, the friendly owner, knows all her customers and dishes up five varieties of empanadas (US$1) as well as a stomach-filling selection of well-prepared casados (US$2.50). Look for a sign that says Taquería Las Flautas and you will have found the place.

Café de Artistas (☎ 228 6045, 288 5082; dishes US$4-7; 🕑 8am-6pm Tue-Sat, 8am-4pm Sun) A great selection of local art (some for sale) graces the walls and shelves, and the snacks, sandwiches, light meals, veggie specialties and coffee are good. On Sunday, there is a nice brunch featuring dishes such as Eggs Benedict along with live music.

Parrilladas Argentinas El Che (Calle L Cortés, south of Carretera JF Kennedy; steaks US$8-10; 🕑 noon-midnight) A small outdoor patio fronts a lively pub and Argentine-style steaks sizzle on the outdoor grills. Don't come without a carnivorous appetite – it has excellent hamburgers and tender steaks, but little else.

Órale (Calle L Cortés, south of Autopista Próspero Fernández; 🕑 5pm-2am) Situated in the Centro Comercial Trejos Montealegre, Órale serves a variety of Mexican and Tex-Mex dishes but is more renowned for its popular bar, which has drink specials on Friday nights. Credit cards accepted.

Restaurante Cerutti (☎ 228 4511, 228 9954; Calle L Cortés, south of Carretera JF Kennedy; dishes US$10-20; 🕑 noon-2:30pm, 6-11pm Wed-Mon) This recommended and well-reviewed Italian restaurant in San Rafael de Escazú serves authentic dishes featuring lots of fresh seafood and homemade pastas. The raviolis with ricotta and mushrooms (US$14) are a favorite and the variety of risottos keeps the locals coming back. Credit cards accepted.

Perro Loco (Centro Comercial El Cruce, cnr Calle L Cortés & Carretera JF Kennedy; hot dogs US$2-3; 🕑 noon-8pm Mon-Tue, noon-4am Wed-Sat, 4-10pm Sun) After too much drinking, this is an ideal place for a little grease to soak it all up. The menu consists of 10 internationally themed hot dogs, all with plentiful toppings; recommended is the Chihuahua dog, which comes loaded with guacamole.

Samurai (☎ 228 4124; Calle L Cortés; 🕑 noon-3pm & 6:30-10pm) This upscale Japanese restaurant has a little bit of a Benihana chain-restaurant feel, but the Japanese garden ambience is pleasant and the sushi fresh. Japan-trained chefs prepare a variety of sushi and sashimi dishes (US$5 to US$12) as well as teppanyaki meat, fish and seafood grills (US$15 to US$27). Credit cards accepted.

Embrujo Limeño (☎ 228 4876; Av 23; meals US$7; 🕑 11am-2:30pm & 6:30-10:30pm) This pleasant Peruvian restaurant is a recent addition to the neighborhood and is situated adjacent to the Apartotel María Alexandra.

Los Anonos BBQ (☎ 228 0180; dishes US$7-18; 🕑 noon-3pm & 6-10pm Tue-Sat, 11:30am-9pm Sun) Out on the road approaching Escazú from San José is this well-known woody place catering to the carnivore set. Los Anonos has been dishing up barbecued steaks and chicken for three decades and prices are reasonable. Credit cards accepted.

Restaurant La Cascada (☎ 228 0906, 228 9393; 🕑 6am-11pm) Just west of Los Anonos BBQ and in a similar price range, this is another long-time favorite, with a good selection of seafood as well as grilled steaks and other meats. It's good, but the atmosphere is a little coffee shop-ish. Credit cards accepted.

Self caterers can try Más X Menos in San Rafael de Escazú or the Saretto Supermarket near the Autopista Próspero Fernández.

Drinking & Entertainment

Taberna Arenas (diagonal from the Shell Station, Escazú Centro; 🕑 opens 4pm) is a delightful, old-fashioned little Tico bar with yummy *bocas* (US$1). It's an Escazú institution. Owner Don Israel is a real gentleman and has his photos with various heads of state on the walls, amongst the agricultural implements that are de rigueur in any decent country bar.

Two hearty drinking options reside in the Plaza San Rafael shopping center a few hundred meters east of the soccer field. **Balcony Lounge** (Carretera JF Kennedy; 🕑 noon-1am) is an upscale bar and gringo hangout with a grill, good views, sports on cable TV and a somewhat severe red and black décor. Across the way is the more laid back (but equally gringo) **Henry's Beach Café & Grill** (Carretera JF Kennedy; 🕑 11am-2:30am), which has music, plenty of TVs and a kitchen that stays open until 1am.

On the road into town from San José, you'll find the **Q'tal Club** (Calle L Cortés; 🕑 6pm-2am), which attracts a mixed crowd ready to party on the weekends.

For first-run Hollywood movies, check out the **Cine Colonial 1 & 2** (☎ 289 9000; admission US$3) on the ground floor of the Plaza Colonial Escazú in San Rafael or the **Cinemark** (☎ 288 1111; admission US$3.50) at the Multiplaza Escazú (see below).

Shopping

You will find delicate and high-quality wood craftsmanship in the traditional Pre-Columbian style at the showroom of **Biesanz Woodworks** (☎ 289 4337; www.biesanz.com; 🕑 8am-5pm weekdays, weekends by appointment) in Bello Horizonte. A variety of bowls and other decorative containers are all beautifully produced, the majority using a traditional crafting method in which the natural lines and forms of the wood determine the shape and size of the bowl. This makes every piece unique. The products are expensive (starting at US$50 for a palm-sized bowl), but they are well worth it. Interested shoppers can take a tour of the workshop and learn about how the craftsman selects, ages and prepares the wood for years before he even begins to cut it. A lake, botanical garden and native hardwood nursery are on the property. Call well ahead to make weekend appointments.

Multiplaza Escazú (☎ 289 8984; www.multiplazamall.com; 🕑 10am-8pm Mon-Sat, 10am-7pm Sun) is a full-scale suburban-style mall that has just about everything you need (or don't) – from clothes to eyeglasses to shoes. There is also a food court. Of particular interest to travelers is the **Cemaco** (☎ 289 7474), a K-Mart style department store that sells basic fishing and camping supplies, including propane gas for portable stoves. If you're coming from San José the mall can be reached by taking any bus marked 'Escazú Multiplaza.' (See p100 for more details on these buses.)

Getting There & Away

Frequent buses between San José and Escazú cost US$0.30 and the run takes roughly 15 minutes. All buses depart in San José from a stop just east of the Coca-Cola bus terminal and take one of several routes: buses labeled 'San Antonio de Escazú' go all the way up the hill to the southern end of Escazú and end their run near the San Antonio de Escazú church; others labeled 'Escazú' end up in the main plaza in Escazú Centro; and yet others, called 'Guachipelín' head west on the Carretera John F Kennedy and pass the Costa Rica Country Club. All of these buses go through San Rafael.

CARIARI COUNTRY CLUB & AROUND

Lining the road between San José and the international airport in Alajuela are numerous hotels – most of which are top end – that cater to big-budget and business travelers. Many of these hotels are clustered around the Cariari Country Club. Most travelers who stay in this area arrive and depart by rented car since this isn't an area that is conducive to walking.

Once a coffee plantation, the **Cariari Country Club** (☎ 293 3211; cariari@racsa.co.cr) is an 18-hole championship golf course (6590 yards, par 71). It is one of Costa Rica's most venerable greens and was designed by George Fazio. Rates are US$40 per day plus a US$20 caddie fee; golf carts (US$25) are also available. Guests of top-end hotels such as the Meliá Cariari and Hotel Herradura (see later) can get greens privileges on a space-available basis. Reservations can be made in the USA through **Costa Rica Golf Adventures** (☎ 877-258 2688; www.golfcr.com).

The **Ojo de Agua** springs (p117) are nearby.

Both **Hotel Herradura** (☎ 293 0033; noon-7am) and **Best Western Irazú** (☎ 232 4811) have casinos.

Sleeping & Eating

Belén Trailer Park (☎ 239 0421; lasutter@racsa.co.cr; tent & small vehicle US$8, larger motor home US$12) The trailer park is a full-service camping area in San Antonio de Belén. There are full hookups for camper vehicles, as well as safe, grassy tent areas for backpackers. Hot showers, laundry facilities (US$1.30 per load), public phone, local information and nearby public buses to San José are all available. The camping ground is 2km west of the San Antonio-Heredia intersection with the Interamericana, near the Meliá Cariari Hotel; there are signs.

All the following top-end places accept credit cards.

Meliá Cariari Hotel (☎ 239 0022; www.solmelia.com; d superior/deluxe US$175/181, ste US$269-527; P) This luxurious hotel has a presidential suite that isn't presidential in name only: foreign leaders have stayed here during trips to Costa Rica. The 221 spacious, carpeted rooms and suites all come with air-con, cable TV, phone and minibar, and many have a private balcony. Amenities include a large pool, sauna, children's play area, convention facilities, casino, shopping mall, restaurants (24-hour room service) and bars. In addition, guests receive privileges at the neighboring Cariari Country Club. Check the website for inexpensive, last-minute bookings. It's a nice hotel, except for the ragged-looking caged scarlet macaws in the lobby.

Best Western Irazú (☎ 232 4811; www.bestwestern.com; Km 3 on Autopista General Cañas; s/d US$92/104, superior US$120/132, child under 18 free; P) For those who would like to visit Costa Rica without feeling like they've left the USA, this is the place. The complex features a 24-hour Denny's restaurant and Burger King or Pizza Hut room service. There are 325 rooms and the usual laundry list of nice hotel amenities: air-con and cable TV plus lighted tennis court, pool and sauna, exercise room, casino, bar, Internet service, laundry service and free airport transfers. Superior rooms have two queens or a king-size bed and a private balcony.

Hotel Herradura (☎ 293 0033; www.hotelherradura.com; s/d US$152/164, ste US$269-930; P) This place has privileges at the neighboring country club as well as ample convention facilities. A travel desk will make arrangements for fishing charters and other tours. A shuttle service to the airport is available. The hotel features 234 carpeted rooms and suites, with air-con and cable TV. There are three pools, including one with waterfalls and a swim-up bar, five Jacuzzis, a casino, sauna, concierge service, three restaurants and two bars. One of its restaurants, **Sakura** (☎ 293 0033; meals from US$10; 11:30am-3pm & 6-11pm Tue-Sun), is one of the top locally recommended Japanese places in the San José area. The menu has traditional dishes, including sushi, sashimi and teppanyaki.

Marriott Hotel (☎ 298 0000, in the USA 800-228 9290; www.marriotthotels.com; d US$268, ste US$585; P) This attractive Spanish colonial-style chain hotel is in the village of San Antonio de Belén, 5km south of the airport. The hotel features a pool, Jacuzzi, tennis courts, gym, sauna, nearby spa and a golf driving range. There are six restaurants and bars. The 248 rooms and seven suites all offer the comforts of a top-notch luxury hotel: air-con, cable TV, minibar, safe, bathrobes and hairdryer. Free airport transportation is offered. Weekend rates are cheaper and include breakfast.

Getting There & Away

Buses between San José and Alajuela can drop you off at the entrances to most of the hotels mentioned in this section. Just let the bus driver know where you will be getting off.

Most travelers who stay in the area prefer to rent cars at the airport or through the travel desks at the hotels.

Central Valley & Highlands

CONTENTS

The fertile soil of this country's sunny heart was cultivated for centuries before the Spanish recognized its graces and found respite here from the sweltering, malaria-ridden coasts. They called it the 'Meseta Central,' or Central Plateau, a name that hints neither at the waterfalls and river valleys secreted throughout, nor the veiled gray peaks that rumble at its borders.

And though the silhouettes of mighty Volcanes Irazú, Poás, Barva and others stand eternal watch over glistening fincas (plantations) of coffee that have fueled this nation's ambitions, the region's English moniker, 'Central Valley', seems a disservice among rolling hills that rise above 3000m to this place of purer light and cool winds.

Perhaps this natural bowl of rivers and rich earth, heaved toward the heavens by malcontent tectonic plates, simply has too many landscapes to be properly labeled. To the north it is bordered by the Cordillera Central mountain range and to the south by the Cordillera de Talamanca and Fila de Bustamante. Between them lies the beautiful Río Reventazón, the historic liquid link between San José and the Caribbean Coast. To the west the plateau falls off into the Pacific lowlands.

Roads are generally excellent and public transportation inexpensive, frequent and comfortable. Hotels, however, apart from in Alajuela with its easy airport access, are rare and tend to be either upscale or on the rustic side. Most visitors use San José as a base for day trips. A bus ride of no more than two hours will get you to national parks, active volcanoes, relaxing hot springs, the Patron Saint of Costa Rica, enormous coffee fincas and some of the best white-water rafting in the world – and it'll cost you next to nothing.

This chapter is arranged in a roughly west-to-east sequence, around San José.

HIGHLIGHTS

- Whooping it up on white-water descents of **Río Reventazón** and **Rio Pacuare** (p145)
- Gazing into the active craters of Volcanes **Irazú** (p140) or **Poás** (p129)
- Descending with the numerous cascades of **Los Jardines de la Catarata La Paz** (p131)
- Shopping for highly polished hardwood handicrafts (or an oxcart-minibar combo) in **Sarchí** (p126)
- Watching **Alajuela's** own La Liga *futból* team score a gooooooooooaaaaal! (p123)

ALAJUELA & THE NORTH OF THE VALLEY

ALAJUELA

Clean and modern, cradled by the gentle undulations of coffee fincas and tamed jungle parks, the provincial capital of Alajuela lies about 18km northwest of San José. Originally known as Villa Hermosa, it's still a very 'pretty city' not to mention the country's second largest, with a population just over 185,000. Though the town center seems like a slightly scaled-down version of the capital's busy market areas, it enjoys a less hurried pace that that of San José, plus a slightly warmer climate, making this a relaxing base for exploring the Central Valley.

Alajuela is also much closer to Juan Santamaría international airport, about 3km away – handy for people with early flights.

Information & Orientation

The map shows the streets and avenues but, as in most Costa Rican towns, street addresses are rarely used (see p453). There's no tourist office, although **Instituto Costarricense de Turismo** (ICT; ☎ 442 1820) has a desk at the airport. There are probably a dozen banks where you can change money, including **Scotiabank** (☎ 443 2168; cnr Av 3 & Calle 2; 🕑 8am-5pm Mon-Fri, 8am-4pm Sat) with an ATM on the Cirrus network. Internet access is available at **BYTE** (☎ 441 1142; cnr Calle 3 & Av 1, 2nd fl; per hour US$0.75; 🕑 Mon-Sat).

The **Hospital San Rafael** (☎ 441 5011; Av 9 btwn Calles Central & 1) and the 24-hour **Clínica Norza** (☎ 441 3572; Av 4 btwn Calles 2 & 4) provide basic medical services.

Sights

The shady **Parque Central**, recently landscaped for a fresh new look, is a pleasant place to relax beneath the mango trees. It is surrounded by several 19th-century buildings, including the **cathedral**, which suffered severe damage in the 1991 earthquake. The hemispherical cupola is unusually constructed of sheets of red corrugated metal. The interior is spacious and elegant rather than ornate; two presidents are buried here.

A more baroque-looking church (though it was built in 1941) is the **Iglesia La Agonía**, six blocks east of the Parque Central.

Two blocks south of the Parque Central is the rather bare **Parque Juan Santamaría**, where there is a statue of the hero in action, flanked by cannons.

MUSEO JUAN SANTAMARÍA

Alajuela's main claim to fame is that it's the birthplace of national hero Juan Santamaría, for whom the nearby international airport was named and to whom this small **museum** (☎ 441 4775; cnr Av 3 & Calle 2; admission free; 🕑 10am-6pm Tue-Sun) is devoted.

Santamaría was the drummer boy who volunteered to torch the building being defended by North American filibuster William Walker in the war of 1856 (see p23). Santamaria died after succeeding with his quest. The museum was once the town jail, and now contains maps, paintings and historical artifacts related to the war with Walker, as well as a rotating art exhibit. There is a small auditorium where performances are occasionally staged.

OJO DE AGUA

About 6km south of Alajuela are the **Ojo de Agua** (☎ 441 2808; admission US$2; 🕑 8am-5pm) springs, a pretty working-class resort that's packed on weekends with folks from San José and Alajuela. Twenty thousand liters of water gush out from the spring each minute, filling swimming pools and an artificial boating lake before being piped down to Puntarenas, for which it is a major water supply. There are also snack stands, game courts and a small gym. From San José, drivers can take the San Antonio de Belén exit off the Interamericana; Ojo de Agua is just past San Antonio.

Courses

There are two Spanish-language schools in town: Castillian House and Fundación Castillo. See the boxed text on p122 for more details.

Festivals & Events

The anniversary of the **Battle of Rivas**, April 11, is particularly celebrated in Alajuela, the hometown of the battle's young hero, Juan Santamaría. There is a parade and civic events.

The **Fiesta de Los Mangos** is held every July, lasts over a week, and includes an arts and crafts fair, parades and some mild revelry.

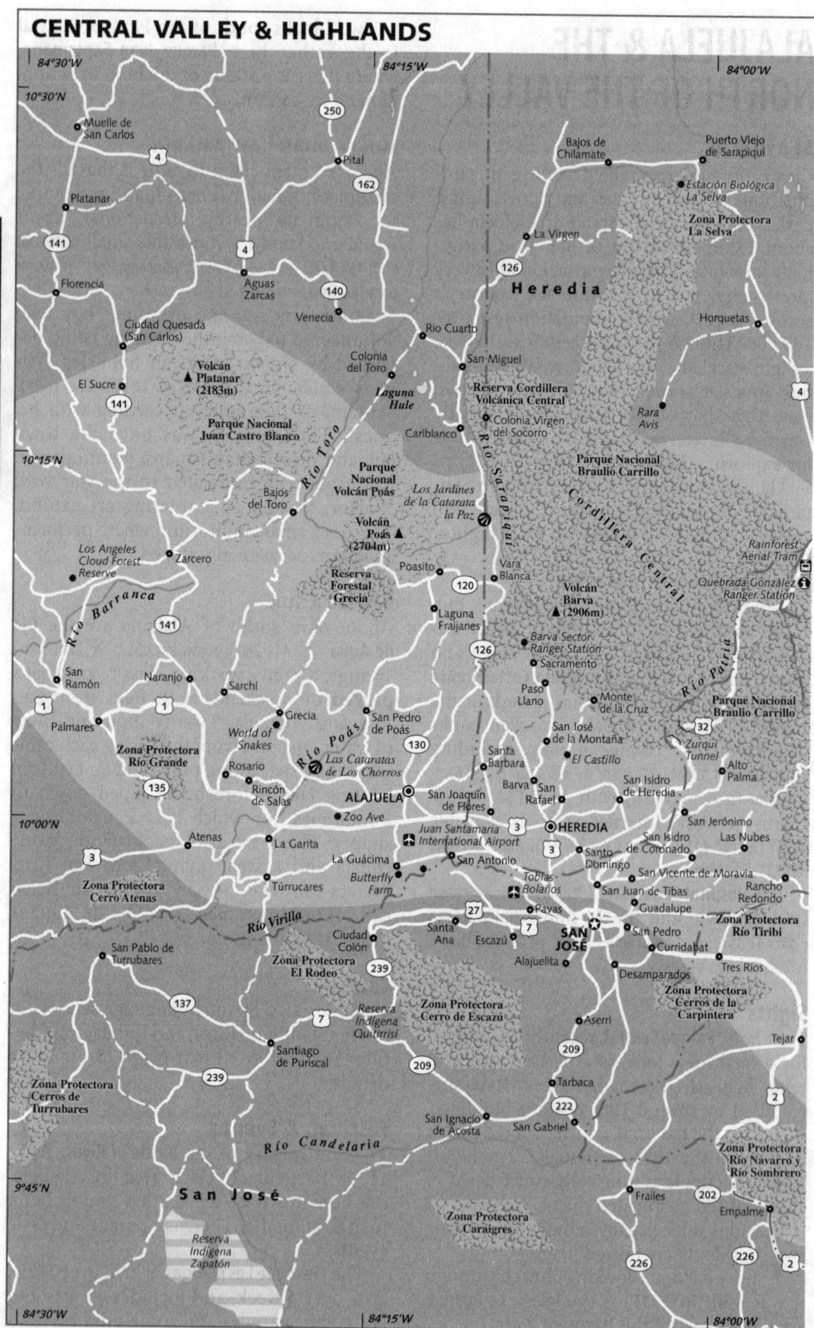
CENTRAL VALLEY & HIGHLANDS
84°30'W
84°15'W
84°00'W
10°30'N
10°15'N
10°00'N
9°45'N
Muelle de San Carlos
Pital
Bajos de Chilamate
Puerto Viejo de Sarapiquí
Estación Biológica La Selva
Zona Protectora La Selva
Platanar
La Virgen
Florencia
Aguas Zarcas
Venecia
Heredia
Horquetas
Ciudad Quesada (San Carlos)
Rio Cuarto
Colonia del Toro
San Miguel
El Sucre
Volcán Platanar (2183m)
Laguna Hule
Reserva Cordillera Volcánica Central
Rara Avis
Colonia Virgen del Socorro
Cariblanco
Parque Nacional Juan Castro Blanco
Río Toro
Río Sarapiquí
Parque Nacional Braulio Carrillo
Parque Nacional Volcán Poás
Los Jardines de la Catarata la Paz
Bajos del Toro
Cordillera Central
Volcán Poás (2704m)
Los Angeles Cloud Forest Reserve
Zarcero
Rainforest Aerial Tram
Poasito
Vara Blanca
Reserva Forestal Grecia
Quebrada González Ranger Station
Volcán Barva (2906m)
Río Barranca
Laguna Fraijanes
Barva Sector Ranger Station
Sacramento
San Ramón
Naranjo
Sarchí
Río Patria
Paso Llano
Monte de la Cruz
Parque Nacional Braulio Carrillo
Palmares
Grecia
San Pedro de Poás
San José de la Montaña
Zurquí Tunnel
World of Snakes
Río Poás
Zona Protectora Río Grande
Santa Barbara
El Castillo
Alto Palma
Rosario
Las Cataratas de Los Chorros
Barva
San Rafael
San Isidro de Heredia
Rincón de Salas
ALAJUELA
San Joaquín de Flores
Zoo Ave
HEREDIA
San Jerónimo
Juan Santamaria International Airport
San Isidro de Coronado
Las Nubes
Atenas
La Garita
Santo Domingo
La Guácima
San Antonio
San Vicente de Moravia
Butterfly Farm
Tobías Bolaños
Zona Protectora Cerro Atenas
Túrrucares
San Juan de Tibas
Rancho Redondo
Guadalupe
Río Virilla
Pavas
Zona Protectora Río Tiribí
Santa Ana
SAN JOSÉ
San Pedro
Ciudad Colón
Escazú
Curridabat
San Pablo de Turrubares
Alajuelita
Zona Protectora El Rodeo
Tres Ríos
Desamparados
Zona Protectora Cerros de la Carpintera
Reserva Indígena Quitirrisí
Zona Protectora Cerro de Escazú
Aserrí
Santiago de Puriscal
Tejar
Tarbaca
Zona Protectora Cerros de Turrubares
San Ignacio de Acosta
San Gabriel
Río Candelaria
Zona Protectora Río Navarro y Río Sombrero
San José
Frailes
Empalme
Zona Protectora Caraigres
Reserva Indígena Zapatón
250
4
162
141
126
140
120
1
130
135
3
27
7
239
137
209
222
32
2
202
226

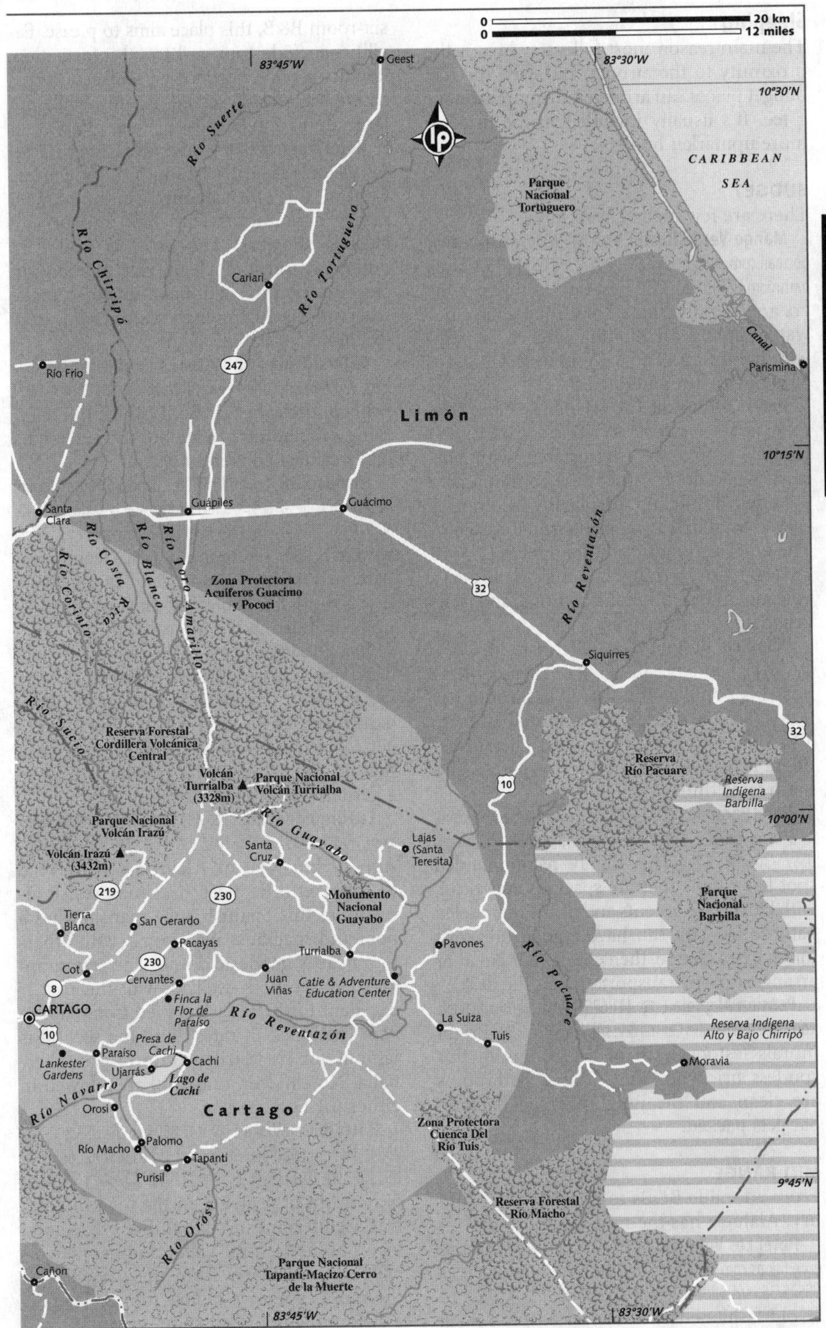
0 20 km
0 12 miles
83°45'W
83°30'W
10°30'N
10°15'N
10°00'N
9°45'N
CARIBBEAN SEA
Parque Nacional Tortuguero
Canal
Parismina
Geest
Río Suerte
Río Chirripó
Río Tortuguero
Cariari
247
Río Frio
Limón
Santa Clara
Guápiles
Guácimo
Río Costa Rica
Río Corinto
Río Blanco
Río Toro Amarillo
Zona Protectora Acuíferos Guacimo y Pococi
32
Río Reventazón
Siquirres
Río Sucio
Reserva Forestal Cordillera Volcánica Central
Volcán Turrialba (3328m)
Parque Nacional Volcán Turrialba
Reserva Río Pacuare
Reserva Indígena Barbilla
10
Parque Nacional Volcán Irazú
Volcán Irazú (3432m)
Río Guayabo
Santa Cruz
Lajas (Santa Teresita)
219
230
Monumento Nacional Guayabo
Parque Nacional Barbilla
Tierra Blanca
San Gerardo
Pacayas
Turrialba
Pavones
Río Pacuare
Cot
Cervantes
Juan Viñas
Catie & Adventure Education Center
8
CARTAGO
Finca la Flor de Paraíso
Río Reventazón
La Suiza
Tuis
Reserva Indígena Alto y Bajo Chirripó
Presa de Cachí
Paraíso
Cachí
Moravia
Lankester Gardens
Ujarrás
Lago de Cachí
Río Navarro
Orosi
Cartago
Zona Protectora Cuenca Del Río Tuis
Palomo
Río Macho
Tapantí
Purisil
Reserva Forestal Río Macho
Río Orosi
Parque Nacional Tapantí-Macizo Cerro de la Muerte
Cañon

Sleeping

The main reason most folks stay here is the proximity to the airport, and even the real budget places can arrange transportation for a fee. It's usually included in the price at more upmarket hotels.

BUDGET

There are few really cheap hotels.

Mango Verde Hostel (☎ 441 6330; mirafloresbb@hotmail.com; Av 3 btwn Calles 2 & 4; s/d US$10/15, s/d with bathroom US$15/25) The best deal in town: owners are friendly, shared bathrooms have hot water, there's an inviting kitchen, a patio with hammocks and a TV lounge. Units are bare but well-maintained.

Hotel Cortéz Azul (☎ 443 6145; Av 5 btwn Calles 2 & 4; per person without/with bathroom US$11/15; P) Homey rooms are comfortable, with polished wood floors, and a fine common area includes a kitchen displaying sculptures carved by affable owner Eduardo Rodríguez. The hotel also rents mountain bikes (US$10 for two hours), arranges outings to the area's volcanoes and other attractions and sells original art at reception.

Villa Real Hostel (☎ 441 4022; cnr Av 3 & Calle 1; dm US$10, r per person US$15; P) This sky-blue hostel is popular: the shared bathroom has hot water and there's a communal kitchen, TV room and laundry service. The atmosphere is festive, but rooms are spartan and mattresses thin.

Hotel Pacandé (☎ 443 8481; www.hotelpacande.com; Av 5 btwn Calles 2 & 4; s US$20, d without/with bathroom US$25/30; P 💻) This highly recommended spot has rooms that are spacious and clean, with hardwood accents and nicely remodeled bathrooms. You can have a good breakfast for an extra charge, then check your email or arrange airport transportation at the desk.

Pensión Alajuela (☎ 441 6251; www.pensionalajuela.com; Av 9 btwn Calles Central & 2; s/d US$20/25; P) Bright murals festoon each of the rooms in this spotless brick building. Shared bathrooms are clean and the jungle-themed bamboo bar gets packed.

MID-RANGE

From adorable B&Bs to business-class luxury, Alajuela has the mid-range covered.

Hotel Los Volcanes (☎ 441 0525; www.montezumaexpeditions.com/hotel.htm; Av 2 btwn Calles Central & 2; s/d US$25/35, s/d with bathroom US$35/45; P ⊠ 💻) In an old-fashioned home converted into a small six-room B&B, this place aims to please. Facilities include tour and travel information, laundry service, hot showers and a courtyard where breakfast is served. Rooms, while not large, do have two beds, TV and phone.

Hotel Alajuela (☎ 441 6595; Calle 2 btwn Avs Central & 2; s/d US$25/35; P) Just south of the Parque Central, this old-fashioned building has 50 rather dark rooms with fans and private electric showers. The hotel is well run, quiet, central and clean, not to mention close to the international airport, so make reservations during high season. Long-stay discounts available.

La Guaria Inn (☎ 440 2948; laguariahotel@netscape.net; Av 2 btwn Calles Central & 1; s/d US$35/40; P) Frilly and clean, this B&B has all the trimmings, including private hot showers and a big breakfast cooked to order.

Islands B&B (☎ 442 0573; islandsbb@hotmail.com; Av 1 btwn Calles 7 & 9; s/d incl continental breakfast US$40/50; P) This unpretentious property, 50m west of Iglesia La Agonía, has 10 clean rooms with private hot showers and two beds. A living room has cable TV, and airport pick-up is included in the price.

Tuetal Lodge (☎ 442 1804; islandnet.com/~tuetal/tuetal.html; d cabins without/with kitchenettes US$42/53; P) This Canadian-run lodge is about 4km north of the city, which allows you to get away from it all without missing your flight. Cute cabinas with porches are set in a garden with a pool.

Las Orquídeas Inn (☎ 433 9346; www.orquideasinn.com; s/d US$75/95, ste US$135-200; P ⊠) About 5km west of Alajuela on the road to San Pedro de Poás (call for precise directions) this Spanish-style mansion has a pool and spacious, airy rooms, with others in a nearby geodesic dome. The restaurant and bar are both well known: the first is excellent for breakfast, served from 8am to 9am (included in rates), and the second is famous for its Marilyn Monroe paraphernalia. No children under 10 are allowed in either the hotel or bar.

Hotel Buena Vista (☎ 442 8595; in the USA 800-506 2304; www.hotelbuenavistacr.com; s/d US$85/96, junior ste US$106, ste US$125-150; P ⊠ 💻) About 5km north of Alajuela on the road to Poás, this Mediterranean-style edifice offers good views of the Central Valley and nearby volcanoes, particularly from the balconies of the more expensive deluxe rooms. There is a swimming pool, gift shop, restaurant and

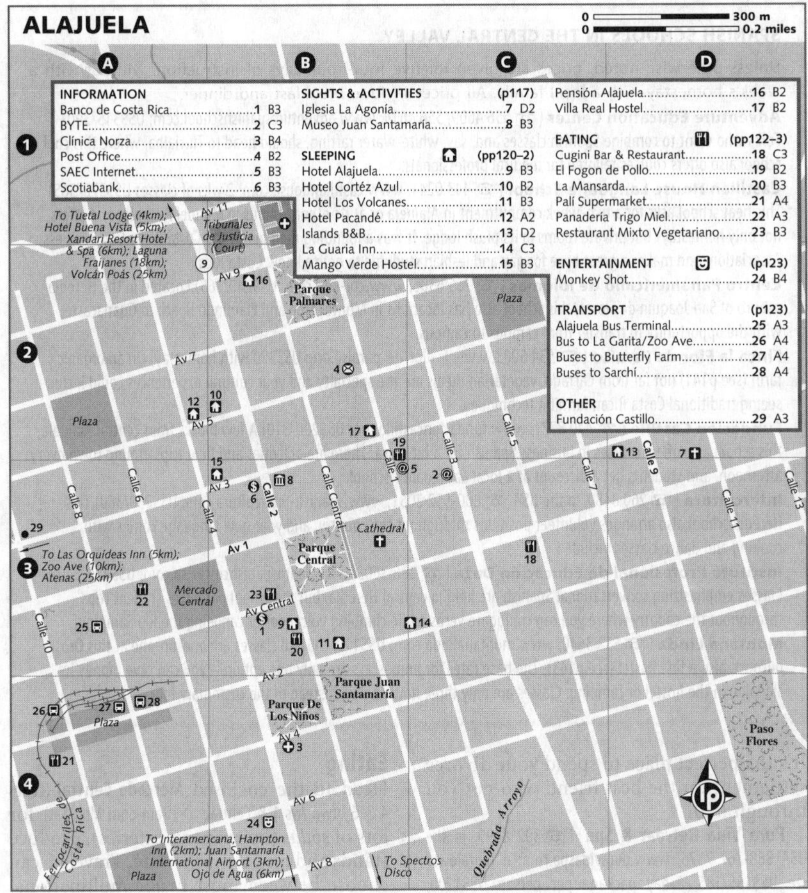

bar, and rates include breakfast and airport transfer.

Hampton Inn (☎ 443 0043, toll free in Costa Rica & USA 800-426 7866; www.hamptonhotel.co.cr; s/d US$111/118, extra person US$8; P ⊠ ⁂ ⛍) Americans worried that they'll experience culture shock should book a room here, where everything is exactly like a Hampton Inn in the USA, except the price, which is much higher. Little soaps and shampoos, in-room coffee makers, continental breakfasts involving plastic-wrapped pastries and easy airport shuttles (only two minutes!) all mean convenience. Folks on tight flight schedules will love that it's only 1km north of the airport on the Interamericana, about five minutes south of downtown Alajuela.

TOP END

Xandari Resort Hotel & Spa (☎ 443 2020; www.xandari.com; s/d villa US$155/185, s/d ultra-villas US$240/262; P ⊠ ⁂ ⛍) Set in a coffee plantation overlooking the Central Valley about 6km north of Alajuela, this relaxed resort seems like it would make for an even better chick trip than a romantic holiday. Rooms are predictably plush and views are postcard perfect, with 3km of private trails and various waterfalls running through them. But the Xandari also offers visitors fitness classes and full spa packages, from facials and pedicures to exotic massages, plus two swimming pools, a Jacuzzi and the real clincher – a gourmet restaurant that specializes in low-fat and vegetarian meals.

SPANISH SCHOOLS IN THE CENTRAL VALLEY

Unless otherwise noted, prices are given for five four-hour days of instruction, without/with a week's homestay with a local family. All prices include breakfast and dinner.

Adventure Education Center (☎ 556 4609, 556 4614; www.adventurespanishschool.com; US$315/390) Folks who want to combine Spanish classes and, say, white-water rafting, should head to Turrialba, where this cool school also offers courses tailored for medical professionals.

Castilian House Language School (☎ 443 0241; www.castilianhouse.com; 2 wks of classes US$370/565) This neat school asks for a two-week commitment in Alajuela or at its other campus in Manuel Antonio, and offers not only homestays but private rooms in its plush lodge. It was a founding member of the Costa Rican Gay Business Association, and makes a great base for gay and lesbian students to get to know Costa Rica.

Centro Panamericano de Idiomas (☎ 265 6306; www.cpi-edu.com; US$240/365) Located in the Heredia suburb of San Joaquín de Flores, this school also has locations in Monteverde and Flamingo Beach in Guanacaste, with the opportunity to transfer from campus to campus.

Finca la Flor de Paraíso (☎ 534 8003; www.la-flor-de-paraiso.org; US$370 with homestay) On an organic farm (see p141) not far from Cartago, vegetarian meals are the specialty and your cultural experiences could include seeing traditional Costa Rican farming techniques.

Fundación Castillo (☎ 440 8771; www.fundacioncastillo.org; US$200/310) A few blocks from central Alajuela, this school also offers courses in business Spanish for a bit extra. There are activities and field trips around town every afternoon, and students get a discount at a local Latin dance school.

Intercultura (☎ 260 8480, in the USA ☎ 800-552 2051; www.spanish-intercultura.com; US$250/360) This Heredia school also arranges volunteer positions throughout the country, and your new language comes with cooking and dance classes included.

Instituto Profesional de Educación Daza (☎ 238 3608; www.learnspanishcostarica.com; US$225/320) Classes emphasizing conversational Spanish are held in central Heredia, but the school organizes student trips throughout the country where you can conjugate verbs while climbing volcanoes or canoeing the Río Sarapiquí.

Montaña Linda (☎ 533 3640; www.montanalinda.com; US$119/145) All classes are one-on-one at this Orosi outpost, also a fine hostel (see p143). The base rates for homestays are only one option – you can save money by sleeping in the hostel or camping. Classes are only three hours a day, instead of the customary four.

It's the perfect place to spend your divorce settlement on the best friend who got you through it all.

Pura Vida Retreat & Spa (☎ 392 8099, in the USA 888-767 7375; www.puravidaspa.com; d tentalows/ste US$165/185; 7-day package per person US$1200; P ⊠) Rates include two daily yoga classes, which is your first clue that this is a very different resort. A renowned yoga and alternative-health center that's a destination in itself, the retreat puts guests up in plush but zen 'tentalows' or more comfortable indoor suites, and offers classes and organized outings that usually include a spiritual or alternative-healing angle. Therapies, including lots of different massages and holistic therapies, are also included in the package deal, as are all meals at the onsite restaurant, which specializes in vegetarian and macrobiotic cuisine. Depending on your best friend, this might be a better choice than the Xandari. It's about 7km north of Alajuela on the road to Carizal, signed from the Estadio.

Eating

Head to the enclosed **Mercado Central** (Calles 4 & 6 btwn Avs 1 & Central; 7am-6pm Mon-Sat) for lots of *sodas* (inexpensive eateries), produce stands and much, much more. Travelers can choose between most major multinational fast-food chains, with outlets downtown,

Panadería Trigo Miel (Av 1 btwn Calles 6 & 8; 6am-5pm) Follow your nose to this excellent bakery and find all types of homemade breads as well as eye-popping pastries and cakes.

El Fogón de Pollo (☎ 443 1362; Calle 1 btwn Avs 1 & 3; mains US$2-4; 7am-8pm Mon-Sat) Why go to KFC when you can get excellent fried chicken and other quality fast food right here, for about half the price?

La Mansarda (☎ 441 4390; Calle 2 btwn Avs Central & 2, 2nd fl; meals US$3-6; 11am-11pm) The top place for Costa Rican fare is this casual balcony restaurant overlooking the street milieu, where fresh seafood dishes and better-than-average casados (set meals) can be complimented by something special from the wine list.

Restaurant Mixto Vegetariano (☎ 440 0413; Av Central btwn Calles 2 & 4; casado US$2.25; ⏲ 7:30am-7pm Mon-Sat) Vegetarians will want to make the trip from San José for casados complete with various soy-based meat substitutes, big veggie burgers and other tasty options.

Cugini Bar & Restaurant (☎ 440 6893; meals US$2-10; cnr Av Central & Calle 5; ⏲ noon-midnight Mon-Sat) This Italian-Irish-Tico-American restaurant does excellent American-style pizza, plus pastas and other Italian specialties in a sports-bar atmosphere, which true to form serves beer and cocktails until late.

You can also stock up at the **Palí supermarket** (cnr Av 2 & Calle 10; ⏲ 8am-8pm).

Entertainment

The perennial Costa Rican soccer champions, Alajuela's own La Liga, play at the Estadio Morera Soto at the northeast end of town on Sundays during soccer season. If you can't get seats, stop by Cugini Bar & Restaurant (see above) and you can catch the game over a brew or two.

On Calle 4, south of the center, **Monkey Shot** (⏲ 6pm-6am) is a huge indoor-outdoor bar that sometimes has live music, as well as male and female strippers on certain nights. Bottoms up!

Spectros Disco (Calle 2 btwn Avs 10 & 12; ⏲ 8pm-4am Wed-Mon) has the biggest dance floor in town, and DJs come from all over the country to rock the party.

Getting There & Away

For details of flights to Juan Santamaría international airport, see p97.

There are several bus stops in Alajuela, the largest being the **Alajuela bus terminal** (Calle 8 btwn Avs Central & 1) for buses to San José, the international airport, Volcán Poás and other destinations.

Butterfly Farm US$0.40; 30 minutes; departs from cnr Calle 8 & Av 2 at 6:20am, 9am, 11am & 1pm.
La Garita/Zoo Ave US$0.40; 30 minutes; departs from cnr Calle 10 & Av 2 every 30 minutes from 6am to 9pm.
Laguna de Fraijanes US$0.40; 30 minutes; departs from Alajuela terminal at 9am, 1pm, 4:15pm & 6:15pm.
San José (Tuasa) US$0.60; 45 minutes; departs from Alajuela terminal every 15 minutes from 5am to 11pm.
Sarchí US$0.40; 30 minutes; departs from Calle 8 btwn Avs Central & 2 every 30 minutes from 5am to 10pm.

You can also take a taxi (US$2) to the airport from Parque Central.

BUTTERFLY FARM

Built in 1983, back when tourism was just a small sector of the country's economy, the **Butterfly Farm** (☎ 438 0400; www.butterflyfarm.co.cr; adult/student/child 5-12 yrs US$15/10/7; ⏲ 8:30am-5pm) originally opened as the first commercial butterfly farm in Latin America. This means that in addition to the informative multilingual plaques, every Monday and Thursday (from March to August) visitors can watch thousands of pupae being packed for export all over the world.

The butterflies are busiest when it's sunny out, particularly in the morning, so try to get there early. Your entrance fee includes a guided two-hour tour, where you can learn about the stages of the complex butterfly life cycle, and the importance of butterflies in nature. Tours in English, German, Spanish or French run three times daily, more often when it's busy.

The complex also has other attractions, primarily gardens devoted to bees, orchids and other tropical species, although you could take a traditional oxcart ride with the obligatory glossy photo: a colorful reward for kids who toughed it out through all those educational videos.

The Butterfly Farm also offers several one-day package tours (adult/student/child US$25/20/13) that include transportation from any San José hotel, lunch and a tour of the farm, plus a Coffee Tour at the Café Britt finca (see p134) and any number of other side trips.

Drivers can reach the Butterfly Farm by heading 12km south of Alajuela to the village of Guácima; it's located almost in front of the well-signed El Club Campestre Los Reyes. The farm provides a round-trip shuttle service from San José hotels for US$10 per person, or you can take a direct bus from Alajuela (see earlier).

WEST TO ATENAS

The road west from Alajuela to Atenas, a small village about 25km away, passes through tiny La Garita, a pilgrimage-worthy destination for folks who really appreciate corn. You'll also pass a small collection of very nice hotels, all within a half-hour ride to the airport, and one worthwhile off-the-beaten-track destination.

Zoo Ave (☎ 433 8989; www.zooave.org; adult/child US$9/1; ⏲ 8:30am-5pm) gets some 60,000 visitors a year, yet this excellent zoo, 10km west of Alajuela, is largely undiscovered by foreign tourists. It's primarily a collection of tropical birds, with more than 80 Costa Rican species on colorful, squawking display in a relaxing park-like setting. All four Costa Rican species of monkey are also on view, as are lots of other critters. There are volunteer opportunities here as well.

Buses (US$0.40, 30 minutes) run between Alajuela and La Garita, via Zoo Ave, every half hour. If you're driving, take the Atenas exit off the Interamericana, then go 3km east to Zoo Ave.

Sleeping

Any of these hotels in and around Atenas can arrange transportation to the airport.

Ana's Place (☎ 446 5019; d incl breakfast US$45; P) Perfectly acceptable rooms with private bathroom take second billing to the population of large exotic birds hopping through the backyard. It's close to the Atenas bus station and about four blocks southwest of the Atenas Parque Central.

Vista Atenas B&B (☎ 380 3252; vistaatenas@hotmail.com; s/d US$35/45, d cabins incl breakfast US$55; P) Just south of Atenas and reachable only by car, this B&B has a few modern rooms plus cabinas with kitchenette, a small pool and views over the Central Valley. Owners speak English and French, and can organize local excursions.

Hotel Colinas del Sol (☎ 446 4244; www.hotelcolinasdelsol.com; d US$45; P) About 4km west of Atenas, bungalows populate a hilly and tranquil 6-hectare property where you'll swim in a nice pool surrounded by farmland. The airport is only 20 minutes away and pick-up can be arranged. Each unit has a kitchenette, terrace and private bathroom with hot water.

El Cafetal Inn B&B (☎ 446 7361; www.cafetal.com; s/d standard US$75/85, d luxury incl breakfast US$100-120; P) Follow the signs to this sweeping coffee plantation 5km north of Atenas, where you can stay the night or simply stop by to sample the local specialty – that'd be coffee. There's a large garden (with two easy trails to waterfalls), a pool, and several attractive rooms that vary in size and amenities, but all with lots of light and great country views. The onsite restaurant **Mirador del Cafetal** (light meals US$1-5; 7am-5pm) sells its own brand of coffee, La Negrita, as beans or in an outstanding selection of beverages, drunk hot or cold while gazing across the entire Central Valley. Sandwiches, pastries and souvenirs are also on the menu.

Martino Resort & Spa (☎ 433 8382; www.hotelmartino.com; s/d standard US$149/178, s/d deluxe US$222/244; P) Couples who can't decide between Las Vegas and Central America can compromise here, amidst over-the-top, Roman-style luxury, complete with 'Costa Rica's most elegant casino.' Gourmet organic Italian meals, an outrageous spa, huge pools, sauna and full gym are all on offer, just 2km north of the Alajuela exit from the Interamericana, about 15 minutes from the airport. Tailored packages can revolve around golf, turtle-watching in Parque Nacional Tortuguero (p393), or 'plastic surgery recovery,' making it the perfect vacation spot for the whole family.

Eating

Sodas and Chinese restaurants abound in town; there are also a couple of small grocery stores. It's well worth stopping in La Garita, Costa Rica's cornbread basket, where scientists from all over the world come to study maize. Everyone else comes to one of two unusual restaurants to do their own tasty investigation.

La Fiesta del Maíz (☎ 487 7057; mains US$1-5; 6am-9:30pm) About 1km from the Interamericana in La Garita, this understated spot is famed for its wide variety of corn concoctions, as well as fried pork skins.

Delicias del Maíz (☎ 433 7206; mains US$3-9; 8am-9:30pm) About 2km farther toward Monolo, this spot is more upmarket with a nice dining room and grill, and also adapts just about every possible recipe to include corn. Iowa, eat your heart out.

Rancho Típico La Trilla (☎ 446 5637; mains US$3-8) In Atenas, opt for the caffeine theme at the 'coffee mill', 75m east of the gas station, a pleasantly touristy spot with rustic ambiance, typical food and good coffee.

La Casa del Viñedo (☎ 487 6086; mains US$4-15; 11am-11pm) This vineyard, also near La Garita, produces small batches of seven different wines, all of which you can sample alongside their recommended steak, Argentine or American style, or Italian offerings (to go with the wine).

Getting There & Away

Frequent buses from San José to Atenas do not stop at Zoo Ave or La Garita, so you'll need to change buses in Alajuela (see p123).

NORTHWEST TO SARCHÍ

Scattered across the carefully cultivated hills to the northwest of Alajuela are a string of villages that, until not too long ago, were relatively isolated farming communities. Though growing along with San José, the towns of Grecia (22km), Sarchí (29km), Naranjo (35km) and Zarcero (52km) still have charm to spare, excellent coffee and a subdued collection of eccentric attractions, from the country's most famous bushes to the arts-and-crafts capital.

The region lends itself to weekend escapes from San José. Though geographically close to the capital's pavements and smog, here the deep jade coffee plants are shaded by flowering trees and interspersed with jungle, rimmed all around with distant gray volcanoes. It's romantic and the lodge owners know it, many providing 'honeymoon suites' for when you want to go that extra mile.

Grecia

Centered on the incongruous, bright-red metal **Catedral de la Mercedes**, which was boxed up in Belgium and shipped to Costa Rica in 1897, Grecia is a modern town spiced up with a fair dash of Costa Rican folklore. The small **Casa de Cultura** (☎ 444 6767; ⌚ vary) has the official version, with Spanish colonial artifacts plus articles about Grecia's 'Cleanest Little Town in Latin America' award. There's also an impressive insect collection.

INFORMATION

The Ministerio del Ambiente y Energía or **Minae** (Ministry of Environment and Energy; ☎ 494 0065; ⌚ 8am-4pm Mon-Fri) theoretically has information about the surrounding parks. The town has several simple restaurants and bars plus most services, including banks with 24-hour ATMs, a post office and Internet access at **Hotel Aero Mundo** (☎ 494 0094; per hour US$2), two blocks from the church, which can also arrange tours.

SIGHTS

Check out the **18th-century rock bridge** south of town connecting the hamlets of Puente de Piedra and Rincón de Salas. Grecians say that the only other rock bridge like this is in China, and some tales tell it was built by the devil. In 1994 it was declared a National Site of Historical Interest.

The premier attraction, however, is **World of Snakes** (☎ 494 3700; adult/child US$12/7; ⌚ 8am-4pm), 1.5km southeast of the town center, a well-done attraction with an endangered-snake breeding program. More than 150 snakes are displayed in comfortable-looking cages as 'Snakes of the World' or 'Snakes of Costa Rica', representing more than 40 species in all. Rounding things out are frogs, caimans, crocodiles and other assorted cold-blooded critters. Informative tours in English, German or Spanish may include the chance to handle certain snakes if there's time. Any bus to Grecia from Alejuela can drop you at the entrance.

Mariposario Spirogyra (adult/child US$5/3; ⌚ 8am-5pm), 150m from the church, is a small but pretty butterfly garden with a few informative plaques. Guided tours are included with the price. About 5km south of Grecia, toward Santa Gertrudis, are **Las Cataratas de Los Chorros** (admission US$4; ⌚ 8am-5pm), two gorgeous waterfalls and a swimming hole surrounded by picnic tables.

SLEEPING

Hotel Aero Mundo (☎ 494 0094; aerotess@co.cr; s/d US$30/40, apt incl breakfast US$50; P 💻) Right in the center of town, immaculate rooms have bathrooms with hot water and big TVs; there's also three apartments with kitchenettes.

Healthy Day Country Inn Resort (☎ 444 5903; healthyday@racsa.co.cr; s/d incl breakfast US$45/55; P ⊠ ❄ 💻 🏊) Still close to the city center, 800m northeast of the red church on the main road, this is both a good mid-range option and great chance to slim down: a tennis court, gym and Jacuzzi are complimented by less taxing weight-loss opportunities including homeopathic therapies, massages and macrobiotic meals. The rooms are cute and decent value, with ceiling fan, telephone and cable TV.

Vista del Valle Plantation Inn (☎ 450 0800; www.vistadelvalle.com; s/d US$100/120, ste incl breakfast US$155-200; P ⊠ 🏊) In the village of Rosario, about 7km southwest of Grecia as the parrot flies, this choice property with a regular airport shuttle (one-way/round trip US$20/30, 20 minutes) may well be one of the swankiest jungle lodges in Costa Rica.

Elegant garden cottages scattered throughout the luxuriously landscaped botanical garden have balconies that overlook the Río Grande, various volcanoes and even San José city lights. Trails lead past a 90m-high **waterfall** into the adjoining **Zona Protectora Río Grande,** a cloud forest reserve at about 800m. Horseback tours (for experienced riders) and massage therapy (by appointment) are available, as are a pool and Jacuzzi for soaking off the hike. A class act.

GETTING THERE & AWAY

The bus terminal is about 400m south of the church, behind the *mercado*.

San José US$0.40; one hour; departs every 30 minutes from 5:30am to 10pm.

Sarchí, connecting to Naranjo US$0.30; one hour; departs every 25 minutes from 4:45am to 10pm.

Sarchí

There's just one problem with vacationing in Costa Rica: lousy souvenir shopping. Blame the whole ecotourism thing – it just seems wrong to buy a plastic bauble commemorating your visit to some of the last untouched rain forests in the world. But here it is, the end of your trip, and you've got to face jealous friends and family who won't care that you spotted a rare three-wattled bellbird while you were shivering waist-deep in mud in the middle of pristine cloud forest. Nope, they want presents.

Welcome to Sarchí, Costa Rica's most famous crafts center, where artists showcase the country's deeply ingrained woodworking tradition, honed through generations of warm evenings whittling away at precious hardwoods. Quality is high, prices are reasonable and you can be fairly sure that any tour you book in the region will include a stop somewhere in town.

For some tourists that 45-minute break in the bus ride will be more than enough time – some uncharitable souls would classify Sarchí as a tourist trap, albeit one with free coffee. But keep in mind as you browse the traps that there are more than 200 workshops scattered around the pretty countryside, many of which invite you to come and talk to the artists, or just watch as wood is transformed into fine tableware, jewelry boxes or furniture. Elegantly polished or brightly painted, Sarchí work is unmistakable.

ORIENTATION & INFORMATION

Sarchí is divided by the Río Trojas into Sarchí Norte and Sarchí Sur and is rather spread out, straggling for several kilometers along the main road from Grecia to Naranjo.

At the Plaza de la Artesanía in Sarchí Sur is an information booth with maps and brochures. In Sarchí Norte you'll find the main plaza with the typical twin-towered church, a hotel and some restaurants. There is also a **Banco Nacional** (☎ 454 4262; 8:30am-3pm Mon-Fri).

SLEEPING & EATING

A great farmers' market happens Fridays behind Taller Lalo Alfaro, with homemade snacks, palmetto cheese and lots of produce. Otherwise, there are a few well-stocked markets, bakeries and basic *sodas* in town.

Cabinas Mandy (☎ 454 2397; s/d US$8/11; P) Close to the fire station in Sarchí Norte, this is a good budget option, with small clean rooms furnished with TV and private hot shower.

Hotel Daniel Zamora (☎ 454 4596; d US$35; P) On a quiet street east of the soccer field, this is a friendly, decent choice, with spotless rooms with ceiling fan and cable TV.

Hotel Villa Sarchí (☎ 454 3029; Calle Rodriguez; s/d US$30/40, s/d with air-con US$40/50; P) A bit out of town, this nicer spot has newer furniture, private hot showers and a pool.

Super Mariscos (☎ 454 4330; mains US$4-9) In Sarchí Norte, this is a recommended spot for seafood, particularly rice with shrimp.

Restaurante Típico La Finca (☎ 454 1602) At the north end of Sarchí Norte, you can enjoy a variety of casados while relaxing in a tranquil garden – a nice break from all that shopping.

Las Carretas (☎ 454 1636; mains US$5-10; 11am-9pm) If you're lucky, this is where your tour bus will stop for lunch, and anyone can drop by for elegantly presented Costarricense classics in the attractive dining room.

SHOPPING

If you're interested in investing in the pricier items on sale, or just learning more about the culture (many top artisans are part of renowned woodworking families), you could spend days exploring the arts scene around here. Among the best-known crafts are the *carretas*, elaborately painted oxcarts that you'll still sometimes see in use, particularly on roads designated 4WD-only. Painting the elaborate mandala designs requires a steady hand and active imagination, and is a process well worth watching.

Though pricier models are ready for the road (oxen sold separately), most are scaled-down versions designed for display in gardens and homes, while others have been customized to function as indoor tables, sideboards and minibars. Smaller models are, of course, suitable for every budget and backpack.

In addition to *carretas*, the unofficial souvenir of Costa Rica (and official symbol of the Costa Rican worker), shoppers in the know come to Sarchí for leather-and-wood furniture, specifically rocking chairs that collapse Ikea-style for shipping. Other items you won't find elsewhere include gleaming wooden bowls and other tableware, some carved from rare hardwoods that Green Party members might feel guilty about buying. Workshops are usually open 8am to 4pm daily, and accept credit cards and US dollars.

Plaza de la Artesanía (☎ 454 3430), in Sarchí Sur, is the top choice for connoisseurs of kitsch. It's a shopping mall with more than 30 souvenir stores selling everything from truly beautiful furniture to mass-produced key chains. There's also a food court complete with local musicians playing marimbas. Nearby, on the main road, are several factories specializing in rocking chairs and other furniture, including **Los Rodríguez** (☎ 454 4097), **La Sarchiseño** (☎ 454 3430) and **El Artesano** (☎ 454 4304).

Fábrica de Carretas Joaquín Chaverri (☎ 454 4411; www.sarchicostarica.com), the oldest and best-known factory in Sarchí Sur, is where you can watch those incredible patterns being emblazoned on the oxcarts by artisans from the old school of transportation aesthetics.

Taller Lalo Alfaro (2 blocks north of the church) is Sarchí's oldest workshop, where they still make working oxcarts using machinery powered by a waterwheel.

Pidesa Souvenirs (☎ 454 4540), by the main plaza, is a spot that specializes in hand-painting local souvenirs Sarchí style, including full-size milk cans. Get a couple for that person who already has everything.

GETTING THERE & AROUND

Driving, you can take the unpaved road northeast from Sarchí to Bajos del Toro and on through Colonia del Toro to the northern lowlands at Río Cuarto. The main attraction of this route is the beautiful waterfall north of Bajos del Toro. Look for local signs for the 'Catarata'.

Even the bus station is artsy.

Alajuela (Tuasa) US$0.40; 30 minutes; departs every 30 minutes from 6am to 11pm.

Grecia US$0.20; 20 minutes; departs every 30 minutes from 6am to 11pm.

San José US$0.50; 1½ hours; departs 12:15pm, 5:30pm & 6pm.

PALMARES

From Sarchí the road continues west to Naranjo, where it divides. You can then continue 13km southwest, through Palmares, to San Ramón, or 17km north to Zarcero. Alternatively, driving west along the Interamericana (Hwy 1) between the exits to Naranjo and San Ramón, you'll see a turnoff to Palmares, which is a few kilometers south of the highway.

Palmares' main claim to fame is the annual **Las Fiestas de Palmares**, a 10-day extravaganza in mid-January with carnival rides, parades, a *tope* (horse parade), big-name bands, small-name bands, fried food, beer stands and bullfights (the bull is never killed in Costa Rica). It's one of the biggest events in the Central Valley and is widely covered on local TV.

The town triples in size, at least at this time and **Cabinas Sueca** (☎ 453 3353; r per person US$9.50), with basic rooms and private bathrooms close to the center of town, is probably booked for the Fiestas through to January 2008. It makes a nice place to stay in other months. There are a few *sodas* scattered around the muted gray church.

SAN RAMÓN

Though small, San Ramón has been no wallflower in the pageant of Costa Rican history. The 'City of Presidents and Poets' has sent five men to the country's highest office, including ex-president Rodrigo Carazo, who currently owns a tourist lodge a few kilometers to the north, which is also the gateway to Los Angeles Cloud Forest (see following).

Stories of the other four, plus poets and more, can be found on plaques around town or at the **Museo de San Ramón** (☎ 437 9851; admission free; 🕑 8:30-11am Wed-Sat & 1-5pm Mon-Fri), on the north side of the Parque Central.

It's worth working around the museum's schedule to see life-size dioramas depicting colonial Costa Rica and well-done exhibits on the area's impressive history.

The Saturday **farmers' market** is a big one, with smaller markets on Wednesday and Sunday.

Sleeping

There are a few basic, inexpensive cabinas where seasoned budget travelers will sleep just fine, plus two excellent high-end properties about 20km from town.

Hotel Gran (☎ 445 6363; s US$5; d with bathroom US$7) Three blocks west of the park, this is among the nicest of the cabina crowd. Clean rooms surround a courtyard with TV.

Hotel la Posada (☎ 445 7359; s/d incl breakfast US$15/40) This is a great hotel, 100m south and 50m east of the hospital, with eclectically decorated common areas and small single rooms – the doubles are much better.

Getting There & Away

There are two daily buses between San Ramón and San José. There are also buses between San Ramón and Ciudad Quesada via Zarcero.

LOS ANGELES CLOUD FOREST RESERVE

This **private reserve** (☎ 661 1600; per person US$15), about 20km north of San Ramón, is centered on a lodge and dairy ranch owned by ex-president Rodrigo Carazo. Some 800 hectares of primary forest have a short boardwalk and longer horse and foot trails that lead to substantial waterfalls and misty cloud forest vistas.

Bilingual naturalist guides are available to lead hikes (US$20 per person) and you can also rent horses (US$15 per hour) or take to the zip lines on a canopy tour (US$40 per person). Tours of the reserve are arranged through Carazo's Hotel Villablanca (see next), and guests get in for free. A taxi to the reserve and hotel costs US$10 from San Ramón, and the turnoff is well signed from the highway.

Sleeping & Eating

Hotel Villablanca (☎ 228 4603; www.villablanca-costarica.com; s/d US$108/124) has a large main lodge and restaurant with about 30 whitewashed, red-tiled, rustic adobe cabins scattered around, all surrounded by the cloud forest. Comfortable cabins have a refrigerator, hot water, bathtub, fireplace and electric kettle, and there's a fine onsite restaurant. The big perk here is free and easy access to the Los Angeles Cloud Forest Reserve, adjacent to the hotel property, with its relatively undisturbed wildlife and lots of trails.

Valle Escondido Lodge (☎ 231 0906; www.valleescondido.com; s/d US$80/105), not to be outdone, is an upscale address, about halfway between Hotel Villablanca and the village of La Tigra, and is adjacent to its own private reserve with 20km of cloud forest trails, plus it's a working ornamental plant and citrus fruit farm. With more than 100 hectares of preserved forest, this whole place is good for birding, and nonguests can pay US$8 just for day use of the trails. There is also a pool, Jacuzzi and a locally popular restaurant with Italian specialties.

ZARCERO

North of Naranjo the main road climbs about 20km along one of the most scenic drives in Costa Rica, winding toward Zarcero's 1736m perch at the western end of the Cordillera Central. The mountains are gorgeous and climate famously fresh, but the reason you've come is evident as soon as you pull into town.

Parque Francisco Alvarado, in front of the already off-kilter pink and blue 1895 Iglesia de San Rafael, was just a normal plaza until the 1960s (of course). Gardener Evangelisto Blanco became suddenly inspired to shave the ordinary, mild-mannered bushes into bizarre abstract shapes and, over the years, everything from elephants to bull fights.

Today the trippy topiary is certainly the town's top sight, but space-age trees aren't the only thing growing in Zarcero: this is a center for Costa Rica's organic-farming movement, and you can find unusual heirloom varieties of pesticide-free goodies all over town. It's also home to two cheese factories, plus lots of independent operations with signs reading '*queso palmito*' out the front. This fresh, light cheese has a delicate taste that goes well with fresh tomatoes and basil; you'll often get a few slices with your casado or *gallo* (tortilla sandwich) around here.

If you brought your swimsuit, stop into **Piscinas Apamar** (☎ 463 3674; per person US$2), 500m west of the parque on the road to Guadalupe, where there's not only a huge swimming pool, but also three hot tubs and a Jacuzzi.

Sleeping & Eating

Hotel Don Beto (☎ 463 3137; s/d US$30/35; P), just north of the town church, is an immaculate option, with well-kept and sunny rooms with private bathrooms. Breakfast is available, the owner has lots of local information, and tours, rafting, horseback riding and airport transfers can be arranged. The hotel also organizes trips to the nearby Bajos del Toro waterfalls, and Termales del Bosque (also known as Ciudad Quesada).

The roads are lined with places selling picnic supplies. But at **Bernardita and Gustavo's Cow's Country** (☎ 463 1211), close to the Piscinas, you can not only buy locally made products, but catch your own trout and have it cooked for you. There are a few *sodas* with good park views: try **Restaurante El Heguirón** (☎ 463 1708; 6:30am-8pm; fast food US$1-3) with Tico standards and fried chicken.

Getting There & Away

Hourly buses traveling between San José and Ciudad Quesada stop at Zarcero, though some buses may be full by the time they reach Zarcero, particularly on weekends. There are also buses from Alajuela and San Ramón.

PARQUE NACIONAL JUAN CASTRO BLANCO

This 143 sq km **park** (admission US$6; camping US$2) was created in 1992 to protect the slopes of Volcán Platanar (2183m) and Volcán Porvenir (2267m) from logging. The headwaters for five major rivers originate here as well, making this not only an important watershed but also a magnet for trout fishers, among the few people who visit.

The park is still in limbo, federally protected but still privately owned by various plantation families; only those parts that have already been purchased by the government are technically open to the traveler. As of yet, there is almost no infrastructure for visitors, though there is a **Minae office** (☎ 460 7600; 8am-4pm) in El Sucre, next to the only official entrance, where you can pay fees for camping or day-use. Here you can take a three-hour hike to abandoned mines, sulfur pools and the lagoons of Pozo Verde.

PARQUE NACIONAL VOLCÁN POÁS

Just 37km north of Alajuela by a winding and scenic road, this popular **park** (entry US$7; 8am-3:30pm) is a must for anyone who wants to peer into an active volcano – without the hardship of hiking up the side of one. The park's dramatic scenery, easy access and short, well-maintained trails make it a popular destination for locals and visitors alike. It is one of the country's best-known parks.

The centerpiece of the park is, of course, Volcán Poás (2704m), which had its last blowout in 1953. This event formed the eerie and enormous crater, which is 1.3km across and 300m deep. The volcano continues to be active to varying extents with different levels of danger. The park was briefly closed in May 1989 after a minor eruption sent volcanic ash spouting more than a kilometer into the air. Lesser activity closed the park intermittently in 1995.

In recent years the bubbling and steaming cauldron atop this denuded peak has posed no imminent threat, and the park has been steadily open for years. Occasionally, when the wind and rain conditions are just right, the fumes from the crater can cause acidic moisture that closes the park briefly.

Geyser-type eruptions take place periodically, with peaceful interludes lasting minutes or weeks. Because of toxic sulfuric-acid fumes, visitors are prohibited from descending into the crater. A more common hazard for visitors is the veil of clouds that the mountain gathers around itself almost daily, even in the dry season, starting at around 10am. Even if the day looks clear, get to the park as early as possible or you won't see much.

Apart from Volcán Poás, there's a dwarf cloud forest near the crater, one of the best examples of this kind of habitat in all the national parks. Here you can wander about looking at bromeliads, lichens and mosses clinging to the curiously shaped and twisted trees growing in the volcanic soil. Birds abound, especially the magnificent fiery-throated hummingbird, a high-altitude specialty of Costa Rica. Other highland specialties to look for include the sooty robin, and even the quetzal has been sighted here.

Information

Some 250,000 people visit the park annually, making it one of the most packed national park in the country; weekends in particular can be busy. The visitor center has a coffee shop, souvenirs and informative videos hourly from 9am to 3pm. A small **museum** offers explanations in both Spanish and English. There's no camping at the park.

The best time to go is in the dry season, especially early in the morning before the clouds roll in and obscure the view. Nevertheless, even in late afternoon and during the rainy season you may be lucky enough to see a muddy eruption as clear as in summertime. If it's clouded in, don't despair! Winds may blow the clouds away, so walk around the cloud forest and keep checking back on the crater.

Overnight temperatures can drop below freezing, and it may be windy and cold during the day, particularly in the morning, so dress accordingly. Poás receives almost 4000mm of rain a year, so be prepared for that, too.

There are well-marked trails in the park. It's an easy walk (about 1km) to the active crater lookout for spectacular views; the trails through the cloud forest are somewhat steeper but still not very difficult or long. The main trail to the crater is paved and is wheelchair accessible.

Tours

Numerous companies offer tours almost daily. Typically, they cost US$40 to US$100 per person and you arrive at the volcano by about 10am, about when the obscuring clouds start rolling in. Some tours spend very little time at the crater, so ask.

The cheaper tours are large group affairs providing only transportation, park entrance, and limited time at the crater. The more expensive tours feature smaller group sizes, bilingual naturalist guides and lunch. You can also visit the volcano quite easily using public transportation from San José.

Sleeping

There's no camping in the park, but there are a few places right outside. The following are listed according to their distance from the park. Bring your own bottled water, as proximity to primordial seepage has rendered the tap water undrinkable. On sunny days the road to Poás is lined with stands selling fruit, cheese and snacks: it's worth picking up picnic supplies, as the coffee shop has a limited menu.

La Providencia Lodge (☎ 389 5842, 380 6315; d incl breakfast US$55, cabins per person US$20; Ⓟ) High up on the southwestern flanks of the volcano, this lodge sits on a 572-hectare working dairy ranch and primary forest adjoining the national park. Six small, rustic cabins, some of them quite isolated, have private hot showers and porches with views that both birders and geologists will love.

Three-hour horseback tours (US$35) with a resident biologist guide are available with advance reservations, and there are several private trails that are a bit more challenging than those at the park. You reach the lodge by taking a 2.5km dirt road (normally passable to cars) leaving from the paved highway about 2km from the national-park entrance.

Lagunillas Lodge (☎ 389 5842; s/d US$25/35; Ⓟ) A signed turnoff about 2.5km after the park exit sends you along a steep 1km dirt road that may require a 4WD – call ahead. The collection of cute cabinas includes some small single rooms, all surrounded by good trails. There's a fish pond out back where you can catch dinner, and the **restaurant** (mains US$4-10) will prepare it – with side dishes. You can also rent horses or arrange a guided ride up to the crater.

Lo Que Tu Quieres Lodge (☎ 482 2092; cabins US$25; Ⓟ) Just over 5km after the park entrance, the name of this place translates to 'Whatever You Want Lodge.' It has three basic little cabins, with private hot showers, that sleep up to three people. There is a small restaurant and sweeping views of the valley; the owners are friendly and may allow camping.

Poás Volcano Lodge (☎ 482 2194; www.poasvolcanolodge.com; s/d US$45/55, s/d with bathroom US$55/75, junior ste US$65/90; Ⓟ 💻) About 16km east of the volcano near Vara Blanca, this high-altitude dairy farm frames the attractive stone building, which blends architectural influences from Wales, England and Costa Rica (the original owners were English farmers). Trails radiate from the eclectically decorated rooms, and common areas include a billiard room ('pool' doesn't do it justice). There's a sitting area with a sunken fireplace and books and board games to while away a stormy night. The hotel offers Internet access from its office, free local calls and breakfast included in the rate.

Bosque de Paz Rain/Cloud Forest Lodge & Biological Reserve (☎ 234 6676; www.bosquedepaz.com;

s/d US$126/218; (P)) Tastefully decorated in rustic luxury, rates for large rooms with private hot showers include all meals, vegetarian by request, and access to a privately owned, 1000-hectare biological reserve. This excellent splurge offers access to what forms a wild corridor between Parque Nacional Volcán Poás and Parque Nacional Juan Castro Blanco: not your average lodge grounds. There are 22km of trails, sometimes used by researchers from all over the world, and the owners can arrange guided hikes as well as tours and transportation to other area attractions. If driving north from the Interamericana through Zarcero, take a right immediately after the church and head north about 15km; just before the last bridge to Bajos del Toro, the reserve will be on your right.

Getting There & Away

You can take a taxi to the park for around US$80 from San José, US$40 from Alajuela. Most visitors using public buses come from San José. Get to the terminal early.

From San José (US$4, five hours) Tuasa buses depart 8:30am daily from Av 2 between Calles 12 and 14, stopping in Alajuela at 9:30am, and returning at 2:30pm.

LOS JARDINES DE LA CATARATA LA PAZ

La Paz waterfall gardens (☎ 265 0643; www.waterfallgardens.com; 8:30am-5:30pm; adult/child & student US$21/10) are built around an almost impossibly scenic series of waterfalls formed as Río La Paz cascades almost 1400m in less than 8km, down the flanks of Volcán Poás. The lowest, whose name means 'Peace Waterfall,' is perhaps the most famous in Costa Rica.

As if that weren't enough, this interesting complex also boasts Costa Rica's largest butterfly garden, botanical and birding exhibits, and a few upscale accommodations.

Visitors, many on tours from San José, begin with a short video that describes facilities at the 30-hectare gardens. Then 3.5km of trails wind past butterflies, hummingbirds, orchids and a fern trail before plunging steeply down alongside five waterfalls. The trails are well-maintained (graveled or paved) and wooden hiking staffs are provided.

A shuttle bus meets hikers at the bottom of the falls and drives back up to the visitor center. Small children, city slickers and active seniors won't have any problems with this adventure, and the views of the waterfalls are excellent (and damp). The restaurant does a decent **buffet** (adult/child US$10/5) alongside a huge fireplace that provides welcome respite from the weather on a rainy day.

HEREDIA AREA

HEREDIA

This rather elegant town and provincial capital (population 80,000) was once seriously considered for the seat of federal government. It retains a pleasantly small-city feel despite being just 11km north of the capital's grit and grime. The cosmopolitan bustle comes courtesy of the many multinational corporations, primarily high-tech, who have their Central American headquarters here. More bohemian stylings radiate from the Universidad Nacional, on the east side of town.

Despite outward appearances and a convenient location, this isn't just a suburb of San José. Since the late 1990s Heredia has come into its own as the high-tech capital of Costa Rica – microchips produced here have suddenly become the country's most important export. Career opportunities make this a magnet for this highly educated nation's tech heads – and considering that the historic coffee center also produces some of the world's strongest brew, there's absolutely no reason to stop computer coding. Ever.

Information

Though there's no tourist office, most other services are readily available. **Scotiabank** (☎ 262 5303; Av 4 btwn Calles Central & 2; 8am-5pm Mon-Fri, 8am-4pm Sat) is just one place that changes money, and has a 24-hour ATM that dispenses US dollars. Fast Internet access is everywhere. **PlanetWeb** (Av 1 btwn Calles 6 & 8; per hour US$0.50; 9am-10pm) is among the cheapest. **Hospital San Vicente de Paul** (☎ 261 0001; Av 8 btwn Calles 14 & 16) is nearby.

Sights

The city was founded in 1706, and in true Spanish Colonial style has several lovely, or at least interesting, old landmarks arranged around the **Parque Central**. To the east is the **Iglesia de la Inmaculada Concepción**, built in 1797 and still in use. Opposite the church steps you can take a break and watch old men playing checkers at the park tables while

weddings and funerals come and go. The church's thick-walled, squat construction is attractive in a Volkswagen Beetle sort of way. The solid shape has withstood the earthquakes that have damaged or destroyed almost all the other buildings in Costa Rica that date from this time.

To the north of the park is an 1867 guard tower called simply **El Fortín** (the small fortress). This area is a national historic site, but passageways are closed to the public, so don't get excited about climbing up. The beautifully landscaped **Universidad Nacional** campus, six blocks east of Parque Central, is worth a stroll. Check out the marine biology department's **Museo Zoomarino** (☎ 277 3240; admission free; 🕑 8am-4pm Mon-Fri), where more than 2000 displayed specimens give an overview of Costa Rica's marine diversity.

At the park's northeast corner the **Casa de la Cultura** (☎ 262 2505; cnr Calle Central & Av Central; www.heredianet.co.cr/casacult.htm, in Spanish; admission free; 🕑 varied), formerly the residence of President Alfredo González Flores (1913–17), now houses permanent historical exhibits as well as rotating art shows and other events. It also has information on other historic buildings in the area, and can recommend walking tours.

Courses

There are three Spanish-language schools in town: Centro-Panamericano de Idiomas, Intercultura and Instituto Profesional de

Educación Daza. See the boxed text on p122 for more details.

Sleeping

With San José so close, most travelers just stay there. Many of the budget hotels in town cater to students, with cheaper monthly rates and paper-thin walls.

Hotel Valladolid (☎ 260 2905; valladol@racsa.co.cr; cnr Calle 7 & Av 7; s/d incl continental breakfast US$64/75) The best hotel in town is this five-story building, which features a sauna, Jacuzzi and solarium on the top floor with good views of the surrounding area. The 12 rooms are attractive, with air-con minibar, cable TV, phone and hot private shower.

Hotel Verano (☎ 237 1616; Calle 4 btwn Avs 6 & 8; d US$7.50) It's in the seedy, noisy area by the bus termional, but is reasonably clean and cheap with cold showers.

Hotel Colonial (☎ 237 5258; Av 4 btwn Calles 4 & 6; s/d US$7.50/10; Ⓟ) Clean and homey (literally, in a home) with shared hot-water bathrooms; you can always spend your spare time hanging out with the dogs or granny in her rocking chair.

Hotel Heredia (☎ 238 0880; Calle 6 btwn Avs 3 & 5; s/d/tr US$10/15/20; Ⓟ) It's in a nice part of town, the rooms are clean as are the private bathrooms, and there's a TV in the lounge. (Don't confuse with the 'Hotel Heredia' near the *mercado,* which is an old apartment building.)

Hotel Las Flores (☎ 261 147, 260 8147; Av 12 btwn Calles 12 & 14; s/d US$12/18; Ⓟ) A quick walk from the center, this family-run place has cool marble floors, hot-water showers and absolutely immaculate sunny rooms

Casa de Huespedes Ramble (☎ 238 3829; Av 8 btwn Calles 10 & 12; r per person US$12.50; Ⓟ) This attractively painted place has shining private bathrooms and a shared kitchen.

Hotel Manolo (☎ 226 3508; Av 12 btwn Calles 2 & 4; s/d US$15/21; Ⓟ) Cheerful, rambling rooms are a bit frayed around the edges, but all have fans and cable television.

Hotel América (☎ 260 9292; Calle Central btwn Avs 2 & 4; s/d incl continental breakfast US$29/41) Acceptable rooms are a good size, sunny, and have hot water and cable TV. There is a 24-hour restaurant and bar. Airport transfers are available.

Eating

In the grand tradition of university towns worldwide, Heredia offers plenty of spots for pizza slices and cheap vegetarian grub, not to mention one branch of every fast-food outlet imaginable. You can fill up for a few hundred colones at the **Mercado Municipal** (Calle 2 btwn Avs 6 & 8; ⌚ 6am-6pm), with *sodas* to spare and plenty of very fresh groceries. **Más X Menos** (Av 6 btwn Calles 4 & 6; ⌚ 8:30am-9pm) has everything else.

Restaurant Fresas (☎ 262 5555; cnr Av 1 & Calle 7; mains US$3-8; ⌚ 8am-midnight) Near the university, this spot specializes in fresh fruit shakes and salads, some involving ice cream and/or chocolate. Casados and other typical meals complete the menu.

Azzura Heladería y Cafetería Italiana (cnr Calle 2 & Av 2; gelati US$1-2, light meals US$3-4; ⌚ 7am-10pm) After a hard morning of designing software, re-rev your engine with a high-octane coffee or yummy gelato. Healthier souls can indulge in salads, quiche or sandwiches.

Vishnu Mango Verde (☎ 237 2526; Calle 7 btwn Avs Central & 1; daily specials US$3; ⌚ 9am-6pm Mon-Sat) This inexpensive eatery does solid vegetarian fast food that's cheap and healthy. The veggie burger and natural fruit drink combo is a great deal.

Gran Chaparral (☎ 237 1010; Av Central btwn Calles Central & 1; dishes US$3-6; ⌚ 11am-11pm) Not far from the Parque Central, this is a top spot for chop suey, shrimp fried rice and a long list of other Chinese and Tico dishes.

El Restaurante Sabroso (Av 6 btwn Calles 6 & 8; mains US$4-6; ⌚ 11am-11pm) Another popular place for Chinese food, this place specializes in seafood.

Drinking & Entertainment

There is no shortage of places to drink near the university. **La Choza**, **El Bulevar** and **El Rancho de Fofo** (cnr Calle 7 & Av Central) are three popular and recommended bars a catty corner from each other (just follow the noise). They all serve *bocas* and beer and host live music. **Bar Oceano** (Calle 4 btwn Avs 2 & 4) is more mellow, with good music and cheap beer. Ask locally about shows.

Getting There & Away

There is no central terminal, and buses leave from bus stops near the Parque Central and market areas. Buses for Barva leave from nearby the **Cruz Roja** (Red Cross; Calle Central btwn Avs 1 & 3). Buses to San José de la Montaña and Sacramento, with connections to Volcán Barva in Parque Nacional Braulio Carrillo,

MICROCHIP REPUBLIC

When industry leaders in Heredia heard that Intel, the world's largest microchip manufacturer, was shopping around for a Latin American base of operations, they decided to invite execs down for a quick *cafecito*.

Costa Rica hadn't even made the list, which included Mexico, Brazil and Chile: it was considered too small, too laid-back and too expensive (per capita earnings are among the hemisphere's highest) for the job. But this little country, famed for exotic wildlife and erupting volcanoes, was conveniently right on the way south. Besides, who wouldn't want to take a 'business trip' here?

The pitch was a pleasant surprise: half a century of investment in schools rather than soldiers had resulted in a highly educated and relatively computer-literate workforce. Costa Rica's track record as a peaceful democracy sat well with the insurance people, and learning that a large percentage of locals already spoke English got human resources' vote. Perhaps most importantly, Intel reps noticed that almost everyone they met was already online, a convenience quite rare in other countries being considered. The tech giant was charmed.

Eager for this massive influx of foreign investment, Heredia officials emailed Intel an offer that included a lovely former finca and some very generous tax breaks. Increased access to computers (subsidized by Intel) and English classes in public schools was also part of the deal.

On some things, however, Heredia would not budge. Microchip production is both water-intensive and ferociously toxic, and Costa Ricans are famously protective of their landscape. Intel finally agreed to ship all waste products out of the country for disposal; moreover, the most environmentally damaging processes continue to take place in the USA, with the final product assembled here.

Pentium processors began rolling out in March 1998, and within three years microchip exports were worth three times as much as bananas and coffee combined. Today Intel products account for 8% of Costa Rica's total GDP and 40% of all exports. The Heredia facility, where local talent is now also responsible for cutting-edge product development and software design, brings in more than US$1 billion annually.

Many other high-tech companies, including Oracle and Microsoft, have since opened up shop in the region hoping to repeat Intel's success, transforming the area into Central America's very own Silicon Valley – but without Starbucks. Their coffee just couldn't compete around here.

leave from Avenida 8 between Calles 2 and 4. Ask around the market for information on other destinations.

Alajuela US$0.25; 20 minutes; departs from cnr Av Central & Calle 9 every 15 minutes from 6am to 10pm.
Barva US$0.25; 20 minutes; departs from Calle Central btwn Avs 1 & 3 every 30 minutes from 5:15am to 11:30pm.
Puerto Viejo de Sarapiquí US$2; 3½ hours; departs from cnr Av Central & Calle 9 at 11am, 1:30pm & 3pm.
Sacramento & Volcán Barva in Parque Nacional Braulio Carrillo departs from Calle 4 across from the *mercado* at 6:30am, 11am & 4pm.
San José US$0.50; 20 minutes; departs from Av 4 btwn Calles Central & 1 every 20 to 30 minutes from 4:40am to 11pm.
San José de la Montaña US$0.50; 20 minutes; departs from Av 8 btwn Calles 2 & 4 every 20 to 30 minutes from 4:40am to 11pm.
Santa Bárbara US$0.50; 20 minutes; departs from Av 6 btwn Calles 6 & 8 every 10 to 30 minutes from 5:15am to 11:30pm.

Taxis are plentiful and can take you to San José (US$5) or the airport (US$8).

BARVA

The small colonial town of Barva, 2.5km north of Heredia, was founded in 1561 and remains centered on the **Iglesia San Bartolomé**, completed in 1575. The city center, packed with 17th- and 18th-century buildings, has been declared a national monument and makes for a very interesting stroll. Grocery stores, several *sodas* and restaurants, a Banco Nacional with 24-hour ATM and Internet cafés can be found close by.

Sights

Café Britt Finca (☎ 277 1600; www.coffeetour.com, www.cafebritt.com; admission US$20; 🕒 tours 11am year-round, 9am & 3pm in high season), about 1km north of Barva, not only turns out organic shade-grown coffee, it shows you how they do it.

Begin your tour with an informative video, then move on to the plantation and processing center for a short and interesting tour. The payoff comes as complimentary coffee beverages. Get tips on making the perfect brew, then buy beans so you can practice on your own. Café Britt operates a daily shuttle that will pick you up from major San José hotels – call for a reservation. If you drive or take the bus, you can't miss the signs between Heredia and Barva.

Museo de Cultura Popular (☎ 260 1619; admission US$2; ⏲ 9am-4pm), in Santa Lucía de Barva, about 1.5km southeast of Barva, is usually seen in conjunction with a Britt tour, though it's worth checking out independently. It recreates Spanish colonial Costa Rica in a century-old farmhouse, restored with period pieces and ingenious tools. If you're lucky, docents in period costumes may use the beehive-shaped ovens to make typical Tico foods, which you can purchase anytime at their **garden café** (US$2-5; ⏲ 11am-2pm), along with Britt's finest.

In 1989 **INBio** (☎ 507 8107; www.inbio.ac.cr/inbioparque; adult/student/child US$15/12/8; ⏲ 7:30am-4pm) was formed to help conserve Costa Rica's biodiversity. Rather than bringing in researchers, the private, nonprofit El Instituto Nacional de Bioversidad (National Bioversity Institute) trained locals, who were already familiar with area wildlife, as parataxonomists, who study and inventory species. Similar to paramedics, parataxonomists do the essential work of data collection and stabilization quickly and inexpensively before passing the information on to the experts.

INBio is modeled after US National Park visitor centers, with an introductory video, state-of-the-art interactive demos, maps of the entire Costa Rican national-park system, exhibits of plants and insects, and three well-signed, wheelchair-accessible trails totaling 2km. The price is a little steep, but you're helping a good cause.

Sleeping

Barva proper doesn't have any lodgings, but there are some truly spectacular country hotels outside of town.

Finca Rosa Blanca (☎ 269 9392; www.fincarosablanca.com; s US$187-281, d US$198-315, additional person US$35; P) Just outside Santa Bárbara, this honeymoon-ready confection of gorgeous garden villas and architecturally outstanding suites, cloaked in fruit trees that shade trails and cascading rivers, ranks as one of the most exclusive hotels in Costa Rica. Breakfast is included in all rates.

Rooms with balconies overlooking the rain forest are individually and lavishly appointed: one tops a tower with a 360° view, reached by a winding staircase made of a single tree trunk. Shower in an artificial waterfall, take a moonlight dip in the sculpted garden pool and hot tub, or have a recommended romantic dinner (US$32), four courses of French-method, often-organic fine dining. Leftovers will be dutifully recycled, and owners happily offer tours of their many other conservation systems, perfect for newlyweds with social consciences.

A few kilometers north of Barva, in **San José de la Montaña**, there are three comfortably rustic high-altitude havens on the slopes of the volcano, all with hot showers and extra blankets to ward off the night's chill. **Las Ardillas Resort** (☎ 260 2172; d with breakfast US$74; P) has cozy cabins sleeping up to four, each with its own fireplace. **Hotel El Cypresal** (☎ 237 4466; s/d US$44/58; P) has rooms with fabulous terrace views, plus a pool and horse rental, while **Hotel El Pórtico** (☎ 266 1000; s/d US$42/56) has well-appointed, heated (!) rooms and arranges area tours.

Hotel Chalet Tirol (☎ 267 6222; www.costaricabureau.com/hotels/tirol.htm; d standard/presidential ste US$91/139; P) Between Monte de la Cruz and Club Campestre El Castillo, you'll find this recommended small country hotel, formerly the residence of Costa Rican president Alfredo González Flores. The cloud-forest enclave is rustic-chic, with comfy chalets arranged around open-air common spaces, including the onsite pizza parlor, where you can relax and watch the mist drift by.

Hotel Bougainvillea (☎ 244 1414; www.bougainvillea.co.cr; s/d US$68/78, junior ste US$113; P) In Santo Domingo de Heredia, about halfway between Heredia and San José, this luxury property has it all. Very comfortable, wood-accented rooms (some wheelchair accessible) and bigger suites come with balconies overlooking either the mountains or lights of San José. Several private trails wind through the jungle and fruit orchards, passing the swimming pool, restaurant and tennis courts en route to the hills. Best of all, this rural wonderland comes with free hourly shuttles to downtown San José.

Getting There & Around

About 1km north of Barva the road forks. To the right lies the village of **San José de la Montaña**, with a clutch of country inns, at a nippy 1550m (bring a jacket) on the southern slopes of Volcán Barva.

Transporte Barveños buses stop at the national park; ask around to make sure you're on the correct corner.

Heredia US$0.25; 20 minutes; departs every 30 minutes from 4:45am to 11pm.
Parque Nacional Braulio Carrillo US$0.30; 30 minutes.
San José de la Montaña US$0.15; 20 minutes; departs every 30 minutes from 4:45am to 11pm.

PARQUE NACIONAL BRAULIO CARRILLO

Thick virgin forest, countless waterfalls, swift rivers and deep canyons – it will be difficult to believe that you are only 30 minutes north of San José when you're walking around this underexplored park. Braulio Carrillo has an extraordinary biodiversity attributable to the steep range of altitudes, from the misty 2906m cloud-forest campsites atop massive Volcán Barva, to the lush, humid 50m lowlands stretching toward the Caribbean Sea. Its watershed is San José's most important water source.

The park's creation was a compromise between conservationists and developers. San José's only link to Puerto Limón was long limited to the crumbling railway and a slow, rural road. Government and industry agreed that a sleek, modern highway was required to link the nation's capital and most important port.

The only feasible route, through a low pass between Volcán Barva and Volcán Irazú, was still virgin rain forest, primarily because access had historically been so difficult. Conservationists were concerned that the road would change all that, and demanded that the jungle be protected. Parque Nacional Braulio Carrillo (named after Costa Rica's third chief of state) was established in 1978, off-limits to development beyond a single major highway to bisect it.

The San José–Guápiles highway was completed in 1987, effectively cutting the area into two smaller preserved areas, but it is considered one national park. Driving through it will give you an idea of what Costa Rica looked like prior to the 1950s: rolling hills cloaked in mountain rain forest. About 75% of Costa Rica was rain forest in the 1940s; now less than a quarter of the country retains its natural vegetative cover.

On the steepest roadside slopes are stands of distinctive huge-leafed Gunnera plants, which quickly colonize steep and newly exposed parts of the montane rain forest. The large leaves can protect a person from a sudden tropical downpour – hence the plant's nickname is 'poor folks' umbrella'. A walk into the forest will give you a chance to see the incredible variety of orchids, ferns, palms and other plant life, although the lushness of the vegetation makes viewing the many species of tropical animals a challenge. You will certainly hear and see plenty of birds, but the mammals are more elusive.

The park is traversed by several rivers, among them the Río Sucio ('Dirty River') whose yellow waters carry volcanic minerals, and the crystal clear Río Hondura. The two rivers intersect right next to the main highway, and it's fascinating to see the difference in colors. Volcán Barva is located at the southwestern corner of the park.

Orientation & Information

The most popular hiking area is accessed on the north end of the park at the **Quebrada González ranger station** (22km past Zurquí tunnel; admission US$7; 8am-3:30pm Tue-Sun), on the right side of the highway. There is a guarded parking lot, toilets and well-marked trails. Hourly buses between San José and Guápiles can drop you off at the entrance, but it's a 2km walk back along the highway to reach the restaurant where returning buses stop.

People who want to climb Volcán Barva on a day trip or camp overnight can stop by

WARNING

Unfortunately, there have been many reports of thefts from cars parked at entrances to some trails in Parque Nacional Braulio Carrillo, as well as armed robbers accosting tourists hiking on the trails or walking along the highway. Readers have reported hearing shots fired on the trails, and hitchhikers have reported being told it is a dangerous area. Stay alert. Don't leave your car parked anywhere along the main highway unless there is a park ranger on duty, such as at Quebrada González.

the **Barva Sector ranger station** (☎ 261 2619; 8am-4pm high season), which may or may not be manned. It can be reached by following the decent paved road north from Heredia through Barva and San José de la Montaña to Sacramento; a signed, 3km-long, 4WD-only trail leads north from Sacramento to the Barva station. **Camping** (per person US$2) is only allowed in basic campsites near the chilly but impossibly scenic summit; you may need to bring your own drinking water. Toilets are close to the ranger station.

There's more information on the **Minae website** (www.minae.go.cr/accvc/braulio.htm, in Spanish).

Climbing Volcán Barva

Climbing Volcán Barva is a good four- to five-hour round-trip adventure along a well-maintained trail. Because of its relative inaccessibility (folks taking a bus have an extra 8km hike to the ranger station) there is a good chance you can commune with the volcano solo. Begin on the western side of the park at the Sacramento entrance, north of Heredia. From there the signed track climbs to the summit at a leisurely pace. Trails are often muddy and you should be prepared for rain at any time of year.

The track leads to three lagoons – Lagos Danta, Barva and Copey – at the volcano's summit, and several spur trails lead to burbling waterfalls and other scenic spots along the way. If you wish to continue from Barva north into the lowlands, you will find that the trails are not marked and not as obvious. It is possible, regardless, to follow northbound 'trails' (overgrown and unmaintained) all the way through the park to La Selva near Puerto Viejo de Sarapiquí. A Tico who has done it reported that it took him four days and it is a bushwhacking adventure only for those used to roughing it and able to use a topographical map and compass.

The best time to go is the supposedly 'dry' season (from December to April), but it is liable to rain then, too. If you're going on a day trip, get there as early as possible as the mornings tend to be clear and the afternoons cloudy. The night-time temperatures can drop to several degrees below freezing.

Getting There & Away

There are two main entrances to the park. **San José de la Montaña**, with access to Volcán Barva, is served by regular buses (US$0.50, 20 minutes) from Heredia. From here, you can get irregular local buses to Sacramento; ask the driver to drop you at the track leading to Volcán Barva. It's another 8km hike to the park entrance.

Quebrada González ranger station, close to almost all other trailheads, is more accessible by car than the San José de la Montaña entrance. The entrance is signed from Hwy 32, and you could theoretically ask any bus connecting San José to Puerto Limón to drop you off, but pickup on the major freeway will be dangerous and difficult.

A little-used third way into the park begins on a slightly improved 19th-century oxcart trail between Puerto Limón and San José. The unnamed 4WD road now runs through Guayabal, Paracito, San Jerónimo and Alto Palma to Bajo Hondura, near the park entrance. The dirt road continues a few kilometers into the park.

RAINFOREST AERIAL TRAM

The brainchild of biologist Don Perry, a pioneer of rain forest canopy research, the **Rainforest Aerial Tram** (☎ 257 5961; www.rainforesttram.com; ride only adult/student & child US$50/25, package US$79/54) is a highly recommended splurge to the heights of the cloud forest in an airborne gondola.

The pricey package is worthwhile, as it includes a trained guide who can point out all the small and important things you'll otherwise miss, and who also leads the optional hike through the 400-hectare reserve, contiguous with Parque Nacional Braulio Carrillo. Although the area is rich with wildlife, the sheer density of the vegetation makes observing animals difficult.

The 2.6km aerial tram ride takes 40 minutes each way, affording a unique view of the rain forest and unusual plant-spotting and birding opportunities. Amazingly, the whole project was constructed with almost no impact on the rain forest. A narrow footpath follows the tram and all 250,000kg of construction material was carried in on foot or by a cable system to avoid erosion, with the exception of the 12 towers supporting the tram that were helicoptered in by the Nicaraguan Air Force (since Costa Rica has no armed forces).

From the parking lot a truck takes you about 3km to the tram loading area, where there is a small exhibit area, restaurant and gift shop. Here you can see an orientation video, and there are short hiking trails that you can use for as long as you want. Tram riders should be prepared for rain – although the cars have tarpaulin roofs, the sides are open to the elements.

Driving from San José, the well-signed turnoff to the tram is just past the national park entrance, on your right. To get here by public transport from San José, take the bus for Guápiles from Terminal Caribe (US$1.50, 1¼ hours), departing hourly from 6:30am to 7pm, and ask the driver to let you out at the *teleferico*. Tram staff will help you flag down a return bus.

MORAVIA

This village is named San Vicente de Moravia or San Vicente on many maps, but is known as Moravia by the locals. It's about 7km northeast of San José and used to be the center for the area's coffee fincas. Today the village is famous for its handicrafts, especially leather, but also ceramics, jewelry and the ubiquitous wood.

Around and nearby the spacious and attractive Parque Central are several stores. Some started as saddle shops but now sell a variety of leather and other goods. Look for **Artesanía Bribrí**, which sells work made by the Bribrí Indians of the Caribbean slope, and the pleasant **Mercado de Artesanías Las Garzas**, a festive complex with arts and crafts stores, a few *sodas* and clean toilet facilities. It's 100m south and 75m east of the *municipio* (town hall).

Local buses to Moravia depart San José from Av 3 btwn Calles 3 & 5.

CARTAGO AREA

CARTAGO

The stunning riverbank setting was handpicked by Spanish Governor Juan Vásquez de Coronado, who said that he had 'never seen a more beautiful valley.' Cartago was founded as Costa Rica's capital in 1563, and Coronado's successors endowed their seat of government with the country's finest Spanish colonial architecture, most of which was subsequently destroyed during the 1723 eruption of Volcán Irazú, with remaining landmarks taken care of in the earthquakes of 1841 and 1910.

After the rubble was cleared, no one bothered to rebuild the city to its former quaint specifications – though it is an attractive modern city, in a heavily reinforced sort of way. The seat of government had moved to San José in 1823, leaving Cartago relegated to backwater status. Despite retaining its standing as a provincial capital (it now has a population of 127,000), you'll be touring sites such as the once-important Iglesia del Convento, destroyed in 1910, as ruins.

There is one major exception: the Basílica de Nuestra Señora de Los Ángeles, the holiest shrine in Costa Rica, has been religiously rebuilt after each of the city's trials and tribulations. This latest version is the result of a 1926 makeover that followed its near total destruction in the 1920 earthquake.

Information

There is no tourist office. Several banks in the town center change money: try **Banco Nacional** (cnr Av 4 & Calle 5). You can check email 50m east of Las Ruinas at **Internet Café Las Ruinas** (cnr Calle 4 & Av 2; per hour US$1; ⏲ 9am-9pm). **Hospital Max Peralta** (☎ 550 1999; Av 5 btwn Calles 1 & 3) offers emergency health care.

Sights

The most important site in Cartago is the **Basílica de Nuestra Señora de los Ángeles** (cnr Av 2 & Calle 16), currently boasting a rather formal Byzantine grace and airy spaciousness with fine stained-glass windows. Though the façade has changed since 1635, the relic that so many walls have crumbled around remains safe inside.

La Negrita, 'The Black Virgin,' is a small, probably indigenous, representation of the Virgin Mary, found on this spot on August 2, 1635, by a native woman. When she tried to take the statuette with her, however, it miraculously reappeared back where she'd found it. Twice. Finally, she and the other townspeople gave up and built a shrine here, where La Negrita was originally found. The statuette has since been stolen twice, and returned each time. The statuette was declared Costa Rica's Patron Saint in 1824, the year after the capital was moved. Each August 2, on the anniversary of the statuette's miraculous discovery, pilgrims from every corner of the country and world walk the 22km from San José to the Basilica to say their most serious prayers on bent knees.

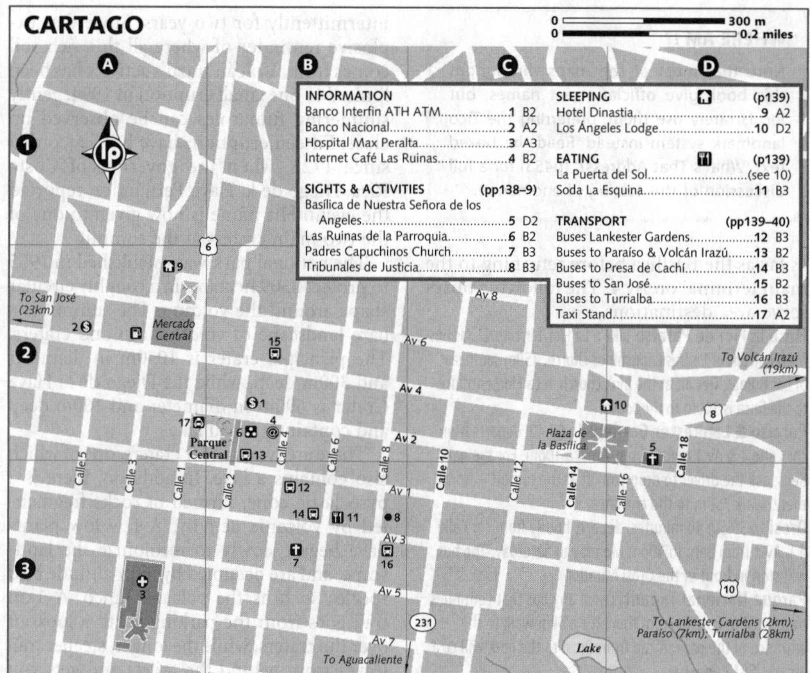

A staircase descends into a small room where *milagrosos*, metal charms representing the body part petitioners hope to have healed, surround the rock upon which the statuette keeps reappearing. This place is absolutely jammed during pilgrimages and holy days.

Las Ruinas de la Parroquia (cnr Av 2 & Calle 2), or Iglesia del Convento, was first destroyed by the earthquake of 1841 and rebuilt. It took another beating in the 1910 earthquake and was never repaired. The solid walls of the church now house a pretty garden, a pleasant spot to sit on a park bench and watch people go about their business.

Sleeping & Eating

Restaurant options are limited, and lodging rarer still. Your best bet for food is to just stroll along Avenidas 2 and 4 downtown, where *sodas* and bakeries congregate.

Hotel Dinastía (☎ 551 7057; cnr Calle 3 & Ave 6; s/d US$8.75/11.25, s with bathroom US$17) Slightly less sketchy than surrounding dives here in the heart of Cartago's red-light district, stuffy rooms come with cable TV to drown out the neighbors, if need be, and cold showers if that doesn't work.

Los Ángeles Lodge (☎ 551 0957, 591 4169; Ave 4 btwn Calles 14 & 16; s/d incl full breakfast US$36/42; P) With it's balconies overlooking the Plaza de la Basílica, this sweet B&B stands out with spacious and comfortable rooms, hot showers and a big breakfast made to order by the cheerful owners.

La Puerta del Sol (Av 4, opposite the Basilica; mains US$3-6; 8am-midnight) With a nicer dining room than a lot of *sodas*, this place does your choice of cooked-to-order casado and other typical food.

Soda La Esquina (cnr Av 3 & Calle 6; mains US$2-4; 24hr) The big draw at this basic place is that it's always open for business.

Getting There & Away

While Cartago may not be a hotbed of excitement, the surrounding areas provide plenty to do – from botanical gardens, serene mountain towns and organic farms to an active volcano – all easy to reach via local buses and never more than an hour or two away. Most buses arrive along Av 2 and go

WHERE AM I?

Note that most of the maps throughout this book give official street names, but locals rarely use them, preferring the Tico landmark system instead. Read the boxed text 'What's That Address?' (p453) for a full discussion of this testing phenomenon.

as far as the Basílica before returning to the main terminal on Av 4. The following buses serve area destinations.

Finca la Flor de Paraíso Take a La Flor/Birrisito/El Yas bus from in front of Padres Capuchinos church, 150m southeast of Las Ruinas. Get off at the pink church in La Flor; entrance to the finca is 100m to the south.

Paraíso & Lankester Gardens US$0.40; departs from cnr Calle 4 & Av 1 hourly from 7am to 10pm. For the gardens, ask the driver to drop you off at the turnoff – from there, walk 750m to the entrance.

Orosi US$0.50; 40 minutes; departs hourly from cnr Calle 4 & Av 1 from 8am to 10pm Monday to Saturday. The bus will stop in front of the Orosi Mirador.

Parque Nacional Tapantí Catch any bus that continues past Orosi to Purisil. From there it's a 5km walk to the entrance of the park. A cab from Orosi to the park will cost about US$12 one way.

San José US$0.50; 45 minutes; departs every 15 minutes from Av 4 btwn Calles 2 & 4, north of Parque Central.

Turrialba US$1; 1½ hours; departs from Av 3 btwn Calles 8 & 10 (in front of Tribunales de Justicia) every 45 minutes from 6am to 10pm weekdays, 8:30am, 11:30am, 1:30pm, 3pm & 5:45pm weekends.

Volcán Irazú US$4; one hour; departs only on weekends from Padres Capuchinos church, or near Las Ruinas. The bus originates in San José at 8am, stops in Cartago at about 8:30am and returns from Irazú at 12:30pm.

PARQUE NACIONAL VOLCÁN IRAZÚ

Looming quietly, but not too quietly, 19km northeast of Cartago, this is the largest and highest (3432m) active volcano in Costa Rica. Its last major eruption occurred on March 19, 1963, welcoming the visiting US President John F Kennedy with a rain of hot volcanic ash that blanketed San José, Cartago and most of the Central Valley – it piled up to a depth of over 0.5m in places.

The agricultural lands northeast of the volcano were temporarily uninhabitable due to the rocks and boulders that were hurled out of the crater. Not only was the farming economy devastated, but waterways were clogged with ash, which flooded the region intermittently for two years. Since that explosive reminder of where all this rich soil comes from, Volcán Irazú's activity has been limited to one small eruption in 1994; gently simmering fumaroles can be observed up close. Fifteen eruptions have been recorded since 1723, when the governor of Costa Rica, Diego de la Haya Fernández, reported the event. His name is now given to one of the two main craters at the summit.

The national park was established in 1955 to protect 2309 hectares in a roughly circular shape around the volcano. The summit is a bare landscape of volcanic ash and craters. The principal crater is 1050m in diameter and 300m deep, while the Diego de la Haya Crater is 690m in diameter and 100m deep and contains a small lake.

There are two smaller craters, one of which also contains a lake. In addition, there is a pyroclastic cone, formed of rocks fragmented by volcanic activity. A few low plants have begun slowly to recolonize the landscape, and are occupied by high-altitude bird species such as the volcano junco. A 1km trail goes from the parking lot to a lookout over the craters, while the longer, steeper trail leaves from behind the toilets and gets you closer to the craters.

From the summit it is possible to see both the Pacific and the Caribbean, but it is rarely clear enough. The best chance for a clear view is in the very early morning during the dry season (January to April). It tends to be cold, windy and cloudy on the summit, and there's an annual rainfall of 2160mm. Come prepared with warm and rainproof clothes as well as food.

Information

There's a small **information center** (☎ 551 2970; admission to park & center US$7; 🕑 8am-4pm) and basic café, but no accommodations or camping facilities. Note that cloud cover starts thickening, even under the best conditions, by about 10am, about the same time that the weekend bus rolls in. If you're on one of those buses, do yourself a favor and don't dally – head straight for the crater. Folks with cars will be glad that they made the extra effort to arrive early.

Tours

Tours are arranged by a variety of San José operators and cost between US$30 and

US$60 for a half-day tour, or up to US$88 for a full day combined with visits to Lankester Gardens and the Río Orosi valley, plus lunch. Ask at your hotel.

Tours from hotels in Orosi (US$25 to US$40) can also be arranged: these may include lunch and visits to the Basilica in Cartago or sites around the Río Orosi valley.

Getting There & Away

Barring a 20km hike, there are three ways to get here on weekdays: an organized tour; a US$30 taxi from Tierra Blanca, which includes the driver waiting for you at the park for a few hours; or by car. Drivers can take Hwy 8 from Cartago, which begins at the northeast corner of the plaza and continues 19km to the summit.

Frustratingly, the only public transport to Irazú departs San José (US$4.50, 1½ hours) on Saturday and Sunday. It stops in Cartago (US$4, one hour), departing about 8:30am. The bus departs Irazú at 12:30pm.

LANKESTER GARDENS

The University of Costa Rica now runs this exceptional **botanical garden** (☎ 552 3247; jbl@cariari.ucr.ac.cr; admission US$3.50; 🕑 8:30am-4:30pm), once privately grown by British orchid enthusiast Charles Lankester. Orchids are the big draw, with 800 at their showiest from February to April. In addition, lush areas of bromeliads, palms, secondary tropical forest, heliconias and other tropical plants are seen from the paved trails winding through the gardens.

With many plant species labeled and informative plaques throughout the unbelievable grounds, this is a shady introduction to Costa Rica's wealth of flora before you hit the wilder (and unlabeled) national parks. This is also one of the very few places where foreigners can legally purchase orchids to take home. Guided walks through the gardens are offered on the half hour from 8:30am to about 2:30pm daily.

The gardens are 3km east of Cartago on the highway to Paraíso.

FINCA LA FLOR DE PARAÍSO

Get your hands a little dirty at this nonprofit organic farm, operated by ASODECAH (Association for the Development of Environmental and Human Consciousness). Located 7km northeast of Paraíso on the road to El Yas, **Finca La Flor** (☎ 534 8003; www.la-flor-de-paraiso.org; dm with 3 veg meals US$20) offers highly recommended volunteer-work programs that provide hands-on instruction in sustainable agriculture and reforestation. The meals, Tico specialties that are animal-free, are a big draw.

There are hiking trails and Spanish study (US$5 an hour) is available. Its website has more detailed information; advise the finca well before your intended arrival. If there's room, you can stay in the dorms provided for volunteers.

RÍO OROSI VALLEY

This river valley and renowned road trip southeast of Cartago is famous for its resplendent mountainous vistas, colonial churches (one in ruins), hot springs, a lake formed by a hydroelectric facility, and one truly wild national park. Most people visit the valley briefly by taking a tour from San José or in their own cars – the 60km drive is considered one of Costa Rica's best cruises – but many parts are easily accessible by taking a public bus.

The first bustling little town you come to is **Paraíso**, 8km southeast of Cartago, where you can grab lunch at one of several *sodas* (some roadside stands have incredible views). Then choose to either head east to Ujarrás and the lake formed by the Presa de Cachí (Cachí Dam), or south to Orosi (p142).

From Cartago, buses go to both the village of Orosi and the Presa de Cachí. The two paved roads are linked by a gravel road passable to any car, which makes this into a seriously scenic loop. If you are traveling by public bus, however, you'll have to do one leg of the trip and then backtrack in order to do the other.

East of Paraíso

On the way to Ujarrás, you'll first pass a good lookout point for the artificial **Lago de Cachí**. The hydroelectric dam, among the country's largest, is at the northeastern corner of the lake. The Cachí bus will drop you off at the entrance to **Ujarrás**, about 7km east of Paraíso.

Driving, you'll find Ujarrás at the flat bottom of a long, steep hill – a couple of stores with the word 'Ujarrás' tell you that you've arrived. Turn right at a sign for Restaurant La Pipiola to head toward the old village (about 1km), which was damaged by the flood of 1833 and abandoned.

The waters have since receded, revealing the ruins of the 1693 **Iglesia de Nuestra Senora de la Limpia Concepción**, once home to a miraculous painting of the Virgin discovered by a local fisherman. Using similar tactics as La Negrita (see p138), the relic refused to move, forcing area clerics to build the church here. In return, the Virgin helped locals defeat a group of marauding British pirates in 1666. After the floods and a few earthquakes, however, the painting conceded to move to Paraíso, leaving the ruins to deteriorate photogenically in an overgrown park. Every year, usually on the Sunday closest to April 14, there is a procession from Paraíso to the ruins where Mass, food and music help celebrate the day of La Virgen de Ujarrás. The church's grassy grounds are a popular picnicking spot on Sunday afternoons.

About 2km south of the Cachí Dam is the **Casa del Soñador** (Dreamer's House; ☎ 577 1186; admission free; 🕑 8am-6pm), a whimsical house designed and built by renowned Tico carver Macedonio Quesada. Every detail of the construction, built largely of coffee branches and bamboo, is elaborately chiseled to divine effect. Quesada's sons, who have managed the workshop since Macedonio's death in 1995, continue the family woodworking tradition, and carvings of local *campesinos,* religious figures and other characters, some life-size, are on display. Some are available for sale. A taxi from Orosi costs about US$7.

At **La Casona del Cafetal Restaurant** (☎ 533 3280; mains US$5-15; 🕑 11am-6pm), about 3km southeast of the dam, you can enjoy a really fresh cup of coffee (or a recommended meal) while watching the next batch being picked (November to March). It's popular on Sunday, when families with kids go for short horseback or horse-drawn cart rides, also available here.

Paraíso to Orosi

Mirador Orosi, a few kilometers down the road to Orosi, is the official scenic overlook, with toilets, a parking lot and lots of photo opportunities. There are a couple of places to stay along the way.

Sleeping & Eating

Cabañas de Montaña Piedras Albas (☎ 577 1462; www.cabinas.co.cr/costa_rica1.htm; s/d US$47/55; Ⓟ) Follow the signed turnoff past La Casona to these well-equipped cabins, where you can pretend you're roughing it on the private trails, then relax in front of the cable TV, fix some dinner in the kitchen and perhaps arrange a tour at the desk.

Mirador Sanchirí (☎ 533 3210; www.sanchiri.com; d incl breakfast US$48; Ⓟ 💻) About 2km south of Paraíso, this is more than just a nice collection of rather dark wooden cabins in paradise: this is a full-blown tourist center, with an incredible view of the Río Orosi Valley, **butterfly garden** (adult/child US$5/3), good restaurant and picnic area. You can also rent horses or just explore the trails on foot.

OROSI

This town was named for a Huetar Indian chief who lived here at the time of the conquest. Spanish colonists quickly became enamored of the town's wealth of water, from lazy hot springs to bracing waterfalls, perfect climate and rich soil. So they decided to take property off the original Orosi's hands.

This is one of the few colonial towns to survive Costa Rica's frequent earthquakes, which have left the 1743 **Iglesia de San José Orosi** the oldest church still in use in Costa Rica; the carved wooden altar is certainly worth a look. It's on the west side of town. Adjacent to the church is a small **museum** (☎ 533 3051; 🕑 9am-noon & 2-5pm Tue-Fri, 9am-5pm Sat-Sun; adult/child US$1/0.25) with some interesting examples of Spanish colonial religious art and artifacts.

And while the attractive town (population 9000) has thus far managed to avoid the more rattling aspects of living in a volcanic region, it's got two big perks: **Los Balnearios** (☎ 533 2156; admission US$1.25; 🕑 7:30am-4pm), on the southwest side of town next to the Orosi Lodge, is the closest thermal bath to town; the other, **Los Patios** (☎ 533 3009; admission US$1.60; 🕑 8am-4pm), about 1.5km south of town, is a bit less convenient but offers a few more pools. Both claim to have the hottest water, but they're about the same temperature: warm, but not super hot.

Information

Oficina de Información Turística, (OIT; ☎ 533 3825; 2 blocks south of the park; 🕑 9am-4pm Mon-Sat) can arrange tours to area attractions, make lodging and transport reservations, and rent mountain bikes (US$7.50 per day). Both the

Montaña Linda hostel and Orosi Lodge (see below) provide similar services, as do most major tour companies based in San José (p72). **Minae** (☎ 533 3082; ⏰ 8am-4pm Mon-Fri) hopes to eventually offer maps and other information about area parks. **PC Orosi** (☎ 533 3302; per hour US$1.25; ⏰ 8am-7pm) has a fast Internet connection.

Sleeping

Montaña Linda (☎ 533 3640; www.montanalinda.com; dm US$5.50, s/d US$8/12, camping per person US$3.50; P 💻) Two blocks south and three blocks west of the bus stop, by the soccer field, this is a great budget option, with a festive hostel environment, hot showers and kitchen privileges (US$1) or excellent cheap home-cooked meals (US$1 to US$3). Accommodations are in dorms, but there are a few doubles for couples. The owners also organize a variety of outings to surrounding volcanoes and hot springs for the traveler on a budget, as well as a great deal on Spanish lessons (see p122). Ask about guided walks (US$10), camping and overnight stays at private **Monte Sky Reserve** (per person including meals US$25).

Media Libra Cabinas (☎ 533 3838; s/d US$23/34; P) Clean, modern rooms sleeping three are two blocks west of the OIT, close to town, and come with a nice collection of creature comforts: cable TV, hot water shower, fridge and phone.

Orosi Lodge (☎ 533 3578; www.orosilodge.com; s/d US$40/53; P) This small, comfortable hotel has nice rooms with excellent views of Orosi and volcanoes beyond. Rooms include a private hot shower, a wet bar with minifridge and coffeemaker, and a shared balcony or patio. A small garden separates the rooms from the reception area in the highly recommended **Cafetería Orosi** (mains US$4-8; ⏰ 7am-7pm) where guests have Internet access. Los Balnearios hot springs is just a few steps away.

Getting There & Away

All buses stop about three blocks west of the football (soccer) field; ask locally about specific destinations. Buses from Cartago (US$0.50, 40 minutes) depart Calle 6, between Avenidas 1 and 3, close to the church, hourly.

Cachí Dam & Ruinas US$0.25; 20 minutes; departs every 30 minutes from 6am to 9pm.

Cartago US$0.50; 40 minutes; departs every 45 minutes from 5am to 9pm.

SOUTH OF OROSI

The Orosi bus usually continues about 4km south of Orosi, through the villages of **Río Macho** and **Palomo**. Río Macho has a power plant on the river of that name, and there is good fishing here.

Parque Purisil

Anglers have already been eyeing the area's crystal-clear collection of sparkling streams hopefully – and yes, they are indeed full of tasty trout. If you can't take the temptation any longer, head about 10km southeast of Orosi, en route to Parque Nacional Tapantí-Macizo Cerro de la Muerte, to a **park** (☎ 228 6630; adult/child with fishing gear US$5/2; ⏰ 8am-5pm) that was made just for you. Happily, designers and Mother Nature conspired to include other attractions – several short trails, a waterfall and swimming hole, plus lots of wildlife, including the occasional quetzal – allowing you to convince nonfishing members of your group to satisfy your addiction. After the onsite **restaurant** (mains US$4-10; ⏰ 10am-4pm) prepares your catch to order, they'll be glad they came along. There's not yet any bus service, and a taxi costs about US$7 each way.

Sleeping & Eating

Hotel Río Palomo (☎ 533 3128; d standard/with kitchen US$21/26; P) Close to the *balneario*, this quiet lodge near Palomo has pleasantly rustic cabins with private hot showers, a big swimming pool and access to a trout stream – the onsite restaurant can cook your catch.

Kiri Lodge (☎ 592 0638; s/d incl breakfast US$32/43) About 3km beyond Purisil, this is the closest lodging to Parque Nacional Tapantí (see below). It sits on 50 mossy hectares with free trails behind the property leading into the Río Macho Forest Preserve, adjacent to the park and inhabited by much of the same wildlife. Six simple cabins have hot showers, there's a trout-fishing pond (per kilo US$6) and a **restaurant** (mains US$3-6; ⏰ 7am-9pm) specializing in…trout.

PARQUE NACIONAL TAPANTÍ-MACIZO CERRO DE LA MUERTE

The **park** (admission US$6; ⏰ 6am-4pm), with the unwieldy name and a rainy claim to fame – this is the wettest park in the system – was greatly expanded in 2000 and now covers 583 sq km. The main entrance is a few kilometers south of Orosi.

The park protects the wild and mossy country on the rain forested slopes of the Cordillera de Talamanca, drained by literally hundreds of rivers. Waterfalls abound, vegetation is thick and the wildlife is prolific, though not easy to see because the terrain is rugged and the trails are few. Rainfall is reportedly about 2700mm in the lower sections but reaches more than 7000mm in some of the highest parts of the park – pack an umbrella. Nevertheless, Tapantí (as it remains locally known) is a popular destination for dedicated birders, and it opens at 6am to accommodate them.

Quetzals are said to nest on the western slopes of the valley, where the park information center is located. More than 200 other bird species have been recorded, including eagles and hummingbirds, parrots and toucans, and difficult-to-see forest-floor inhabitants such as tinamous and antbirds. A number of reptiles and warm-blooded critters have also been sighted.

There are three signed trails leading from the information center, the longest a steep 4km round trip, while a well-graded dirt road runs through a northern section of the park and is quite popular with mountain bikers.

Information

There is an **information center** (6am-4pm) near the park entrance and a couple of trails leading to various attractions, including a picnic area, a swimming hole and a lookout with great views of a waterfall. Fishing is allowed in season (from April to October; permit required), but the 'dry' season (from January to April) is generally considered the best time to visit. Camping is not permitted.

Several tour companies in San José do day trips. Some of the best are with bilingual naturalist guides from Costa Rica Expeditions or Horizontes (see p474). Cheaper tours are available in Orosi; see p142.

Getting There & Away

If you have your own car, you can take a good gravel road passable to all cars from Orosi through Río Macho and Purisil to the park entrance.

Buses are a bit trickier. From Cartago, take a Paraíso bus and switch there for a bus to Orosi. For Tapantí, catch any bus from Cartago to Purisil. From there, it's a 5km walk to the entrance. A **cab** (☎ 771 5116, 551 2797) from Orosi to the park will cost about US$12 one way.

TURRIALBA AREA

TURRIALBA

Along the otherwise impassable Caribbean slope of the Cordillera Central, at an elevation of 650m above sea level, the Río Turrialba, which flows into the Reventazón, has gouged a pass in the mountain. In the 1880s it allowed the Jungle Train between San José and Puerto Limón to roll through. Later, the first highway between the cities used the same hydrogeological quirk to unite the country. Turrialba thrived.

After the 1991 earthquake shut down the nation's rail system, however, and the construction of the smooth, straight (boring) stretch of Hwy 32 that shortened drive-time between the capital and the Caribbean by precious hours, Turrialba (population 72,400) found itself suddenly off the beaten path. No one wanted to move away – it's gorgeous here – so folks fell back on coffee production, of course, and oddball industries such as baseball manufacturing. San Francisco Giants fans should know that the instrument of Barry Bonds' 73rd home run was born right here.

But by the late 1980s, white-water rafters from all over the world were already whispering about Turrialba, an undiscovered mountain stronghold with access to some of the best white-water rafting on the planet. A cottage river-running industry sprang up in the hills, and by the time the ICE, the national power company, began making good on plans to dam the scenic waterways, the town united with conservation groups to fight (see p150): so far, it looks like they're winning. Fair enough – Turrialba has sacrificed enough to the bulldozers of progress.

The pleasant town also makes a good, low-key base for several nearby excursions, including the archaeological site at Guayabo (p148) and climbing Volcán Turrialba (p148). And the old highway, scenic still, links San José to the sea through mountain and valley, a perfect trip into rural Costa Rica that you just can't get along the beaten path.

ERIC L WHEATER

Milkman pushing his cart, San José (p65)

STEPHEN SAKS

Alfresco dining, San José

Women processing bananas, San José (p65)

ULRIKE WELSCH

ROB RACHOWIECKI

Los Jardines Catarata de La Paz (p131), Parque Nacional Volcán Poás

TOM BOYDEN

Active crater, Parque Nacional Volcán Poás (p129)

TOM BOYD

Tropical rain forest, Los Jardines Catarata de La Paz (p131)

Volcán Irazú's huge crater, Parque Nacional Volcán Irazú (p140)

ALFREDO MAIQU

Information

There's no official tourist office, but better hotels and most white-water rafting outfits can organize tours, accommodations and transportation throughout the region. There are several banks with 24-hour ATMs, and you can check your email at **Café Internet** (per hour US$1; 9am-9pm), one block southwest of Parque Central.

White-water Rafting

Sure, Turrialba's a cute town with strollable streets, stunning scenery and the only volcano in Costa Rica with crater access, but that's not why you're here, is it? This is the unofficial White-water Capital of Costa Rica, close to the famously sublime scenery of Río Pacuare (p151) and the superb challenges and sunny floats of Río Reventazón (p149), arguably the two finest white-water experiences in Costa Rica.

Dozens of operators, both in Turrialba and throughout the country, arrange a variety of trips down both rivers in rafts or kayaks. Children must be at least nine years old for most trips, older for tougher runs. There's a friendly competition among tour operators over who serves the best picnic lunch, which only benefits you.

Day trips usually raft the Class III-IV Lower Pacuare or Class III Flamingo segment of Río Reventazón, both boasting easy-access put-ins that reduce your travel time. These leave San José, Puerto Viejo de Limón, La Fortuna and other destinations at around 6am, returning late afternoon, with almost two hours of drive time in either direction. Exploradores Outdoors (see p413) will transport you between cities free of charge, but ask other operators as well. Prices range from US$80 to US$110, depending on transportation (it's usually about US$15 cheaper from Turrialba) and what you're getting for lunch.

There are other runs, however, including the less accessible (and less crowded) Upper Pacuare and Pascua segment of Reventazón, which folks willing to spend more time in a car will find rewarding. These should be arranged in advance. Most operators also offer rafting on other area rivers, including Río Sarapiquí (p439), the Class IV Río Chirripó, white-water-free Río Pejibaye, and others.

Two-day trips are offered by almost every operator, usually including a very comfortable campsite or a fairly plush lodge, optional guided hikes and those borderline gourmet meals. Prices vary widely depending on amenities, but expect to pay around US$170 to US$300 per person. Unless you want to spend two very short days on the water, make sure the operator puts in well above the day trippers.

Most larger agencies in San José (see p473) offer these trips, including Costa Rica Expeditions, Horizontes, Aventuras Naturales and Ríos Tropicales, which operates a foundation to stop the Siquirres Hydroelectric Project (see p150). Exploradores Outdoors has operations in San José and Puerto Viejo de Talamanca (see p413).

There are also quite a few operations based in Turrialba:

Costa Rica Ríos Aventuras (☎ 556 9617; 25m north of evangelical church; www.costaricarios.com) A small and recommended outfitter that can customize lessons and trips all over the country, and also offers kayak and mountain-bike excursions.

Jungla Expeditions (☎ 556 2639; www.junglaexpeditions.com) Provides a broad range of adventure services including canyoning down waterfalls, kayak lessons and combo hiking-biking-rafting custom trips.

Loco's (☎ 556 6035) An independent company that prefers to work with small groups, and also offers guided hikes and horseback tours around Volcán Turrialba.

Rain Forest World (☎ 556 2678; in the USA 888-513 2808; www.rforestw.com/welcome2.cfm) In addition to the standard tours, offers an overnight in the Cabecar Indigenous reserve while running the river, as well as horseback trips into area national parks and volcano snorkeling trips. Yep, you snorkel in a volcano.

Tico's River Adventures (☎ 556 1231; www.ticoriver.com) In addition to all the Pacuare and Reventazón tours, offers a trip down the Class IV Río Chirripó from June through November.

Sleeping

Whittingham's Hotel (☎ 550 8927; Calle 4 btwn Avs 2 & Central; d without/with bathroom US$7/10) Seasoned budget travelers won't mind the cool, clean (just like the showers) and cavernous rooms, all of which have private sinks and fans.

Hotel La Roche (☎ 556 7915; Calle 4 btwn Avs 2 & Central; d US$9; P) Though a bit frayed around the edges, brightly painted rooms surrounding a private courtyard are quite cheerful, and the upstairs rooms have nice balconies.

Hotel Interamericano (☎ 556 0142; www.hotelinteramericano.com; Av 1; s US$10, s/d with bathroom US$24/36; P) On the south side of the

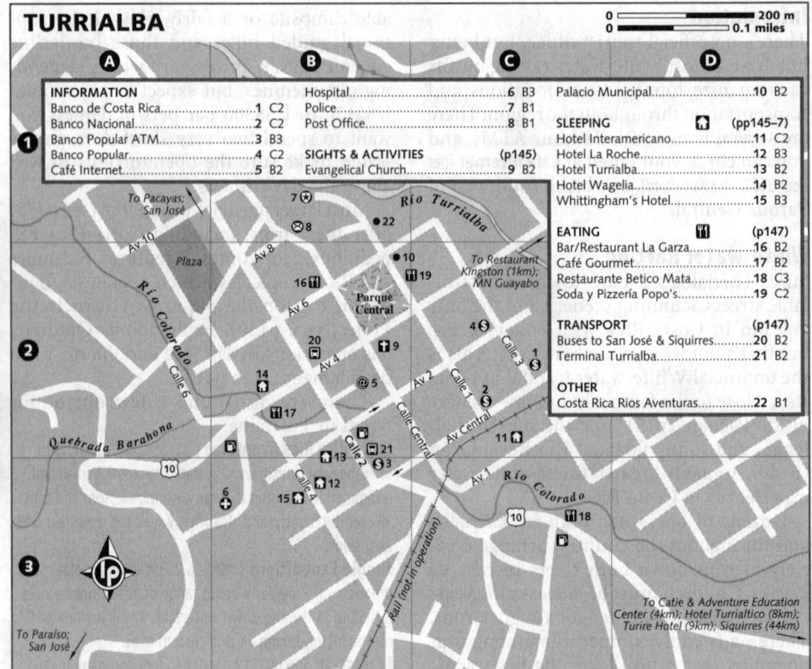

old railroad tracks is a good budget option, and breakfast is available for another US$3. Rooms with big windows, some sleeping four, are clean, as are the shared bathrooms with hot water; laundry service and luggage storage are both available. There is a nightclub nearby so bring earplugs – especially on karaoke night.

Hotel Turrialba (☎ 556 6654; Av 2 btwn Calles 2 & 4; s/d US$13/18; Ⓟ) Small rooms with warm wooden accents have cable TV, fan and private hot-water bathroom. The onsite restaurant is recommended, and there's a lounge with a pool table.

Hotel Wagelia (☎ 556 1566; Av 4 btwn Calles 2 & 4; www.hotelwagelia.com; s/d incl breakfast US$62/78; Ⓟ ❄) Folks looking for a bit more luxury in town will be pleased to find this fine spot, set in a landscaped garden with lots of amenities. Pretty rooms come with air-con, so you can actually enjoy the private hot-water shower, plus phone, big TV and a pleasant sitting area.

There are several small but pleasant country hotels to be found several kilometers east of Turrialba:

Hotel Turrialtico (☎ 538 1111; www.turrialtico.com; s/d incl breakfast US$52/63) An excellent option for either lodging or dinner (see opposite), this lovely, if not extravagant, lodge has been run by the García family since 1968. It's about 8km from town on the road to Siquirres and Limón, making it a fine midway stop for road-trippers plying the old highway to the Caribbean. There are 14 rustic rooms, all with great views, in a nice old building with wooden floors. Outside there's a tiny kids playground. The staff arranges river-running trips, among other things.

Pochotel (☎ 538 1010; s/d incl breakfast US$55/65) About 11km from Turrialba, also on the road to Siquirres, this is a favorite of local river guides. The hotel is above the village of Pavones, and there is a sign for it in the village. A very steep 1.5km dirt road reaches the hotel, which has great views: a lookout tower takes in Irazú and Turrialba volcanoes above (weather permitting) and a newly dammed lake below, plus a small playground for kids. The 10 rooms have hot electric showers; some have tubs and clock radios. Reservations are recommended.

Casa Turire Hotel (☎ 531 1111; www.hotelcasaturire.com; d US$148, ste US$165-280) More upscale than neighboring Turrialtico, this elegant three-story mansion features wide, shady verandahs and is set in well-landscaped grounds with sugarcane, coffee and macadamia nut plantations nearby. There is a swimming pool, tennis court and a game room with a pool table. Children under 16 years old are not accepted. The spacious rooms, most with private balcony, have hot water, phone and cable TV, and four suites have a refrigerator and king-size bed. The most expensive suite has two floors, a balcony that takes up the whole side of the building, and a spa. Horse and mountain-bike rental and guided walks in the rain forest or plantations are available. This is about as nice as hotels get in Costa Rica.

Eating

There are several *sodas,* Chinese restaurants, bakeries and grocery stores in town.

Café Gourmet (☎ 556 9689; cnr Calle 4 & Av 4; snacks US$1-3; 🕑 7am-7pm Mon-Sat) This cute little café sells Turrialba's best coffee done up as dozens of different beverages, plus light meals and excellent pastries.

Restaurante Betico Mata (☎ 556 8640; Hwy 10; US$1-3; 🕑 11am-midnight) At the south end of town, this clean and well-known hole-in-the-wall is a great place to hang out in the evenings. Carnivores will go crazy over excellent *carne asada* (grilled steak), tacos and ice cold beer.

Soda y Pizzería Popo's (☎ 556 0064; Calle 1 btwn Avs 4 & 6; daily specials US$2; 🕑 11am-11pm) This *soda* not only packs the small dining area with quality Tico, Mexican and Italian grub, but it also delivers!

Bar/Restaurant La Garza (Cnr Av 6 & Calle Central; mains US$3-6; 🕑 10am-10pm) This venerable eatery has been serving good seafood, chicken and other meat dishes to happy customers for years.

Restaurant Kingston (☎ 556 1613; mains US$3-10) On the outskirts of town on the road to Puerto Limón, this restaurant has long had a good reputation in Turrialba and has meals mostly at the higher end of the price range. The locally well-known chef is Jamaican trained.

Hotel Turrialtico (☎ 556 1111; mains US$4-10; 🕑 7am-9pm) Great views come with excellent food and a dining room showing off the García family's woodworking prowess; try the fresh trout.

Getting There & Away

The main **bus terminal** (Av 4) is 100m west of Parque Central. Buses from San José (US$1.80, 1¾ hours) depart Calle 13 between Avenidas 6 and 8 on an hourly basis from 8am to 8pm. **Terminal Turrialba** (cnr Av 2 & Calle 2) serves nearby villages, with several buses daily to La Suiza, Tuis, Santa Cruz and other little towns. Buses to Monumento Nacional Guayabo give you about two hours to enjoy the ruins before making the return run.

Monumento Nacional Guayabo US$0.50; one hour; departs from cnr Av 2 & Calle 2 at 11am & 5:15pm Mon-Sat, 9am Sun.

San José US$1.80; 1¾ hours; departs from Av 4 almost hourly from 5am to 9pm.

Siquirres, for transfer to Puerto Limón US$1.25; 1¾ hours; departs from Av 4 every two hours.

AROUND TURRIALBA

Centro Agronómico Tropical de Investigación y Enseñanza (Catie; Center for Tropical Agronomy Research & Education; ☎ 556 6431; www.catie.ac.cr; admission free; 🕑 7am-4pm), about 4km east of Turrialba and known throughout Costa Rica by its acronym of Catie (which is just as well), is comprised of about 1000 hectares dedicated to tropical agricultural research and education. Agronomists from all over the world recognize this as one of the most important agricultural stations in the tropics.

You need to make reservations for a guided tour of the various agricultural projects, including one of the most extensive libraries of tropical agricultural literature anywhere in the world, laboratories, greenhouses, a dairy, an herbarium, a seed bank and experimental plots. Or you can simply take a sedate stroll through the gardens or visit the central pond, where waterbirds such as the purple gallinule are a specialty. Another good birding area is the short but steep trail descending from behind the administration building to the Río Reventazón.

Pick up a map at the main building for a free self-guided tour. You can walk or get a taxi (US$2) from Turrialba.

About 10km east of Turrialba, in the village of Pavones (500m east of the cemetery) is **Parque Viborana** (☎ 538 1510), known for its serpentarium. Here you can see a variety of

CENTRAL VALLEY & HIGHLANDS

Costa Rican snakes, including some unusual albino specimens and several boas, one of which weighs as much as a good-size person. The serpentarium has a rustic visitors area with educational exhibits. Stop by if you're driving east of Turrialba.

MONUMENTO NACIONAL ARQUEOLÓGICO GUAYABO

Guayabo lies 19km northeast of Turrialba and contains the largest and most important archaeological site in the country. Although interesting, it's not as flashy as Mayan and Aztec archaeological sites – don't expect pyramids. Nevertheless, excavations have unearthed some sophisticated infrastructure, as well as mysterious petroglyphs that interested visitors can examine. Polychromatic pottery and gold artifacts found here are also exhibited at the Museo Nacional in San José (see p77).

The aqueduct system, which may have served more than 10,000 people in AD 800, the height of the city's prominence, is particularly impressive. It uses enormous stones hauled in from far-off Río Reventazón along an 8km road that's still in pretty good shape, by Costa Rican standards. The extra effort was worth it – the cisterns still work, and (theoretically) potable water remains available onsite, which you can enjoy among various unearthed structures and unexcavated but suspicious-looking mounds.

The site, which may have been occupied as early as 1000 BC, was mysteriously abandoned by AD 1400: the Spanish conquistadors, explorers and settlers left no record of having found the ruins. Though underfunded archaeologists as yet can only toss about hypotheses about Guayabo's significance or the circumstances surrounding what appears to have been a mass exodus, most believe it was an important cultural, religious and political center.

In 1968 Carlos Aguilar Piedra, an archaeologist with the University of Costa Rica, began the first systematic excavations at the site. As its importance became evident, it was obviously necessary to protect it. The site became a national monument in 1973, with further protection decreed in 1980.

The monument is small, some 232 hectares, and most of these ruins are yet to be excavated. The remaining 90% of the area is premontane rain forest. The monument is important because it protects some of the last remaining rain forest of this type in the province of Cartago. However, because of its small area, there aren't many animals to be seen. The few that do live in this rain forest, though, are interesting.

Particularly noteworthy among the avifauna are the oropendolas, which colonize the monument by building sacklike nests in the trees. Other birds include toucans and brown jays – the latter are unique among jays in that they have a small, inflatable sac in the chest, which causes the popping sound that is heard at the beginning of their loud and raucous calls. Mammals including squirrels, armadillos and coatis can also be seen.

Information

There's an information and **exhibit center** (☎ 559 0099; www.minae.go.cr/accvc/guayabo.htm, in Spanish; admission US$7; 🕑 8am-3pm), but many of the best pieces are on display at the Museo Nacional in San José (p77). The archaeological site is worked on during the week, and sections may be closed to visitors. Guided tours are not currently available, but it's worth asking around in Turrialba or at the ranger station about independent local guides.

Camping (per person US$2) is permitted, and services include latrines and running water. Keep in mind that the average annual rainfall is about 3500mm; the best time to go is during the January to April dry season, though it might still rain.

Getting There & Away

The last 3km of the drive to the monument may be passable to normal cars, if it's dry and you're careful. As always, your life will be made much easier with a 4WD. Buses from Turrialba (US$0.50, one hour) depart from the corner of Avenida 2 and Calle 2 at 11am, 3:15pm and 5:15pm Monday through Saturday, and at 9am Sunday. Buses return at 12:45pm and 4pm. Buses and most taxis (about US$10 one way from Turrialba) drop you at the turnoff to the park, from where it's a 4km hike.

PARQUE NACIONAL VOLCÁN TURRIALBA

This rarely visited national park highlights an active volcano (3328m) that is actually part of the Irazú volcanic massif, but it is more remote and difficult to get to than Irazú. The name of the volcano was coined by early Spanish settlers, who named it Torre Alba (white tower) for the plumes of smoke pouring from its summit in early colonial days. The volcano is only about 15km northwest of Turrialba as the crow flies, but more than twice as far by car then foot.

The last eruption was in 1866, which means the crater is considered safe enough to explore – a unique opportunity in Costa Rica. The summit has three craters, of which the middle one is the largest. This is the only one that still shows signs of activity with fumaroles of steam and sulfur. From the rim there are views of Volcáns Irazú, Poás and Barva, weather permitting. Below the summit is a montane rain and cloud forest, dripping with moisture and mosses, full of ferns, bromeliads and even stands of bamboo. The average temperature up here is only about 15°C, so dress accordingly.

At time of writing, there was neither ranger station nor admission fee, but this may change. There is a picnic table and a trail part of the way around the crater. Volcán Turrialba Lodge (see below) arranges a variety of guided hikes and horseback rides through the park.

Sleeping

Volcán Turrialba Lodge (☎ 273 4335; www.volcanturrialbalodge.com; per person with 3 meals US$45; Ⓟ), about 14km northwest of Santa Cruz, is accessible by 4WD only. You can get directions or arrange a shuttle from San José or other nearby towns when you make your reservation. Perched between the Turrialba and Irazú volcanoes, great views and comfortable rooms are augmented by interesting, well-guided hikes and horseback rides (this is a working cattle ranch) to Volcán Turrialba. There are several package deals. Friendly owner Tony Lachner speaks English. The rustic hotel has a blazing wood stove in the bar-restaurant and sitting room, with TV and board games. The cozy rooms have electric heaters; some have wood stoves. Excellent food is served buffet-style and tends toward Tico with an international flair. It definitely gets cold and wet up here, but the place is recommended for travelers looking for some cool highland adventure. Quetzals nest on the property from February to April.

Getting There & Away

To climb Turrialba, take a bus to Santa Cruz, from where an 18km road climbs to the summit. The road is paved for the first 10km, then becomes increasingly rough and a 4WD is necessary to reach the summit. (You can get a 4WD taxi from Santa Cruz for about US$20 each way; you can arrange for the taxi to wait or pick you up later.) There are signs along the way, and this is the official route into the national park.

Another approach is to take a bus from Cartago to the village of San Gerardo on the southern slopes of Volcán Irazú. From here a rough road continues to Volcán Turrialba – it's further than from Santa Cruz, but San Gerardo, at 2400m, is a higher starting point than Santa Cruz is at 1500m. The rough road goes about 25km, then there are a few kilometers of walking, but this route is unsigned.

RANCHO NATURALISTA

This 48-hectare **ranch** (☎ 297 4134; www.ranchonaturalista.com; 7-day package per person with 3 meals US$840-1200; Ⓟ 💻) is about 20km southeast of Turrialba, just past the village of Tuis (4WD needed). The Spanish-style five-bedroom lodge and six duplex cottages are popular with naturalists. The North American owners are avid birders who have recorded over 400 species of birds in the area – over 200 species have been recorded from their balcony alone. Hundreds of species of butterflies can be found on the grounds as well. The ranch lies at 900m above sea level in montane rain and wet forest and there is a trail system.

Prices include three home-cooked meals a day and a variety of tours that range from guided birding trips and horseback riding on the low end to plush overnight adventures in Parque Nacional Tortuguero.

RÍO REVENTAZÓN

From the northeast end of Lago de Cachí flows one of the top white-water rafting destinations in Costa Rica, Río Reventazón. It has one of the most difficult runs in the country, though with more than 65km of rapids to choose from, you can choose your challenge. The Presa de Cachí across the Río Reventazón created the artificial lake Lago de Cachí, from which the river

DAMMING THE RIVERS?

Considered one the most beautiful white-water rafting trips in the world, in 1985 the wild Río Pacuare became the first federally protected river in Central America. Two years later, Instituto Costarricense de Electricidad (ICE), Costa Rica's national energy and communications provider, unveiled plans to build a 200m gravity dam at the conveniently narrow and screamingly scenic ravine of Dos Montañs.

This dam would be the cornerstone of the massive Siquirres Hydroelectric Project, proposed to include four dams in total, linked by a 10km-long tunnel that will divert water from the Río Reventazón to the Río Pacuare. If built, rising waters on the Pacuare would not only flood 12km of rapids, up to the Tres Equis put-in, but also parts of the Awari Indigenous Reserve and a huge swath of primary rain forest where some 800 animal species have been recorded.

When the project was first proposed, ICE was in debt and struggling to keep up with rapidly increasing power demands (tourists, after all, must have their air-conditioning). Costa Rica uses fossil fuels only for vehicles: all other power is generated using renewable resources, including geothermal, solar and wind energy, with a whopping 81% of its power produced by a dozen hydroelectric dams. Technically this is a renewable resource; in practice, dams not only interrupt rivers and wash away ecosystems, they have long-term impacts not completely understood.

As the project moved from speculation toward construction, a loose coalition of local landowners, indigenous leaders, conservation groups and, yep, white-water rafting outfits were already organizing a resistance movement. They filed for the first Environmental Impact Assessment (EIA) in history, an independent audit of such projects that the Central American Commission for Environment and Development first proposed in 1989. The paper-shuffling didn't come to much legally, but it stalled the dam's construction and earned the Río Pacuare's plight international attention.

Today Costa Rica is a net exporter of electricity (not including oil), primarily to Panama and Nicaragua. Because of new geothermal plants built since the dam was proposed, as well as coordinated national efforts to reduce electrical usage, the dam is not currently needed. For now.

Plans for the project have not been abandoned, not by a long shot. Siquirres would be relatively easy to build, and could generate a tremendous amount of income and electricity in a country modernizing more rapidly than most. Pressure from international conservation groups is holding ICE at bay, while growth in white-water rafting has helped the Pacuare prove its worth on a spreadsheet somewhere in San José, protecting it for another day.

The neighboring Río Reventazón, however, has not been so lucky: the (in)famous Class V Peralta section has already lost one-third of its Class V rapids to the first phase of the Siquirres Project. Don't put your white-water rafting trip off until the next time you make it down to Costa Rica.

now tumbles, starting at 1000m above sea level and running down the eastern slopes of the mountains to the Caribbean lowlands. It is a favorite river of rafters and kayakers.

Water levels stay fairly constant year-round because of releases from the dam. Note that there are no water releases from the dam on Sunday and, although the river is runnable, this is considered the worst day. Minimum age for rafters is usually nine.

Tour operators divide into four sections between the dam and take-out, below Siquirres. **Power House** (Las Máquinas) is a Class II-III float that's perfect for families, while **Florida**, the final and most popular segment, is a scenic Class III with a little more white water to keep things interesting. For information on Siquirres, see p383.

The **Pascua** section, with 15 Class IV rapids featuring names like 'The Abyss,' is considered the classic run, with huge waves and volcano views. The Class V **Peralta** segment is the most challenging white water in the country, and is most definitely not for beginners.

Single-day and multiday river trips are offered by several agencies in San José, with day trips costing between US$88 and US$100 per person, including lunch and transportation, or you can arrange the same trips for a bit less in Turrialba, closer to the put-in.

RÍO PACUARE

The Río Pacuare is the next major river valley east of the Reventazón, and offers arguably the most scenic rafting river in Costa Rica, if not Central America. The river plunges down the Caribbean slope through a series of spectacular canyons clothed in virgin rain forest, through runs named for their fury and separated by calm stretches that enable you to stare at the near-vertical green walls towering hundreds of meters above the river – a magnificent and unique river trip.

The Pacuare can be run year-round, though June to October are considered the best months. The highest water is from October to December, when the river runs fast with huge waves. In March and April the river is at its lowest and, though waves aren't as big, the river is still very rocky and challenging.

The Class III-IV **Lower Pacuare** is the more famous and more accessible run: 28km through rocky gorges and isolated canyons, past an indigenous village, untamed jungle and lots of wildlife curious as to what the screaming is all about. The run usually costs between US$85 and US$100 per person, depending on transportation.

The **Upper Pacuare** is also classified as Class III-IV, but there are a few sections that can go Class V depending on conditions. You'll need to drive two hours to the put-in. Some operators charge by the boat (US$500 for six people), which means you'll either need to wait around for a group or form your own. It's worth it – you'll have the prettiest jungle cruise on earth all to yourself.

Northwestern Costa Rica

CONTENTS

NORTHWESTERN COSTA RICA

With an unrivalled collection of national parks and wilderness areas, awash in hot springs and waterfalls, cloud forests of quetzals and endless savannah that explodes into raucous color come rainfall, there is no end to this region's gifts.

From the Interamericana's efficient blaze through the Northwest's most important towns, Cañas and Liberia, then north to the border with Nicaragua, turnoffs of earth and gravel wind from ranch land up the fertile slopes of myriad volcanoes, where Martian landscapes of bubbling fumaroles and lavishly landscaped commercial hot springs await.

The Cordillera de Guanacaste, which together with the Cordillera de Tilarán forms the region's backbone, is a spectacular string of dormant or gently active volcanoes. Volcán Arenal, spewing lava almost nightly since 1968, is the unabashed star of the show, tempting visitors to its shifting slopes with the promise of unforgettable fireworks and the charms of La Fortuna below. Across sparkling Lake Arenal, luxuriating at its base, the impossibly lovely Monteverde–Santa Elena ecoplex of organic farms, unusual and generally recyclable attractions and untouched cloud forest are another world entirely.

To the west of the mountains lies the Península Santa Elena, a rare remaining thatch of dry tropical forest that surrounds those who make the isolated descent to beautiful Bahía Salinas and the outstanding and historic Parque Nacional Santa Rosa, with its beach to end all beaches. And folded elsewhere into this dramatic landscape are wilder places, made remote by lousy public transportation along rough roads where even 4WD cars are tested.

HIGHLIGHTS

- Taking a hike up **Rincón de la Vieja** (p190), one of the few active volcanoes safe to climb
- Soaking your sore muscles afterward in one of the mild to wild hot springs welling up from the slopes of **Volcán Miravalles** (p182)
- Watching wildlife on empty shores or in the dry forest, and riding wicked waves at Witch's Rock at unequalled **Santa Rosa** (p193)
- Windsurfing – or kitesurfing! – **Laguna de Arenal** (p218) and **Bahía Salinas** (p197), shimmering beneath some of the world's best wind
- Braving the mud and mists of **Monteverde** (p174) and **Santa Elena** (p177) reserves in search of a cloud forest of ecodreamers and quetzals

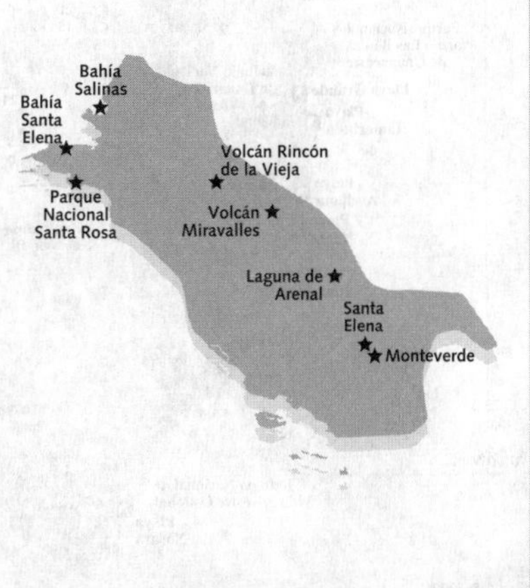

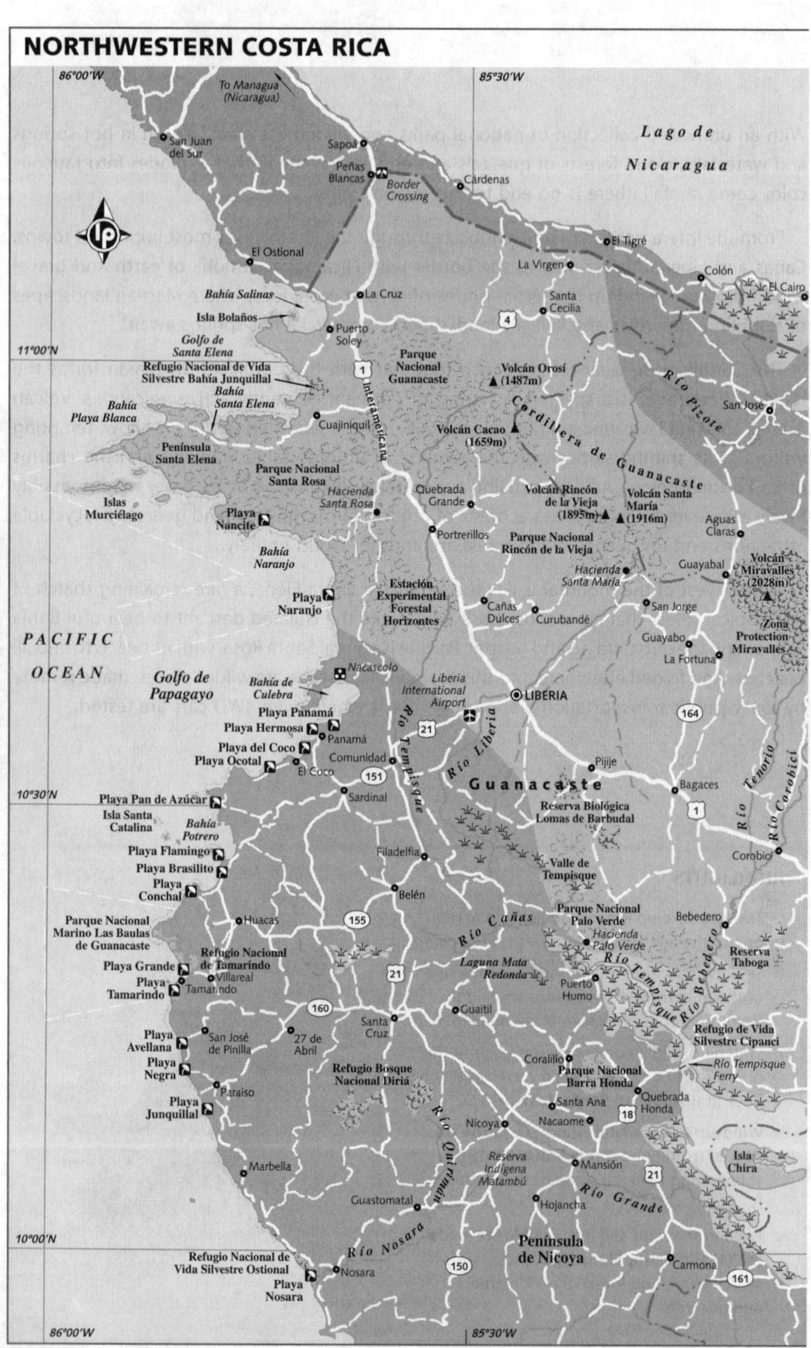
NORTHWESTERN COSTA RICA
Lago de Nicaragua
PACIFIC OCEAN
Golfo de Papagayo
Golfo de Santa Elena
Bahía Salinas
Isla Bolaños
San Juan del Sur
Sapoá
Peñas Blancas
Border Crossing
Cárdenas
El Ostional
La Cruz
Puerto Soley
La Virgen
El Tigré
Colón
El Cairo
Santa Cecilia
Parque Nacional Guanacaste
Volcán Orosí (1487m)
Volcán Cacao (1659m)
Cordillera de Guanacaste
Río Pizote
San José
Refugio Nacional de Vida Silvestre Bahía Junquillal
Bahía Santa Elena
Bahía Playa Blanca
Península Santa Elena
Cuajiniquil
Interamericana
Parque Nacional Santa Rosa
Hacienda Santa Rosa
Islas Murciélago
Playa Nancite
Quebrada Grande
Portrerillos
Volcán Rincón de la Vieja (1895m)
Volcán Santa María (1916m)
Parque Nacional Rincón de la Vieja
Aguas Claras
Bahía Naranjo
Playa Naranjo
Estación Experimental Forestal Horizontes
Cañas Dulces
Curubandé
Hacienda Santa María
Guayabal
Volcán Miravalles (2028m)
San Jorge
Zona Protection Miravalles
Guayabo
La Fortuna
Nacascolo
Bahía de Culebra
Liberia International Airport
LIBERIA
Río Tempisque
Río Liberia
Playa Panamá
Playa Hermosa
Panamá
Playa del Coco
Playa Ocotal
Comunidad
El Coco
Sardinal
Guanacaste
Pijije
Bagaces
Río Tenorio
Río Corobicí
Playa Pan de Azúcar
Isla Santa Catalina
Bahía Potrero
Reserva Biológica Lomas de Barbudal
Playa Flamingo
Playa Brasilito
Playa Conchal
Filadelfia
Valle de Tempisque
Corobicí
Belén
Parque Nacional Marino Las Baulas de Guanacaste
Huacas
Río Cañas
Parque Nacional Palo Verde
Hacienda Palo Verde
Bebedero
Río Bebedero
Reserva Taboga
Refugio Nacional de Tamarindo
Playa Grande
Villareal
Playa Tamarindo
Laguna Mata Redonda
Puerto Humo
Guaitil
Santa Cruz
Playa Avellana
San José de Pinilla
27 de Abril
Refugio de Vida Silvestre Cipanci
Río Tempisque Ferry
Playa Negra
Refugio Bosque Nacional Diriá
Coralillo
Parque Nacional Barra Honda
Paraiso
Playa Junquillal
Santa Ana
Quebrada Honda
Nicoya
Nacaome
Río Quirimán
Reserva Indígena Matambú
Mansión
Isla Chira
Marbella
Río Grande
Guastomatal
Hojancha
Río Nosara
Península de Nicoya
Refugio Nacional de Vida Silvestre Ostional
Nosara
Playa Nosara
Carmona
86°00'W
85°30'W
11°00'N
10°30'N
10°00'N
1
4
21
151
155
160
164
18
150
161

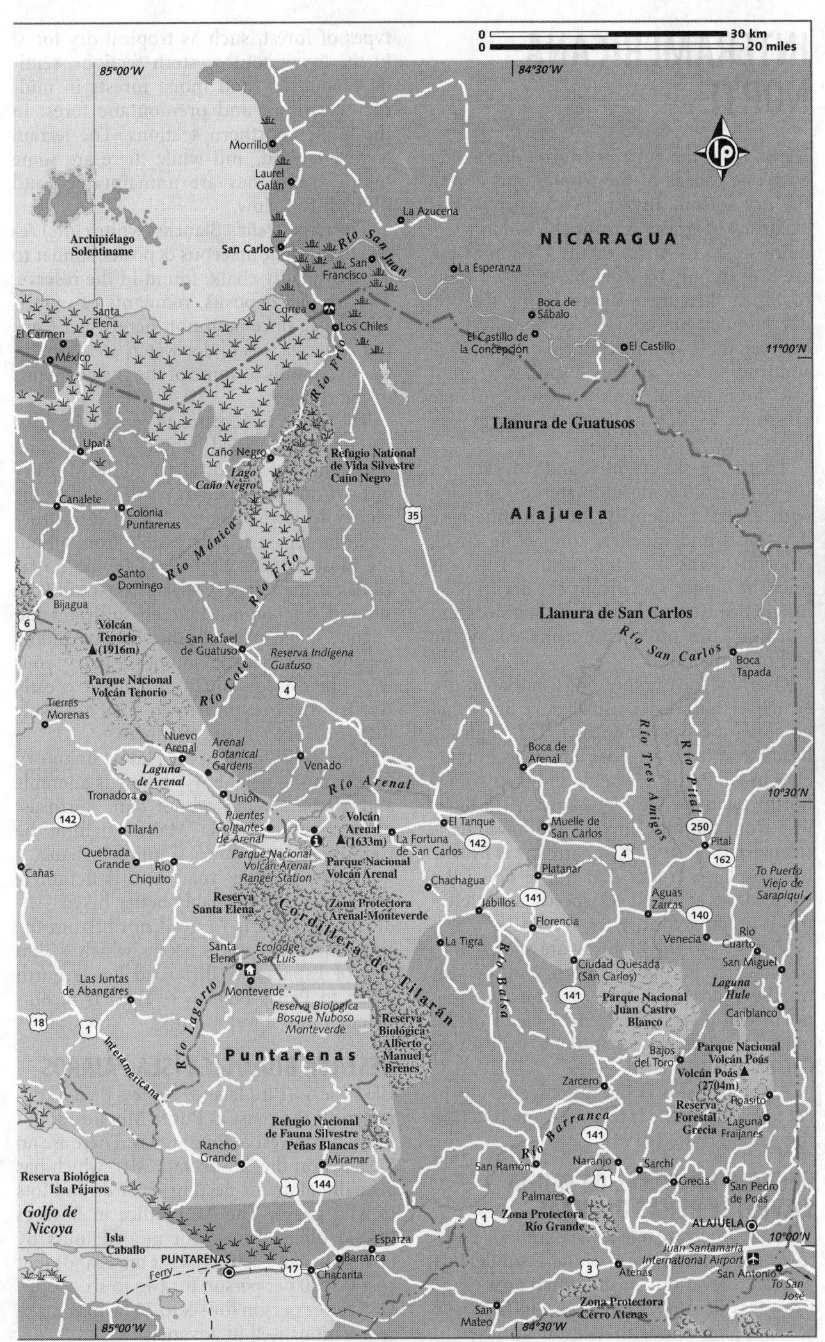

NORTHWESTERN COSTA RICA

INTERAMERICANA NORTE

Views from the Interamericana don't offer everyone's ideas of the tropics, not during the dry season, anyway. Vistas across vast expanses of grassy savannah, which seem more suited to Africa or the US southwest, are broken only by wind-blown trees, some of which shed their leaves during the hot, dry summer. But complex communications between these seemingly dormant giants will suddenly inspire an entire species to erupt into fountains of pink, yellow or orange blossoms, welling up from the dry grasses in astounding syncopation.

This is big-sky country, and you can spot the rivers from some kilometers off, snaking with emerald intensity through otherwise dry fincas and ranches, connecting small, colorful towns of some means. This was once the jungle; specifically the dry tropical jungle, a shrinking habitat of songbirds and sunshine, too often compromised by the will of humankind.

Overland travelers heading from San José to Managua, Nicaragua, usually take buses that go along the Interamericana. This highway heads west from San José almost to Puntarenas in the Pacific lowlands and then swings northwest to the Nicaragua border. The highway from the highlands to the lowlands is steep, winding, and often narrow, yet heavily used by large trucks that hurtle down the steep curves at breakneck speeds. Stay alert – this is no place for drivers to relax.

Views from the highway are spectacular, particularly at the northern end. A seat on the right-hand side of a bus heading north will give you excellent views of the magnificent volcanoes in the Cordillera de Guanacaste.

A popular, slower but more scenic way to get to Cañas on the Interamericana is to take the Arenal route (p199).

REFUGIO NACIONAL DE FAUNA SILVESTRE PEÑAS BLANCAS

This 2400-hectare **refuge** (admission US$7) clings to a steep southern arm of the Cordillera de Tilarán. Elevations in this small area range from less than 600m to over 1400m above sea level, variations that result in different types of forest, such as tropical dry forest in the lower southwestern sections, semideciduous dry and moist forests in middle elevations, and premontane forest in the higher northern sections. The terrain is very rugged, and while there are some hiking trails, they are unmaintained and difficult to follow.

The name Peñas Blancas (white cliffs) refers to the diatomaceous deposits, similar to a good-quality chalk, found in the reserve. The whitish deposits, remnants of unicellular algae once common here when Central America was under water, are found in the steep walls of some of the river canyons in the refuge.

The refuge was created to protect the plant species in the varied habitats as well as an important watershed, and until the Ministry of Environment & Energy (Minae) gets the money to develop some tourist infrastructure, the region is inaccessible from all but the most diligent visitors. There are no facilities at the refuge. **Camping** (per person US$2) is allowed, but you must be self-sufficient and in good shape to handle the very demanding terrain. There's no obvious place to pay your fees. The dry season (from January to early April) is the best time to go – it's not likely that you'll see anyone else there.

The closest town to the almost unknown (even among neighbors) refuge is adorable and scenic **Miramar**, about 8km northeast of the Interamericana. Make a right at the Catholic church onto Camino Sabana, a bone-jarring, 6km 'road' that is definitely 4WD only, but probably better hiked. Another approach is to head north from the Interamericana at Macacona, which is 3km east of Esparza. A dirt road heads north 20km to Peñas Blancas – 4WD is recommended in the wet months.

RESERVA BIOLÓGICA ISLA PÁJAROS

Isla Pájaros (Bird Island) lies less than a kilometer off the coast at Punta Morales, about 15km northwest of Puntarenas. There are no facilities on the 3.8-hectare islet, which has a small colony of nesting seabirds and lots of wild guava. The ACT office in Bagaces (p183) offers three-hour guided tours by boat (you can't actually visit the island) that cost US$30 per person for two to six people, US$25 per person for six to 20 people; make reservations well in advance.

JUNTAS

Las Juntas de Abangares (its full name), a small town on the Río Abangares, used to be a major gold-mining center in the late 19th and early 20th centuries, attracting fortune seekers and entrepreneurs from all over the world who wanted a part of mine-owner Minor Keith's (p24) other golden opportunity. The gold boom is over, but an ecomuseum opened in 1991, and currently a small tourist industry based on the sleepy town's plethora of hot springs is being developed.

Orientation & Information

The town of Las Juntas is centered on the Catholic church, with some very nice stained glass, and the small but bustling downtown is about 300m north of the church, with a Banco Nacional and several *sodas* (inexpensive eateries) and small markets. The Ecomuseo is 3km from the main road.

Mina Tours (☎ 662 0753; www.minatur.com), behind the church, is a family-run tour outfit that can arrange transportation and accommodations reservations, and offers several gold-themed tours, including the Ecomuseo and abandoned mines, beginning at about US$30 per person for day trips and more for overnight excursions.

Ecomuseo de las Minas de Abangares

Five kilometers beyond Juntas is this small **mining museum** (☎ 662 0129; admission US$1.50; 7am-3pm Tue-Fri, 7am-5pm Sat-Sun) with a few photographs and models depicting the old mining practices of the area. On the grounds outside the museum are a picnic area and children's play area; trails above the museum lead to mine artifacts, such as bits of railway. There's good birding (and iguana-ing) along these beautiful trails – it's very quiet here and the animals are rarely disturbed.

From the Interamericana, take the paved road 100m past the Parque Central, turn left, cross a bridge, then turn right at the 'Ecomuseo 4km' sign. A couple of kilometers past Juntas, the road forks – a sign indicates a road going left to Monteverde (30km) and to the right to the Ecomuseo (3km).

Sleeping & Eating

The really big news in town at the time of research was an almost-completed luxury resort with natural hot springs, Turkish baths, and a huge pool close to the museum; contact **Gold Mine Adventures** (☎ 662 0033) or Hotel Fonda Vela (p171) in Monteverde to see if it's open.

Cabinas Las Juntas (☎ 662 0153; 200m south of Bombero; r per person US$6-20; P) Basic but clean, small, tiled rooms come standard with a cold private shower; some rooms have hot shower and TV. América, the proprietor, will fix breakfast for US$2 extra.

Cabinas y Balniero Cayuco (☎ 662 0868; 200m north of Mining Statue; r per person without/with TV US$10/20; P) Though geared toward Tico tourists, this hotel has simple rooms with private cold showers and one big bonus: in addition to the cool pool and locally popular outdoor bar, there's a small natural hot spring on the site. Nonguests can also use the **pools** (admission US$1.25; 8am-close).

Hospedaje El Encanto (☎ 662 0153; d US$20; P) On the way to the Ecomuseum, the nice rooms with private, hot-water bathroom are much nicer inside than out.

Delicias de Trigo (50m south of Bombero; snacks US$0.50-2; 5am-9pm) This place can get you caffeinated in time for the first ferry – the coffee is complimented by pastries and breads.

Restaurante Los Mangos (☎ 662 0410; mains US$3-6; 11am-2pm Wed-Mon) The nicest restaurant in town is right on the main road, with good *ceviche*, fried chicken, and a full bar.

Getting There & Away

Buses from Cañas (US$0.50, 45 minutes) depart at 9:30am and 2:15pm. There are no buses to the Ecomuseo, but a taxi will cost you about US$4, one way.

Drivers can take the turnoff from the Interamericana, 27km south of Cañas at **Irma's Restaurant** (☎ 662 0348; mains US$2-5; 7am-9pm) a locally popular eatery where you can flag down buses between Liberia and San José. Monteverde is 30km from Las Juntas on a rough dirt road, passable to normal cars in dry season, at least.

MONTEVERDE & SANTA ELENA

Strung between two lovingly preserved cloud forests that their inhabitants have guarded for decades, this slender corridor of civilization connecting the Tico village of Santa Elena and Quaker settlement of Monteverde is one of Costa Rica's most popular destinations.

You have to work just to get here: part of the ongoing effort to preserve these lands has been active resistance to paved roads. But do not be dissuaded by the rough, bumpy ride, or curse the rocks and potholes. They have effectively created a moat around a precious experiment in sustainable ecotourism, where humans are learning to make their living from the rain forest without destroying it. The balance here remains fragile, and is one that ease of access too early on would have most certainly tipped toward overdevelopment.

Instead, the cloud forest sets a fine stage for this attempt to live comfortably within the natural order of things, alive with ruby-red poison dart frogs and sapphire quetzals, arrayed against the misty emerald green. And within this jungle, made mystical in light muted by the 100% humidity, ecologically minded businesses showcase organic farming techniques, area wildlife, solar energy and other technologies geared toward salvaging our planet.

It is something of an education center, with institutes specializing in this same task at hand, and a place where artists come to interpret this world. If you look, there's a lot of wisdom to be found here beneath the ever-multiplying zip lines.

There's certainly an understated theme-park vibe to the scene – it's touristy. Ecotouristy. It also attracts a fair number of expats, who like most locals seem intent on perfecting the practical aspects of those philosophies that say we're supposed to take care of Eden. English is widely spoken, and when conversation turns to conservation, as it so often does in these fair hills, it's worth listening. A blueprint for existing in harmony with nature is being drawn up right here, a piece of which might make a far more enduring souvenir in your home country than anything you could possibly buy.

Orientation

Driving from either of the Interamericana's first two turnoffs to the region, you'll first arrive in Santa Elena, a bustling little community with lots of budget hotels, restaurants and attractions, making it the most convenient place for pedestrians to stay. A road beginning at the northern point of the triangle leads to Juntas and Tilarán, with a turnoff to Reserva Santa Elena. From the westernmost point of the triangle (to the right as you enter town) you can access a scenic and heavily rutted 6km road to the Monteverde reserve.

This road forms the backbone of this spread-out community, and is lined with hotels and restaurants displaying varying degrees of adorableness. About 2km from Santa Elena, the neighborhood of Cerro Plano has another neat nucleus of cute businesses centered on Casem and the Monteverde Cheese Factory. Almost 5km from town, a turnoff leads three steep kilometers to San Luis Biological Station and Waterfall. Roads are generally paralleled by pedestrian trails.

Information

BOOKSHOPS

Chunches Coffeeshop (☎ 645 5147; ⏲ 8am-6pm Mon-Sat), in Santa Elena, is a bookstore and coffee shop with a fine selection of books (many in English), including travel and natural history guides and some US newspapers. There's laundry service (US$5 to wash and dry) and its bulletin board is a good source of information. Also see Bromelia's books (p163).

EMERGENCY

Police (☎ 645 5127)

INTERNET ACCESS

Internet access is widely available and all of the following places charge US$2 per hour.

Internet Café (☎ 645 6940; ⏲ 8am-9pm) In Cerro Plano.

Internet Pura Vida (☎ 361 1365; ⏲ 10am-9pm) Has free coffee.

Internet Taberna Valverde (☎ 645 5825; ⏲ 9am-8pm) Fast computers.

Tranquilo.com (☎ 645 5831; ⏲ 9am-8pm) On the western outskirts of Santa Elena.

MEDICAL SERVICES

Santa Elena also has a small **clinic** (☎ 645 5076; ⏲ closed 3pm Fri-7am Mon). The **Red Cross** (☎ 645 6128), just north of Santa Elena, is open 24 hours.

MONEY

There is a **Banco Nacional** (☎ 645 5027; ⏲ 8:30am-3:45pm Mon-Fri) in Santa Elena, open weekdays. Euros, US dollars and traveler's checks in amounts under US$100 can be exchanged at Hotel Camino Verde (p167), with fairly steep commission.

WHO HAS SEEN THE GOLDEN TOAD?

One animal you used to be able to see so often that it almost became a Monteverde mascot was the golden toad *(Bufo periglenes)*. Monteverde was the only place in the world where this exotic little toad appeared. The gold-colored amphibian used to be frequently seen scrambling along the muddy trails of the cloud forest, adding a bright splash to the surroundings. Unfortunately, no one has seen this once-common toad since 1989, and what happened to it is a mystery.

During an international conference of herpetologists (scientists who study reptiles and amphibians), it was noted that the same puzzling story was occurring with other frog and toad species all over the world. Amphibians once common are now severely depleted or simply not found at all. The scientists were unable to agree upon a reason for the sudden demise of so many amphibian species in so many different habitats.

One of several theories holds that degenerating air quality is the culprit. Amphibians breathe both with primitive lungs and through their perpetually moist skin, and they're more susceptible to airborne toxins because of the gas exchange through their skin. Another theory is that deforestation and global warming pushed the frogs ever higher, until there was no higher altitude for them to go. Yet another theory is that their skin gives little protection against UV light, and increasing UV light levels in recent years have proven deadly to amphibians. Perhaps they are like the canaries that miners used in the old days to warn them of toxic air in the mines. When the canary keeled over, it was time for the miners to get out!

Are our dying frogs and toads a symptom of a planet that is becoming too polluted?

TOURIST INFORMATION

There's no general information office, but most tour operators (p167) and some hotels can help with accommodations, transportation and other quandaries. **Pensión Santa Elena** (p169; www.monteverdeinfo.com) is a great source of information geared to the budget traveler, and its website is probably the most comprehensive source of information about the region available.

Sights

The best thing about this particular cloud forest is that it straddles the continental divide, which means that there are two different ecosystems each boasting several distinct species, most of which you probably won't be able to see. If you'd like a good look at any particular critter, however, there are plenty of places in town where your view won't be obscured by all those pesky trees.

BUTTERFLY GARDEN

One of the most interesting activities is visiting **El Jardín de las Mariposas** (☎ 645 5512; adult/student US$7/5; 🕑 9:30am-4pm). Admission entitles you to a guided, naturalist-led tour (in Spanish, English, or German) that begins with an enlightening discussion of butterfly life cycles and the butterfly's importance in nature. A variety of eggs, caterpillars, pupae and adults are examined. Then visitors are taken into the greenhouses, where the butterflies are raised, and on into the screened garden, where hundreds of butterflies of many species are seen. The tour lasts about an hour, after which you are free to stay as long as you wish. There are excellent opportunities to photograph the gorgeous butterflies. There are good volunteer opportunities here.

RANARIO

With all this mist, it's no wonder that so many amphibians call Monteverde home, and the **Frog Pond** (☎ 645 6320; ranariomv@racsa.co.cr; 🕑 9am-8:30pm; adult/student US$8/6) has about 30 species on display, including newts and salamanders in addition to the wide assortment of frogs and toads. Guides lead tours in English or Spanish through the well-maintained terrariums, and point out the often poisonous frogs with flashlights. One you won't find, no matter how hard you look, however, is the golden toad (see the boxed text above), though they've got a spot waiting should it ever again be found.

If you're lucky (tips are as always appreciated) your guide may also imitate frog calls, or give you the lowdown on local folklore. Many resident amphibians are more active by night, so if you'd like to see them in action, you're welcome to come back in the evening with the same ticket.

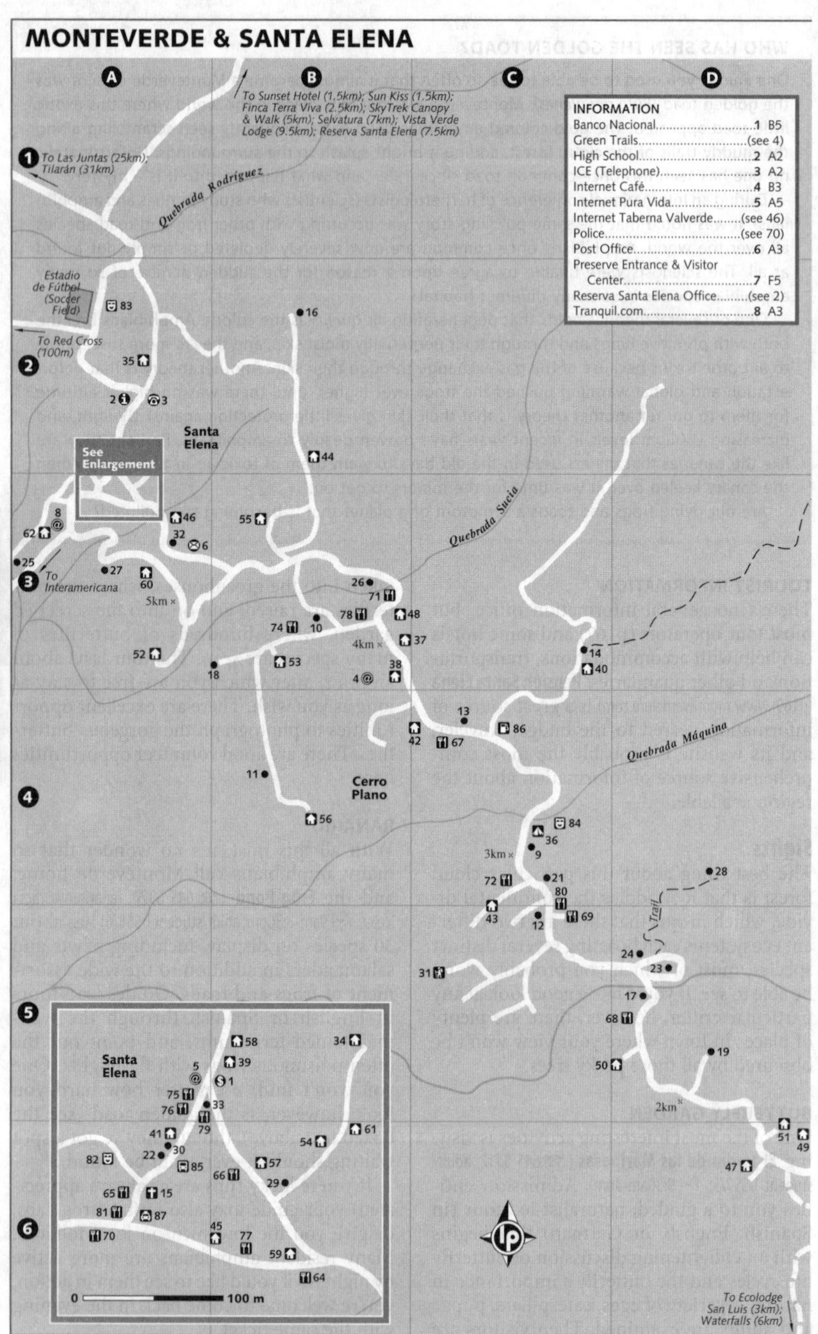
MONTEVERDE & SANTA ELENA
INFORMATION
Banco Nacional....1 B5
Green Trails....(see 4)
High School....2 A2
ICE (Telephone)....3 A2
Internet Café....4 B3
Internet Pura Vida....5 A5
Internet Taberna Valverde....(see 46)
Police....(see 70)
Post Office....6 A3
Preserve Entrance & Visitor Center....7 F5
Reserva Santa Elena Office....(see 2)
Tranquil.com....8 A3
To Sunset Hotel (1.5km); Sun Kiss (1.5km); Finca Terra Viva (2.5km); SkyTrek Canopy & Walk (5km); Selvatura (7km); Vista Verde Lodge (9.5km); Reserva Santa Elena (7.5km)
To Las Juntas (25km); Tilarán (31km)
Quebrada Rodríguez
Estadio de Fútbol (Soccer Field)
To Red Cross (100m)
Santa Elena
See Enlargement
To Interamericana
5km
4km
3km
2km
Quebrada Sucia
Quebrada Máquina
Cerro Plano
Trail
To Ecolodge San Luis (3km); Waterfalls (6km)
Santa Elena
0
100 m

NORTHWESTERN COSTA RICA

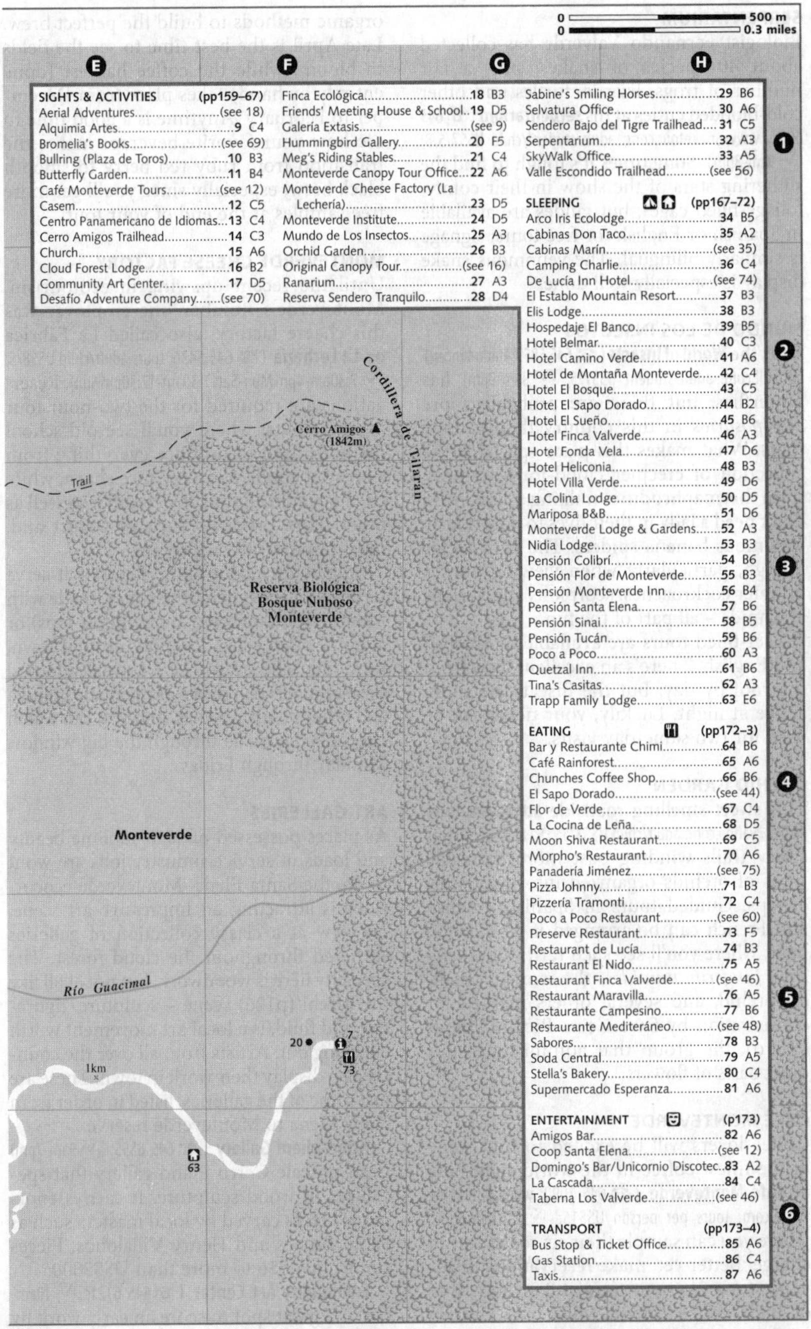

0 500 m
0 0.3 miles

E F G H

SIGHTS & ACTIVITIES (pp159–67)
Aerial Adventures (see 18)
Alquimia Artes 9 C4
Bromelia's Books (see 69)
Bullring (Plaza de Toros) 10 B3
Butterfly Garden 11 B4
Café Monteverde Tours (see 12)
Casem 12 C5
Centro Panamericano de Idiomas 13 C4
Cerro Amigos Trailhead 14 C3
Church 15 A6
Cloud Forest Lodge 16 B2
Community Art Center 17 D5
Desafío Adventure Company (see 70)
Finca Ecológica 18 B3
Friends' Meeting House & School 19 D5
Galería Extasis (see 9)
Hummingbird Gallery 20 F5
Meg's Riding Stables 21 C4
Monteverde Canopy Tour Office 22 A6
Monteverde Cheese Factory (La Lechería) 23 D5
Monteverde Institute 24 D5
Mundo de Los Insectos 25 A3
Orchid Garden 26 B3
Original Canopy Tour (see 16)
Ranarium 27 A3
Reserva Sendero Tranquilo 28 D4
Sabine's Smiling Horses 29 B6
Selvatura Office 30 A6
Sendero Bajo del Tigre Trailhead 31 C5
Serpentarium 32 A3
SkyWalk Office 33 A5
Valle Escondido Trailhead (see 56)

SLEEPING (pp167–72)
Arco Iris Ecolodge 34 B5
Cabinas Don Taco 35 A2
Cabinas Marín (see 35)
Camping Charlie 36 C4
De Lucía Inn Hotel (see 74)
El Establo Mountain Resort 37 B3
Elis Lodge 38 B3
Hospedaje El Banco 39 B5
Hotel Belmar 40 C3
Hotel Camino Verde 41 A6
Hotel de Montaña Monteverde 42 C4
Hotel El Bosque 43 C5
Hotel El Sapo Dorado 44 B2
Hotel El Sueño 45 B6
Hotel Finca Valverde 46 A3
Hotel Fonda Vela 47 D6
Hotel Heliconia 48 B3
Hotel Villa Verde 49 D6
La Colina Lodge 50 D5
Mariposa B&B 51 D6
Monteverde Lodge & Gardens 52 A3
Nidia Lodge 53 B3
Pensión Colibrí 54 B6
Pensión Flor de Monteverde 55 B3
Pensión Monteverde Inn 56 B4
Pensión Santa Elena 57 B6
Pensión Sinai 58 B5
Pensión Tucán 59 B6
Poco a Poco 60 A3
Quetzal Inn 61 B6
Tina's Casitas 62 A3
Trapp Family Lodge 63 E6

EATING (pp172–3)
Bar y Restaurante Chimi 64 B6
Café Rainforest 65 A6
Chunches Coffee Shop 66 B6
El Sapo Dorado (see 44)
Flor de Verde 67 C4
La Cocina de Leña 68 D5
Moon Shiva Restaurant 69 C5
Morpho's Restaurant 70 A6
Panadería Jiménez (see 75)
Pizza Johnny 71 B3
Pizzería Tramonti 72 C4
Poco a Poco Restaurant (see 60)
Preserve Restaurant 73 F5
Restaurant de Lucía 74 B3
Restaurant El Nido 75 A5
Restaurant Finca Valverde (see 46)
Restaurant Maravilla 76 A5
Restaurante Campesino 77 B6
Restaurante Mediteráneo (see 48)
Sabores 78 B3
Soda Central 79 A5
Stella's Bakery 80 C4
Supermercado Esperanza 81 A6

ENTERTAINMENT (p173)
Amigos Bar 82 A6
Coop Santa Elena (see 12)
Domingo's Bar/Unicornio Discotec 83 A2
La Cascada 84 C4
Taberna Los Valverde (see 46)

TRANSPORT (pp173–4)
Bus Stop & Ticket Office 85 A6
Gas Station 86 C4
Taxis 87 A6

Cordillera de Tilarán
Cerro Amigos (1842m)
Trail
Reserva Biológica Bosque Nuboso Monteverde
Monteverde
Río Guacimal
20
7
73
1km
63

1 2 3 4 5 6

NORTHWESTERN COSTA RICA

SERPENTARIUM

Biologist Fernando Valverde has collected about 40 species of snakes, plus a fair number of frogs, lizards, turtles and other cold-blooded cuties at his **serpentarium** (☎ 645 6002; www.snaketour.com; adult/student/child US$7/5/3; ⌚ 9am-8pm). Sometimes it's tough to find the slithering stars of the show in their comfy, foliage-filled cages, but guides are available in Spanish or English for free tours; signage is similarly bilingual. The venomous snake display is especially well done.

MUNDO DE LOS INSECTOS

Sure, the **World of Insects** (☎ 645 6859; klatindancer@hotmail.com; adult/student US$7/5; ⌚ 8am-9pm) has butterflies, but there are probably more *mariposarios* in this country than canopy tours. What makes this place special is the collection of creepier cloud-forest critters, from hermaphroditic walking sticks who don't need a lady in their lives to notoriously venomous banana spiders. The yuck factor is high, particularly when viewing hordes of water cockroaches, scorpions and various arachnids – all part of the fun.

Fact-filled tours are available in Spanish and English. There's an excellent view from the roof by day, but the insects are more active at night. Luckily, your ticket can be used for two same-day visits.

ORCHID GARDEN

This sweet-smelling roadside **attraction** (gabyorchid@yahoo.com; adult/child US$3/5; ⌚ 8am-5pm) has shady trails winding past more than 400 types of orchids organized into taxonomic groups. Guided tours in Spanish, English and French can be arranged if it's not too busy, where you'll see such rarities as *Plztystele jungermannioides*, the world's smallest orchid, and several others marked for conservation by Save Costa Rican Orchids (Sacro), the group that administrates this quiet oasis of flowers.

CAFÉ MONTEVERDE

Coffee lovers will be excited to find some of the finest coffee in the world right here at **Café Monteverde** (☎ 645 7090; www.cafemonteverde.com; tours per person US$15; ⌚ 7:30am-6pm), where you can sample their six roasts free of charge. Better yet, make reservations in advance for a 2½ hour tour (at 8am and 1pm) of their coffee fincas, which use entirely organic methods to build the perfect brew. Late April is the best time to see the fields in bloom, while the coffee harvest (done entirely by hand) takes place from December to February. Anytime is a good time to see how your favorite beverage makes the transition from ruby red berry to smooth black brew, especially since you'll get more free samples at the end of your tour.

MONTEVERDE CHEESE FACTORY

Until the recent upswing in ecotourism, Monteverde's number one employer was this cheese factory, also called La Fábrica or **La Lechería** (☎ 645 5436; tours adult/child US$8/5; ⌚ 7:30am-4pm Mon-Sat, 7:30am-12:30pm Sun). Reservations are required for the two-hour tour of operations, where you'll see old-school methods used to produce everything from a creamy gouda to a very nice sharp, white cheddar, sold all over the country, as well as other dairy products such as yogurt and, most importantly, ice cream.

Stop by for a cone of the almost soft-serve scrumptiousness here (the coffee, made with Monteverde's own organic grind, is tops) or at a few other select locations around town, including Sabores (p172). The small attached shop also sells deli meats, homemade granola and other picnic goodies, and you can watch cheese being made through the big window Monday through Friday.

ART GALLERIES

As places possessed of such sublime beauty and loads of service-industry jobs are wont to do, the Santa Elena–Monteverde ecocorridor is attracting an impressive art scene, on view at a classy collection of galleries scattered throughout the cloud forest. The specialty here is woodwork, but not at all like the Sarchí (p126) scene – sculpture, figurative and fluid, is a local art movement worth checking out. Artists from all over the country also display their work in town. These are just some of the galleries, listed in order from Santa Elena to Monteverde reserve.

Atmosphera Gallery (☎ 645 6555; ⌚ 9am-7pm) is an upscale Cerro Plano gallery that specializes in wood sculpture. It carries enormous pieces carved by local masters such as Fabio Brenes and Henry Villalobos. Pieces run from US$6 to more than US$5000.

Community Art Center (☎ 645 6121; ⌚ 10am-6pm) is a great spot to score an early work by

THE QUAKERS OF MONTEVERDE

The story of the founding of Monteverde is an unusual one. It begins in Alabama with four Quakers (a pacifist religious group also known as the 'Friends') who were jailed in 1949 for refusing to register for the draft in the USA.

After their release from jail, they, along with other Quakers, began to search for a place to settle where they could live peacefully. After searching for land in Canada, Mexico and Central America, they decided on Costa Rica; its peaceful policies and lack of army matched their philosophies. They chose the Monteverde area because of its pleasant climate and fertile land, and because it was far enough away from San José to be (at that time) a relatively cheap place to buy property.

Forty-four original settlers (men, women, and children from 11 families) arrived in Monteverde in 1951. Many flew to San José. They loaded their belongings onto trucks, which a few of them drove from Alabama to Monteverde, a journey that took three months. If you think the roads to Monteverde are bad now, imagine what they must have been like over five decades ago! In 1951, the road was an ox-cart trail, and it took weeks of work to make it barely passable for larger vehicles.

The Quakers bought about 1500 hectares and began dairy farming and cheese production. Early cheese production was about 10kg per day; today, Monteverde's modern cheese factory produces more than 1000kg of cheese daily, which is sold throughout Costa Rica. The Cheese Factory (La Lechería; p162) is now in the middle of the Monteverde community and can be visited by those interested in the process.

There has been talk of paving the really rough road from the Interamericana to Monteverde. However, many locals don't want this to happen, and are rightly concerned that a paved road would dramatically change the area for the worse.

Note that due to the Quaker influence and the high level of tourism, much of the local population speaks English, and many local places are named in English as well as Spanish. Also remember that there were a few rural Costa Rican families in the area before the Quakers arrived.

a soon-to-be-renowned Costa Rican artist – local kids make much of the pottery, jewelry and other artwork and they staff the place. Ask about their interesting gray-water treatment project.

Galería Extasis I & II (☎ 645 5548; 🕓 9am-6pm), about 100m apart, separate an exquisite collection. Galería I focuses on woodwork, including pieces by Fabio, Marco and Tulio Brenas, part of a family of wood sculptors who carve exceptional and usually figurative pieces with a fluidity that's impressive in this material, and animals created by David Villalobos. Paintings, primarily in Galería II, are all from Monteverde-area artists.

Alquimia Artes (☎ 645 5837; 🕓 8:30am-6pm) has work that is a tad more affordable – check out the jewelry by Tarcicio Castillo from the Ecuadorian Andes – but this doesn't mean this collection of work by artists from throughout Costa Rica isn't astounding. Don't miss Helen Rodas' brightly colored portraits of women on banana paper and Justo Aguilar's surreal scenes.

Casem (Cooperativa de Artesanía Santa Elena Monteverde; ☎ 645 5190; 🕓 8am-5pm Mon-Sat, 10am-4pm Sun high season) began in 1982 as a women's cooperative representing eight female artists. Today it has expanded to include almost 150 area artisans, eight of which are men. Embroidered and hand-painted clothing, polished wooden tableware, handmade cards and other work, some priced even for budget souvenir shoppers, make for an eclectic selection.

Don cute felt shoes before entering **Bromelia's Books** (☎ 645 6272; 🕓 10am-5:30pm), with its polished-wood Cerro Plano expanse of local arts and crafts, including some intricate batik. There are also books about the region, in particular natural history, in English and Spanish, plus lots of Costa Rican music. At press time, the owners were completing an all-natural sauna made from a type of adobe structure (with windows made of glass bottles and a niche near the heat source that also bakes bread) that should be open to the public by the time this book hits the shelves. It's owned by the same folks as the Hummingbird Gallery.

Just outside Monteverde reserve, **Hummingbird Gallery** (☎ 645 5030; 🕑 8:30am-5pm) has beautiful photos, watercolors, art by the indigenous Chorotega people of Guanacaste and, best of all, feeders that constantly attract several species of hummingbird. Great photo ops include potential hot shots of the violet sabrewing (Costa Rica's largest hummer) and the coppery-headed emerald, one of only three mainland birds endemic to Costa Rica. An identification board shows the nine species that are seen here. If you'd like a closer look, slides and photographs of the jungle's most precious feathered gems (and other luminous critters) by the renowned British wildlife photographers Michael and Patricia Fogden are on display; the smaller prints are for sale.

Activities

Don't forget your hiking boots, bug spray and copy of the movie *Vertigo* – there's plenty to do outdoors around here, including lots of action in the jungle canopy.

HIKING

The best hikes are at the two cloud-forest reserves bookending the main road, Reserva Biológica Bosque Nuboso Monteverde (p174) and Reserva Santa Elena (p177), both covered later in the chapter.

If you've ever gotten cynical about schoolchildren asking for money to save the rain forest, then you really must stop by **Bosque Eterno de los Niños** (Children's Eternal Forest; ☎ 645 5923; adult/student day use US$5/4, guided night hike US$15/10; 🕑 7:30am-5:30pm) and see what they purchased with all that spare change. Keep in mind, however, that this enormous 22,000-hectare reserve, which dwarfs both the Monteverde and Santa Elena reserves, is largely inaccessible. The international army of children who paid the bills decided that it was more important to provide a home for local wildlife among the primary and secondary forest (and to allow former agricultural land to be slowly reclaimed by the jungle), than to develop a lucrative tourist infrastructure. Kids today, what can you do?

The effort has allowed for one fabulous trail (which hooks into a system of unimproved trails that are primarily for researchers), the 3.5km **Sendero Bajo del Tigre** (Jaguar Canyon Trail), which offers more open vistas than do those in the cloud forest, so spotting birds tends to be easier. Make reservations in advance for the popular night hikes, which set off at 5:30pm for a two-hour trek by flashlight through a sea of glowing red eyes. The San Gerardo Biological Station at the end of the trail has dorm beds for researchers and students, but you may be able to stay overnight with prior arrangements.

Finca Ecológica (Ecological Farm; ☎ 645 5363; www.fincaecologicamonteverde.com; adult/student US$7/5; 🕑 7am-5pm) has four loop trails (the longest takes about 2½ hours at a slow pace) offering hikes of varying lengths through private property comprising premontane and secondary forest, coffee and banana plantations, and past a couple of waterfalls and lookout points. Coatis, agoutis, and sloths are seen on most days, and monkeys, porcupines, and other animals are sometimes seen as well. Birding is also good. Guided tours (three hours, US$15, excluding admission) are available throughout the day, and you'll see even more animals on the guided night tours (5:30pm to 7:30pm, adult/student US$14/9).

Valle Escondido (Hidden Valley Trail; ☎ 645 5156; day use US$5, night tours adult/child US$15/10; 🕑 7:30am-5:30pm) is a pretty path beginning at the Pensión Monteverde Inn (p168) and winds through a deep canyon and into an 11-hectare reserve. It can be wandered at will during the day, but make reservations for the guided, two-hour night tours.

Take a free hike up **Cerro Amigos** (1842m) for good views of the surrounding rain forest and, on a clear day, of Volcán Arenal, 20km away to the northeast. The trail leaves Monteverde from behind Hotel Belmar and ascends roughly 300m in 3km; from the hotel, take the dirt road going downhill, then the next left.

SAN LUIS WATERFALL

Allow six hours for the round-trip hike to this gorgeous ribbon of water streaming from the cloud forests into a series of swimming holes just screaming for a picnic. The walk there is steeply graded downhill; if you want a ride coming back, you can call a taxi at the Ecolodge San Luis (p178) for US$12, which is probably worth it.

Drivers will need 4WD to ford the little river and climb the muddy road out. Cross the river, then make a left at the *pulpería* on the other side. You can park (US$6 per car) at a private farm, from where it's a short hike the falls. Several horseback riding companies offer excursions to the falls (US$50 per person), but note that much of the road is now paved and this is hard on the horse's knees. ATVs (see Monteverde Off-Roader, p167) also make the trek.

CANOPY TOURS

Wondering where the whole 'canopy tour' euphemism was coined? Santa Elena is the site of Costa Rica's first zip lines, today eclipsed in adrenaline by the 80-some imitators who have followed, many of which are right here in town. Sure, the only way you're going to see a quetzal on one of these things is if you run smack dab into the poor bird, and the US$35 to US$45 price tag is absolutely ridiculous, but what the heck. They really are fun. And there are plenty of other ways up into the clouds, too, should you actually want to see some wildlife.

Aerial Adventures & Natural Wonders Tram (☎ 645 5960; naturalwonders@racsa.co.cr; tram adult/child US$15/8, hike US$7, tram & hike US$20) is essentially a ski lift, offering a 1.5km journey in electrically propelled gondola chairs along rails attached to towers; heights reach 12m. The ride lasts between one and 1½ hours; you have the option of pausing your car briefly to look around. Lacking the thrills offered by the zip-line tours, this quieter tour offers similar views and probably a better chance of seeing birds and wildlife.

You can also rent golf carts (US$30 per car) that hold up to three people for cruising around the trails afterward, a great choice for folks with limited mobility who want to get out in the woods on their own.

Tired of canopy tours that clutter the grounds with educational attractions? **Aventura** (☎ 645 6959; mauaventura@hotmail.com; adult/student US$35/28; 7am-2:30pm) has 16 cables spiced up with rope swings and rappelling. About 3km north of Santa Elena on the road to the reserve, a well-signed turnoff brings you here; transportation from your hotel is included in the price.

On the grounds of Cloud Forest Lodge, **Original Canopy Tour** (☎ 291 4465; www.canopytour.com; adult/student/child US$45/35/25; 7:30am-2:30pm) has the fabled zip lines that started an ecotourism movement of questionable ecological value, nevertheless generating an estimated US$120 million annually for Costa Rica, pesticide-free (of which builder Darren Hreniuk would like a bigger cut, see p165). These lines aren't as elaborate as the others, but with 14 platforms, rappelling and 5km of private trails worth a wander afterward, you can enjoy a piece of history that's far more entertaining than most museums.

NORTHWESTERN COSTA RICA

CANOPY FIGHTING *Carolina A Miranda*

All is not well in the world of zip-line operators. As competition has come to a boil between the 80-plus canopy tour operators around the country, the founder of The Original Canopy Tour decided to patent his concept and the words 'canopy tour' with Costa Rica's National Registry. After receiving the title, Darren Hreniuk, the Canadian behind the tour, has claimed that all other operators are running 'pirate tours' and has demanded that they pay him licensing fees or shut down.

The title has been largely ignored by other operators, who insist that the idea of crossing trees on a cable-and-pulley system is hardly a new one. (There is a painting dating back to 1858 in the Museo Nacional that shows people transporting themselves on ropes tied between trees.) Hreniuk insists otherwise. 'I am the inventor of the canopy tour,' he told the *Tico Times* in August of 2003, 'if people like that or not, it is irrelevant.'

The National Registry supported his claim and provided Hreniuk with a cease-and-desist order that demanded that all other tours close up shop. Armed with this, Hreniuk visited more than a dozen tour sites in April and December of 2003 and attempted to shut them down.

At the time of research, the cease-and-desist order had been frozen by the government, which wants to study the matter further. Locally, Hreniuk's legal moves are poorly regarded. Many Ticos view his patent and subsequent enforcement of it as an attempt to create a foreign monopoly on an activity that more than a quarter of all tourists who go to Costa Rica participate in.

Either way, this is the kind of legal wrangling that can take all the fun out of traveling. Let's just hope that the person who 'invented' rafting doesn't try to do the same.

The makers of eco-fun really went all out at **Selvatura** (☎ 645 5929; www.selvatura.com; adult/child canopy tour US$45/38, package US$75/60; 7:30am-4pm), just 150m from Reserva Santa Elena. It's worth getting the package deal: in addition to 2½ hours on what claims to be the longest canopy tour in the country (seriously, though, by the time you finished measuring them, six more would have opened), you get access to all their attractions, most of which can be viewed separately for US$10 each.

The sizable butterfly and hummingbird gardens are pleasant and very photogenic, but it's the slightly overwhelming **Jewels of the Rainforest Exhibition**, with lots of insect and butterfly specimens artfully arranged in various patterns, that takes the cake. There's also a 3km hike that includes a series of eight suspension bridges (admission US$25 separately) through the canopy, slowly this time around. A guide is US$30 extra, per group, and the trails are wheelchair-accessible. Prices include transportation from your hotel, and the operators don't mind if you take the early shuttle, go visit the nearby reserve and come back for your tour.

Considered by many to be the wildest ride in town, **SkyTrek** (☎ 645 5796; www.skywalk.co.cr; adult/student Skytrek US$40/32, Skytrek & SkyWalk US$45/36; 7:30am-5pm) is an ecotourism complex that has been recommended for screaming canopy action along 11 separate cables over the roads (they don't bother with trees for the big thrills, relying instead on steel towers) and through 'tunnels of forest views.'

If you'd like a closer look at those views, get the package that includes **SkyWalk**, with several suspension bridges through the canopy at a more leisurely pace. There's also a combo deal with the Serpentario in town (adult/student US$48/38), and transportation is free from your hotel.

SkyTrek is only 2km from Reserva Santa Elena, and you could certainly see both in the same day. Folks considering a canopy tour for vertigo therapy should note that the first two platforms are close to the ground, giving you a chance to chicken out after the first cable without being forced to rappel down. There are no refunds, but you may get a T-shirt.

HORSEBACK RIDING

Until recently, this region was most easily traveled on horseback, and considering the roads around here, that's probably still true. Several operators offer you the chance to test this theory, with guided horseback rides ranging from two-hour tours to five-day adventures. Shorter trips generally run about US$15 per hour, while an overnight trek including meals and accommodations runs between US$150 and US$200.

Some outfitters also make the trip to La Fortuna, an intriguing transportation option with several caveats (US$60 to US$100; see p174). Some outfitters may charge less, but remember you (or more likely, the horse) get what you pay for.

Caballeriza El Rodeo (☎ 645 5075) does local tours on private trails, as well as trips to San Luis Waterfall and a sunset tour to a spot overlooking the Golfo de Nicoya, all two-hour treks that cost US$20 per person (two-person minimum).

Desafío Adventure Company (☎ 645 5874; www.monteverdetours.com) does local treks for groups and individuals around town, day trips to San Luis Waterfall (six hours, per person US$50) and several multiday rides, as well as the Lake Trail to La Fortuna. This established outfitter will arrange rides on the Castillo Trail if the weather is perfect and the riders are experienced. The company also arranges white-water rafting trips on the Ríos Toro, Sarapiquí and others, and can help with transport and hotel reservations.

Meg's Riding Stables (☎ 645 5560; www.guanacaste.com/sites/stellas/stables.htm) takes folks on private trails nearby plus treks to San Luis Waterfall. Kid-sized saddles are also available. Their horses are well looked after, and this is the longest-established operation in Monteverde.

Sabine's Smiling Horses (☎ 645 6894; www.horseback-riding-tour.com), run by Sabine, who speaks English, French, Spanish and German, offers a variety of treks, from US$15 per hour day trips to specialty tours including a Full Moon Ride (US$50 per person, five hours). Several multiday treks are also on offer, and Sabine may also take experienced riders on El Castillo Trail, weather permitting. This outfitter has been highly recommended by readers.

Courses

Monteverde Institute (☎ 645 5053; www.mvinstitute.org) is a nonprofit educational institute, founded in 1986, that offers interdisciplinary courses in tropical biology, conserva-

NORTHWESTERN COSTA RICA

tion, sustainable development, and Spanish, among other topics. These courses are occasionally open to the general public – check the website. There is also a volunteer-placement program for people who wish to teach in local schools or work in reforestation programs.

The institute's short courses (US$800 to US$1800, two weeks) teach both high school and college students about conservation and land use in the Monteverde area. Long courses (US$4000; 10 weeks) are university-accredited programs for undergraduates and they emphasize tropical community ecology.

The institute also administrates **Monteverde Studios of the Arts**, which offers a variety of classes and workshops, sometimes open to visitors, covering everything from woodworking to papermaking, with a special emphasis on pottery.

Centro-Panamericano de Idiomas (☎ 265 6306; www.cpi-edu.com; classes without/with homestay US$240/365) also has locations in Heredia (p131) and Playa Flamingo in Guanacaste (p231), with the opportunity to transfer from campus to campus.

Clave Spanish School (☎ 645 5023; clave@monteverdeconnection.net; classes per wk, without/with homestay US$175/275) is a new entry on the Spanish school circuit and offers five days of four-hour classes and an optional homestay including all meals, or you could just schedule a six-hour, one-time immersion course for US$75.

Yoga classes (☎ 645 5906; elyhawking@yahoo.com; per person US$6; ⏲ 9-10:30am) are offered at Bromelia's Books (p163).

Tours

There are several tour outfits around town, though your hotel can probably arrange any area tour.

La Asociación de Tour Operadores de Monteverde (Atom; ☎ 645 6565) publishes the useful *What to Do in Monteverde* booklet, available free just about everywhere. It also offers custom package deals that let you choose two or more attractions around town; you can save several dollars off each admission fee, which you can arrange at any participating attraction (most of them).

Pensión Santa Elena (☎ 645 5051; www.monteverdeinfo.com) is an excellent source of information about almost anything going on in town. The staff also arrange a variety of tours and transportation options with the budget traveler in mind; their website is probably the best source of information on the area anywhere.

Green Trails (☎ 364 1710; greentrailsgt@yahoo.com) specializes in group tours, usually arranged outside the country, but this experienced outfitter also arranges city tours (US$55 per person) with visits to the Ranario, Butterfly Garden and more. These folks can help you with everything from plane tickets to budget lodging throughout the country.

Have you had enough of the organic vegetables already? Hop on an ATV from **Monteverde Off-Roader** (☎ 645 5023; quadadventures@ad.com; tours per ATV US$35-100) and head out to San Luis Waterfall and other semipristine destinations.

Hotel Camino Verde (☎ 645 5204; www.monteverdeinfocenter.com; ⏲ 6am-9pm) books every possible tour and transport option, including the US$2 shuttle to Reserva Santa Elena, and also offers Internet access (US$3 per hour) and exchanges euros, dollars and traveler's checks (with fairly steep commissions).

Pensión Tucán (p168; ⏲ 6am-9pm) and Albergue El Banco (p168) also arrange all the tours.

Festivals & Events

The **Monteverde Music Festival** (www.mvinstitute.org) is held annually on variable dates from late January to early April. It's gained a well-deserved reputation as one of the top music festivals in Central America. Music is mainly classical, jazz, and Latin, with an occasional experimental group to spice things up. Concerts are held on Thursday, Friday and Saturday, at different venues all over town. Some performances are free, but most events ask US$5 to US$15 for each performance; proceeds go toward teaching music and the arts in local schools.

Sleeping

During Christmas and Easter, many hotels are booked up weeks in advance. During the January-to-April busy season, and also in July, hotels tend to be full often enough that you should telephone before arriving to ensure yourself a room in the hotel you want. You may have to book well in advance to get the dates and hotel of your choice. If you're flexible, however, you can almost always find somewhere to stay.

BUDGET

Competition has kept costs low and even budget spots usually offer warm(ish) showers. Pensión Santa Elena (see opposite) is the author's choice for budget accommodations.

Camping Charlie (☎ 645 6962; per person US$3) With a few tiny but picturesque campsites by a burbling river, plus bathrooms and cold showers, this would be a fine spot to pitch a tent even without the opportunity to watch owner Carlos Méndez weld his spacey sculptures using only found objects.

Hotel Camino Verde (☎ 645 5204; www.monteverdeinfocenter.com; dm without/with bathroom US$8/5) Clean basic dorms with kitchen privileges and clean, shared hot-water showers are centrally located; owners also arrange all local tours.

Pensión Colibrí (☎ 645 5682; r per person without/with bathroom US$5/10; P) Down the street and up a very quiet lane, this family-owned pension feels like it's perched among the trees. The larger rooms with private bathrooms and little balconies overlook the woods, and everyone can use the shared kitchen.

Pensión Sinai (☎ 645 5343; lucreciajc@yahoo.com; r without/with bathroom US$5/10) Brand new tiled rooms in this homey family-owned pension are pristine.

Hospedaje Giaconda (☎ 645 5461; r per person US$5) Five neat little rooms share a bathroom behind Hospedaje Giaconda *soda*.

Pensión Tucán (☎ 645 5017; r per person without/with bathroom US$5/10) Small wooden rooms are clean and comfortable enough, but right by a 'major' Santa Elena intersection, street noise can go late, particularly on weekends. Breakfast (US$3) is available, and there's a tour office downstairs.

Tina's Casitas (☎ 820 4821; www.tinascasitas.de; dm US$5, r US$20) West of the La Esperanza supermarket this terrific budget place has spotlessly maintained rooms that feature hand-carved furniture, firm beds and private bathroom. There's a shared kitchenette.

Albergue El Banco (☎ 645 5204; r without/with bathroom US$7/10; P 💻) In addition to clean and cute basic rooms, laundry service and an onsite **Internet cafe** (per hr US$2; 🕑 6am-9pm), this spot arranges lots of tours.

Cabinas Marín (☎ 645 5279; cabmarin@racsa.co.cr; r incl breakfast without/with bathroom US$8/12; P) On a hill about 50m north of the high school, this very clean spot has small wooden rooms with great big windows.

Manakín Lodge (☎ 645 5835; www.manakinlodge.com; incl breakfast r per person without/with bathroom US$12/32, d cabinas US$50; P 💻) This fine Cerro Plano spot is simple but friendly, with hot showers and Internet access, and the owners can arrange a variety of personalized tours for US$50 per group. Some of the rooms come with little balconies, and cabinas have full kitchens.

Pensión Flor de Monteverde (☎ 645 5236, www.flormonteverde.com; r without/with bathroom incl breakfast US$12/15, all meals US$15 extra; P) Further out than the others, this is a small, clean, friendly, family-run, and helpful place. Owner Eduardo Venegas Castro has worked at both the Monteverde and Santa Elena reserves and was director of the latter. Tours and transportation can be arranged.

Pensión Monteverde Inn (☎ 645 5156; s/d US$14/24; P) In a remote part of Cerro Plano is this friendly place, also the trailhead for the Hidden Valley Trail, which goes into a deep canyon and through an 11-hectare reserve. Rooms are Spartan but adequate and have private hot showers; breakfast is available on request for US$5, and the owners can pick you up at the bus stop if you have a reservation. The remote and very quiet location is the main attraction here.

Hotel El Sueño (☎ 645 6695; s/d incl breakfast US$15/25; 💻) Huge, newly renovated wooden rooms all have private hot showers. Upstairs rooms are airier, and the rooms out back better still. A new terrace overlooks the hills.

MID-RANGE

Arco Iris Ecolodge (see the boxed text opposite) is the best mid-range choice.

Finca Terra Viva (☎ 645 5454; www.terravivacr.com; r US$30; P 💻) About 3km out on the road toward Reserva Santa Elena, this 135-hectare finca is being gradually returned to the forest; about 60% is already there. In the meantime, a passel of cattle, pigs, goats, horses and chickens offer guests a typically Costa Rican rural experience – kids love this place. Each of the four rustic, wooden rooms sleeps up to four and has a private hot shower; for an extra US$5 per person there's access to a full kitchen. Or, they'll whip up three Costa Rican meals per day for an additional US$15 per person. Owner Federico is a well-known naturalist and guide who has long envisioned living in a finca that combines education, conservation and farming, and this is the

THE AUTHOR'S CHOICE

Budget

Pensión Santa Elena (☎ 645 5051; www.monteverdeinfo.com; dm US$5, d without/with bathroom US$15/25, camping per person US$3; P) This full-service shoestringer's hostel is *the* place to stay in the area with several small rooms and little houses with a cute courtyard, some with private bathroom and non-electric hot shower. Other amenities include a message board, shared kitchen, cozy, communal atmosphere and coffee all day. Caffeinated and multilingual proprietor Jacques is a frenzied and busy source of information, and can always answer questions and make a variety of transportation and tour arrangements geared toward the budget traveler.

Mid-range

Arco Iris Ecolodge (☎ 645 5067; www.arcoirislodge.com; r US$33-65; P) This clutch of pretty cabins is on a little hill overlooking Santa Elena and the surrounding forests, through which several private trails wend, including one to a lookout point where, on a clear day, you can see to the Pacific. The multilingual owners are helpful and make an excellent breakfast (US$7), sometimes with organic vegetables grown right here. The cheap cabin is just big enough to hold two bunk beds and a private hot shower; the pricier cabins are not only spacious, but sweet.

Top end

Vista Verde Lodge (☎ 380 1517; www.info-monteverde.com; d incl breakfast US$75, additional person US$12; P) When you really want to get away from it all, take the signed side road just east of Selvatur and head 2.5 rough kilometers (4WD only) to this marvelous lodge. Huge picture windows take in views of Volcán Arenal and the lake from the 10 huge, pretty wooden rooms or from the comfy common area, with TV and fireplace. Some 4km of trails through the primary forest surrounding the gorgeous spot can be explored by horseback; tours further into the forest can be arranged at the desk. The staff may be able to pick you up in Santa Elena, but if not it's a US$15 taxi ride from town, or you could take the bus to Selvatur and walk the rest of the way.

result. Horseback riding can be arranged, and you can try your hand at milking cows and making cheese.

Quetzal Inn (☎ 645 6076; victorgl@costarricense.co.cr; d incl breakfast without/with bathroom/with balcony US$22/35/42; P) Smallish rooms have high ceilings and lots of pretty wood, and the common area has cable TV, air-con and a fireplace.

Elis Lodge (☎ 645 5609; elislodge@yahoo.com; d without/with bathroom US$23/39; P) This cozy home with lots of cutesy personal touches has clean, bright rooms and a comfortable common area with a cable TV and fireplace.

Cabaña Lodge (☎ 245 5844; s/d small US$24/29, s/d large US$29/35; P) This new, all-wood hotel just outside of Santa Elena proper is a quiet option; the big rooms are spacious. The front desk can arrange tours.

Mariposa B&B (☎ 645 5013; umfamilia@costarricense.cr; s/d incl breakfast US$20/35; P) Just 1.5km from the reserve, this friendly family-run place has simple but very nice rooms with private warm showers. In addition to breakfast (other meals can be arranged), you can enjoy kitchen privileges and a little balcony out back for observing wildlife, which at the time of research included a passel of *pizotes* waving their long tails around while begging for potato chips.

Cabinas Don Taco (☎ 645 5263; www.cabinasdontaco.com; d standard/cabina incl breakfast US$25/30; P) With big porches, great murals and an outdoor dining/chill-out area, this spot, just north of Santa Elena proper, is fabulous. Cabinas come with TV, fridge and a balcony overlooking the Golfo de Nicoya.

Sunset Hotel (☎ 645 5228; s/d/tr US$26/38/48; P) About 1.5km out of Santa Elena toward Reserva Santa Elena, this is a small, well-kept place with a quiet location and great views of the Golfo de Nicoya. Clean, standard rooms with porches have two little luxuries: real hot showers (not suicide machines), and toilets with enough pressure to flush paper. German and English are spoken.

Hotel El Bosque (☎ 645 5221, bosquelodge@racsa.co.cr; s/d/tr US$30/37/45; P) Behind popular Pizzería

Tramonti (see p172), this excellent midrange choice has little paths through expansive grounds to spacious, simple rooms with big windows and hot showers.

Nidia Lodge (☎ 645 6082; s/d US$35/40; P) The proprietor of Pensión Flor de Monteverde, Eduardo Venegas Castro, has a beautiful new inn named for his wife. The area is peaceful and just steps away from the Finca Ecológica. The accommodations are first rate, with hot water and private balconies upstairs, plus there's a nice restaurant. Eduardo, an expert naturalist, clearly revels in offering guided walks of area forests.

Hotel Finca Valverde (☎ 645 5157; www.monteverde.co.cr; s/d US$46/64, ste US$68/82; additional person US$12; P) Outside Santa Elena, this is a working coffee farm. Cabins each have two clean and spacious (if rather bare) units with private hot-water showers, an upstairs loft, and a balcony. Junior suites have full baths and cable TV. A simple but pleasant **restaurant** (mains US$4-11; 6am-9:30pm) serves good fish and meat dishes; try Don Miguel's tenderloin for dinner. The attached bar is locally popular.

De Lucía Inn Hotel (☎ 645 5976; www.costa-rica-monteverde.com; s/d/tr US$47/58/69; P) Owned by the same friendly folks as the famed Restaurante de Lucía, this entry has pretty cedar-walled rooms with almond-wood floors and a nice common area with TV; upstairs rooms are carpeted.

La Colina Lodge (☎ 645 5009; www.lacolinalodge.com; d/tr US$42/54, d/tr with bathroom US$49/61; per person camping US$5) This is the former 'Flor Mar' opened in 1977 by Marvin Rockwell, one of the area's original Quakers, who was jailed for refusing to sign up for the draft in 1949 and then spent three months driving down from Alabama. The new owners have renovated the rooms, some with balconies and all have cozy Central American bedspreads. The recommended private **restaurant** (meals US$11) announces an internationally inspired meal, usually with Mediterranean flair, each morning. The owners speak English and German and offer a book exchange in their comfy TV room, which has a great selection of DVDs. Prices include breakfast.

Swiss Hotel Miramontes (☎ 645 5152; www.swisshotelmiramontes.com; s/d US$50/70; P) Just outside Santa Elena on the road to Juntas is this pleasantly situated place with nine rooms of varying size, all with fabulous private hot baths. Kids love the expansive landscaped grounds, with trails through the well-stocked orchid garden (US$5 for nonguests) and everyone enjoys the huge, pretty chalets. The **restaurant** (mains US$4-10; 1-10pm) specializes in Swiss treats such as *geschnetzeltes* with *rostï*, made with locally grown manioc instead of potatoes, and *café fertig*, coffee with real Swiss schnapps.

Sun Kiss (☎ 645 6984; www.hotels.co.cr; d/tr US$55/70, ste US$75; P) This serene and comfy outpost, just north of Santa Elena proper, has a B&B feel (though breakfast is US$4 extra) and grand views of the Golfo de Nicoya. Rooms are huge, showers are hot and the suite is something special.

Hotel Villa Verde (☎ 645 5025; s/d/tr incl breakfast US$57/75/93; P) Geared toward student groups on package tours, rooms surround a pool bedecked with some really cool murals and a fire pit perfect for relaxing with a beer. Rooms are dark and comfortable, but not luxurious by any stretch. Internet access is available (US$3 per hour).

Hotel Poco a Poco (☎ 645 6000; www.hotelpocoapoco.com; s/d/tr US$58/75/88; P) A short walk from the village of Santa Elena, this lovely spot has sparkling rooms sleeping three, with full hot baths, big cable TVs and phones; one room is wheelchair-accessible. The best perk, however, is the excellent **restaurant** (mains US$6-11; 6:30-9am & noon-9:30pm), also open to the public, with barbecue that gets raves and good seafood.

Trapp Family Lodge (☎ 645 5858; www.trappfam.com; s/d/tr r US$69/80/94; s/d cabin US$94/11, additional person US$13; P) The closest lodge to the reserve entrance (just under 1km away) has 20 spacious rooms with high wooden ceiling, big bathroom, and fabulous views from the picture windows overlooking either gardens or cloud forest. New cabins come complete with TV and fridge, and there's no smoking anywhere. There's a homey **restaurant** (mains US$10-16) for guests only; a bar and sitting room with cable TV is open till 10pm. The friendly owners can arrange tours and transportation.

Hotel Belmar (☎ 645 5201; hotelbelmar.net; s/d US$79/91, s/d chalet US$69/79; P) This is a real ecoresort, where typically pretty upscale rooms are decked out in artwork from Casem (see p163), and water from the mountainside Jacuzzi and pool is reused in the organic gardens, which provides veggies for the good

NORTHWESTERN COSTA RICA

restaurant (mains US$5-12). Minibars in the rooms, a TV lounge, and transportation from the bus stop are all part of the deal, but the biggest bonus is right out back: this is the trailhead for Cerro Amigos (p164).

TOP END

Many of the pricier hotels are taking it upon themselves to experiment with alternative technologies, from solar-heated showers to elaborate gray-water systems. Owners are usually more than happy to offer impromptu tours with full explanations of how these technologies work, and can offer suggestions to folks who'd like to implement similar systems back home.

Vista Verde Lodge (see p169) is the author's choice for this price range.

Hotel Fonda Vela (☎ lodge 645 5125, reservations 257 1413; www.fondavela.com; s/d US$88/98, junior ste US$98/110, additional person US$9; P ⊠) A little more than 1.5km away from the reserve, this classy retreat has 2km of trails through the 14-hectare grounds (offering good birding), and on-site stables that mean there's no wait to rent a horse. Even the standards are spacious and light, with wood accents and large windows, while suites include minibar, bathtub, balcony and sitting room with huge TV. Many rooms are wheelchair-accessible. The **restaurant** (mains US$8-16; 6:15-9am, noon-2pm & 6:30-8:30pm), open to the public, serves excellent food – try the tilapia – in a beautiful building; the owners' father, Paul Smith, is a well-known local artist whose work, along with others', graces the walls.

Hotel de Montaña Monteverde (☎ 645 5046; www.monteverdemountainhotel.com; d standard/superior/deluxe US$73/96/120; P) Opened in 1978 as the first top-end hotel in Monteverde, this comfortably rustic spot has a variety of rooms (the nicer ones including view, minibar and hairdryer) in addition to the fabulous views to the Golfo de Nicoya, and a good **restaurant** (mains US$6-17; 6am-9:30pm) specializing in seafood, as well as a cozy adjoining bar and a TV lounge. The spacious gardens and forests of the 15-hectare property are pleasant to walk around. A sauna and Jacuzzi can be used for US$1 per hour by reservation (for privacy) from 4pm to 9pm. All the local tours and activities are arranged.

Hotel Heliconia (☎ 645 5109, www.hotelheliconia.com; s/d standard US$87/94; junior ste US$89/105; P) About 4 km from the reserve, this attractive, wooden, family-run lodge and bungalows spread out across the mountainside. Standard rooms have breezy views while junior suites are ridiculously luxurious with two double beds, full baths and stained glass. Owners arrange all the usual tours, and operate a spa with four Jacuzzis (US$7 per hour per person) and an endless list of beauty treatments, all open to the public, as well as the reader-recommended **Restaurante Mediterráneo** (mains US$7-10; 6:30am-9pm), with Italian and seafood specialties.

El Establo Mountain Resort (☎ 645 5110; hotelestablo.com; incl breakfast d US$87, ste junior/deluxe US$156/212; P ⊠) This seriously upscale lodge has a few standard rooms adjacent to the parking lot that aren't so outrageous, but some huge suites with balconies overlooking the pool, mountains and Golfo de Nicoya also include personal flagstone-trimmed Jacuzzis. This being Monteverde, the new deluxe property comes complete with solar power, gray-water systems, a well-insulated underground electrical network and a good restaurant where buffet-style meals usually include locally grown produce. It's a steep hike to the best rooms, but the resort runs a shuttle by request.

Hotel El Sapo Dorado (☎ 645 5010; www.sapodorado.com; d/ste US$89/99, additional person US$17; P ⊠) This hotel is owned by long-time residents who are active in the community, promoting sustainable tourism and other values. There are 30 spacious rooms mostly in duplex cabins. All have two queen-size beds, a table and chairs, and private hot showers. Various deluxe suites, named for their incredible views, have minibars, fridges, and French doors that open to a private terrace with views down to the Golfo de Nicoya. Light sleepers should opt for the sunset terrace suites, which have thicker walls than the mountain suites.

The private forest behind the hotel has trails, and the **restaurant-bar** (mains US$10-20; 6:30-9am, noon-3pm & 6-9pm) always offers vegetarian options. Professional massage services are available for US$45 per hour.

Monteverde Lodge & Gardens (☎ 257 0766; www.costarica.com; s/d US$115/138, additional person US$22; P ⊠) A progressive recycling strategy, a solar-energy system, and a huge solar-powered – but nice and hot – Jacuzzi are among this nonsmoking hotel's noteworthy environmentally sound practices. Large rooms with coffee makers, full bathrooms, and picture windows have garden or forest views. The large lobby is graced by a huge fireplace.

The grounds are attractively landscaped with a variety of native plants, emphasizing ferns, bromeliads, and mosses, and a short trail leads to a bluff with an observation platform at the height of the forest canopy, with good views of the forest and a river ravine. Most folks are here on all-inclusive package deals that include three meals, served à la carte and featuring quality international cuisine, as well as guided tours and transportation from San José.

Eating

Pricier hotels often have good (if similarly pricey) restaurants; many are open to the public. Santa Elena has most of the budget eateries. Well-stocked **Supermercado Esperanza** (☎ 758 7351; 7am-8pm) has organic groceries, too. **Coop Santa Elena** (7:30am-6pm) in Cerro Plano has a smaller selection, but profits are reinvested in the community.

These restaurants are listed from Santa Elena to the Monteverde preserve.

Restaurante El Nido (mains US$3-7; 8:30am-9pm) Enjoy top-quality typical food including casados of every sort, plus burgers and snacks, while watching the street scene below. Downstairs, **Panadería Jiménez** (5am-6:30pm Mon-Sat, 5-10am Sun) has the best baked goods in town, plus coffee for folks booked on the early bus.

Café Rainforest (light meals US$2-3; 8am-8pm) Grab the best cup of coffee in town (which is saying something) with a pastry or sandwich to mellow the buzz.

Restaurante Maravilla (mains US$2-5; 6am-9pm) You'd never guess from the white-plastic-table ambience that this place had some of the best *soda* food around; try the seafood soup (US$4) or various *ceviches* (US$1 to US$5).

Restaurante Campesino (mains US$2-8; 9am-11pm) Relax beneath about 80 stuffed animals won from machines by the dexterous owner, who also serves up amazing casados, beautiful salads and lots of good seafood with a smile. Recommended.

Morpho's Restaurant (☎ 645 5607; mains US$4-8; 7:30am-9:30pm) This romantic spot, complete with candles in the elegant dining room, does delicious typical food with gourmet flair. The special of the day (think sea bass in orange sauce) comes with your choice of a nice selection of wine, or a natural drink.

Bar y Restaurante Chimi (☎ 645 6330; mains US$3-8; 11am-11pm) Pull up a stool to a highly polished tree stump and tell your vegetarian friends you'll see them later – this place specializes in meat, specifically steak, although seafood and lots of beer is also on offer.

Sabores (10am-9pm; cones US$0.30-3) With longer hours than at La Lechería, this place serves Monteverde's own ice cream, plus coffee and other desserts.

Pizza Johnny (☎ 645 5066; pizza US$8-12, other mains US$4-12; 11:30am-9:30pm) Make dinner reservations during high season for a candlelit table, preferably on the outdoor patio overlooking the jungle. There's a full bar, pasta is made in-house (try the raviolis) and all veggies are organic when available.

Restaurant de Lucía (☎ 645 5337; 11am-8:30pm; mains US$6-12) On the same road as the Butterfly Garden, this Chilean-owned place is one of Monteverde's best restaurants, though not very expensive at about US$20 for a meal for two people. The specialty is Italian food: Try the vegetarian lasagna or fish in garlic sauce.

Flor de Vida (☎ 645 6081; mains US$2-6; 7am-9:30pm) This popular vegetarian restaurant makes everything in-house, from recommended lasagna to cruelty-free casados, but start with the spicy potato wedges. Still hungry? Try the mango pie or heavenly *tiramisu*.

Pizzería Tramonti (☎ 645 6120; mains US$5-11; 11:30am-3pm & 5:30-10pm, closed Mon in low season) This popular spot is probably most famous for its pizzas, but also does an assortment of Italian-style dishes, from pasta to seafood.

Stella's Bakery (☎ 645 5560; 6am-6pm; mains US$2-5) Order your choice of sandwich on any of their delicious homemade breads with a convenient order form (one side is in English), and don't skimp on the veggies, many of which are grown organically behind the bakery. You can also get soups, salads, savory pastries stuffed with meats and cheeses, and lots of tempting sweet pastries.

Moon Shiva Restaurant (☎ 645 6270; dishes about US$4-8; 10am-10pm) On a rise in Cerro Plano with fine forest views, this bohemian eatery does mostly vegetarian dishes with Mediterranean and Middle Eastern flair by day, but turns into a very danceable live music venue – think rock, jazz and salsa – after the sun goes down.

La Cocina de Leña de Doña Flory (☎ 645 5306; mains US$4-6; 🕑 8am-8pm Sun-Fri) On a tiny turnoff close to La Colina Lodge, this 'Restaurante Rustico' is indeed simple, as you'd expect anything owned by Marvin Rockwell, one of the area's original Quaker settlers, to be. The outdoor *soda* serves up typical fare, with recommended tamales anytime, and their own special stew on Sunday.

Entertainment

Monteverde and Santa Elena's nightlife generally involves a guided hike into one of the reserves, but there are a few places for more inebriating amusements.

La Cascada is a popular dance club in Cerro Plano that's open Thursday to Sunday nights; there may be a cover charge, or try Domingo's Bar/Unicornio Discotec, a local hangout next to the soccer field at the northern end of Santa Elena.

Popular bars also include Amigos Bar in Santa Elena, a great place to drink and shoot pool, and the Taberna Los Valverde, which has a dance floor and attracts a healthy mix of visitors and locals, all ready to shake what their mamas gave them.

Getting There & Away

The government has been planning to build a series of bridges across the several rivers that feed Laguna de Arenal's southwestern shore for about 20 years; lately there's actually been some construction work going on. If completed, this will provide a road connection between Monteverde and La Fortuna. But don't hold your breath.

BUS

All intercity buses stop at the **bus terminal** (☎ 645 5159; 🕑 6-11am & 1:30-5pm Mon-Fri, closes 3pm Sat & Sun) in downtown Santa Elena, and most continue on to La Lechería in Monteverde. On the trip in, keep an eye on your luggage, particularly on the San José–Puntarenas leg of the trip, as well as on the Monteverde–Tilarán run.

Purchase tickets to Reservas Monteverde and Santa Elena at Hotel Camino Verde (p167), which can also make reservations for pricier trips with private companies. Destinations, bus companies, fares, journey times and departure times are as follows:

Las Juntas US$2; 1½ hours; departs from the bus station at 4:45am.

Managua, Nicaragua (Nica Bus) US$10; eight hours; departs from the bus station at 6am.

Reserva Monteverde US$1; one hour; departs from front of Banco Nacional at 6:15am & 1:15pm; returns 11am & 4pm.

Puntarenas US$2; three hours; departs from the front of Banco Nacional at 6am.

San José (TransMonteverde) US$4.25; 4½ hours; departs from La Lechería at 6:30am & 2:30pm, with pick-up at the bus station in Santa Elena.

Reserva Santa Elena US$2; departs from front of Banco Nacional at 6:45am & 11am; returns 10:30am & 3:30pm.

Tilarán, with connection to La Fortuna US$1.75; three to four hours; departs from the bus station at 7am.

CAR

While most Costa Rican communities regularly request paved roads in their region, preservationists in Monteverde have done the opposite. All roads here are shockingly rough, and 4WD is necessary all year, especially in the rainy season. Many car-rental agencies will refuse to rent you an ordinary car during rainy season if you admit that you're headed to Monteverde.

There are four roads from the Interamericana: coming from the south, the first turnoff is at Rancho Grande (18km north of the Puntarenas exit); a second turnoff is at the Río Lagarto bridge (just past Km 149, and roughly 15km northwest of Rancho Grande). Both are well signed and join one another about a third of the way to Monteverde. Both routes boast about 35km of steep, winding, and scenic dirt roads with plenty of potholes and rocks to ensure that the driver, at least, is kept from admiring the scenery.

A third road goes via Juntas (p157), which starts off paved, but becomes just as rough as the first two a few kilometers past town, though it's about 5km shorter than the previous two. Finally, if coming from the north, drivers could take the paved road from Cañas via Tilarán (p217) and then take the rough road from Tilarán to Santa Elena.

HORSE

There are a number of outfitters (p166) that offer transportation on **horseback** (5-6hrs; per person US$65-100) to La Fortuna, usually in combination with jeep rides. The Castillo Trail has long been the source of some hand-wringing on the part of animal lovers and guidebook writers, but today there are three different

TO RIDE OR NOT TO RIDE?

Though the top two tourist destinations in the region, La Fortuna and Monteverde/Santa Elena, are only about 25km apart, there are a few roadblocks that have thus far stopped anyone from paving a direct route between them: an erupting volcano, the country's largest lake, seven rivers, and the Cordillera de Tilarán for starters, not to mention mountains of bureaucratic red tape in San José. Currently, it takes several very bumpy hours by bus to make the trip.

In the mid-1990s, local entrepreneurs began offering transportation on horseback between the towns, calling it 'the shortest and most convenient connection.' The idea enchanted tourists and quickly became a booming business; as demand for the scenic trip grew, so did the number of outfitters. The result was severe price-cutting, and someone had to suffer for the savings. It was usually the horses.

Unethical practices such as buying cheap old horses and literally working them to death were reported: Lonely Planet received scores of horrified letters describing thin, diseased mounts that could barely make it through the mud; at least one overworked animal died on the Castillo Trail. Author Rob Rachowiecki wrote about the problem, angering local business people who complained that his 'job was to write a guidebook, not harass them.' But the letters kept coming, so Rachowiecki kept reporting. Many companies went out of business.

Today, standards are high for reputable operators (see p166), in part (we like to think) because of informed tourists who asked hard questions and insisted on examining their horses before setting out, two precautions we still ask you to take. Although incidents of abuse are still reported, these are happily the exception rather than the rule. Costs have risen, the

trails available of varying difficulty. Use your own best judgment (see the boxed text).

JEEP & BOAT

The fastest route between Monteverde/Santa Elena and La Fortuna is a jeep-boat-jeep combo (US$25, three hours), which can be arranged through almost any hotel or tour operator in either town. A 4WD jeep taxi takes you to Río Chiquito, meeting a boat that crosses Laguna de Arenal, where a taxi on the other side continues to La Fortuna.

RESERVA BIOLÓGICA BOSQUE NUBOSO MONTEVERDE

When Quaker settlers first arrived, they agreed to preserve about a third of their property in order to protect the watershed above Monteverde. By 1972, however, encroaching squatters began to threaten the region. The community joined forces with organizations such as the Nature Conservancy and the World Wildlife Fund to purchase 328 hectares adjacent to the already preserved area. This was called the Reserva Biológica Bosque Nuboso Monteverde (Monteverde Cloud Forest Biological Reserve), which the Centro Científico Tropical (Tropical Science Center) began administrating 1975.

In 1986 the Monteverde Conservation League (MCL) was formed to buy land to expand the reserve. Two years later they launched the International Children's Rainforest project, which encouraged children and school groups from all over the world to raise money to buy and save tropical rain forest adjacent to the reserve. Today the reserve totals 10,500 hectares.

The most striking aspect of this project is that it is the result of private citizens working for change rather than waiting around for a national park administered by the government. The reserve relies partly on donations from the public (see Information opposite). Considering how the ridiculously underfunded Minae struggles to protect the national-park system, enterprises like this are more important than ever for maintaining cohesive wildlife corridors.

Visitors should note that some of the walking trails are very muddy, and even during the dry season (late December to early May) the cloud forest tends to drip. Rainwear and suitable boots are recommended if you plan on going a long distance. Many of the trails have been stabilized with concrete blocks or wooden boards and are easier to walk. During the wet season, the unpaved trails turn into quag-

advertising revolves around how healthy the horses are, and most operators offer mellower alternatives.

There are now three main routes: The gorgeous and infamous **Castillo Trail** (5hr hike, 3hr horseback), also called the 'Mountain Trail' or 'Mirador Trail,' crosses the fierce Caño Negro three times. It's still in use, but should only be done during the dry months (if then) from mid-March through May (assuming that it's actually dry) by experienced riders. Some businesses offer the trek year-round, as it saves operators about US$25 per person in transport costs compared to other options – but don't do it in the rainy season, no matter what your operator says.

The **Chiquito Trail** (6hr hike, 4hr horseback) is still scenic and slippery, but doesn't require crossing the deepest rivers. This trail should also be avoided during wet weather, particularly by inexperienced riders. Finally, the flat and somewhat-less-scenic **Lake Trail** (6hr hike, 2½hr horseback) is fine year-round, great for newbies, and basically skirts Laguna de Arenal between the boat taxi and jeep taxi that provide the actual transportation.

A good operator will never guarantee these or any other horseback trip, particularly along the Castillo Trail, as safety for both you and the horse depends completely on the weather. If they aren't offering some kind of refund in the event of rain, and/or an alternate lake trail or jeep-boat option, something's wrong. Also note that some hotels will imply that they are booking you through an established operator, but actually deliver you to a pal's independent company: ask if anything seems fishy.

And yes, budget travelers, you can find cheaper rides or even bargain reputable operators down by a few dollars in the low season. Hey, it's your choice. But consider this: When you save US$5, it's got to come out of someone's hide. Whose do you think it will be?

mires, but there are usually fewer visitors then.

Because of the fragile environment, the reserve will allow a maximum of 160 people at any given time. During the dry season this limit is almost always reached by 10am, which means you could spend the better part of a day waiting around for someone to leave. The best strategy is to get there before the gates open, or better (and wetter) to come during the off season, usually May through June and also September through November.

Information

The **information office** (☎ 645 5122, www.cct.or.cr; entry to the park adult/student US$13/6.50, child under 6 free; 🕑 7am-4pm) is adjacent to the gift shop, where you can get information and buy trail guides, bird and mammal lists, and maps. The gift shop also sells T-shirts, beautiful color slides by Richard Laval, postcards, books, posters and a variety of other souvenirs, and rents binoculars (US$10) and rubber boots (US$2); you'll need to leave your passport. The annual rainfall here is about 3000mm, though parts of the reserve reportedly get twice as much. It's usually cool (high temperatures around 18°C/65°F), so wear appropriate clothing.

It's important to remember that the cloud forest is often cloudy (!) and the vegetation is thick. This combination cuts down on sound as well as vision; also keep in mind that main trails in this reserve are also among the most trafficked in Costa Rica. Some readers have been disappointed with the lack of wildlife sightings. The best bet is, as always, to hire a guide.

Donations to the **Friends of Monteverde Cloud Forest** (friends@cct.or.cr; www.cloudforestalive.org) are graciously accepted at the following address: PO Box 1964, Cleveland, OH 44106, USA.

Hiking

There are currently 13km of marked and maintained trails; a free map is provided with your entrance fee. The most popular of the nine trails, suitable for day hikes, make a rough triangle (El Triángulo) to the east of the reserve entrance. The triangle's sides are made up of the popular **Sendero Bosque Nuboso** (1.9km), an interpretive walk (booklet US$0.75 at gate) through the cloud forest that begins at the ranger station, paralleled by the more open, 2km **El Camino**, a favorite of bird-watchers. The **Sendero Pantanoso** (1.6km) forms the far side of El Triángulo, traversing swamps, pine forests and the continental divide. Returning to the entrance,

Sendero Río (2km) follows the Quebrada Cuecha past a few photogenic waterfalls.

Bisecting the triangle, gorgeous **Chomogo Trail** (1.8km) lifts hikers 150m to 1680m, the highest point in the triangle, and other little trails criss-cross the region, including the worthwhile **Sendero Brillante** (300m), with birds' eye views of a miniature forest. There's also a 100m suspension bridge about 1km from the ranger station.

There are also more substantial hikes, including trails to the three backcountry shelters (see later) that begin at the far corners of the triangle; if you're strong enough, these trails are highly recommended. The shorter trails are among the most trafficked in the country, despite valiant efforts to contain crowd sizes, and wildlife learned long ago that the region is worth avoiding unless they want a good look at hominids indigenous to Africa.

Even longer trails, many of them less developed (read: wear rubber boots) stretch out east across the reserve and down the Peñas Blancas river valley to lowlands north of the Cordillera de Tilarán. Some of these trails enter the Children's Rainforest (see p164). Ask at the reserve regarding hiking through.

The bird list includes more than 400 species that have been recorded in the area, but the one most visitors want to see is the resplendent quetzal (see the boxed text, opposite), which is most often spotted during the March and April nesting season, though you could get lucky anytime of year.

Tours & Guides

Although you can hike around the reserve on your own, a guide is highly recommended, and not just by us but by dozens of readers who were inspired by their adventures to email us. The park runs a variety of guided tours: make reservations *at least* one day in advance. As size is limited, groups should make reservations several months out for dry season and holiday periods. Guides speak English and are trained naturalists, and proceeds from the tours benefit environmental-education programs in local schools.

The reserve offers guided **natural history tours** at 7:30am daily (☎ reservations 645 5112; admission US$15, excl entry fee), and on busy days at 8:30am as well. Participants meet at the Hummingbird Gallery (p164), where a short 10-minute orientation is given. A half-hour slide show from renowned wildlife-photographers Michael and Patricia Fogden is followed by a 2½- to three-hour walk. Once your tour is over, you can return to the reserve on your own, as your ticket is valid for the entire day.

The reserve also offers recommended two-hour **night tours** (admission without/with transportation & incl entry fee US$13/15) at 7:15pm nightly. These are by flashlight (bring your own for the best visibility), and offer the opportunity to observe the 70% of regional wildlife with nocturnal habits.

Guided **birding tours** (5hr; per person incl entry fee US$40-50) in English begin at Stella's Bakery at 6am, and usually sight more than 40 species. There's a two-person minimum and six-person maximum. Longer tours go on by request at a higher fee, and usually more than 60 species are seen.

Several local businesses can arrange for a local to guide you either within the reserve or in some of the nearby surrounding areas. Pensión Santa Elena (p169) organizes **guided tours** (day/night 3½/2hr, per person US$15/13); meet at 7:15pm at the reserve, no reservations needed for the night tours. Staff can also recommend **private guides** (guide@monteverdeinfo.com), or ask at your hotel or any tour operator.

The reserve can also recommend excellent guides, many of which work for them, for a private tour. Costs vary depending on the season, the guide, and where you want to go, but average about US$60 to US$100 for a half day. Entrance costs may be extra, especially for the cheaper tours. Full-day tours are also available. The size of the group is up to you – go alone or split the cost with a group of friends.

Sleeping & Eating

Near the park entrance are **dormitories** (dm US$10) with 43 bunks and shared bathrooms. These are often used by researchers and student groups but are often available to tourists – make reservations. Full board can be arranged in advance.

There are also three **backcountry shelters** (dm US$3.50), with drinking water, showers, propane stoves, and cooking utensils. You need to carry a sleeping bag, candles, food and anything else (toilet paper?) you might need. **El Valle** (6km, 2hr) is the closest, **La Leona** (8km, 4hr) is near a cable car across Río Peñas Blancas, and

DAVID M WATSON

Waterfall, Reserva Biólogica Lomas de Barbudal (p185)

Elfin forest, Reserva Biólogica Bosque Nuboso Monteverde (p174)

DAVID M WATSON

Playa Naranjo, Parque Nacional Santa Rosa (p194)

LUKE HUNTER

MARK NEWMAN

Beach scene, Montezuma (p262)

RALPH LEE HOPKINS

Squirrel monkey *(Saimiri oerstedii),* Parque Nacional Manuel Antonio (p303)

CHRIS BART

Firey sunset, Península de Nicoya (p220)

Kayaking down the estuary, Isla Damas (p283)

ROBERTO SONCIN GEROMETTA

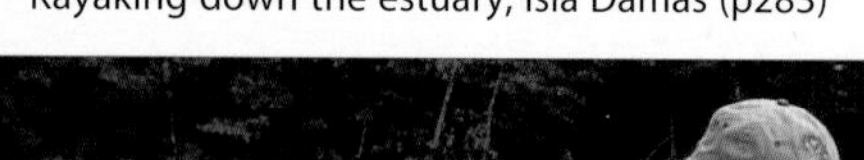

TAIL OF THE RESPLENDENT DECOY

Perhaps the most sought-after sighting in Monteverde is a glimpse of the iridescent and notoriously shy quetzal, Guatemala's national bird, to the eternal frustration of the Costa Rican tourist bureau who do not have rights over it.

Though there are probably better spots in the country to see them (eg Cerro de la Muerte, p320), this is the most famous and easily accessible, so shorter trails see a lot of camera-snapping traffic. But there's more remote country just a steep and muddy few kilometers away, and most quetzals simply prefer the clouds to the crowds.

Obviously, this is a problem for guides hired by tourists who have been fooled by the photos at the back of their guidebooks into thinking that successful birding is a day in the park, rather than a long, wet slog into the heart of the rain forest. Take this tale with as many grains of salt as you'd like (we were unable to get confirmation), but according to the story, one group of local entrepreneurs came up with an ingenious solution.

A decoy quetzal, by some accounts wooden and by others stuffed, but always quietly resplendent in his borrowed electric blue-and-green plumage, was mounted in a tree fairly far from an area road, on safely gated private land. 'If you don't see anything,' guides-in-the-know whispered to one another, 'drive by this spot.' Tourists were thrilled, tips rose exponentially, and word got around.

The ruse worked for about a week, but the folks responsible had wholly underestimated the tenacity of bird-watchers intent on taking the top prize. One morning they got a call from property owners: their fence had been surreptitiously snipped during the night, and the yard was infested with khaki-clad tourists sneaking around the grounds, hiding behind trees and under bushes, and covertly snapping pictures of the suspiciously still bird.

Eyes rolling, the hucksters apologetically escorted excited birders back to the road, fixed the fence, and sighed. The quetzal came down, and most park visitors have since had to make do with photos of hummingbirds, unless they're either lucky or persistent. And the resplendent decoy? That's a 'tail' that will hopefully make another appearance, so keep your eyes open.

Eladios Hut (13km, 6hr) is the nicest, with separate dorm rooms and a nice porch. Trails are muddy and challenging, scenery mossy and green, and the tourist hordes who inundate the day hikes a far-off memory. This may be the best way to appreciate the reserve.

If you don't have reservations, show up by 1pm on the dot to stay at any of the park facilities.

Getting There & Away

Public buses (US$2, 45 minutes) depart the Banco Nacional in Santa Elena at 6:15am and 1pm daily; only the morning bus runs on Sunday in low season. Buses return from the reserve at 11am and 4pm. You can flag down the buses from anywhere on the road between Santa Elena and the reserve; ask at your hotel about what time they pass by. Taxis (US$5) are also available.

The 6km walk from Santa Elena is uphill, but lovely – look for paths that run parallel to the road. There are views all along the way, and many visitors remark that some of the best birding is on the final 2km of the road.

RESERVA SANTA ELENA

Though Monteverde Reserve gets all the attention, this exquisitely misty entry, at 310 hectares just a fraction of that other forest's size, has plenty to recommend it. While Monteverde Crowd…er…Cloud Forest entertains almost 200,000 visitors annually, many of whom spend peak-season mornings waiting around to meet strict quotas before entering, Santa Elena sees fewer than 20,000 tourists each year, which means its dewy trails through mysteriously veiled forest are usually far quieter. It's also a bit cheaper, plus your entry fee is helping support another unique project.

One of the first community-managed conservation projects in the country, this cloud-forest reserve was created in 1989 and opened to the public in March 1992. It is now managed by the Santa Elena High School board and bears the quite unwieldy official name of Reserva del Bosque Nuboso del Colegio Técnico Profesional de Santa Elena. You can visit the **reserve office** (☎ 645 5693; 🕑 8am-4pm Wed-Fri) at the high school.

The reserve is about 6km northeast of the village of Santa Elena. This cloud forest is slightly higher than, but otherwise similar to, Monteverde. There's a stable population of spider monkeys and sloths, many seen on the road to the reserve. And because some of the forest is second-growth, there are sunnier spots for spotting birds and other animals throughout.

This place is moist, and almost all the water comes as fine mist, and more than 25% of all the biomass in this forest are epiphytes – mosses and lichens – for which this place is a humid haven. Though about 10% of species here won't be found in Monteverde, which is largely on the other side of the continental divide, you can see quetzals here too, as well as Volcán Arenal exploding in the distance – theoretically. Rule No 407 of cloud forests: it's often cloudy.

Information

You can visit the **reserve** (☎ 645 5390; www.monteverdeinfo.com/reserve-santa-elena-monteverde; adult/student US$9/5; 7am-4pm) on your own, but just as at Monteverde, a guide will enhance your experience tenfold (see below).

There's a simple restaurant, coffee shop and gift store. Note that all proceeds go toward managing the reserve and to environmental education programs in local schools. Donations are most graciously accepted.

If you've got more time than money, there's a good volunteer program here. You're expected to make at least a one-week commitment, and very basic (no electricity, very cold showers) dorm-style accommodations are available free to volunteers, though all but the most rugged will prefer a US$10 per day homestay, including three meals.

Hiking

More than 12km of trails are currently open, featuring four circular trails offering walks of varying difficulty and length, from 45 minutes to 3½ hours (1.4km to 4.8km) along a stable (though not 'concrete blocked') trail system. Rubber boots (US$1) can be rented at the entrance.

Tours & Guides

The reserve offers guided **daylight tours** (3hr; per person not incl admission US$15) at 7:30am and 11:30am daily; try to make the earlier hike. Popular **night hikes** (1½hr; per person excl admission US$13) leave at 7pm nightly. Tours have a two-person minimum and six-person maximum, so reservations are recommended for both tours during the dry season. The reserve can also arrange three-day private tours through various guides for US$20.

Getting There & Away

At the time of writing, regular bus service between the village of Santa Elena and the reserve had been suspended; check at any hotel to see if it's been reinstated. In the meantime, a daily shuttle (US$2 each way) makes the 8km trek, departing from Banco Nacional in town at 6:45am and 11am, returning at 10:30am and 3:30pm. A taxi from Santa Elena costs US$8.

You can also book a pricey trek through the nearby SkyTrek (2km from the reserve; see p166) or Selvatur (see p166), 150m from the park entrance, which include transportation from any Monteverde or Santa Elena hotel to their operations, from where it's an easy walk to the reserve.

ECOLODGE SAN LUIS & BIOLOGICAL STATION

Formerly a tropical biology research station, this facility now integrates research with ecotourism and education. It is administrated by the University of Georgia, and volunteer opportunities are available to folks with relevant degrees and in excellent physical condition. There are also comfortable **accommodations** (☎ 645 8049; www.ecolodgesanluis.com; dm US$58, s/d cabin US$95/90, bungalow US$74/69; P) for anyone interested in learning about the cloud-forest environment and experiencing a bit of traditional, rural Costa Rica. Rates include all meals.

The 70-hectare site is on the Río San Luis and adjoins the southern part of the Monteverde reserve. Its average elevation of 1100m makes it a tad lower and warmer than Monteverde, and birders have recorded some 230 species attracted by the slightly nicer weather. Many mammals have been sighted as well, and visitors have a good chance of spotting coatis, kinkajous, tayras, sloths, monkeys, and others. There are a number of trails into primary and secondary forest, and there's also a working farm with tropical fruit orchards, and a coffee harvest from November to March.

Three types of lodging are available. Near the center's dining room, lecture hall, and library are four bunkhouse rooms with 30 beds and shared hot-water baths. Bungalows have private hot baths and sleep up to five, while 12 larger cabins also include a balcony and views from porches overlooking the Río San Luis. There are a host of day and night hikes guided by biologists, as well as slide shows, seminars, horseback rides and even an introduction to research activities. Discounts can be arranged for students, researchers, large groups, and long stays.

From the main road between Santa Elena and Monteverde, it's a steep 3km walk from the signed road where the bus will drop you off. A 4WD taxi from town runs about US$12 each way, and the lodge can also arrange transportation from San José in advance.

PUENTE LA AMISTAD

About 23km south of Cañas on the Interamericana is a turnoff to the Puente La Amistad, 25km to the west. For more details, see p248. (Prior to that, drivers used to take a ferry.)

CAÑAS

If you're cruising north on the Interamericana, this is the first town of any size (population 25,200) in Costa Rica's driest and dustiest province, Guanacaste. *Sabanero* (p187) culture is evident on the sweltering and quiet streets, where full-custom pickup trucks share the road with wizened cowboys on horseback, fingering their machetes with a swagger you just don't see outside the province. It's a typically Latin American town, where everyone walks slowly and businesses shut down for lunch, all centered on the Parque Central and Catholic church – which are most definitely not typical.

Information

You can find public phones, a post office, library and a Banco Nacional, as well as many simple *sodas* and hotels here. The **emergency clinic** (☎ 669 0092; cnr Av Central & Hwy 1; 🕑 7am-4pm Mon-Fri) has 24-hour on-call service.

Internet Ciberc@ñas (Av 3 btwn Calles 1 & 3; per hr US$1.25; 🕑 8am-9pm Mon-Sat, 2-9pm Sun) has fast computers, air-con and, if you get here at 8am, two hours for the price of one.

The Cañas **Minae/ACT office** (☎ 669 0533; Av 9; 🕑 8am-4pm Mon-Fri) has limited information about nearby national parks and reserves.

Sights & Activities

Though most visitors simply use the town as a base for visits to nearby **Parque Nacional Palo Verde** (p184) or rafting the **Río Corobicí**, it's worth the trip just to see the Catholic church's **psychedelic mosaics** designed by famed local painter Otto Apuy: sinewy vines and colorful starbursts that have enveloped the modern church's once clean lines are enhanced by jungle-themed stained glass that's completely different from anything on offer at the Vatican. In **Parque Central** opposite, park benches and the pyramid-shaped bandstand are equally elaborate.

RAFTING

Gentle rafting trips down the Río Corobicí can be made with **Safaris Corobicí** (☎ 669 6091, www.safariscorobici.com). Bookings can be made at their office on the Interamericana about 4.5km north of Cañas. The emphasis of these trips is wildlife observation rather than exciting white water. The river is Class I-II (in other words, pretty flat) but families and nature-lovers enjoy these trips. Swimming holes are found along the river.

Safaris Corobicí offers departures from 7am to 3pm daily. A two-hour float costs US$37 per person, a three-hour birding float covering 12km costs US$45 per person, and a half-day 18km float including lunch costs US$60 per person. All prices are based on a two-person minimum; children under 14 are half price. The company also rents out a little guesthouse nearby.

LAS PUMAS

Safaris Corobicí also has access to **Las Pumas** (☎ 669 6044; admission by donation; 🕑 8am-5pm), a wild-animal shelter directly behind its office. Started in the 1960s by Lilly Hagnauer, a Swiss woman, it is said to be the largest shelter of its kind in Latin America. Pumas, jaguars, ocelots, and margays, plus peccaries and a few birds that were either orphaned or injured are taken care of here and it has clearly been a labor of love to save and raise them. Unfortunately, Lilly herself died in 2001, but now Safaris Corobicí is running Las Pumas with obviously high standards. Las Pumas is not officially

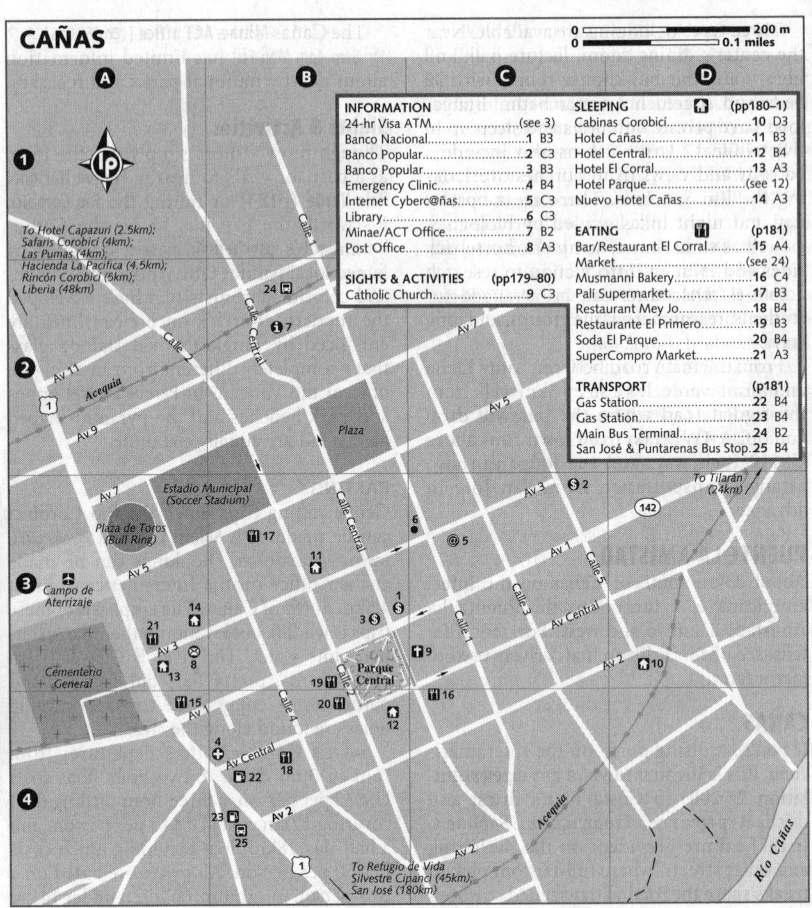

funded and contributions help offset the high costs of maintaining the shelter.

REFUGIO DE VIDA SILVESTRE CIPANCI

New in 2001, this small wildlife refuge is at the confluence of the Ríos Tempisque and Bebedero, at the southern end of Parque Nacional Palo Verde. Local fishers offer passenger boats for tours on these two rivers. A three-hour guided tour costs around US$20 per person (US$150 minimum), and can usually be arranged at the docks; show up early.

The Minae/ACT office in Cañas has more information on the park. Boats leave from the Níspero dock, just north of the Tempisque ferry.

Sleeping

Cañas is a cheaper place to stay than Liberia, which may be why so many long-haul truck drivers spend the night here. Get in by mid-afternoon for the best choice of rooms.

Hotel Central (☎ 669 1101; s/d US$3.50/7, s/d with bathroom US$9/14) Right on Parque Central, dark rooms (ask for one with windows) have a high-school-gym ambience but are quite clean, as are the shared showers, and all front a little balcony overlooking the street and a lobby with a couple of rocking chairs and a TV.

Hotel Parque (☎ 669 2213; r per person US$3.50) Rooms are smaller, grungier and a little sunnier than Hotel Central, next door. All have shared bathrooms.

Cabinas Corobicí (☎ 669 0241, cnr Av 2 & Calle 5; r per person US$9; P) At the southeastern end of town, this is a better budget option, where the friendly management maintains comfortable, good-sized rooms with private showers.

Hotel Cañas (☎ 669 0039; hotelcanas@racsa.co.cr; cnr Calle 2 & Av 3; s/d US$12/20, with TV & air-con US$17/28; P) Basic rooms surrounding the parking lot are dark and clean, with private cold showers. Bonus: guests are welcome to use the pool at Nuevo Hotel Cañas.

Hotel El Corral (☎ 669 1467; s/d US$17/27) Right on the Interamericana, ask for your absolutely standard room (some with air-con, hot shower and/or TV) in the back, away from the highway noise.

Nuevo Hotel Cañas (☎ 669 5118; hotelcanas@racsa.co.cr; Av 3 btwn Calle 4 & Hwy 1; s/d US$28/45; P) This is the nicest hotel in town, and comfortable rooms have air-con and TV. There's also a pool and Jacuzzi.

Hotel Capazuri (☎ 669 6280; capazuri@racsa.co.cr; d without/with air-con incl breakfast US$36/41; P) About 3km northwest of Cañas on the Interamericana, this fine spot has rather frilly rooms, most sleeping three, with TV and private bathroom. There's also a festive, onsite restaurant and, best of all, a huge pool (admission US$1.25 for nonguests).

Eating

There's an enormous **SuperCompro supermarket** (8am-8pm) right on the Interamericana.

Soda El Parque (7am-9pm; mains US$2-4) Right on the park, this typical *soda* also serves ice cream.

Bar/Restaurant El Corral (mains US$2-5; 6am-10pm) Enjoy basic *soda* fare overlooking the Interamericana, where you can watch (and smell) the big rigs blast by.

Restaurante El Primero (mains US$2-4; 11am-10pm) Some say it's the best Chinese restaurant in town, and directly across from the church it's certainly got one of the best views.

Restaurant Mey Jo (Av Central btwn Calle 4 & Hwy 1; mains US$3-5; 11am-9pm) This bright place with pink tables serves good chop suey and rice dishes.

Hotel Cañas (☎ 669 0039; mains US$2-6; 6am-9pm Mon-Sat, 7am-2pm Sun) Not just a hotel restaurant, excellent breakfasts attract some of the town's important people to sit around and plan the day's events. Other entrees, from casados to chicken cordon bleu and beef stroganoff, are cooked on a wood stove.

Hacienda La Pacífica (☎ 669 6050; mains US$7-12; 7am-9pm) Once a working hacienda and nature reserve, this elegant restaurant is 5km north of Cañas on the Interamericana and is now part of a private hotel for researchers. Many of the ingredients are grown right here on experimental organic plots, including the only large-scale organic rice cultivation in the country.

Rincón Corobicí (☎ 669 6162; mains US$3-10; 8am-8pm) This attractive Swiss-run restaurant, affiliated with Safaris Corobicí, is 5.5km north of Cañas on the banks of the Río Corobicí. A terrace provides pretty river and garden views, and a short trail follows the riverbank (people swim off the rocks). English, French, and German are spoken here.

Getting There & Away

All buses arrive and depart from **Terminal Cañas** (8am-1pm & 2:30-5:30pm) at the northern end of town. There are a few *sodas* and snack bars, and you can store your bags (US$0.25) at the desk. There's a taxi stand in front. Destinations and departure times for buses include:

Juntas US$0.50; 1½ hours; departs 9am & 2:15pm.

Liberia US$1.35; 1½ hours; 6:45am, 8:30am, 9am, 10:30am, 1pm, 2pm, 3pm & 5:30pm.

Puntarenas US$2; two hours; 6am, 6:40am, 9:30am, 10:30am, 11:30am, 12:30pm, 1:45pm; 3:30pm & 4:30pm.

San José US$3; 3½ hours; 4am, 4:50am, 6am, 9:30am, 12:30pm, 1:40pm & 5pm.

Tilarán US$0.50; 45 minutes; 6am, 8am, 9am, 10:30am, noon, 1:45pm, 3:30pm & 5:30pm.

Upala US$2; two hours; departs five times from 6:20am to 5pm.

VOLCÁN TENORIO AREA

The 58km paved highway to Upala goes north from the Interamericana about 6km northwest of Cañas. This road passes in between Volcán Miravalles (2028m) to the west and Volcán Tenorio (1916m) to the east. Tenorio is an active volcano, though activity is limited to fumaroles, hot springs, and mud pots.

Parque Nacional Volcán Tenorio, among Costa Rica's newest national parks and part of the Area de Conservación Arenal (ACA), is one of the true gems of the system. Though the hiking trails are still being developed (there may be more by the time you read this), grab a map at the **ranger station** (☎ 200 0135;

admission US$6; 7am-4pm) to two of the finest short hikes in Costa Rica.

On the northeast flanks of the volcano, the **Río Celeste**, just 1.5km from the ranger station, is famed for the blue created by many minerals dissolved in its waters. Its thermal headwaters contain springs and boiling mud pots – take great care not to scald yourself when you're exploring the area. Another 3km hike through epiphyte-laden cloud forest takes you to another hot spring.

There's no camping unless you plan to do the two-day trek up to the top of the volcano, where a small lake makes your evening just surreally beautiful. Make reservations two weeks in advance for this hike or, better, go through one of the lodges listed below; it's recommended that you go with a guide.

There's no public transport to the park, well signed from Hwy 6 east of Bijagua, but a taxi from Bijagua, about 33km north of the Interamericana and 25km south of Upala, costs about US$12 each way.

Sleeping & Eating

There are a few simple *sodas* in Bijagua, but other than that, you'll probably be eating at the lodge.

Finca Recreativa el Angel (☎ 466 8393; camping with tilapia fishing US$7; P) Typical of national tourist fincas, this beautiful farm just west of Bijagua doesn't charge for camping per se, but instead invites you to fish in their tilapia pond, then stay the night. The on-site restaurant cooks you fish to order, with all the trimmings; the campground has toilets and cold showers. Otilio, the owner, can arrange horseback tours of the volcano, and there's an on-site motocross track.

Heliconia Ecotourist Lodge (☎ 248 2538; www.agroecoturismo.net; s/d/tr US$35/45/55) About 3km east of Bijagua on an unpaved road, this lodge has sweeping views and a few private trails, including one with three impressive hanging bridges. Guests can visit local farms or go on locally guided hikes and horseback rides to waterfalls, hot springs, and rivers in Parque Nacional Volcán Tenorio. Tours cost US$20 to US$30 per person. Six simple, comfortable cabins have private hot showers. From the **restaurant** (mains US$3-7) you can see the valley, Volcán Miravalles, and (on a clear day) Lago de Nicaragua. The signed turnoff to the lodge is by Bijagua's Banco Nacional, where you can change money.

Posada Cielo Roto (☎ 352 9439, 466 8692; r per person with 3 meals & horseback rides US$40; P) On expansive grounds with horse stables and several kilometers of private trails, owner Mario Tamayo, who speaks English, has built several lovely, rambling houses with shared kitchens that are just perfect for groups. Some rooms are doubles, but most are dorm-style, all with private bathrooms and lots with big windows overlooking the stunning scenery. There's no electricity, but kerosene lamps and candles are provided. Mario accepts walk-ins, but it's better to make reservations so he can bring in food, ice and whatnot for your stay. Horseback riding is free, and guided treks can be arranged.

La Carolina Lodge (☎ 380 1656; www.lacarolinalodge.com; r per person night/week with 3 meals US$70/315; P) Six kilometers north of Bijagua, a sign points east to this lodge, about 7km east of the highway toward the village of San Miguel. The remote location means no electricity – it's candles only (provided) and your amazing meals are cooked over an outdoor wood-burning stove. Showers are warm, however, and there's a hot spring, right next to a scenic river and swimming hole. Rooms are a bit nicer, though still pretty basic, in the main lodge; the separate upper house is serene. Rates include guided horseback tours of the volcano and Río Celeste. Recommended. A taxi from Bijagua costs about US$12.

VOLCÁN MIRAVALLES AREA

Volcán Miravalles (2028m) is the highest volcano in the Cordillera de Guanacaste. Although the main crater is dormant, there is some geothermal activity at **Las Hornillas** (a few bubbling mud pools and steam vents), at about 700m above sea level on the southern slope of the volcano. There are no guardrails around the vents and mud pools – stay away from their edges, which occasionally collapse.

This isn't a national park or refuge, though the volcano is afforded a modicum of protection by being within the Zona Protectora Miravalles. You can visit the government-run Proyecto Geotérmico Miravalles, north of Fortuna, an ambitious project inaugurated in 1994 that uses geothermal energy to produce electricity, primarily for export to Nicaragua and Panama. A few bright steel tubes from the plant snake along the flanks of the volcano, adding an eerie touch to the remote landscape. There are small signs for both the project and Las Hornillas along the road.

But the geothermal energy most people come here to soak up comes in liquid form, at two neighboring, and fabulous, developed hot springs just north of Fortuna.

Thermo Manía (☎ 673 0233; admission US$4; 🕒 8am-10pm) has seven developed springs of different (some very hot) temperatures, shapes and décor are connected by all manner of waterslides, heated rivers, waterfalls and whatnot. But there weren't enough for the very friendly owners. Nope, there are little boats for kids, a playground, go-cart racing and a 170-year-old colonial cabin furnished with museum-worthy period pieces, just to give folks a glimpse into Costa Rica's pre-banana culture. The **restaurant-bar** (mains US$4-10) can cook up the tilapia you catch in the pond, or fix fine seafood, steak and snacks. Oh, and for an extra US$2, you can hike up and see unimproved springs so hot that they'd kill you if you fell in – careful!

If you're in the mood to relax, however, **Yökö Hot Springs** (☎ 673 0410; adult/child US$4/2; 🕒 7am-10pm) is a more established spot, with four attractively landscaped springs and a relatively sedate waterslide and waterfall, may be more your speed. Extra amenities include a Jacuzzi, sauna and **restaurant** (mains US$2-10) serving everything from burgers to filet mignon. The real draw, however, is the four rather elegant **cabinas** (s/d/tr US$30/50/65), with huge bathrooms and gleaming wood floors, where you can relax after soaking all day. The staff also arrange guided tours of the geothermal facility and hikes to area lagoons and petroglyphs.

You could also stay at **Cabinas Las Brisas** (☎ 673 0333; s/d/tr US$7/11/16; Ⓟ). A couple of kilometers north of Guayabo, these huge cabinas with private bathroom are fairly simple – except for the wall-sized mirrors facing the double beds. The **restaurant** (mains US$3-7; 🕒 7:30am-close) cooks up good, simple Tico-Cuban cuisine, and there's also a full bar here.

Volcán Miravalles is 27km northeast of Bagaces and can be approached by a paved road that leads north of Bagaces through the communities of Salitral and Torno, where the road splits. From the left-hand fork, you'll reach **Guayabo**, with a few *sodas* and basic cabinas; to the right, you'll find **Fortuna** (not to be confused with La Fortuna, see p200), with easier access to the two hot springs. The roads reconnect north of the two towns for a rough trek north toward Upala (p434), and also make a great scenic loop.

Though the region is relatively remote, it's well served by buses from Bagaces.

BAGACES

This small town is about 22km northwest of Cañas on the Interamericana. The main reason to stop here is to visit the national park and reserve offices.

Bagaces is the headquarters of the **Area de Conservación Tempisque** (ACT; ☎ 200 0125; 🕒 8am-4pm Mon-Fri) which, in conjunction with Minae, administers Parque Nacional Palo Verde, Reserva Biológica Lomas de Barbudal, and several smaller and lesser-known protected areas. The office is on the Interamericana opposite the signed main entry road into Parque Nacional Palo Verde. The office is mainly an administrative one, though sometimes rangers are available. The staff is friendly and will try to help – you can ask them to call Palo Verde to get information directly from the rangers.

Eating

Soda La Fuente (600m north of ACT/Minae; mains US$2-5; 🕒 6:30am-9pm) is a recommended *soda* that does all the typical delicacies right.

It's just not Costa Rica without chop suey, and **Restaurante El Hambo** (Parque Central; mains US$2-5; 🕒 11am-10pm) is a Chinese restaurant that gets raves.

Getting There & Away

The bus terminal is 100m north of the Parque Central. Pullmitan buses to Liberia from San José (US$4, four hours) depart hourly, and can drop you off in Bagaces. Eleven daily buses to Cañas from Liberia (US$1, one hour) stop in Bagaces. Let your driver know in advance. You can flag a bus from the Interamericana. There are local buses to the Volcán Miravalles region. Also there's:

Guayabo US$0.50; 45 minutes; almost hourly from 6am to 5pm.

La Fortuna US$0.50; 45 minutes; depart every 30 minutes from 6am to 5pm.

PARQUE NACIONAL PALO VERDE

The 18,417-hectare Parque Nacional Palo Verde lies on the northeastern banks of the mouth of Río Tempisque at the head of the Golfo de Nicoya. A large number of different habitats are represented, ranging from mangrove swamps, marshes, and lagoons to a variety of seasonal grasslands and forests. A number of low limestone hills provide lookout points over the park. The dry season, from December to March, is very marked, and much of the forest dries out. During the wet months, large portions of the area are flooded.

Palo Verde has the greatest concentrations of waterfowl and shorebirds in Central America, as well as many forest birds. Birders come to see the large flocks of herons (including the country's largest nesting colony of black-crowned night herons on Reserva Biológica Isla Pájaros (p156), storks (including the only Costa Rican nesting site of the locally endangered jabiru stork), spoonbills, egrets, ibis, grebes, and ducks. Inland, birds such as scarlet macaws, great curassows, keel-billed toucans, and parrots may be seen. Approximately 300 bird species have been recorded in the park. Other possible sightings include crocodiles (reportedly up to 5m in length), iguanas, deer, coatis, monkeys, and peccaries.

The best time for a visit is September to March because of the huge influx of migratory and endemic birds. September and October are very wet, and access may be limited. From December to February, during the dry season, trees lose their leaves and the massed flocks of birds that tend to congregate in the remaining lakes and marshes become easier to observe. There are also far fewer insects in the dry season, roads and trails are more passable, and mammals are seen around the water holes. Take binoculars or a spotting scope if possible.

Information

The **park entrance** (☎ 200 0125; admission US$13) is 28km from the Interamericana. Optional, guided, half-/full-day visits are available for adults (US$15/30) and children (US$10/20); make reservations through the Hacienda Palo Verde Research Station (see later). The station also offers horseback tours (US$6 per person, per hour).

The ACT office in Bagaces can be contacted for information about the park, but the research station is the best source of information.

Sleeping & Eating

Overnight visitors should make reservations, and remember you'll need to pay the US$13 entry fee, too.

Camping (per person US$7) is permitted near the Palo Verde ranger station, where toilets and hot-water showers are available.

Palo Verde ranger station (☎ 200 0125; dm US$13) Fans, mosquito nets, and showers are provided in six rooms, each with six beds. These may be occupied by student groups, so call ahead. Meals are available here for US$7 each, preferably by advance arrangement.

Hacienda Palo Verde Research Station (☎ 661 4717; www.ots.ac.cr; s/d US$55/100) The research station is run by the Organization of Tropical Studies (OTS), which conducts tropical research and teaches university graduate-level classes. Researchers and those taking OTS courses get preference for dormitories with shared bathrooms. A few two- and four-bed rooms with shared bathrooms are also available. Meals are US$9 each. The research station is 8km from the park entrance; several trails lead from the station area into the national park.

Getting There & Away

It's a 28km walk from the bus terminal, so consider renting a car, hiring a taxi in Bagaces (US$15 one way) or booking a day trip from San José (around US$75 to US$100 per person, including transportation, guide and meals). You can also hire boats in Puerto Humo or Puerto Chamorro, two tiny towns on the Río Tempisque.

The easiest way here is by car. The main road to the entrance, usually passable to ordinary cars year-round, begins from a signed turnoff from the Interamericana, opposite Bagaces. The 28km gravel road has tiny brown signs that usually direct you when the road forks, but if in doubt, take the fork that looks more used. Another 8km brings you to the limestone hill, Cerro Guayacán (and the OTS research station), from which there are great views; a couple of kilometers further are the Palo Verde park headquarters and ranger station. You can drive through a swampy maze of roads to the Reserva

Biológica Lomas de Barbudal without returning to the Interamericana.

Buses connecting San José and Liberia (see p183) can drop you at the ACT office, opposite the turnoff to the park. If you call the ACT office in advance, rangers may be able to pick you up in Bagaces. If you're staying at the Hacienda Palo Verde Research Station, the staff can also arrange to pick you up in Bagaces.

RESERVA BIOLÓGICA LOMAS DE BARBUDAL

The 2646-hectare Lomas de Barbudal reserve forms a cohesive unit with Palo Verde, and both are administrated by the ACT/Minae office in Bagaces (see p183). About 70% of the area is deciduous forest that contains several species of endangered trees, such as mahogany and rosewood, as well as the common and quite spectacular corteza amarilla. This tree is what biologists call a 'big bang reproducer' – all the yellow cortezes in the forest burst into bloom on the same day, and for about four days the forest is an incredible mass of yellow-flowered trees. This usually occurs in March, about four days after an unseasonal rain shower.

During the dry season, many of the trees shed their leaves just as they do in autumn in temperate lands. This kind of forest, known as tropical dry forest, was once common in many parts of the Pacific slopes of Central America, but very little of it now remains. In addition to tropical dry forests, there are riparian forests along the Río Cabuyo (which flows through the reserve year-round) and small areas of other types of forest.

Some people call this 'Insect Park' for its abundant and varied wasps, butterflies, moths and other insects. There are about 250 different species of bee in this fairly small reserve – representing about a quarter of the world's bee species. Bees here (and in nearby Palo Verde) include the Africanized 'killer' bees – if you suffer from bee allergies, this is one area where you really don't want to forget your bee-sting kit.

There are more than 200 bird species, including the great curassow, a chicken-like bird that is hunted for food and is endangered. Other endangered species found locally are the king vulture, scarlet macaw, and jabiru stork. Mammals you may see include white-tailed deer, peccaries, coatis, and howler and white-faced monkeys.

Orientation & Information

At the reserve entrance, there's a small **information center** (entry to the park US$6; 7am-4pm). The actual reserve is on the other side of the Río Cabuyo, behind the museum. The dry season is from December to April, and it can get very hot then – temperatures of 38°C (100°F) are sometimes reached. During the rainy season it is a little cooler, but insects are more abundant; bring repellent.

Getting There & Away

The turnoff to Lomas de Barbudal from the Interamericana is near the small community of Pijije, 14km southeast of Liberia or 12km northwest of Bagaces. It's 7km to the entrance of the reserve. The road is unpaved but open all year – some steep sections may require 4WD in rainy season. Buses between Liberia and Cañas can drop you at the turnoff to the reserve.

LIBERIA

The capital of sunny Guanacaste Province, Liberia is at a crossroads – geographically and politically. It lies on the corner of the Interamericana, connecting the capital with both borders, and Hwy 21, Nicoya's main road providing access to the country's finest beaches. Though the city has long been the standard bearer of Costa Rica's *sabanero* culture (see the boxed text, p187), serving a widespread community of ranching operations and still enamored of cowboy hats and machetes, there are other opportunities on the horizon.

Some 50km away, the Golfo de Papagayo (p228), tagged by hopeful tourist-industry magnates as 'the new Cancún,' is undergoing unprecedented development. Liberia's airport is slated to become the most important entry point for package tourists in search of a tan, and the city itself is scheduled to become a service community for this strange new world. Though most of the power players are multinational corporations, locals are not about to be left out of the game.

Liberia has long been a base for visiting such attractions as Parques Nacionales Santa Rosa, Guanacaste, and Rincón de la Vieja, all to the north, as well as Parque Nacional

LIBERIA

0 — 300 m
0 — 0.2 miles

INFORMATION
Banco de Costa Rica....................1 B4
Banco de Costa Rica....................2 C3
Banco Nacional....................3 B3
Banex....................4 B4
Cyberm@nia....................5 C3
ICE (Telephone)....................6 B4
Planet Internet....................7 D4
Post Office....................8 B3
Sabanero Art Market & Tourist Information Centre....................9 D4
Tourist Office....................10 D4
Western Union....................(see 6)

SIGHTS & ACTIVITIES (p187)
Church of La Agonía....................11 D2
Iglesia Inmaculada Concepción de María....................12 C3
La Gobernación....................13 D4
Museum....................(see 10)
Sabanero Monument....................14 B4

SLEEPING (pp188–9)
Best Western Hotel El Sitio....................15 A4
Hospedaje Condega....................16 C4
Hospedaje La Casona....................17 C4
Hospedaje Real Chorotega....................18 C4
Hostal Ciudad Blanca....................19 D3
Hotel Boyeros....................20 B4
Hotel El Bramadero....................21 B4
Hotel Guanacaste....................22 B3
Hotel La Siesta....................23 C4
Hotel Liberia....................24 D4
Hotel Primavera....................25 D4
La Posada del Tope....................26 C3

EATING (p189)
Café Liberia....................27 B3
Food Mall de Burger King....................28 A4
Heladería Diaz....................29 B3
La Copa de Oro....................30 D4
Las Tinajas....................31 C3
Market....................32 B3
Musmanni Bakery....................33 C3
Palí Supermarket....................34 C3
Panadería Pan y Miel....................35 C3
Panadería Pan y Miel....................(see 38)
Paso Real....................36 D4
Pizza Pronto....................37 C3
Pizzería Da Beppe....................38 B4
Restaurante Elegante....................39 D4
Soda Rancho Dulce....................40 D4
SuperCompro....................41 C3

ENTERTAINMENT (p189)
Discoteque Kuru Kuru....................42 A4
Pooles Liberia....................43 D4

TRANSPORT (pp189–90)
Main Intersection (Gas Stations)....................44 B4
Terminal Liberia....................45 A3
Terminal Pulmitan (Buses to San José)....................46 B3

Palo Verde and Reserva Biológica Lomas de Barbudal to the south. But this new development raises the stakes: already, grassroots groups have been pressuring the government to enforce strict regulations on new resorts, even as Liberia ramps up its own infrastructure to make sure local talent will guide the city's all-but-inevitable transformation.

The public schools have expanded the number of English courses on offer, a huge hospital that will also cater to foreigners is under construction, and some folks are even looking into renovating the 150-year-old downtown with a full face-lift and expanded pedestrian mall. What will the future bring? Part of that depends on the Papagayo Project, sure, but this trail will be blazed *sabanero* style.

Information

INTERNET ACCESS

Cyberm@nia (Av 1 btwn Calles 2 & Central; per hr US$1.10; 8am-10pm) Also good for cheap long-distance calls, charging US$0.25 a minute to most parts of the world.

Planet Internet (Calle Central btwn Avs Central & 2; per hr US$1; 8am-10pm) Has speedy machines in spacious air-conditioned cubicles, making this one of Costa Rica's finest emailing experiences.

MEDICAL SERVICES

Hospital Dr Enrique Baltodano Briceño (☎ 666 0011, emergencies ☎ 666 0318) is behind the stadium on the northeastern outskirts of town.

THE SABANERO *John Thompson*

The open, dry cattle country of Guanacaste is Costa Rica's equivalent of the USA's West – and the *sabanero* is Guanacaste's cowboy. But in keeping with Costa Rica's peaceful self-image, the *sabanero* tends to be a figure of dignity rather than of fist-fighting rambunctiousness. A *sabanero* carries himself with an air that will remind you as much of a samurai or knight as of a cowboy. You'll see *sabaneros* riding along roads in Guanacaste, and will recognize them by their straight-backed posture, casual hand on the reins, holster-slung machetes, and the high-stepping gait of their horses. This gait is a signature of *sabanero* culture – it demands endurance and skill from both horse and rider. Every year *sabaneros* show off their horsemanship at the local *tope*.

A tope is a mix of Western rodeo and country fair. Food stalls, music, and bull riding – the bulls are not wounded or killed – are all central features. The bull-riding spectacle is where youthful wild oats are sown. A macho young man turning pale and crossing himself as the bullring door is thrown open is a sight to remember. For comic relief, there are always a few drunks willing to volunteer as rodeo clowns, dancing around the ring to distract the bull as fallen riders scramble to safety. The horseback riding of the *sabaneros* is the high point of the day. Almost every little town has a *tope*; the dates change, so ask locally in any region you're visiting about when the next one will be held.

MONEY

Most hotels will accept US dollars, and may be able to change small amounts. If not, Liberia probably has more banks per square meter than any other town in Costa Rica.

Banco de Costa Rica (cnr Calle 2 & Av 1; 8:30am-3pm Mon-Fri) Has a 24-hour ATM.

Banex (cnr Calle 10 & Av 25 de Julio; 9am-8pm Mon-Fri, 9am-12:30pm Sat) Has an ATM that accepts MasterCard.

Coopmex Liberia (cnr Calle 8 & Av 2) Home to ICE and Western Union.

Mutual Alajuela (cnr Calle 2 & Av 5; 8am-5pm Mon-Fri, 8am-noon Sat)

TOURIST INFORMATION

A **tourist office** (☎ 666 4527; cnr Av 6 & Calle 1) has hours that remain a mystery. One local explained it this way: 'Sometimes it's open. Sometimes it's closed.' Travelers will be better off seeking guidance at the **Sabanero Art Market & Tourist Information Center** (☎ 362 6926; Calle 8 btwn Avs Central & 1; www.elsabanero.8k.com). It has bus schedules, information on tours and lodging and will arrange taxi pick-ups.

Sights & Activities

There are a number of good hotels, restaurants, and bars, and the main activity is relaxing in one of them as you plan your next trip to a beach or volcano.

The tourist office has a tiny **museum** of local ranching artifacts – cattle raising is a historically important occupation in Guanacaste. There has been talk of re-opening a museum of *sabanero* culture in **La Gobernación**, the old municipal building at the corner of Avenida Central and Calle Central, but it was still being renovated at the time of research.

In the meantime, a **statue** of a steely-eyed *sabanero*, complete with an evocative poem by Rudolfo Salazar Solorzano, stands watch over Avenida 25 de Julio, the main street into town. The blocks around the intersection of Avenida Central and Calle Central contain several of the town's oldest houses, many dating back about 150 years.

The pleasant Parque Central frames a modern church, **Iglesia Inmaculada Concepción de María**. Walking six blocks northeast of the park along Avenida Central brings you to the oldest church in town, popularly called **La Agonía** (though maps show it as La Iglesia de la Ermita de la Resurección). Strolling to La Agonía and around the surrounding blocks makes a fine walk.

Tours

Hotel Liberia and La Posada del Tope (see p188) can arrange one of a variety of tours, including day trips to Parques Rincón de la Vieja (US$10 per person), Palo Verde (US$40 per person), and Santa Rosa (US$16 to park, US$100 camping at Witch's Rock/ Playa Naranjo), as well as great deals on rental cars.

Festivals & Events

Día de Guanacaste, on July 25, is actively celebrated here in the capital of the province with a *tope* (horse parade), cattle auction, bullfight (the bull is never killed in Costa Rica), music, and rural fair. Ask at the tourist information office about *topes* and other events in small towns in the area – they happen frequently though irregularly.

Sleeping

The town is busy during the dry season, so you make reservations, particularly at Christmas, Easter, Día de Guanacaste and on high-season weekends. Conversely, the upmarket hotels give discounts in the wet season. Note that although streets are labeled on the map, very few of them are signed, especially once you get away from Parque Central (see boxed text, p453).

BUDGET

Hospedaje Real Chorotega (☎ 666 0898; cnr Av 6 & Calle 2; r per person US$5) This basic budget entry has small, windowless rooms with shared bathroom, plus a little lobby with rocking chairs if you start to feel claustrophobic.

Hospedaje Condega (☎ 666 1165; Av 6 btwn Calles 4 & 6; r per person without/with bathroom US$3.75/7.50) Clean, yet unremarkable, this is a slightly better option. Be prepared to shout at the owner – he is hard of hearing

Hotel Liberia (☎ 666 0161, www.hotelliberia.com; Calle Central btwn Avs Central & 2; s/d US$5/10, s/d with bathroom US$8/16; P) Rooms in this rambling, century-old building are well maintained, but pretty darned basic (especially the ones with shared bathroom), but the genial vibe and an outdoor lounge with a pool table, TV and hammocks make this a winner. Rooms in the back wing are brighter. They offer a highly recommended overnight trip to Rincón de la Vieja (US$15 per person), and other budget tours as well.

La Posada del Tope (☎ 666 3876; www.posadadeltope.com; Calle Central btwn Avs Central & 2; r per person US$5-12; P ⊠) This mid-19th-century house, with an attractive front and lobby, has pretty, threadbare rooms with mosquito nets, shared bathrooms, and thin walls. The annex across the street, Hotel Casa Real, has rooms with private bath and TV. The vivacious English-speaking owner offers a variety of tours and services (see p187).

Hotel Guanacaste (☎ 666 0085; www.hicr.org; cnr Av 3 & Calle 12; dm US$6, s/d with bathroom US$10/18; P) This HI-affiliated hostel near the bus terminal has dorm-style bunk rooms that may remind you of summer camp. The restaurant is popular with riders of the TransNica bus, which stops here on its way to Managua.

Hospedaje La Casona (☎ 666 2971; marijozuniga@hotmail.com; cnr Calle Real Av 6; s/d US$7/10, d with bathroom US$15; P ❄) This is a good choice. A pink, wooden house contains plain rooms sharing three bathrooms, while a new annex has tidy rooms (one with air-con) with bathroom. Laundry service is available (US$2 per kg).

MID-RANGE

Hotel Primavera (☎ 666 0464; Av Central btwn Calles Central & 2; s/d US$23/33; P ❄) Right on the Parque Central, the small, appealing rooms are a little worn, but come furnished with microwave, cable TV and a little table. The room with air-con costs US$5 more.

Hotel La Siesta (☎ 666 0678; hotellasiesta@hotmail.com; Calle 4 btwn Avs 4 & 6; s/d incl breakfast US$25/38, P ❄ 🏊) Clean, standard rooms with cable TV and private cold showers are arranged around a pretty garden inset with a small and inviting pool. Slightly larger upstairs rooms have air-con and cost US$5 more.

Hostal Ciudad Blanca (☎ 666 3962; Av 4 btwn Calles 1 & 3; s/d US$30/50; P ❄) This small hotel – one of Liberia's most attractive – occupies a mansion. Guest rooms have air-con, fan, cable TV, nice furnishings, and private (hot water) bathroom. There is a charming little restaurant-bar.

Hotel El Bramadero (☎ 666 0371; bramdero@racsa.co.cr; cnr Interamericana & Hwy 21; s/d/tr US$29/37/43; P ❄ 🏊) Conveniently located at the crossroads of both major highways, this *sabanero*-themed spot is not only a hotel and good **restaurant** (mains US$3-10; 🕑 6am-10pm), specializing in steak, of course, but also the Tica Bus agency. Plain, clean rooms have private bathroom, cable TV, air-con and access to a cool pool.

Hotel Boyeros (☎ 666 0995; www.hotelboyeros.com; cnr Interamericana & Av 2; s/d/tr US$40/46/52; P ⊠ ❄ 🏊) Near the intersection of the Interamericana and the main road into Liberia, this is the largest hotel in town, with air-conditioned rooms featuring cable TV; ask for one of the upstairs balcony rooms. Amenities include a 24-hour restaurant, adults' and kids' swimming pools and one very nicely tiled water slide.

TOP END

Top end in Liberia is strictly business class.

Best Western Hotel Las Espuelas (☎ 666 0144; espuelas@racsa.co.cr; s/d incl breakfast US$64/76; P ⊠

) This hotel is on the east side of the Interamericana, about 2km south of the main road into Liberia. It has pleasant grounds, a pool, restaurant-bar, and gift shop. Rooms come with private bathroom, TV, telephone and air-conditioning.

Best Western Hotel El Sitio (666 1211; htlsitio@racsa.co.cr; s/d incl breakfast US$64/76, additional person US$12;) On the road to Nicoya about 250m west of the Interamericana, this hotel offers spacious air-conditioned rooms with TV and private (hot water) bathroom. It has a decent restaurant-bar, a spa, and adults' and kids' pools. The hotel arranges car rental and tours to beaches and national parks.

Eating

There are lots of inexpensive *sodas* around town, or you could grab groceries at the **SuperCompro** (Av Central btwn Calles 4 & 6; 8am-8pm Mon-Fri, 8am-6pm Sat & Sun).

Café Liberia (Calle 8 btwn Avs 25 de Julio & 2; snacks US$1-3; 10am-6pm Mon-Fri) Espresso beverages and light snacks get the day started right, if a bit late.

Heladería Diaz (cnr Av 25 de Julio & Calle 10; treats US$0.50-3; 1-9pm) Not just your average ice-cream shop, this progressive place also serves soy ice cream, yogurt and lots of fruitier options.

Panadería Pan y Miel (cnr Calle 2 & Av 3; snacks US$1-3; 6am-8pm) This branch of this fine local bakery sticks to the basics, with the earliest cup of coffee in town and lots of sweets and eats (and some elaborate birthday cakes) to go with it.

Musmanni Bakery (Calle 2 btwn Avs 3 & 5; light meals US$1-4; 5am-9pm) A bit more ambitious than your average Musmanni, this place adds sandwiches and other goodies to the standard pastry line-up.

Restaurante Elegante (Calle Real btwn Av Central & 2; dishes US$3) You'll find ample portions of fried rice and other Chinese fare at this spot.

Soda Rancho Dulce (Calle Central btwn Avs Central & 2; mains US$2-4; 7:30am-10pm) Sometimes a casado is more than a casado, and this outstanding *soda*, with groovy wooden tables and good *batidos*, serves some of the best.

Pan y Miel (665 3733; Av 25 de Julio btwn Calles 8 & 10; mains US$2-5; 7am-8pm Mon-Fri, 7am-2pm Sat) The best breakfast in town can be had at the second branch of this bakery, which serves its excellent bread as sandwiches and French toast, or alongside a long list of salads, pastas and other entrees.

Pizza Pronto (cnr Av 4 & Calle 1; pizzas from US$5) Situated in a handsome 19th century house, this place is ideal for scrumptious pizza cooked in a Guanacaste clay oven.

Pizzeria Da Beppe (666 0917; cnr Av Central & Calle 10; mains US$ 2-10; 7:30am-10:30pm) Enjoy the attractive outdoor patio over fresh pasta and good pizza, but keep in mind that the daily special – think fresh seafood, or quality steak – is always tops. There's also a full bar (with a decent wine list) that stays open until 11:30pm, at least.

Las Tinajas (Calle 2 btwn Avs Central & 1; meals US$4-7) This is an ideal place to watch the town mutts run around while sipping a cold beer.

Paso Real (666 3455; Av Central btwn Calles Central & 2; mains US$6-20; 11am-10pm) Liberia's fanciest restaurant has a breezy balcony overlooking Parque Central, where you could start with a *ceviche* (US$4 to US$8) before moving on to other well-prepared catches of the day.

Food Mall de Burger King (cnr Interamericana & Hwy 21; 7am-11pm) Homesick? Take a trip through the Burger King drive-thru, or come inside for Church's Chicken and Papa John's Pizza. Junk-food junkies should note that a 24-hour Subway, TCBY, Pizza Hut and Pollo Campero are all nearby.

Entertainment

Liberia isn't what you'd call a wild nightspot, but both Casa Romana Jalija and Las Tijanas (see above) are fine places to have a drink; Las Tijanas sometimes has live music.

Pooles Liberia (Calle Central btwn Avs Central & 2; 11am-11pm) lets you enjoy a cold brew and a hot game inside the historic Calle Real building. **Discoteque Kuru Kuru**, across from the Best Western El Sitio, lets the DJs do their thing Thursday through Sunday nights.

Getting There & Away

AIR

Since 1993, Aeropuerto Internacional Daniel Oduber Quirós (LIR), 12km east of Liberia, has served as the country's second international airport, providing easy access to all those beautiful beaches without the hassle of dealing with less-than-pristine San José. It's a tiny airport, jam-packed with increasing traffic, and a serious (and potentially schedule-busting) overhaul is planned for the 'near future.' All international flights are through the USA.

NatureAir and Sansa both make regular runs between Liberia and San José, with connections all over the country, for about US$90 one way, US$170 round trip.

There are no car rental desks at the airport; make reservations in advance, and your company will meet you at the airport with a car. There are plans to open a tourist information desk, but at press time, there weren't even racks of flyers available. A taxi to Liberia costs US$10.

American Airlines (☎ 800-421 0600; www.aa.com) Fights to/from Miami, Florida.
Continental (☎ 800-231 0856; www.continental.com) To/from Houston, Texas.
Delta (☎ 800-241 4141; www.delta.com) To/from Atlanta, Georgia.
NatureAir (☎ 220 3054; www.natureair.com) To/from San José four times daily.
Sansa (☎ 668 1047; www.flysansa.com) To/from San José three times daily.

BUS

Buses arrive and depart **Terminal Liberia** (Av 7 btwn Calles 12 & 14) and **Terminal Pullmitan** (Av 5 btwn Calles 10& 12). Routes, fares, journey times and departures are as follows:

Cañas US$1; 1¼ hours; departs Terminal Liberia 5:45am, 1:30pm, 4:30pm & 5:10pm.
La Cruz/Peñas Blancas US$1.25; 1½-two hours; departs Pullmitan 5:30am, 8:30am, 9am, 11am, noon, 2pm, 4:45pm & 8pm.
Managua, Nicaragua US$9; five hours; departs Pullmitan 8:30am, 9:30am & 1pm (buy tickets one day in advance).
Nicoya, via Filadelfia & Santa Cruz (Alfaro Buses) US$1.25; two hours; departs Terminal Liberia roughly every 30 minutes from 5am to 7pm.
Playa del Coco US$0.75; one hour; departs Pullmitan 5:30am, 12:30pm, 2pm & 4:30pm.
Playa Hermosa, Playa Panamá (Tralapa) US$0.75; 1¼ hours; departs Terminal Liberia 7:30am, 11:30am, 3:30pm, 5:30pm & 7pm.
Playa Tamarindo US$1; two hours; departs Terminal Liberia 5:15am & 2:30pm.
Puntarenas US$1.40; 2½ hours; seven services depart from 5am to 3:30pm.
San José US$4; four hours; depart Pullmitan hourly 6:20am to 7:20pm.

CAR

Liberia lies on the Interamericana, 234km north of San José and 77km south of the Nicaraguan border post of Peñas Blancas. Highway 21, the main artery of the Nicoya Peninsula, begins in Liberia and heads southwest. A dirt road, passable to all cars in dry season (4WD is preferable), leads 25km from Barrio la Victoria to the Santa María entrance of Rincón de la Vieja; the gravel road to the Las Pailas entrance begins from the Interamericana 5km north of Liberia (passable to regular cars, but 4WD recommended).

There are several rental car agencies in the region (none of which have desks at the airport), that charge about the same amount as those in San José. Most can arrange pickup in Liberia and drop-off in San José, though they'll try to charge you extra. Rental agencies are on Highway 21 between Liberia and the airport, but should be able to drop off your car in town. La Posada de Tope (p188) arranges the cheapest car rental in Liberia. Some rental agencies in town include:

Avis (☎ 666 7585; www.avis.co.cr)
Ada (☎ 668 1122)
Budget (☎ 668 1024; www.budget.com)
Dollar (☎ 668 1061; www.dollarcostarica.com)
Economy Rent-A-Car (☎ 666 2816)
Elegante (☎ 668 1054; www.eleganterentacar.com)
Europcar (☎ 668 1022; www.europcar.co.cr)
National (☎ 666 5595; www.natcar.com)
Poas Rent-a-Car (☎ 667 0214; www.carentals.com)
Payless (☎ 257 0026; www.paylesscr.com)
Sol Rent-A-Car (☎ 666 2222; solcar@sol.racsa.co)
Toyota Rent a Car (☎ 666 8190; www.carrental-toyota-costarica.com)

PARQUE NACIONAL RINCÓN DE LA VIEJA

This 14,161-hectare national park is named after the active Volcán Rincón de la Vieja (1895m), the steamy main attraction, but within the same volcanic massif are several other peaks, of which Volcán Santa María (1916m) is the highest. The region bubbles with multihued fumaroles, lukewarm hot springs, lively mudpots hurling clumps of ashy gray mud in flatulent (the sulfur smell in these hills is strong) Dr Seuss–style fun, a young and feisty *volcancito* (small volcano), plus a cacophony of popping, hissing holes in the ground. All these can be visited on well-maintained but sometimes steep trails.

The park was created in 1973 to protect the 32 rivers and streams that have their sources within the park, an important watershed. Its relatively remote location means that wildlife, rare elsewhere, is out in force here, with the major volcanic crater a rather dramatic backdrop to the scene. Volcanic activity has occurred many times since the late 1960s, with the most recent eruption of steam and ash in 1997. At the moment, however, the volcano is gently active and does not present any danger (ask locally to be sure).

Elevations in the park range from less than 600m to 1916m, so visitors pass through a variety of different habitats as they ascend the volcanoes. Many tree species are found in the forests. And the area has the country's highest density of Costa Rica's national flower, the purple orchid (*Cattleya skinneri*), locally called *guaria morada.* (See the boxed text, p37, for more on the fate of this flower.)

Because of its relative remoteness, the park is not heavily visited, but several lodges just outside the park provide access, and transportation is easy to arrange from Liberia. Rincón de la Vieja is the most accessible of the volcanoes in the Cordillera de Guanacaste.

Orientation & Information

There are two main entrances to the park, each with its own ranger station, where you sign in and get free maps. Most visitors enter through the **Las Pailas ranger station** (☎ 661 8139; admission US$7; 🕑 7am-4pm) on the western flank. Trails to the summit and the most interesting volcanic features begin here.

The **Santa María ranger station** (☎ 661 8139; admission US$7; 🕑 7am-4pm), to the east, is in the Casona Santa María, a 19th-century ranch house with a small public exhibit that was reputedly once owned by US President Lyndon Johnson. It's closest to the sulfurous hot springs and also has an observation tower and a nearby waterfall.

Wildlife Watching

The wildlife of the park is extremely varied. Almost 300 species of bird have been recorded here, including curassows, quetzals, bellbirds, parrots, toucans, hummingbirds, owls, woodpeckers, tanagers, motmots, doves, and eagles – to name just a few.

Insects range from beautiful butterflies to annoying ticks. Be especially prepared for ticks in grassy areas – long trousers tucked into boots and long-sleeve shirts offer some protection. A particularly interesting insect is a highland cicada that burrows into the ground and croaks like a frog, to the bewilderment of naturalists.

Mammals are equally varied; deer, armadillos, peccaries, skunks, squirrels, coatis, and three species of monkey are frequently seen. Tapir tracks are often found around the lagoons near the summit. Several of the wild cat species have been recorded here, including the jaguar, puma, ocelot, and margay, but you'll need patience and good fortune to observe one of these.

Hiking

A circular trail east of Las Pailas (about 8km in total) takes you past the boiling mud pools (Las Pailas), sulfurous fumaroles, and a miniature volcano (which may subside at any time). Trails lead 8km (one way) to the summit and the **Laguna de Jilgueros**, which is reportedly where you may see tapirs – or more likely their footprints, if you are observant. This trail, much of it along the top of a ridge, is known for being extremely windy and cloudy – come prepared for the weather. About 700m west of the ranger station is a swimming hole.

Further away are several waterfalls – the largest, **Catarata La Cangreja**, 5km west, is a classic, dropping straight from a cliff into a small lagoon where you can swim. Dissolved copper salts give the falls a deep blue color. This trail winds through forest, then onto open grassland on the volcano's flanks, where you can get views as far as the Golfo de Nicoya. The Cangreja Trail is among the best-recommended on the mountain. The slightly smaller **Cataratas Escondidas** (Hidden Waterfalls) are 4.3km west on a different trail; there are cliff views and swimming.

From the Santa María ranger station, a trail leads 2.8km west through the 'enchanted forest' and past a waterfall to sulfurous **hot springs** with supposedly therapeutic properties. Don't soak in them for more than about half an hour (some people suggest much less) without taking a dip in one of the nearby cold springs to cool off. An observation point is 450m east of the station.

Sleeping & Eating

INSIDE THE PARK

Both ranger stations have **camping** (per person US$2). Each campground has water, pit toilets, showers, tables, and grills. There is no fuel available, so bring wood, charcoal, or a camping stove. Mosquito nets or insect repellent are needed in the wet season.

Camping is allowed in most places within the park, but you should be self-sufficient and prepared for cold and foggy weather in the highlands – a compass is very useful. The wet season is very wet (October is the rainiest month), and there are plenty of mosquitoes then. Dry-season camping in December, March, and April is recommended; January and February are prone to strong winds.

OUTSIDE THE PARK

Note that all of these places are a long way from a restaurant, so you're stuck with paying for meals at your hotel restaurant. Two lodges – the Hacienda Lodge Guachipelín and Rincón de la Vieja Mountain Lodge – lie near the Las Pailas sector (see p191), and require a US$2 entrance fee because the road crosses private property with a toll booth.

Rinconcito Lodge (☎ 666 2764, leave a message in English for 'Rinconcito' ☎ 224 2400; www.rinconcitolodge.com; s/d US$12/22, s/d with bathroom US$17/28; camping per person US$2; P) Just 3km from the Santa María sector of the park, this incredible budget option offers attractive, rustic cabins with electricity and cold showers, surrounded by some of the prettiest pastoral scenery imaginable. The private stable offers horses for rent (half/full day US$12/18) with an optional guide (US$18) who'll take you to hot springs, mud pots or into the volcanic crater itself. They offer several inexpensive package deals that include transport from Liberia (one way/round trip per person for up to four people US$18/35) guided hikes and horseback rides, and meals (breakfast US$4, lunch and dinner US$6). Transport can also be arranged from San José and other destinations in advance. Recommended.

Hacienda Lodge Guachipelín (☎ 666 8075; www.guachipelin.com; s/d US$42/61, with 3 meals US$67/110;) On the site of a 19th-century ranch, parts of which are incorporated into the current hacienda, this fine place sits on some 1200 hectares of primary and secondary forest, along with a working cattle ranch. Most accommodations are in 30 spacious, light duplex cabins with large private bathrooms (hot water) and porches. A **restaurant** (mains US$7-13) is close to the rustic barn, with a bar and relaxation room, behind which is a swimming pool.

Rincón de la Vieja Mountain Lodge (☎ 661 8198; www.rincondelaviejalodge.com; d/tr standard US$67/80, d/tr cottage US$80/101, additional person US$17; P) Closest to the Las Pailas entrance to the park, this popular spot has spacious standard rooms, some with wildly painted walls or rustic beamed roofs, and even larger cottages with balconies. All have private, nicely tiled hot showers. There's 24-hour electricity courtesy of their private hydroelectric project, a pool, Internet access, a small lending library, butterfly garden, and a canopy tour (US$50/82 day/night). The lodge also rents mountain bikes (US$5 per hour) and horses (US$30/45 half/full day, guide US$15). It is about 2km from the mud pools and 5km from the fumaroles described earlier. Meals (US$6 to US$10) are available from the restaurant, and transportation can be arranged from Liberia separately or as part of a multi-day package.

Hotel Borinquen (☎ 666 0363; www.borinquenresort.com; s/d incl breakfast US$207/249; P) The most luxurious of area resorts, elegant and air-conditioned bungalows with decks, minibars and satellite TV are connected by a steep trail system that you can negotiate with golf carts if you're too drained from soaking in the on-site hot springs and mud baths to walk. Rates include options like guided hikes to area waterfalls, horseback and ATV trips and, of course, a canopy tour.

Getting There & Away

The Las Pailas sector is accessible via a good, 20km gravel road beginning at a signed turnoff from the Interamericana 5km north of Liberia; a private road is needed to reach the park and costs US$2 per person. The Santa María ranger station, to the east, is accessible via a rougher road beginning at Barrio La Victoria in Liberia. Both roads are passable to regular cars in dry season, but 4WD is required in the rainy season and highly recommended at all other times (or it will take you twice as long). There's no public transportation, but any of the above lodges can arrange transport from Liberia for around US$15 per person with a two or three person minimum, or from San José and other locations for more.

Hotels and tourist information spots can arrange transport for similar prices; Hotel Guanacaste and Posada del Tope (p188), are your best bets. Alternately, you can hire a

4WD taxi for about US$25 to Las Pailas, or US$45 to Santa María, each way.

PARQUE NACIONAL SANTA ROSA

Among the oldest (established in 1971) and largest national parks in Costa Rica, Santa Rosa's sprawling 38,674 hectares of the Península Santa Elena is home to a variety of attractions that are unique in the nation. The shady campsite near the ranger station is one of the finest in the national-park system, with beachside camping also a worthwhile (but pricey, considering transport) option.

Santa Rosa covers most of the Península Santa Elena, which juts out into the Pacific at the far northwestern corner of the country. The park is named after the Hacienda Santa Rosa, where a historic battle was fought on March 20, 1856, between a hastily assembled amateur army of Costa Ricans and the invading forces of the North American filibuster William Walker. In fact, it was mainly historical and patriotic reasons that brought about the establishment of this national park in the first place. It is almost a coincidence that the park has also become extremely important to biologists.

Santa Rosa protects the largest remaining stand of tropical dry forest in Central America, and it also protects some of the most important nesting sites of several species of sea turtle, including endangered ones. Wildlife is often seen, especially during the dry season when animals congregate around the remaining water sources and the trees lose their leaves. The dry season also has fewer biting insects and the roads are more passable. But this is also the 'busy' season when, particularly on weekends, the park is popular with Ticos in search of their often hard-to-find history. It's always fairly quiet, though, compared to parks such as Volcán Poás or Manuel Antonio.

In the wet months from July through December, particularly September and October, you can observe the sea turtles nesting and often have the rest of the park virtually to yourself. An increase in package tours to see the turtles nesting prompted a closure of **Playa Nancite** (the best-known turtle-nesting beach) to large groups, though individuals and small groups can sometimes obtain a permit.

The park is also famous for **Playa Naranjo**, specifically spectacular Witch's Rock, legendary among the surfing set.

Orientation & Information

Parque Nacional Santa Rosa's entrance is on the west side of the Interamericana, 35km north of Liberia and 45km south of the Nicaragua border. The **park entrance** (☎ 666 5051; admission US$6, camping per person US$2; 🕑 8am-4pm) is close to the Interamericana, and it's another 7km to park headquarters, with the administrative offices, scientists' quarters, an information center, campground, museum, and nature trail. This office administers the Area de Conservación Guanacaste (ACG).

From this complex, a 4WD trail leads down to the coast, 12km away. It's closed to cars from May to November (wet season). Horses and walkers can use the road all year. There are several beaches, and a camping area lies at the southern end of Playa Naranjo. Rangers can and will shut down the beaches to all visitors during turtle nesting season. There are also other jeep, foot, and horse trails that leave the main visitor complex and head out into the tropical dry forest and other habitats.

The park's Sector Murciélago (Bat Sector) encompasses the wild northern coastline of the Península Santa Elena. A ranger station and camping area are here; a short trail leads to a swimming hole. You can't get there from the main body of the park; you'll need to return to the Interamericana and travel further north.

Sights & Activities

LA CASONA

The historic La Casona (the main building of the old Hacienda Santa Rosa) was destroyed by arson in May 2001 and rebuilt in 2002 using historic photos and local timber. The battle of 1856 was fought around this building, and the military action, as well as the region's natural history, are described with the help of documents, paintings, maps, and other displays, most in Spanish only. If you remember your dictionary, this will be an inspiring (and perhaps humbling) history lesson in how not to invade a country.

The arson was set by a local father-son team of poachers who were disgruntled at being banned from hunting here by park rangers. They were caught and sentenced to 20 years in prison for torching a building of national cultural and historical value.

Behind La Casona, a short trail leads up to the **Monumento a Los Héroes** and a lookout platform. There are also longer trails through the dry forest, including a gentle 4km hike to the Mirador, with spectacular views of Playa Naranjo, which is accessible to hikers willing to go another 9km along the deeply rutted road to the sea. The main road is lined with short trails to small waterfalls and other photogenic natural wonders as well.

WILDLIFE WATCHING

Near La Casona is **El Sendero Indio Desnudo,** a 1km trail with signs interpreting the ecological relationships among the animals, plants and weather patterns of Santa Rosa. The trail is named after the common tree, also called *gumbo limbo*, whose peeling orange-red bark can photosynthesize during the dry season, when the tree's leaves are lost, resembling either a naked Indian or sunburned tourist, depending on the guide.

Also seen along the trail is the national tree of Costa Rica, the guanacaste (*Enterolobium cyclocarpum*). The province is named after this very large tree species, which is found along the Pacific coastal lowlands. You may also see birds, monkeys, snakes, iguanas, and petroglyphs (probably pre-Columbian) etched into some of the rocks on the trail.

The wildlife is certainly both varied and prolific. More than 250 bird species have been recorded, including the raucous white-throated magpie jay, unmistakable with its long crest of maniacally curled feathers. The forests contain parrots and parakeets, trogons and tanagers, and as you head down to the coast, you will be rewarded by sightings of a variety of coastal birds.

Bats are also very common; about 50 or 60 different species have been identified in Santa Rosa. Other mammals you have a reasonable chance of seeing include deer, coatis, peccaries, armadillos, coyotes, raccoons, three kinds of monkey, and a variety of other species – about 115 in all. There are also many thousands of insect species, including about 4000 moths and butterflies.

Reptile species include lizards, iguanas, snakes, crocodiles, and four species of sea turtle. The olive ridley sea turtle is the most numerous, and during the July to December nesting season, tens of thousands of turtles make their nests on Santa Rosa's beaches. The most popular beach is **Playa Nancite**, where, during September and October especially, it is possible to see as many as 8000 of these 40kg turtles on the beach at the same time. The turtles are disturbed by light, so flash photography and flashlights are not permitted. Avoid the nights around a full moon – they're too bright and turtles are less likely to show up. Playa Nancite is strictly protected and entry restricted, but permission may be obtained from park headquarters to observe this spectacle.

The variety of wildlife reflects the variety of habitat protected within the boundaries of the park. Apart from the largest remaining stand of tropical dry forest in Central America, habitats including savanna woodland, oak forest, deciduous forest, evergreen forest, riparian forest, mangrove swamp, and coastal woodland.

Surfing

Playa Naranjo, the next major beach south of Playa Nancite, is near the southern end of the national park's coastline. The surfing here is world-renowned, especially near **Witches Rock** or at **Ollie's Point** Witches Rock is famous for its totally tubular 3m curls and great camping in between taking rides. Ollie's Point is near the old airstrip that was used to smuggle goods to the Nicaraguan Contras in the 1980s. This is a popular place to camp and surf, but you'll need to pack everything in – surfboards, tents, food, and drinking water (though brackish water is available for washing off after a day in the waves). The hike in takes several hours. Surfing and boat tours to Witches Rock are offered from Playa del Coco (p224) and Playa Tamarindo (see p235), and can be arranged by tourist agencies in Liberia as well. There's a 25 person, two-night limit for campers.

Sleeping & Eating

There is a shady developed **campground** (per person US$2) close to the park headquarters, with picnic benches, grills, flushing toilets and cold-water showers. Playa Naranjo has pit toilets and showers, but no potable water – bring your own. Other camping areas in the park are undeveloped. There's a 25-person, two-night maximum for camping at Playa Naranjo.

Make reservations in advance to stay at the **research station** (dm US$20), with eight-bed bunk rooms, cold showers and electricity.

Researchers get priority, but there's usually room for travelers. Good meals (US$3 to US$7) are available, but make arrangements the day before. There's also a snack bar.

Getting There & Away

The well-signed main park entrance can be reached by public transport: Take any bus between Liberia and the Nicaragua border and ask the driver to set you down at the park entrance; rangers can help you catch a return bus. You can also arrange transportation from Liberia at Hotel Liberia (see p188) for about US$15 per person round-trip.

To get to the northern Sector Murciélago of the park, go 10km further north along the Interamericana, then turn left to the village of Cuajiniquil, with a couple of *sodas* and a *pulpería*, 8km away by paved road. Keep your passport handy, as there may be checkpoints. The paved road continues beyond Cuajiniquil and dead-ends at a marine port, 4km away – this isn't the way to Sector Murciélago but goes toward Refugio Nacional de Vida Silvestre Bahía Junquillal. It's about 8km beyond Cuajiniquil to the Murciélago ranger station by poor road – 4WD is advised in the wet season, though the road may be impassable. You can camp at the Murciélago ranger station, or continue 10km to 12km on a dirt road beyond the ranger station to the remote bays and beaches of Bahía Santa Elena and Bahía Playa Blanca.

REFUGIO NACIONAL DE VIDA SILVESTRE BAHÍA JUNQUILLAL

This 505-hectare wildlife refuge is part of the Area de Conservación Guanacaste, administered from the park headquarters at Santa Rosa. There is a **ranger station** (☎ 679 9692; admission US$6, camping per person US$2; 🕑 7am-4pm) in telephone and radio contact with Santa Rosa; the admission fee covers entrance to both parks.

The quiet bay and protected beach provide gentle swimming, boating, and snorkeling opportunities, and there is some tropical dry forest and mangrove swamp. Short trails take the visitor to a lookout for marine birding and to the mangroves. Pelicans and frigatebirds are seen, and turtles nest here seasonally. Volcán Orosí can be seen in the distance. Campers should note that during the dry season especially, water is at a premium and is turned on for only one hour a day. There are pit latrines.

From Cuajiniquil, continue for 2km along the paved road and then turn right onto a signed dirt road. Continuing 4km along the dirt road (passable to ordinary cars) brings you to the entrance to Bahía Junquillal. From here, a poorer 700m dirt road leads to the beach, ranger station, and camping area.

PARQUE NACIONAL GUANACASTE

This newest part of the ACG was created on July 25 (Guanacaste Day), 1989. The park is adjacent to Parque Nacional Santa Rosa, separated from it by the Interamericana, and is only about 5km northwest of Parque Nacional Rincón de la Vieja.

The 34,651 hectares of Parque Nacional Guanacaste are much more than a continuation of the dry tropical forest and other lowland habitats found in Santa Rosa. In its lower western reaches, the park is an extension of Santa Rosa's habitats, but the terrain soon begins to climb toward two volcanoes: Volcán Orosí (1487m) and Volcán Cacao (1659m). Thus it protects animals moving between the coast and the highlands, allowing ancient migratory and hunting patterns to continue as they have for millennia that these animals might thrive.

Not all the preserved areas are natural forest. Indeed, large portions are ranch land. But researchers have found that if the pasture is carefully managed (much of this management involves just letting nature take its course), the natural forest will reinstate itself in its old territory. Thus, crucial habitats are not just preserved, but in some cases they are also expanded.

For information on this park, contact the **ACG headquarters** (☎ 666 5051) in Parque Nacional Santa Rosa.

Research Stations

Research is an important part of Guanacaste, and there are three biological stations within its borders. They are all in good areas for wildlife observation or hiking.

MARITZA BIOLOGICAL STATION

This is the newest station and has a modern laboratory. From the station, at 600m above sea level, rough trails run to the summits of Volcán Orosí and Volcán Cacao (about five to six hours). There is also a better trail to

NORTHWESTERN COSTA RICA

a site where several hundred Indian petroglyphs have been found, about two hours away. Another trail goes to Cacao Biological Station.

To get there, turn east off the Interamericana opposite the turnoff for Cuajiniquil. The station is about 17km east of the highway along a dirt road that may require a 4WD vehicle, especially in the wet season.

CACAO BIOLOGICAL STATION

High on the slopes of Volcán Cacao (about 1060m), this station offers access to rough trails that lead to the summit of the volcano and to Maritza Biological Station. Cacao Biological Station is reached from the southern side of the park. At Potrerillos, about 9km south of the Santa Rosa park entrance on the Interamericana, head east for 7km on a paved road to the small community of Quebrada Grande (marked 'Garcia Flamenco' on many maps). A daily bus leaves Liberia at 3pm for Quebrada Grande. From the village plaza, a 4WD road that is often impassable during the wet season heads north toward the station, about 10km away.

PITILLA BIOLOGICAL STATION

This station is a surprise – it lies on the northeast side of Volcán Orosí, and because it lies on the eastern side of the continental divide, the surrounding forest is more like that found on the Caribbean slopes than on the Pacific.

To get to the station, turn east off the Interamericana about 12km north of the Cuajiniquil turnoff, or 3km before reaching the small town of La Cruz. Follow the paved eastbound road for about 28km to the community of Santa Cecilia. From there, a poor dirt road heads 11km south to the station – you'll probably need 4WD. (Don't continue on the unpaved road heading further east – that goes over 50km further to the small town of Upala.)

Sleeping & Eating

INSIDE THE PARK

If there's space, you may be able to reserve dorm-style accommodations at **Maritza** or **Cacao** (☎ 666 5051; dm US$20); Pitilla is the province of research biologists and students. The stations are all quite rustic, with room for about 30 people, and shared cold-water bathrooms. Meals are also available for US$3 to US$7, and should be arranged in advance.

You can also **camp** (per person US$2) near the stations, though there aren't any facilities.

OUTSIDE THE PARK

Hacienda Los Inocentes (☎ 679 9190; www.losinocentesranch.com; d without/with 3 meals US$39/89) This ranch, on the north side of Parque Nacional Guanacaste, is owned by folks interested in wildlife and conservation as well as ranching; they promote recycling and solar energy and host scientists engaged in environmental research. The hacienda building itself is a very attractive, century-old wooden house converted into a comfortable country lodge. The setting below Volcán Orosí is quite spectacular. About two-thirds of the 1000-hectare ranch is forested (mainly with secondary forest), and bird- and animal-watching opportunities abound.

The staff arrange trips into Parque Nacional Guanacaste (US$60 per person), climbs up Volcán Orosí (US$40) looming high on the horizon about 7km to the south, and horseback rides (US$60). The lodge building has 11 spacious wooden bedrooms with private (but separate) bathroom, plus several larger separate cabins. The upper floor is surrounded by a beautiful, shaded, wooden verandah with hammocks and also volcano views – a good spot for sunset/moonrise.

The hacienda is 15km east of the Interamericana on the paved road to Santa Cecilia. Buses from San José to Santa Cecilia pass the lodge entrance at about 7:30pm, returning at around 4:15am. Taxis from La Cruz charge about US$10.

LA CRUZ

Though this is the closest town to the main border crossing with Nicaragua, it's actually a rather pleasant (if potentially boring) spot to spend the night, by border-town standards, with above-average accommodations and a handful of *sodas*, good-sized markets and bars arranged around the grassy Parque Central. Its best feature is the location on a small hill overlooking Bahía Salinas in the distance – there are incredible views of the coast.

Information

Banco Nacional (☎ 679 9296) is at the junction of the short road into the center and the Interamericana. The **Banco Popular** (☎ 679 9352) is in the center. It's reportedly easier to change money at the border post. There is a small **clinic** (☎ 679 9116).

Sleeping

Cabinas Maryfel (☎ 679 8173; s/d US$5/8.75; P) This fairly clean, basic, budget choice, in the unmarked pink house opposite the bus station, is a favorite of migrant workers.

Cabinas Santa Rita (☎ 679 9062; s/d US$5/8, s/d with bathroom US$12/20, air-con US$19/23 P) This clean, well-run hotel has dark, basic rooms with shared bathroom, popular among migrant workers, and frillier options with private bathroom, plus cable TV, hot showers, and air-con. Across the street, a newer annex provides similar rooms at the same rates.

Hostal de Julia (☎ 679 9084; s/d US$23/35 P) North of the gas station on the road going into town from the Interamericana, this place has a dozen clean, motel-like rooms (with fans and private hot bath) around a white-washed courtyard.

Amalia's Inn (☎ 679 9618; s/d US$20/35; P) Not just the best hotel in town, but one of the finest nonresort accommodations in the region, this spot offers seven enormous rooms furnished with 1980s-style leather modular couches, comfy beds and lots of absolutely incredible paintings by the deceased North American husband of Amalia, the Tica owner. The mural by the pool and fabulous views of the gulf through each room's huge picture windows make this a great reason to spend the night in a border town. Go figure.

Hotel Colinas del Norte (☎ 810 6986; d incl breakfast US$40; P) About 6km north of La Cruz this attractive ranch with 10km of private trails arranges local tours, from horseback riding and volcano visits to trips around Isla Bolaños (p197). Rooms are wood trimmed, rustic and spacious, but ask for one far from the disco, which goes until at least 1am on Friday and Saturday.

Eating

It's not the gastronomic capital of Costa Rica, but you can always get a good *gallo* (tortilla sandwich).

Soda Santa Marta (mains US$1-3; 6am-6pm) This cheerful little *soda*, about 50m from the Parque Central, specializes in steak and *carne asada* with its huge casados.

Soda Candy (mains US$1-3; 6am-8pm) There's no menu at this basic *soda* across from the bus terminal, but in addition to casados and *gallos* 'made with a lot of love,' Candy knows all the bus schedules by heart and can fill you in if the station is closed.

Bar/Snacks Pizotes (bocas US$1, mains US$2-4; 11am-10pm) More inviting than the other very basic bars around town, this spot serves cheap *bocas* (savoury snacks) and a selection of light meals.

Pollo Rico Rico (mains US$2-4; 10am-10pm) Folks who love fried chicken should stop by this spot, right on the park, or try their roasted chicken, which is even tastier.

Restaurant Las Orquideas (☎ 679 9316; mains US$1-5; 8am-10pm) Right on the Interamericana, this friendly spot is part bus stop, where you can get good coffee in a basic dining room with a big TV, and part nice restaurant, where red tablecloths and a pleasant ambience make the casados, seafood and rice dishes rather elegant.

Getting There & Away

A **Transportes Deldú counter** (7am-1pm & 3-5:30pm) sells tickets and stores bags. To catch a TransNica bus to Peñas Blancas, you'll need to flag a bus down on the Interamericana. Local buses to Bahía Salinas (US$0.50, one hour) depart at 10:30am and 1:30pm.

Liberia (Transportes Deldú) US$1.25; 1½-two hours; departs 7am, 10am, noon, 3:30pm & 5:30pm.
Peñas Blancas US$1; 45 minutes; 5am, 7am, 7:45am, 10:45am, 1:20pm & 4:10pm.
San José (Transportes Deldú) US$5.50; 4½ hours; 5:45am, 8am, 11:15am, 12:30pm & 4pm.

BAHÍA SALINAS

A dirt road (normally passable to cars) leads down from the lookout point in La Cruz past the small coastal fishing community of Puerto Soley and out along the curve of the bay to where there are a couple of newer resorts. Boats can be rented here to visit **Isla Bolaños** (you can't land, but you can approach and view the nesting seabird colonies) and other places; try **Frank Schultz** (☎ 827 4109; franks diving@costaricense.co.cr), who also organizes fishing and diving trips. The bay is becoming something of a windsurfing spot, and there is a windsurfing school where you can rent boards and get lessons.

Windsurfing & Kiteboarding

This is the second-best place in Costa Rica (after Laguna de Arenal) for windsurfing, and because vegetation around the lake can be dangerous for folks in the air, is arguably the best place for kiteboarding. The strongest and steadiest winds blow from December through March, but it blows pretty well year-round here. The shape of the hills surrounding the bay funnel the winds into a predictable pattern, and the sandy, protected beaches make this a safe place for beginners and experienced board riders alike.

Tico Wind (☎ 692 2002; www.ticowind.com; half-/full-day rentals US$38/68) is a recommended windsurfing company at Ecoplaya Beach Resort. Like its flagship operation on Laguna de Arenal (p213), it maintains the same high standards, with new equipment purchased every year and top-notch instruction.

If windsurfing too tame for you, try **Kitesurf School 2000** (☎ 672 0218; Nov-May; www.suntourssandfun.com/kitesurfing.htm) a sporty combination of wind and waves (which school instructors insist is much easier to learn than regular surfing) where you are attached to a large kite, seriously, then pulled across the bay by the breeze, allowing more advanced students to do flips and other aerial acrobatics above the froth and swells – way cool. If you want to give this a try, make reservations a couple of days in advance for 10 hours of lessons (US$225) or just equipment rental (basic gear US$45 per day). It's about 12km from La Cruz. If they aren't full of grinning students, the school rents **basic dorms** (dm US$12.50) with hot showers and a shared kitchen.

NORTHWESTERN COSTA RICA

Sleeping & Eating

Playa Copal (☎ 676 1055; www.progettopuravida.com) Though geared toward long-term stays, this agency rents several wicker-furnished apartments and houses for US$45 to US$100 per night, depending on the size and amenities, which may include a pool or, perhaps, a bidet (they're Italian-owned); all overlook as fine a stretch of beach as you'd want. If you stay for five days, you generally get two days free; monthly stays are an even better deal.

Restaurant Copal (☎ 676 1006; mains US$4-7; 5pm-party is over) Though there's not much competition, that doesn't stop this excellent eatery from turning out top-quality seafood, salads and other beautifully prepared entrees; try the *pizza del mar*, with shrimp and the catch of the day – outstanding. It's popular with folks escaping Ecoplaya, about 3km away.

Ecoplaya Beach Resort (☎ 676 1010; www.ecoplaya.com; d standard/junior/master/luxury US$80/110/160/195; P) About 16km from La Cruz, you're really getting away from it all on this isolated stretch of paradise, where bungalows range from upscale elegance (big bathroom, nice furniture) to full luxury (minibar, sitting room, private porch). Between the kayak and mountain bike rental, fishing tours, diving trips, windsurfing lessons, horseback riding, pool with a swim-up bar, and perfect beach, there's plenty to ward off the boredom. There's also an on-site, thatch-roofed **restaurant** (mains US$5-11).

Getting There & Away

Buses along this road depart the La Cruz bus terminal at 10:30am and 1:30pm daily. A taxi to either beach area costs about US$11, and you can usually catch a colec-

GETTING TO RIVAS, NICARAGUA

Peñas Blancas is a busy border crossing, and it's good to get there early, if only to avoid the sliding entry fee into Nicaragua, which runs US$7 until noon, US$9 afterward; your car will cost another US$22. You won't be charged to enter Costa Rica, but leaving Nicaragua costs US$2, payable in US dollars only. (There are banks on either side that will change local colones and córdobas for dollars, but not for each other, though independent money changers will happily make the exchange at a ridiculous rate.) And those are just the base fees.

The border posts, open 6am to 8pm daily, are 1km apart; if you're feeling saucy you can hire a golf cart (US$2) to make the run. Hordes of totally useless touts will offer to 'guide' you through the simple crossing; if you let them carry your luggage, they will charge you whatever they want. And, should you have any hard currency left, there's a fairly fabulous duty-free shop, with fancy makeup and lots of liquor, waiting for you on the Nicaraguan side.

Relax with your purchases on the 37km bus ride (US$0.50, 45 minutes), departing every 30 minutes, to Rivas, a quiet town with a few hotels and bus connections throughout the country.

tivo (US$3.50) from La Cruz, close to the taxi stand, though you may have to wait a while for it to fill up.

PEÑAS BLANCAS

On the border with Nicaragua, Peñas Blancas is a border post, not a town. There isn't anywhere to stay, although meals and money changing are available.

See the boxed text on p198 for border-crossing details.

ARENAL ROUTE

Sure, the Interamericana is the fastest way around the region, but then there's this route, the road less traveled, probably because of all the potholes. The Arenal route takes you through several fine towns: Ciudad Quesada (San Carlos), where the almost constant drizzle makes lounging in the area's hot springs all the more enjoyable; La Fortuna, famed for its explosive views of Volcán Arenal; and the tiny and terrific Tico towns of Nuevo Arenal and Tilarán, with their exquisite lake and volcano (if you're lucky) views. From there, you can connect to Cañas or even head to the hills of Santa Elena and Monteverde; either way the scenic beauty just keeps on coming.

Though all these spots are well-served by public transportation, this is a five-star road trip just made for folks lucky enough to have rented their own vehicle. This vista-packed trip is lined with lakeside picnic spots, wacky art galleries, wonderful restaurants and weird hotels galore, all just waiting to be explored by folks with a little time on their hands.

CIUDAD QUESADA (SAN CARLOS)

The official name of this small city is Ciudad Quesada (sometimes abbreviated to 'Quesada'), but all the locals know it as San Carlos, and local buses often list San Carlos as the destination. It's long been a bustling ranching and agricultural center, known for its *talabaterías* (saddle shops). They make and sell some of the most intricately crafted leather saddles in Costa Rica; a top-quality saddle can cost US$1000.

Today, however, it's growing into a more urban experience (31,000 residents) with traffic clogging roads around pretty Parque Central, though hotels still get packed for the **Feria del Ganado** (cattle fair and auction) held every April and the biggest such event in the country. The fair is accompanied by the usual carnival rides and a *tope* (horse parade).

There's not really any other reason for the average tourist to stop by, except to change buses or visit one of the area's fine hot springs. In addition to two resorts, just outside town is a public park and recreation area, **Aguas Termales de la Marina** (☎ 460 1692; admission US$2), referred to as 'El Tucanito' by the locals, with the best deal on hot water in town.

Check your email at **Internet Café** (100m north of parque; per hr US$1; 🕑 8am-9pm Mon-Sat, 3-7pm Sun). **Banco de San José**, 200m north of the parque, and the **Mutual de Alajuela** across the street both have ATMs on the Cirrus and Plus systems.

Sleeping

Hotel del Norte (☎ 460 1959; 200m north of Banco Nacional; s/d US$6.25/10, s/d with bathroom US$9.75/14.75) Small, clean rooms with TV and thin walls (so pray that you like what your neighbor is watching) are made marvelous by the excellent security and service, better than some four-star hotels.

Hotel del Valle (☎ 460 0718; 100m north of Banco Popular; s/d US$10/15) This place is another good budget choice, with private bathroom and cable TV.

Hotel Lily (☎ 460 0616; r per person US$6.25) Located 100m to the west, this homey option has nicely appointed rooms and a friendly owner.

Hotel Don Goyo (☎ 460 1780; 100m south of Parque Central s/d US$12/22; Ⓟ) This is about as fabulous as it gets in San Carlos proper, with hot showers and small, pleasant, salmon-colored rooms. Mornings are a good time to sit in the restaurant and watch birds feed near the river.

Termales del Bosque (☎ 460 4740; www.termalesdelbosque.com; s/d incl breakfast US$37/49; Ⓟ) Several airy cottages are arranged around the jungly grounds at this resort designed with Tico tourism in mind. There's a good restaurant and the obligatory canopy tour (US$42 per person), but the real reason you're here are the seven natural hot and warm springs, set in a quiet, forested valley populated by morpho butterflies and other wildlife, arranged along a cool and scenic river. It's low-key luxuriating that comes highly recommended, though the springs are about 1km from the hotel on a good dirt road.

El Tucano Resort & Thermal Spa (☎ 460 6000; www.costaricareservation.com/tucano.htm; d US$105, ste US$157-221; P) This posh Mediterranean-style resort, 8km northeast of Ciudad Quesada comes complete with an Italian restaurant, swimming pool, Jacuzzi, and sauna, plus various sports facilities ranging from tennis courts to miniature golf. Nearby thermal springs are tapped into three small hot pools where you can soak away your ills. The on-site **spa** (☎ 460 0891) provides massages, mud baths and more to guests and nonguests (who can also use the pools here for US$11 per person). A variety of package deals include spa treatments and various guided tours.

Eating

There aren't many fine restaurants, but you certainly won't starve. Apart from the hotel restaurants, there are several places to eat on or near the park.

Musmanni Bakery (Parque Central; 5am-9pm) The old standard has the usual selection of baked goods.

Charlie's Burger (Parque Central; mains US$2-4; 11am-10pm) When you really need a burger (or casado) this place delivers.

Restaurant Los Geranios (100m south of the church; mains US$2-5) On a 2nd-story terrace, the local twentysomethings pack into this relatively hot spot for cheap food and beer.

Restaurant El Imperial (100m south of parque; mains US$2-6; 10:30am-11pm) For big servings of shrimp fried rice and chop suey with everything, this is the place.

Restaurant El Parque (50m north of parque; mains US$3-6; 11am-9pm) This *soda* specializes in Italian food; try the lasagna.

Getting There & Away

The new Terminal Quesada is about 2km from the center of town. Taxis (US$1) and a twice-hourly bus (US$0.20) make regular runs between town and the terminal. (Walking there is fine if you don't mind hauling your luggage uphill.) Popular bus routes (and their bus companies) from Ciudad Quesada are:

La Fortuna (Coopatrac) US$0.70; 1½ hours; depart 6am, 10:30am, 1pm, 3:30pm, 5:15pm & 6pm.

Los Chiles (Chilsaca) US$2.25; two hours; 5am, 6:30am, 9am, 10am, 11am, noon, 1pm, 1:30pm, 2:45pm, 3pm, 4pm & 5pm.

Puerto Viejo de Sarapiquí (Empresarios Guapileños) US$1.50; 2½ hours; 4:40am, 6am, 9:15am, 10am, 3pm & 5:30pm.

San José (Autotransportes San Carlos) US$2.25, 2½ hours; 5am, 6:40am, 7:10am, 8:15am, 9:20am, 11:40am, 1pm, 2:30pm, 3:30pm, 5:35pm & 6:15pm.

Tilarán (Transportes Tilarán) US$4; 4½ hours; 6:30am & 4pm.

LA FORTUNA

pop 8000

Even without an active volcano spewing smoke and fireworks overhead, the quiet, charismatic town of La Fortuna would be a relaxing place to while away a few days – which is good luck, since you may have to wait that long for the star attraction to unveil itself. The town's official name is La Fortuna de San Carlos, to distinguish it from Fortuna (p182) about 70km northwest of here. But since it is always called La Fortuna, or Fortuna for short, confusion is inevitable.

In addition to a fantastically wild waterfall and fabulously landscaped hot springs, La Fortuna is close to crossroads connecting three very different regions: shimmering Laguna de Arenal, the cloud forests of Monteverde and Santa Elena reserves, and the otherwise isolated attractions of the northern lowlands. Transport is convenient (and unusual, in the case of Monteverde), the lodging is cheap, and you just can't beat the view, assuming you're in luck.

More than that, despite the influx of tourists who have swollen the economy in recent years, La Fortuna still retains that *sabanero* vibe and real Tico feel, probably because it's quite consciously holding on to it. Brilliant flowers, not fences, still guard the edges of jungle that echo with the cries of howler monkeys and frame this friendly collection of family-run restaurants, hotels and businesses, as yet untouched by booming resort mania.

And above it all, Volcán Arenal. Is it so easy to accept that this looming gray mountain, ominous in its symmetry and spilling the planet's boiling lifeblood with unpredictable fury, is just 6km away? But like moths, visitors are drawn to its fiery display, humbled and exhilarated as they watch it renew these fertile lands. These views are incredible, but this is not a free show: Arenal has called in its debt before, taking even tourists at supposedly secure overlooks (see p211).

But it's worth whatever risk nature demands of her most ardent devotees for one clear night, illuminated in streams of glowing lava that tumble down the mountain, accompanied by low rumbles and clouds of smoke subtly obscuring the stars above. And as you tremble at Arenal's magnificence, please just try to remember one thing: flash photography is futile! You'll just get a blurry picture of the trees.

Orientation & Information

Although streets in La Fortuna have recently been named and (poorly) signed, locals can give you better directions using landmarks. It's still a small town, centered on the pretty Parque Central, where the Costa Rican flag is proudly flown from a small, cement, erupting volcano in the center. Both the bus stop and taxi stand are adjacent to the square.

The clinic, police station, and post office are shown on the La Fortuna map.

Masajes Serenity (☎ 479 8261; 50m southeast of Parque Central; massages (US$20-65); ⌚ 9am-10pm) treats weary muscles with a variety of massages, and skin with a selection of facials and spa treatments.

INTERNET ACCESS

Adventure Center (per hr US$1.75) Air-conditioned.
Destiny Internet & Tours (per hr US$2.50)
Hotel Colinas (per hr US$1.25)
Internet La Parada (across from Parque Central; per hr US$1.25; ⌚ 9am-10pm Mon-Sat) Also sells a few English-language magazines.

LAUNDRY

Lavandería La Fortuna (across from school; per load US$2.50; ⌚ 8am-9pm) Do-it-yourself laundry; for US$1.25 extra you get the full fluff-and-fold treatment.

MONEY

Despite being a relatively touristy town, some hotels and restaurants won't accept US dollars, only colones. Banco de Costa Rica has a Visa Plus ATM.

TOURIST INFORMATION

There are probably a dozen private tour operators (p203) with information veering toward enlightened self-interest, and almost every hotel in town can arrange tours, transportation and accommodations anywhere in the country. See p203 for details of some tour operators.

Lunatíca (☎ 479 8255; across from the school; ⌚ 9:30am-7:30pm) has information on the odd cultural offering in town, as well as work from some 30 area artists on display, including baskets, masks and jewelry made by Muleka Indians.

Sights & Activities

For details on white-water rafting, hiking and mountain biking in the area, see Tours, p203.

HOT SPRINGS

What's the best thing about volcano country, particularly if you can't see the volcano? Why, hot springs, of course, and La Fortuna has some doozies.

If Aaron Spelling ever needed a set for the Garden of Eden sequence in Genesis, **Tabacón Hot Springs** (☎ 256 1500; www.tabacon.com; adult/child US$29/17, after 7pm US$19/17; ⌚ 10am-10pm) is what it would look like. Enter through the gratuitously opulent ticket counter, flanked by an outrageous buffet (adult/child US$12/9 extra) on one side and glittering gift shop on the other. Then, with a thundering announcement, rare orchids and more florid tropical blooms part to reveal, oh yes, a 40°C waterfall pouring over a cliff, concealing naturalish-looking caves complete with camouflaged cup holders. And lounged across each well-placed stone, in various stages of sweat-induced exhaustion, relax reddening tourists all enjoying what could be called a hot date.

But wait, there's more. Probably a couple of kilometers of trails crisscross the surreal landscape, connecting an in-pool bar with more secluded pools, and there's even a cold spring hidden away in the back. The views can only be described as explosive, especially on a clear night when your soak is enhanced by periodic fireworks from Arenal, just overhead. The spa is actually on the site where a volcanic eruption ripped through in 1975, killing one local (there weren't any tourists here in those days). The resort (see p211) itself, on the other side of the road and up a hill, is out of the danger area.

Baldi Thermae Hot Springs (☎ 479 5691; per person US$14; ⌚ 10am-10pm) can only be considered understated in comparison to Tabacón.

NORTHWESTERN COSTA RICA

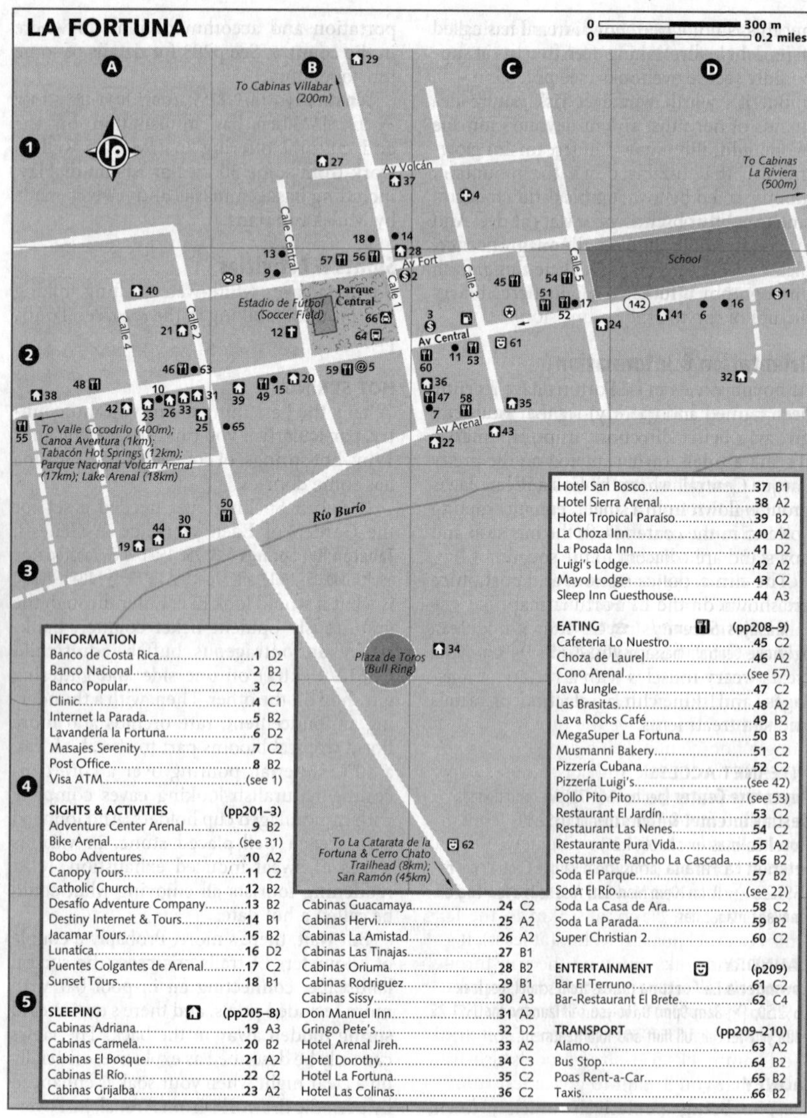

With 10 springs, including one with a bar, this still has a bit of the Roman orgy feel, but without quite so many people.

Eco-Termales (☎ 479 9819; admission US$14; ⏲ 10am-10pm by reservation only) On an unsigned road that begins across from Volcán Look, these somewhat simpler springs, with large pools and a more relaxed, natural ambiance, are limited to 100 visitors at a time. Make reservations at least a few hours in advance.

VALLE COCODRILO

Part crocodile conservation program, part seat-of-its-pants tourist attraction, this locally operated **crocodile ranch** (☎ 479 9279; 700m west of church; admission US$2; ⏲ 8am-6:30pm) receives no government aid for feeding the ferocious collection, so feel free to tip.

Enter through the cavernous cement scale model of Volcán Arenal, complete with lava, to view more than 50 crocs and caimans, from adorably scaly babies to 4m monsters. They're arranged in various fenced-in ponds and creeks that thread the property, and there's usually someone at the desk who can give you a guided tour (in Spanish), with insight into not only the crocs' natural history, but also their plight here in Cost Rica. It's *so* worth the admission fee.

LA CATARATA DE LA FORTUNA

Even if you can't see Arenal, La Fortuna has another natural wonder that pales only in comparison with an erupting volcano: **La Catarata de la Fortuna** (admission US$6; 8am-5pm), a sparkling 70m ribbon of clear water pouring through a sheer canyon of dark volcanic rock arrayed in bromyliads and ferns. It's photogenic, and you don't have to descend the canyon – a short, well-maintained, and almost vertical hike paralleling the river's precipitous plunge – to get the shot, though you do have to pay the steep entry fee.

It's worth the climb out (think Stairmaster with a view) to see the rare world at the jungle floor. Though it's dangerous to dive beneath the thundering falls, a series of perfect swimming holes with spectacular views tiles the canyon in aquamarine – cool and inviting after the hike or ride here. Keep an eye on your backpack.

Though the signed turnoff from the road to San Ramón claims it's 5km to the falls, this is a cruel hoax. It's 7km (at least), it's all uphill, and folks enjoying the trip through pastureland and papaya trees will appreciate a stop at **Neptuno's House of Hammocks** (479 8269; hammocks US$50-150), which sells soft drinks and hammocks (cat-sized models also available) that you'll want to give a test run.

You can also get to the *catarata* on horseback (US$20 to US$30 per person) or by car or taxi (US$7 one way); several outfits also offer overpriced tours that include a shuttle. A handful of snack and souvenir stands are at the entrance to the falls, but it's worth packing your own lunch and making a day of it.

The falls are also the trailhead for the steep, five-hour **Cerro Chato** climb, a seriously strenuous trek to a lake-filled volcanic crater, where you can see two Arenals fuming for the price of one.

Can't handle the hike? Just past the turnoff to the *catarata*, at the third bridge as you leave La Fortuna for San Ramón, there's a short trail on the left leading to a pretty swimming hole just under the road, with a rope swing and little waterfall of its own, thank you very much.

Courses

The **Adventure Education Center** (556 4609, 556 4614; www.adventurespanishschool.com, 1 week without/with homestay US$315/390) is an unusual Spanish school offering various guided hikes and outdoor adventures as part of the curriculum (most adventures cost a little extra). There's another campus in Turrialba (p144).

Tours

La Fortuna is well situated for not only the obligatory Volcán Arenal trip, Laguna de Arenal and visits to various hot springs, but also for several otherwise hard-to-reach attractions in the northern lowlands. Luckily, you won't have to walk more than 100 meters to find someone willing to arrange any trip. Just make sure that your agency has a permanent address, as ripping off tourists (see p204) is an industry that's been elevated to an art form around here.

There's usually a two-person minimum for any trip, though you're always welcome to pay double. Groups can work out discounts in advance with most outfitters. Almost any hotel can arrange tours through these agencies, tacking on something like US$5 per person commission for most trips; some places undercut the market by foregoing this fee, which saves you a little cash.

The most popular Volcán Arenal trips are generally afternoon excursions to either the national park or a private overlook to appreciate the mountain by day, combined with a trip to one of the hot springs and usually dinner. Then it's off to another overlook, where lucky souls will see some lava. Prices vary widely, but generally run US$25 to US$55 per person. Make sure your tour includes entry fees to the park and hot springs, which could easily add another US$25 to the total. Remember that there's a better than even chance that Arenal will remain demurely wrapped in cloud cover for the duration of your trek, and there are no refunds if you can't see anything.

Other popular trips include excursions into the wild northern lowlands, treks to the Venado Caves (p433; US$35 to US$45 per person) and Caño Negro (p435), with agencies offering outings including naturalist tours (US$50 to US$100 per person) in motorboats, canoes or kayaks, or sport fishing (US$150 to US$400 per person), usually including all tackle. Other fishing trips are arranged on Laguna de Arenal (US$150 to US$300).

White-water rafting on the Ríos Toro, Peñas Blancas and Sarapiquí are also convenient day trips, and several outfitters offer Class I or Class II floats down the Peñas Blancas (US$45 to US$65 per person), while agencies that specialize in rafting handle the Class IV Río Toro (US$85 to US$100 per person). Kayaking trips (US$60 to US$100) are also popular on the Peñas Blancas. Class III rides down the Río Sarapiquí (US$100 per person) require a lot more time in the shuttle van. Rates usually include breakfast or lunch and a riverside snack.

There are also canopy tours, canyoning down waterfalls, and guided hiking/biking/horseback treks of every sort, all of which can be customized into multiday adventure tours. Most agencies can also arrange transportation by jeep, boat and/or horseback to Monteverde (see p157). These are just some of the outfitters available.

Aventure Center Arenal (☎ 479 9052, 479 8585; 50m north of church; www.arenal-adventure.com; Internet per hr US$1.75) specializes in white-water rafting and extreme hikes, but also organizes most other tours plus visits to the Maleku Indian reserve, which can include a ceremonial fire, drums and the works.

Bike Arenal (☎ 479 9454; www.bikearenal.com; Don Manuel Inn) rents bicycles and offers guided half-day rides (US$48) on the relatively flat route around Laguna de Arenal, and full-day treks (US$65) that also take in the more mountainous national park. The trips include a bilingual guide, shuttle vans and snacks.

Selim Rodríguez López at **Bobo Adventures** (☎ 479 9390; www.boboadventures.com) offers personal guided tours of the Venado Caves.

The highly recommended **Canoa Aventura** (☎ 479 8200), about 1km west of town on the road to Arenal, does one thing: canoe trips. Most are geared toward wildlife watching, in particular birds, certain species of which (green macaws, rosette spoonbills, honeycreepers etc) are the focus of various tours. The most popular paddles include the full-day tri-colored heron trip to Caño Negro (US$90) and the four-hour, early-morning tanager paddle on Río Fortuna (US$45), but overnights (US$250) are also on offer.

Canopy Tours (☎ 479 9769; www.crarenalcanopy.com; per person US$45) offers a 45-minute horseback ride and rappelling, in addition to the zip lines.

NORTHWESTERN COSTA RICA

SCAMS

If you're taking the bus to La Fortuna, they start before you even get there, boarding a few kilometers out of town, then working the crowd: 'That hotel is overpriced, but I have a friend…' You know this scam, right? But it gets worse.

In addition to steering travelers to poor hotels, which discredits reputable hoteliers who meet the bus because they can't afford flashy brochures and still charge US$5 per room, there's a family in La Fortuna who'll also book you on 'half-price tours.' Usually, you'll just show up for your tour and learn that your receipt is invalid – one French traveler we met paid US$45 to a scammer for a birding tour to Caño Negro, and not only lost his money, but wasted a day scrambling to make other arrangements. We've also heard about folks taken to pricey hot springs, then abandoned without transportation or their entry fees paid as promised.

After milking a batch of tourists, family members trade off between La Fortuna, Monteverde and other hot spots for a couple weeks; it's worked hassle-free for years. Why haven't the police done anything? That's a good question, but basically it comes down to the fact that no one wants to wait around for months to bring these folks to trial. Any police report you file will be for insurance purposes, period.

It's worth going through a reputable agency or hotel to book your tours around here. You may pay twice as much, but at least you'll get to go.

Horseback rides and white-water rafting take top billing at **Desafío Adventure Company** (☎ 479 9464; 150m north of church; www.desafiocostarica.com), but the company can also arrange a variety of tours, including multiday extreme adventures, including rappelling. This company treats their horses well and has been recommended for the trek to Monteverde, with a couple of caveats (see p174).

Destiny Internet & Tours (☎ 479 9850; www.destinytours.com; Internet per hr US$2.50) offers a free hour of Internet access with all the usual tours.

Ecotourism, shmeekotourism – sometimes you just want to get on get on a four-wheeler and roar through jungles and fincas to pristine waterfalls (ooh) and butterfly farms (ahh). **Fourtrax Adventures** (☎ 479 8444; www.fourtraxadventure.com) charges US$75 per ATV for the three- to four-hour tour, and each little monster can carry two.

Long-standing **Jacamar Tours** (☎ 479 8039, www.arenaltours.com) offers a wide variety of tours.

Puentes Colgantes de Arenal (Hanging Bridges of Arenal; ☎ 479 9686; www.hangingbridges.com; 8am-8pm; adult/senior/student US$20/15/10, child under 12 free) organizes daily tours of this recommended outing close to Laguna de Arenal (p213), there are also 6am birding trips and guided night walks with volcano views.

Coming highly recommended **Sunset Tours** (☎ 479 9800; www.sunsettourcr.com; 6:30am-9pm) is La Fortuna's most experienced tour company, offering a variety of high-quality tours with bilingual guides (one speaks Russian) and all the trimmings.

Festivals & Events

The big annual bash is **Fiestas de la Fortuna,** which is held in mid-February and features two weeks of Costa Rican-rules bullfights, colorful carnival rides, greasy carnival food, craft stands and unusual gambling devices. It's free, except for the beer (which is cheap) and you'll have a blast trying to decide between the temporary disco with go-go dancers getting down to Christina Aguilera or the rough and wild tents next door with live ranchero and salsa.

Sleeping

La Fortuna is popular among foreign and domestic travelers alike, all eager for a glimpse of the famous erupting volcano. Try to make reservations in advance on weekends and during Costa Rican holidays. Almost any hotel can arrange tours, transportation and whatever else you might need.

The great thing about La Fortuna is the number of small, family-run places, usually a few simple rooms with electric showers and maybe a private bathroom, offering meals by arrangement and good conversation. Some aren't well signed, and you may hear about them through word of mouth. These places will help arrange local tours and are a good way to help locals cash in on the tourism boom. Hotel touts meet the buses and are a little more aggressive with their wares than in most of Costa Rica; not all are trustworthy (see the boxed text, p204).

Note that hotels beyond the town center and on the road to Arenal are listed separately (see p210).

IN TOWN

Budget

La Fortuna is a budget traveler's bonanza, with everything from festive youth hostels to quality cabinas, rooms are generally much nicer than your colón usually buys.

Gringo Pete's (☎ 479 8521; gringopetes2003@yahoo.com; 100m south of school; dm US$3, r per person without/with bathroom US$4/5, camping per person US$2; P) With a clean and cozy hostel vibe from the comfy dorms sleeping four and the breezy covered common areas (with free coffee all day), this is a great spot to hook up with other budget travelers. Pete, from Washington State, can point you toward cut-rate tours and store your bags for you while you're on them. There's also a book exchange, and lockers in every room.

Cabinas Adriana (☎ 479 9474; 300m west of Mega Super; dm US$4, r per person US$6) Hey, it's not the Ritz, but the ageing pink wooden house has clean and very basic dorms, plus rooms with air-con and private cold showers, and a couple of big perks: Adriana herself, who does a homemade breakfast for US$2, and a few older mountain bikes renting for US$1 per hour.

La Choza Inn (☎ 479 9091; 100m west of Parque Central; solarenal@racsa.co.cr; dm without/with bathroom US$5/8; P) This is a great option for backpackers. Big rooms, a shared kitchen and a pleasant lounge come with free (though limited) Internet access.

La Posada Inn (☎ 479 9793; across from school; r per person without/with bathroom US$5/6, camping per person

NORTHWESTERN COSTA RICA

US$1.50; (P)) This welcoming place is popular with young backpackers. Rooms are small and basic, showers are hot and the camping area is rather private; a good choice.

Sleep Inn Guesthouse (☎ 394 7033; 250m west of MegaSuper; carlossleepinn@hotmail.com; r per person US$5) Three basic rooms with shared bathroom are cared for by Carlos, who speaks English really well, and his wife Cándida, who'll let you use their kitchen and big cable TV, though you might find yourself out on the porch watching the comings and goings at the tamale stand across the street instead. Recommended.

Cabinas Villabar (☎ 479 9363, 399 3234; 400m north of Parque Central; r per person without/with bathroom US$5/9) Cute and fairly clean, three rooms with fridges and rocking chairs, separated from the main house, come with a good breakfast for US$1 more.

Hotel Dorothy (☎ 479 8068; next to bullring; noelsamuelsdouglas@hotmail.com; www.geocities.com/costarica; r per person US$6; (P)) This recommended spot has neat, cheap and quiet (well, except during fiestas and bullfights) rooms with private showers; larger units have full kitchens. It's below the river, east of the bullring, which congenial owner Noel once noticed had caught fire – when it was being used to temporarily detain scores of undocumented workers from Nicaragua. He got the fire department there just in time, saving the day. Noel speaks English and arranges tours.

Hotel Las Colinas (☎ 479 9305; www.lascolinasarenal.com; r per person incl breakfast without/with bathroom US$7/16) Rooms with shared bathroom are old and underground, but clean. The nicer rooms have sunny windows, two double beds, and balconies with volcano views (check out Nos 33 and 27).

Cabinas Sissy (☎ 479 9256, 479 9356; r per person with shared bathroom US$6, per person without/with TV US$8/10, camping per person US$4; (P)) These excellent-value budget units have a screened-in private dining area, shared kitchen, nice grounds, laundry service and some rooms with coffee makers. The rooms with shared bathrooms are in an older building that's not as plush, but comfy just the same.

Don Manuel Inn (☎ 479 9585; donmanuelinn@racsa.co.cr; south of church; r per person without/with bathroom US$9/12; (P)) Huge, shiny, wood-paneled rooms with big windows are sweet, the continental breakfast a nice bonus. Recommended.

Mid-Range

Cabinas El Río (☎ 479 9341; 100m south of Parque Central; d US$14.50) Sunny basic rooms with private bathroom come with one big perk: they're upstairs from one of the best restaurants in town (p208).

Hotel La Fortuna (☎ 479 9198; lacasonasc@yahoo.com; s/d/tr incl breakfast US$15/24/30) This very basic hotel had just been bought out by La Casona, a very nice hotel, with plans to renovate dark but clean rooms for a more luxurious feel – and probably higher price. The attached restaurant is getting ready for the same transformation.

Mayol Lodge (☎ 479 9110; 100m east of Soda El Río; s US$15-26, d US$32; (P) (pool)) This bright spot off the beaten track offers sunny yellow rooms with fans and coffee makers, plus a cool blue swimming pool with volcano views. Some of the single rooms are quite small.

Cabinas Oriuma (☎ day 479 9111, night 479 9070; mathiew@racsa.co.cr; northeast cnr of parque; s/d/tr US$17/28/40, with TV US$5 extra) You've never seen a bathroom sparkle quite like they do at this family-run place above the hardware store. Orderly rooms with double bed and private hot shower should be reserved in advance on Sunday, when the hardware store is closed and they need to leave the key next door.

Cabinas La Amistad (☎ 479 9364; r per person US$15; (air-con)) Great rooms – some with any combination of kitchenette, air-con, balcony and/or cable TV, so ask – are even cheaper for groups.

Cabinas El Bosque (☎ 479 9365; 100m west of Parque Central, s/d US$20/24; (P)) Has more comfortable rooms with TV, tiled floor, private bathroom and hot water than the overgrown grounds might suggest. The real bonus here is the gracious and helpful host Edwin who offers information and arranges tours anywhere in the area.

Cabinas Grijalba (☎ 479 9129; d with fan/TV/air-con & TV US$20/25/30; (P) (air-con)) Mirrors and windows make the big rooms seem even bigger at this relatively plush spot to lay your weary head.

Cabinas Hervi (☎ 479 9430; 25m west of church; d US$20) Big, tiled rooms all come with cable TV, and there are apartment setups that let you lock your own room and share a kitchen; some large rooms can be rented by groups of more than four for US$6 per person.

Hotel Sierra Arenal (☎ 479 9751; 300m west of the church; d without/with air-con US$25/40, q US$60; (P) (air-con))

At the edge of town on the road to the volcano, this very comfortable mid-range option has good beds, big cable TVs, and mountain bikes for rent (US$5); upstairs rooms have air-con, and big balconies with volcano views. It's recommended.

Cabinas La Riviera (☎ 479 9048; 800m east of Banco Nacional; s/d/tr incl breakfast US$20/30/40, camping per tent US$6; P) A pretty 10-minute walk (and world away) from town, this recommended spot has nine basic, fan-cooled cabinas scattered around absolutely fantastic gardens, where fruit trees attract all manner of birds and the fruit is used in your very fresh juice at breakfast. The friendly staff has a bird list for free and mountain bikes for rent (half/full day US$12/18). Since it's a bit off the beaten path, campers will sleep a little easier.

Hotel Tropical Paraíso (☎ 479 9222, paraisotropical_ras@hotmail.com; s/d US$30/42, upstairs extra US$5; P) All the rooms are just beautiful, with nice furniture and big windows, and come with thoughtful amenities such as an electric jug and microwave in addition to a phone and air-con.

Hotel Arenal Jireh (☎ 479 9004; 150m west of Parque Central; www.arenalexperience.com; s/d/tr US$35/45/55; P) You definitely want the upstairs rooms, with balconies and volcano views, but all six are quite nice, with cable TV, fridge, phone and coffee maker. The pool has a kiddie section.

Cabinas Las Tinajas (☎ 479 9308, d US$39; P) You can appreciate your homey room, with fans and cable TV, on this quiet residential street, from the rocking chairs parked right outside.

Top-End

Top end is relative around here; local interests have thus far resisted the probably inevitable spread of fabulous resorts to La Fortuna proper. These are all excellent places, but true luxury lovers will want to head toward the volcano and the fine hotels clinging to its side.

Hotel San Bosco (☎ 479 9050; www.arenal-volcano.com; s/d/tr US$40/47/54; P) This hotel is plush and centrally located, with balcony views of Arenal, a garden with a pool and Jacuzzi, and a guarded parking lot. Rooms, which can sleep up to five, are spacious and comfortable with cable TV and big bathroom. Two furnished houses, each with kitchen, cost US$80 (six beds, fans, one bathroom, maximum eight people) and US$100 (10 beds, air-con, two bathrooms, maximum 14 people).

Cabinas Rodríguez (☎ 479 9843; lorcum@costarricense.cr; 200m north of Banco Nacional; s/d incl breakfast US$40/50; P) Frilly and fancy, this immaculate option has a lady's touch, obvious from the moment you see the bedspreads. Some rooms have TV, and one sleeps five people for US$70; you can use the elegant owners' refrigerator if you ask nicely.

Cabinas Carmela (☎ 479 9010, 50m south of church; cabinascarmela@racsa.co.cr; s/d/tr/q US$40/47/58/64; P) There are 22 super-clean, well-appointed rooms, all with fridge, private hot shower, phone, air-con, microwave and cable TV; two are wheelchair-accessible. There's also a shared kitchen, and some of the upstairs rooms have balconies (no volcano views, however). You can't beat the location, across from the bus terminal.

Cabinas Guacamaya (☎ 479 9393, www.cabinasguacamaya.com; s/d/t/q incl breakfast US$41/47/58/69; P) Good-sized and very nice but spartan rooms have fridge, private bathroom, and hot water, but the real draw is the pretty garden patio with volcano views.

Luigi's Lodge (☎ 479 9909; www.luigislodge.com; s/d/tr incl breakfast US$59/70/83; P) Twenty-four carpeted, air-con rooms have ceiling fan, cable TV, fridge with tempting minibar, and shower/tub bathroom with hair dryer. Some rooms have TV, and many open onto an upstairs balcony with good volcano views (though La Fortuna is not the side with the most lava). There's a good-sized swimming pool and a gym (US$4 a day for nonguests). A good Italian restaurant, Pizzería Luigi's (see p209), is attached.

EAST OF TOWN

Hotel Las Cabañitas (☎ 479 9400; www.cabanitas.com; d standard/deluxe US$92/102; P) Almost 1.5km east of La Fortuna, this resort has two pools, a tour desk, restaurant, bar, and 30 spacious individual cabins, all with ceiling fan and porch and many with great volcano views. Newer deluxe rooms have TV and air-con.

Hotel Rancho Corcovado (☎ 469 1818; s/d US$35/45; P) In the village of El Tanque de la Fortuna, 7km east of La Fortuna, this clean and comfortable and helpful place has a swimming pool, pool table, restaurant overlooking the river and horse rental. Groups can work out package deals that include meals and tours.

SOUTH OF TOWN

Arenal Country Inn (☎ 479 9670; www.arenalcountryinn.com; s/d incl breakfast US$104/110; P) About 1km south of town on the paved road to San Ramón, this manicured old ranch is now home to 20 spacious, modern, air-con rooms, all with two queen-size beds, cable TV and private patio. The restaurant-bar is an interesting open-air affair, housed in a restored cattle corral. There are adults' and children's pools, volcano views, and a river running through the property. This is a quiet and relaxing hotel, with friendly, helpful staff.

Villas Josipek (☎ 430 5252; www.villasjosipek.com; d US$69, q US$89; P) About 8km (a US$2 taxi ride) from La Fortuna along the road to San Ramón, these attractively rustic cabins, outfitted with kitchens and coffee makers, are surrounded by private rain forest trails with fabulous volcano views and access to the Children's Eternal Rainforest (p164). Groups can arrange meals in advance, served beside the substantial outdoor pool, and anyone can book horseback riding tours throughout the region.

Chachagua Rainforest Lodge (☎ 239 6464; d US$96, additional person US$10) Request the older, Frank Lloyd Wright-esque wooden cabins, with indoor jungles and low windows for watching the birds, rather than the more comfortable, but less charming new cinderblock edifices. Even if you're in the new cabins, scattered around this exquisitely landscaped property abutting the Children's Eternal Rainforest, you're sure to enjoy the wonderful pool – with waterfall! – and choice of two **restaurants** (breakfast US$8, other meals US$14) – one with a horse show at breakfast! Tours can be arranged and there are on-site facilities for meetings and retreats.

Eating

For groceries, **Super Christian 2** (southeast corner of Parque Central; 7am-9pm) has the best selection, but **Megasuper La Fortuna** (7:30am-9pm) has better prices.

Cafetería Lo Nuestro (200m east of Parque Central; fancy coffee beverages US$0.50-2; 8am-5pm) Across from Las Nenes, espresso beverages (liquor booster shots are available) come with homemade pastries and a side of local art.

Pizzería Cubana (300m east of Parque Central; US$1-3) Recommended as the best cheap meal in town, this pizza place does it by the pie or slice.

Java Jungle (south of Hotel Las Colinas; mains US$1-4) In addition to supplying a serious java jolt, this place fries up a massive 'Huevos McGringo' breakfast sandwich that could raise the dead.

Soda La Casa de Ara (100m south of gas station; mains US$1-4; 6am-10pm) With a steam table laden with freshly cooked food (the turnover here is high!) and probably a dozen different salads, this spot gets packed with lunchers in the know and on the go.

Soda el Río (6am-10pm; mains US$2-5) Great casados and *gallos* are typically delicious at this quality *soda*, with outdoor tables and excellent natural drinks. Recommended.

Soda La Parada (50m south of church; mains US$1-5; 24hr) Across from the bus terminal, this place stays open serving great steak casados, decent pizza and a couple of bizarre Tico health drinks, *chan* (slimy) and *linaza* (good for indigestion), to after-hours revelers and folks waiting for their buses.

Cono Arenal (north side of parque; ice cream US$1-3; 8am-9pm Mon-Thu, 8am-11pm Fri-Sun) The pun ('Arenal Cone,' it works in Spanish, too) is reason enough to stop by, but there's also excellent ice cream and a small playground for any subsequently wired youngsters.

Restaurante El Jardín (☎ 479 9360; 100m east of the parque; mains US$2-8; 5am-1pm) You can either relax over a shrimp pizza in the pleasant dining room, or order at the window outside beneath the **Pollo Pito Pito** sign, which has roast chicken that's popular with budgeters.

Restaurante Rancho La Cascada (☎ 479 9145; breakfast US$2-4, dinner US$4-15; 7-11am, 6pm-2am) This thatch-roofed landmark is probably a better bet for drinks than food, although wines imported from France, Italy and California could come with seafood or Italian specialties.

Restaurant Las Nenes (☎ 479 9192; 200m east of Parque Central; mains US$3-12; 10am-11pm) Start with the *ceviche* (US$3) at Fortuna's best recommended fine dining option, where steak and seafood, in particular the shrimp dishes, are a specialty.

Lava Rocks Café (mains US$2-6; 7:30am-10pm) Big breakfasts, casados with broiled chicken and various salads are all big draws at this popular café.

NORTHWESTERN COSTA RICA

Choza de Laurel (150m west of church; mains US$4-7; 6am-10pm) In the thatch-roofed hut at the western end of town, this place is on the pricey side and worth it for dishes such as *arroz volcán*, with veggies, chicken, ham and egg, as well as big breakfasts, espresso beverages and great ambiance.

Pizzería Luigi's (479 9909; breakfast US$5, dinner US$6-15; 7-9:30am & 11am-11pm) Formal enough to justify lipstick at least, this spacious Italian spread does a decent buffet breakfast, but a better bet are the pizzas, calzones and pastas – including many vegetarian options – and variety of fancy cocktails and imported wines. The bar stays open till 3am or so.

Las Brasitas (479 9819; mains US$5-15; 11am-11pm) Sometimes you just need some good Mexican food – nothing against Lizano sauce, but there's just no burn. Check out this breezy but elegant open-air spot with good fajitas (US$6) and something called a *choriqueso*, sort of like a sausage fondue. Hey, if you're going to have a heart attack, go happy.

Restaurante Pura Vida (300m west of church; dishes US$3-6 11am-11pm) This solid Chinese restaurant does a good *chop suey seco* and shrimp fried rice, served up just as you leave town toward Arenal.

Entertainment

You can dance in the nightclub over the **Restaurante Rancho La Cascada**, but it is usually empty except on weekends. They show videos here sometimes.

Just south of town on the road to San Ramón, **Bar-Restaurant El Brete** (479 9982; mains US$2-6; 11am-close) has ladies' nights and other specials on cheap beer. Otherwise, there's not much in the way of entertainment in Fortuna apart from hanging out with other travelers or locals over a beer. **Bar El Terruño** is a basic local drunks' bar that serves *bocas*.

Volcán Look (479-9690/1), 5km west of the town, is supposedly the biggest discotheque in Costa Rica outside of San José. It's usually dead except on weekends and holidays.

Getting There & Away

Although flights have not yet resumed between San José and La Fortuna following a 2000 airplane crash, there are still plenty of unusual transport options if you're sick of the bus.

The trip between Monteverde/Santa Elena and La Fortuna involves either a very scenic road trip (taking the longer route, around Laguna de Arenal, is highly recommended), a long and bumpy, roundabout bus ride, or a trip across the lake and through the mountains.

The jeep-boat combo (US$17 to US$25; three hours) is the least expensive and quickest option, involving a taxi to the lake, quick boat trip across and then a 4WD taxi for the scenic haul over the mountains. It can be arranged by any hotel or tour company in town.

Several companies also make the trip partially by horseback, including Desafío Adventure Company (p205). There are a few other options, one of which is not always recommended. See the boxed text, on p174, for a full description of the trip.

BUS

All buses currently stop at Parque Central, though there are plans to build a real terminal about 400m west. Keep an eye on your bags, particularly on the weekend San José run.

Ciudad Quesada (Auto-Transportes San José-San Carlos) US$1; one hour; departs 5am, 8am; 12:15pm & 3:30pm.

Monteverde US$2; four hour; 8am (change at Tilarán at 12:30pm for Monteverde).

San José (Auto-Transportes San José-San Carlos) US$3; 4½ hours; 12:45pm & 2:45pm.

Tilarán (Auto-Transportes Tilarán) US$1.40; 3½ hours; 8am & 5:30pm.

Getting Around

BICYCLE

Some hotels rent bikes to their guests, and **Bike Arenal** (479 9454; www.bikearenal.com; half day US$6-12, full day US$9-18), in the Don Manuel Inn, has a variety of bikes available. It also offers guided bike tours (p206). Cycling after dark is illegal in La Fortuna.

The classic mountain-bike trip to La Catarata (p203) is a fairly brutal, if nontechnical, 7km climb, though it was successfully tested by a pack-a-day smoker who managed, barely, by walking the worst bits. Another good trip for which La Fortuna makes a fine base is the Laguna de Arenal loop, a paved and scenic four-hour ride on the other side of a serious hill that is thankfully covered by the shuttle, which is included in your fee.

CAR & SCOOTER

La Fortuna is easy to access by public transport, but nearby attractions such as the hot springs, national park and Laguna de Arenal require a bit more effort without internal combustion. Luckily, you can rent cars at **Alamo** (☎ 479 9090; www.alamocostarica.com; ⏰ 7:30am-6pm) or **Poas Rent-a-Car** (☎ 479 8418; 100m west of church; www.carentals.com) for similar rates to those in San José or in Liberia.

Scooters for Rent (☎ 479 8103; per hr/day US$5/25; ⏰ 8am-9pm) has scooters, which are perfect for tooling around between the waterfalls and hot springs.

ROAD TO ARENAL

The road west from La Fortuna seems to climb toward Volcán Arenal, but instead skirts its base steeply before descending to the shores of Laguna de Arenal. Paved and picturesque, the road is line with upscale accommodations, restaurants and a disco named for its volcano views, not to mention some very nice hot springs (see p201).

Sleeping & Eating

Cerro Chato Lodge (☎ 479 9494; cerrochato@racsa.co.cr; r per person US$13, camping US$2; P) It's off the beaten track (the turnoff to the dirt road leading to the lodge, south of the main road, is easy to miss; look for the faded 'Mariposario' sign), but owner Miguel Zamora can arrange transportation from La Fortuna. Rooms are immaculate, simple and sweet, with fan, huge bathroom, hot water and electricity until 11pm; the neighborhood is rural, the surroundings jungle and the views awesome. Campers will love the solitude and security and everyone will want breakfast (US$2); other meals can be arranged. Miguel also leads naturalist tours in English and Spanish.

Hotel Arenal Rossi (☎ 479 9023; www.hotelarenalrossi.com; d standard/deluxe US$61/72, additional person US$10; P) Excellent rooms with two double beds, private hot showers and all the extras come with air-con and cable TV for a few dollars more. Everyone gets to use the palm-shaded pool in the gardens, and there's a little playground for kids. Older toy-lovers can rent scooters (US$35 per day) from the exceedingly professional and efficient staff.

Cabinas Las Flores (☎ 479 9307; r per person incl breakfast US$15, camping per person US$5; P) Some of the clean rooms with hot bathrooms are even nicer than the others, with attractive wood paneling. It's already a great deal, and the owner may give discounts if things are slow.

Restaurante Neo-Latino La Vaca Muca (☎ 479 9186; dishes US$6-12; ⏰ 11am-11pm) Start with the *ceviche* and perhaps a glass of wine before moving on to a list of Latin-fusion dishes incorporating recipes from Argentina to Mexico. There's an orchid garden out back and good vibes inside.

El Vagabondo (☎ 479 9565; mains US$3-10) Popular with the rafting guides and known for its 'killer pizza,' this is a more mellow dining experience, dude.

Restaurante Arenas Steak House (☎ 479 9023; mains US$5-12; ⏰ 6:30am-10pm) For a big breakfast before you hit the trail or a fine steak dinner after you unwind from volcano watching, this nice spot does *churrasco* (steak) just right.

Lomas del Volcán (☎ 479 9000; www.lomasdelvolcan.com; d incl breakfast US$88; P) This quiet collection of simple but comfy hardwood cabins may not have hot springs, but the Jacuzzi has better volcano views than the Tabacón. There's a simple restaurant, and monkeys in the trees.

Mirador Arenal Kioro (☎ 461 1700; admission US$3; mains US$3-8; ⏰ 6am-midnight) With blockbuster volcano views from the hillside and a rather elegant outdoor restaurant serving international cuisine, this is a top tour-bus stop for volcano viewing, though you're more than welcome to drop by for dinner. The admission is waived as long as you spend US$6 on dinner.

Hotel Los Lagos (☎ 479 8000; www.hotelloslagos.com; s/d standard US$47/57, cabinas US$57/67 P) About 6km west of La Fortuna this is a lodge for adventurous types: nicely landscaped gardens come with a crocodile farm, hot springs and two swimming pools (one heated) connected by a scary concrete water slide that goes underground. There's also a swim-up bar, a restaurant, gift shop, and pleasant air-conditioned rooms and cabins (for up to five people) with cable TV, phone, minifridge, and private hot shower. Breakfast is included. From the entrance area, a dirt road with scenic views climbs steeply to two lakes in the foothills of the volcano, about 3km away from the entrance. Above here, two tourists and their guide were caught in a gaseous eruption in August 2000; only one person survived. Some of the upper trails are now closed, and the lower area, where the hotel is, lies in a valley that might be covered by deadly gaseous or volcanic flows in the event of a major eruption.

Volcano Lodge (☎ 460 6080; www.volcanolodgecostarica.com; d/tr incl breakfast US$93/100; P) With about two dozen modern rooms arranged around a rather spare central yard, this hotel gets points for its excellent volcano views from both its patios and picture windows. Each room has two double beds and a hot shower, as well as rocking chairs to relax in while gazing at Arenal. A restaurant, large pool, and Jacuzzi are available.

Montaña de Fuego Inn (☎ 460 1220; www.montanadefuego.com; d standard/deluxe incl breakfast US$95/121, additional person US$25; P) Nine kilometers west of town, pretty wooden duplex cabins all have patio and picture windows facing the volcano. The deluxe rooms are larger, with both front and back decks – the back one giving views of the forested hillside. All rooms sleep up to four and have views, hot showers, and air-con. Amenities include a pool with swim-up bar, a Jacuzzi, a spa with sauna, massage rooms, mud baths, and a small gym. Lunches and dinners are pricey at about US$25 to US$30. Horseback riding and other local excursions can be arranged.

Tabacón Resort (☎ 256 1500; www.tabacon.com; d/ste incl breakfast US$151/203; P) Rates include unlimited access to Tabacón Hot Springs (p201), 400m away. The hotel is 12km from La Fortuna and offers modern, large, but uninspired air-con rooms with cable TV, hair dryer, coffee maker, and private patio or balcony, most with volcano views; nine larger, junior suites are available. There is a tour desk, and mountain bikes are available for rent. Within the hot springs complex, the **Iskandria Spa** offers a multitude of treatments such as massages, volcanic mud masks, manicures, and aromatherapy.

Further west you pass the entrance to Parque Nacional Volcán Arenal; there are more places to stay beyond the volcano and around Laguna de Arenal (see p213).

PARQUE NACIONAL VOLCÁN ARENAL

Arenal was just another dormant volcano surrounded by fertile farmland from about AD 1500 until July 29, 1968, when something snapped. Huge explosions triggered lava flows that destroyed two villages, killing about 80 people and 45,000 cattle. The cone's perfect slopes, now ashen instead of green, were evacuated and roads were closed. Eventually, the lava subsided to a relatively predictable flow and life got back to normal. Sort of.

Despite this massive eruption, the volcano retained its picture-perfect silhouette, now even more dramatic beneath the streamers of molten rock that form its crown. Occasionally, it quiets down for a few weeks or even months, but generally Arenal has been producing menacing ash columns, massive explosions, and glowing red lava flows almost daily since 1968.

The degree of activity varies from year to year and week to week – even day to day. Sometimes it can be a spectacular display of flowing red-hot lava and incandescent rocks flying through the air; at other times the volcano subsides to a gentle glow. During the day, the lava isn't easy to see, but you might still see a great cloud of ash thrown up by a massive explosion. Between 1998 and 2000, the volcano was particularly active (which is when many of those spectacular photos you see in tourist brochures were taken), and while the lava of late hasn't been quite that photogenic, it's still an awe-inspiring show.

The park was created in 1995. Along with Tenorio, Miravalles, and the Monteverde Cloud Forest reserve, among other regions, it is part of the Area de Conservación Arenal, which protects most of the Cordillera de Tilarán. This area is rugged and varied, and the biodiversity is high; roughly half the species of land-dwelling vertebrates (birds, mammals, reptiles, and amphibians) known in Costa Rica can be found here.

Every once in a while, perhaps lulled into a sense of false security by a temporary pause in the activity, someone tries to climb to the crater and peer within it. This is very dangerous – climbers have been killed and maimed by explosions. The problem is not so much that the climber gets killed (that's a risk the foolhardy insist is their own decision) but rather that the lives of Costa Rican rescuers are placed at risk.

The best night-time views of the volcano are usually from its northern side, although activity can sometimes be seen from any direction. Still, most visitors drive or take a tour around to the north side in hope of catching these most impressive views.

Be aware that clouds can cover the volcano at any time, and tours don't guarantee a view (though sometimes you can hear explosions). Also be aware that on cloudy, rainy days, a tour can be a miserably cold affair. Thank goodness for all those hot springs (see p201).

Orientation & Information

The **ranger station** (☎ 461 8499; admission to the park US$7; 🕒 8am-4pm) is on the west side of the volcano. Most people arrive as part of a group tour, but you can reach it independently. Drivers can head west from La Fortuna for 15km, then turn left at the 'Parque Nacional' sign and take a 2km dirt road to the entrance. A road continues 1.4km toward the volcano, where there is a parking lot.

You can also take an 8am bus toward Tilarán (tell the driver to drop you off at the park) and catch the 2pm bus back to La Fortuna. From the 'Parque Nacional' sign off the main road, a 2km dirt road leads to the ranger station and information center. From there, trails lead 3.4km toward the volcano. Rangers will tell you how far you are allowed to go. Currently, this area is not in a danger zone. There isn't a great deal of hiking right here, but there are trails at Arenal Observatory Lodge (US$7 day use), and guided treks on the Silencio Trail (US$25 to US$35, arranged by most tour agencies) that also skirt the mountain.

It should be noted that this route gets you close to the volcano, but as a result, the view is foreshortened. Many visitors prefer more distant views from some of the lodges west of the volcano or from Laguna de Arenal. However, the explosions do sound loud from here!

Arenal Observatory Lodge

Originally a private observatory, chosen for its proximity to the volcano and safe location on a ridge, it was established in 1987 on a macadamia nut farm on the south side of Volcán Arenal. Volcanologists from all over the world, including researchers from the Smithsonian Institute in Washington, DC, have come to study the active volcano. A seismograph operates around the clock. The lodge is the only place inside the park where you can legally bed down (see following).

The observatory lodge, just over 2km from the volcano, is a good base for exploring the nearby countryside. The volcano views and sounds of eruptions are excellent, although most lava flows are on the north side while the hotel is on the west. Laguna de Arenal is visible in the other direction.

There are 6km of trails, accessible to nonguests for US$7 per day. A handful of short hikes include views of a nearby waterfall, while sturdy souls could check out recent lava flows (2½ hours); old lava flows (three hours); or the climb to Arenal's dormant partner, Volcán Chato, whose crater holds an 1100m-high lake only 3km southeast of Volcán Arenal (four hours). For the best nighttime views, a guided hike is suggested. Maps and local English-speaking guides are available for these hikes.

Sleeping & Eating

INSIDE THE PARK

No camping is allowed inside the park, though people have camped (no facilities) off some of the unpaved roads west of the volcano by the shores of the lake.

Arenal Observatory Lodge (☎ reservations 290 7011, lodge 692 2070; www.arenal-observatory.co.cr; day use US$7; P ⊠ 💻) has a variety of rooms spread throughout the property, five of which are wheelchair-accessible (along with the pool and several trails – this lodge hasn't slouched). Rates include a buffet breakfast and guided hike. **La Casona** (s/d/tr/q US$52/67/85/103) is about 500m away in the original farmhouse. It now houses four rustic double rooms sharing two bathrooms; there are volcano views from the house porch. **Standard rooms** (s/d/tr/q US$73/95/109/127), adjacent to the main lodge, were originally designed for researchers but have been renovated to acceptably plush standards. **Smithsonian rooms** (s/d/tr/q US$102/128/138/149), accessible via a suspension bridge over a plunging ravine, are the best and have the best views. The **White Hawk Villa** (8 people for US$375), with a kitchen and several rooms, is perfect for groups.

The lodge also offers massages (US$60), guided hikes and all the usual tours at good prices. You can swim in the pool, wander around the macadamia nut farm or investigate the pine forest that makes up about half of the 347-hectare site. Horse rental costs US$7 per hour. A tiny **museum** (admission free) on the old observation deck has a seismograph and some cool newspaper clippings. The **restaurant** (lunch/dinner US$15/20) is pricey,

NORTHWESTERN COSTA RICA

but the jars of venomous snakes in formaldehyde out front make up for it.

You can arrange for free pickup in La Fortuna at 1pm daily, with reservations. A taxi will run about US$20. Drivers from La Fortuna should turn left on the road toward Parque Nacional Volcán Arenal and drive about 9km to the lodge. There's only one major fork (after about 5.5km) where you go left – there are several signs.

OUTSIDE THE PARK

If you follow the road past the ranger station to the fork described above and turn right (instead of left), you'll come to three other hotels. While a regular car might be able to pass, this is pretty much 4WD country, particularly the last two lodges. A taxi from La Fortuna can get you here for about US$20.

Linda Vista (☎ 380 0847; www.lindavistadelnorte.com; s/d/tr standard US$60/70/80, ste US$90/100/110; Ⓟ) Just more than 3km beyond the fork, across two small bridges, you reach this honeymoon-worthy lodge. It has 11 simple but smashing rooms with fan, fridge, coffee maker and private hot shower. Breakfast is included. Set up on a ridge, the rooms take in the forest and lake, but only a few have volcano views. However, the restaurant-bar has a huge picture window and outdoor terrace where you can watch all the eruptive action. They have the usual selection of tours at competitive prices.

Cabanitas El Castillo Dorado (☎ 383 7196, 692 2065; r per person US$15; Ⓟ) About 2km further (after the road slowly deteriorates through the tiny community of El Castillo), make a signed left at the bridge and climb the ridge to these ultra-cute cabinas in the sky. They're simple, sleep four and have a fan and TV, and the breezy **restaurant** (mains US$2-6) has knock-out views of the lake and volcano. Staff can arrange most of the tours, but specialize in fishing trips to Laguna de Arenal. The owners also have a friend in town who does in-room massages (US$45) and facials (US$7 to US$18). Recommended.

Arenal Vista Lodge (☎ 221 0965; www.arenalvistalodge.com; s US$76, additional person US$12; Ⓟ) Continue past El Castillo to Pueblo Nuevo, the next teeny community, for a more typical resort experience. This attractive place has 25 spacious rooms, all with fan, private hot shower, balcony, and volcano views. Buffet-style **meals** (breakfast US$7.50, lunch US$10, dinner US$12.50), a conference room, pool, and a volcano-viewing room are on offer. Horseback rides to a waterfall and lava flow (US$25) and other places are offered, and fishing and other excursions can be arranged.

LAGUNA DE ARENAL AREA

It's about an 18km drive west from La Fortuna, past Tabacón and the national park road, to the 750m-long causeway across the dam that created this 88-sq-km lake. The dam was built in 1974, flooding several small towns including Arenal and Tronadora. Laguna de Arenal is Costa Rica's largest lake and supplies water for Guanacaste and hydroelectricity for the region.

The road continues around the north and west shores of the lake, past the village of Nuevo Arenal to the small town of Tilarán. It's a classic bicycle ride or road trip, but folks relying on public transport will best enjoy the spectacular views from the jeep and boat trip to Monteverde (see p209).

The road, famed for its rambunctious *pizote* population (who, in the event that part of the road washes out, will come right to your stalled car to beg for food), is lined with odd and elegant businesses, many run by foreigners who have fallen in love with the place. Shopping, dining and particularly sleeping are rarely done without some attention to detail around here. The exception is the village of Nuevo Arenal, a remaining Tico outpost in this sparkling world. Distances given are from the dam.

Winds are usually strong and steady, especially at the western end during the dry season, and the lake is recommended for **sailing** and **windsurfing**. Rainbow bass (locally called *guapote*) weighing up to 4kg are reported by anglers, who consider this a premier **fishing** spot; 10 species of fish are now found here. Boats and guides can be hired for fishing expeditions – ask at any of the major hotels in the area.

While most of the road is supposedly paved, repairs have been infrequent, and there are some huge potholes. Don't expect to drive this stretch quickly. Buses run about every two hours; hotel owners can tell you when to catch your ride.

Dam to Nuevo Arenal

There are several places of interest, and fantastic accommodations along this road that takes you west from the dam. This is cloud-forest scenery, so places can look wonderful in sunshine and dreary in the rain. They are described here in the order you will pass them.

HANGING BRIDGES OF ARENAL & AROUND

The **Puentes Colgantes de Arenal** (Hanging Bridges of Arenal; ☎ 479 9686; www.hangingbridges.com; adult/senior/student US$20/15/10, child under 12 free; 🕑 8am-8pm) are probably what you imagined the first time you heard the term 'canopy tour,' before realizing that those were mere carnival rides. Here, about 4km west of La Fortuna, some 4km of trails and bridges across canyons silently lift you into the trees. The entrance is well signed from the road just as you cross the dam.

While you can go independently if you have a car (it's a 3km climb from where the Tilarán bus would let you out), which saves about US$20 per person from La Fortuna on a package, be sure to make reservations if you want a guided tour (US$30). In addition to regular tours led several times daily, there are also 6am birding trips and guided 6pm night walks with volcano views.

Climb the paved but incredibly steep road 2.5km to **Arenal Lodge** (☎ 228 3189; www.arenallodge.com; 400m west of dam; s/d standard US$73/80, junior ste US$130/136, chalet US$134/143, additional person US$23) for exceptionally fine volcano views, and wildlife-watching opportunities that the forests surrounding the attractive grounds provide. The lodge has a Jacuzzi with a volcano view, a billiards room, a pricey **restaurant** (mains US$5-13), and a variety of accommodations. Standard rooms are pretty standard, but junior suites are spacious, tiled and have wicker furniture, a big hot-water bathroom and a picture window or balcony with volcano views. Ten chalets sleep four and have kitchenettes and good views. Complimentary mountain bikes, US$5 shuttles to Tabacón and US$10 per person horseback rides around the cloud forest are just a few of the extras.

UNIÓN AREA

There are places to stay, eat or sip coffee around here.

Hotel Los Heroes (☎ 692 8012/3; www.hotelloshereos.com; 14km west of the dam; d without/with balcony US$55/65, apt US$115; (P) (🅧)) You can't miss this slightly incongruous Alpine chalet, complete with carved wooden balconies and Old World window shutters – and that's just on the outside. Large, immaculate rooms with wood paneling and private hot bathrooms are decorated in thickly hewn wood furniture that may get Swiss-Germans a little homesick, particularly when viewing paintings of tow-headed children in Leiderhosen smooching innocently. There are also three apartments (each sleeps up to six) with full kitchen, huge bathroom and balcony overlooking the lake. It's a great deal already. Breakfast is included.

Facilities include a Jacuzzi, swimming pool and chapel with an unusual mural worth a stop in itself. A good European-style **restaurant** (mains US$4-11; 🕑 7am-3pm & 6-8pm) gets Swiss folks on the road too long to indulge in good Zuercher Geschnetzelts, and the fondues are supposed to be tops. Bonus: there's a miniature train that gives daily one-hour tours at 9am, 11am and 1:30pm for US$3, which is already cool. And at the time of research, the owners were completing what may be the first rotating restaurant in the country, accessible only by the train, which makes this a true can't-miss stop.

Toad Hall (☎ 692 8020; www.toadhall-gallery.com; 16km west of dam; mains US$3-8; 🕑 8am-5pm) Quite simply a great place to stop for coffee (espresso drinks or regular) and one of their heavenly macadamia chocolate brownies, Costa Rica's best! The restaurant overlooks the forest and serves a short, delicious and beautifully presented menu that tends toward California cuisine, with homemade focaccia, spectacular sandwiches and hot dishes, all made with organic veggies grown outside; don't skip the yummy fruit drinks. While there, you can browse the **art gallery,** which has a small but very high-quality collection of local and indigenous art and jewelry, as well as a bookstore (travel and wildlife guides in English) and the *pulpería*, where local farmers stop for sundries.

Just beyond Toad Hall, a dirt road to the right goes to the **Venado Caves** (p433) that can be explored with guides.

La Mansion Inn Arenal (☎ 692 8018; www.lamansionarenal.com; 17km west of dam; champagne-breakfast cottages US$165, deluxe cottages US$195, ste US$265; (P) (🅧) (✱)) Rates for these colorful, gorgeous rooms – works of art, really – also include a fruit basket, welcome cocktail, canoe access and horseback rides, all conspiring with the magnificent views to make this the most romantic inn in the region. An ornamental garden features Chorotega Indian pottery and an infinity swimming pool that appears to flow into the lake. The Belgian owners speak several European languages. The inn has a good, if pricey **restaurant** (4-course dinner excl wine US$35), a pool table, and a cozy bar shaped like the prow of a ship that invites lingering. Huge split-level rooms, each with private terrace and lake view, feature high ceilings, Italianate painted walls, and louvered, arched, bathroom doors. The deluxe cottages also have a TV and minibar with free drinks. The two spacious suites have kitchens (and bigger bathrooms). Fishing trips on the lake cost US$100 per half day for two people, and other excursions are arranged.

La Ceiba Tree Lodge (☎ 692 8050, 385 1540; www.ceibatree-lodge.com; 21km west of dam; s/d incl breakfast US$39/64; Ⓟ) Beneath the shade of a most impressive ceiba, this wacky spot has five spacious, cross-ventilated rooms and one apartment (US$99), all decorated with original paintings and entered through Mayan-inspired carved doors. Breakfast is served on the expansive patio. Mountain bikes are available and tours can be arranged. Lake views from the tree are pretty, and the grounds have a collection of 70 local orchids and good birding possibilities. The friendly owners will cook dinner for you with advance notice. English and German are spoken.

ARENAL BOTANICAL GARDENS & AROUND

About 25km west of the dam, the **gardens** (☎ 694 4305; www.junglegold.com; adult/child US$8/4; 9am-5pm Mon-Sat, 10am-2pm Sun) were founded in 1991 as a reserve and living library of tropical and subtropical plants. Well-laid-out trails lead past 1200 varieties of tropical plants from Costa Rica and all over the world, and guide booklets in English, German, and Spanish describe what you see. Plenty of birds and butterflies are attracted to the gardens, which feature a butterfly sanctuary and small serpentario all accessible along trails through primary forest. This is a great spot for families to take a breather and stretch their legs for a while.

Restaurante Lajas (☎ 694 4780; mains US$2-8; 8am-9pm) is designed for tour groups but with food that gets raves from locals, this unassuming spot makes a great place for fish with veggies or perhaps some souvenir coffee.

Villa Decary B&B (☎ 694 4330, 383 3012; www.villadecary.com; s/d US$90/100, d with kitchen US$145, additional person US$15) is an all-round winner with bright, spacious, well-furnished rooms, delicious full breakfasts included, and fantastic hosts. Five rooms have private hot showers, a queen and a double bed, bright Latin American bedspreads and artwork, and balconies with excellent views of woodland immediately below (good birding from your room!) and of the lake just beyond. There are also three separate *casitas* (small houses) with a kitchenette. Credit cards are not accepted. Paths into the woods behind the house give good opportunities for watching wildlife, including howler monkeys that might wake you in the morning (though rooms have clock radios as well). Guests can borrow binoculars and a bird guide to identify what they see. Jeff, one of the US owners, has gotten the bird bug and can help out with identification. His partner, Bill, is a botanist specializing in palms (Decary was a French botanist who discovered a new palm).

Nuevo Arenal

This small village, sometimes simply called Arenal, replaced an earlier Arenal and other villages that were flooded by the lake formed after 1974. The old Arenal is now 27m underwater; 3500 people were displaced. The new Arenal is 29km west of the dam and is the only good-sized town between La Fortuna and Tilarán. Arenal has a gas station, a Banco Nacional, and a bus stop near the park.

SLEEPING & EATING

Nuevo Arenal (camping per tent US$5) Just a few kilometers beyond the Villa Decary B&B, on the left side of the highway from this direction, you can camp at the lakeside park, with bathrooms and cold showers.

Cabinas Rodríguez (☎ 694 4237; r per person without/with bathroom US$5/10) This friendly place, close to the Aurora, has clean, dark rooms (some with bigger windows) and a shared kitchenette.

Cabinas Catalina (☎ 694 4015; d/tr US$20/25; Ⓟ) Sterile and new, these rooms make a fine mid-range option.

Hotel Aurora Inn (☎ 694 4245; aurorainn@hotmail.com; s/d incl breakfast US$41/54; Ⓟ) Located on

NORTHWESTERN COSTA RICA

the shoreline and next to the soccer field, this inn has a swimming pool, restaurant, Jacuzzi, sports bar, and big rooms with porches and digital cable. Fishing trips on the lake can be arranged.

Restaurant Típico Arenal (☎ 694 4159; mains US$2-5; 🕑 10am-9pm) In between the Aurora and Cabinas Rodríguez, this place does quality Tico food with a view.

Bar y Restaurant Bambú (☎ 694 4048; mains US$2-4; 🕑 6am-10pm) In addition to doing good casados and *gallos* (not to mention another round of beer on Friday night when there's live music), owner Randall has tourist information and can arrange tours including fishing trips, guided hikes and horseback rides.

Tom's Pan (☎ 694 4547; mains US$1-6, d incl breakfast US$52; 🕑 7am-4pm Mon-Sat; P) German bread, from strudels and plum cake to pumpernickel, is just the beginning at this Nuevo Arenal establishment. Big German breakfasts, goulash with homemade noodles, and a deli stocking Leiberkäs and Weibwurst are also on the menu. Behind the restaurant, is a cozy room for rent with huge windows and an outdoor Jacuzzi. Ask about waterskiing on the lake.

Pizzeria e Ristorante Tramonti (☎ 694 4282; dishes US$3-8; 🕑 11:30am-3pm & 5-10pm Tue-Sun) Also in Arenal, this pizzeria is a classy Italian-run place with a wood-burning pizza oven, attractive outdoor patio, and good-value Italian meals.

NORTHWESTERN COSTA RICA

Nuevo Arenal to Tilarán

Continue west and around the lake from Nuevo Arenal, where the scenery gets even more spectacular just as the road gets progressively worse. Tilarán is the next 'big' city, with a reasonable selection of hotels and restaurants, plus roads and buses that take you to Cañas, Monteverde and beyond.

SLEEPING & EATING

Chalet Nicholas (☎ 694 4041, www.chaletnicholas.com; s/d incl breakfast US$45/69; ⊠ P) Two kilometers northwest of Arenal, Chalet Nicholas is an attractive little place. Owners Catherine and John Nicholas are helpful and knowledgeable hosts; their co-owners are Great Danes (don't be alarmed when they come bounding out to greet you). The two downstairs rooms have private bathrooms; the upstairs loft has two linked bedrooms (for families or groups) sharing a downstairs bathroom. On clear days, all rooms have views of the volcano at the end of the lake, 25km away. The owners enjoy natural history and have a living collection of dozens of orchids. Birding is good too – one guest reported seeing 80 bird species in four days. Smoking is not allowed, and credit cards aren't accepted. This place has many repeat guests.

Caballo Negro Restaurant (☎ 694 4515; mains US$3-10; 🕑 8am-8pm high season, 8am-5pm low season) Three kilometers west of Nuevo Arenal, the Caballo Negro (Black Horse) serves recommended vegetarian and European fare handcrafted by owner Monica, who speaks English and German (hence the excellent schnitzel). The cozy restaurant has forest and lake views, and you can look for iguanas, turtles, and birds while you are dining. Also here is the fabulously quirky **Lucky Bug Gallery**, which features high-quality work from local and national artisans, not least of whom are Monica's teenage triplets, Kathryn, Alexandra, and Sabrina Krauskopf. The talented girls turn the profits of their work toward an animal-rescue project – the whole family is passionate about animals, their gallery, and their restaurant. The artistry really is outstanding, and should you fall in love with a painting of a bug or something bigger, they can ship it for you.

Four or five kilometers west of Arenal is a sign for the next establishment.

Lago Coter Ecolodge (☎ 440 6768; www.ecolodgecostarica.com; buffet meals US$8-20; d standard/cabin US$55/70; P) A 3km unpaved but OK road leads to the lodge near Lago Coter, where most visitors come on complete packages that include meals, rental equipment, and activities led by naturalist guides. The emphasis is on natural history and adventure. There are trails through the nearby cloud forest, and other amenities include naturalist guides for hiking and birding, canoes (US$15 per half day), kayaks (US$25 per half day), and horses (US$20 per half day). The handsome wood-and-stone lodge has a large fireplace and a relaxation area with billiards, TV and a small library. Buffet meals are plentiful; standard rooms, in the main lodge, are small but comfortable. A few hundred meters away, 14 larger cabins with coffee makers and hot showers feature a mix of red-tiled and carpeted floors, white walls, paneled windows, and good lake views.

Hotel el Cielo (☎ 694 4290; d/tr US$20/30; P) Murals on the walls of the large, comfortable rooms and porches with lake and volcano views – where the mellow Tico owners will serve your typical breakfast – make this rather basic budget option something special. Recommended.

Rock River Lodge (☎ 695 5644, www.rockriverlodge.com; d r/bungalow US$52/76, additional person US$10; P) This fabulous option for outdoorsy sorts has six rooms in a long, rustic-looking wooden building with a porch and lake/volcano views. Separate bungalows have larger rooms with saltillo tiles, excellent (if small) tiled tubs, and private terraces. The staff specializes in arranging mountain biking (rental US$40 a day with guide) and windsurfing (US$35 per day), facials and massages (US$25 per half-hour), and can arrange other excursions. The lodge tends to close down the windsurfing outside of the December-to-April high-wind season. The good **restaurant** (breakfast US$6, dinner US$12, no lunch) is open to the public and gets raves; the bar, with brilliant views and a warm fireplace, is a great place to chill.

Equus Bar-Restaurant (mains US$4-8; 11am-close) Four kilometers beyond Rock River is a popular bar-eatery specializing in barbecued meats. There's live music some nights – ask at your hotel.

Mystica Resort (☎ 692 1001; mystica@racsa.co.cr; s/d incl breakfast US$60/70; P) This place has great views of the 30km-long Laguna de Arenal and the volcano puffing away just beyond the end of it. It's also a good **pizzeria** (7:30am-9:30pm, US$5-10) with a wood-burning oven on the premises, and the bar-restaurant is cozy and has a fireplace. Each of the six comfortable, uniquely decorated, good-size rooms has hot showers and opens up onto a long shared balcony with garden and lake views. All the usual sporting and touring options can be arranged.

Almost 6km beyond the Tierras Morenas turnoff and 9km north of Tilarán, a sign points to the **Hotel Tilawa** (☎ 695 5050; www.hotel-tilawa.com; s/d garden view US$48/58, lake view US$58/68, r with kitchenette US$88; P) And now, for something completely different: architecture reminiscent of the Palace of Knossos in Crete – frescoes, columns, and other Grecian extras – play backdrop to the best collection of amenities on the lake. A skateboard park for guests, for starters, complements more standard offerings such as a pool, tennis courts and free use of bikes. Better yet, between Volcán Arenal and its reflection, you have two water sports to try: There's not only world-class windsurfing (see p213) including classes and equipment rental at competitive prices, but also, for guests and nonguests, **kiteboarding** (2hr lessons US$55) with equipment rentals once you hit your glide. There's a 12m yacht for up to 20 passengers, if you'd rather relax. Rooms are huge, cool and carry on the Classic theme, right down to the full bathroom in some rooms.

TILARÁN

This small town, near the southwestern end of Laguna de Arenal, is a ranching center near the northern end of the Cordillera de Tilarán. There's a **rodeo** the last weekend in April, popular with Tico visitors, and another fiesta on June 13 dedicated to patron San Antonio – with more rodeos and bullfights. The nearby lake (6km away) has consistently high winds that attract experienced windsurfers and operate all those windmills – more than 200 of them – generating the area's electricity. With a friendly Western feel, Tilarán town makes a refreshingly tourist-free stopover between La Fortuna and Monteverde.

It's easy to check email while waiting for your bus at **Cicsa** (☎ 695 6619; 25m west of bus terminal; per hr US$1.25; 8am-10pm Mon-Sat), which has computers with speedy connections. Next to the bus terminal, **Tilatur Info** (☎ 695 8671; 8:30am-5pm) stores backpacks (US$1) and sells fishing trips.

Sleeping & Eating

Cheap meals can be found in the *mercado*, beside the bus terminal, or pop into the **SuperCompro** (8am-8pm), just across from the park, for groceries.

Hotel y Restaurant Mary (☎ 695 5479; r per person US$5, s/d with bathroom US$11/20) Clean but somewhat tattered rooms share shiny hot-water showers. Plan on street noise in the park-side rooms, or just enjoy it from the balcony. The attached **restaurant** (mains US$1-5; 6am-midnight) does decent Chinese food.

Hotel Tilarán (☎ 695 5043; r per person US$5; d US$11.25) On the west side of Parque Central, this is an excellent budget choice. Small rooms are clean and those in the rear face

WORLD-CLASS WINDSURFING

Some of the world's most consistent winds blow across northwestern Costa Rica, and this consistency attracts windsurfers from all over the world. Laguna de Arenal is rated one of the three best windsurfing spots in the world, mainly because of the predictability of the winds. From December to April, the winds reliably provide great rides for board sailors who gather on the southwest corner of the lake for long days of fun on the water. Windsurfing is possible in other months, too, but avoid September and October, which are considered the worst.

The best company for windsurfing is **Tico Wind** (☎ 692 2002; www.ticowind.com), which sets up a camp every year during the December 1 to April 15 season. It has state-of-the-art boards and sails that are replaced every year; rentals cost US$38 for a half day or US$68 for a full day, including lunch. There are 50 sails to allow for differing wind conditions, experience, and people's weights, but it rents only 12 at a time so that surfers can pick and choose during the day as conditions change – a class act. Staff will arrange nearby hotel accommodations. Serious surfers book boards weeks ahead of time; newbies and those wishing to improve their skills can take lessons. Tico Wind also offers rentals and lessons through Ecoplaya Beach Resort (p198) on the Bahía Salinas, Costa Rica's second windsurfing destination.

Hotel Tilawa (p217) also has an excellent selection of sailboards for rent at comparable rates. The hotel has a windsurfing school. Lessons during the first day begin on land with stationary boards so you can learn what to do before going out on the water.

Some folks think that the high winds, waves, and world-class conditions are too much for a beginner to handle. The folks at Tilawa disagree, and say that if you don't enjoy your first day of lessons and can't get at least a short ride by the end of the day, they'll refund your money. After the first day, lessons become more expensive and cater to all skill levels – once you've learned the basics, self-motivated practice with short instructional periods is the best way to learn.

It gets a little chilly on Laguna de Arenal, and rentals usually include wet suits, as well as harnesses and helmets (serious boarders bring their own for the best fit, just renting the board and sail). For a warm change, head down to Bahía Salinas on Costa Rica's far northwestern coast. Resorts here offer windsurfing year-round, and though the wind may not be quite as world-class as at Lake Arenal, it comes pretty close. The seasons are the same as for the lake.

a quiet garden. Units with TV cost more. The park-view restaurant serves home-cooked meals.

Hotel Naralit (☎ 695 5393; d US$18, s/d with minifridge US$18/26; Ⓟ) South of the church, the Naralit ('Tilarán,' reversed!) has clean rooms with fan, private bathroom, hot water and cable TV; some have minifridges. Older, smaller doubles are a bargain for pairs.

Hotel El Sueño (☎ 695 5347; s/d standard US$15/35, s/d with balcony US$20/30) Beautiful in an ageing, baroque sort of way, smaller standard rooms come with private bathroom, hot water, fan and cable TV, while the three much nicer balcony rooms have all that plus antiques. This friendly, clean place is a block from the bus terminal and the Parque Central and has free coffee and tea. (A restaurant downstairs is convenient but not part of the hotel.) A balcony has views of the Tenorio and Miravalles volcanoes, and parking is available.

Hotel & Restaurante y Cafetería Guadalupe (☎ 695 5943; d US$22) Quiet rooms sleeping three are all upstairs and arranged around a few nice common areas for rocking and reading. The attached **restaurant** (🕒 6am-9pm Mon-Fri, 7am-5pm Sat; mains US$2-6) comes highly recommended by locals for its solid casados and even better desserts.

La Carreta (☎ 695 6593; ppiedra_z@yahoo.com; s/d standard US$30/55, s/d near garden US$45/55; Ⓟ) The standard rooms are fine, but the bigger rooms surrounding the garden, home to their toucan, Sam, are worth the extra cash. All have TV and fan, and as an added bonus are attached to a good **restaurant** (🕒 10am-9pm; mains US$2-8), where the specialty is tilapia and the atmosphere is 'ladies who lunch.' This is probably the only place in town that sells souvenirs.

Restaurante El Parque (☎ 695 5425; mains US$3-5; 🕒 7am-11pm) Under Cabinas El Sueño, this cool, dark spot smells great and allegedly has the best chop suey in town. Discriminating bar flies also appreciate the selection of good *bocas*.

Getting There & Away

Tilarán is usually reached by a 24km paved road from the Interamericana at Cañas. The route on to Santa Elena and Monteverde is unpaved and rough, though ordinary cars can get through with care in the dry season.

Buses arrive and depart from the terminal, half a block west of Parque Central. Be aware that Sunday afternoon buses to San José may be sold out by Saturday. The route between Tilarán and San José goes via Cañas and the Interamericana, not the Arenal–La Fortuna–Ciudad Quesada route. Buses offer regular service to the following locations:

Arenal US$0.50; 1¼ hours; departs 5am, 6am, 10am, 2:30pm & 4:30pm.

Cañas US$0.50; 45 minutes; 5am, 6:40am, 7:30am, 9am, 10am, 11:30am, 3:30pm.

Ciudad Quesada, via La Fortuna US$1.50; four hours; 7am & 12:30pm.

Liberia US$1; 1¾ hours; 6am, 7:30am, 9am, 10:30am, 11:30am, noon, 2:30pm, 3:50pm & 5pm.

Puntarenas US$2.50; two hours; 6am & 1pm.

San José (Auto-Transportes Tilarán) US$2.50; three hours; 5am, 7am, 7:45am, 2pm & 4:55pm.

Santa Elena US$1.75; three to four hours; 12:30pm.

Península de Nicoya

CONTENTS

Some of Costa Rica's most beautiful beaches line the western coast of this rugged peninsula that juts out from the country's northwest. It is a land of stark contrasts: beach bums and surfer dudes on the coast coexist with cowboys and ranchers inland while monkeys make their way through the remaining patches of tropical dry forest. The bridge over the Río Tempisque, which opened in 2003, has made transport to the area much easier. However, there are still many towns lacking paved roads and access remains difficult – especially in the rainy season when rivers must be forded at every turn. But travelers will be abundantly rewarded for their efforts. The peninsula has everything: small nature reserves, word-class resorts, enjoyable rural towns, prime surfing and striking Pacific sunsets.

It may not seem logical, but the peninsula is split between the Guanacaste province in the north and Puntarenas in the south. The main peninsular highway (21) begins in Liberia (p185) – also in Guanacaste – where the airport has flights to and from the USA.

The highway is the main artery through the center of the peninsula, and side roads (most in poor condition) branch out to the beaches. There is no good coastal road connecting one beach town to the next; this usually requires backtracking to the central highway and coming back out on another road. If you have a sturdy 4WD vehicle, it might be possible to more or less follow the coast on these dirt roads (none of which have bridges) – but this can only be contemplated in the dry season.

As with beach areas throughout the country, reservations are recommended, especially during dry-season weekends, Semana Santa (Easter week) and the oh-so-popular week between Christmas and New Year's.

HIGHLIGHTS

- Spelunking into the little-explored caves at **Parque Nacional Barra Honda** (p247)
- Surfing the killer waves at **Playa Avellana** (p241) and **Santa Teresa** (p267)
- Visiting Costa Rica's first wildlife park, **Reserva Natural Absoluta Cabo Blanco** (p269)
- Inspecting prize bulls at the **Santa Cruz rodeo** (p243) held during one of their many fiestas
- Becoming mesmerized by spectacular beach sunsets (and potent cocktails) in **Playa Tamarindo** (p234)

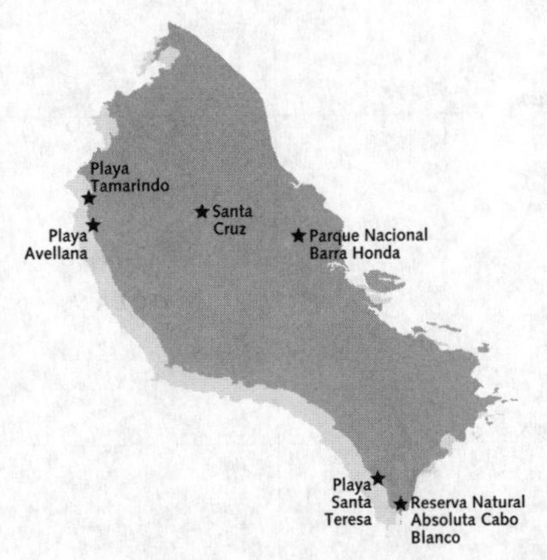

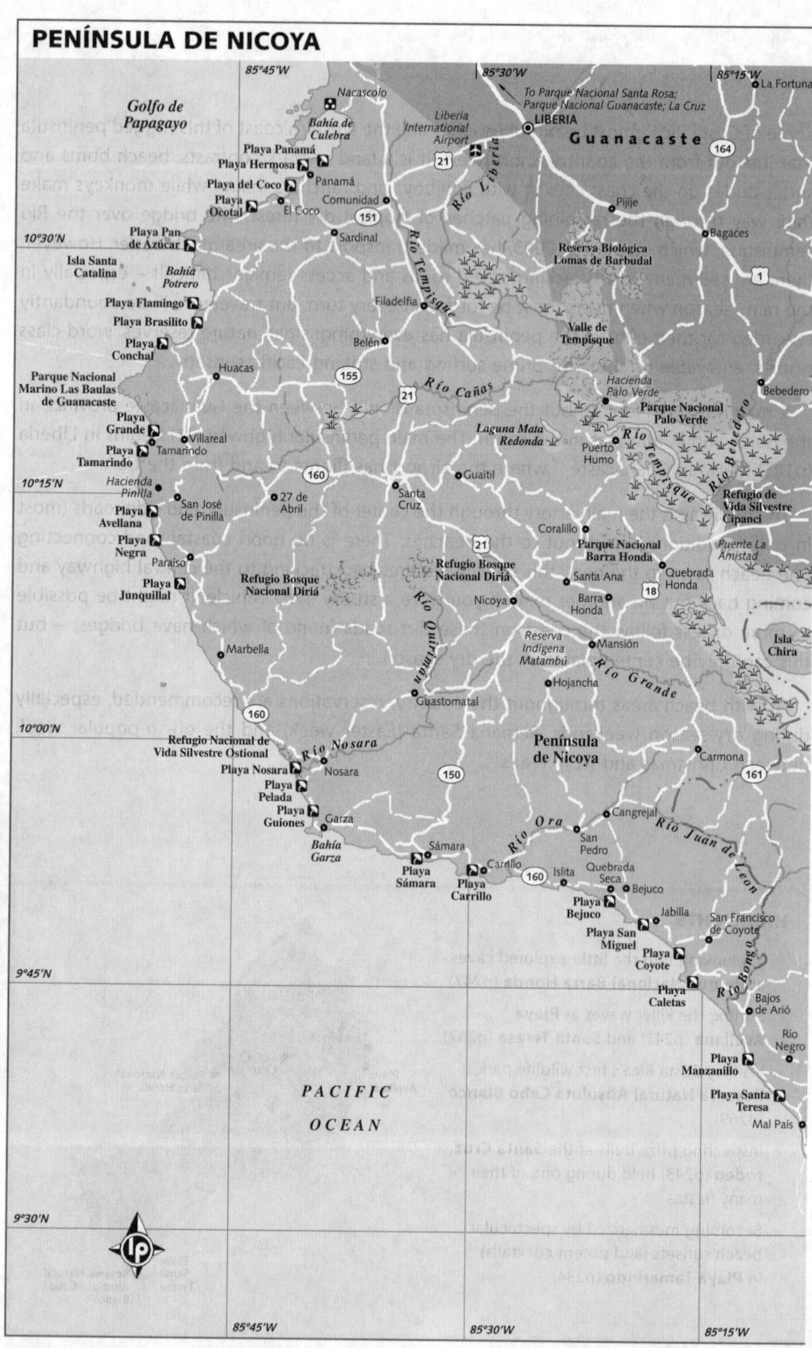
PENÍNSULA DE NICOYA
85°45'W
85°30'W
85°15'W
10°30'N
10°15'N
10°00'N
9°45'N
9°30'N
Golfo de Papagayo
Nacascolo
Bahía de Culebra
To Parque Nacional Santa Rosa; Parque Nacional Guanacaste; La Cruz
LIBERIA
Liberia International Airport
Guanacaste
La Fortuna
Playa Panamá
Playa Hermosa
Playa del Coco
Panamá
Playa Ocotal
El Coco
Comunidad
Río Liberia
Pijije
Sardinal
Río Tempisque
Bagaces
Playa Pan de Azúcar
Isla Santa Catalina
Bahía Potrero
Reserva Biológica Lomas de Barbudal
Playa Flamingo
Playa Brasilito
Filadelfia
Playa Conchal
Belén
Valle de Tempisque
Parque Nacional Marino Las Baulas de Guanacaste
Huacas
Río Cañas
Hacienda Palo Verde
Bebedero
Parque Nacional Palo Verde
Playa Grande
Villareal
Laguna Mata Redonda
Río Tempisque
Río Bebedero
Puerto Humo
Playa Tamarindo
Tamarindo
Hacienda Pinilla
San José de Pinilla
27 de Abril
Santa Cruz
Guaitil
Refugio de Vida Silvestre Cipanci
Playa Avellana
Coralillo
Playa Negra
Parque Nacional Barra Honda
Puente La Amistad
Paraíso
Refugio Bosque Nacional Diriá
Santa Ana
Quebrada Honda
Playa Junquillal
Refugio Bosque Nacional Diriá
Río Quirimán
Nicoya
Barra Honda
Reserva Indígena Matambú
Mansión
Isla Chira
Marbella
Río Grande
Hojancha
Guastomatal
Refugio Nacional de Vida Silvestre Ostional
Río Nosara
Península de Nicoya
Carmona
Playa Nosara
Nosara
Playa Pelada
Playa Guiones
Garza
Bahía Garza
Cangrejal
Río Ora
San Pedro
Río Juan de León
Sámara
Playa Sámara
Carrillo
Playa Carrillo
Islita
Quebrada Seca
Bejuco
Playa Bejuco
Jabilla
San Francisco de Coyote
Playa San Miguel
Playa Coyote
Río Bongo
Playa Caletas
Bajos de Arió
Río Negro
Playa Manzanillo
PACIFIC OCEAN
Playa Santa Teresa
Mal País
21
151
164
1
155
160
18
150
161

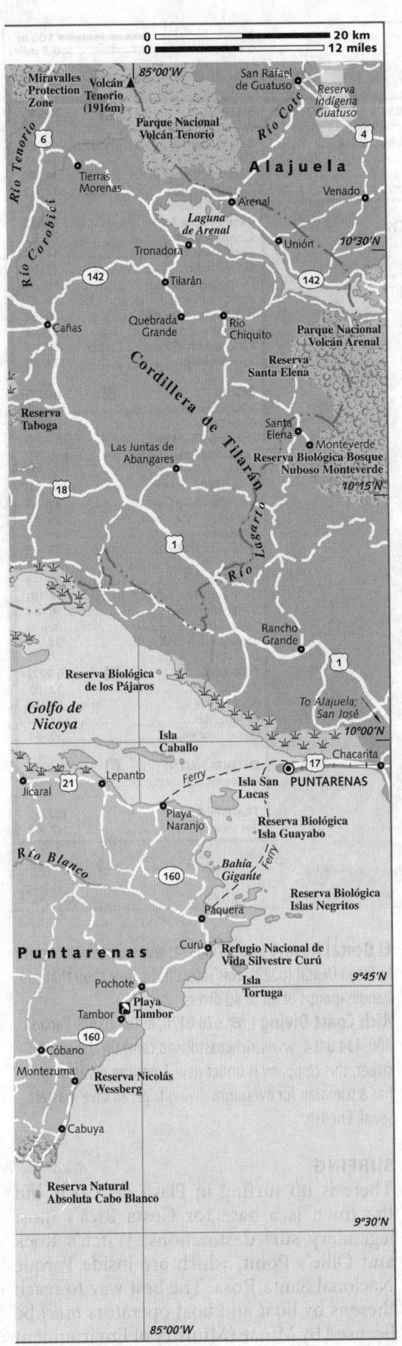

NORTHERN PENINSULA

FILADELFIA

Filadelfia is about 32km from Liberia and saddles the peninsular highway. It serves as a small transportation hub for the northern part of the peninsula. The population of the town and the surrounding district is about 7100.

About 100m north and 150m west of the Parque Central, you'll find **Cabinas Amelia** (☎ 688 8087; s/d US$12/22; tr with air-con US$26; P). Rooms are clean, small and have private bathroom. Also, try the basic **Cabinas Tita** (☎ 688 8073; r per person US$12) nearby; units have private bathroom. Get typical local fare at **Soda Gaby** (casados US$2.50) on the park.

The bus terminal, half a block from the park, has several buses a day to San José, and hourly buses pass through en route to Nicoya or Liberia.

PLAYA DEL COCO

Thirty-seven kilometers west of Liberia and connected by good roads to San José, El Coco is the most easily accessible of the peninsula's beaches. It is attractively set between two rocky headlands, with a small village and some nightlife, though the beach itself is not as inviting as others on the peninsula. (Visitors who take 10 minutes to walk past the rocky headland to the south will be rewarded with a small sandy white beach and tranquil, clear blue waters.)

The town is a growing scuba-diving center, and divers from all over come to gaze at local marine life. It's also a popular resort for young Ticos, and on weekends the town is consumed with a small-time beach-party atmosphere (which can get loud if you don't choose your accommodations carefully).

Information

Surf the Internet (US$1.25 per hour), get your laundry done (US$1.25 per kg) and drink fresh juice (US$2) at **Internet Jugo Bar** (🕑 8am-9pm), on the main road into town. It even rents mountain bikes (US$7 per day).

Email access and English-language newspapers are available at Hospedaje Catarino (see p225). Banco Nacional will exchange US dollars and traveler's checks.

The police station and post office are both on the southeast side of the plaza by the

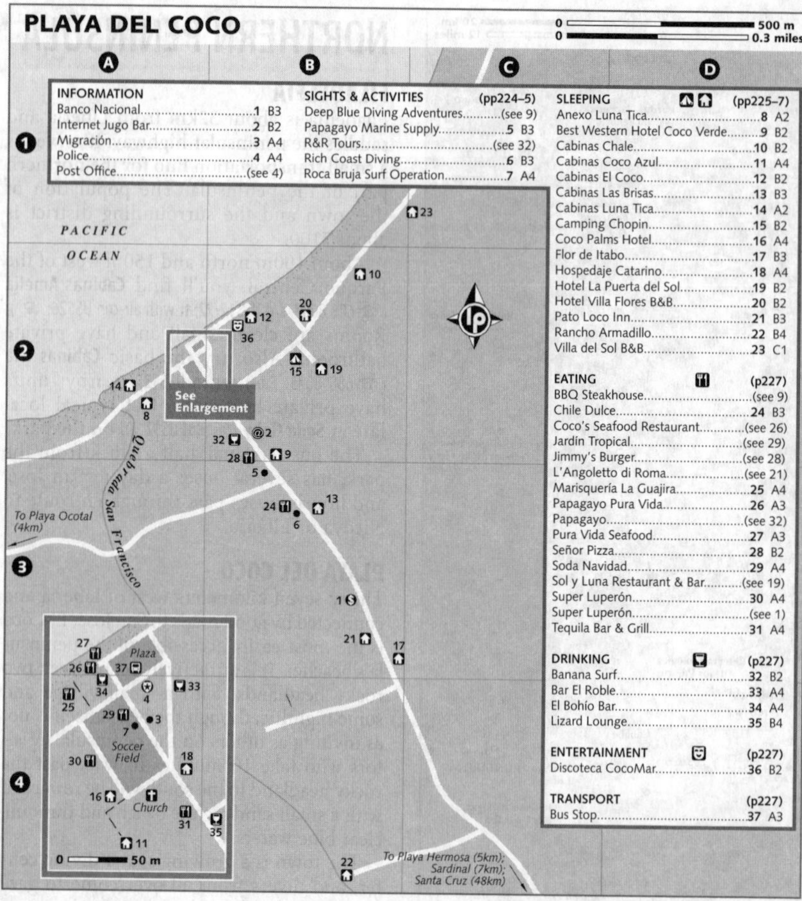

beach. The few people arriving at Playa del Coco by boat will find the migración office just southeast of the police station.

Activities

DIVING & SNORKELING

All of the listed agencies are recommended and are located in Playa del Coco unless otherwise stated.

Bill Beard's Diving Safaris (☎ 672 0012, in the USA 877-853 0538, 954-453 5044; www.billbeardcostarica.com) Situated inside the Villa Sol in Playa Hermosa (p228), these folks have been scuba diving and snorkeling here since 1970.

Deep Blue Diving Adventures (☎ 670 0201; www.deepblue-diving.com) Inside the Best Western (p226), this is one of the cheaper outfitters in town and has received several reader recommendations.

El Ocotal Resort (☎ 670 0321; www.ocotalresort.com) In Playa Ocotal (p229), this resort has a dive shop that can handle groups of up to 40 divers.

Rich Coast Diving (☎ 670 0176, in the USA & Canada 800-434 8464; www.richcoastdiving.com) On the main street, this company is under new American ownership. It has a trimaran for overnight diving trips; all dive masters speak English.

SURFING

There is no surfing in Playa del Coco, but the town is a base for Costa Rica's most legendary surf destinations: Witch's Rock and Ollie's Point, which are inside Parque Nacional Santa Rosa. The best way to reach these is by boat and boat operators *must* be licensed by Minae (Ministry of Environment

SCUBA DIVING

The northern area of the peninsula is one of the best and most easily accessible sites in the country for diving. There's no good beach diving in this area, so dives are made either around volcanic rock pinnacles near the coast, or from a boat further off at Isla Santa Catalina (about 20km to the southwest) or Isla Murciélago (40km to the northwest near the tip of Península Santa Elena).

Diving here is not like diving the Caribbean – do not expect to see colorful hard coral on the scale of Belize. Conditions can be mediocre from a visibility standpoint (9m to 15m visibility, and sometimes up to 20m) but makes up for it in other ways: namely, the abundant marine life. The richness, variety and sheer number of marine animals is astonishing. This is the place to catch sight of large groupings of manta rays, spotted eagle rays, sharks, whales, dolphins, turtles, as well as moray eels, starfish, crustaceans and huge schools of native tropical fish. Most of the dive sites are less than 25m deep, allowing three dives a day.

The so-called Papagayo winds blow from early December to late March and make the water choppy and cooler, cutting down on visibility, especially for the four days around the full moon. June and July are usually the best months for visibility.

Isla Catalina and **Isla Murciélago** both boast a rich variety of marine life living and cruising around these rocky outcrops. Manta rays have been reported from December to late April and at other times you can expect to spot eagle rays, eels, Cortez angelfish, hogfish, parrot fish, starfish, clown shrimp and other bottom dwellers. The far point of Murciélago is known for its regular sightings of groups of bull sharks (for advanced divers only). **Narizones** is known as a good deep dive (about 27m). For inexperienced divers, **Punta Gorda** is considered one of the easier descents.

and Energy) to enter the park. **Roca Bruja Surf Operation** (☎ 381 9166; www.rocabruja.50g.com) is a local, licensed operator. An eight-hour tour to both breaks is US$200 for five people. (See also Witch's Rock Surf Camp in Tamarindo, p235, which also offers tours to both.)

OTHER ACTIVITIES

Sportfishing, sailing and sea kayaking are other popular activities. Many places will rent sea kayaks.

Papagayo Marine Supply (☎ 670 0354; papagayo@infoweb.co.cr) offers bounteous information and supplies for anglers. Nearby, **R & R Tours** (☎ 670 0573) offers fishing charters and has day trips to Parque Nacional Palo Verde (p184) for US$65. **Cool Runnings** (☎ 395 6090, 834 1875; discovercostarica@yahoo.ca) has a 50-foot trimaran, a 65-foot schooner, a 38-foot Benateau and a 50-foot Drums of Bora luxury teak sailing yacht available for charters.

Just outside Playa del Coco, **El Ocotal Resort** (see opposite) offers fishing charters (it has six boats) and offers kayak rentals. Complete fishing packages are also available. In Playa Hermosa, **Hotel El Velero** (☎ 672 0036, 672 0016; www.costaricahotel.net) has a yacht and offers daily sunset cruises (minimum four people). Also in Hermosa, **Aqua Sport** (☎ 672 0050) has boats for fishing, water tours and snorkeling.

Festivals

In late January the town hosts a **Fiesta Cívica**, with bullfights, rodeos, dancing and plenty of drinking. But the biggest festival in El Coco is the **Fiesta de la Virgen del Mar**, celebrated in mid-July with a vivid religious-themed boat procession in the harbor and a horse pageant.

Sleeping

BUDGET

All lodgings listed below have cold-water showers unless otherwise noted.

Hospedaje Catarino (☎ 670 0156; d US$20; 🖳) On the main road, two blocks in from the beach, this place has six small and tidy doubles that come with fan and private bathroom. There is an Internet café.

Cabinas Coco Azul (☎ 670 0431; r per person US$10; P) These homey, family-owned cabinas in a quiet part of town are super clean and come with private bathroom. Each room also has a small outdoor deck with a table and hammocks. This is a great budget choice.

Cabinas Luna Tica (☎ 670 0127; d/tr/q US$25/30/37.50; P) Rooms in the main hotel and the

PENÍNSULA DE NICOYA

Anexo Luna Tica (across the street) are clean, but the tired-looking bathrooms have peeling paint. The ocean-side location partly makes up for this.

Cabinas Las Brisas (☎ 670 0155, 213 3292; d US$25; P) There isn't much of a breeze in these doubles beside a row of almond trees. The rooms are clean, but dark.

Cabinas Chale (☎ 670 0036; d US$33; P) About 50m from the beach and 600m from town, this simple place is to the right as you arrive (there are signs). The 25 fan-cooled rooms are clean but uninspiring; some have a fridge, and there's a big pool.

Camping Chopin (☎ 391 5998; per person US$3; P) Bathroom facilities and water are available at this small campground.

MID-RANGE

Coco Palms Hotel (☎ 670 0367; hotelcocopalm@racsa.co.cr, cocopalms@hotmail.com; d US$36; P) Spic-and-span, nicely decorated rooms all have fan and private bathroom with hot water. The hallways are light and airy and have high ceilings but some interior rooms are a little dark. An outdoor deck is a great place to hang out and there's an L-shaped pool.

Cabinas El Coco (☎ 670 0110; s/d US$32/39; P) Just right of the park, this sprawling place on the beach has clean rooms (with air-con) that are nothing special. Only at the far end does the crashing surf override the thumping disco.

Pato Loco Inn (☎ 670 0145; patoloco@racsa.co.cr; d/tr US$47/59, with air-con US$59/70; P) This small, European-style hotel is owned by a Dutch/Italian couple who also speak English, French, and Spanish. Their inn has four rooms, each with a fan and hot-water bathroom; two have air-con. All local activities can be arranged. The well-reviewed L'Angoletto di Roma restaurant (p227) is here.

Villa del Sol B&B (☎ 670 0085, in the USA 866-815 8902, in Canada 866-793 9523; www.villadelsol.com; d standard/villa US$64/76; P) This quiet, French Canadian–run place is 1km north of the main road and offers seven large, clean rooms, five with private bathroom. Standard rooms have hot water, five have air-con and rates include breakfast. Six villas include a full kitchen, cable TV and phone (no breakfast); upstairs units have incredible views. The hotel is about 100m from the beach, which is little visited at this end.

Hotel Villa Flores B&B (☎ 670 0787; www.hotel-villa-flores.com; d/tr standard US$64/76, d/tr/q deluxe US$74/84/94; P) The new American owners have updated this B&B just 200m north of the main road. Each of the nine rooms has been brightly painted, tile floors sparkle and there is air-con and a private bathroom in every unit. Upstairs quarters have nice terraces overlooking the grounds, and larger deluxe units have cable TV. Rates include breakfast. Credit cards accepted.

TOP END

In addition to hotels listed here, see also listings under Playa Ocotal (4km to the south, p229) and Playa Hermosa (7km to the north, p228).

Best Western Hotel Coco Verde (☎ 670 0494/544; www.bestwestern.com; s/d/tr incl breakfast US$76/94/105; P) This hotel has 33 big, modern, rooms with air-con, cable TV, phone and private hot shower. There's a pool, the BBQ Steakhouse restaurant (opposite), a sports bar and a small **casino** (7pm-2am). Fishing and diving packages are offered. Credit cards are accepted.

Flor de Itabo (☎ 670 0011/292/455; www.flordeitabo.com; d bungalow US$45, r standard/deluxe US$70/90, apt US$120-140; P) This low-key place is 1.3km before the beach, on the right-hand side as you arrive. Standard units sleep two and have air-con, cable TV, phone, mini-fridge and coffee maker, while deluxe units also have whirlpool tubs and accommodate four. Apartments sleep four or six and have full kitchens. There's a restaurant serving Italian-international food, a casino and a bar that attracts anglers.

Hotel La Puerta del Sol (☎ 670 0195; s/d/tr US$60/80/100, ste US$110; P) Only a five-minute walk from town, this comfortable, small hotel offers eight spacious, brightly painted, modern rooms, each with a small sitting area, cable TV, phone, air-con, fan, and private bathroom with hair dryer and hot water. Larger suites also come with a refrigerator, coffee maker, and balcony. The well-manicured grounds have a putting green, pool and minigym and the Sol y Luna Bar & Restaurant (opposite). All rates include continental breakfast.

Rancho Armadillo (☎ 670 0108; www.ranchoarmadillo.com; s/d US$111/122, ste US$171; P) Near the entrance to town, this place is on an incredible hillside about 600m off the main road (all paved). The view from the common areas is the best in town, and the seven rooms are light, spacious and nicely decorated. Units have coffee makers, mini-fridges, individually crafted furniture and large bathrooms. Suites sleep four; some have two bathrooms and two entrances. There's a pool, outdoor gym, and plenty of decorative armadillos. The American owners arrange fishing, sailing, diving and surfing trips. Gourmands will enjoy comparing recipes with chef/owner Rick Vogel and using the fully equipped professional kitchen.

Eating

Soda Navidad (gallo pinto US$2) On the west end of the soccer field, this local favorite offers cheap counter breakfasts.

Jardín Tropical (casados US$3), around the corner, has a wide selection of reasonably priced meals, including Tico specialties and pizza (US$6) and fish (US$6).

On the water, **Papagayo Pura Vida** and **Coco's Seafood Restaurant** (fish dinners US$7) have tasty red snapper and excellent fresh *ceviches*. One block away, **Marisquería La Guajira** (dishes US$6) ladles out hearty shellfish chowder.

Papagayo (dishes US$10) is a very good seafood restaurant, but go for the food, not the ambience, which is that of a noisy roadside diner.

For a Mex fix (at a price), amble over to **Tequila Bar & Grill** (dishes US$6-11; ⌚ evenings only), where you can pick up fajitas and *tortas* (Mexican sandwiches).

On the main road into town, **Chile Dulce** (sandwiches US$4-5, main courses US$8; ⌚ 12:30-10:30pm) whips up well-reviewed and highly inventive sandwiches, energy shakes, veggie specials and seafood courses. (Try the dorado in citrus-spiced coconut milk.)

Italian food is big in Playa del Coco. **Sol y Luna Restaurant & Bar** (in Hotel Puerto del Sol; dishes US$7.50) is considered the best Italian of the bunch. Also worth a try (and in a similar price range) are the **Pizzería** (in Flor de Itabo Hotel) and **L'Angoletto di Roma** (⌚ 6-9pm) at the Pato Loco Inn.

Señor Pizza (pizza US$5) has small pies and nachos and is open until 11:30pm for late-night noshing. **Jimmy's Burger** (burgers US$2), nearby, has gut-filling cheeseburgers.

BBQ Steakhouse (adjacent to the Best Western; steaks US$7-14; ⌚ 6am-10pm) grills up steaks in a rustic, semi-open-air setting. An ample breakfast buffet (US$4) is a good deal.

Two branches of the Super Luperón market offer plenty of choices for self-caterers.

Drinking & Entertainment

Beach-party life doesn't tend to be about lasting commitments, and hip spots come and go. A quick walk around will let you know what's in vogue.

The restaurants around the plaza double as bars, with El Bohío Bar the long-standing favorite. The open-air Bar El Roble is preferred by locals, while the Lizard Lounge attracts a steady stream of global partyers. One of the top places for liver damage is Banana Surf, serving perennial favorites such as Jaegermeister and Red Bull. Tequila Bar & Grill is the spot for margaritas.

Boogie 'til the break of dawn at Discoteca Cocomar on the beach, which attracts a steady stream of young Ticos ready to party on.

Getting There & Away

All buses arrive and depart from the main stop on the plaza, across from the police station.

Filadelfia, for connection to Santa Cruz US$0.75; 45 minutes; depart 11:30am & 4:30pm.

Liberia US$0.75; one hour; 5:30am, 7am, 9am, 11am, 1pm, 3pm, 5pm & 6pm.

San José (Pullmitan) US$5.25; five hours; 4am, 8am & 2pm.

A taxi from Liberia to Playa del Coco costs US$15. Taxis between Playa del Coco and Playa Hermosa or Ocotal cost between US$5 and US$7.

Note that there's no gas station in town; the nearest one is in Sardinal, about 9km before Playa del Coco.

PLAYA HERMOSA

This gently curving and tranquil beach is about 7km (by road) north of Coco. At the moment, it's quiet and less crowded than other beaches, although the ongoing development of the Papagayo Project beginning at the next beach (see Playa Panamá, p228) may change this dramatically. Don't confuse this beach with the surfing beach of the same name on the central Pacific coast.

For information on fishing, surfing, scuba diving and sailing in the area, see Activities (p224). Food and other basic supplies are available at Mini Super Cenizaro, on the paved road into town.

Sleeping & Eating

Thefts have been reported at some of these hotels, so keep your valuables under lock and key while you're at the beach.

Hotel Playa Hermosa (☎ 672 0046; s/d/tr US$41/53/59, with air-con US$59/76/82; P) Right on the southern end of the beach (via the first entrance road), this quiet hotel has new owners and has received a recent remodeling. The 20 rooms all have private bathroom with hot water, and cable TV is on the way. Hammocks are strung up on palm trees and there is a good Tico **restaurant** (casados US$4; 7am-9:30pm).

On the second (or northern) entrance to the beach, you'll find several other lodging options.

Iguana Inn (☎ 672 0065; per person US$17;) Set 100m back from the beach, this rambling terracotta place has 10 simple, slightly beat-up rooms with private bathroom. Newer apartments have a kitchen, two bedrooms, and a foldout sofa. There is a pool, and laundry service is available.

Villa Huetares (☎ 672 0081/52; standard/villa US$60/90; P) This locally run and well-maintained hotel has 15 small, nicely decorated 'villas' with air-con, kitchenette, dining area and private bathroom. Brand new standard rooms in the back are comfy and have cable TV. Units sleep four to six people.

Hotel El Velero (☎ 672 0036/16, 672 1017; www.costaricahotel.net; r US$84; P) Just steps from the beach, this place has 22 spacious, light rooms decorated with woodwork and colorful spreads. Each unit has air-con, private hot shower, a coffee maker and two double beds. There's a pool, a patio lounge and a restaurant serving US-style bar food. The hotel yacht provides guests with a variety of cruises (see p225). Credit cards accepted.

Playa Hermosa Inn (☎ 672 0063; www.costarica-beach-hotel.com; d with fan/air-con US$50/60, 2-bedroom apt US$70, additional person US$10, child under 12 US$5; P) Nine simple rooms have private bathroom, hot water and fan; five have air-con. A fully equipped 2nd-story apartment can house seven people. All rates include breakfast and credit cards are accepted.

Cabinas La Casona (☎ 672 0025; d US$34; P) Seven small, clean, whitewashed rooms with kitchenette are available at this friendly place. All units have private bathroom and hot water. One room sleeping five costs US$53.

A variety of recommended seafood specialties are served at the pleasant **Restaurant Pescado Loco** (☎ 672 0017; dishes US$5-14). For drinking, visit **Monkey Bar** (5pm-midnight Mon-Sat, noon-midnight Sun), between the first and second entrances (on the east side of the road) to Playa Hermosa that offers good sunset views.

Villas Sol Hotel (☎ 257 0607; www.villassoltc.com; d US$144, villa US$283-361; P) This resort is perched on a hill overlooking Playa Hermosa and offers more than 100 units. Standard rooms have private bathroom with hot water, hair dryer, cable TV, air-con, minifridge, coffee maker and safe; rates include breakfast. Pricier villas have up to three bedrooms, a kitchen and come with or without pools. There are also tennis courts, a restaurant and a bar. The owners can arrange all types of activities. Bill Beard's Diving Safaris (p224) is based here. Credit cards accepted.

Many Ticos camp for free near the main beach; there are some good, shady spots but no facilities.

Getting There & Away

There is a daily bus from San José, but you can always take a bus to Liberia and switch for more frequent buses to Playa Hermosa once you're there.

Buses to Liberia and San José depart from the main road on the northern end of the beach and make a stop in Sardinal.

Liberia US$0.75; 1¼ hours; depart 5am, 6am, 10am, 4pm & 5pm.

San José (Empresa Esquivel) US$4; five hours; 5am.

A taxi from Liberia costs about US$15, and a taxi from Coco costs about US$5. If you're driving from Liberia, take the signed turnoff to Playa del Coco. The entire road is paved.

PLAYA PANAMÁ & THE PAPAGAYO PROJECT

The protected dark-sand beach that lines the Golfo de Papagayo was once a rural beach, scattered only with a few campers and local families. Recently, the area has been colonized by a crew of luxury resorts geared to the traveler who wants the best of the best.

The beach is part of the so-called Papagayo Project, a tourism development plan for the gulf that the ICT hatched in 1976.

Initially, no environmental impact studies were done and tropical dry forest was to be razed to make way for golf courses and more than 15,000 hotel rooms. Thankfully, there have been improvements made to the plan. An environmental analysis was done and, as a result, up to 70% of the Papagayo Gulf area is slated to remain tropical dry forest. The number of hotel rooms was reduced by more than half and planned golf courses were relocated to former cow pasture, instead of in forested areas.

But there are still bumps in the road. At the time of research, a controversy had arisen over the right to camp in a beach area in front of the Four Seasons Hotel. (Camping is a time-honored tradition on many Costa Rican beaches.) Since there are no camping facilities here, it is unclear whether the letter of the law allows it. The ICT claims it isn't; local and environmental groups argue otherwise. The courts will determine who has the law on their side.

Either way, the resorts are here, and they're here to stay – and it's worth noting that some locals appreciate the extra jobs (though they're primarily in the service sector). Certainly, the hotels are beautiful, extravagant (and whatever other superlatives you can think of) and they're ready and waiting to accept your gold card.

Sleeping & Eating

The following places have the usual luxury amenities: air-con rooms, suites and villas with private bathroom and hot water; restaurants; bars; casinos; pools; tennis courts; saunas and spas; ocean views and activities. Other options in the area can be found through the project's website: www.papagayo-info.com.

Four Seasons (☎ 696 000/98, in the USA 212-688 2440; www.fourseasons.com; r US$462-1229; P) Get ready to pay! This hotel, at the end of the road on Península de Papagayo, has the honor of being the most expensive in the country. The hotel's policy of the customer being right has led some staff being reluctant to stop guests from feeding the local animals. Please respect nature by not feeding the animals.

Occidental Allegro Papagayo (☎ 690 9900, in the USA & Canada 800-858 2258, in Europe 800-6460 6460; www.occidentalhotels.com/allegropapagayo/; r per person US$105, additional person US$80, child under 12 US$40) Rates are based on double occupancy and include all meals.

PLAYA OCOTAL

This attractive but small beach is 4km southwest of Coco by paved road. It's the cleanest, quietest beach in the area, offering good swimming and snorkeling (especially at the southern end of the beach) and is a good base for dive trips.

See Activities (p224) for information on excursions.

Sleeping & Eating

Villa Casa Blanca (☎ 670 0518/448; www.costa-rica-hotels-travel.com; d standard/honeymoon/condo incl breakfast US$94/123/146, additional person US$10; P) Between Playa del Coco and Ocotal, this attractive villa is on a pleasant hilltop just a few minutes' walk from the beach. There are 10 lovely rooms, each with private bathroom, ceiling fan, and air-con. They are beautifully decorated; some have Victorian motifs and others are more modern. Three honeymoon suites are larger and feature a step-up bathtub and ocean views. Two fully equipped condos with kitchens are available. The pool is crossed by a garden bridge and has a swim-up bar. Local tours can all be arranged. This is a recommended and relaxing place to stay.

El Ocotal Resort (☎ 670 0321; www.ocotalresort.com; s/d/tr US$129/146/176, junior ste US$211/234/270; P) Perched on an ocean-side cliff with spectacular views, rooms have air-con, cable TV, phone, ceiling fan, coffee maker, and huge picture windows opening onto a private terrace with ocean view. Bathrooms have hair dryer and hot shower, but are a bit small. There are roomier ocean-view suites as well, some with Jacuzzi and sitting room. A restaurant showcases the views and serves up a full American breakfast (included in the rate). The resort has a fully equipped, five-star gold PADI dive center and can offer fishing charters (see p224). Complete diving and fishing packages are available. Sea kayaks and mountain bikes can be rented. Credit cards accepted.

Apart from eating at the hotels, there's **Father Rooster Restaurant** (dishes US$5-10), adjacent to El Ocotal near the beach. Inexpensive and fun, it has a variety of grilled dishes, including fish, snacks and burgers. The staff makes a good margarita and a killer frozen cocktail called the 'kamikaze.'

BEACHES SOUTH OF PLAYA OCOTAL

It's possible to reach the set of beaches south of Ocotal by taking a poor dirt road from Sardinal to Potrero. This requires 4WD and you should ask locally about how good this road is before setting out. However, if you want to avoid the rough roads, return to the main peninsular highway then head south through Filadelfia and on to Belén (a distance of 18km). From here, a paved road heads 25km west to Huacas (where there is a gas station) and where short paved roads radiate to a number of popular beach areas.

The first 9km stretch of the poor dirt road isn't too bad and ends at the town of Artola where you'll find the **Congo Trail Canopy Tour** (☎ 666 4422; US$45). Hotels in Playas del Coco, Hermosa and Ocotal can all book this tour for you. After this point, the road deteriorates.

From Santa Cruz, further south on the peninsular highway, a 16km paved road heads west to the tiny community of 27 de Abril, where roads radiate to several beaches. Huacas is connected with 27 de Abril by a potholed road. Thus, all the beaches described below are accessible from Santa Cruz.

The road from Huacas hits the ocean at the village of Brasilito. Turn right and head north and you'll pass Bahía Potrero (opposite) and head onto Playa Pan de Azucár (p232). If you make a left instead and head south, you will end up at Playa Conchal (p233).

Buses from San José, Liberia or Santa Cruz can get you to most of the beaches as well.

Playa Brasilito

Brasilito has a few small stores and restaurants and the cheapest accommodations in the area. There's a tranquil beach, but other beaches nearby are better. On weekends, buses from the capital roll in and the place fills up.

Brasilito Excursiones (☎ 654 4237; www.brasilito.com), which operates out of Hotel Brasilito (see later), can book two-hour guided horseback rides (US$25), sunset sails (US$60) and two-tank dives ($75).

SLEEPING & EATING

Brasilito Lodge (☎ 654 4452; www.brasilito-conchal.com; per person US$9, camping per person US$3, child under 6 free; Ⓟ) Run by a German family, this lodge is just off the beach, about 200m from the plaza in the direction of Conchal. Showers, a kitchen area and shade trees are available for campers. Basic cabins have kitchenette, fan and cold shower.

Cabinas Ojos Azules (☎ 654 4346; r downstairs per person US$5; d upstairs US$35; Ⓟ) This somewhat ramshackle place is 200m south along the main road and has big, comfy beds complete with saucy mirrored headboards. Fancy doubles are upstairs and simpler downstairs quarters fit up to eight people. All units have private bathroom, some with hot water.

Hotel Brasilito (☎ 654 4237; www.brasilito.com; d/tr/q US$30/35/40, d/q with view US$40/50; Ⓟ) On the beach side of the plaza in Brasilito, this recommended hotel has 15 simple, clean, screened rooms with fan and private hot shower. Sea-view rooms are pricier. Staff speak German and English and will help arrange tours. Credit cards accepted.

Cabinas Nany (☎ 654 4320; www.apartotelnany.com; d US$50, additional person US$15; Ⓟ) Between Playas Brasilito and Conchal, this remodeled hotel has large rooms painted in cheerful tropical colors. Each unit has two bedrooms, a fully equipped kitchen, private cold shower and cable TV. Air-con is available for US$10 per night. A small restaurant provides meals all day. The hotel is managed by the López family, who have been in the area for four decades. The staff can book all tours. The cabinas are walking distance from Brasilito and Conchal.

Perro Plano (dishes US$3-12), the restaurant attached to Hotel Brasilito, serves various specialties and is run by the amiable Charlie, an Irishman who recently moved to Costa Rica and had the whole adventure documented by the BBC.

Restaurant Happy Snapper (☎ 654 4413; meals US$6-10) Nearby, on the beach side of the plaza, this cheerful restaurant serves steaks and seafood and has occasional live music. Several other cheap eateries lie around the plaza.

Restaurante y Bar Camarón Dorado (☎ 654 4028; dishes US$3-17) This large beachfront place, a couple of blocks north of the school, is the top place for seafood in Brasilito. Tables are right on the beach and if you're on a tight budget, a fish casado will only cost you US$3. You can get your catch cooked here as well.

Il Forno (☎ 654 4125; dishes US$5-6) The pasta and pizza are recommended at this Italian eatery.

GETTING THERE & AWAY

See Playa Flamingo (see later) for details on getting to Brasilito.

Playa Flamingo

Three kilometers north of Brasilito, the road comes to Playa Flamingo, a pretty white-sand beach. The area's original name was Playa Blanca, but it's taken its new name from the Flamingo Beach Resort. The country's original upscale resort, it has been developed for sportfishing and boating and is a popular stop on the gringo trail.

There are many luxurious private houses and villas, but there's no village as such.

Banco de Costa Rica (☎ 654 4984; 🕑 8:30am-3:30pm), across from the Flamingo Marina Resort, can exchange US dollars and traveler's checks. The **Super Massai** (on the main north-south road) is good for all kinds of food supplies and toiletries.

SIGHTS & ACTIVITIES

Next door to the Super Massai, check out the **Wishbone Gallery** (☎ 654 4195; www.wishbonegallery.com), a great little space displaying and selling works of art.

At the entrance to Flamingo beach, the **Edge Adventure Company** (☎ 654 4946, 350 3670; www.costaricaexotic.com) offers a full range of rentals and tours. A two-tank dive costs US$75, and snorkeling gear, bikes and body boards are available for rent. Fishing charters are also available.

Samonique III (☎ 388 7870) is a 52-foot ketch available for sunset cruises for US$60 per person (minimum four). Overnight tours are available by arrangement. You can find their office at the Mariner Inn.

Centro Panamericano de Idiomas (☎ 645 5002, www.cpi-edu.com) has a Spanish school here. Prices for courses start at US$240 per week without homestay.

SLEEPING & EATING

Guanacaste Lodge (☎ 654 4494; d/tr/q US$45/50/55; P ✱ ☒) At the edge of town, this hotel has 10 clean rooms, each with two double beds, private hot shower, air-con and cable TV. The pleasant shaded grounds feature a nice pool. There's a popular restaurant serving grilled specialties and casados (US$4.30). This is good value. Credit cards accepted.

Flamingo Marina Resort (☎ 654 4141; www.flamingomarina.com; d US$99, ste US$170, condo US$328; P ✱ ☒) This hotel is up on a hill and has good ocean views. The 22 standard rooms have air-con, ceiling fan, satellite TV, phone and balcony views. The eight suites also have kitchenette and Jacuzzi tub. Condos have one or two bedrooms and fully equipped kitchens. There's a tennis court, dive shop, restaurant, bar, tour agency, and the nearby marina with plenty of sportfishing boats. Credit cards accepted.

Flamingo Beach Resort (☎ 654 4444; www.resortflamingobeach.com; r US$140, ste US$263; P ✱ ☒) The granddaddy of the area's resorts, this 91-room complex on the beach has a 1950s air about it. Quarters have air-con, cable TV, private bathroom, hot water and safe. The hotel has a large pool and all the activities you can handle. It also has two restaurants and two bars.

Apart from the hotel restaurants, there are few other places to eat.

Marie's (🕑 6:30am-9:30pm) One of the longest-established eateries in town offers a variety of snacks and meals. The breakfast pancakes are locally famous, and this is the best place in town for a big hamburger.

Amberes (☎ 654 4001) A dinner place with a casino, disco, and live music on some weekends.

GETTING THERE & AWAY

Air

You can fly to Tamarindo (p240), which has regular scheduled flights and is about 8km away by paved road.

Bus

Buses depart from the Flamingo Marina on the point and travel through Brasilito on the way out. Schedules change often so ask locally about departure times as well as the best place on the road to wait for the bus.

Liberia US$1.20; two hours; depart 5:30am & 2:30pm.

San José (Tralapa) US$5.80; five hours; 2:45am, 9am & 2pm Mon-Sat, 10:30am Sun.

Santa Cruz US$1.30; one hour; eight buses depart from 5:45am to 10pm.

Bahía Potrero

This stretch of bay is 7km north of Brasilito and is separated from Playa Flamingo by a rocky headland. There's a small community at **Potrero,** just beyond the northern end of the beach. This is where the bus line ends; although the beaches here don't get the weekend rush found at Brasilito. While upscale Playa Flamingo is visible across the bay, this is still an area where monkeys can be heard in the trees.

Several beaches are strung along the bay. The black-sand beach is **Playa Prieta**, the white-sand beach is **Playa Penca**, and **Playa Potrero**, the biggest, is somewhere in between – these names, it should be noted, are used loosely. Hotels on the beaches rent water-sports equipment. The rocky islet 10km due west of Playa Pan de Azúcar is **Isla Catalina**, a popular diving spot (see p225 for details).

SLEEPING & EATING

Mayra's (☎ 654 4213, 654 4472; d/tr/q US$25/30/43, camping per person US$3.50; P) Right on the southern beach, this friendly, tranquil place has shady camping with beach showers and five rustic rooms with cold shower, fan, fridge and kitchenette. A small *soda* (basic eatery) prepares meals. Mayra is helpful and friendly, and her husband Álvaro, a retired journalist, is well stocked with stories.

Cabinas Isolina (☎ 654 4333; www.isolinabeach.com; d/tr/q US$47/58/70, d/tr/q villa US$94/117/140; P) Set back from the northern end of the beach, but with easy access to it, Isolina has 11 attractive rooms surrounded by hibiscus. All units come with a double bed and bunk bed, tiled hot shower, ceiling fan, cable TV and air-con. Villas have two bedrooms and a kitchen. Rates include continental breakfast, and a restaurant serves Tico-Mediterranean specialties. Italian and English are spoken.

Cabinas Cristina (☎ 654 4006; www.cabinascristina.com; d/q US$35/58, d/q with kitchen US$47/70, apt US$58-94; P) It's about 700m away from the sea near the northern end. Rooms vary from simple doubles with fan and bathroom to fully equipped mini-apartments with air-con and kitchenette. There is a small pool and local tours and boat rentals can be arranged. Credit cards accepted.

Bahia Esmeralda (☎ 654 4480; www.hotelbahiaesmeralda.com; d/tr/q US$53/58/63, apt US$98, villa US$117; P) About 50m east of the village center, this mustard-colored place is good value. Standard rooms are small, but clean, and apartments sleeping up to four have foldout futons and a kitchen. The villas sleep six. All 20 units have private hot shower and air-con. A pool and an **Italian restaurant** (breakfast & dinner) are on the premises. English and Italian are spoken and all local tour activities can be arranged. Credit cards accepted.

Hotel Montecarlo Beach Resort (☎ 654 5048; 4-/6-person villa US$94/140; P) This bright yellow beachside hotel has comfy villas that come with cable TV, air-con, private hot shower and a kitchenette with microwave oven. There is an ocean-side pool and a pleasant outdoor **restaurant** (mains US$7-10) serving Mediterranean cuisine.

There are a couple of restaurants other than the ones inside the hotels. About 50m inland the Bahía Potrero Resort, you'll find **Hardens Gardens & Bakery** (dishes US$5-8), serving pizzas, pastries, and sandwiches.

Las Brisas Bar & Grill (☎ 654 4047; casados US$3.75) At the far end of the bay past the village, this locally popular place has *bocas* (appetizers) and typical Tico dishes. The pool table is popular with villagers and the open-air bar is a great place to watch the sunset.

GETTING THERE & AWAY

Many buses begin their route in Potrero on the southeast corner of the soccer field. See Playa Flamingo (p231) for schedules. Ask locally before setting out, not every bus goes all the way into Potrero.

Playa Pan de Azúcar

This small white-sand beach, 3km north of Potrero, is the last beach reachable by a rough dirt road. (Take a 4WD in the wet season.) The waters are protected by rocky headlands at either end of the beach and offer good snorkeling.

Hotel Sugar Beach (☎ 654 4242; www.sugar-beach.com; d standard/deluxe US$129/162, ste US$193, apt US$222, beach house US$409-526; P) This small and lovely hotel above the beach is long-established and offers excellent service. It has 22 modern, brightly painted rooms, each with individually carved wooden doors, air-con, private hot-water bathroom, phone, safe, and cable TV; deluxe units have ocean views. There are also four two-bedroom apartments and two beach houses (with two or three bedrooms sleeping 10 to 12). The restaurant has great views. All area tours can be arranged. Credit cards accepted.

Buses only come as far as Potrero, 3km away.

Playa Conchal

About 2km south of Brasilito you'll find the wide and pristine Playa Conchal, so called for the many *conchas* (shells) that pile up on the beach. The clear water makes for decent snorkeling. A huge hotel has been built on the northern stretch of the beach, which makes beach access difficult unless you are staying there.

SLEEPING & EATING

Condor Lodge & Beach Resort (☎ 654 4050; www.condorlodge.com; d standard/deluxe US$88/104, ste US$130; P) At the southern end of the beach, accessible from the main road, this hotel has rooms with air-con, fan, minifridge, cable TV, and private hot-water bathroom. There's a restaurant, bar, two pools, and a tennis court, all with good views. Rates include breakfast, and golfing and fishing packages are available. Credit cards accepted.

Hotel Meliá Playa Conchal (☎ 654 4123; www.paradisusplayaconchal.com; s/d ste US$321/536; P) This walled compound at the northern end has all the usual amenities, including an over-the-top free-form pool and a championship golf course. There are more than 300 suites, seven restaurants and three bars. All the usual amenities are included: private bathroom, hot water, cable TV, phone, minibar, safe and air-con. Rates listed above are all-inclusive and credit cards are accepted. Check the website for specials.

GETTING THERE & AWAY

If you're staying in Conchal, it's best to catch buses in Brasilito. See Playa Flamingo (p231) for further details.

If you're driving, note that the gas station between Playa Brasilito and Playa Flamingo is the only one in the area.

PLAYA GRANDE

Playa Grande, southwest of Huacas, consists largely of a few hotels strung along the northern end of Parque Nacional Marino Las Baulas on an aptly named large, wide beach. (These places are actually within the limits of the park.) The **surfing** is tops here but the area is quiet, so if you came to Costa Rica for a party, stay in Tamarindo (p234).

Sleeping & Eating

Centro Vacacional Playa Grande (☎ 653 0834; camping per person US$2; r US$35; P) A few hundred meters back from the beach on the main road, this place is popular with vacationing Tico families and surfers. Basic rooms have fan and cold shower, and some have kitchenette. There's a pool and a cheap restaurant that serves tasty food.

Villa Baula (☎ 653 0644/493; www.hotelvillabaula.com; d/tr US$70/94, bungalow US$117-146, additional person US$10; P) At the southern end of the park, just across the estuary from Tamarindo, this pleasantly rustic beachfront complex has 20 rooms and five bungalows of various sizes. More expensive bungalows have a kitchenette and air-con. Surfboards, body boards, kayaks, and bikes are available. Surf instruction is available, as are a variety of tours.

Hotel Cantarana (☎ 653 0486; www.hotelcantarana.com; s/d US$60/80; P) This pretty, well-kept hotel near the estuary has 10 air-con rooms with private hot showers and cable TV. There's a good European restaurant, massage services, and kayak rental, and there's a large free-form pool. The German owners also speak French and English and can arrange local tours.

Hotel Las Tortugas (☎ 653 0423; www.cool.co.cr/usr/turtles; d US$76, ste US$105, apt US$30-105; P) Eleven spacious rooms with air-con have private bathroom with hot water, plus thick walls and small windows to enable daytime sleep after a night of turtle-watching. There's a pool, Jacuzzi, a popular restaurant, and all tours can be arranged. The owner, Louis Wilson, was instrumental in organizing protection for the turtles and designed the hotel so that the lights, which are quite dim, shine away from the beach area. Surfboards, body boards, sea kayaks, snorkels, and horses are rented. The hotel also has two apartments with kitchens for rent up the hill.

Getting There & Away

There are no buses to Playa Grande. You can drive to Huacas and then take the paved road to Matapalo followed by a 6km dirt road to Playa Grande. If you don't have your own car and are staying in Playa Grande, call ahead and the hotel owners can arrange for a pickup from the Matapalo turnoff (where the bus from San José can drop you off). You can also get a local boat captain to take you across the estuary from Tamarindo to the southern end of Playa Grande (see Getting Around, p241).

PARQUE NACIONAL MARINO LAS BAULAS

This seaside protected area just north of Tamarindo village includes Playa Grande, one of the most important nesting sites in the entire world for the *baula* (leatherback turtle). Formerly a national wildlife refuge, this national marine park was created in 1991 to control unregulated tourism and poaching and covers about 379 hectares on the north side of the Río Matapalo estuary. In addition, 22,000 hectares of ocean are also protected. Most of the land is mangrove swamp containing all six of the mangrove species found in Costa Rica.

All this creates a great habitat for caimans and crocodiles, as well as numerous bird species, including the beautiful roseate spoonbill. Other creatures to look for when visiting are howler monkeys, raccoons, coatis, otters, and a variety of crabs. But as is to be expected, the main attraction is the nesting of the world's largest turtles, which can weigh in excess of 300kg. Nesting season is October to March, when up to a dozen leatherbacks lay their eggs on a given night.

Playa Grande is also a favored surfing beach, its break touted as one of the most consistent in Costa Rica.

Turtle Watching

Visitors must watch the activities from specified areas, accompanied by a guide, and no flash photography or lights of any kind are allowed. The **park office** (☎ 653 0470; 🕑 9am-6pm) is by the northern entrance. The US$7 admission fee is charged only for night-time turtle tours.

A good way to begin your tour is with a visit to **El Mundo de la Tortuga** (☎ 653 0471; admission US$5; 🕑 4pm-dawn), a small and informative self-guided exhibit about leatherback turtles near the northern end of the park.

Many Tamarindo hotels and tourist agencies can book tours that include transport to and from Playa Grande, admission to the exhibit and the park and the guided tour. The whole package costs US$35. This is the best way to go.

The leatherback is critically endangered from overhunting, a lack of protected nesting sights, and coastal overdevelopment (beachside lights disorient the turtles when they come up to nest). It is believed that more than 1000 turtles used to come to nest every season, but now the area draws between 50 and 200 *baulas* annually. Because of this, guidelines for the tours are very strict. Tourists are not allowed on the beach until the turtles have made it to dry sand. Guards with two-way radios are posted on the beach and they will alert your guide when a turtle is ready for its close-up. As a group, you are only allowed to watch one turtle.

Naturally, there is no guarantee that you will see a turtle. This is nature, not the San Diego Zoo. This also means that you may wait for 10 minutes before a turtle shows up, or you could be there for five hours. A small stand at the exhibit sells snacks and *sodas*, but bring a (thick) book or a deck of cards for entertainment. It could be a very long night – but well worth it.

PLAYA TAMARINDO

The surfing is first-rate, the beaches are beautiful, the town is laid-back and there's no shortage of things to do. Nature buffs will enjoy watching leatherback turtles nest at the nearby national park (see earlier) and adventurers will get a thrill out of good waves, sunset ATV tours and zip-line adventures. Tamarindo is one of the most popular destinations on the peninsula and it is well served by accommodations, restaurants, and equipment-rental outlets. This beach has better access by public transport than most of the beaches in the area and is bustling with small-scale development. It's no wonder that US residents have moved here in droves, leaving us to wonder if the town shouldn't be renamed 'Tamagringo.'

The town is south of the village of Huacas off a paved road and east of Santa Cruz on a partly paved road. During the dry months, especially February, winds can make the beach a bit gritty.

Information

Tourist information is available from any of the tour operators in town. A helpful website is www.tamarindobeach.org.

Shark Bite Deli (near the police station) has one of the best book exchanges in Costa Rica, so if you're desperate for some reading material (other than this guidebook) this is the place to get it.

Check email at @ **Internet** (per hr US$4.50; 🕑 9am-9pm), which has speedy connections, friendly service and free coffee.

Lavandería Mariposa and **Lavandería Punto Limpio** (both Mon-Sat) charge US$1.25 per kg for wash and dry.

Banco Nacional (☎ 653 0366; 8:30am-3:30pm) exchanges US dollars cash and traveler's checks, but will not give advances on credit cards. The Best Western (p239) has an **ATM** (7am-10pm) on the Cirrus network that is open to the public (though it's often out of service). The **Super Tamarindo** (7:30am-9pm) will cash traveler's checks for a fee (and it's a good place for groceries).

Calls can be made from pay phones on the main road and around the rotunda at the southern end of town.

Dangers & Annoyances

Unfortunately, the tourist invasion has left the town grappling with a growing drug problem. Vendors openly ply their wares on the main road by the rotunda and some bars can get rough at closing time when everyone has had a little too much of everything. In conjunction with this, thefts are on the rise. Leave your hotel room locked, make use of room safes, don't leave valuables on the beach and never leave anything in your car.

Activities

HORSEBACK RIDING

Innumerable independent horse owners are available to provide guided beach and hillside riding. Most of these local entrepreneurs station themselves on the beach-side area just south of the Witch's Rock Surf Camp office and solicit passersby. While some of them are honorable and offer good riding experiences, others have overworked-looking horses that are forced to take tourists up and down the beach at a full gallop all day. Choose your horse and your guide carefully.

If you wish to gallop on the beach, make sure that your guide takes you to one of the more abandoned beach areas to the north or south. Too many guides are letting travelers with little or no riding experience gallop full throttle through sunbathers on the main beach area, leaving startled travelers and plenty of horse excrement in their wake. See also tours, p237.

SPORTFISHING

None of the following outfitters have offices so you'll have to book excursions by phone or online.

Capullo Sportfishing (☎ 653 0048, 837 3130; www.capullo.com) Has a 36-foot custom Topaz and a 22-foot Boston Whaler; both inshore and offshore trips are available for half-day (US$275 to US$500) and full-day (US$400 to US$900) charters.

Lone Star Sportfishing (☎ 653 0101; www.lonestarsportfishing.com) Captain Gaylord Townley has a 30-foot Palm Beach boat available for half-day/full-day charters (US$450/750).

Tantrum Sportfishing (☎ 653 0357; www.tamarindofishingcharters.com) Captain Philip Leman has a 26-foot Boca Grande custom sportfisher available for half-day/full-day charters (US$375/600).

SAILING

For sunset and day-long sailing excursions book in advance via phone or online with one of the following outfits:

Captain Brian King (☎ 653 0405, 833 0713; kingfishcr@hotmail.com) Has a panga available for hire for about US$45 per hour.

Mandingo Sailing (☎ 653 0623, 831 8875; www.tamarindosailing.com) A gaff-rigged schooner is available for snorkeling and sunset sails for US$45 to US$65 per person.

Osprey (☎ 653 0162, 835 8500; osprey@racsa.co.cr) A 31-foot Rampage piloted by Captain Brock Menking is available for half-day/full-day charters for US$500/850.

SURFING

Smaller breaks in town are cluttered with beginners from surf academies learning to pop up. More advanced surfers will appreciate the bigger, faster and uncrowded waves at Playas Langosta, Avellana, Negra and Junquillal to the south and Playa Grande to the north. Note that the best months for surfing coincide with the rainy season.

A number of surf schools and surf tour operators line the main stretch of road in Tamarindo. Surf lessons hover at around US$30 for 1½ to two hours and most operators will let you keep the board for a few hours beyond that to practice. All outfits can organize day-long and multiday excursions to popular breaks and almost all rent equipment. Try:

Chica Surf (☎ 827 7884; chicasurfschoolcr@hotmail.com) Specifically created for 'girls who wanna learn to rip.'

Costa Rica Best Tours (☎ 653 0918; besttours@costarricense.cr) Locally owned and operated, it offers the cheapest lessons in town: US$20 for two hours.

Iguana Surf (☎ 653 0148; www.iguanasurf.net) There are two outlets – one on the beach and one in town; surf taxi service to neighboring beaches is available

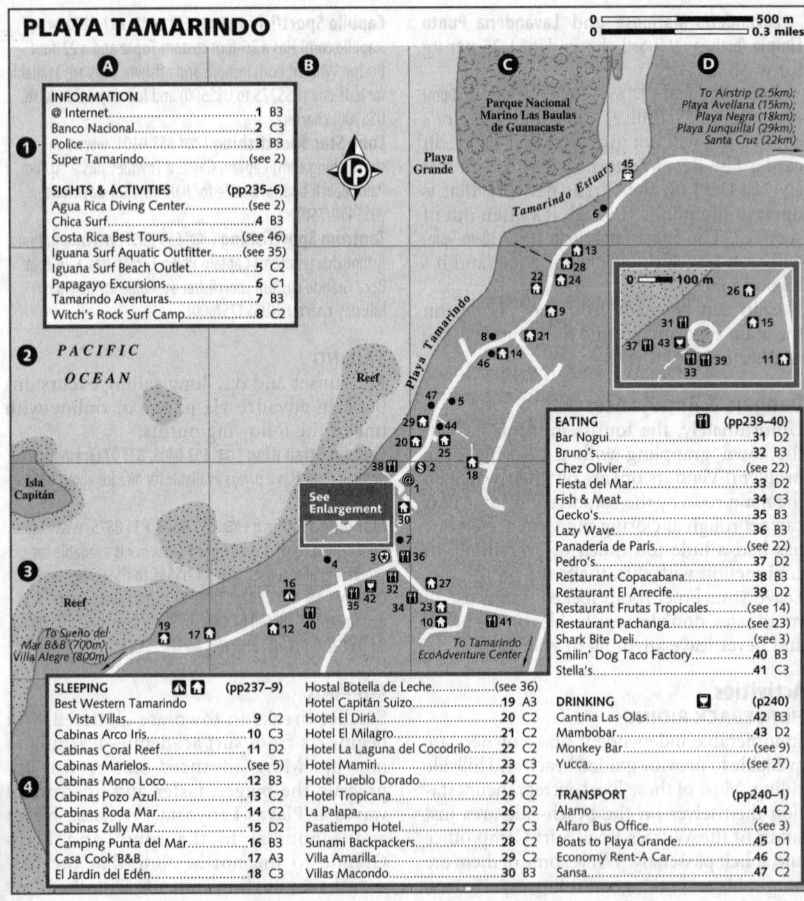

(US$10 per person to Playa Grande, US$25 per person to Playa Negra).

Robert August Surf Shop (☎ 653 0114; rasurfshop@yahoo.com) Based in the Best Western Tamarindo Vista Villas (p239); boards and lessons are available.

Tamarindo Aventuras (☎ 653 0108; www.tamarindoadventures.net) The folks here rent boards, sell gear and give lessons.

Witch's Rock Surf Camp (☎ 653 0239; www.witchsrocksurfcamp.com) Board rentals, surf camps, lessons and regular excursions to Witch's Rock and Ollie's Point (p194) are available; there are beach-side accommodations for surfers who sign up for multiday packages.

OTHER ACTIVITIES

Agua Rica Diving Center (☎ 653 0094; www.aguarica.net), the area's scuba-diving experts offers snorkeling and an assortment of dives, including diving certification classes.

Just outside Tamarindo, near the village of San José de Pinilla, lies a new residential development project that boasts one of the finest **golf** courses in Central America. **Hacienda Pinilla** (☎ 680 7000; www.haciendapinilla.com) has a 7500-yard par 72 course that was designed by noted architect Mike Young. Greens fees are US$105/125 per person during the low/high season and golf carts are available for US$20 per day. Watch out when looking for stray balls, there's a boa living in a swamp near the 9th hole. Call ahead for tee times and directions.

Yoga classes are available at Cabinas Arco Iris (see opposite).

Tours

Boat tours, ATV tours, snorkeling trips and scooter rentals can be arranged through one of the various tour agencies in town. Many also rent equipment. The most reputable ones include the following:

Papagayo Excursions (☎ 653 0254; www.papagayo excursions.com) The longest-running outfitter in town organizes a variety of aquatic and horseback tours, as well as visits to turtle nesting sites.

Tamarindo Aventuras (☎ 653 0108; www.tamarindo adventures.net; scooters US$25 per hr, ATVs US$60 per 4hr, dirt bikes US$34 per 4hr) Also rents water-sports equipment, including kayaks and snorkeling gear.

Tamarindo EcoAdventure Center (☎ 653 0939/26; www.tamarindoecoadventurecenter.com) On the outskirts of town, this center operates a zip line and offers horseback riding and boat excursions.

Sleeping

BUDGET

See the boxed text (p238) for details of Hostal Botella de Leche, the author's choice for budget accommodations.

Cabinas Roda Mar (☎ 653 0109; per person without/with bathroom US$8/10; P) Concrete doubles and triples with private bathroom are spacious and clean, though dark and airless. It's best to spring for the better rooms – its older rooms are rundown and the shared toilets look spent.

Cabinas Pozo Azul (☎ 653 0280; d fan/air-con US$29/48; P) Popular with Tico families, it has 17 basic, large whitewashed rooms on bare grounds. All have private cold-water bathroom, kitchenette and shaded patio, with a choice of fan or air-con. There's a pool.

Cabinas Marielos (☎ 653 0141; d US$30;) Comfortable rooms have firm beds, fan and private bathroom; some cabins have decks facing a garden. Air-con costs US$5 more.

Cabinas Coral Reef (☎ 653 0291; s/d/tr US$7.50/12.50/15; P) The cheapest place in town has reasonably clean though disheveled small, wooden cabins packed full of surfers. Bathrooms are shared and Swedish massage is available.

Sunami Backpackers (☎ 653 0956; s/d US$14.50/19; P) At the northern end of town, spartan units all have private showers with cold water. The rooms are spacious, though musty.

Villa Amarilla (☎ 653 0038; carpen@racsa.co.cr; d US$25, d with bathroom US$40, additional person US$10) This small, French-owned place is right on the beach and features four units with private bathroom, air-con and cable TV as well as three cheaper units with shared hot-water shower. All have a fridge and safe, and share an outdoor kitchen. Credit cards accepted.

Camping Punta del Mar (per person US$3) This basic campground has toilets, showers, water and electricity and it's open all year.

MID-RANGE

The author's choice for this price range is Villas Macondo (see the boxed text on p238).

Cabinas Arco Iris (☎ 653 0330; www.hotelarcoiris.com; d US$45-50; P) A cluster of four pretty, hillside cabinas make up this imaginatively decorated, Italian-owned place. Every unit has a private bathroom (with hot water), fan and fridge and there's a communal open-air kitchen. The hotel offers weekday yoga classes on its shaded deck. The hotel is 500m from the beach.

Hotel Mamiri (☎ 653 0079; www.hotelmamiri.com; d/tr US$35/45; P) This peaceful, charming place has 10 different rooms with walls attractively painted with Indonesian-style motifs. The showers are hot.

Hotel Mono Loco (☎ 653 0238; d with fan/air-con US$35/45;) This recommended place has comfortable, nicely decorated rooms (with private hot-water shower) surrounding an agreeable garden courtyard. The pretty yellow building has a thatched roof. Breakfast service is available.

Hotel La Laguna del Cocodrilo (☎ 653 0255; www.lalagunadelcocodrilo.com; dm US$14, d/tr/q in the back US$40/45/55, d/tr/q upstairs US$50/60/70, d/tr with terrace US$55/65; P) There are rooms of varying sizes, locations and amenities at this pleasant French-run inn. All of the clean, well-kept units have private bathroom with hot water; some face the back, while others have air-con and overlook the grounds or the ocean/estuary. The two bunk rooms that rent as dorms are a good deal. There's a good French Restaurant, Chez Olivier (p240). Credit cards accepted.

La Palapa (☎ 653 0362; www.lapalapa.info; r US$60, apt US$85; P) The entrance might seem crowded and noisy, but the units at this hidden little beachfront hotel are not. Well-appointed cabins (sleeping two or three) and loft-style apartments (sleeping two to four) are beautifully furnished and have ocean views. All units come with private bathroom, hot water, coffee makers, fridge and air-con.

THE AUTHOR'S CHOICE

Budget

Hostal Botella de Leche (☎ 653 0944; www.labotelladeleche.com; per person US$15;) This is, without a doubt, the best place to stay if you're on a budget. Spotless dorm-style rooms and bathrooms are bright and airy. A comfy lounge has a big-screen TV and there's a palatial communal kitchen. The Argentinean owner speaks English, French and Italian. Laundry service is available and there is plenty of space to store surfboards.

Mid-range

Villas Macondo (☎ 653 0812; www.villasmacondo.com; d/tr US$35/40, d/tr with air-con US$50/55; 2-/4-person apt US$80/100, additional person US$5;) Only 200m from the beach, this quiet, German-run establishment is one of the best deals in Tamarindo. Fresh concrete rooms are brightly painted, well kept and come with private solar-heated shower, powerful ceiling fan and furnished deck with hammocks. Apartments are equipped with kitchen, cable TV and air-con. There's a pristine communal kitchen, a pool and the helpful, friendly owners book tours. Credit cards accepted.

Top end

Sueño del Mar B&B (☎ 653 0284; www.sueno-del-mar.com; d standard/honeymoon US$155/195, casita US$170-185;) This memorable place has the air of a Spanish *posada*. There are six rooms in the beautifully decorated house, a honeymoon suite, and two *casitas* (sleeping four). The rooms have four-poster beds, artfully placed crafts, and garden showers. The honeymoon suite has a wraparound window with sea views. A delicious breakfast is included and access to the beach is through a pretty garden. Handcrafted rocking chairs, hammocks and a cozy living room make the setting unforgettable. All tours can be arranged. No children aged under 12 allowed. Credit cards accepted.

Apartments have fully equipped kitchens. Credit cards accepted.

Cabinas Zully Mar (☎ 653 0140, 226 4732; www.tr506.com/zullymar; d/tr US$55/66, d/tr with air-con US$65/78, additional person US$12;) Near the rotunda, this long-standing local favorite has 38 basic, whitewashed rooms with private hot shower and minifridge. The cheaper units come with fan, but can seem a little overpriced. More expensive units have air-con. Credit cards are accepted and the front desk will exchange US dollars (for guests).

Hotel Tropicana (☎ 653 0503/261, www.tropicanacr.com; s/d/tr US$70/80/90, s/d/tr with air-con US$80/90/100;) This large, peaceful hotel has 40 clean, simply decorated rooms, all with fan, writing desk, and private bathroom (with hot water). Most rooms have air-con and there's a garden, a big pool, Jacuzzi, and a tower that provides views of the sea. The restaurant charges US$5 for breakfast. English and Italian are spoken. Credit cards accepted.

Hotel Pueblo Dorado (☎ 653 0008; s/d/tr US$58/70/88;) All the 26 super-clean, bright rooms at this tranquil hotel have air-con, private bathroom and hot water. There's a small pool, and sportfishing and tours can be arranged. Credit cards accepted.

TOP END

See the boxed text (above) for details on Sueño del Mar B&B, the recommended option for this price range.

Villa Alegre B&B (☎ 653 0270; www.villaalegrecostarica.com; r US$140-158, villa US$216,) This quaint beachside B&B has five rooms of various sizes, each lovingly decorated with different themes. All have private bathroom, hot water, air-con and fans. Two larger and more expensive villas have a kitchen and living room as well. There's an honor bar, a comfortable guest living room and plenty of games for children. Bounteous breakfasts (included in the rates) are served on the deck and the friendly owners can make tour arrangements. Two units are wheelchair-accessible; credit cards are accepted.

Casa Cook B&B (☎ 653 0125; www.tamarindo.com/cook; d fan/air-con US$180/190, additional person US$20;) This exquisitely kept little inn in a private house is owned by a hospitable US couple. Four cabinas feature completely equipped kitchens, ceiling fans, and cable TV. A sitting room has foldout couches for extra guests. There's a pool, and a garden leads to the beach, where hammocks hang and body boards are available for guests.

El Jardín del Edén (☎ 653 0137/11; www.jardindeleden.com; s regular/large US$94/117, d US$140, apt US$152, additional adult/child under 12 US$20/15; P ❄ ♿) On a hill overlooking Tamarindo, this luxurious, French-run hotel has 18 beautiful rooms, each with a sitting area and private patio or balcony (and some of Tamarindo's best views). All rooms have fan and air-con, fridge, cable TV, phone, and private bathroom with hot water and hair dryer. All rates include breakfast. There are two apartments (sleeping five) with kitchenette. There's a Jacuzzi, and a nice pool with swim-up bar. All the usual local tours can be arranged, and a professional massage therapist is available. The recommended **restaurant** (mains US$12-25) specializes in French and Italian seafood. Credit cards accepted.

Hotel El Diriá (☎ 653 0031/2, in San José 291 2821, in the USA 510-315 1294; www.eldiria.com; d garden/ocean/premium US$137/158/180; P ❄ ♿) In town next to the beach, this large place was Tamarindo's first luxury hotel and has a faithful clientele. Regular renovations and expansions have kept it in good shape and the grounds are dotted with indigenous art, providing a setting of casual elegance. There are three pools, a Jacuzzi, a good restaurant and bar. The 115 modern rooms with air-con have fan, cable TV, phone and hot-water bathroom. Cheaper units face the garden, while more expensive units provide varying views of the ocean. The helpful staff can make all tour arrangements. Credit cards are accepted.

Pasatiempo Hotel (☎ 653 0096; www.hotelpasatiempo.com; d standard/grande/ste incl breakfast US$81/92/99, additional person US$12; P ❄ ♿) The 16 standard and larger 'grande' rooms have comfortable beds, hot-water bathroom, fan, and air-con. Walls are painted in pastels with murals depicting local beaches, and each room has a little patio with a hammock. Suites have a living room with foldout couch and are good for families. There's a pool, and the popular Yucca bar and restaurant (p240). English is spoken. Credit cards accepted.

Hotel El Milagro (☎ 653 0042; www.elmilagro.com; d with fan/air-con US$88/99, additional person 10 & over/under 10 US$10/5; P ❄ ♿) The 32 bungalows are a bit close together, but each room has its own little patio and private hot shower. There's a small pool, restaurant and bar and all tours can be arranged. Rates include breakfast, and credit cards are accepted.

Best Western Tamarindo Vista Villas (☎ 653 0114; www.tamarindovistavillas.com; d/tr US$104/116, ste US$163-257; P ❄ ♿) Perched up on a hill overlooking the entrance to Tamarindo, this popular surfer outpost has 33 rooms and suites with air-con, phone, cable TV, VCR, coffee maker, and hair dryer. A variety of suites have kitchen, patio or balcony, and living room with foldout futon. Some sleep four, while larger two-bedroom units have two bathrooms and sleep eight. The hotel has an ocean-view pool, the popular Monkey Bar (p240), a dive shop, the Robert August Surf Shop (p236), and a tour desk. Rates include continental breakfast, and credit cards are accepted.

South of the hotel, the road continues about 1km, leading to Playa Langosta.

Hotel Capitán Suizo (☎ 653 0075/353; www.hotelcapitansuizo.com; d with fan/air-con US$146/170, bungalow/apt US$205/462, additional person US$23; P ❄ 💻 ♿) On the beach towards the southern end, this excellent Swiss-run hotel has a cheerful garden and expert staff. There are 22 spacious rooms on two levels; the lower 11 have air-con, and the upper 11 have fan and cooling sea breezes. All units have a minifridge, phone and a terrace or balcony. There are eight larger bungalows with huge sunken bathtub and fan (no air-con) and one four-bedroom apartment that sleeps eight. Rates include breakfast (except the apartment). The free-form pool is right next to the beach and there's an excellent restaurant and bar. Kayak hire, horse riding, surf lessons and massages can all be arranged. Credit cards accepted.

Eating

Panadería de París (in Hotel Laguna del Cocodrilo; pastries US$0.50-1; 🕑 6am-7pm) The breakfast is entrancing at this Parisian-style bakery that serves fresh pastries, croissants and bread.

Restaurant Frutas Tropicales (breakfasts US$2-4) This roadside *soda* is great for cheap breakfasts, including granola (muesli), fruit salads and fresh juices.

Witch's Rock Surf Camp Café (dishes US$4-7) The best snack in town is at this American-run surf camp, where you can order 'nachos as big as your ass' while sucking down cold ones on the outdoor deck until 2am. Sweet!

Smilin' Dog Taco Factory (tacos US$1.75, burritos US$3.25) Mexican foodies will appreciate the offerings at this popular eatery – all easy on the pocket.

Shark Bite Deli (sandwiches US$5; 8am-8pm) This deli has delicious, heaping sandwiches that are perfect for picnics on the beach.

A number of places line the rotunda at the southwestern end of town. **Fiesta del Mar** (dishes US$3.75-12; 24hr) is an attractive place serving good steaks and seafood, as well as plenty of midnight snacks for area revelers. The popular (with gringos) and pricier **Bar Nogui** (dishes US$6-11) offers first-rate sandwiches for lunch, grilled fish and chicken for dinner. Come early for dinner or you'll have to wait. You can't go wrong with the fish in garlic sauce at **Pedro's** (dishes US$5), about 100m behind Nogui on the beach.

Restaurant Arrecife (casados US$4) This is a good place for inexpensive typical Costa Rican food, including good whole fish (US$5) and *arroz con pollo* (US$3.50).

On the main road, the pricier **Restaurant Copacabana** (dishes US$5-10) prepares upscale daily specials, but it's best for a beachside sunset cocktail.

Fish & Meat (dishes from US$12) Can't stomach another night of rice and beans? This delectable place has grilled steaks with mesmerizing garlicky potatoes and incredibly fresh tuna and salmon sushi. Oh, and don't forget the chocolate cake.

Lazy Wave (☎ 653 0737; dinner entrees US$9-15; 11am-11pm) The menu here changes nightly and features a constantly rotating variety of braised meats and fresh seafood. The dining patio is built around a huge tree and at night, the atmosphere is nothing less than excellent. No wonder so many readers recommend it.

Bruno's (pizzas US$5-8) For delicious pizza, this place is tops. Thin-crust pies are baked in an outdoor brick oven.

Gecko's (dishes US$8; 5:30pm-close) Inside the Iguana Surf Aquatic Outfitter complex, this popular and well-reviewed eatery serves a variety of Italian and international plates and is good value.

Stella's (☎ 653 0217; entrees US$7-23; Mon-Sat) This is Tamarindo's most elegant restaurant, with white tablecloths and sparkling glassware in a semi-rustic building. Seafood and Italian are the specialties here, though there are plenty of other choices.

Restaurant Pachanga (☎ 653 0021; entrees US$11-17; 6-10pm Mon-Sat) This mellow little place is a Tamarindo favorite, with a small menu featuring a combination of Mediterranean and Asian specialties.

Chez Olivier (inside Hotel La Laguna del Cocodrilo; dishes US$7-12; 6-11pm) This French establishment serves seafood and meats in a pleasant outdoor dining room. At 5pm daily you can nibble on fine cuisine as the caimans and crocodiles gather in the estuary nearby to have dinner themselves.

Drinking

Yucca, inside Pasatiempo Hotel, has live music jams on Tuesday nights and the nearby Hotel Kalifornia is a good place for a drink.

The wild spot in town is Mambobar, which attracts a dedicated young crowd who are into sex, drugs and rock 'n' roll. Cantina Las Olas is hot for ladies' night on Wednesday, which starts at 9pm and keeps going 'til the break of dawn. The Monkey Bar, inside Best Western Tamarindo Vista Villas, has a mellower ladies' night on Friday evening.

Getting There & Away

AIR

The airstrip is 3km north of town; a hotel bus is usually on hand to pick up arriving passengers or you can take a taxi. NatureAir (one way/round trip US$80/150) has three daily flights to and from San José, while Sansa (US$66/132) has five. **Sansa** (☎ 653 0012) has an office on the main road, and the travel desk at Hotel El Diriá can book trips on NatureAir. The airstrip belongs to the hotel and all passengers must pay a US$3 departure tax to use it.

BUS

Buses from San José (US$5.50, five hours) depart from the Empresas Alfaro office next to the police station (at 3:30am and 5:45am Monday to Saturday, 5:45am and 12:30pm Sunday). Buy tickets well in advance, these buses are crowded.

Catch the following buses at any point on the main road:

Liberia US$1; two hours; depart 5:30am, 9am, 11:30am, 1pm, 2pm & 4:30pm.

PENÍNSULA DE NICOYA

Santa Cruz US$0.70; 1¼ hours; 6am, 9am, noon, 2:30pm & 4:15pm.

CAR & TAXI

If driving to Tamarindo, the better road is from Belén to Huacas and then south. It's also possible to drive from Santa Cruz to 27 de Abril on a paved road and then northwest on a dirt road for 19km to Tamarindo; this route is rougher, though passable to ordinary cars. A taxi from Santa Cruz costs about US$20 and twice that from Liberia.

Getting Around

Boats on the northern end of the beach can be hired to cross the estuary for daytime visits to the beach at Playa Grande. The ride is roughly US$1.25 per person, depending on the number of people.

Many people arrive in rental cars. If you get here by air or bus, you can rent bicycles and dirt bikes from tour operators (see p237). There isn't a gas station, though you can buy expensive gas from drums at the hardware store near the entrance of town. (It's cheaper to fill up in Santa Cruz or at the station in Huacas). Cars are available for rent from the following agencies:

Alamo (☎ 653 0727)
Budget (☎ 653 0756; inside Hotel Zullymar)
Economy Rent-a-Car (☎ 653 0752)

PLAYAS NEGRA & AVELLANA

These popular surfing beaches have some of the best, most consistent waves in the area, made famous in the film *Endless Summer II*. (One part of Avellana is known as 'Pequeño Hawaii' for its fast, hollow breaks.) The beaches begin 15km south of Tamarindo and are reached by a dismal dirt road requiring 4WD at all times of the year. (In the wet season, there are three rivers to cross.) The difficult access keeps the area refreshingly uncrowded. Avellana is a long stretch of white sand and Negra, a few kilometers further south, is a darker beach broken up by rocky outcrops that offers exciting **surfing**.

If you're not coming from Tamarindo, head west on the paved highway from Santa Cruz, through 27 de Abril to Paraíso, then follow signs or ask locals.

Café Playa Negra (☎ 658 8348; 7am-9pm) offers laundry service (US$7 per load), Internet access (US$2.50 per hour) and a small book exchange.

Sleeping & Eating

The following places to stay and eat are very spread out and are listed approximately from north to south.

Cabinas Las Olas (☎ 658 8315; www.cabinaslasolas.co.cr; s/d/tr US$55/65/75; P) On the road from San José de Pinilla into Avellana, this pleasant hotel is set on spacious grounds only 200m from the beach. Ten airy, individual bungalows have shiny woodwork, stone detailing, hot-water showers and private decks. There's a restaurant and a specially built boardwalk leads through the mangroves down to the beach (good for wildlife spotting). Kayaks and surfing gear are for hire.

Cabinas El León (☎ 658 8318; d US$36) About 250m from the beach, the three bright and clean rooms at this popular place come with private hot shower and fan. There's cable TV in the dining area and the Italian owners also speak English.

The shoestring crowd can be found at **Cabinas Gregorios** (☎ 658 8319; per person US$5, camping US$3.75), which has minuscule open-air stalls with shared bathroom (bring repellent) and campsites. **Rancho Iguana Verde** (☎ 658 8310; per person US$10) nearby has six dark, but reasonably clean rooms. Both of these cabinas have *sodas* that serve basic meals.

Lola's on the Beach (pizzas US$7-8) is a simple and beautiful establishment serving fruit juice, pizza and beer all within view of the crashing surf.

More or less between Playas Avellana and Negra, you'll find **Mono Congo Surf Lodge** (☎ 658 8261; www.monocongolodge.com; dinner US$7-18, d with breakfast US$35; P) This large open-air, ranch-style building is surrounded by monkey-filled trees. Polished wood rooms are exquisite and private bathrooms have hot water and Spanish tile. A patio has hammocks and a star-watching deck on the roof provides 360° views of the area. A variety of French/international meals are available from the gourmet kitchen.

In Playa Negra to the south, there are a variety of surfer-oriented places.

Aloha Amigos (☎ 658 8023; per person US$10, d with bathroom US$30, 6-person cabin US$50) has basic rooms that share bathrooms, or more expensive doubles with private bathroom and kitchenette. Meals are available. Next door, **Juanito's Ranchitos** (☎ 658 8038; per person US$25) has basic and clean rooms, free bikes, surfboards and snorkeling equipment.

Hotel Playa Negra (☎ 658 8034; www.playanegra.com; s/d/tr/q US$64/77/88/98; P) On the beach, this charming hotel offers 10 spacious, circular bungalows all painted bright tropical colors. Each cabin has a queen-sized bed, two single beds and a private bathroom with hot water. Tours and rentals are available.

Cabinas Pablo Picasso (☎ 658 8158; per person US$10-20; P) This brightly painted surfer outpost has an assortment of rooms in several price ranges. Upstairs units share a bathroom, while pricier downstairs quarters have their own. There are two apartments, which have kitchenette with fridge as well as air-con. Take on the restaurant's half-kilo 'burger as big as your head.'

For everything else, head to **Café Playa Negra** (☎ 658 8348; 7am-9pm; dishes US$3-6;), a local eatery serving Tico/Peruvian food. There's also a bakery, laundry service and Internet access.

Getting There & Away

There is no public transportation to Avellana or Negra, though surf outfitters in Tamarindo (p235) organize trips. If you want to get there, local driver **Rodolfo Valerín** (☎ 834 4075; per person US$25, minimum 3 people) does the route on a regular basis. He also has a board rack on his roomy 4WD.

PLAYA JUNQUILLAL

This is a 2km-wide, wild beach, with high surf, strong riptides, many tide pools and few people. Ridley turtles nest here, but in smaller numbers than at the refuges. There is barely a village to speak of (the nearest is **Paraíso**, 4km inland), but there are several places to stay.

Sleeping & Eating

The following places are listed in order as you drive in from Paraíso and most are well signed.

Hotel Iguanazul (☎ 658 8124; www.iguanazul.com; s/d/tr US$70/82/94, with ocean view US$82/94/105, with air-con US$94/105/117; P) This brightly painted, friendly hotel is the best in the area. There are 24 clean and cool tiled rooms with garden or ocean views and some have air-con. Amenities include a pool, games room, volleyball, and a restaurant-bar with killer views. The beach is rocky and there are tide pools for exploration. Sportfishing, diving, horseback rides, dolphin tours and other excursions can be arranged and a massage therapist is on-call. All rates include breakfast and credit cards are accepted.

Just south of the Iguanazul, **Camping Los Malinches** (☎ 658 8429; per person US$5) has a pretty campground with toilets, showers, electricity until 9pm and ocean views.

Hotel El Castillo Divertido (☎ 658 8428; www.costarica-adventureholidays.com; d US$35; P) On a hilltop about 500m down the road, you'll find the entrance to this quirky, seven-room inn owned by an affable German/Tica couple. The hotel's rooftop bar has panoramic views – a breezy place to laze in a hammock. Paulo, one of the owners, will play his guitar for guests during sunsets. Tiled rooms are clean and have private hot showers; three have ocean views. Meals are available and it's less than 1km to the beach.

Guacamaya Lodge (☎ 658 8431; www.guacamayalodge.com; s/d US$59/65, villa US$140, apt US$250 per week; P) Next door to El Castillo, this quiet little Swiss-run place has six bungalows with fan and private hot-water bathroom. There's also a two-bedroom villa with a kitchen, and an apartment with balcony views (both sleep four). There's a pool and a good restaurant-bar. The owners speak six languages. Credit cards accepted.

Hotel Tatanka (☎ 658 8426; www.crica.com/tatanka/; d/tr US$45/55; P) Another 500m or so brings you to this simple hotel housing clean rooms (with private bathroom) around a pool. The restaurant serves pizzas from a wood-burning oven in the evenings. Credit cards accepted.

Hotel Hibiscus (☎ 658 8437; d US$40) Almost opposite Hotel Playa Junquillal, this charming Tica/German-run hotel has five spotless rooms with fans surrounding a garden. There's a restaurant serving international cuisine. All rates include breakfast.

El Lugarcito (☎ 658 8436; ellugarcito@racsa.co.cr; d US$50-60; P) This hospitable, Dutch-run three-room B&B has clean, homey rooms in a variety of sizes. The owners will rent snorkeling gear and can arrange horseback and mangrove tours.

Closer to the beach, **Hospedaje El Malinche** (☎ 653 0433; d without/with bathroom US$10/12.50) has very basic rooms that are nothing marvelous, but they're the cheapest around.

On the beach, the somewhat overpriced **Hotel Playa Junquillal** (☎ 653 0432, in the USA 888-666 2322; www.playa-junquillal.com; d US$37.50; P) has dark, basic cabins with fan and hot-water shower. Hammocks and body boards are available and the restaurant-bar is the very popular (especially on Saturday nights).

Playa Junquillal Surf Camp (☎ 658 8089; www.playajunquillalsurfcamp.com; camping per person US$5) Towards the end of the road, a bare bones surf camp has protected tent platforms for camping and outdoor garden showers – and a beach break on its doorstep. Guests can bring their own tents, or you're welcome to string up a hammock and mosquito net and call it a night. There's a communal kitchen and meals are provided with advanced reservation. Santiago, the owner, is an experienced surfer and can provide lessons and excursions to area breaks.

Apart from the hotels, there's nowhere to eat unless you return 4km to the village of Paraíso, where there are a few simple local restaurants, *sodas*, and bars.

Getting There & Away

Buses arrive and depart from in front of Hotel Playa Junquillal. Daily buses to Santa Cruz depart at 5:45am, noon and 4pm.

If you're driving, it's about 16km by paved road from Santa Cruz to 27 de Abril, and another 17km by unpaved road via Paraíso to Junquillal. From Junquillal, you can head south by taking a turnoff about 3km east of Paraíso on a road marked 'Reserva Ostional.' This is for 4WD only and may be impassable in the rainy season. There are no gas stations on the coastal road and there is little traffic, so ask before setting out. It's easier to reach beaches south of Junquillal from Nicoya (p244).

A taxi from Santa Cruz to Junquillal costs about US$25.

SANTA CRUZ

A stop in Santa Cruz provides a local flavor missing from foreign-dominated beach towns. This small *sabanero* (cowboy) town, 57km from Liberia and 25km south of Filadelfia, is on the main peninsular highway and is often an overnight stop for people visiting the peninsula. A paved road leads 16km west to 27 de Abril, from where dirt roads continue to Playa Tamarindo, Playa Junquillal, and other beaches.

About three city blocks in the center of town burned to the ground in a devastating fire in 1993. The **Plaza de Los Mangos**, once a large grassy square with three mango trees, has since been not much more than a vacant lot. However, it is an important landmark. The attractive and shady **Parque Bernabela Ramos**, a new park, has opened 400m south of here. Across from a ruined clock tower, there is a modern **church** with interesting stained-glass windows.

The population of Santa Cruz and the surrounding district is about 17,500.

Information

The **Kion** (southwest corner of the plaza), a K-Mart–style department store, sells English-language newspapers and other sundries. Check email at **Ciberm@nia** (100m north of Parque Ramos). Change money at **Banco de Costa Rica** (☎ 680 3253), three blocks north of Plaza de Los Mangos.

Sights & Events

Nearby villages (see the boxed text, below) are famous as Chorotega pottery centers.

There is a rodeo and fiesta during the second week in January and on July 25 for **Día de Guanacaste** (p457). At these events, you can check out the *sabaneros*, admire prize bulls and drink plenty of beer while listening to ear-popping music.

GUAITIL

An interesting excursion from Santa Cruz is the 12km drive by paved road to the small pottery-making community of Guaitil. Attractive ceramics are made from local clays, using earthy reds, creams and blacks in pre-Columbian Chorotega Indian style. Ceramics are for sale outside the potters' houses in Guaitil and also in San Vicente, 2km beyond Guaitil by unpaved road. If you ask, you can watch part of the potting process.

Get there by taking the main highway toward Nicoya and then following the signed Guaitil road to the left, about 1.5km out of Santa Cruz. This road is lined by yellow corteza amarilla trees and is very attractive in April when all of them are in bloom. There reportedly are local buses from Santa Cruz (p244).

If you don't have time to get to Guaitil, visit the small *déposito* (outlet) selling ceramics on the peninsular highway, about 10km north of Nicoya on the eastern side of the road.

Santa Cruz is considered the folklore center of the region and is home to a long-time marimba group, Los de la Bajura. The group plays traditional *bombas*, a combination of music with funny (and off-color) verses. Keep an eye out for wall postings announcing performances or ask hotel staff.

Sleeping

Any directions that mention the 'plaza' are making reference to Plaza de Los Mangos. All showers are cold.

Pensión Isabel (☎ 680 0173; 400m south & 50m east of the plaza; per person US$5) Bare whitewashed rooms with firm beds come with shared bathroom and a friendly owner.

Hotel Anatolia (☎ 680 0333; 100m west & 200m south of the plaza; d/tr US$7.50/10) Basic, musty, wooden boxes are available at this blue boardinghouse with a restaurant.

Cabinas Permont (☎ 680 0425; s/d US$12.50/18.75, with air-con US$17.50/25; P ❄) On the road out of town to the north, you'll find this friendly place. Very clean, concrete rooms have bathroom and cable TV. This is good value, even if it's a little out of the way.

Hotel La Estancia (☎ 680 0476; 100m west of Plaza; s/d US$13.75/19.75, with air-con US$17.50/27; P ❄) You'll find 16 very clean rooms with fans, TV and private bathroom set around a motor court. The annex, **Estancia del Este** (☎ 680 2115; 50m south of the school; P ❄) has 15 rooms (all with air-con) at the same price.

Hotel La Pampa (☎ 680 4586; 50m west of the plaza; s/d US$20/30, with air-con US$24/36; P ❄) This terracotta-colored building houses 33 simple and clean modern rooms, all with private bathroom and cable TV.

Hotel Diriá (☎ 680 0080/402; hoteldiria@hotmail.com; 500m north of the plaza; s/d US$30/44; P ❄ 🏊) On the northern outskirts of town you'll find this long-standing hotel on the intersection with the peninsular highway. This is the best hotel in town and has a landscaped garden, adult and children's pools, a restaurant and 50 rooms with air-con, private bathroom, cable TV and phone. Credit cards accepted.

Eating

Feast on tasty, inexpensive casados at **La Fábrica de Tortillas** (700m south of the plaza; casados US$2.50; 🕐 6am-6:30pm), also referred to by its official name, Coopetortillas. It's a huge corrugated-metal barn that looks like a factory. Inside are plain, communal wooden tables, and you eat whatever's available – all of it cooked right in front of you in the wood-stove kitchen.

El Milenio (100m west of the plaza; dishes US$3-6) serves colossal portions of fried rice and decent stir-fries. There is blessed air-con and a big-screen TV. **Restaurant Jardín La Luna** (northeast corner of Parque Ramos; 🕐 10am-3pm & 5:30-11pm), dishes up similarly inexpensive portions of Chinese food.

Getting There & Away

Some buses depart from the terminal on the north side of Plaza de Los Mangos.

Liberia (La Pampa) US$0.90; 1½ hours; 16 buses from 5:30am to 7:30pm.
Nicoya (La Pampa) US$0.40; one hour; 17 buses from 6am to 9:30pm.
San José US$5.25; 4¼ hours; Tralapa nine buses from 3am to 5pm; Empresas Alfaro depart 5:30am, 7:30am, 10am, 12:30pm & 3pm. (For Alfaro, buy tickets at the Alfaro office, 200m south of the Plaza, but catch the bus on the main road north of town.)

Other local buses leave from the terminal 400m east of the plaza. The schedules to these destinations seem to fluctuate constantly, so ask around.

Bahía Potrero US$1.50; 1¼ hours; depart 4am, 6am, 9am, 11am, 2:30pm & 7pm.
Playa Brasilito US$1.40; one hour; 4am, 6am, 9am, 11am, 5pm & 7pm.
Playa Flamingo US$1.40; one hour; noon, 2pm & 5pm.
Playa Junquillal 10am, 2:30pm & 5pm.
Playa Tamarindo 4:20am, 5:30am, 8:30am, 10:30am, 1:30pm, 3:30pm & 7pm.

There are supposedly six buses a day to Guaitil, but no one seems to know what time they arrive or depart. You might be better off with a taxi; catch one by Plaza de Los Mangos. A round-trip to Guaitil can be arranged for about US$10 to US$15, depending on how long you decide to stay.

CENTRAL PENINSULA

NICOYA

pop 21,000

Nicoya is a commercial center for the cattle industry and the political capital and transportation hub of the peninsula. Situated 23km south of Santa Cruz, it was named after an indigenous Chorotega chief, who welcomed

Spanish conquistador Gil González Dávila in 1523. (A gesture he no doubt regretted, see p22.) The Chorotegas were the dominant Indian group in the area at the time of the conquest, and many local inhabitants are at least partly of Indian descent.

The town is pleasant to visit and is a good base to visit Parque Nacional Barra Honda (p247), to the east.

Information

For Internet access, head to **Ciber Club** (50m south of Parque Central; per hr US$1; 🕘 9am-9pm Mon-Sat, 1-8pm Sun), which has air-con and roughly a dozen terminals with very good connections.

The main hospital on the peninsula is **Hospital La Anexión** (☎ 685 5066), north of town. For lesser illnesses, visit **Clínica Médica Nicoyana** (☎ 685 5138).

Both **Banco de Costa Rica** (🕘 8:30am-3pm Mon-Fri) and **Banco Popular** (🕘 9am-4:30pm Mon-Fri, 8:15-11:30am Sat) will exchange US dollars. There's a 24-hour **ATH ATM** (A Toda Hora ATM; 100m east & 100m north of Parque Central) that accepts cards on the Cirrus system.

The office of the **Area de Conservación Tempisque** (ACT; ☎ 685 5667; 🕘 8am-4pm Mon-Fri) can help with accommodations and cave exploration at Parque Nacional Barra Honda.

Sights & Events

In Parque Central, a major town landmark is the attractive white colonial **Iglesia de San Blas**, which dates back to the mid-1600s.

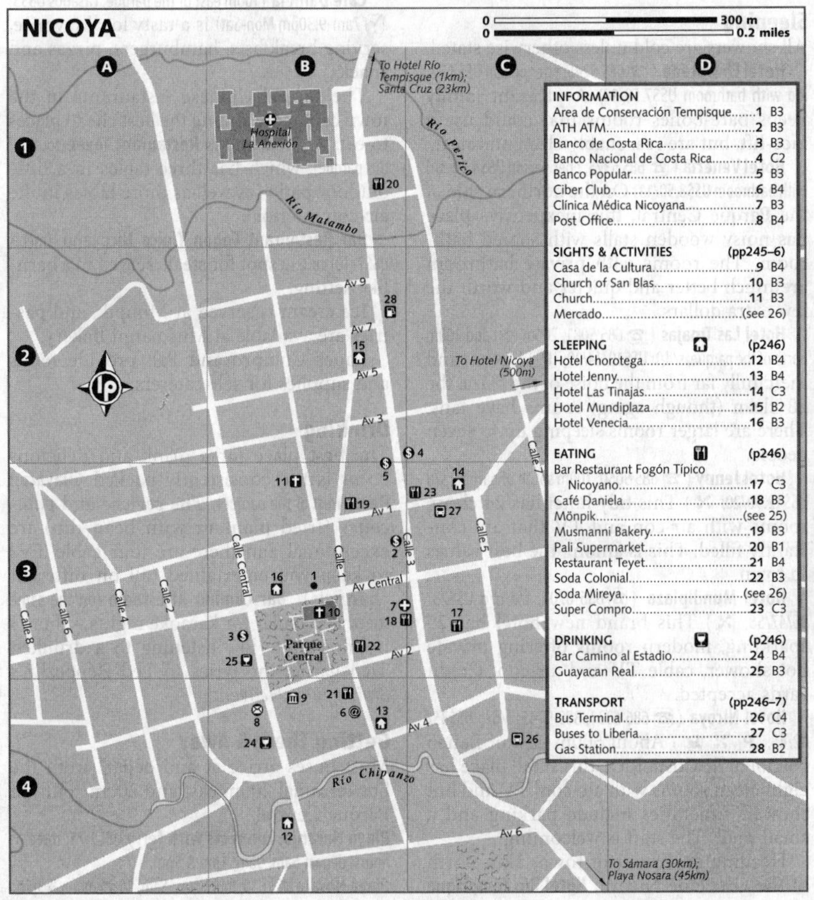

The church, whose mosaic tiles are crumbling, is under continuous restoration, but can be visited. It holds a small collection of colonial religious artifacts and the wooden-beamed church is appealingly peaceful. The park outside is an inviting spot to stroll and people-watch.

On the opposite side of the parque is **La Casa de la Cultura**. This small exhibit area has cultural exhibits a few times a year and features work by local artists. The exhibit schedule and hours of operation are erratic, but it's worth a peek if there doors are open.

The town goes crazy for **Día de Guanacaste**, on July 25, so expect plenty of food, music and beer in the town plaza to celebrate the province's annexation from Nicaragua.

Sleeping

All showers are cold unless otherwise stated.

Hotel Chorotega (☎ 685 5245; r per person US$3.75, s/d with bathroom US$7.50/10) A pleasant family keeps bare-bones rooms that could use a face-lift, but are reasonably clean and neat.

Hotel Venecia (☎ 685 5325; r per person US$4.50, s/d with bathroom US$8.50/11) On the northern side of the Parque Central, this inexpensive place has noisy wooden stalls with shared bathroom. The rooms with private bathroom are much better and quieter and worth the few extra dollars.

Hotel Las Tinajas (☎ 685 5081, 200m east and 100m north of the parque; s/d/tr US$10/14/19; P) Decent and mercifully far from the noise of the plaza, the 28 clean (though aging) rooms have fans. There are larger rooms sleeping up to seven people.

Hotel Jenny (☎ 685 5050; 100m south of parque; s/d US$12.50/20; ❄) This tidy hotel has 24 clean, rooms with air-con and TV that are constantly filled. This is among the best values in town.

Hotel Mundiplaza (☎ 686 6704; s/d/tr/q US$23/35/47/58; ❄) This brand new hotel has 25 sparkling, modern rooms offering private hot shower, cable TV and air-con. Credit cards accepted.

Hotel Nicoya (☎ 686 6331, 389 9745; s/d/q US$35/42/45; P ❄ 🏊) About 500m east of Banco Nacional de Costa Rica, this small place has eight clean rooms with air-con, TV and hot shower. Amenities include parking and a small pool. The staff is welcoming.

Heading north out of town, 1km north of the Cruce de Nicoya, **Hotel Río Tempisque** (☎ 686 6650; d/tr/q US$43/53/60; P ❄ 🏊) is bustling with Tico families enjoying a good getaway. Thirty clean and modern tiled rooms come with private hot shower, air-con, cable TV, minifridge and microwave. It fills up on high-season weekends. Credit cards accepted.

Eating

There are a number of cheap *sodas* in the *mercado* that are good for a cheap eat. The very clean **Soda Mireya** (🕑 from 6:30am) is good for *gallo pinto* or a *tortilla con queso* (tortilla with cheese) while you're waiting for your bus. Another good *soda* is **Soda Colonial** (east side of Parque Central), serving inexpensive dishes with delicious freshly made tortillas.

Café Daniela (100m east of the parque; casados US$3; 🕑 7am-9:30pm Mon-Sat) is a tasty local favorite, serving breakfasts, hamburgers, pizzas and snacks.

The several Chinese restaurants in the town center are among the best cheap places to eat. A good one is **Restaurant Teyet** (south of the parque), which has three tables in a little outdoor patio (as well as more tables in the air-con interior).

Bar Restaurant Fogón Típico Nicoyano (meals US$7-10) is the spot for steak, served in a barn-like setting.

Ice cream is served at Mönpik, and pastries are available at Musmanni Bakery.

Super Compro and Palí provide foods and supplies for self-caterers.

Drinking

The best place for a drink and delicious *bocas* is the consistently packed **Guayacan Real** (west of the parque). The *ceviche* and *patacones* (fried plantain with bean dip) are exceptional and there are four cable TVs to keep you entertained (all on different channels). **Bar Camino Al Estadio** (on the same street) is popular for karaoke nights – there's nothing quite like listening to a drunken Tico garble the lyrics to Led Zeppezlin's *Stairway to Heaven*.

Getting There & Away

Most buses arrive at and depart from the bus terminal 200m east and 200m south of Parque Central.

Playa Naranjo, connects with ferry US$1.75; three hours; depart 5am, 9am, 1pm & 5pm.
Playa Nosara US$1.50; four hours; 5am, 10am, noon & 3pm.

Puntarenas 7:35am & 4:20pm.
Sámara US$1; two hours; 6am, 7:45am, 10am, noon, 2:30pm, 4:20pm, 3:30pm, 6:30pm & 9:45pm.
San José, via Liberia (Empresas Alfaro) US$6; five hours; depart five times daily.
San José, via Río Tempisque bridge US$5.25; 3½ hours; Empresas Alfaro seven buses from 3am to 5:20pm; Tralapa depart 3:20am, 5:20am, 6:50am, 10:45am & 1:45pm.
Santa Ana, for Barra Honda depart 8am, 12:30pm & 3:30pm (there is no bus on Sunday).

Other buses depart from the terminal 100m north and 200m east of the parque. Buses for Santa Cruz, Filadelfia and Liberia depart every 30 minutes from 3:50am to 8:30pm.

For taxis, call **Cootagua** (☎ 686 6490, 686 6590) and **Taxis Unidos de Nicoya** (☎ 686 6857).

PARQUE NACIONAL BARRA HONDA

Located midway between Nicoya and the mouth of the Río Tempisque, this 2295-hectare national park protects a vast underground system of more than 40 caves. A combination of rainfall and erosion has created the caverns, some of which are more than 200m deep. Only 19 of the caves have been explored, so Barra Honda is of special interest to speleologists looking for something new.

The caves come with the requisite cave accoutrement: stalagmites, stalactites, and a host of beautiful formations with intriguing names such as fried eggs, organ, soda straws, popcorn, curtains, columns, pearls, flowers, and shark's teeth. Cave creatures, including bats, sightless salamanders, fish, and a variety of invertebrates, live in the underground system. Pre-Columbian human skeletons have also been discovered.

There are also some hiking options here.

Information

The dry season is the best time for caving. (Though hiking is good any time of year.) In the dry season, carry several liters of water and let the rangers know where you are going. Two German hikers died at Barra Honda in 1993 after getting lost during a 90-minute hike. They had no water, and died of dehydration. Sneakers are necessary if you will be caving.

The **ranger station** (☎ 659 1551; 8am-4pm) in the southwest corner of the park takes the US$6 admission fee and provides information.

Sights & Activities

You can explore caves only on guided tours. Permits can be obtained at least one day in advance from the headquarters of the **Area de Conservación Tempisque** (☎ 685 5667) in Nicoya (p244). A guide charges about US$17 for a group of up to four cavers, US$20 for five to eight people, and US$24 for groups larger than nine. Equipment rental is an additional US$12 per person. The descent involves using ladders and ropes, so you should be reasonably fit.

A guide service is available for hiking the trails within the park and also for descending into the most popular caves. Guides speak Spanish, though a few of the rangers speak some English.

The only cave with regular access to the public is the 62m-deep **La Terciopelo**, which has the most speleothems – calcite figures that rise and fall in the cave's interior; the most well known of these is **El Órgano** which produces several notes when lightly struck. Scientists and other visitors are required to get permits from the park service to enter other caves. These include Santa Ana, the deepest (249m); Trampa (Trap), 110m deep with a vertical 52m drop; Nicoya, where human remains were found; and Pozo Hediondo (Stinkpot), which has a large bat colony.

Caves cannot be entered after 1pm.

Above the ground, the Barra Honda hills have well-marked trails and are covered with the deciduous vegetation of a tropical dry forest. The top of **Cerro Barra Honda** boasts a lookout with a view that takes in the Río Tempisque and Golfo de Nicoya. There are waterfalls (adorned with calcium formations) in the rainy season and animals year-round. Howler and white-faced monkeys, armadillos, coatis, and white-tailed deer are regularly spotted. Striped hog-nosed skunks and anteaters are frequently sighted.

Sleeping & Eating

At the entrance to the park, there is a **camping area** (per person US$2) with bathrooms and showers. There is also a small park-administered area that has three basic dorm-style **cabins** (per person US$12), each with a shower and six beds. Meals can also be prearranged: breakfast (US$1.75), lunch and dinner (US$3). Reserve accommodations and meals through the ACT office in Nicoya or by calling the ranger station. Spanish is necessary.

Getting There & Away

The easiest way to get to the park is from Nicoya. No bus goes directly to the park, however buses to Santa Ana (1km away) will get you close. These leave Nicoya at 8am, 12:30pm and 3:30pm. Return buses leave Santa Ana at 1pm and 6pm. There are no buses on Sunday. The better option is to take a taxi from Nicoya, which will cost about US$10. You can arrange for your driver to pick you up later at a specified time.

If you have your own vehicle, take the peninsular highway south out of Nicoya towards La Mansión and make a left at Tony Zecca's restaurant on the access road leading to Puente La Amistad. From here, continue another 1.5km and make a left on the signed road to Barra Honda. The dirt road will take you to the village of Barra Honda and will then wind to the left for another 6km before ending up at the entrance to the national park. The community of Santa Ana is passed en route. The road is clearly marked and there are several signs along the way indicating the direction of the park. After the village of Barra Honda, the road is unpaved, but in good condition. There is no telling, however, what the next rainy season will do to it, so ask locally before setting out.

If you are coming from Puente La Amistad you will see the access road to Barra Honda signed about 16km after leaving the bridge. From this point, follow the directions listed above.

PUENTE LA AMISTAD

Once crossed exclusively by ferry (car and passenger), the trip over the Río Tempisque has been completely transformed by the recent construction of a brand new 780m bridge, now the largest in Costa Rica (but tiny by US standards). The Puente La Amistad (Bridge of Friendship) was built with Taiwanese financial support and opened in July 2003. There is a small parking area and observation platform on the western side of the river so that you can admire it and take photos (as the locals proudly do).

PLAYA NOSARA

The attractive white-sand beach of Playa Nosara is backed by a pocket of luxuriant vegetation that attracts birds and wildlife. The area has seen little logging, partly because of the nearby wildlife refuge and partly because of real-estate development – an unlikely sounding combination. It also attracts a steady stream of surfers to consistent breaks that supply plenty of power and speed.

The permanent occupants are mainly foreign (especially North American) retirees. The expat community is keen on protecting some of the forest, which makes Nosara an attractive area to live in, and you can see parrots, toucans, armadillos and monkeys just a few meters away from the beach. So far, there's been a reasonable balance between developing the area and preserving enough habitat to support wildlife.

Orientation

The accommodations options are spread out along the coast and a little inland (making a car or a rented bike a bit of a necessity) and are set unobtrusively into the forest.

The village (where you'll find supplies and gas) and the airport are 5km inland from the beach.

There are three distinct beaches here. The southernmost is **Playa Guiones**, a long, calm stretch of white sand with corals and the best snorkeling; **Playa Pelada**, in the middle, is a small crescent with shady trees; **Playa Nosara**, north of the river and hardest to access, has surf. There are many unidentified little roads. This makes it hard to get around if you don't know the place – look for hotel and restaurant signs and ask for help. Also you can log on to **Nosara Travel's website** (www.nosaratravel.com/map.html) for a handy map.

Information

Expensive Internet access is available at **Mini Super Delicias del Mundo** (per hr US$6; 8:45am-1pm & 2:30-6:15pm), on the second access road to Playa Guiones.

Laundry Mat Nosara (9am-1pm & 1-5pm), in a small shopping center west of Café de Paris, has do-it-yourself (US$7 per load) and drop-off service (US$12 per load).

There is no bank or ATM, but the **Super Nosara** (8am-7pm Mon-Sat, 8am-3pm Sun), located 300m west and 400m south of the soccer field, will change US dollars and traveler's checks. This is also a good place to stock up on supplies – and cheaper than anything by the beaches.

The **post office** (7:30am-noon & 1-6pm), **police** (682 0317) and Red Cross are all next to one another on the southeast corner of the soccer field in the village center. There is a public phone by Sodita Vanessa.

By the soccer field in the village, the Dutch-run **Tuanis** (☎ 682 0249; tuanisart@racsa.co.cr) serves as an unofficial tourist information center. It also has bike rentals (US$8 per day), a notice board, local crafts, a book exchange and Internet access.

Paula White at **Nosara Travel** (☎ 682 0070; www.nosaratravel.com) is the local travel agent and can arrange charter flights, book NatureAir tickets and arrange car rentals and hotel reservations.

Activities & Tours

Most hotels and cabinas offer tours or can hook you up with one. The most popular area tour is a visit to **Ostional** (p251) to watch olive ridley turtles nest.

If you enjoy hiking and wildlife, then head to the private **Reserva Biológica Nosara** behind Lagarta Lodge (p251). Trails lead directly from the lodge through the reserve and down to the river (five minutes) and beach (10 minutes). Nonguests can visit the reserve for US$5.

Arrange horseback excursions (US$45 per person) with some fine-looking steeds at **Boca Nosara Tours** (☎ 682 0610; www.holidaynosa.com), also near Lagarta Lodge. The same company also operates Tony's River Tours & Fishing, which can arrange wildlife-watching expeditions on the Río Nosara and Río Montaña in their silent, electric motor boat. The crew can also arrange deep-sea fishing trips.

On the main road into Guiones, past Café de Paris, **Nosara Surf 'n' Sport** (☎ 682 0186; www.nosarasurfshop.com; 7am-6pm) rents ATVs (US$35 to US$50), repairs surfboards and arranges surf lessons and tours.

In the Guiones shopping center, the **Nosara Yoga Institute** (☎ 682 0071; www.nosarayoga.com) offers yoga classes and massage.

Sleeping & Eating

IN THE VILLAGE

The cheapest accommodations are inland, in the village.

Cabinas Chorotega (☎ 827 4142; d without/with bathroom US$12/30; P) This cheapie has a courtyard balcony and clean rooms with fan and tidy shared bathroom. More expensive rooms have private shower and air-con. The hotel can be noisy: the restaurant-bar next door features regular karaoke.

Cabinas Agnnel (☎ 682 0142; per person US$6; P) Just west of the soccer field is a nice quiet row of clean, basic and well-maintained cabins with private cold shower and fan.

Sodita Vanessa (casados US$2.50), on the soccer field, dishes out the standard Tico fare and is popular for breakfast and lunch. **Rancho Tico** (dishes US$3.50-6), to the west, has good Tico specialties and tasty garlic fish.

NEAR THE BEACHES

These places are listed roughly in order as you drive into town from south to north.

Café de Paris (☎ 682 0087; www.cafedeparis.net; d without/with kitchen US$57/81, bungalow US$116, villa US$140, additional person US$10; P) This pleasant hotel is located on the corner of the main road and the first access road that leads to Playa Guiones. Shiny, clean rooms feature plenty of polished woodwork, a private bathroom and air-con. Bungalows accommodate four people, while villas have ocean views and sleep up to six. The bakery-café is perfect for breakfast and an outdoor restaurant has cable TV. Credit cards accepted.

Marlin Bill's (☎ 682 0548; dinners US$8-19; 11am-2:30pm & 6pm-late Mon-Sat) Across the main road, you'll find this popular local bar with a decidedly American menu. Go at lunchtime when the ocean views are fantastic and the prices are lower.

Further down the road and across the street (beyond the Nosara Surf 'n' Sport), you'll see **Hotel Villas Taype** (☎ 682 0333/280; www.villataype.com; d econo/standard US$53/94, bungalow US$135, villa US$140, ste US$152-158; P) This pretty, Spanish hacienda-style hotel has a variety of clean, tiled rooms at a wide range of prices. The cheapest are four econo doubles (with private bathroom and fan) and 12 standard units (with fridge and air-con). Pricier bungalows and villas sleep five or six; suites sleep two and four. There's a restaurant and English and German are spoken. Rates include breakfast and credit cards are accepted.

The road bends to the left as it hits the shore, coming to the **Harbor Reef Lodge** (☎ 682 0059; www.harborreef.com; d US$87, Pelada/Guiones ste US$105/128, casa per wk US$850-1050, additional person US$10; P). Cool tiled rooms have wood detailing and attractive Latin American textiles. Units have private bathroom, air-con, hot water and fridge. Suites are bigger and more expensive ones have full kitchens. There are also two- and three-bedroom *casas* (houses) available for rent. They are pristine and guests can use the hotel's facilities. Credit cards accepted.

On the main road and north of Marlin Bill's is **Giardino Tropicale** (☎ 682 0258; www.giardinotropicale.com; tr standard US$58-76, tr deluxe US$64-82; P). This place has four cool, white-walled cabins of various sizes and views with fan and private hot shower. The pleasant quarters all look out onto a lawn shaded by a huge tree. There's also a rambling, rustic **restaurant** (pizzas US$5, pastas US$7-9) with a wood-burning stove that produces tasty pizzas.

Off the main road, there is a second access road into Guiones that has a few lodging options. On the north side of this intersection on the main road, you'll find **Rancho Congo** (☎ 682 0078; d/tr with breakfast US$30/40;). Here, you'll find two spacious rooms with fan and hot shower. One of the rooms is wheelchair-accessible. German, English, Spanish and French are spoken.

Down the road towards the beach and past the Mini Super Delicias del Mundo is **Blew Dog's Surf Camp** (☎ 682 0080; www.blewdogs.com; dm US$10, d rancho/cabin US$35/45) on the right-hand side. Just a five-minute walk to the beach, this lodge has four small ranchos with a double bed and hot shower, and three larger cabins with two beds and a kitchenette. There's also dorm-style accommodation in the 'flop house,' which has four beds. A restaurant-bar serves American-style food and the Reggae Bar plays a continuous stream of surf videos.

A little further down is **Gilded Iguana Bar & Restaurant** (☎ 682 0259; www.gildediguana.com; d small/big US$53/64, ste US$76-94, additional person US$10; P) This place is popular with fishermen and surfers and has rooms of various sizes and amenities. Tiled units are well furnished and come with private hot shower, fan, coffee maker, fridge and toaster. Fishing charters can be arranged and kayaking, snorkeling and nature tours are offered by the congenial, English-speaking **Joe** (☎ 682 0450). The tasty restaurant will grill your catch for you – and don't miss the incredible dorado in avocado sauce! The bar is a popular gringo hangout. Credit cards accepted.

Casa Romántica y Hotel Casita Romántica (☎ 682 0019; www.hotelcasaromantica.com; d Casa US$70-76, Casita US$82-94; P) Right next to Playa Guiones is this highly recommended lodge made up of two little hotels. Rooms with private bathroom and hot-water shower are spic and span. The Casita has newer, more expensive units with kitchenette. These units accommodate three, four and five people and air-con can be requested for an extra US$10 per night. Friendly Swiss owners Rolf and Angela speak English, German, Italian, and French and run a popular international **restaurant** (entrees US$8-12; Mon-Sat). Wellbeing services (yoga, massage) and tours can be arranged. Rates include breakfast and credit cards are accepted.

Back to the main road, another kilometer of winding turns takes you to a left-hand turnoff for Playa Pelada. Turn right at the fork in the road and you will come to another winding road that leads to several other sleeping and eating options.

The first hotel you'll come across is **Almost Paradise** (☎ 682 0173; www.nosaravacation.de; d incl breakfast US$45; P), which is housed in a vintage wooden building high on a hill overlooking Playa Pelada. The six pleasant rooms have plenty of character and are decorated with Tico crafts. A balcony gives fine ocean views, and there's a good restaurant-bar.

Follow the road all the way down and left and you'll reach the unusual **Hotel Playas Nosara** (☎ 682 0121; d US$70; P). With its whitewashed minaret-style tower, this is the most visible of Nosara's hotels. Situated between Playas Pelada and Guiones, the hotel has existed for over two decades and it's architecture is part *1001 Nights* and part Salvador Dalí painting. (Check out the giant hand looming over the reception desk.) Balconied rooms offer beautiful beach views and there's a restaurant and pool, but the place feels strangely abandoned.

La Luna (11am-11pm; dishes US$9-12) On the beach and to the right of the hotel, you'll find this cool stone building housing this trendy restaurant-bar. The international menu has Asian flourishes and the views (and the cocktails) are intoxicating.

A few hundred meters to the north, on a separate side road, lies ever-popular **Olga's Bar & Restaurant** (casados US$3). This Tico-owned joint whips up cheap, yummy casados and very reasonable fish dinners (US$6).

From Olga's the road continues to the north. Make a left in front of Mariposa

Bakery and follow the road to the left another 200m to the end. **Rancho Suizo Lodge** (☎ 682 0057; www.nosara.ch; s/d/tr US$38/55/87; P) is only a few minutes' walk from Playa Pelada and is run by René and Ruth, a charming Swiss couple. The lodge has 11 pleasant, tiled bungalows with fan, and five larger, newer units, all with private bathroom. Horse and other tours can be arranged on request. Their Piratabar is a popular spot for drinking and beachside barbecues.

Lagarta Lodge (☎ 682 0035; www.lagarta.com; s/d/tr US$70/76/82; P) Further north, a road dead-ends at this seven-room hotel, a recommended choice high on a steep hill above the private 50-hectare Reserva Biológica Nosara. Birding and wildlife spotting is good here – and you can watch from the comfort of the hotel balcony or see many more species if you go on a hike (p249).

Rooms aren't large but have high ceilings, fan, hot shower, and a small private patio or balcony. There's Internet access, a pool and massages, and tours can be arranged. The balcony **restaurant** (breakfast & lunch US$6, dinner US$12) is worth a sunset visit. The menu is a rotating selection of international and Tico specialties. Visa is accepted.

Getting There & Away

AIR

Both Sansa (one way/round trip US$71/142) and NatureAir (one way/round trip US$80/150) have two daily flights to and from San José. The **Sansa office** (☎ 682 0168; 8am-noon & 2-6pm) is just west of the soccer field in the village.

BUS

Local buses depart from the *pulpería* by the soccer field. Traroc departs for Nicoya (US$1.50, four hours) at 5am, 7am, 12:25pm and 3pm.

Empresas Alfaro buses going to San José (US$5.50, seven hours) depart from Sodita Vanessa by the soccer field at 12:30pm.

For US$0.25, any of these buses will drop you off at the beach. To get to Sámara, take any bus out of Nosara and ask the driver to drop you off at *la bomba de Sámara* (Sámara gas station). From there, catch one of the buses traveling from Nicoya to Samara. It's also easy to hitch at this point. (See Hitching, p472, for tips.)

CAR

From Nicoya, a paved road leads towards Playa Sámara. About 5km before Sámara (signed), a windy, bumpy (and in the dry season, dusty) dirt road leads to the village (4WD recommended). It's also possible to continue north (in the dry season), to Ostional, Paraíso and Junquillal, though you'll have to ford rivers. Ask around before trying this road in the rainy season, when the Río Nosara becomes all but impassable.

The nearest gas station is on the paved road leading to Sámara. Otherwise, vendors in Nosara sell gas from drums around town.

TAXI

Clemente (☎ 682 0142) at Cabinas Agnnel (see p249), by the soccer field, has taxi service.

REFUGIO NACIONAL DE FAUNA SILVESTRE OSTIONAL

This coastal refuge includes the beaches of Playa Nosara and Playa Ostional, the mouth of the Río Nosara, and the beachside village of Ostional. The small reserve is 8km long and a few hundred meters wide. The main attraction is the annual nesting of the olive ridley sea turtles, which arrive July to November with a peak from August to October. (This coincides with the rainy season, so bring appropriate gear.) This beach and Playa Nancite in Parque Nacional Santa Rosa (p193) are the most important nesting grounds for these turtles in Costa Rica.

Apart from turtles, there are iguanas, crabs, howler monkeys, coatis, and many birds. Some of the best bird-watching is at the southeastern end of the refuge, near the mouth of the Río Nosara, where there's a small mangrove swamp. The rocky **Punta India** at the northwestern end of the refuge has tide pools that abound with marine life, such as sea anemones, urchins and starfish. Along the beach thousands of almost transparent ghost crabs go about their business, as do the bright red Sally Lightfoot crabs. The vegetation behind the beach is sparse and consists mainly of deciduous trees.

Beware of very strong currents off the beach – it's not suitable for swimming.

Turtle Viewing

The turtles tend to arrive in large groups of hundreds or even thousands. The mass arrivals, or *arribadas*, occur every three or four weeks and last about a week, usually on dark nights preceding a new moon. You can see turtles in lesser numbers almost any night during nesting season.

Coastal residents used to harvest both eggs and turtles indiscriminately, and this made the creation of a protected area essential for the turtles' continued survival. An imaginative conservation plan has allowed the inhabitants of Ostional to continue to harvest eggs from the first laying. Most turtles return to the beach several times to lay new clutches, and earlier eggs frequently become trampled or damaged by later layings. Thus, it seems reasonable that locals harvest the first batches and sell them. Leatherback and green turtles also nest here in smaller numbers.

Many of the upmarket hotels and tour operators in the region offer tours to Ostional during nesting season.

Sleeping & Eating

In the village of Ostional, **Hospedaje Guacamaya** (☎ 682 0430; per person US$4) has several small and dark rooms with shared cold shower. It's likely to be full during turtle-nesting nights. The same folks run the attached *pulpería*, which can sell you basic supplies.

Across the street, **Cabinas Ostional** (☎ 682 0428; r per person US$6) has better rooms with private cold-water shower and a cozy garden.

Rancho Brovilla (☎ 839 2327; d US$81; 🅟) Situated in the hills above the refuge, Brovilla is a more upscale lodging option, complete with shiny-wood guestrooms with private hot-water bathroom. There's a restaurant and bar. All tours can be arranged.

Camping (per person US$3) is permitted behind the centrally located Soda La Plaza, which has a portable toilet available. The *soda* is open for breakfast, lunch and dinner.

Getting There & Away

Ostional village is about 8km northwest of Nosara village. During the dry months, there are two daily buses from Santa Cruz (times change so ask around), but at any time of the year the road could get washed out by rain. Hitching from Nosara is reportedly easy.

If you're driving, plan on taking 4WD as a couple of rivers need to be crossed. From the main road joining Nosara beach and village, turn north just before Supermercado La Paloma. Continue north for about 400m and you will see a pedestrian bridge over the Río Nosara. The river becomes deep in the rainy season, so approach it with respect. (See the boxed text, p471, before driving through rivers.) After the bridge, there's a T-junction; take the right fork and continue 1.2km to another T-junction where you take the left fork. From here, continue on the main road north to Ostional, about 6km away. Drivers arriving at Ostional should slow down; three of the most vicious speed bumps in the country greet you at the entrance to town.

Beyond Ostional, the dirt road continues onto Marbella before arriving in Paraíso, northeast of Junquillal (p242). Ask carefully before attempting this drive and use 4WD.

PLAYA SÁMARA

This beautiful, gentle, white-sand beach is one of Costa Rica's safest and prettiest, and one of the most accessible on the peninsula. Former president Oscar Arias had a vacation house near here, as do many other wealthy Ticos. It's also a favorite beach for tourists and has good bus and air service.

The beach lies about 35km southwest of Nicoya and the paved road leading all the way to the water makes it popular with vacationing Tico families. The village has a few stores and discos and several hotels, restaurants, and bars. Some hotels are on the outskirts, so a rental car or bicycle might be advisable.

Information

Check email at **Tropical Latitude** (☎ 656 0120; 100m east of main road; 🕑 Tue-Sun). Drop the dirty shirts off at the **Lava Ya** (☎ 656 0059; 75m east of the main road, 100m north of beach; 🕑 8am-5pm). The amiable American owner can provide you with information on everything there is to do in town.

An informative website is www.samarabeach.com.

Sights & Activities

The personable Jesse at **Jesse's Samara Beach Gym & Surf School** (☎ 656 0055; whiteagle@racsa.co.cr; 500m east of police station on the beach) has taught wannabe surfers, aged five to 62. If you need a workout, his gym has machines and free weights (US$3 per day). His daughter, Sunrise, does massage.

Next door, visit Jaime at the **Koss Art Gallery** (☎ 656 0284). He frequently displays his richly hued works around his outdoor studio in the high season. Call ahead for a viewing.

The local zip-line adventure is available through **Wingnuts** (☎ 656 0153; US$40) on the eastern outskirts of town off the main paved road. Several kilometers west in Playa Buenavista, the **Flying Crocodile** (☎ 656 8048; www.flying-crocodile.com) offers ultralight flights for US$60.

Ciclo Sámara (☎ 656 0438; adjacent to Soda El Ranchito, 100m west of Cabinas Arenas) rents bicycles – but check their condition carefully before riding off. Rentals are US$2.50 an hour or US$12 per day.

Courses

Next to Marisquería El Dorado (p254) **Centro de Idiomas Intercultura** (☎ 656 0127; www.interculturacostarica.com) has language courses that begin at US$180 a week without homestay.

Tours

Tío Tigre (☎ 656 0098; www.samarabeach.com/ps35.html) and **Carrillo Tours** (☎ 656 0543; www.carrillotours.com), on opposite sides of the street near the Super Sámara, offer all kinds of excursions: snorkeling, dolphin watching, kayaking and horseback riding. In high season they also offer turtle tours to Ostional. The latter company also has an office in Carrillo (p255).

Sleeping

BUDGET

Showers are all cold unless otherwise noted.

Cabinas El Ancla (☎ 656 0254; r per person US$7.50) On the beach on the eastern side of the main road, this budget place is quite reasonable. Woody rooms are simple (though slightly musty) and all have private bathroom (though the water pressure in 2nd-story rooms is nonexistent on busy weekends). There's a mellow bar overlooking the water. Be forewarned that the area is patrolled by a rooster who likes to wake his charges up early.

Cabinas Playa Sámara (☎ 656 0190; per person US$5) Off of the soccer field, this locally popular hotel has reasonably clean lime-green rooms with private bathroom and questionable water pressure. It's a good deal if you don't mind the pounding nightclub next door.

The following two places have the best campgrounds in town.

Bar Restaurant Las Olas (☎ 656 0187; camping per person US$3; d cabin US$15, d thatched hut US$25, additional person US$5) This place is about 200m west of Soda Sherif Rustic on the beach and offers the most unique accommodations in town: one- and two-story thatched indigenous huts with private bathroom. There are no screens, so plan on bugs. It also offers camping and there are several regular cabinas as well. As the name implies, there is a cool bar and restaurant complete with a *foosbal* table.

Bar Restaurant El Lagarto (camping per person US$2) Next door, this beachside place offers camping and a popular bar. The restaurant serves up a nightly barbecue after 6pm.

Cabinas Arenas (☎ 656 0320; per person US$9) On the main drag you'll find this unremarkable, though clean, place. Rooms all come with private bathroom and fan. Rates are based on double occupancy so the owners will only rent to solo travelers if there is plenty of space available.

MID-RANGE & TOP END

Entre Dos Aguas B&B (☎ 656 0641; www.samara.net.ms; d/q incl breakfast US$39/54; P 💻 🏊) This fantastic hilltop inn, on the way into town, is what one reader accurately describes as 'Mercedes Benz accommodations on a Toyota budget.' Seven freshly painted rooms have private stone showers with hot water. There is a well-manicured garden surrounding the pool and there's free Internet access, and bike rental is available (US$5 a day). Laundry service is also available (US$2.50 per load).

Hotel Giada (☎ 656 0132; www.hotelgiada.net; s/d/tr/q incl breakfast US$40/50/60/70; P ❄ 🏊) On the main road down to the beach, the Giada is one of the nicer places in town. Plants and bamboo give it a tropical feel and the 13 large, clean, tiled rooms have private bathroom and hot water. The hotel arranges all local tours, and there's a bar and laundry service. Their restaurant serves OK pizza and pasta and the management speaks Italian, English, and German. Credit cards accepted. Sansa has an office in the lobby.

Hotel Sámara Beach (☎ 656 0218; www.hotelsamarabeach.com; d/tr/q incl breakfast US$85/95/105; P ❄ 🏊) Across the street, this hotel has 20 whitewashed and tiled rooms all with private hot-water shower. A dozen units have air-con and there is a garden with a pool. Credit cards accepted.

Hotel Casa del Mar (☎ 656 0264; www.casadelmarsamara.com; s/d/tr US$35/41/52; d/tr/q with bathroom

PENÍNSULA DE NICOYA

US$58/70/82; P) Just east of the Super Sámara and close to the beach, is this agreeable two-story hotel with 18 spacious, very clean, pleasant rooms with fan. Twelve units have private bathroom while six share. Air-con is available for an extra US$11 per night and there's a Jacuzzi. The French-Canadian owners speak French and English. Continental breakfast is included and credit cards are accepted.

Casa Valeria B&B (656 0511; casavaleria_af@hotmail.com; d US$20-30, bungalows US$40-55) This intimate little place is right on the beach about 100m east of the main road. The rooms and bungalows are of varying size and location and can accommodate two or three people. All have private hot shower and fan and there's a garden for quality hammock time. A communal kitchen is available and the owners can arrange tours.

Hotel Belvedere (656 0213; www.samara-costarica.com; d/tr/q US$52/60/65, d bungalow US$60, additional person US$5; P) Set in a breezy garden with nice views on the northern end, the 10 spotless rooms here all have solar-heated private shower, fan, cable TV and a small terrace; most have air-con. Two larger bungalows include a kitchenette. The German owners also speak English. All rates include breakfast, and credit cards are accepted.

Hotel Mirador de Sámara (656 0044; www.miradordesamara.com; d US$90, additional person US$10; P) Near the center, this blue-and-white place is perched on a hill, and its tall tower looms prominently over the town, offering dizzying views of the area. Five spacious and neatly appointed, airy rooms have private hot shower, fan, kitchen and sleep up to five. Credit cards accepted.

Hotel Fenix (656 0158; fenix@samarabeach.com; d/q US$76/82; P) Near the beach and about 1.5km east of the town center, this charming hotel has six small apartments, each with a kitchenette, hot shower, and a balcony overlooking the pool. English is spoken.

Hotel Las Brisas del Pacífico (656 0250; www.brisas.net; d hill without/with air-con US$82/105, d beach without/with air-con US$99/123; P) Nearby, you'll find this popular place. There's an assortment of 34 rooms on a hill and the beach. All of the clean, tiled units come with private hot shower. There are two pools (one shaped like a clover-leaf) and a restaurant. The hotel rents boats and surfboards and tours can be arranged. Credit cards are accepted.

Eating & Entertainment

Soda Sherif Rustic (west of the post office, on the beach) has fine and filling breakfasts for only US$2.

The best cheap eats in town are at **Cevichera** (11:30am-6:30pm), on the main road, an outdoor restaurant making the most unbelievable Argentinean empanadas (US$1) and Peruvian *ceviche*. Its fresh hot sauce will bring tears (of joy) to your eyes.

El Dorado (pizza US$3-6, meals US$5-10; 2-10pm) This delicious place serves seafood and some of the best pizza in Costa Rica. In addition, the freshly baked, melt-in-your-mouth desserts are not to be missed. Ask the owner to show you his naughty business cards.

Ananas (656 0491; dishes US$2-5; 7am-5pm) Near the entrance to town, this is the place for sandwiches, snacks and ice cream, as well as cakes baked fresh by Tica owner Beatriz.

Bar Restaurant El Lagarto and Bar Restaurant Las Olas (see p253) are recommended for meals as well as lodging. (And are even better for an evening beer.)

Campers can stock up on supplies at the Super Sámara Market, east of the main road.

La Gondola (on the main road; 9am-late) is a fun, late-night nightspot with pool, darts and an unlikely mural of Venice. **Tutti Frutti Discotheque** (on the beach) keeps the music pumping hard most weekends of the year.

Shopping

Numerous vendors sell crafts and handmade jewelry at stands along the main road. Worth a stop is Mama Africa, a unique shop selling beaded leather sandals from Kenya. The Italian owners work directly with a Masai collective that crafts the beautiful sandals and purchases support this work.

Getting There & Away

AIR

The airport is between Playa Sámara and Playa Carrillo (actually closer to the latter) and serves both communities. Sometimes the airport is referred to as Carrillo. Sansa (one way/round trip US$71/142) flies daily to and from San José. It has an office in Hotel Giada (p253).

BUS

Empresas Alfaro has a bus to San José (US$5, five hours) that departs from the main road at 8:45am. There is an added departure at

3pm on Sunday. (The office is located across and down the street from Ananas.)

Traroc buses to Nicoya (US$1, two hours) depart from the *pulpería* by the soccer field at 4:15am, 5:30am, 7am, 8:45am, 11:45am, 1:45pm, 5pm and 6pm.

TAXI

Unofficial taxis regularly gather outside the *pulpería* by the beach. For licensed service, call **Jorge González** (☎ 830 3002). He does trips around the area in his 4WD truck.

PLAYA CARRILLO

This beach begins about 4km southeast of Sámara and is a smaller, quieter, less developed version. With its clean sand, rocky headlands, and curving boulevard of palm trees, Carrillo is a postcard-perfect tropical beach. During holiday periods such as New Year's and Semana Santa (Easter week), the beach has been popular with Tico families who descend from San José and Nicoya to enjoy the sun.

The town is located on a hillside above the beach and attracts a trickle of surfers working their way down the coast as well as schools of American sportsfishermen chasing billfish. The road is paved from Sámara to Carrillo.

Carrillo Tours (see below) offers Internet access for US$3 per hour.

Activities & Tours

Popos (☎ 656 0086; www.poposcostarica.com) offers exciting, well-orchestrated, and reasonably priced kayak tours, including a few designed for families. Prices start at US$55.

Carrillo Tours (☎ 656 0543; www.carrillotours.com; 🕓 8am-7pm), on the road up the hill, organizes snorkeling, dolphin watching, kayaking, horseback riding and trips to Palo Verde (p184).

Sportfishing is the main activity for many foreign travelers to the area. **Kingfisher Sportfishing** (☎ 656 0091; www.costaricabillfishing.com) is a well-known local outfit, offering full-day offshore excursions for US$850. **Kitty Cat Sportfishing** (☎ 656 0170; www.sportfishcarrillo.com) is another reputable operation, with full-day charters at US$750.

Sleeping & Eating

All of the following hotels are situated up on the eastern end of the beach on a hill. The beach is a five- to 10-minute walk down from most of these places.

Casa Pericos (☎ 656 0061; dm US$9, d US$25, camping per person US$5; P) This laid-back place is to the left up the hill. It has four dorm beds and three double rooms with views, private bathroom, and fan. There's a deck with amazing views, a living room, and communal kitchen. The welcoming owners speak German and English and offer surfing, diving and horseback trips.

Cabinas El Colibrí (☎ 656 0656; www.hotelcabinaselcolibri.com; d incl breakfast US$25-35; P) This place, which is Argentine-run, has six tiled cabins with fan, private bathroom and hot water; five come with kitchenette. A **restaurant** (🕓 5pm-midnight) serves traditional Argentinean *parrilladas* (grilled meats).

Hotel Esperanza B&B (☎ 656 0564; www.hotelesperanza.com; d incl breakfast US$48, additional person US$10; P) The brightly painted rooms at this cheerful, recommended B&B have fan and private hot shower, and can accommodate up to five people. The restaurant, **El Ginger** (🕓 5:30-9pm), is popular for fresh fish and banana flambé desserts. The multilingual French Canadian owner can arrange massages and all tours.

Guanamar Beach Resort (☎ 656 0054; www.guanamar.com; d garden/ocean views US$88/111, ste US$187; P ❄ 🏊) On the eastern side of the road, this resort is popular with US sportfishermen. The tiled units have cable TV, phone, air-con and private hot shower. Rates include breakfast, and credit cards are accepted.

Carrillo Club (☎ 656 0316; www.carrilloclub.com; d incl breakfast US$55, apt US$75; P 🏊) This pleasant yellow inn has spectacular views and four well-appointed double rooms with private hot shower and fan. An apartment has a kitchen and sleeps four. There's a pool, spa and group-exercise classes.

At the western end of the beach, you'll find the basic **Camping Mora** (☎ 656 0118; per person adult/child US$2.50/2; P), with showers, bathrooms, electricity and potable water. Just beware of the paralytic dog – she's not a happy camper.

Pizzería Restaurant y Bar El Tucán (dishes US$3-6.50; 🕓 5:30-10:30pm Thu-Tue) This local Italian joint serves pizza and other Italian food. **El Yate** (dishes US$3), at the top of the hill, has arresting views that make the OK seafood taste that much better.

ALONG THE SOUTH COAST BY 4WD

If you are truly adventurous, have a lot of time on your hands and have lots of experience driving in places where there is nary a road, then you might be ready to take on the southern Pacific coast of Península de Nicoya. Make sure, though, that you have a 4WD with a high clearance. Do not attempt this drive during the rainy season.

Cóbano, Mal País, Montezuma and Cabo Blanco are most frequently reached by the road that follows the eastern part of the peninsular coast and connects with the ferry from Puntarenas in Playa Naranjo (p258). However, if you are keen it's possible to take a 4WD from Playa Carrillo (p255) along the southeast coast to Islita, Playa Coyote (p257) and beyond. Don't even *think* of trying to do any of this in a regular car.

Headed south, it's 70km of very rough road from **Playa Carrillo** to the town of **Cóbano**. Allow at least five hours for the trip, provided you encounter no delays. Several rivers have to be forded, including the Río Ora about 5km east of Carrillo. This river is impassable at high tide during the dry season – even to 4WDs; check tide schedules. During the rainy season, it's rarely crossable.

From Coyote, drivers will pass Playas Caletas, Arío, and Manzanillo (camp at any of these places if you're self-sufficient) before heading inland via Río Negro to get to Cóbano, Mal País, Montezuma, and Cabo Blanco. There are hairy river crossings in this stretch, so check with 4WD taxi drivers before setting out. In some cases, the road doesn't cross directly through the river and you'll have to drive up the river a bit to find the egress. In these cases, it is best to walk the river first, double check the egress and then drive in so that you don't plunge your rental car into thigh-deep mud or onto a pile of rocks. Many a rental vehicle has been lost to this stretch of road, so it pays to be cautious (see p471 about driving through rivers). Note that this journey requires driving on the beach (there's no road) and there are no facilities, few villages and few other travelers on the route. The road is unsigned, so getting lost will be part of the deal. Take a jerry can of gas and if you break down, plan on spending some quality time on your own.

For good reason, Costa Rica's tourist office recommends *against* undertaking this journey.

Getting There & Away

Regularly scheduled Sansa flights arrive at the airstrip just northwest of the beach. Some Traroc buses from Nicoya to Sámara continue on to Playa Carrillo; check with the driver first. (See p254, for more detailed information.)

Adolfo Badilla (☎ 390 0681) is the town's one licensed taxi driver. (Call well ahead for longer excursions in the high season. He gets booked up!) Adolfo can do the route from Carrillo to Punta Islita (US$25), Playa San Miguel, Playa Bejuco and San Francisco de Coyote (all three US$60). This may cost more if the roads are flooded and he has to backtrack through the peninsula. During the dry season he also does the little-traveled beach-side route to Mal País and Montezuma (US$140). Add US$5 extra if you plan to depart from Sámara. Prices also fluctuate depending on the number of passengers.

ISLITA AREA

It's possible to continue southeast beyond Playa Carrillo, more or less paralleling the coast, to reach the southeastern tip of the peninsula (see boxed text, above). Although Punta Islita is less than 10km by road southeast of Playa Carrillo, the road is wicked and requires some river crossings that are impossible in the wet season. (During this time, cut back inland and approach the area on a separate dirt road.)

The coast southeast of Playa Carrillo remains one of the most isolated and wonderful stretches on the peninsula. There are various small communities, but accommodations and public transportation are minimal.

Sleeping & Eating

You can **camp** on many of the beaches (without facilities) if you have a vehicle and are self-sufficient. Otherwise, the few hotels are listed in order heading southeast from Playa Carrillo.

Hotel Punta Islita (☎ 661 3324/32, in San José 231 6122; www.hotelpuntaislita.com; d/ste US$228/386, villa US$468-819; P ❄ 💻 🏊) is a luxury resort done right! The hilltop hotel offers 40 elegant rooms with private bathroom, cable TV, air-con, hair dryer, coffee maker, terrace and above all, staggering views. Some of the pricier units have private Jacuzzis overlooking the ocean. A fine **restaurant** (dishes US$8-20) is open to the public and serves a rotating array of specialty *ceviches* and seafood and the dining room is decorated with artifacts from the set of the movie *1492*. The owners can arrange surf lessons, snorkeling, biking, tennis, and boating and fishing excursions. Credit cards accepted.

Most importantly, the hotel has worked hard to integrate the rural community of Islita into its development. It sponsored the construction of a new church and instituted a community arts project. The hotel brought renowned San José artists to work with residents to develop saleable arts and crafts. In addition, artists teamed up with villagers to create a dazzling display of outdoor mosaics, sculptures and murals around Islita, creating an incredible 'outdoor gallery.' The hotel provides maps for a self-guided tour. Small works of art are all for sale in the hotel's shop.

On the crest of a hill about 2km southeast of the hotel, you'll find **Restaurant Mirador Barranquilla** (dishes US$3-5; 11am-10pm Wed-Mon), which provides breathtaking 180° views of Punta Islita and Playas Bejuco and San Miguel. This place is tops for a sunset beer.

Getting There & Away

AIR

NatureAir flies between San José and Punta Islita once daily (one way/round trip US$80/160).

BUS

The closest you can get to Islita by bus is Empresa Arza's two daily buses from San José that go through San Francisco de Coyote, and on to Playa San Miguel and Bejuco. See Playa San Miguel to Playa Coyote, later, for more details. Keep in mind, though, that from Bejuco there is still a long uphill hike to Islita – and hitching is almost impossible due to the lack of traffic.

CAR

To get to Islita and other places southeast of Playa Carrillo. the 'easiest' route (if you're driving), is to head inland from Playa Carrillo through the communities of San Pedro, Soledad (also known as Cangrejal) and then down to Bejuco on the coast. From there, you can head to Islita (to the northwest).

TAXI

Adolfo Badilla in Playa Carrillo does the route from Carrillo to Punta Islita (US$25) and further down the coast. For more details, see opposite.

PLAYA SAN MIGUEL TO PLAYA COYOTE

Playa San Miguel is southeast of Bejuco and offers wide, open and isolated sunbathing, swimming and surfing. This is definitely off the tourist trail and with little to do in the evenings, it offers a tranquil option to some of the crowded tourist beaches to the north and south.

Here you'll find the quirky **Blue Pelican** (☎ 390 7203, 655 8046; www.amtec.co.cr/bluepelican; d US$24; P). A purple wooden house with a pelican carving on the roof, it has doubles with canopy beds, fan and private bathroom. Good food and ice-cold beer are available.

Beyond the Blue Pelican, lies **Azul Plata B&B** (☎ 655 8080; azul-plata@gmx.net; d incl breakfast US$30, studio US$45; P). This homey, German-run inn has five renovated rooms, all with hot shower. A larger studio has a living room and a deck overlooking the ocean.

Hotel Arca de Noé (☎ 655 0065; arcanoe@racsa.co.cr; d incl breakfast US$64, d surfer US$20, additional person US$5; P) Inland from the beach, this pleasant complex has 10 attractive doubles with private hot shower, air-con and fan. Five cheap 'surfer' rooms have bunk beds and cold-water shower – and also include breakfast. There is an Italian restaurant and a bar. Activities can all be arranged.

San Francisco de Coyote, a small village 4km inland from Playa Coyote, is tourist-free and you'll find a few locally popular accommodations in 'town.'

Soda Familiar y Cabinas Rey (☎ 655 1055; s/d/tr/q US$5/10/13/17; P) The family that administers the *soda* offers clean, basic, concrete-and-wood cabinas that sleep up to four. Behind here, **Coyote Online** (per hr US$1.50; 2-6pm Mon, Tue, Thu, Fri) has Internet access.

About one block east, you'll find **Rancho Loma Clara** (☎ 655 1027/68/69; s/d/tr US$6/12/18, large cabina US$29; P), with nine clean rooms with cold shower. One large cabina sleeps eight and has a kitchenette. The attached **restaurant** (casados US$2.50) serves tasty typical dishes. **Bar Francis** (on the corner) offers old-world ambiance, cold beer, plenty of *guaro* and a pool table that looks like it could be carbon-dated.

Getting There & Away

BUS

Empresa Arza has two daily buses from San José that cross the Golfo de Nicoya on the Puntarenas ferry and continue through Jicaral to San Francisco de Coyote, and on to Playa San Miguel and Bejuco. Buses depart San José at 6am and 3pm, pass through San Francisco de Coyote at about 11:30am and 10pm and arrive at Playa San Miguel at noon and 10:30pm. Return buses leave Bejuco at 2am and 12:30pm, pass through Playa San Miguel at around 2:30am and 1pm, and San Francisco de Coyote at 3am and 2pm. This service is sketchy in the rainy season and the trip may take longer if road conditions are bad.

There aren't any other buses to this area from Nicoya or any other peninsular towns. In addition, there is no bus service (because there is barely a road) going south along the coast between Playa Coyote and Mal País. See under Jicaral & Lepanto (below) for details on accessing the southeastern part of the peninsula by public transportation.

CAR

See Islita Area (p256) for details of heading north along the coast from here. See the boxed text, p256, for details on how *possibly* to go further south along the coast.

TAXI

See p256 for details.

SOUTHEASTERN PENINSULA

JICARAL & LEPANTO

From Nicoya, buses travel 72km on a combination paved/dirt road southeast through Jicaral and Lepanto to the car-ferry terminal at Playa Naranjo. From Jicaral, you can get buses to Playas Coyote and San Miguel (above). To travel beyond Playa Naranjo into Paquera and the eastern part of the peninsula, you need your own transportation since all buses either end at the car ferry or cross over to Puntarenas. (Taxis are available to make this journey, see later, or you could do it by taking two ferries, see later.)

In Jicaral, there are a couple of cheap and basic places to stay and eat. Near Lepanto, salt pans are visible from the road. This is a good place to stop and look for waders – you may see roseate spoonbills here.

PLAYA NARANJO

This tiny village is the terminal for the Puntarenas car ferry. It isn't terribly exciting and most travelers just come through here on their way through to Nicoya or Puntarenas.

Sleeping & Eating

A few hotels offer lodging for those waiting for a ferry; they can all arrange horseback or water-based tours.

Hotel El Ancla (☎ 661 3887; d without/with air-con US$25/30; P ❄ 🏊), just 200m from the pier, has nine bright rooms with air-con and outdoor hammocks. There is a pool and a restaurant.

At the dock there are a couple of *sodas*.

Getting There & Away

All transportation is geared to the arrival and departure of the Puntarenas ferry. (Don't worry if either is running late – the other will wait.)

BOAT

The **Coonatramar ferry** (☎ 661 1069; passenger US$1.60, car US$11; 1½ hours) to Puntarenas operates daily at 5:10am, 8:50am, 12:50am, 5pm and 9pm and accommodates both cars and passengers. If traveling by car, get out and buy a ticket at the window, reboard your car and then drive onto the ferry. You must have a ticket before driving on. Show up at least an hour early on holidays and busy weekends as you'll be competing with a whole lot of other drivers to make it on.

BUS

Buses meet the ferry and take passengers to Nicoya (US$1.75, three hours). Departures are at approximately 5:15am, 9am, 1pm, 5pm and 9pm. There are no buses that go southeast from here.

If you're on a budget and want to get to Paquera, cross the Golfo de Nicoya on the car ferry to Puntarenas and then recross the gulf on the Puntarenas–Paquera ferry. Regular buses ride from Paquera to Montezuma.

CAR & TAXI

It is possible to get to Paquera via a scenic, bumpy and steep dirt road that offers some great vistas of Bahía Gigante. For this 4WD is recommended, especially in the rainy season when there are rivers. The only public transportation option is to take a 4WD taxi costing about US$25 depending on the number of passengers and road conditions.

BAHÍA GIGANTE

This isolated bay is about 9km southeast of Playa Naranjo and has a slightly abandoned feel to it. (Ideal if you're looking to *really* get away from it all.) A rental 4WD is recommended; there is no public transportation.

Horseback riding, sportfishing, water skiing and kayaking in the gulf's tranquil waters are the main activities, which the hotels below can arrange.

The well-maintained and newly renovated **Hotel Paradiso** (☎ 641 8193; www.hotelparadisocr.com; r per person incl breakfast US$25; P ✣ 🏊) has clean, brightly painted rooms with air-con and private hot-water shower.

Another 3km south along the road is **Hotel Bahía Luminosa Resort** (☎ 641 0386, www.bahialuminosa.com; d with fan/air-con US$58/64, q US$88; P ✣ 🏊). Overlooking the beach, this place is set on a little hill and has 15 rooms, some of which have been newly renovated. There are hammocks for lounging and a restaurant. Visa is accepted.

ISLANDS NEAR BAHÍA GIGANTE

The waters in and around Bahía Gigante are studded with islands, 10 large enough to be mapped on a 1:200,000 map, and many smaller little rocks and islets that attract a variety of sightseers on kayaks and boats.

The biggest of these islands is the 600-hectare **Isla San Lucas**, which is about 4km northeast of Bahía Gigante and 5km west of Puntarenas. Here lie the remains of one of Latin America's most notorious jails that serves as the basis of Costa Rica's most internationally famous memoir: *La isla de los hombres solos* (available in English as *God was Looking the Other Way*) by José León Sánchez (see p33). Visitors to the island can expect to see the overgrown remains of the prison (closed in 1992) and some of the prison cells, some of which are more than 100 years old. (When taking the ferry to Puntarenas, sit on the right side of the boat for views of the island.)

A few hundred meters off the coast, **Isla Gitana** (shown on most maps as Isla Muertos because of the Indian burial sites found here) is in the middle of Bahía Gigante. The almost 10-hectare island once served as a rustic resort but is now up for sale.

Isla Guayabo and **Islas Negritos** are two protected biological reserves and well-known seabird sanctuaries. For the protection of the birds, no land visitors are allowed except researchers with permission from the park service. The reserves can be approached by boat and you can observe the colonies of frigatebirds and brown boobies from afar. The Paquera ferry is the cheapest way to get fairly close or you can charter a boat.

The best-known island in the area is **Isla Tortuga**, which consists of two uninhabited islands about 5km southwest of Islas Negritos. The islands have beautiful beaches for snorkeling and swimming and can be reached by daily boat tours (see below).

Tours

The most popular tour goes to Isla Tortuga for **snorkeling**, swimming and hiking. These can all be arranged from Paquera (p259), Montezuma (p264), Puntarenas (p275) or Jacó (p283).

The most luxurious excursion is with **Calypso Tours** (☎ in San José 256 2727; www.calypsotours.com). The company transports passengers to the island in a luxurious 70-foot motorized catamaran called the *Manta Raya*. It's all flash with this boat, which has air-con, a couple of outdoor Jacuzzis and an underwater viewing window. Tours start at US$99 per person and include transport from San José via private bus. (Calypso can also arrange the trip from Puntarenas.) The fee includes breakfast, lunch and snacks – all highly regarded culinary affairs. Go midweek to avoid the crowds and bring a towel and sunblock. Fun, but touristy.

Some agencies offer tours of **Isla San Lucas** on demand. Calypso Tours has a sailing excursion that makes a stop at the island (US$150 per person). Otherwise, check with the tour agencies in the towns mentioned above.

PAQUERA

About 25km by road from Playa Naranjo and 4km from the Paquera ferry terminal is the tranquil village of Paquera. Most travelers pass straight through on their way to Montezuma – but a little bit of recent development is giving travelers reason to spend an evening or two here.

Banco Popular (8:15am-4pm), on the side street, can change US dollars and traveler's checks.

On the main road, across from the gas station, you'll find the new **Turismo Curú** (641 0004; luisschutt@hotmail.com; 7am-9pm), operated by the knowledgeable Luis Schutt of the Curú refuge (see later). There's Internet access (US$3 per hour) here and he offers a two-in-one tour that combines a visit to Curú and a snorkeling excursion to Isla Tortuga for US$20 per person. (This good deal alone is reason enough to stay in Paquera.)

Sleeping & Eating

Cabinas & Restaurant Ginana (641 0119; s/d US$8.50/10, d/tr with air-con US$20/30; P) This is the best place in town, offering 28 simple and clean rooms with private bathroom and fan; 20 of these have air-con. There is a pleasant restaurant on-site and management is cordial.

North of the Ginana are **Cabinas Jardín** (641 0003; per person with fan US$7.50, s/d with air-con US$11/16; P). A variety of simple rooms have bunks, single and double beds. The units are clean, and most have private bathroom. The owner is friendly.

Getting There & Away

All transportation is geared to the arrival and departure of the Puntarenas ferry. (Don't worry if either is running late – the other will wait.)

BOAT

Ferry Peninsular (641 0118/515, 661 8282; passenger US$1.60, car US$11; 1 hour) operates daily at 4:30am, 6:30am, 8:30am, 10:30am, 1pm, 2:30pm and 5:30pm and accommodates both cars and passengers. If traveling by car, get out and buy a ticket at the window, reboard your car and then drive onto the ferry. You must have a ticket before driving on. In addition, show up at least an hour early on holidays and busy weekends as you'll be competing with a whole lot of other drivers to make it on.

BUS

Buses meet passengers at the ferry terminal and take them to Paquera, Tambor and Montezuma. The bus can be crowded so try to get off the ferry early to get a seat.

Most travelers take the bus from the terminal directly to Montezuma (US$2.25, two hours). Many taxi drivers will tell you the bus won't come, but this isn't true. There are no northbound buses.

TAXI

Getting several travelers together to share a cab is a good option since the ride will take half as long as the bus. The ride to Montezuma is about US$7 per person and to Mal País it's about US$10 – provided you can get enough people together.

A 4WD taxi to Playa Naranjo costs about US$25.

REFUGIO NACIONAL DE VIDA SILVESTRE CURÚ

This small 84-hectare refuge is a wilderness gem in the largely deforested peninsula. Situated at the eastern end of the peninsula and only 6km south of Paquera, the tiny Curú holds a great variety of habitats and is now part of a larger protected area of almost 1500 hectares.

Day visitors can show up any time during operating hours and pay the US$6 day fee to hike the trails and visit the reserve. In addition, a variety of tours are available – from horseback riding, to kayaking through the estuary to snorkeling and guided hikes.

Seventeen different trails can take you through deciduous and semideciduous forests with large forest trees, mangrove swamps with five different mangrove species, beaches fringed by palm trees, and rocky headlands. The forested areas are the haunts of deer, monkeys, agoutis, and pacas, and three species of cats have been recorded. Iguanas, crabs, lobsters, chitons, shellfish, sea turtles, and other marine creatures can be seen on the beaches and in the tide pools. Birders have recorded more than 232 species of birds on the reserve, but there are probably more. The reserve has three beaches and the snorkeling and swimming are good.

The refuge is privately owned by the Schutts, a Tico family whose roots in the area go back more than 70 years. They have long been active in environmental efforts and were instrumental in having the area designated a wildlife refuge. They are currently working to reintroduce species such as scarlet macaws and spider monkeys to the area.

For visitors who want to stay in the reserve, there is rustic **lodging** (☎ 641 0004; curuturism.com; per person with 3 meals US$30; 🕑 7am-3:30pm) in one of six cabinas. Stays must be arranged in advance through the office in Paquera (opposite). There is no electricity, so take a flashlight and batteries.

The Schutts can arrange transport to the reserve and travel agencies in Montezuma will arrange guided day tours. The entrance to the refuge is clearly signed on the paved road between Paquera and Tambor.

PLAYAS POCHOTE & TAMBOR

These two long beaches are protected by Bahía Ballena, the largest bay on the southeastern peninsula coastline. This is a good spot to spend quiet beach time or to use as a base for hiking in Curú or snorkeling in Isla Tortuga. The beaches are safe for swimming and whales are sometimes sighted in the bay. There isn't much of a town to speak of and the area is comprised primarily of a few resorts and teeny villages on either end.

The beaches begin 14km south of Paquera, at the community of Pochote, and stretch for about 8km southwest to Tambor. They're divided by the narrow and wadable estuary of the Río Pánica.

Sleeping

BUDGET

At the southern end of the bay in the village of Tambor is **Hotel Dos Lagartos** (☎ 683 0236; aulwes@costarica.net; d without/with bathroom US$20/29; Ⓟ). This clean, simple hotel has beach views, a nice restaurant and a garden. Seventeen tidy rooms share clean bathrooms, while five pricier units have private bathroom. Tours can be arranged to nearby areas.

Cabinas Tambor Beach (☎ 683 0057; q US$19) has neat, tiled blue rooms with private bathroom, some of which have hot water. There is a patio with hammocks and a **restaurant** (🕑 6:30am-9pm Mon-Sat) provides inexpensive meals.

Cabinas Cristina (☎ 683 0028; d/tr with shared bathroom US$14.50/20, q with bathroom US$24) has nine simple but spotless, tiled rooms. There's a restaurant and the congenial owners can book tours.

CLAMOR IN TAMBOR

There are times when 'eco' is less than green. Few sites have been better examples of this than Playa Tambor. In 1991 Spanish hotel chain Grupo Barceló began construction on a massive beachside resort on this tranquil bay that was to include 2400 hotel rooms, a golf course and a marina. The following year, Barceló and the regional government overseeing the project were challenged by grass roots groups alleging environmental violations – from the draining of mangrove swamp to the removal of sand and gravel from a nearby riverbed (causing erosion). The hotel chain was ultimately fined the sum of US$14,000 for its actions, which many regard as paltry. But the project proceeded – though the plans were significantly scaled down – and Hotel Barceló Playa Tambor opened its doors to the public in 1992. (Ironically, the hotel's website now touts the resort as ideal for 'nature lovers.')

The small fine outraged Noemi Canet, a Costa Rican biologist who was active in Ascona (Costa Rican Association for the Protection of Wildlife), an organization that helped lead the charge against Barceló. But for her, the main issue shouldn't be one hotel chain's alleged actions, but the compliant attitude of her own government, which opens the door for other developers to do the same thing.

Canet says that a number of things need to improve. For one, all tourism projects should require an environmental impact study conducted by a biologist knowledgeable about the area. In addition, she reports that the permit process is so Byzantine that sometimes it's difficult to know who is in charge of what, much less enforce environmental laws. Unfortunately, groups such as Ascona are fighting a continuing battle – one that pits the influence of money against the interests of local communities. 'This belongs to the people of Costa Rica,' says Canet of the country's natural wonders. 'It's a national treasure – we should start treating it as such.'

As the massive developments at the equally controversial Papagayo Project (p228) develop on the northern Península de Nicoya, it's easy to be skeptical about whether this will happen soon enough.

MID-RANGE & TOP END

Hotel Costa Coral (☎ 683 0105; www.costacoral.com; d without/with air-con US$53/65; P) Ten colorful villas have cable TV, kitchenette, coffee maker, fan, phone and optional air-con. Showers are cold and each room can accommodate up to four people. There's a restaurant and bar. Rates include breakfast, and credit cards are accepted.

Tango Mar Resort (☎ 683 0001; www.tangomar.com; d US$209, ste with ocean-front US$270, villa US$526-1168, additional person US$20; P) This attractive and secluded resort is 3km south of Tambor village. The hotel and adjacent country club have two spring-fed pools, a nine-hole golf course, two tennis courts, a soccer field, two bars and a world-class seafood restaurant, **Cristobal** (dishes US$15-25). Horseback riding, nature trails, a cliffside waterfall, natural pools, and a secluded beach are just some of the attractions. All rates include breakfast, and credit cards are accepted.

Tambor Tropical (☎ 683 0011, in the USA 503-365 2872; www.tambortropical.com; d incl breakfast US$176-205; P) This is one of the newest resorts and offers 10 spacious, shiny wooden rooms in five split-level cabins on the beach. Each room has a fully equipped kitchen, fan, veranda and a large, hot-water bathroom. There's a restaurant and all activities can be arranged. Children aged under 16 are not allowed. Credit cards accepted.

One of the most controversial hotels in the history of Costa Rican tourism is **Hotel Barceló Playa Tambor** (☎ 683 0303; www.barcelo.com; d US$211). See the boxed text, p261.

Most hotels have their own restaurants. There are also some beachfront *sodas*.

Getting There & Away

The airport is just north of the entrance to Hotel Barceló Playa Tambor. Hotels will arrange pickup at the airport for an extra fee. Sansa (one way/round trip US$58/116) and NatureAir (US$66/132) have two daily flights each.

Paquera–Montezuma buses pass through here.

CÓBANO

Though most travelers tend to head straight to Montezuma, Cóbano is the most important community in the far south of the peninsula, with a post office, shops, and other services.

Information

Banco Nacional (☎ 642 0210)
Emergencia 2000 (☎ 642 0630, 683 0338; 24hr)
Gas/service station (☎ 642 0072)

Sleeping & Eating

Villa Grace (☎ 642 0225; per person US$10; P), 50m beyond the Mega Super on the road to Montezuma, has 17 cabinas with private bathroom, some with hot water and kitchenette. All have TV, new tile floors and renovated bathroom.

The most popular restaurant with tourists and locals, is **Restaurant Caoba** (casados US$3.75), which packs in the crowds day and night. There are numerous cheap *sodas*.

Getting There & Away

The beaches are served by the Paquera–Montezuma bus. Buses to Mal País leave at 10:30am and 2:30pm. A 4WD taxi to Montezuma costs US$6.

During the dry season, **Doristur** (☎ 821 6277) books seats on overland transfers by minivan to destinations such as Tamarindo and Sámara for about US$30 to US$45 per person. Also during the dry season it's also possible (though very difficult) to reach Cóbano by 4WD along the south coast from Playa Carrillo. See the boxed text, p256.

MONTEZUMA

This charming village, near the tip of the peninsula is close to Costa Rica's first nature reserve. The town is exceedingly popular with young foreign travelers who enjoy the laid-back atmosphere, fueled partially by the consumption of marijuana. For other nature enthusiasts, the village is also a good base for visiting Reserva Natural Absoluta Cabo Blanco (p269), Isla Tortuga (p259) and the Curú wildlife reserve (p260).

Because of the town's carefree 'hippie' feel, topless and (sometimes) nude sunbathing have become *de rigueur* on some beaches. No one is likely to say anything to you if choose to sunbathe topless, but keep in mind that Ticos are fairly conservative and many residents find the whole scene disrespectful of their town.

On the whole, this is one of the more popular destinations on the coast and its mellow vibe, pretty beaches, cheap hotels and good restaurants tend to hold travelers for longer than they ever intended to stay.

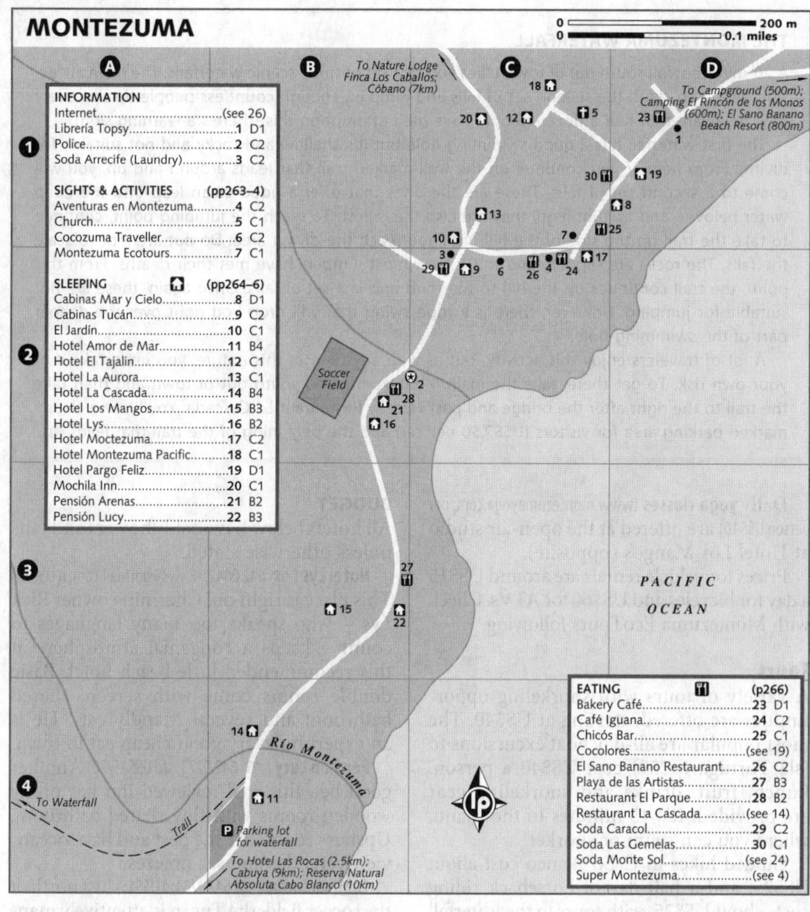

Parking can be a problem so walking is the best way to get around.

Information

Librería Topsy (8am-4pm in high season) has American newspapers and magazines, and a large lending library in several languages. It also serves as the unofficial post service, selling stamps and making regular mail drops at Cóbano's post office. Internet is available at El Sano Banano (p266) and Aventuras en Montezuma (p264) for about US$4 an hour.

Laundry service is available at Soda Arrecife, Soda Caracol and Pensión Lucy, all for about the same price (US$1.50 per kg).

The nearest bank is in Cóbano. For money exchange, CocoZuma Traveller (p264) will take US dollars, euros or traveler's checks (the latter for a fee), while Aventuras en Montezuma will exchange US dollars cash.

A couple of good web resources are www.nicoyapeninsula.com and www.playamontezuma.net.

Activities

Nice **beaches** are strung out along the coast, separated by small rocky headlands and offering great beach-combing and tide-pool studying. The surf is strong and the rip tide is ferocious, so ask the locals for advice before going for a swim and take care. Snorkeling gear and body boards can be hired from tour agencies (following) for about US$10 per day.

THE MONTEZUMA WATERFALL

A 20-minute stroll south out of town takes you to a set of three scenic waterfalls. The main attraction here is to climb the second set of falls and jump in. Though countless people do this every day, be aware that half a dozen people have died attempting this (there's a warning sign).

The first waterfall has a good swimming hole but it's shallow and rocky and not suitable for diving. From here, if you continue on the well-marked trail that leads around and up, you will come to a second set of falls. These are the ones that offer a good clean leap into the deep water below – and at 10m high, they are also the tallest. To reach the jumping point, continue to take the trail up the side of the hill until you reach the diving area. Do *not* attempt to scale the falls. The rocks are slippery and this is how most jumpers have met their deaths. From this point, the trail continues up the hill to the third and last set of falls. Once again, these are not suitable for jumping. However, there is a rope swing that will drop you right over the deeper part of the swimming hole.

A lot of travelers enjoy this activity, but as with anything of this nature, you undertake it at your own risk. To get there, take the main Montezuma road south out of town and then take the trail to the right after the bridge and past Hotel y Restaurant La Cascada. You'll see a clearly marked parking area for visitors (US$2.50 per car) and the beginning of the trail that leads up.

Daily **yoga classes** (www.montezumayoga.com; per person US$10) are offered at the open-air studio at Hotel Los Mangos (opposite).

Prices for vehicle rentals are around US$15 a day for bicycles and US$60 for ATVs. Check with Montezuma EcoTours following.

Tours

A variety of tours with snorkeling opportunities are offered, starting at US$40. The most popular are all-day boat excursions to Isla Tortuga (p259) cost US$40 a person. Lunch, fruit, drinks and snorkeling gear are provided. It's 45 minutes to the island, where you can swim or snorkel.

Guided hikes in Cabo Blanco cost about US$25, and a half-day of horseback riding costs about US$25, with tours to the waterfall offered (see boxed text, p264).

The following agencies are recommended:

Aventuras en Montezuma (☎ 642 0050; avenzuma@racsa.co.cr; 🕑 8am-8pm) Can also book and confirm flights.

CocoZuma Traveller (☎ 642 0911; www.cocozuma.com)

Montezuma EcoTours (☎ 642 0467; www.playamontezuma.net) Check with Deanne about horseback riding; it also runs a shuttle bus to Cabo Blanco (see p266).

Sleeping

The high season gets crowded, especially if you arrive late on Friday when single rooms are scarce. (Still, with so many hotels dotting such a small town, you're bound to find something.) High-season prices are listed throughout.

BUDGET

All hotels below have cold showers and fans unless otherwise stated.

Hotel Lys (☎ 642 0642; ricklys@hotmail.com; d US$15) This place is right on! Charming owner Rick Lys – who speaks too many languages to count – keeps a congenial atmosphere at this recommended little beach hotel. Basic double rooms come with screen, shared bathroom and several friendly cats. He is an expert on every good cheap eat in town.

Pensión Lucy (☎ 642 0273; s/d US$15/20) Another good bet, this well-reviewed inn has pretty wooden rooms with tiny shared bathroom. Upstairs rooms are the best and have ocean-view verandas and sea breezes.

Cabinas Tucán (☎ 642 0284; d US$15) Just north of the soccer field, the Tucán is attentively managed by the crotchety Doña Marta. Rooms are spotless as are the communal showers.

Pensión Arenas (☎ 642 0306; per person US$5) On the beach, it has basic, small rooms with shared bathroom. Upstairs rooms are airier. The service could be better, but the beachside location makes up for it.

Hotel Moctezuma (☎ 642 0058; s/d/tr US$10/20/30) Twenty-one worn-out rooms are spacious and clean and come with private hot or cold shower. Credit cards accepted. The loud (and I mean L-O-U-D) bar next door won't allow for any beauty rest.

Mochila Inn (☎ 642 0030; per person US$10) An amiable owner rents attractive rooms with fridge and gas range. The outdoor toilets offer a thin curtain between you and nature.

(Bring binoculars and watch nature from the throne.) The rooms are on a quiet hillside that requires a mildly challenging walk.

Cabinas Mar y Cielo (☎ 642 0261; d US$30-40) On the beach, the clean rooms here all have fans and views. Upstairs rooms have ocean breezes and some units accommodate up to six. The place is set back from the street; the desk inside Chico's Souvenirs serves as the reception area.

Hotel Pargo Feliz (☎ 642 0064/5; d US$25-30) Next to the recommended Cocolores restaurant, this hotel has eight well-kept rooms with fans on the northern end of town. Upstairs rooms are more expensive.

A 10-minute walk north on the beach leads to a small, shaded **campground** (per person US$1.25) next to a blue house. There are bathrooms and cold showers. Better yet, try the peaceful **Camping El Rincón de Los Monos** (☎ 642 0048; momaya@gmx.ch; per person US$3), 50m further along, which has grills, showers, locks and laundry service; it sells beer and soft drinks.

Camping on the beaches is illegal.

MID-RANGE

Hotel La Aurora (☎ 642 0051; www.playamontezuma.net/aurora.htm; d US$25-50, additional person US$5, house per wk US$250; P ❄) Up on the hill as you come into town is one of Montezuma's first hotels. La Aurora has been around for more than 20 years and the pretty, vine-covered yellow building houses an assortment of 15 clean and pleasant rooms. All of the units come with fan and mosquito net, and others come with varying degrees of cold or hot water and air-con. There's a communal kitchen and plenty of hammocks for chilling. The hotel rents a roomy wooden house on the road leading up to the waterfalls; the house can accommodate up to six people – the price above is for two people and each additional person is charged US$25. Credit cards accepted.

Hotel El Tajalin (☎ 642 0061; www.tajalin.com; d/tr US$58/70; ❄) Fifteen quiet, clean, spacious rooms have polished-wood floors, private hot shower, fan and air-con and some have a fridge. The owners speak English and Italian. Rates include breakfast in the high season and credit cards are accepted.

Hotel Montezuma Pacific (☎ 642 0204; d/tr US$35/40; ❄) Next door you'll find this tranquil place with decent rooms with air-con and hot showers. Decoratively, it's nothing exciting, but the rooms are clean and a good value. Some units have balconies. Credit cards accepted.

El Jardín (☎ 642 0548; www.hoteleljardin.com; d with cold-/hot-water bathrooom US$60/70, with air-con US$80, villa US$120, additional person US$10; ❄ 🏊) Near the entrance to town, this agreeable hotel has 15 shiny wooden cabinas of various sizes, hot water and fan; some have air-con and balcony. Some have stone bathrooms, others have nice ocean views and a villa accommodates four people. Credit cards accepted.

Hotel La Cascada (☎ 642 0056/7; d US$40, per person for 3-5 people US$20) This hotel is situated by the river en route to the waterfalls. The 19 clean rooms come with fan, private bathroom (cold water), and ocean views; some sleep up to five. A 2nd-floor deck has plenty of hammocks for lounging. The Tico management is helpful. Credit cards accepted.

Hotel Los Mangos (☎ 642 0076; www.hotellosmangos.com; d without bathroom US$35, tr bungalow US$82; P 🏊) This is a charming hotel offering double rooms with shared bathroom in the main building and bungalows scattered around the spacious grounds, dotted with mango trees. The brightly painted units have been renovated and come with fan. Each of the wooden bungalows has a private hot shower and a verandah with hammocks.

Hotel Amor de Mar (☎ 642 0262; shoebox@racsa.co.cr; d US$41-88) At the southern end of town, this quiet place has a well-manicured garden and a beautiful shorefront with a tide pool big enough to swim in. There are 11 rooms of varying size and location with cold or hot shower; two units share bathrooms. A 2nd-floor balcony area overlooks the sea and a restaurant serves a Sunday brunch.

El Sano Banano Restaurant (d incl breakfast US$65; ❄) A dozen well-appointed rooms are available for travelers who don't want to hoof it out to the beach resort (see p266). They're all spotless and comfy, but a little dark. All come with private hot shower, cable TV and air-con and some have mountain views.

Around Montezuma

Nature Lodge Finca Los Caballos (☎ 642 0124; www.naturelodge.net; s/d/tr US$73/82/94, d bungalow US$94, additional person US$10; P 🏊) Another 1.5km up the hill you'll find this well-run ranch with great views. There are eight pleasant rooms with private bathroom and patio and one two-bedroom bungalow. The Canadian owner prides herself on having some the best-looked-after horses in the area. Apart from riding, you can rent bikes, arrange tours or splash around the infinity pool. There's a restaurant.

Hotel Las Rocas (☎ 642 0393; d US$30, d apt US$50, additional person US$10; P) About 2.5km south of Montezuma on the road to Cabuya, this simple, quiet spot near rocky tide pools has a few basic doubles with shared bathroom, mosquito net and nice ocean breezes. Rustic one-bedroom apartments have private bathroom, kitchen, a terrace with hammocks and a little garden. There are free bikes, body boards and snorkeling gear for guests to use. Visa is accepted.

El Sano Banano Beach Resort (☎ 642 0638; www.elbanano.com; d standard/ste US$105/130, bungalow US$150-180, additional adult/child 6-12 US$25/15, child under 6 free;) About a 15-minute walk north of town along the beach (past El Rincón del Los Monos), you'll find this resort. (You can't drive to it; they'll bring your baggage for you.) Here you'll find 14 quiet, beautifully appointed rooms and polygonal bungalows with private hot shower, fan and fridge. Suites have lofts with views of the ocean and four have kitchenette. Rates include breakfast and dinner, and credit cards are accepted.

Eating & Drinking

The best cheap eat in town is **Soda Las Gemelas** (casados US$3), where you can get a heaping and delicious fish casado and good *batidos* (fruit shakes). **Restaurant El Parque**, on the beach, also has reasonable seafood dishes at similar prices. **Soda Monte Sol** (breakfast US$2) has bountiful traditional and American breakfasts.

Café Iguana (sandwiches US$4-5) Next door, this cheerful place has good cappuccinos, sandwiches and fresh juices.

Bakery Café (banana bread US$1, French toast US$2.50) Has a great outdoor patio and scrumptious baked goods. The banana bread and French toast are exceptional. Pack the tasty homemade whole-grain bread for picnics and long ferry rides.

Other places that serve good meals include **Restaurant La Cascada** (dishes US$4-8), pleasantly located next to a stream. The restaurant specializes in Tico specialties and a 2nd-story bar with superlative views is on the way.

Playa de las Artistas (entrees US$8-10; 10:30am-10:30pm) This artfully decorated beachside restaurant has received positive local reviews. The brief international/Mediterranean menu is constantly changing, though you can always count on fresh seafood.

Soda Caracol (pizza US$3-5, pasta US$5-6; 5pm-late) This unassuming *soda* serves up some of the tastiest fresh pastas and pizzas on the peninsula. Vegetarians will welcome the delicious lasagna and don't miss the garlic bruschetta.

El Sano Banano (☎ 642 0638; dishes US$5-12) This restaurant has a multipage menu that offers everything from yogurt to stir-fry to vegetarian specialties, though some travelers report that the food isn't all that great. The restaurant shows nightly films for US$5 minimum consumption.

Cocolores (☎ 642 0348; dishes US$5-12; 2-9:30pm) This pleasant patio restaurant offers candlelit dinners and heaping portions of French-influenced cuisine.

Self-caterers should head on over to the Super Montezuma for fresh food.

Chico's Bar (in the centre of town) is the spot for a drink. You can have drinks in one of their two bars – one on the street and one under a thatched rancho closer to the beach.

Getting There & Away

BOAT

There is a regular boat service to Jacó, which takes one hour and costs US$30 (minimum of four people). Boats usually depart between 8am and 9:30am, but this may be affected by the tides and weather. Make reservations at any of the tourist agencies in town.

BUS

Buses depart Montezuma from in front of Café Iguana. Buy tickets directly from the bus driver. Buses to Cabo Blanco (US$1.20) depart at 8am, 9:50am, 2:10pm and 6:30pm. Montezuma EcoTours has a shuttle service at 8am and 9.30am. Buses to Paquera (connecting with the Puntarenas ferry, US$2.25, two hours) depart at 5:30am, 8am, 10am, noon, 2pm and 4pm.

CAR & TAXI

During the rainy season, the stretch of road between Cóbano and Montezuma is likely to require 4WD. Colectivo taxis between the two towns cost US$6 and can take up to five people. A 4WD taxi from Montezuma to Paquera will cost about US$30, to Cabo

Blanco about US$12, and to Mal País or Tambor airport about US$25. There aren't many taxis around; but you can reserve one at Aventuras en Montezuma (p264) or with licensed driver **Luis Delgado** (☎ 825 6008). His wife and daughters run Soda Las Gemelas and they can phone him for you.

MINIVAN

During the dry season, many travel agencies offer overland transfers by minivan to destinations such as Tamarindo and Sámara (saving at least one day of travel). Departures depend on demand and road conditions, but can cost US$30 to US$45 per person. Check with any of the travel agencies in Montezuma or with **Doristur** (☎ 821 6277) in Cóbano.

MAL PAÍS & SANTA TERESA

The road from Cóbano meets the beach road next to Frank's Place (see below) on the western side of the peninsula. To the left lies Mal País (south) and to the right, the road continues another 6km north through the area known as Santa Teresa.

The coastal strip begins just 4km north of Cabo Blanco and is increasingly popular with surfers and vacationers who want to get away from it all. The Mal País end of the beach is rockier, emptier, and good for tide-pool exploration; the Santa Teresa end is sandier and better for **surfing**. There is no town; the area is just a loose straggle of lodges and hotels and a few remaining local residences.

Information

Tuanis (☎ 640 0370; 2km north of Frank's) has Internet access, various gifts and sundries, and can help book taxi service around the area.

Super Santa Teresa (300m north of Frank's place), on the road to Santa Teresa, will change cash US dollars and traveler's checks.

Just west of Frank's, **Surf Shop Malpaís** (☎ 640 0173) rents and fixes boards.

A useful website is www.malpais.net.

Sleeping & Eating

MAL PAÍS

Frank's Place (☎ 640 0096; www.frankplace.com; per person US$12, d/tr US$28/54; P) This popular place serves as the local surf outpost. The helpful owners have information on local tours and activities and there's a patio **restaurant** (casados US$4) with cable TV. Roomy, tiled-floor cabinas are all well kept. Cheaper units share bathrooms, while more expensive doubles have private bathroom and triples have kitchenette. There are plenty of hammocks for lounging.

On the road that leads down to the beach from Frank's, you'll pass Surf Shop Malpaís, followed by **Playa Carmen restaurant** (pizzas US$3-8) a locally recommended eatery dishing up a good variety of pizza and pasta.

You'll find all of the following places heading south into Mal País; all distances are in relation to Frank's Place.

Ritmo Tropical (☎ 640 0174; ritmo.malpais.net; 100m south; d US$50; P) The six bright, white and well-kept cabinas with private hot-water bathroom are a good deal. A restaurant serves Tico-Italian food. Credit cards accepted.

The Place (☎ 640 0001; www.theplacemalpais.com; 200m south; d US$69-81, additional person US$10; P) Beautiful, airy cabins of various sizes are modeled on African, Asian, and Mediterranean motifs. Quarters have private hot showers and the restaurant serves Mediterranean-style seafood by candlelight in the evenings. The Swiss owners are multilingual and can arrange surfing lessons and tours.

Malpaís Surf Camp & Resort (☎ 640 0061; www.malpaissurfcamp.com; 500m south; d/q bunk US$25/35, d villa US$65, additional person US$10; camping per person US$7; P) This great lodge has cozy (read: small) bunks in spotless rooms. Larger bungalows are immaculate and nicely decorated; some sleep up to five. There is a restaurant-bar that keeps the surfer dudes coming back for more – it must be the pool, satellite TV and surf videos. Horseback riding and other tours can be arranged.

Blue Jay Lodge (☎ 640 0089; www.bluejaylodgecostarica.com; 1km south; d incl breakfast US$80, additional person US$20; P) This traveler-recommended Tico-owned lodge has seven stunning private bamboo bungalows, each with huge, screened half-walls (protected with an awning), a fan, hot shower, two beds, and a large veranda with a view. Some bungalows are high in the forest and require a short walk. There is a restaurant and bar and guided tours in Spanish, French, and English are available. Credit cards accepted.

Cabinas Bosque Mar (☎ 640 0074; bosquemar@racsa.co.cr; 1.5km south; q US$36; P) It has a very friendly Tico owner and large, shining rooms, some with kitchenette. There's also a pool and a restaurant. This is good value.

Mary's (about 2km south; dishes US$5-8; 5-10pm) Just before the road to Cabuya, this locally owned café serves good pizza and plenty of seafood specialties.

Star Mountain Eco Resort (640 0102; www.starmountaineco.com; 5.5km south; s/d incl breakfast US$65/75, additional person US$20; P) This place is off the rough road (4WD only) between Mal País and Cabuya, alongside the Cabo Blanco reserve (follow the signs). The small lodge was built without cutting down trees and the forest abounds with wildlife. The property is half forested and half old pasture and has trails with good birding and a viewpoint overlooking both sides of the peninsula. There are four hillside rooms, each painted in cool tropical pastels. The multilingual Belgian managers will prepare excellent dinners on request for US$15 per person.

SANTA TERESA

The following are described by their distance north of Frank's.

Tropico Latino Lodge (640 0036; www.tropico.malpais.net; 800m north; d without/with ocean view US$85/95; P) The beautifully decorated and roomy wooden bungalows are painted in bright colors and come with air-con, king-size bed, fan and private hot-water bathroom. Each unit also has a patio with hammocks. There's a dreamy pool right next to the beach and a surfside **restaurant** (dishes US$4-8) serves Italian food. Tours can be arranged.

Rancho Itáuna (640 0095; www.malpais.net; 1.6km north; q without/with kitchen US$50/60; P) Rooms in this bright yellow structure are in one of two octagonal towers and each of them come with a double bed, a bunk bed, private hot shower and a fridge. The rooms are meticulously maintained and some have kitchenette. A good **restaurant** (dishes US$5-7) serves Brazilian food and barbecue.

Funky Monkey (640 0317; www.funky-monkey-lodge.com; 2km north; q US$40; 4-/8-person bungalow US$65/110; P) Up the hill from Tuanis, this new well-recommended lodge has attractive rustic-style rooms and well-finished bungalows that sleep four or eight. Bungalows built out of bamboo have garden showers and ample decks with hammocks and views. Smaller, more basic rooms have four beds each. A popular **sushi restaurant** (rolls US$4.25-8) packs in the crowds with good raw fish and excellent sunsets.

Cabinas & Restaurant Santa Teresa (640 0137; 2.8km; cabin US$25-30; P) This place has nine sherbet-colored, tiled cabins, each sleeping two or four and some with kitchenette. All have private bathroom.

Cecilia's B&B (640 0115, in the USA 619-224 1238; www.casacecilia.com; 3.6km north; d incl breakfast US$70; P) Under new American ownership, this spotless little house has four pleasant, simple rooms with private hot-water shower and fan. Hammocks are strung on palm trees on the beach for maximum relaxation.

On the beach, **Roca Mar** (3.8km north; per person US$3; P) and **Paraíso Azul** (per person US$2.50; P) both offer camping and shared bathrooms with cold showers.

Milarepa (640 0023; www.milarepahotel.com; 4.1km north; d US$116-140; P) This beachfront hotel has elegant, spacious, bamboo-and-wood bungalows with Indonesian teak furniture. Bathrooms are private and have garden showers. The French owners run a good **restaurant** (mains US$6) serving southern French cuisine.

Hotel Flor Blanca (640 0232; www.florblanca.com; 4km north; 1-/2-bedroom villa incl breakfast US$339-573; P) This intimate and luxurious hotel is nothing less than marvelous. Ten large and romantic villas with air-con have been scattered around three hectares of land next to a pristine white-sand beach. About half of the villas have ocean views (US$50 extra) and all units boast garden showers with roomy sunken tubs. Yoga and Pilates classes are offered as well as guided tours. Its restaurant, **Nectar** (dishes US$7-19), is open to the public and serves up a fusion menu that includes many vegetarian, seafood and meat specialties. Credit cards accepted.

Getting There & Away

From Mal País, there's a bus to Cóbano at 7am. From Santa Teresa there are buses at 6:45am and 11am. A taxi to these areas from Cóbano costs about US$18, depending on road conditions.

CABUYA

This tiny village is about 9km south of Montezuma and 2km north of Cabo Blanco. An interesting feature is the local **cemetery**, on Isla Cabuya, just to the southeast. The cemetery can be reached only at low tide because the (otherwise uninhabited) island is cut off from the mainland at high tide.

Ancla de Oro (☎ 642 0369; www.caboblancopark.com/ancla/; d US$20-25, cabin with kitchen US$35-45; Ⓟ) is one of the original places to stay in the area. There are simple thatched-roof huts in a pleasant garden and rooms inside the house. The restaurant serves seafood, and the owners arrange boat, horse, and vehicle tours to local sites of interest.

Hotel Cabo Blanco (☎ 642 0332; www.playamontezuma.net/caboblanco.htm; r with fan/air-con US$35/50; Ⓟ), close to the national park, is a pretty hotel that has nice rooms with private bathroom, TV and the option of fan or air-con. There's a nice bar and restaurant.

Hotel Celaje (☎ 642 0374; celaje@racsa.co.cr; s/d/tr incl breakfast US$35/45/55; Ⓟ), near the park, has rooms with air-con, a pool and a restaurant. The owners can book tours.

For everything else, make a pit stop at **Café Coyote** (dishes US$5-6). The owners serve up pizza, seafood and veggie meals, and they offer Internet access.

RESERVA NATURAL ABSOLUTA CABO BLANCO

Situated on the southeastern tip of Península de Nicoya, this is Costa Rica's oldest protected wilderness area. Cabo Blanco is about 11km south of Montezuma by dirt road, and features an evergreen forest, fine **beaches** and a host of birds and animals among its attractions. The park was originally established by a Scandinavian couple, the late Karen Morgenson and Olof Wessberg, who donated it to Costa Rica several years before a park system had even been created.

The reserve encompasses 1272 hectares of land and 1700 hectares of surrounding ocean and includes the entire southern tip of the Península de Nicoya. Until the late 1980s, Cabo Blanco was called an 'absolute' nature reserve, because no visitors were permitted. Even though the name has remained, now there are trails and visits are allowed, but the reserve remains closed on Mondays and Tuesdays to minimize impact.

Information

Just inside the park, south of Cabuya, is a **ranger station** (☎ 642 0093; admission US$8; 8am-4pm Wed-Sun) with trail maps. Camping is not permitted, and no food or drink is available. Bring water and snacks.

The average annual temperature is about 27°C and annual rainfall is some 2300mm at the tip of the park. The easiest months for visits are from December to April – the dry season.

Activities

WILDLIFE WATCHING

The reserve preserves an evergreen forest, a couple of attractive beaches, and a host of birds and animals. Monkeys, squirrels, sloths, deer, agoutis, and raccoons are among the more common sightings. Armadillos, coatis, peccaries, and anteaters are also present.

The coastal area is known as an important nesting site for the brown booby. Some nest on the mainland, but most are found on **Isla Cabo Blanco**, 1.6km south of the mainland. The island supposedly gains its name (meaning 'white cape') from the guano encrusting the rocks. Other seabirds in the area include brown pelicans and magnificent frigatebirds. The beaches at the tip of the peninsula abound with the usual marine life – starfish, sea anemones, sea urchins, conchs, lobsters, crabs, and tropical fish are a few of the things to look for.

HIKING

A trail (4.5km) leads from the ranger station to the beaches at the tip of the peninsula. The hike takes two hours, and passes through lush forest before emerging at the coast. Travelers report that this trail, which is clearly marked, can get very muddy, making for a long and difficult walk. You can visit two beaches at the peninsula tip and then return by a different trail. The high point of the reserve is 375m, and parts of the trail are steep and strenuous.

Check with park rangers about trail conditions and tides. The trail joining the two beaches at the tip of the reserve may be impassable at high tide.

Getting There & Away

Buses depart from the park entrance for Montezuma at 7:10am, 9:10am, 1:10pm and 4:10pm. **Montezuma EcoTours** (☎ 642 0467), has a twice-daily shuttle (US$1.25 per person) departing for Montezuma at 8am and also 9:30am.

A 4WD taxi (for six passengers) from Montezuma to the park costs about US$12. You can pre-arrange for a pickup if you so desire.

Central Pacific Coast

CONTENTS

Small coastal villages, palm-oil plantations and well-developed resort towns clutter this stretch of coastline. Surfing, sunbathing and sportfishing are the main attractions, though many travelers come to enjoy the wildlife. Rare scarlet macaws can be seen inside Parque Nacional Carara, and the appealing beaches inside the national park at Manuel Antonio further south invite swimming and snorkeling. Bounteous bars assure that all visitors remain well lubricated.

Paved roads leading west all the way from San José to Puntarenas and then due south make this area easy to get to. This also means that the region can occasionally suffer from an overdose of tourists – though thankfully some tranquil pockets remain.

There are marked wet and dry seasons along this coast. The rains begin in April, and you can expect regular precipitation from May to November, with September and October being the rainiest months. The wet eases in December, and the dry season continues through April. The dry season, naturally, is the high season and rates for this season have been given throughout. Reservations are recommended for this time but become absolutely essential for Easter and the week between Christmas and New Year's. Travelers who venture here during the off-season will be rewarded with low-season rates at some hotels that can represent savings of up to 50%. Average temperatures on the coast, year-round, range from about 22°C to about 32°C.

HIGHLIGHTS

- Watching squirrel monkey troops hustle around **Parque Nacional Manuel Antonio** (p303)
- Surfing the breaks at **Playa Hermosa** (p289) and **Dominical** (p307)
- Clambering up the canopy platform to admire wildlife and the views at **Hacienda Barú** (p306)
- Taking a tranquil dip at the quiet beach at **Matapalo** (p305)
- Appreciating the culinary delights of an iguana burger at **Iguana Park** (p278)

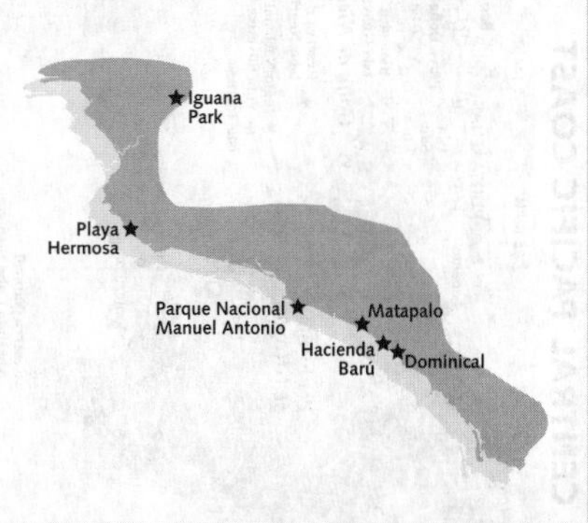

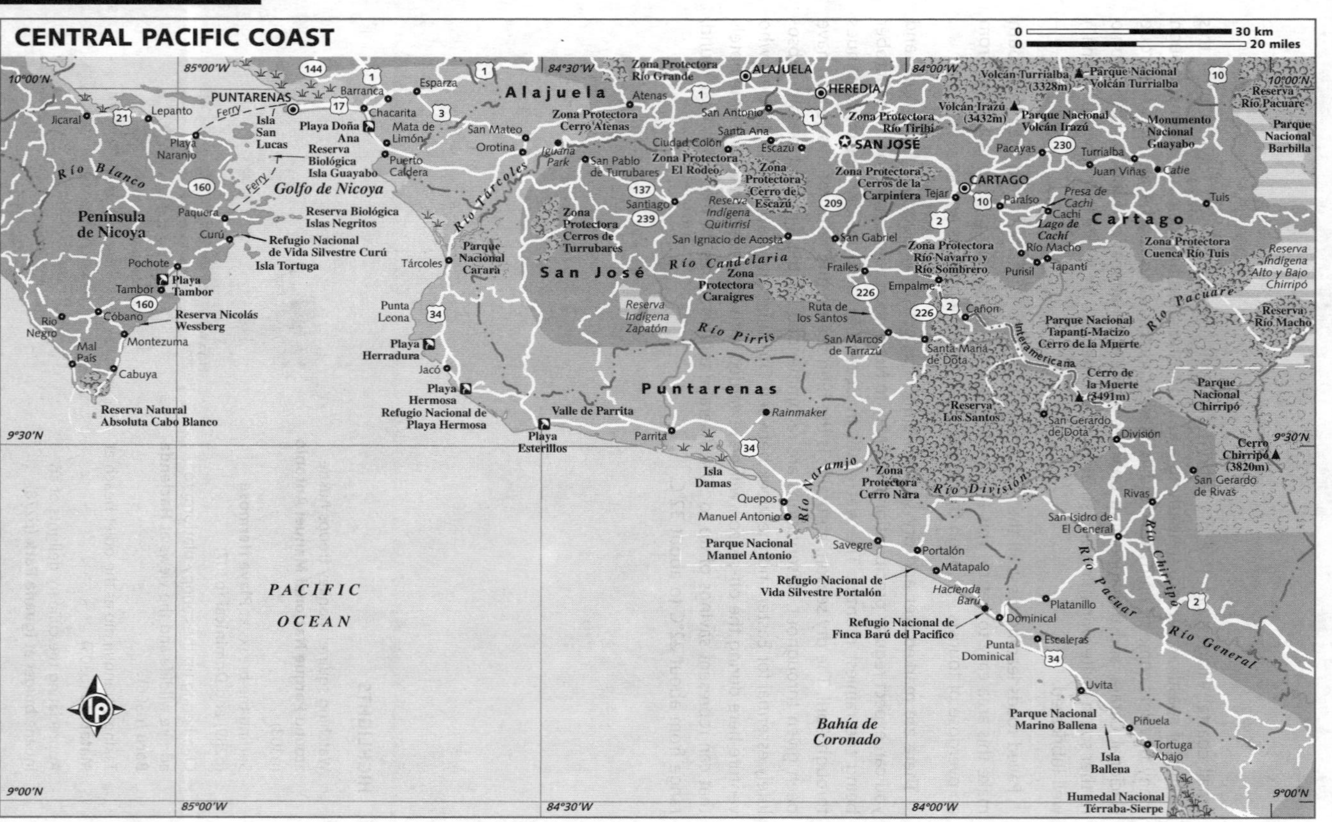

CENTRAL PACIFIC COAST

PUNTARENAS

Situated at the end of a sandy peninsula (8km long but only 100m to 600m wide), Puntarenas is Costa Rica's most significant Pacific coastal town and is just 110km west of San José by paved highway. This city of about 50,000 inhabitants is the capital of the province of Puntarenas and once served as the country's biggest port. In the 19th and early 20th centuries, goods such as coffee were hauled by ox cart from the highlands down the Pacific slope and then shipped off around Cape Horn to Europe. After the railway to Puerto Limón was built, Puntarenas declined in importance, but was still the major port on the Pacific coast. This all changed in 1981 when a bigger port was opened at Puerto Caldera, about 18km southeast of Puntarenas, and the town turned to its current means of economic survival: tourism.

Despite the loss of shipping, Puntarenas (locally referred to as the 'Pearl of the Pacific') is a bustling place during the dry season – foreigners arrive to catch ferries to the Península de Nicoya, and Tico vacationers land in droves to visit the beaches. (It is, after all, the closest coastal town to San José and good for a quick getaway.) Unfortunately the water here is polluted – though the south side of the point is reportedly OK for swimming. The beaches themselves are regularly cleaned and the views across the Golfo de Nicoya are scenic. You can stroll along the beach or the aptly named Paseo de los Turistas, stretching along the southern edge of town. Cruise ships make day visits to the eastern end of this road, and a variety of souvenir stalls and *sodas* are there to greet passengers. During the wet months, the city is much quieter.

The city has 60 calles running north to south but only five avenidas running west to east at its widest point. As in all of Costa Rica, street names are largely irrelevant and landmarks are used for orientation (see p453).

Information

INTERNET ACCESS

Internet Café Puntarenas (across from the church; per hour US$1.30)
Cibercafé Millenium (cnr Paseo de los Turistas & Calle 17; per hour US$2)
Coonatramar (cnr Calle 31 & Av 3; per hour US$1.50; 8am-5pm) Has three computer terminals with speedy connections. This is a good place to check email while waiting for the car ferry.

MEDICAL SERVICES

Hospital Monseñor Sanabria (663 0033; 8km east of town)

MONEY

The major banks along Avenida 3, to the west of the market, exchange money and are equipped with 24-hour ATMs. **Banco de San José/Credomatic** (cnr Av 3 & Calle 3) is on the Cirrus network.

TOURIST INFORMATION

Puntarenas tourism office (Catup; 8am-5pm Mon-Fri) is opposite the pier on the` 2nd floor above the Báncredito. It closes for lunch.

Sights & Activities

La Casa de la Cultura (661 1394; Av Central btwn Calles 3 & 5) has an art gallery with occasional exhibits as well as a performance space offering seasonal cultural events. Behind the Casa is the **Museo Histórico Marino** (661 5036, 256 4139, www.museocostarica.com; admission free; 8am-1pm & 2-5pm Tue-Sun). The museum describes the history of Puntarenas through audiovisual presentations, old photos and artifacts.

A block away, the old stone **church** is one of the town's most attractive buildings and is definitely worth a peek inside. At the time of research, it was receiving a much needed renovation.

The **Puntarenas Marine Park** (adult/child under 12 US$7/1.50; 9am-5pm Tue-Sun) has an aquarium that showcases manta rays and other creatures from the Pacific. The park sits on the site of the old train station and has a tiny splash pool, snack bar, gift shop and information center – but, frankly, it's overpriced

FIVE AGAINST THE SEA

In January 1988 five fishermen from Puntarenas set out on a trip that was meant to last seven days. Just five days into the voyage, their small vessel was facing 30-foot waves triggered by northerly winds known as El Norte. Adrift for 142 days, they would face sharks, inclement weather, acute hunger and parching thirsts. They were finally rescued – 7200km away – by a Japanese fishing boat. *Five Against the Sea* by American reporter Ron Arias, recounts in gripping detail the adversities they faced and how they survived.

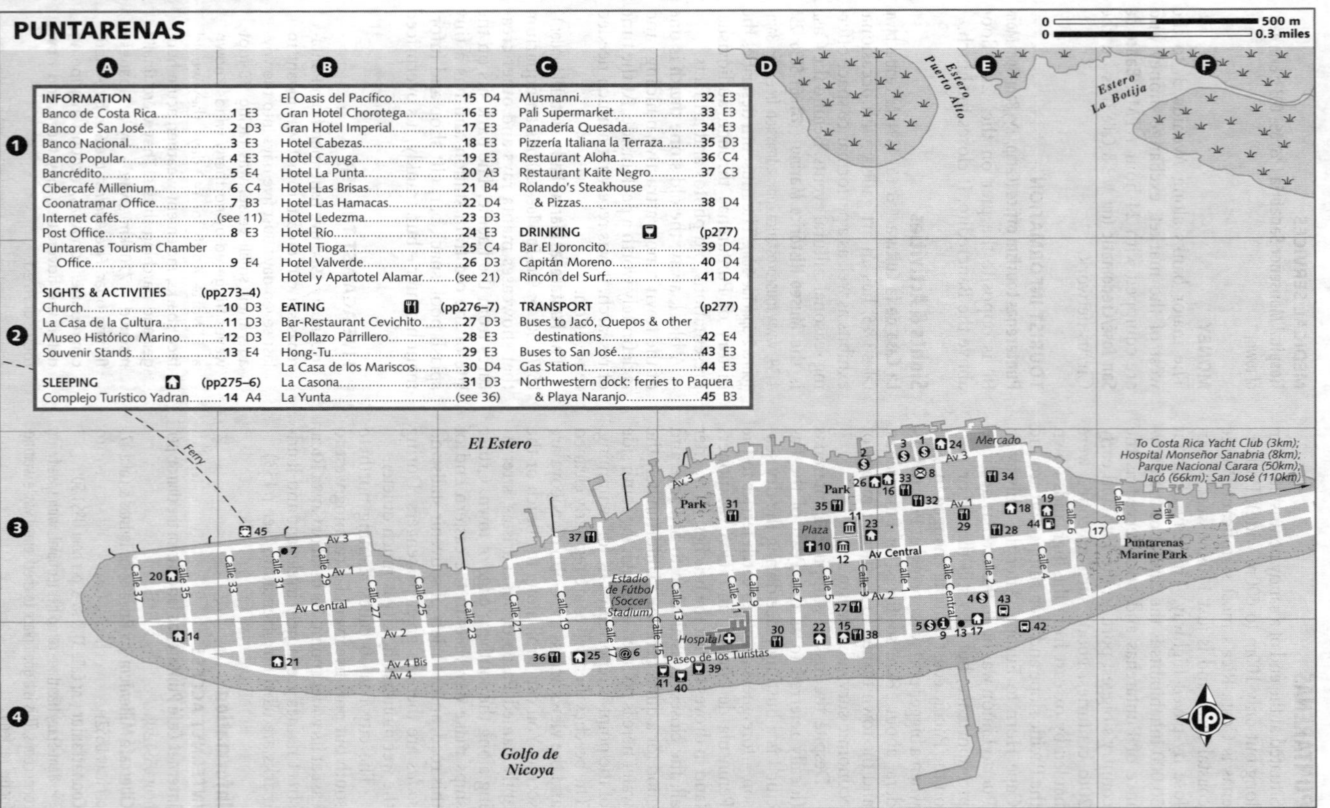
PUNTARENAS
0 500 m
0 0.3 miles
INFORMATION
Banco de Costa Rica....1 E3
Banco de San José....2 D3
Banco Nacional....3 E3
Banco Popular....4 E3
Bancrédito....5 E4
Cibercafé Millenium....6 C4
Coonatramar Office....7 B3
Internet cafés....(see 11)
Post Office....8 E3
Puntarenas Tourism Chamber Office....9 E4
SIGHTS & ACTIVITIES (pp273–4)
Church....10 D3
La Casa de la Cultura....11 D3
Museo Histórico Marino....12 D3
Souvenir Stands....13 E4
SLEEPING (pp275–6)
Complejo Turístico Yadran....14 A4
El Oasis del Pacífico....15 D4
Gran Hotel Chorotega....16 E3
Gran Hotel Imperial....17 E3
Hotel Cabezas....18 E3
Hotel Cayuga....19 E3
Hotel La Punta....20 A3
Hotel Las Brisas....21 B4
Hotel Las Hamacas....22 D4
Hotel Ledezma....23 D3
Hotel Río....24 E3
Hotel Tioga....25 C4
Hotel Valverde....26 D3
Hotel y Apartotel Alamar....(see 21)
EATING (pp276–7)
Bar-Restaurant Cevichito....27 D3
El Pollazo Parrillero....28 E3
Hong-Tu....29 E3
La Casa de los Mariscos....30 D4
La Casona....31 D3
La Yunta....(see 36)
Musmanni....32 E3
Pali Supermarket....33 E3
Panadería Quesada....34 E3
Pizzería Italiana la Terraza....35 D3
Restaurant Aloha....36 C4
Restaurant Kaite Negro....37 C3
Rolando's Steakhouse & Pizzas....38 D4
DRINKING (p277)
Bar El Joroncito....39 D4
Capitán Moreno....40 D4
Rincón del Surf....41 D4
TRANSPORT (p277)
Buses to Jacó, Quepos & other destinations....42 E4
Buses to San José....43 E3
Gas Station....44 E3
Northwestern dock: ferries to Paquera & Playa Naranjo....45 B3
Estero Puerto Alto
Estero La Botija
El Estero
Ferry
Mercado
Park
Plaza
Av 3
Av 1
Av Central
Av 2
Av 4 Bis
Av 4
Calle 37
Calle 35
Calle 33
Calle 31
Calle 29
Calle 27
Calle 25
Calle 23
Calle 21
Calle 19
Calle 17
Calle 15
Calle 13
Calle 11
Calle 9
Calle 7
Calle 5
Calle 3
Calle 1
Calle Central
Calle 2
Calle 4
Calle 6
Calle 8
Calle 10
Estadio de Fútbol (Soccer Stadium)
Hospital
Paseo de los Turistas
Puntarenas Marine Park
To Costa Rica Yacht Club (3km); Hospital Monseñor Sanabria (8km); Parque Nacional Carara (50km); Jacó (66km); San José (110km)
Golfo de Nicoya

for what it is. There's a **pool** at El Oasis del Pacífico (p276), where the kiddies can take a dip with hordes of local children any time between 8am and 5pm for under US$2.

Tours

Several companies can take you via boat to visit island beaches near Bahía Gigante (p259).

Coonatramar (☎ 661 9011, 661 1069; www.coonatramar.com; cnr Av 3 & Calle 31) runs tours around the estuaries and mangroves of Puntarenas and to nearby islands, including Isla Tortuga. It can also organize fishing charters. Fares range from US$6 to US$15 per person, with a minimum of five to eight people, depending on the tour.

Festivals & Events

Puntarenas is one of the seaside towns that celebrate the **Fiesta de La Virgen del Mar** (Festival of the Virgin of the Sea) on the Saturday closest to July 16. Fishing boats and elegant yachts are beautifully bedecked with lights, flags, and all manner of fanciful embellishments as they sail around the harbor, seeking protection from the Virgen as they begin another year at sea. There are also boat races, a carnival, and plenty of food, drink, and dancing.

Sleeping

BUDGET

Make sure your room has a decent fan or you'll not only be sweltering, but contending with mosquitoes. All of the following hotels have cold showers unless otherwise stated.

Hotel Cabezas (☎ 661 1045; Av 1 btwn Calles 2 & 4; s/d US$7/14, s/d with bathroom US$10/20; Ⓟ) This is the best budget choice. Rooms are calm, clean, freshly painted and have functional overhead fan and screened windows. Parking in the locked lot costs US$3.

Gran Hotel Imperial (☎ 661 0579; Paseo de los Turistas btwn Calles Central & 2; r per person US$11; Ⓟ) Well situated near the bus stations, this dilapidated and rickety wooden structure still manages to retain a little old-world charm. Cavernous rooms with several beds include shower and overhead fan. Upstairs rooms have balcony.

Hotel Ledezma (☎ 661 1919; Calle 3 btwn Avs Central & 1; r per person US$7) This quiet hotel is situated just opposite the Casa de Cultura. Rooms are gloomy, though reasonably clean, with shared bathroom.

Gran Hotel Chorotega (☎ 661 0998; cnr Av 3 & Calle 1; s/d US$9/15, d with bathroom US$25) This is a more upscale choice, offering decent rooms with clean, tiled floor, overhead fan and TV.

Hotel Valverde (☎ 661 2731; r per person US$5) Extremely basic white and mint-green stalls with shared bathroom are clean enough. Not recommended for solo women.

Hotel Río (☎ 661 0331; 100m west of the market) The rooms are like cells, but they're clean and secure. And if the wind is blowing just right, you won't smell the fish market next door. Watch out for street crime at night.

MID-RANGE

All showers are cold-water unless otherwise stated.

Hotel La Punta (☎ 661 1900, 661 0696; cnr Av 1 & Calle 35; s/d with fan US$25/32, with air-con US$40/48; 🅂 ❄) At the far-western end of town, you'll find this decent little hotel. There's a pleasant bar, small pool, and restaurant, and all the rooms have hot water, fan and balcony.

Hotel y Apartotel Alamar (☎ 661 4343; www.alamarcr.com; tr/q standard US$94/105, d/q apt US$105/141; Ⓟ ❄ 🅂) This brand new, bright yellow complex is a good option for families. Rooms are all spotless, with tiled floor, private hot shower, cable TV and air-con. Apartments have fully equipped kitchen that includes coffee maker and rice cooker. There are two pools (one for kids) and all rates include breakfast. Credit cards accepted.

Hotel Las Brisas (☎ 661 4040; hbrisas@racsa.co.cr; cnr Paseo de los Turistas & Calle 31; s/d US$47/66; 🅂) Also near the west end, this is a quiet, clean hotel with friendly management, a good restaurant and pool. All rooms have fan, air-con, TV and private hot shower but seem a little expensive for what they have to offer.

Hotel Tioga (☎ 661 0271; www.hoteltioga.com; Paseo de los Turistas btwn Calles 17 & 19; d standard/deluxe/balcony US$64/82/99; Ⓟ ❄ 🅂) Opened in 1959, this is the most established of the Puntarenas hotels. There are 52 rooms, all of which have air-con and private bathroom. Standard rooms have cold shower, while more expensive units have hot water. The most expensive rooms have a balcony with a sea view; all others face the courtyard, which has a pool. Rates include breakfast in an upstairs dining room with ocean views. Making a reservation is highly recommended during the high season, and credit cards are accepted.

Hotel Cayuga (☎ 661 0344; Calle 4 btwn Avs Central & 1; d US$19, s/d with TV US$25/33; P ❄) This hotel has efficient air-con and clean but uninspiring rooms with faded carpet, private shower and phone. The bar-restaurant attached to the hotel is good, though not cheap. There is a locked parking lot.

El Oasis del Pacífico (Paseo de los Turistas btwn Calles 3 & 5; s/d US$22/35, d with air-con US$40; P ❄) This place has a pool, disco, restaurant and bar and is popular with Tico families. The simple rooms are somewhat rundown but have private hot shower. Be prepared to listen to the DJ's musical selection from your bedroom all night.

Hotel Las Hamacas (☎ 661 0398, Paseo de los Turistas btwn Calles 5 & 7; s/d/tr/q US$18/37/45/53, d/tr/q with air-con US$43/53/59; ❄) Popular with younger Ticos, this place has seen better days. Basic rooms are dark and come with peeling paint and 'private' bathroom separated from the sleeping area by a thin curtain. Definitely overpriced.

Complejo Turístico Yadran (☎ 661 2662; www.puntarenas.com/yadran; cnr Paseo de los Turistas & Calle 35; d standard/superior US$76/88; P ❄) Near the end point of the sand spit, this bland-looking place has a restaurant, bar, casino, disco and two pools. Comfortable rooms have air-con, cable TV and phone. Pricier superior units have a balcony overlooking the ocean.

Costa Rica Yacht Club (☎ 661 0784; cryacht@racsa.co.cr; s/d US$30/45, s/d with air-con US$38/53, villa US$82; P ❄) Some 3km east of downtown, this uninteresting but comfortable place is at the narrowest portion of the peninsula, near the eastern end. The club caters to members of both local and foreign yacht clubs as well as the public. There's a decent restaurant-bar and a pool, and the 20 rooms are spartan but spotless. Villas accommodate a gaggle of five fishermen – a good value. Credit cards accepted.

Eating

The cheapest food for the impecunious is in the *sodas* around the market area. This area is also inhabited by sailors, drunks and prostitutes, but it seems raffish rather than dangerous – during the day, at least. Restaurants along the Paseo de los Turistas are, predictably, filled with *turistas*.

There's a row of fairly cheap *sodas* on the beach by the Paseo de los Turistas, Calle Central and Calle 3. They are good for people-watching and serve snacks and nonalcoholic drinks.

Pizzería Italiana La Terraza (Av 1, west of Calle 3; pizza from US$3; noon-9pm Mon-Sat & 5-9pm Sun) This pleasant corner restaurant on a small plaza is a good place for a personal-sized pie, pasta or cheap lunch special (US$2). It displays artwork, all for sale.

La Casona (cnr Av 1 & Calle 9; casados US$2) This bright yellow house isn't marked with a sign, but it's an incredibly popular lunch spot, attracting countless locals who jam onto the large deck and into the interior courtyard. Portions are heaping, and soups are served in bathtub-sized bowls. Bring your appetite.

La Casa de los Mariscos (Paseo de los Turistas btwn Calles 7 & 9; entrees US$5-10) This is a popular and friendly place serving mostly seafood.

Bar-Restaurant Cevichito (cnr Calle 3 & Av 2) This place has well-prepared sea bass for under US$5 – a good deal.

On the other side of the peninsula, **Los Delfines** (at Complejo Turístico Yadran; cnr Paseo de los Turistas & Calle 35) may not look terribly remarkable, but it serves a darn good *arroz con camarones* (rice and shrimp).

Rolando's Steakhouse & Pizzas (cnr Paseo de los Turistas & Calle 3; dishes US$4-12) True to its name, this place serves the requisite steak and pizza, and seafood, too. There's a popular bar serving a long list of *bocas*.

Restaurant Aloha (☎ 661 0773; Paseo de los Turistas btwn Calles 19 & 21; meals US$6-14) This eatery is great for seafood, offering everything from simple rice dishes to fish and lobster. Cheap specials (US$2) at lunchtime make it worthwhile. Next door, **La Yunta** (entrees US$6-9) is another good bet for seafood.

Restaurant Kaite Negro (☎ 661 2093; cnr Av 1 & Calle 17; dishes US$2-9) On the north side of town, this is a rambling restaurant popular with the locals. It serves good seafood and generous *bocas*. There's music and dancing on weekends.

Hong-Tu (Av 1 btwn Calles Central & 2; dishes US$3-7) It's good for Chinese food – and will make a vegetarian stir-fry on request.

El Pollazo Parrillero (cnr Av Central & Calle 2; half chicken US$3.50; 11am-10pm) Grills up tasty chicken 'butterflied' over coals.

Panadería Quesada (casados US$2; Mon-Sat) Tasty fresh-baked goods and cheap lunch specials make this a popular lunch spot. The *enchilados* (pastries with meat) are delicious and surprisingly spicy.

For more baked goods, there's always the omnipresent **Musmanni** (Av 1 btwn Calle Central & 1) and self-caterers can head to the **Palí supermarket** (Calle 1 btwn Av 1 & 3) to stock up on just about anything.

Entertainment

Countless bars line Paseo de los Turistas, each one much like the next. The current hot spot for shaking some booty is **Capitán Moreno's** (Paseo de los Turistas at Calle 13) on the beach. On this same bend in the street, you'll find **Bar El Joroncito** and **Rincón del Surf**, two other popular waterfront bars offering cheap beer and loud music. Another older, but still popular, spot is **El Oasis del Pacífico** (cnr Paseo de los Turistas & Calle 5), which has a lengthy bar and a warehouse-sized dance floor. Discos may close or have shorter hours in the low season.

Getting There & Away

BOAT

Car and passenger ferries bound for Paquera and Playa Naranjo depart several times a day from the **northwestern dock** (Av 3 btwn Calles 31 & 33). (Other docks are used for private boats.) If you are driving and will be taking the car ferry, arrive at the dock early to get in line. The vehicle section tends to fill up quickly and you may not make it on. In addition, make sure that you have purchased your ticket from the walk-up ticket window *before* driving onto the ferry. You will not be admitted onto the boat if you don't already have a ticket.

Schedules change seasonally and can be affected by inclement weather. Check with the ferry office by the dock for any changes. Many of the hotels in town also have up-to-date schedules posted. The free publication *Península de Nicoya* includes the schedule.

To Playa Naranjo (for transfer to Nicoya and points west) **Coonatramar** (☎ 661 1069; northwestern dock; passenger US$1.60, car US$11; 1½ hours) departs at 3:15am, 7am, 10:50am, 2:20pm and 7pm.

To Paquera (for transfer to Montezuma and Mal País) **Ferry Peninsular** (☎ 641 0118, 641 0515; northwestern dock; passenger US$1.60, car US$11; one hour) departs at 4:30am, 6:30am, 8:30am, 10:30am, 12:30pm, 3:30pm, 5:30pm and 8:30pm.

BUS

Buses for San José depart from the large navy blue building on the north corner of Calle 2 and Paseo de los Turistas. Book your ticket ahead of time on holidays and weekends.

Buses for other destinations leave from across the street, on the beach side of the paseo.

Cañas & Tilarán US$2.30; 1½ hours; departs 11:45am & 4:30pm.

Costa de Pájaros US$0.40; 1½-two hours; 5:50am, 10:45am, 1:15pm & 5pm.

Jacó/Quepos US$1.50/3; 1½/3½ hours; 5am & 11am, 2:30pm & 4:30pm.

Liberia US$1.40; 2½ hours; 4:40am, 5:30am, 7am, 8:30am, 9:30am, 11am, 2:30pm & 3pm.

Nicoya, Santa Cruz & Filadelfia three to five hours; 6am & 3:45pm.

San José US$2.30, 2¼ hours; depart frequently from 4:15am to 9pm.

Santa Elena, Monteverde US$2; three hours; 1:15pm & 2:15pm.

Getting Around

Buses marked 'Ferry' run up Avenida Central and go to the ferry terminal, 1.5km from downtown. The taxi fare from the San José bus terminal in Puntarenas to the northwestern ferry terminal is about US$2.

Buses for the port of Caldera (also going past Playa Doña Ana and Mata de Limón) leave from the market about every hour and head out of town along Avenida Central.

PUNTARENAS TO IGUANA PARK

Playa Doña Ana

About 13km southeast of downtown Puntarenas, Playa Doña Ana is the first clean beach you'll find. There are actually two beaches a few hundred meters away from each other: Boca Barranca and Doña Ana. **Surfing** is decent, especially at Boca Barranca, where you can get a left-hand break coming out of the river mouth. The Doña Ana beach has seen a little tourism development, though the area retains an isolated and unhurried feel. You can expect crowds from Puntarenas on weekends during the high season.

On the Costanera Sur (coastal highway) you'll see a sign that says 'Paradero Turístico Doña Ana.' At the beach entrance there is a parking lot (US$0.60). Day-use fees for the beach are US$1.50 for adults (half that for children), and the beach is open 8am to 5pm. There are snack bars, picnic shelters and changing areas, and the swimming is good.

Mata de Limón & Beyond

This sleepy little place has long been popular with locals from Puntarenas and the Central Valley. It's near the port of Caldera, and the buses from Puntarenas to Caldera will get you to Mata de Limón. The turnoff is 5.5km south of Playa Doña Ana.

The village is situated around a mangrove lagoon that is good for **birding** (especially at low tide), though not very good for swimming. It's divided by a river, with the lagoon and most facilities on the south side.

The major port on the Pacific coast is **Puerto Caldera**, which you pass soon after leaving Mata de Limón. The beach is unremarkable, though it is of interest to the occasional surfer. Further south, **Playa Tivives** and **Playa Valor** are also of interest to surfers, offering beach breaks at the river mouth. Any Puntarenas-Jacó bus can drop you at the turnoffs – but you may have to walk 500m or more to find your waves.

Iguana Park

This **park** (admission US$15; 🕑 8am-4pm) is an interesting nonprofit project administered by the **Fundación Pro Iguana Verde** (☎ 240 6712; iguverde@racsa.co.cr), which protects the endangered green iguana through breeding and release programs. This animal is endangered in part because it's good to eat (locals refer to it as *gallina de palo,* 'chicken of the tree') and has been severely over-hunted. The foundation has developed breeding programs that have returned more than 80,000 lizards into the wild and provided income for local breeders who 'farm' iguanas for food. It seems odd that to protect the iguana it has to be farmed, but thus far this has proven the best way to stop illegal poaching and provide locals with much-needed income.

The park has a visitor center where you can see exhibits and videos, and a restaurant where you can taste the world's only 'iguana burger' (yup, tastes like chicken). There's a petting zoo area where you can 'cuddle' an iguana and a souvenir store sells iguana-leather products – we strongly advise against buying iguana skins anywhere else in Costa Rica. The 400-hectare park is set in a tropical forest 14km east of Orotina. There are 4km of well-maintained trails in an area of transitional forest between the dry tropical forest of the northern lowlands and the tropical rain forest of the south. Entrance fees at Iguana Park go toward supporting the foundation and tours are available (US$10 per person).

From Orotina, buses to the park (US$0.50, 30 minutes) depart at 5:30am, noon and 4:30pm. If you're driving, look for a road to the east just south of Orotina signed 'Coopebaro, Puriscal.' This road goes over a wooden suspension bridge to the park, and there are signs. It's about 9km, and half the road is paved. Call the Fundación for up-to-date directions and to make sure that the gates are open. The park closes sporadically.

PARQUE NACIONAL CARARA

Situated at the mouth of the Río Tárcoles, the 5242-hectare park is only 50km southeast of Puntarenas by road or about 90km west of San José via the Orotina highway. Its significance cannot be understated. This reserve is at a crucial meeting point between the dry tropical forests to the north and the wet rain forests to the south. Surrounded by pasture and agricultural land, it forms a necessary oasis for the area's wildlife. There are also archaeological remains of various indigenous burial sites that you can see only with a guide – though they're tiny and unexciting compared to anything you might see in Mexico or Guatemala. (For more on the area's indigenous history, see the boxed text, p23.)

A variety of forest birds inhabit the reserve but can be difficult to see without an experienced guide. The most exciting bird for many visitors to see, especially in June or July, is the brilliantly patterned scarlet macaw. Other birds to watch for include guans, trogons, toucans, motmots and many other forest species. Monkeys, squirrels, sloths and agoutis are among the more common mammals present.

The dry season from December to April is the easiest time to go, though the animals are still there in the wet months. March and April are the driest months. Rainfall is almost 3000mm annually, which is less than in the rain forests further south. It's fairly hot, with average temperatures of 25°C to 28°C – but it's cooler within the rain forest. An umbrella is important in the wet season and occasionally needed in the dry months. Make sure you have insect repellent.

If you're driving from Puntarenas or San José, pull over to the left immediately after crossing the Río Tárcoles bridge, also known as the **Crocodile Bridge**. Basking crocodiles are often seen along the muddy banks below the bridge. Binoculars help a great deal. A variety of water birds may also be seen: herons, spoonbills, storks and anhingas.

Some 600m further south on the left-hand side is a locked gate leading to the Laguna Meandrica trail. Another 2km brings you to the **Carara ranger station** (admission US$8; 7am-4pm), where you can get information and enter the park. There are bathrooms, picnic tables and a short nature trail. Guides can be hired for US$15 per person (two minimum) for a two-hour hike. About 1km further south are two loop trails. The first, Sendero Las Araceas, is 1.2km long and can be combined with the second, Sendero Quebrada Bonita (another 1.5km).

Vehicles parked at the trailheads have been broken into. There may be guards on duty, but drivers are advised to leave their cars in the lot at the Carara ranger station and walk along the Costanera Sur for 2km north or 1km south. Go in a group and don't carry unnecessary valuables (there have been muggings reported here). Alternately, park by Restaurante Ecológico Los Cocodrilos (see below).

Sleeping & Eating

Camping is not allowed, and there's nowhere to stay in the park, so most people come on day trips.

Restaurante Ecológico Los Cocodrilos (☎ 661 8261; d US$12), on the Costanera, to the north side of the Río Tárcoles bridge, is the nearest place to stay and eat. It has clean roadside cabins, but most travelers just stop to eat at the **restaurant** (casados US$3; 6am-8pm). Otherwise, the nearest hotels and restaurants are in Tárcoles, 3km south of the park. Readers have recommended staying in Tárcoles and getting to the park early in the morning before tours begin to arrive.

Getting There & Away

There are no buses to Carara, but any bus between Puntarenas and Jacó can leave you at the entrance. You can also catch buses headed north or south in front of the Restaurante Ecológico Los Cocodrilos. This may be a bit problematic on weekends, when buses are full, so go midweek if you are relying on a bus ride. If you're driving, the entrance to Carara is right on the Costanera and is clearly marked.

TÁRCOLES AREA

Two kilometers south of the Carara ranger station is the Tárcoles turnoff to the right (west) and the Hotel Villa Lapas turnoff to the left. To get to Tárcoles, turn right and drive for a kilometer, then go right at the T-junction to the village, with cabins and a beach. To reach the mudflats of the Río Tárcoles, continue past the village for 2km or 3km; this is a prime area for birders looking for shorebirds, particularly at low tide.

Sights & Activities

A 5km dirt road past Hotel Villa Lapas (p280) leads to the 70-hectare **Jardín Pura Vida** (☎ 637 0346; admission US$10; 8am-5pm) in the town of Bijagual. This private botanical garden in primary forest offers hiking and incredible vistas of one of the country's tallest waterfalls. It's about 200m high – and claims to be the highest in the country – and to see it in its full glory you need to clamber down a steep trail (45 minutes) and then climb back out (90 minutes). It'll probably take you four hours, or longer if you stop to examine poison-dart frogs and the many birds above, and pause at various lookout points. The falls are more dramatic in the rainy season, when they're fuller. At the bottom, the river continues through a series of natural swimming holes. A **camping** area and outhouse are located at the bottom. You can also arrange horseback riding and other activities.

If you want to get the adrenaline pumping, check out a crocodile tour. Bilingual guides in boats will take you out in the river for croc spotting and some hair-raising croc tricks. And you know it's going to be good when the guide gets *out* of the boat and *into* the water with these massive beasts. It's *Crocodile Hunter* without the Australian accent. Both **Crocodile Man** (☎ 637 0427; crocodileman@hotmail.com) and **Jungle Crocodile Safari** (☎ 637 0338; www.costaricanaturetour.com) have offices in the town. Some travelers are not pleased that the crocodiles are fed by hand by the tour guides; others say that these tours may not be worth it if you've already been to Tortuguero (p394). Tours usually cost US$25 per person for two hours.

Sleeping & Eating

The Tárcoles area can be almost deserted midweek in the wet season, when finding a restaurant can be problematic.

Hotel Carara (☎ 637 0178; d US$50; P) Situated in the village and right on the beach, this pink building has 30 decent rooms that are clean but in need of a facelift. The units are spacious and upstairs rooms have views of the ocean, but it's overpriced. Rates include breakfast and dinner.

Hotel Villa Lapas (☎ 637 0232; www.villalapas.com; d US$93; P) This Spanish colonial-style hotel is 500m inland from the Tárcoles turnoff. Fifty five well-maintained and spacious tiled rooms have private hot shower, air-con, coffee maker and nice terrace. A pool and gardens are surrounded by forested hillside. There is good birding along trails that wind up the Río Tárcoles in a private reserve. The **restaurant** (7am-9pm) is open to the public and the bar area has a pool table. Credit cards accepted.

Tarcol Lodge (Costa Rica ☎ 433 8278, 433 5634, in the USA & Canada 888-246 8513; www.ranchonaturalista.com; r per person with 3 meals US$99; P) This homey lodge is on the south bank of the Río Tárcoles, at the northwestern end of the village. At low tide, a huge expanse of mudflats attracts thousands of shorebirds during migration, and hundreds at other times – and plenty of avid birders who come to gaze upon them. Definitely bring binoculars.

The lodge is run by the Erb family, the same folks who run Rancho Naturalista near Turrialba (p149). The focus is on birding and Tarcol provides rustic, comfortable lodging and good food. This is highly recommended for birders; a three-day visit will usually yield at least 150 species, and more than 400 are recorded on the lodge list. Well-appointed wood rooms have fan, and the shared bathrooms have hot water. Rates are based on a three-day minimum stay and include access to an expert bird guide, admission into Parque Nacional Carara and transport to and from local birding areas.

PUNTA LEONA AREA

This tiny headland is about halfway between Tárcoles and Jacó. There are a couple of upscale places to stay with super views.

US-based **JD's Watersports** (☎ 256 6391; www.jdwatersports.com) operates a complete watersports center inside Hotel Punta Leona and offers sportfishing packages, scuba diving trips, half-day jungle river cruises, sunset cruises and ocean-kayak rental. Other gear and boat charters to various destinations are also available.

Sleeping & Eating

Hotel Punta Leona (☎ 231 3131; www.hotelpuntaleona.com; s/d/tr US$84/96/108, apt US$170-240; P) About 6km south of Tárcoles, a guarded gate lets guests onto the 4km dirt road that leads to this complex. The bland-looking rooms and apartments all come with the usual top-end amenities. The beaches lining the property are exquisite, but unfortunately the hotel has, in the past, tried to shut down public access to them. This is illegal in Costa Rica, where beaches are public property. In addition, the overzealous security at the gate will make you wonder if you're entering a prison compound. (After much questioning, they let me in for 15 minutes.) Credit cards accepted.

Hotel Villa Caletas (☎ 637 0606; www.hotelvillacaletas.com; r US$160-400; P) This luxurious place is 3km south of the Punta Leona entry and 8km north of the Jacó turnoff from the Costanera. A steep 1km paved road leads to the beautiful hotel, which is perched on a dramatic hillside overlooking the Pacific. The hotel is lovingly decorated with art and antiques. There is a French-influenced restaurant, a beautiful infinity pool and a private 1km trail leading to the beach. There are 35 units in various styles on the steep, forested property, each with private balcony, cable TV, phone, minibar and coffee maker. À la carte meals cost about US$11 for breakfast and US$25 for lunch or dinner. Although tours and activities can be arranged, many guests just do nothing more strenuous than relax. Credit cards accepted.

PLAYA HERRADURA

The Herradura turnoff is on the Costanera Sur, 3.5km north of the turnoff to Jacó. A paved road leads 3km west to Playa Herradura – a quiet, sheltered, palm-fringed, black-sand beach. Until the mid 1990s, this was a rural beach, popular mainly with campers. Now it's home to a marina, hotel and condominium complex that is one of the largest new tourism developments in the country. Regardless, it still attracts a slew of locals who come to take a dip in the tranquil waters.

A few hundred meters before the beach on the main road is a large grass campground, **Campamento Herradura** (per person US$3.30), which has showers and basic facilities.

About 500m from the beach on the main road, **Cabinas del Río** (☎ 643 8891; s/d US$10/20, additional person US$10; Ⓟ) is a German-owned place with six cabins of varying comfort and size spread out around a tiny creek. It costs slightly more for the four cabins with kitchen.

Los Sueños Marriott Beach & Golf Resort (☎ 630 9000; www.lossuenosresort.com; d mountain/ocean/premium US$328/363/421; Ⓟ) is a US$40 million hotel-and-condo project at the northern end of the bay. It features a 250-slip marina, golf course, tennis courts, pool, shopping center, casino, sportfishing, and enough other stuff that'll hopefully make the US$300+ room rate seem worth it. The **golf course** (green fee guest/nonguest US$95/140) is one of the principal attractions. The hills above the bay have been bulldozed to make way for million-dollar homes (that only a foreigner could afford). And while the whole Spanish colonial-style complex is breathtakingly beautiful, it also reeks of a manufactured sameness that'll make you wonder if you're in Costa Rica, or Orange County, California.

On the beach are many locally popular seafood restaurants. The best one on the row is **Marisquería Juanita** (dishes US$3-6), which attracts locals in the know.

JACÓ AREA

Jacó is a flat, nondescript resort town and the closest developed beach resort to San José. It mainly attracts surfers, seeking consistent year-round breaks. The more appealing **Playa Hermosa**, 5km south and with bigger and faster curls, attracts a more determined crew of wave chasers.

For everyone else, the area is *the* party destination on the central Pacific coast and attracts a slew of sportfishing enthusiasts, spring-breakers, ocean-liner types (who disembark in Puntarenas) and vacation package visitors who all come to paint the town red at night and pass out on the beach during the day. In the past few years, drug dealing and prostitution have become a bigger part of the local scene, and on a Sunday morning the streets are usually littered with the detritus of a big Saturday night party (empty beer bottles, food wrappers, hungover gringos). In response, hoteliers and tourist-industry personnel have gotten together to help keep the area clean and regularly sponsor trash pickups along the shoreline.

Despite its reputation as a 'party beach,' Jacó is definitely more sedate than its overdeveloped North American counterparts. And the town, which is popular with Central Valley Ticos looking for a little fun and sun, still manages to attract a healthy dose of local and foreign families, especially during January and February.

Jacó is expensive and during the high season it's jam-packed with tourists. The beach itself is average (unless you're a surfer). Swimming is possible, but riptides are common and you should avoid the areas nearest the estuaries, which are polluted.

Orientation

Playa Jacó is about 2km off the Costanera, 3.5km past the turnoff for Herradura. The beach itself is about 3km long, and hotels and restaurants line the road running behind it. The areas on the northern and southern fringes are the most tranquil and attractive and are the cleanest.

In an effort to make foreign visitors feel more at home, the town has placed signs with street names on most streets. These names are shown on the map, but the locals continue to use the traditional landmark system (see p453).

Information

There's no unbiased tourist information office, though several tour offices will give information. Look for the free monthly *Jaco's Guide* which includes tide charts and up-to-date maps.

There are pay phones on the main street. If you're on the beach and your bladder needs relief, there are public toilets (US$0.30) just north of Hotel Balcón del Mar (p285). For a fee (US$1.50) the staff will also let you check in belongings.

Aquamatic Coin Laundry (Map p284; 7:30am-12:30pm & 1-5pm) The best place to get the skivvies clean; do-it-yourself and drop-off service.

Banco de San José (Map p284; Av Pastor Díaz, north of Calle Cocal; 8am-5pm Mon-Fri & 8am-noon Sat) Has a Cirrus ATM open during bank hours on the 2nd floor of the Il Galeone shopping center.

Banco Popular (Map p284; Av Pastor Díaz at Calle La Central) Exchanges US dollars and traveler's checks.

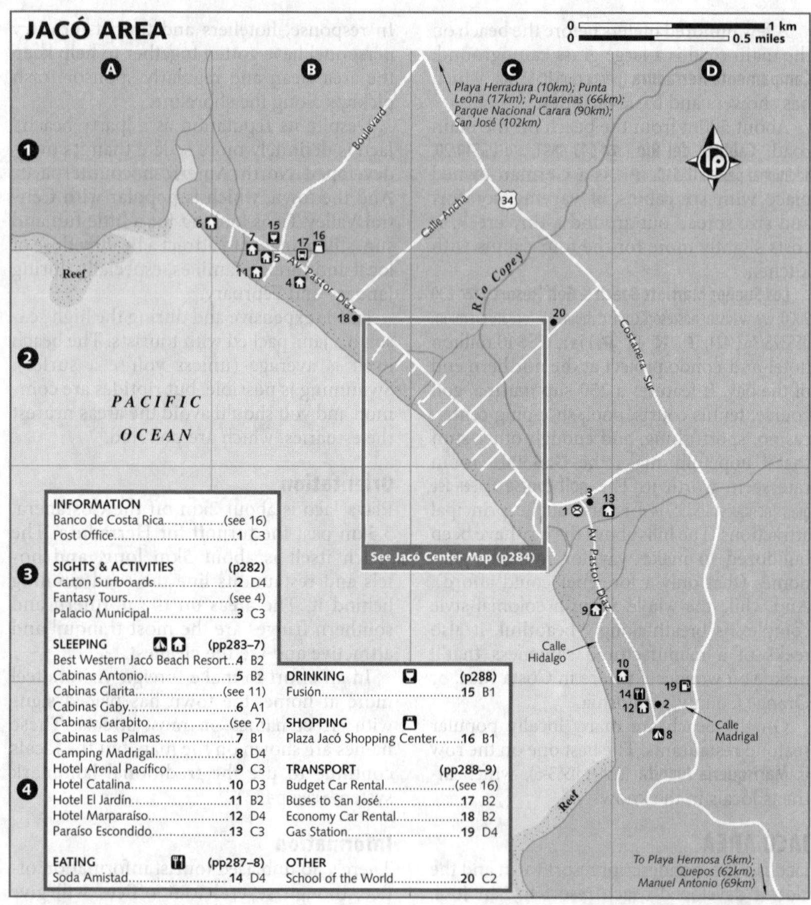

Books & Stuff (Map p284; Av Pastor Díaz btwn Calles Las Olas & Bohío) Has books in several languages as well as US newspapers.

Flaco Internet (Map p284; Av Pastor Díaz btwn Calles Las Olas & Bohío; per hour US$1; 9am-9pm Mon-Sat & 10am-8pm Sun) The best place to check email; has eight terminals with good connections, and air-con.

Red Cross (Map p284; 643 3090, Av Pastor Díaz btwn Calles El Hicaco & Las Brisas)

Activities

SURFING

With consistent breaks all year, it's no wonder that Jacó serves as the surfing capital of Costa Rica. (The rainy season is considered best for Pacific coast surfing.) In addition, Jacó is quickly and easily reached from the capital and provides a ready infrastructure of hotels, restaurants and surf shops.

La Chosita del Surf (Map p284; 643 1308; www.surfoutfitters.com; Av Pastor Díaz, north of Calle Anita) repairs and rents boards and provides surfing information. Owner Chuck Herwig is one knowledgeable dude and runs Chuck's Cabinas around the corner (p283). In the center of town, **Mango Surf Shop** (643 1916; Av Pastor Díaz at Calle El Hicaco) has supplies. At the southern end, **Carton Surfboards** (Map p282; 643 3762; cnr Calle Madrigal & Av Pastor Díaz) makes custom boards and offers rentals, ding repair and lessons.

Courses

City-Playa Language Institute (Map p284; 643 2123; www.costarica-spanishschool.com; Av Pastor Díaz btwn

Calle Las Palmeras & Calle Las Olas) offers inexpensive courses in Spanish. Ask about group rates.

School of the World (Map p284; ☎ 643 1064; www.schooloftheworld.org; 1-4 week packages US$540-1900; Ⓟ) is a popular school and cultural-studies center offering classes in Spanish, surfing, art and photography. It's in the process of adding yoga and Latin American cooking. The sweet new building also houses a café and art gallery. Rates include kayaking and hiking field trips and on-site lodging. Spanish and surfing are the most popular programs.

Tours

Tours around the area include visits to Parque Nacional Carara (US$41) as well as longer-distance trips around the country. One new destination is Isla Damas – you can organize tours here or in Quepos (p291), further south. Isla Damas is not 100% an island, but the tip of a pointed mangrove forest that juts out into a small bay just south of Parrita. During high tide, as the surrounding areas fill with water, this point becomes an island – offering an incredible opportunity for birders and other wildlife watchers. Boating tours can be arranged from Jacó for US$60 per person, but more avid adventurers can opt for a sea-kayaking expedition with Amigo Tico Complete Adventure Tours in Quepos.

Check in at the following agencies to book tours:

Fantasy Tours (Map p282; ☎ 220 2126; www.fantasy.co.cr; inside the Best Western lobby)

King Tours (Map p284; ☎ 643 2441, 388 7810; www.kingtours.com; Av Pastor Díaz, north of Calle Cocal)

Solutions Travel Agency (Map p284; ☎ 643 3485; www.jacotour.com; Il Galeone Shopping Center) Handles tour bookings as well as airline reservations.

Sleeping

The center of town, with its many bars and discos, can mean that noise will be a factor in where you choose to stay. The far northern and southern ends of town have more relaxed and quiet accommodations. Reservations are highly recommended during dry-season weekends and become critical during Easter and the week between Christmas and New Year's. If you plan on a lengthy stay (more than five days), ask about long-term rates.

The rates given are high-season rates, but low-season rates could be as much as 30% to 40% lower. Hotels below are listed from north to south.

BUDGET

Hotel de Haan (see the boxed text on p286) is the author's choice for this price range.

Cabinas Antonio (Map p282; ☎ 643 3043; cnr Av Pastor Díaz & Boulevard; d US$14; Ⓟ) At the northern end of town, basic cabins here are clean and come with private cold shower and cable TV. This is an overall good deal.

Cabinas Garabito (Map p282; ☎ 643 3321; d US$20; Ⓟ) Off a small road just west of Cabinas Antonio at the far northern end of town you'll find these basic cold-water cabins run by a local family. Units are all clean and have private bathroom.

Cabinas Clarita (Map p284; ☎ 643 2615; western end of Boulevard; r per person US$8.80; Ⓟ) This squat pink motor court on the beach offers concrete rooms with private bathroom. There is a bar and restaurant.

Chuck's Cabinas (Map p284; ☎ 643 3328; chucks@racsa.co.cr; Calle Anita; r per person US$7.50, d/tr/q with bathroom US$25/30/35; Ⓟ) This cool, budget hangout is usually packed to the gills with surfers from all over. Concrete-block rooms are small and clean and come with high-powered fan. A couple of larger rooms come with private bathroom. Owner Chuck is a fount of knowledge on the area and runs La Chosita del Surf (p282).

Cabinas Emily (Map p284; ☎ 643 3513; Av Pastor Díaz btwn Calles Anita & Bri Brí; d US$12.50; Ⓟ) Situated right behind Wahoo's, this is another great budget option and comes well recommended. The owner is friendly and helpful and the rooms are clean and have big beds.

Cabinas Mar de Plata (Map p284; ☎ 643 3580; Calle Las Olas; d US$20) These tidy concrete cabins with tile floors have private cold shower.

Cabinas Roble Mar (Map p284; ☎ 643 3173; Calle Bohío; d US$20) Comfy doubles here come with private bathroom. A room for five with a kitchenette is US$38. Also available are small, dank rooms with tired-looking shared bathroom; rates vary.

Cabinas Jacomar (Map p284; ☎ 643 1934; Calle Bohío; d/tr US$20/25) Well-scrubbed, brightly painted rooms have private cold shower, shared kitchen and an attached *soda* serving cheap breakfasts. The owner is not known for her charm, but she's this way with everyone, so don't take it personally.

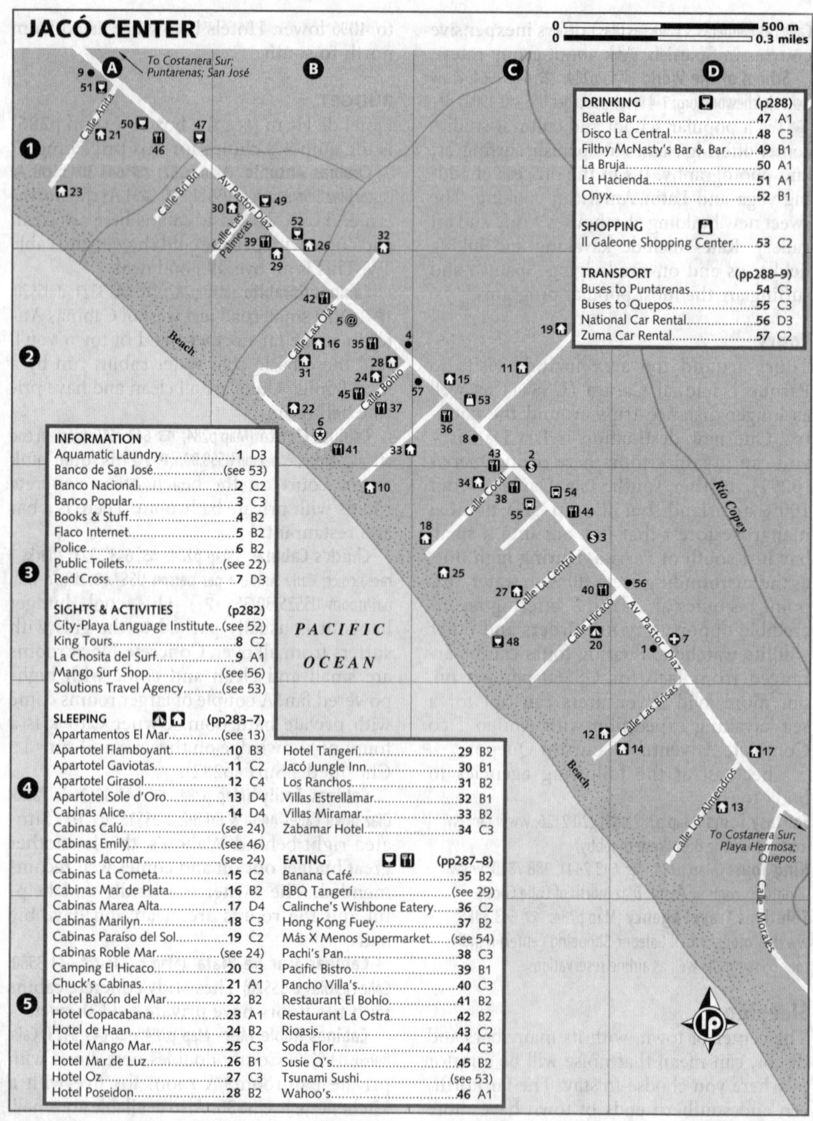

Cabinas Calú (Map p284; ☎ 643 1107; Calle Bohío; d US$25) Comfortable and spacious clean doubles have tiled floor, fan and private bathroom and have been recommended by readers. The owners are friendly.

Cabinas La Cometa (Map p284; ☎ 643 3615; Av Pastor Díaz, south of Calle Bohío; d without/with bathroom US$22/32) Rooms are fresh and clean at this calm, French Canadian–run inn. Four units share a clean bathroom with cold shower, while another three have private restroom with hot water. There is a spotless shared kitchen. Good value.

Cabinas Marilyn (Map p284; ☎ 643 3215; Calle Cocal; q US$20) Bare rooms here are seriously musty and not at all well kept, but are cheap. All come with private bathroom, and a couple of units have fridge.

Cabinas Marea Alta (Map p284; ☎ 643 3554; Av Pastor Díaz near Calle Los Almendros; tr US$29;) This friendly, 2nd-story place has basic cabins with fan and cold private shower. Some rooms have a fridge for a few dollars more.

Camping El Hicaco (Map p284; ☎ 643 3004; Calle Hicaco; per person US$3.30;) The best campground in town: there are picnic tables, bathrooms and a lockup for gear. (Don't leave valuables in your tent.)

Camping Madrigal (Map p282; Calle Madrigal; per person US$2.50) South of the center, this tranquil grassy campground has a bar-restaurant next door and easy access to the beach.

MID-RANGE

See also Hotel Mar de Luz, which is the author's mid-range choice, in the boxed text on p286.

Villas Estrellamar (Map p284; ☎ 643 3102; www.estrellamar.com; eastern end of Calle Las Olas; d US$51, d villas US$61-112;) Twenty-eight spacious, pristine rooms have massive bathroom with hot-water shower, cable TV, fridge, lock box, air-con, phone and private balcony. Villas accommodate from two to seven people and have equipped kitchen with coffee maker. There's a pool and Jacuzzi and the French management is congenial. (English and Spanish are also spoken.) Worthwhile off-season rates are available. Credit cards accepted.

Cabinas Gaby (Map p282; ☎ 643 3080; d with air-con US$40;) At the far northern end of town, this bright yellow place is popular with Tico families and has pleasant rooms with kitchenette, hot water and a choice of fan or air-con. There's a small pool and a shady garden. A cabin with fan sleeps five.

Cabinas Las Palmas (Map p282; ☎ 643 3005; northern end of Av Pastor Díaz; s/d US$24/29, d with air-con US$40, apt US$36-44) Twenty-three mint-green units have clean tile floors and are set around a pleasant garden, which has a small pool. Older rooms have cold water and fan, while newer, bigger units have hot water and kitchenette. This place is popular with families.

Hotel El Jardín (Map p282; ☎ 643 3050; western end of Boulevard; s/d US$36/43;) This friendly, French-owned place is known for its good restaurant. Simple rooms are well maintained and come with hot water and fan. There's a pool.

Jacó Jungle Inn (Map p284; ☎ 643 1631; cnr Av Pastor Díaz & Calle Las Palmeras; d US$50, ste from US$70;) This friendly place has plain, clean rooms with private hot shower, air-con and cable TV. Bigger and more expensive suites include coffee maker and fridge. There is a pool and Jacuzzi.

Los Ranchos (Map p284; ☎ 643 3070; Calle Las Olas; d without/with kitchen US$40/52, bungalow US$92;) This popular place is near the beach and attracts many repeat clients from Europe. It has a newly refinished pool, pleasant garden, small paperback library and friendly staff offering information on local tours and surfing. Rooms are clean, well kept and quiet and all have fan and private bathroom with hot water. Larger bungalows sleep up to seven. Credit cards accepted.

Hotel Balcón del Mar (Map p284; ☎ 643 3251; next to police station btwn Calles Las Olas & El Bohío; d/tr US$88/98;) This beachfront place has a prime location and rooms all have hot-water shower, private balcony, ocean view, minifridge, air-con and cable TV. There's a pool and a good restaurant. Credit cards accepted.

Villas Miramar (Map p284; ☎ 643 3003; villasmiramar@racsa.co.cr; d US$60;) Set in a nicely landscaped and quiet garden, this terracotta-colored inn has 12 spacious cabinas that are clean and comfy and come with spacious bathroom. Units all have kitchenette, fridge, hot water and fan. Long-term rates available.

Apartotel Flamboyant (Map p284; 643 3146; flamboya@racsa.co.cr; s/d/tr US$35/50/60, apt US$88;) Just steps from the beach, this place has eight clean and pleasant studio rooms (sleeping two), four cabins (for three or more) and one fully equipped apartment (for up to seven). All have fan, hot shower, kitchenette and little patio, and they're a good value. Amenities include a barbecue area and a pool. Credit cards accepted.

Cabinas Paraíso del Sol (Map p284; ☎ 643 3250; www.paraisodelsolcr.com; d/q US$40/55, 6-bed r US$75;) Eleven clean rooms here are equipped with air-con, kitchenette and hot water. There's a pool and a bar with cable TV, table tennis and surf videos. Credit cards accepted.

Apartotel Gaviotas (Map p284; ☎ 643 3092; r US$85;) Here you'll find 12 spacious and modern apartments with kitchenette, fridge, sitting area, cable TV, fan and hot water.

THE AUTHOR'S CHOICE

Budget

Hotel de Haan (Map p284; 643 1795; www.hoteldehaan.com; Calle Bohío; r per person US$10, child under 10 free;) This new Dutch/Tico outpost is one of the top budget bets in town. Freshly tiled rooms with hot-water shower are clean. There's a shared kitchen with fridge, a pool and free Internet. Ask about long-term rates.

Mid-Range

Hotel Mar de Luz (Map p284; 643 3259; mardeluz@racsa.co.cr; Av Pastor Díaz btwn Calles Las Palmeras & Los Olas; d/tr/q incl breakfast US$67/75/85; P) This recommended place has tidy and attractive air-con rooms with patio, hot-water shower, microwave, fridge and coffee maker. Several larger stone rooms in the back are also a good option. There are two pools and barbecue grills for guests to use. The friendly Dutch owners also speak Spanish, English, German and Italian and are knowledgeable. Credit cards accepted.

Top End

Hotel Arenal Pacífico (Map p282; 643 3419, Av Pastor Díaz, north of Calle Hidalgo; r standard/ocean incl breakfast US$93/110; P) The entrance doesn't look like much, but you'll be pleasantly surprised once you step into this pretty, wooded hotel which has 26 rooms with private hot shower, air-con and cable TV. Standard rooms surround a lagoon and pricier ocean-view units line the beach. All units are priced for two adults and two children. There is an ocean-front pool.

They sleep five. There's a fine pool and a TV room. Significantly lower rainy-season rates are available.

Zabamar Hotel (Map p284; 643 3174; Calle Cocal; q US$55; d/q with air-con US$40/77; P) Twenty tidy, pleasant whitewashed and tiled rooms here each have air-con and private cold-water shower. Upstairs rooms are more private. The owners are friendly and there is a pool. Rates include breakfast, and credit cards are accepted.

Hotel Mango Mar (Map p284; 643 3670; Calle Cocal; d US$55, apt US$95-115; P) Also on the beach, this whitewashed hotel has a dozen air-con rooms with kitchenette, hot water, and balcony overlooking the pool and Jacuzzi. It also has two fully equipped apartments that can accommodate up to six. Credit cards accepted.

Cabinas Alice (Map p284; 643 3061; Calle Las Brisas; d with fan/air-con US$36/46, q with kitchen US$67; P) Here you'll find decent, clean rooms with private bathroom, hot water and fan or air-con. The beach is steps away. Credit cards accepted.

Apartamentos El Mar (Map p284; 643 3165; Calle Los Almendros; d/tr/q US$35/45/55; P) Spacious rooms here surround a courtyard with a pool. Apartments are clean and have hot water, kitchenette and fan. They can sleep up to five and are a good deal. Credit cards accepted.

Apartotel Sole d'Oro (Map p284; 643 3172; Calle Los Alemendros; d with fan/air-con US$72/96; P) Rooms here are clean, modern and spacious, with kitchenette, hot water and fan or air-con. All of them sleep three or four, and there's a pool and Jacuzzi.

Hotel Paraíso Escondido (Map p282; 643 2883; www.hoteljaco.com; d with fan/air-con US$30/35, additional person US$7; P) This pleasant hotel is nestled into the woods a couple of blocks from the beach. Ten pretty rooms (some with canopy beds) in a Spanish-style building have private hot-water bathroom. Some quarters have a kitchenette and others accommodate up to six – a good value. Visa accepted.

Hotel Catalina (Map p282; 643 3217; www.hotelcatalina.net; Calle Hidalgo; r per night/month US$55/700, with air-con per night/month US$70/900; P) Large and spotless tiled rooms overlook a garden courtyard and have private hot shower, fan, kitchenette and a small balcony or patio. Several units have air-con and there is a barbecue grill available for guest use. Monthly rates are available.

Hotel Marparaíso (Map p282; 643 1947, 643 3277; www.hotelmarpariso.com; southern end of Av Pastor Díaz; d/tr/q US$68/78/88; P) Twenty clean rooms come with private hot shower, cable

TV and air-con at this refurbished bright yellow hotel. The grounds are well landscaped and the hotel is situated at the end of the road (where you just might see wildlife). There are adult and kiddie pools and a pleasant restaurant-bar overlooking the ocean. Some units sleep six. Credit cards accepted.

TOP END

See also Hotel Arenal Pacífico, which is the author's choice, in the boxed text on p286). All of the hotels below accept credit cards. Listings are from north to south.

Best Western Jacó Beach Resort (Map p282; ☎ 643 1000; www.bestwestern.com; Av Pastor Díaz btwn Boulevard & Calle Ancha; s/d $112/125; P) This hotel offers all the amenities of a full-service beach resort: more than 100 rooms have air-con, cable TV, private bathroom, hot water and, of course, the laundry list of resort activities – from biking, surfing and horseback riding to lounging by one of the hotel's pools. There's a restaurant and bar. Nice, but totally uninteresting.

Hotel Tangerí (Map p284; ☎ 643 3001; www.hoteltangeri.com; Av Pastor Díaz btwn Las Palmeras & Las Olas; d/tr/q US$88/102/124, villa US$144, chalet US$150; P) This pleasant resort complex is in the middle of it all, but manages to remain pleasantly tranquil. The grounds are well manicured and there are three pools. Rooms have air-con, cable TV, private hot shower and fridge; villas sleep up to five people and come with fully equipped kitchen; chalets accommodate eight. All rates include breakfast, and there is a restaurant, BBQ Tangerí, attached (p288). Green-season rates available.

Hotel Copacabana (Map p284; ☎ 643 1005; hotcopa@racsa.co.cr; Calle Anita; d US$89, ste US$149; P) This Canadian-run hotel is on the beach. Standard tile-floor rooms have fan, hot shower and air-con. Suites sleep up to four people and have kitchenette and private balcony. The owners will help arrange car rental and tours to nearby national parks. There's a pool, restaurant and sports bar with satellite TV and pool table.

Hotel Poseidon (Map p284; ☎ 643 1642; www.hotel-poseidon.com; Calle Bohío; d economy/standard/premium US$76/94/105;) This modern place has 14 sparkling, attractive rooms with bathroom and hot water. Some units have cable TV, and hair dryers are available. There's an elegant open-air restaurant, pool, bar, Jacuzzi and private parking. French, Spanish, English and German are spoken.

Hotel Oz (Map p284; ☎ 643 2162; Calle La Central; d/tr/q US$75/100/125;) The 12 rooms in this brand-new yellow building are a good size and each has a massive bathroom with hot shower, a safe, air-con and cable TV. There is a popular bar.

Apartotel Girasol (Map p284; ☎ 643 1591; www.girasol.com; Calle Las Brisas; d/tr/q US$99/126/138, d/tr/q per week US$725/794/864; P) This brand-new place has units surrounding a landscaped garden with private access to the beach. All units have private bathroom, hot water and a fully equipped kitchen with fridge.

Eating

Plenty of restaurants busily cater to the crowds and new ones open (and close) every year. Hours fluctuate in the rainy season, so eat early.

Soda Flor (Map p284; Av Pastor Díaz, north of Calle La Central; casados US$2) This is the best deal for budget travelers. Food is fresh, tasty and cheap and you can get good fresh fish for only US$4.

Soda Amistad (Map p282; southern end of Av Pastor Díaz; dishes US$2-4; 7am-9pm Tue-Sat, 7am-2pm Sun) At the far southern end, this cheap *soda* mainly attracts locals and has both good service and good meals. A bargain!

Banana Café (Map p284; Av Pastor Díaz btwn Calles Las Olas & Bohío; breakfast US$2-3) This is the place for breakfast, serving up heaping platters of truly sublime banana pancakes.

Wahoo's (Map p284; Av Pastor Díaz btwn Calles Anita & Bri Bri) This place is all the rage for fresh *ceviche* (US$3.80) and excellent sea bass (US$6).

Tsunami Sushi (Map p284; Av Pastor Díaz, north of Calle Cocal; sushi & rolls US$3-11; 5-10pm) If you've got a hankering for raw fish, don't miss Tsunami. This modern, lively, beautifully decorated restaurant serves up an exquisite assortment of sushi, sashimi and rolls.

Pacific Bistro (Map p284; Av Pastor Díaz, south of Calle Las Palmeras; entrees US$7-11) This popular place offers Southeast Asian fusion-style dishes. Noodle dishes are good, but one local claims he can't live without the shrimp in spicy Thai sauce.

Hong Kong Fuey (Map p284; Calle Bohío) Decent Chinese food is a good deal here.

Rioasis (Map p284; cnr Calle Cocal & Av Pastor Díaz; medium pizza US$5) This place is good for beer and pizza from a wood-burning oven, all on the outdoor deck.

Calinche's Wishbone Eatery (Map p284; Av Pastor Díaz, south of Calle Bohío; meals US$5-10) Overseen by the charming Calinche, this is a good pizza option and has a spacious, shady patio. Pita sandwiches, stuffed potatoes and grilled seafood are also specialties.

Restaurant El Bohío (Map p284; Calle Bohío; dishes US$5-8) This frequently packed place has good food and sea views. It's open all day and has a popular bar.

Susie Q's (Map p284; dishes US$6-9; 5-9pm Tue-Sun) Carnivores will find some decent ribs and other barbecue dinners here.

BBQ Tangerí (Map p284; Av Pastor Díaz btwn Calles Las Palmeras & Las Olas; dishes US$10) For more upscale grilled meats and seafood, try this place attached to the hotel of the same name. Specialties include filet mignon and a variety of grilled and fried fish dishes.

Restaurant La Ostra (Map p284; cnr Av Pastor Díaz & Calle Las Olas; dishes US$6-10) This is a good mid-priced restaurant serving up fresh seafood on a patio.

Pancho Villa's (Map p284; dishes US$8) The greasy food here is hardly worth the price, but the kitchen is open until the wee hours (depending on the crowd) and the dining room consistently picks up the overflow from the rowdy strip club upstairs.

Pachi's Pan (Map p284; Av Pastor Díaz, south of Calle Cocal) Pick up steaming fresh bread, good cinnamon rolls and decent empanadas here and make your own picnic on the beach.

Drinking & Entertainment

There are several dance clubs and in this fast-changing town it's definitely worth asking around to find the latest hot spots. Foam parties are popular in the high season; ask about locations if you're feeling sudsy.

All of these places (unless otherwise stated) are located on Avenida Pastor Díaz and only cross street information is provided.

Filthy McNasty's Bar & Bar (Map p284; at Calle Las Palmeras) This unfortunately named bar is one of the strip's rowdier spots. Read the warning sign before entering.

Onyx (Map p284; south of Calle Las Palmeras) At the time of research, this was the trendy place in town for beer and music. The 2nd-story terrace offers good views of the main drag.

La Bruja (Map p284; south of Calle Anita) Also in the center of town, La Bruja is an old standby that offers a mellow atmosphere for downing a few beers.

Beatle Bar (Map p284; at Calle Las Palmeras) This place is renowned for its high number of single men and prostitutes.

Disco La Central (Map p284; Calle La Central) This disco sets the volume at eleven, whether or not there's anyone on the dance floor.

La Hacienda (Map p284; north of Calle Anita) This popular dance club is currently *the* place to go for locals and travelers alike.

Fusión (Map p282; cnr Boulevard & Av Pastor Diaz) This new dance spot (with air-con) is at the northern end.

Getting There & Away

BOAT

There are boats to Montezuma daily. The one-hour trip costs US$35. Reservations can be made at Solutions Travel Agency (p283). It's a beach landing, so wear the right shoes.

BUS

Buses for San José (US$2.50, three hours) stop at the Plaza Jacó mall, north of the center. Buy tickets well ahead of time at the office of **Transportes Jacó** (7am-noon & 1-5pm). Buses depart at 5am, 7:30am, 11am, 3pm and 5pm.

The bus stop for other destinations is opposite the Más X Menos supermarket. (Stand in front of the supermarket if you're headed north; stand across the street if you're headed south.) Buses to Puntarenas (US$1.50, 1½ hours) depart at 6am, 9am, noon and 4:30pm. Buses to Quepos (US$2, 1½ hours) depart at 6:30am, 12:30pm, 4pm and 6pm. These are approximate departure times since buses originate in Puntarenas or Quepos. Get to the stop early!

If you're heading on to Nicaragua or points north after your stay in Costa Rica, Solutions Travel Agency (p283) can book tickets for the Tica bus. The bus doesn't come into Jacó, but the agency can reserve a seat for you from San José.

Getting Around

BICYCLE & SCOOTER

Several places advertise bike rentals. These usually cost about US$2 an hour or US$6.50 a day. Mopeds and small scooters cost from US$35 to US$50 a day (many places ask for a cash or credit card deposit of about US$200); look for signs in the center.

CAR

There are several rental agencies in town, so shop around for the best rates.

Budget (☎ 643 2665; Plaza Jacó mall; 8am-6pm Mon-Sat, 8am-4pm Sun)
Economy (☎ 643 1719; Av Pastor Díaz, south of Calle Ancha; 8am-6pm)
National (☎ 643 1752; Av Pastor Díaz at Calle El Hicaco; 7:30am-6pm)
Zuma (☎ 643 3207; Av Pastor Díaz, south of Calle Bohío; 7am-noon & 1-5:30pm Mon-Sat)

TAXI

Taxis to Playa Hermosa from Jacó cost about US$3. To arrange for a pickup, call **Taxi 30-30** (☎ 643 3030).

PLAYA HERMOSA

The beach at Playa Hermosa begins about 5km south of Jacó and has its own small cluster of hotels and restaurants. This beach stretches for about 10km and has a strong break that draws expert surfers; there's an annual contest in August.

Diana's Trail Rides (☎ 838 7550) offers one- to three-hour horse rides for US$25 to US$45.

Sleeping & Eating

All of the following hotels (listed north to south) offer easy access to waves.

Terraza del Pacífico (☎ 643 3222; www.terraza-del-pacifico.com; tr US$102; P) Right on the beach, this bright yellow hotel has modern, spacious tile-floor rooms with ocean view, air-con, cable TV, phone and private bathroom with hot water. There are two pools and a restaurant-bar, and all the usual tours are available. Credit cards accepted.

Hotel Fuego del Sol (☎ 643 3737; www.fuegodelsolhotel.com; d incl breakfast US$78.50; P) Head south on the Costanera and make a right at the Jungle Surf Café (later) to find this complex, which includes a pool, restaurant and beachside bar. The whitewashed rooms have small balcony, air-con, hot water and phone. Tours and transportation to surfing spots can be arranged. Credit cards accepted.

Villa Hermosa Hotel (☎ 643 3373; taycole@racsa.co.cr; d/tr US$45/60; P) This cool, beachside spot has 13 nice rooms with private bath, air-con and kitchenette. There are a few units accommodating up to six for US$80 – good value. There's a garden-shaded pool and a happening poolside bar. Credit cards accepted.

Cabinas Rancho Grande (☎ 643 3529; s/d US$15/20, additional person US$10; P) Further down the Costanera, this surfer joint is run by a friendly couple from Florida. There are eight rustic cane-paneled rooms with private hot shower and cable TV. An A-frame room on the top floor has killer views and some units sleep up to seven. There's an outdoor communal kitchen.

Costanera B&B (☎ 643 1942; d incl breakfast US$30-50; P) This Italian-run B&B is situated in a beautiful, mustard-colored building. There are five rooms of various sizes, some with garden and others with ocean view. A small Italian restaurant is open for dinner.

Cabinas Las Olas (☎ 643 3687; d with fan/air-con US$40/50, larger r per person US$20; P) A whitewashed three-story building and several nice bungalows here have kitchen, fan and hot water. Some larger rooms sleep up to six. It has a pool and a good **restaurant** (breakfast US$3, burgers US$6). Friendly and helpful staff will provide transportation to the best local surfing spots.

Cabinas Vista Hermosa (☎ 643 3422; d/tr with shared bathroom US$35/45, r for 6/8 people with bathroom US$100/140, r for 2/4/6 persons with air-con & bathroom US$50/80/120; P) These plain oversized concrete-block quarters with screens pack in surfers from all over. There's a beachfront restaurant and two pools. All rates include breakfast.

Jungle Surf Café (dishes US$4; 7am-3pm & 6-10pm Thu-Tue). Don't miss this locally recommended spot. Specialties include burritos and some serious fish tacos.

PLAYA HERMOSA TO QUEPOS

The paved Costanera continues southeast from Playa Hermosa to Quepos, 60km away. The road parallels the Pacific coastline but ventures down to it only a few times. The route has a few good beaches (some with surf) that are rather off the beaten track and most easily visited by car, though you could disembark from buses going to Quepos or Manuel Antonio and walk down to them.

Esterillos Area

Esterillos Oeste, Esterillos Centro and Esterillos Este are about 22km, 25km and 30km southeast of Jacó, respectively; all are a couple of kilometers off the Costanera. Between them, **Playa Esterillos** stretches for a few deserted kilometers and there are several surfing spots. The Esterillos area is undiscovered and little visited; there are a few cheap and basic cabins and camping areas that are used by surfers for off-the-beaten-path relaxation.

On the beach in Esterillos Este, there are a couple of tranquil and charming spots to stay.

Formerly the Auberge de Pelican, **Hotel El Pélicano** (☎ 778 8105; www.aubergepelican.com; d without/with air-con US$30/60; P) was recently purchased by enthusiastic American owners who have retained its homey look. Rooms have air-con and private hot shower. Two smaller, cheaper, more rustic doubles have fan. All rooms have new beds and fresh linen. There's a pool, a restaurant serving American and Tico specialties all day, and plenty of hammocks for lounging. Surfboards, body boards and bikes are available for guests; boat tours can be arranged.

Just south of El Pélicano, you'll find the lovely French Canadian-run **Flor de Esterillos** (☎ 778 8045, 778 8087; pages.infinit.net/taus/; tr per night/week US$60/360; P). Ten comfortable cabins of various sizes have tiled floor, colorful detailing, fan, kitchenette and pristine bathroom with hot shower. A great choice!

Rarely visited beaches to the south of Esterillos include **Playa Bejuco** (good surfing) and **Playa Palma**, which is two beautiful, wide beaches that are reached by short side roads from the Costanera. (Watch out for riptides if you're swimming here.)

In Bejuco, you'll find **Hotel El Delfín** (☎ 778 8054; esuperglide@yahoo.com; s/d US$53/76; r deluxe with air-con US$94)), a whitewashed building at the end of the beach road. The hotel is owned by an American family that has given the building a hefty renovation. The simple, whitewashed rooms have been completely refurbished and deluxe units feature teak accents. The owners are preparing to open a restaurant and bar on site.

Parrita

Parrita, a bustling little banana town on the river of the same name and just 40km south of Jacó, has a couple of basic hotels, many restaurants and *sodas*, two gas stations and two banks. At the eastern end of town, you'll see a sign for **Beso del Viento B&B** (☎ 779 9674; www.besodelviento.com; d/q US$70/150; P), which leads 6km to Playa Palo Seco. All four apartments have private tiled bathroom, a kitchen and fans. There's a pool and the uncrowded beach nearby offers surfing. Kayaks, bikes and horses can be rented. French and English are spoken.

After Parrita, the coastal road dips inland through countless African oil-palm plantations on the way to Quepos. The road is a mix of a badly potholed pavement and stretches of dirt, with several rickety one-way bridges.

Rainmaker Aerial Walkway

Rainmaker was the first aerial walkway through the forest canopy in Central America and its tree-to-tree platforms offer spectacular views. From the parking lot and orientation area, visitors walk up a beautiful rain forest canyon with a pristine stream tumbling down the rocks. A wooden boardwalk and series of bridges across the canyon floor lead to the base of the walkway. From here, visitors climb several hundred steps to a tree platform, from which the first of six suspension bridges spans the treetops to another platform. The longest span is about 90m, and the total walkway is about 250m long. At the highest point, you are some 20 stories above the forest floor.

In addition, there are short interpretive trails that enable the visitor to identify some of the local plants, and some long and strenuous trails into the heart of the 2000-hectare preserve. Keep your eye out for countless birds, poison-dart frogs and various insects. Tours with naturalist guides leave hotels in Manuel Antonio and Quepos daily except Sunday; reservations can be made at most hotels or by calling the **Rainmaker office** (☎ in Quepos 777 3565, 288 0654; www.rainmakercostarica.com). Tours cost US$65 and include a light breakfast and lunch. Binoculars are invaluable for watching wildlife. Bring sun protection and water.

A large colorful sign marks the turnoff for Rainmaker on the Costanera at the northern end of Pocares (10km east of Parrita or 15km west of Quepos). From the turnoff, it is 7km to the parking area.

QUEPOS

This town gets its name from the seaside Quepoa Indian tribe, a subgroup of the Borucas, who inhabited the area at the time of the conquest. As with many indigenous subgroups, the Quepoa population declined because of European diseases and slavery. By the end of the 19th century, no pure-blooded Quepoa were left, and the area began to be colonized by farmers from the highlands.

Quepos first came to prominence as a banana-exporting port in the early 20th century. But the crop has declined precipitously in recent decades because of disease and labor issues (underpaid workers had the gall to demand raises). African oil-palms, which stretch towards the horizon in dizzying rows around Quepos, have replaced bananas as the major local crop, but, unfortunately for the locals, generate a lot less employment.

Consequently, Quepos has not been able to recover as a major shipping port. Instead, it has become important as a sportfishing center and as the gateway to Parque Nacional Manuel Antonio, which is only 7km away. There are regularly scheduled flights and buses from San José, and Quepos has gradually developed a new economic niche for itself as a year-round tourism destination, with tour companies, bars and cafés rounding out the attractions.

Information

INTERNET ACCESS

You can check email at the very pleasant **Arte Net** (per hour US$1.30; 🕑 8am-8pm Mon-Sat), where eight computers have good connections.

LAUNDRY

Lavandería Yara (per load US$5; 🕑 8am-5:30am Mon-Sat) has inexpensive same-day service. **Aquamatic Laundry** (per load US$4.50; 🕑 8am-noon & 1-5pm Mon-Sat) offers self-service machines or they'll do it for you for an additional US$1.

MEDICAL SERVICES

The hospital **Dr Max Teran Vals** (☎ 777 0200) provides emergency medical care for the Quepos and Manuel Antonio area. It's on the Costanera Sur en route to the airport. However, this hospital doesn't have a trauma center and seriously injured patients are evacuated to San José. There is also the **Red Cross** (☎ 777 0118).

MONEY

Banco de San José and Coopealianza both have 24-hour ATMs on the Cirrus and Plus systems. Other banks will all change US dollars and traveler's checks.

TOURIST INFORMATION

The latest happenings are listed in the free English-language monthly magazine, **Quepolandia** (www.quepolandia.com), found in many of the town's businesses.

Dangers & Annoyances

The town's large number of easily spotted tourists has attracted thieves. In response, the Costa Rican authorities have greatly increased police presence in the area, but travelers should always lock hotel rooms and never leave cars unattended on the street – use guarded lots instead. The area is far from dangerous, but the laid-back atmosphere should not lull you into a false sense of security.

In addition, women should keep in mind that the town's bars attract rowdy crowds of plantation workers on weekends. So walking around town in your swimsuit will most certainly garner the wrong kind of attention.

Note that the beaches in Quepos are polluted and not recommended for swimming. Go over the hill to Manuel Antonio instead.

Activities

SPORTFISHING

Sportfishing is big in the Quepos area. Offshore fishing is best from December to April, when sailfish are the being hooked. Some of the main charter outfits are listed below. Not all charters have offices in Quepos, so it's usually best to call ahead. If you don't have a reservation, any hotel in the area can help put you in contact with a charter outfit.

Bluefin Sportfishing Charters (☎ 777 1676, 777 2222; www.bluefinsportfishing.com)
Blue Water Sportfishing (☎ 777 1596; www.sportfishingincostarica.com)
High Tec Fishing (☎ 777 3465, 388 6617)
Luna Tours (☎ 777 0725; www.lunatours.net; in Best Western Hotel Kamuk)

Tours

There are numerous reputable tour operators in the Quepos area.

Amigo Tico Complete Adventure Tours (☎ 777 2812; www.puertoquepos.com) Offers a range of tours, including rafting, walks in national parks, mountain biking and fishing. A full day of rafting on the Savegre is US$95 and this outfit also offers boat and kayaking tours of Isla Damas (see p283).

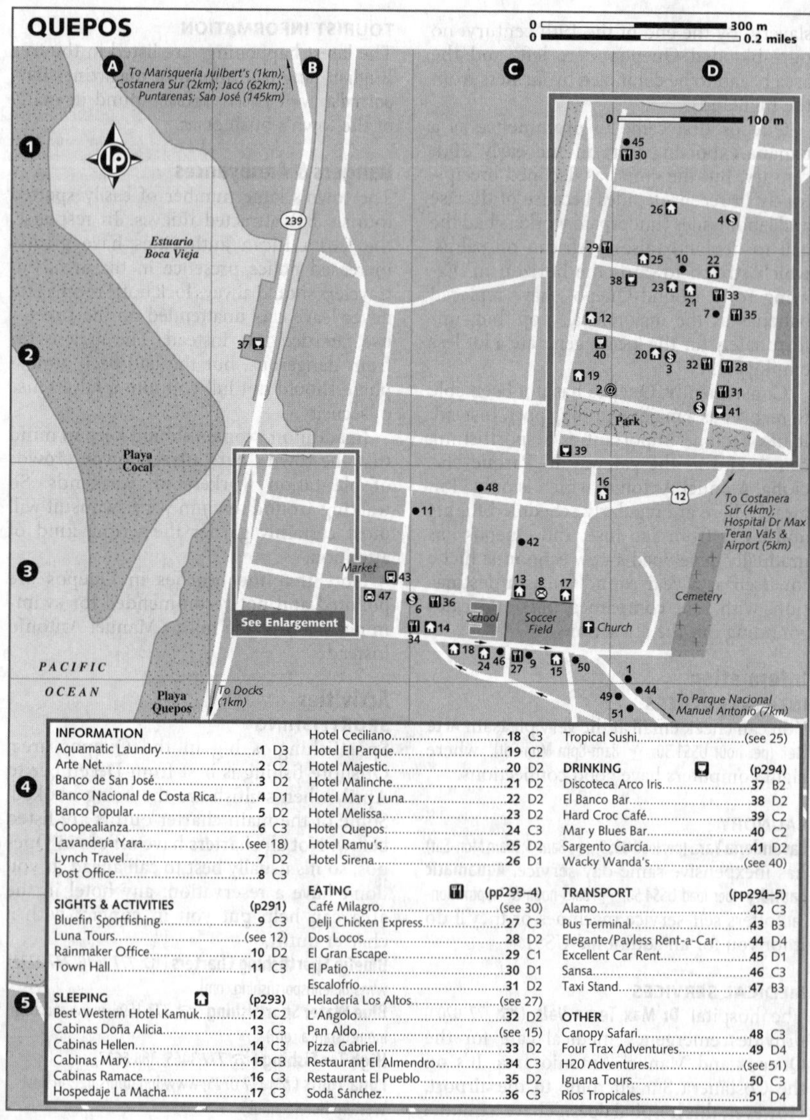

Brisas del Nara (☎ 779 1235; www.horsebacktour.com) Locally recommended for horseback-riding tours; half-day tours are US$45 and include pickup at your hotel and breakfast. Brisas doesn't have an office in Quepos; book by phone or through your hotel.

Canopy Safari (☎ 777 0100) The obligatory canopy tour costs US$75 and includes all transfers to and from their site, which is 45 minutes inland.

Four Trax Adventures (☎ 777 1825; www.fourtrax adventure.com) Four-hour ATV tours are US$95 per person.

H2O Adventures (☎ 777 4092; www.aventurash2o.com) All things watery. A half-day of sea kayaking is US$65.

Iguana Tours (☎ 777 1262; www.iguanatours.com) An adventure travel shop offering river rafting, sea kayaking, horseback rides, mangrove tours and dolphin-watching excursions.

Lynch Travel (☎ 777 1170; www.lynchtravel.com) From airline reservations to fishing packages to rain forest tours, this travel shop has it all.

Ríos Tropicales (☎ 777 4092; www.riostropicales.com) The venerable Costa Rican rafting company (p475) now has an office in Quepos.

Sleeping

Staying in Quepos offers a cheaper alternative to the sky-high prices at many lodges on the road to Manuel Antonio. Reservations are recommended during high-season weekends and are necessary during Easter and the week between Christmas and New Year's. High-season rates are listed, but many places have less expensive green-season rates.

BUDGET

All these hotels have cold-water showers unless otherwise stated.

Hotel El Parque (☎ 777 0063; r per person US$6.30) A popular budget option with thin walls; rooms are basic but clean, and the shared bathrooms are acceptable.

Hotel Mar y Luna (☎ 777 0394) In the same price range, this is the best budget deal in town; owner Alvaro is friendly, rooms are clean (though small) and the bathrooms have hot showers.

Hotel Melissa (☎ 777 0025; r per person US$10) Decent, bland rooms here have private bathroom.

Hotel Ramu's (☎ 777 0245; r per person US$7) Dark and tidy rooms with bathroom and fan; some travelers have complained of poor service.

Hospedaje La Macha (☎ 777 0216; r per person US$6, d with bathroom US$16) Small but clean stalls share decent restrooms here. Rooms with private bathroom are much better.

Cabinas Mary (☎ 777 0128; cabins per person US$7.50) On the south side of the soccer field, this is an excellent value and very secure; freshly painted units with private bathroom are spic and span – if a little dark – and the owners are friendly.

Hotel Majestic (☎ 777 1045; r per person US$2.50) This is a decrepit wooden hotel with gloomy stalls, dark shared bathrooms and no chance of ever living up to its stately name.

Cabinas Doña Alicia (☎ 777 0419; s/tr US$10/16.50) These quarters are small and dim but reasonably clean.

Hotel Quepos (☎ 777 0274; d US$15) Rooms are small but fairly clean; ask for lodging in the back or you'll be enjoying the loud TV near reception.

Hotel Hellen (☎ 777 0504; d US$18) This homey pension has neat rooms that come with private shower and a fridge.

MID-RANGE & TOP END

Hotel Malinche (☎ 777 0093; d US$20, s/d with air-con US$30/50; Ⓟ ❄) This is a good choice for various budgets. A pretty mustard building lined with balconies has older, more basic rooms which are good for budget travelers. Newer, more expensive units have tiled floors and come with private hot shower, air-con and cable TV.

Hotel Ceciliano (☎ 777 0192; per person US$12, d with bathroom US$22) Comfortable doubles, friendly owners and hot showers: a perfect combo.

Cabinas Ramace (☎ 777 0590; s/d US$30/45; Ⓟ) Sparkling rooms offer private bathroom with hot water and a fridge. The owner is helpful.

Hotel Sirena (☎ 777 0528; d US$50; Ⓟ ❄ 🏊) Here you'll get modern, air-con rooms that are sort of dark but clean and come with private hot shower. Continental breakfast is included in the rate and there's a small pool. The hotel arranges horseback tours and sportfishing.

Best Western Hotel Kamuk (☎ 7770379; www.kamuk.co.cr; d standard/superior incl breakfast US$70/94, additional person US$10; Ⓟ ❄ 🏊) The most upscale hotel in town has air-con rooms with hot water and phone. Amenities include a bar, 3rd-floor restaurant (with good views), pool and casino. There are standard rooms, and pricier superiors with balcony and ocean view. Credit cards accepted.

Eating

The town is packed with eating possibilities.

Soda Sánchez (meals US$2-3) is a good option for cheap casados and greasy snacks. For inexpensive broiled chicken, stop by the brightly lit **Delji Chicken Express** (combos US$3).

Restaurant El Almendro (dishes US$3-6) and **Restaurant El Pueblo** (dishes US$3-5) are two good 24-hour eateries. They quieten down during the day but do brisk business after dark.

El Patio (breakfast US$3-4, dinner entrees US$8-15; 🕑 6am-10pm) This colorfully painted restaurant is the top place in town for a meal. Cooking is Nuevo Latino (a welcome relief from pizza and burgers) and the changing menu is innovative. Various meats and seafood are marinated, grilled and served with homemade salsas. Breakfast offerings include dreamy French toast.

Café Milagro (🕒 6am-10pm Mon-Fri) Serving great cappuccino, espresso and baked treats, this is a good place to relax and read English-language newspapers that are available.

L'Angolo (dishes from US$3) This excellent Italian deli is great for sandwiches and other to-go treats for picnics. There is a tiny indoor café with a few tables if you want to eat there.

Pizza Gabriel (pizzas US$3-5) Just west of the market, this locally popular pizza joint has decent food.

Escalofrío (ice cream US$1.50, meals US$3-6; 🕒 Tue-Sun) Here you'll find 20 flavors of ice cream and a spacious seating area, as well as espresso, cappuccino and delicious Italian food. Another good ice-cream shop is **Heladería Los Altos** (desserts US$1-2.50), on the soccer field, where you can get everything from a scoop to a sundae.

El Gran Escape (☎ 777 0395; dishes US$7.50-12; 🕒 6am-11pm) This restaurant caters primarily to gringo anglers and their palates. The food is overrated, but they do whip up some fiery chicken wings (US$3) that are damn fine eating.

Dos Locos (☎ 777 1526; dishes US$4-14; 🕒 7am-11pm Mon-Sat, 11am-10pm Sun) This popular Mexican place has been recommended for its steaks, though others say it's overpriced. Expect live bands on Wednesday and Friday nights in the high season.

Tropical Sushi (sushi rolls US$3.50-10, sashimi per portion US$4; 🕒 5-10pm) For Japanese, try this colorfully decorated restaurant; it has a handful of tables and serves sushi rolls and sashimi.

Pan Aldo (south side of soccer field) It's a tasty bakery serving good cappuccino, excellent empanadas and gooey cinnamon rolls. Pick up fresh bread here for a picnic.

Marisquería Juilbert's (dishes US$3-10) This place is about 1km north of town, and locals report that it has the best seafood around.

Drinking & Entertainment

The mellow **Mar y Blues** (🕒 10am-2am) is good for a beer and chit-chat, while **Wacky Wanda's** will chill you out with cheap cocktails and air-con. **Hard Croc Café** is a lively waterfront bar with a wonderfully ironic name. For the best hangout in town, head to **Sargento García**, which is packed with determined young dudes eyeing the girls during ladies' night on Thursdays.

The bar at **El Gran Escape** restaurant (p294) is the place for swapping fish tales, and **El Banco Bar** (🕒 3pm-close) around the corner is good for sports on satellite TV. And, if you feel like giving away your cash, there's the **casino** (p292; 🕒 7pm-3am) at the Best Western Hotel Kamuk. The industrial-sized **Discoteca Arco Iris** brings out the locals with thumping dance beats.

Shopping

Café Milagro and nearby El Patio (p293) both sell roasted coffee, as well as other assorted souvenirs. Arte Net (p291) has a worthwhile selection of local arts and crafts.

Getting There & Away

AIR

The airport is 5km out of town and taxis make the trip for US$3 to US$5 (depending on traffic). Sansa has six daily flights between San José and Quepos (one way/round trip US$44/88), and NatureAir (US$50/95) has four. In Quepos, **Sansa's office** (☎ 777 0683) is on the soccer field, and **NatureAir** (☎ 777 2548) is on the 2nd floor above Iguana Tours.

Lynch Travel (p293) can book charter flights to and from the Quepos area.

Flights are packed in the high season, so book (and pay) for your ticket well ahead of time and reconfirm often.

BUS

All buses arrive and depart from the main terminal in the center of town. Buy tickets for San José well in advance at the **Transportes Morales ticket office** (☎ 777 0263; 🕒 7-11am & 1-5pm Mon-Sat, 7am-1pm Sun). Buses from Quepos depart for the following destinations:

Puntarenas, via Jacó US$3; 3½ hours; departs 4:30am, 7:30am, 10:30am & 3pm.

San Isidro, via Dominical US$2; four hours; 5am & 1:30pm.

San José (Transportes Morales) US$4; four hours; 5am, 8am, 10am, noon, 2pm, 4pm & 7:30pm.

Uvita, via Dominical US$2.30; 4½ hours; 10am & 7pm.

Getting Around

BUS

Buses between Quepos and Manuel Antonio (US$0.25) depart roughly every 30 minutes from the main terminal between 6am and 7:30pm, and less frequently after

7:30pm. The last bus departs Manuel Antonio at 10:25pm. There are more frequent buses in the dry season.

CAR

The following car rental companies operate in Quepos; reserve ahead and reconfirm to guarantee availability:

Alamo (☎ 777 3344; 🕑 7:30am-noon & 1:30-5:30pm)
Elegante/Payless (☎ 777 0115; 🕑 7:30am-5pm Mon-Fri)
Excellent (☎ 777 3052; 🕑 7:30am-5pm Mon-Sat)

TAXI

Colectivo taxis between Quepos and Manuel Antonio will usually pick up extra passengers for about US$0.50. A private taxi will cost about US$5. Call **Quepos Taxi** (☎ 777 0425/734) or catch one at the taxi stand south of the market.

QUEPOS TO MANUEL ANTONIO

From the port of Quepos, the road swings inland for 7km before reaching the beaches of Manuel Antonio village and the national park. The winding, forested road goes over a series of hills with picturesque views of the ocean. Along this stretch, every hilltop vista has been commandeered by a hotel that lists 'ocean views' as a major attraction. This is also one of Costa Rica's more popular gay destinations, with gay-friendly establishments lining the road.

This is also perhaps one of the most publicized destinations in all of Central America. Visitors might expect pristine nature, but the Manuel Antonio area has been discovered by the masses and is not the unspoiled gem it was as recently as the 1980s. The proliferation of hotels in an area where the sewage system is primitive at best has led to serious threats of marine pollution. The famous national park can be overwhelmed by visitors, and hotel prices tend to be much higher here than in the rest of the country. (If you visit at the beginning of the rainy season – June or July – accommodations will be far less crowded and much cheaper.)

Note that the road is steep, winding and very narrow; local bus drivers love to careen through at high velocities. There are almost no places to pull over in the event of an emergency. Drive and walk with care.

See the Manuel Antonio Area map (p301) for locations mentioned in this section.

Information

INTERNET ACCESS

Cantina Internet Café (opposite Hotel Costa Verde)
El Chante Internet (per hour US$2; 🕑 8am-10pm) Adjacent to Hostal Vista Serena.
TicoNet (Centro Comercial Si Como No)

MONEY

Banco Promerica (across from Restaurant Barba Roja; 🕑 8am-5pm Mon-Fri, 9am-1pm Sat) Has a 24-hour ATM on the Cirrus network and can exchange US dollars.

TOURIST INFORMATION

La Buena Nota (p302) in Manuel Antonio is a good source of tourist information for this area.

The booking and information office for the **Rafiki Safari Lodge** (p305; ☎ 777 2250; www.rafikisafari.com) is across the street from the Kekoldi Beach Hotel/Dorado Mojado.

Sights & Activities

Equus Stables (☎ 777 0001) offers horse rental and a variety of excursions.

You can relax after a day's activities at the **Serenity Spa** (☎ 777 0777, ext 220; inside the hotel Si Como No), a good place for couples massages, sunburn-relief treatments, coconut body scrubs and tasty coffee.

Belonging to the Hotel Si Como No and situated just across the street is **Fincas Naturales** (www.butterflygardens.co.cr; US$15), a private rain forest preserve and butterfly garden. About three dozen species of butterfly are bred here. The garden has a sound-and-light show at night (US$40 per person) and is surrounded by nature trails.

Courses

Escuela de Idiomas D'Amore (☎ 777 1143, in the USA 310-435 9897, 262-367 8589; www.escueladamore.com) has Spanish immersion classes at all levels; local homestays can be arranged. Two-week classes start at US$845 without homestay.

Centro de Idiomas del Pacífico (☎ 777 0805; www.cipacifico.com) provides personalized Spanish tutorials and offers a variety of housing options. One-week classes (four hours of class time) start at US$290 without homestay.

Sleeping

This stretch of winding, forested road has mostly top-end hotels, but there are a few mid-range and budget options as well. Some places require that you pre-pay your stay – so choose carefully (see the boxed text, p449). High-season rates are provided throughout, and reservations are a must for weekends. Low-season rates can be as much as 40% lower in some hotels.

Hotels listed below are in the order they're passed traveling from Quepos to Manuel Antonio. Also check out the author's choices in the boxed text on p297.

Cabinas Pedro Miguel (☎ 777 0035; www.cabinaspedromiguel.com; d/tr/q US$29/41/76; P) Just up the hill and out of Quepos is this friendly, family-owned hotel on the right-hand side of the road. The 18 spic-and-span rooms are nicely decorated. Larger units sleep four and five people and have a kitchenette. There's a pool and breakfast is available upon request. Long-term rates are available and credit cards are accepted.

Mimo's Hotel (☎ 777 0054; www.mimoshotel.com; d US$76, junior ste US$99, additional person US$15, child under 12 free; P) This pretty, white-washed hotel has colorful murals in its spacious, clean, terracotta-tiled rooms. All units have an ample bathroom, hot water, air-con, kitchenette and cable TV. There's a pool, Jacuzzi and **restaurant-bar** (entrees US$10; open to the public) serving Italian-influenced dishes. The Italian owners speak half a dozen languages and can book tours. Credit cards accepted.

Hotel Mono Azul (☎ 777 1548; www.monoazul.com; s/d/tr/q US$53/59/64/70, r deluxe add US$15, d villa US$135, additional person US$10, child under 12 free; P) This place is a good value. There are 27 pleasant rooms, all of which have private hot shower and ceiling fan. Deluxe units also have air-con and patio, and villas have two bedrooms and a kitchen. There are three pools, sunning decks, a games room with cable TV, a small gym, Internet access and a good restaurant (p297). Credit cards accepted.

The Mono Azul is home to 'Kids Saving the Rainforest' (KSTR), started by two local schoolchildren who were concerned about the endangered *mono tití* (Central American squirrel monkey). Many monkeys were run over on the narrow road to the national park, or electrocuted on overhanging electrical cables, so KSTR purchased and erected seven monkey 'bridges' across the road (you can see them, often in use, as you head to the park). Ten percent of hotel receipts are donated to the organization. (To learn how you can work with other worthwhile local organizations to support protection and conservation of the *mono tití*, see the boxed text, p299.)

Hotel California (☎ 777 1234; www.hotel-california.com; d standard/deluxe US$123/146; P) Look for a driveway to the left to find this quiet hotel, which is well set back from the road and has 10km of hiking trails into rain forest surrounding the property. The 22 rooms are cool, spacious and comfortable. They all feature hardwood floors, light-colored walls with attractive hangings, air-con, cable TV, telephone, minibar and a large bathroom with hot shower. The deluxe rooms are slightly larger and have a private terrace with ocean views. There's a pool with a waterfall, and the adjacent restaurant has views. Credit cards accepted.

Hotel Las Tres Banderas (☎ 777 1284/521; d standard/superior US$70/76, d ste US$111, apt US$176; P) About 2.5km south of Quepos, this place is owned by a Polish-born US citizen who lives in Costa Rica – hence Tres Banderas (three flags). There's a pool, terrace and huge Jacuzzi. Alongside is a wooden bar named Pod Popugami. Fourteen attractive, spotless doubles and three suites have air-con, large bathroom, hot water, cable TV and private balcony. Suites have bathtub, microwave and fridge. A two-bedroom apartment accommodates eight and has air-con, cable TV and kitchen. Credit cards accepted.

La Colina (☎ 777 0231; www.lacolina.com; d US$64, ste US$99.50; P) Down the road, this pleasant American/Brazilian-owned hotel has magnificent ocean views. There are five small, clean, colorfully decorated air-con rooms with hot water and fan, and six air-con suites with cable TV, small private terrace and ocean views. Two units have kitchenette. There is a mosaic pool with swim-up bar, as well as a popular restaurant, Bruno's Sunset Grill (p299). A big breakfast is included in the price and credit cards are accepted.

Hotel Flor Blanca (☎ 777 5050, 777 1620; d incl breakfast US$65; P) This locally run place has 10 simple, clean rooms with air-con, private hot-water shower, cable TV and fridge. While the units are nothing special, it is a good value for the area. Laundry service is available (US$7 per load).

Tulemar Bungalows (☎ 777 1325; www.tulemar.com; bungalows incl breakfast US$275; P) This luxurious place has 20 modern bungalows

THE AUTHOR'S CHOICE

Budget

Hostal Vista Serena (☎ 777 5162; www.vistaserena.com; dm US$15, d US$40; P) In an area that is hopelessly overpriced, it's a relief to find a great budget hostel. Perched on a hillside, this hostel allows guests to enjoy spectacular, ocean sunsets from a hammock-filled terrace. The white-tiled dorms are spic-and-span, shared bathrooms have hot water and there's a communal kitchen. There are a couple of neighboring doubles with shared bathroom and kitchen. A lounge has cable TV and there is laundry service (US$4 per load). Sonia, the super-helpful Tica owner, is fully bilingual. A café serves cheap meals. A small trail leads down through a farm to a remote beach.

Mid-Range

Hotel Plinio (☎ 777 0055, www.hotelplinio.com; d without/with air-con US$70/82, duplex US$99; jungle house US$140; P) This cozy hotel is nestled in the rain forest and has large rooms with super-high ceilings. Larger duplex units are two stories and have great polished-wood decks for lounging. (Duplexes don't have air-con, but the high ceilings keep rooms fresh.) Attractive units have private hot shower and there are plenty of hammocks. A jungle house accommodates five. The grounds boast 10km of trails into the forest, where you'll find a 17m-high lookout tower (open to the public). There is a highly recommended restaurant (p299) and the staff is friendly. Rates include breakfast during the high season. Visa is accepted.

Top End

Makanda by the Sea (☎ 777 0442; www.makanda.com; studio/villa incl breakfast US$310/468, additional person US$29; P) About 1km down the steep gravel road, this place is memorable for peaceful luxury and attentive, helpful staff. There are nine contemporary studios and larger villas, and a beautiful infinity pool and Jacuzzi with a superb view. Villa 1 (the largest) will take your breath away – the entire wall is open to the rain forest and the ocean. Several of the units can be interconnected and all of them have kitchen, fridge, minibar, hair dryer, coffee maker, cable TV and robes. Every room (except Villa 1) has air-con, and breakfast is delivered to your room. You can reach the remote beach by taking the 552 steps down the side of the mountain. Children under 16 years are not admitted. There is an exclusive poolside restaurant, the Sun Spot (p300). Credit cards accepted.

that sleep six. Each has air-con, huge picture windows with great views, two queen-sized beds, sitting room with two more foldout queen-sized beds, well-equipped kitchenette, phone, TV, VCR and hair dryer. There's an infinity pool and you can hike 15 minutes to the beach, where complimentary kayaks and snorkeling gear are available for guests' use. Credit cards accepted.

Hotel Divisimar (☎ 777 0371; d standard/superior US$88/105, master ste US$152, additional person US$15; P) This architecturally unremarkable hotel is popular with families and has 12 standard doubles and 12 larger superior units with fridge and extra bed. A couple of master suites sleep four. Clean, tiled units all have air-con and hot water, but are nothing special decor-wise. This hotel also has a pool, Jacuzzi and restaurant. The friendly Tico owners will book all tours. Credit cards accepted.

El Parador (☎ 777 1411, in the USA 800-648 1136; www.hotelparador.com; d standard/deluxe/premium US$205/269/304, junior ste US$357, additional person US$30; P) Just beyond the Divisimar, a side road heads to this hotel, which was created for the admirers of lavish excess, à la *Lifestyles of the Rich and Famous*. It is situated on a formerly forested hilltop that was dynamited away to build the 68-room, 10-suite complex, complete with a private helicopter landing pad, two Jacuzzis, an infinity pool with swim-up bar, a sauna, a tennis court and minigolf. Splendiferous rooms of various types and sizes have all the usual goodies: private terrace, cable TV, phone, air-con, hot water and minibar. Security here is at code orange at all times, so don't think you can just drop by for a visit. Rates include breakfast; credit cards accepted.

Hotel La Mariposa (☎ 777 0355/456; www.lamariposa.com; d standard/deluxe US$181/205, ste US$252-363, penthouse US$439; P ✱ ♿) This internationally acclaimed hotel was the area's first luxury accommodation. Fifty-seven pristine rooms of various sizes are elegantly decorated with hand-carved furniture and cool, tiled floors. All quarters come with one king-sized or two double beds, private bathroom, hot water, air-con, phone and private terrace or balcony. The penthouse suite has a terrace Jacuzzi. The grounds and pools are meticulously kept and there are hammocks for lounging. Staff will arrange all tours and activities. Credit cards accepted. The hotel's restaurant, Le Papillon (p300), is recommended.

Kekoldi Beach Hotel/Dorado Mojado (☎ 777 0368; www.kekoldibeachhotel.com; d US$70, villa US$94; ✱ ♿) Back on the Quepos–Manuel Antonio road, this lovely little hotel has five simple, prettily decorated rooms that come with air-con and hot-water shower. Three villas have fully equipped kitchen. There's a pool and the helpful staff can arrange local tours. The hotel is gay-friendly. Credit cards accepted.

Si Como No (☎ 777 0777, in the USA ☎ 800-237 8201; www.sicomono.com; d standard/superior/deluxe US$187/210/227, ste US$261-290, additional person US$29, child under 6 free; P ✱ 💻 ♿) This fabulous, architecturally arresting hotel was built to incorporate the rain forest. The hotel has two pools (one with a slide for kids; one for adults only; both with swim-up bars), two solar-heated Jacuzzis and two restaurants. Rooms are insulated for comfort and use energy-efficient air-con units; water is recycled into the landscape, and solar-heating panels are used. Units have private balcony or picture window, as well as queen- or king-sized bed and spacious hot-water bathroom. Standard rooms are spacious; superior suites have wet bar or kitchen, and there are larger deluxe suites, some with stained-glass windows. Standard features include minibar, hair dryer, phone, alarm clock, iron, coffee maker and air-con. Rates include breakfast; credit cards accepted.

La Plantación (☎ 777 1332, 777 1115, in the USA & Canada 800-477 7829; www.bigrubys.com; d standard/deluxe/apt/house incl breakfast US$181/199/600/1111; P ♿) This exclusive hotel caters primarily to gay men. The 24 lovely rooms are cool, light and spacious with large bathroom, fan, air-con, cable TV and VCR, and big mosquito nets over king-sized beds. There are eight standard rooms as well as a handful of larger deluxe rooms with patio overlooking the gardens and free-form pool. Two deluxe rooms have sea views and share a private pool with a luxurious two-bedroom apartment. A larger three-bedroom house has every amenity imaginable. There's a pool and clothing-optional sundeck and an adjacent bar. Staff will arrange all tours. Rates include a cocktail hour. Credit cards accepted.

Hotel Casitas Eclipse (☎ 777 0408, 777 1738; www.casitaseclipse.com; d standard/junior ste US$140/180; P ✱ ♿) This pure white complex is unmistakable and comprises a good restaurant, three swimming pools and nine attractive split-level houses. The bottom floor of each house is a spacious junior suite with air-con, queen-sized and single beds, bathroom with hot water, living room, kitchen and patio. The upper floor is a standard room with queen-sized bed, bathroom and terrace. These have a separate entrance but a staircase (with lockable door) combines the two and, voilà, you have a house sleeping five. There are also 11 unconnected rooms and suites. There's an excellent Italian restaurant, Gato Negro (p300), on the premises. Credit cards are accepted.

Hotel Costa Verde (☎ 777 0700, 777 0584, 777 0187; www.costaverde.com; efficiency US$108, studio/studio-plus US$144/177; P ✱ 💻 ♿) This is the sister hotel of the Costa Verde Inn in Escazú (p107) and has been recommended by several readers. The attractive, tile-floor rooms have fan, kitchenette, fridge, private bathroom, hot water and air-con. Efficiency units have two queen-sized beds, while studios have partial ocean views and more expensive 'studio-plus' rooms have full ocean views. Some rooms in the adults-only section have screens and no windows and there is a swim-up pool bar with ocean views. Internet access is available (US$6 per hour) and there is a popular restaurant and bar. The helpful staff will arrange local tours and activities. Credit cards accepted.

Hotel Karahé (☎ 777 0170/52; www.karahe.com; d US$90-130; P ✱ ♿) On the final hill before you reach Manuel Antonio, you'll find this hotel. You could easily walk to the national park entrance from here in about 20 leisurely minutes. There's a pool, spa, restaurant and three levels of rooms. The oldest cabins have superb views and are reached by climbing a flight of steep stairs. All have hot water

SAVING THE SQUIRREL MONKEY

With its expressive eyes and luxuriant coat, the *mono tití* (Central American squirrel monkey) is one of the most beautiful of Costa Rica's four monkey species. Unfortunately, it is also in danger of extinction. Roughly 1500 of these charming animals are left in the Manuel Antonio area, one of their last remaining habitats. Unfortunately, the area is in constant environmental jeopardy due to overdevelopment. To remedy this problem, the folks at **Ascomoti** (Asociación para la Conservación del Mono Tití, Association for the Conservation of the Titi Monkey; ☎ 224 5703; www.ascomoti.org) have begun to take measures to prevent further decline.

The organization is creating a biological corridor between the hilly Cerro-Nara biological protection zone in the northeast and the Parque Nacional Manuel Antonio on the coast. To achieve this, they are reforesting the Río Naranjo, a key waterway linking the two. Already more than 10,000 trees have been planted along 8km of the Naranjo. This not only has the effect of extending the monkeys' habitat, but also provides a protected area for other wildlife. Scientists at the Universidad Nacional de Costa Rica have mapped and selected sites for reforestation and the whole project is supported financially by business owners in the area. (Ascomoti's website has a list of all the local businesses supporting this valuable effort.)

If you want to volunteer, Ascomoti is looking for individuals interested in planting trees or tracking monkey troops. Volunteers must be able to devote at least one month. The cost is US$350 per person per month to cover room and board. Inquire months ahead of your desired travel date as opportunities are not always immediately available.

and air-con; rates depend on the location of your room and include breakfast. Credit cards accepted.

A few minutes' walk further, the beach level is reached; there are more accommodations along here and in Manuel Antonio village (p302).

Eating

Many hotels mentioned earlier have good restaurants open to the public, and there are also several good independent places; the following are particularly recommended. Reservations are a good idea in the high season. Restaurants are also listed from north to south.

Hotel Plinio (☎ 777 0055; dishes US$7-12) The restaurant at this popular hotel has an incredible Southeast Asian menu that includes a smattering of Italian and German specialties. The food is, without a doubt, inventive and delicious. The Asian *bocas* menu allows you to put together a multitude of tapas-sized dishes to make a main course of your choosing.

Next door, the restaurant **Bambú Jam** (in Hotel Mirador del Pacífico) is the hot new music and drinking spot every Friday night, when there are live bands. The restaurant serves 'French exotic' cuisine.

Hotel Mono Azul (☎ 777 1548; dishes US$5-12; 🕑 6am-10pm) There's pizza take-out and delivery service all over Manuel Antonio from this cozy restaurant with a menu featuring Tico and American food. Vegetarian selections are available.

Jungle Room (☎ 777 1645; dishes US$4-10; 🕑 5-10pm) This place features salads, Italian dishes, snacks, meat and seafood. It becomes a disco and bar after 10pm, so you can eat first and dance the calories off later.

Ronny's Place (☎ 777 5120; mains about US$5-12; 🕑 7:30am-10pm) Head 800m west from the main drag, on the good, well-signed dirt road opposite Manuel Antonio Experts, to sip some of the best *sangría* in the country alongside big burgers or fabulously fresh seafood, all the while overlooking two pristine bays and 360° of jungle absolutely atwitter with wildlife. Ronny's was about to open for breakfast soon after we were there.

Bruno's Sunset Grill (☎ 777 0231; La Colina; dishes US$8-11) Bruno's has a good Italian-influenced menu including an assortment of seafood and meats and an international wine list. Lunches are significantly cheaper. There is live music on Thursday and Saturday nights.

Restaurant Mar Luna (dishes US$5-10) A consistently good restaurant with a Tico and international menu and a good bar.

Café Milagro (breakfast US$3-4, sandwiches US$4-6) This café, which is next to Hotel Divisimar, has the same great cappuccino, baked treats and tranquil atmosphere you find in the Quepos outlet. It also serves a full breakfast.

Restaurant Barba Roja (☎ 777 0331; dishes US$3-8; ⏰ 4-10pm Mon, 10am-10pm Tue-Sun) Here you can eat North American food (hamburgers, sandwiches, Mexican dishes, steak and seafood), and there's a great view. In the evenings, the 'margarita sunsets' pack in the crowds.

Bar Restaurante Karola's (☎ 777 1557; dishes US$5-15; ⏰ 11am-10pm) Behind Barba Roja is this outpost serving Mexican dishes, steaks, ribs and seafood in an attractive garden setting. Try the coconut margaritas and the macadamia nut pie for local flavor.

Restaurant Gato Negro (☎ 777 0408, 777 1738; Hotel Casitas Eclipse; dishes US$6-21) This pleasant terrace restaurant specializes in Italian-influenced seafood and meats. Some dishes with lobster and jumbo shrimp can cost as much as US$35. One traveler reports that it's 'hands down the best food in the area.'

Le Papillon (☎ 777 0355/456; Hotel Mariposa; lunch dishes US$6-10, dinner entrees US$12-38) This beautiful restaurant overlooking the rugged shoreline has sunsets that are spectacular and food that's even better (largely continental cuisine). If the dinners are too rich for you, indulge in the cheaper lunch menu, recommended by several travelers.

Sun Spot (☎ 777 0442; Makanda by the Sea; dishes US$7-10) This exclusive little poolside restaurant has breathtaking forest and ocean views and whips up delicious seafood, sandwiches and salads. Reservations are required at all times if you are not a guest at the hotel. No children under 16 allowed.

Rico Tico Bar 'n Grill (☎ 777 1548) This restaurant at the Si Como No hotel provides some informal dining options.

Claro Que Si! (entrees US$10-20; ⏰ dinner only) This more upscale place presents seafood specialties in a fine-dining environment. Accepts guests aged over 18 only.

El Avión (☎ 777 3378; sandwiches US$6, dishes from US$7) See 'bombs away' boxed text.

Super Josette and Super Manuel Antonio, next door to each other, are the best grocery and sundries stores on the road.

Also see Manuel Antonio (p303) and Quepos (p293) for nearby eating suggestions.

BOMBS AWAY!

On the Quepos to Manuel Antonio road, you'll find **El Avión** (☎ 777 3378), an airplane bar constructed from the body of a 1954 Fairchild C-123. The plane was originally purchased by the US government in the '80s for the Nicaraguan Contras, but it never made it out of its hangar in San José because of the ensuing Iran-Contra scandal that embroiled Oliver North and his cohorts in the US government. (The plane is lovingly referred to as 'Ollie's Folly.') In 2000 the enterprising owners of El Avión purchased it for US$3000 and then proceeded to cart it piece by piece to Manuel Antonio. It now sits on the side of the main road, where it looks as if it had crash-landed into the side of the hill. It's now a great spot for a beer, guacamole and a Pacific sunset, and on evenings in the dry season there is live music.

Getting Around

Many visitors who stay in this area arrive by private or rented car (see p295 for rental agencies in Quepos). Drive carefully on this narrow, steep and winding road – and keep an eye out for pedestrians. There's no shoulder, so everyone walks in the street.

Buses between Manuel Antonio and Quepos (US$0.25) run every 30 minutes between 6am and 7:30pm, and less frequently after 7:30pm. The last bus departs Manuel Antonio at 10:25pm. Taxis going to Quepos will usually pick up extra passengers for about US$0.50.

MANUEL ANTONIO

This village at the national park entrance is frequently packed with young international travelers who are drawn here by the park's universal appeal. Reservations are a must for the high season, especially weekends, and lengthy advance planning is needed for Easter week.

There's a good beach, **Playa Espadilla**, but swimmers should beware of rip currents. There are some lifeguards working at this beach (but not at the others in the area). At the far western end of Playa Espadilla, beyond a rocky headland (wear sneakers), there's a gay beach frequented primarily by young men and offering nude sunbathing. This point is inaccessible one hour before and after the high tide, so time your walk well or you'll get cut off.

As with many beach towns that have grown too much and too quickly, the usual

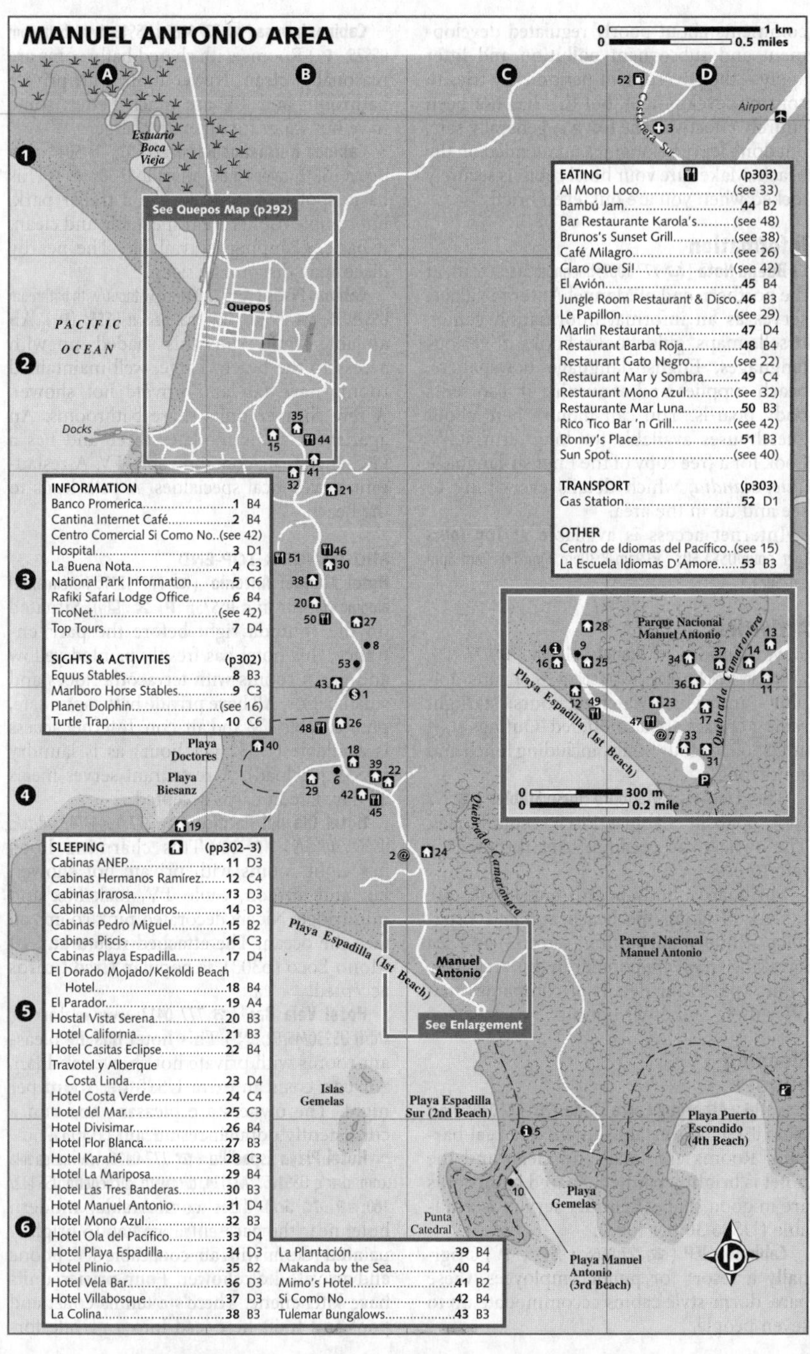
MANUEL ANTONIO AREA
0 1 km
0 0.5 miles
A
B
C
D
1
2
3
4
5
6
Estuario Boca Vieja
See Quepos Map (p292)
Quepos
PACIFIC OCEAN
Docks
Costanera Sur
Airport
Playa Doctores
Playa Biesanz
Playa Espadilla (1st Beach)
Quebrada Camaronera
Parque Nacional Manuel Antonio
Manuel Antonio
See Enlargement
Islas Gemelas
Playa Espadilla Sur (2nd Beach)
Playa Puerto Escondido (4th Beach)
Playa Gemelas
Punta Catedral
Playa Manuel Antonio (3rd Beach)
0 300 m
0 0.2 mile
EATING (p303)
Al Mono Loco (see 33)
Bambú Jam 44 B2
Bar Restaurante Karola's (see 48)
Brunos's Sunset Grill (see 38)
Café Milagro (see 26)
Claro Que Si! (see 42)
El Avión 45 B4
Jungle Room Restaurant & Disco 46 B3
Le Papillon (see 29)
Marlin Restaurant 47 D4
Restaurant Barba Roja 48 B4
Restaurant Gato Negro (see 22)
Restaurant Mar y Sombra 49 C4
Restaurant Mono Azul (see 32)
Restaurante Mar Luna 50 B3
Rico Tico Bar 'n Grill (see 42)
Ronny's Place 51 B3
Sun Spot (see 40)
TRANSPORT (p303)
Gas Station 52 D1
OTHER
Centro de Idiomas del Pacífico (see 15)
La Escuela Idiomas D'Amore 53 B3
INFORMATION
Banco Promerica 1 B4
Cantina Internet Café 2 B4
Centro Comercial Si Como No (see 42)
Hospital 3 D1
La Buena Nota 4 C3
National Park Information 5 C6
Rafiki Safari Lodge Office 6 B4
TicoNet (see 42)
Top Tours 7 D4
SIGHTS & ACTIVITIES (p302)
Equus Stables 8 B3
Marlboro Horse Stables 9 C3
Planet Dolphin (see 16)
Turtle Trap 10 C6
SLEEPING (pp302–3)
Cabinas ANEP 11 D3
Cabinas Hermanos Ramírez 12 C4
Cabinas Irarosa 13 D3
Cabinas Los Almendros 14 D3
Cabinas Pedro Miguel 15 B2
Cabinas Piscis 16 C3
Cabinas Playa Espadilla 17 D4
El Dorado Mojado/Kekoldi Beach Hotel 18 B4
El Parador 19 A4
Hostal Vista Serena 20 B3
Hotel California 21 B3
Hotel Casitas Eclipse 22 B4
Travotel y Alberque Costa Linda 23 D4
Hotel Costa Verde 24 C4
Hotel del Mar 25 C3
Hotel Divisimar 26 B4
Hotel Flor Blanca 27 B3
Hotel Karahé 28 C3
Hotel La Mariposa 29 B4
Hotel Las Tres Banderas 30 B3
Hotel Manuel Antonio 31 D4
Hotel Mono Azul 32 B3
Hotel Ola del Pacífico 33 D4
Hotel Playa Espadilla 34 D3
Hotel Plinio 35 B2
Hotel Vela Bar 36 D3
Hotel Villabosque 37 D3
La Colina 38 B3
La Plantación 39 B4
Makanda by the Sea 40 B4
Mimo's Hotel 41 B2
Si Como No 42 B4
Tulemar Bungalows 43 B3

comments about poorly regulated development and subsequent pollution and litter apply – the government periodically tries to control development, but this has not been entirely effective. The town is generally safe, but don't leave belongings unattended on the beach. Make sure your hotel room is securely locked when you are out, even briefly.

Information

La Buena Nota (☎ 777 1002; buennota@racsa.co.cr), at the northern end of Manuel Antonio village, serves as an informal information center. It sells maps, guidebooks, books in various languages, English-language newspapers, beach supplies and souvenirs; it also rents body boards. You can inquire here about guesthouses available for long-term stays. Look for a free copy of the English-language *Quepolandia*, which details everything to see and do in the area.

Internet access is available at **Top Tours** (per hour US$1.50; 9am-8:30pm Mon-Fri, 9am-6pm Sat-Sun).

Activities

Steve Wofford at **Planet Dolphin** (☎ 777 2137; www.planetdolphin.com; inside Cabinas Piscis) runs dolphin- and whale-watching tours; starlight sailing cruises are also offered. Outings start at US$65 for four hours, including lunch and snorkeling.

The Tico-run **Marlboro Horse Stables** (☎ 777 1108), opposite Cabinas Piscis, rents horses. The owners can organize trips through the rain forest.

Surfboards, body boards and kayaks are rented all along the beach at Playa Espadilla. White-water rafting (see p53) and sea kayaking (p55) are popular in this area – see Tours (p473) for details of companies that offer these and other options.

Sleeping

BUDGET

Travotel y Albergue Costa Linda (☎ 777 0304; r per person US$8) This establishment is a real bargain. Rooms are small and clean and the hotel is brightly painted. Shared bathrooms are in good shape. Laundry service is available (US$6.30 per load).

Cabinas ANEP (☎ 777 0565; r US$35; P) Originally a resort for public employees, these bare, dorm-style cabins accommodate up to seven people.

Cabinas Irarosa (☎ 777 5085; r US$10, d with bathroom US$25; P) Rooms with shared bathrooms are reasonably clean. Newer units with private bathroom and TV are much better; some have hot water for an extra charge.

Cabinas Hermanos Ramírez (☎ 777 5044; r per person US$12, camping per person US$2.50; P) This basic spot looks a little like a trailer park, but double rooms are respectable and clean, if basic. Camping is available. The nearby disco may discourage sleep.

Cabinas Piscis (☎ 777 0046; d without/with bathroom US$29/35, apt US$65, additional person US$5; P) An amiable family runs this shaded inn with access to the beach. Large, well-maintained rooms have fan and private hot shower. A few cheaper units share bathrooms. An apartment accommodates three and has a kitchenette, air-con and cable TV. A restaurant serves local specialties. A path leads to the beach.

MID-RANGE & TOP-END

Hotel Manuel Antonio (☎ 777 1237; hotelmanuelantonio@racsa.co.cr; d US$75; P) Situated on the rotunda right before the park entrance, this hotel has freshly painted yellow and green rooms with terracotta floors and small patios. All have private bathroom, safe, phone, cable TV and air-con. Internet access is available (US$2 per hour) as is laundry (US$5 per load). A restaurant serves meals all day. Credit cards accepted.

Hotel Ola del Pacífico (☎ 777 1944/74; s/d/tr/q US$60/70/85/95; P) This charming hotel has eight rooms with private hot shower, fan and air-con, cable TV, lock box and minifridge. Nicely decorated pink rooms all face the ocean. The attached restaurant, Al Mono Loco (p303), is popular. Credit cards accepted.

Hotel Vela Bar (☎ 777 0413; www.velabar.com; s/d/tr US$30/45/52) This hotel has 19 pleasant rooms with private hot shower and fan. Air-con costs an extra US$8 per room per night. The owners are pleasant and run a consistently popular restaurant (p303).

Hotel Playa Espadilla (☎ 777 0416; www.espadilla.com; d/tr/q US$125/143/174, d/tr with kitchenette US$142/160; P) This comfortable, modern hotel near the park entrance has 16 brightly painted rooms with air-con, cable TV, phone and private hot shower. Four pricier units have kitchenette. There's a tennis court and pool and trails here lead into a private forested area. Rates include breakfast and credit cards are accepted.

Situated just a bit down the street and under the same management, are the recommended **Cabinas Playa Espadilla** (d/tr/q US$79/85/99, d/tr/q with air-con US$84/91/104; P), which are slightly cheaper. The hotel has its own pool and cheaper units without air-con have small kitchenette. Rates do not include breakfast, but credit cards are accepted.

Hotel Villabosque (☎ 777 0463; www.hotelvillabosque.com; d US$82; P) This attractive place has decent, tiled air-con rooms with balcony and private hot-water bathroom. There are 15 rooms, pool, restaurant and guided tours into the national park. Credit cards accepted.

Cabinas Los Almendros (☎ 777 0225, 777 5137; tr fan/air-con US$40/50;) This place, managed by the friendly Doña Emilia, has 21 large, quiet, pleasant rooms with hot-water bathroom. There's a pool, and a decent restaurant is attached. Internet is available (US$2.50 per hour). This is a good value.

Hotel del Mar (☎ 777 0543; d without/with air-con US$58/69, d with queen bed US$81; P) This place has 12 spacious, clean rooms that are nicely maintained, each with private hot shower. The lush grounds provide a nice tranquil option away from the main drag. The hotel is gay-friendly.

Eating & Drinking

Al Mono Loco (casados US$6) Just north of the rotunda, Al Mono Loco sits under a thatched *rancho* and serves Tico and international specialties, including pasta (US$7) and burgers (US$4).

Marlin Restaurant (breakfast US$2-4.50, fish dishes US$6-7.50; 7am-10pm) This is popular with gringos, who pack in for the fresh fish dishes and good breakfasts.

Hotel Vela Bar (dishes US$7-15) Has the best and priciest restaurant in Manuel Antonio. It specializes in seafood, but there are other items, including vegetarian entrees, available.

The slightly cheaper restaurant at **Hotel Villabosque** (dishes US$5-16) and the steakhouse in **Cabinas Los Almendros** (dishes US$2-8) are also good.

Restaurant Mar y Sombra (casados US$3 and fish dinners US$6) The atmosphere at this place just up the beach is good, but the food isn't so great. On weekends it's a popular waterside nightclub.

Getting There & Away

All flights for Manuel Antonio land at the airport in Quepos (p294).

Buses depart Manuel Antonio for San José at 6am, 9:30am, noon and 5pm. These will pick you up in front of your hotel if you are on the road to flag them down or from the Quepos bus terminal, after which there are no stops. Buy tickets well in advance at the Quepos bus terminal. This bus is frequently packed and you will not be able to buy tickets from the driver. Buses for destinations other than San José also leave from the main terminal in Quepos (see p294 for more details).

PARQUE NACIONAL MANUEL ANTONIO

At the end of an easily navigable paved road, Manuel Antonio has many obvious attractions – beautiful forest-backed tropical beaches, rocky headlands with ocean and island views, prolific wildlife and a clearly marked trail system. This makes it one of the most popular parks in Costa Rica. Unfortunately, this has led to intense pressure on the park and the area: too many visitors, too many hotels and too much impact on the wildlife and environment.

Parque Nacional Manuel Antonio was declared a national park in 1972, preserving it (with minutes to spare) from being turned into yet another dull and expensive beach resort. (The developer who had purchased the land had even begun razing trees from the site to build condos!) Manuel Antonio was enlarged by about 1000 hectares in 2000, but at 1625 hectares, it remains the country's second-smallest national park.

Clearly, large numbers of people in such a small area tend to detract from the experience of visiting the park. Idyllic and romantic beaches have to be shared with many others, wildlife is either driven away or – worse still – taught to scavenge for tourist handouts, and there are inevitable litter and traffic problems.

Fortunately, several steps have been taken to minimize pressure on the park. Camping is no longer allowed, vehicular traffic is prohibited and the park is closed on Mondays. In addition, the number of visitors is limited to 600 during the week and 800 on weekends and holidays. (To avoid the crowds, go early in the morning, midweek or in the rainy season.)

Nonetheless, Manuel Antonio is a wonder to see. Squirrel monkeys still fly through the trees while sloths lounge in the branches and its tranquil beaches offer ample opportunities for snorkeling or restful sunbathing.

Orientation & Information

Visitors must leave their vehicles in the parking lot near the park entrance; the charge is US$3. However, the road here is very narrow and congested and it's suggested that you leave your car at your hotel and take an early-morning bus to Manuel Antonio and then walk in. The **park entrance** (US$7; 7am-4pm Tue-Sun) is a few meters south of the rotunda. To reach it, you'll have to wade through the Camaronera estuary, which can be anywhere from ankle to thigh deep, depending on the tides and the season. Here you can hire naturalist guides to take you into the park.

The park ranger station and **information center** (☎ 777 0644) is just before Playa Manuel Antonio. Drinking water is available, and there are toilets, beach showers, picnic tables and a refreshment stand. There is no camping and guards will come around in the evening to make sure that no one has remained behind.

The beaches are often numbered – most people call Playa Espadilla (outside the park) 'first beach,' Playa Espadilla Sur 'second beach,' Playa Manuel Antonio 'third beach,' Playa Puerto Escondido 'fourth beach,' and Playa Playita 'fifth beach.' Some people begin counting at Espadilla Sur, which is the first beach in the park, so it can be a bit confusing trying to figure out which beach people may be talking about. The refreshment stand is at third beach.

The average daily temperature is 27°C and average annual rainfall is 3875mm. The dry season is not entirely dry, merely less wet, so you should be prepared for rain (although it can also be dry for days on end). Make sure you carry plenty of drinking water, sun protection and insect repellent. Pack a picnic lunch if you're spending the day.

Hiking

After the park entrance, it's about a 30-minute hike to **Playa Espadilla Sur**, where you'll find the park ranger station and information center; watch for birds and monkeys as you walk. West of the station, follow an obvious trail through forest to an isthmus separating Playas Espadilla Sur and Manuel Antonio. This isthmus is called a tombolo and was formed by the accumulation of sedimentary material between the mainland and the peninsula beyond, which was once an island. If you walk along Playa Espadilla Sur, you will find a small mangrove area. The isthmus widens into a rocky peninsula, with forest in the center. A trail leads around the peninsula to **Punta Catedral**, from where there are good views of the Pacific Ocean and various rocky islets that are bird reserves and form part of the national park. Brown boobies and pelicans are among the seabirds that nest on these islands.

You can continue around the peninsula to **Playa Manuel Antonio**, or you can avoid the peninsula altogether and hike across the isthmus to this beach. At the western end of the beach, during the low tide, you can see a semicircle of rocks that archaeologists believe were arranged by pre-Columbian Indians to function as a **turtle trap**. (Turtles would swim in during high tide, but when they tried to swim out after the tide started receding, they'd be trapped by the wall.) The beach itself is an attractive one of white sand and is popular for bathing. It's protected and safer than the Espadilla beaches.

Beyond Playa Manuel Antonio, the trail divides. The lower trail is steep and slippery during the wet months and leads to the quiet Playa Puerto Escondido. This beach can be more or less completely covered by high tides, so be careful not to get cut off. The upper trail climbs to a **lookout** on a bluff overlooking Puerto Escondido and Punta Serrucho beyond – a stunning vista. Rangers reportedly limit the number of hikers on this trail to 45.

Tours & Guides

Hiring a guide costs US$20 per person for a two-hour tour. The only guides allowed in the park are members of Aguila (a local association governed by the park service) who have official ID badges, and recognized guides from tour agencies or hotels. This is to prevent visitors from getting ripped off and to ensure a good-quality guide – Aguila guides are well trained and most are bilingual. (French-, German-, or English-speaking guides can be requested.)

DON'T FEED THE MONKEYS!

However tempting it might be, feeding monkeys is prohibited because it has the serious side effects of making them susceptible to human illnesses and overly aggressive. In addition, just imagine what those Cheetos will do to the digestive system of a wild animal raised on a natural diet of leaves and raw fruit. (It's not a pretty sight.) This has become a serious problem in Manuel Antonio and the Minae, and businesses in the area support an initiative in which the names (and sometimes photos) of violators are published in the local press. So, before your photo ends up in the paper, you have ample warning. *Don't feed the monkeys.*

Wildlife Watching

Monkeys abound in the park, and it's difficult to spend a day walking around without seeing at least some. White-faced monkeys are the most common, but rarer squirrel monkeys are present and howler monkeys can usually be seen (and heard). Apart from monkeys, sloths, agoutis, peccaries, armadillos, coatis, and raccoons are also spotted quite regularly. More than 350 species of bird are reported in the park and surrounding area, and a variety of lizards, snakes, iguanas and other animals may be observed.

All the trails within the park are good for wildlife watching, but it's always wise to ask the rangers about recent sightings. Some trails may limit the number of hikers to minimize disturbance of the animals. There's a small coral reef off Playa Manuel Antonio, but the water is rather cloudy and the visibility limited. Despite this, snorkelers can see a variety of fish, as well as marine creatures such as crabs, corals, sponges and sea snails.

Immediately inland from the beaches is an evergreen littoral forest. This contains many different species of tree, bush and other plants. Watch out for the *manzanillo* tree *(Hippomane mancinella)*. It has poisonous fruits that look like little crab apples, and the sap exuded by the bark and leaves is toxic, causing the skin to itch and burn. Warning signs are prominently displayed beside examples of this tree near the park entrance.

MANUEL ANTONIO TO DOMINICAL

To continue further south along the coast from Manuel Antonio, you have to backtrack to Quepos and from there head 4km inland to the Costanera Sur. It's 44km from Quepos before you reach the next village of any size, Dominical. The road is bone-shaking gravel, easily passable in the dry season but requiring care to negotiate with an ordinary car in the wet. Residents of this area have long complained to the government that the Costanera Sur should be paved. The government repeatedly promises to pave and improve this road (as they do with every road in Costa Rica), though this has yet to happen.

The drive is through kilometer after kilometer of African oil-palm plantation, with identical-looking settlements along the way. These are minor centers for the palm-oil extracting process. Each has a grassy village square, institutional-looking housing, a store, church and bar.

Rafiki Safari Lodge

About 15km south of Quepos you'll come to the town of Savegre. From here a 4WD dirt road parallels the Río Savegre and leads 7km inland, past the towns of Silencio and Santo Domingo, to the **Rafiki Safari Lodge** (☎ 777 2250, 777 5327; www.rafikisafari.com; s/d with 3 meals US$132/225, child under 5 free; P). Nestled into the rain forest, with a prime spot right next to the river, the lodge combines all the comforts of a hotel with the splendor of a jungle safari – all with a little bit of African flavor. The owners, who are from South Africa, have constructed 11 luxury tent cabins equipped with private concrete bathroom and hot water. All units are screened in and have private porches and electricity. There's a springwater pool and activities include horseback riding, bird-watching (more than 350 species have been identified), hiking and white-water rafting. There's a well-equipped bar and a rancho-style restaurant serving Tico and South African specialties.

The lodge has an office on the Quepos to Manuel Antonio road (p295). Packages are available, including combination specials with Bahari Beach Bungalows in Matapalo (p306). Credit cards accepted.

Matapalo

Matapalo offers a mainly unvisited stretch of beach with long vistas, palm trees and safe swimming. (Nope, this isn't a surfing beach.) If you are looking for a slice of oceanside tranquility, go no further. The surf is calm, the beach is clean and the town was recently awarded its first Bandera Azul Ecológica (see p453 for more on this honor).

The turnoff to this tiny village from the main road is at the **Restaurant Express Deli del Pacífico** (dishes US$4-8), where you can nosh on pizzas, quiche, burgers and chili con carne.

The well-kept **El Coquito del Pacífico** (☎ 787 5028, 384 7220; www.elcoquito.com; s/d/tr/q US$45/55/65/75; P) about 1km from the main road, has spacious, whitewashed cabins in a shady spot next to the beach. Units have private bathroom and hot water and there's a pool, restaurant and bar. The German owners speak English and can arrange tours and massages.

Just down the road on the beach side, **Dos Palmas B&B** (☎ 787 5037; d US$47, additional person US$5; P) is a tiny, bright-yellow inn with two large rooms, each with private hot shower, minifridge and a king-sized bed. (Extra beds can be added on request.)

The American-owned **Jungle House** (☎ 787 5005, 777 2748; www.junglehouse.com; d incl breakfast US$65; P) provides the epitome of relaxation, with five polished-wood quarters that are all nicely decorated and come with private bathroom, cable TV, air-con, kitchenette and hammock. The bamboo 'honeymoon' cabin in the back is a large open-air unit with incredible views of the hills. Charlie, the friendly owner, is active locally and supports local education initiatives and trash pickup efforts on the beach. A pool table provides a great gathering spot.

Almost next door, **La Piedra Buena** (☎ 787 5020; lapiedra_buena@hotmail.com; dishes US$7-10; d/q US$35/65; P) is a restaurant-bar offering delicious food – a kind of gourmet Swiss-international blend with a good selection of veggie dishes. They have a handful of wood cabins which are basic but spotless with private bathroom and hot water. Credit cards accepted.

At the end of the road you'll find the new **Bahari Beach Bungalows** (☎ 787 5057/14; andrealudwig10@hotmail.com; d cabin US$45, d tent US$80; P) with four safari-style beachfront tents and two cabins. All of the tents are fully furnished and have electricity, tiled private bathroom with hot shower, hand-painted sink and ocean views. The cabins, across the road, are also beautifully decorated and come ornamented with fresh flowers. There's a pool overlooking the ocean and a restaurant. Credit cards accepted.

There's a **campsite** on the beach by the main access road, but it gets quite crowded on high-season weekends.

Buses between Quepos and Dominical can drop you off at the turnoff to the village; from there it's a couple of kilometers to the beach.

Hacienda Barú National Wildlife Refuge

South of Matapalo, about a kilometer before reaching the Río Barú, is the private nature reserve, Hacienda Barú. It covers only 336 hectares but manages to pack in more than 349 species of bird, 69 species of mammal (including 24 bats) and 94 types of amphibian and reptile – in addition to the many frogs, toads and snakes yet to be identified. It's also a great place to see the activities of leaf-cutter ants.

This impressive collection of wildlife results from its location on the steep coastal hills that encompass a variety of habitats, including beach, mangroves, the Río Barú, pasture, plantations and lowland and hilly rain forest up to 320m above sea level. In addition, the reserve contains several pre-Columbian cemetery sites and petroglyphs.

Owners Jack and Diane Ewing are active conservationists and have lived (and raised their family) here since 1970. The Ewings, along with co-owner Steven Stroud, have begun a nonprofit foundation to establish biological corridors between Corcovado and the more northern Pacific regions of Costa Rica.

There is an **information center** (☎ 787 0003; www.haciendabaru.com) near the junction of the road from San Isidro and the Costanera, at the southern end of the Hacienda property, 3km north of Dominical. Here you can make reservations for tours or accommodations. You can inquire about volunteering opportunities via email (hacbaru@racsa.co.cr).

The El Ceibo gas station, 1.7km north of the hacienda, is the only one for a good way in any direction. Groceries, fishing gear, tide tables, and other useful sundries are available, and there are clean toilets.

TOURS

There are several guided tours offered. These include a lowland **birding walk** (US$20,

2½ hours), a **rain forest hike** (US$35 incl lunch, 5½ hours), a **mangrove and beach hike** (US$20) and an **overnight jungle or beach tour** (US$60 incl meals and comfortable camping). These prices are for one person, and there's a two-person minimum. Horseback rides and kayak tours are also available.

There's also a **canopy platform** (US$35) about 32m above the ground, built in a tree that is reached after a 15-minute hike through the forest. Here visitors can get magnificent treetop views of the forest canopy and its abundant wildlife. If this isn't enough adventure, try a **tree-climbing tour** (US$35), where you rope climb into some of the reserve's bigger trees (more strenuous). And, naturally, there's the adrenaline rush of a zip-line tour, the so-called **Flight of the Toucan** (US$35).

During weekends and school holidays, local school children knowledgeable about ecology will lead your tour for a tip. Other activities include **self-guided hikes** (US$6) on the reserve's many trails.

SLEEPING & EATING

There are six simple but spacious two- and three-bedroom **cabins** (d incl breakfast US$68, additional person US$10; P). Each has a kitchenette, refrigerator, fans in every room, hot shower, sitting room and insect screens. There's also a **restaurant** (lunch US$7.50, dinner US$8.50).

GETTING THERE & AWAY

The Quepos–Dominical–San Isidro bus stops outside the hacienda entrance. The San Isidro–Dominical–Uvita bus will drop you at the Río Barú bridge, 2km from the hacienda office. A taxi from Dominical costs US$4.

DOMINICAL

Dominical is a mellower surfing alternative to Costa Rica's other central Pacific beaches. A long beach with big waves assures a steady stream of advanced surfers. The nearby Hacienda Barú (p306) provides peaceful hiking and wildlife observation, and Parque Nacional Marino Ballena to the south is a tranquil seaside alternative with good swimming. Despite the slower pace, Dominical is fast becoming a stop on the tourist trail and the town can get full on weekends. The town is 44km south of Quepos by a partially paved road and 34km from San Isidro by a steep paved, but potholed, road.

Orientation & Information

The main Costanera highway bypasses Dominical; the entrance to the village is immediately past the Río Barú bridge. There's a main road through the village, where many of the services mentioned are found, and a parallel road along the beach.

You can check email at **Internet Colibrí** (per hour US$4.50; 9:30am-7pm Mon-Sat) above the San Clemente Bar & Grill and have laundry done at **Lavandería Las Olas** (7am-9pm), inside the minisuper of the same name.

There are no banking facilities, but San Clemente Bar & Grill (see Sleeping, p308) will exchange both US dollars and traveler's checks. It has a postal service upstairs.

For emergencies, phone the local **police** (☎ 787 0011).

Dangers & Annoyances

Waves, currents and riptides in Dominical are very strong and many people have drowned at the local beaches. Watch for red flags (which mark riptides), follow the instructions of posted signs and swim at beaches with lifeguards. For information on what to do if you're caught in a riptide, see Ocean Hazards (p453).

In addition, because of the heavy-duty party crowd Dominical is attracting, there is a burgeoning drug problem and some of the bars can get a little rough at night.

Sights & Activities

The **Green Iguana Surf Camp** (☎ 815 3733; www.greeniguanasurfcamp.com), on a side road leading to the beach, is run by experienced surfers Jason and Karla Butler. It offers a variety of surf lessons and tours as well as seven- to 10-day surfing camps.

Dominical is emerging as a base for day trips to Parque Nacional Corcovado (about US$95), Parque Nacional Marino Ballena (US$55), Isla Caño (US$95) and local kayaking and snorkeling trips (US$55). Get details at **Southern Expeditions** (☎ 787 0100; www.costarica-southern-expeditions.com) at the entrance to the village. The staff can also organize trips to the Guaymi indigenous reserve near Boruca.

About 10km along the road to San Isidro, just before Platanillo, an entrance to the right leads to **Centro Turístico Cataratas Nauyaca** (☎ 787 0198, 771 3187; www.ecotourism.co.cr/nauyacawaterfalls/index.html). There's no vehicle access to this tourist center, but you can hire horses for a guided ride to two waterfalls that plunge into a deep swimming hole. With a day's notice, a tour can be arranged, including the guided ride, swimming, and country meals with the local family. Tours leave at 8am, take six to seven hours and cost US$40 per person. A campground with dressing rooms and toilets is available.

The San Clemente Bar & Grill rents bicycles and surfboards.

Courses

Adventure Spanish School (☎ 787 0023, in the USA & Canada 800-237 730; www.adventurespanishschool.com) runs one-week Spanish-language programs starting at US$315, without homestays. Private lessons are available.

Sleeping

The hotels listed here are in the main village and have cold-water showers unless noted otherwise.

Posada del Sol (☎ 787 0085; s/d US$25/40; P) This quiet, pleasant hotel is one of the better places in town and worth the price. Well-decorated rooms come with clean bath and hot water and the friendly Tica owners are very helpful.

Tortilla Flats (☎ 787 0033; s/d US$21/24, s/d with air-con US$24/31;) On the beach, this beautifully maintained lodge has brightly painted rooms with private hot-water bathroom and patio hammock, and a tasty restaurant. More expensive units have air-con and face the beach.

San Clemente Bar & Grill (☎ 787 0026; r per person US$8; P) This has basic rooms above the restaurant on the main road, though readers report that the bathrooms are dingy. It also operates the **San Clemente Hostel** (dm US$10) at the northern end of the beach. There are bunks, shared bathrooms with hot water, and a communal kitchen and living room with cable TV. Next door, and footsteps from the beach, is the **San Clemente Inn** (d US$25-60;). Shiny wooden units of various sizes are spacious and clean; pricier ones have air-con and ocean views. Credit cards accepted. All reservations must be paid up front.

Sundancer Cabinas (☎ 787 0189; d US$21; P) This is definitely a quieter option: clean rooms with shared hot-water shower are situated in a pleasant family home. There is a shared kitchen and a swimming pool.

Cabinas Coco (☎ 787 0235; d US$12.50, camping per person US$3.80, r with bathroom US$34; P) Adequate doubles have fans and shared or private bathroom – just don't expect friendly service. The adjacent disco may interfere with beauty sleep.

Cabinas Thrusters (☎ 787 0127; d US$25) A steady stream of surfers and skaters fill these simple and clean wood cabins. The bar downstairs is raucous, so retire late.

Hotel DiuWak (☎ 787 0087; www.diuwak.com; d with fan/air-con US$65/80; P) On the road to the beach, DiuWak has eight clean, spacious rooms with fan and hot water, and eight bright, nicely tiled air-con units with kitchenette and fridge. There is a restaurant, bar, Jacuzzi, minimarket and Internet access (US$4.30 per hour).

Río Lindo Resort (☎ 787 0028; www.riolindo.com; d without/with air-con US$53/64; P) This hotel is on the outskirts of Dominical. Rooms are tiled and attractively painted. Five units have hot-water shower and air-con; others have fan and cold water. There's an attached **restaurant-bar** (pizza & pasta under US$10). Credit cards accepted.

Antorchas Camping (☎ 787 0307; camping per person US$3, s/d US$9/12; P) Just a few meters from the beach, this campground provides lockers and showers. It rent out tents for US$1 per night and there are six basic rooms sharing cold showers. For an extra fee of US$3 per stay, basic kitchen privileges are available.

Camping Piramis (☎ 787 0196; camping per person US$2.30, tr US$10; P) At the beach's southern end, this unexceptional campground has decent (though dark) concrete rooms with an unusual Egyptian theme.

The following places are a few minutes out of town by car:

Hotel Villas Río Mar (☎ 787 0052; www.villasriomar.com; s/d/q US$70/82/123; P) Just beyond the edge of town, a sign points under the bridge to this hotel about 800m from the village. It has 40 pretty, polished-wood bungalows, each with a terrace, hot-water shower, mini-fridge, hair dryer, fan and phone. Room service is available and for an extra US$15 a day per person, you can have breakfast and dinner. There's a pool, Jacuzzi, tennis court, restaurant and bar. The hotel can arrange all local tours and has surfboards for rent. Credit cards accepted.

Hotel y Restaurante Roca Verde (☎ 787 0036; www.rocaverde.net; r US$75; P) Overlooking the beach about 1km south of the village, this hotel has 12 air-con, tropical-theme rooms which can accommodate up to three or four people, with pretty murals and hot showers. There is a good restaurant-bar (this page) and a pool.

For other accommodations see the area southeast of Dominical (p310).

Eating & Drinking

Soda Nanyoa is the cheapest eatery in town, serving casados for about US$2. (Stick to casados; the spaghetti and burgers don't live up to the promising descriptions.)

San Clemente Bar & Grill (dishes US$3-8) This large restaurant has big breakfasts, Tex-Mex bar food and a weekly club night on Fridays. There is a pool table and *foosball*.

Fish Lips (dishes US$9; 11am-9:30pm Thu-Tue) Just down the street, this popular new seafood eatery has a long list of choice fish dishes.

Tortilla Flats (dishes US$4-7) Here you'll find a great beach-side atmosphere, highly drinkable margaritas as well as a tangy chicken-parmesan sandwich.

Thrusters Bar (at Cabinas Thrusters) The local party people congregate here for beer and skateboarding around the pool tables. Patrons have evidently spent quality time at the tattoo parlor upstairs, conveniently situated if you feel the need to drink and redecorate yourself.

Hotel y Restaurante Roca Verde (in Hotel Roca Verde; dishes US$4-8) This restaurant has an international menu, as well as a big bar and plenty of cold beer. On Saturday nights there's music and dancing and on Sundays you can recover with an all-you-can eat brunch (US$12).

Getting There & Away

BUS

Buses all arrive and depart at the end of the road next to Cabinas Coco. These schedules change regularly, so ask about times before setting out. (Most hotel owners have current schedules.)

Ciudad Cortés US$2.50; 1¾ hours; departs 4:15am & 10am (maybe later if the driver stops for breakfast).
Palmar 4:30am & 10:30am.
Quepos US$2; four hours; 5:25am, 8:15am, 1:40pm & 2:45pm.
San Isidro US$1; one hour; 6:45am, 7am, 2:40pm & 3:30pm.
Uvita US$0.60; one hour; 10am, 11:30am, 5:15am & 9pm.

TAXI

Taxis to Uvita cost US$10, while the ride to San Isidro costs US$20 and the ride to Quepos is US$50. Cars can accommodate up to five people. Minivans for up to 28 passengers can also be arranged. For service call **Del Tabaco Real & Taxi Dominical** (☎ 814 444), which can arrange pickups and drop-offs anywhere in the region.

ESCALERAS AREA

Heading south out of Dominical along the Costanera, you'll pass the turnoff for the road to San Isidro on your left. Just over 2km to the south, a sign points towards a steep and narrow dirt road that heads east up the mountain and winds its way back down to the Costanera in a loop through the area known as 'Escaleras' (Staircase). A 4WD vehicle is an absolute necessity (the locals weren't kidding when they named it Escaleras). The rough ride will be worth it – the views are absolutely breathtaking.

Sleeping & Eating

Bellavista Lodge & Ranch (☎ 388 0155, in the USA 800-909 4469, access code 01; www.bellavistalodge.com; d US$53, d cabin upper/lower fl US$55/65, additional person US$5; P) Perched at the top of the Escaleras road, you'll find this lodge owned by long-time resident Woody Dyer, who has a wealth of stories about his many years in the area. The remote lodge is in a revamped farmhouse surrounded by a balcony providing superb ocean views. Accommodations are in four shiny wood rooms with private, solar-heated shower. A two-floored private cabin comes with a kitchen and living room and accommodates six. Rates include breakfast or an evening snack of beer and chips. Tasty home-cooked meals (and pies!) are available (breakfast and lunch US$5, dinner US$10). The ranch has electricity 24 hours a day. There are guided horseback excursions to waterfalls (US$35 to US$55). If you don't have a 4WD, Woody will pick you up in Dominical for US$10.

Villa Escaleras (☎ 823 0509, in the USA 773-279 0516; www.villa-escaleras.com; villas for 4/6/8 people US$240/280/320; P) About another kilometer up the Escaleras road, this spacious villa has gorgeous views and a pool and is a great getaway spot for a large family or a group of friends. There are four bedrooms, five bathrooms, an equipped kitchen, cathedral ceilings and Spanish tiled floors. Weekly maid service, coffee supplies and a wraparound balcony make the setting complete. Local tours can be arranged and there are special weekly rates available.

Finca Brian y Emilia (☎ 396 6206; r per person without/with US$36/50; P) Also on the Escaleras road, this small, isolated, working farm is surrounded by rain forest. It has screened cabins that sleep up to six and come with shared or private bathroom. Rates include meals and a short hiking tour. There's a heated rock pool to soak in. There are volunteer opportunities if you can commit to two weeks.

Pacific Edge (☎ 381 4369; www.exploringcostarica.com/pacificedge/; s/d US$52/58, bungalow 2/3/4 people US$87/105/128; P) The Escaleras road drops back down towards the Costanera past this friendly place. Four cabins are perched on a knife-edge ridge about 200m above sea level and have solar-heated hot shower, balcony, coffee maker and fridge. Family bungalows accommodate up to six and have kitchen. You can add breakfast and dinner to the rate for US$25 per person. There's a pool and local tours can be arranged. Reserve through Selva Mar in San Isidro (p322).

Sun Storms Mountain (☎ 305 2414; d US$30; P) This is the budget option on the mountain and easiest to reach via the second entrance to Escaleras. Basic wood cabins are clean and rooms have private bathroom with hot water. The hotel is most popular for its bar, the **Jolly Roger** (till 1am), run by American pirate, er, proprietor, Roger.

SOUTHEAST OF DOMINICAL

Just southeast of Dominical, the paved road continues through lush vegetation another 17km towards Uvita. If you're driving, note that the smooth tarmac has speed bumps at inopportune and unmarked places, and the rainy season regularly produces ditch-sized potholes.

The attractive, tranquil and comfortable **Costa Paraíso Lodge** (☎ 787 0025; www.costaparaisodominical.com; d US$90-105, additional person US$12; P) is about 2km south of town, nestled on the northern end of Dominicalito beach. Here you'll find five rooms of various sizes housing up to four people. All units have private bathroom, living room and porch overlooking the ocean. Several rooms have air-con and a couple come with kitchenette. Credit cards accepted.

Cabinas Punta Dominical (☎ 787 0016/34, 787 0241; puntadominical@racsa.co.cr; q incl breakfast US$60, additional person US$6; P), about 4km south of Dominical and then to the right on a dirt road to the beach, are situated high on the rocky Punta Dominical. The four attractive cabins are isolated yet comfortable and have fan, private bathroom, electric shower and a porch. Each cabin will sleep up to four people and reservations are recommended. Boat trips can be arranged. Credit cards accepted. **Restaurant La Parcela** (meals US$6-16; 7am-9:30am), the eatery on the premises, is widely regarded as one of the best in the area. Come for sunset views and good steak.

About 2km further on, **Las Casitas de Puertocito** (☎ 393 4327, 200 0139; www.lascasitashotel.com; d/tr incl breakfast US$54/72, additional person US$18; P) has eight pretty cabins. All rooms are beautifully appointed and have private hot shower, fan and patio. One unit has a kitchenette and fridge. There's a pool, bar, Italian restaurant and beach access nearby. Lara, the manager, speaks Italian, English, Spanish and French. Guests can rent horses and arrange hiking, snorkeling, diving and boat trips.

A few kilometers before reaching Uvita, you'll see a signed turnoff to the left on a rough dirt road (use 4WD) that leads 3.5km up the hill (look over your shoulder for great views of Parque Nacional Marino Ballena) to **Reserva Biológica Oro Verde** (☎ 743 8072, 843 8833; P). This private reserve is on the farm of the friendly Duarte family, who have homesteaded the area for more than three decades. About two-thirds of their 150-hectare property is rain forest and they offer guided hikes (US$15 per person), horseback tours (US$25) and birding walks (US$30). The birding walks take three hours and depart at 5am and 2pm.

Opposite the turnoff to Oro Verde is **La Merced National Wildlife Refuge**, a 506-hectare national wildlife refuge (and former cattle ranch) with primary and secondary forests and mangroves lining the Río Morete. Here, you can take guided nature hikes (US$25), horseback tours to Punta Uvita (US$35) and half-day birding walks (US$35). The latter can be turned into full-day tours with lunch for an extra US$20.

You can stay at La Merced in a 1940s **farmhouse** (r per person with 3 meals US$60), which can accommodate 10 people in double rooms of various sizes. There is a separate cabin that has space for up to seven people. Rooms are very well maintained and all of them share hot-water bathrooms, a living room and porch. Electricity is available by generator from 6pm to 9pm. Rates include a guided tour. Book through Selva Mar (p322).

UVITA

This hamlet, 17km south of Dominical, will give you an idea of what Costa Rican beach towns must have looked like before the tourist boom descended on the country's coasts. The town is a loose straggle of farms, houses and *sodas* and the entry point for Parque Nacional Marino Ballena. The area off the main highway is referred to locally as Uvita, while the area next to the beach is called Playa Uvita and Playa Bahía Uvita (the southern end of the beach).

The beach area is reached through two parallel dirt roads that are roughly 500m apart. The first entrance is just south of the bridge over the Río Uvita and the second entrance is the dirt road that runs next to Cabinas Gato (p312). This area is popular with Ticos looking for a place to swim. This is not a surfing area. (Sorry, dudes.)

At low tide you can walk out along Punta Uvita, but ask locally before heading out so that you don't get cut off by the tides.

Banco Coopealianza (☎ 743 8231) will change small amounts of US dollars. Steve at Hotel Toucan will exchange traveler's checks for a 3% service charge.

The **Jardín de Mariposas** (admission US$4; 8am-4pm) is in Playa Uvita (just follow the signs). This Tico-run outfit raises butterflies for export and education and this is a good opportunity to get up-close-and-personal with breeds such as the morpho. Go early in the morning when butterflies are at their most active. Admission includes a guided tour.

Sleeping & Eating

The main entrance to Uvita leads inland, east of the highway, where you'll find the following places. All showers are cold unless otherwise stated.

Hotel Toucan (☎ 743 8140; www.tucanhotel.com; 100m east of main road; dm US$7, d without/with bathroom US$16/18, tr without bathroom US$16, camping per person US$4;) Located 100m inland of the main highway in Uvita, the hotel offers Internet access (US$2.50 per hour), laundry service (US$3 per load, wash and hang dry), free luggage storage, communal kitchen, movie nights and Sunday spaghetti dinners. Excitable American owner Steve is just bursting at the seams with news on the area and his clean rooms are a bargain.

Cabinas Los Laureles (☎ 743 8235; d US$17.50, r for 6 persons US$29; P) About 200m up the road you'll find this pleasant, locally run place which has eight clean, polished wood cabins with private bathroom. The family can arrange horseback tours and any other activities you might be interested in.

Cabinas El Coco Tico (☎ 743 8032; d US$17.50; P) Another 100m up on the left-hand side you'll find this very similar hotel, which has seven concrete units and a *soda*. The owners can also help out with local tour arrangements.

Cascada Verde (www.cascadaverde.org; dm US$7, shared loft per person US$9, s/d house US$10/16, s/d lodge US$20/36) About 2km inland and uphill from Uvita is this alternative-living organic permaculture farm. Accommodations include rooms in a communal house and separate wood lodge. Rooms are simple and bathrooms are all shared. The owners request that guests bring fully biodegradable soap and shampoo. A restaurant serves vegetarian, raw-food specialties. A taxi here will cost about US$3 from the highway area.

By Playa Uvita, you'll find several other accommodations.

Cabinas Hegalva (☎ 743 8016; r per person US$8, camping US$2; P) This is run by the gracious Doña Cecilia, who offers clean rooms with private bathroom. A restaurant serves breakfast upon request.

Cabinas Dagmar (☎ 743 8181; r per person without/with breakfast US$14.50/18, camping per person US$2.50; P) This place next door has fresh mint-green rooms and a very congenial owner. Rooms come with private bathroom and hot-water shower. One unit has a kitchenette.

Cabinas María Jesús (☎ 743 8121; r per person US$10; P) A little further from the beach, but still within walking distance, is this more rural place located on a farm. Six dark, but very tidy, wood cabins come with private bathroom and fan.

Cabinas Punta Uvita (☎ 771 2311, 743 8015; d/tr/q US$12/14/19, cabin for 5 persons US$24; d with bathroom US$14.50, camping per person US$2; P) Close to the beach on the southern access road to Playa Uvita, this pleasant family-run establishment has a variety of rooms, most of which have shared bathroom. There is camping.

Cabinas Gato (☎ 818 2484; d/tr US$17/24; P) Continue 500m past the bridge over the Río Uvita and on the right-hand side you'll find these brand-new units, which all come with tiled floors, private bathroom and plenty of parking. It's on the main road, so it's not scenic, but it's still pleasant.

Villas Bejuco (☎ 743 8093; meals US$2.50-4; d/tr US$47/59; P) Just 2km south of the bridge, a clearly signed turnoff leads up a concrete driveway to this comfortable lodge 500m from the beach. There are 10 cabins with private shower and screen. There's a bar and an inexpensive restaurant.

La Colonia (☎ 743 8021; tr/q US$12/29; P) A few hundred meters further down the Costanera, you'll see a dirt road leading to the beach. Here you'll find this family-run establishment, which has basic and spacious cabins with private bathroom. More expensive units for four people also have kitchenettes. The helpful owners can arrange transport around the area.

Across the street from Hotel Toucan, you'll find the cheap and tasty **Soda Salem** (casados US$2), which serves up hearty lunchtime meals. There's no menu; just sit at the counter and ask what's cooking.

For a bigger splurge and a lengthy Southeast Asian menu, head to the highly recommended **Balcón de Uvita** (dishes average US$8; 11am-9pm Tue-Sun). The turnoff is on the east side of the Costanera, just south of the gas station.

Getting There & Away

Most buses depart from the two sheltered bus stops on the Costanera in the main village.

Ciudad Cortés/Palmar US$1/1.30; one/1½ hours; buses originate in Dominical and pick up passengers in Uvita at about 4:45am and 10:30am (times depend on whether the driver stops for breakfast).

San Isidro de El General, via Dominical US$1.30; 1½ hours; departs 6am & 2pm.

San José, via Dominical & Quepos US$4.80; seven hours; 5am & 1pm.

PARQUE NACIONAL MARINO BALLENA

This tranquil park protects coral and rock reefs in more than 5300 hectares of ocean and 110 hectares of land around Isla Ballena, south of Uvita. The island has nesting seabird colonies as well as plenty of lizards. Humpback whales migrate through the area from December to March and common and bottle-nosed dolphins are found here year-round. Olive ridley and hawksbill turtles nest here from May to November, with a peak in September and October.

From Punta Uvita, heading southeast, the park includes 13km of sandy and rocky beaches, mangrove swamps, estuaries and rocky headlands. All six kinds of Costa Rican mangrove occur within the park.

The **ranger station** (☎ 743 8236; admission US$6) is in Playa Bahía, the seaside extension of Uvita. While there's a set admission, the guards at the gate will often charge less because of the limited number of visitors. The station is run by Asoparque (Association for the Development of the Ballena Marine National Park), a joint protection effort launched by local businesses in conjunction with the Minae. It has worked hard at installing services, so be considerate and don't litter; cook with driftwood and use biodegradable soap when bathing.

From the station, you can walk out onto Punta Uvita and snorkel (best at low tide). Boats from Playa Bahía to Isla Ballena can be hired for US$30 per person for a two-hour snorkeling trip. The park has a free **campground** just 300m from the entrance, with toilets and showers. There is no electricity.

SOUTHEAST OF UVITA

Beyond Uvita, the road (all paved) follows the coast as far as Palmar, almost 40km away. There are several remote beaches along here that are becoming discovered as hotels begin opening their doors to visitors who travel the Costanera all the way through. This route provides a coastal (and less congested) alternative to the Interamericana. Daily buses between Dominical/Uvita and Cortés/Palmar can drop you near any of the places described below. Telephone links here are poor; be patient when sending messages, faxes and emails.

About 5km south of Uvita, you'll see a sign on the beachside for the attractive **La Cusinga** (on Finca Tres Hermanas; ☎ 770 2549, www.lacusingalodge.com; per person with 3 meals US$94; P). The grounds have a small stream that provides hydroelectricity, a farm growing organic crops, five cabins with two to four beds, and two dorms sleeping eight. Each unit has a private hot shower. Food served is 'rural Tico' and includes fish, vegetarian options, and chicken, but no beef. Boat trips to the national park, hiking on several kilometers of trails, birding, snorkeling, surfing and other activities are offered.

On the inland side of the road, you'll see a signed dirt road leading to **Finca Bavaria** (no phone; www.finca-bavaria.de; d US$69, additional person US$12; P), a quaint rain-forest inn which has five spacious, clean, tiled rooms with private bathroom. There's a hilltop pool with views of the ocean, and meals (cooked on request) are served in an open-air *rancho*. The owners speak German and English and can book local tours.

About 7km south of Uvita is **Playa Bahía Ballena**, which is within the marine boundaries of the park. There's no village here but there are a number of small places to stay along the road, all of them near the beach.

Cabinas Flamingo (☎ 743 8145, 835 7222; cabin US$29; P) has six simple, clean cabins with tiled floor and private bathroom. In addition, there is a restaurant under a thatched *rancho* where live music is played on some weekend nights. Surfing, kayaking and horseback riding are all available.

About 10km beyond Uvita at the far southeastern corner of Parque Nacional Marina Ballena is **Playa Piñuela**, followed 1.5km later by **Playa Ventanas** just outside the park. At the southern end of this beach in a strip mall is the **Mystic Dive Center** (☎ 788 8636; www.mysticdivecenter.com), a PADI operation offering scuba and snorkeling trips. Parque Nacional Marina Ballena and Isla del Caño are among the destinations featured.

About 14km south of Uvita is **Playa Tortuga**. The beach is called Turtle Beach by expats (though it's listed as Tortuga Abajo on many maps), but locals refer to it as Ojochal, after the small town located slightly inland. In this area you'll find several spread-out hotels and restaurants, all offering plenty of rest and relaxation. This area is best reached and navigated by car; buses are scarce and taxis nonexistent.

Diving trips of all types are offered at **Crocodive** (☎ 382 0199; www.crocodive.com; 8:30am-5pm Mon-Sat). It is situated across from the police station and behind the Ventana del Pacífico real estate office. The French owners also speak Spanish, English and German.

Be aware that Playa Tortuga has a fierce riptide.

A signed turnoff on the eastern side of the road leads to the beautiful hilltop **Lookout at Turtle Beach** (☎ 350, 9013, 378 7473; www.hotelcostarica.com; d US$70-80; P) The hotel has 12 brightly painted rooms with hot shower, fan, and private balcony. A large deck in a tower above the pool is excellent for morning birding or general lounging. The views from the hotel are incredible and the open-air lounge is an ideal place to sit and read. The hotel caters mostly to large groups (family reunions, retreats etc), but the pleasant California and South African owners will take drop-in guests from December to May. All local tours can be arranged. Rates vary, depending on the number of people in the group and the length of stay.

Along the beach side of the road is the beautifully kept **Hotel Villas Gaia** (☎ 256 9996, 282 5333, 382 8240; www.villasgaia.com; d US$70, large bungalow US$129; P). Set in tranquil forested grounds, 12 shiny wooden cabins are all decorated with tropical colors; each has a private terrace, hot water and ceiling fan. There is a restaurant, a bar and a hilltop pool with staggering views. The beach is a 20-minute hike down the hill. Tours of all kinds can be arranged. Credit cards are accepted.

A few hundred meters south of the Gaia, **Villas El Bosque** (☎ 398 2112; www.villaselbosque.com; d US$50, cabin with kitchen per wk US$300; P) is a friendly little place perched on a hilltop; it has three spotless rooms with hot shower, patio and ocean views. There are two private cabins with kitchen and hot shower. The management can book tours and a 15-minute hike leads to the beach below. All rates include breakfast; credit cards are accepted.

Just south and inland is the charming hilltop **El Perezoso** (☎ in the USA fax 435-518 8923; www.elperezoso.net; d incl breakfast US$55-70; P) with great views, a pool, and seven rooms in a small vine-covered villa. The British owner, Roger, is helpful and will pick guests up at the Palmar airport with prior arrangement. All units have fan and private, hot-water bathroom; a few have balcony views. Rates vary according to the size and location of the room. A room in the 'tower' is the most expensive and has the most incredible views. A small restaurant and bar are on the premises.

Just past the office for Ventana del Pacífico real estate on the eastern side of the road, you'll see signs for the low-key **Rancho Soluna** (☎ 788 8351/210; solunacr@yahoo.com; s/d US$25/30, camping per person US$5-7, additional person US$5; P). There is a small bar-restaurant (open from Wednesday to Sunday) in an open-air patio with a thatched roof and mosquito netting. Two brightly painted rooms have private hot shower and larger cabins have a kitchenette and deck with hammock. The latter are available by the week. This is a good value.

For hearty lasagna, head into the town of Ojochal and eat at **El Jardín de Tortuga** (no phone; theturtlegarden@yahoo.com; dishes US$5-7; P). The multilingual German owner, Stefan, serves up delicious food in a pretty outdoor garden next to a river. He also has three **cabins** (d US$25, additional person US$10) that sleep up to five people. There is a natural swimming hole nearby.

Southern Costa Rica

CONTENTS

Southern Costa Rica

Mist-shrouded peaks descend dramatically into agricultural lowlands and lush, isolated beaches. The towns are small, the people friendly, and thankfully much of this part of the country remains off the main tourist trail.

From San José the Interamericana (Hwy 2) cuts east toward Cartago before dipping south and traversing Cordillera de Talamanca located 100km to the south. The highway climbs steadily until it reaches its highest point, near the staggering Cerro de La Muerte (Mountain of Death; 3491m) – the name becomes foremost on your mind when you see the way buses speed through the spine-tingling hairpin bends. The road then drops steeply into San Isidro de El General (702m), the entry point to nearby Parque Nacional Chirripó, home to the nation's highest mountains.

From San Isidro the Interamericana winds its way southeast through hillside agricultural towns, where side roads (bad ones) lead to some of the more remote protected areas in the country – including the difficult-to-get-to Parque Internacional La Amistad.

The Interamericana then dips to sea level at Palmar, where the scenery is dominated by African palm plantations. From this point the Panamanian border lies a little more than 100km away. This unremarkable stretch of highway offers access to the magnificent wilderness contained in Parque Nacional Corcovado on the Peninsula de Osa, the primary destination in the region for most visitors.

Note that the yellow-topped, numbered posts along the Interamericana south of San José are kilometer markers and are referred to in the chapter text.

HIGHLIGHTS

- Peering into the cloud forest mist in search of quetzals near **San Gerardo de Dota** (p319)
- Making the 16km trek up **Cerro Chirripó** (p326)
- Staying at **Reserva Biológica Durika** (p329) and hiking into **Parque Internacional La Amistad** (p337)
- Enjoying the clean mountain air in **San Vito** (p334) and the nearby **Wilson Botanical Garden** (p336)
- Doing the jungle camp circuit at **La Amistad Lodge**, Costa Rica's third largest private reserve (p337)

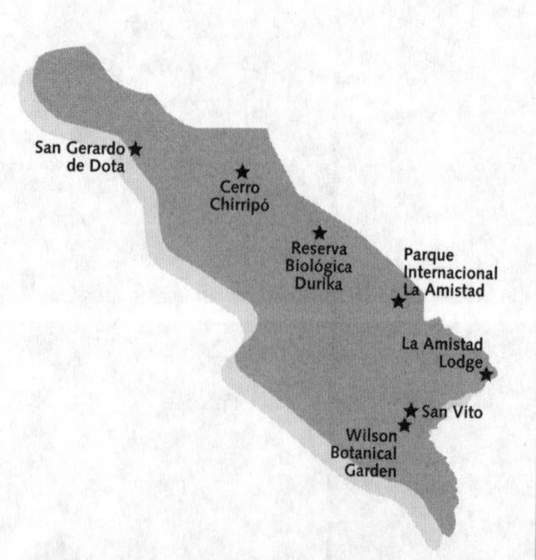

RUTA DE LOS SANTOS

Also called Zona Santa, or 'Saint's Route,' this region of redolent coffee plantations and cool cloud forests isn't exactly a destination, but rather a collection of highland villages at the heart of relaxed, rural Costa Rica. They famously bear sainted names: San Pablo de León Cortés, Santa María de Dota, San Marcos de Tarrazú, San Cristóbal Sur, San Gerardo de Dota and others, and are all ensconced in the positively divine Cordillera de Talamanca.

Though regular buses serve these small towns, the Zona Santa makes for a classic road trip: in less than an hour the Interamericana delivers you from the cosmopolitan cityscape of San José onto narrow, steep roads twisting through the spectacular high-altitude scenery – green and inviting or dark and forbidding, depending on the weather. You'll also have the dubious opportunity of driving the country's most dangerous road along the way (see p320).

This trek crosses the Continental Divide, and in the space of mere kilometers might go from stormy gray to glorious sunshine. Oh, and this is quetzal country (particularly April through June), so keep your eyes open for what Steve Friedman at Genesis II poetically termed 'stained glass in flight.'

Leave the highway just south of Cartago, from which good roads loop through highland villages before heading back to San José. The towns are all small, with inviting parks or plazas worth a wander; those with hotels and restaurants are detailed under Sleeping & Eating following.

Santa María de Dota is a small town centered on a green, grassy soccer field and surrounded by lavish plantations. It's a great place to stretch your legs, though it's so quiet you can practically hear the coffee drying.

A Banco Nacional and post office are next to the soccer field, as is the **Artesanías Café Almancer** (☎ 541 1616; ⌚ irregular), which offers handcrafts, coffee and snacks.

San Marcos de Tarrazú bustles a bit more than Santa María, and has a wider range of hotels and restaurants, as well as bars advertising karaoke nights and drink specials.

At about 2360m above sea level, **Genesis II** (☎ 381 0739; www.genesis-two.com; admission adult/student US$10/5), a private nature reserve situated in the Cordillera de Talamanca, covers 38 hectares, almost all of which are virgin cloud forest (or technically, tropical montane rain forest). There are about 3.5km of private trails; rubber boots are provided for exploring. The 'dry' season is from January to May, but annual rainfall is 2300mm, so rainwear and warm clothes are essential any time of year. Not surprisingly, sighting frogs and other amphibians is a specialty. Also onsite is the **Talamanca Treescape canopy tour** (guests/nonguests US$25/35), which offers a suspension bridge, two zip lines, three platforms and a naturalist guide – the idea is education as much as adrenaline. The reserve also offers accommodations (see below).

The turnoff for Genesis II is at the Cañón church, just south of Km 58 on the Interamericana. Turn east and follow the rough road 4km to the reserve.

San Gerardo de Dota, a spread-out little farming community on the western slopes of Cerro de La Muerte, is famous for excellent highland birding. Quetzals are spotted frequently every April and May (during breeding season) but are seen all year. The trout fishing in the Río Savegre is good: the seasons are May and June for fly-fishing and December to March for lure-fishing.

Sleeping & Eating

SANTA MARÍA DE DOTA

Cabinas Restaurante Dota (☎ 541 1874, 546 7466; s/d US$9/13; Ⓟ) is a good budget option. Clean, sunny rooms come with cable TV and hot-water shower (one room, sleeping five, has a kitchenette) and guarded parking.

Mi Megasuper (⌚ 8am-8pm) is your best bet for groceries, and there are a handful of *sodas* including **Soda la Casona** (☎ 541 2258; mains US$2-4; ⌚ 6am-7pm Mon-Sat), 50m from the soccer field, with daily specials and inexpensive casados.

SAN MARCOS DE TARRAZÚ

Hotel Zacatecas (☎ 546 6073; s/d US$7/9, s/d with bathroom US$11/14) Across from the church and right upstairs from a popular bar and restaurant in the town center, this spot has good rooms with clean shared bathrooms.

Hotel Tocayos (☎ 546 6898, after 10pm 546 6236; s/d US$7/11) Clean, secure rooms with air-con and TV are underground; some have small windows.

Hotel La Cascada (☎ 546 6239; s/d US$12/18; Ⓟ ❄) On the outskirts of town, this hotel has modern, basic rooms and a parking area.

SOUTHERN COSTA RICA
84°00'W
83°30'W
9°30'N
9°00'N
8°30'N
Zona Protectora Cerro de Escazú
Aserrí
CARTAGO
Tejar
Presa de Cachí
Cachí
Ujarrás
Orosi
Palomo
Tapantí
San Ignacio de Acosta
Tarbaca
San Gabriel
Ruta de los Santos
Frailes
Zona Protectora Caraigres
Zona Protectora Río Navarro y Río Sombrero
Empalme
Genesis II
Cartago
Tuis
Moravia
Reserva Indígena Alto y Bajo Chirripó
Zona Protectora Cuenca Río Tuis
Río Pacuare
Río Chirripó
Río Estrella
Reserva Río Macho
Limón
Parque Nacional Tapantí-Macizo Cerro de la Muerte
San Marcos de Tarrazú
Santa María de Dota
Río Pirrís
Cerro de la Muerte (3491m)
San José
San Gerardo de Dota
Parque Nacional Chirripó
Cerro Chirripó (3820m)
División
Avalon Reserva Privada
Herradura
San Gerardo de Rivas
Canaán
Rivas
Reserva Los Santos
Zona Protectora Cerro Nara
To Puntarenas
Río División
Parque Internacional LaAmistad
Cordillera de
Cerro Durika (3280m)
Quepos
San Isidro de El General
Parque Nacional Manuel Antonio
Savegre
Portalón
Matapalo
Reserva Biológica Durika
Reserva Indígena Ujarrás
Ujarrás
Platanillo
Río Convento
Refugio Nacional de Finca Barú del Pacifico
Dominical
Escaleros
Punta Dominical
Reserva Indígena Salitre
Río Ceibo
Buenos Aires
Río Cabagra
Uvita
Río General
Valle del General
Parque Nacional Marino Ballena
Piñuela
Tortuga Abajo
Isla Ballena
Reserva Indígena Térraba
Reserva Indígena Boruca
Boruca
Paso Real
Curré
Palmar Norte
Ciudad Cortés
Palmar Sur
Río Grande de Térraba
Reserva Indígena Curré
Bahía de Coronado
Valle de Diquis
Humedal Nacional Térraba-Sierpe
Sierpe
Puntarenas
PACIFIC OCEAN
Isla Violín
Río Sierpe
Chacarita
Río Chocuaco
Laguna Sierpe
Rancho Quemado
Reserva Golfo Dulce
Parque Nacional Piedras Blancas
Reserva Biológica Isla del Caño
Bahia Drake
Drake
Agujitas
Rincón
Gamba
Reserva Indígena Guaymí de Osa
La Palma
Playa San Josecito
Golfo Dulce
Punta Gallardo
Playa Llorona
Laguna Corcovado
Península de Osa
Dos Brazos
Ferry
Puerto Jiménez
Playa Corcovado
Parque Nacional Corcovado
Reserva Golfo Dulce
Carate
Cabo Matapalo
84°00'W
83°30'W

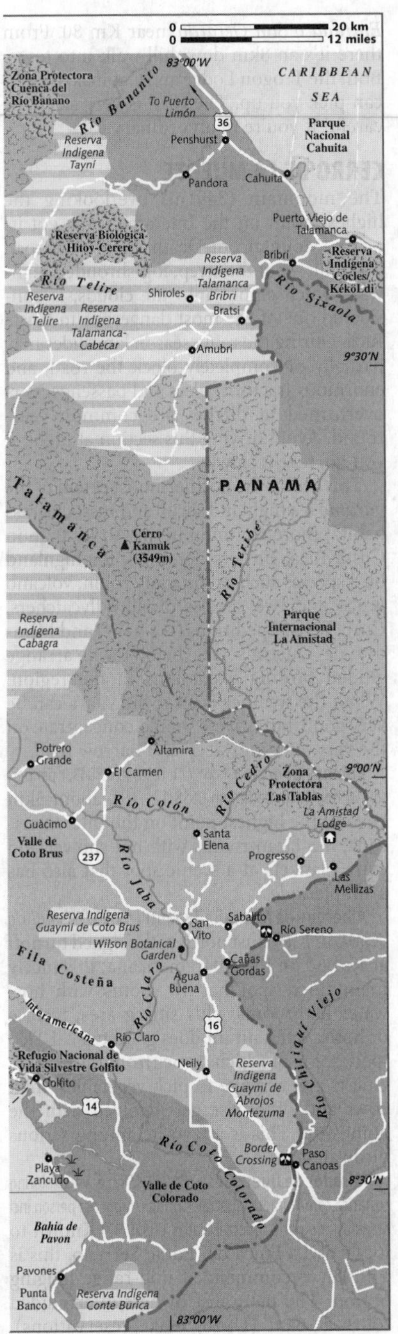

There are at least a dozen *sodas*, many with Chinese food, lining the main drag. **Yogui Restaurant** (☎ 546 5061; gallos US$1-2, casados US$2-3; 6am-10pm) is a groovier-than-average place with cozy, dark décor and cheap Tico specialties.

CAÑON AREA

Cerro Alto Hotel de Montaña (☎ 382 2771, 571 1010; s/d US$44/58; P) On the Interamericana, 3km north of the Empalme junction, this place has eight rustic but comfortable cabins, all of which sleep up to four and have hot shower, fireplace and kitchenette. If you are returning to San José by road from southern Costa Rica, Cerro Alto is probably the last lodging option before Cartago.

El Toucanet Lodge (☎ 541 1435; www.eltoucanet.com; s/d incl breakfast US$45/58; P) Take the well-signed turnoff from the Interamericana at Cañón (near Km 58) and go 8km south to Copey de Dota to find this quaint country lodge at 1850m. Overlooking a (very) cold river, lovely double cabins with hot shower are sequestered in a quiet rural location. Birding is good, and with five hours' notice the owners will fire up a wood-burning outdoor spa. One cabin sleeps five and has a kitchenette and fireplaces.

Close to the turnoff, **Cafetería la Ruta del Café** (☎ 571 1118) serves the local specialty as espresso or fancier beverages, as well as light meals and pastries.

Genesis II (☎ 381 0739; www.genesis-two.com; adult/student US$10/5; camping per person US$5, r per adult/student US$95/50, house with kitchen US$105/65) Rooms at this private reserve are basic, with shared hot shower and small windows. The house with a kitchenette, and the tent sites are sweet, and the grounds are beyond gorgeous. The main attractions are the hiking and Talamanca Treescape canopy tour (see p317). There is also a volunteer program, which allows you to build trails and keep tabs on wildlife for US$600 per month, including all food and lodging. If traveling by bus, get off at the Cañon church: the owners will pick you up if you make arrangements, or you can walk. Round-trip transportation from San José can also be arranged.

SAN GERARDO DE DOTA

Trogon Lodge (☎ 740 1051; in San José 223 2421; www.grupomawamba.com; s/d US$55/70; P) Almost 7km from the Interamericana is the turnoff for Trogon Lodge, which caters mainly to package tourists escaping the coastal heat in the cloud forest, complete with a stocked trout-fishing pond (the onsite restaurant will prepare your catch for dinner). Hardwood-accented rooms in attractive wooden cabins come with heaters (not air-con) and lots of extra blankets. Guided tours, including some on horseback, can be arranged.

Cabinas El Quetzal (☎ 740 1036; r per person US$35; Ⓟ) About 1km after the Trogon Lodge turnoff, this good mid-range choice has six rooms with fireplace and hot shower. Because of the lower elevation, quetzals can be seen here from December to March.

Cabinas Chacón (☎ 771 1732; www.costaricaexpeditions.com/lodging/savegre; r per person with meals & transport US$78; camping per person US$7; Ⓟ) Also known as the Albergue de Montaña Savegre, this recommended hotel was carved out of the wilderness by Don Efraín Chacón in 1957 and is still in the same family, overseen by the patriarch himself. The 400-hectare farm is now part orchard, part dairy ranch, and 250 hectares remain as virgin forest, threaded by trails winding past waterfalls and a small lake stocked with trout where the owners allow camping. Rooms are cozy and plush, with wood accents and extra blankets.

The owners are enthusiastic about their birds, and usually know where the quetzals hang out. Often, they'll put up telescopes so guests can get a close look at nearby nests. They have also set up the Quetzal Education & Research Center in cooperation with US scientists.

Getting There & Away

Most drivers take the Interamericana south to Empalme, a gas station and *soda* (simple eatery) stop almost 30km from Cartago. Just south of the station a signed turnoff leads west along a paved road and turns toward Santa María de Dota (about 10km away), San Marcos (7km further) and San Pablo (4km further). From here, a choice of paved roads takes you back to the Interamericana via San Cristóbal, or winding north through San Gabriel and other villages to San José.

Some buses from San José (p99) to Santa María de Dota (US$2.75, 2½ hours) go via San Marcos de Tarrazú.

Buses between San José and San Isidro de El General (US$3.75, three hours) can drop you off at San Gerardo de Dota. Ask for '*La Entrada a San Gerardo*' near Km 80. From there it's an 8km downhill walk into town. Both the Trogon Lodge and Cabinas Chacón can pick you up. The road is very steep: be careful if you're in an ordinary car.

CERRO DE LA MUERTE

The mountain (3491m) overlooking the highest point on the Interamericana got its name 'Mountain of Death' before the road was built – but the steep, fog-shrouded highway, which climbs into the clouds, is considered one of the most dangerous in Costa Rica. During the rainy season landslides may partially or completely block the road, and enormous tractor trailers and passenger cars overturned in ditches are common year-round. Avoid driving this section at night; if you do, take it slowly.

This area is the northernmost extent of the *páramo* – a highland shrub and tussock grass habitat more common in the Andes than in Costa Rica. Birders here look for highland bird species such as the sooty robin, volcano junco and two species of silky flycatchers. Costa Rica Expeditions (see p474) and Mirador de Quetzals (see below) will arrange guided birding excursions in the region. When the weather is clear the views can be very good, but drivers should concentrate on the very winding, steep and narrow road.

Cabinas Georgina (☎ 771 1299, 770 8043; r per person without/with bathroom US$8/12; Ⓟ), about 5km beyond the highest point on the Interamericana, has clean rooms with hot shower and extra blankets at a scenic spot that also has a simple *soda*.

Albergue de Montaña Tapantí (☎ 232 0436; d/tr/q US$40/55/70; Ⓟ) Just north of the signed turnoff at Km 62 on the Interamericana, this nicely maintained spot has 10 rooms with hot-water bathrooms, plus sitting area, terrace or both. A restaurant does good typical Tico food, some of which comes from the garden. Guests can arrange to pick vegetables, milk cows and otherwise get involved with the goings-on. This is a favorite among serious birdwatchers.

Mirador de Quetzales (☎ 771 4582; www.exploringcostarica.com/mirador/quetzales.html; r/cabin per person incl breakfast, dinner & 'quetzal watch' US$29/37) Known to locals as La Finca del Eddie Serrano, this is a highly recommended mid-range lodging option. The naturalist owners offer guided tours at 6am (US$6, make reservations), available for nonguests too, where you may see quetzals and will most definitely stop to smell the orchids.

The finca is about 1km west of a signed turnoff near Km 70 on the Interamericana. Quetzals are most frequently seen from November to April, but are year-round residents, as happy guests will attest. Four simple rooms with two bunk beds each share hot showers, while roomier cabinas with private bathroom include four doubles and two triples; there are larger cabins with kitchenettes. The accommodations are rustic but clean and have good views. A lookout point above the lodge gives glimpses of up to five volcanoes on a clear day.

AVALON RESERVA PRIVADA

About 3.5km west of the Interamericana by way of the tiny community of División, just past Km 107, is the 170-hectare **Avalon Reserva Privada** (☎ 771 7226; dm US$10, d without/with bathroom US$45/55). This stunning mountain-top reserve has 150 hectares of primary growth cloud forest and plenty of hiking trails ideal for spotting high-altitude birds and toucanets. Guided hikes start at US$10 per person. Any bus between San José and San Isidro can drop you off in División. You can walk to the reserve – but it's mostly uphill. Check in at the roadside *pulpería* (grocery store) for a taxi ride.

SAN ISIDRO DE EL GENERAL

pop 45,000

Lively and fairly modern, San Isidro de El General is the most important town on the southern Interamericana. Set within the agricultural valley of the Río General, it's a transportation hub and commercial center for the coffee fincas, cattle ranches and fruit plantations that dot the surrounding slopes.

The town is also a gateway to numerous activities and sites of interest. A road to the southeast leads towards Parque Nacional Chirripó (p326), another to the southwest leads to Dominical on the Pacific coast (p307). This allows you to make a loop from San José to Dominical up to Manuel Antonio (p295) and back to San José without retracing your steps.

The locals refer to San Isidro, situated 136km south of San José, as Pérez (the county is Pérez Zeledón). Though labeled on the map, streets are poorly signed and everyone uses landmarks to orient themselves (see p453).

Information

BTC Internet (Av 2 btwn Calles Central & 1; per hour US$1.25) and **Brunc@ Net Café** (☎ 771 3235; Av Central btwn Calles Central & 1; per hour US$1.50) both offer Internet access Monday through Friday.

Several banks exchange US dollars and traveler's checks. The **Banco de San José** (Av 4 btwn Calles Central & 1) gives cash advances on credit cards. **Banco Cuscatlán** (Av 2, east of Calle 3) and two branches of the **Banco Coopealianza** (Av 4 btwn Calles 2 & 4; Av 2 btwn Calles Central & 1) have 24-hour ATMs on the Cirrus network.

Medical services are available at the **Clínica El Labrador** (☎ 771 7115, 771 5354; Calle 1 btwn Avs 8 & 10), which has 10 private doctors in a variety of specialties. The **post office** (Calle 1 btwn Avs 6 & 8) is two blocks south of the park and there are numerous pay phones in the Parque Central.

For travel information there's the well-organized **Ciprotur** (☎ 770 9393; www.ecotourism.co.cr; Calle 4 btwn Avs 1 & 3; 🕑 7:30am-5pm Mon-Fri, 8am-noon Sat).

There is a **Minae park service office** (Sinac; ☎ 771 3155, 771 4836, 771 5116; Calle 2 btwn Avs 2 & 4; 🕑 8am-noon & 1-4pm Mon-Fri) where you can make reservations for the mountaintop hostel at Chirripó. Reservations must be made between 8am and noon weekdays. You can also get information from this office about Parque Internacional La Amistad (p337).

Sights

Rancho La Botija (☎ 770 2146, 770 2147; labotija@racsa.co.cr; admission US$5; 🕑 8:30am-5pm Tue-Sun) is a 12-hectare recreation center which is popular for day trips. A working coffee and sugar finca, it lies 6km from San Isidro, on the highway to San Gerardo de Rivas. The grounds afford nice views of the valley, and hiking trails lead to an archaeological site with petroglyphs (there is a daily guided walk). The daily rate includes use of the pool and trails. Kayak rentals (for the onsite lake) are available at an extra rate. There is also lodging (see p323) and a restaurant.

Fudebiol Reserve (☎ 771 4131; admission US$6), another day trip destination, is 7km northeast of San Isidro – the acronym stands for Fundación para el Desarrollo del Centro Biológico Las Quebradas (Foundation for the Development of the Biological Center

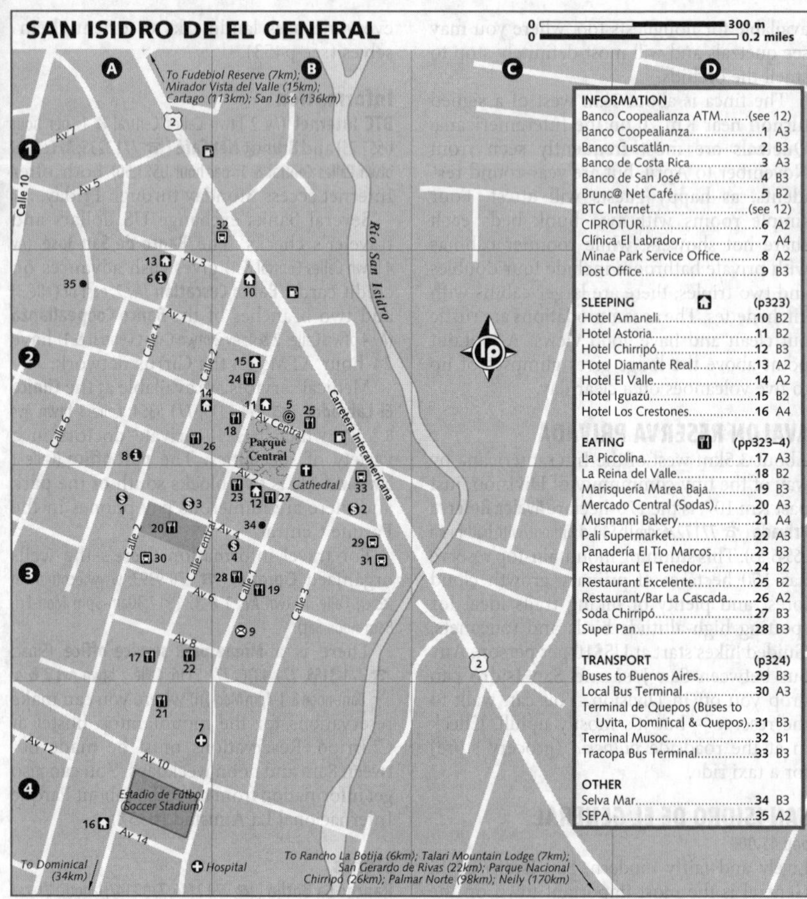

at Las Quebradas). This is a community-run reserve along the Río Quebradas (a source of local drinking water) and there are several trails, picnic areas, camping spots and lookouts. There is lodging (see p323) as well. The Ciprotur office can provide you with additional information.

Tours

Selva Mar (☎ 771 4582, 771 4579; www.exploringcostarica.com; Calle 1 btwn Avs 2 & 4; 🕐 8am-noon & 1:30-6pm) is a helpful travel agency that books tours for a number of activities in the area – some of which are outlined above. The office also serves as a reservation service for more than a dozen hotels in the San Isidro area, as well as Dominical and the Peninsula de Osa. The office can arrange all kinds of tours and book airline tickets.

Headquartered inside the Selva Mar, **Costa Rica Trekking Adventures** (www.chirripo.com) offers guided excursions to Chirripó. Its 'Urán Trek' does a loop around the park and includes camping (US$499 per person). **Birding Escapes** (www.birdwatchingcostarica.com), also at Selva Mar, is a popular birding outfit that has birding trips for all budgets.

Ríos Tropicales (☎ 233 6455; www.riostropicales.com) has river-running trips on nearby Río General from May to December. These include transportation from San José, gear, tents for camping, expert river guides and meals. Costs start at about US$350 per person for a three-day trip. This is a Class III-IV river.

Courses

SEPA (☎ 770 1457; western end of Av 1; www.sabalolodge.com/programs.html) provides Spanish-language programs for US$195/323 per week without/with homestays .

Events

If you time it right, your trip to San Isidro can coincide with that of a whole lot of livestock. In early February prize cattle are displayed at the annual **agricultural fair,** and on May 15 farmers bring their animals into town to have them blessed in honor of San Isidro, patron saint of farmers.

Sleeping

Hotel Iguazú (☎ 771 2571; cnr Av 1 & Calle Central; s US$8.80, s/d with bathroom US$12.50/20) Spacious and clean tiled rooms have mercifully hot showers, fans and cable TV. Units on the higher floors have a bit of a view. It's good value.

Hotel El Valle (☎ 771 0246; Calle 2 btwn Avs Central & 2; s/d US$6.30/10.50, s/d with hot-water bathroom & TV US$8.80/15.30; Ⓟ) This is the best budget bet in town. Small rooms are clean and bare and have sturdy furniture. Units with bathrooms are spacious and airier.

Hotel Astoria (☎ 771 0914; Av Central btwn Calles Central & 1; r per person US$4.30, d with bathroom & TV US$20; Ⓟ) It looks like a cell block in a state sanatorium, but the place is spotless. Rows of tidy stalls share cold showers while those with bathrooms have hot water.

Hotel Chirripó (☎ 771 0529; Av 2 btwn Calles Central & 1; s/d US$5/8.50, s/d with bathroom US$7.50/12) Popular with budget travelers, here you'll find bare, white-washed rooms that are stark but dirt-free. Cheaper rooms share tepid showers, but the others have (sort of) hot water.

Hotel Amaneli (☎ 771 0352; cnr Calle 2 & the Interamericana; r per person US$7.50) Thirty dark but clean rooms share similar-looking hot-water bathrooms. Ask for a room away from the Interamericana or you'll be enjoying the roar of trucks. The owners are installing cable TV; expect prices to go up.

Hotel Los Crestones (☎ 770 1200, 770 1500; www.hotelloscrestones.com; Calle Central at Av 14; s/d US$30/40, s/d with air-con US$40/45, additional person US$10; Ⓟ ✱) Just west of the stadium, this clean motor court–style hotel has 20 good rooms. Nine have air-con and all have hot shower, fan and cable TV. Credit cards are accepted.

Hotel Diamante Real (☎ 770 6230, 770 6233; cnr Av 3 & Calle 4; d/tr US$47/53; ste master/Jacuzzi US$59/70; Ⓟ ✱) This brand-new hotel is the nicest in town. The 22 rooms come with hot-water bathroom, air-con and phone with voice mail. They're all painted bright yellow and feature shiny black lacquered furniture. A larger master suite accommodates four, as does a special suite with a whirlpool tub. There is a restaurant and credit cards are accepted.

AROUND SAN ISIDRO

Mirador Vista del Valle (☎ 384 4685; Km 119 on the Interamericana; s/d incl breakfast US$41/47, additional person US$10; Ⓟ) Overlooking San Isidro from 15km to the north is this small restaurant and inn with inspiring views. The inn has rustic, well-appointed wood cabinas and comfortable beds with bright spreads. The restaurant specializes in locally caught trout.

Fudebiol Reserve (☎ 771 4131; r per person US$25; Ⓟ) This popular reserve has a small lodge that accommodates up to 35. Shiny wood rooms with bunk beds share hot showers. The rate includes breakfast, lunch and dinner.

Rancho La Botija (☎ 771 2146, 771 2147; labotija@racsa.co.cr; s/d incl breakfast US$32/63; Ⓟ ⊠ ✱) This recreation center (p321) on the road to San Gerardo has good lodging. Eleven comfortable tiled rooms have firm beds, hot shower and a sitting area. The place is nonsmoking.

Talari Mountain Lodge (☎ 771 0341; www.talari.co.cr; s/d/tr incl breakfast US$36/52/72; Ⓟ ✱) This well-recommended place is 7km southeast of San Isidro, en route to San Gerardo de Rivas (just before the village). Owners Pilar and Jan, a multilingual Tica/Dutch couple, run this attractive place, which specializes in customized birding tours led by their biologist son, Pieter. They can also arrange treks up Chirripó and horseback rides. The eight-hectare property has a small river, pool, restaurant and piano bar (Jan is an accomplished pianist). Rooms are clean and tiled and come with solar-heated shower. Lunch (US$7.50) and dinner (US$10) are available on request. Credit cards are accepted. The hotel is closed from September 15 to October 31.

Eating

Travelers watching their colones should head for the inexpensive *sodas* in the **Mercado Central** (Av 4 btwn Calles Central & 2), though the restaurants in town are quite reasonable.

Soda Chirripó (cnr Calle 1 & Av 2; dishes US$2-4; 6:30am-6pm) The bustling corner *soda* adjacent to Hotel Chirripó has tasty *gallo pinto* and lunch specials for US$3. Do not confuse it with Restaurant Chirripó next door which is more expensive.

La Reina del Valle (cnr Calle Central & Av Central; dishes US$3-5) The 2nd-floor of this informal eatery is where it's at. There's a popular bar with cheap *bocas* (appetizers) and great views of Parque Central at sunset.

Marisquería Marea Baja (Calle 1 btwn Avs 4 & 6; dishes US$4-7) Mammoth and cheap portions of fresh fish and other specialties are served in a cavernous restaurant with a bar that packs in the twenty-somethings.

Restaurant/Bar La Cascada (cnr Calle 2 & Av 2; dishes US$3.50-9) This trendy balcony has a menu consisting primarily of *bocas*, though you can get steak and seafood. Area hipsters spend quality time here, getting to know the beer, burgers and each other.

Restaurant El Tenedor (Calle Central btwn Avs Central & 1; dishes US$1-7; 10am-11pm) Next to Hotel Iguazú, El Tenedor has a balcony overlooking a busy street and serves hamburgers for US$1 as well as other meals. Pizzas (from US$3.50) and Italian dishes are a specialty.

La Piccolina (Calle Central btwn Avs 8 & 10; dishes US$5; 11am-10pm Wed-Mon) A pleasant outdoor restaurant across the street from the Palí supermarket serves a variety of pizzas (US$3.50 to US$5), pastas and Tico food.

Restaurant Excelente (Av Central btwn Calles Central & 1; dishes US$4-6) Chinese and Tico food are indeed excellent at this local favorite.

For baked goods there's **Panadería El Tío Marcos** (Av 2 btwn Calles Central & 1) or **Super Pan** (Calle 1 btwn Avs 4 & 6), which sells highly delectable cheese loaves.

Getting There & Away

BUS

In San Isidro the local bus terminal on Avenida 6 serves nearby villages. Long-distance buses leave from various points near the Interamericana and are frequently packed, so buy tickets early.

From Tracopa Terminal

The following buses originate in other destinations and pick up passengers on a space-available basis. The Tracopa terminal is on the Interamericana, just southwest of Avenida Central. Times are approximate, so get there early.

Agua Buena departs 9:30am, 11:30am, 2:30pm & 5:45pm.
Ciudad Cortés 11:30am & 5:30pm.
Coto 47 1:30pm.
David, Panama 10:30am.
Golfito 10am & 6pm.
San José US$3; three hours; departs 7:30am, 8am, 9:30am, 10:30am, 11:30am, 1:30am, 4pm, 5:45pm & 7:30pm.
San Vito 9:30am, 11:30am, 2:30pm & 5:45pm.

From Terminal Quepos

Terminal Quepos is on the side street south of the Tracopa terminal. Buses originate in San Isidro.

Dominical US$1; one hour; departs 7am & 1:30pm.
Palmar Norte/Puerto Jiménez US$2/4; three/six hours; 6am, 9am & 3pm.
Quepos US$3; three hours; 7am & 1:30pm.
Uvita US$1.25; 1½ hours; 9am & 4pm.

From Other Bus Stops

These buses all originate in San Isidro:

Buenos Aires (Gafeso) US$1.10; one hour; departs 5:15am, 6am, 7:20am, 8:30am, 10am, 11:30am, 12:15pm, 1:30pm, 3pm, 4pm & 5pm from north of Terminal Quepos. Note: the 5:15am & 12:15pm buses don't run Sunday.
Palmar Norte/Neily/Paso Canoas (Tracopa) US$2.50/3/4; three/four/4½ hours; depart from Interamericana southwest of Av Central 8:30am, 4:30pm, 7:30pm & 9pm.
San Gerardo de Rivas, for Parque Nacional Chirripó US$1; two hours; departs from Parque Central at 5am & from the main terminal on Av 6 at 2pm.
San José US$3; three hours; departs from Terminal Musoc on Interamericana btwn Calles 2 & 4 every 30 minutes from 5:30am to 5:30pm.
San Vito (Tracopa) US$3.50; three hours; departs from Interamericana southwest of Av Central 5:30am & 2pm.

TAXI

A 4WD taxi to San Gerardo de Rivas will cost at least US$17. A taxi all the way up to Albergue Urán (p326) will cost US$20. (As always, these rates vary depending on road conditions.)

SAN GERARDO DE RIVAS

About 22km northeast of San Isidro, this small village centered around its soccer field nestles in a scenic valley. It serves as the entry point to Parque Nacional Chirripó. It is 1350m above sea level, so the climate is pleasant and there are hiking and birding opportunities. You can inquire for bilingual birding guides in the Selva Mar offices in San Isidro (p322) or with the folks at Talari Mountain Lodge (p323).

About 2km north of San Gerardo de Rivas are some very welcome **thermal hot springs** (US$2; 7am-6pm). Walk north out of town until you see the cement bridge and then turn left. From here a paved road leads towards the town of Herradura. After about 1km you see the sign for Parqueo Las Rosas, turn right and take the rickety suspension bridge over the river. A switchback trail (yes, that'd be uphill all the way) will lead you another 1km to a house with a *soda*, where you will be charged admission.

Orientation & Information

The **Chirripó ranger station** (Sinac; 200 5348; 6:30am-4:30pm) is about 1km below the soccer field on the road from San Isidro. Just above the ranger station the road forks: take the right one to San Gerardo de Rivas; the left leads 3km to Herradura, passing the hot springs en route.

The village *pulpería*, by the soccer field and Hotel y Restaurant Roca Dura Café (see later), has a public phone.

Sleeping & Eating

Hotels are all situated along the narrow road that runs parallel to the river. They are listed in order as you go uphill.

Río Chirripó Retreat (377 3557; www.riochirripo.com; s/d/tr US$39/59/69; P) About 1.5km below the ranger station, in the community of Canaán, this is the most upscale lodge in the area. An inviting Santa Fe–style communal area is used during yoga retreats and there are mats available for anyone wishing to practice on their own. You can hear the gurgle of the river from eight beautifully decorated cabins, all of which have a balcony, bathroom and hot water. Breakfast is included in the rate, and vegetarian dinners are available for another US$10. There's a restaurant, bar and heated swimming pool. Hiking trails lead to the river.

Hotel y Refugio Albergue El Pelicano (382 3000; www.hotelelpelicano.net; cabinas per person without/with bathroom US$10/13; P) About 200m below the ranger station, the El Pelicano is owned by Rafael Elizondo, a late-blooming local artist who sculpts whimsical pieces out of wood and stone – worth a look even if you aren't staying here. His studio is open for viewing, though pieces aren't for sale. (Don't miss the wood motorcycle.) The well-designed wood lodge has 10 spotless, simple rooms that share heated showers and a balcony overlooking the river valley. New cabinas have bathrooms with hot water. There's a recreation room and pool. All rates include transport to the park entrance. Meals are available upon request.

Cabinas La Marín (308 6735; r per person without/with bathroom US$6/12) Just below the ranger station, this basic place has eight stuffy rooms with hot showers. Those with bathrooms are a hair better and sport tiled floors. There is a small **restaurant** (5:30am-8pm), a mini-supermarket and a public phone.

Cabinas El Bosque (771 4129; r per person US$7, d with bathroom US$14) You'll find sunless rooms with shared bathrooms as well as newer units with hot showers here. There is some camping equipment available for rent and non-guests can store luggage for US$2 per day. There's a restaurant and bar with a pleasant outdoor deck overlooking the river.

Cabinas y Restaurante El Descanso (771 7962, 369 0067; camping per person US$3.50, r per person without/with bathroom US$7/10; P) Past the ranger station is this place with 12 small wood rooms, which are all clean and come with hot showers. There's a small garden with chairs for hanging out and upstairs rooms have a balcony with a view. The Elizondo family is helpful; transport to the park entrance for trekkers is included in the rate. Meals are available on request.

Hotel y Restaurant Roca Dura Café (771 1866; camping per tent US$4, r per person without/with bathroom US$5/7.50; P) This charming and rustic lodge is built into the sides of several giant boulders right in the center of town. Bright murals lighten up eight stone rooms. All showers are hot. A camping ground with a cold shower is behind the hotel, by the river. There's a restaurant-bar which offers live music some evenings and is a popular local pit stop. The hotel offers free storage if you need to leave gear while hiking the park.

Vista al Cerro Lodge (373 3365; r per person US$8, camping per person US$2; P) This lodge is just 300m above the soccer field and offers simple and clean rooms as well as a rough camping ground overlooking the river. There are shared hot showers and room 3 has a bunk bed built into a boulder. Breakfast for early hikers is available on request.

Albergue Urán (☎ 388 2333, 771 1669; www.hoteluran.com; dm US$9, d US$35) Just 50m below the trailhead, this recommended lodge has 11 simple, spotless rooms with one or two beds (or bunks) and shared hot showers. Spiffy new doubles have bathrooms and majestic views. There's a good restaurant, though no beer or cigarettes are sold (bring your own if you wish). The owner is incredibly friendly and this is a convenient location for an early start on climbing Chirripó.

Getting There & Away

Buses to San Isidro depart from the soccer field at 7am and 4pm (US$1, two hours). Any of the hotels can call a taxi for you.

If you're driving in from San Isidro, head south on the Interamericana and cross the Río San Isidro at the southern end of town. About 500m further cross the Río Jilguero and look for a steep turn up to the left, about 300m beyond the Jilguero. A small wooden sign with yellow lettering indicates the turn-off for the park; more visible is a large, red sign for the Universidad Nacional. If you are coming from the south, note that there are two entrances to this road, both most easily identified by the university's signs. If you cross the Río Jilguero you've gone too far.

The ranger station is about 18km up this road from the Interamericana. The road is paved as far as Rivas but beyond that it is steep and graveled. It is passable to ordinary cars in the dry season, but 4WD is recommended. The road leading up from the village of San Gerardo de Rivas to Albergue Urán is in poor condition and is 4WD only.

PARQUE NACIONAL CHIRRIPÓ

This breathtaking national park is named after Cerro Chirripó (3820m), Costa Rica's highest peak. At 502 sq km, this is Costa Rica's principal mountain park and one of the country's largest protected areas. It holds three peaks over 3800m, including Cerro Chirripó, and most of the park lies at more than 2000m above sea level. Of all the Central American countries, only Guatemala has higher mountains.

The park entrance is at San Gerardo de Rivas, which lies 1350m above sea level; from here the summit is 2.5km straight up! An easy-to-follow 16km trail leads all the way to the top, and no technical climbing is required. Almost all visitors use this trail to reach the summit, though alternatives are discussed on p328. Walking at the lower elevations is also rewarding, with excellent views and opportunities for good birding and butterfly observation. A hostel (see p328) near the summit accommodates trekkers (with advance reservation).

The climb is fascinating and takes you through constantly changing scenery, vegetation and wildlife. After passing through the pastureland outside the park, the trail leads through several types of vegetation at various altitudes. Emerging above the main canopy (25m to 30m high) are oak trees reaching almost 50m in height.

These highland forests are home to birds such as the flame-throated warbler and buffy tuftedcheek, to name but two. Small brown frogs and lime-colored caterpillars thickly covered with stinging hairs make their way across the trail, and spider monkeys and Baird's tapirs lurk in the thick vegetation (though you aren't likely to see them). Eventually the trail climbs out of the rain forest and into the bare and windswept *páramo*.

The Chirripó massif is part of the Cordillera de Talamanca, which continues to the northwest and southeast. The eastern boundary of the national park coincides with the western boundary of the huge and largely inaccessible Parque Internacional La Amistad (p337).

Information

The dry season (from late December to April) is the most popular time to visit. On weekends, and especially during Easter week, the park is crowded with Tico hiking groups and the mountaintop hostel will likely be packed. February and March are the driest months, though it may still rain. The park is closed in May.

The early months of the rainy season are still good for climbing since there are fewer visitors and the torrential rains don't really start pouring until September. For the most part it doesn't rain before 1pm, but it is worth remembering that as much as 7000mm of annual rainfall has been recorded here. Temperatures can drop below freezing at night, so warm clothes (including a hat and gloves), rainwear and a good sleeping bag are necessary. The ranger station outside San Gerardo de Rivas is a good place to check weather conditions.

Before beginning the climb you have to make a reservation for the mountaintop hostel (p328) at the San Isidro park service office. This can be done over the telephone (Spanish necessary), and during the dry season it should be done at least one month ahead of time.

Once you arrive in San Gerardo de Rivas for your climb, you will need to check in at the **Chirripó ranger station** (Sinac; ☎ 200 5348; 🕑 6:30am-4:30pm) to confirm your reservation and pay the entry fee. You must do this the day *before* you set out. Do not call the Chirripó ranger station to reserve a slot at the hostel: it does not book them. The park entrance fee for two days is US$15, plus US$10 for each additional day. Excess luggage can be locked up here during your park stay at no extra charge.

There may be no-shows and it is always possible to fill one of these slots. For these it's best to stay in San Gerardo and check in daily at the ranger station for cancellations. Travelers may find that the hostel is indeed full – but space will usually become available if you can wait a day or two. The park is usually packed on Semana Santa and the chances of getting a slot are slim; there are rarely problems at other times of the year.

You can hire a pack horse to carry your belongings to the hostel during the dry season for US$18; there is a weight limit of 35kg. (You cannot ride the horse.) Porters are also available – at any time of year – to carry up 14kg worth of belongings for a fee of US$17. Get ready to feel embarrassed about your mountaineering abilities when you watch these guys fly up the mountain loaded down with your stuff.

It's a good idea to place everything in your pack in plastic bags in case of rain. Also, make sure that you have everything you will need for the climb in your day pack. When luggage is sent with porters or horses up or down the mountain you will not see it until you get to the destination point.

Because of fire hazards (a major forest fire in 1976 destroyed much of the *páramo* vegetation in the area), cigarette smoking is not permitted on the trail. There are designated smoking areas at the lodge.

MAPS

The maps available at the ranger station are fine for the main trails. Good topographical maps from the Instituto Geográfico Nacional de Costa Rica (IGN) are available in San José bookstores (p67). Note that the hostel, shelters and trails are not marked on these maps. Chirripó lies frustratingly at the corner of four separate 1:50,000-scale maps, so you need maps 3444 II San Isidro and 3544 III Durika to cover the area from the ranger station to the summit of Chirripó, and maps 3544 IV Fila Norte and 3444 I Cuerici to cover other peaks in the massif. Topographical maps are useful but not essential.

Climbing Chirripó

From the ranger station it is a 16km climb straight up to the mountaintop hostel; from there it's another 5km to the summit. Allow seven to 14 hours to reach the hostel, depending on how fit you are. The trailhead lies 50m beyond Albergue Urán in San Gerardo de Rivas and the main gate is open from 4am to 10am to allow climbers to enter; no one is allowed to begin the ascent after 10am. Inside the park the trail is clearly signed at every kilometer.

The open-sided, insect-ridden hut at Llano Bonito, halfway up, can provide shelter and water – but it is intended for emergency use, not overnight stays. Rangers recommend that hikers on day trips don't ascend beyond this

CHIRRIPÓ EQUIPMENT CHECKLIST

Costa Rica might be in the tropics, but Chirripó lies at some chilly altitudes. Don't get caught without the necessities when hiking Costa Rica's highest mountain.

- Biodegradable soaps and shampoos
- Flashlight and matches (there's no electricity for much of the evening at the mountaintop hostel)
- Food (including snacks for the hike)
- Gloves and a hat (temperatures can dip below freezing)
- Good sleeping bag (optional)
- Rain gear (even if it's not raining, the summit is misty)
- Sun block (temperatures on the summit can reach 29°C at noon)
- Warm jacket
- Water

point. Carry water on the trail: during the dry season the only place to get water before reaching the lodge is Llano Bonito.

Reaching the hostel is the hardest part. From there the hike to the summit is on relatively flatter terrain: allow at least two hours if you are fit, but carry a warm jacket, rain gear, water, snacks and a flashlight just in case. One reader suggests leaving the hostel at 3am and arriving at the summit just in time to watch the sun rise. A minimum of two days is needed to climb from the ranger station in San Gerardo to the summit and back; this gives you little time for resting or visiting the summit. Three days is a better bet. Some travelers report that the trip down is harder than the trip up, so get ready for a long haul.

OTHER TRAILS

Almost every visitor to the park climbs the main trail to Chirripó and returns the same way. Other nearby mountains can also be climbed via fairly obvious trails leading up from the lodge. These include Cerro Ventisqueros (3812m) and several other peaks. Some maps show rarely used, unmaintained wilderness trails leading north and south out of the park: these are extremely difficult to find and are not recommended. Check with the rangers before setting out.

For hard-core adventurers an alternative route is to take a guided three-day loop trek that begins in Herradura, goes up Chirripó and descends through San Gerardo. This trip requires camping and you must be accompanied by a local guide at all times. Check with Costa Rica Trekking Adventures inside Selva Mar in San Isidro about this journey (the 'Urán Trek', p322) or make the arrangements through **Cabañas Río Blanco** (☎ 352 0916, 771 0804) in Herradura.

Alternatively, you can call the **pulpería** (☎ 771 1199) in Herradura (Spanish necessary) and ask for Fabio Badilla or Rodolfo Elizondo, who are active members of the guide association and speak some English. They will help with arrangements.

Sleeping

Centro Ambientalista El Páramo (dm US$10), also known as Base Crestones, looks like a monastery and can house up to 60 people in dorm-style bunks. The basic stone building has a solar panel which provides electric light from 6pm to 8pm and sporadic heat for showers. (The water tends to be less frigid in the afternoon, so bathe then.) The lodge rents a variety of gear including sleeping bags (US$1.25), blankets (US$0.75) and cooking equipment (US$0.75); all rates are per day. Camping gas canisters are another US$2. See the Information section for details on how to make reservations for the hostel.

Getting There & Around

See details under San Gerardo de Rivas (p326) for directions on how to get here. From opposite the ranger station, in front of Cabinas El Bosque, there is free transportation to the trailhead at 5am. Also, several hotels offer early-morning trailhead transportation for their guests.

BUENOS AIRES

This small village is 64km southeast of San Isidro and 3km north of the Interamericana. It is reachable via a good asphalt road, just south of the Del Monte plant. There's a tree-filled plaza, a couple of banks, a gas station, a disco and other services.

Buenos Aires is in the center of an important pineapple-producing region (hence Del Monte) and is also an entry point for the rarely visited Reserva Biológica Durika, several Indian reserves (Ujarrás, Salitre and Cabagra) to the north, the Reserva Indígena Boruca to the south and the Parque Internacional La Amistad. You will not see many other tourists in this area.

There is a Banco Nacional on the southeast corner of the Parque Central and a new travel agency, **Geomar Viajes** (☎ 730 0805, 813 7588; geomarviajes@hotmail.com), has just opened on the 2nd floor of a shopping center just north of Ferretería El Pueblo. The friendly proprietors provide all sorts of local travel information and can help with arrangements to the Boruca indigenous reserve.

Also in town is a new **Fundación Durika office** (☎ 730 0657; www.durika.org), which administers the lodge and finca inside Reserva Biológica Durika (p329). Here you can make reservations and arrange transport. The office is 400m south and 100m east from Banco Nacional

Sleeping & Eating

Cabinas Violeta (s/d US$6/8.50; P) and **Cabinas Fabi** (☎ 730 1110; s/d/tr US$8.50/11/13; P) on the northern end of town both offer similar motor court-style lodging in clean, concrete rooms with cold showers. Ask at the **Ferretería El Pueblo** (hardware store; ☎ 730 0104), at the northwest corner of the park, about rooms for Cabinas Violeta.

On the road into town and 100m north of the clinic you'll find **Cabinas Mary** (☎ 730 0187; d/q US$7.50/13; P), which has a friendly owner and decent rooms with TV sets. West of here you'll find **Cabinas Kanajaka** (☎ 730 0207; s/d US$8.50/10; P), marked by an orange and red sign that says 'cabinas.' Rooms come with fan, wood floor and curtained-off bathroom. Both have cold showers.

A number of *sodas* operate out of the Mercado Central, and you'll find a Musmanni bakery on the north side.

Getting There & Away

Gafeso buses from San Isidro depart regularly to Buenos Aires, or you can take any bus headed to Palmar Norte or San Vito and ask to be let off at the turnoff. From here you can walk the 3km in or find a taxi.

If traveling from Buenos Aires to San Isidro, San José or San Vito, you can also wait for buses in transit on the Interamericana. Southbound buses stop in front of Soda El Paraíso about one hour after leaving San Isidro, and northbound ones stop in front of Restaurante de la Sabana two hours after leaving San Vito or Palmar. Some buses may be full, especially on weekends and holidays. There is no marked bus shelter, so be sure that you are visible so the bus driver knows to stop for you.

The following buses (except San Isidro) leave from the *mercado*:

Boruca US$1.25; 1½ hours; departs at 11:30am & 3:30pm.
San Isidro US$1.10; one hour; depart from the Gafeso terminal, diagonally opposite the *mercado* at 5:30am, 6am, 6:30am, 7:30am, 8am, 10am, 11am, 12:15pm, 2pm, 2:45pm & 5pm. Note: the 7:30am & 12:15pm buses don't run Sunday.
San José (Tracopa) Buses from Neily stop here around 9:15am & 4:30pm.

RESERVA BIOLÓGICA DURIKA

This 75-sq-km private biological reserve is 17km north of Buenos Aires on the flanks of Cerro Durika in the Cordillera de Talamanca, and is within the Parque Internacional La Amistad. Within the Durika reserve is the **Finca Anael,** where a couple of dozen people live in a more or less independent and sustainable manner. Community members are committed to local conservation; most are Tico, but there are a few foreigners.

The reserve opened to tourism in 1992: there is a lodge, and birding and hiking are the main activities. Day hikes, overnight tours and camping trips are offered to nearby waterfalls, the Continental Divide and local farms. A six-day hike and climb of Cerro Durika (3280m) in Parque Internacional La Amistad is also possible. There is a sauna and small Jacuzzi; classes may be offered in yoga, vegetarian cooking and meditation.

In addition, staff here can arrange forays to the Cabecar Indian village of **Ujarrás,** where crafts such as string bags are sold. There isn't much in the village to see, but if you want a glimpse of contemporary indigenous life in Costa Rica, this is a good place. As with excursions to any indigenous settlement, wear conservative attire and be respectful of the locals by asking permission before taking photographs.

There are 10 cabins of various sizes sleeping two to eight people (US$35 per person). All the cabins have a bathroom and porch with mountain views. Rates include reader-recommended organic vegetarian meals made from locally grown foods. Some short guided walks are included in the price. If driving to the finca on your own (not recommended), a 4WD is necessary.

There are special nightly rates for large groups, students (US$25) and also volunteers (US$15). Reservations and information are available from the **Fundación Durika office** (☎ 730 0657; www.durika.org) in Buenos Aires. The office can arrange transport to the reserve (US$30 for up to five passengers). Make reservations at least 10 days in advance.

A trip to this reserve is for adventurous travelers.

RESERVA INDÍGENA BORUCA

This reserve is centered on the village of **Boruca,** about 20km south of Buenos Aires. It is one of the few Indian reserves where there is any kind of infrastructure (however minimal) to welcome visitors on a limited basis. This is perhaps because Boruca is only some 8km west of the Carretera Interamericana.

The Boruca indigenous group is known for its carvings, including balsa wood masks and decorated gourds. The women use pre-Columbian back-strap looms to weave cotton cloth and belts, which can sometimes be purchased locally. Residents here support themselves primarily through agriculture.

If you are driving through the area on the Interamericana, you can stop at the community of Curré, where a small cooperative sells handicrafts.

Festivals & Events

The three-day **Fiesta de los Diablitos** (*diablitos* means 'little devils') is held in Boruca from December 31 to January 2 and in Curré from February 5–8. About 50 men wearing wooden devil masks and burlap costumes take the role of the Indians in their fight against the Spanish conquerors. The Spaniards, represented by a man in a bull costume, lose the battle. The Borucas may charge visitors photography fees and require photographers to wear a pass indicating they've paid.

Another festival, **La Fiesta de los Negritos**, held during the second week of December, celebrates the Virgin of the Immaculate Conception and involves costumed dancing and traditional Indian music (played mainly on drums and bamboo flutes).

Sleeping & Eating

The village *pulpería* in Boruca has a few basic rooms for rent, or can help you find a place to stay if they're already full. But it isn't set up for tourism. Camping is probably the easiest option. You can check in at Geomar Viajes in Buenos Aires for lodging options as well.

During the Fiesta de los Diablitos the town gets packed and locals will likely arrange for you to stay at somebody's home.

Traveling to Boruca is for culturally sensitive travelers (dress modestly) who can respect and appreciate the local lifestyle – not for individuals who will suffer without a swimming pool and CNN.

Getting There & Away

Buses (US$1.25, 1½ hours) leave the central market in Buenos Aires at 11:30am and 3:30pm daily, traveling to Boruca via a very poor dirt road. Drivers will find a better road that leaves the Interamericana about 3km south of Curré – look for the sign. It's about 8km to Boruca; a 4WD is recommended.

PALMAR NORTE & PALMAR SUR

This unremarkable, flat town lies right in the center of the banana-growing region of the Valle de Diquis. It is divided into north and south sections by the Río Grande de Térraba and serves primarily as the northern gateway to Parque Nacional Corcovado. Situated strategically between San Isidro (125km to the north) and the Panamanian border (95km to the southeast), Palmar is also a key transportation hub in any north-south migrations. Palmar Norte has banks, buses and hotels; Palmar Sur has the airport.

Lack of charm aside, Palmar is one of the best sites in the country to see the **granite spheres** *(esferas de piedra)* a legacy of pre-Columbian cultures – some of which exceed 2m in diameter (see p21 for more on these). You'll find them scattered all over town, but some of the largest and most impressive are in front of the peach-colored school *(el colegio)* on the Interamericana.

To get from Palmar Norte to Palmar Sur, take the Interamericana southbound over the Río Grande de Térraba bridge, then take the first right beyond the bridge.

Information

The **Internet café** (per hour US$2; 8:30am-6pm Mon-Sat), next to Coopealianza, has five decent terminals for checking email. Banks include **Banco Coopealianza** (8am-5pm Mon-Fri, 8am-noon Sat) on the Interamericana, which has an ATM on the Cirrus network, and the **Banco Popular** (786 7033), nearby, which changes traveler's checks and cash.

In the same complex you'll find **Osa Tours** (786 6534, 786 7825; catuosa@racsa.co.cr; 8am-noon & 2-6pm), which is both the home of the local tourist board and a good place to arrange tours into the Península de Osa.

Sleeping & Eating

The best values for budget travelers are on the Interamericana: **Cabinas Tico Alemán** (786 6232; d US$11, d with air-con US$16; P) and **Cabinas & Restaurante Wah Lok** (786 6262; s/d US$6.25/8.75; P) both have clean rooms with bathroom and fan.

Brunka Lodge (786 7944; brunkalodge@costaricense.cr; s/d US$8.80/17.50, s/d with air-con US$22/25;) This mid-range option on the Interamericana has immaculate bungalows with hot showers and cable TV. There is a decent pool and a popular restaurant.

Hotel Vista al Cerro (786 7744, 786 6663; s/d US$15/20, with air-con US$24; P) This hotel is on the western outskirts of town and offers 20 rooms, six with air-con. All are clean with fan

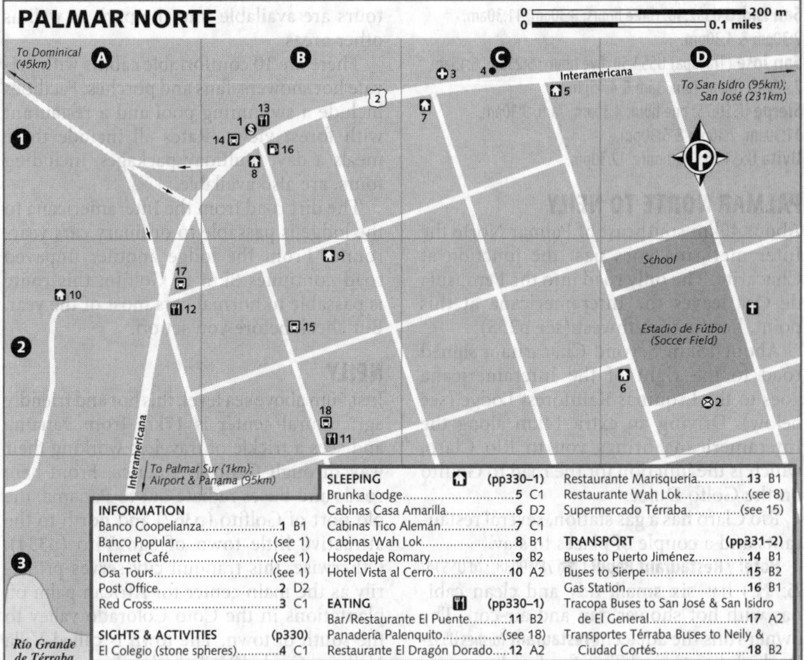

and basic cold shower. There is a restaurant and Internet access (US$2 per hour).

Hospedaje Romary (☎ 786 6459, 786 6300; d US$19, tr with air-con US$23; ❄) About 100m east of the Tracopa bus stop on the right hand side, this lodge has seven clean and cool tiled rooms with cable TV and cold shower; all have a fan, some have air-con. A small apartment sleeps up to four (rates vary with length of stay).

Cabinas Casa Amarilla (☎ 786 6251; s without/with bathroom US$3/6.30, s/d with bathroom & TV US$10/13; P) Very basic wood rooms with gloomy toilets are located in town, opposite the soccer field. Newer concrete doubles at the back are significantly cheerier and come with bathroom.

Bar/Restaurante El Puente (dishes US$2.50-4), in town, serves one tasty *arroz con pollo*. **Restaurante Marisquería** (dishes US$3-4) by Banco Coopealianza is another locally popular choice, serving good seafood and plenty of rice dishes.

On the highway, **Restaurante El Dragón Dorado** (dishes US$3-5) and **Restaurante Wah Lok** (dishes US$3-5) serve simple Chinese food.

Getting There & Away

AIR

Sansa has two daily flights to and from San José (US$66/132 one-way/round trip), while NatureAir has one (US$73/145).

Taxis meet incoming flights and charge about US$3 to Palmar Norte and US$12 to Sierpe. Otherwise, the infrequent Palmar Norte–Sierpe bus goes through Palmar Sur – you can board it if there's space available.

BUS

Buses to San José and San Isidro stop on the east side of the Interamericana. Other buses leave from in front of Panadería Palenquito or Supermercado Térraba a block apart on the town's main street. The bus ticket office is inside the Palenquito.

Ciudad Cortés (Transportes Térraba) six buses depart from 6:30am to 6:30pm.

Dominical 8am.

Neily (Transportes Térraba) 5am, 6am, 7am, 9:30am, noon, 1pm, 2:20pm & 4:50pm.

Puerto Jiménez departs from in front of Banco Coopealianza at 8am, 11am & 5pm. (These buses originate in San Isidro, so pick-up times are approximate.)

San Isidro US$2.50; three hours; 8:30am, 11:30am, 2:30pm & 4:30pm.
San José (Tracopa) US$4.50; five hours; 5:25am, 6:15am, 7:45am, 10am, 1am, 3am & 4:45pm.
Sierpe US$0.75; one hour; 4:30am, 7am, 9:30am, 11:30am, 2:30pm & 5:30pm.
Uvita US$1.25; 1½ hours; 12:30pm.

PALMAR NORTE TO NEILY

About 40km southeast of Palmar Norte the Interamericana goes past the junction at Chacarita. The only road into the Península de Osa leaves the Interamericana at this point, heading southwest (see p355).

About 15km beyond Chacarita a signed road to the right of the Interamericana goes to the Esquinas Rainforest Lodge (see below). Driving an extra 14km along the Interamericana brings you to Río Claro, which is the junction for the road to Golfito on the Golfo Dulce.

Río Claro has a gas station, several restaurants and a couple of places to stay.

Hotel y Restaurant Papili (☎ 789 9038; s/d US$16/25; ❄) has six small, tidy and clean cabinas with hot shower, fan and air-con. The owner runs the adjacent **restaurant** (dishes US$2-5) which has typical Tico food and pizza.

Nearby, **Hotel, Cabinas y Restaurant Impala** (☎ 789 9921; s/d US$14/20, s/d with air-con US$22/25; P ❄) has clean, white-tiled rooms with pink bedspreads. All units have hot shower and cable TV.

Any bus between Neily and Golfito can drop you off in Río Claro. If you're traveling to Golfito and don't want to wait for the bus, semi-regular collective taxis usually cruise through town soliciting passengers for the ride which costs US$1.50 per person if you have a full car.

Esquinas Rainforest Lodge

In the village of Gamba, less than 6km south of the Interamericana and above the Parque Nacional Piedras Blancas (formerly part of Parque Nacional Corcovado), is **Esquinas Rainforest Lodge** (☎ 775 0901; www.esquinaslodge.com; cabin per person US$95; P), which is Austrian-funded. This project embodies ecotourism in the truest sense: Most of the employees are from Gamba, and profits from the lodge are reinvested in community projects.

The lodge is surrounded by 120 hectares of rain forest. Bus, boat, horse and hiking tours are available into the park as well as other areas.

There are 10 comfortable cabins with private hot showers, fans and porches. Facilities include a swimming pool and a restaurant with forest views. Rates all include three meals a day; multiday packages, including tours, are also available.

The dirt road from the Interamericana to the lodge is passable to ordinary cars year-round. From the lodge another unpaved road continues 8km to Golfito; this route is passable to normal cars most of the year. But check before you set off.

NEILY

Just 50m above sea level, this hot and friendly agricultural center is 17km from Panama and sees a trickle of travelers working their way through Central America. From here roads and buses radiate out to Panama, the old port of Golfito (p362) and north to the attractive little town of San Vito (p334). Otherwise, this tranquil city serves primarily as the main center for African palm oil plantations in the Coto Colorado valley to the south of town. The town is called Villa Neily or Ciudad Neily by locals.

Information

Check email at **Technoplanet** (per hr US$1.25), 200m north of the school, or **Neurotec** (per hr US$1.25), southwest of the *mercado*. There is a public hospital about 2km south of town on the Interamericana. Any bus to Paso Canoas can drop you off there.

Banco Coopealianza, southwest of the *mercado*, has a 24-hour ATM on the Cirrus network. **Banco de Costa Rica** (🕑 8am-3pm Mon-Fri), near the Interamericana, and **Banco Popular** (☎ 783 3076; 🕑 8am-5pm Mon-Fri, 9-11:30am Saturday), opposite the school, will change US dollars and traveler's checks.

Caving

Just 3km north of Neily on the road to San Vito (turn off at the bridge that leads to the Río Corredore) there is a network of newly explored **caverns** on a privately owned banana plantation. The site isn't developed for tourism but it is possible to visit. La Purruja Lodge in Golfito (p366) is currently running tours for guests to the site (US$35 per person), but at least two days notice is needed. Alternatively, you can hire a 4WD

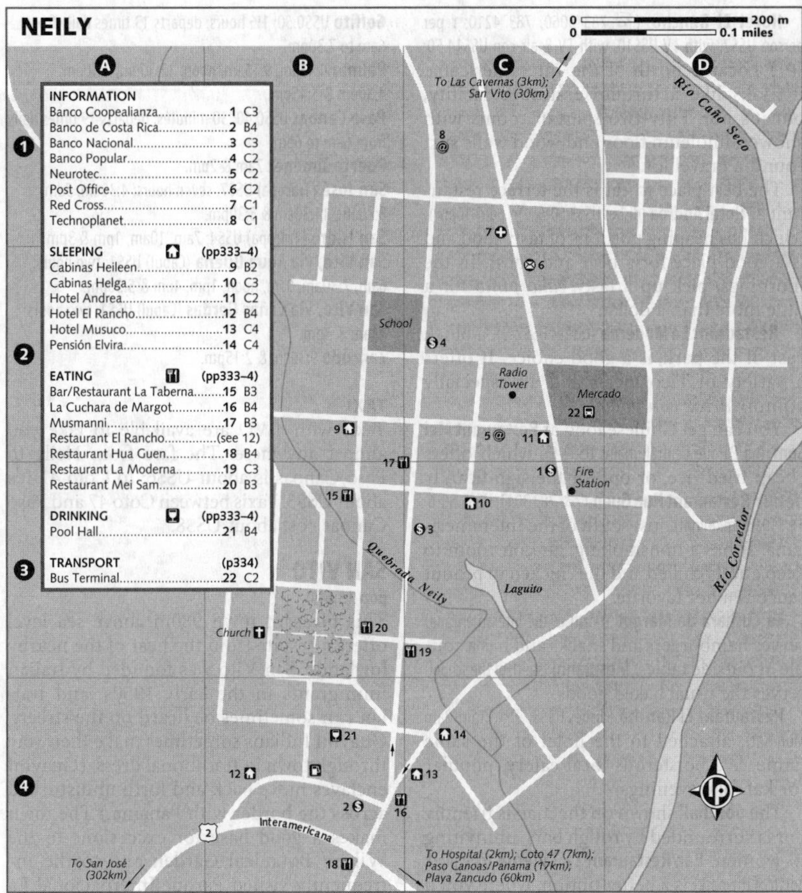

taxi to get you there (US$6 one way): Tell them you're going to *'las cavernas de San Rafael'*. Be aware that since this site is not geared to tourism there is no guarantee that the gate will be open or that there will be anyone there to admit you if you arrive. Entry fees vary.

Sleeping, Eating & Drinking

All hotels have cold showers unless otherwise mentioned.

Hotel Andrea (☎ 783 3784; s/d/tr US$19/20/24, s/d/tr/q with air-con US$23/24/26/28; P) Diagonally opposite the *mercado*, this is the top place in town and the rooms are good value. Thirty-nine super clean, white-tiled units sparkle and upstairs ones have a terrace with views; all have hot shower and cable TV. Credit cards are accepted.

Pensión Elvira (☎ 783 3057; r US$5, d with bathroom US$7.50; P) Southeast of the park, this hotel has small, dark turquoise rooms that are sort of clean; bathrooms could be better.

Hotel Musuco (☎ 783 3048; r per person without/with bathroom US$3.50/5.50) Down the road from Elvira, this is a better deal: clean and secure, though not inspiring.

Cabinas Helga (☎ 783 3146; d US$17.40; P) Southwest of the bus station, with spacious, clean rooms with cable TV and bathroom, this is good value.

Cabinas Heileen (☎ 783 3080; s/d US$7.50/12; P) North of the school, this family-owned pension is a little dark, but tidy and well run.

Hotel El Rancho (☎ 783 3060, 783 4210; r per person US$7, with TV US$10, with TV & air-con US$14.50; P) Located north of the Interamericana, it looks like a turquoise storage facility, but it's not. Fifty-two spartan rooms with shower, linoleum floor and wood walls surround a gravel lot.

The best place to eat is the terrace restaurant at **Hotel Andrea** (dishes US$3.50-5; 6am-10pm), which has heaping portions of tasty food and is a good place for a beer and *bocas*. In the mornings, pick up a tasty *gallo pinto* for a little more than a dollar.

Restaurant La Moderna (dishes US$2-6), a block east of the park, is a good choice. It offers a variety of Tico meals and an especially yummy *arroz con pollo*.

You can get Chinese food at **Restaurant Mei Sam** (on Parque Central; mains US$2-5), which offers cheap fried rice, or opt for the significantly better **Restaurant Hua Guen** (☎ 783 3041; US$2.50-6; 10am-midnight), just south of the Interamericana. It has a nonsmoking, air-con room to keep guests chilled and the chicken in peanut sauce is a hot favorite.

La Cuchara de Margot (north of the Interamericana) serves hamburgers and snacks and has a couple of outside tables. **Musmanni** (south of the school) serves the usual baked goods.

Restaurant El Rancho (dishes US$3; 11am-2am Mon-Sat), attached to the hotel of the same name, is a boisterous local eatery, popular for karaoke evenings.

The **pool hall** shown on the map is friendly but is surrounded by rough bars, uninviting to women. **Bar/Restaurant La Taberna** (one block north of the park) is a better option, where you'll find a mixed crowd admiring the monster television.

Getting There & Away

AIR

Sansa has a daily flight (US$71/142 one-way/round trip) between San José and Coto 47, the airport located 7km southwest of Neily. The bus to Finca 40 makes a stop by the airport (see below).

BUS

These buses leave from the main terminal on the east side of town:

Ciudad Cortés departs 4:45am, 9:15am, noon, 12:30pm, 2:30pm, 4:30pm & 5:45pm.
Finca 40 (airport) US$0.25; 9:15am, 11:30am, 1:15pm, 3:15pm, 4:30pm & 6pm.
Golfito US$0.50; 1½ hours; departs 13 times daily from 6am to 7:30pm.
Palmar 4:45am, 9:15am, noon, 12:30pm, 2:30pm, 4:30pm & 5:45pm.
Paso Canoas US$0.40; 30 minutes; departs 19 times daily from 6am to 6pm.
Puerto Jiménez 7am & 2pm.
San José (Tracopa) US$7; seven hours; 4:30am, 5am, 8:30am, 11:30am & 3:30pm.
San Isidro (Tracopa) US$4; 7am, 10am, 1pm & 3pm.
San Vito, via Agua Buena (Capul) US$1; two hours; 6am, 7:30am, 9am, noon, 1pm, 4pm & 5:30pm.
San Vito, via Cañas Gordas (Capul) US$1; two hours; 11am & 3pm.
Zancudo 9:30am & 2:15pm.

TAXI

Taxis with 4WD are available to take you almost anywhere. The fare from Neily to Paso Canoas is about US$6; to Coto 47 it's about US$3. Taxis between Coto 47 and Paso Canoas cost about US$8.

SAN VITO

pop 15,000

This pleasant town 980m above sea level offers a respite from the heat of the nearby lowlands. San Vito was founded by Italian immigrants in the early 1950s, and Italian can sometimes be heard on the streets. Guaymí Indians sometimes make their way through town in traditional dress. (Guaymí enclaves move back and forth undisturbed across the border with Panama.) The town makes a good base for excursions to the Wilson Botanical Garden and to the infrequently visited Parque Internacional La Amistad.

The drive north from Neily is a scenic one, with superb views of the lowlands dropping away as the road climbs the steep and winding hillside. The road is steep, narrow and full of hairpin turns. You can also get to San Vito from San Isidro via the Valle de Coto Brus – an incredibly scenic and lesser-used route offering fantastic views of the Cordillera de Talamanca to the north and the lower Fila Costeña to the south. The narrow, swooping road is paved.

The two banks will exchange US dollars and are open between 8:30am and 3:30pm on weekdays. In addition, the **Centro Cultural Dante Alighieri** (across from the park), has tourist information and historical information on Italian immigration, but opening hours

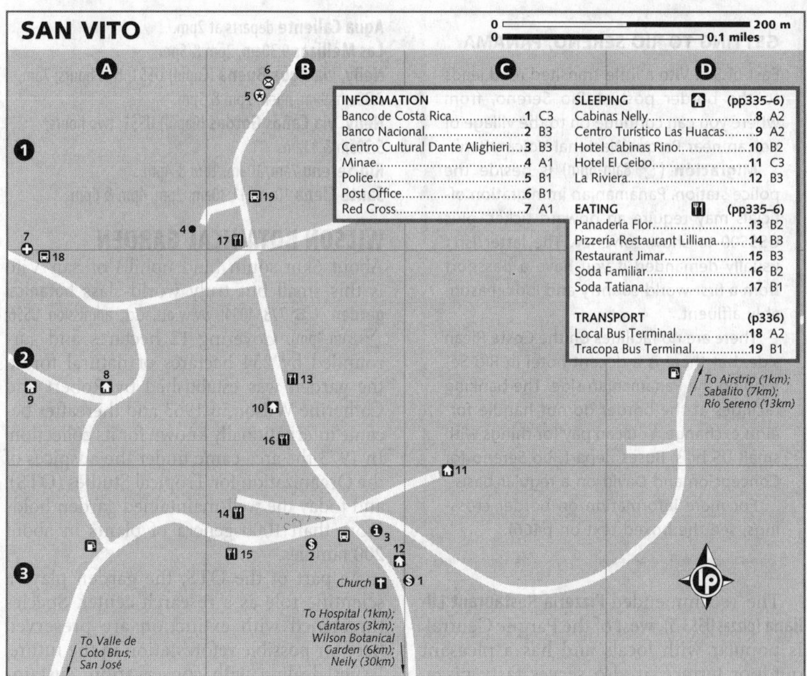

are erratic. Behind the center look for the bombed-out Jeep that served in Italy during WWII.

A **Minae parks office** (☎ 773 4090; 9am-4pm), at the northern end of town, can provide information on travel to Parque Internacional La Amistad (p337).

There's a hospital 1km south of the town center.

Sights & Activities

Cántaros (☎ 773 3760; admission US$0.90; 9:30am-5pm Tue-Sun), about 3km away en route to Wilson Botanical Gardens, has a pleasant recreation center and gift shop (there is no admission fee to enter the gift shop). Housed in a pretty and well-maintained cabin built by early area pioneers and now restored, Cántaros stocks a small but carefully chosen selection of local and national crafts. The center has a small park with a lake, trails and a lookout.

Sleeping & Eating

All rooms have a private bathroom with hot water unless otherwise noted.

Centro Turístico Las Huacas (☎ 773 3115; s/d US$8/12.50; P) On the west side of town, this hotel has pretty, well-maintained rooms.

Cabinas Nelly (☎ 773 4735; r per person US$6.30) Across the street and just east of Las Huacas, this place has dark wood cabins that are a bit musty. Bathrooms are shared and hot water is tepid at best.

Hotel Cabinas Rino (☎ 773 3071, late-night 773 4030; s/d US$10/17; P) Travelers have good things to say about the pleasant and comfortable whitewashed rooms surrounding a 2nd-story courtyard. It's located on the main road; rooms all come with TV sets.

La Riviera (☎ 773 3305; s/d US$13.80/25) Next to the Dante Alighieri center, the Riviera has small, clean carpeted rooms and cable TV. The ones at the back have sensational views.

Hotel El Ceibo (☎ 773 3025; d/tr US$35/45; apapilic@racsa.co.cr; P) Further east you'll find El Ceibo, the best hotel in town. The 40 rooms are well manicured and have cable TV and fan. Some have pretty forest views; others face the parking lot which is less scenic. A **bar-restaurant** (dishes US$4-5) has good Italian/Tico fare.

GETTING TO RÍO SERENO, PANAMA

East of San Vito a little-transited road leads to the border post at Río Sereno, from where you can continue on to the village of Volcán near Parque Nacional Volcán Barú.

Migración (8am-6pm) is beside the police station. Panamanian immigration officials may require an onward ticket, plus US$500 to show solvency. The latter isn't usually demanded if you have a passport from a first-world country and look reasonably affluent.

There are no facilities on the Costa Rican side, but there is a decent hotel in Río Sereno on the Panamanian side. The banking facilities at the border do not handle foreign exchange. You can pay for things with small US bills. Buses depart Río Sereno for Concepción and David on a regular basis.

For more information on border crossings, see the boxed text on p466).

The recommended **Pizzería Restaurant Lilliana** (pizzas US$3-5), west of the Parque Central, is popular with locals and has a pleasant outdoor terrace; it also serves tasty pizza. Both **Soda Familiar** and **Soda Tatiana** (casados US$2 at both), on the main road, have cheap Tico fare.

The recommended **Restaurant Jimar** (dishes US$2-3) has a terrace with good views and serves burgers, casados and sandwiches.

Do not miss **Panadería Flor** (main road), which has truly amazing and marvelously gooey cinnamon raisin rolls (US$0.30).

Getting There & Away

AIR

You can charter light aircraft to and from the San Vito airstrip, 1km west of town. Otherwise, the nearest airports with scheduled services are at Coto 47 near Neily and in Golfito (p367).

BUS

The main Tracopa terminal is located on the northern end of the main street.

San Isidro US$3.50; three hours; departs 6:45am & 1:30pm.
San José US$7; six hours; 5am, 7:30am, 10am & 3pm.

A local bus terminal on the northwest end of town runs buses to Neily and other destinations as follows:

Agua Caliente departs at 2pm.
Las Mellizas 9:30am, 2pm & 5pm.
Neily, via Agua Buena (Capul) US$1; two hours; 7am, 7:30am, 9am, noon, 2pm & 5pm.
Neily, via Cañas Gordas (Capul) US$1; two hours; 5:30am & 11am.
Río Sereno 7am, 10am, 1pm & 4pm.
Santa Elena 10am, 11:30am, 2pm, 4pm & 6pm.

WILSON BOTANICAL GARDEN

About 6km south (and uphill) of San Vito is this small but truly world-class **botanical garden** (773 4004; www.ots.ac.cr; admission US$6; 8am-4pm). Covering 12 hectares and surrounded by 254 hectares of natural forest, the garden was established by Robert and Catherine Wilson in 1963 and thereafter became internationally known for its collection. In 1973 the area came under the auspices of the Organization for Tropical Studies (OTS), and today the well-maintained garden holds more than 1000 genera of plants in about 200 families.

As part of the OTS, the garden plays a scientific role as a research center. Species threatened with extinction are preserved here for possible reforestation in the future. Issues dealing with conservation, sustainable development, horticulture and agroecology are primary research topics and students and researchers stay here to use the greenhouse and laboratory.

The gardens are well laid out, many of the plants are labeled and a trail map is available for self-guided walks. You can show up at any time during operating hours for these. Guided nature walks (in English) cost US$10/25 for a half-/full-day and US$8/10 for children aged under 12. Reservations for guided hikes and visits can be made via the OTS website (look for information under the 'Las Cruces' link in the biological stations section of the site). The staff speak English and Spanish.

Overnight guests can be accommodated if reservations are made (far) in advance through the OTS website; otherwise, consider staying in San Vito.

About a dozen comfortable cabins come with phone, hot shower and balcony with great views. Rates are US$62.50 per person for double occupancy; children under 12 sharing with adults are charged US$25. The rates include meals and entry to the gardens.

Getting There & Away

Buses between San Vito and Neily pass the entrance to the gardens several times a day. Make sure you take the bus that goes through Agua Buena; buses that go through Cañas Gordas do not stop here. A taxi from San Vito to the gardens costs US$3.

PARQUE INTERNACIONAL LA AMISTAD

This huge 1950-sq-km park is by far the largest single protected area in Costa Rica. It is known as an international park because it continues across the border into Panama, where it is managed separately. The Panamanian side of the park is another 2070 sq km.

Combined with two adjoining national parks and a host of indigenous and biological reserves, La Amistad is part of a huge biological corridor protecting a great variety of tropical habitats ranging from rain forest to *páramo*, and has thus attracted the attention of biologists, ecologists and conservationists worldwide. In 1982 Unesco declared La Amistad to be a Biosphere Reserve, and in 1983 it was given the status of a World Heritage Site.

The park has the nation's largest population of Baird's tapirs, as well as giant anteaters, all six species of Neotropical cats – jaguar, puma (mountain lion), margay, ocelot, oncilla (tiger cat) and jaguarundi – and many more common mammals. More than 500 bird species have been sighted (more than half of the total in Costa Rica); 49 of these exist only within the biosphere reserve. In addition, 115 species of fish and 215 different reptiles and amphibians have been listed. There are innumerable insect species.

The backbone of this park is the Cordillera de Talamanca, which not only includes the peaks of the Chirripó massif but has many mountains over 3000m high. The thickly forested northern Caribbean slopes and southern Pacific slopes of the Talamancas are also protected in the park, but it is only on the Pacific side that ranger stations are found.

Within the park, development is almost nonexistent, which means trekkers are limited to their own resources. Hiking through steep, thick and wet rain forest is difficult and not recommended without taking a guide (see p352).

Orientation & Information

Information is available at local **Minae offices:** San Vito (☎ 773 4090) San Isidro (☎ 771 3155, 771 4836, 771 5116; Calle 2 btwn Avs 4 & 6). Only the San Vito office can make reservations at the park hostels and arrange for guides (Spanish necessary). Admission to the park costs US$6 per day and camping is US$2.

Park headquarters is at **Estación Altamira** (☎ 200 5355), now manned at all times. This is the best-developed area of the park and has a small exhibit room covering the local flora and fauna, a camping area, showers and drinking water, electric light and a lookout tower. There are several trails, some passing through primary forest and others sharing panoramic views or leading to tiny communities along the border of the park. Wear long pants – grasses can get waist deep on some trails.

The longest trail (20km) – known as the **Valle del Silencio** – departs from the Estación Altamira and winds its way through pristine (and hilly) primary forest, before ending up at a camping area and refuge at the base of Cerro Kamuk. The walk takes anywhere from eight to 12 hours, provided you are in very good physical condition. It is reportedly spectacular and traverses one of the most isolated areas in all of Costa Rica. A local guide is required to make the journey.

The refuge is very basic and provides little more than shelter, toilets, water and 20 bunk-style beds. All other supplies must be taken in: compass, sleeping bags, food, cooking equipment (stove and gas canisters), candles, flashlight etc.

There is a lesser-used park service post at Estación Santa María de Pittier, a few kilometers south of Altamira on the slopes of Cerro Pittier. Here you'll find another basic 30-person bunk bed hostel that has fresh water, toilets and not much else. As with the other stations, take in all your own supplies. There is a trail that connects this station to Altamira. Hiring a guide is highly recommended.

Sleeping & Eating

Apart from camping near the ranger stations, and the two refuges mentioned above, there are two lodges close to the park. Also see Reserva Biológica Durika (p329).

La Amistad Lodge (☎ in San José 289 7667, 200 5037; www.laamistad.com; r per person US$88) Situated about

3km by poor dirt road from the village of Las Mellizas (not near Altamira), this was the first tourist lodge to open up in the area. It is situated on a combined 100 sq km of wilderness and organic farm that constitutes Costa Rica's third-largest reserve. The congenial Montero family has lived here for generations and do a good job balancing the needs of development with protecting the environment. The lodge has 10 double rooms in tropical hardwood, seven with bathroom (all showers are hot). The lodge has also set up three jungle tent camps (with a fourth on the way) at different altitudes and in different vegetation zones that allow the visitor to do a multiday trek around the area without having to leave the comforts of a solid bed and good cooking. Each camp is about 7km apart. The staff will transport your belongings from one site to another and provide meals at each camp, which has full-sized walk-in tents, toilets and running water. The birding is excellent and other tours are available.

Rates include three meals a day and the entry fee into the park. Electricity is available for most hours of the day, but pack a flashlight. Buses to Las Mellizas can get you close to the lodge, but the owners will come get you if you call ahead. For reservations call the San José number.

Monte Amuo Lodge (☎ 265 6149; r per person with 3 meals US$75) Set on 50 hectares bordering La Amistad, this is another good facility near the park. It's reached by driving northwest from San Vito on the Valle de Coto Brus road. About 4km past the Río Grande de Térraba (44km north of San Vito), a signed road leads to Potrero Grande (5km); Monte Amuo is 10km beyond here on signed roads (4WD necessary). Accommodations here are in rustic cabins with private hot showers. Electricity is available for only part of the night.

Getting There & Away

Taxis with 4WD can usually be hired to get you (sort of close) to the park stations. You may have to do a bit of asking around before finding someone who knows the way. Regardless, the roads – if they can be called that – are grueling, and even the hardiest 4WD can have a tough go of it. If you are driving here, inquire about road conditions at the Minae office in San Vito prior to departing. This is a trip only for adventurers who have days to spare.

TO ESTACIÓN ALTAMIRA

From San Isidro or San Vito you can take any of the buses that run between these two towns and get off in the town of Guácimo (written up in some guides as Las Tablas). Ask the driver to let you know when the stop comes up. From Guácimo two buses daily travel to the town of El Carmen – and if the road conditions permit, they go all the way to the town of Altamira (but this is iffy). There is a *soda* and some cheap cabinas in El Carmen, if for some reason you have to spend the night. From here it's

GETTING TO DAVID, PANAMA

Paso Canoas is the major border crossing with Panama and is generally quite crowded. At the time of writing, the border station was in the process of being demolished and rebuilt. Until the new station is complete, you'll find Costa Rican migración on the eastern side of the highway north of the Tracopa bus terminal. After securing an exit visa, walk 400m east to the Panamanian immigration post, located somewhat inconspicuously behind the Centro de Copias Joamy (photocopy center) 50m north of the highway. Here you can purchase the necessary tourist card (US$5) to enter Panama, though they have been known to run out. You might be asked for an onward ticket and evidence of financial solvency. Presenting a credit card should usually do, but this border station is known for giving travelers a hard time for not having one. From here dozens of minivans go to David, 1½ hours away (US$1.50 per person).

If driving into Panama in a private vehicle (or if you're coming from Panama into Costa Rica), you must have your car fumigated (US$3.50). Keep a copy of the fumigation ticket as roadside checkpoints often request it. If you don't have it, you'll be dispatched back to the border until your car is doused. The border is open 24 hours. The Panamanian currency is the *balboa*, which is on par and interchangeable with US dollars.

For more information about border crossings, see (p466).

a 4km walk on a windy road to the town of Altamira, from where you can follow the Minae sign (near the church) leading to the steep 2km hike to the ranger station.

TO ESTACIÓN SANTA MARÍA DE PITTIER

This station is accessible in the dry season only. To reach it, catch the bus that departs San Vito for Agua Client. If the road is in poor condition – which is highly likely – you may only make it as far as Santa Elena. From Santa Elena it is a 5km walk uphill to the station. This station is not always manned, so it is important to make reservations at the hostel prior to departing.

PASO CANOAS

This small town is the main port of entry between Costa Rica and Panama and, like most border outposts, is largely devoid of charm. (Neily, only 17km away, is far more pleasant.) Hotels are often full of Tico bargain hunters looking for duty-free specials, especially on weekends and holidays. Most of the shops and hotels are on the Costa Rican side.

Accredit (8am-4:30pm) near Costa Rican migración changes traveler's checks and there is an ATM on the Visa Plus system near the border. Moneychangers have acceptable rates for converting US dollars into colones or balboas. Rates for converting excess colones into dollars are not good. Colones are accepted at the border, but are difficult to get rid of further into Panama.

The **Instituto Panameño de Turismo** (727 6524; 6am-11pm), by the Panamanian border post, has information on travel to Panama. If you are arriving in Costa Rica, you'll find tourist information and maps (sometimes) at a small ICT office by the departures line at the Costa Rican migración office. Hours are irregular.

Sleeping & Eating

The hotels in Paso Canoas aren't particularly good, but there are a few decent options. All showers at the following places are cold.

Cabinas Romy (732 1930; d US$20; P) Shiny new rooms in a bright yellow building are spotless, with tiled floors and private bathrooms. Wooden doors all have decorous wood carvings.

Hotel Azteca (732 2217; r per person US$5, with air-con US$7.50;) On the western side of town, this good, clean, well-run bright-red hotel has 57 rooms with private showers and is among the town's best. More expensive rooms with air-con have TVs and there's an onsite restaurant.

Cabinas Interamericano (732 2041; s/d US$5/10, s/d with air-con US$6.30/15;) Of the cheapies, this is the best deal in town. Rooms are dark but clean and all have showers.

Hotel Real Victoria (732 3586; s/d US$10/13.75; P) A secure place with a pool and clean, air-con rooms with showers.

Cabinas Jiménez (732 2258; s/d US$9/12, s/d with air-con US$15/18) Eighteen decent rooms in a peach-colored house all have TV and

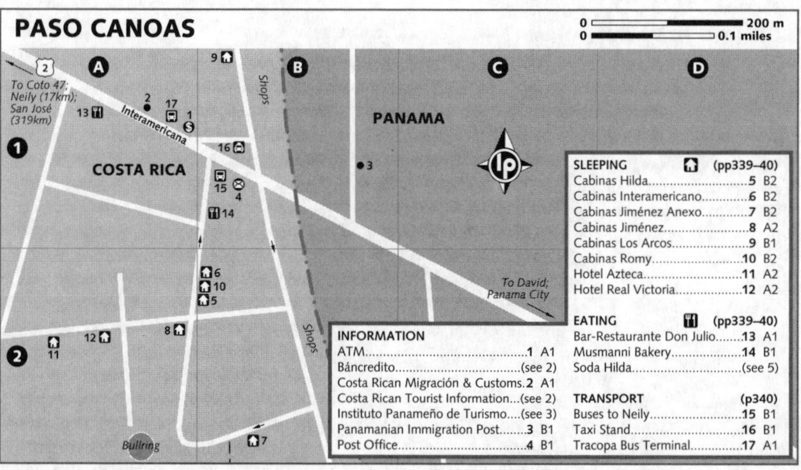

shower. The anexo, at a separate location, is slightly cheaper but significantly gloomier and very basic.

Cabinas Hilda (☎ 732 2873; d US$10, d with air-con US$17.50;) These cabinas have bathrooms, but are musty and rather dark; the attached *soda* is good.

Cabinas Los Arcos (☎ 732 1632; r per person US$6; P) Situated on a quiet end of town, Los Arcos has dark, somewhat scruffy, concrete cabinas that are reasonably clean and have a bathroom and fan.

Dining options include a number of cheap *sodas*. The best of these is **Soda Hilda** (casados US$3). It is one of the cleaner, nicer and more family-friendly places in town. **Bar-Restaurante Don Julio** (casados US$4), on the Interamericana, is marked with a sign that says Brunca Steak House and serves a variety of Tico and Chinese specialties. **Musmanni** (US$0.30-3.00) has baked goods.

Getting There & Away

Tracopa buses (☎ 732 2119; US$7; 8hr) leave for San José at 4am, 8am, 9am and 3pm. The bus office, or window really, is north of the border post, on the east side of the main road. Sunday afternoon buses are full of weekend shoppers, so buy tickets. Buses for Neily (US$0.40, 30 minutes) leave from in front of the post office at least once an hour from 6am to 6pm. Taxis to Neily cost about US$6 and to the airport at Coto 47 about US$8.

Península de Osa & Golfo Dulce

CONTENTS

Home to the best remaining strands of Central America's Pacific coastal rain forest, the largely inaccessible Península de Osa also boasts the Parque Nacional Corcovado, which protects some of Costa Rica's most spectacular natural wonders. This protected area attracts countless visitors who arrive by boat, bus, car and plane, ready to explore its many riches – from flocks of scarlet macaws to colonies of monkeys to elusive animals such as the jaguar. Snorkeling enthusiasts can take day trips to the Reserva Biológica Isla del Caño (about 20km west of the peninsula) and snorkel the clear, body-temperature waters.

The Osa protects the Golfo Dulce from the powerful Pacific, attracting groups of whales and dolphins during mating season and while they're raising their newly born offspring in the gulf's tranquil waters. At the southern end, surfers descend on Pavones for the country's longest left-hand break, while beach lovers head to the quieter waters of Zancudo.

There are several ways to get to the peninsula: one way is to take a boat from Sierpe to Bahía Drake from where you can walk or boat into Corcovado. Another option is to go to the peninsula's biggest town, Puerto Jiménez, reachable by air, bus, car, or a boat from Golfito. From there, a rough road continues around the end of the peninsula to the southeast entrance of the national park at Carate.

HIGHLIGHTS

- Traversing the incomparable **Parque Nacional Corcovado** (p351)
- Surfing one of the continent's longest left-hand waves at **Pavones** (p374)
- Enjoying the isolation of hilly rain forests in a **Río Nuevo tent camp** (p355)
- Lounging on the tranquil beaches of **Zancudo** (p371)
- Visiting the botanical wonders of the **northern Golfo Dulce** (p362), especially at **Casa de Orquídeas** (p369)

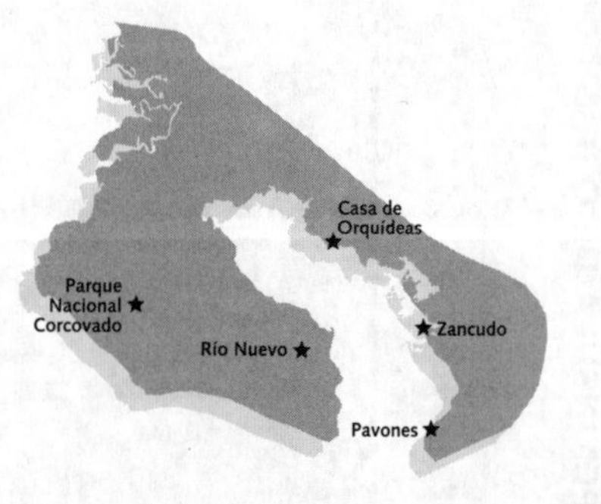

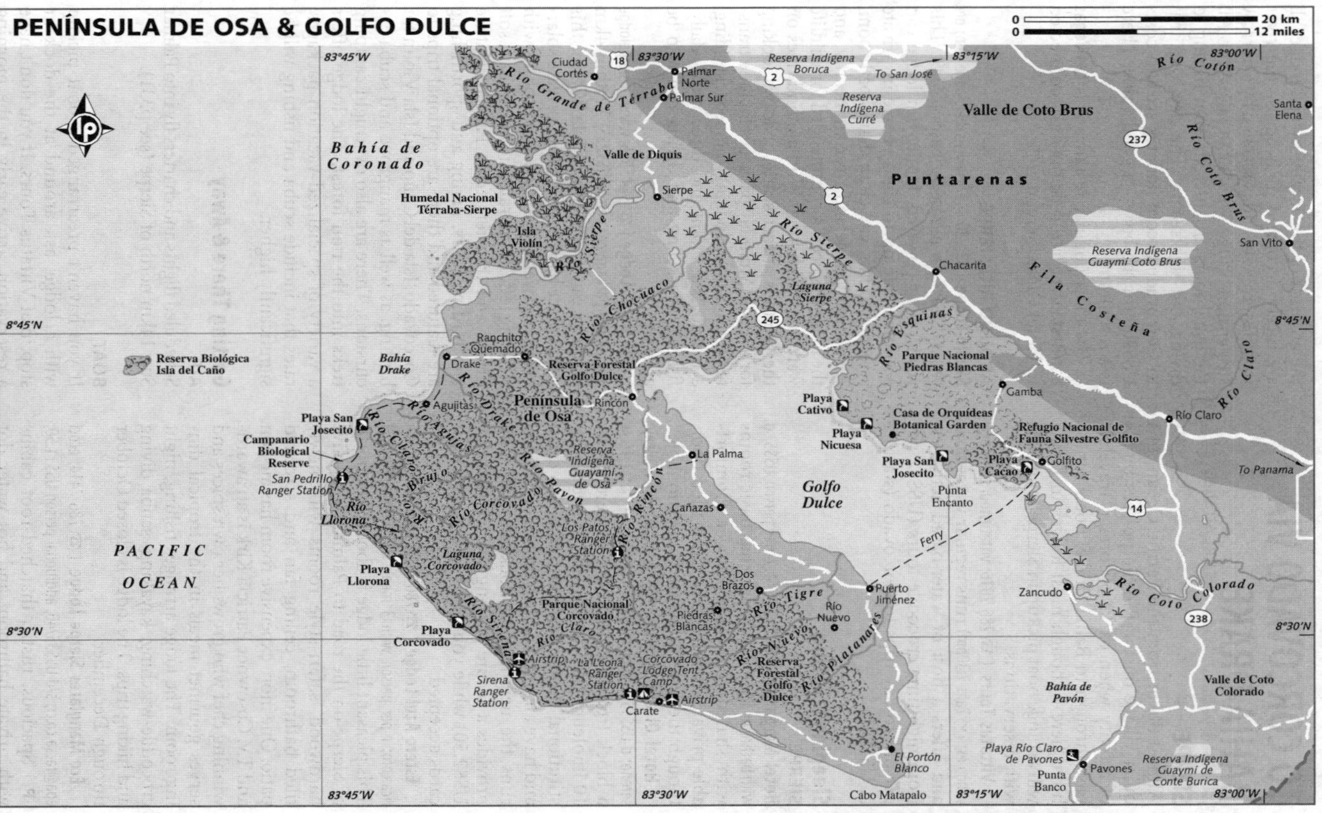

PENÍNSULA DE OSA & GOLFO DULCE

TO CORCOVADO VIA BAHÍA DRAKE

SIERPE

Almost 30km from the Pacific Ocean, this quiet village on the Río Sierpe sees bursts of activity when packs of foreign travelers pass through to Bahía Drake. Boats can be hired here – though most lodges in Drake will arrange boat pickup in Sierpe for guests with reservations.

Vittatus Tours (☎ 786 7016; vittatustouroperator@yahoo.es; 🕒 7am-7:30pm) runs regular water taxis and offers a host of water-based activities, from nighttime crocodile tours (US$12 per person) to day trips to Corcovado (starting at US$80).

Sleeping & Eating

SIERPE

Hotel Margarita (☎ 786 7574; r per person US$5, d with bathroom US$10) This place has basic rooms with shared cold-water shower. Comfortable private doubles have clean tiled floor, though the water pressure is questionable.

Hotel Oleaje Sereno (☎ 786 7580; www.oleajesereno; d US$35, additional person US$10; P ❄) Just a block from the dock, Oleaje Sereno has 10 linoleum-tiled rooms, all painted an institutional turquoise. The rooms are clean and have air-con and hot shower. The hotel runs the neighboring dockside *soda* and provides a secure parking service (per day US$2.50) while you travel to Drake. Credit cards accepted.

Estero Azul Lodge (☎ 786 7422; www.samplecostarica.com; r per person with 3 meals US$90-94; P ❄) This pleasant little lodge is about 2km north of Sierpe on the road to Palmar. It has five hardwood, safari-style rooms with newly tiled bathroom, ceiling fan and screened patio. One more expensive room has air-con and TV. Co-owner Patricia Kirk is an award-winning chef who grows her own spices and serves gourmet meals in the tropical dining room. The lodge arranges fishing, night crocodile-watching, kayaking, scuba diving and hiking trips. The lodge is closed October through December.

Eco Manglares Sierpe Lodge (☎ 786 7414; ecociepa@racsa.co.cr; s/d US$35/40, additional person US$11.50; P) Spacious, rustic, thatched-roof cabins with private bathroom and hot water dot the grounds of this family-owned lodge; all are nicely decorated. It is across the river from Estero Azul and is reached by a narrow suspension bridge, which can take a car. All the usual tours are offered: from fishing to diving and sightseeing. The day-long trip to Corcovado accommodates six and costs US$200 for the boat – a good value. There is a restaurant.

The most popular restaurant is **Las Vegas Bar/Restaurant** (next to the boat dock), connected to Hotel Oleaje Sereno.

AROUND RÍO SIERPE

Sábalo Lodge (☎ 770 1457; www.sabalolodge.com; per person US$55; 4-day package per person US$349) This rustic, solar-powered, family-run lodge can accommodate up to eight people in private screened rooms with clean shared bathroom. A swimming hole and river are nearby, and the lodge has been recommended for wildlife watching and hiking. Wild almond trees on the grounds attract scarlet macaws looking for a snack. Multiday packages include transfer from Sierpe, lodging, horseback riding, a trip to Isla Violín and three meals daily; fishing, snorkeling and diving can also be arranged.

Río Sierpe Lodge (☎ 384 5595; www.riosierpelodge.com; 4-day package per person US$255) Within 4km of the ocean and south of Isla Violín, this rustic place has 17 rooms with private solar-heated shower and six two-story rooms with sleeping loft. Room rates include meals, soft drinks and transfers from Palmar. Nature and birding tours, diving and sportfishing are featured and there are optional trips to Corcovado, Isla del Caño and Isla Violín for birding, as well as mangrove and scuba excursions. There are also overnight camping treks into the rain forest. The lodge offers a variety of specialized vacation packages; rates that include scuba and fishing will be significantly higher.

Getting There & Away

AIR

Scheduled flights and charters fly into Palmar Sur, 14km north of Sierpe (see p331).

BOAT

If you haven't prearranged a boat pickup with a lodge, ask around at the dock or stop in at Vittatus Tours. If you don't have a reservation, arrive early in the morning

(8am-ish), when boats from Drake drop off passengers. The going rate to Bahía Drake is US$15 per person, with a minimum of four. The trip takes 90 minutes or more, depending on the size of the boat engine and the tides.

The trip to Drake is scenic and – without a doubt – quite entertaining. Boats travel first along the river through rain forest and then through the mangrove estuary. Captains then pilot boats through tidal currents and surf the river mouth into the ocean. The river mouth has a reputation for being dangerous, and in a small dugout it is. The larger boats with strong engines used by experienced operators don't have any problems (though the ride is sure to provide everyone on board with a good adrenaline rush). Most hotels in Drake have beach landings, so wear reef-walkers.

BUS & TAXI

Buses to Palmar Norte (US$0.75) depart from in front of the Pulpería Fenix at 5:30am, 8:30am, 10:30am, 1:20pm, 3:30pm and 6pm. A taxi to Palmar costs about US$12.

BAHÍA DRAKE

Bahía Drake town is nestled between the thick jungle of the Parque Nacional Corcovado and Bahía Drake (the bay), on the western side of Península de Osa. The 'town' is actually composed of two tiny towns: **Drake** and **Agujitas**, which are joined by a thin and arduous dirt road that runs north-south along the coast between the airport and the soccer field. Simply called 'Drake' locally (pronounced 'DRA-cay' in Spanish), this area is rich in history. Sir Francis Drake himself supposedly visited the bay in March 1579 during his global circumnavigation in the *Golden Hind*, and there's a monument at Punta Agujitas to this effect. The town is not easy to do on the cheap, since it's reachable almost exclusively by boat, but the proximity to the incredible Corcovado will assure that your time, effort and money were well spent.

Agujitas, the southernmost village on the bay, has a *pulpería*, a public phone, a clinic, a school and a couple of cheapish cabins. Though most travelers tend to be sequestered in their resorts, the village is quite pleasant

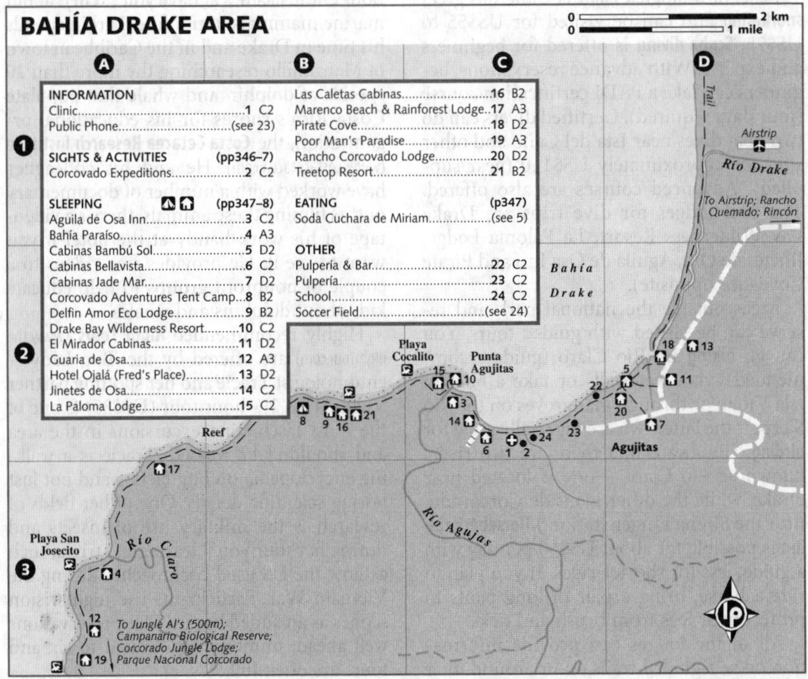

and it's worth picking up a drink at the *pulpería* while you watch the kids coming home from school.

Activities & Tours

The variety of activities offered in this area will keep visitors busy for days. Most companies offer the same tours and usually will set you up with another lodge if, for some reason, they can't provide you with your choice. Tours are priced competitively among the more expensive lodges, with cheaper tours offered by Corcovado Expeditions, the independent company in town (listed at the end of this section). All prices quoted for tours below are per person.

Probably the most popular tour is the trip to Parque Nacional Corcovado. It includes a boat ride (almost one hour) to the north end of the park and a hike. The hike can be short and easy or long and difficult – let the lodge know what you want. The tours (US$50 to US$75) may or may not include the US$8 park fee; all include lunch. It's possible to go to the Sirena ranger station (US$100) as well.

Reserva Biológica Isla del Caño has great **snorkeling** and can be visited for US$55 to US$75. **Scuba diving** is offered for beginners and experts. With advance reservations, beginners can take a PADI certification course (four days required). Certified divers can do two boat dives near Isla del Caño and other sites for approximately US$110 (gear supplied). Advanced courses are also offered. The best lodges for dive trips are Drake Bay Wilderness Resort, La Paloma Lodge, Jinetes de Osa, Aguila de Osa Inn and Pirate Cove (see opposite).

Areas outside the national park and reserve can be visited with guided tours. You can go **hiking** up Río Claro (guide recommended), visit waterfalls or take a boat to Isla Violín or through mangroves on the Río Sierpe – the latter two are especially good for **birding**. (Be aware that there are two rivers known as Río Claro – one is located near Drake, while the other is inside Corcovado, near the Sirena ranger station.) **Horseback riding** is possible for about US$60 per day with a guide, less for shorter rides. If you plan to ride a horse, bring a pair of long pants to protect your legs from brush and ticks.

All of the lodges can provide information on self-guided trails on or around their grounds, or you can choose to hike along the beach trail towards Corcovado by yourself (see p349).

Sportfishing is available, starting at US$35 an hour in small boats and costing US$800 a day in a fully equipped 9m boat. The best lodge for dedicated offshore anglers is Aguila de Osa, though all of them arrange fishing. Poor Man's Paradise and Hotel Ojalá are especially good places for fisherpeople on a budget.

Canoeing on the river and **sea kayaking** on more serious trips can be arranged at most lodges. Drake Bay Wilderness Resort is the best bet for sea-kayaking tours.

A variety of lodges offer **whale-watching** and **dolphin encounter tours** in the area. Tours are geared at people who want to admire and/or interact directly with these animals and who are comfortable with swimming in the ocean several kilometers offshore. Tours generally cost about US$100 per person, with a minimum of four people. The best place for this tour is Drake Bay Wilderness Resort (see p348), where you'll be guided by marine biologist Shawn Larkin, whose infectious enthusiasm will have you excited about marine mammals in no time. Larkin spends his time in Drake and in the Caribbean town of Manzanillo researching the more than 20 species of dolphin and whale that populate Costa Rica's shores for his educational organization, the **Costa Cetacea Research Institute** (www.costacetacea.com). He and his colleagues have worked with a number of documentary outfits filming these animals; there's a videotape of his work handy at the hotel if you want to see it. He provides free videos to a couple of nonprofit groups to help educate kids about dolphins and whales.

Highly recommended **Night Tours** (www.thenighttour.com) are offered by the 'Bug Lady' – entomologist Tracie and her spotting partner Victor. This 2½-hour tour (US$35) is one of the most fascinating excursions in the area and shouldn't be missed. Tracie is a walking encyclopedia on bug facts – and not just boring scientific details. One of her fields of research is the military use of insects and during her tour you'll learn great trivia, such as how the US used cockroaches during the Vietnam War. Participants use night-vision scopes as an added bonus. Make reservations well ahead; numbers are limited to six and tours are often full.

Corcovado Expeditions (☎ 818 9962, 396 7774; corcovadoexpeditions@hotmail.com), the independent tour company in town can provide any of the popular area tours, including multiday trips into Corcovado or other areas.

Away from the village, over the hill dominated by La Paloma Lodge (see p348), a path leads to Playa Cocalito, a small, pretty beach. Most of the shoreline in the nearby area is rocky, and this little beach is the best bet for ocean **swimming**, though not at high tide.

Sleeping & Eating

Lodging – much like everything else – doesn't come cheap in Bahía Drake. In addition, the town doesn't have electricity, so some of the cheaper places may not have power at night. (Pack a flashlight.) Reservations are recommended in the dry season (mid-November to the end of April), and high-season prices are given throughout. All of the rates given below include three meals a day unless otherwise stated.

Phones are an iffy proposition in this area and most lodges communicate by radio phone or short-wave radio. You may not be able to get through the first time, but keep trying. For other accommodations, check out the area from Bahía Drake to Corcovado, beginning on p349.

BUDGET & MID-RANGE

Hotel Ojalá (Fred's Place; ☎ 380 4763, 815 1080; drake@racsa.co.cr; per person US$50) This is at the northern end of town, about 5km from the airstrip. Fred's Place, as it's locally known, specializes in sportfishing. But all of the other usual tours can be arranged.

Cabinas Jade Mar (☎ 384 6681; per person US$45) This family-run place up a hill has comfy wood cabins with private bathroom, fan, and hammocks on the patio. There's electricity from 6pm to 9pm. Doña Marta, the owner, can arrange the transfer from Sierpe.

El Mirador Cabinas (☎ 836 94156, 356 4758; www.mirador.co.cr; per person US$35) This friendly place, up a steep path at the north end of Bahía Drake, has eight rustic wood rooms with private bathroom and superb views of the bay. There's no electricity, but candles are available. The Elizondo family also operates the new and very basic **Cabinas Bambú Sol** (per person incl breakfast US$15) on the main road in town. The **Soda Cuchara de Miriam** (next door) provides other meals.

Cabinas Bellavista (☎ 829 1482; incl 2 meals US$30) This ramshackle, bare green building was being remodeled at the time of research, though it should be open by mid-2004. There will be a killer bar up on the hill with views – which should be perfect for sunset beers.

Rancho Corcovado Lodge (☎ 786 7903; camping/unit per person US$10/40) The González family runs this newly remodeled place, offering seven rooms with private bathroom. Each unit sleeps two to four; campers can set up a tent in the yard and are permitted to use the bathrooms. There is electricity at night.

Jinetes de Osa (☎ 371 1598, in San José 236 5637, in the USA 800-317 0333; www.costaricadiving.com; r/unit per person US$65/70) The hotel has nine well-appointed rooms, some of which boast views of the bay. Four pricier, superior units are larger and have fan, decoratively tiled hot shower and a shared balcony. Three smaller quarters (some with shared bathroom) are equally appealing. The hotel is nicely situated on the water, and has easy access into town by foot and there is a sociable bar. Credit cards accepted. Jinetes is a PADI dive facility and offers certification courses as well as two-tank dives at Isla del Caño (US$85). Beginners can opt for a 'resort course' for US$140, which includes two dives. All equipment is provided.

Pirate Cove (☎ 234 6154, 393 9449, 934 1226; www.piratecovecostarica.com; 4-day package standard/luxury US$350/400) Well-appointed screened tent cabins and bigger 'luxury suites' dot the grounds of this relative newcomer. Cheaper rooms share bathrooms and all cabins have a balcony with views and a safe. There is no electricity in the rooms at night. This hotel is another PADI dive facility offering scuba trips around the area. The hotel's website has a handy list of local dives sites. All of the usual tours are offered, and rates are based on double occupancy.

TOP END

Many of the top-end lodges offer multiday packages in addition to nightly stay options, though the last day usually involves leaving early in the morning. All of the following hotels have river docks and include three meals a day in their prices unless otherwise stated.

Aguila de Osa Inn (☎ 296 2190; www.aguiladeosa.com; 4-day package per adult/child under 12 US$543/275) On the east side of the Río Agujas, this upscale lodge specializes in sportfishing and scuba diving. The roomy quarters have shining wood floors and high ceilings and are situated on a hillside above the lodge's main restaurant. The 11 standard rooms and two suites all have attractive view, 24-hour electricity, fan, tiled bathroom with hot water and beautifully carved doors. The restaurant is one of the main attractions. The comfortable, yet elegant, open-air *rancho* dining room overlooks the bay and has one of the more lively bars (and best *bocas*) in all of Drake. (Rooms are far enough away from the bar that its late hours don't preclude sleep.)

The lodge has 10m and 11m boats for fishing trips. Deep-sea fishing is US$800 per day per boat (four people); inshore trips are cheaper. The kitchen will prepare your catch – grilled or as sashimi. Scuba diving and local tours are available. You'll see some incredible wildlife here, including the owner's dog 'smiling' for guests. Packages include transfer from Palmar; credit cards accepted.

Drake Bay Wilderness Resort (☎ 770 8012, in the USA 561-371 3437; www.drakebay.com; tent/cabin per person US$65/95, standard 4-day package per person US$780;) This resort is run by a congenial American-Tica couple, Herb and Marleny, and it has the best piece of real estate in all of Drake, situated on a point. You can explore the tide pools, swim in the ocean or paddle up the Río Agujas. All local tours are offered and this is where Shawn Larkin of Costa Cetacea (see p346) and Gulf Islands Kayaking (see p475) have their base. The standard package includes two guided tours (to Corcovado, Isla del Caño or the mangroves) and there are also specialized kayaking, fishing and diving packages. The lodge is especially popular with families. Most of the accommodations are in 19 comfortable cabins, all of which have one or two double beds, fan, private solar-heated tiled shower, and patio with ocean view. During the high season (December to April) there are several cheaper, furnished tent cabins with electricity and shared bathroom. Meals are served in a communal dining hall and the food comes from the family's organic farm (tour available). Save room for Marleny's scrumptious cinnamon rolls and chocolate-chip cookies. An airy bar is perfect for watching sunsets and there's an ocean-fed pool. A generator provides 24-hour electricity and there is free same-day laundry service (a blessing). Credit cards accepted.

La Paloma Lodge (☎ 239 2801; www.lapalomalodge.com; 4-day package per person standard/deluxe/sunset deluxe US$825/935/995;) This highly recommended lodge is perched on a lush hillside, providing guests with incredible views of the ocean and forest. For scuba enthusiasts the lodge has a compressor and dive shop. It also has an 11m pontoon boat that makes fast time to Isla del Caño and is currently the most comfortable dive boat in Drake. There is a pool with ocean views and tours with English-speaking guides are available. Kayaks are available at no extra charge. The rooms are all superlative. Four spacious standard rooms, each with a queen and single bed, have plenty of closet space and nice ocean breezes. Beds are draped with huge mosquito nets and spotless, tiled private bathroom have shoulder-high walls that provide rain-forest views. Each room has a large balcony with a hammock. In addition, there are five secluded, spacious, tiled-roof deluxe *ranchos* sporting wide, wraparound balcony with incredible views. These can sleep two to five people on two levels and are great for families. Excellent meals are served in the beautiful dining room, which has a high thatched roof and a spacious balcony for sipping cocktails and watching breathtaking sunsets. Electricity is available 24 hours and a massage therapist can be scheduled with a few hours' notice. All rates include air transfer from San José. Credit cards accepted.

Drake Bay Rainforest Chalet (☎ 382 1619; www.drakebayholiday.com; 4-/7-day package per person US$760/1150, additional night per person US$100) This luxurious house in the jungle features a decadent two-person spa, satellite TV and spacious modern accommodations with a fully stocked, mosaic-tiled, self-catering kitchen. A king-sized bed with giant mosquito net makes for romantic nights, and two queen-sized beds can be added on request. Packages include round-trip air, taxi and boat transfers from San José and Sierpe and full-day guided tours of Corcovado and Isla del Caño, as well as the famous Night Tour (see p346). Chef service is available at an extra charge. A two-adult minimum is required; children pay 50%.

Getting There & Away

AIR

From San José NatureAir (one way/round trip US$85/170) has three flights daily and Sansa (US$73/146) has two flights daily. The airstrip is 2km north of most lodges. From the airstrip, you'll be transported to Bahía Drake either by boat (prepare for wet feet), by jeep or by a combination of both. Hotels can arrange pick-ups at the airstrip.

BOAT

All of the hotels offer boat transfers between Sierpe and Bahía Drake. **Gringo** (☎ 812 4558), **Serrapa** (☎ 384 6681) and **Rafael** (☎ 824 3710) all provide the service for US$15 per person (two-person minimum).

BUS & CAR

A bad dirt road links Agujitas with Rancho Quemado (a tiny community to the east). This road continues on to Rincón, from where you can head south to Puerto Jiménez or north to the Interamericana. A 4WD is required and, even so, the road becomes impassable in the rainy season (June to November). There are several deep river crossings, the one at Río Drake being the most significant. (Locals fish many a water-logged tourist vehicle out of the river, see p471).

If you want to journey overland to the other side of the peninsula, **Cabinas Golfo Dulce** (☎ 775 0244) in Rincón (see p355) has a sturdy, high-clearance 4WD vehicle that can be booked.

HIKING

From Bahía Drake, it's a four- to six-hour hike along the beachside trail to San Pedrillo ranger station at the north end of Corcovado. Trekkers can hike through Parque Nacional Corcovado to or from Bahía Drake, but you must have lodging reservations at the ranger stations inside the park (see p352).

If you have a reservation at a Drake lodge, staff can arrange pick-up and drop-off in San Pedrillo for the hike through the park. If you backpack into Drake, any of the lodges will help you find a boat to Sierpe.

BAHÍA DRAKE TO CORCOVADO

Lining the stretch of craggy shore from Drake to Corcovado is a series of inlets hugged by luxuriant rain forest. As with Drake, this area is for travelers who want a restful vacation experience. There are no towns, bars or nightclubs.

It's not difficult to hike from Bahía Drake to Corcovado along the coast. It takes four to six hours to reach the San Pedrillo ranger station, and trails continue through the park from there. Low tide is the best time to go since the trail goes through beach areas; tides may cut you off or delay you, so ask before departing.

The route is easy to follow for much of the way, though it tends to get more overgrown as you get closer to the park. Walk along the beach or, where a headland cuts you off, look inland for a trail over or around the headland, paralleling the coast. This route is hiked often, so if the trail appears overgrown you're probably on the wrong one. Walk back a bit and try again.

Sleeping & Eating

Places to stay and eat along this section of coast can all be reached by boat from Sierpe or Bahía Drake, or on foot from Drake. None of these hotels have docks, so all landings are on the beach.

Hotels are described in the order they're passed when hiking west and then south from Bahía Drake towards Corcovado. Not all lodges have electricity. Reservations are recommended for the high season (December through April). All rates include three meals daily unless otherwise stated.

Treetop Resort (☎ in the USA 310-450 1769, 310-748 6844; www.drakebayresort.com; per person US$65) Three rustic wooden rooms in the main house and one small separate cabin all have their own cold shower. The pleasant beachside cabins were built using fallen trees, so there was no extensive chopping to build this lodge.

Las Caletas Cabinas (☎ 381 4052, 826 1460; www.caletas.co.cr; d/tr/q US$120/165/200) Owned and operated by a friendly Swiss-Tico family, this intimate little hotel has received several recommendations from guests. Jolanda and David are warm hosts and their well-appointed wooden duplex cabins are cozy. All quarters come with private tiled bathroom, balcony with view and hammocks for relaxing. Solar panels provide 24-hour electricity. Tours can be arranged, and German, English and some Italian are spoken.

Delfín Amor Eco Lodge (☎ 394 2632; www.divinedolphin.com; d per person US$85, 4-day package from US$770) A 30-minute walk west from Bahía Drake, this small lodge has five well-appointed, screened-in cabins with private bathroom. The hotel specializes in dolphin encounter tours through its company, the Divine Dolphin, but other tours are available. Packages include transfer from the Bahía Drake airport, a dolphin tour and one tour to Isla del Caño or Corcovado. One reader has complained that this resort is not 'eco' enough and the two frayed macaws scratching around the dining room don't do much to dispel the notion.

Corcovado Adventures Tent Camp (☎ 384 1679; www.corcovado.com; per person US$55) Less than an hour's walk from Drake brings you to this pretty, family-run spot. There are 17 large, walk-in platform tents with a double and single bed and nightstand. (Some have three beds.) There are seven bathrooms and a dining room/bar with 24-hour solar power. The rate includes use of body boards and snorkeling gear. Waves suitable for body boards are a few minutes' walk away, while good snorkeling at Playa San Josecito is about a 1½-hour walk away. All the usual activities and tour options are available (at extra cost).

Marenco Beach & Rainforest Lodge (☎ 258 1919, in the USA 800-278 6223, 305-908 4169; www.marencolodge.com; d bungalow US$75, additional person US$10) Marenco lies about 5km west of Bahía Drake and 5km north of Corcovado. Once a biological station, it's now a private 500-hectare tropical forest reserve set up to protect part of the rain forest. The reserve is set on a bluff overlooking the Pacific. There are 4km of trails and many of the plant, bird and other animal species seen in Corcovado can be found here. There are eight small cabins and 17 more spacious bungalows. Accommodations are rustic, but rooms are well appointed and come with private bathroom. Meals (not included in the rate) are served family style. Overall, the lodge is very nice, but service could be better. Credit cards accepted.

Bahía Paraíso (☎ 538 1414; www.bahiaparaiso.com; per person in tent camp US$57, in cabins US$65-85, camping without meals US$15) A pleasant inlet on San Josecito beach with prime snorkeling is home to this 17-hectare hotel. Clean, simple cabins all have screens, private bathroom with cold-water shower, and ample patio with hammocks. An adjacent platform tent camp has 12 fully furnished walk-in tents and clean shared bathroom. A beachside kitchen serves traditional fare; campers pay US$5 for breakfast and US$8 for lunch and dinner. There is electricity from dusk until 10:30pm. Tours are offered and horseback riding is available, but the horses look tired. Credit cards accepted.

Guaria de Osa (☎ in the USA 510-235 4313; www.experientials.org; 8-day package per person US$1000) This exquisite Asian-style lodge on San Josecito beach serves primarily as a group retreat center and offers wellness programs such as yoga, spiritual study, shamanism and more. Rates include transfers from Sierpe as well as tours of Corcovado and Isla del Caño and guided walks. Other tours can also be booked. Guaria de Osa accepts payments via PayPal, check and money order. All reservations must be made at least 60 days in advance.

Poor Man's Paradise (☎ 786 7642; www.mypoormansparadise.com; camping/tent camp per person US$7/40, cabin per person without/with bathroom US$50/63) About 3km south of Marenco in Playa Rincón is this lodge owned by Pincho Amaya, a well-known local sportfisherman. It is on the beach, about a 20-minute walk from Playa San Josecito, where there is good snorkeling, and two hours from Parque Nacional Corcovado. Eight furnished tent cabins are built on sturdy wood platforms and two other cabins share a bathroom; the rest have private facilities. There's a camp site and meals for campers are US$7 (breakfast or lunch) and US$10 (dinner). There's electricity from dusk till 9pm and local tours can be arranged; Pincho can also take guests sportfishing. Credit cards accepted.

Jungle Al's (www.jungleals.com; camping per person incl 3 meals US$20, 5-day package US$610) Just down the beach from Poor Man's is this new lodge aimed at anglers as well as campers. There are five comfortable wood cabins, and tents and camping equipment are available for rent. Tours to the park and fishing excursions can be arranged. A beachside restaurant and bar is coming soon. All rates include air-taxi-boat transfers from San José and Sierpe as well as free rain-forest tours, use of snorkeling equipment and boogie boards, horseback rides on the beach and an open beer bar.

Campanario Biological Reserve (☎ 258 5778; www.campanario.org; 4-day package per person US$359) This reserve has a biology field station, a library, dorms with tiled shower, a kitchen/dining area, and five large platform tents, each sleeping two and with a separate private outdoor bathroom. The main accommodations complex is behind a lawn on the beach and has good views. The reserve is 150 hectares and climbs up to 155m above sea level behind the lodge. The basic package includes transportation from Sierpe, meals, a visit to Parque Nacional Corcovado and a guided introductory hike into the reserve. All other activities can be arranged at extra cost; multiday excursions are available. See the website for details of longer visits, courses and volunteer or research opportunities.

Casa Corcovado Jungle Lodge (☎ 256 3181, 256 8825, in the USA 888-896 6097; radio channel 14; www.casacorcovado.com; 4-day package US$855;) A spine-tingling boat ride will take you to this comfortable place on 175 hectares of rain forest right on the national-park boundary. The main facilities are a steep climb up from the beach (a tractor hauls luggage and visitors), and trails from the property enter Corcovado (a 40-minute walk away). The 14 roomy bungalows are screened all the way around for cross breezes and good views and each has a ceiling fan, a safe, tiled bathroom with hot shower and private patio with hammocks. The restaurant-bar has forest views, and a pool a short walk below. There's a bigger pool by the reception office. Halfway between the lodge and the beach is the Margarita Sunset Bar, serving up 25 different types of 'rita and great sunset views over the Pacific. Packages include transfer by air-bus-boat from San José and tours of Corcovado and Isla del Caño. Children under 10 pay 25% less. The lodge has 24-hour electricity and credit cards are accepted.

RESERVA BIOLÓGICA ISLA DEL CAÑO

This 326-hectare island is 17km west of Bahía Drake and is the tip of numerous underwater rock formations. About 2700 marine hectares of ocean are part of the reserve, and the body-temperature waters are an enormously popular marine habitat – as much with fish and marine mammals as with snorkelers, divers and biologists.

So far, 15 different species of coral have been recorded, as well as threatened animal species that include a native lobster and a giant conch. The sheer numbers of fish attract dolphins and whales, frequently spotted swimming in outer waters. The water is much clearer here than along the mainland coast (though not crystalline) and scuba divers can enjoy one of four dive sites. There's a small beach (inundated at high tide) with an attractive rain-forest backdrop. A trail leads inland, through evergreen rain forest to a ridge at about 110m above sea level.

Near the top of the ridge there are several pre-Columbian **granite spheres**. Vegetation on the island includes milk trees (also called 'cow trees' after the drinkable white latex they exude), rubber trees, figs and a variety of other tropical species. Birds include coastal and oceanic species, as well as rain-forest inhabitants, but wildlife is not as varied or prolific as on the mainland.

Camping is prohibited, and there are no facilities except a ranger station by the landing beach. Admission is US$6 per person for land visits and US$3.50 per person per day for scuba diving. Most visitors arrive on tours arranged by the nearby lodges.

PARQUE NACIONAL CORCOVADO

This breathtaking national park is the last great original tract of moist tropical forest in Pacific Central America. The humid rain forest is home to Costa Rica's largest population of scarlet macaws as well as more than 500 species of tree and countless animal species, including jaguars, coatis, toucans and snakes. Its great biological diversity has long attracted the attention of tropical ecologists, as well as a devoted stream of visitors who pour in from Drake and Puerto Jimenez to enjoy the scenery.

The 42,469-hectare park is nestled in the southwestern corner of the peninsula and protects at least eight distinct habitats. Because of its remoteness, it remained undisturbed until the 1960s, when logging began. This was halted in 1975 when the area was established (with much controversy) as government-administered parklands. The early years were a challenge as park authorities, with limited personnel and resources, sought to deal with illegal clear-cutting, poaching and gold-mining, the latter of which was causing severe erosion in the park's rivers and streams. Many of the miners were evicted in 1986, but some still continue to work clandestinely – and many can be seen working the neighboring Reserva Forestal Golfo Dulce, where mining is not illegal.

Unfortunately, poaching remains a severe problem and some experts have warned that because of this the jaguar population could be extinct by 2005. The government has responded with all-night police patrols, but it remains to be seen whether this action is another case of too little, too late.

Information

There are three ranger stations on the park boundaries, and a fourth, the headquarters at Sirena, is on the coast in the middle of the park. There's also an airstrip at Sirena. Trails link Sirena with all other ranger stations – San Pedrillo, La Leona and Los Patos – and all permit camping, provided you have a reservation.

Park fees are US$8 per day. Camping costs US$4 per person per day at any station; facilities include freshwater and latrines. (There are no shelters or hostels for tourists.) Remember to bring a flashlight or a kerosene lamp, because the camp sites are pitch black at night. Meals can be arranged in advance (US$8 breakfast, US$11 lunch or dinner). Food and cooking fuel have to be packed in, so reserve at least 15 to 30 days in advance through the **Área de Conservación Osa office** (☎ 735 5036) in Puerto Jiménez. Camping is not permitted in areas other than the ranger stations. Sirena has a biological station that houses scientists carrying out research and they get preference over travelers for accommodations and meals. Some areas may be off-limits, or trees and sites might be marked with tags. Do not disturb these sites if you come across them. One traveler reports that the station now rents canoes for up to four people for US$5 an hour for river exploration.

Because Corcovado is the only rain-forest park with such extensive, cross-park trails, it attracts a fair number of backpackers. If you plan on doing the cross-park hike, make all arrangements with plenty of advance notice. During the wettest months (June to November), parts of the trail system (the route between San Pedrillo and La Sirena) close to the public; during this time, check with the Jiménez office to see if there are other closures.

Wildlife Watching

The wildlife within the park is varied and prolific. In addition to being home to the scarlet macaw (*lapa* in Spanish), the park protects many other important or endangered rainforest species: tapirs, five local feline species, crocodiles, peccaries, giant anteaters, monkeys and sloths. The rare harpy eagle, almost extinct in Costa Rica, may still breed in remote parts of Corcovado, and almost 400 bird species and about 140 mammal species have been spotted here. However, it's only fair to say that these animals are difficult to spot – because of timidity or camouflage or because they're nocturnal.

Hiking

One of the most exciting aspects of Corcovado for visitors is the park's long-distance trails. Paths are primitive and the hiking is hot, humid and insect-ridden, but it can be done. The best bet is to hire a local guide, who will know the trails well and can avoid the unmitigated disaster of getting lost. (Using the sun or stars to navigate in the rain forest is impossible since you can barely see through the canopy.) Otherwise, travel in a small group. Traveling alone is not recommended. One reader who did

VISITING THE WILDERNESS

The rain forest is beautiful, the animals are enchanting and the vegetation is gorgeous. But the fact is that this is 100% wilderness and the dangers should not be underestimated. Every season, numerous travelers to Parque Nacional Corcovado become injured or ill – and some even die.

Most hikers suffer from heat exhaustion and dehydration because they don't carry enough water and set out on hikes for which they are not prepared. This is a regular phenomenon: visitors who barely exercise in their daily lives arrive in the jungle and attempt to undertake 23km hikes in the blistering tropical sun. This is foolish. Build up to it by starting with small day hikes (6km to 8km) and take it from there.

In addition, the river crossing at Sirena is quite dangerous. Hikers have tried to cross the river at high tide and been swept away by the current. Others have been attacked by crocodiles and bull sharks. Yet others have been bitten by poisonous snakes.

If you are planning to hike across Parque Nacional Corcovado, it is highly recommended that you hire a knowledgeable guide (especially if you have limited wilderness experience). Guides are familiar with the park and can help you spot animals, such as bull sharks in river bottoms. It may cost more, but you'll save lots of trouble in the long run – and maybe even your life.

LUKE HUNTER

Páramo (montane) vegetation, Parque Nacional Chirripó (p326)

Hikers crossing a creek, Parque Nacional Chirripó (p326)

LUKE HUNTER

TOM BOYDEN

Blue-gray tanager *(Thraupis epicopus)*, San Gerardo de Dota (p317)

RALPH LEE HOPKIN

Tropical rain forest, Parque Nacional Corcovado (p351)

Sunset through the palms, Parque Nacional Corcovado (p351)

MARK NEWMAN

View through the rain forest, Refugio Nacional de Fauna Silvestre Golfito (p368)

DAVID M WATSO

so claims he was chased by peccaries and robbed by a gang of youths; he ended his trip uncomfortably with hundreds of itchy bug bites after losing his insect repellent. Not the way to go.

Travel is best in the dry season (from December to April), when there is still regular rain but all of the trails are open; at this time of year you can avoid slogging around in calf-deep mud. The largest herds of peccaries are on the Sirena to Los Patos trails, and if you climb about 2m off the ground you'll avoid being bitten in the unlikely event of running into a surly bunch.

You can hike in from the north, south or east side of the park (see the map, p343) and exit a different way. Note that times listed are fairly conservative. Fit hikers with light packs can probably move faster, though if you spend a lot of time birding or taking photos, it'll be longer.

SAN PEDRILLO TO SIRENA

It's at least a 10- to 15-hour hike between San Pedrillo and Sirena, and the route is for people who are in *very* good physical condition. The first few hours take you through coastal rain forest, before the trail drops to the beach. This is where things get difficult. The total route between San Pedrillo and Sirena is 23km, but 18 of these are beach hiking – during the heat of the day and with a heavy pack, walking through loose sand is grueling. A number of people have suffered heat exhaustion on this particular stretch of coast. Pack a hat and plenty of water and don't overdo it.

En route you'll pass a beautiful waterfall plunging onto the wild beach of Playa Llorona. A few hundred meters south of the waterfall, a small trail leads inland to a cascading river and a refreshing swimming hole. At this point, you'll have to ford the Río Llorona. At Playa Corcovado, two or three hours later, the Río Corcovado must also be crossed. And about a kilometer before reaching Sirena, you must ford the Río Sirena, which can be chest-deep at low tide – it's the largest river on the hike and it's the neighborhood hang for sharks and crocodiles. Do not try to cross further up, the river only gets deeper. Ask the rangers at San Pedrillo about tide tables and conditions before departing; you should time your arrival at the Río Serena to coincide with low tide.

Local guides recommend doing this hike from Sirena to San Pedrillo, rather than the other way around. In this direction, it is easier to time it to the tide tables, leaving less chance that you will become stranded. To do this, depart Sirena about two hours before low tide.

This trail is only open from December through April, since heavy rains can make the Río Sirena impassable.

LA LEONA TO SIRENA

This is another hot beach hike. From La Leona, it's a six- to seven-hour hike to Sirena, but, as always, check the tide schedule as there are several rocky headlands to cross, and tides can cut you off. If you look carefully, you can usually find trails going inland around the headlands. Often, these inland trails offer the best chances opportunities to see mammals, though jaguars have been seen loping along the beach – keep your eyes open for paw prints.

The entire distance from Carate to Sirena is about 16km, but much of it is on loose sand, making this stretch a sizzler. Pack plenty of water and look for shady sections in the forest behind the beach. Also, keep an eye out for crocodiles at the Río Claro crossing – travelers report that our amphibian friends like to congregate by the river banks.

LOS PATOS TO SIRENA

Unlike the other two main beach trails, the route from Los Patos goes through 18km of rain forest and affords the hiker an opportunity to pass through plenty of dense primary forest. The trail undulates steeply through the hilly forest for two or three hours but flattens out once it reaches Laguna Corcovado. You'll then have to wade the Río Sirena and, further on, the Río Pavo before reaching Sirena. This latter part of the hike is through secondary forest. Total walking time is roughly eight hours.

Check with rangers about changes in trail and river conditions. If you don't plan on traversing the park, doing a 6km day hike from Los Patos to the Laguna Corcovado is a good option. (This requires spending two nights at Los Patos.) If you hike out of the park through Los Patos, the rangers can help you call a jeep-taxi to take you out at least part of the way.

PARQUE NACIONAL ISLA DEL COCO

In the opening minutes of the film *Jurassic Park*, a small helicopter swoops over and around a lushly forested island with dramatic tropical peaks descending straight into clear blue waters. That island is Isla del Coco and that scene turned Costa Rica's most remote national park into more than a figment of our collective imaginations.

Isla del Coco is more than 500km southwest of the mainland in the eastern Pacific and is often referred to as the Costa Rican Galapagos. Spanish explorer Joan Cabezas 'discovered' the island in 1526 and it was noted on a map drawn by French cartographer Nicolas Desliens in 1541. It's extremely wet, with about 7000mm of annual rainfall, and thus attracted the attention of early sailors, pirates and whalers, who frequently stopped for freshwater and coconuts. Legend has it that a band of pirates buried a huge treasure here, but despite more than 5000 treasure-hunting expeditions, it's never been found.

The island is rugged and heavily forested, with the highest point at Cerro Iglesias (634m). Because of its remote nature a unique ecosystem has evolved, earning the island the protective status of national park. More than 70 animal species (mainly insects) and 70 plant species are endemic, and more remain to be discovered. Birders come to see the colonies of seabirds, some of which are endemic and many of which nest on Cocos. There are also two endemic lizard species. The marine life is also varied, with sea turtles, more than 18 species of coral, 57 types of crustacea, three types of dolphin and tropical fish in abundance. Needless to say, the diving is excellent and the main activity in the area.

Settlers who lived on the island in the late 19th and early 20th centuries left behind domestic animals that have since converted into feral populations of pigs, goats, cats and rats. Today it's the pigs that are the greatest threat to the unique species native to the island since they uproot vegetation, cause soil erosion and contribute to sedimentation around the island's coasts, which damages coral reefs. Unregulated fishing and hunting pose further, more ominous, threats. The Servicio de Parques Nacionales (Sinac) is aware of the problem, but a lack of funding has made regulation of these illegal activities difficult, if not impossible.

Information & Tours

There's a park station, and permission is needed from the park service to visit it. (The dive operator that you use will arrange for the necessary permission.) There are some trails, but camping or spending the night on the island is not allowed. Visitors are required to stay on their boats and there's a US$35 daily per-person park fee. Note that these trips are for advanced, certified divers; beginners' lessons and basic certification are not offered.

In Costa Rica, **Undersea Hunter** (☎ 228 6613, in the USA 800-203 2120; www.underseahunter.com) specializes in 10-day dive trips. The typical cost of a 10-day tour from San José (including seven days of diving with three or four dives a day) is US$3245 per person, plus US$35 per day in park fees. Longer trips are available.

The US-owned **Okeanos Aggressor** (☎ in the USA 985-385 2628, in the USA & Canada 800-348 2628; www.aggressor.com) also offers eight- and 10-day dive cruises on their 36m namesake ship. Prices start at US$2795 per person for an eight-day trip.

Getting There & Away

From Bahía Drake you can arrange with any lodge for a boat ride to San Pedrillo or Playa Llorona in the northern part of the park. Otherwise, you can walk the jungle trail that leads from Drake to San Pedrillo. (Allow at least four hours for this hike.) Alternatively, you can also arrange a boat ride directly from Drake to Sirena.

There are two ways to access the park from Puerto Jiménez. From the north you can enter the park through Los Patos. One of several buses a day departs Jiménez for La Palma. From here you can catch a 4WD taxi or walk the 10km to the ranger station. The road is passable to 4WD vehicles and it crosses the river about 20 times in the last 6km before Los Patos. It's easy to miss the right turn shortly before the ranger station, but locals can advise you.

Heading south and then west from Puerto Jiménez, a road heads about 45km around the peninsula to Carate, where you can access the park through La Leona. A 4WD jeep-taxi leaves Puerto Jiménez daily (see p359) or you can hire a private vehicle.

You can also arrange to fly into the Sirena airstrip by chartered aircraft from San José, Golfito or Puerto Jiménez. (Charter flights start at US$220 for four passengers.)

TO CORCOVADO VIA PUERTO JIMÉNEZ

THE INTERAMERICANA TO PUERTO JIMÉNEZ

A 78km road links the Interamericana (at Chacarita) with Puerto Jiménez. The road is paved for 45km to the miniscule town of **Rincón**, which consists of a *pulpería*, a few homes and a hotel. Here, you'll find the waterside **Cabinas Golfo Dulce** (☎ 775 0244; d or tr US$18.75, d or tr with bathroom US$21.25; Ⓟ). Situated behind the *pulpería,* these wood cabins are basic but well maintained, and the owners and their pet cockatiels are friendly. Meals are available. There are kayaks for expeditions around the Golfo Dulce, which is a good place to spot dolphins and whales in the dry season.

From Rincón, a poor and potholed dirt road heads west towards the Pacific, passing Rancho Quemado (unmarked on most maps) and continuing to Bahía Drake. Beyond Rancho Quemado, the road is passable only to high-clearance 4WD vehicles – and only in the dry season. If you want to make it overland to Drake, the folks at Cabinas Golfo Dulce have a sturdy, high-clearance 4WD vehicle that can be booked for the trip. (It's usually US$60 per group, but rates vary depending on road conditions.) Buses between Puerto Jiménez and San José can drop you off in Rincón.

Beyond Rincón, 33km of gravel road continues to Puerto Jiménez. About 9km to the southeast is the village of **La Palma**, from where a rough road goes to the Los Patos ranger station. The women of La Palma run a tourist office of sorts, with homemade souvenirs and coffee available. There are restaurants, *pulperías* and cheap hotels, all clustered around a right-angle turn in the main road. Note that a couple of travelers have reported getting mugged on the road from La Palma to Los Patos, so keep your eyes peeled. It's best to travel in a group.

About 12km beyond La Palma is the town of **Cañazas**. Four kilometers further, on the left-hand side, you'll find **Jardín de Aves Lodge** (www.safariosa.com; per person camping US$5, cabin per person US$25-45, house per week US$250). Tucked into the jungle are two cabins accommodating up to six people. Both have private cold shower, though a shared hot shower is available. A fully equipped house has a kitchen and hot-water heater. This place is suited to birding and getting away from it all. Rates vary according to the number of people in your party and the cabin you choose to stay in. All fees include breakfast and use of the kitchen; meals are available at an extra charge. There is no phone, so make reservations online.

About 21km beyond La Palma and 4km before Puerto Jiménez, a right turn leads 8km to **Dos Brazos**, a gold-mining and farming village. A couple of kilometers beyond Dos Brazos, you'll find the private sanctuary and lodge **Bosque del Río Tigre** (☎ 383 3905, in Puerto Jiménez 735 5725, in the USA 888-875 9453; www.osaadventures.com; per adult/child under 12 US$88/50). Run by naturalists Elizabeth Jones and Abraham Gallo, the lodge has four well-appointed rooms with forest views and clean shared bathroom; one cabin has a private bathroom. All showers have hot water. You can arrange horseback rides, kayaking excursions and hikes to the national park and the gold-mining town of Piedras Blancas; the birding is excellent. Rates are based on double occupancy and include three meals. If you're driving, you'll need a 4WD to cross a river right before the lodge. Buses for Dos Brazos leave Puerto Jiménez from the Super 96 at 5:15am, 11am and 4pm and drop you off 400m from the lodge. Buses return to Puerto Jiménez from Dos Brazos at 6am, noon and 5pm. Schedules vary on weekends, so ask around.

Just before entering Puerto Jiménez, a turn-off in the road leads 16km to the hamlet of **Río Nuevo**. About 2km beyond the town is the **Río Nuevo Lodge** (☎ 735 5407; www.rionuevolodge.com; US$50), a popular new tent camp offering hiking and wildlife watching in primary and secondary forests; horseback riding is also available. A good trail network through the uncrowded countryside that borders Parque Nacional Corcovado leads to spectacular mountain viewpoints, some with views of the gulf. Birding is very good, and visitors can expect to see the many species they would find in Corcovado: everything from scarlet macaws to toucans in abundance. The lodge is situated at the juncture of the Río Nuevo and the Quebrada La Lucha, which provide restorative dips at the end of a long day.

Guests sleep in large, walk-in tents on protected platforms, with access to shared cold-water showers and toilets. Tasty meals are served family style in a thatched *rancho* with hammocks. The communal areas have solar-powered electricity, but tents do not. The lodge is owned by the Aguirre family, who are from the area and employ local guides – some of whom are former gold miners. Rates include three meals daily and transfer from Puerto Jiménez; tours are billed separately. Credit cards accepted. The lodge has an office next to Restaurant Carolina in Jiménez. Do not try to drive here yourself, as the road is punishing – even in the best of 4WD vehicles. It is impassable in the rainy season, requiring part of the journey to be done on horseback.

PUERTO JIMÉNEZ

With about 7000 inhabitants, Puerto Jiménez is the only town of any size on the peninsula. Until the 1960s, this was one of the most remote parts of the country. With the advent of logging in the '60s and the subsequent discovery of gold in the local streams, Jiménez became a small boomtown. The logging industry still operates in parts of the peninsula, but the gold rush has quieted down in favor of the tourist rush. Even so, Port Jim (as the gringos call it) retains a frontier feel. Now, instead of gold miners descending on the town's bars on weekends, it's the area's naturalist guides, who come to have a shot of *guaro* and brag about the snakes, sharks and alligators they've allegedly tousled with.

This steamy town also has some pleasant and still isolated beaches nearby, but its main attraction is its closeness to Parque Nacional Corcovado, which has an administration and information office here.

Information

Doña Isabel at **Osa Tropical** (☎ 735 5062, 735 5722; www.osaviva.com) is the NatureAir agent and the best and most reputable source of local travel information. She handles hotel and transportation arrangements of all kinds and has a radio that reaches all the lodges on the peninsula and in the Golfo Dulce areas.

There's Internet access and tour information at **Osa Natural** (☎ 735 5440; www.osanatural.com; 8am-9pm) and **Cafenet El Sol** (☎ 735 5717, 735 5718; 7am-10pm) for about US$2 an hour.

The **Oficina de Area de Conservación Osa** (☎ 735 5036, 735 5580; 8am-4pm with a lunch break) has information about Corcovado, Isla del Caño, Parque Nacional Marino Ballena (see p312) and Golfito parks and reserves. You can make reservations here to camp in Corcovado – do so at least 15 days in advance.

Emergency medical treatment can be obtained at the Clínica CCSS, or call the **Red Cross** (☎ 735 5109).

Banco Nacional de Costa Rica (8:30am-3:45pm Mon-Fri) exchanges cash dollars. **Colectivo Transportation** (☎ 735 5539; tonsa@hotmail.com; 200m south of the bus station) will exchange US dollars and euros when the bank is closed.

Tours

Escondido Trex (☎ 735 5210; www.escondidotrex.com) has an office inside the Restaurant Carolina. It does half-day to 10-day tours, primarily kayaking for all levels of experience, but also guided hikes, mangrove paddles and dolphin-watching.

Naturalist Andy Pruter runs **Everyday Adventures** (☎ 353 8619; www.everydaycostarica.com) in Cabo Matapalo and specializes in sea kayaking and rain-forest treks, including hikes up a hollow strangler fig tree and increasingly popular waterfall-rappelling tours. Most of the tours cost between US$45 and US$75. Call ahead or make reservations online.

Another popular local guide is 'Crocodile Mike' Boston of **Osa Aventura** (☎ 735 5670; www.osaaventura.com), a charming Irish adventurer who loves things that go bump in the night: namely snakes, crocodiles, bull sharks and anything potentially lethal. Mike specializes in a countless number of multiday adventure tours up and down the Osa. Mike doesn't have an office, so ring ahead.

Taboga Aquatic Tours (☎ 735 5265) is run by local fisherman Marco Loaiciga, who has been recommended for fishing and snorkeling trips. **Cacique Tours** (☎ 735 5440; www.osanatural.com) is run by the affable Oscar Cortés, who speaks English and specializes in Corcovado, birding and crocodile tours. **Aventuras Tropicales** (☎ 735 5195, www.aventurastropicales.com)

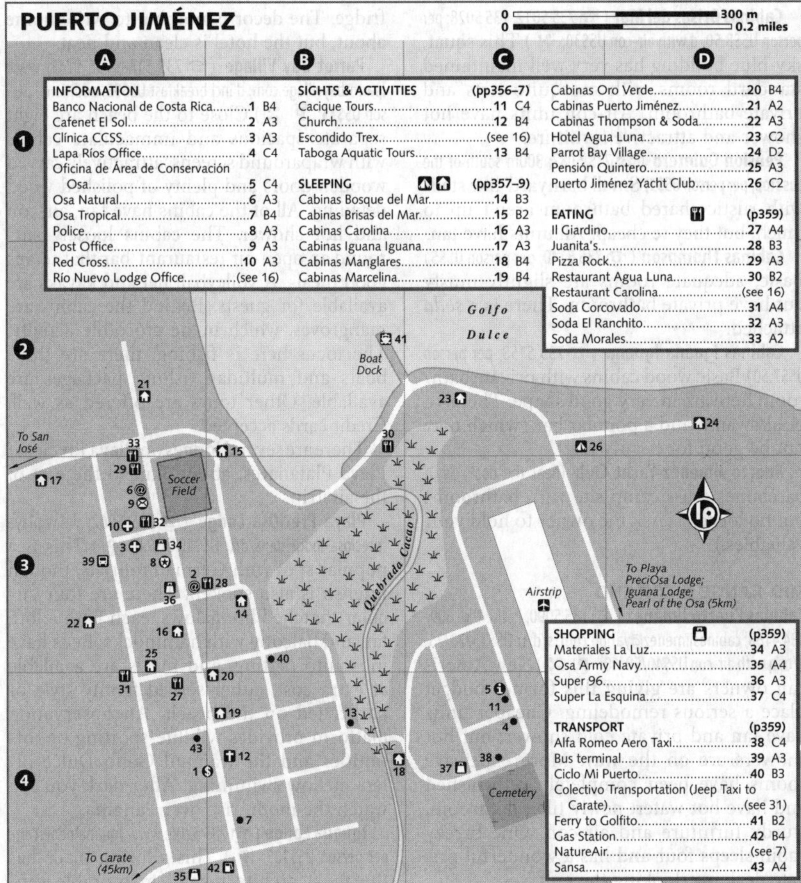

has a variety of kayaking tours around the Golfo Dulce. Call ahead to book tours.

Sleeping

During Semana Santa (Easter week) and dry-season weekends many hotels may be full, so call ahead to make reservations. Rates below are for the high season.

BUDGET

Puerto Jiménez has a good selection of budget accommodations, most of which have cold-water showers (unless otherwise stated).

Cabinas Oro Verde (☎ 735 5241; per person US$7) Roomy, simple and clean – this is a great budget deal. All units have private bathroom and fan. You may get a wake-up call from the rooster next door.

Restaurant y Cabinas Carolina (☎ 735 5185; 200m west of Banco Nacional; d US$11.30;) Five clean doubles here have the usual amenities: private bathroom and fan. Two newer quarters have air-con.

Cabinas Marcelina (☎ 735 5007; cabmarce@hotmail.com; per person US$15, d with air-con US$42;) Remodeled in 2002, this HI-affiliated hotel has immaculate white-tiled rooms, hot water and fluffy towels.

Cabinas Bosque del Mar (☎ 735 5681; per person US$8, d/tr with air-con US$30) These clean and simple cabins are an excellent value. Rooms come with fan and private hot shower. Three air-con doubles are more expensive.

Cabinas Brisas del Mar (☎ 735 5012, 735 5028; per person US$8.50, d with air-con US$30; ❄) This squat, sky-blue building has very well maintained standard rooms with mosquito nets and private bathroom. Air-con units have hot shower and attractive furniture.

Pensión Quintero (☎ 735 5087; 300m south of the bus stop; per person US$3) Small barnyard-like stalls with rustic shared bathroom aren't up to much, but they're cheap. All units have fan.

Cabinas Thompson (☎ 735 5140; per person US$5) Basic, adequate rooms are slightly musty but have private bathroom. There is a *soda* attached.

Cabinas Iguana Iguana (☎ 735 5158; per person US$7.50) Basic wood cabins with private bathroom here are in very good shape. There's a pool/swamp and a popular bar (which may not be good for beauty rest).

Puerto Jiménez Yacht Club (near the dock) is a barebones grass camp site with bathrooms but no lockers. (Ask the owner to hold your valuables.)

MID-RANGE & TOP END

Cabinas Puerto Jiménez (☎ 735 5090, in the USA 609-884 4163; cabinasjimenez@yahoo.com; s/d/tr US$15/20/25, d/tr/q with air-con US$40/50/60; P ❄) New American owners are giving this former budget place a serious remodeling. Cheaper units have fan and private cold shower, but hot showers are on the way. More expensive rooms have been completely refurbished and have hot water, newly tiled bathroom, sturdy furniture and air-con. One breezy cabin sleeps four and has a wonderful private deck overlooking the gulf.

Away from the town center is **Cabinas Manglares** (☎ 735 5002; www.manglares.com; per person incl breakfast US$30; P ❄) This pleasant, Tico-run place has eight rooms with air-con, private hot-water shower and super-firm beds. The place has been updated, and small, pretty rooms are decorated with Peruvian textiles. It's a good value. Behind the hotel is a mangrove area, ideal for looking for frogs and other wildlife.

Hotel Agua Luna (☎ 735 5393; osanatural.com; s/d US$20/40, with TV US$25/45, with TV & bathtub US$40/55; ❄) Near the boat dock, this whitewashed hotel has three types of room – all of which are spacious and tiled and feature air-con (which is rather loud) and hot-water shower. Mid-priced units have cable TV, while more expensive rooms come with tub, phone and fridge. The decor is nothing to write home about, but the hotel is clean and neat.

Parrot Bay Village (☎ 735 5180, 735 5748; www.parrotbayvillage.com; d incl breakfast US$95, additional person US$15; P ❄) Close to the beach are eight separate spacious and immaculate cabins with wraparound screens, attractively carved wooden doors and plenty of polished wood detailing. All of the cabins have fan, air-con and hot shower. The cabins loosely surround an open-air restaurant-bar that serves good meals. A volleyball net and kayaks are available for guests. Behind the cabins are mangroves, which invite crocodile activity. The focus here is fishing: there are three boats and multiday fishing packages are available. Other tours are offered as well. Credit cards accepted.

There are several lodges on Playa Preciosa/Playa Platanares, about 5km to the east of the airstrip.

Playa PreciOsa Lodge (☎ 735 5062; www.playa-preciosa-lodge.de; s/d/tr US$40/50/60; P) This is a popular spot with German tourists, though English is also spoken. There are four circular thatched bungalows, each with a loft, fan and balcony with hammocks. Beds have mosquito netting, and meals are available at extra cost, either served family style or barbecued on the beach. An observation platform provides wildlife-spotting opportunities and the tranquil Golfo Dulce offers mellow swimming. After dark you can watch the moon rise over Panama.

Iguana Lodge (☎ 735 5205; www.iguanalodge.com; per person US$105; P) This alluring place has the most architecturally memorable cabins in the area. Four beautifully appointed, airy, two-story hardwood units provide guests with huge decks, comfortable beds and lovely hot-water bathroom with garden shower. Rates include three tasty meals a day, which are served under a huge thatched *rancho* where guests relax with board games and beer. The American owners have children, and families are welcome. All of the usual tours can be arranged, from bird-watching to waterfall rappelling. Massage, acupuncture, and salsa-dancing lessons are available on request.

Pearl of the Osa (www.thepearloftheosa.com; d US$76-88; P) Near to and owned by Iguana Lodge, this beachside place has eight pretty, brightly colored rooms – and rates that are a smidgen cheaper (for folks who can't afford the Iguana). Room prices depend on views and all include breakfast. Other meals are available at an extra charge in the airy patio dining room. It offers the same tours as Iguana Lodge.

Eating & Drinking

Restaurant Carolina (dishes US$3-8) is *the* hub for just about everything in Puerto Jiménez. Expats, nature guides, tourists and locals all gather here for food, drinks, gossip and plenty of carousing. The food is decent and the service indifferent, but it does serve a delicious yogurt-granola-fruit platter that goes down well for breakfast.

Soda El Ranchito (on the soccer field) dishes up tasty *gallo pinto* and colossal fruit salads, while **Soda Morales** (⌚ 2-10pm) has a highly recommended *ceviche*. Cheaper places include Soda Katy and Marly's Soda by the main bus stop, both of which are OK. **Soda Corcovado** (200m south of the bus terminal) is good for very early breakfasts for passengers departing on the jeep-taxi to Carate, which stops right in front.

Restaurant Agua Luna (dishes US$4-6) has a creative mix of Tico and Chinese food. It's not anything exceptional, but the views are very nice and it's the popular local spot for a date. One reader reports that it has the best piña colada in Central America.

Pizza Rock (pizzas US$3-6) produces good pizza in its wood-burning oven. If you're looking for more atmosphere, try **Il Giardino** (dishes US$4-6; ⌚ 10am-2pm & 5-10pm), a cozy garden restaurant with pretty furnishings and a variety of well-prepared Italian specialties.

You can get greasy, rather unappetizing Mexican food at Juanita's, but it's better to stick to the beer.

Iguana Iguana, at the cabins of the same name, is a popular watering hole, especially on weekends. One local swears it's 'the' place to be in Puerto Jiménez on New Year's Eve.

There are several other male-dominated, rowdy bars on the main street across from Carolina's.

Shopping

You can stock up on food items, bug repellent and other necessities at the **Super La Esquina** (near the airstrip) or the smaller **Super 96 Store** (main drag). The **Osa Army Navy** (⌚ 8am-7pm Mon-Sat, 9am-4pm Sun) has sportswear, boogie boards, fishing gear, bug nets, knives, backpacks and a selection of Costa Rican arts and crafts. Expect to pay American prices. **Materiales La Luz** (⌚ Mon-Sat), the electrical supply shop on the main street, sells fishing line, batteries and camping fuel.

Getting There & Around

AIR

To and from San José **Sansa** (☎ 735 5017; one way/round trip US$71/142) has three flights daily and **NatureAir** (☎ 735 5062, 735 5722; at Osa Tropical; US$84/168) has four flights daily. Both offices are closed on Sunday.

Alfa Romeo Aero Taxi (☎ 735 5353) has charter flights. Five-seater aircraft fly to Sirena inside Corcovado (US$220), Golfito (US$100), Drake (US$285) and San José (US$607); book two days in advance.

BICYCLE

Ciclo Mi Puerto (☎ 735 5297) rents bikes; they're well used, so check them thoroughly before you rent.

BOAT

The **passenger ferry** (US$2.50; 1½hr) to Golfito leaves at 6am. **Taboga Aquatic Tours** (☎ 735 5265) runs water taxis to Zancudo for US$15 per person. Other journeys can be arranged.

BUS

Most buses arrive at the new peach-colored terminal on the west side of town. All of these pass La Palma (23km away) for the eastern entry into Corcovado. Buy tickets to San José in advance; these buses are packed.

Neily US$3; four to six hours; departs 2pm.
San Isidro US$4; six hours; 1pm.
San José, via San Isidro (Autotransportes Blanco Lobo) US$6; eight hours; 5am & 11am.

TRUCK & TAXI

Colectivo Transportation (☎ 735 5539; tonsa@hotmail.com; 200m south of the bus terminal) runs a collective jeep-taxi service to Matapalo (US$3) and Carate (US$6) on the southern tip of the national park. Departures are from the Soda Corcovado at 6am and 1:30pm, returning at 8:30am and 4pm. At other times, you can hire a 4WD taxi for about US$60 for the ride to Carate, US$25 for the ride to Matapalo and US$100 for the overland trek to Drake. **Olman Alaníz Rodríguez** (☎ 735 5270, radio channel 8) is recommended and has a rugged, high-clearance 4WD truck.

PUERTO JIMÉNEZ TO CARATE

It's 45km by dirt road around the tip of Península de Osa to the end of the road at Carate near Parque Nacional Corcovado. All places in this section can be reached by taxi from Puerto Jiménez, or the scheduled jeep-taxi between Carate and Puerto Jiménez. There are a couple of river crossings, so use a 4WD – even in the dry season.

About 16km from Puerto Jiménez is the trendy, tropical Buena Esperanza Bar, where you can get a cold beer and snacks until about midnight (or whenever the party dies down). A kilometer beyond, on the left and slightly set back from the road, is a white cement gate (called 'El Portón Blanco') that leads into a hilly area above the coast with dirt roads accessing several small lodges.

Cabo Matapalo

This area attracts well-to-do surfers who come to chase waves at a number of popular breaks (all point or reef breaks). Note that some places have minimum stays of two or three days.

Casa Bambú (☎ in the USA 512-263 1650; www.casabambu.addr.com; d US$125, additional person US$25, 6 or more people per week US$1350) This attractive and rustic two-story wooden house is set back 100m from the beach and each of its three bedrooms has a double bed, indoor bathroom and open-air shower. Rooms are all open-air and beds have mosquito screen. There is a kitchen, dining room, covered porch and fan. All power is solar. Meals are available at lodges within walking distance, and maid service is offered.

Encanta La Vida (☎ 735 5678, in the USA 805-969 4270; www.encantalavida; per person with 3 meals US$75-87) The grounds of this homey property offer several different vacation options. La Casona, the biggest unit, is a 2½-story house with four bedrooms and three bathrooms. The Pole House has three bedrooms and two bathrooms and the Honeymoon Cabin is a small, white, Spanish-style structure with a queen-sized bed, sitting area and table. All are beautifully kept and have hammocks. There is beach access nearby and sea kayaks are available for all guests.

Hacienda Bahía Esmeralda (☎ 381 8521; www.bahiaesmeralda.com; per person with 3 meals US$120; 🍴) This place is within walking distance of some of the more popular surfing areas (and their website tells you everything you need to know about local breaks). Two large rooms in the main lodge are screened and have private bathroom and fan. Three bungalows also have private terraces and great views. All beds are queen sized. There is a spring-fed pool and the owners can arrange rafting, kayaking, jungle trekking and other tours. Massage and yoga are available upon request.

Matapalo to Carate

Past El Portón Blanco and beginning 19km from Jiménez you'll find other very good lodging options.

Ojo del Mar (☎ 735 5062; ojodelmar@yahoo.de; per person US$35-60) Three very rustic, thatched open-air huts dot lush beachfront grounds here. Rooms have mosquito nets and a private bathroom with garden. Meals are available and there is a small library area with hammocks. A deck overlooking the ocean serves as an outdoor yoga studio. There is no electricity, so bring a flashlight. The reservation number listed here is for Osa Tropical in Jiménez, which takes their bookings. Rates include breakfast.

Lapa Ríos (☎ in Puerto Jiménez 735 5130; www.laparios.com; s/d/tr per person with 3 meals US$328/214/206, child under 10 US$111; P 🍴) A few hundred meters beyond El Portón Blanco, on the right, you'll find this fabulous, top-of-the-line wilderness resort. Situated in a 400-hectare private nature reserve, Lapa Rios combines the right amount of luxury with rustic, tropical ambience. Sixteen spacious, shiny wooden bungalows are scattered over the site. Each unit has a large bathroom with two sinks and hot water. There is electricity, fan and two queen-sized beds with mosquito nets, along with screened windows and ample decks. There's also a pool, bar, reading room, and restaurant with wonderful views. A spiral staircase climbs three stories to an observation deck near the roof. A massage therapist is on hand. Traveler feedback for this place has been nothing short of glowing. Tours are available and you can hike on the reserve's extensive trail system. Other activities include swimming, surfing, snorkeling and soaking in tide pools 500m from the lodge, and there are horseback tours. The owners have a commitment to conserve and protect the environment and the hotel has helped build a school for local children through the nonprofit Asociación de Educación de Escuela Carbonera. You can make arrangements to visit the school or make a donation. Check the website to see what kinds of supplies the kids need. The lodge has an office next to the airport in Puerto Jiménez and it can arrange all transfers. Credit cards accepted.

Bosque del Cabo (☎ 381 4847, in Puerto Jiménez 735 5206; www.bosquedelcabo.com; per person standard/deluxe US$140/155; 2-/3-bedroom houses US$260/350; P) From Lapa Ríos, a signed turn to the left leads 2km to this wilderness lodge. It is set on 200 hectares, half of it virgin forest. There are nine rustic, attractive thatched-roof bungalows set on a bluff with ocean views, comfortable beds and sun-warmed garden shower. The bungalows are spaced apart and come with ocean or forest views. A few (sleeping four and six) are lit only by candles and each has a private hot-water bathroom, kitchen and hydroelectric energy. The houses are rented for a three-day minimum, and meals are not included; rates for these are per house, not per person. Rates for the bungalows are all based on double occupancy and include three meals a day. Hiking, riding and other excursions can be arranged. Massage is also offered. Credit cards accepted.

El Remanso Rainforest Beach Lodge (☎ 735 5569; www.elremanso.com; per person US$90-154; P) Just 20m beyond Bosque del Cabo on the left-hand side, you'll find this pristine and excellent lodge on the ocean. Constructed entirely from fallen tropical hardwoods, the luxurious, spacious and very private cabins have shiny wood floors and beautifully finished fixtures. All of the units and the main house are powered by solar or hydroelectric power, and the owners (rightly) take a great deal of pride in not using pesticides. (Each cabin has a tiny moat around it that prevents ants from entering the room, and bedroom areas are screened.) Several units have folding French-style doors that open to provide unimpeded vistas of the foliage and the ocean in the distance. Activities include waterfall rappelling, tree climbing and various guided nature hikes. Three meals a day are included in the rate and credit cards are accepted.

CARATE

The 'village' of Carate consists of the airstrip and the *pulpería* and not much else other than the few lodges that line the coast. This is the beginning of the road if you're departing from Corcovado, or the end of the road if you're arriving at the park from Puerto Jiménez. The *pulpería* is the gathering center of sorts – attracting a colorful mix of locals, travelers, nature guides and gold miners, who all descend on the shop for rowdy beer-drinking sessions.

If you're driving, you can leave your car here (US$4.50 per night) and hike to a tent camp (less than an hour) or the La Leona ranger station (1½ hours).

Sleeping & Eating

Communication is often through Puerto Jiménez, so faxes, telephone messages and emails may not be picked up for several days; book well in advance.

The **pulpería** (per person US$15) has very basic singles and doubles with cold shower. Ask about camping here. Meals are available.

Terrapin Lodge (☎ 735 5062, 845 7982; correovielka@hotmail.com; per person US$82; P) From Puerto Jiménez, this Tico-owned lodge is about 2km before the airstrip on the right-hand side. Five cabins have private bathroom and two have ocean views. The rooms are small, basic and very private. There is a pool and a waterfall on eight hectares of land. Free kayaks are available for guests. Credit cards are accepted if you reserve and pay in advance through Osa Tropical (p356) in Jiménez.

Lookout Inn (☎ 735 5431; www.lookout-inn.com; per person US$99; P) A little closer to the airstrip, this solar-powered inn has four rooms and two private cabins, all with hand-carved wooden doors and private hot shower. Quarters are tastefully decorated and there is a roomy observation deck with coastal and rain-forest views, a pool and hot tub. It also has a wine cellar, and meals are served on an outdoor terrace with incredible vistas. Hiking is available, and kayaking, fishing and horseback riding can be arranged. A wood stairway behind the inn leads straight up the side of the mountain to a trail that leads to two waterfalls. (Get ready to climb stairs, though; this thing is never-ending. The owner likes to refer to it as the 'stairway to heaven.') Rates include three meals a day; credit cards accepted.

Luna Lodge (☎ 380 5036, 358 5848, in the USA 888-409 8448; www.lunalodge.com; tents/cabins per person US$88/146; P) Just beyond the airstrip and behind the *pulpería*, the Río Carate comes steeply out of the rain-forested coastal hills.

Prior to the *pulpería,* you'll see a signed turn-off for this wonderful place. A steep 4WD-only road goes through a river and 2km up the valley to this superb hotel and retreat center. The hillside location offers fantastic forest views reaching to the ocean in the distance; a high-roofed, open-sided restaurant takes full advantage of this. The seven spacious, beautifully decorated hardwood cabins each have a huge private garden shower and personal patio. Five secluded tents have two single beds each. An open-air yoga and meditation studio at the top of the hill is nothing less than incredible. (Call the lodge or visit their website for class and retreat schedules.) A massage bungalow offers an equally marvelous environment. Meals include plenty of organically grown food from the lodge garden. Three meals a day and waterfall hikes are included in the rates; other tours and activities are available at extra charge. Credit cards accepted.

La Leona Eco-Lodge & Tent Camp (☎ 735 5704; www.laleonalodge.com; per adult/child under 8 US$70/35) A 30-minute, 1km hike along the beach will bring you to this new tent camp. Thirteen comfy walk-in tents are nestled on platforms between palm trees, facing the beach. The common areas and kitchen are lit by solar power in the evenings, but you'll need a flashlight for your tent as there is no electricity. There is hiking on the 30 hectares of virgin rain-forest property behind the accommodations, offering many opportunities to view the peninsula's abundant wildlife. Boogie boards are available free to guests, and guided hikes, horseback, crocodile and waterfall tours can all be booked for an extra fee. Rates are based on double occupancy and include three meals a day; credit cards accepted.

Corcovado Lodge Tent Camp (☎ in San José 227 0766, 222 0333; www.corcovadolodge.com; s without meals US$47, s/d with meals US$87/126). Just 500m from the southern border of Parque Nacional Corcovado, 1.7km west of Carate along the beach, is this comfortable and renowned place. Owned and operated by Costa Rica Expeditions (see p474), it makes an excellent base from which to explore Corcovado in reasonable comfort, and serves as a restful spot for those who have already hiked through the national park. The lodge has 20 walk-in tents with shared bathrooms, a dining room and a bar/lounge area. A small generator provides electricity to the dining room and bathhouses only – a flashlight is needed in the tents. Walk-in tents have two beds with linen. Food is served family style and is excellent and plentiful. A sandy beach fronts the camp and a steep trail leads to the rain forest 100m away, where a 160-hectare private reserve is available for hiking and wildlife observation. Guided and self-guided hikes around here will provide you with good views and encounters with lots of birds and monkeys. Horseback riding is also available. A mere 30-minute hike into the reserve is a canopy platform in a 45m-tall guapinol tree that can be accessed for day/overnight trips (US$69/125). The platform is reached by a hand-operated rope and pulley system. (Not for acrophobes.) Guides are trained in platform safety and are well versed in ecology and wildlife spotting and identification. This is a popular option; book ahead. Packages from San José are available through Costa Rica Expeditions. Reservations are encouraged, though the lodge will take travelers on a walk-in basis if there is room.

NORTHERN GOLFO DULCE AREA

GOLFITO

Formerly a bustling banana port, the fading town of Golfito is now being slowly reclaimed by the jungle behind it. From 1938 to 1985, it was the headquarters of United Fruit's operations in the southern part of Costa Rica, but a combination of declining foreign markets, rising Costa Rican export taxes, worker unrest and banana diseases led the agricultural conglomerate to pack its bags for cheaper pastures (such as Ecuador). Some of the plantations now produce African palm oil, but this has not alleviated the economic hardship caused by United Fruit's departure. (Palm-oil production requires far less manpower.)

In an attempt to boost the region's economy, the federal government built a duty-free facility *(depósito libre)* in the northern part of Golfito. ('Duty free' is a misnomer, because items for sale are still heavily taxed and do not offer significant savings for foreign tourists.) Nevertheless, prices are substantially lower than elsewhere in Costa Rica and this lures Ticos from all over the country into visiting Golfito on 24-hour shopping sprees for microwave ovens and TVs. This puts hotel rooms at a premium on weekends, especially near vacation season.

Locals also make a living through the trickle of tourism that passes through as visitors embark on boats to destinations around Golfo Dulce and Península de Osa. It is also a key departure point for journeys to the beach communities of Zancudo and Pavones. There are no beaches in Golfito itself (Playa Cacao, across the gulf, is the closest). The town also attracts a few sportfishers who come to dock their vessels while they catch up on their beer drinking and tale-telling. (This does little for the local economy as many of the marinas are foreign owned and operated.)

For those who linger, a visit to Refugio Nacional de Fauna Silvestre Golfito (p368) will reward you. This little-visited rain-forest park on the steep hills backing the town has wonderful birding and wildlife-spotting opportunities. Likewise, a trip to nearby Casa de Orquídeas botanical garden (p369) will provide you with spectacular vistas.

Orientation

Golfito is named after a tiny gulf that emerges into the much larger Golfo Dulce, a large Pacific Ocean gulf just west of Panama. The town is, superficially, two towns strung out along a coastal road with a backdrop of steep, thickly forested hills. The southern part of town is where you find most of the bars and businesses – including a seedy red-light district that is popular with local and foreign drunks. Warner Brothers chose this site to film *Chico Mendes*, the true story of a Brazilian rubber tapper's efforts to preserve the rain forest. One of the few remnants of the movie set is an old steam locomotive that graces the park. Nearby, is the so-called Muellecito (Small Dock), where the ferry to Puerto Jiménez departs on a daily basis.

Old banana-worker houses are scattered just south of here. They are recognizable by their industrial uniformity.

The northern part of town was the old United Fruit Company headquarters (the so-called 'Zona Americana'), and it retains a languid, tropical air with its large, well-ventilated homes with verandas and attractively landscaped surroundings. Several of these houses now offer inexpensive accommodations. The airport and duty-free zone are also at this end.

The port is a well-protected one, and a few foreign yachts on oceanic or coastal cruises are usually anchored here as well as the occasional freighter looming above the local taxi boats and fishing launches.

Information

Land Sea Tours (☎ 775 1614; landsea@racsa.co.cr), on the shoreline at Km 2, can book Sansa tickets and lodgings; it is also a good source of local real-estate information. Katie Duncan knows just about everything about the area and she is an enthusiastic advocate for Golfito; if she can't connect you with what you're looking for, she'll know who can. There is also a small selection of Guaymí and Boruca handicrafts, all produced by local collectives.

Arriving sailors will find the **port captain** (☎ 775 0487; 🕑 7:30-11am & 12:30-4pm Mon-Fri) opposite the large Muelle de Golfito, also known as the Muelle Bananero (Banana Company Dock). **Migración** (☎ 775 0423; 🕑 8am-4pm) is situated away from the dock, in a 2nd-story office above the Soda Pavas, near the Tracopa bus terminal.

Many places around Golfito communicate with one another by VHF radio. If you need to reach someone by radio, ask at Land Sea Tours, Las Gaviotas Hotel or one of the marinas to borrow their radio. Alternatively, call Doña Isabel at **Osa Tropical** (☎ 735 5062) in Puerto Jiménez, who can put you in radio contact with lodges on the Golfo Dulce. (She doesn't work on Sunday.)

The best place to check email is **@Internet** (🕑 8am-9pm; per hour US$1.30), below Hotel Golfito, where the connections are speedy and there is delicious air-con. Hotel Samoa del Sur also offers Internet access to the public, but at twice the price. Laundry service is available at **Ilona's Laundry** (🕑 8am-5pm; per kilo US$2) next to Hotel Delfina.

Emergency medical attention can be obtained at the **Hospital de Golfito** (☎ 775 0011). A recommended local physician is **Dr Guillermo Torres Álvarez** (☎ 775 2135, 775 0822; 🕑 9am-noon & 5-8pm Mon-Fri) in the center of town (see 'doctor's office' on the map).

Banco Coopealianza (🕑 8am-5pm Mon-Fri, 8am-noon Sat) has a 24-hour ATM that accepts cards on the Cirrus network. There is a Western Union office inside. Other local banks will change US dollars and traveler's checks. The

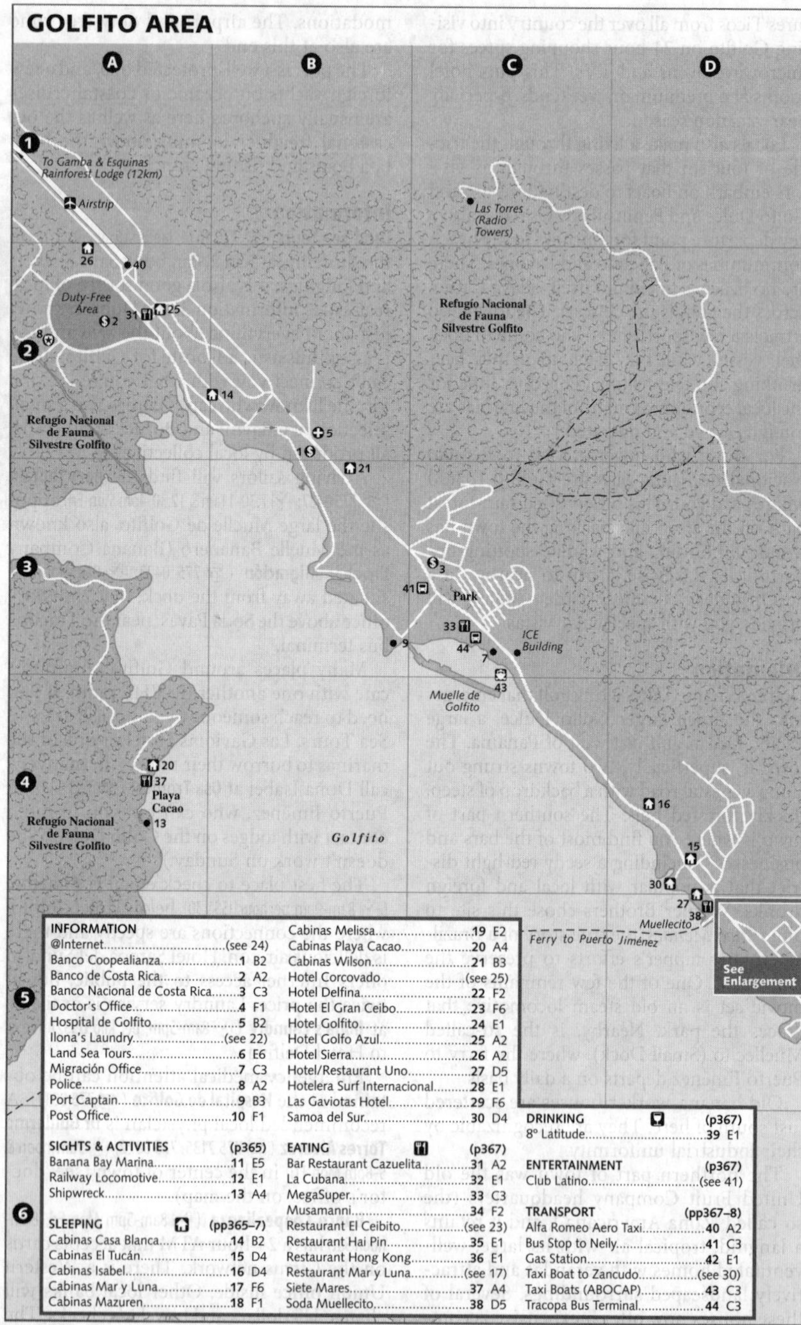
GOLFITO AREA
A
B
C
D
1
2
3
4
5
6
To Gamba & Esquinas Rainforest Lodge (12km)
Airstrip
Duty-Free Area
Las Torres (Radio Towers)
Refugio Nacional de Fauna Silvestre Golfito
Refugio Nacional de Fauna Silvestre Golfito
Refugio Nacional de Fauna Silvestre Golfito
Park
ICE Building
Muelle de Golfito
Playa Cacao
Golfito
Muellecito
Ferry to Puerto Jiménez
See Enlargement
INFORMATION
@Internet.....(see 24)
Banco Coopealianza.....1 B2
Banco de Costa Rica.....2 A2
Banco Nacional de Costa Rica.....3 C3
Doctor's Office.....4 F1
Hospital de Golfito.....5 B2
Ilona's Laundry.....(see 22)
Land Sea Tours.....6 E6
Migración Office.....7 C3
Police.....8 A2
Port Captain.....9 B3
Post Office.....10 F1
SIGHTS & ACTIVITIES (p365)
Banana Bay Marina.....11 E5
Railway Locomotive.....12 E1
Shipwreck.....13 A4
SLEEPING (pp365–7)
Cabinas Casa Blanca.....14 B2
Cabinas El Tucán.....15 D4
Cabinas Isabel.....16 D4
Cabinas Mar y Luna.....17 F6
Cabinas Mazuren.....18 F1
Cabinas Melissa.....19 E2
Cabinas Playa Cacao.....20 A4
Cabinas Wilson.....21 B3
Hotel Corcovado.....(see 25)
Hotel Delfina.....22 F2
Hotel El Gran Ceibo.....23 F6
Hotel Golfito.....24 E1
Hotel Golfo Azul.....25 A2
Hotel Sierra.....26 A2
Hotel/Restaurant Uno.....27 D5
Hotelera Surf Internacional.....28 E1
Las Gaviotas Hotel.....29 F6
Samoa del Sur.....30 D4
EATING (p367)
Bar Restaurant Cazuelita.....31 A2
La Cubana.....32 E1
MegaSuper.....33 C3
Musamanni.....34 F2
Restaurant El Ceibito.....(see 23)
Restaurant Hai Pin.....35 E1
Restaurant Hong Kong.....36 E1
Restaurant Mar y Luna.....(see 17)
Siete Mares.....37 A4
Soda Muellecito.....38 D5
DRINKING (p367)
8º Latitude.....39 E1
ENTERTAINMENT (p367)
Club Latino.....(see 41)
TRANSPORT (pp367–8)
Alfa Romeo Aero Taxi.....40 A2
Bus Stop to Neily.....41 C3
Gas Station.....42 E1
Taxi Boat to Zancudo.....(see 30)
Taxi Boats (ABOCAP).....43 C3
Tracopa Bus Terminal.....44 C3

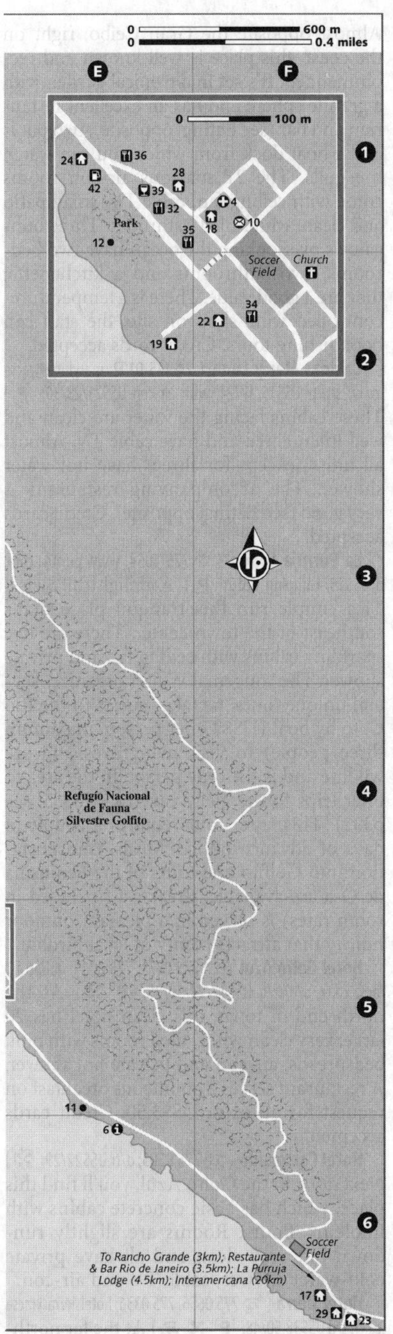

gas station (locally called La Bomba) changes US dollars, provided there are enough colones on hand.

Sportfishing & Boating

Sportfishing is a highlight of the Golfo Dulce area, with operators leaving both from here and from the more southern Zancudo. You can fish year-round, but the best season for the sought-after Pacific sailfish in the Golfito area is from November to May.

Banana Bay Marina (☎ 775 0838; www.bananabaymarina.com), run by Bruce Blevins, has a floating dock marina accommodating up to 155 yachts with a full range of services. Charters can be arranged; a full day of all-inclusive fishing on a 6m or 17m boat starts at US$750 a day.

Land Sea Tours (☎ 775 1614; see Information previous) has a dock and provides 'boat-sitting' for sailors wanting to visit inland Costa Rica. It can also organize fishing charters that vary in price by length of trip and the type of fish sought.

You can hire local sailors for tours of the gulf at any of the docks (see p368).

Sleeping

Note that the area around the soccer field in town is Golfito's red-light district.

BUDGET

Cabinas El Tucán (☎ 775 0553; per person US$5, with air-con US$14.50; Ⓟ) This hotel is actually comprised of Hotel Tucán #1 and Tucán #2. Both have clean, spacious, tiled-floor rooms with private cold shower. More expensive rooms have air-con and cable TV. There are units that can accommodate six or even 10 people. The hotel is a good value all around, though the rooms in Tucán #2 are newer and nicer. Credit cards accepted.

Cabinas Melissa (☎ 775 0443; per person US$5) Situated behind the Delfina, this is a much better deal – and one of the best budget options in town. Clean, quiet units with private bathroom overlook the water.

Hotel/Restaurant Uno (☎ 775 0061; r per person US$2) Near the ferry dock, this ramshackle wood building has windowless stalls without fan, and dingy shared bathroom – but it's got to be one of the cheapest places in the country; not a good choice for solo women.

Cabinas Mazuren (☎ 775 0058; per person US$5) The doting Doña Luz runs a secure house with a hodgepodge of seven clean rooms of various sizes. Dark and woody rooms, all painted blue, are reasonably clean and well kept. All units have fan and bathroom.

Hotelera Surf Internacional (☎ 775 0034; s/d US$5/7, d with air-con US$14.50) This dark and rambling old hotel has 22 rooms, many of which either lack windows or have only a skylight – get ready for some serious mustiness. Single units share bathrooms, which resemble the pit of despair. Doubles have private cold shower; all units have fan. There are three rooms with air-con and hot shower. A seedy bar is open all day, for those who prefer a beer breakfast. Not recommended for solo women travelers.

Hotel Delfina (☎ 775 0043; per person US$5) Minimally ventilated rooms with and without grungy private bathroom are spread out through a dilapidated wood building.

Hotel Golfito (☎ 775 0047; d US$10, d with air-con US$21; P ⊠) Concrete doubles are bare but have firm beds, industrial-strength fan and private bathroom; they are well lit. This is a good value and it is conveniently situated by the Muellecito.

Cabinas Isabel (☎ 775 1774; s/d US$3.50/7) Here you'll find decent rooms in an attractive old house, but it's a little out of the way. Staff can arrange local tours.

Cabinas Casa Blanca (☎ 775 0124; s/d US$5/10) At the northern end, this family-run place has clean, concrete cabins with fan and private bathroom.

Cabinas Wilson (☎ 775 0795; s/d US$5/10) Just to the south, you'll find these decent, basic cabins, which come with fan and private bathroom with cold shower.

MID-RANGE

Hotel El Gran Ceibo (☎ 775 0403; www.soldeosa.com/granceibo; d/tr US$17/21, d with air-con US$28; P ⊠ ⊡) About 3km southeast of Golfito, this hotel has 15 modern, clean rooms with fan and cold-water bathroom, and 12 cabins with air-con and hot water. All have cable TV and can sleep up to four or six. Rooms overlooking the swimming pool are best, and a restaurant, El Ceibito, (see Eating, opposite) is attached. The management is friendly and can help you arrange any tours. The local Golfito bus ends its run at a bus stop right outside, so getting here is easy. Credit cards accepted.

Las Gaviotas Hotel (☎ 775 0062; gaviotas@racsa.co.cr; d/tr/q US$42/48/54, bungalow US$84; P ⊠ ⊡) Almost opposite the Gran Ceibo, right on the coast, this place is well known and recommended. It's set in a tropical garden with a granite sphere and has an excellent restaurant and bar (see Eating, opposite), two pools and a boat dock from which you can watch the gulls. The 21 spacious air-con rooms come with ceiling fan, cable TV, small patio and clean, white-tiled bathroom. Three bungalows overlooking the ocean have two bedrooms, two bathrooms and a kitchenette; they are a good value. There is a temperature-controlled wine shop on site; the staff can book fishing tours. Credit cards accepted.

Cabinas Mar y Luna (☎ 775 0192; maryluna@racsa.co.cr; s/d/tr US$15/17/24, with air-con US$21/23/30; P) These cabins facing the water are clean and well maintained and have cable TV. Almost all units (except for three) have hot water shower. The accompanying restaurant is very good (see Eating, opposite). Credit cards accepted.

La Purruja Lodge (☎ 775 1054, www.purruja.com; d US$25, camping US$2; P) A delightful Swiss/Tica couple run this tranquil place that's southeast of the town center. There are five sparkling cabins with ceiling fan and private shower. The congenial Walter organizes several unique tours: he takes guests to the Río Coto by boat (US$25 per person, maximum three people) to visit mangroves and see wildlife and is the only person in the area to offer trips to the Neily caverns (US$35; see p332). This latter tour requires a couple of days of advance notice. Meals, transportation into Golfito and tours of the Península de Osa are available. Breakfast (included in room rates) is served in a pleasant outdoor *rancho* that attracts plenty of local birdlife.

Hotel Golfo Azul (☎ 775 0871, 775 0004; golfazul@racsa.co.cr; s/d/tr/q US$17/24/30/36; P ⊠) At the north end of town, this clean hotel has 20 large, very clean white-tiled rooms with pink bedspreads, air-con and private hot shower. A restaurant serves a bounteous breakfast on request for an extra US$3.50. Credit cards accepted.

Hotel Corcovado (☎ 775 0505; d/tr US$22/29; ⊠) Next door to the Golfo Azul, you'll find this place, which has basic concrete cabins with linoleum floors. Rooms are slightly run-down but very clean and all have private cold-water shower, cable TV and air-con.

Hotel Sierra (☎ 775 0666, 775 0336; hotelsierra@racsa.co.cr; s/d US$38.50/48; P ⊠ ⊡) At the far northern end of town, convenient to the airport, this two-story modern hotel has 72 clean rooms with tiled floor, cable TV, air-con, bathroom and hot shower. There are two pools (worth the price on a really hot day) in a courtyard, and a restaurant. The hotel can organize fishing excursions. Credit cards accepted.

Samoa del Sur (☎ 775 0233, 775 0264; www.samoadelsur.com; r US$50, RV US$10; P ✈ 💻) This large, pyramid-roofed building is just north of the town center. It has a hotel, restaurant facilities and a small dock. There are 14 well-appointed, spacious air-con rooms, each with two queen-sized beds, fan, TV and hot water; each room sleeps up to four people. Parking and hook-up prices for RVs (recreational vehicles) include use of shared bathrooms and showers. Apart from the restaurant, which has decent food (though the pizza is a cheesy bomb), it has a bar with a pool table, darts and *foosball*. It also has a darts club on Monday and Wednesday nights, when you can try beating some of the local champs. Laundry service (per kg US$2) is available and the hotel provides Internet access (per hour US$2.50) and faxing services. There's a book exchange, gift shop and a shell museum (open to the public). The staff can arrange any local tour and Spanish, English and French are spoken. Credit cards accepted. The weekday taxi-boat to Zancudo departs from the hotel's dock.

Eating

Hotel/Restaurant Uno (see Sleeping, p365; dishes US$2) This place has been around for decades and serves up decent (and very cheap) Chinese food.

Soda Muellecito (by the ferry dock), is popular for early breakfasts, as is **La Cubana** (casados US$3) in the center of town. The food at the latter establishment isn't the greatest, but the views and strong coffee mitigate that.

Restaurant Hai Pin (dishes US$3-7) Down the same street, you can get decent Chinese food at this clean and well-lit place.

Restaurant Hong Kong (dishes US$3-8) This eatery nearby looks a little sketchier.

Bar Restaurant Cazuelita (dishes US$3-6; 🕒 noon-1pm Tue-Sun) In the northern zone, this place has decent Chinese and Tico meals.

Las Gaviotas Hotel (see Sleeping opposite; meals from US$8; 🕒 6am-10pm) This popular restaurant serves a variety of pricier food, popular with North American and European guests.

Restaurant Mar y Luna (dishes US$3-6) This excellent waterfront spot is a great place for some tasty fish, cold beer and a good seat from which to admire the sunset. Friendly and prompt service make the whole deal even better.

Restaurant El Ceibito (casados US$2.50; 🕒 6am-10pm) Attached to Hotel El Gran Ceibo, but under separate ownership, this pleasant eatery offers cheap and tasty Tico food. There are especially good fresh tortillas and a variety of fresh fruit *batidos*.

Rancho Grande (dishes US$5-12) Almost 3km further out of town, this rustic, thatched-roof place serves country-style Tico food cooked over a wood stove. Margarita, the Tica owner, is one of Golfito's established characters. Her hours are erratic, so stop in during the day to let her know you're coming for dinner.

Restaurante & Bar Río de Janeiro (☎ 775 0509; dishes US$2-12) Almost 1km further, this nice roadside bar has a dart board. It's small, but a changing menu ranges from cheap cheeseburgers to US$12 steaks. You have to ask the staff what they have – there's no written menu.

Musmanni offers the usual fresh-baked goods and the MegaSuper has plenty of food and other sundries.

Drinking & Entertainment

Drinking can be an interesting proposition in Golfito. A lot of travelers hang out at their respective hotel bars and avoid the local scene altogether. Samoa del Sur, Banana Bay Marina and Las Gaviotas all offer ample opportunities to swig with expats.

And the local scene, well, it's a bit rough – especially around the town's red-light district near the soccer field, where drunks and prostitutes are a regular part of the panorama. Around here, the best place for a drink is **8° Latitude** (northwest of the soccer field), which is laidback and frequented by Americans into sportfishing (including some women).

Club Latino (north end of town) is the place for dancing, especially on weekends, and is popular with Ticos.

Getting There & Away

AIR

The airport is 4km north of the town center. Sansa flies four times a day to and from San José (US$71/142 one way/round trip); Nature-Air has one flight (US$84/168).

Alfa Romeo Aero Taxi (☎ 775 1515) has light aircraft (three and five passengers) for charter flights to Puerto Jiménez, Parque Nacional Corcovado and other areas.

BOAT

There are two main boat docks for passenger service: the Muellecito is the main dock in the southern part of town and frequently has independent sailors with whom you can negotiate the fare for a trip. There is a smaller dock north of the Muelle Bananero (opposite the ICE building) where you'll find the **Asociación de Boteros** (Abocap; ☎ 775 0357), a taxi-boat association that can provide service anywhere in the Golfo Dulce area. Rates are affected by the number of passengers, distance and weather conditions.

Boats to Playa Cacao depart from the Abocap dock (though you can get boatmen to take you from the Muellecito as well). The fare is US$5 minimum or US$1 per person.

The daily passenger ferry to Puerto Jiménez (US$2.50, 1½ hours) departs at 11:30am daily from the Muellecito. (Be aware: life jackets are an iffy proposition on this boat.) Weekday taxi boats for Playa Zancudo (US$3.75, 45 minutes) leave from the dock at Samoa del Sur at 11am (roughly), returning to Golfito at 7am the next day.

The vast majority of destinations around the Golfo Dulce require beach landings. Be ready to get your feet wet.

BUS

Buses depart from several points around Golfito.

Neily (bus stop in front of Club Latino) US$0.50; 1½ hours; departs hourly from 6am to 7pm.

Pavones (bus stop in front of the Muellecito) three hours; departs 10am & 3pm; may be affected by road and weather conditions, especially in the rainy season.

San José, via San Isidro (Tracopa; from the terminal near Muelle Bananero) US$5.80; eight hours; departs 5am & 1:30pm.

Getting Around

City buses travel up and down the main road of Golfito and begin their journey at the Hotel El Gran Ceibo. A ride costs US$0.20.

If you don't want to wait for the bus, colectivo taxis travel the same stretch of the main road from the airport down to Hotel El Gran Ceibo. Just flag one down if it has a seat. The set fare is US$0.60. Colectivos will take you beyond El Gran Ceibo for an additional US$0.50 to US$1.

A private taxi from downtown to the airport costs about US$2.

PLAYA CACAO

This small local beach is opposite Golfito, and the view of the bay, port and surrounding rain forest is worth the short boat ride out here. As for swimming, although it's cleaner than the polluted waters just off the town, the water isn't exactly pristine. This is not the Golfo Dulce proper, and though efforts have been made to clean up trash, you're still near a dock visited by freighters.

Cabinas Playa Cacao (☎ in San José 221 1169; www.kapsplace.com; d US$40) This place has six spacious cabins, screened in, with high thatched roofs and tiled floors. Each unit has a fan, microwave, fridge, kitchenette and bathroom. The owners have also added a larger, fully equipped communal kitchen that overlooks the gulf. This place is right on the beach, and with Golfito across the water, it is a tranquil spot from which to enjoy the old port. The cabins are run by the personable Doña Isabel Arias, whose energetic daughter Karla owns Kap's Place in San José.

The restaurant **Siete Mares** (dishes US$4-8; 🕑 8am-8pm) is a popular gathering spot for Golfito residents, who come in for the good beachside atmosphere, plenty of beer, garlic fish and good *ceviche* (US$2.50). This place is good for inexpensive breakfasts, lunches and dinners. The bar will stay open as long as there is a crowd.

The five-minute boat ride from Golfito costs US$1.30 per person for a group of four or more people. Boats can be hired by the Muelle Bananero. You can also get to Playa Cacao by walking or driving along a dirt road west and then south from the airport – about 6km total from the airport. A 4WD vehicle is recommended.

REFUGIO NACIONAL DE FAUNA SILVESTRE GOLFITO

This small, 2810-hectare refuge was originally created to protect the Golfito watershed. It encompasses most of the steep hills surrounding the town, and while the refuge has succeeded in keeping Golfito's water clean and flowing, it has also had the wonderful side effect of conserving a number of rare and interesting plant species. These include a species of Caryodaphnopsis, which is an Asian genus otherwise unknown in Central America, and Zamia, which are cycads. (Cycads are called 'living fossils' and are among the most primitive of plants. They were abundant before the time of the dinosaurs, but relatively few species are now extant.)

Other species of interest include many heliconias, orchids, tree ferns, and tropical trees including copal, the kapok tree, the butternut tree and the cow tree.

The vegetation attracts a variety of birds such as parrots, toucans, tanagers, trogons and hummingbirds. Although the scarlet macaw has been recorded here, poaching in this area has made it rare. Peccaries, pacas, raccoons, coatis, and the four types of monkeys are among the mammals that have been sighted here.

The refuge administration is in the Oficina de Area de Conservación Osa in Puerto Jiménez (see p356). There is usually no one around to collect the admission price of US$6. Camping is permitted in the refuge, but there are no facilities – most people stay in Golfito.

Rainfall is very high: October, the wettest month, receives more than 700mm. January to mid-April is normally a dry time.

Getting There & Away

About 2km south of the center of Golfito, before you come to Las Gaviotas Hotel, a gravel road heads inland, past a soccer field, and winds its way up to some radio towers (Las Torres), 7km away and 486m above sea level. This is a good access road to the refuge (most of the road actually goes through the middle of the reserve). You could take a taxi up first thing in the morning and hike down, birding as you go (the most popular option). A few trails lead from the road down to the town, but there's so little traffic on the road itself that you'll probably see more from the cleared road than from the overgrown trails. The descent takes about three hours (if you're birding), depending on your physical condition.

A very steep hiking trail leaves from almost opposite the Samoa del Sur hotel. A somewhat strenuous hike (allow about two hours) will bring you out on the road to the radio towers. The trail is in fairly good shape, but easier to find in Golfito than at the top. Once you reach the radio tower road, return the way you came or, for a less knee-straining descent, head down the road.

Another option is to take the poor dirt road to Gamba and the Esquinas Rainforest Lodge (see p332). This road begins a couple of kilometers northwest of the duty-free area and crosses through part of the refuge. You'll probably need 4WD. A local bus stops at the beginning of this dirt road – ask for the bus that goes to the road for Gamba or Esquinas. From where the bus leaves you, it's about 10km to Gamba, so you could walk and bird-watch.

Finally, there are several trails off the road to Playa Cacao. Two trails are reached by taking the right-hand fork in the road (coming from Golfito), which leads to a forked trail, each leading to a different waterfall. Further along the main trail, another 2km trail leads to a ridge that provides views of the Golfo Dulce. Trails are often obscured, so ask before setting out.

NORTH TO PLAYA CATIVO

Boat taxis can take you up along the northeast coast of the Golfo Dulce, past remote beaches and headlands interspersed with several jungle lodges. The backdrop to the coastline is largely virgin rain forest, protected by **Parque Nacional Piedras Blancas**. It can be visited from the coastal lodges, although this park has no facilities and only limited trails.

Casa de Orquídeas

This private **botanical garden** (admission & tour US$5; ⏲ tours at 8:30am Sat-Thu), surrounded by primary rain forest, is a veritable Eden. The garden's plants have been lovingly collected and tended by Ron and Trudy MacAllister, who have lived in this remote region since the 1970s. They first planted fruit trees simply to survive and soon became interested in plants. Self-taught botanists, they've amassed a wonderful collection of tropical fruit trees, bromeliads, cycads, palms, heliconias, ornamental plants and more than 100 varieties of orchid, after which their garden is named.

Guided tours last about two hours and are fascinating – touching, smelling, feeling and tasting is encouraged. One seasonal highlight is chewing on the pulp surrounding a 'magic seed' whose effect is to make lemons taste sweet instead of sour; another is the smell of vanilla. You might also see bats hanging out in a 'tent' made from a huge leaf, insects trapped in bromeliad pools, or torch ginger in flower – available treats vary according to season.

Casa de Orquídeas is at the west end of Playa San Josecito and can be reached from the lodges on that beach by foot. Otherwise, it's accessible only by boat. Transport can be arranged with all the area's lodges (if you're staying in one), or through Abocap, the sailors' association in Golfito (see p368).

Sleeping

The following places are difficult to contact directly; you may have to call a local agent and ask for a radio link (all of them are on radio channel 68), or leave a message. All of the places below have beach landings; expect to get your feet wet.

PLAYA SAN JOSECITO

Golfo Dulce Lodge (☎ 821 5398, in San José 232 0400; www.golfodulcelodge.com; per person standard/deluxe US$95/105;) This Swiss-owned place is set back 250m from the rocky beach on the edge of a 275-hectare property, much of which is rain forest. The owners are well informed about local flora and fauna and support a nearby wildcat rehabilitation project. Their deluxe units consist of five individual wooden cabins, each with a large veranda containing a rocking chair and hammock. Three standard adjoining rooms with smaller verandas surround the spring-fed pool. All have private bathroom with sun-warmed shower. A minimum two-night stay is required, and various packages and excursions are available. Round-trip boat transfers from Golfito/Puerto Jiménez are US$20/30 per person. Rates are based on double occupancy.

Dolphin Quest (☎ 775 1742; www.dolphinquestcostarica.com; s/d camping US$30/55, cabins US$60/100, house US$70/120) This jungle lodge offers as much privacy as a mile of beach and 280 hectares of mountainous rain forest can offer. Three round, thatched-roof cabins sleeping two and a larger house sleeping up to seven are spread out around two hectares of landscaped grounds. Camping is also an option. Meals are served communally in an open-air pavilion near the shore, and the food is good; many ingredients are grown organically on the property. Various activities are available at an extra fee, including horseback rides, kayaking, motorboat excursions, a butterfly garden, snorkeling, scuba diving, dolphin tours and plenty of hiking. Access to the trails is free after an introductory tour outlining the beauties and dangers of the forest (US$10). A red-macaw release program is hosted here, and Casa de Orquídeas is a short walk down the beach. Other options include massage, a work-exchange program for skilled people who want to stay awhile (in a bunkhouse), and local pickup for soccer games; there's a small library. Cash is preferred, though traveler's checks are accepted for a fee.

PLAYA NICUESA

Playa Nicuesa Rainforest Lodge (☎ 735 5237, in the USA 866-348 7610; www.nicuesalodge.com; per person guesthouse/cabins US$130/150) North of Casa de Orquídeas you'll find this lodge, a spectacular addition to the Golfo Dulce bunch. Nestled into a 65-hectare private rain-forest reserve, this lodge is barely visible from the water (though its dock gives it away). The accommodations are all superbly decorated and maintained and feature four rooms in the main guesthouse and four private cabins. All rooms are open air and are beautifully appointed with indigenous textile spreads; they have private hot-water bathroom with garden shower, and lockbox. Meals are served in a thatched *rancho,* featuring a sparkling, polished wood bar. Prices include three meals daily made from fresh local ingredients, one guided hike and the use of kayaks and fishing rods. A freshwater creek runs through the property, and electricity is provided through solar power. Several trails go into Piedras Blancas, and the lodge can arrange guided hikes at an extra price, as well as sunset boat tours and trips to Casa de Orquídeas. Credit cards are accepted at an extra charge. The lodge is closed October 1st through November 15th.

PLAYA CATIVO

Rainbow Adventures Lodge (☎ in the USA 800-565 0722, 503-690-7750; www.rainbowcostarica.com; s/d US$225/345, penthouse US$250/375, beachfront cabins US$275/395, additional adult/child 4-10 yrs US$95/80;) This private 400-hectare reserve bordering Parque Nacional Piedras Blancas is ideal for hiking, snorkeling and swimming. The all-wood, wide-balconied, rustic appearance of the lodge belies the elegance within – handmade furniture, silk rugs, early-20th-century antiques and fresh flowers make this a special place. The first level is the dining room, lounge and library, which has air-con and contains a collection of more than 8000 natural-history publications (in English). Guests are welcome to relax and read.

Two upper floors have double rooms and the penthouse suite. They're partially exposed to the elements to allow unimpeded views of the rain forest, beach and gulf. Beds have mosquito nets and bathrooms have hot shower and hair dryer. (A hydroelectric system on the property provides power.) There are also two equally attractive cabins, each with two bedrooms sleeping up to five, a bathroom and a veranda. Truly exquisite!

The price includes three scrumptious meals cooked by the truly skilled Juana (who makes an unbelievable flan). Prices also include beer and wine with meals, nonalcoholic drinks, snacks and transportation to and from the Golfito airport. Also included is a short tour of the nearby jungle, snorkeling gear and jungle boots. There's laundry service, a pool table and a pretty spring-fed pool that is drained daily. Management is friendly. Kayak rental, birding and fishing tours and guided hikes are available. Credit cards are accepted for lodging, but all tours must be paid in cash.

NORTH OF PLAYA CATIVO

Caña Blanca Beach & Rainforest Lodge (☎ 813 3803; canablan@racsa.co.cr; per person US$150) About 2km (by boat) north of Playa Cativo and Rainbow Adventures is a small beach with three well-designed, breezy, comfortable hardwood cabins. Each cabin has a spacious veranda and cold-water garden shower with forest views (hot water is on the way). The cabins are well laid out so you don't see the others. Guests have access to 10km of rain-forest trails that have excellent birding and a waterfall. Owner Carol is from the San Francisco area and cooks gourmet veggie and seafood meals. Rates are based on double occupancy and a three-night minimum stay. (Special rates can be set for extended stays.) Included are transport from Puerto Jiménez, three meals, hors d'oeuvres and rum cocktails, wine with dinner and use of kayaks and snorkels. Other tours can be arranged on request. All rates are based on double occupancy and credit cards are accepted.

SOUTHERN GOLFO DULCE AREA

ZANCUDO

This pretty dark-sand swimming beach, 15km south of Golfito, is popular with locals, especially in the dry season, when single rooms are scarce. The surf is gentle, and at night the water sometimes sparkles with bioluminescence, tiny phosphorescent marine plants and plankton that light up if you sweep a hand through the water – the effect is like underwater fireflies. Hotels are scattered along the shore and locals report that seeing another person on the beach means it's 'crowded.'

There are also mangroves in the area around the river mouth that offer wildlife-watching possibilities, even on the boat-taxi ride from Golfito. Look for crocodiles, monkeys and birds.

The largest store in town is the **Super Bellavista** (opposite Cabinas Tío Froylan). There's a public phone here. Near Cabinas y Restaurant Tranquilo and Roy's Zancudo Lodge, you'll find the smaller Mini-Super Tres Amigos.

Activities

The best sportfishing is from December to May for sailfish, though you can catch something almost any month. Most of the outfits listed below have a variety of multiday fishing packages that include lodging in San José, all transfers to Zancudo, and meals, lodging and fishing while in Zancudo. All of the companies below can customize your itinerary.

Arena Alta Sportfishing (☎ 766 0115; www.costaricasailfish.com) Run by Dar Randall, Arena Alta has three-/seven-day fishing packages for one person that cost US$3500/6480, for two US$4300/7950.

Golfito Sportfishing (☎ 776 0007; www.costaricafishing.com) Captain Bob Baker's outfit has offshore fishing packages for three/seven days for one person costing US$2490/4950, for two US$3970/7650.

Roy's Zancudo Lodge (☎ 776 0008; www.royszancudolodge.com) All-inclusive three-/six-day fishing packages for one person cost US$2650/4480, for two US$4520/6830. Lodging is also available (see p372).

Zancudo Boat Tours (☎ 776 0012; www.loscocos.com), which is run by the folks at Cabinas Los Cocos, have three- and four-hour boat tours to a variety of destinations around the area.

PENÍNSULA DE OSA & GOLFO DULCE

One trip involves power boating and kayaking in the mangroves and estuary of the nearby Río Coto (US$40 per person). It also organizes excursions to the Península de Osa (US$65) and Casa de Orquíideas (US$40). Kayaks can be rented.

Surfing lessons are available; just ask at any hotel to be hooked up with one of several local instructors. **Horseback riding** is available through Zancudo Beach Club (see opposite).

Sleeping & Eating

Businesses are strung out along 5km of beach (so plan on lots of walking). During the high season there are few rooms available and reservations become critical (especially on weekends). Most hotels have a restaurant attached. Places here are listed heading south from the main dock.

Macondo (☎ 776 0157; d/tr US$30/36, tr with air-con US$45; P) Four large cabins with tiled floors all have their own bathroom and are very clean. Overlooking the garden, there is a pleasant balcony which serves as a popular **Italian restaurant** (dishes US$5-10), whipping up fresh-made meals and excellent espressos and cappuccinos.

Rancho Coquito (☎ 776 0128, 776 0142; per person US$5) This place is a concrete block of 16 rather stuffy rooms painted an unappetizing institutional green. The windowless rooms are alleviated somewhat by ceiling fan and a private cold shower. A **soda** (casados US$3) serves inexpensive meals and there is a pool table.

Cabinas Tío Froylan (☎ 776 0128; per person US$7) Plain and cheap whitewashed rooms with private cold shower and fan attract a loyal Tico following. Some of the rooms have four or five beds. There's a shady patio, a garden, beach access and an attached restaurant and disco with a pool table. Expect to hear the disco from your room on weekend nights.

Bar/Cabinas Sussy (☎ 776 0107; s/d US$5/10) About a 15-minute walk from the dock, this place is one of the cheapest in town and offers clean rooms (some of which sleep up to seven people) and a restaurant. The bar, which has a pool table, is *the* late-night hang in Zancudo, attracting locals and travelers.

Soda Katherine (dishes US$2-4) This is small, typical, open-air *soda* with just five tables is full of locals and savvy visitors enjoying fresh fruit juices, *gallo pintos* and casados.

La Puerta Negra (dishes US$7-15; dinner only Tue-Sun). Eating here is an experience. Alberto, who is chef, waiter, maitre d' and musical entertainer, cooks delicious seafood and fresh pasta dinners and will consume bottles of good wine right along with you. Stop in during the day to check on the daily special and make a reservation.

Cabinas Los Cocos (☎ 776 0012; www.loscocos.com; banana/thatch cabin US$64/70; P) This beachfront place is about 1km south of the public dock and is also the home of Zancudo Boat Tours, the boat-taxi and tour service owned by Susan and Andrew Robertson. Both are artists, and Andrew's sculptures, some of which showcase his wry sense of humor, decorate the grounds. Two cabins used to be banana company homes in Palmar and were transported in pieces to Zancudo, reassembled and completely refurbished. These sleep three. Two larger thatched-roof cabins sleeping four are a little more expensive. All are attractively designed with bathroom, kitchenette, hot water, fridge, fan, body boards, porch with hammocks, and a faithful clientele that rents them out by the week for a 10% discount. Each cabin is quite private, with beach access and an outdoor shower to wash off the sand. Susan works in property management, so if you're looking for a long-term rental, definitely check with her. The pair have two large rustic houses of their own that can be rented by the week or month.

Cabinas Sol y Mar (☎ 776 0014; www.zancudo.com; camping US$3, d economy/standard/deluxe US$29/41/46, additional person US$5; P) Just south of Los Cocos on the beach, this popular place is run by the congenial Rick and Lori, both of whom are a good source of local information. They have several kinds of cabin: the economy dwelling is the smallest of the bunch, while standard units are larger and share a common terrace. A couple of solo deluxe units stand on their own, offering the most privacy. All of the airy and spacious cabins are nicely finished and have pleasant, private stone-pebbled hot shower. The **restaurant** (dishes US$5-8) has good food and Rick's Friday night barbecue is not to be missed, especially if you're carnivorous. There is a nice bar in a thatched *rancho* that serves as the gathering spot for expats. Wednesday and Sunday there are competitive horseshoe matches and Saturday it's all about the volleyball. Fishing and other excursions can be arranged. They have a rental house for US$750 a month – book well in advance. Visa credit cards accepted.

Latitude 8 (☎ 776 0168; www.latitude8lodge.com; d US$60, additional person US$10; P) These two spacious, shiny, well-furnished cabins are some of the nicest in town. Known locally as 'Ty's Place,' they both have a huge hot-water shower, pretty floral sink, and refrigerator stocked with drinking water. There is also an outdoor kitchen and barbecue grill that's wonderful for whipping up a beachside meal. Fishing packages can be arranged.

Cindy's Cabin (☎ 776 0151; cyndykasket@yahoo.com; d US$45; P) This is a small, white unsigned bungalow. Fully furnished, it has a queen-sized bed and is very clean, private and charmingly decorated.

Coloso del Mar (☎ 776 0050; www.coloso-del-mar.com; d US$40, additional person US$3) Four simple and pretty wood cabins here have a fan, hot shower and good-sized deck. There's a good **restaurant** (7am-midnight) and a cozy bar. The owners speak Dutch, English and German.

Cabinas y Restaurant Tranquilo (☎ 776 0131; per person US$5, s/d with bathroom US$7.50/12.50) Known locally as 'María's Place,' this simple lodge has small, clean rooms, some with shared cold-water shower, some with a bathroom. A pleasant terrace restaurant serves delicious local specialties.

Zancudo Beach Club (☎ 776 0087; www.zancudobeachclub.com; d cabin/villa downstairs/villa upstairs US$60/50/75; P) Across the street, and near the entrance of the beach if you're driving in, this place is run by Gary and Debbie. It has three attractive, spacious wooden cabins, each with cool tiled floors, solar-heated shower, a fridge, coffee maker, ceiling fan and patio. A brand-new villa offers more private accommodations. The international **restaurant** (lunches US$6, dinners US$10-15) with a view is excellent; so are the mixed drinks. Nightly specials vary from Tex-Mex to Asian and weekend pizza nights draw in the locals. It has a dozen horses on a farm at La Virgen, 7km away, and can arrange 6am rides over the hills, down to the beach and back to the hotel for a full breakfast at 10am (US$50 per person). The surf gets slightly bigger at this end of the beach, which makes surfing possible. Credit cards accepted.

Roy's Zancudo Lodge (☎ 776 0008; www.royszancudolodge.com; per person US$115; P) North of the dock you'll find one of the oldest places in Zancudo. Its faithful clientele consists primarily of anglers. (The lodge holds more than 50 world records for fishing.) Clean but bland rooms have air-con, hot-water bathroom, fan and phone. There's a pool, hot tub, bar and restaurant, and reputable owner Roy Ventura has a fleet of 11 fishing boats. The lodge is closed mid-September to mid-November for maintenance. Rates include three meals a day and credit cards are accepted. For information on the fishing packages, see Activities p371.

Getting There & Away

BOAT

The boat dock is near the north end of the beach on the inland, estuary side (1km or more from many of the hotels). The weekday taxi boat to Golfito departs at 7am from this dock. **Zancudo Boat Tours** (☎ 776 0012; www.loscocos.com) at Cabinas Los Cocos can provide private taxi boat service to and from Puerto Jiménez (US$15 per person, three person minimum) and Golfito (US$12.50, two person minimum).

BUS

A bus to Neily leaves from the *pulpería* near the dock at 5:30am and the bus for Golfito leaves at 5am for the three-hour trip, with a ferry transfer at the Río Coto Colorado. Service may be suspended, or the hours changed, in the wet season; ask locally.

CAR

It's also possible to drive to Golfito by taking the road south of Río Claro for about 10km and turning left at the Rodeo Bar, then following the road another 10km to the Río Coto Colorado ferry, which carries three vehicles (US$1 per car) and runs all day except during the lowest tides. From there, 30km of dirt roads brings you to Golfito. To get to Pavones, take a right at the first major intersection, instead of a left. A 4WD is necessary, especially in the rainy season.

TAXI

There is no regular taxi service in Zancudo, but local resident **James Morgan** (southernticotours@yahoo.com) has a sturdy vehicle and can take you where you need to go for a price. Rick and Lori at Sol y Mar can track him down for you or you can email him in advance to set up a pick-up.

PAVONES

About 15km south of Zancudo is the Bahía de Pavón, which has some of the best **surfing** on the Pacific side of Central America. The name Pavones is used locally to refer to the area comprising both Playa Río Claro de Pavones and, 5km southwest, Punta Banco.

The beach at Pavones is rockier than at Punta Banco, which is sandier and has fewer surfers. The best season is from April to October, when the waves are at their biggest and the famous long left can reportedly give a three-minute ride. (Legend has it that the wave passes so close to the Esquina del Mar Cantina that you can toss beers to surfers as they zip by.) Parents with small children will want to stick to the beaches further south, which offer lots of tranquil tidal pools for exploration. Note that the best season for surfing coincides with the rainy months, so getting here will offer an adventure of its own. A 4WD vehicle is needed year-round.

Information & Activities

Run by the helpful Candyce Speck, **Arte Nativo** (⌚ 1-5pm Mon-Sat) across from the Esquina del Mar restaurant in the 'center' on the beach sells a good selection of local art and Indian crafts. **Sea Kings** (inside Arte Nativo; seakings@racsa.co.cr) sells and rents surfboards and offers ding repairs. In addition, it can book boat tours and jungle hikes.

Daily yoga classes and karate are available at the **Shooting Star Studio** (www.yogapavones.com), which is located 400m south of the point. Check in locally about schedules.

Note that phone lines are poor and there is no bank.

Sleeping & Eating

There are several basic places to stay and eat stretched out along a few kilometers of beach.

Esquina del Mar Cantina (☎ 844 9454; per person US$6; Ⓟ) This popular, central place is quite literally the heart of Pavones. Three breezy upstairs rooms have incredible views and are clean and well maintained. There aren't any mosquito screens, so bring your own or some repellent. The owner also manages six similar, though significantly quieter, rooms across the street. All units have shared, cold-water shower. An attached **restaurant** (dishes US$3-6; ⌚ 6:30am-9pm) serves good food and a delicious fish sandwich. The bar is open until 1am on weekends, so if you're staying here, plan on staying up too.

Café de la Suerte (breakfast US$4) Across the road you'll find this new veggie restaurant offering delicacies such as guacamole sandwiches (US$3), and daily lunch specials.

Hotel Maureen (per person US$8; Ⓟ) Seven basic wood cabins here are very clean and come with fan and shared cold-water shower. Three upscale rooms with bathroom and balcony were being built at the time of research.

Cabinas Willy Willy (per person US$15; Ⓟ ❄) Around the corner and on the soccer field you'll find this place behind the *pulpería* of the same name. Three brand-new, basic concrete cabins with cold-water shower have tiled floors and air-con.

Cabinas Mira Olas (☎ 393 7742; www.miraolas.com; d/tr rustic US$28/34, d deluxe US$45, additional person US$8, child under 10 free; Ⓟ) A bad road and a steep walk up a hill gets you to this 4.5-hectare farm full of wildlife and fruit trees. Situated inland by the Río Claro, this spot also offers ample opportunities for dips in various natural pools. Two high-ceilinged cabins have a kitchen, bathroom and porch hammocks; a smaller, more rustic cabin is a little cheaper. The friendly English-speaking owners arrange horseback rides and hikes into Reserva Indígena Guaymí Conte Burica, among other excursions. This place is best reached by private car.

Casa Siempre Domingo (☎ 820 4709, 775 0932; per person incl breakfast US$25, child under 12 free; www.casa-domingo.com; Ⓟ) The most unbelievable views of the gulf are from this luxurious private home high in the hills of Pavones. Lodging is elegant and simple and the cathedral ceilings give the whole place a wonderful sense of openness. Four rooms sleep up to four people each and one sleeps five. There's also a nice family room with a TV set (but who needs that, when you've got these views!). This place is best reached by private car.

Cabinas La Ponderosa (☎ 824 4145, in the USA 954-771 9166; www.cabinaslaponderosa.com; per person US$45, with air-con US$50; Ⓟ) This is a great place to stay near the south end of the beach, just 1.5km from the point. Five clean rooms have huge screened windows, electricity, fan and hot-water bathroom (external to the room to eliminate humidity); some units have air-con. Super-helpful owners, Brian, Marshall and Angela, surf every day (they really know their stuff) and will arrange a horseback ride or fishing for a change of pace. The cabins are set on 5 hectares, with well-groomed hiking trails through primary forest. There's a comfortable dining room and lounge with table tennis, satellite TV and videos. Surfers who hang out here for weeks can request special long-stay rates.

Sotavento (☎ 3913468; www.sotaventoplantanal.com; Casa Poinsetta US$60, Casa Vista Grande US$80; P) After the soccer field and near the end of the road, you'll see signs for these two tropical hardwood, furnished houses. The rustic, open-air architecture takes advantage of the breeze and the views, and each home comes with comfy beds with mosquito nets, kitchen, electricity and even satellite TV in the cozy living room. Casa Poinsetta and the larger Casa Vista Grande are nestled in a pepper and cacao plantation and managed by personable American surfer Harry, who makes his own boards. Both homes are walking distance from the beach (though Vista Grande is perched higher on the hill and is easier to access by car). It's a great deal if you can get a pack of friends together to split costs.

Rancho Burica (www.ranchoburica.com; s/d/tr US$5/10/15, d with bathroom US$15; P) This is literally the end of the road in Punta Banco. The rustic lodge is a friendly and youthful Dutch-run outpost with various clean wood cabins with concrete floors – some of which can sleep up to 20 people. Garden showers are the rule; units with bathroom also have balcony. Activities include hiking to a nearby waterfall and *mirador*, as well as snorkeling, surfing, volleyball and horseback riding. A small kitchen serves breakfast (US$5) and dinner (US$7) and an honor bar dispenses plenty of beer and soda. Hammocks interspersed around the property offer ample opportunity for chilling out.

Camping on the beach is possible, but watch your stuff. Thefts from tents have been reported. Don't leave your camp site unattended.

Getting There & Away

You can book private water taxis at **Sea Kings** (inside Arte Nativo; seakings@racsa.co.cr) to various destinations, but plan on paying dearly for it. A boat to Puerto Jiménez will cost about US$150. No regular boat service exists.

There are two daily buses to Golfito: the first leaves at 5am and departs from the end of the road at Rancho Burica; the second leaves at 12:30pm and leaves from the Esquina del Mar Cantina. Buses from Golfito to Pavones depart at 10am and 3pm from the stop at the Muellecito.

A 4WD taxi will charge about US$50 from Golfito. You can drive here (see p373). About halfway between the ferry and Zancudo, a signed turnoff goes left to Pavones.

TISKITA JUNGLE LODGE

Only 6km south of the Esquina del Mar Cantina in Pavones and 10km from the border with Panama, Tiskita is a wonderful combination of private biological reserve and experimental fruit farm. Set on a verdant hillside, the property consists of 100 hectares of virgin forest which drops down to an idyllic 1km-long coastline, complete with tidal pools suitable for swimming. The remaining land area supports the orchard, which produces more than 100 varieties of tropical fruit from all over the world. Guests are able to sample dozens of seasonal exotic fruits, and fruit drinks are served during their visit to the lodge.

There are trails in the surrounding rain forest, which contains waterfalls and freshwater pools suitable for swimming. (Guided hikes in English are available.) The tide pools are home to a variety of marine life such as starfish, sea urchins, anemones, tunicates, crabs and many shells.

Birders will find that the combination of rain forest, fruit farm and coastline produces a long list of birds. About 300 species have been recorded here, depending on who's counting. The fruit farm is particularly attractive to frugivorous (fruit-eating) birds such as parrots and toucans, which can be more easily observed in the orchard than the rain forest. Nature trails into the forest help enthusiasts see more reticent species such as yellow-billed cotingas, fiery-billed aracaris, green honeycreepers and lattice-tailed trogons, to name a few. Monkeys, sloths, agoutis, coatis and other mammals are often seen. Of course, insects and plants abound. Ask for booklets describing the rain-forest trail, the tide pools and the land crabs, and for a butterfly list.

Run by personable conservationist (and conversationalist) Peter Aspinall, the lodge also oversees the Tiskita Foundation, which has worked to protect ridley turtle nesting sites and helped reintroduce the scarlet macaw to the area. The foundation also support education initiatives in local schools, where volunteers teach youngsters about the environment and the dangers of poaching. There are also health initiatives in the local community. Check its website for volunteer opportunities.

You can stay at the **Jungle Lodge** (☎ in San José 296 8125; www.tiskita-lodge.co.cr; s/d/tr US$145/240/315, child under 12 US$60; Ⓟ) Accommodations are in one of 16 beautiful, shiny wood rooms, all of which overlook the Pacific Ocean. Private bathrooms have hot water, stone garden shower and one unit even has a garden toilet with pretty forest views. (You won't need magazines; just binoculars.) Rooms are in eight rustic, well-maintained cabins of one to four rooms each. An informal relaxation and library area has pretty views and the dining room serves fresh, home-cooked meals. There's a hillside pool with ocean views. Daily rates include meals and guided walks through the fruit orchard and the rain forest. Various other tours are available, including chartered air trips from Tiskita to the Sirena station in Parque Nacional Corcovado (US$150 per person; two person minimum). Some body boards, snorkeling gear and horse rental are also available. Reservations are essential. Be aware that the lodge is closed from mid-September to mid-October.

It is possible to drive (4WD only), but many people opt to fly to the nearby private airstrip that's a five-minute walk from the lodge. It is also possible to get here by taking the 3pm bus from Golfito to Pavones, which passes the lodge entrance. Directions are very unwieldy, but you can find them posted on the lodge's website, or call the San José office for details.

Caribbean Coast

CONTENTS

Upon arriving at Costa Rica's Caribbean Coast, visitors come to a delicious realization – they've somehow got into two countries for the price of one. This is a different world, where the jungle meets the sea in a smooth arc of sandy beaches interrupted only by mangrove swamps and river deltas where a wealth of wildlife is rarely disturbed.

More than a quarter of the coast is officially protected, and Parque Nacional Cahuita and the Gandoca-Manzanillo refuge guard this coast's last living coral reefs. You'll need to take to scenic canals in search of Parque Nacional Tortuguero, Costa Rica's mini-Amazon, where more green turtles are born than anywhere else on earth, while more adventurous souls pull on rubber boots and hike Hitoy Cerere reserve, a mossy dreamscape that is perhaps the rainiest reserve in the system.

Which brings up one reason why this coast sees less tourism than other parts of the country: it's probably going to rain while you're here. The dry season, from February to April, is strictly theoretical, particularly north of Puerto Limón. On the upside, the sun shines year-round as well; during the Pacific coast's rainy season (August to November), the Caribbean is actually somewhat drier than usual.

The coast is home to a true melting pot of cultures: the highest concentration of Chinese Costa Ricans is found in Puerto Limón, while further south, the indigenous communities of Cocles/KéköLdi, Talamanca Cabecar and Bribrí are among the last remaining native groups in Costa Rica.

Most famously, the Caribbean Coast is home to the country's large and vibrant Afro-Caribbean population. More than one-third of the region's inhabitants still celebrate their Jamaican heritage with reggae and calypso backbeats, wild carnivals and exotically spiced seafood cooked in rich coconut milk – that by itself is worth the trip.

HIGHLIGHTS

- Observing wildlife in **Parque Nacional Tortuguero** (p392) – where there's turtles, monkeys, and birds galore!
- Surfing the gnarly 'Salsa Brava' off **Puerto Viejo de Talamanca** (p413)
- Hanging out on the white-sand beach at **Cahuita** (p408)
- Learning about and touring **indigenous reserves** with ATEC (p411)
- Supporting sloth rehabilitation and research at **Aviarios del Caribe** (p400)

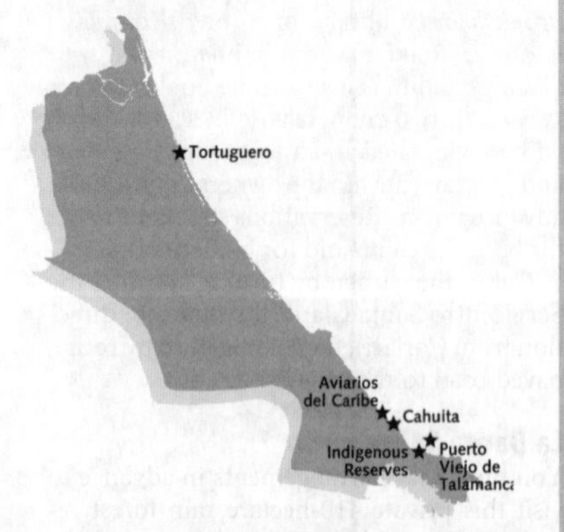

HIGHWAY 32 TO PUERTO LIMÓN

GUÁPILES & AROUND

This pretty, prosperous town in the northern foothills of the Cordillera Central is the transport center for the Río Frío banana-growing region. Some 60km northeast of San José, it's the first town of any size on the San José–Puerto Limón highway. It's a good base for visiting the Rainforest Aerial Tram (p137), 20km away, and there's a lively agricultural market on Saturday, but for the most part, there is little of interest in Guápiles itself.

Guápiles is about 1km from Highway 32. The two major streets are one-way, running parallel to each other. Most of the city's wide range of services – banks, huge grocery stores, restaurants and hotels – are located on the loop these streets make through the busy downtown. You bypass the town completely if you're headed to Limón or Cariari.

Jardín Botánico Las Cusingas

This is not a typical **botanical garden** (☎ 710 2652). The owners Jane Segleau and Ulyses Blanco emphasize education on a variety of subjects, including medicinal plants, rural Costa Rican life, conservation, the ethical use of plants for profit and other nature-related subjects, on two-hour tours (US$5), in English or Spanish. Eighty medicinal-plant species, 80 orchid species, 30 bromeliad species and more than 100 bird species have been recorded on their 20-hectare property. There are several easy trails, courses, research projects and a library, open to visitors. Jane is also a Reiki master (hands-on natural-healing) and massages can be booked.

A rustic two-room **cabin** (q US$30; P) comes with a living area and a wood-burning stove and you can eat with the owners' family, with advance notice. Reservations should be made for both the cabin and for guided tours.

Get to the garden by turning south at the Servicentro Santa Clara (the opposite direction from Cariari), then going 4km by rough paved road to the signed entrance.

La Danta Salvaje

You must make arrangements in advance to visit this private 410-hectare rain forest reserve, **La Danta Salvaje** (The Wild Tapir; ☎ 750 0012; www.greencoast.com/ladanta/ladantasalvaje.htm; 3-night package per person US$210). On the Caribbean slope at 800m above sea level, contiguous with Parque Nacional Braulio Carrillo (p136), this waterfall-packed property and jungle lodge can be reached only by a rough 4WD road, followed by a three-hour hike. Visitors must be in good physical shape.

There is no electricity, but there are flush toilets, hot showers and a fireplace. Owner David Vaughan arranges guided visits to the remote reserve about twice a month, with a four-person minimum and eight-person maximum.

Sleeping

Though basic cabinas for long-term workers are the norm, the town boasts a few nicer accommodations.

Hotel y Cabinas Wilson (☎ 710 2217; s/d US$8/12; P ❄) On the left as you enter town, this clean, basic spot has relatively well-appointed rooms, including TV and air-con.

Hotel Cabinas Lomas del Toro (☎ 710 2934; d US$9-15; P ❄) If you'd rather not brave Guápiles proper, this ramp motel right off Hwy 32 is spotless, efficient and easy to find at night.

Cabinas Irdama (☎ 710 7034/177; s/d US$10/13, apt per night/month US$19/300; P) Here you'll find 21 decent, bright rooms with cold shower. Apartments have two double beds, kitchenette and warm shower. There's an attached *soda* (basic eatery).

Cabinas Quinta (☎ 710 7016; d with fan/air-con US$32/42; P ❄) Much nicer than the average cabina, 10 large, spotless rooms with cable TV, hot shower, good beds and stocked fridge, are on the road to Cariari just as you leave Guápiles. The 19-hectare grounds have private trails, two rivers, horses and a motocross track.

Hotel Suerre (☎ 710 7551; www.suerre.com; s/d US$87/102, ste US$130-155; P ⊠ ❄) Join banana executives and other VIPs at this relatively swish spot with 50 spacious, tiled, air-conditioned but bland rooms and suites, 2km north of the Servicentro Santa Clara. It has a restaurant, Olympic-sized pool, two tennis courts, and a sauna and spa for guests.

Casa Río Blanco (☎ 382 0957; crblanco@racsa.co.cr; s/d/tr incl breakfast US$60/72/90) This small, environmentally conscious B&B and reserve is famed for its five cabins perched 20m above the Río Blanco, offering great rain-forest

CARIBBEAN COAST

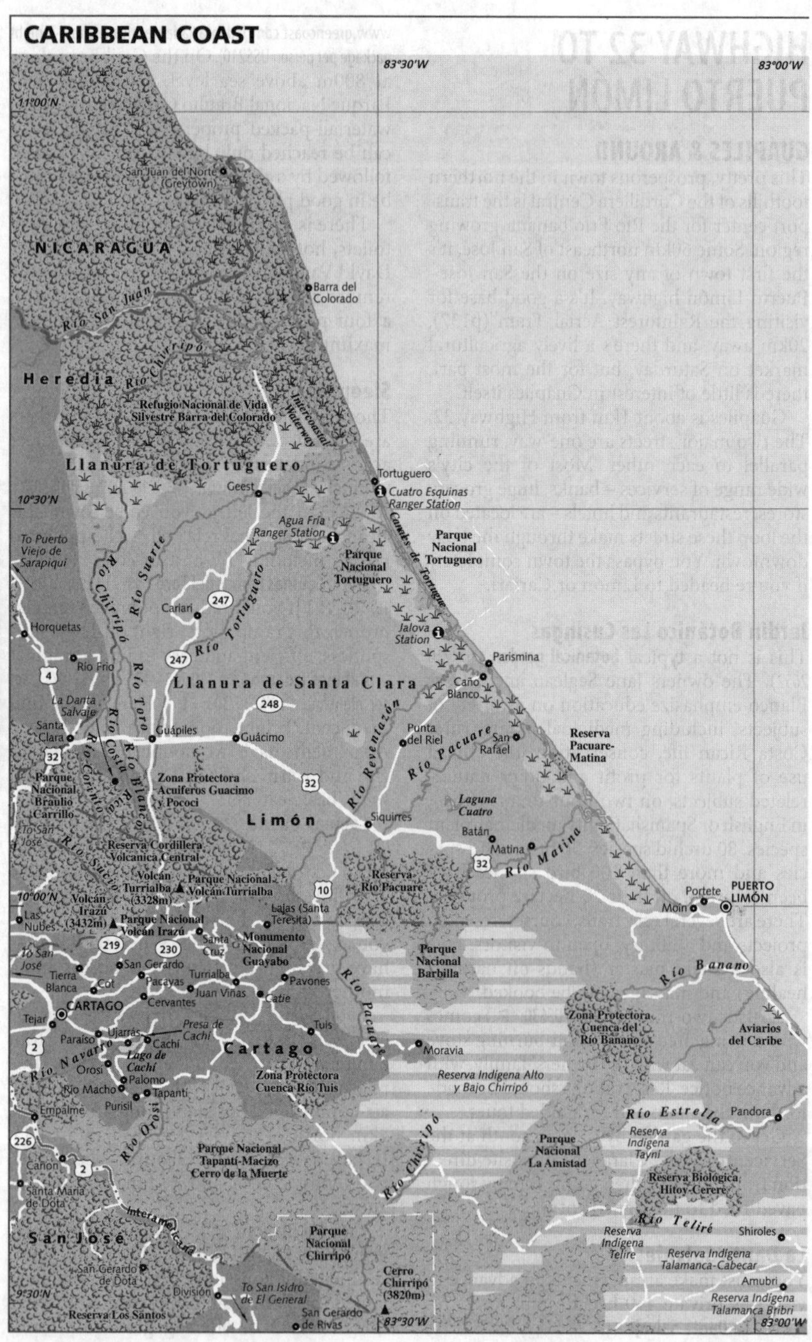

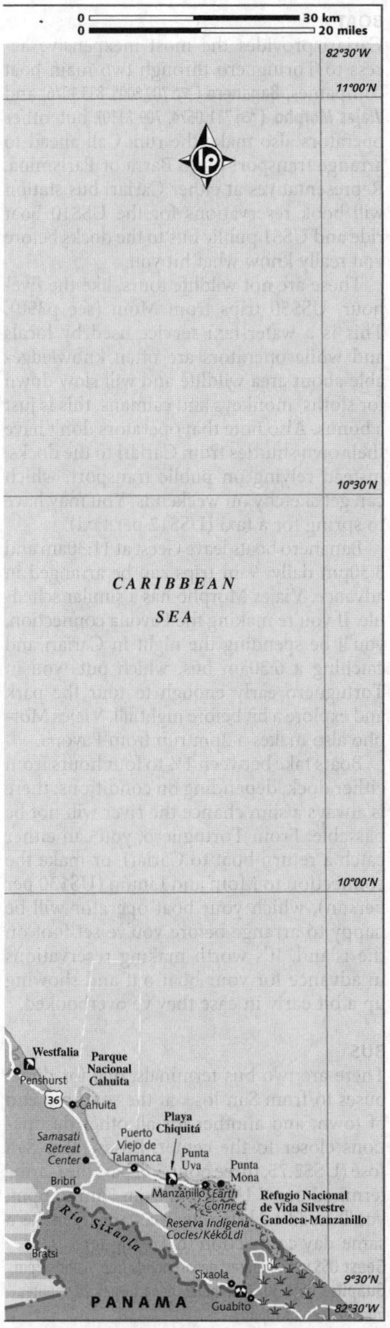

canopy views with excellent birding and other wildlife watching. Kerosene lanterns illuminate comfortably rustic interiors and there is solar electricity in the private hot-water bathrooms. Rates include guided hikes (with complimentary rubber boots) on private trails.

The turnoff to Casa Río Blanco is 5km west of Guápiles on the west side of the Río Blanco bridge. From here it's about 1.5km south to the site. Buses can drop you at **Restaurant La Ponderosa** (☎ 710 7144; mains US$3-10; 🕑 11am-midnight), 300m west of the entrance road, and next to the Ranchito de Hoss van, where you can arrange to get picked up. Enjoy *bocas* and a beer, or perhaps a steak while you wait, beneath Ben Cartwright's steady gaze.

Eating

There are an assortment of *sodas*, bakeries and fast-food joints in town, plus a huge **Más X Menos supermarket** (200m from the bus terminal; 🕑 9am-9pm).

Soda Buenos Aires (☎ 710 1768; Hwy 32; mains US$1-3; 🕑 6am-10pm) On your way out of town, stop at a top-quality *soda* with great breakfasts and brewed coffee.

Happy's Pizza (☎ 710 2434; 100m from the Catholic church; mains US$1-5; 🕑 10am) More than just pizza, this place anchors a food court with all sorts of independent fast food.

Getting There & Away

The Guapileños bus terminal is just south of downtown.

Cariari US$0.30; 20 minutes; depart every 20 minutes from 6am to 10pm.

Puerto Limón via Guácimo & Siquirres US$2; two hours; depart hourly from 6:30am to 7pm.

Puerto Viejo de Sarapiquí US$1; 45 minutes; depart every 1½ hours from 6am to 5pm.

San José US$1.50; 1¼ hours; depart every 30 minutes from 6:30am to 7pm.

CARIARI

Due north of Guápiles (the turnoff is about 1km east, at the Servicentro Santa Clara), Cariari is a blue-collar banana town, rough around the edges but with a festive feel when the sun comes out and an impromptu market springs up on the sidewalks. There's a gas station, a Banco Nacional and two bus stations, one handling traffic from San José, the second handling all other traffic, all within a few blocks of the main road.

BANANA TRAINS

Bananas, Costa Rica's most important agricultural export, used to be loaded onto steam trains and hauled to the Caribbean coast. Today, trucks have superseded trains for transporting bananas, though small sections of track remain for hauling banana cargo in the Caribbean lowlands.

The reason why most tourists cruise through is to catch a boat to Tortuguero (p382), which can usually be accomplished without spending more than a couple of hours in town. Folks who miscalculate bus schedules, however, or who want to take the early trip via Pavona, which requires catching a 6am bus, may need to spend the night.

Sleeping & Eating

Hotel Central (☎ 767 6890; r per person US$10) Conveniently located close to the bus terminals, this is your best bet in Cariari. Spotless rooms with antiseptic shared hot-water bathroom all come with cable TV, continental breakfast, balcony overlooking the street, guarded parking and a security gate. Better yet, the proprietor Patricia can store bags and cars for a fee while you're in Tortuguero, as well as make transportation and hotel reservations there, La Fortuna, Monteverde and elsewhere in the country.

There are also a few basic cabinas catering primarily to workers; ask about hourly rates.

You'll find several tempting bakeries, or you can grab Chinese food at **Restaurante Chino Fu Kong** (☎ 767 7163; mains US$3-6; 🕐 11am-9pm, bar open later) or casados at a dozen places.

Marisquería Acuario (☎ 767 7161; bocas US$1.25, seafood mains US$3-15; 🕐 9:30am-midnight) Just 100m from the San José bus terminal, this downright elegant little gem has a relaxed bar, fine *ceviche* and other great, inexpensive seafood – shrimp is the specialty.

Getting There & Away

The turnoff to the excellent paved road to Cariari is about 1km east of Guápiles, at the Servicentro Santa Clara. Drivers headed to Tortuguero can arrange to leave their cars in unguarded lots for free through the boat companies, while Hotel Central can store your car in a guarded lot for a daily fee.

BOAT

Cariari provides the most inexpensive access to Tortuguero through two main boat companies, **Bananero** (☎ 709 8005, 833 1076) and **Viajes Morpho** (☎ 711 0674, 709 8110), but other operators also make the run. Call ahead to arrange transport on to Barra or Parismina. Representatives at either Cariari bus station will book reservations for the US$10 boat ride and US$1 public bus to the docks before you really know what hit you.

These are not wildlife tours, like the five-hour, US$50 trips from Moín (see p390). This is a water-taxi service used by locals and while operators are often knowledgeable about area wildlife and will slow down for sloths, monkeys and caimans, this is just a bonus. Also note that operators don't have their own shuttles from Cariari to the docks, instead relying on public transport, which can get sketchy on weekends. You may have to spring for a taxi (US$12 per taxi).

Bananero boats leave Geest at 11:30am and 3:30pm daily; 9am trips can be arranged in advance. Viajes Morpho has a similar schedule. If you're making the Pavona connection, you'll be spending the night in Cariari and catching a 6:30am bus, which puts you in Tortuguero early enough to tour the park and explore a bit before nightfall. Viajes Morpho also makes a 2pm run from Pavona.

Boats take between 1½ to four hours from either dock, depending on conditions; there is always a slim chance the river will not be passable. From Tortuguero, you can either catch a return boat to Cariari, or make the connection to Moín and Limón (US$30 per person), which your boat operator will be happy to arrange before you've set foot on the island. It's worth making reservations in advance for your boat out and showing up a bit early in case they've overbooked.

BUS

There are two bus terminals, one for direct buses to/from San Jose, at the southern end of town, and another for all other destinations closer to the center. Buses from San José (US$2.75, three hours) depart the Caribe terminal every 1½ hours from 7am to 6pm; you'll need to leave by 10:30am to make a same-day connection to Tortuguero.

Geest US$1; 40 minutes; depart hourly from 6am to 7pm.

Guápiles US$0.30; 20 minutes; depart every 20 minutes from 6:30am to 10pm.

CARIBBEAN COAST

Pavona US$1; 45 minutes; depart hourly from 7am to 6pm.
Puerto Limón US$2.25; 2½ hour; depart 4:30am, 8:30am, noon & 3pm.
San José US$2.75; three hour; depart hourly 6:30am to 7pm.

GUÁCIMO

This small town, 12km east of Guápiles, is the home of **Escuela de Agricultura de la Región Tropical Húmeda** (Earth; ☎ 713 0000; www.earth.ac.cr). A private, not-for-profit university, it attracts students from around the world to research sustainable agriculture in the tropics. An integrated four-year program stresses ecosystems ecology, learning from actual farmers as well as accredited professors, and 'an entrepreneurial spirit'. And, true to this philosophy, it offers tours of the 3300-hectare campus, which includes various experimental plots, hectares of jungle and a plantation where researchers continue their quest for a less chemical-dependent commercial banana (see p440).

Tours and lodging are run by **Earthbirding** (www.earthbirding.org; r standard/package per person US$106/242; P ⛐ 💻 🍽), which specializes in spotting some of the 350 bird species recorded – you can go on horseback, by riverboat or as part of a guided hike. Natural history, local culture and orchid tours are also available. Package deals include transportation from San José, three buffet meals and various tours, plus pleasant rooms with hot showers and shiny wood floors that are far nicer than at other research facilities in Costa Rica.

Costa Flores (☎ 717 6439; 🕓 8am-7pm) A popular destination of the Limón cruise ship crowd is a tour of this 120-hectare tropical flower farm that claims to be the largest in the world. It is huge – 120 hectares of showy blossoms tough enough to ship to the USA, Switzerland and elsewhere, an interesting process in itself.

Hotel Restaurant Río Palmas (☎ 760 0330, 760 0305; www.hotelriopalmas; d without/with air-con US$45/50; P ⊠ ⛐ 🍽) Some 600m east of Earth, this hotel stands out with its exceptional garden and very comfortable rooms with cable TV, hot shower and other amenities. It's an excellent deal, in the middle of nowhere.

SIQUIRRES

Siquirres has served as an important transportation hub since the early 20th century, being on the old highway that connected San José with Puerto Limón via Turrialba. Highway 10, as it is known, was largely replaced in 1970 by the faster, more efficient Hwy 32 to the north – but Siquirres managed to stay on this path and retain its important status. (Though the old route is slower, it's more scenic – good for those with a little time on their hands.)

Even before the roads, Siquirres administered the most important junction in the San José–Limón railway, and not just in terms of banana tonnage (significant). The town delineated, for the first part of the 20th century, Costa Rica's western internal border that blacks were barred from crossing, without special permission (see p29). Until the constitution of 1949 outlawed racial discrimination, black conductors and engineers would change places with their Spanish counterparts here, then head back into Limón Province.

Today, Siquirres still seems to mark the moment when Costa Rica proper takes a dip into the Caribbean – and it's not just the food, either. The lack of infrastructure to the east of Siquirres is subtle, but you'll certainly notice when you're charged twice as much for painfully slow Internet access, then spend half a day locating an ATM to pay for it. Oh, and this is also the most easterly point where it's considered 'safe' for tourists to drink the tap water.

Siquirres is the last major town on the main highway before Puerto Limón, 58km further east. Most travelers go straight through or maybe stop at the small but bustling center, where there are a few interesting-looking buildings (look out for the round church) and a few cheap and basic hotels. This is also the major access point for the Ríos Reventazón and Pacuare (p149), but it's generally easier to make arrangements for white-water rafting trips in Turrialba (p144) and elsewhere.

PUERTO LIMÓN

This is the great city of Costa Rica's Caribbean Coast, birthplace of United Fruit and capital of Limón Province. It's in so many ways still removed from San José's sphere of influence. Around here, business is measured by the truckload of bananas, not busload of tourists, so don't expect much pampering. Cruise ships do deposit passengers here almost daily from October through May and observers can only hope that they weren't expecting to spot a quetzal.

Most travelers simply pass through on their way to more user-friendly destinations, as this hard-working port city certainly doesn't float everyone's boat. But if you're one of those rare people inclined to a little urban exploration, Limón, as locals call it, is an interesting place. Sloths in the trees (allegedly) and a growing music scene help offset the peeling paint and creative scam artists, while the dilapidated 'charm' (to be charitable) is giving way to more modern growth as federal funds are slowly invested in this side of the country.

Some urban renewal programs have already been implemented, such as extending the pedestrian mall from the market to the sea wall, with more improvements scheduled for when somebody gets around to them. But Limón, both port and province, have a long and difficult history of complications with the capital, and locals don't expect their city to get a full federally funded face-lift anytime soon. (This might not seem such a bad thing for visitors who need a break from the zip-line economy anyway.)

History

Although Christopher Columbus first dropped anchor in Costa Rica at Isla Uvita (p387) in 1502 (for only 17 days), Spanish settlement really began on the Pacific coast. This left Atlantic beaches and indigenous towns sheltered from the incursion by the almost impassable Cordilleras Central and Talamanca. The most frequent visitors until the 1850s were pirates, who used Limón's natural deep-water port as a hideout.

With coffee production soaring in the Central Valley, however, the small port on the Río Sarapiquí, the historical link between the plantations and Atlantic, was experiencing a pricey shipping bottleneck. A plan was hatched to build a major port right on the Caribbean, with an ambitious railroad connecting the highlands to the sea. In 1867 Limón was chosen as the site, only accessible through some 150 unexplored kilometers of dense jungles, malaria-ridden swamps and steep, muddy mountainsides. To the Costa Rican government, that looked like a job for subcontractors.

New York–born railway scion Minor C Keith (p24) got the bid, which eventually came to include 300,000 hectares of land – some 7% of the country – to sweeten the deal. The work was obscenely dangerous: thousands, including Keith's two brothers, died during the nine years it took to lay the first 110km of track. Locals stopped applying for jobs early on, which forced the company to come up with creative staffing solutions.

Convicts from the USA and indentured servants from China suffered mortality rates approaching 90%, malaria being the worst culprit. Eventually, Keith began bringing in recently freed and unemployed slaves from Jamaica, which seemed to work out. The railroad nevertheless went way over budget, so Keith had begun to grow banana trees along the tracks as a cheap food source for his workers.

The railroad's completion was no end to Keith's financial woes; coffee and passengers simply couldn't fill all the cars. In 1878 he packed the empties with conveniently located bananas, which he sent to New Orleans as part of a desperate experiment. They were a hit and by 1900 bananas had eclipsed coffee as Costa Rica's most lucrative export. By the time Keith consolidated the thriving company as United Fruit in 1909, he was not only a gazillionaire, but the most influential man in Central America.

American businesspeople intent on a piece of the 'banana republic' preferred an English-speaking workforce and continued hiring Jamaicans (by this time full British citizens with education and skills) for every aspect of the rapidly expanding banana economy. United Fruit slyly exploited racial tensions between Costa Rican and immigrant workers by implementing a two-tiered pay schedule, with blacks making slightly more. The friction that resulted successfully undermined any attempts to unionize, which kept costs low. This clever strategy has also left a legacy of racial problems that the country continues to struggle with today.

Pressured by Spanish-speaking Ticos to act, San José began handing down increasingly strict visa regulations, which eventually restricted everyone of Afro-Caribbean ancestry to Limón Province; even a quick vacation required difficult-to-secure permissions. In 1913 when a banana blight known as 'Panama disease' shut down many Caribbean fincas, most banana jobs moved to the Pacific coast – where black workers

ERIC L WHEATER

Children on a verandah, Puerto Limón (p383)

Boys playing football, Puerto Limón (p383)

ERIC L WHEATER

Picture-postcard beach, Puerto Limón area (p383)

PATRICK HORTON

LUKE HUNTER

Observing wildlife in the canopy, Parque Nacional Tortuguero (p392)

LUKE HUNTER

Yellow-crowned night-heron *(Nyctanassa violacea)*, Parque Nacional Tortuguero (p392)

Transport along the canals, Parque Nacional Tortuguero (p392)

ROB RACHOWIEC

were forbidden to follow. Stranded and unemployed in the least-developed part of the country, many turned to subsistence farming, fishing or work on cocoa plantations. Others joined the communist party.

Under the name 'Workers and Peasants Bloc,' disillusioned former employees of United Fruit joined communists throughout Latin America organizing a series of often bloody strikes against the company. The movement culminated in Puerto Limón in August 1934 with the largest protest in Costa Rica's history.

Thousands staged a general strike: the docks shut down, federal troops were called in, shots were fired and negotiations held. In a victory duplicated nowhere else in Central America, United Fruit capitulated, forgiving debts to the company store and promising to improve worker conditions. Blacks were not given the freedom to travel or work outside the province, however, and in 1940, the communist party was instrumental in ousting President León Cortés Castro, who had made his fortune in bananas and railroads.

Limón later provided key support to José Figueres during the 40-day civil war of 1948 and afterward the new president actually lived up to his promises of equality under the law. The 1949 constitution allowed blacks to work and travel freely throughout Costa Rica, though most have chosen to remain here, along the Caribbean.

Although the official boundary at Siquirres (see p383) has been erased, Limón Province remains the poorest in the nation, though its vast cultural wealth is helping change all that as more tourists discover the Caribbean's charms. *What Happen: A Folk-History of Costa Rica's Talamanca Coast* and *Wa'apin man: la historia de la costa talamanqueña de Costa Rica, según sus protagonistas,* by Paula Palmer, are both excellent oral histories of the region.

Orientation

Streets are poorly marked and most do not have signs (see p453). Calles and avenidas go up one number at a time (Calle 1, Calle 2, etc) instead of going up in twos, as they do in most other towns. This system hasn't really caught on and locals can give you better directions using city landmarks such as the market, old Radio Casino and Parque Vargas.

Avenida 2 begins as the pedestrian mall, stretching from the sea wall past Parque Vargas to the market, where it becomes one of the city's main streets. Several banks, bars, restaurants and hotels are within a few blocks, as is the main bus terminal.

Information

There is no tourist office. For information on tours, ask at better hotels or in the souvenir shops fronting Parque Vargas. Between October and May, you can find enterprising young men near the cruise ship terminal, who offer a variety of tours for widely varying prices.

INTERNET ACCESS

Internet Café (☎ 798 0128; per hr US$1; 🕑 8am-7pm) is conveniently located upstairs at Terminal Caribeño; you can get high on bus fumes while using one of five fairly fast computers.

MEDICAL SERVICES

Hospital Tony Facio (☎ 758 2222), on the coast at the northern end of town, serves the entire province. **Centro Médico Monterrey** (☎ 798 1723, emergency 297 1010), with several private doctors, is opposite the cathedral.

MONEY

Banks are a rarity in other parts of the Caribbean Coast, so whether you're headed north or south, stock up here on as many colones as you think you're going to need. There are several banks, but **Scotiabank** (☎ 798 0009; cnr Av 3 & Calle 2; 🕑 8:30am-4:30pm Mon-Fri & 8:30am-3:30pm Sat) is tops. It exchanges cash and traveler's checks and has a 24-hour ATM on the Plus and Cirrus systems that dispenses US dollars. **Banco de Costa Rica** (☎ 758 3166; cnr Av 2 & Calle 1) also exchanges cash US dollars.

Dangers & Annoyances

Limón is what you'd call gritty: take precautions against pickpockets during the day, particularly in the market. People do get mugged here, so stick to well-lit main streets at night, avoiding the sea wall and Parque Vargas. Park in a guarded lot after dark and remove anything even remotely tempting from the car, as vehicle break-ins are common.

Women traveling solo probably won't feel comfortable walking around after dark, so consider getting a room with TV. This is one

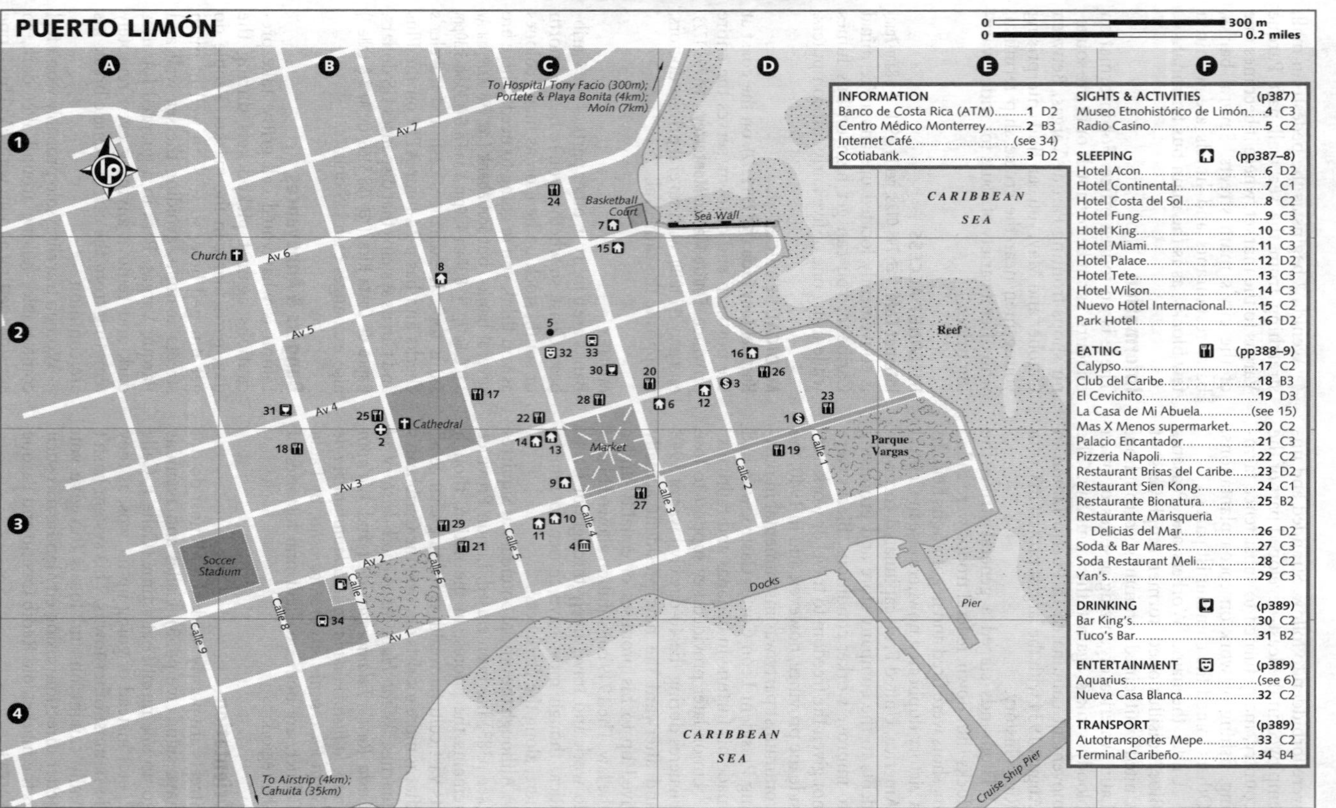
PUERTO LIMÓN
0 300 m
0 0.2 miles
INFORMATION
Banco de Costa Rica (ATM) 1 D2
Centro Médico Monterrey 2 B3
Internet Café (see 34)
Scotiabank 3 D2
SIGHTS & ACTIVITIES (p387)
Museo Etnohistórico de Limón 4 C3
Radio Casino 5 C2
SLEEPING (pp387–8)
Hotel Acon 6 D2
Hotel Continental 7 C1
Hotel Costa del Sol 8 C2
Hotel Fung 9 C3
Hotel King 10 C3
Hotel Miami 11 C3
Hotel Palace 12 D2
Hotel Tete 13 C3
Hotel Wilson 14 C3
Nuevo Hotel Internacional 15 C2
Park Hotel 16 D2
EATING (pp388–9)
Calypso 17 C2
Club del Caribe 18 B3
El Cevichito 19 D3
La Casa de Mi Abuela (see 15)
Mas X Menos supermarket 20 C2
Palacio Encantador 21 C3
Pizzeria Napoli 22 C2
Restaurant Brisas del Caribe 23 D2
Restaurant Sien Kong 24 C1
Restaurante Bionatura 25 B2
Restaurante Marisqueria Delicias del Mar 26 D2
Soda & Bar Mares 27 C3
Soda Restaurant Meli 28 C2
Yan's 29 C3
DRINKING (p389)
Bar King's 30 C2
Tuco's Bar 31 B2
ENTERTAINMENT (p389)
Aquarius (see 6)
Nueva Casa Blanca 32 C2
TRANSPORT (p389)
Autotransportes Mepe 33 C2
Terminal Caribeño 34 B4
CARIBBEAN SEA
CARIBBEAN SEA
Reef
Parque Vargas
Pier
Cruise Ship Pier
Docks
Sea Wall
Basketball Court
Market
Cathedral
Church
Soccer Stadium
To Hospital Tony Facio (300m); Portete & Playa Bonita (4km); Moín (7km)
To Airstrip (4km); Cahuita (35km)
Calle 1
Calle 2
Calle 3
Calle 4
Calle 5
Calle 6
Calle 7
Calle 8
Calle 9
Av 1
Av 2
Av 3
Av 4
Av 5
Av 6
Av 7

town where it's worth paying a little more for a hotel that doesn't offer hourly rates.

Sights & Activities

The city's main attraction is the waterfront **Parque Vargas**, an incongruous expanse of bench-lined sidewalks beneath a lost little jungle of tall palms and tropical flowers, centered on an appealingly decrepit bandstand. Its claim to fame is a contingent of sloths hanging out in the trees; if you can't find one, children will happily point one out for about 100 colones; a good deal considering entry fees to the parks. Other wildlife attracted to this shady oasis include migrating birds, colorful butterflies, morose teens, stressed-out office workers and passed-out drunks.

From here, you can head inland along the **pedestrian mall**, along Avenida 2, where shops still sell more tools and maternity clothing than souvenirs. A few vendors also set up here; keep an eye out for folks selling home-burned CDs by local bands – Limón is getting a reputation for its growing hip-hop and Latin-reggae fusion scenes. You'll end up at the colorful **mercado central**, which has a variety of *sodas* (cheap eateries) and plenty of bustling activity. Two blocks away, the **Museo Etnohistórico de Limón** (Calle 4 btwn Avs 1 & 2; entry free), on the 2nd floor of the post office, was closed for renovations at press time, but considering that past shows have included area artifacts of Afro-Caribbean culture and paintings by renowned Costa Rican artists, this small museum is worth checking out if it's re-opened.

From the park, it's a pleasant walk north along the **sea wall**, where views of the rocky headland are set to a steady baseline of waves from the Caribbean crashing against the concrete. After dark, it's a popular mugging and make-out spot.

Although there are no beaches for swimming or surfing in Limón, **Playa Bonita** (see p389), 4km northwest of town, has a sandy beach. Serious surfers and adventurers can hire a boat for the 20-minute, 1km trip to **Isla Uvita**, a largely undeveloped destination with good birding and heavy waves.

Festivals & Events

Limón's big claim to fame is **El Día de la Raza** (October 12). Also known as Columbus Day, it is celebrated here with more than the usual enthusiasm because of Columbus' historic landing on Isla Uvita. Thousands of mainly Tico visitors stream into town for a carnival of colorful street parades and dancing, music, singing, drinking and some general carrying-on that lasts four or five days. Book your hotel in advance.

Festival Flores de la Diáspora Africana is a celebration of Afro-Caribbean culture held in late August. While it is centered in Puerto Limón, the festival sponsors events throughout the province and San José showcasing African heritage in Costa Rica and throughout the world. Guests, including the Harlem Ballet and the Steel Band of Trinidad and Tobago, join local artists and musicians for a serious party, with parades, dances and, yes, cricket matches, something the British Ambassador won't miss.

Sleeping

Hotels all along the Caribbean coast are in demand on weekends and vacations, when prices rise. Reserve ahead if possible during those periods.

BUDGET

There are lots of cheap hotels in Limón, generally designed with migrant workers in mind and sometimes used by prostitutes and their clients, which, while not generally dangerous, can make for a restless night. Those listed here are on the more wholesome end of the spectrum, but ask to see a room and check security.

Hotel Palace (☎ 798 2604; Calle 2 btwn Avs 2 & 3; s/d US$11/17) On the 2nd floor of what once must have been a beautiful building, this woman-owned spot has somewhat frayed but freshly painted quarters with cold private shower and good security; ask for a room on the balcony. A 'student dorm' with five single beds is available to groups for US$7 per person.

Hotel King (☎ 758 1033; Av 2 btwn Calles 4 & 5; s/d US$4/8, with bathroom US$8/10) Conveniently located 250m from the bus station, dark but clean rooms that are quieter toward the back are a good budget choice.

Hotel Fung (☎ 758 3309; Calle 4, opposite market; s/d US$4/8, with bathroom US$7/11) Basic rooms with paint-peeled walls are clean enough for the seasoned budget traveler, but it's definitely worth the extra cash for a private shower.

Hotel Costa del Sol (☎ 798 0707; cnr Calle 5 & Av 5; per person without/with bathroom US$4/5; Ⓟ ❄) A

CARIBBEAN COAST

fair budget alternative, this place takes credit cards for small rooms with fan; women will probably want the one with a bathroom.

Hotel Wilson (☎ 758 5028; Av 3 btwn Calles 4 & 5; s/d US$9/13, d with air-con US$18;) Friendly management and small, neat rooms all with warm-water bathroom, and there's a TV lounge out front, which could be a good or bad thing.

Nuevo Hotel Internacional (☎ 798 0545, 798 7532; Av 5 btwn Calles 2 & 3; s/d with fan US$7/11, with air-con US$10/15; P) Reasonably clean rooms with paper-thin walls all have private hot shower, but only some have windows, so ask. The same family runs **Hotel Continental** (across the street) with the same prices for slightly less comfortable accommodations (except for rooms 26 and 27, which have excellent balcony windows).

MID-RANGE

Limón proper offers nothing remotely upscale, although these spots should suffice at a pinch. The really nice hotels are located north of town (p389) on the road to Moín, closer to the area's prettiest stretch of beach.

Hotel Miami (☎ 758 0490; Av 2 btwn Calles 4 & 5; s/d US$19/28;) Perhaps the most comfortable and secure option in Limón, this fine spot has spacious, attractively lit pink rooms with cable TV and industrial-strength fans.

Hotel Tete (☎ 758 1122; Av 3 btwn Calles 4 & 5; s/d with fan US$12/20, with air-con US$20/26; P) Nicer inside than out, clean and pleasant rooms come with amenities like hot water and cold air.

Hotel Acon (☎ 758 1010; Av 3 btwn Calles 2 & 3; s/d US$25/30; P) Rooms are large and fairly clean, with air-con, TV and phone. The real draw, however, is the popular dance club on the 2nd floor (see Entertainment, opposite), where you can drink to your heart's content as your room is just meters away.

Park Hotel (☎ 798 0555, 758 3476; Av 3 btwn Calles 1 & 2; d US$40; P) This is downtown Limón's best stab at upscale, where clean but plain rooms with high ceilings come with TV, air-con, guarded parking and private hot-water bathroom. Spacious rooms with sea views and little balconies cost US$5 more.

Eating

A budget traveler's best bet is the **mercado central** (6am-8pm Mon-Sat), with several *sodas* and plenty of groceries. There's also a big **Más X Menos** (8am-9pm) across the avenue. Puerto Limón is well known for its Chinese cuisine, so don't skip the chop suey.

Calypso (Calle 5 btwn Avs 3 & 4; mains US$1-3; 10am-7pm Mon-Sat) Attached to the hair salon of the same name, this place offers a 'plate of the day' (think seafood stew or Caribbean-style chicken with rice) for less than US$2 and yummy empanadas for US$0.50.

Soda Restaurant Meli (Av 3 btwn Calles 3 & 4; meals US$2-4) On the north side of the market, this cheap, popular establishment dishes out loads of fried rice and casados.

Yan's (Av 2 btwn Calles 5 & 6; mains US$1-5; 11am-11:30pm) Limón's answer to fast food, the formica tables and big-screen TV go best with burgers or rice dishes.

Club del Caribe (Calle 7 btwn Avs 3 & 4; mains US$3-6) Next to a pool hall, this homey eatery is chock-full of Creole flavor. A bowl of cow's foot soup and a cold beer can be had for US$3.

La Casa de Mi Abuela (mains US$3-7; 11am-11pm), a Chinese restaurant, is downstairs at Nuevo Hotel Internacional (see earlier).

Restaurante Bionatura (Calle 6 btwn Avs 3 & 4; mains US$2-5; 8am-8pm Mon-Sat) In a town where everything seems deep-fried, this new entry stands out with its focus on healthy vegetarian cuisine, from fresh fruit salads to veggie burgers and 'bistek de soya' casados. There's a health-food store next door.

Restaurante Marisquería Delicias del Mar (Av 3 btwn Calles 1 & 2; mains US$3-7; 7am-8pm) A step above your average *soda*, this spot specializes in *ceviche* and shrimp soup.

Restaurant Brisas del Caribe (mains US$3-5; 7am-11pm Mon-Fri, 10am-11pm Sat & Sun) The best view in town isn't over the waves: right by the park, outdoor tables make for excellent people-watching over big plates of basic food from the very long menu. There's also a buffet.

Pizzería Napoli (☎ 758 3371; Av 3 btwn Calles 4 & 5; mains US$3-6; large pizza US$10; 10am-11pm) Upstairs at the Plaza Caribe, this place caters to students and budget travelers with large portions of good pizza and pasta.

El Cevichito (Av 2 btwn Calles 1 & 2; mains US$4) The outdoor patio attracts local customs agents, who gather here to guzzle beer, discuss soccer and devour tasty garlic fish.

Soda & Bar Mares (Av 2 btwn Calles 3 & 4; dishes US$3-7; 9am-3am) One of those places where you might find Indiana Jones making contact with a seedy antiquities dealer, this place does stiff drinks, good *bocas* and suspect Chinese food and casados.

Palacio Encantador (Av 2 btwn Calles 5 & 6; mains US$3-9; 11am-11pm) This recommended spot for quality Chinese cuisine is about two blocks from the market.

Restaurant Sien Kong (cnr Av 6 & Calle 3; dishes US$5-10; 11am-10pm) Further from the center, this place is worth the walk for some of the best Chinese food in town.

Drinking & Entertainment

No one in Limón need ever go thirsty, considering the wide selection of bars. Those by Parque Vargas and a few blocks west are popular hangouts for a variety of coastal characters: sailors, ladies of the night, entrepreneurs, boozers, losers and the casually curious. The standard warnings for solo women travelers go double here and this is a lousy town for getting blotto drunk – keep your wits about you.

Somewhat tamer entries include **Soda & Bar Mares** (see Eating, opposite) that has a sizeable contingent of foreigners and a few blocks away, **Tuco's Bar**, a cozy place with good *bocas* and cheap beer. **Bar King's** (Calle 3 btwn Avs 3 & 4) has a distinctly Latin flavor and attracts a few local women.

Nueva Casa Blanca (cnr Calle 4 & Ave 4) is packed from about 5pm on with a primarily male clientele who listen to loud reggae, sometimes played by live bands on weekends. Aquarius is the hottest disco in town, with salsa, reggae and pop spinning on different nights.

Getting There & Away

Puerto Limón is the transportation hub of the Caribbean coast.

AIR

The airstrip is about 4km south of town; a taxi costs about US$4 to the bus terminals and US$10 to Moín. **NatureAir** (☎ 220 3054; www.natureair.com; one way/round trip US$66/110) can drop you in Limón on its San José–Tortuguero run.

BOAT

Cruise ships occasionally dock in Limón, but most boats providing transportation use the major port at Moín, about 7km west of Limón. For information on boats to Tortuguero, see p390.

BUS

Buses to and from San José, Moín, Guápiles and Siquirres arrive at **Terminal Caribeño** (Av 2 btwn Calles 7 & 8) on the west side, walking distance from hotels. Buses to points south all depart from **Autotransportes Mepe** (Mepe; Av 4 btwn Calles 2 & 4).

Bribrí & Sixaola (Mepe) US$2.25; three hours; 10 buses daily.

Cahuita (Mepe) US$1; 1½ hours; depart hourly from 5am to 5pm.

Guápiles (Empresarios Guapileños; Terminal Caribeño) US$2; two hours; depart hourly 6:30am to 7pm.

Manzanillo (Mepe) US$2.50; 2½ hours; depart 6am, 2:30pm & 6pm.

Moín, for boats to Tortuguero (Tracasa; Terminal Caribeño) US$0.25; 20 minutes; depart hourly 5:30am to 6:30pm.

Puerto Viejo de Talamanca (Mepe) US$2; two hours; depart hourly 5am to 5pm.

San José (Autotransportes Caribeños; Terminal Caribeño) US$3.25; three hours; depart every 30 minutes from 5:30am to 7pm.

Siquirres (Empresarios Guapileños; Terminal Caribeño) US$2; two hours; depart hourly from 6:30am to 7pm.

CAR

If you are driving, note that south of Limón there is only one gas station on the coast, at the crossroads just north of Cahuita.

AROUND PUERTO LIMÓN

Portete & Playa Bonita

While not the finest beaches in the Caribbean, Portete and Playa Bonita both offer sandy stretches of seashore and good swimming convenient to Limón. Bonita has decent waves and a picnic area, made lovely by the backdrop of tropical scenery. The city's best hotels are close by and most can arrange trips to attractions along the coast.

SLEEPING & EATING

The road between Limón proper and Moín is home to its prime accommodations. You're fairly far from town, which most folks consider a perk. Limón–Moín buses will drop you at your hotel.

Cabinas Cocori (☎ 758 2930; s/d US$34/44; P) About 4km out of Limón and 2.5km from the Moín dock, these cute, clean cabinas, complete with kitchenette, air-con and fridge are the best deal on the beach.

Hotel Matama (☎ 795 1123, 759 1409; www.matama.com; d without/with air-con $46/55; P) Across the road, this place is a little further

CARIBBEAN COAST

from the beach but has a pool and Jacuzzi set in colorful tropical gardens to make up for it. Some of the hot-water bathrooms are miniature jungle gardens; some rooms have kitchenette. Breakfast is included.

Hotel Maribú Caribe (☎ 758 4010/543; www.costaricabureau.com/maribu.htm; s/d incl breakfast US$74/85; P ✂ ☻) About 3km northwest of Puerto Limón, several comfortable, air-con bungalows arranged atop a small hill catch ocean breezes and enjoy good views, as does the Afro-Caribbean restaurant. There's a pool with an outdoor bar.

Cabinas Maeva (☎ 758 2024; moyso@racsa.co.cr; s/d US$17/28) Just east of the Maribu Caribe these pleasant, quiet cabins have unheated showers. There's a restaurant on the premises.

Springfield Restaurant (☎ 758 1203; mains US$4-9) One of Limón's more renowned culinary experiences, this beachside spot serves quality rice and beans and seafood dishes to a packed house in the evenings.

Moín

The reason you're here is probably to catch a boat through the canals to Parque Nacional Tortuguero, and perhaps on to Refugio Nacional de Fauna Silvestre Barra del Colorado. There have always been a series of natural waterways north of Limón as far as Barra del Colorado, but they could only be used during the rainy season, and even then could often be used only by small canoes, dangerous when crossing the straits. In 1974, canals linking the system were completed, eliminating the need for boats to go out to sea when traveling north from Moín.

When canals north of Moín are blocked by water hyacinths or logjams, the route might be temporarily closed.

TOURS

If you'd like a closer look at the region's copious collection of wildlife (recommen-ded!), scores of tour agencies throughout Costa Rica offer five-hour guided canal tours (around US$60/90 per person, one-way/round trip) en route to Tortuguero, including a naturalist guide, lunch and perhaps transportation from San José. Tours usually take place on the Moín to Tortuguero leg of the trip; make reservations in advance if you'd like a guide in the other direction. Independent captains at the docks can usually provide similar guide service, with a personal touch.

These trips often come as part of a package tour that includes lodging, meals, turtle-watching (in season) and/or a guided boat trek through the national park. **Riverboat Francesca Nature Tours** (☎ 226 0986; www.tortuguerocanals.com) has been highly recommended; packages that include lodging, meals and guided tours of the park start at US$185 per person. See p395 for other tour agencies.

GETTING THERE & AWAY

Boat

This is the main departure point for boats to Tortuguero, and transportation can also be arranged from here to Parismina and Barra de Colorado, with connecting boats to destinations throughout the Caribbean coast and northern lowlands during rainy season. Several companies and independent operators offer service to Tortuguero, which falls into two general categories. One category, tours, are described above.

Water taxi service, is offered by **Bananero** (☎ 709 8005; 833 1076) and **Viajes Morpho** (☎ 711 0674; 709 8110), as well as several independent captains who are easily contracted at the docks (get there early), and basically costs US$30 per person for a two-hour straight shot through the canals. Operators usually can't resist pulling over for the perfect photo-op, wildlife permitting, but that's just a tip-worthy extra.

You can get to Tortuguero more cheaply from Cariari (p381), or arrange a transfer to Cariari from Tortuguero when you arrive. Most package tours offer a standard round-trip service, but should be able to send you on to Cariari instead, if you wish.

Please keep in mind that this isn't a Disneyland ride. Particularly after a hard rain, boats can flip when skirting the powerful river mouths; tourists have been known to drown, something that can happen no matter how much you paid for the trip. Make sure your boat has life jackets and wear one. No joke. (See p469 for more on this.)

Bus & Car

Tracasa buses from Puerto Limón (US$0.25, 20 minutes) depart the Terminal Caribeño hourly from 5:30am to 6:30pm. You can park your car in the unsecured lot at the Moín dock overnight, but it's worth the small fee charged by area hotels to use their guarded lots.

NORTHERN CARIBBEAN

PARISMINA

At the mouth of the Río Parismina, accessible only by a specially arranged boat or water taxi, lies a village that serious anglers spend years saving up to stay at: Parismina, about as remote as it gets in Costa Rica, and where wildlife abounds – in particular, record-breaking Atlantic tarpon and snook.

Top tarpon season is from January to mid-May, while big snook are caught from September to November. However, all the locals will tell you that the fishing is good any month of the year because these fish don't migrate. There's also an offshore reef where folks looking for a change of bait can hook up something different and your fabulous lodge will certainly offer other options.

Most visitors come here on expensive, all-inclusive fishing retreats with optional eco-trips to Tortuguero for bored spouses. But there are several intriguing budget options, which may be reserved in advance during turtle season. Though not as famed (or as crowded) as the beaches of Tortuguero, Parismina is the preferred breeding ground of hundreds of discriminating leatherback, green and hawksbill turtles.

A locally grown conservation group, **Asociación Salvemos Las Tortugas de Parismina** (Save the Turtles of Parismina; ☎ 390 9963; www.costaricaturtles.com), working with the Costa Rica Coast Guard, has built a guarded turtle hatchery to deter increasing numbers of poachers and egg thieves. You can volunteer as a turtle guard for US$130 a week, including a homestay with a local family and all meals; US$200 per week with Spanish lessons; and a little more with Latin dance lessons and/or guided tours. It also arranges inexpensive accommodations for other visitors.

Sleeping & Eating

Even the expensive lodges are pretty rustic.

Alex Periera (camping per person without/with kitchen use US$2/3, cabina per person US$5) Alex at the hardware store offers sheltered tent sites with access to showers, bathrooms and a kitchen for a small charge, as well as simple cabinas.

Asociación Salvemos Las Tortugas de Parismina (☎ 390 9963; www.costaricaturtles.com; s/d US$20/30) Although volunteers get first choice of accommodations, this organization can arrange homestays, including three meals, with a local family for anyone.

Iguana Verde (☎ 393 5481; per person US$10) Three clean rooms with private bathroom are fronted by a popular bakery and coffee shop that serves sandwiches and other light meals. It's also the general store, rents kayaks and can organize guided hikes in English or Spanish.

Cariblanco Lodge & Doña Esther's Cantina (☎ 393 5481; d US$20) Ten clean rooms with private bathrooms come in various configurations and you can admire the ocean from the on-site Caribbean restaurant and bar. There's sometimes live music.

La Rosa Espinoza (☎ 390 9963, 710 1479; elizabetpark@hotmail.com; r per person US$12) With pretty gardens and a white picket fence, this place gives you a lot of charm for your colón, as well as private bathrooms and family-style meals for an additional charge. The owners can also arrange fishing tours.

Jungle Tarpon Lodge (☎ 380 7636, in the USA 800-544 2261; www.jungletarpon.com; per person 3-day US$1200-2000, 7-day US$2400-3000) Plush cabanas with hardwood accents make this a pleasant base for a variety of outings, most involving tarpon, though offshore boats are provided for folks who prefer snapper or tuna. Eco-tours are also offered as part of a variety of packages, all of which include meals and transportation from San José.

Caribbean Expedition Lodge (232 8118, in the USA 361-884 4277; www.costaricasportfishing.com; r per person 5/7 day US$1345/1745) Six very comfortably rustic cabins are designed to keep anglers happy between quests for huge tarpon. A variety of guided tours, including visits to a local banana plantation, are offered.

Río Parismina Lodge (☎ 229 7597, in the USA 800-338 5688, 210-824 4442; www.riop.com; s/d 3-day US$2050/3700, 7-day US$3350/6200; ⊠ ⊡) Everything is included at this comfy fishing lodge, where reduced rates and nature tours are available for nonfishers humoring lucky companions in their scaly version of paradise. Private trails lead through 20 hectares of jungle and there's a pool, Jacuzzi and, of course, great seafood at the restaurant. Absolutely everything is provided in the lodge's all-inclusive fishing packages (except tips for fishing guides and lodge staff), which include a night in a 1st-class San José hotel at either end of your lodge stay, plus air or land transfers from San José.

Getting There & Away

Parismina is only accessible by boat. You can arrange boats from Moín, Cariari or Tortuguero, but the only regular service is through Caño Blanco, via Siquirres. From San José, Líneas Nuevo Atlántico departs for Siquirres from the Caribe Terminal almost hourly from 6:30am to 6pm. You arrive at the new bus terminal which is two blocks from the old one, where the **Caño-Aguilar bus** (☎ 768 8172) departs at 5am and 12:30pm Monday through Friday, 6am and 2pm Saturday and Sunday, schedule subject to change (US$1, two hours). Taxis make the run for US$40.

The tiny outpost of Caño Blanco has one *soda* and no other services, so be sure to get there before 6pm, when the last boat (US$2.50, 15 minutes) departs to Parismina. It's much easier to arrange transportation from Parismina to Tortuguero and other destinations than the other way around.

PARQUE NACIONAL TORTUGUERO

This 31,187-hectare coastal park (plus about 52,000 hectares of marine area) is the most important breeding ground for the green sea turtle (*Chelonia mydas*) in all of the Caribbean. There are eight species of marine turtles in the world; six nest in Costa Rica and of those, four lay their eggs right here in Tortuguero.

These black-sand hatching grounds also gave birth to the sea turtle conservation movement: the Caribbean Conservation Corporation (p394). The first program of its kind in the world, it has continuously monitored turtle populations here since 1955. Today, green sea turtles are increasing in numbers along this coast, but both the leatherback and hawksbill turtles are in decline.

Parque Nacional Tortuguero, despite being such a popular ecotourism destination, is being encroached upon by squatters, loggers, plantations and even some tourist developments. An illegal road bulldozed by such interests now connects the region, officially accessible only by boat, to the highway system. Only a narrow swath of jungle along some of the canal banks hides this development from tourists on their scenic boat tours.

Regardless, the famed Canales de Tortuguero are quite the introduction to this important park. Created to connect a series of naturally lazy lagoons and meandering rivers, in 1969 this engineering marvel finally allowed inland navigation between Limón and the coastal villages in something sturdier than a dugout canoe (though you'll still see plenty of those). There are regular flights, sure, but a leisurely ride through the banana plantations and wild jungle sets a fine tone for your whole visit.

And it's more than just turtles: as you wander the park's beaches and muddy jungle trails, or take a guided boat trip through the rivers and canals, you'll see rows of red mangroves standing sentinels along the way, guarding the wealth of wildlife within. From iguanas and howler monkeys in the treetops, to the tiny frogs and, on occasion, endangered manatee, that call the roots home, this place is thick with life.

Orientation & Information

Park headquarters is at **Cuatro Esquinas** (admission US$7; 🕒 8am-4pm), a few minutes' walk from Tortuguero village. It has maps, information and access to a 2km loop nature trail that's muddy, even in the dry season. This trail hooks into a system of other, less-maintained trails that go further into the park. **Jalova Station**, on the canal at the south entrance to the national park, has a short nature trail, a bathroom and drinking water.

SLOW AND STEADY WINS THE RACE

Thanks to information collected by the CCC (see p394), scientists realized in the 1980s that fewer than 3000 female green turtles were nesting in Tortuguero annually, compared to tens of thousands in earlier decades. The alarming data helped them convince a coalition of public and private groups to initiate long-term conservation efforts geared toward bringing the turtles back. Today, more than 20,000 of the lovely ladies show up on these shores to breed during the year.

The tale of the green turtle's perilous rebound and the conservation projects built to help out is told in two popular books by Archie Carr, a herpetologist who was instrumental in getting Tortuguero protected: *The Windward Road: Adventures of a Naturalist on Remote Caribbean Shores* and *The Sea Turtle: So Excellent a Fishe*.

'Humid' is the driest word that could truthfully be used to describe Tortuguero. With annual rainfall of up to 6000mm in the northern part of the park, it is one of the wettest areas in the country. There is no dry season, although it does rain less in February, March and September, so dress accordingly. If it's sunny, note that swimming is not recommended due to strong undertows and large sharks. Bring insect repellent either way – you'll use it.

Turtle Watching

Visitors are allowed to check out the turtle rookeries at night from February to November (late July through August is prime time) and observe eggs being laid or hatching. Park fees for two-hour night tours are US$5, while several local lodges operate these tours for between US$10 and US$30 per person. Local guides charge about US$15. A guide must accompany all visitors.

Artificial lights, including flash photography, are prohibited by law, as they disturb the egg-laying process and attract predators. Some readers say that certain guides have used bright flashlights and disturbed eggs to give visitors a closer look at the turtles, which pretty much defeats the whole purpose of the refuge. Should your guide offer to go that extra mile, make it clear that you aren't *that* kind of tourist.

If unable to visit during the green turtle breeding season, the next best time is February to July, when leatherback turtles nest in small numbers (the peak is from mid-April to mid-May). Hawksbill turtles nest sporadically from March to October, and loggerhead turtles are also sometimes seen. Stragglers have been seen every month of the year. Only the green turtle nests in large numbers; the other species tend to arrive solo.

Other Wildlife Watching

Great wildlife viewing and birding opportunities can be had both from the few trails within the park and on boat trips. Three local species of monkeys (howler, spider and capuchin), sloths, anteaters and kinkajous are often seen. Manatees, peccaries, tapirs and various members of the cat family have also been recorded, but you have to be exceptionally lucky to see them.

Also of great interest are the area's reptiles and amphibians. Apart from the sea turtles, there are seven species of freshwater turtle. You may also see lizards, caimans, crocodiles and snakes, including the deadly fer-de-lance (a pit viper). About 60 species of amphibian, including tiny poison-dart frogs, have been recorded here, as have more than 400 bird species. These include oceanic species, such as the magnificent frigatebird and royal tern; shorebirds such as plovers and sandpipers; river birds such as kingfishers, jacanas and anhingas; and inland forest species such as hummingbirds and manakins.

More than 400 tree species and at least 2200 species of other plants have been recorded, but there are undoubtedly more to be identified.

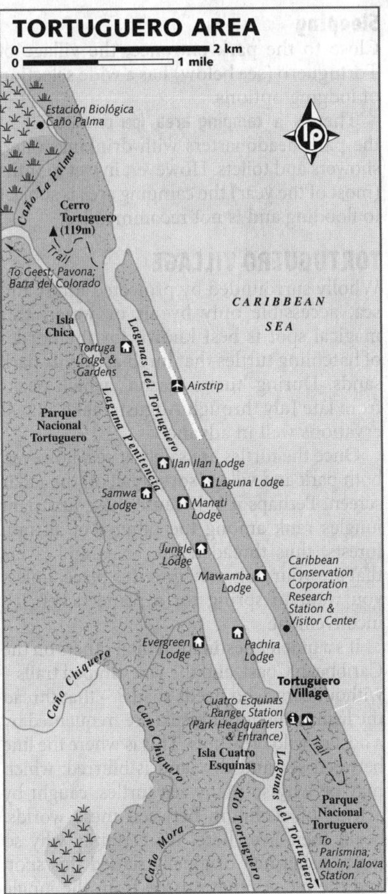

Sleeping

Close to the park entrance, the village of Tortuguero (see below) has a wide selection of lodging options.

There's a **camping area** (per person US$2) at the park headquarters with drinking water, showers and toilets. However, in wet months (most of the year) the camping area is subject to flooding and is not recommended.

TORTUGUERO VILLAGE

Wholly surrounded by protected forest and sea, accessible only by air or water, this magical spot is best known for the hordes of hatchling turtles that lurch across its dark sands. During 'turtle season', which peaks from late July through August, make all reservations well in advance.

Once the turtles are safely at sea, however, both park and village sort of fall off the radar screen. Perhaps it is because these luxuriant jungles rank among the rainiest of all rain forests, thus threaded by canals and rivers that are your only way into this place, unless you want to spring for a plane ticket. It's inconvenient.

It's a quieter destination than others on the Caribbean Coast, and the vine-draped trails – without cars, who needs roads? – that thread the lush, slender peninsula are frequented by a host of wild creatures. This is where the line between sea and dry land is blurred, which may be why so many sea turtles, caught by a trick of evolution between these worlds, begin their lives here. It's certainly why so many fishermen originally settled this spot, and the recipes they stirred from the jungle and ocean are still served up faithfully by folks around town.

Information

Almost any business in town can offer up-to-date information on transportation schedules, tours and qualified guides for everything from medicinal plant expeditions to group kayak trips. There are several independently operated tourist centers, including **Tortuguero Information** (☎ 709 8955; tortuguero@flysansa.com; across from Catholic church), which can make reservations on Sansa Airlines, and **Paraíso Tropical Store** (☎ 710 0323), which sells souvenirs and NatureAir tickets and is also the only place in town to cash traveler's checks.

The **Caribbean Conservation Corporation** (CCC; ☎ 709 8091, in the USA 800-678 7853; www.cccturtle.org; admission US$1; 🕑 10am-noon & 2-5pm Mon-Sat, noon-5pm Sun) operates a research station about 1km north of Tortuguero village. The station has a small visitor center and **museum** with exhibits on all things turtle-related, including a short video (in English or Spanish) about the history of local turtle conservation. The research station teaches courses in various biological fields – contact the CCC for information. Visitors may be able to stay in the CCC's dorms if they're not full.

From March through October there are volunteer programs for people interested in assisting scientists with turtle tagging and research. Volunteers pay US$1400 to US$2700 for seven to 21 days, including a dorm bed, all meals and transportation from San José. There are also bird-migration programs from March through May, and August through October costing US$1245 to US$1975 for seven to 21 days. These are popular projects and advance reservations must be made through the US office of the CCC.

Activities

CANOEING

You'll see signs all over Tortuguero, just north of the entrance to the park, announcing boats for hire. You can paddle yourself in a dugout canoe for about US$2 per person per hour, or go with a guide for a little more. Recommended guides include **Chico** (ask at Miss Miriam's) or **Castor Hunter Thomas** (☎ 709 8050; ask at La Caribeña) two experienced local guides who offer canoe tours for around US$15 for three to four hours, not including park admission. Miss Junie's rents canoes, as do several other places around town. This is the best way to see nature since motorboats disturb wildlife and canoes allow you to get into the nooks and crannies of the park.

HIKING

Apart from visiting the waterways and beaches of the park, hikers can climb the 119m **Cerro Tortuguero**, about 6km north of the village within the Refugio Nacional de Fauna Silvestre Barra del Colorado. You need to hire a boat and guide to get there and the 45-minute hike to the top is muddy and steep. But it is the highest point right on the coast anywhere north of Puerto Limón and offers good views of the forest, canals, sea, birds, monkeys and other wildlife. Bring your insect repellent.

COTERC

The Canadian Organization for Tropical Education and Rainforest Conservation (Coterc) is a nonprofit organization with many local education, research and conservation activities. Coterc operates the Estación Biológica Caño Palma in the Caño La Palma area just north of Cerro Tortuguero and about 7km north of Tortuguero village. Although the biological station is actually within the southern boundary of Refugio Nacional de Fauna Silvestre Barra del Colorado, access is easiest from Tortuguero.

The station accommodates researchers, student groups and volunteers who pay a nominal fee for food and board, help with the upkeep of the station and assist ongoing research projects. Other guests (nature tourists) are accepted when space is available. The buildings are 200m from the Caribbean, but separated from it by a river. Rivers, streams and lagoons can be explored and there is a trail system into the rain forest. Researchers, volunteers and visitors stay in simple dormitories with bunks and bedding, and outdoor showers and bathrooms. There is also a covered area with four hammocks, a study area, and a kitchen and dining area. The rate is US$65 per person per day including three meals and use of the trails. Guided boat excursions can be arranged.

You can reach the station by hiring a boat from Tortuguero. If you make prior arrangements, the staff will pick you up either at Tortuguero airport or the village for US$10.

Coterc relies on members and donors to run its programs. Members receive the quarterly newsletter, *Raphia*. For further information and reservations, contact **Coterc** (☎ in Canada 905-831 8809; www.coterc.org). Drop-in visitors can usually find space.

Tours

Many travel agencies offer package tours of the Tortuguero area, one night for US$130 to US$250 per person, two nights for US$200 to US$300 per person. These usually include some or all meals, lodging and transportation (flying costs about US$150 more). Costs vary widely depending on accommodations and options; make sure the riverboat portion of your ride includes a guided nature tour (making for a five-hour ride in one direction), where you'll likely see more wildlife than in the park itself.

Once in the village, you can arrange all sorts of tours at several independent operations, including **Soda El Muellecito** (across from Super Morpho Pulpería; mains US$2-4; 🕑 6:30am-8pm), which serves up guided hikes and canoe trips over good breakfasts. Often, the best (and most economical) guides are local people with signs outside their homes or businesses advertising their specialties. Several companies offer unusual and recommended tours.

Caño Blanco Marina (☎ 259 8216, 256 9444; tucanti@racsa.co.cr) Fly into Tortuguero for a ride through the jungle in style.

Learning Trips (☎ 258 2293, 396 1979; www.costa-rica.us) Specializes in the natural and social history of the region.

Riverboat Francesca Nature Tours (☎ 226 0986; www.tortuguerocanals.com) Fran and Modesto Watson operate highly recommended custom tours on the Riverboat Francesca.

Tortuguero Wildlife Tours (☎ 833 0827, 392 3201; safari@racsa.co.cr) Operated by biologist Daryl Loth, excellent guided tours include boat trips through the canals (US$15) and sea turtle excursions (US$10, July to October). Loth also leads guided hikes and lectures on the area's natural history.

Sleeping

TORTUGUERO VILLAGE

There are a wide range of budget and mid-range options here.

Tropical Lodge (☎ 826 6246; d US$15) This colorful and classically Caribbean setup behind Tienda Bambú has cute cabinas right on the river.

Cabinas Tortuguero (☎ 709 8114, 839 1200; r per person US$10) This festive spot has spacious rooms with rather elegant wood floors, pretty gardens and plenty of hammocks. The owner Bonnie Scott also leads turtle and canoe tours, and operates an **restaurant** (breakfast US$3, seafood US$7).

Cabinas Maryscar (☎ 711 0671; s/d US$5/8) This quiet spot has basic but bright rooms, some with private hot-water bathroom. A good breakfast costs US$2.

Cabinas Sabina (Green bldg east of Mini-Super; d/tr US$10/15, d with bathroom US$15) It's the biggest place in town and the last resort, with 31 rickety rooms overlooking the ocean.

Spring for the private bathroom or you'll be taking some long midnight walks to the outhouse.

Cabinas Aracari (☎ in Puerto Limón 798 6059; r per person US$6) A good deal, with Spanish-tiled floors in rooms sleeping two or three.

Cabinas Miss Miriam (at the soccer field; s/d US$15/20) A top choice, Miss Miriam has new tiled rooms with good beds, private hot showers and upstairs rooms with balcony and fine views. There's also an annex, with equally nice rooms, a bit closer to the beach.

Miss Junie's (☎ 711 0684; s/d incl breakfast US$17/27, 2-night package per person US$200) At the northern end of the village, Miss Junie's clean rooms are comfortable, with big beds, fans and a porch outside for relaxation. The package includes transportation, a park tour and, best of all, all meals. But this is not your usual buffet: Miss Junie is also Tortuguero's best-known cook (see Eating, opposite). After, you'll need to rent a canoe (US$5 for two hours) to work it all off.

Casa Marbella (☎ 392 3201; across from the Catholic church; safari@racsa.co.cr; s/d US$35/55) One of the nicest lodging options in town, this four-room B&B features light, airy rooms with private solar-heated showers and a full breakfast, perhaps out by the shady patio overlooking the dock. Owner Daryl Loth also organizes excellent area tours (p395).

NORTH OF THE VILLAGE

Lodges north of town cater primarily to groups who have arranged a package deal, usually including transportation from San José, all meals and a guided tour through the park. Air-conditioners don't last long in this humidity, so even the priciest places may have only fans. Note that lodges on the west side of the lagoon don't have beach – or turtle – access. All these lodges will accept walk-ins if they aren't full, but only the first two can actually be walked to; you'll want to call ahead to the others so they'll send a boat. Per person rates are all based on double occupancy.

Mawamba Lodge (293 8181, in San José 223 2421; www.grupomawamba.com; d US$98, 2-night package per person US$252;) Rooms are airy and spacious, with fan and hot shower, all fronted by a veranda with hammocks and rocking chairs. There's a beach and a pool but the real draw is that you can walk to town, unlike guests at the other lodges.

Laguna Lodge (☎ 709 8096, 391 0937; www.lagunalodgetortuguero.com; per person US$55, 2-night package US$243;) Sparkling clean, nicely appointed rooms are hewn from beautiful hardwood, with tiled bathroom mirrors that match the wild mosaics spicing up already pleasant grounds, in particular the very nice pool. But the most outstanding feature – generous CEOs hoping to encourage corporate creativity take note – is the truly trippy conference room, constructed according to a Gaudí design with conch-shell motif, more wild tiles, lots of aquariums and, oh yes, a small waterfall. Synergy, anyone?

Manati Lodge (☎ 383 0330; s/d US$25/35) Run-down rooms in paradise certainly are away from it all, so be sure to arrange your meals (not included) in advance.

Ilan Ilan Lodge (☎ 255 2031/262; www.mitour.com; r per person US$40, 2-night package US$219;) Smallish, fan-cooled rooms with hot-water bathroom are arranged around a rather overgrown courtyard that the birds just love.

Jungle Lodge (☎ 233 0133; www.grupopapagayo; r per person with 3 meals US$55, 2-night package US$240;) The best thing about this lodge is the excellent outdoor bar and the pool has a nice view (as well as a sort of anemic waterfall). Rooms are clean and comfortable, but rather basic for the price.

Pachira Lodge (☎ 256 2780, 382 2239; www.pachiralodge.com.cr; r per person US$55, 2-night package US$259) With attractively Flintstones-themed rocky paths through nicely landscaped jungle grounds, it's a pleasant walk from the beautiful buffet-style restaurant to your pastel room in the rain forest, with fan and hot water. The lodge also operates the nearby **Evergreen Lodge**, across Laguna Penitencia. It has more privacy but smaller rooms, as well as its very own **canopy tour** (US$25) with nine cables and two hanging bridges – the only one in the region at press time.

Tortuga Lodge & Gardens (☎ 710 8016, 222 0333; www.costaricaexpeditions.com; s/d US$99/119, 2-night package per person US$379) This was the first comfortable lodge built in the area and remains the cushiest place to stay. Superior rooms are spacious, screened, cross-ventilated and have ceiling fans and large tiled bathrooms with hot showers. Rocking chairs and hammocks await invitingly in covered walkways outside all the rooms. An airy bar-restaurant is right on the riverside and there's veranda dining next to the water.

Beyond the restaurant, an inviting free-form swimming pool edged by boulders flows serenely by, mirroring the languid movement of the canals. The lodge has won numerous awards for supporting the local community through sustainable development, hiring locals and supporting local conservation projects. The staff and guides are helpful, well trained and many speak English. The lodge is on 20 hectares of landscaped gardens, with private trails and a quiet pond that often has a caiman floating lazily in it or a toad hiding nearby.

Eating

One of Tortuguero's unsung pleasures is the cuisine, where welcoming restaurants lure you in from the rain with steaming platters of Caribbean-style seafood. Grab groceries at the **Super Morpho Pulpería** (☎ 709 8110; 🕑 6:30am-9pm Mon-Sat, 8am-8pm Sun).

Darling Bakery (☎ 845 6389; snacks US$1; 🕑 6am-8pm) Outstanding homemade breads and pastries baked fresh every day get you even more wired when combined with good coffee and espresso beverages. It's cozy.

La Caribeña (☎ 709 8050; across from Super Morphos Pulpería; dishes US$2-5; 🕑 7am-9pm) *Soda*-style breakfast and big casados are the specialties here.

Miss Miriam's (at the soccer field; mains US$3-5, lobster US$7) It's worth blowing off your lodge's meal plan and getting a boat into town just for this fine food, from delicious rice and beans to whole lobsters served up by the friendly and fabulous Miss Miriam.

La Casona (at the soccer field; mains US$4-7; 🕑 11am-10pm) Next door and also highly recommended is this spot, which does a garlic-laden hearts of palm salad that is too scrumptious to be believed.

Miss Junie's (☎ 711 0684; mains US$6-10) The thing about really high-quality Caribbean-style meals – and this place is Tortuguero's best-known restaurant – is that the longer seafood and veggies simmer in coconut sauce, the better they taste. This is why you should order dinner early in the day (though Miss Junie asks only two hours at a pinch). It's worth it.

Drinking

La Culebra, the town nightclub, is a good place for a waterside beer and perhaps a *boca*. The whole village, including the town mutts, turn out on Saturday nights.

Punto D'Incontro (☎ 710 6716; 🕑 11:30am-close), adjacent to Tropical Lodge, also gets packed, especially when there's live music.

Getting There & Away

AIR

The small airstrip is 4km north of Tortuguero village. **NatureAir** (☎ 710 0323; one way/round trip US$66/125) and **Sansa** (☎ 709 8955; across from the Catholic church; tortuguero@flysansa.com; one way/round trip US$60/116) both have daily flights to and from San José. Many hotels can arrange chartered flights.

BOAT

The most popular way to reach Tortuguero is from Moín (p390), where most people on package tours, or those who have booked a guided tour en route to Tortuguero, embark. Two companies, **Viajes Morpho** (☎ 711 0674, 709 8110) and **Bananero** (☎ 709 8005, 833 1076) offer water taxi service between Tortuguero and Moín for about US$30; independent operators charge similar prices.

It costs a lot less to get to Tortuguero from Cariari (see p381) using the bus service to docks at Pavona and Geest; the same operators charge US$10 per person for this shorter and just as scenic run.

Tortuguero is also a good spot for finding boats to Parismina and Barra del Colorado.

BARRA DEL COLORADO AREA

At 90,400 hectares, including the frontier zone with Nicaragua, **Refugio Nacional de Fauna Silvestre Barra del Colorado** (admission US$6), locally called Barra, is the biggest national wildlife refuge in Costa Rica and forms a regional conservation unit with the adjacent Parque Nacional Tortuguero.

Barra is much more remote than Tortuguero, and more expensive and difficult to visit. Despite the incredible wildlife-watching opportunities, fishing is still the bread and butter of most of the area's lodges. Anglers go for tarpon from January to June and snook from September to December.

Fishing is good year-round, however, and other tasty catches include barracuda, mackerel and jack crevalle, all inshore; or bluegill, rainbow bass (*guapote*) and machaca in the rivers. There is also deep-sea fishing for marlin, sailfish and tuna, though this sort of fishing is probably better on the Pacific. Dozens of fish can be hooked on a good day, so 'catch and release' is an important conservation policy of all the lodges.

The northern border of the refuge is the Río San Juan, the border with Nicaragua. This area was politically sensitive during the 1980s, which contributed to the isolation of the reserve. Today many residents are Nicaraguan nationals. Since the relaxing of Sandinista–Contra hostilities in 1990, it has become straightforward to journey north along the Río Sarapiquí and east along the San Juan, technically entering Nicaragua (p399).

Orientation & Information

Barra del Colorado village lies near the mouth of the Río Colorado and is divided by the river into Barra del Norte and Barra del Sur. There are no roads. The airstrip is on the south side of the river, but more people live on the north side. The area outside the village is swampy and travel is almost exclusively by boat, though some walking is possible around some of the lodges.

The Servicio de Parques Nacionales (SPN) maintains a small **ranger station** (south side of the Río Colorado) near the village. However, there are no facilities here. From the airport, only the Tarponland and Río Colorado Lodges (see opposite) are accessible if you're on foot. All other lodges require a boat ride (a boat operator will be waiting for you at the airport if you have a reservation).

Barra-born **Eddie Brown Silva** (☎ 382 3350, 383 6097), who holds a world fishing record for

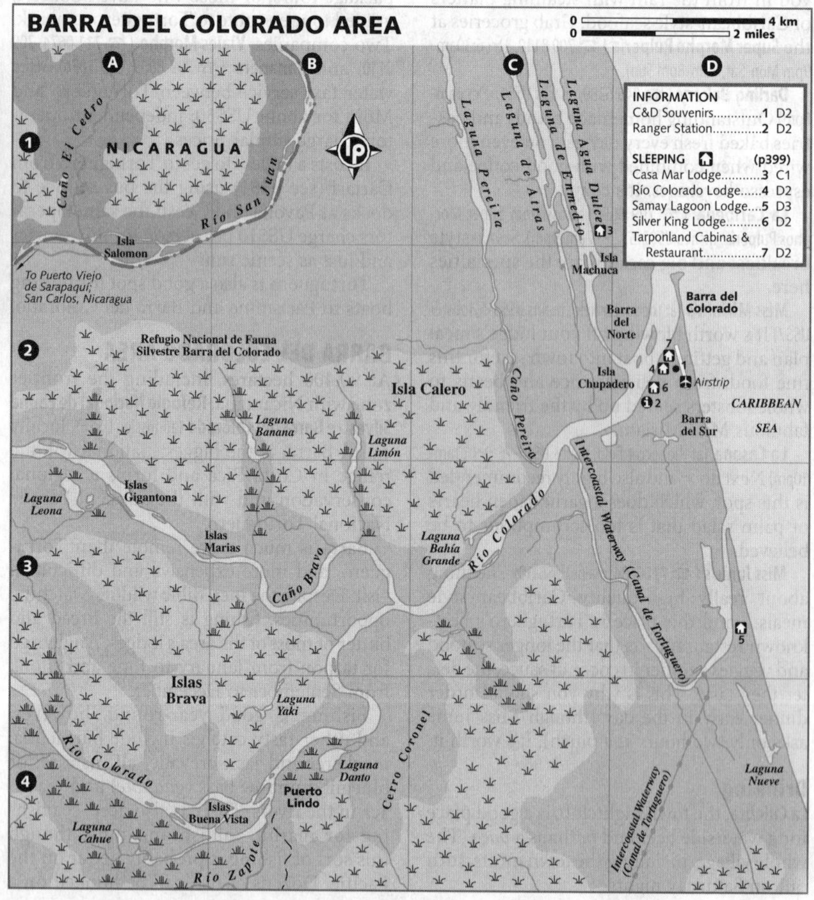

cubera snapper, and other fishing records for Costa Rica, is well known and in great demand as a fishing captain.

C&D Souvenirs (☎ 710 6592), close to the airport, has a public telephone and fax and also offers tourist information.

ENTERING NICARAGUA

Day trips along the Río San Juan and some offshore fishing trips technically enter Nicaraguan territory. Carry your passport and US$9, in the unlikely event that you are stopped and checked.

San Juan del Norte, the Nicaraguan village at the mouth of the Río San Juan, has no services, but is linked with the rest of Nicaragua by irregular passenger boats sailing up the San Juan to San Carlos, on the Lago de Nicaragua. This is not an official entry point into either country but inquire locally about the possibilities.

Sleeping & Eating

Visitors to Barra del Colorado are allowed to **camp** (per person US$2) in the refuge, but there are no facilities.

Tarponland Cabinas & Restaurant (☎ 710 2141, 710 1271; s/d US$30/45, d with sportfishing US$250;) This is it as far as budget lodgings go in Barra. Walking distance from the airport, these basic but cozy hardwood rooms come complete with a pool and a good on-site restaurant.

Samay Lagoon Lodge (☎ 384 7047, 390 9068; www.samay.com; 2-night package per person US$278, double occupancy;) This mid-range option, with a good restaurant and bar, includes meals (which get rave reviews), transportation from San José and tours including guided hikes through the parks and horseback riding. It's a nice spot, but could be spruced up a bit.

Casa Mar Lodge (☎ 433 8834; www.casamarlodge.com; per person 3-night US$1325-1700, 7-night US$2675-3550, charter airfare US$145 extra) When CEOs hang a 'gone fishing' sign on the office door, you can bet this is the type of place they've gone to. Luxurious cabins with nicely tiled hot showers and home-cooked meals are set in a pleasant 2.8-hectare garden that attracts lots of birds; ecotourists stay here for that reason. But the real drawcards are the big-engine boats, English-speaking guides and of course the impressive 75kg tarpon that make the covers of all those sportfishing magazines. Packages include transfers from the Barra del Colorado airport, all fishing, accommodations, meals and an open bar. Trips of other lengths can be arranged.

Río Colorado Lodge (☎ 232 4063; www.riocoloradolodge.com; r per person without/with fishing US$90/360) Built in 1971, this is the longest-established lodge on the Caribbean coast and is well known. The rambling tropical-style buildings near the mouth of the Río Colorado are constructed on stilts, double-roofed for a natural cool, with covered walkways that make a lot of sense in the rain forest. Rooms are breezy and pleasant, with air-con and hot showers. Two rooms have wheelchair access. The food is all-you-can-eat, served family-style. For relaxation after a day of fishing, the lodge features a happy hour with free rum drinks, a lounging area with a pool table and other games, a breezy outdoor deck and a video room with satellite TV. This is the only upscale lodge from which you can walk to the airport, and as a result, a local crowd can stop by and hang out – this place has a reputation for being a 'party lodge,' and it is. Most guests are anglers, but nonfishing visitors can stay here. Package rates include boats, bilingual guides, all meals and transportation.

Silver King Lodge (☎ 381 1403, in the USA 800-847 3474; silverkinglodge.net; r US$144, s/d 3-day package US$2320/3700, 5-day package US$3600/5100) This is quite simply the best sportfishing lodge on this coast. Large rooms are truly comfortable, with big bathrooms and a coffee maker. Other amenities include a pool with waterfall, indoor Jacuzzi, great restaurant and, best of all, a 24-hour bar with river views and free cocktails. Boats and other fishing equipment are state of the art and included in the package, but they'll take you fishing in a dugout canoe if you'd like. Nature tours are also available. The lodge is usually full during the busiest months (mid-January to mid-May); you should book several months in advance to get the dates you want. This lodge closes in July and December.

Getting There & Away

The easiest way to Barra by far is by air, and both Sansa and NatureAir will drop you off here on their daily Tortuguero run (p397) for about US$75/125 one way/round trip.

There is no regular boat service to Barra, although you can arrange boat service from Tortuguero (US$50 per boat), Puerto Viejo de Sarapiquí (p442; US$60 per boat) and

Cariari (p381). It's also possible to hire a boat in Moín, but that's a long haul, so get started early. Most lodges can arrange to pick you up here. Bring your passport, as you'll be on the water near the border.

SOUTHERN CARIBBEAN

This is the heart and soul of Costa Rica's Afro-Caribbean community, where Jamaicans brought here by United Fruit to build the backbone of the original banana republic finally learned to call this country home. For more than half a century, the communities of the Southern Caribbean existed almost independent of the rest of the country, turning to subsistence farming and fishing when the banana plantations, and later cacao fincas, fell to devastating blights.

And so these still very Jamaican communities found good neighbors instead among the ancient indigenous towns, now encompassed by the nearby Cocles/KéköLdi, Talamanca Cabecar and Bribrí reserves. The two peoples, isolated, far from the goings-on of mainstream Costa Rica, exchanged the ancient wisdom of medicinal plants, agriculture and jungle survival. And thrived.

Though the racial borders fell in 1949, electricity, roads and phones all came late to this perfect stretch of beachfront property; just 30 years ago, the four-hour bus ride from San José to Puerto Viejo required a solid week of hard travel. The effect of all this isolation is a culture still largely independent of mainstream Costa Rica, though increased access to roads and other infrastructure, as well as a rapidly growing tourism industry, are inexorably wearing away the cultural quirks that many folks come to experience.

But not to worry, not yet: the music of the islands is everywhere, reggae and calypso pouring from homes and businesses into the streets. The cuisine is extraordinary, where even the simplest rice and beans are simmered in rich coconut milk and exotic spices, conjuring the flavors of both Jamaica and Africa. And while most residents speak Spanish, a patois of English remains common, if a little bit difficult to decipher for folks unused to it. For example, 'All right' means 'Hello' and 'Okay' means 'Goodbye,' although folks can and will sacrifice such poetry for clarity in order to help out a confused tourist.

In the meantime, two of the country's most beautiful and accessible protected coasts, Cahuita National Park and the Gandoca-Manzanillo wildlife refuge, are waiting in sandy anticipation.

Dangers & Annoyances

The southern Caribbean has received, generally unfairly, a bad rap for danger, theft and drugs. But as in the rest of Costa Rica, it is wise to take the usual precautions you would take in any tourist area. Keep your hotel room locked and the windows closed, never leave gear unattended on beaches when swimming, don't walk the beaches alone at night. Don't give money for a service in advance, as you might not see the person again, and always count your change.

Most residents are not happy with young travelers who come to the area in search of drugs. Remember that buying drugs is illegal as well as dangerous (dealers may be crooked or collaborating with the police).

AVIARIOS DEL CARIBE

About 1km north from where the coastal highway crosses the Río Estrella, 31km south of Limón, is this small wildlife sanctuary, B&B and **sloth research center** (☎ 750 0775; www.ogphoto.com/aviaros; d US$80-105; Ⓟ). On an 88-hectare island in the delta of the Río Estrella, the owners have recorded about 320 bird species – and are still counting. Guestrooms are spacious, with fans, comfortable beds, restful décor, flower vases and well-designed bathrooms with hot water. If you call for reservations, keep trying; it can be difficult to get through on the phone.

The center offers a variety of local naturalist excursions, including the recommended three-hour canoe tour (US$30) through the Estrella delta, getting you close to a variety of birds and animals. Look for monkeys, caimans, river otters and, of course, sloths.

The now-famous orphaned sloth named Buttercup reigns over the grounds. Buttercup's mother was killed by a car, so Luis and Judy raised the youngster, only about five weeks old when they found it. This gave rise to a passion for sloths and now Aviarios del Caribe has a sloth rescue sanctuary that doubles as a sloth research center. The owners' passion for sloths is palpable and there are about 10 animals here at any one time. Visits and informative guided tours (in English) of

CARIBBEAN COAST

the sloth center are available for US$20 to US$30. There is a volunteer program here.

Any bus to Cahuita will drop you off at the entrance to Aviarios del Caribe.

RESERVA BIOLÓGICA HITOY CERERE

This 9950-hectare **reserve** (☎ 758 5855; admission US$6; 🕑 8am-4pm) is 60km south of Limón by road, but only half that distance as the vulture glides. The route takes you through the Río Estrella valley, a long-established banana- and cacao-growing area. There are plantations producing several other types of tropical fruit as well.

Although not far from civilization, it is one of the most rugged and rarely visited reserves in the country. There is a ranger station, but there are no other facilities – no camp sites or information booths. A 9km trail leads south from the ranger station, but the steep and slippery terrain and dense vegetation make it a possibility only for the most fit and determined hikers. Hiking is permitted throughout the reserve; walking along a streambed is the best way to get through the dense vegetation. This may be one of the wettest reserves in the parks system; its evergreen forests are typically inundated with 4000mm to 6000mm of rain annually.

Though few people come to Hitoy Cerere, that is no reason to ignore it. The reserve is a fascinating place and, being so rarely visited, offers a great wilderness experience in an area that has been little explored. Heavy rainfall and broken terrain combine to produce many beautiful streams, rivers and waterfalls, as well as the park's trademark soft carpeting of mosses. The reserve lies at elevations between about 100m and 1025m on the south side of the Río Estrella valley, surrounded by indigenous reserves.

Getting There & Away

The reserve is most easily reached by car (4WD recommended) via a signed turnoff to the west on the signed road to Valle de la Estrella and Penhurst just south of the bridge over the Río Estrella. Another small sign at the bus stop sends you down a good dirt road about 15km to the reserve.

You can also get there by public transport: catch a bus to Valle de la Estrella from Limón, and from the end of the bus line (Fortuna/Finca 6) you can hire a taxi to take you the rest of the way and pick you up at a pre-arranged time (US$25). You can also arrange taxis and guided hikes, including transportation, from Cahuita.

CAHUITA

While neighboring Puerto Viejo is rapidly developing into a can't-miss hit on the groovier travel circuit, Cahuita has managed to maintain a more relaxed relationship with folks discovering the Caribbean Coast. It's beautiful. The unusual black sand, which makes certain Caribbean beaches so warm and perfect for sea turtles incubating their eggs, gives the very swimmable Playa Negra (it boasts a blue flag; see p453) an unusual and ethereal presence.

An itinerary in this relaxed paradise would almost certainly include, among the excellent meals and quality beach time, a wander into neighboring Cahuita National Park (p408), a five minute walk from 'downtown.' Here are even more perfect beaches (with mostly white sand), not to mention trails through protected jungle and one of Costa Rica's two living coral reefs, with exceptional snorkeling from March through May, September and October. Oh, and at this entrance, the park's entry fees are 'by donation,' rather than US$6 at the other gate. And that pretty much covers a fancy seafood dinner.

Information

Internet access, slow throughout the Caribbean region, is sporadically available at some businesses and hotels for about US$3 an hour, including **Centro Turístico Brigitte** (☎ 755 0053; www.brigittecahuita.com; per hr US$3; 🕑 7am-6pm) and **Cabinas Seaside** (☎ 755 0210/027; spencer@racsa.co.cree; per hr US$3).

There are no banks in Cahuita – the closest are in Puerto Limón and Bribrí – but most hotels and tour companies take US dollars. **Mercado Safari** (🕑 6am-4pm) changes US and Canadian dollars, euros, Swiss francs, British pounds and traveler's checks but has a steep commission.

Dangers & Annoyances

Cahuita has something of a reputation, primarily because of the highly publicized murders of two North American women in 2000. The perpetrators are now serving long sentences and Cahuita, if anything, is safer than many destinations on the Caribbean Coast. Take normal precautions, of course,

CAHUITA

0 — 500 m
0 — 0.3 miles

To Westfalia Surf Beach
Playa Negra
CARIBBEAN SEA
School
Parque Central
Soccer Field
To Aviaros del Caribe (5km); Puerto Limón (36km)
To Puerto Viejo de Talamanca (18km)
Kelly Creek
Kelly Creek Entrance Station
Río Suárez (Kelly Creek)
Parque Nacional Cahuita
See Enlargement
0 — 300 m
0 — 0.2 miles

INFORMATION
Internet Access (Cabinas Seaside)....(see 31)
Internet Access (Centro Turístico Brigitte)....(see 5)
Mercado Safari....1 A3
Public Phone (Abastidor La Amistad)....2 A1
Public Phone (Soda Uvita)....3 A3

SIGHTS & ACTIVITIES (p403)
Cahuita Tours....4 A3
Centro Turístico Brigitte....5 C3
Ciclo Safari....6 A3
Mariposario de Cahuites....7 C4
Mister Big J Tourist Service....8 B4
Roberto's Tours....9 B4
Turistica Cahuita....10 A4
Willie's Tours....11 B3

SLEEPING (pp404–7)
Alby Lodge....12 E4
Atlantída Lodge....13 C3
Bungalow Aché....14 E4
Cabinas Algebra....15 A1
Cabinas Arrecife Reef....16 A3
Cabinas Atlantic Surf....17 E4
Cabinas Bobo Ashanti....18 B3
Cabinas Brisas del Mar....19 B3
Cabinas Iguana....20 C3
Cabinas Jardín Tropical....21 C3
Cabinas Jenny....22 B3
Cabinas Mambo....23 C3
Cabinas Nirvana....24 C3
Cabinas Palmer....25 B3
Cabinas Rhode Island....26 E4
Cabinas Riverside....27 E4
Cabinas Safari....28 B3
Cabinas Smith....29 A3
Cabinas Sol y Mar....30 B4
Cabinas Spencer Seaside....31 B3
Cabinas Surfside (Annex)....32 B3
Cabinas Surfside (Main Site)....33 A3
Cabinas Tito....34 D3
Cabinas Vaz....35 B4
Cabinas Villa Delmar....36 E4
Centro Turístico Brigitte....37 C3
Chalet Hibiscus....38 A1
Cuartos Jibaru....39 B3
El Encanto B&B....40 D3
Hotel National Park....41 B4
Kelly Creek Hotel....42 B4
La Piscina Natural....43 B2
Linda's Secret Garden....44 E4
Magellan Inn....45 A1
Reggae Cabinas....(see 52)

EATING (pp407–8)
Bluespirit....46 D3
Café del Parquecito....47 B3
Cha Cha Cha!....48 A3
Chau's Paradise....49 C3
Elizabeth Pastry Shop....(see 25)
Kelly Creek Restaurant....(see 42)
La Casa de Creole....(see 45)
Miss Edith's....50 A3
Pizzería El Cactus....51 D3
Reggae Restaurant....52 C3
Restaurant Bananas....(see 15)
Restaurant Cahuita National Park....(see 41)
Restaurant El Palenque....53 A3
Restaurant Relax....54 B4
Restaurant Sobre Las Olas....55 D3
Restaurant Típico Cahuita....56 A4
Restaurant Vista del Mar....57 B4
Roberto's Restaurant....58 B4
Rosa's....59 C3
Soda Bella Horizante....60 D3
Soda Café Caribbean Flavor....61 B3
Yoli's Restaurant....62 A3

DRINKING (p408)
Bar Hannia....63 A3
Chau's Paradise....(see 49)
Coco's Bar....64 A4
Ricky's Bar....(see 54)

TRANSPORT (p408)
Bus Stop....65 B4

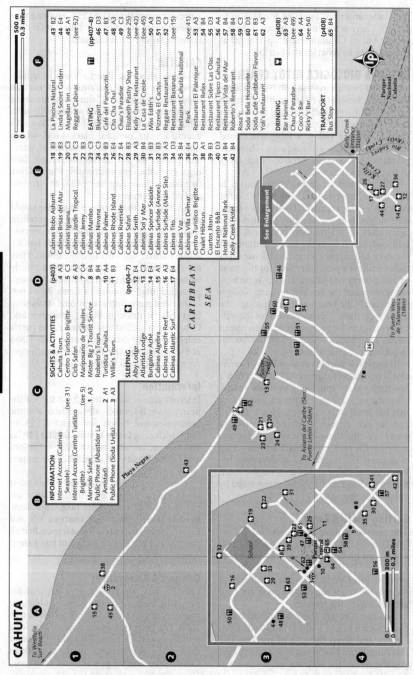

but don't worry too much – the worst thing that happens to most visitors is that they're politely offered a lousy deal on marijuana. Be careful with your cash.

Women should know that the town enjoys a free-love reputation and evidently some female travelers do come here for a quick fling. Be prepared to pay your gent's way around town and bring (and use!) your own condoms. Male visitors should consider purchasing flowers for their girlfriends while in Cahuita, 'for no special reason except that I love you.'

Sights

Three **beaches** are within walking distance of the village. At the northwest end of Cahuita is **Playa Negra**, a long, black-sand beach flying the *bandera azul ecológica* (see p453 for more on this). Some people think that the black-sand beach has better swimming than the white-sand beach at the entrance to the national park (see p408), though ask about conditions at both. A trail through the jungle behind that beach leads to a third stretch of sand, about 6km away and separated from the others by a rocky headland with a coral reef offshore that is suitable for snorkeling. Incidence of theft in broad daylight at the two beaches closer to town have been reported, so why not store your stuff – anything from passports to backpacks, at Mister Big J Tourist Service (above) for US$4 per day?

Mariposario de Cahuites (☎ 750 0361; admission US$7; 🕑 9am-4pm) is a well-maintained garden that lets you walk among the butterflies and cool caterpillars such as the Toas, which sticks out little red horns when owner Francoise pets it. Tours are offered in English, German, French and Spanish, as are posted descriptions of the residents. A beautiful fountain surrounded by stunningly carved wooden benches makes a pleasant place to relax.

Activities & Tours

A number of places rent equipment and arrange tours. Snorkeling is best from March through May and from September through November. You should shop around for the best deals – the prices listed here are subject to change depending on the season and size of your group.

Centro Turístico Brigitte (☎ 755 0053; www.brigittecahuita.com), also a good place to stay (see p406), specializes in horseback riding tours (three/six hours per person US$30/40) and can also arrange fishing trips, surfing lessons, guided hikes and just about anything else. Brigitte also offers Internet access, bicycle rentals (per hour US$1) and laundry service.

Mister Big J Tourist Service (☎ 755 0328; 🕑 8am-7pm) is run by Big 'J' who is Mr Joseph Spencer, a man who has been leading tours by horse, boat and on foot throughout the area for years. Larger groups can make deals for guided horseback rides along the beach (US$30 for three hours) or to a private waterfall (US$40 for six hours); snorkeling trips in Parque Nacional Cahuita (US$20 for three hours); fishing expeditions (US$45) and all manner of guided hikes. You can also arrange one- or two-night trips to Tortuguero at varying costs, depending on your choice of accommodations.

Roberto's Tours (☎ 755 0117) arranges four-hour snorkeling trips (US$15) and dolphin tours (US$25) in the national park. Roberto's real claim to fame, though, is sportfishing. For US$35 per person (minimum two), you can take a four-hour cruise closer to shore in search of mackerel and snapper. For US$300 per person (minimum two) you get eight hours of deep-sea fishing for tarpon, tuna and sailfish. Bonus: after all your hard work, Roberto can have your haul cooked for dinner in his recommended restaurant.

Willie's Tours (☎ 843 4700; williestours@hotmail.com) is run by Willie, who speaks German and English, and specializes in tours to a Bribrí village (US$35), where you'll meet a family he's known for years, then visit a butterfly garden, iguana farm and waterfall. He also offers 72-hour excursions to Panama's Bastimentos Island (US$130), perfect if your visa is about to expire.

Cahuita Tours (☎ 755 0000/101; cahuitat@racsa.co.cr) is one of the oldest established agencies in town and offers guided hiking and snorkeling tours (US$25) in the park and traditional fishing trips (US$65) in a dugout canoe around the reef, among other tours. It also has a Western Union. Another place is **Turística Cahuita** (☎ 755 0071; dltacb@racsa.co.cr).

The **Asociación Talamanqueña de Ecoturismo y Conservación** (ATEC; see p409), based in Puerto Viejo de Talamanca, offers guided hikes through the old cacao plantations and into the rain forest around Cahuita with an emphasis on Afro-Caribbean lifestyle plus natural history.

CORAL REEFS

The monkeys and other forest creatures are not the only wildlife attractions of Parque Nacional Cahuita. About 200m to 500m off Punta Cahuita is the largest living coral reef in Costa Rica (though very small compared to the huge barrier reef off Belize, for example). Corals are tiny, colonial, filter-feeding animals (cnidarians, or, more commonly, coelenterates) that deposit a calcium carbonate skeleton as a substrate for the living colony. These skeletons build up over millennia to form the corals we see. The outside layers of the corals are alive, but, because they are filter feeders, they rely on the circulation of clean water and nutrients over their surface.

Since the opening up of the Caribbean coastal regions in the last couple of decades, a lot of logging has taken place and the consequent lack of trees on mountainous slopes has led to increased erosion. The loosened soil is washed into gullies, then streams and rivers and eventually the sea. By the time the coral reef comes into the picture, the eroded soils are no more than minute mud particles – just the right size to clog up the filter-feeding cnidarians. The clogged animals die and the living reef dies along with them.

After deforestation, the land is often given over to plantations of bananas or other fruit. These are sprayed with pesticides which, in turn, are washed out to sea and can cause damage to animals that need to pass relatively large quantities of water through their filtering apparatus in order to extract the nutrients they need.

The 1991 earthquake, which was centered near the Caribbean coast, also had a damaging effect on the reef. The shoreline was raised by over a meter, exposing and killing parts of the coral. Nevertheless, some of the reef has survived and remains the most important in Costa Rica.

It is important never to step on or touch corals. A reef is not just a bunch of colorful rocks. It is a living habitat, just as a stream, lake, forest, or swamp is a living habitat. Coral reefs provide both a solid surface for animals such as sponges and anemones to grow on and a shelter for a vast community of fish and other organisms – octopi, crabs, algae, bryozoans and a host of others. Some 35 species of coral have been identified in this reef, along with 140 species of mollusk (snails, chitons, shellfish and octopi), 44 species of crustacean (lobsters, crabs, shrimps and barnacles), 128 species of seaweed and 123 species of fish. Many of these seemingly insignificant species represent important links in various food chains. Thus logging has the potential to cause much greater and unforeseen damage than simply destroying the rain forest.

On a more mundane level, the drier months in the highlands (from February to April), when less runoff occurs in the rivers and less silting occurs in the sea, are considered the best months for snorkeling and seeing the reef. Conditions are often cloudy at other times.

The best way to reach the reef is to hire a boat in Cahuita and snorkel from a boat.

Sleeping

There are two possible areas in which to stay. Within the town, hotels are generally cheaper, noisier, and close to many restaurants and the national park. Northwest of town, along Playa Negra, you'll find more expensive hotels and a few pleasant cabinas, which offer more privacy and quiet but a limited choice of restaurants unless you travel the one or two kilometers into town.

BUDGET

There's no shortage of accommodations in town and along Playa Negra. Most are clean and basic, geared for folks content with a cold shower and décor revolving around mosquito nets. There are a few more luxuriously appointed places hidden away in the jungle.

Cabinas Smith (☎ 755 0068; s/d/tr US$12/15/18; Ⓟ) With much nicer rooms than the basic exterior would indicate, this recommended spot offers neat, freshly painted quarters with lots of shelf space overlooking a pleasant garden.

Cabinas Vaz (☎ 755 0218; s/d US$15/20) A good choice: spotless and pleasant rooms with good beds are much quieter in the back of the building.

Cuartos Jibaru (no phone; per person US$7) This family-run place isn't fancy, but you get your own clean, dark room with a fan and busy shared bathroom for cheap.

Cabinas Surfside (☎ 755 0246; evadarling1930@yahoo.com; d without view US$18, s/d US$20/25; Ⓟ) The less expensive concrete-block rooms are clean, with fans and private hot-water bathrooms surrounding a nice courtyard, while slightly pricier rooms face the waterfront. There's also a shared kitchen and parking.

Reggae Restaurant & Cabinas (☎ 755 0515; s/d US$15/20, apt US$35, camping per person US$4.50; P) A bit off the beaten track, these basic cabinas right across from Playa Negra have big windows, cold showers and mosquito nets. Cold showers are also available to campers.

Cabinas Atlantic Surf (☎ 755 0116; s/d/tr US$20/25/30; P) This sweet spot has six pleasant, wooden rooms with semi-private porches, offering a nice change from the mainly concrete-block construction of many of Cahuita's hotels. Rooms have fans, hot showers and, of course, hammocks.

Cabinas Brisas del Mar (☎ 755 0011; r per person US$10) Sparkling rooms with hot water and homey touches surround charmingly overgrown gardens with parrots and hammocks.

Cabinas Rhode Island (☎ 755 0264; d/tr US$12/15; P) Good-sized, reasonably clean rooms with comfy chairs and cold showers surround a grassy parking lot.

Cabinas Villa Delmar (☎ 755 0392/75; s US$12, d US$18-30; P ❄) Ten rooms in various sizes and configurations, from a very small single to a large apartment with air-con and a full kitchen sleeping six, are clean and for the most part spacious spots not far from the main drag.

Cabinas Jenny (☎ 755 0256; d US$20-25, additional person US$5; P) A stones throw from the advancing waves, this basic place has great views from the porches, nice rooms with hot water and shelves, and bigger, more private rooms upstairs for a few dollars more.

Cabinas Seaside (☎ 755 0210/027; spencer@racsa.co.cr; d US$16-20; P 💻) With hammocks strung beneath the coconut palms fronting cabinas with cool murals and great bathrooms, this is a good place to relax and chat or just watch the waves roll in. The upstairs rooms are even nicer and about half have hot water.

Cabinas Bobo Ashanti (☎ 755 0128, 829 6890; tr US$21; P) Rooms are a good deal if you can fill the beds at this reggae-flavored spot, fully equipped with hammocks for napping and a basic outdoor kitchen with fridge for preparing inexpensive munchies.

Cabinas Palmer (☎ 755 0046; cabinaspalmer@racsa.co.cr; s/d incl breakfast US$15/25) This recommended place has 13 spotless, comfortable rooms with private bathroom, and a neat raised porch above the garden hung with hammocks. Double bonus: on-site are both **Elizabeth Pastry Shop** (light meals $3-5; 🕑 6am-7pm) with sunny tables and excellent snacks, and **Centro Oasis Massage Therapy** (per hr US$25) to get you relaxed after too much coffee.

Cabinas Safari (☎ 755 0405; s/d/tr/q US$15/18/22/25) Tiled, well-maintained basic rooms with a few frilly details all have fans and the helpful owners also provide parking and money-changing services. Big breakfasts are worth the extra US$2 charged. Next door, the owners also manage **Cuartos Jabiru** (per person US$7) with seven simple rooms sharing bathrooms.

Linda's Secret Garden (☎ 755 0327; s/d US$18-30; P) The garden really is lovely, as are the communal outdoor kitchen and spacious, attractively decorated rooms with private hot-water showers nestled inside. It's an excellent value.

Cabinas Algebra (☎ 755 0057; s/d $18/33; P 💻) This brightly colored option features friendly rooms with kitchenettes and hot showers and is most certainly well away from it all. The recommended on-site **Restaurant Bananas** (meals US$5-10) serves good Creole food. It's about 2km from town, but transport can be arranged in advance.

Cabinas Nirvana (☎ 755 0110; d US$20-35) Out toward Playa Negra, this is a good budget choice with a variety of options. Built by a friendly Italian, all the wooden cabins are nice and have private hot showers, cross ventilation and floor fans. There are two small cabins, two midsize ones (one with kitchenette) and a larger one sleeping four with a kitchenette. Though this place is tucked down a side road several hundred meters from the beach, coral juts up from the grassy lawn area.

La Piscina Natural (no phone; d US$20; P) This gem is about 2km out of town and 100% worth the walk (or cab ride) to the right sort of person: rooms are basic and very well kept, but it's the gorgeous grounds fronting an unbelievably scenic stretch of beach, not to mention the best picnic table in Cahuita, that make the place. Check out the neat natural pool for which the complex, which also includes a breezy bar, is named.

Cabinas Tito (☎ 755 0286; www.cabinastito; s/d incl breakfast US$20/25; P) Surrounded by enormous gardens, bright rooms furnished in wicker with jungly accents and mosquito nets make this atmospheric spot a good value. Bonus:

there's a small banana finca right on the property.

Cabinas Arrecife Reef (☎ 755 0081; d US$20-25; P) Plain but comfortable rooms have silent fan and hot shower, and the breezy, shaded porch has good sea views. There's also a teeny pool surrounded by hammocks.

You can camp in Parque Nacional Cahuita (p408) or just north of town at Reggae Restaurant & Cabinas. Also ask at Chau's Paradise, across the street.

MID-RANGE

Cabinas Jardín Tropical (☎ 755 0033; jardintropical@racsa.co.cr; cabins US$30, house US$50; P) Quiet and out of the way, this pleasant place rents two nice cabins with hot water, fans, fridge and porch hammocks; there's also a larger house available.

Hotel National Park (☎ 755 0244; s/d/tr US$20/30/35, f US$60-100; P) Almost at the entrance to Parque Nacional Cahuita, the less expensive rooms have beautiful hardwood paneling and porches; views are best from the 2nd floor. The family rooms are outstanding, with separate bedrooms, full kitchen, TV and air-con. A popular restaurant (see opposite) is attached.

Cabinas Mambo (☎ 375 0723; jardintropical@racsa.co.cr; d/tr US$30/40) Four really nice rooms with huge, beautiful hot showers and a relaxing hardwood porch are on offer by the same fine folks who run the Jardín Tropical, above.

Cabinas Iguana (☎ 755 0005, 355 1326; www.cabinas-iguana.com; d US$17, cabin US$25-60; P) Three nice rooms with shared warm shower and several even nicer rooms and cabins with private bathroom, hot water and kitchenette sleep two to six people. The swimming pool is pretty sweet and there is also a book exchange, a few trails, and sinks to do your laundry.

Centro Turístico Brigitte (☎ 755 0053; www.brigittecahuita.com; s/tr US$28/39; P) The small single rooms are fairly basic, but the larger rooms have air-con and fridge. The **restaurant** (mains US$5; 7am-noon) serves breakfast only.

Kelly Creek Hotel & Restaurant (☎ 755 0007; www.hotelkellycreek.com; d US$58, additional person US$10; P) Right by the entrance to Parque Nacional Cahuita, this hotel offers four attractive and spacious rooms with big, white-tiled hot shower. Each room is on a corner and has slatted windows for excellent light and cross-ventilation. High ceilings keep the place cool and it's a good deal. There's a fine restaurant here, too (see Eating).

Alby Lodge (☎ 755 0031; alby_lodge@racsa.co.cr; d incl breakfast US$30-50; P) Near Kelly Creek Hotel, this fine, German-run place has pleasant grounds with attractive thatched wooden cabins built on stilts. All have high ceiling, hot shower, fan, mosquito nets and a porch with a hammock.

Bungalows Aché (☎ 755 0119; www.bungalowsache.com; s/d/tr US$40/45/50; P) Beautiful, spacious wooden bungalows have almost every amenity, including an electric jug, fridge, hot water and mosquito nets, and one is designed for folks in wheelchairs, although anyone would appreciate the larger bathroom.

TOP END

El Encanto B&B (☎ 755 0113; www.elencantobedandbreakfast.com; s/d US$54/64, apt US$87, house incl healthy breakfast US$147; P) This hospitable place, run by charming French-Canadian artists Pierre and Patricia, is set in lovingly landscaped grounds, with statuettes and nooks reflecting the creative and peaceful nature of the owners. An Asian-style pavilion has hammocks and lounge chairs – yoga classes are given here; massages are also available. A meditation room is provided for use from 5:30am to 6:30am, and again in the evening.

Attractive wooden bungalows have hot water, ceiling fan and private patio. The two-room apartment and house, with three bedrooms, come with a fully equipped kitchen. The open-sided breakfast room can be used during the day; there are drinks on the honor system, and cable TV if you really need it. The owners can refer you to several good local guides.

Chalet Hibiscus (☎ 755 0021; www.hotels.co.cr/hibiscus.html; d US$40-50, chalets US$100-120; P) The double rooms are fine, with mosquito nets, hot showers and a few artsy touches; the chalets, with two floors, full kitchens and in the priciest a Jacuzzi, are truly fabulous. Amenities include a pool and a games room with pool table.

Atlántida Lodge (☎ 755 0115/213; www.atlantida.co.cr; s/d US$53/66; P) With lots of bamboo, an attractive pool and good restaurant, these 30 rooms surrounded by pleasant gardens have fan and hot shower. It's about 1km from town – if you have a reservation the staff will pick you up. They can also arrange transport through Fantasy Bus from San José (US$25).

Magellan Inn (☎ 755 0035; magellaninn@racsa.co.cr; d incl breakfast US$75, additional person US$12; P) About 2km northwest of Cahuita at the northern end of Playa Negra, this elegant, upscale inn isn't really within a casual stroll of town, but is worth the extra effort: comfortable, classy rooms with Asian rugs on the wooden floors face a well-designed garden formed from an ancient coral reef surrounding a pretty swimming pool. The restaurant **La Casa de Creole** (mains US$7-20; 6-9pm Mon-Sat) serves fine French fusion cuisine with an emphasis on seafood; try the shrimp martiniquaise, in a caramelized garlic-ginger sauce.

Eating

Restaurante y Café del Parquecito (breakfast US$3-5; 6:30am-noon) Early risers and crepe lovers alike gather here to wake up over granola (muesli), good coffee and some of the hugest, most beautiful crepes you'll ever eat, wrapped around fresh fruit and many other fillings.

Soda Café Caribbean Favor (mains US$2-5; 6am-9pm) This popular spot specializes in good Caribbean-style Tico standards, particularly fresh juices and rice and beans, at excellent prices.

Reggae Restaurant (mains US$4-9; 7-11am & noon-9pm) Caribbean-style *soda* standards from inexpensive casados to the house specialty, shrimp in coconut milk, sometimes come with a side of live music.

Bluespirit (pastas US$5-7, seafood US$9-15) Overlooking a small, sheltered beach (you could ask to have your romantic dinner on the gently lit beachside patio), this sweet spot boasts good barbecues and Italian classics as well as piña coladas. It plans to offer homemade gelato, and three really nice bungalows on the same pretty shore for about US$20 per person.

Miss Edith's (dishes US$7-12; 8am-10pm) Undoubtedly the most famous and arguably the best restaurant in town is Miss Edith's. (As local people earn respect in the community, they are called Miss or Mister, followed by their first name – hence, Miss Edith. You wouldn't refer to a young person in this way.) Stopping for mouthwatering, cooked-to-order Caribbean cuisine is *de rigeur*; don't miss the potatoes in garlic sauce.

Restaurant El Palenque (dishes US$5-8) Tasty vegetarian fare as well as fish and meat dishes are cooked Caribbean Creole style (mildly spicy, sometimes with coconut or mango flavors). Casados are available, too.

Yoli's Restaurant (mains US$3-7; 10am-10pm) Its great prices on well-prepared, health-conscious food (don't skip your shot of noni juice, a Costa Rican-grown panacea) would be enough to recommend this spot, but the Colombian flare with fajitas and other standards make this spot stand out.

Cha Cha Cha! (mains US$6-9; noon-10pm Tue-Sun) In a corner veranda of an old, blue-painted clapboard house, this attractive eatery offers recommended *'cuisine del mundo.'* Well-prepared dishes range from Jamaican jerked chicken to Tex-Mex cuisine; there's always a vegetarian special and tofu can be substituted almost anywhere. It's all savored against a background of world music and jazz.

Roberto's Restaurant (☎ 755 0117; seafood dishes US$3-8; 7am-10pm) Owned by one of the top fishing guides (see p403) in the region, you know the seafood is fresh – try the red snapper in coconut milk (US$7) for first-hand experience. The restaurant uses organic ingredients whenever possible and does not serve artificial concoctions such as Coca Cola, so fresh juices will just have to do.

Pizzería El Cactus (pizzas US$8, other mains US$6-12; 5pm-close) On a side road northwest of downtown, this eatery serves pizzas (which will feed three people), pastas and barbecue, seafood and meat dishes.

Soda Bella Horizonte At the northwestern end of town is this popular beachfront shop, which offers delicious fresh-baked bread, cakes and pies and has picnic tables by the shore – a good place for a snack while being cooled by ocean breezes.

Restaurant National Park (casados US$3-5, seafood US$8-15; 11am-10pm) This restaurant by the entrance to Parque Nacional Cahuita has the best view in town, as well as good steak and shrimp dishes.

Restaurant Vista del Mar (fish US$3-6; 11am-10pm) Across the street, this recommended Chinese restaurant does an excellent chicken in ginger sauce.

Chau's Paradise (☎ 755 0421; seafood mains US$6-10; 11am-close) It's worth the short beachside jaunt out of town to enjoy the catch of the day simmered in spicy Chau sauce. The open-air restaurant/bar also has a pool table and live reggae and calypso music some nights. Bonus: you can get your nails done by Chau's wife at her salon next door.

Kelly Creek Restaurant (dishes US$8-10; 6:30pm-close Thu-Tue) Right by the park entrance, this recommended place at the Kelly Creek Hotel specializes in paella (US$9 per person, two minimum) and other Spanish cuisine, authentically prepared by Spanish owners.

Restaurant Relax (dishes US$4-8; 11am-close Wed-Mon) Inexpensive pastas and spicy fajitas courtesy of the Italian-Mexican owners are served alongside seafood dishes.

Restaurant Típico Cahuita (mains US$4-8, seafood US$5-15; 8am-close) A block off the main drag, this spacious spot beneath a *palapa* does everything from good rice and beans to lobster by weight and imported stone crabs.

Drinking

Though low-key, Cahuita certainly has some fine spots for a few drinks or even live music.

Cocos Bar, in the middle of town, has a nice conversational bar, but pounds to the sounds of Caribbean disco or the occasional salsa night. **Ricky's Bar** (☎ 755 0228; 1pm-midnight or so), next door, has a jungly vibe, outdoor seating and a nice dance floor. This place really gets hopping on Wednesday and Saturday nights at 9pm, when live bands take the stage.

Bar Hannia, a block away is a more relaxed local hangout. A quick walk up the beach to Playa Negra gets you to **Rosa's,** a laid-back option for beer and music, and **Chau's Paradise** (see p407), with live calypso and good seafood.

Getting There & Away

All buses arrive and depart from the parque central.

Puerto Limón/San José (Autotransportes Mepe) US$0.75/5; 1½/four hours; depart 7am, 8am, 9:30am, 11:30am & 4:30pm, additional bus at 2pm on weekends.

Puerto Viejo de Talamanca & points south US$1; 30 minutes; depart hourly from 7am to 9:30pm, three continue to Manzanillo and the rest to Bribrí/Sixaola.

Getting Around

The best way around Cahuita's mellow attractions is on foot or by bicycle, which you can rent at **Ciclo Safari** (☎ 755 0013/20; bikes hr/day US$1/6; 7am-6pm), where the staff also change currency, rent snorkeling gear (US$4.50 per day) and arrange taxis. If you're hankering for a little internal combustion, **Cahuita Center** (☎ 379 9974, 755 0045) rents scooters for US$10 an hour, including helmet and gas.

PARQUE NACIONAL CAHUITA

This small park of 1067 hectares is one of the more frequently visited national parks in Costa Rica. The reasons are simple: easy access and nearby hotels combined with attractive beaches, a coral reef and coastal rain forest with many easily observed tropical species, including sloths.

The park is most often entered from the southeastern end of Cahuita village, through the 'donate what you want' Kelly Creek entrance station. A steep increase of national park fees to US$15 several years ago (since reduced to US$6 or US$7) had the locals up in arms because they thought that travelers would refuse to fork out US$15 to sit on the beach and would go elsewhere. So villagers closed the park entrance booth and encouraged visitors to use the beach for free. The then Minister of National Resources, René Castro, blamed the situation upon drug-taking budget travelers! Be aware that you'll have to pay US$6 at the Puerto Vargas entrance.

Almost immediately upon entering the park, you'll see a 2km-long white-sand beach stretching along a gently curving bay to the east. About the first 500m of beach has signs warning about unsafe swimming, but beyond that, waves are gentle and swimming is safe. (It is unwise to leave clothing unattended when you swim; take a friend. Near the entrance, Mister Big J Tourist Service stores valuables in individual security boxes for US$1 per day.)

A rocky headland known as Punta Cahuita separates this beach from the next one, Playa Vargas. At the end of Playa Vargas is the Puerto Vargas ranger station. It's about 7km from Kelly Creek if you go this way, via a trail through the coastal jungle behind the beaches and headland. The trail ends at the southern tip of the reef, where it meets up with a paved road leading to the ranger station. At times, the trail follows the beach; at other times hikers are 100m or so away from the sand. A river must be forded near the end of the first beach and the water can be thigh-deep at high tide. Snorkeling is an option at Punta Cahuita (see the boxed text, p404).

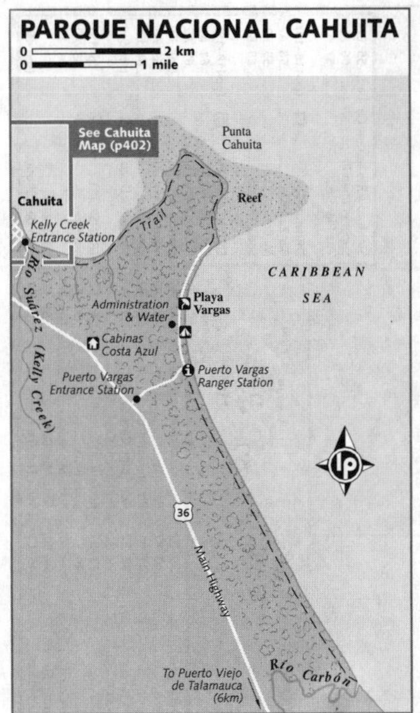

Information

The **Kelly Creek station** (admission by donation; 6am-5pm) is convenient to the town of Cahuita, while 1km down Hwy 32 takes you to the well-signed **Puerto Vargas station** (admission US$6; 8am-4pm), where you must enter if you're camping. No one stops you from entering the park on foot before or after these opening hours at Kelly Creek.

Camping (per person US$2) is permitted at Playa Vargas, less than 1km (which you can drive) from the Puerto Vargas ranger station, with outdoor showers, drinking water and pit latrines at the administration center near the middle of the camping area.

PUERTO VIEJO DE TALAMANCA

This is one of those remarkable places you wonder if a glowing recommendation in a guidebook won't ruin, a decidedly Caribbean concoction of perfect beaches, spectacular surfing and laid-back attitude spiced up with the best music, nightlife and restaurant scene on the coast. It's touristy – not to mention packed with expats, which may offer you the opportunity to discuss sports teams back home with your waitress – but if you can let go of getting in touch with 'the real Costa Rica' for a moment (it's here, but you'll need to look for it) you'll have a blast.

Puerto Viejo is most certainly a party town. But the road to Manzanillo is strewn with mellow bungalows and empty beaches if you would rather watch wildlife protected by the Gandoca-Manzanillo refuge (see p424) then come into town to get wild on Reggae Night at Bambú (see p418). Thanks to the newly paved road between the two towns, bicycles are the best way around, which just makes the whole vibe that much groovier.

Do keep in mind that as tourism grows, a cottage industry of sketchy drug dealers and irritating touts is growing with it. Most folks are fabulous, but it just takes one moron to ruin your vacation. Stay alert late at night, choose your own accommodations (and use the hotel safe!) and always remember that an ounce of caution is worth more than a pound of weed.

Information

INTERNET ACCESS

There are several places in town with Internet access, all of them expensive and slow.

ATEC (see Tourist Offices, p411) Charges a little more, but cost is figured by the minute, not the half-hour.

Internet Cafe (☎ 750 0633; per hr US$2; 9am-9pm) Has somewhat speedier machines than Videomundo.

Videomundo Internet (☎ 750 0653; per hr US$2; 7am-10pm) Conveniently allows you to buy large blocks of time for significant discounts on their painfully slow computers.

LAUNDRY

Lavandería Flash & Book Trade (☎ 750 0467; fluff & fold US$6; 9am-5pm) Lets you drop off your clothes and pick up a good book.

Lavandería Puerto Viejo (no phone; wash US$3, dry US$3; 7am-7pm Mon-Sat, 10am-2pm Sun) Has self-service machines, or you can tip a little extra for full service.

MONEY

Although Banco de Costa Rica plans to open opposite Mercado el Buen Precio, the closest bank at the time of research is in Bribrí (see p426). In town try either:

Cabinas Almendras (☎ 750 0235) Changes Canadian and US dollars, British pounds and euros at 1% commission, 2.5% on traveler's checks.

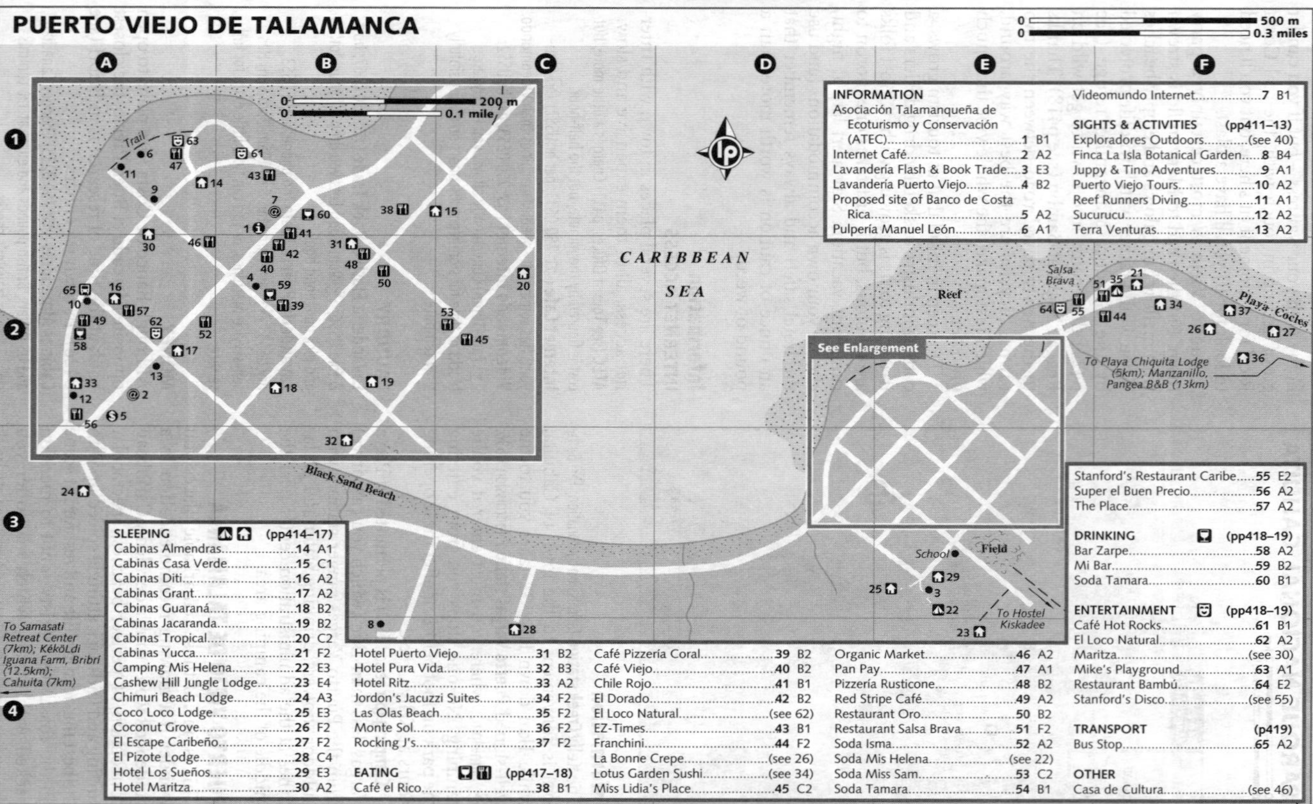
PUERTO VIEJO DE TALAMANCA
0 500 m
0 0.3 miles
0 200 m
0 0.1 mile
CARIBBEAN SEA
Trail
Reef
Salsa Brava
Playa Cocles
Black Sand Beach
See Enlargement
School
Field
To Playa Chiquita Lodge (5km); Manzanillo, Pangea B&B (13km)
To Hostel Kiskadee
To Samasati Retreat Center (7km); KéköLdi Iguana Farm, Bribri (12.5km); Cahuita (7km)
INFORMATION
Asociación Talamanqueña de Ecoturismo y Conservación (ATEC)....1 B1
Internet Café....2 A2
Lavandería Flash & Book Trade....3 E3
Lavandería Puerto Viejo....4 B2
Proposed site of Banco de Costa Rica....5 A2
Pulpería Manuel León....6 A1
Videomundo Internet....7 B1
SIGHTS & ACTIVITIES (pp411–13)
Exploradores Outdoors....(see 40)
Finca La Isla Botanical Garden....8 B4
Juppy & Tino Adventures....9 A1
Puerto Viejo Tours....10 A2
Reef Runners Diving....11 A1
Sucurucu....12 A2
Terra Venturas....13 A2
SLEEPING (pp414–17)
Cabinas Almendras....14 A1
Cabinas Casa Verde....15 C1
Cabinas Diti....16 A2
Cabinas Grant....17 A2
Cabinas Guaraná....18 B2
Cabinas Jacaranda....19 B2
Cabinas Tropical....20 C2
Cabinas Yucca....21 F2
Camping Mis Helena....22 E3
Cashew Hill Jungle Lodge....23 E4
Chimuri Beach Lodge....24 A3
Coco Loco Lodge....25 E3
Coconut Grove....26 F2
El Escape Caribeño....27 F2
El Pizote Lodge....28 C4
Hotel Los Sueños....29 E3
Hotel Maritza....30 A2
Hotel Puerto Viejo....31 B2
Hotel Pura Vida....32 B3
Hotel Ritz....33 A2
Jordon's Jacuzzi Suites....34 F2
Las Olas Beach....35 F2
Monte Sol....36 F2
Rocking J's....37 F2
EATING (pp417–18)
Café el Rico....38 B1
Café Pizzería Coral....39 B2
Café Viejo....40 B2
Chile Rojo....41 B1
El Dorado....42 B2
El Loco Natural....(see 62)
EZ-Times....43 B1
Franchini....44 F2
La Bonne Crepe....(see 26)
Lotus Garden Sushi....(see 34)
Miss Lidia's Place....45 C2
Organic Market....46 A2
Pan Pay....47 A1
Pizzería Rusticone....48 B2
Red Stripe Café....49 A2
Restaurant Oro....50 B2
Restaurant Salsa Brava....51 F2
Soda Isma....52 A2
Soda Mis Helena....(see 22)
Soda Miss Sam....53 C2
Soda Tamara....54 B1
Stanford's Restaurant Caribe....55 E2
Super el Buen Precio....56 A2
The Place....57 A2
DRINKING (pp418–19)
Bar Zarpe....58 A2
Mi Bar....59 B2
Soda Tamara....60 B1
ENTERTAINMENT (pp418–19)
Café Hot Rocks....61 B1
El Loco Natural....62 A2
Maritza....(see 30)
Mike's Playground....63 A1
Restaurant Bambú....64 E2
Stanford's Disco....(see 55)
TRANSPORT (p419)
Bus Stop....65 A2
OTHER
Casa de Cultura....(see 46)

Pulpería Manuel León Change US dollars and euros with 'El Chino,' who charges 1.5% commission on cash and more on traveler's checks.

TOURIST OFFICES

Asociación Talamanqueña de Ecoturismo y Conservación (ATEC; ☎ 750 0191, 750 0398; atecmail@racsa.co.cr; www.greencoast.com/atec.htm; 🕑 8am-9pm, depending on scheduling) The headquarters of this progressive and worthwhile organization is your one-stop shop for information on local culture and environment; the office has a large flier board posting general tourist information and the staff can field most questions. Regional books on culture, wildlife and birding are available here, as are international phone cards and **Internet access** (per hr US$2).

ATEC, a nonprofit grassroots organization, began in the 1980s. Its purpose is to help promote environmentally sensitive local tourism in a way that supports local people and enhances their communities. Staff can provide you with information ranging from the problems caused by banana plantations to how to arrange a visit to a nearby indigenous reserve. ATEC is not a tour agency, but will arrange visits to local areas with local guides. Most trips involve hiking – they range from fairly easy to difficult, and trips on horseback can also be arranged.

If you want to visit nearby indigenous communities you can request guides who will focus on anything from medicinal plants to area artisans; or ask about visiting the Bribrí iguana farm, where lizards are legally raised for food, or a spectacular waterfall nearby. All sorts of trips can be geared toward the visitor's interests, be they natural history, bird-watching (more than 350 bird species have been recorded in the area; one group reported 120 species sighted on a two-day trip), Afro-Caribbean cultures, environmental issues, adventure treks, snorkeling, or fishing.

Although these trips aren't dirt cheap, they are a fair value. The idea is to charge the traveler less than the big tour companies, but to pay the guides more than they might make working for those companies. A percentage of fees goes toward supporting community activities. Prices start at about US$20 per person for half-day trips, early-morning birding hikes and night walks. Day trips cost about US$30, and various overnight trips are available, priced depending on your food and lodging needs. Group numbers for outdoor activities are limited to six.

ATEC can arrange talks about a variety of local issues for around US$45 per group. Also, staff can arrange meals in local homes for various prices, depending on the meal required.

Sights

INDIGENOUS RESERVES

There are several reserves on the Caribbean slopes of the Cordillera de Talamanca, including the Reserva Indígena Cocles/KéköLdi, which comes down to the coast just east of Puerto Viejo; the Talamanca Cabecar reserve, which is the most remote and difficult to visit; and the Bribrí reserve, where locals are a bit more acculturated and tolerant of visitors. Access should be arranged with a guide; ATEC (opposite) is a comprehensive source of information.

There are several outfitters who offer tours to the reserves, but keep in mind that there is a little bit of discomfort on the part of at least some indigenous folks about the way certain operations are run. Visitors are welcome, as many people would love to diversify the economy away from bananas. But at present, tensions are being caused by tour operators who have reportedly failed to pay indigenous guides out of your ticket price (instead working only for tips) and others who have actually skipped paying the entrance fee, which helps support local schools.

These are still recommended trips, but let your tour operator know that you'd rather not cut corners, even if it means a more expensive trip. Note that most indigenous people wear modern clothes and speak Spanish in addition to their own languages. Please ask permission before snapping photos.

FINCA LA ISLA BOTANICAL GARDEN

To the west of town is the **Finca La Isla Botanical Garden** (☎ 750 0046; www.greencoast.com/garden.htm; admission US$2; 🕑 10am-4pm Fri-Mon), a working tropical farm where the owners have been growing local spices, tropical fruits and ornamental plants for over a decade. Part of the farm is set aside as a botanical garden, which is also good for birding and wildlife observation (look for sloths and poison-dart frogs). There is a picnic area. An informative guided tour (in English) costs US$5 (including admission, fruit tasting and finishing with a glass of homemade juice), or you can buy a booklet for a self-guided tour for US$2.

Activities

SURFING

Kurt Van Dyke, owner of the Hotel Puerto Viejo (see p414) in the village, is a local surfing expert and many surfers stay at his place. The famed 'Salsa Brava', outside the reef in front of Stanford's Restaurant Caribe, is known as the country's best wave. The reef here is shallow, so if you lose it, you're liable to smash yourself and your board on the reef; this is not for beginners.

Almost as impressive are the less damaging waves at Playa Cocles, about 2km east of town (an area known as 'Beach Break' after a local restaurant), or 'The Barge' (sometimes called 'Escuelas' as this was once within view of distracted students), actually the grassy remains of the old dock, near the bus station. North of Cahuita, Playa Negra and Westfalia also have good surfing. For the truly adventurous, a 20-minute boat trip from Puerto Limón to undeveloped Isla Uvita puts you in the path of some serious surf. Ask around for other places and up-to-date conditions.

The waves are generally best here from December to March, and there is a mini-season for surfing in June and July. From late March to May, and in September and October, the sea is at its calmest.

> **SOUTH CARIBBEAN MUSIC & ARTS FESTIVAL**
>
> Organized by Wanda Patterson, owner of Playa Chiquita Lodge, this **festival** (☎ 750 0062; wolfbiss@racsa.co.cr) fills weekend nights in March and April with eclectic offerings, all home grown on the Caribbean Coast: calypso to jazz, reggae to Celtic and even classical artists perform; dancing troupes take the stage with Jamaican and African flair; and Costa Rican-produced films and shorts are shown. This is a family-oriented event.
>
> Dates for the festival vary but are usually weekends in March and April (for about five weeks before Easter) and performances are held at the Playa Chiquita Lodge (p415). Tickets cost US$5 and proceeds go to music programs for children along the southern Caribbean coast.

There are several surf schools around town, more or less independent operations charging about US$25 for an hour of lessons and you'll generally get to keep the board all day. Rocking J's is just one place that can arrange classes. Note that Puerto Viejo isn't really the best spot for true beginners to pick up the sport – the Pacific coast has smaller, more user-friendly waves – but folks with some experience will benefit from local advice before tackling the big breaks. It's not a bad deal considering that boards rent for about US$10 to US$15 per day at several places around town.

DIVING & SNORKELING

The waters from Cahuita to Manzanillo are protected by Costa Rica's only two living reef systems, which form a naturally protected sanctuary, home to some 35 species of coral and more than 400 species of fish, not to mention dolphins, sharks and, occasionally, whales. Generally, underwater visibility is best when the sea is calm; ie, when surfing is bad, snorkeling is good. The best snorkeling reefs are at Cahuita, Punta Uva and by Manzanillo – the latter has the greatest variety of coral and fauna. You can arrange snorkeling trips with operators in Cahuita, Puerto Viejo and Manzanillo, sometimes in conjunction with guided hikes into Parque Nacional Cahuita or the Gandoca-Manzanillo reserve.

Reef Runners (☎ 750 0480; arrecifes55@hotmail.com; 🕑 7am-8pm) offers a range of diving options. Introductory courses start at US$75 for three hours, and one-/two-tank boat dives cost US$40/60. You don't need PADI certification – a US$35 temporary license is available – but for US$285 you can get fully certified right here. **Aquamor Talamanca Adventure** (p423) in Manzanillo, which has helped coordinate reef research as well as compile data on nearby dolphin communities, also offers diving trips and courses, sea kayaking, and snorkeling.

SWIMMING

The safest swimming around is along Playa Negra, also an excellent body-boarding spot, or in the natural sea pools in front of Pulpería Manuel León and Stanford's. For about 10 smooth kilometers east on the main road are some of the most beautiful beaches imaginable, the sort you see in movies and wonder if they aren't computer-generated.

CARIBBEAN COAST

SALSA BRAVA

It's the biggest break in Costa Rica, for expert surfers only and dangerous even then: Salsa Brava, named for the heaping helping of 'sauce' it serves up on the sharp, shallow reef, continually collecting its debt of fun in broken skin, boards and bones. There are a couple of take-off points and newbies waiting around to catch the popular North Peak should keep in mind that there are plenty of people in this town who gave up perks like mom's cooking and Wal-Mart just to surf this wave regularly. Don't get in their way.

In a sense, it was the Salsa Brava that swept Puerto Viejo into the relaxed limelight it enjoys today. Although discrimination against the primarily black residents of the Southern Caribbean was officially outlawed in 1949, the development of little luxuries such as paved roads, electricity and telephone lines came more slowly here than elsewhere in Costa Rica. Most tourists – nationals and foreigners – still spend most of their beach time on the more accessible and developed Pacific coast.

But surfers are a special breed and would not be dissuaded even 30 years ago by the bumpy bus rides and rickety canoes that hauled them and their boards from San José on the week-long trip (assuming that the bus didn't get stuck in the mud for a night or two) to this once remote outpost. Bemused locals first opened their homes, then basic cabinas and *sodas*, to accommodate those rugged souls on their quest.

In the wake of the wave riders came other intrepid explorers, eager to see those storied sunrises over perfect coastlines and monster curls; residents, who were by this time surfing with the best of them, happily developed a grassroots tourist infrastructure to keep everyone happy – *pura vida*, baby.

And though today's visitors enjoy Internet access, fine dining and a paved route that's shortened travel time by several orders of magnitude, the magnificence of Salsa Brava and its attendant waves still flood Puerto Viejo with tanned troopers on a mission.

So if you find yourself wondering what stirred up this marvelous mix of Caribbean culture and tourist trappings amidst all this natural beauty, grab a beer at the Stanford and watch the wave roll in.

This really is where the jungle meets the sea: picturesque sandy beaches (quite slender at high tide) are caressed by smaller waves perfect for swimming and body surfing, all (of course) fringed with swaying coconut palms. Plus you're as likely to see toucans, monkeys and sloths right here as anywhere in the country.

A gorgeous 6km bicycle ride east of town is **Punta Uva**, named for the small peninsula with a natural cave and home to some of the best beaches of all. It's convenient to good restaurants and home to several cabinas perfect for the budget traveler. It, along with Playas Negra, Cocles, Chiquita and, on the eastern end of the Gandoca-Manzanillo refuge, flies that coveted blue flag (see p453).

Swimming is not recommended in Manzanillo east to Punta Mona, a three- to four-hour hike into the reserve, because of strong undertows. Be cautious at all beaches, particularly if the waves are high and ask at any business area if you're unsure about current conditions at a particular beach.

RAFTING

Puerto Viejo provides easy access (two hours to the put-in) to the Río Pacuare (p151) courtesy of **Exploradores Outdoors** (☎ 222 6262; www.exploradoresoutdoors.com), a recommended outfit with a booth in front of Café Viejo. The one-day trip down the Class III-IV Pacuare (per person US$88) is the most popular excursion. It leaves at 6:30am and returns at 4:30pm and includes great meals. The company also arranges more challenging and/or remote trips on the Pacuare, Río Reventazón, including two-day adventures with an overnight at their comfortable camping ground.

Bonus: this company can pick you up at your hotel in either Puerto Viejo or San José, take you rafting, then transport you, free of charge, to the other city. Sweet.

Tours

Tour operators generally require a minimum of two people on any excursion and these prices are per person. Larger groups can often arrange discounts.

Terra Venturas (☎ 750 0750/489; www.terraventuras.com; 🕑 8am-7pm) is a block from the bus terminal. It offers overnights in Tortuguero (US$90), guided hikes (US$35), snorkeling in Cahuita (US$40), dolphin tours in Manzanillo (US$40), white-water rafting (US$85) and more, plus their very own 18-platform, 2.1km long canopy tour (US$40), with a Tarzan swing.

Puerto Viejo Tours (☎ 750-0411, 755 0082; 🕑 7am-7pm Tue-Sun), located close to the bus stop, can arrange rental cars, Fantasy Bus tickets and a variety of tours, including snorkeling (US$40), guided hikes (around town US$20, in Gandoca-Manzanillo refuge US$60), fishing trips (US$60), Bribrí indigenous reserve tours (US$45 to US$60), horseback riding (US$400), white-water rafting (US$75 to US$85) and dolphin encounters (US$50). It also sells inexpensive raincoats.

Juppy & Tino Adventures (☎ 750 0621/761; juppytinoadventures@yahoo.com) allows you to rent your own kayak (hour/day US$5/18) or arrange a guided kayak tour through the Gandoca-Manzanillo refuge or Talamanca Indigenous Reserve (US$60). It also offers guided hikes (US$35), snorkeling (US$40), dolphin watching (US$40) and a hike to the Bribrí waterfall (US$35).

Sucurucu (☎ 841 5578; 🕑 8am-6pm) is the place if you're tired of resorts masquerading as 'nature reserves' yet they don't recycle; or 'canopy tours' that are a blur of green? Go euphemism-free on a four-hour guided ATV tour (s/d per person US$70/50), where you'll tear through gorgeous mountains and jungle and may even see deaf wildlife. Sucurucu also rents scooters (three/24 hours US$15/30), a great way to get around the beach towns; you must be 18 years old and leave either a passport, credit card or US$200 deposit.

Sleeping

Standards for accommodations in Puerto Viejo are almost universally high; even the most basic places tend to be not only clean and comfortable, but have a certain flair, as well as a relaxing outdoor spot to read when the weather isn't cooperating. For the more luxuriously inclined, the slim selection of mostly disappointing resorts is easily eclipsed by a strand of beautiful bungalows between Puerto Viejo and Manzanillo.

During Costa Rica's December to April high season, the Christmas and Easter vacations, and the Caribbean Carnival period in August, you'll be paying the high-season rates listed here and reservations may be necessary for the most popular spots. Most places offer low-season and long-term rates, and many allow camping on their grounds.

BUDGET

Cold water is the norm in budget places, but you'd have to have the air-con on at full blast to appreciate a hot shower anyway. The majority of hotels will provide either mosquito nets or fans; a breeze fanning the bed will help keep mosquitoes away.

The author's choice for this price range, Rocking J's, is described in the boxed text opposite.

Cabinas Jacaranda (☎ 750 0069; www.cabinasjacaranda; s/d US$15/22, s/d with bathroom US$25/30; P) In the land of quickly constructed concrete cabanas, this colorful spot surrounded with flowers proves that personal touches and attention to detail make a place feel more luxurious than a private bathroom. This sexier-than-average option suggests that magic inhabits each uniquely decorated room, but with hot showers, lovely gardens and shared kitchen, it's a good deal no matter what goes on under mosquito netting.

Hotel Puerto Viejo (☎ 750 0620; r per person without/with bathroom US$6/9, d with air-con US$25; tent US$3.50; P ✖ 💻) 'No shoes, no shirt, no problem,' dude, and that goes for the clean, functional rooms with hot showers, the shared kitchen and Internet terminals. Boards can be hung in the reception area, where talk revolves

BUS STOP MADNESS

Expect to be greeted at the bus terminal in Puerto Viejo by a crew of local solicitors offering sweet deals on hotel rooms. Some are honest people representing their businesses, while others will say just about anything to get you to the hotel that pays them the highest commission. You might be told that, shockingly, your chosen accommodation is teeming with rats and scabies, or coincidentally, your new friend is a representative from that very place and sadly, it's overbooked. Don't believe everything you hear. And if you have any doubts about your hotel, simply ask to see a room before agreeing to stay.

THE AUTHOR'S CHOICE

Budget

Rocking J's (☎ 750 0657; www.rockingjs.com; tent/rent-a-tent US$4/6, hammock US$5, dm/d US$7/20, treehouse US$60; Ⓟ) Amenities at this backpackers' mecca include a 'hammock hotel' with sheets, pillows and mosquito nets, tent rentals, private rooms, some with mirrors on the ceiling, community kitchen, rigorous security, TV salon with 300 movies, beachside bonfires, oh and a free slushy when you walk in the door. Pretend that you're the professor on *Gilligan's Island and* climb 30m into your fully equipped (but basic) treehouse, dumbwaiter included. Perhaps the most incredible thing about this complex is the mosaic work – art supplies are available to guests with artistic urges. The result is incredible: shared bathrooms are gorgeous, common areas outrageous. It's worth booking a beachside massage (US$15 to US$30) as an indulgent excuse to check it all out. J's also rents kayaks (US$5 per hour), bikes (US$4 per day) and other fun stuff.

Mid-range

Playa Chiquita Lodge (☎ 750 0408; www.playachiquitalodge.com; d incl breakfast US$55, additional person US$12, house per night/wk US$60/275; Ⓟ) East of Puerto Viejo, this is more than just your average fabulous beachfront lodge. Nestled on a quiet stretch of beach in Playa Chiquita, the lodge is run by community-oriented owners Wolf Bissinger and Wanda Paterson. Wanda is active in the community and organizes the Music & Arts Festival (p412). Rooms with overhead fans and private bathrooms are simple but spacious and nicely designed. Anyone can make reservations for an 'internationally influenced Caribbean-style' dinner for US$6 to US$10 per person (worth it). Tours can be arranged; massage is available for US$40 per hour. Ask about the tree shower. A fully equipped four-room house is nearby.

Top end

Viva (☎ 750 0089; www.puntauva.net; d night/wk US$175/500; Ⓟ ❄) There are plenty of luxurious jungle bungalows between Puerto Viejo and Manzanillo, but these elegantly constructed cabins are something special. Enormous, gorgeously constructed and fully furnished hardwood houses, each with tiled hot-water shower, kitchen, two bedrooms and a wrap-around veranda are set in a semiformal garden with a croquet lawn (you can borrow a mallet and balls), near the beach.

around surfing big waves, a topic about which owner Kurt Van Dyke is a respected local expert.

Hotel Ritz (☎ 750 0176; d/q US$10/20) It's basic – maybe check out the room first – but has character to spare courtesy of long-time proprietor Vincente, with tales aplenty about the history of this very interesting old port.

Cashew Hill Jungle Lodge (☎ 750 0256; cashewhilllodge.co.cr; tr US$25) Set on a hectare of land, this recommended establishment has two cabins with shared hot showers, a covered patio, hammocks and a communal kitchen. Newer, bigger bungalows are on the way.

Las Olas Beach (☎ 750 0424; masterservicios@yahoo.com; d/tr/q US$30/40/50, tents per person US$3.75; Ⓟ) Watch the big waves roll in from your rather rustic room's porch hammock or sandy tent site.

Hotel Los Sueños (☎ 750 0369; hotellossuenos@hotmail.com; s/d US$10/20; Ⓟ) A bit removed from the milieu but still in town, this clean, cozy Swiss-run spot has four relaxing rooms with fan and mosquito net, sharing two nice bathrooms with hot showers and a fine porch.

Cabinas Diti (☎ 750 0311; s/d US$10/14) Rooms are standard but fine; a bike-rental (US$2.50 per day) and a souvenir-clothing store is attached.

Hotel Pura Vida (☎ 750 0002; www.hotelpuravida.com; s/d US$15/19, s/d with bathroom US$25/30) This attractive and clean place has 10 decent rooms with fans. Those without bathrooms have sinks, and shared hot showers are down the hall. A kitchen is available for guest use and there's parking and a pleasant garden to hang out in. German and English are spoken.

Cabinas Grant (☎ 758 2845, 750 0292; per person weekday/weekend US$10/15; Ⓟ) This place has decent rooms, some sleeping six, with cold-water bathrooms, fans, porches and a locked parking area. The attached **restaurant** (breakfast

US$3.25, other meals US$4-9; 7am-10pm) has a long menu of seafood and standard meals, including tasty salads such as the Caribbean-style shrimp and avocado.

Cabinas Guaraná (750 0244; www.cabinasguarana.com; s/d/tr US$23/33/40; P) offers a spacious shared kitchen plus lots of personal touches, hot water, ceiling fans, writing desks and balconies with hammocks. There are wheelchair-accessible options, plus a great tree house at the back worth exploring.

Chimuri Beach Lodge (750 0119; chimuribeach@racsa.co.cr; d/q US$35/40; P) Located in a residential area on the west side of Puerto Viejo by the black-sand beach, this lodge is run by Mauricio Salazar, a local authority on indigenous culture. The cabins are secluded and come with private bathroom, kitchen, hot shower and balcony.

Cabinas Yucca (750 0285; cabinas-yucca@yahoo.de; s/tr US$25/30; P) Immaculate, well-designed rooms overlook the ocean. During high season, owner Christel serves breakfast on an outdoor thatched patio.

Cabinas Almendras (750 0235/46; flchwg@racsa.co.cr; s US$20, d without/with air-con US$35/50, apt US$55, additional person US$10; P) Centrally located with guarded parking and satellite TV in the much larger doubles, this place is comfortable. Three apartments sleeping six boast separate rooms and small kitchens.

Monte Sol (750 0098; montesol@racsa.co.cr; d US$20; P) Simple, stylish cabins lie away from the noise of the main road. Private showers have hot water and filtered water is available free to guests.

Coconut Grove (750 0093; s/d US$15/20, s/d/tr with bathroom US$20/25/30; P) Pleasant and clean with hot water, mosquito nets, fans and hammocks overlooking the street, these lovely rooms (the ones with private bathroom are nicer) have two big perks downstairs: a great shoe store and **La Bonne Crepe** (crepes US$1-2; 7am-9pm), with fancy coffees and cheap, delicious crepes to start your day right.

Camping Mis Helena (750 0580; tent spaces US$5, rent-a-tent US$6) Off the main drag, this mellow camping spot is quieter and more family-oriented and there's a covered area in case of rain. Bonus: it's right by the excellent **Soda Mis Helena** (mains US$2-4; 7am-6pm Tue-Sun), serving inexpensive Caribbean/Tico standards and daily soup specials made over a wood-burning stove, best washed down with a cool glass of spicy homemade ginger ale.

Several hotels offer camping, including Rocking J's, with covered tent sites and Las Olas Beach, with sandy spots right on the waves. There's also camping in the Gandoca-Manzanillo Refuge (see p424)

MID-RANGE

Playa Chiquita Lodge, see the boxed text on p415, is the author's choice for this price range.

Pangea B&B (759 9204; pangeacr@racsa.co.cr; r per person incl breakfast US$35; P) Tucked away in gorgeous gardens hidden within Refugio Nacional de Vida Gandoca-Manzanillo Wildlife Refuge, this small, ecologically minded B&B is worth a stay. It has two pretty rooms surrounded by extravagant gardens and uses mainly organic produce (grown on-site) and fresh, locally caught seafood, though you'll need to arrange dinner in advance. The helpful owner can arrange local guides for the refuge and region.

Hotel Maritza (750 0003; per person without/with bathroom US$15/30) Extremely nice rooms with private bathrooms may be more comfortable, but the older, wood-paneled rooms are cozier. The hammock hangout area wins, however.

Cabinas Casa Verde (750 0015; www.cabinascasaverde.com; s/d US$28/32, s/d with bathroom US$45/52; P) Tiled walkways lead through lovely gardens hung with hammocks to 14 sparkling, beautifully painted rooms, with ceiling fans, mosquito nets, balconies and hammocks. Bikes are available (US$6 a day) and breakfast is served daily except Monday.

Cabinas Tropical (750 0283; www.cabinastropical.com; s/d US$25/30; P) Eight spotless rooms with mosquito nets, large private hot showers, nice breakfast nooks and fridges are just part of the appeal: the personable German owner, Rolf, has written and illustrated German-language guidebooks to the plants and fruits of Central America. He leads jungle hikes for birders from dawn until about 11am (per person US$30, three minimum, breakfast provided).

Coco Loco Lodge (750 0281; www.cocolocolodge.de; s/d US$30/35; P) On the quiet edge of town, this place has five bungalows with hot water, set on spacious, pleasant grounds. Breakfast is available for US$5 and German and English are spoken.

El Escape Caribeño (750 0103; www.escapecaribeno.com; s/d US$45/55; P) About 500m east of town, this recommended spot has a variety of bungalows with fan, private hot-water bathroom, fridge, bar and porch with hammocks. Most sleep one to four people but one has seven beds in two bedrooms and is suitable for students or large families. A rancho in the garden is available for breakfast (separate cost). Italian, English, French and German are spoken.

El Pizote Lodge (☎ 750 0227; pizotelg@racsa.co.cr; d standard US$56, d bungalows US$76-90; P ✕) About 1km west of town on a quiet backroad, this is a relatively comfortable place. The rooms are large and clean, while nicer wooden bungalows with private bathrooms are more private. The lodge is set in a garden and you can rent bicycles, horses and snorkeling gear; boat and snorkeling tours are also available.

Jordon's Jacuzzi Suites (☎ 750 0232; s/d US$70/80; P ✕) Simple but elegant Japanese-style cabinas come with, yes, in-room Jacuzzis! To complete the mood, neighboring **Lotus Garden Sushi** (3-11pm) offers and all-you-can-eat sushi special for US$14.

TOP END

The author's choice for this price range, Viva, is described in the boxed text on p415.

Samasati Retreat Center (☎ 750 0315; www.samasati.com; s/d per person US$90/69, s/d with bathroom & meals US$162/107) Set on a lush hillside north of Puerto Viejo, this well-built, attractive complex affords sweeping views of the coast – the village is just visible far below. German and English are spoken and daily programs of different meditation techniques are offered in its large open-air meditation/group room. There is a calendar of special events and instruction is available in, among other things, yoga, bodywork, herbalism and nutrition. Tasty vegetarian meals are served buffet-style on a wooden terrace with ocean views. There are nine private bungalows with cool, wraparound screened walls, or you can stay in a guesthouse with five rooms sharing four bathrooms, all with hot showers. A yoga class (open to everyone) costs US$12, a meditation session US$5, and a massage US$60. Packages and long-stay discounts are available and tours of the area can be arranged. There is a sign for the retreat center about 1km north of the fork on the main highway where the road splits southeast to Puerto Viejo and west to Bribrí. From here it's a 1km drive to the entrance and another 1.6km to the center itself.

Eating

Cooking up the most impressive restaurant scene on the coast, Puerto Viejo has the cure for casado overkill (although there are plenty of great *sodas* dishing up *gallos* galore, not to worry), with outstanding Asian and Italian entries in particular. You'll pay for your fine meal, but there are also plenty of solid budget options the next day.

The best spot for groceries is **Super el Buen Precio** (6:30am-8:30pm). Don't miss the weekly **Organic Market** (6am-6pm Sat), when area vendors and growers sell snacks typical of the region, including the red, pear-shaped 'water apple,' a light and not-too-sweet treat that's hard to find elsewhere.

Café El Rico (8am-4pm) Rich and excellent coffee – iced, even – is served alongside light breakfasts and lunches. Bonus: you get a free cappuccino when you do your laundry (US$5 for 4kg) on-site. Bikes can be rented here, too.

Pan Pay (light meals US$2-4; 7am-7pm Thu-Tue) Another excellent spot for strong coffee also comes with some of the best baked goods in town (check out the chocolate croissants), as well as sandwiches, quiches and other tasty fare.

Soda Miss Sam (mains US$2-6) Perhaps the best recommended *soda* in town, Miss Sam has been stunning locals and tourists alike for years with her Caribbean flavors and renowned rice and beans.

Franchini (mains US$3-6; 7am-4am) After a long night of drinking and dancing, cruise by this hot spot for fabulous fried chicken, good seafood and fine breakfasts – often it just stays open all night, allowing early birders to start their checklist with a look at night owls finishing one last beer.

Café Pizzería Coral (☎ 750 0051; breakfast US$2-3, pizza US$4-6; 7am-noon & 5:30-9:30pm Tue-Sun) Beloved for healthy breakfasts and homemade wholemeal bread, this community standard now serves excellent pizza including lots of seafood and vegetarian options.

Miss Lidia's Place (mains US$2-6) Another well-recommended local spot does all the *soda* standards, Caribbean-style of course, but with lots of vegetarian options.

Soda Tamara (breakfast US$2-4, seafood dinners US$6-10; 7am-10pm) Popular for breakfast overlooking the street and good seafood meals throughout the day is this friendly place – don't skip the coconut bread. The same folks also rent basic cabinas.

Red Stripe Café (🕐 7am-10pm) Close to the bus terminal, this recommended local spot run by a cool surfing couple does good breakfasts, fresh juices, falafel, breads and pastries, but specializes in homemade *helados* featuring locally grown ingredients – try the lemongrass sorbet or coffee ice cream.

EZ-Times (mains US$5-9; 🕐 10am-2:30am) Step into this beach-bum's paradise for pizza, pasta, salads and live music on Friday nights. Too relaxed to even leave the bungalow? Call for delivery until 2:30am!

The Place (mains US$3-7; 🕐 11am-10pm) Even though local fans love the curries and extensive vegetarian menu, the staff says that the daily chalkboard specials are always tops.

Pizzería Rusticone (mains US$4-7; 🕐 11am-close) This small and certainly rustic spot wins raves for its excellent pizza.

Restaurant Oro (mains US$4-10) This mellow local spot with a great outdoor seating area and relaxed vibe serves typical dishes and fresh seafood at great prices.

El Dorado (dishes US$3-6; 🕐 11am-close) Stop by for a burger or seafood (also see Drinking later).

El Loco Natural (mains US$4-8; 🕐 6-11pm) Vegetarian and other healthy meals are served with Caribbean flair at this 2nd-floor musical café, boutique and crafts store overlooking the street scene. It's a great place to hang out anytime and there's live music at 8:30pm Thursday and Saturday.

Chile Rojo (mains US$6-10; 🕐 noon-10pm) The promise of truly excellent Thai, Middle Eastern and other Asian food packs this small and highly recommended restaurant, but the curries are worth whatever wait might be required

Stanford's Restaurant Caribe (mains about U$5-14; 🕐 8am-10pm) Folks who have been returning here for decades marvel at how little this community landmark has changed – the beer is still cold, the seafood is still spectacular and the views remain absolutely perfect.

Restaurant Salsa Brava (☎ 750 0241; mains US$6-12; 🕐 11am-11pm) This well-recommended hotspot specializes in seafood and open-grill cooking in an intimate atmosphere. The owner promises that the on-site 'juice joint' will be returning with its signature healthy breakfasts.

Café Viejo (☎ 750 0817; mains US$6-15; 🕐 11am-close) Elegant and a little bit pricey, this fine Italian restaurant gets high marks for the excellently dressed fresh pastas and good cocktails, while the upscale, romantic ambiance makes it a definite date spot if you've got someone to impress.

Drinking

Restaurants often metamorphose into rollicking bar scenes after the tables are cleared. Try **Soda Tamara** (see Eating, earlier) for some people-watching over a beer, or **Café Viejo** for being seen over a fancy cocktail. **Mi Bar**, basically a row of brightly painted seats topped with equally colorful characters at a narrow bar near the post office, is also a fine spot.

El Dorado (🕐 11am-close) is quieter and more relaxed than many bars in town. Grab a beer and sidle up to the town's only pool table.

Bar Zarpe (🕐 11am-2:30am) It's not fancy, but the sunsets from this centrally located spot are spectacular and there's live calypso on Saturday night.

Entertainment

As you might expect from such a hip town, there are plenty of goings on after the sun sets. So put away that surfboard and fluff those dreadlocks – Puerto Viejo is an entirely different sort of paradise after dark.

CINEMA

Cine Playa Cocles (☎ 750 0128, 750 0507) At Cabinas El Tesoro (see opposite), this popular big screen shows a cool selection of camp, cult and classic movies plus plenty of Hollywood blockbusters at 7pm nightly; admission is free, but each table must purchase at least US$4.50 of beer and grub. Children are welcome at special 5:30pm showings on weekends.

Café Hot Rocks (☎ 750 0525; meals $3-8; 🕐 11am-2:30am) In a big red tent in the center of town, this place shows fine flicks for free most evenings and also hosts live (and often new) calypso, reggae and rock bands. Try their specialty dish – a granite hot plate and meats and veggies of your choice delivered to your table, where you can stir-fry everything yourself.

LIVE MUSIC & DANCING

Restaurant Bambú A humble sandwich and snack shop by day, Puerto Viejo's claim to fame stays open until the wee hours on Monday and Friday for Reggae Night, where DJs get irie and party people cruise in from up and down the coast to dance all night.

Mike's Playground Better known as Johnny's (its name for years), this place is at its most hopping on Thursday, when DJs spin reggae, hip-hop, salsa and more and patrons light beach bonfires outside.

Cabinas El Tesoro (☎ 750 0128/507) has been hosting an open-mic night at their bar and restaurant every Wednesday for more than 300 weeks straight.

Although returning surfers say the bar with the best view in town hasn't changed in 30 years, on Saturday the disco at **Stanford's** becomes the hottest dance spot in town.

Maritza (p416) has live Calypso on Sunday afternoon and **El Loco Natural** sometimes has mellow live music.

Getting There & Away

Buses arrive and depart at the main stop in town by the beach.

Bribrí/Sixaola US$0.50/2.50; 30 minutes/1½ hours; depart 6:15am, 8:15am, 9:15am, 11:15am, 2pm, 2:30pm, 5:15pm, 5:30pm & 7:30pm.

Cahuita/Puerto Limón US$1/1.10; 30 minutes/1½ hours; 6am, 9am, 11:45am, 1:45pm, 4pm, 4:30pm, 5pm & 5:30pm.

Manzanillo US$1.20; 30 minutes; 7:15am, 4pm & 7:15pm.

San José US$5.50; 4¼ hours; 6am, 10am, 1:30pm & 3:30pm.

Getting Around

Places renting bicycles tend to come and go, but there are usually several in operation. Look for signs, and shop around for bike quality and price – rust works fast on the coast. For horse rental, ask at ATEC.

EAST OF PUERTO VIEJO DE TALAMANCA

The 13km road heading east from Puerto Viejo was paved for the first time in 2003, dramatically shortening the time it takes to drive or bike past the sandy, driftwood-strewn beaches and rocky points, through the small communities of Punta Uva and Manzanillo, through sections of Reserva Indígena Cocles/KéköLdi, and ending up in Refugio Nacional de Vida Silvestre Gandoca-Manzanillo.

The road is still considered the property of folks without internal combustion, and drivers should be particularly careful at night, as cyclists and pedestrians make their way between the different bars, restaurants and lodges. Hitching is quite common on this stretch, but remember that you're taking a small but real risk every time you stick out your thumb (see p472).

This road more or less follows the shoreline and a variety of places to stay and eat can be found along the way. The paving is sure to inspire increased efforts by developers eagerly snapping up this prime real estate, and at least one resort has been accused of creating an artificial lagoon with, yep, dynamite. Luckily for local monkeys, wild boars and other wildlife, the southern stretch of road is within the Gandoca-Manzanillo refuge, which has even stricter rules for development than the rest of the beachfront.

Remember that all beaches in Costa Rica are public; you may be legally barred from using paths through private property to find the palm-fringed slice of heaven you've been dreaming about, but the sand is free to all.

Sights & Activities

The region's biggest draws involve surf, sand, wildlife-watching and attempts to get a decent tan between downpours. **Playa Cocles** is known for great surfing and an organized lifeguard system, which helps offset the dangers of the frequent riptides, while **Punta Uva** features the best and safest beaches for swimming. **Manzanillo**'s beaches have a serious riptide, but as part of the **Refugio Nacional de Vida Silvestre Gandoca-Manzanillo** (p424), are a haven for wildlife. A hike or snorkeling trip into the refuge is sure to be the highlight of any visit.

Mariposario (☎ 750 0086; adult/child under 10 US$5/free; ⏲ sunrise to sunset), in Punta Uva, is an unusual butterfly farm as it's only secondarily a tourist attraction – there aren't any informative displays, for example. This is a reproduction center, where some 70 species of butterfly are bred annually, including four species they claim exist in captivity nowhere else in the world: Prepona, Filaetinias, Mintorio and Inmanius. What you'll see depends on the time of year. Lydia, the biologist in charge of the project, can lead interesting guided tours in Spanish by request.

Sleeping & Eating

PLAYA COCLES

Known for big waves, this stretch, beginning 1.5km south of Puerto Viejo, caters to

CARIBBEAN COAST

budget travelers (with boards) and is liberally sprinkled with good, cheap *sodas* serving big, typical meals. Or enjoy fine dining at one of the country's best restaurants and retire to a hardwood cabina in your own private jungle.

Cabinas El Tesoro (☎ 750 0128; www.puertoviejo.net; dm US$9, r per person US$10-20; P) has a range of accommodations from the basic 'surf lodge' with shared bathroom and bunk beds, to a variety of other dorms and private room configurations plus two 'executive suites' (US$55) with air-con and TV. This festive spot serves coffee all day alongside free Internet access, community kitchens and more. What more? Try movies every night at 7pm and live music on Wednesday. Oh yeah, and there's the beach. Recommended.

La Isla Inn (☎ 750 0109; islainn@racsa.co.cr; d US$40, additional person US$10, air-con US$20; P) New and beautiful rooms with views and some unusually lovely furniture (made with the slightly curved outer boards discarded during lumber processing) make this a sweet stay by the sea.

Cabinas Garibaldi (☎ 750 0101; d/tr US$8/12; P) Many surfers stay at this place, which has reasonably clean quarters with private bathrooms and sea views.

Cabinas Beach Break (☎ 750 0326; d US$32 P) Like, this place has pretty basic rooms for the price, but dude – it's right across from some totally gnarly waves and rents surfboards, too.

Cariblue (☎ 750 0518; www.cariblue.com; d US$79, bungalow US$93, house incl breakfast US$190; P) This complex, set in lovely gardens with a swimming pool, has nine standard cabins with fans, hot water and high ceilings that keep them airy, quiet and cool. Four spacious hardwood bungalows with bathrooms (each with different mosaic tiling) have a porch and hammock. The house sleeps seven and has two bedrooms, two bathrooms and a kitchen.

Azania Bungalows (☎ 750 0540; www.azania-costarica.com; s/d with breakfast US$58/68; P) Spacious thatch-roofed bungalows sleeping four have mezzanines, porches with hammocks and neato hot-water bathrooms, all hidden away in landscaped jungle beauty.

La Costa de Papito (☎ 750 0704; www.greencoast.com/papito.htm; d US$48-60, additional person US$8; P) Relax in Rasta luxury as you reflect on a mellow philosophy of life. Five large hardwood bungalows with two double beds, carved tables, porches, high ceilings and fans all feature artistically tiled hot showers; two smaller bungalows have one bed, and all access the sculpture-studded jungle grounds. For an extra US$5 you can have breakfast delivered to your table (or hammock) on the porch – a nice way to start your day. You can also rent bikes, body boards and snorkeling equipment.

Río Cocles Cabinas (☎ 750 0142; riococles@racsa.co.cr; d/bungalow US$30/85; P) The rooms are fine, with hot water, fans and pleasant surroundings, but the fabulous bungalow, which sleeps four, is outstanding.

Bungalow & Rooms Yaré (☎ 750 0106; www.hotelyare.com; d US$40-60, cabin US$90-100; P) Between Playa Cocles, Playa Chiquita and perhaps Alice's Wonderland, vine-strewn covered walkways connect fanciful, brightly painted, high-ceilinged rooms and cabanas, some with outdoor kitchen. At night, the air is filled with the music of frogs, which drifts across the complex to the pleasant **restaurant** (mains US$3-6; 7am-9pm) from the surrounding jungle.

Casa Camarona (☎ 283 6711, 750 0151; www.costaricabureau.com/casacamarona.htm; s/d US$45/70, with air-con US$13; P) This modern and shady beachside spot has 18 rooms with tiled, hot-water bathroom and private little patio. A trail leads through a tree-filled garden to the beach, which at press time was flying that coveted blue flag.

El Rinconcito Peruano (mains US$3-9; noon-10pm Wed-Sun) For something a bit different, stop at this Peruvian restaurant renowned for its seabass *ceviche*, but justly proud of its spicier-than-usual salsas and cooked to order fresh seafood.

La Pecora Nera (☎ 750 0490; mains US$10-15; 11am-close, closed Mon in low season) Arguably the region's finest dining, this well-recommended spot is marvelously free of pretensions as you savor starfruit-and-shrimp carpaccio, fresh pasta dishes, steak and seafood perfectly prepared by amicable Italian chef Ilario. No menu makes an appearance; the chef or a server will come to your table and discuss what you'd like to eat and make suggestions. Wash your dinner down with some imported Italian wine and add an appetizer and dessert. It will make it an expensive evening – but it's worth it.

PLAYA CHIQUITA

It isn't exactly clear where Playa Cocles ends and Playa Chiquita begins, but conventional wisdom applies the name to a series of beaches about 4km to 7km east of Puerto Viejo.

Cabinas Olé Caribe (☎ 750 0455; q US$36; P) It's further from the beach than other entries, but the cute, clean rooms with fans are a deal if you can fill the double and bunk beds.

Villas del Caribe (☎ 750 0202, in San José 233 2200; www.villascaribe.net; d US$92; P) This is the most luxurious place on this beach. Here you'll find a dozen nice beachfront apartments (all sleeping up to five people) with sea view, separate rooms, hot shower, full kitchen, outdoor barbecue, and fan. This is also an excellent spot to arrange trips into nearby indigenous reserves.

Cabinas Slothclub (☎ 750 0358; d US$20, with kitchen US$25; P) Five clean wood cabins have great views, beach access and a snorkeling reef out the front.

Cabinas Yemanya (☎ 750 0110; www.yemanya.tk; q US$30, small house per month US$350) This basic affair is reasonably clean, has cold showers, an outdoor kitchen and a great vibe, with splashy colors and little trails running through the wild unkempt jungle growing right up to your door.

Hotel Punta Cocles (☎ 750 0338; www.puntacocles; d US$81; P) This rather bleak mod ern resort has all the amenities, including swimming pool, Jacuzzi, restaurant, games room, playground and activities, which make it popular with families and package tours.

Kashá (☎ 750 0205; www.costarica-hotelkasha.com; US$76; P) Though lovely and very comfortable, the small rooms with fans and hot showers are pretty standard – except for the bathrooms, which are works of art. Furnishings are fabulous. The grounds are also grand, with pool and Jacuzzi and the **Magic Ginger Restaurant** (mains US$5-10; 6am-10pm Tue-Sun) does gourmet French cuisine; try the ginger salad or grilled salmon.

Miraflores Lodge (☎ 750 0038; www.mirafloreslodge.com; dm/d US$10/46, additional person US$10) Dorms, sleeping four, are simple and clean with access to the shared outdoor kitchen, while eight private rooms with fridge, hot water, hammocks and nice décor are tucked away on the beautiful grounds. Owner Pamela Carter has been living in the area since 1988 and has gradually financed the construction of the lodge by growing and selling exotic flowers. She is knowledgeable about local botany and wildlife and can organize trips to visit Bribrí farming families or indigenous-medicine practitioners. A number of interesting healing and local-culture workshops are available. Breakfast (included) consists of seasonal fruits grown on the grounds. Reservations are recommended.

Bar y Restaurante Elena Brown (☎ 750 0265; mains US$4-7; 8am-11pm) The culinary-gifted Brown family scores high marks once again with Elena's famed whole red snapper, shrimp dishes and big breakfasts. The rice and beans get raves. The bar is festive and features a big TV and occasionally live music.

Shawandha Lodge (☎ 750 0018; www.shawandhalodge.com; d incl breakfast US$105, extra person US$22; P) This upscale lodge has 10 large, airy bungalows, all with fabulous bathroom mosaics – a feature that seems to represent a minor cultural movement along this stretch of coast. The elegant French-Caribbean **restaurant** (mains US$5-14; 7am-9:30pm) adds flambé panache and Provencial flavorings to Caribbean classics.

PUNTA UVA

About 7km east of Puerto Viejo is the Punta Uva area, known for the region's most swimmable beaches, each lovelier than the next, along which are strung several lodging options ranging from budget beauties to memorable extravagances. Or just stop by for a tranquil dip and the region's first micro-brewed beer, La Jungla, made right here.

Tree House (☎ 750 0706; www.costaricatreehouse.com; house US$99; P) Among the most intriguing accommodations in the region is this 'tree house', built from found (not cut) hardwood ingeniously constructed around a living Sangrio tree. The house sleeps six, and a similar beach house sleeping five also boasts impressive (though non-photosynthesizing) architecture, hot showers, beach access and an adjacent iguana farm (p422). Reservations recommended.

Cabinas Itaitá Villas (☎ 750 0414; labvaeo@racsa.co.cr; d US$41; P) Huge, no-nonsense rooms with a scenic view and festive furnishings feature fine porches for catching a coastal breeze.

Selvin's Cabins (no phone; d without/with bathroom US$10/14, d with kitchen US$20; P) Basic rooms with a mellow vibe, right on the beach, are just part of the experience; Selvin is a member of the extensive Brown family, noted for their charm and unusual eyes, which have attracted them both romantic and scientific attention. Even sweeter, the **restaurant-bar** (mains US$4-12; 8:30am-8pm Wed-Sun) is considered one of the region's best, specializing in shrimp, lobster and chicken *caribeño*.

Albergue Walaba (750 0147; per person from US$10) This groovy spot is pretty darned basic, but colorful rooms and dorms decorated like hippy havens in their own personal jungle, plus a handy outdoor kitchen, give it character to spare.

Viva (750 0089; www.puntauva.net; d per night/wk US$175/500; P) See Author's Choice, p415.

Ranchito Beach Restaurant (759 9048; mains US$3-8; 10am-6pm) Fronting a fine, palm-lined swimming beach, this mellow outpost features a thatch-roofed outdoor bar and a few romantic little tables scattered about beneath their own personal *palapas*. Mixed drinks involving fruit, pizzas, fresh pastas and of course fish (try the *carpaccio de marlin*, US$6) are happily served to folks in swimsuits with sandy feet.

Cabinas Angela (759 9092; s/d US$10/16, with kitchen US$15/23) It's certainly not fancy, but Angela (who speaks English, German and Spanish) has been keeping her four spacious cabins clean for decades, plus they have hot water and are right across from the beach.

Cabinas Morpho (759 9044; cabins US$50; P) Two lovely older houses, each with two floors sleeping three (and they can add beds), kitchen, TV, mosquito net, balcony and lots of rustic Caribbean charm, seem designed for long-term stays.

Bar & Marisquería Arrecife (759 9200; seafood dishes US$4-10; 7am-9pm) is a breezy beach-side bar specializing in the catch of the day, convenient to the previous two cabinas.

Two neighboring resorts catering primarily to tour groups: **Hotel Suerra** (759 9065; www.suerre.com; d US$95; P) made with mustard-colored concrete, and **Hotel Las Palmas** (759 9090; www.minotelcr.com; d US$90; P) with slightly nicer rooms in orange concrete, somehow have all the luxuries – pools, fancy restaurants, beach views – without seeming luxurious at all.

MANZANILLO

This idyllic destination has long been a bit off the beaten track – until 2003, the 13km road from Puerto Viejo de Talamanca was still a rutted, bumpy affair that could take 45 minutes by car or bus. Today, however, a paved road has cut drive time down to 15 minutes, as well as making bicycling

CHICKEN OF THE TREE

As the Caribbean Coast heats up each February and March, plump pregnant green iguanas make ready to lay their eggs, anticipating a new generation of young lizards to rule the jungle canopy. At the same time, local kids eager for a real treat set out with slingshots, hoping to bring a tasty 'chicken of the tree' to the family table. Although hunting iguanas is now federally forbidden (except for indigenous folks), some residents believe that they are still legally entitled to harvest one iguana each year. The results of these traditional hunts have been devastating.

According to Edsart Besier, a Dutch conservationist who founded **Iguanaverde** (750 0706; www.iguanaverde.com) in 2001, there are only between 500 and 2000 green iguanas left in the Southern Caribbean, at most a third of what researchers at the National University of Costa Rica consider a stable population. The species is found from Northern Mexico down into South America, but are becoming increasingly rare throughout the range. Climate change and loss of habitat, along with barbecues, have probably contributed to the crisis.

Iguanaverde, which began collecting eggs and endangered lizards in cooperation with Minae, now boasts an 800-sq-m enclosure stocked with the trees and plants iguanas enjoy in the wild. Besier has been raising and releasing the camouflaged critters into the protected refuge, often with the help of local schoolchildren who are in turn educated about the iguanas' plight. Bessier, who has largely funded the project out of his own pocket, offers supporters the chance to 'adopt an iguana' for US$15 (entitling you to a certificate and email updates on the project) and at press time planned to offer public tours (adult/child US$8/5) of the facilities at least two days a week; call for details.

the gorgeous stretch of perfect, palm-lined beaches a smooth option.

Though some worry that the easier access will funnel too many tourists in from Puerto Viejo, this region remains among the most pristine on the coast, thanks to ecologically minded locals and the 1985 establishment of the Refugio Nacional de Vida Silvestre Gandoca-Manzanillo, which actually encompasses the village and imposes strict regulations on further development of the region.

Wildlife, not nightlife, is the main attraction on this end of the road, where folks wake up early to take advantage of the fog-shrouded beauty of jungle, swamp and sea while Puerto Viejo is still rocking out. (Though Manzanillo does have its moments, courtesy of Maxi's.) Beaches are pristine and postcard perfect, but note that the stretch from the Almonds & Coral Lodge all the way to Punta Mona has potentially deadly riptides. Swimmers are strongly cautioned to be aware of them.

Water Sports

Aquamor Talamanca Adventures (☎ 759 9012; aquamor@racsa.co.cr) is a unique diving outfit that's run by the Tico-American Larkin family and devoted as much to conservation as recreation. Scuba diving ranges from US$30 for a one-tank beach dive to US$55 for a two-tank boat dive; rates include equipment and guide. PADI open-water certification courses cost around US$300. Kayak rentals for sea and river trips cost US$6 per hour, snorkeling gear is US$8 per day and various discounts are offered for all-day or overnight kayaking, diving, camping and snorkeling adventures. Dolphin-watching tours by boat or kayak are available for US$25 to US$55. Many guides speak English as well as Spanish, but ask about other languages.

This is also a great spot to come for general information about the refuge (particularly if you don't speak much Spanish), with an informative display of articles and tips about enjoying the park and reef, as well as the many conservation programs on the coast. People interested in the **Talamanca Dolphin Foundation** (☎ 759 0715/612; www.dolphinlink.org), dedicated to the study and preservation of local dolphins through outreach programs including a four-day, all-inclusive tour (US$380 per person), can get more details here.

Sleeping & Eating

Maxi's Restaurant & Cabinas (☎ 759 9073; deluxe/basic q US$35/15; Ⓟ) This family-owned landmark close to the entrance of the park has two sets of cabinas: the older portion with rustic, cold-water, rather ramshackle (but clean and cozy) rooms; the newer, much nicer rooms with TV, hot water and fridge, set back a bit further. **Maxi's Soda** (mains US$2-3; 6am-close) and famed **seafood restaurant & bar** (seafood US$4-10; noon-10pm at least), featuring inexpensive red snapper casados and extravagant fresh lobster served by weight. It's all topped off with good mixed drinks, local color and occasional live music, plus it's a fine spot to ask around about trail conditions and local guides.

Cabinas y Soda Las Veraneras (☎ 759 9050; s/d with fan US$10/17, with air-con US$12/20; Ⓟ) In a quiet residential neighborhood, small but pretty rooms have either cold water and fans or air-con, hot water and TV. A family room sleeping five has a kitchen ($50). The pleasant **soda** (breakfast US$2, other meals US$4-8; 7am-9pm), serves Caribbean and Tico standards plus, when available, lobster specials.

Cabinas Something Different (☎ 759 9014/97; s/d/q US$15/30/35; Ⓟ) New and spacious rooms with hot water, coffee maker, fridge and minibar are fronted by pleasant porches perfect for watching the sloths amble by. The small single rooms skip the extras (but do have hot water).

Pangea B&B (☎ 759 9204; pangeacr@racsa.co.cr; r per person incl breakfast US$35; Ⓟ) See Sleeping under Puerto Viejo de Talamanca on p416.

Congo Bongo (☎ 759 9016; mvleevwenzegueld@wxs.nl; d/q US$50/80; Ⓟ) Four fully equipped houses – with upstairs bedrooms, kitchen, fan, balcony with hammocks – sit among seven hectares of reclaimed chocolate plantation, now jungle, with several private trails including one to the beach.

Almonds & Corals Lodge Tent Camp (☎ in San José 272 2024; www.almondsandcorals.com; s/d/tr per person US$81/65/53; Ⓟ) This unusual option features roomy, comfortable tents on raised wooden platforms with amenities such as mosquito nets, fans, lights, tables and hammocks. A central lodge provides family-style **dining** (breakfast US$9, other meals US$14-16) and there are hot showers, toilets and a swimming pool. Guided hikes, snorkeling, bicycle rental, birding and horseback riding are offered and you can rent all manner of sports equipment. The surrounding area is undeveloped and full of wildlife – insects and frogs call all night and howler monkeys wake you at dawn. Guests and visitors alike can pay US$30 to walk private trails and see the onsite butterfly garden.

El Colibrí Lodge (☎ 759 9036; www.elcolibrilodge.fr.fm; d US$75; P) Designed with romance in mind, six bright and comfortable rooms open onto a terrace surrounded by gardens alive with interesting insects and the colorful birds who love them; for US$5 you can have your breakfast here or in your room, before walking the 300m trail to the beach.

Carnes Cuca 2 (⌚ 5am-9pm) This solid little grocery store supplies all your picnic needs.

Soda Rinconcito Alegre (casados US$2-5; ⌚ 7am-7pm) This cheerfully painted spot serves up seafood casados (try the marlin), spaghetti and rice dishes with a smile.

Restaurante Manzanillo (seafood mains US$4-8; ⌚ 11am-close) Sharp seafood at this expansive (but not expensive) spot right off the main drag.

Getting There & Away

There are three buses daily between Cahuita and Manzanillo, via Puerto Viejo de Talamanca. For Bribrí and Sixaola, change buses at Puerto Viejo.

REFUGIO NACIONAL DE VIDA SILVESTRE GANDOCA-MANZANILLO

This relatively new refuge (called Regama for short) protects nearly 70% of the Southern Caribbean Coast, extending from Manzanillo southeast to the Panama border. It encompasses 5013 hectares of land plus 4436 hectares of sea, making this the ultimate in surf and turf exploration.

The park was created in 1985, with special provisions for folks already living here, and the dry (well, drier) land portion provides an enormous variety of species with various habitats, not least of which is farmland. This was once a productive cocoa-growing region, but after a devastating blight swept through, the monoculture was replaced by a patchwork of fincas, ranches and re-encroaching jungle. The little village of Manzanillo is actually within the boundaries of the refuge, which also features rain forest, and some of the most beautiful **beaches** on the Caribbean, protected by rocky headlands.

Information

In the green wooden house as you enter town, **Minae** (☎ 759 9901; ⌚ 8am-4pm) is more useful than the average Minae office and has maps of the refuge and trails, as well as information about trail conditions, turtle watching and local guides; this is also where you pay to camp. Aquamor Talamanca Adventures (p423) also has information about the refuge. An excellent book of photos featuring local flora and fauna, including the folks who live here, with commentary in Spanish and English, is *Refugío Nacional de Vida Silvestre Gandoca-Manzanillo* by Juan José Puccí, available locally and online.

Sights & Activities

HIKING & SNORKELING

There is a coastal trail leading 5.5km from Manzanillo to Punta Mona, where swimming and snorkeling are considered safer than on beaches closer to town. South of this trail is an unusual 400-hectare swamp containing holillo palms and sajo trees, one of the country's most extensive. Another more difficult trail leaves from just west of Manzanillo and skirts the southern edges of this swamp, continuing to the small community of **Gandoca**, roughly 9km away. Unless visitors are knowledgeable about local flora and fauna, a local guide is well worth the modest cost, although experienced hikers could follow the Punta Mona trail without one.

The undersea portion of the park cradles one of two living coral reefs in the country – the other is at Cahuita, just a few kilometers away. Comprising five different types of coral, the reefs begin in about 1m of water and extend 5km offshore to a barrier reef that local fishers have long relied on and researchers have only recently discovered. You can easily arrange a trip by boat into the thick of this colorful undersea world, or start snorkeling right offshore to enjoy schools of some 400 different species of fish and crustaceans who make this natural coral aquarium their home, plus dolphins or whales if you're lucky.

WILDLIFE WATCHING

The variety of vegetation and the remote location of the refuge attract many tropical birds; sightings of the rare harpy eagle have been recorded here. Other birds to look for include the red-lored parrot, the red-capped manakin and the chestnut-mandibled toucan, among hundreds of others. The birding here is considered very good; one volunteer talked about flocks of toucans soaring overhead as their crew photographed a tribe of monkeys that had taken over two trees. The area is also known for incredible raptor migrations, with more than a million birds flying overhead in the fall.

Beyond Punta Mona, protecting a natural oyster bank, is the only red mangrove swamp in Caribbean Costa Rica. In the nearby Río Gandoca estuary there is a spawning ground for Atlantic tarpon, and caimans and manatees have been sighted. The endangered Baird's tapir is also found in this wet and densely vegetated terrain.

Marine turtles, especially leatherbacks but also green, hawksbill and loggerheads, all endangered, nest on the beaches between Punta Mona and the Río Sixaola. Leatherbacks nest from March to July, with a peak in April and May. Local conservation efforts are underway to protect these nesting grounds – the growth in the human population of the area has led to increased theft of turtle eggs and has contributed to the declining local population.

The **Asociación Nacional de Asuntos Indígenas** (ANAI; ☎ 759 9100; www.anaicr.org), or National Association of Indigenous Affairs, is a grassroots organization that works with locals to protect the sea turtles. During turtle season, knowledgeable staff are always available at their offices in Gandoca, accessible via a three- to five-hour hike or rough drive via Bribrí; at other times, it might be worth calling ahead. If you are interested in sea turtle conservation, you can volunteer to collect nesting and size data, patrol beaches and move eggs that are in danger of being destroyed by high tides or predation. Volunteering involves long hours, no pay, hot and humid conditions, and a chance to help sea turtle conservation while seeing a remote part of Costa Rica. If this appeals to you, contact **ANAI** (☎ in San José 277 7549; tortugas@racsa.co.cr; Apartado 170-2070, Sabanilla de Montes de Oca, San José, Costa Rica). Or write to the office in the USA, 1176 Bryson City Rd, Franklin, NC 28734, requesting information. If you can't volunteer, contributions are welcome.

Tours & Guides

Sure, you can explore the refuge on your own (if you've made it to Manzanillo, you already are), but without a guide you'll probably be missing out on the refuge's incredible diversity of medicinal plants, exotic birds and earthbound animals. Most guides charge US$20 to US$30 per person for a four- to five-hour trek, depending on the size of the group. If you can't get through on the phone, ask around at Maxi's. Prepare to get muddy and wet and don't forget your binoculars.

Florentino Grenald (☎ 759 9043, 841 2732), who used to serve as the reserve's administrator, has been highly recommended for birding and nature hikes. **Ricky Alric** (☎ 759 9020) has also received rave reviews and specializes in birding and medicinal plants. **Abel Bustamonte** (☎ 759 9043) is another recommended area guide. A local boat captain, Willie Burton, will take you boating and snorkeling from Manzanillo. Horses and guides can also be hired locally.

ATEC in Puerto Viejo de Talamanca (see p409) offers a variety of tours into the refuge, including day and overnight trips on foot, horseback, or by boat.

Sleeping & Eating

Accommodations for the ANAI volunteers ranges from camping to housing with local families; a minimum stay of seven days is required and volunteers must contribute to the cost of meals and housing (from US$7 to US$15 per day, depending on how much comfort you want). The project runs from early March to late July each year and there is a US$30 registration and training fee.

ANAI also has a volunteer tracking program based in the Cocles/KéköLdi reserve, with accommodations in their Hone Creek office near Puerto Viejo. This project runs during migrations from March to June and August to December; registration is US$160 and accommodations are US$150 a month.

Finally, ANAI also has an agroforestry and crop experimentation project at nearby Finca Lomas, where volunteers can stay for US$90 a month, plus a one-time US$160 registration fee. Most volunteers stay one to four months.

Punta Mona (www.puntamona.org; 5km south of Manzanillo; dm US$20 per person, incl 3 meals; 💻) is a unique experiment in permaculture design and sustainable living that covers some 40 hectares. More than 200 varieties of edible fruits and veggies are grown here, which make up about 85% of your huge vegetarian meals, also available for US$6 separately.

You can visit Punta Mona on a guided day trip (US$6 per person), stay overnight as a guest or, if you make arrangements in advance and are willing to work, volunteer for US$200 per month, which pays for room and board. Accommodations are fairly basic, but you can't beat the view – beach and jungle are accessible only by boat or on foot.

It's best to contact Punta Mona by email before you arrive, and the staff can organize a boat from Manzanillo (US$10 per person each way for guests, US$15 per person as part of a tour) for a minimum of three people, or arrange guides for the 5km hike from Manzanillo, or 2km hike from Gandoca, just south of Puerto Viejo on the other side of the park.

Camping is permitted on a donation basis (US$3 per person is suggested), but there are no organized facilities unless you are volunteering with ANAI. Reportedly, camping on the beach is best, as there are fewer insects and more breezes, and there are camping areas near the Gandoca entrance as well; the town also has a couple of *sodas* and cabinas. Most visitors take day hikes, though, and stay between Manzanillo and Puerto Viejo.

Getting There & Away

The Gandoca-Manzanillo reserve is accessible from Manzanillo by trail or by boat.

BRIBRÍ

You'll find this small, pleasant village en route from Cahuita to Sixaola and the Panama border, at the end of the paved (and badly potholed) coastal road. From Bribrí, a 34km gravel road takes the traveler to the border. It's a lively little town, with little to offer the casual tourist except for a handful of good restaurants, a few accommodation options and the closest bank to Puerto Viejo (Banco Nacional de Costa Rica), though this may change.

Bribrí is the center for the local indigenous communities in the Talamanca mountains, and though it is convenient to these interesting villages as well as a fine waterfall, all these sights are currently most easily accessed by organized tour from Cahuita or Puerto Viejo.

These indigenous communities are only now coming to terms with this sort of tourism and are currently organizing for a larger slice of the pie – at present, locals don't always see too much of your tourist colón (p411). However, about 1km from the bus stop, **Artesenias Bribrí** (8am-4pm) has begun organizing tours by Timotheo and Carlos Jackson; stop by or ask around for more information.

The Ministry of Health operates a clinic in Bribrí that serves both Puerto Viejo and the surrounding communities.

Sleeping & Eating

There are a couple of basic lodging options, a good-sized supermarket and some restaurants, including the requisite Musmanni Bakery, in Bribrí. Accommodations tend to fill up on market days (Monday and Tuesday).

Cabinas El Piculino (751 0130; d US$7-20; P) Fifteen clean, pleasant rooms have private hot showers; some have TV and air-con. A recommended **soda** (mains US$2-3; 7am-10pm Mon-Sat) run by the same family serves a fine *sopa consomé de pollo* and good rice dishes.

Complejo Turístico Mango (751 0054/155; s/d/tr/q US$7/10/12/14; P) Various configurations of basic rooms, some with hot water, are adjacent to a large restaurant on the outskirts of town.

Delicias de Mi Tierra (mains US$2-5; 6am-9pm Mon-Sat) You can't miss this wide-open and popular spot close to the bus terminal, with a steam table and quality local meals.

Soda Restaurant Bribri (mains US$2-5; 5am-5pm Mon-Sat) A bit more plush, this restaurant not only serves good casados, *gallos* and recommended fried plantains, but is also an excellent place to ask about tours to indigenous villages.

Getting There & Away

Buses to and from Sixaola usually stop in front of Restaurante Bribrí. Buses going north then continue to Puerto Viejo de Talamanca and Cahuita.

SIXAOLA

This is the end of the road as far as the Costa Rican Caribbean is concerned. Sixaola marks the country's secondary border crossing with Panama, though most foreign tourists travel overland via Paso Canoas on the Carretera Interamericana. But the crossing here is relaxed and popular among expats without residency visas who take their required 72-hour vacation on the lovely islands of Bocas del Toro, Panama.

GETTING TO GUABITO & BOCAS DEL TORO, PANAMA

With a reputation as one of Costa Rica's most relaxed border crossings, Sixaola is popular among folks embarking on their three-day 'visa vacation' to the islands of Bocas del Toro. The picturesque archipelago of jungle islands has more than a dozen beaches, home to everything from endangered red frogs and leatherback turtles to a dilapidated *Survivor* set, plus a range of accommodations, all accessible by convenient water taxis. Paradise.

Get to Sixaola as early as possible; the border is open from 7am to 5pm (8am to 6pm in Guabito, Panama, which is an hour ahead of Costa Rica) and one or both sides may close for lunch at around 1pm. Begin crossing the high metal bridge over the Río Sixaola, stopping at **migración** (☎ 754 2044) to process your paperwork. Cars (US$4) can cross here, but be prepared for a long wait. Fees vary widely to enter Panama, depending on your nationality; the most charged is US$5, which should be paid in US dollars.

Entry into Costa Rica is free. If you're asked to show a return ticket and don't have one, you can purchase a bus ticket (US$5) at the pharmacy. Make sure to get your visa stamp at migración.

Guabito has no hotels or banks, but it does have taxis (US$3) to Changuinola, which has a couple of basic hotels if you get stuck. Take another taxi to Finca 60 (US$1), where you can catch a water taxi (US$9) to Bocas del Toro on Isla Colón.

'Bocas' has the widest range of hotels and restaurants, from a basic bed over the water at **Tranquilo Inn** (no phone; r per person without/with private bathroom US$5/7), right behind the recommended Indian restaurant Om Café, to luxurious **Swan's Cay Hotel** (☎ 757-9090; www.swanscayhotel.com; d US$60-90; ⊠ ❄), with lots of amenities and diving packages.

The car-free island of Bastimentos (boat taxi US$2) is even more relaxed, with excellent and inexpensive accommodation options including the cheapest sleep on the islands, **Magic Beach** (no phone; 1.2km from Bastimentos; hammocks US$2, tent space per person US$2, rent-a-tent US$4) on almost undeveloped Wizard Beach, a steep and gorgeous half-hour hike from town. Other islands offer ample opportunity for exploration.

Sixaola is centered on the optimistically named Mercado Internacional de Sixaola, a gravelly square where you can find taxis, the bus stop, a handful of *sodas* and several small stores selling a wide selection of rubber boots. The *mercado* is about two blocks from the border crossing.

For details on crossing the border at this point, see the Getting to Garabito & Bocas del Toro, Panama, boxed text above.

Sleeping & Eating

While it's not exactly a layover in Tokyo, there are worse places to be stuck if you miss immigration hours – accommodations and restaurants are basic, but certainly acceptable for any seasoned budget traveler. Still, it's best to get here as early as possible and get to Changuinola, a US$3 taxi ride from the Panama border town of Guabito.

Hotel Doris (☎ 754 2207; s/d US$5/7) Reasonably well-maintained rooms with shared cold-water bathroom, fans and mosquito nets are above the bar, which features Karaoke on Monday night. It's one block off the main strip, turn at the Castañeda DiscoBar.

Hotel Imperio (☎ 754 2289; d without/with bathroom US$7/9) Cleaner and quieter, this basic motel's biggest selling point is its location, right across the street from the police checkpoint.

Soda Martha (mains US$2-4; 🕑 5am-5:30pm) Right on the Mercado Internacional, this hole-in-the-wall does good casados and an excellent *pollo en salsa* with rice.

Soda Navi (mains US$2-4; 🕑 6am-9pm) Around the corner, this pleasant spot with crocheted décor specializes in pintos and fried fish casados.

Restaurante Las Cabinas (mains US$2-5; 🕑 7am-9:30pm) This is as upscale as it gets in Sixaola, with pretty checkered tablecloths, fried chicken and to-go food.

Getting There & Away

All buses stop at the Mercado Internacional. Buses to either San José or Puerto Limón all stop at Bribrí and Cahuita, but only some go through Puerto Viejo.

Puerto Limón US$2.50; three hours; departs seven times daily.

San José US$7; five hours; departs at 6am, 10:30am, 1:30pm & 3:30pm.

Northern Lowlands

CONTENTS

Those who worry that the 'real' Costa Rica is becoming hopelessly entangled in an ever-expanding web of zip lines really must make their way to this rugged region, where folks are more likely to know how to saddle a horse than what the latest dollar-to-colon exchange rate is.

The name of the game here is agribusiness, and from the Atlantic slopes of the Cordillera Central, through rich tropical plains stretching to the Nicaragua border, farmers coax from red earth important crops – staples such as corn and beans. The big money-earners, however, are rice, sugarcane and cattle.

In the more remote areas, particularly near Nicaragua, each rainy season floods vast hectares of pastureland, creating ephemeral swamps and lakes that define the rhythm of an entire ecosystem. When the rivers swell, flat-bottomed boats set out across the temporarily widened waterways with gusto. Though human interests have devoured much of this world, some wetlands have been protected in the Refugio Nacional de Vida Silvestre Caño Negro. Here you can observe the rituals of the seasons, as the Río Frío grows from a meandering stream into a sea of creatures who spend each hot summer waiting for paradise to return.

In human terms this area has low population density and relatively little in the way of tourist facilities. The luxuriant jungle surrounding Puerto Viejo de Sarapiquí is the major exception: this small city remains a regional hub, with good bus (and boat) services and a range of accommodations. The area also provides access to spelunking in the Venado Caves, rafting and visiting Caño Negro.

Foreign tourists don't venture far into this region despite intriguing opportunities for adventure, not the least of which is taking the back way into Nicaragua by riverboat, a satisfying way to explore so much of Costa Rica's last frontier.

HIGHLIGHTS

- Watching raptors and spoonbills frolic at **Refugio Nacional de Vida Silvestre Caño Negro** (p435)
- Taking a dugout canoe along the **Río San Juan**, the remote boundary between Costa Rica and Nicaragua (p444)
- Visiting **Estación Biológica La Selva** (p445), one of the country's best-known tropical research centers
- Dangling on the 267m-long suspension bridge between **Centro Neotrópico Sarapiquís** (p441) and **Tirimbina Rainforest Center**
- Spotting spiders and bats (aren't you tired of butterfly gardens?) at the spectacular **Venado Caves** (p433)

NORTHERN LOWLANDS

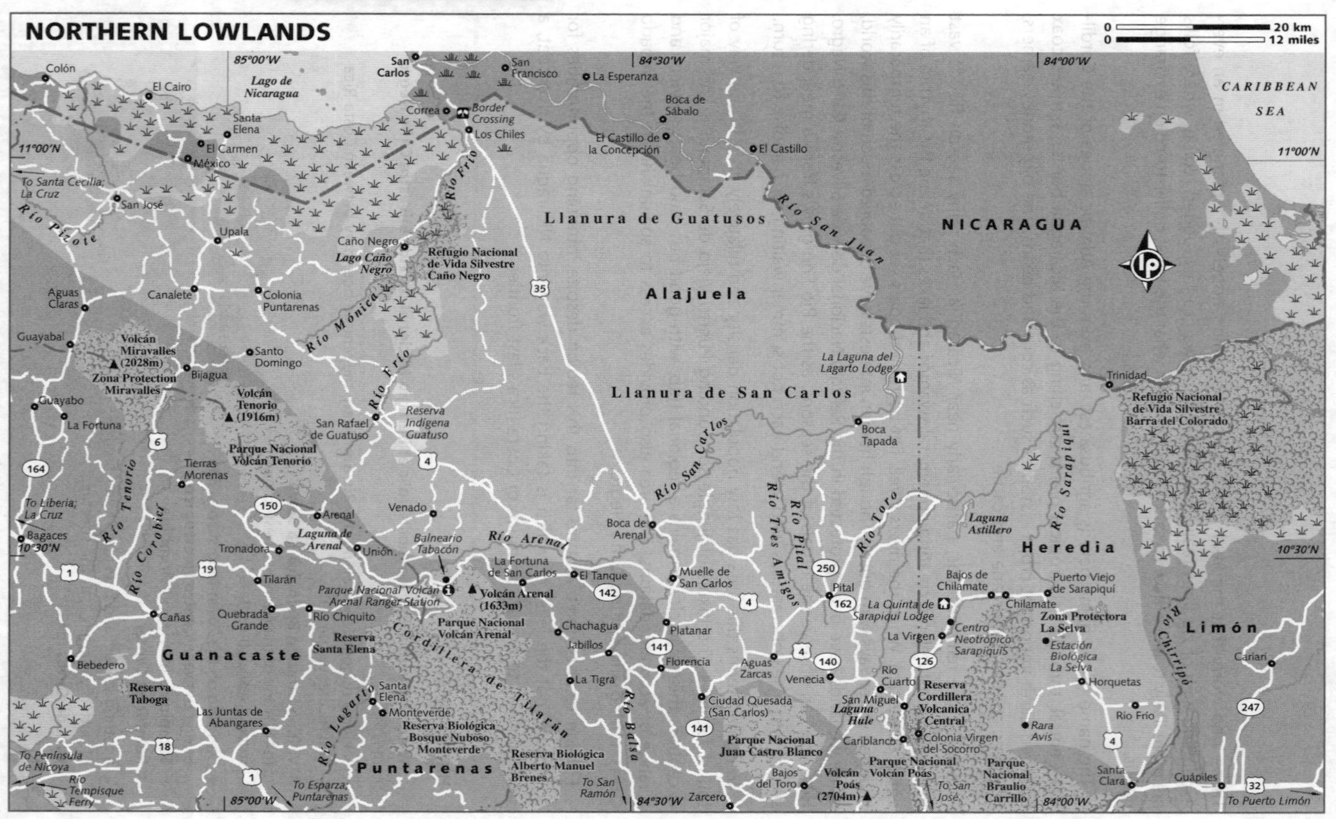

HIGHWAY 126 TO SAN MIGUEL

There are four main ways to access the northern lowlands. The main access route is to go north along Hwy 126 from San José, passing through Heredia, Vara Blanca and Catarata La Paz to reach San Miguel. This route, from Vara Blanca, is described below. Other routes include taking Hwy 141 by passing through Alajuela and Grecia to Ciudad Quesada (San Carlos), from where the lowlands can be reached by either continuing north to Muelle de San Carlos or northeast to Aguas Zarcas and beyond. See San Miguel to the Caño Negro Area, p435, for more details of destinations reached by these two routes. The fourth route involves going north along the Hwy 4 from Santa Clara, via Horquetas to Puerto Viejo de Sarapiquí (see p445). The four routes allow the southeastern area of the lowlands to be explored as a round trip without backtracking.

Buses from San José head to Puerto Viejo de Sarapiquí via Hwy 126.

VARA BLANCA & AROUND

Hwy 126 is spectacular and a favorite of tour companies. After leaving Heredia it continues over a pass in the Cordillera Central between Volcán Poás to the west and Volcán Barva to the east (see p136). The steep and winding mountain road climbs to over 2000m just before the tiny community of Vara Blanca.

A couple of kilometers past the highest point is a turnoff to Poasito and Volcán Poás, followed by a dizzying descent with beautiful views. People on tours or with their own vehicles can stop for photographs or for high- and middle-elevation birding.

About 8km north of Vara Blanca, the Río La Paz is crossed by a bridge on a hairpin bend; to your left is an excellent view of the spectacular Catarata La Paz (see p131). Several other waterfalls may be seen, particularly on the right-hand side (heading north) in the La Paz river valley, which soon joins with the Sarapiquí river valley.

COLONIA VIRGEN DEL SOCORRO & AROUND

About 6km beyond Catarata La Paz is a turnoff that leads to Colonia Virgen del Socorro, a small community several kilometers away across the river. This road (which may require 4WD) is famous among birders, who often spend several hours here looking for unusual species; a forest, a river, clearings and changes in elevation all contribute to species diversity in this one spot.

Barely a kilometer north of Virgen del Socorro is a turnoff to the left that leads along a poor dirt road to the attractive **Laguna Hule**. The 9km road is just passable to ordinary cars in the dry season, but 4WD is necessary during the wet season. The lake is the remnant of a volcanic crater and is set amid luxuriant rain forest – though away from the lake most of the forest is gone.

About 7km north of the Virgen del Socorro turnoff, the road forks at the community of San Miguel. The westbound fork goes to Ciudad Quesada, about 35km away by paved road, and the north fork heads for Puerto Viejo de Sarapiquí to the northeast.

SAN MIGUEL TO LOS CHILES

The papaya-plantation and jungle-trimmed route from San Miguel to Muelle twists and turns; drivers should pay close attention to sometimes overgrown road signs pointing the way. But just as the patchwork of fincas and wildflowers gives way entirely to sugarcane, the region's predominant crop, the road opens to a long, straight and usually steaming-hot stretch across the lowlands to the border crossing at Los Chiles.

VENECIA & AROUND

The westbound road hugs the northern limits of the Cordillera Central, and there are occasional views of the northern lowlands. About 14km west of San Miguel along this road is the village of Venecia, where the unmissable 'Medieval castle' of **Torre Fuerte Cabinas** (☎ 472 2424; s/d US$9/15; P) offers clean, basic rooms with private bathroom. Halfway between San Miguel and Venecia is the hamlet of Río Cuarto, from where an unpaved road heads southeast past the beautiful **waterfall** near Bajos del Toro, through Parque Nacional Juan Castro Blanco, and on to Zarcero (see p128).

LA LAGUNA DEL LAGARTO LODGE

One of the most isolated places in the country, this **lodge** (☎ 289 8163; www.lagarto-lodge-costa-rica.com; s/d US$43/57, s/d with bathroom US$53/70, breakfast US$6, other meals US$12) is surrounded by 1300 hectares of virgin rain forest and is something of a legend among birders. Simple but pleasant screened rooms, some with private bathroom, have fan and large veranda. Package tours include transportation from San José, all meals and guided tours.

Most of the 500-hectare 'grounds' of the lodge is rain forest. Some is swamp, some is lagoon, and canoes are available to explore it all. There are also about 10km of foot trails, and horseback trips and boat tours down along the Nicaraguan border can be arranged. This is one of the few places where the increasingly rare great green macaw, subject of an on-site study, can be seen frequently.

To get here by car, take the paved road to Pital (north of Aguas Zarcas) and continue on a decent gravel road 29km to the tiny community of Boca Tapada, from where it's 7km further to the lodge (there are signs). Buses from San José (US$4.30, five hours) depart the Atlántico Norte terminal twice daily, with a connection to Boca Tapada, where you will be picked up on prior request. The lodge can also arrange round-trip transportation from San José for US$90 per person (two-person minimum).

MUELLE DE SAN CARLOS

This small crossroads village is locally called Muelle, which means 'dock,' seemingly because 'Cañas' was already taken – this is sugarcane country. Breaks in the sweet scenery include huge sugarcane-processing facilities, always interesting to ponder over a Coke, and very slow sugarcane-hauling trucks, so drive carefully. This was, actually, an important dock (hence the shipping infrastructure still here) as it's the most inland spot from which the Río San Carlos is navigable.

The main tourist activity in Muelle is pulling over to have a look at the map. A 24-hour gas station lies at the intersection of Hwy 4 (which connects Ciudad Quesada and Upala) and Hwy 35 (running from San José to Los Chiles). From Hwy 4 you can easily catch Hwy 32, the main artery serving the Caribbean coast. Can't decide? A range of accommodations will let you sleep on it, and they're convenient to just about everything.

Sleeping & Eating

Cabinas Beitzy (☎ 469 9153; s/d US$7/11; P) This basic hotel, right at the crossroads, has clean rooms with private cold shower; a fine option if you just need somewhere to crash.

La Quinta Lodge (☎ 475 5260, 475 5921, 817 9679; s/d US$30/35; P) About 5km south of Muelle in the tiny community of Platanar, this rustic inn has a B&B feel thanks to the eclectic antiques splashed around, plus a pool with a small waterslide and sauna. It's run by the Ugaldes, a friendly Tico couple who taught in the USA for years and who both speak excellent English. Birds have adopted the grounds, and there's a small river behind the inn where fish and caimans can be seen.

Hotel La Garza (☎ 475 5222; d US$80; P) Also near Platanar, this attractive, upscale lodge sits on a 600-hectare working dairy ranch and citrus plantation with views of the Río Platanar and far-off Volcán Arenal. Visitors enter the landscaped compound via a graceful suspension footbridge, and 12 polished wooden bungalows with big porch, ceiling fan, telephone and good-size private bathroom await. Tennis, basketball and volleyball courts are available, as are 4km of private trails, a swimming pool and Jacuzzi. Meals are served in the adjoining farmhouse (US$9 for breakfast, US$15 for lunch and dinner). A number of tours are available, including horseback rides through the extensive grounds (US$25/40 for two/four hours).

Tilajari Resort Hotel (☎ 469 9091; www.tilajari.com; s/d incl breakfast US$92/104, ste incl breakfast US$104/114, additional person US$12; P) This luxury resort is remarkable for its wide range of tours, all of which are just a short shuttle ride away. Once a country club, the hotel is surrounded by landscaped grounds. Very comfortable rooms in modern buildings have private hot shower, ceiling fan and telephone; the suites have living room, TV and refrigerator. All include a terrace, some with views of the Río San Carlos. A few of the rooms and private trails are wheelchair accessible. Other amenities include pools, racquetball and tennis courts, a restaurant, sauna, spa and **butterfly garden** (admission US$3), plus access to the neighboring 400-hectare private rain-forest reserve with several trails. Horseback riding is available. Tours are offered on a sliding scale: the more people who join the tour, the cheaper it is. Just some of the offerings include tours to **Volcán Arenal and the Tabacón Hot Springs** (per person with 1/2/3 people US$120/60/50), the **Venado Caves** (per person with 1/2/3 people US$90/45/30) and **guided boat trips at Caño Negro** (per person with 2-person minimum US$75). You can also go rafting, kayaking, hiking or just about anything else. These activities are also available to nonguests, as long as they call ahead to make arrangements. The resort is located 800m west of the intersection at Muelle, on the road to Ciudad Quesada.

Restaurant/Bar La Subasta (☎ 467 8087; mains US$3-7; 11am-11pm) Right at the crossroads and overlooking a bullpen, this expansive spot serves cold beer and big casados (set meals). There's a small supermarket next door.

SAN RAFAEL DE GUATUSO AREA

Despite its four-star location, surrounded by highland jungle and volcano views, and its convenience to a variety of attractions including the Venado Caves about 15km away, the small town of Guatuso (shown on some maps as San Rafael) remains a low-key, local affair. This settlement of 7000 people is on the Río Frío, 19km northeast of Nuevo Arenal (see p215) via a decent dirt road, or 40km northwest of La Fortuna (see p200) by paved road. The latter has good views of Volcán Arenal smoking away to the south.

Venado Caves

Four kilometers south of Venado (Spanish for 'deer') along a good dirt road, the **Venado Caves** (☎ 478 8071; admission US$7; 7am-4pm) are a popular rainy-day attraction that can be organized as a day trip from La Fortuna, San José and many other cities for US$45 to US$65 per person, including transportation and lunch. You can visit by yourself much more cheaply, although bus service is inconvenient.

The caverns, an eight-chamber labyrinth of lit-up limestone, get rave reviews from folks fond of giant spiders, bats and getting wet and muddy: obviously a big hit with certain families. A guide takes you through the caves, including a few tight squeezes, pointing out various rock formations and philosophizing about what they sort of look like.

Drop-ins are welcome, but it's best to make reservations so you don't need to wait around for a group. You're provided with a guide (some speak English), lights, helmets and showers afterward. It's strongly recommended that you bring an extra set of clothes. There's a small *soda* on site, and a few nicer spots for a snack in Venado, but no lodging.

A 1pm bus from Ciudad Quesada drops you off at a steep 4km slog from the cavern entrance at about 2pm, with pickup at 4pm – hurry! A taxi from Guatuso will cost from US$15 to US$20.

Sleeping & Eating

There are several clean, basic cabinas in San Rafael de Guatuso, sometimes used on a long-term basis by workers, as well as a good selection of *sodas* and stores.

Cabinas Milagro (☎ 464 0037; s/d US$6/8; P) This quiet, family-run place on the edge of town is a tranquil budget option. From the center, go past the church toward the Río Frío bridge and turn right just past the soccer field. Rooms have cold shower and fan.

Cabinas Tío Henry (☎ 464 0344; r per person US$9; P ❄) Big, clean, air-conditioned rooms here are relatively plush, with cable TV and private hot shower. Reception is at the vet and feed store next door, and staff can arrange tours for large groups in advance.

Cabinas El Bosque (☎ 464 0335; s/d with fan US$7/11, s/d with air-con US$10/15; P ❄) Just a bit north of town, this 10-room hotel has clean, simple rooms, some with cable TV, and a locked parking lot.

Soda La Macha (☎ 464 0393; mains US$3; 6am-9pm) You don't exactly get a menu at this fine *soda*, located on the main road, across from the bus stop. Everything here is cooked using a wood-fired oven. Just request your casado or *gallo* (tortilla sandwich) preferences and they'll be made on the spot.

Restaurante El Turiste (☎ 464 1000; mains US$2-4; 6am-10pm) Despite the name, locals pack into this inexpensive *soda* for its brewed coffee and big servings of rice dishes and typical Tico food. It's located on the main road, close to the bus stop.

Rancho Ukurin (☎ 464 0308; mains US$4-8; 11am-10pm) You'll pay a little extra to dine in this attractive, open-air restaurant just past the Río Frío bridge en route to Upala; it's also a fine spot for a beer.

Getting There & Away

Guatuso lies on Hwy 4, about 40km from either Upala, to the northwest, or Muelle, to the southeast. Buses leave about every two hours for either Tilarán or Ciudad Quesada, some of which continue to San José. Ciudad Quesada is the most frequent destination.

UPALA

Just 9km south of the Nicaraguan border, in the northwestern corner of the northern lowlands, Upala is a small but thriving town that serves a widespread community of some 15,000 people. A center for the area's cattle and rice industries, Upala is linked to the Interamericana by an excellent paved road and regular bus service, and it enjoys some apparent affluence. Most visitors are Costa Rican businesspeople, so accommodations are unexpectedly nice, and there's a small but choice selection of restaurants around the grassy plaza, which also serves as a soccer field. A paved bicycle path runs from the plaza to the hospital, attracting joggers in the morning.

If you're not negotiating for a truckload of grain, however, there's not really any special reason to stop by. The few foreign travelers who do pass through generally use it as a comfortable base for visiting Caño Negro, perhaps before crossing the border at Los Chiles. But it's worth coming up with some excuse – you've always wanted to hear Nicaraguan radio, for example – just to enjoy an evening relaxing into this oasis of Costa Rican *sabanero* (cowboy) culture.

Sleeping

Rooms tend to fill up during the week, so consider calling ahead, particularly if you're going to arrive later in the evening. Showers are cold, and you probably won't mind a bit.

Cabinas Ebenezer (☎ 837 6920; r per person US$8; P) Just down the bike path from town, this cozy spot has basic rooms with fan and private bathroom.

Cabinas del Norte (r US$5) This place is conveniently located above the bus terminal. Folks seeking somewhat sooty and cement-block ambience to inspire the next scene in their screenplay need look no further.

Hotel Rosita (☎ 470 0198; s/d US$7/11; P) Across from the bridge, this place is basic but much cleaner and more comfortable than Cabinas del Norte.

Hotel Upala (☎ 470 0169; s/d with fan US$9/12, s/d with air-con US$12/15; P) You can watch the soccer games from the porch of your bright, spotless room with private cold shower, fan and cable TV. The owner is nice and reception is open 24 hours.

Cabinas Maleku (☎ 470 0142; s/d with fan US$10/16, s/d with air-con US$16/21; P) Big, high-ceilinged rooms have folksy furniture, including really cute Sarchí-style rocking chairs in front of the rooms, and large cable TV.

Eating

The busy market, just behind the bus terminal, opens early with several nice *sodas* dishing up good *gallos*, *empanadas* (meat or chicken turnovers) and just about everything else; there are a few Chinese restaurants and produce vendors here as well.

Soda Norma (☎ 819 7048; mains US$2-4; 6:30am-9pm) With outdoor tables overlooking the park, this is a seriously top-notch *soda*, serving some of the most beautiful casados, with all the trimmings, you've ever seen.

Rancho Don Horacio (☎ 470 0905; mains US$5-7; 11am-10pm) Right off the plaza and far more atmospheric is this romantic restaurant with red tablecloths, mood lighting and a nice bar; the specialty is steak.

Heladería Baloons (☎ 470 0041; ice cream US$0.75; 8am-9pm) After dinner, grab your favorite flavor of ice cream and relax.

Restaurant Buena Vista (☎ 470 0063; mains US$3-6; 11am-9pm) This breezy spot where you can eat yummy chow mein and shrimp fried rice, lives up to its name, with wonderful river views.

Rancho Verdun (across from the hospital; mains US$3-7; 11am-late) A bit out of town, this place cooks up all those cows you've been seeing to juicy perfection, and it's a nice place for just a beer even if you're a vegetarian.

Just further down the street, **Waka's Discoteque** (9pm-late) does dancing, rave-style parties and sometimes live music, while Bar El Mundo is more a conversational bar.

Getting There & Away

Upala is connected to the Interamericana north of Cañas by Hwy 6, an excellent paved road, and also to La Fortuna and Laguna de Arenal by the somewhat more potholed Hwy 4. A rough, unpaved road, usually passable to all cars, skirts the Refugio Nacional de Vida Silvestre Caño Negro on the way to Los Chiles, the official border crossing with Nicaragua.

Other dirt roads cross the Nicaraguan border, 9km away, but these are not official entry points into either Costa Rica or Nicaragua. Sometimes there's a passport check by the bridge at the south end of Upala (coming from San Rafael de Guatuso) and another near Canalete (coming from the Carretera Interamericana on the paved road from Cañas). Make sure you have your passport accessible.

The bus terminal is right off the park; a **ticket booth** (4:30-5:15am & 7:30am-1pm, 6:45-8pm Mon-Sat) has information and can store bags for US$1. Taxis congregate just outside the Upala bus terminal, by the park.

Caño Negro US$1; one hour; departs 11am & 4pm.
Los Chiles US$2; two hours; 5am & 4pm.
San José, via Cañas US$5.50; four hours; 5am, 2pm & 4:30pm.
San José, via Ciudad Quesada/San Carlos US$5.50; four hours; 9am & 3:30pm.

REFUGIO NACIONAL DE VIDA SILVESTRE CAÑO NEGRO

Because of the region's relative remoteness (although this has changed in recent years with the improvement of roads), this 102-sq-km refuge has long been frequented primarily by two sorts of specialists. Anglers come in search of that elusive 40-pound snook, though they abandon ship April through July, when the park is closed to fishing (a good time to bargain at nearby lodges). Birders flock here each year from January through March to spot an unequalled assortment of waterfowl including anhingas, roseate spoonbills, storks, ducks and herons, as well as the largest Costa Rican colony of the olivaceous cormorant. The refuge is the only place in Costa Rica where the Nicaraguan grackle regularly nests. During the dry season water levels drop, with the effect of concentrating the birds (and fish) in photogenically (or tasty) close quarters. From January to March, when migratory birds land in large numbers, avian density is most definitely world class.

The refuge is also of great interest to illegal logging operations, poachers and squatters, but they tend to stay on the other side of the park, well away from the official entrance and handful of rangers. Despite these incursions, pumas, jaguars and tapirs have been recorded here more often than in many of the other refuges.

WILL THE REAL CAÑO NEGRO PLEASE STAND UP?

Thanks to improved roads, dozens of tour operators are now able to offer relatively inexpensive trips to Caño Negro from all over the country. There's a lot of competition, and certain entrepreneurs have figured out how to shave a few dollars – that US$6 entrance fee, for starters – off the bottom line. These folks evidently take you to swampy private property that is by all accounts lovely, complete with wildlife and boat rides, but which is *not* Caño Negro.

If you want to be sure that you're slapping mosquitoes in the real protected refuge, book your trip through a reputable operator. If you still have your doubts, take a look at a map before leaving and pay attention while you ride. And should you indeed find yourself elsewhere, please do us a favor: ask your tour operator to point out where in the heck you are, then email us the location – we're dying to know.

The Río Frío defines the landscape. During the wet season the river breaks its banks to form an 800-hectare lake, and then contracts during the dry months from January through April, when water levels drop to the point where the river is no longer navigable. By April it has almost completely disappeared – until the May rains begin.

During the dry season the lake is accessible only from Caño Negro village, but when the water rises you can catch a boat here from Los Chiles or Puerto Viejo de Sarapiquí. There are also some foot and horse trails during the dry season, but you'll likely spend most of your visit on the water.

Orientation & Information

The refuge is part of the Area de Conservación Arenal-Huetar Norte and is accessible primarily by boat. Close to the park entrance (that'd be the dock) is the tiny community of Caño Negro, which has no grocery stores, banks or gas stations, though there is a **Minae office** (☎ 471 1309; 8am-4pm), where you pay your entrance fees (US$4).

You can get all other information and arrange guided tours at the **ranger station** (☎ 471 1309; 8am-4pm), located at the dock. In addition to administering the refuge, rangers are contact points for local guides and a few community projects, including a butterfly garden put together by a local women's association (Asomucan). You can camp (US$2 per person) by the river, or stay in the rangers' house for US$6 with advance reservations. There are cold showers, and meals can be arranged.

Local guides for fishing and ecological tours can be arranged in advance at the Los Chiles **subregional office** (☎ 460 6484, 460 0644), as well as at Soda La Palmera, Cabinas Martín Pescador (owned by recommended guides Carlos and Antonia Sequera, who also rent horses) and most businesses in town. Other local guides who have been recommended are Elgar Ulate and Vicente Mesa. You can usually find a guide (US$10 to US$20 per hour) on short notice, but they can get booked up during peak fishing and birding seasons.

Tours

This is an inconvenient spot to visit independently, so most people come here on an organized day trip from La Fortuna (see p200) or San José; you can arrange similar tours at upmarket hotels anywhere within 150km. These are generally geared toward wildlife watching, and reservations should be made early during peak birding season (January through March). People looking to do a little sportfishing should either go through the lodges or arrange a local guide when they get here.

The key is to get to the refuge as early in the morning as possible, when wildlife is still active, and it's worth paying extra for an overnight adventure that puts you in the water early. Folks staying in town basically have the refuge to themselves at daybreak, with boat-trippers from Puerto Viejo de Sarapiquí and Los Chiles arriving by 9am.

Sleeping & Eating

There are a few budget lodging options in town, plus a handful of nicer accommodations down the road, most of which are geared toward fishing – they're still pretty rustic by ecolodge standards. Businesses are listed according to their distance from the park; none is more than 1.5km from the dock.

Soda La Palmera (☎ 816 3382; mains US$3-10; 6am-9pm) Located right at the entrance to the refuge, this pleasant *soda* serves Tico standards and fresh fish, including your personal catch of the day. The staff can also arrange local guides for fishing excursions (US$10 per hour, up to three people) or ecological tours (US$40, two hours, up to three people), though the two could probably be combined. Advance reservations are a good idea in high season.

Cabinas Martín Pescador (☎ 471 1369; per person US$10; P) These clean, fairly rustic cabins with shared bathroom are about 100m from the town center and come with a couple of big perks: the spot is owned by recommended refuge guides and boat captains Carlos and Antonio Sequera. Carlos speaks English, while his brother Antonio rents horses. A third brother, English-speaking guide Napoleon Sequera, is semi-retired. Two-hour fishing or naturalist trips for up to five people cost US$40.

Caño Negro Natural Lodge (☎ 471 1426; www.canonegrolodge.com; s/d incl breakfast US$91/102; P) Perched on land that becomes a virtual island in the Río Frío during the high-water season, this family-run lodge offers package deals that include fishing and/or ecological trips, various guided hikes and mountain biking. Reasonably plush rooms with private hot-water shower and ceiling fan surround a pleasant pool, Jacuzzi and game room. Its restaurant is open to the public, and anglers often stop for a beer or a bite.

Caño Negro Fishing Club (☎ 471 1021; www.welcometocostarica.com; d incl breakfast US$55; P) Set in a lakeside orchard of mango and citrus trees, this lodge is all about the fishing. The restaurant will cook up your fresh tarpon and bass, caught on a variety of organized outings to secret fishing holes. And after a hard day of fighting monster fish, relax in clean, light rooms with ceiling fan and private hot shower. You can rent any combination of boats, guides and fishing equipment here, as well as kayaks and horses (US$10 per hour) at the well-stocked tackle shop. There's also a **restaurant** (mains US$7-12; 7-9am, noon-2:30pm & 6-8:30pm) specializing in, you guessed it, fish.

Caño Negro Villas (☎ 471 1023, 471 2053; www.canonegrovillas.com; d US$50, q cabin US$100; P) This Spanish-owned spot has comfortable bungalows with kitchen and barbecue, and is surrounded by 32 hectares of former finca undergoing a bit of redecorating: some is returning to jungle, but there are also small plots of pineapples, bananas and endangered trees. There are a few kilometers of private trails on the property, and the owner guides tours through the park, primarily from the wildlife-watching angle, though he can work in some fishing if you so desire.

Getting There & Away

The village of Caño Negro and entrance to the park lie on the rough road connecting Upala and Los Chiles, which is passable to all cars during the dry season. Two buses daily run past the park entrance from both Upala (see p434) and Los Chiles (see below), and during the rainy season you can catch a boat here from Los Chiles.

LOS CHILES

Seventy sweltering kilometers north of Muelles on a smooth, paved road through the sugarcane, and just three dusty, red and heavily rutted kilometers south of the Nicaraguan border, lies the sleepy farming and fishing town of Los Chiles (population 8000), not usually considered Costa Rica's top attraction.

The humid lowland village, arranged with dilapidated grace around a grassy soccer field and along the unmanicured banks of the leisurely Río Frío, is pleasant enough – almost charming by border-town standards. It was originally settled by folks who worked river traffic along the nearby Río San Juan, much of which forms the Nicaragua–Costa Rica border. Ever since rail and road became the principal arteries of trade, the port has primarily supported fishing boats and small-scale tourism, though it still buzzes with that nervous tension you so often find this close to an international crossing.

There are two reasons to stop by. The first is to enjoy the scenic route to Caño Negro, an often early-morning excursion by small motorized boat that's an adventure in itself. The second big draw is the scenic route to Nicaragua, a one- to two-hour boat ride across a border little used by foreign tourists, who usually go through Peñas Blancas (see p199). Just because it's remote doesn't mean it's relaxed, so make sure your papers are in order. Otherwise, it's a hassle-free border.

In the 1980s Los Chiles was on an important supply route for the Contras in Nicaragua, and a strong US military presence set up shop here as well. Until 1990 this crossing was closed except to Costa Rican and Nicaraguan nationals, but today anyone can cross. It's still considered a bit dodgy, so checkpoints are plentiful along both roads and rivers. Keep your passport handy.

Information & Orientation

The last stretch of paved road along Hwy 35 is home to a few restaurants, the post office, a gas station and the **Minae office** (☎ 460 6484; 8am-4pm Mon-Fri), on the right side of the main highway coming into town, which may have information regarding Caño Negro. If you continue north past Los Chiles on the rutted dirt road, you'll find yourself in the dusty no-man's-land en route to a border crossing you probably won't be allowed to use.

Drivers must head west through town to reach the town center and the docks of the Río Frío, close to the bus station. It's a small town. Banco Nacional, close to the central park and soccer field, changes money. Folks headed to Nicaragua must stop at **migración** (☎ 471 1223; 8am-5pm), about 100m east of the park, on the way to the dock.

Tours

Although organized tours to Caño Negro can be arranged from more convenient places, using Los Chiles as a base gets you on the river early, which means you'll probably see more wildlife than folks being shuttled in from La Fortuna and San José. The port is also a good base for exploring the Lago de Nicaragua.

Rancho Tulípan (☎ 471 1414; cocas34@hotmail.com), which is also a nice hotel, offers tours including a three-hour Caño Negro trip (US$60 for two, US$20 per person for more). The staff can also arrange transportation to Nicaragua and almost anywhere else, plus accommodations when you get there.

Cabinas Jabirú (☎ 471 1055), run by friendly Manfred Vargas Rojas, has been in the area for a while. In addition to the well-known Caño Negro trips, it runs tours to the nearby private reserve of Medio Queso, with opportunities for horseback riding, to observe traditional farming techniques, and a typical farm lunch – it's a chance to see some of rural Costa Rica. Other tours and guided camping trips go to the islands in Lago de Nicaragua.

At the boat dock you can also hire individual boat captains to take you up the Río Frío during the dry season and all the way into Lago Caño Negro during the rainy season, as well as to San Carlos, Nicaragua. Three- to four-hour trips cost about US$45 to US$80 for a small group, depending on the size and type of boat.

Viajes y Excurciones Cabo Rey (☎ 471 1251, 839 7458) provides a boat service to the refuge (US$45 per group) as well as to El Castillo and the Solentiname islands in Nicaragua. Cabo himself can usually be found by the dock.

Sleeping & Eating

There's no real grocery store in town, though a couple of well-stocked markets should do the trick.

Rancho Tulípan (☎ 471 1414; cocas34@hotmail.com; s/d incl breakfast US$25/30) Easily the nicest hotel in town, this air-conditioned lodge has largish, comfortable rooms with private hot shower, and an on-site travel agency; it is also conveniently just steps away from migración and the docks. The on-site **restaurant** (mains US$3-7; 7am-10pm), with good breakfasts and recommended sea bass and Chinese dishes, is also popular.

Cabinas Jabirú (☎ 471 1055; s/d US$7/9; P) Conveniently located near the bus terminal, this top budget option has spacious, clean rooms with cable TV. Internet access is US$2 per hour.

Hotel Río Frío (☎ 471 1127; r per person US$3) Old plank rooms arranged in a row, with shared cold shower at the end, are kept sparkling clean at this very basic budget option. The new owners plan to spruce it up a bit.

Restaurant El Parque (☎ 471 1373, 471 1090; mains US$3-5; 6am-9pm) This solid spot is probably where your tour bus will take you to eat: go for the *pollo a la plancha* (grilled chicken) or steak with mushroom sauce. The self-serve coffee bar is a hit with the early birds.

Restaurant Central (mains US$2-5; 7am-10pm), nearby, caters to a more local crowd.

Getting There & Away

You can charter a plane to a nearby landing strip, but there is currently no regular passenger service.

Drivers usually get here via Hwy 35 from Muelle, about 70 smooth, straight kilometers where huge trucks completely ignore the posted 40km/h signs, except when confronted with awkward sugarcane-hauling contraptions lurching along at 20km/h. Skid marks do break up the monotony of endless sugarcane plantations. More scenic, if harder on your chassis, is the decent dirt road running 50km to Upala, through Caño Negro, passable to normal cars in the dry season.

Note that you can't drive across the border at the Los Chiles checkpoint without special permission, arranged in San José.

All buses arrive and leave from the stop on the main street, across from the park.

Ciudad Quesada US$2.25; two hours; departs 12 times daily from 5am to 7:15pm.
San José US$4; five hours; departs 5:30am & 3:30pm.
Upala via Caño Negro US$2.25; 2½ hours; departs 5am & 2pm.

GETTING TO SAN CARLOS, NICARAGUA

Although there's a 14km dirt road between Los Chiles and San Carlos, Nicaragua, using this crossing requires special permission generally reserved for federal employees. Most folks go across by boat, which is easily arranged in Los Chiles proper. You must first have your paperwork processed at **migración** (☎ 471 1223; 8am-5pm), 100m west of the dock, which is also your first stop when entering from Nicaragua.

Regular boats (US$7, 1½ hours) leave Los Chiles at 1pm and 4pm daily, with extra boats at 11am and 2:30pm if demand is high. Boats reliably leave San Carlos for Los Chiles at 10:30am and 1:30pm, with extra boats scheduled as needed. Nicaragua charges a US$5 entry fee before 11am; US$7 to US$9 afterward, which means you'll be paying a little extra unless you charter a boat before 11am, clever bastards. Fees should be paid in US dollars.

Border officials are generally patient with travelers making day trips to Lago de Nicaragua or El Castillo, and those folks probably won't be charged the fee for entering Nicaragua – probably. Bring your passport and a few US dollars, just in case.

From San Carlos, which has a similar range of services as Los Chiles, you can arrange bus, boat and plane transportation to Managua, Granada and other destinations in Nicaragua. For more information about border crossings, see the boxed text (p466).

NORTHERN LOWLANDS

Regular boat transport is limited to shuttles across the Nicaraguan border (US$7) and various day trips throughout the region. When the water is high enough, however, boats can be arranged to Caño Negro (about US$65), Barra del Colorado and Tortuguero (US$250 to US$300) and just about everywhere else with a dock in northeastern Costa Rica.

SAN MIGUEL TO PUERTO VIEJO DE SARAPIQUÍ

The road north from San Miguel drops for 12km to the village of La Virgen (not Colonia Virgen del Socorro, mentioned previously), which is truly in the northern lowlands. The now-flat road goes mainly through agricultural country for an additional 13km to Bajos de Chilamate, and then 6km on to Puerto Viejo de Sarapiquí.

The buses linking either San José or Ciudad Quesada with Puerto Viejo de Sarapiquí are the main means of public transportation along this route.

LA VIRGEN

Tucked into the densely forested shores of the wild and scenic Río Sarapiquí, which tumbles down the Atlantic slope's dramatic descent from windswept highlands into the humid jungle, the tiny town of La Virgen has long been a center of banana-related commerce. In recent years, however, the locals have diversified.

Today it's a home base for several white-water rafting companies, who offer good deals on the big thrills of the Río Sarapiquí; it isn't the country's wildest white water (that'd be the Pacuare) but it will still get your heart racing. And yes, you can go down in a kayak, too.

Most tourists arrange day trips from San José or La Fortuna, including lunch and round-trip transportation, which tacks a reasonable US$20 to US$30 onto the price. Or you could just stay in La Virgen, enjoying an off-beat (if not exactly off-the-beaten-track) destination where even the most budget accommodations boast flawless river views.

As an added bonus, three luxurious lodges east of town incorporate interesting attractions – museums, trails and even an archaeological site – into the mix, which nonguests can enjoy for a fee.

Information

Most of La Virgen's businesses are strung along the highway, including a gas station, a Banco Nacional with 24-hour ATM, a couple of small supermarkets and many bars. **Internet Café** (☎ 761 1107; per hour US$1.25; 🕑 8am-9pm Mon-Sat, 2pm-9pm Sun) has fairly fast computers.

Sights & Activities

RÍO SARAPIQUÍ TRIPS

You can run the Sarapiquí year-round, but July through December are considered peak months. Although it's possible to get a rafting trip on short notice, it's far better to make reservations at least two days in advance. Several tour operators in San José, including Costa Rica Expeditions, Horizontes and Ríos Tropicales, can organize trips (see Getting Around, p473).

There are three basic runs offered by several companies, and all have a minimum age of nine or 10; prices and times vary a bit, but the following are average. The Class I-II Chilamate put-in (US$40 per person, three hours) is a gentle float more suited to younger kids and wildlife watching. The Class III-IV Lower Sarapiquí (US$45 to US$50 per person, three hours) puts in close to La Virgen and is a scenic and challenging trip that's a good choice for healthy people without white-water experience. The Class IV-V Upper Sarapiquí (US$75, five hours) is seven screaming miles of serious white water, perfect for thrill-seekers.

Sarapiquí Outdoor Center (☎ 761 1123; sarapaquioutdoor@hotmail.com) is a well-established, family-run operation that offers top-quality rafting trips, as well as camping and good budget accommodations.

Aguas Bravas (☎ 292 2072, 229 4837; www.aguas-bravas.co.cr), in addition to offering rafting trips from La Virgen, San José and La Fortuna, can also arrange horseback rides and bike tours. Bunk beds in simple dorms with shared bathroom are primarily for rafters, but if there's space you can sleep here for US$8 per person.

Aventuras del Sarapiquí (☎ 766 6768; www.sarapiqui.com), in Puerto Viejo, and **Pozo Azul Adventures** (☎ 438 2616, 761 1360) also arrange rafting trips.

TALLYING BANANAS' TRUE COST *Beth Penland*

Banana cultivation, the second-largest industry (trailing tourism) in Costa Rica, began in 1878 when Minor Keith, the American entrepreneur contracted to build the Atlantic Railway (see p24), planted those first Panamanian cuttings to provide cheap food for his workforce. The sweet crop was a surprise hit in the USA and, after the completion of the Atlantic Railway in 1890, the banana boom began in earnest.

Mostly foreign investors bought and cleared the land that would become the 'banana coast.' In 1909 Keith consolidated his holdings as United Fruit, a banana empire that would influence Central American affairs for the next half century.

The industry has had a profound effect on Costa Rica's environment, as it has created an enormously lucrative monoculture that has historically been susceptible to a variety of parasites and other diseases, including a series of blights that swept through the region in the early 20th century, decimating banana crops throughout the northern lowlands and Caribbean coast. To combat these diseases and other parasitic organisms that might compromise the bottom line, growers use an arsenal of ecologically destructive methods to guarantee a profitable harvest.

For example, while still on the trees, bananas are wrapped in blue plastic bags impregnated with petrochemicals that shield them from pests while also inducing the fruit to ripen more quickly. Although growers are required by law to dispose of these baggies appropriately, they often end up in streams and canals built around the fincas. The bags are a pollutant that can kill wildlife directly by suffocation, or indirectly by contaminating the environment with a host of chemicals. Moreover, runoff from the fincas, which are kept free of weeds and other undergrowth that could naturally stop serious erosion, is enriched with fertilizers that often inspire radically increased growth in some plants, potentially denying space and light to organisms less capable of using the fertilizers for themselves. These synthetic products can also affect humans.

At least 280 pesticides are authorized by the government for use in the cultivation of the fruit, including five that the World Health Organization (WHO) ranks as 'extremely hazardous.' Plantation owners and chemical companies have faced lawsuits from more than 24,000 Latin American workers over the effects of Dibromochloropropane (DBCP), which has been linked to birth defects, tissue damage and sterility in male workers. Although it was banned in 1977 by the USA, where it is manufactured, it was used here until 1990.

In Costa Rica the right to acceptable working conditions is protected under the Declaration of Human Rights, but this does not include protection from hazardous toxins. Workers had to petition US courts (a legal nightmare) to seek recourse against the producers and distributors of DBCP. Though Nicaraguan courts ordered US corporations in 2002 to pay out US$490 million to 583 workers affected by DBCP (a Dow Chemical representative called the ruling 'unenforceable'), most of the 9000 Costa Rican workers who claim to have been rendered sterile are still waiting for a settlement.

Conditions for many Costa Rican banana workers are still poor: wages of US$4 per 11-hour day are common, particularly among the underregulated indigenous workforce along the Caribbean Coast – and Costa Rica isn't exactly a third-world country, as budget travelers have noted. Efforts to organize the labor force, also protected by federal law, have reportedly resulted in the blacklisting of union representatives. The chemical paraquat, banned in several European countries because of links to problems including blurred vision, tissue damage and death, is still used to the tune of 65kg per worker annually.

In the late 1990s a loose coalition of organizations began certifying bananas as 'Fair Trade;' these labeled, premium-priced fruits are usually grown on smaller farms, and companies must prove that they pay living wages and offer workers minimal protection from agrochemicals. This increased focus on social responsibility is finally moving US corporations such as Chiquita Brands to work with auditors including the Rainforest Alliance, European Good Agriculture Practices and Social Accountability International to meet labor, human-rights and food-safety standards.

Despite efforts towards change, the long-term ecological damage done by the banana trade will be evident throughout Costa Rica for years to come. Fortunately, socioeconomic and sustainable growth in the industry are seemingly on the right track.

SERPENTARIO

What to do between rafting trips? Why, look at lots of cool snakes, of course. This newish **'snake garden'** (☎ 761 1059; adult/student US$5/3; ⏲ 9am-6:30pm), on the main road, offers quite clear views of some 60 reptiles and amphibians, including poisonous frogs, as the smallish cages aren't yet furnished with much in the way of greenery.

Highlights at this family-run attraction include an 80kg Burmese python, an anaconda that seems petite only by comparison, and Lydia, the fabulous owner, who can give impromptu tours and take certain snakes out of their cages for big hugs and memorable photo ops. The mural outside is most definitely tattoo-worthy.

Sleeping & Eating

Sarapiquí Outdoor Center (☎ 761 1123; sarapaquioutdoor@hotmail.com; camping per person US$4, r per person US$8; Ⓟ) Excellent camp sites here overlook the river, the focal point of an ongoing landscaping project that would put the Mayans to shame, and have access to showers and bathrooms. Rooms are simple and a fair value with river views from some windows. There's a communal kitchen and a covered terrace in case of rain. In addition to (of course) rafting trips, the owners can arrange horseback rides and guided hikes to a nearby waterfall.

Rancho Leona (☎ 841 5341; www.rancholeona.com; dm US$9) The most unusual accommodations in town are on a particularly photogenic stretch of river. Simple dorm beds have shared solar-heated shower and access to a hot tub and sweat lodge. The laid-back spot also features a pleasant common area overlooking the river where all visitors are welcome to order light meals (US$3 to US$7), including healthy salads and made-to-order nachos. **Kayaking trips** (per person including lunch US$75; 6hr) and guided hikes can also be arranged on an ad hoc basis. The reason why you really must stop by, however, is to see the owner's outrageous Tiffany-style stained glass made with a copper-foil technique. The on-site workshop is a dazzling display of glass hangings, windows, and, especially, lampshades, all of which are custom-designed.

Restaurante y Cabinas Tía Rosita (☎ 761 1032, 761 1125; mains US$2-5, s/d/tr US$7/11/17; ⏲ 8am-9pm; Ⓟ) Not only is it the most highly recommended *soda* in town, with excellent spaghetti, *chiles rellenos* (stuffed chilies) and fish dishes, it also rents four clean, cute cabinas with private hot shower, TV and fan. Both rooms and meals are very popular with truckers.

Hotel Claribel (☎ 761 1190; d US$16; Ⓟ) Simple, largish rooms here are more comfortable than those at the cheaper places, and come with cable TV and hot shower.

Restaurant La Costa (☎ 761 1117; mains US$3-8; ⏲ 11am-9pm) On the eastern edge of town, the specialty here is Chinese-style seafood dishes.

Restaurant Mar y Tierra (☎ 761 1603; mains US$3-10) La Virgen's favorite finer-dining (but still very relaxed) option is this comfortable seafood and steak restaurant; the shrimp dishes are a tad more expensive because they're worth it.

LA VIRGEN TO PUERTO VIEJO DE SARAPIQUÍ

This scenic stretch of Hwy 4 is home to some of the loveliest lodges in the country, which are not only wonderful places for the well-heeled to stay; they also allow nonguests to see unusual attractions and private trails for a fee. Any bus between La Virgen and Puerto Viejo de Sarapiquí can drop you at the entrances, while a taxi from La Virgen (or Puerto Viejo for Selva Verde) will cost from US$4 to US$6.

Centro Neotrópico Sarapiquís

Two kilometers east of the village of La Virgen is this unique ecotourism project (☎ 761 1004; www.sarapiquis.org; s/d standard US$81/97, s/d deluxe US$90/110; Ⓟ ⊠), which is much more than just a clutch of luxuriously appointed hardwood rooms with huge solar-heated bathroom and private terrace in Palenque-style, thatch-roofed buildings modeled after a 15th-century pre-Columbian village.

You don't have to stay to enjoy the center's real claims to fame, which include the **Alma Ata Archaeological Park**, **Chesters Field Botanical Gardens** and **Museum of Indigenous Cultures** (adult/child over 8/child under 8 US$19/10/free; ⏲ 9am-5pm). Petroglyphs and pottery have been found at Alma Ata, where some 70 Maleko Indian tombs are being excavated. There's no visually spectacular pyramid, but it's fascinating nonetheless. The museum chronicles the history of the rain forest (and of human interactions with it) through a mixture of displays and videos. An on-site **restaurant** (mains US$7-20; ⏲ 7am-2pm & 5-9pm) serves meals incorporating spices and edible flowers used in indigenous cuisine, and many of the vegies are grown right here.

The gardens also boast the largest scientific collection of medicinal plants in Costa Rica. Best of all, following the museum tour, visitors enter the **Tirimbina Rainforest Center** (☎ 761 1418; www.tirimbina.org), a 300-hectare reserve reached from the center by two suspension bridges, 267m and 111m long, spanning the Río Sarapiquí. Halfway across, a spiral staircase drops down to a large island in the river. The reserve has more than 6km of trails, some of which are paved or woodblocked.

La Quinta de Sarapiquí Lodge

About 5km north of the village of La Virgen, this pleasant family-run **lodge** (☎ 761 1300, 761 1052; www.laquintasarapiqui.com; s/d/tr US$58/70/81; P ♿), on the banks of the Río Sardinal, has covered paths through the landscaped jungle connecting cool thatch-roofed hangout spots, stocked with hammocks and wildlife guides, to beautiful bungalows. All the rooms have terrace, ceiling fan and private hot shower; four rooms are wheelchair accessible.

Owner Beatriz Gámez is active in local environmental issues and helps administer the Cámara de Turismo de Sarapiquí (Cantusa), which works to balance conservation and tourism in the area. Activities at the lodge include swimming in the pretty pool or river (there's a good swimming hole near the lodge), horseback riding, fishing, boat trips, mountain biking and birding, and you can spend time in the large **butterfly garden** or hike the 'frog land' trail where poison-dart frogs are commonly seen. Fishing and horseback riding are free for lodge guests. You can also get meals in the lovely **restaurant** (mains US$8-13).

La Galleria (admission US$8.50, free for lodge guests), on the hotel grounds, features an eclectic collection of regional ephemera, including an extensive collection of insect specimens such as La Machaca, famously possessed of a venom with an odd antidote: women bitten by the odd-looking critter must make love within 24 hours…or die.

Even more interesting are the unusual exhibits on Costa Rican history. Indigenous artifacts, including some worthwhile copies of the area's more important archaeological finds, are a treat. The collection of Spanish-colonial relics is even more impressive, featuring not only antiques collected by the owners, but interesting family heirlooms as well? Gámez's great-grandmother was pen pals with famed Nicaraguan poet Rubén Darío. The fee also includes access to the lodge's private trails and gardens but, sadly, not the pool.

Selva Verde

In Chilamate, about 7km west of Puerto Viejo, this former finca is now an **elegant lodge** (☎ 766-6800, in the USA 800-451 7111; www.selvaverde.com; s/d/tr/q with 3 meals US$90/144/180/196, child 12-15 US$37). Just getting the room saves you US$24, exactly the cost of three buffet-style meals at the restaurant.

The attractive complex is set on 200 hectares of mostly forested land, with 45 rustic but very comfortable double rooms with private hot shower. Large communal verandas have hammocks and jungle views. The lodge works closely with Elderhostel (a tour company for over-55s; see p473) and offers educational opportunities, guided tours and other interesting diversions, many of which nonguests can enjoy for a fee.

There are several kilometers of walking trails through the grounds and into the premontane tropical wet forest; you can either get a trail map or can hire a bilingual guide from the lodge (US$15 per person, three hours). There's also a garden of medicinal plants, as well as a **butterfly garden** (admission US$5, free for lodge guests).

Various boat tours on the Río Sarapiquí are also available, from rafting trips to guided canoe tours; locally guided horseback rides (US$20 for two to three hours) can also be arranged.

The Holbrook family, who own the lodge, also funds the nonprofit Sarapiquí Conservation Learning Center nearby, where guests can visit, buy their arts and crafts, chat with locals and perhaps make a donation.

PUERTO VIEJO DE SARAPIQUÍ & AROUND

At the scenic confluence of Río Puerto Viejo and Río Sarapiquí, Puerto Viejo de Sarapiquí was once the most important port in Costa Rica. Boats laden with coffee plied the Sarapiquí as far as the Nicaraguan border, then turned east on the Río San Juan to the sea. After railways built in the 1880s connected shiny new Puerto Limón with the rest of the country, the 'old port' became something of a backwater.

Despite its distance from Nicaragua, Puerto Viejo (the full name distinguishes it from Puerto Viejo de Talamaca on the Caribbean coast) feels like a jungle border town – slightly seedy in a film-noir sort of way. Migraciónes is near the small wooden dock, sometimes avoided by visiting Nicaraguans who share the river with local fishers and visiting birders. Adventure-seekers can still travel down the Sarapiquí in motorized dugout canoes.

There is no dry season, but late January to early May is the less wet season. On the upside, when it rains there are fewer mosquitoes.

Banco Popular has an ATM and changes money. **Internet Sarapiquí** (☎ 766 6223; 🕑 8am-10pm) is at the west end of town. **Souvenir Río Sarapiquí** (☎ 766 6727), on the main street, has tour information on birding, kayaking, white-water rafting and zip lining.

Activities

Grassroots environmental activity is strong in this area. Local guide Alex Martínez, owner of the Posada Andrea Cristina B&B (see p443), maintains an **ecotourism center** (☎ 766 6265; 🕑 8am-3pm), which focuses on conservation activities and wilderness tours – birding trips in particular. You can also arrange transportation and make other reservations here, as well as learn about worthwhile volunteer opportunities in the region.

Sleeping & Eating

The region boasts a huge range of accommodations, from budget bunks, designed for local long-term plantation workers, situated in town, to several extraordinary lodges on the outskirts, the most exclusive of which are on the road to La Virgen (see p439). Lodges in the area north of Puerto Viejo are also listed, including one in the river town of Trinidad, on the Nicaraguan border.

There's a **Palí Supermarket** (west end of town; 🕑 8am-9pm) and several *sodas* in Puerto Viejo de Sarapiquí, including the excellent **Soda Judith** (mains US$2-4; 🕑 6am-7pm), a block off the main road, where early risers grab brewed coffee and big breakfasts or an *empanada* to start their day. The resorts generally include some or all meals as part of package stays.

BUDGET

Mi Lindo Sarapiquí (☎ 766 6281; s/d US$12/20; Ⓟ) This place, on the south side of the soccer field, has the nicest budget rooms in town: simple but spacious and clean, with private hot shower and fan. The on-site **restaurant** (mains US$4-9; 🕑 8am-10pm) is on the upscale side, with good seafood.

Cabinas Restaurant Monteverde (☎ 766 6236; s/d US$4/8 Ⓟ) Fairly dark and dingy rooms here are the cheapest in town, while the attached restaurant, with similarly low prices, serves great typical Tico food.

Hotel Gonar (☎ 766 6055; r per person without/with bathroom US$4/8) Above a hardware shop called Almacén Gonar, this place has 18 bare rooms with fan, some with private cold shower.

Trinidad Lodge (no phone on site, bookings ☎ in San José 213 0661, 259 1679; s/d US$15/20) Situated on the Río San Juan in the community of Trinidad, this budget travelers' lodge is right across from the Nicaraguan border post. It is accessible only by boat (US$5), which departs at 11am from the main dock of Puerto Viejo de Sarapiquí (35km away) and returns at 2pm. It's a working ranch, and several rustic cabins sleeping three comfortably have private bathroom. Home-cooked meals (US$4 to US$8) are available, and you can arrange horse rentals and also boat tours at the desk.

MID-RANGE

Hotel El Bambú (☎ 766 6359; www.elbambu.com; s/d incl continental breakfast US$53/64; Ⓟ 🏊) You really can't miss the sign for downtown Puerto Viejo's finest lodging, with nicely appointed and very clean rooms. A balcony overlooks the street, and there's a big pool. The large and modern **restaurant** (🕑 7am-10pm; mains US$4-10) is popular.

Posada Andrea Cristina B&B (☎ 766 6265; cabins per person, including big, home-cooked breakfast US$20) About 1km west of the center, this fine family-run place has six quiet little cabins in its garden, each with fan and a private hot-water bathroom. The owner, Alex Martínez, is an excellent and charming guide and a passionate frontline conservationist. He arrived here 30 years ago as a tough young hunter exploring what was virgin forest and saw the jungle's rapid destruction in the hands of humankind. He changed his philosophy and is now a volunteer game warden – who will abandon a Saturday-night soccer match to chase down poachers on the river. He helped found Asociación para el Bienestar Ambiental de Sarapiquí (ABAS), a local environmental-protection and education agency. Alex, who speaks English and runs an on-site ecotourism center (see p439), can tell you as much as you want to know about environmental issues in the area.

Los Cuajipales (☎ 283 9797, 766 6608; camping per person US$10, r per person US$17-25; Ⓟ) About 3km north of town on a good gravel road, this rustic complex is geared toward Tico tourists. Comfortable thatch-roofed cabañas sleeping up to five were designed according to Huetar Indian techniques that keep them naturally cool (cable TV and private cold showers are less authentic). All rates include meals at the casually elegant restaurant and access to the rather extravagant pool, ping-pong and billiards tables, 4km of private trails and tilapia pond.

El Gavilán (☎ 766 6743; www.gavilanlodge.com; s/d incl breakfast US$52/58; Ⓟ) Sitting on a 100-hectare reserve about 4km northeast of Puerto Viejo, this former cattle hacienda is gradually returning to the jungle. Birders can watch the colorful action in the attractive gardens from the porches of spacious cabins that have big hot-water shower and fan; some have river views. The grounds feature 5km of private trails and a good restaurant, plus a nice outdoor Jacuzzi to relax in after the hike. Multiday package deals include meals, tours and transportation from San José.

Boat trips are the big attraction, and range from short jaunts down the Río Sarapiquí (US$15 per person, two-person minimum, two hours) to day tours on the Río San Juan (US$280 for up to three people) and overnights on the Barra del Colorado or Tortuguero (US$400 one way, several people can go for this price). Rafting, horseback riding and tours to Volcán Arenal can also be arranged.

A taxi or boat from Puerto Viejo costs US$4. There's a signed turnoff from Hwy 4 about 2km from town.

Getting There & Away

Puerto Viejo de Sarapiquí has been a transport center longer than Costa Rica's been a country and is easily accessed by paved major roads from San José, the Caribbean coast and other population centers. There is a taxi stop across from the bus terminal, and taxis will take you to the nearby lodges and Estación Biológica La Selva (see p442) for US$3 to US$6.

SAILING TO NICARAGUA *Rob Rachowiecki*

Sailing down the Río Sarapiquí to the Río San Juan is a memorable trip. If the water is low, dozens of crocodiles can be seen sunning themselves on the banks. If the water is high, river turtles climb out of the river to sun themselves on logs. Birds are everywhere. North of Puerto Viejo much of the land is cattle pasture with few trees, but as you approach the Nicaraguan border more stands of forest are seen. In trees on the banks you may see monkeys, iguanas or maybe a snake draped over a branch.

On my trip the boat captain suddenly cut the engine, so I turned around to see what the matter was. He grinned and yelled and it was not until the dugout had gently nosed into the bank beneath the tree that I saw a sloth raise a languid head to see what was going on. How he managed to make out that the greenish-brown blob on a branch (the color is caused by the algae that grows in the fur of this lethargic animal) was a sloth is one of the mysteries of traveling with a sharp-eyed *campesino*.

We continued on down to the confluence of the Sarapiquí with the San Juan, where we stopped to visit an old Miskito Indian fisher named Leandro. He claimed to be 80 years old, but his wizened frame had the vitality of a man half his age. From the bulging woven-grass bag in the bottom of his fragile dugout, Leandro sold us fresh river lobster to accompany that evening's supper.

The official border between Nicaragua and Costa Rica is the south bank of the San Juan, not the middle of the river, so you are technically traveling into Nicaragua when on the San Juan. This river system is a historically important gateway from the Caribbean into the heart of Central America. Today it remains off the beaten tourist track and allows the traveler to see a combination of rain forest and ranches, wildlife and old war zones, deforested areas and protected areas.

BUS

Right across from the park, the **bus terminal** (☎ 233 4242; ⏰ 5am-7pm) sells tickets and stores backpacks (US$1.30).

Ciudad Quesada/San Carlos via La Virgen (Empresarios Guapileños) US$1; three hours; departs 5:30am, 9am, 2pm, 3:30pm & 7:30pm.

Guápiles (Empresarios Guapileños) US$1; one hour; departs eight times daily from 6:20am to 6pm.

San José (Autotransportes Sarapiquí) US$2.30; 1½ hours; departs 5am, 7:30am, 11:30am & 4:30pm.

BOAT

The small port has regular service to the Trinidad Lodge in Trinidad (opposite), and you can arrange transportation anywhere along the river, seasonal conditions permitting, through independent boat captains. Short trips cost about US$10 per hour per person for a group of four, or US$20 per hour for a single person. Serious voyages to Tortuguero or Barra del Colorado and back cost about US$350 for a boat holding five.

SOUTH OF PUERTO VIEJO DE SARAPIQUÍ

After visiting the interesting Puerto Viejo de Sarapiquí area, you can return to San José via the eastern road. About 4km southeast of Puerto Viejo the road passes the entrance to Estación Biológica La Selva. About 15km further is the village of Horquetas, from where it's 15km to the rain-forest preservation project and lodge at Rara Avis.

From Horquetas the paved road continues for about 17km through banana plantations to Hwy 32, which connects San José to the Caribbean coast. The route to San José takes you through the middle of Parque Nacional Braulio Carrillo.

ESTACIÓN BIOLÓGICA LA SELVA

Not to be confused with Selva Verde in Chilamate, the **Estación Biológica La Selva** (☎ 766 6565; laselva@sloth.ots.ac.cr; r per person without/with bathroom US$67/78; Ⓟ) is not a lodge, though you can stay here with advance reservation. The biological station is the real thing, teeming with research scientists and also graduate students using the well-equipped laboratories, experimental plots, herbarium and library. Rooms are basic, with fan and bunk beds (a few have doubles), but rates include all meals and guided hikes.

La Selva is operated by the **Organization for Tropical Studies** (OTS; ☎ 240 6696; www.ots.ac.cr), a consortium founded in 1963 to provide leadership in the education, research and wise use of tropical natural resources. Many well-known tropical ecologists have trained at La Selva. Twice a year OTS offers a grueling eight-week course open mainly to graduate students of ecology, along with various other courses and field trips that you can apply for.

The area protected by La Selva is 1513 hectares of premontane wet tropical rain forest, much of it undisturbed. It's bordered to the south by the 476 sq km of Parque Nacional Braulio Carrillo, creating a protected area large enough to support a great diversity of life. More than 430 bird species have been recorded at La Selva, as well as 120 mammal species, 1900 species of vascular plants (especially from the orchid, philodendron, coffee and legume families) and thousands of insect species.

Hiking

Reservations are required for guided hikes (US$26/40 per person for four/eight hours, children half price; 8am and 1:30pm daily) across the hanging bridge and into 50km of well-developed jungle trails, some of which are wheelchair accessible. Unguided hiking is forbidden, although you'll be allowed to wander a bit after your guided tour. You should make reservations for the popular guided birding hikes, led at 6am and 7pm, depending on demand. Profits from these walks help to fund the research station.

No matter when you visit La Selva, it will probably be raining. Bring rain gear and footwear that's suitable for muddy trails. Insect repellent and a water bottle are also essential.

Getting There & Away

Public buses between Puerto Viejo and Río Frío/Horquetas can drop you off 2km from the entrance to La Selva. It's about 3km from Puerto Viejo, where you can catch a taxi for around US$3.

OTS runs buses (US$10) from San José on Monday. Make reservations when you arrange your visit, and note that researchers and students have priority.

RARA AVIS

When they say remote, they mean remote: this **private reserve** (☎ 764 3131; www.rara-avis.com; Ⓟ), 1335 hectares of high-altitude tropical rain forest on the northeastern slopes of the Cordillera Central, is accessible only to overnight guests willing to make the three-hour tractor ride up a steep, muddy hill to get there.

Rara Avis was founded by Amos Bien, an American who came to Costa Rica as a biology student in 1977. The land borders the eastern edge of Parque Nacional Braulio Carrillo, and has no real dry season. Rainforest birding is excellent, with more than 350 species sighted so far. Many mammals, including monkeys, coatis, anteaters and pacas, are often seen. Visitors can use the trail system alone or on guided hikes included in the cost of lodging. A popular jaunt is the short trail leading from the lodge to **La Catarata** – a 55m-high waterfall that cuts an impressive swath through the forest.

The accommodations, although lovely, are rustic – most don't have electricity, though the kerosene lamps and starry skies are nice. Room prices, which include all meals, transportation and a guided hike, seem high, but it's because of the remote location – you, the groceries and the guides all have to be hauled up that mountain from Horquetas.

Very basic **cabins** (per person US$45) in the woods sleep four and have shared cold-water bathroom, while nicer rooms in the **Waterfall Lodge** (s/d/tr US$70/130/165) have private hot-water shower and balcony overlooking the rain forest. Even when it's pouring outside you can watch birds from your private balcony. The **River-Edge Cabin** (s/d US$85/150) is the nicest spot, with solar-powered electricity, hot water and separate rooms. It's a dark (or romantic, depending on the company) 10-minute hike from the rest of the lodge.

Because access is time-consuming and difficult, a two-night stay is recommended. Buses leave San José (US$4; four hours) from the Atlántico Norte terminal at 7am, and you'll be met in Horquetas, where there's a storage facility for extra luggage, then embark on the famed tractor ride. You can also arrange to be taken by jeep or on horseback, both of which require hiking the last 3km yourself.

Directory

CONTENTS

ACCOMMODATIONS

The hotel situation in Costa Rica ranges from luxurious and sparkling all-inclusive resorts to dingy, I-can't-believe-I'm-paying-for-this barnyard-style quarters. In addition, the sheer number of hotels means that it's rare to arrive in a town and find nowhere to sleep.

In touristy towns, you'll find plenty of cabinas, a loose term for cheap to mid-range lodging. Apartotels are like a hotel room but come with equipped kitchens. This type of accommodation can usually be rented for a cheaper rate for week- and month-long stays.

High season (December to April) prices are provided throughout this book, though many lodges lower their prices during the rainy season. In some popular towns, prices stay the same almost all year-round. Some beach towns will also charge high-season prices in June and July, when travelers from the northern hemisphere arrive in droves. During Semana Santa (Easter Week) and the week between Christmas and New Year, hotels raise their rates beyond what's listed in this book. During this time, make reservations a couple of months ahead. During school-vacation weekends in January and February

PRACTICALITIES

- **Electricity** Electrical current is 110V AC at 60Hz and plugs are two flat prongs (same as USA).
- **Newspapers** The most widely distributed newspaper is *La Nación* (www.nacion.co.cr), followed by *Al Día* (a tabloid), *La República* and *La Prensa Libre* (www.prensalibre.co.cr). The *Tico Times* (www.ticotimes.net), the English-language weekly newspaper, hits the streets every Friday afternoon.
- **Magazines** The Spanish-language *Esta Semana* is the best local weekly news magazine.
- **Television** Cable and satellite TV are widely available for a fix of CNN, French videos or Japanese news, and local TV stations have a mix of news, variety shows and *telenovelas* (Spanish-language soap operas).
- **Radio** 107.5FM is the English-language radio station, playing current hits and providing a regular BBC news feed.
- **Video Systems** Videos on sale use the NTSC image registration system (same as USA).
- **Weights & Measures** Costa Ricans use the metric system for weights, distances and measures.

it's advisable to book your accommodation before arriving at your destination.

If you're traveling in from another part of Central America, note that prices in Costa Rica will generally be much higher than in the rest of the region. The boxed text 'Bargaining' (p460) has more advice about costs.

B&Bs

Almost unknown in the country in the 1980s, the B&B phenomenon has swept Costa Rica. B&Bs vary from mid-range up to top-end options. The **B&B Association** (☎ 289 8638; www.savethemanatee.com/B&B/bandb.shtml; crnow@amnet.co.cr) can help you reserve B&Bs throughout the country.

Camping

Camping is the way many Ticos (Costa Ricans) enjoy the more expensive seaside towns. Most destinations have at least one camp site, and if not, many budget hotels outside San José accommodate campers on their grounds. The sites usually include toilets and cold showers and can be crowded, noisy affairs. Camp sites are available at many national parks as well; take food and supplies in with you.

Camping can be a challenge anywhere because of the bounteous mosquitoes. Pack repellent or you'll be a human buffet. In addition, camping fuel can be difficult to find in remote areas, so stock up in San José. The Cemaco (see p112) in Escazú stocks it. Camping prices in this book are listed per person, per night.

Hostels

There are some Hostelling International (HI) hostels, but offerings in Costa Rica tend to be fairly expensive. Most places will charge US$11 to US$40 per person for a bed. Hostal Toruma (p103) in San José is a member and can make reservations in HI-affiliated hostels around the country.

There are numerous independently run hostels around the country, which are considerably cheaper than the HI ones. San José has several places, as does Manuel Antonio, Puerto Viejo de Talamanca and Tamarindo. Shoestring travelers can also find cheap rooms at basic hotels.

> **HOTEL SECURITY**
>
> Although hotels give you room keys, it is recommended that you carry a padlock for your backpack or suitcase. Don't leave valuables, cash or important documents lying around your room or in an unlocked bag. Upmarket hotels will have safes where you can keep your money and passport. If you're staying in a basic place, take your valuables with you.

Hotels

It is always advisable to ask to see a room – and a bathroom – before committing to a stay, especially in budget lodgings.

BUDGET

For the most part, this guide's budget category covers lodging in which a typical double costs up to US$30. Cheaper places generally have shared bathrooms, but it's still possible to get a double with a private bathroom for US$10 in some towns off the tourist trail. (Note that 'private' in some low-end establishments consists of a stall in the corner of your hotel room.) On the top end of the budget scale, rooms will frequently include a fan and private bathroom that may or may not have hot water. At the cheapest hotels, rooms will frequently be a stall, with walls that don't go to the ceiling.

Hot water in showers is often supplied by electric showerheads (affectionately termed the 'Costa Rican suicide shower'). Contrary to traveler folklore, they are perfectly safe – provided you don't fiddle with the showerhead while it's on. It will actually dispense hot water if you keep the pressure low.

MID-RANGE & TOP END

Mid-range generally covers hotels that charge between US$30 and US$80 (expect to pay less than this in San José). These rooms will be more comfortable than budget options and include a private bathroom with hot water, a choice between fans and air-con, and maybe even cable TV. The better places will offer tour services and many will have an onsite restaurant or bar and a swimming pool or Jacuzzi. In this price range, many hotels offer kitchenettes and even full kitchens. (This is a popular choice for families.)

It is worth noting that, because of popular demand, many places have installed TVs in the rooms. While it may seem like a good

RESERVING BY CREDIT CARD

Some of the pricier hotels will require that you confirm your reservation with a credit card. Before doing so, note that some top-end hotels require a 50% to 100% payment up front when you reserve. Unfortunately, many of them aren't very clear about this rule.

Most times, visitors end up 'reserving' a room only to find out that they have actually paid for it in advance. Technically, reservations can be cancelled and refunded with enough advance notice. (Again, ask the hotel about its cancellation policy.) However, in Costa Rica it's a lot easier to make the reservation than to unmake it. In addition, many hotels charge a 7% service fee for credit card use. So, before you make a single reservation, make sure you understand these policies well.

Also, have the hotel fax or email you a confirmation. Hotels often get overbooked, and if you don't have one, you could be out of a room.

idea to catch a local show, keep in mind that most local hotels have unbearably thin walls so you'll be listening to your neighbor's set as well. (Besides, did you come to get away from it all, or watch CNN?)

Anything more than US$80 is considered top-end and includes all-inclusive resorts, business and chain hotels, in addition to a strong network of more intimate boutique hotels, jungle lodges and upmarket B&Bs. Many such lodging options will include amenities such as hot-water bath tubs, private decks, cable TV, air-con (in some cases), as well as concierge, tour and spa services.

Most mid-range and top-end places charge 16.39% in taxes. This book has attempted to include taxes in the prices listed throughout. Note that many hotels charge per person, rather than per room; read rates carefully. See also the boxed text above.

A good resource for finding smaller, independent lodges is the **Costa Rica Innkeepers Association** (☎ 441 1157; www.costaricainnkeepers.com).

ACTIVITIES

Bungee Jumping

No vacation appears to be complete without a head-first, screaming plunge off a bridge. **Tropical Bungee** (☎ 248 2212, 383 9724; www.bungee.co.cr; one jump US$60), in San José, has been organizing jumps off the Río Colorado bridge since 1992.

Canopy Tours

By this time, most people know that life in the rain forest takes place at canopy level. But with trees extending 30m to 60m in height, the average human has a hard time getting a look at what's going on up there. Enter the so-called 'canopy tour.'

Some companies have built elevated walkways through the trees that allow hikers to stroll through. SkyWalk (p166) near Monteverde and Rainmaker (p290) near Quepos are known for this. You can also take a ski-lift-style ride through the tree tops. Try the Rainforest Aerial Tram near Braulio Carrillo (p137) or the smaller Aerial Adventures in Monteverde (p165).

Other outfitters have built viewing platforms into huge trees. Visitors are winched up 20m or more into the canopy where they lie in wait for the wildlife to swing by (which they often do). Good sites are at Hacienda Barú Coast (p306) and Corcovado Lodge Tent Camp (p362). Pack your binoculars.

And, of course, there's nothing quite like sailing through the rain forest at high speeds á la *George of the Jungle*. On zip-line tours, adventurers are strapped into harnesses and hooked onto a cable-and-pulley system that allows them to traverse from tower to tower. Operators sell this as a great way to see nature, but plan on viewing broccoli-sized trees as you go whizzing past at full throttle.

One of the top zip-line experiences is at SkyTrek (p165) in Monteverde. The Original Canopy Tour (see the boxed text 'Canopy Fighting', p165) operates rides at several locations. Nearly every town has an independent operator to indulge wannabe Tarzans.

Zip-line adventures are not without risk. Travelers have been injured, and in a couple of cases killed. Go with well-recommended tour operators and make sure that you're provided with: a secure harness with two straps that attach to the cable (one is a safety strap), a hard hat and gloves.

Diving & Snorkeling

The numbers and variety of sealife is the country's draw. As a general rule, the worst water visibility occurs during the rainy months, when rivers swell and their outflow clouds the ocean. At this time, boats to locations off-shore offer better viewing opportunities.

The water is warm – around 24°C to 29°C at the surface, with a thermocline at around 20m below the surface, where it drops to 23°C. If you're keeping it shallow, you can skin dive (ie no wet suit).

For snorkelers, many coastal areas have popular reefs. Leading destinations include Manzanillo (p422), Isla del Caño (p351) and Isla Tortuga (p259).

If you want to spend time diving, it's advisable to get diving accreditation ahead of time. Get information from the **Professional Association of Diving Instructors** (PADI; ☎ in the USA 949-858 7234, 800-729 7234, in Canada 604-552 5969, 800-565 8130, in Switzerland 52-304 1414; www.padi.com). **Divers Alert Network** (☎ in the USA 800-446 2671, 919-684 2948; www.diversalertnetwork.org) is a nonprofit organization that provides diving insurance and emergency medical evacuation.

Fishing

Sportfishing of the 'catch-and-release' variety (a small number of fish are kept to eat or mount as trophies, though) is a tremendously popular activity.

Inland, fishing in rivers and lakes is popular. Particularly recommended are the Río Savegre near San Gerardo de Dota for trout fishing (p319) and Laguna de Arenal (p213) for *guapote* (Central American rainbow bass). Check with the local operators about closed seasons.

The ocean is always open for fishing. As a general rule, the Pacific coast is slowest from September to November, though you'll get better fishing on the south coast during that period, while the Caribbean is slowest during June and July.

Sought-after fish include tarpon and snook on the Caribbean side and sailfish and black marlin on the Pacific side. Particularly popular outposts include Barra del Colorado (p397) and Tortuguero (p392) on the Caribbean coast. On the Pacific side, there's Playa Flamingo (p231), Playa Carrillo (p255), Quepos (p290), Golfito (p362), Zancudo (p371) and Puerto Jiménez (p356).

A good resource is **Costa Rica Outdoors** (☎ 800-308 3394; www.costaricaoutdoors.com), a magazine carrying information on adventure travel, with a focus on fishing.

Hiking & Trekking

For long-distance hiking and trekking, it's best to travel in the dry season. In Parque Nacional Corcovado (p351) rivers become impassable and trails are shut down in the wet. The trek up Cerro Chirripó (p326) becomes more taxing in the rain and the bare landscape offers little protection. For more details on trekking opotions see p52.

Be sure to pack a hat, sunscreen, insect repellent and plenty of water – and always carry any waste out with you. The parks have a limited ability to collect trash, so do them and the environment a favor and dispose of your own garbage after leaving the park.

Assaults and robberies have been reported in some parks, namely Carara (p278), Braulio Carrillo (p136) and on the road between La Palma and Los Patos (p355) near Corcovado. Go with a group or a guided tour. For other precautions, turn to Dangers & Annoyances, p453.

Horseback Riding

Wherever you go, you are sure to find someone giving riding trips. Rates vary from US$25 for an hour or two, to US$100 for a full day. Overnight trips with pack horses can also be arranged. If you've never been on a horse, then don't start with a six-day trek. Stick to an hour or two instead or you'll be sporting some serious saddle sores. In addition, riders weighing more than 100kg (221lbs) cannot expect small local horses to carry them very far.

With the increased demand for riding, some unscrupulous owners have worked their horses past breaking point. In the past, the trail between La Fortuna and Monteverde (or vice versa) was a center of such abuse, where overworked horses were forced through muddy trails and chest-deep rivers. Recently, the situation appears to have improved. (For more on this, see p174.) Ask to see the condition of the horses before setting out.

Riding along the beach is popular and possible at any number of beach towns. Guides in some towns (such as at Playa Tamarindo, p235) are allowing travelers with little to no riding experience to ride through crowded beach areas at a full gallop. Isolated beach areas aren't hard to find. Make sure your guide is respectful of this.

Travelers should continue to recommend good outfitters (and give the heads up on bad ones) by writing in to Lonely Planet.

Hot-Air Ballooning

Ballooning is still a fledgling activity in Costa Rica. Serendipity Adventures (p474) has three different take-off spots: Arenal, Turrialba and Naranjo (west of Sarchí). Some rides are available only when the air currents are favorable.

Mountain Biking

Outfitters in Costa Rica and the USA can organize multiday mountain-biking trips around Costa Rica that cover stretches of highland and beach (see p53 for details). Gear is provided on trips organized by local companies, but US outfitters require that you bring your own.

Most international airlines will fly your bike as a piece of checked baggage if you box it. (Pad it well, because the box is liable to be roughly handled.) Other airlines might charge you an extra handling fee. As airline bicycle-carrying policies vary; shop around.

You can rent mountain bikes in almost any tourist town, but the condition of the equipment varies. It is advisable to bring your own helmet and water bottle. For a monthly fee of US$5, **Trail Source** (www.trailsource.com) can provide you with information on trails all over Costa Rica and the world.

River Running & Kayaking

The months between June and October are considered the wildest months for rafting, but some rivers offer good running all year.

Rafters should bring sunblock, a spare change of clothes, a waterproof bag for your camera and river sandals to protect your feet. The regulation of outfitters is poor, so make sure that your guide is well-versed in safety and has had emergency medical training.

River kayaking can be organized in conjunction with rafting trips if you are experienced and sea kayaking is popular year-round.

Specific operators are listed in the Transport chapter (p474). The Adventure Travel chapter has more detailed information on destinations (p53).

Surfing

Most international airlines accept surfboards (properly packed in a padded board bag) as one of the two pieces of checked luggage. However, domestic airlines offer more of a challenge. They will accept surfboards (at an extra charge), but the board must be under 2.1m (7 feet) in length. If the plane is full, there's a chance your board won't make it on because of weight restrictions.

Outfitters in many of the popular surf towns rent short and long boards, fix dings, give classes and organize excursions. Jacó (p281), Tamarindo (p234), Nosara (p248) and Puerto Viejo de Talamanca (p409) are good for these types of activities

For detailed information, including a surf map, turn to p54.

Wildlife- & Bird-watching

The national parks are good places for observing wildlife, as are the many private reserves. Perhaps the single best area for spotting wildlife is the Península de Osa (p341). Parque Nacional Santa Rosa (p193), Tortuguero p392) and Caño Negro (p435) all provide good birding and wildlife-watching opportunities. The areas near the Cerro de la Muerte (p320) and the reserves near Santa Elena (p157) are good for quetzal-watching. A map of the protected areas of Costa rica appears on p38.

Early morning and late afternoon are the best times to see animals, since most are at rest during the heat of the noonday sun. A pair of binoculars – even cheap ones – will improve your powers of observation tremendously. Hiring a guide will vastly improve your chances; a qualified guide is more than worth the expense. For details of tour operators see p473.

Windsurfing

Laguna de Arenal is the nation's undisputed windsurfing center. From December to March winds are strong and steady, averaging 20 knots in the dry season, with maximum winds often 30 knots, and windless days are a rarity. The lake has a year-round water temperature of 18°C to 21°C with 1m-high swells and winds. Get further information on p218.

For warmer water (but more inconsistent winds), try Puerto Solely in the Bahía Salinas (p197).

BUSINESS HOURS

Restaurants are usually open from 7am and serve dinner until 9pm, though in more remote areas hours can be significantly shorter. See other business hours on the inside cover of this book.

For the purpose of this book, count on sights, activities and restaurants to be open daily, unless otherwise stated.

CHILDREN

Children under the age of 12 receive a discount of 25% on domestic airline flights, while infants under two fly free (provided they sit on a parent's lap). Children pay full fare on buses (except for children under the age of three). Infant car seats are not always available at car-rental agencies, so bring your own.

Most mid-range and top-end hotels will have reduced rates for children under 12, provided the child shares a room with parents. Top-end hotels will provide cribs and usually have activities for children.

If you're traveling with an infant, bring disposable diapers (nappies) and creams from home, or stock up in San José. In rural areas, supplies may be harder to find, though plenty of towns stock cloth diapers – which are friendlier to the environment. Also pack baby aspirin, a thermometer and, of course, a favorite toy.

Top destinations for families with small children include the many beach-side communities, particularly Jacó (p281) and Manuel Antonio (p300) on the central Pacific coast and also Sámara on the Península de Nicoya (p252). Other popular activities include gentle float trips at La Virgen (p439) or near Cañas (p179). See also p79 of the San José chapter for some activities in the capital.

For a near-infinite number of travel suggestions, check out Lonely Planet's *Travel with Children*. For some useful Latin American words and phrases, see p491.

CLIMATE

For a small country, Costa Rica's got an awful lot of weather going on. The highlands are cold, the cloud forest is misty and cool, San José and the Central Valley get an 'eternal spring' and both the Pacific and Caribbean coasts are pretty much sweltering year-round. (Get ready for some bad-hair days.)

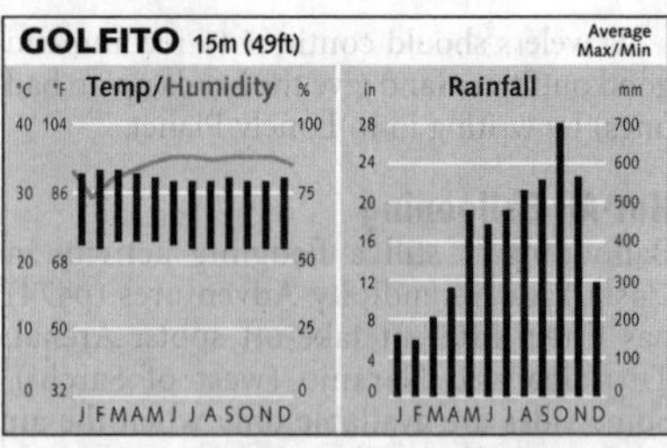

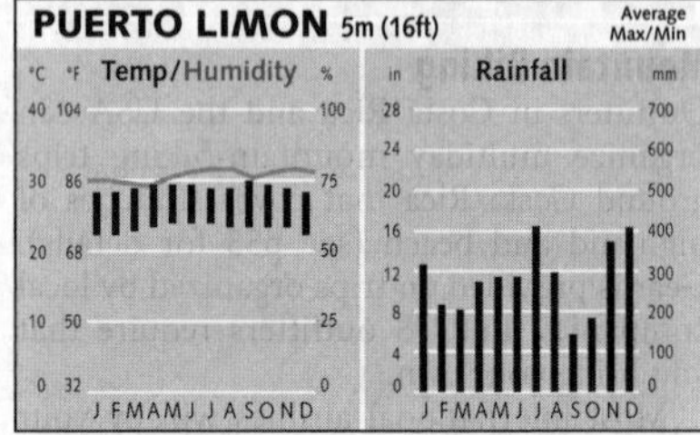

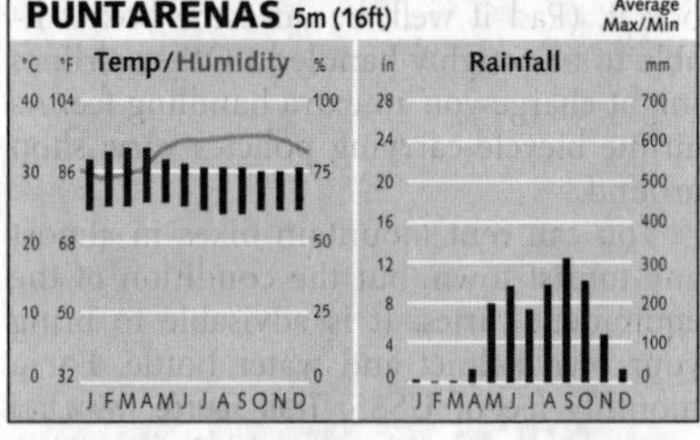

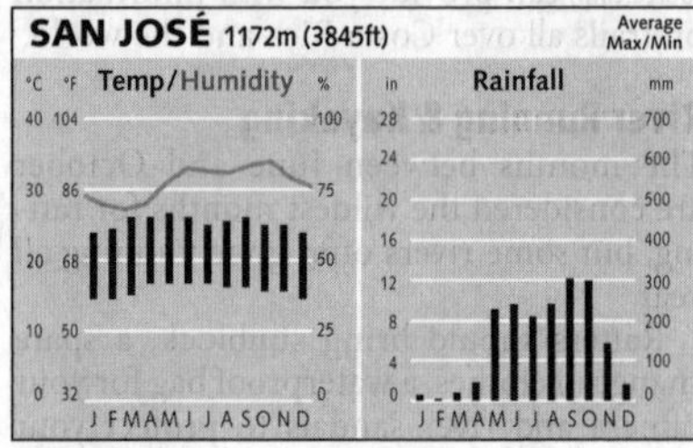

COURSES

A number of Spanish-language schools operate all over Costa Rica and charge by the hour of instruction. Lessons are usually intensive, with class sizes varying from two to five pupils and classes meeting for several hours every weekday.

Courses are offered mainly in central San José (p78) and the suburb of San Pedro (p102), which has a lively university and student scene. In the Central Valley, there are a number of institutions offering courses (see the boxed text 'Spanish Schools in the Central Valley', on p122). Other language schools can be found in Santa Elena, near Monteverde (p166), Playa Flamingo (p231), Sámara (p253), Jacó (p282), Manuel Antonio (p295) and Dominical (p308).

It is best to arrange classes in advance. A good clearing house is the **Institute for Spanish Language Studies** (ISLS; ☎ 258 5111, in the USA 800-765 0025, 626-441 3507, 858-456 9268; www.isls.com, www.teenspanish.com) which represents half a dozen schools in Costa Rica.

CUSTOMS

All travelers over the age of 18 are allowed to enter the country with 5L of wine or spirits and 500g of processed tobacco (400 cigarettes or 50 cigars). Camera gear, binoculars, and camping, snorkeling and other sporting equipment are readily allowed into the country. Officially, you are limited to six rolls of film, but this is rarely enforced. There's seldom a problem bringing in items for personal use.

DANGERS & ANNOYANCES

For the latest official reports on travel to Costa Rica see the websites of the **US State Department** (travel.state.gov/travel_warnings.html) or the **UK Foreign & Commonwealth Office** (www.fco.gov.uk).

Earthquakes

Costa Rica lies on the edge of active tectonic plates, so it is decidedly earthquake prone. Recent major quakes occurred in 1990 (7.1 on the Richter scale) and 1991 (7.4). Smaller quakes and tremors happen quite often, particularly on the Península de Nicoya, cracking roads and knocking down telephone lines.

If you're caught in a quake, the best place to take shelter is under a door frame. If you are in the open, don't stand near walls or telephone poles.

Hiking Hazards

Hikers setting out into the wilderness should be adequately prepared for their trips. First of all, don't bite off more than you can chew. If your daily exercise routine consists of walking from the fridge to the TV, don't start your trip with a 20km trek. There are plenty of 3km and 5km trails that are ideally suited to the couch potato.

> **WHAT'S THAT ADDRESS?**
>
> Though some larger cities have streets that have been dutifully named, signage is rare and finding a Tico who knows what street they are standing on is even rarer. Everybody uses landmarks when providing directions; an address may be given as 200m south and 150m east of a church. (A city block is *cien metros* – literally 100m – so '250 metros al sur' means 2½ blocks south, regardless of the distance.) Churches, parks, office buildings, fast-food joints and car dealerships are the most common landmarks used – but these are often meaningless to the foreign traveler who will have no idea where the Subaru dealership is to begin with. Better yet, Ticos frequently refer to landmarks that no longer exist. In San Pedro, outside of San José, locals still use the sight of an old fig tree (*el antiguo higuerón*) to provide directions.
>
> Confused? Get used to it...

In addition, carry plenty of water, even on short trips. The hiking is hot and dehydration sets in quickly. In Corcovado, at least one hiker every year dies of heat exhaustion on the scorching trail between San Pedrillo and Sirena (p352). Hikers have also been known to get lost in rainforests, so carry maps, extra food and a compass. Let someone know where you are going, so they can narrow the search area in the event of an emergency.

There is also wildlife to contend with. Central America's most poisonous snakes, the fer-de-lance (the 'Costa Rican landmine') and the bushmaster are quite assertive and crocodiles are a reality at many estuaries. Bull sharks love to lounge at the mouth of Río Sirena in Corcovado.

This is no reason to be paranoid. Most animals don't want to mess with you anymore than you want to mess with them, but they will attack if they feel threatened. Hiring a guide can be helpful as they will better know how to spot animals and avoid angst to begin with. To minimize the risk of snake bite, wear sturdy boots.

Ocean Hazards

Approximately 200 drownings a year occur in Costa Rican waters, 90% of which are caused by riptides – a strong current that pulls the swimmer out to sea.

Many deaths in riptides are caused by panicked swimmers struggling to the point of exhaustion. If you are caught in one, float. Do not struggle. Let the tide carry you out beyond the breakers, after which it will dissipate. Then swim parallel to the beach and allow the surf to carry you back in.

Some beaches are polluted by litter, or worse, sewage and other contamination. Beaches are now checked by the local authorities, and the cleanest are marked with a blue flag (the *Bandera Azul Ecológica*).

River Running

River-rafting expeditions may be particularly risky during periods of heavy rain – flash floods have been known to capsize rafts. Reputable tour operators will ensure conditions are safe before setting out; some are listed on p474.

Thefts & Muggings

The biggest danger that most travelers face is theft, primarily from pickpockets. Overall, Costa Rica is safer than neighboring Central American countries, but that doesn't mean you should let your guard down. Some tips:

- in public areas keep your daypack on your back, don't wear a lot of jewelry, and never put your wallet in a back pocket
- keep your passport and money on you at all times – preferably in an inside pocket or money belt. (The latter isn't the coolest accessory, but it works.)
- don't put your daypack containing important documents on the overhead bus rack or leave it unattended on a beach
- don't leave your belongings inside a parked vehicle, even for a few minutes
- bring traveler's checks or credit cards. The former can be refunded if lost or stolen; the latter can be canceled and reissued.
- keep an emergency packet somewhere separate from your documents that includes photocopies of important papers such as your passport, visa, airline tickets and the serial numbers of traveler's checks

Of greater concern are the growing number of armed robberies in San José as well as tourist-heavy areas. See Dangers & Annoyances (p72) so that you'll know what neighborhoods to avoid. In the countryside, don't walk around isolated areas at night by yourself. It is always safest to travel in groups.

Solo women travelers would do best to stay away from red-light districts and male-only *cantinas* (see p461 for more information).

If you are robbed or otherwise attacked, police reports (for insurance claims) should be filed with the **Organismo de Investigación Judicial** (OIJ; ☎ 222 1365; Av 6 btwn Calles 17 & 19, San José) in the Corte Suprema de Justicia (Supreme Court). Bigger towns have police stations that can assist you with this process. If you don't speak Spanish, bring a translator; most policemen do not speak English. It's highly unlikely that the police will be able to recover your property. By law, the tourist board is obliged to represent foreign tourists who are victims of tourist-related crimes in court. Check in with the Instituto Costarricense de Turismo (ICT) in San José (p72) before leaving the country.

For emergency numbers, see the inside cover of this book.

DISABLED TRAVELERS

Independent travel is difficult for anyone with mobility problems. Although Costa Rica has an equal-opportunity law for disabled people, the law applies only to new or newly remodeled businesses and is loosely enforced. Therefore, very few hotels and restaurants have features specifically suited to wheelchair use. Many don't have ramps, while room or bathroom doors are rarely wide enough to accommodate a wheelchair.

Outside the buildings, streets and sidewalks are potholed and poorly paved, making wheelchair use frustrating at best. Public buses don't have provisions to carry wheelchairs and most national parks and outdoor tourist attractions don't have trails suited to wheelchair use. Notable exceptions include Volcán Poás (p129), INBio (p135) and the Rainforest Aerial Tram (p137).

In Costa Rica, **Vaya con Silla de Ruedas** (☎ 391 5045; www.gowithwheelchairs.com) offers specialty trips for the wheelchair-bound traveler. The company has specially designed vans and their equipment meets international accessibility standards. In the USA, **Accessible Journeys** (www.disabilitytravel.com) can organize independent travel to Costa Rica for folks with disabilities.

DISCOUNT CARDS

Students with an ISIC card or a valid ID from a university offering four-year courses are generally entitled to discounts on museum or guided tour fees. Cards supplied by language schools are not honored.

EMBASSIES & CONSULATES

Costa Rican Embassies & Consulates

For a full list of embassies in Spanish, log on to the **Foreign Ministry's website** (www.rree.go.cr) and click on 'Viajando al Exterior'.

The following are the principal Costa Rican embassies and consulates abroad:

Australia (☎ 02-9261 1177; 11th fl, 30 Clarence St, Sydney, NSW 2000)
Canada (☎ 613-562 2855; 325 Dailhouise St, Ottawa, Ontario K1N 7G2)
Denmark (☎ 03-311 0885; Kvasthusgade 3, DK-125 Copenhagen)
France (☎ 01 45 78 96 96; 78 ave Emile Zola, Paris 75015)
Germany (☎ 030-2639 8990; Dessauerstrasse 28-29 D-10963, Berlin)
Israel (☎ 02-2566 6197; Rehov Diskin 13, No 1, Jerusalem 92473)
Italy (☎ 06-442 510 46; Vía Bartolomeo Eustachio, No 22, Interno 6, 00161 Rome)
Japan (☎ 03-3486 1812; Kowa Building No 38, fl 12-24, Nishi-Azabu 4, Chome Minato-Ku, Tokyo, 106-0031)
Netherlands (☎ 070-354 0780; Laan Copes Van Cattenburg 46, The Hague 2585 GB)
Nicaragua (☎ 02-66 2404, 02-66 3986; De la Estatua de Montoya; 200m towards the lake & 200m north, Callejón Zelaya, Managua)
Panama (☎ 264 2980, 264 2937; Calle Samuel Lewis, Edificio Plaza Omega, 3rd fl, next to the Santuario Nacional, Panama City)
Spain (☎ 91 345 9622; Paseo de la Castellana 164, No 17A, Madrid 28046)
Switzerland (☎ 31 37 27 887; Schwarztorstrasse 11, Bern 3007)
UK (☎ 020-7706 8844; Flat 1, 14 Lancaster Gate, London W2 3LH)
USA (☎ 202-234 2945; 2112 S St NW, Washington, DC 20008)

Embassies & Consulates in Costa Rica

Mornings are the best time to go. Australia and New Zealand do not have consular representation in Costa Rica; the closest embassies are in Mexico City. All of the following are in San José. For visa information see p461.

Canada (☎ 242 4400; Oficentro Ejecutivo, 3rd fl, behind La Contraloría, Sabana Sur)
El Salvador (☎ 257 7855; 500m north & 25m west of Toyota dealership that's on Paseo Colón)
France (☎ 234 4167; road to Curridabat, 200m south & 50m west of Indoor Club)
Germany (☎ 232 5533; 200m north and 75m east of ex-president Oscar Arias' residence, Rohrmoser)
Guatemala (☎ 283 2557; Carr a Curridabat, 500m south and 30m east of Pops)
Honduras (☎ 234 9502; 250m east, 200m north then another 100m east from Universidad Las Veritas)
Israel (☎ 221 6011; Edificio Centro Colón, 11th fl, Paseo Colón)
Italy (☎ 234 2326; Calle 33, btwn Avs 8 & 10, 50m west of Restaurant Río, Los Yoses)
Mexico (☎ 234 9171; 250m south of the Subaru dealership, Los Yoses)
Netherlands (☎ 296 1490; Oficentro Ejecutivo La Sabana, Edificio 3, 3rd fl, behind La Contraloría, Sabana Sur)
Nicaragua (☎ 222 2373; Av Central 2540 btwn Calles 25 & 27, Barrio La California)
Panama (☎ 281 2104; 200m south and 25m east from the antiguo higuerón, San Pedro)
Spain (☎ 222 1933; Calle 32 btwn Paseo Colón & Av 2)
Switzerland (☎ 233 0052; Edificio Centro Colón, 10th fl, Paseo Colón btwn Calles 38 & 40)
UK (☎ 258 2025; Edificio Centro Colón, 11th fl, Paseo Colón btwn Calles 38 & 40)
USA (☎ 220 3939; Carretera a Pavas opposite Centro Commercial del Oeste)

EMERGENCIES

Emergency numbers are listed on the inside cover, but may not apply in some remote parts of the country. The ICT in San José (p72) distributes a helpful brochure with up-to-date emergency numbers for every region.

FESTIVALS & SPECIAL EVENTS

The following events are of national significance in Costa Rica:

JANUARY/FEBRUARY

Fiesta de Santa Cruz (Mid-January) Held in Santa Cruz de Nicoya (p243), here is a religious procession, rodeo, bullfight, music, dances and a beauty pageant.

Fiesta de los Diablitos (December 31-January 2 in Reserva Indígena Boruca; February 5-8 in Curré; p330) During the fiesta men wear carved wooden devil masks and burlap masks to re-enact the fight between the Indians and the Spanish. In this version, the Spanish lose.

MARCH

Día del Boyero (Second Sunday of the month) A parade is held in Escazú (p106) in honor of oxcart drivers.

Día de San José (St Joseph's Day; 19th) This day honors the patron saint of the capital.

JUNE

Día de San Pedro & San Pablo (St Peter & St Paul Day; 29th) Celebrations with religious processions held in villages of the same name.

JULY

Fiesta de La Virgen del Mar (Festival of the Virgin of the Sea; Mid-July) Held in Puntarenas (p275) and Playa del Coco (p225), it involves colorful regattas and boat parades.

Día de Guanacaste (July 25) Celebrates the annexation of Guanacaste from Nicaragua. There's a rodeo in Santa Cruz on this day.

AUGUST

Virgen de Los Angeles (August 2) The patron saint is celebrated with a particularly important religious procession from San José to Cartago.

NOVEMBER

Día de los Muertos (All Souls' Day; 2nd) Families visit graveyards and have religious parades in honor of the deceased.

DECEMBER

La Inmaculada Concepción (Immaculate Conception; 8th) An important religious holiday.

FOOD

For this book, you can expect that most main dishes at a basic budget eatery will cost under US$5 and between US$5 and US$12 at mid-range places. Entrees (main course) at top-end restaurants will climb to well over US$12. Many mid-range and top-end places charge an extra 23% in sales and service taxes.

For additional information see Food & Drink (p58).

GAY & LESBIAN TRAVELERS

The situation facing gay and lesbian travelers is poor but improving, though it's better than in most Central American countries. Homosexual acts between two consenting adults (aged 18 and over) are not illegal, but most Costa Ricans are tolerant only at a 'Don't ask; don't tell' level.

In the recent past, there were outward acts of prejudice. In 1998 a gay-and-lesbian festival planned in San José was cancelled following heavy opposition from Catholic clergy. The Church also forced the cancellation of a gay-and-lesbian tour to Manuel Antonio and encouraged the blockade of a coastal hotel hosting a gay group. Things took an embarrassing turn in 1999 when the tourism minister said that Costa Rica should not be a destination for sex tourism or gays. The gay community made it clear that it was against sex tourism, and that linking gay tourism with sex tourism was untrue and defamatory. The official position in Costa Rica then modified toward stating that gay tourism was neither discriminated against nor encouraged.

Thankfully, Costa Rica's gays and lesbians have made some strides. In the 1990s, the Supreme Court ruled against police harassment in gay nightspots and guaranteed medical treatment to people living with HIV/AIDS. And in June 2003, the first ever gay-pride festival in San José drew more than 2000 attendants.

Outside of gay spots, public displays of affection are not recommended.

Meeting Places

In San José, hotels that are gay or gay-friendly include Hotel Kekoldi (p81), Joluva Guesthouse (p80) and Colours (p88). Also, the aforementioned Agua Buena association offers long-term accommodations (p104).

The Pacific resort town of Manuel Antonio (p295) is a popular gay vacation center. Hotels include La Plantación (p298) and Hotel Mariposa (p298).

In San José, there is a good selection of nightclubs, that range from cruising joints to pounding dance clubs to more intimate places (see p94).

Organizations & Resources

A comprehensive resource is **Gay Costa Rica** (www.gaycostarica.com), which provides up-to-the-minute information on nightlife, travel and many links.

The website of the leading activist organization in Costa Rica, **Cipac** (☎ 280 7821; www.cipacdh.org), is a great resource. **Agua Buena Human Rights Association** (☎ 234 2411; www.aguabuena.org) is another. This noteworthy non-profit organization has campaigned steadily for fairness in medical treatment for people living with HIV/AIDS in Costa Rica.

The monthly newspaper *Gayness* and the magazine *Gente 10* (in Spanish) are both available at gay bars in San José (p94).

Tiquicia Travel (☎ 256 9682; www.tiquiciatravel.com; Condominios Pie Montel, La Uruca in San José) can help you make arrangements at gay-friendly hotels.

In the USA, gay-travel specialists **Toto Tours** (☎ in the USA 800-565 1241, 773-274 8686; www.tototours.com) organizes regular trips to Costa Rica, among other destinations. The **International Gay & Lesbian Travel Association** (IGLTA; ☎ in the USA 800-448 8550, 954-776 2626; www.iglta.org) has a list of hundreds of travel agents and tour operators all over the world.

HOLIDAYS

National holidays (*días feriados*) are taken seriously in Costa Rica. Banks, public offices and many stores close. During this time, public transport is tight and hotels are heavily booked. Many festivals involve public holidays as well (see opposite).

New Year's Day January 1

Semana Santa (Holy Week) March or April. The Thursday and Friday before Easter Sunday is the official holiday, though most businesses shut down the whole week. From Thursday to Sunday, bars are closed and alcohol sales are prohibited; on Thursday and Friday buses stop running

Día de Juan Santamaría April 11. Honors the national hero who died fighting William Walker in 1856; major events are held in Alajuela, his hometown.

Labor Day May 1

Día de la Madre (Mother's Day) August 15. Coincides with the annual Catholic feast of the Assumption.

Independence Day September 15

Día de la Raza (Columbus Day) October 12

Christmas Day December 25. The day before is often an unofficial holiday

Last week in December The week between Christmas and New Year is an unofficial holiday; businesses close and beach hotels are crowded.

INSURANCE

In general, signing up for a travel-insurance policy is a good idea. For Costa Rica, a basic theft/loss and medical policy is recommended. Read the fine print carefully as some companies exclude dangerous activities from coverage, which can include scuba diving, motorcycling, even trekking. You may prefer a policy that pays doctors or hospitals directly rather than you having to pay on the spot and make a claim later.

Make copies of all insurance information in the event that the original is lost. For information on health insurance, turn to p476 and for car insurance, see p470.

INTERNET ACCESS

Cybercafés abound in Costa Rica, and for the most part, finding cheap and speedy Internet access is easy for checking your Web-based email. The normal access rate in San José is US$1 to US$2 per hour, slightly more in other large towns, and up to US$5 per hour in the hard-to-reach places. If you do not have Web-based email, Lonely Planet's **ekit** (www.ekno.lonelyplanet.com) provides a free service.

Travelers with a laptop and modem will find that many top-end hotels have RJ-11 phone jacks similar to those used in the USA. However, your Internet service provider will likely not have local dial-in numbers since Web access is managed by a government monopoly. This necessitates having an account with the state telecommunications agency, **Racsa** (☎ 800-628 3427; www.racsa.co.cr).

LEGAL MATTERS

If you get into legal trouble and are jailed, your embassy can offer only limited assistance. This may include an occasional visit from an embassy staff member to make sure your human rights have not been violated, letting your family know where you are and putting you in contact with a Costa Rican lawyer, whom you must pay yourself. Embassy officials will not bail you out and you are subject to Costa Rican laws, not the laws of your own country.

In many beachside towns, police tend to turn a blind eye to casual marijuana use. However, be forewarned that penalties in Costa Rica for possession of even small amounts of illegal drugs are much stricter than in the USA or Europe. Defendants often spend many months in jail before

LEGAL AGE

- Driving: 18
- Voting: 18
- Age at which you can marry: 15
- Drinking age: 18
- Minimum age for consensual heterosexual sex: 18. Sex with anyone under 18 is illegal and penalties are severe.
- Minimum age for consensual homosexual sex: no legal age, but sex with anyone under 18 is not advisable.

they are brought to trial and, if convicted, can expect sentences lasting several years.

Prostitution is legal for women over 18. Although prostitutes carry cards showing how recently they have had a medical checkup, these are quite unreliable.

If you are the victim of a crime, report it to the authorities (see p454 for details).

Drivers & Driving Accidents

Drivers should carry their passport as well as driver's license. In the event of an accident, call the police immediately to make a report (required for insurance purposes) or attend to any injured parties. Leave the vehicles in place until the report has been made and do not make any statements except to members of law-enforcement agencies. Injured people should only be moved by medical professionals.

Keep your eye on your vehicle until the police arrive and then call the car-rental company to find out where you should take the vehicle for repairs (do not have it fixed yourself). If the accident results in injury or death, you could be jailed or prevented from leaving the country until legalities are handled.

Emergency numbers are listed on the inside cover of this book.

MAPS

An excellent map is the 1:330,000 *Costa Rica* sheet produced by **International Travel Map** (ITMB; www.itmb.com; 530 W Broadway, Vancouver, BC, V5Z 1E, Canada) and available around the world. The map includes a San José inset and has just debuted in a waterproof edition.

The **Instituto Costarricense de Turismo** (ICT; see p72) publishes a 1:700,000 Costa Rica map with a 1:12,500 Central San José map on the reverse. These are free at both ICT offices.

Topographical maps, created by the **Instituto Geográfico Nacional** (IGN; ☎ 257 7798; Calle 9 btwn Avs 20 & 22, San José; ⏲ 7:30am-noon & 1-3pm Mon-Fri) are available for sale in their office and San José bookshops (see p67). Don't count on any of the national park offices or ranger stations having maps for hikers. Online, **Maptak** (www.maptak.com) has maps of Costa Rica's seven provinces.

The **Fundación Neotropica** (www.neotropica.org) has published a 1:500,000 map showing national parks and other protected areas. These are available in San José bookstores.

MONEY

ATMs

It's increasingly easy to find ATMs (*cajeros automáticos* in Spanish). The Visa Plus network is the standard, but machines on the Cirrus network, which accept most foreign ATM cards, can be found in San José and in touristy or larger, developed towns.

Some ATM machines will dispense US dollars. Note that some machines (eg at Banco Nacional) will only accept cards held by their own customers.

Cash & Currency

The Costa Rican currency is the colón (plural colones), named after Cristóbal Colón (Christopher Columbus). The symbol for colones is written as ¢ and bills come in 500, 1000, 5000 and 10,000 notes; coins come in denominations of 5, 10, 20, 25, 50 and 100 colones. Older coins are silver, newer ones are gold-colored.

You can pay for tours, park fees, hotel rooms and large-ticket items with US dollars. Meals, bus fares and small items should all be paid with colones.

Paying for things in US dollars should be free of tears.

Credit Cards

Holders of credit and debit cards can buy colones and sometimes US dollars in some banks. Cards are accepted at some mid-range and most top-end hotels, as well as top-end restaurants and some travel agencies. All car-rental agencies accept credit cards.

Visa is the most widely accepted, MasterCard less so and American Express (Amex) rarely. Some hotels might charge a 7% fee for using credit cards, in addition to government and service taxes. Check their policies and prices carefully (for more information, see p449).

Exchanging Money

All banks will exchange US dollars, and some will exchange euros; other currencies are more difficult. Most banks have excruciatingly long lines, especially at the state-run institutions (Banco Nacional, Banco de Costa Rica, Banco Popular). However, they don't charge commissions on cash exchanges. Private banks (Banex, Banco Interfin, Scotiabank) tend to be faster. Make sure the dollar bills you want to exchange are in good condition or they may be refused.

Changing money at hotels and travel agencies is even faster and more convenient, though some only provide these services to their customers and many charge hefty commissions. Changing money on the streets is not recommended, except possibly at land borders. Street changers don't give better rates, and scammers abound.

Non-US travelers should buy US dollars before they arrive in Costa Rica. Carry your passport when exchanging currency and try not to leave the country with many excess colones; it's difficult to buy back more than US$50 at the border or airport.

Tipping

It is customary to tip the bellhop/porter US$0.50 to US$1 per service and the housekeeper (US$1 per day in top-end hotels, less in budget places). On guided tours, tip the guide US$1 to US$5 per person per day. Tip the tour driver about half of what you tip the guide. Naturally, tips depend upon quality of service

Taxi drivers are not normally tipped, unless some special service is provided.

Traveler's Checks

Most banks and exchange bureaus will cash traveler's checks at a commission of 1% to 3%. Many hotels will accept them as payment, but check policies carefully as many hotels do not. US dollar traveler's checks are preferred. It may be difficult or impossible to change checks of other currencies.

Amex checks are the easiest to replace quickly in Costa Rica. If your checks are lost or stolen, call **Amex** (☎ 800-012 0039) to have them replaced.

PHOTOGRAPHY

Camera gear is expensive in Costa Rica and film choice is limited, though basic types of Kodak film are available in San José and in popular tourist towns. Slide film tends to only be available in San José. Check expiration dates carefully before purchase.

Guard your film from the particularly intense X-Ray machines at the international airport in San José.

If you wish to take pictures of people (particularly in indigenous communities), always ask for permission first. If you are refused, do not be offended.

POST

Airmail letters to North America/Europe/Australia cost about US$0.24/0.29/0.31 for the first 20g. Parcels can be shipped at the rate of US$6.75 per kilo. The better hotels will provide stamps for your letters and mail them for you; otherwise there are post offices in the major towns.

You can receive mail at the main post office of major towns. Mail to San José's central post office should be addressed:

Joanne VISITOR, c/o Lista de Correos, Correo Central, San José, Costa Rica.

Use a first and last name only, since two surnames may cause the letter to be misfiled. Letters usually arrive within a week from North America; it takes a little longer from more distant places – up to two weeks from Australia. The post office will hold mail for 30 days from the date it's received; there's a US$0.20 fee per letter. Photo identification is required to retrieve mail and you will only be given correspondence with your name on it. In addresses, *apartado* means 'PO Box'; it is not a street or apartment address.

Avoid having parcels sent to you. They are held in customs and cannot be retrieved until you have paid the exorbitant customs fees and dealt with a whole lot of bureaucracy.

SHOPPING

Alcohol

The most popular purchases are Ron Centenario, the coffee liqueur Café Rica and also *guaro*, the local firewater. All are available at duty-free shops inside the airport, or in supermarkets and liquor stores around the country.

Ceramics

Ceramics are also popular souvenirs and can be found in gift shops all over Costa Rica. The best place for these is Guaitil (p243).

Coffee

Coffee is perhaps the most popular tourist item. It is available at gift shops, the *Mercado Central* in San José (p96) and at any supermarket.

BARGAINING

A high standard of living along with a steady stream of international tourist traffic means that the Latin American tradition of haggling is fast dying out in Costa Rica. The beach communities, especially, have fixed prices on hotels that cannot be negotiated. (Expect some business owners to be offended if you try to negotiate.) Some smaller hotels in the interior still accept the practice.

Negotiating prices at outdoor markets is acceptable though, and some bargaining is accepted when hiring long-distance taxis. Overall, Ticos respond well to courteous manners and gentle inquiries. Don't demand a service for your price or chances are you won't get it.

Handicrafts

Tropical hardwood items include salad bowls, plates, carving boards, jewelry boxes and a variety of carvings and ornaments. The most exquisite woodwork is available at Biesanz Woodworks in Escazú (p112). All of the wood is grown on farms expressly for this purpose, so you needn't worry about forests being chopped down for your salad bowl.

Uniquely Costa Rican souvenirs are the colorfully painted replicas of traditional oxcarts *(carretas)* produced in Sarchí (p126).

Leatherwork includes the interesting wood/leather rocking chairs seen in many tourist lodges. Because of their leather seats and backs, they can be folded for transport, packed two to a carton and checked in as airline luggage.

SOLO TRAVELERS

Costa Rica is a fine country for solo travelers. Inexpensive hostels with communal kitchens encourage social exchange, while a large number of language schools, tours and volunteer organizations will provide every traveler with an opportunity to meet others.

However, it isn't recommended to undertake long treks in the wilderness by yourself (see p352). See also Women Travelers opposite.

TELEPHONE

Public phones are found all over Costa Rica and Chip or Colibrí phonecards are available in 1000, 2000 and 3000 colón denominations. Chip cards are inserted into the phone and scanned. Colibrí cards (the most common) require dialing a toll-free number (☎ 199) and entering an access code. Instructions are provided in English or Spanish. These are the preferred card of travelers since they can be used from any phone. Cards can be found just about everywhere, including supermarkets, pharmacies, newsstands, *pulperías* (corner grocery stores) and gift shops.

The cheapest international calls are direct-dialed using a phonecard. Costs of calls from Costa Rica per minute are approximately US$0.55 to North America and US$0.80 to Europe and Australia. To make international calls, dial '00' followed by the country code and number. Pay phones cannot receive international calls.

Make sure that no one is peeking over your shoulder when you dial your code. Some travelers have had their access numbers pilfered by thieves.

To call Costa Rica from abroad, use the international code (☎ 506) before the seven-digit number. Find other important phone numbers on the inside cover of this book.

TIME

Costa Rica is six hours behind Greenwich Mean Time (GMT), which means that Costa Rican time is equivalent to Central Time in North America. There is no daylight saving time.

TOILETS

Public restrooms are rare, but most restaurants and cafés will let you use their facilities at a small charge – usually between US$0.25 to US$0.50. Bus terminals and other major public buildings usually have lavatories, also at a charge.

If you're particularly fond of toilet paper, carry it with you at all times as it is not always available. Just don't flush it down! Costa Rican plumbing is often poor and has very low pressure in all but the best hotels and buildings. Dispose of toilet paper in the rubbish bin inside every bathroom.

TOURIST INFORMATION

The government-run tourism board, the Instituto Costarricense de Turismo (ICT) has two offices in the capital (see p72). Don't expect to be wowed with any particularly insightful travel advice. It's the staff's job to tell you that it's all good. They speak English.

However, the ICT can provide you with free maps, a master bus schedule and information on road conditions in the hinterlands. Consult the ICT's flashy English-language website (www.visitcostarica.com) for information, or in the US call the **ICT's toll-free number** (☎ 800-343 6332) for brochures and information.

VISAS

Passport-carrying nationals of the following countries are allowed 90 days' stay with no visa: most western European countries, Argentina, Canada, Israel, Japan, Panama, and the USA.

Citizens of Australia, Iceland, Ireland, Mexico, Russia, New Zealand, South Africa and Venezuela are allowed to stay for 30 days with no visa. Others require a visa from a Costa Rican embassy or consulate. Lists of embassies are on p455. These lists are subject to continual change. For the latest info, check the websites of the **ICT** (www.visitcostarica.com) or the **Costa Rican embassy** (www.costarica-embassy.org).

Visa Extensions

Extending your stay beyond the authorized 30 or 90 days is a time-consuming hassle. It is far easier to leave the country for 72 hours and then re-enter. Otherwise go to the office of **migración** (Immigration; ☎ 220 0355; 8am-4pm) in San José, opposite Channel 6 about 4km north of Parque La Sabana. Requirements for stay extensions change so allow several working days.

COMMUNICATING WITH COSTA RICA

Readers have commented that phone messages, faxes, and e-mails sent to Costa Rica can remain unanswered for a week or more. The reason is simply that the remote location of many of the hotels and lodges means that someone must go to the nearest town to recover messages (which might happen once a week or less).

Most commonly, telecommunications systems break down due to bad weather, so you may have to try more than once before you actually get through and someone is able to respond. Some phones do not accept international calls (this is rarely the case for hotels, though).

Just be patient and keep trying.

WOMEN TRAVELERS

Most women travelers in Costa Rica rarely experience little more than a *mi amor* or an appreciative hiss from the local men. But it is worth noting that, in general, Costa Rican men consider foreign women to have looser morals and be easier conquests than Ticas. They will often make flirtatious comments to single women, particularly blondes. Women traveling together are not exempt from this. The best way to deal with this is to do what the Ticas do – ignore it completely. Women who firmly resist unwanted verbal advances from men are normally treated with respect.

In small highland towns, dress is generally fairly conservative. Women rarely wear shorts, and tend to favor jeans, slacks or skirts – though belly baring tops are becoming the rage. On the beach, skimpy bathing suits are acceptable, though topless bathing and nudity are not.

As in any part of the world, the possibilities of rape and assault do exist. Use your normal caution – avoid walking alone in isolated places or through city streets late at night and skip the hitchhiking. Do not take unlicensed 'pirate' cabs (licensed cabs are red and have medallions) as reports of assaults by unlicensed drivers against women have been reported.

And more mundane, yet still an important point: birth-control pills are available at most pharmacies (without prescription) and tampons can be difficult to find in rural areas – bring some from home or stock up in San José.

The **Centro Feminista de Información y Acción** (Cefemina; ☎ 224 3986; www.cefemina.or.cr), in San Pedro, is the main Costa Rican feminist organization. It publishes a newsletter and can provide information and assistance to women travelers.

WORK

Getting a bona fide job necessitates obtaining a work permit, a time-consuming and difficult process. The most likely source of paid employment is as an English teacher at one of the language institutes, which advertise courses in the local newspapers. Naturalists or river guides may be able to find work with private lodges or adventure-travel operators. Don't expect to make more than survival wages from these jobs.

Volunteering

There are numerous volunteer opportunities with placements available around the country:

Asociación de Voluntarios para el Servicio en las Areas Protegidas de Costa Rica (ASVO; ☎ 233 4989; www.asvocr.com) Has 30-day work programs in the national parks; volunteers pay US$14 per day to defray meal costs and a 15-day commitment is required.

Programa Voluntarios para la Conservación del Ambiente (Provca; ☎ 395 0412, 222 7549; www.provca.cjb.net) Offers two-week placements in the national parks; intermediate Spanish is necessary; fees are US$12 per day.

Cross Cultural Solutions (☎ in the USA 800-380 4777, in the UK 0845-458 2781; www.crossculturalsolutions.org) A nonprofit group that partners with grass-roots organizations for volunteer placement; Spanish is a must.

Earthwatch (☎ in the USA 978-461 0081, 800-776 0188; www.earthwatch.org) All-inclusive 10-day turtle-tagging projects; tax deductible.

Habitat for Humanity (☎ 447 2330; www.habitatcostarica.org) Highly regarded international group that has community building projects around the country.

Other organizations look for volunteers who can speak English. These include the Caribbean Conservation Corporation (p394), ANAI (p425), Genesis II (p319), the Reserva Biológica Bosque Nuboso Monteverde (p174) and Ascomoti (p299).

Transportation

CONTENTS

GETTING THERE & AWAY

ENTERING THE COUNTRY

A few people arrive in Costa Rica by sea, either on fishing or scuba charters or as part of a brief stop on a cruise. Others travel in by bus from neighboring countries. But the vast majority of travelers land at the international airport in San José.

Entering Costa Rica is usually hassle-free (with the exception of some long queues). There are no fees or taxes payable on entering the country, though some foreign nationals will require a visa. Be aware that those who need visas cannot get them at the border. For information on visas, see p461.

Passport

Citizens of all nations are now required to have a passport to enter Costa Rica. US and Canadian citizens used to be able to enter with a birth certificate. The law changed in late 2003 and travelers will not be admitted unless they have a passport that is valid for at least six months beyond the dates of the trip.

When you arrive, your passport will be stamped. The law requires that you carry your passport at all times during your stay.

Onward Ticket

Travelers officially need a ticket out of Costa Rica before they are allowed to enter, but the rules are enforced erratically. Those arriving by land can generally meet this requirement by purchasing an outward ticket from the TICA bus company, which has offices in Managua (Nicaragua) and Panama City.

AIR

Airports & Airlines

International flights arrive at Aeropuerto Internacional Juan Santamaría, 17km northwest of San José, in the town of Alajuela. In recent years, Daniel Oduber airport in Liberia (p185) has started receiving international flights from the USA, primarily Delta Airlines flights from Atlanta, Georgia. Daniel Oduber airport is convenient for travelers visiting the Península de Nicoya.

Costa Rica is well connected by air to other Central and Latin American countries, as well as the USA. The national airline, Lacsa (part of the Central American Airline consortium Grupo TACA), flies to numerous points in the USA and Latin America, including Cuba. The Federal Aviation Administration in the USA has assessed Costa Rica's aviation authorities to be in compliance with international safety standards.

Airlines flying to and from Costa Rica include the following. The addresses of airline offices in San José can be found on p97.

Air Canada (no office in Costa Rica; ☎ in Canada 514-393 3333; www.aircanada.ca; airline code AC)

American Airlines (☎ 257 1266; www.aa.com; airline code AA)

> **THINGS CHANGE...**
>
> The information in this chapter is particularly vulnerable to change. Check directly with the airline or a travel agent to make sure you understand how a fare (and ticket you may buy) works and be aware of current security requirements for international travel. Shop carefully. The details given in this chapter should be regarded as pointers and are not a substitute for your own careful, up-to-date research.

America West (no office in Costa Rica; ☎ in the USA 480-693 6718; www.americawest.com; airline code HP)
Avianca see SAM/Avianca.
Continental (☎ 296 4911; www.continental.com; airline code CO)
COPA (☎ 222 6640; www.copaair.com; airline code CM)
Cubana de Aviación (☎ 221 7625, 221 5881; www.cubana.cu; airline code CU)
Delta (☎ 256 7909, press 5 for reservations; www.delta.com; airline code DL)
Grupo TACA (☎ 296 0909; www.taca.com; airline code TA)
Iberia (☎ 257 8266; www.iberia.com; airline code IB)
KLM (☎ 220 4111; www.klm.com; airline code KL)
Lacsa see Grupo TACA.
Mexicana (☎ 295 6969; www.mexicana.com; airline code MX)
SAM/Avianca (☎ 233 3066; www.avianca.com; airline code AV)
TACA see Grupo TACA.
United Airlines (☎ 220 4844; www.united.com; airline code UA)
US Airways (no office in Costa Rica; ☎ toll-free reservations in Costa Rica 800-011 0793, 800-011 4114; www.usairways.com; airline code US)

Tickets

You should purchase tickets more than 21 days in advance for the cheapest deals. In general, fares will be more expensive during the Costa Rican high season (from December through April), with December and January the most expensive months to travel. The prices during the week between Christmas and New Year's are almost prohibitive.

Costa Rica

The best place to buy airline tickets out of Costa Rica is San José, either at airline offices (p97) or travel agencies (p72). Other good areas to book are the tour companies in tourist hubs such as Quepos (p291), Jacó (p283) and Liberia (p187). Top-end hotels usually have travel desks that can assist with travel arrangements.

DEPARTURE TAX

There is a US$26 departure tax on all international outbound flights, payable in cash (US dollars or colones or a mix of the two). At the Juan Santamaría airport you can pay with credit cards, and Banco de Costa Rica has an ATM (on the Plus system) by the departure-tax station.

Other Central & Latin American Countries

American Airlines, Continental, Delta and United all have connections to Costa Rica from several other Central and Latin American countries. Grupo TACA generally offers the greatest number of flights on these routes, though.

Australia & New Zealand

Travel routes from these two countries usually go through the USA or Mexico. Fares tend to go up in June and July (the beginning of the rainy season in Costa Rica).

The following are well-known agents for cheap fares, with branches throughout Australia and New Zealand:

Flight Centre Australia (☎ 133 133; www.flightcentre.com.au) New Zealand (☎ 0800-24 35 44; www.flightcentre.com.nz)
STA Travel Australia (☎ 1300-733 035; www.statravel.com.au) New Zealand (☎ 0508-782 872; www.statravel.co.nz)
Trailfinders Australia (☎ 1300-780 212; www.trailfinders.com.au)

Canada

Most travelers to Costa Rica connect through US gateway cities, though Air Canada has direct flights from Toronto. A good choice for student, youth and budget airfares is **Travel CUTS** (☎ 866-246 9762; www.travelcuts.com). Also see the USA, later, since many of the companies listed can arrange travel from Canada.

Europe

Most flights from Europe connect either in the USA or in Mexico City. High-season fares may apply during the northern summer, which is the beginning of the Costa Rican rainy season.

Some recommended agencies operating across Europe are:

Flightbookers (www.flightbookers.net) Covers all countries in Western Europe.
STA Travel (www.sta.com) Can book travel in more than half a dozen European countries.

THE UK & IRELAND

Discount air travel is big business in London, which means that it's possible to find some bargains here. Advertisements for many travel agencies appear in the weekend broadsheet newspapers, in *Time Out*, the *Evening Standard* and in the free magazine *TNT*. Some recommended agencies are:

Bridge the World (☎ 0870-444 7474; www.b-t-w.co.uk)
Flight Centre (☎ 0870-890 8099; flightcentre.co.uk)
Journey Latin America (JLA; ☎ in London for flights 020-8747 3108; www.journeylatinamerica.co.uk)
North-South Travel (☎ 01245-608 291; www.northsouthtravel.co.uk) North-South Travel donate part of their profit to projects in the developing world.
Quest Travel (☎ 0870-442 3542; www.questtravel.com)
Trailfinders (☎ in London 020-7628 7628, in Glasgow 0141-353 2224, in Dublin 01-677 7888; www.trailfinder.co.uk)
Travel Bag (☎ 0870-890 1456; www.travelbag.co.uk)

CONTINENTAL EUROPE

European travelers will most likely find it cheaper to travel to Costa Rica via London or the USA. Some recommended agencies include:

Airfair (☎ 020-620 5121; www.airfair.nl) Dutch.
Anyway (☎ 0892-893 892; www.anyway.fr) French.
CTS Viaggi (☎ 06-462 0431; www.cts.it) Italian agency that specializes in student and youth travel.
Expedia (www.expedia.de) German.
Just Travel (☎ 089-747 3330; www.justtravel.de) German.
Lastminute France (☎ 0892-705 000; www.lastminute.fr); Germany (☎ 01805-284 366; www.lastminute.de)
Nouvelles Frontières France (☎ 08 25 00 07 47; www.nouvelles-frontieres.fr); Spain (☎ 90 217 09 79; www.nouvelles-frontieres.es)
OTU Voyages (www.otu.fr) French agency that specializes in student and youth travelers.
Voyageurs du Monde (☎ 01 40 15 11 15; www.vdm.com) French.

The USA

More than one-third of all travelers to Costa Rica come from the USA, so finding a nonstop flight from Houston, Miami or New York is quite simple. Schedules and prices are competitive – a little bit of shopping around can get you a good fare.

The following agencies and websites are recommended for bookings:

American Express Travel Services (☎ 800-346 3607; www.itn.com)
Cheap Tickets (www.cheaptickets.com)
Exito Latin America Travel Specialists (☎ 800-655 4053; www.exitotravel.com)
Expedia (www.expedia.com)
Hotwire (www.hotwire.com)
Lowestfare.com (www.lowestfare.com)
Orbitz (www.orbitz.com)
STA Travel (☎ 800-781 4040; www.statravel.com)
Tico Travel (☎ 800-493 8426; www.ticotravel.com)

LAND & RIVER

Bus

Costa Rica shares land borders with Nicaragua and Panama and a lot of travelers, particularly shoestringers, enter the country by bus. An extensive bus system links the Central American capitals and it's vastly cheaper than flying.

If crossing the border by bus, note that international buses may cost slightly more than taking a local bus to the border then another onwards from the border, but they're worth it. These companies are familiar with border procedures and will tell you what's needed to cross efficiently. (Some travelers have reported trying to save money by taking local buses to the border, only to discover upon arrival that they have to return to the capital for a visa.)

There are no problems crossing, provided your papers are in order. If you are on an international bus, you'll have to exit the bus and proceed through both border stations. Bus drivers will wait for everyone to be processed before heading on.

If you choose to take local buses, it's advisable to get to border stations early in the day to allow time for waiting in line and processing. Note that onward buses tend to wind down by the afternoon. See Border Crossings boxed text (pp466-7).

Car & Motorcycle

The cost of insurance, fuel and border permits makes a car journey significantly more expensive than buying an airline ticket. Also, the mountain of paperwork required to drive into Costa Rica from other countries deters many travelers, who prefer to arrive here and then buy or rent a vehicle. Regardless, any number of hardy adventurers undertake the intercontinental trip on the Interamericana every year.

To enter Costa Rica by car, you'll need the following:

- valid registration and proof of ownership;
- valid driver's license or International Driving Permit (see p470);
- valid license plates;
- recent inspection certificate (not required, but a good idea);
- your passport; and
- multiple photocopies of all these documents in case the originals get lost.

BORDER CROSSINGS

There is no fee for travelers to enter Costa Rica. However, the fee for each vehicle entering the country is US$22. For more information on visa requirements for entering Costa Rica, see p461.

Nicaragua – Sapoá to Peñas Blancas

This is the most heavily trafficked border station between Nicaragua and Costa Rica. Situated on the Interamericana, virtually all international overland travelers from Nicaragua enter Costa Rica through here. The border station is open from 6am to 8pm daily on both the Costa Rican and Nicaraguan sides – though local bus traffic stops in the afternoon.

The **Tica Bus** (☎ in Managua 222 6094), **Nica Bus** (☎ in Managua 228 1374) and **TransNica** (☎ in Managua 278 2090) all have daily buses to Costa Rica. The fare is US$10 to US$12 and the trip takes nine hours. From Rivas (37km north of the border) twice-hourly buses depart for Sapoá from 5am to 4:30pm. Regular buses depart Peñas Blancas, on the Costa Rican side, for the nearby towns of La Cruz, Liberia and San José.

The Costa Rican and Nicaraguan immigration offices are almost 1km apart; most people travel through by bus or private car. Travelers without a through bus will find golf carts (US$2) running between the borders, but walking is not a problem. While Costa Rica does not charge visitors to cross the border, Nicaragua does: people leaving Nicaragua pay US$2, while folks entering Nicaragua will be charged US$7 until noon, after which the fee becomes US$9. This is the only official border between Nicaragua and Costa Rica that you can drive across. All fees must be paid in US dollars.

Note that Peñas Blancas is only a border post, not a town, so there is nowhere to stay. For detailed information on crossing the border, see the boxed text, p198.

Nicaragua – San Carlos to Los Chiles

International travelers rarely use this route, though it's reportedly hassle-free. There is no land crossing and you cannot drive between the two points.

Instead, the crossing must be done by boat. The international agreement between the two countries requires boats to be exchanged equally. Be aware that travelers might need to queue several hours for space on a boat. In reality, this rarely happens; this border is simply not that frequently used. Regular **ferries** (US$7; 1½hr) depart San Carlos in Nicaragua and head south along the Río Frío for Los Chiles three times a day. At other times, boatmen can usually be found by the ENAP dock in San Carlos. There is a road that travels from the southern banks of the Río San Juan in Nicaragua to Los Chiles, but it is reserved for federal employees. You will not be able to enter Costa Rica this way (and you certainly will not be able to drive in). Use the river route.

If you are entering Costa Rica, don't forget to get the US$2 exit stamp at the San Carlos migración office, 50m west of the dock. If traveling to Nicaragua, you will need to pay a fee upwards of US$5. For more information, see Los Chiles, p438.

One traveler who has made this journey by vehicle recommends arriving at border stations late in the morning or by noon. Border posts tend to be clogged with commercial trucks in the early hours and you'll end up waiting anyhow.

Sometimes border guards can be zealous when examining a vehicle, so make sure that it doesn't violate any potential existing (or imaginary) safety regulations or you'll likely have to pay a hefty 'fee' (read: bribe) to get it processed. Before departing, check that:

- the head and tail lights, and blinkers are all working properly;
- the spare tire is in good condition;
- there is a jerry can for extra gas (petrol);
- there is a well-stocked toolbox that includes parts, such as belts, that are harder to find in Central America; and
- the car is equipped with emergency flares, roadside triangles and a fire extinguisher.

Another option is to ship a car from Miami to Costa Rica. Costs are US$750 to US$850

Panama – Paso Canoas

This border crossing on the Carretera Interamericana (Pan-American Hwy) is by far the most frequently used entry and exit point with Panama and is open 24 hours a day. The border crossing in either direction is generally straightforward if your documents are in order. Be sure to get your exit stamp from Panama at the migración office, though, before entering Costa Rica. There is no charge for entering Costa Rica. Travelers without a private vehicle should arrive during the day because buses stop running soon after nightfall. Travelers in a private vehicle would do better to arrive late in the morning when most of the trucks have already been processed.

Tica Bus (☎ in Panama City 262 2084) travels from Panama City to San José (US$23; 15 hours) daily and crosses this border post. In David, **Tracopa** has one bus daily from the main terminal to San José (US$9; nine hours). Here, you'll also find frequent buses to the border at Paso Canoas (US$1.50; 1½ hours) that take off every 10 minutes from 4am to 8pm.

If traveling to Panama, you will have to pay US$5 for a tourist card. For further details, see Paso Canoas, p338.

Panama – Guabito to Sixaola

Situated on the Caribbean coast, this is a fairly tranquil and hassle-free border crossing. Immigration guards regularly take off for lunch and you may have to wait a while to be processed. The border town on the Panamanian side is Guabito.

The border is open from 8am to 6pm in Panama and from 7am to 5pm in Costa Rica. (Panama is one hour ahead.) Both sides close for an hour-long lunch at around 1pm, which means that there are potentially two hours each day when you'll be unable to make it across the border quickly. Get to Sixaola as early in the day as possible; while there are a couple of places to spend the night, it probably won't be the highlight of your vacation. Before crossing the bridge, be sure to stop at **migración** (☎ 754 2044) to process your paperwork. Cars can cross here, but be prepared for a long wait. Walking across the bridge is kind of fun, in a vertigo-inducing sort of way.

From the Terminal La Piquera in Changuinola (16km south of the border), take a bus to Guabito (US$0.70; less than 30 minutes). Buses depart every 45 minutes between 7am and 7:45pm. Unless you take a bus by mid afternoon, though, you will not have enough time to cross the border.

For additional details on crossing this border, see Sixaola, p427.

Panama – Río Sereno to San Vito

This is a rarely used crossing in the Cordillera de Talamanca. The small village of Río Sereno on the Panamanian side has a hotel and a place to eat. There are no facilities on the Costa Rican side. Regular buses depart Concepción and David in Panama for Río Sereno (also on the Panamanian side) on a daily basis. After crossing the border, you can catch a local bus to San Vito.

Get additional details under San Vito, p336.

and vary depending on the size of the car and destination. (It's cheapest to ship to Puerto Limón.) For specifics, contact **Latii Express International** (☎ in the USA 800-590 3789, 305-593 8929; www.latiiexpress.com).

Insurance from foreign countries is not recognized in Costa Rica, so you'll have to buy a policy locally. This can be done at the border and costs about US$15 a month. In addition, you'll probably have to pay a US$10 road tax to drive in. You are not allowed to sell the car in Costa Rica. If you need to leave the country without the car, you must leave it in a customs warehouse in San José.

SEA

Cruise-line boats stop in Costa Rican ports and enable passengers to make a quick (and insignificant) foray into the country. Typically, ships dock at either the Pacific port of Caldera (near Puntarenas, p273) or the Caribbean port of Moín (near Puerto Limón, p383). It is also possible to arrive by private yacht.

GETTING AROUND

AIR

Scheduled Flights

Costa Rica's domestic airlines are **NatureAir** (☎ 220 3054; www.natureair.com) and **Sansa** (☎ 221 9414; www.flysansa.com); the latter is linked with Grupo TACA.

Both airlines fly small passenger planes, and you're allocated a baggage allowance of no more than 12kg. If the flight is full, your surfboard or golf clubs might not make it on, and, even if they do, you'll likely be paying extra for excess weight. NatureAir flies from Tobías Bolaños airport, 5 miles west of the center of San José in the suburb of Pavas, and Sansa operates out of the blue building to the right of the international terminal at Juan Santamaría airport. Both airlines fly 14- and 19-passenger aircraft and offer a bumpy ride. These services aren't for people who have phobias about flying. Space is limited and demand is high in the dry season, so reserve and pay for tickets in advance.

Schedules change constantly and delays are frequent because of inclement weather. Be patient: Costa Rica has small planes and big storms. You should not arrange a domestic flight that makes a tight connection with an international one back home.

All domestic flights originate and terminate at San José. Although the Air Routes map has flights between, say, Puerto Jiménez and Golfito, be aware that, on most occasions, flights from both centers will be direct to San José. During the high season, fares range from about US$50 for a one-way trip to Quepos to US$85 for the flight to Bahía Drake. High-season fares are listed throughout this chapter.

Destinations reached from San José include Bahía Drake, Barra del Colorado, Golfito, Liberia, Coto 47/Neily, Palmar Sur, Playa Nosara, Playa Sámara/Carrillo, Playa Tamarindo, Puerto Jiménez, Quepos, Tambor and Tortuguero.

Charters

Tobías Bolaños airport in Pavas caters to small aircraft that can be chartered to fly just

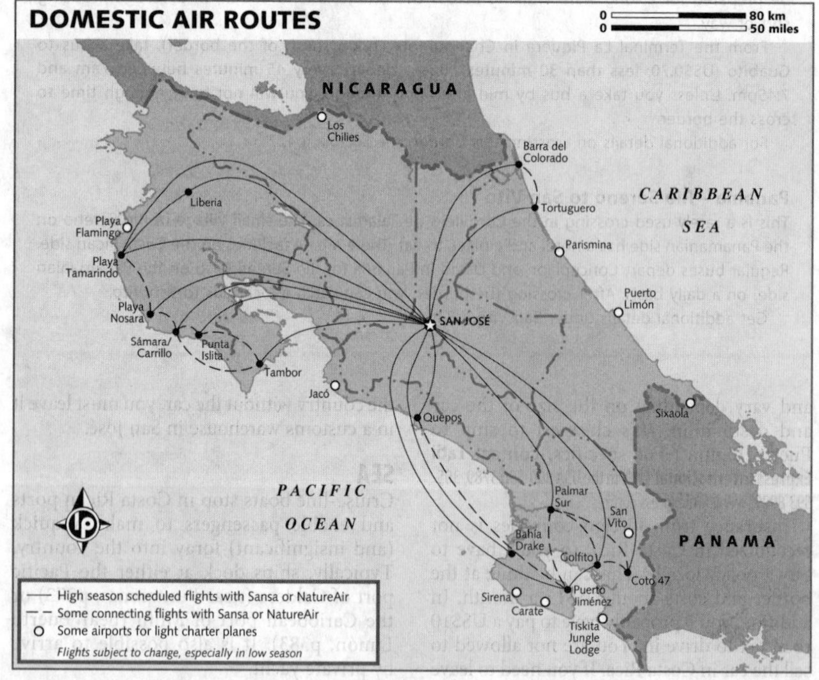

about anywhere in the country. Fares start at about US$300 per hour for three- or four-seater planes, and it takes 40 to 90 minutes to fly to most destinations. You also have to pay for the return flight. Note that luggage space is very limited.

Many tour agencies can book charters, but you can book directly as well. For a list of companies, see San José (p97), Golfito (p367) and Puerto Jiménez (see p359).

BICYCLE

Mountain bikes and beach cruisers can be rented in towns with a significant tourist presence, at the rate of US$8 to US$15 per day. A few companies organize bike tours around Costa Rica (see p53).

BOAT

Ferries cross the Golfo de Nicoya connecting the central Pacific coast with the southern tip of Península de Nicoya. The **Coonatramar ferry** (☎ 661 1069; US$1.60, car US$11) links the port of Puntarenas with Playa Naranjo. The **Ferry Peninsular** (☎ 641 0515; US$1.60, car US$11) travels between Puntarenas and Paquera, for a bus connection to Montezuma.

In the Golfo Dulce, on the southern Pacific coast, a daily passenger ferry links Golfito with Puerto Jiménez on the Península de Osa and a weekday water taxi travels to and from Playa Zancudo. Another small ferry operates on the Río Coto Colorado on the Golfito–Playa Zancudo road. On the other side of the Península de Osa, water taxis connect Bahía Drake with Sierpe.

On the Caribbean, there is also a daily bus and boat service from Cariari to Tortuguero and vice versa. Boats are available for travel between Moín, near Puerto Limón, and Tortuguero. A daily water taxi connects Puerto Viejo de Sarapiquí with Trinidad on the Río San Juan. (The San Juan is Nicaraguan territory, so take your passport.) You can arrange boat transport in any of these towns for Barra del Colorado.

Trips are not without incident. In December of 2003, two European tourists drowned when a boat between Moín and Tortuguero was caught in rough waters and overturned. No one on board was wearing a life jacket. Some boats don't carry life jackets at all, and the ones that do tend to keep them stored up front, doing everyone little good during an emergency. Check that boats are properly equipped – and make sure that you're at least holding on to a life jacket during your ride. Avoid taking boats in bad weather.

BUS

For some Latin American Spanish words and phrases useful for catching buses, see p489.

Local Buses

Local buses are the best (if rather slow) way of getting around Costa Rica. You can take one just about everywhere, and they're frequent and cheap, with the longest domestic journey out of San José costing less than US$9.

San José is the transportation center for the country (see p97), but there is no central terminal. Bus offices are scattered around the city: some large bus companies have big terminals that sell tickets in advance, while others have little more than a stop – sometimes unmarked. (One local bus 'station' in San José consists of a guy with a clipboard sitting on a lawn chair.)

Normally there's room for everyone on a bus, and if there isn't, someone will squeeze you on anyhow. The exceptions are days before and after a major holiday, especially Easter, when buses are ridiculously full. Friday night and Saturday morning out of San José any time of the year can be crowded, as can Sunday afternoon and evening coming back. (Note that there are no buses on the Thursday to Saturday before Easter Sunday.) There are two types of bus: directo and *normal*/colectivo. The directo buses presumably go from one destination to the next with few stops. If only this were so! It is against the instinctual nature of Costa Rican bus drivers not to pick up every single roadside passenger. (Directo buses charge more for this largely non-existent nonstop service.) As for the colectivo, you know you're on one when the kids outside are outrunning your bus.

Trips longer than four hours usually include a rest stop (buses do not have bathrooms). Space is limited on board, so if you have to check luggage, watch that it gets loaded and that it isn't 'accidentally' given to someone else at intermediate stops. Keep your day pack with important documents on you at all times. Thefts from overhead racks are rampant.

Bus schedules should be treated as mere guidelines and certainly not exact. Some routes haven't changed their schedules in years, while others change them regularly. Most times, the brilliantly painted schedules on the station walls haven't been updated…ever. Always ask at the ticket office about departure times, and if there isn't one ask the ladies that take care of the restrooms. They always know the bus schedule – even if they're reluctant to say so. (A tip: buy toilet paper, *then* ask for times.)

If you are catching a bus that picks up somewhere along a road, get to the roadside early. Departure times are estimated and if the bus comes early, it will leave early. Patience is not a virtue of bus drivers, so have your fare ready.

For information on departures from San José, pay a visit to the ICT office (p72) to pick up the sort of up-to-date copy of the master schedule. You can also check hotels and travel offices for *Hop on the Bus*, published by the **Exintur Travel Agency** (☎ 232 8774; www.exintur.com/costarica/hopon.html). It includes bus-terminal locations and departure information for major destinations.

Shuttle Bus

An alternative to the standard intercity buses is the tourist-van shuttle services provided by **Grayline's Fantasy Bus** (☎ 220 2126; www.graylinecostarica.com) and **Interbus** (☎ 283 5573; www.interbusonline.com). Both companies run overland transport from San José to the most popular destinations as well as directly between other destinations (see their websites for the comprehensive list). Fares start at $17 for trips between San José and Puntarenas and climb to $38 for the bumpy ride to Monteverde. These services will pick you up at your hotel and reservations can be made either online or through local travel agencies and hotel owners. The vans are quick and convenient – but will you truly experience what Central America is all about from a hermetically sealed, air-conditioned minivan where you're not besieged by vendors plying ceviche and fried bananas? Probably not.

CAR & MOTORCYCLE

If you plan to drive in Costa Rica, your driver's license from home is normally accepted for up to 90 days. Many places will also accept an International Driving Permit (IDP), issued by the automobile association in your country of origin. After 90 days, you will need to get a Costa Rican driver's license. Most travelers fly into Costa Rica and then rent a car or motorcycle (the latter is less common). If you plan to drive to Costa Rica in your own vehicle, turn to p465).

Gasoline (petrol) and diesel are widely available and 24-hour service stations dot the entire stretch of the Interamericana. The price of gas is generally US$0.65 per liter. In more remote areas, fuel will likely be more expensive and might be sold from a drum at the neighborhood *pulpería* (corner grocery store). (Look for signs that say *Se vende gasolina.*) Spare parts may be hard to find, especially for vehicles with sophisticated electronics and emissions-control systems. Old Toyota 4WD pick-ups are ubiquitous, so finding parts and mechanics to fix them is generally easier.

See p490 for some useful Latin American Spanish words and phrases.

Hire

Most car-rental agencies can be found in San José and in popular tourist destinations on the Pacific coast (Tamarindo, Jacó and Quepos). Car rental is not cheap, and if you are going to be doing even a small amount of driving, invest in a 4WD. Many agencies will insist on 4WD for extended travel, especially in the rainy season, when driving through rivers is a matter of course. Ordinary cars are pointless on most roads, and even if a dirt road is passable, the trip is liable to take twice as long. Most rental vehicles are manual shift.

To rent a car you need a valid driver's license, a major credit card and a passport. The minimum age for car rental is 21. When reserving a car, ask for written confirmation. Carefully inspect rented cars for minor damage and make sure it is noted on the rental agreement. If your car breaks down, call the rental company. Don't attempt to get the car fixed yourself; most companies won't reimburse expenses without prior authorization.

Prices start at US$450 per week for a 4WD and US$270 for an economy car, including unlimited mileage *(kilometraje libre)*. Insurance will cost an additional US$12 to US$20 per day and rental companies won't rent you a car without it. (Foreign policies are not accepted anywhere in Costa Rica.) Even with insurance, there is a high deductible or excess (about US$1500), but you can pay an extra fee (about US$10 per day) to waive this. Note that insurance doesn't cover water damage, so drive with extreme caution (see Driving Through Rivers, below). Some agencies offer discounts if you reserve online. Note that rental offices at the airport charge a 12% fee in addition to regular rates.

Thieves can easily recognize rental cars, and many thefts have occurred from them. *Never* leave anything in sight in a parked car and remove all luggage from the trunk overnight. Many hotels will provide parking areas for cars. Park the car in a guarded parking lot rather than on the street.

Motorcycles (including Harleys) can be rented in San José (p100) and Escazú (p106), and you'll find scooters, dirt bikes and 4-wheel ATVs in towns such as Monteverde, Tamarindo and Montezuma.

Below is a list of the more popular rental agencies:

Adobe (☎ 259 4242; www.adobecar.com)
Alamo (☎ 233 7733; www.alamocostarica.com)
Avis (☎ 239 2806; www.avis.co.cr)
Dollar (☎ 443 2950; wwwdollarcostarica.com
Toyota (☎ 258 5797; www.toyotarent.com)

Road Conditions & Hazards

Overall, driving in Costa Rica is for people with nerves of steel (see p11). The roads vary from quite good (the Interamericana) to barely passable (just about everywhere else), and even the good ones can suffer from landslides, sudden flooding and fog. Most roads are single lane, lack hard shoulders and are winding; others are dirt-and-mud affairs that climb mountains and traverse rivers.

When driving, always expect cyclists, a broken-down vehicle, a herd of cattle, slow-moving trucks or an ox cart around the next bend. Unsigned speed bumps are placed on some stretches of road without warning. (The locals lovingly refer to them as *muertos*, 'dead people.') After hurricanes, earthquakes and heavy rains, expect delays.

Drive defensively.

Most roads (except around the major tourist towns) are inadequately signed and will require at least one stop to ask for directions. Always ask about road conditions before setting out, especially in the rainy season; a number of roads become impassable in the rainy season.

DRIVING THROUGH RIVERS

You know all those great ads where monster trucks or 4WD/SUVs splash through rivers full speed ahead? Forget you ever saw them.

Driving in Costa Rica will likely necessitate a river crossing at some point. Unfortunately, too many travelers have picked up their off-road skills from watching TV, and every season Ticos get a good chuckle out of the number of dead vehicles they help wayward travelers fish out of waterways.

If you're driving through water, follow these rules.

Rule 1: Only do this in a 4WD. Don't drive through a river in a car. (It may seem ridiculous to have say this, but it's done all the time.) Getting out of a steep, gravel riverbed requires 4WD. Besides, car engines flood very easily – adios rental car.

Rule 2: Check the depth of the water *before* driving through. To cross an average rental SUV (usually a Kia Sportage or similar), the water should be no deeper than above the knee. In a sturdier vehicle (Toyota 4-Runner or equivalent), water can be waist deep. If you're not sure, ask a local.

Rule 3: The water should be calm. If the river is gushing so that there are white crests on the water, do not try to cross. Not only will the force of the water flood the engine, it could sweep your car away.

Rule 4: Drive slooooowly. Taxi drivers all over Costa Rica make lots of money towing out tourists who think that slamming through a river at full speed is the best way to get across. This is a huge mistake. The pressure of driving through a river too quickly will send the water right into the engine and you'll be cooking that electrical system in no time. Keep steady pressure on the accelerator so that the tail pipe doesn't fill with water, but take it slow.

Rule 5: Err on the side of caution. Car-rental agencies in Costa Rica do not insure for water damage, so if you drown your vehicle, you're paying – in more ways than one.

TRANSPORTATION

Road Rules

There are speed limits of 100km/h or less on all primary roads and 60km/h or less on secondary roads. Traffic police use radar, and speed limits are enforced with speeding tickets. You can get a traffic ticket for not wearing a seat belt. It's illegal to enter an intersection unless you can also leave it without stopping or make a right turn on a red. At unmarked intersections, yield to the car on your right. Driving in Costa Rica is on the right, and passing is allowed only on the left.

If you are given a ticket, you have to pay the fine at a bank; instructions are given on the ticket. If you are driving a rental car, the rental company may be able to arrange your payment for you – the amount of the fine should be on the ticket. A 30% tax is added to the fine and the proceeds go to a children's charity.

Fines can be expensive: up to US$150 for driving 40km/h over the speed limit, US$70 for running a red light, and US$15 for not wearing a seat belt. Police have no right to ask for money and shouldn't confiscate a car unless the driver cannot produce a license and ownership papers, or the car lacks license plates, or the driver is drunk or has been involved in an accident causing serious injury. (For more on what to do in an accident, turn to Legal Matters, p458).

If you are driving and see oncoming cars with headlights flashing, it often means that there is a road problem or a radar speed trap ahead. Slow down immediately. Police cars are blue with white doors and have a small red light on the roof – they can be sedans or pick-ups. White or red police motorcycles are also in use.

HITCHING

Hitchhiking is never entirely safe in any country, and Lonely Planet doesn't recommend it. Travelers who hitchhike should understand that they are taking a small but potentially serious risk. People who do hitchhike will be safer if they travel in pairs and let someone know where they are planning to go. Single women should use even greater discretion. Talk to the occupants of the car to get an idea of their disposition. Hitch from somewhere (a gas station, store, restaurant, police post) that you can retreat to if you don't like the look of your prospective driver. Hitching for rides from drivers of pick-ups is possibly the best bet, since you don't have to get into a car with anyone.

Hitchhiking in Costa Rica is not common on main roads that have frequent buses. On minor rural roads, hitching is easier. To get picked up, most locals wave to cars in a friendly manner rather than stand around with their thumb out. If you get a ride, offer to pay when you arrive: *¿Cuanto le debo?* (How much do I owe you?) Your offer may be waved aside, or you may be asked to help with money for gas.

TAXI

Taxis are considered a form of public transport in remote areas that lack good public-transportation networks. They can be hired by the hour, the half day or full day, or you can arrange a flat fee for a trip.

Meters are not used on long trips, so arrange the fare ahead of time. Fares can fluctuate due to worse-than-expected road conditions and bad weather in tough-to-reach places. The condition of cabs varies wildly, from basic sedans held together by rust to fully equipped 4WDs with air-con. In some cases, taxis are pick-up trucks with seats built into the back. Most towns will have at least one licensed taxi, but in some remote villages you may have to get rides from whoever is offering. (Ask at *pulperías*.)

Hiring a car with a driver can cost the same or less than renting a car for the day, and it allows someone else (who knows the roads) to do the driving while you enjoy the scenery.

LOCAL TRANSPORTATION

Bus

Local buses operate chiefly in San José, Puntarenas, Golfito and Puerto Limón, connecting urban and suburban areas. Most local buses pick up passengers on the street and on main roads. (If you are confused about where the stop is, the locals will usually help out.) The vehicles in service are usually converted school buses imported from the USA, and they tend to be packed, sweaty affairs. Local fares are usually US$0.25.

Taxi

In San José, taxis have meters, called *marías*, but many drivers try to get out of using them, particularly if you don't speak Spanish. (It is illegal not to use the meter.) Outside San José, most taxis don't have meters and fares tend to be agreed upon in advance; some bargaining is acceptable (see p460). In some towns, there are colectivo taxis that several passengers share. Manual Antonio and Golfito have a collective system in which drivers charge passengers a flat fee of about US$0.50 to take them from one end of town to the other. This service is getting harder to find in Manuel Antonio, where foreign travelers seem reticent to share transportation. (Come on folks, loosen up!)

In rural areas, 4WD jeeps are often used as taxis. A 10-minute ride in one will usually cost about US$2. Taxi drivers are not normally tipped unless they assist with your luggage or have provided an above-average service.

TOURS

More than 200 tour operators are recognized by the Costa Rican tourist board (ICT), with the majority based in San José. Many companies specialize in nature and adventure tours with knowledgeable English-speaking guides. Most operators will take reservations from abroad.

In addition to these, scores of tour operators in North America and a few in Europe run tours to Costa Rica. Some can be convenient for adventure travel requiring specialized itineraries and lots of gear (kayaking, camping etc) or for visitors that don't want to deal with planning. Many outfits will arrange custom itineraries for private groups.

There are also tour companies that cater for gays and lesbians (see p456) as well as disabled people (see p454).

General Sightseeing & Activities

Most of the companies listed below also offer natural-history tours or multi-activity tours suitable for beginners.

COSTA RICAN–BASED COMPANIES

Ecole Travel (☎ 223 2240; www.ecoletravel.com) See p78 for more details.

Green Tortoise Adventure Travel (☎ 838-7677, in the USA 800-807 8647; www.greentortoise.com) Budget camping tours.

Green Tropical Tours (☎ 229 4192, 380 1536, www.greentropical.com)

Swiss Travel Service (☎ 282 4898; www.swisstravelcr.com) See San José, p78.

AUSTRALIAN-BASED COMPANIES

Intrepid (☎ in Australia 1300-360 887; www.intrepid.com; 11 Spring St, Fitzroy, Vic 3065)

CANADIAN-BASED COMPANIES

GAP Adventures (☎ in Canada 1-800-465 5600; www.gap.ca)

Trek Holidays (☎ in Canada 800-661 7265, www.trekholidays.com)

UK-BASED COMPANIES

Condor Journeys & Adventures (☎ in the UK 01700-841 318; www.condorjourneys-adventures.com)

Exodus (☎ in the UK 08772-3822; www.exodus.co.uk; 9 Weir Rd, London, UK SW12 OLT)

Explore Worldwide (☎ in the UK 01252-760144; www.explorewordwide.com; 1 Frederick St, Aldershot, Hants, UK GU11 1LQ)

Journey Latin America (JLA; ☎ in the UK 020-8747 8315; www.journeylatinamerica.co.uk)

Last Frontiers (☎ in the UK 01296-653 000; www.lastfrontiers.co.uk)

US-BASED COMPANIES

Abercrombie & Kent (☎ in the USA 630-954 2944, 800-554 7016; www.abercrombiekent.com)

Adventure Center (☎ in the USA 510-654 1879, 800-228 8747; www.adventurecenter.com)

Ecotour Expeditions (☎ in the USA 401-423 3377, 800-688 1822; www.naturetours.com)

Elderhostel (☎ in the USA 978-323 4141, 877-426 8056; www.elderhostel.org) Tours for travelers aged over 55 (younger companions permitted).

International Expeditions (☎ in the USA 205-428 1700, 800-633 4734; www.internationalexpeditions.com)

Wilderness Travel (☎ in the USA 510-558 2488, 800-368 2794, www.wildernesstravel.com)

Wildland Adventures (☎ in the USA 206-365 0686, 800-345 4453; www.wildland.com)

Customized Itineraries

In addition to the US-based companies below, many Costa Rican–based companies listed earlier can also create custom itineraries.

Costa Rica Connection (☎ in the USA 805-543 8823, 800-345 7422; www.crconnect.com)

Costa Rica Experts (☎ in the USA 773-935 1009, 800-827 9046; www.costaricaexperts.com)

Holbrook Travel (☎ in the USA 352-377 7111, 800-451-7111; www.holbrooktravel.com) See also Selva Verde Lodge, p442.

Preferred Adventures (☎ in the USA 651-222 8131, 800-840 8687; www.preferredadventures.com)

Natural History

The Costa Rican-based companies below have all been in operation a long time and come highly recommended by our readers. These companies can book everything, from gentle hikes to adrenaline-inducing rafting trips to trips to remote wilderness. See also Birding, following.

Costa Rica Expeditions (☎ 257 0766, 222 0333; www.costaricaexpeditions.com)

Costa Rica Rainforest Outward Bound (☎ 278 6058, in the USA 800-676 2018; www.crrobs.org) Multiday adventure courses for academic credit or pure exhilaration.

Costa Rica Sun Tours (☎ 296 7757; www.crsuntours.com)

Expediciones Tropicales (☎ 257 4171; www.costaricainfo.com)

Horizontes (☎ 222 2022; www.horizontes.com)

Birding

COSTA RICAN–BASED COMPANIES

Birding Costa Rica (☎ 229 5922; www.birdscostarica.com) Highly recommended agency that creates special birding itineraries or custom adventure and hiking tours.

Costa Rica Sun Tours See Natural History, above.

UK- & US-BASED COMPANIES

Condor Journeys & Adventures See General Sightseeing, p473.

Elderhostel See General Sightseeing, p473.

Boat Tours

Boat tours can be arranged in just about any seaside town. Standouts include tours of the Golfo de Nicoya (see Puntarenas, p275, and Islands near Bahía Gigante, p259), and the Golfo Dulce (see p368). Boat tours up and down the Canal de Tortuguero are also popular (p389). See also some of the dangers discussed on p469.

More adventurous types should look at Rafting & Kayaking later.

Diving

The following companies are all based in the USA; Undersea can be contacted in Costa Rica.

JD's Watersports (☎ in the USA 970-356 1028, 800-477 8971, www.jdwatersports.com) See also p280.

Okeanos Aggressor (☎ in the USA 985-385 2628, in the USA & Canada 800-348 2628; www.aggressor.com) See the boxed text, p354.

Undersea Hunter (☎ 228 6613, in the USA 800-203 2120; www.underseahunter.com) See the boxed text, p354.

Fishing

These companies, which are all based in the USA, offer sportsfishing tours.

JD's Watersports See Diving, earlier.

Rod & Reel Adventures (☎ in the USA 800-356 6982; www.rodreeladventures.com)

Hiking & Mountain Biking

COSTA RICAN–BASED COMPANIES

Aventuras Naturales (☎ 225 3939, 224 0505, in the USA 800-514 0411; www.toenjoynature.com)

Coast to Coast Adventures (☎ 280 8054; www.ctocadventures.com) Everything from short excursions to 14-day coast-to-coast multisport trips.

Ocarina Expeditions (☎ 229 4278; www.ocarinaexpeditions.com) Also arranges horseback tours.

FRENCH-BASED COMPANIES

Club Aventure (☎ in France 08 25 30 60 32; www.clubaventure.fr) organizes treks.

US-BASED COMPANIES

Backroads (☎ in the USA 510-527 1555, 800-462 2848; www.backroads.com) Also organizes rafting trips.

Serendipity Adventures (☎ in the USA 734-995 0111, 800-635 2325, in Costa Rica 558 1000; www.serendipityadventures.com) Also organizes hot-air ballooning, rafting, climbing and kayaking.

Motorcycling

COSTA RICAN–BASED COMPANIES

Wild Rider (☎ 258 4604; www.wild-rider.com) See San José, p100.

Harley Davidson Rentals (☎ 289 5552; www.mariaalexandra.com) See Escazú, p106.

US-BASED COMPANIES

MotoDiscovery (☎ in the USA 800-233 6564, 830-438 7744; www.motodiscovery.com) organizes tours through Central America – including an annual trip that takes riders from the Río Grande in Mexico to the Panama Canal on their own motorcycles; the company then ships bikes from Costa Rica to Houston and riders fly back.

Rafting & Kayaking

River running or floats down the Ríos Pacuare, Reventazón, Corobicí, Chirripó, and Sarapiquí for one or more days is an option. Refer to p53 for specific details.

CANADIAN-BASED COMPANIES

Gulf Islands Kayaking (☎ in Canada 250-539 2442; www.seakayak.ca) specialize in sea kayaking; see also p346.

COSTA RICAN–BASED COMPANIES

Many companies specialize in kayaking and rafting trips (but will arrange other tours).

Amigo Tico Complete Adventure Tours (☎ 777 2812; www.amigotico.com)

Aventuras Naturales See Hiking & Mountain Biking, earlier.

Coast to Coast Adventures See Hiking & Mountain Biking, earlier.

Costa Rica Expeditions See Natural History, earlier.

Exploradores Outdoors (☎ 280 9544; www.exploradoresoutdoors.com)

H2O Adventures (☎ 777 4092; www.aventurash2o.com)

Ríos Tropicales (☎ 233 6455; www.riostropicales.com)

Safaris Corobicí (☎ 669 6191; www.nicoya.com)

Sarapiquí Aguas Bravas (☎ 292 2072; www.aguas-bravas.co.cr)

US-BASED COMPANIES

The companies listed here offer specialized activities in addition to a number of general natural-history tours.

BattenKill Canoe Ltd (☎ in the USA 802-362 2800, 800-421 5268; www.battenkill.com) Canoeing experts.

Mountain Travel Sobek (☎ in the USA 510-594 6000, 888-687 6235; www.mtsobek.com) Specializes in sea kayaking, river rafting etc.

Surfing

Both of these companies are based in the USA.

Pura Vida Adventures (☎ in the USA 415-465 2162; www.puravidaadventures.com) For women only.

Tico Travel (☎ in the USA 800-493 8426; www.ticotravel.com)

Health

Dr David Goldberg

CONTENTS

Travelers to Central America need to be vigilant about food-borne as well as mosquito-borne infections. Most of these illnesses are not life-threatening, but they can certainly ruin your trip. Besides getting the proper vaccinations, it's important that you bring along a good insect repellent and exercise great care in what you eat and drink.

BEFORE YOU GO

Since most vaccines don't produce immunity until at least two weeks after they're given, visit a physician four to eight weeks before departure. Ask your doctor for an International Certificate of Vaccination (otherwise known as the yellow booklet), which will list all the vaccinations you've received. This is mandatory for countries that require proof of yellow fever vaccination upon entry, but it's a good idea to carry it wherever you travel.

Bring medications in their original containers, clearly labeled. A signed, dated letter from your physician describing all medical conditions and medications, including generic names, is also a good idea. If carrying syringes or needles be sure to have a physician's letter documenting their medical necessity.

INSURANCE

Most doctors and hospitals expect payment in cash, regardless of whether you have travel health insurance. If you develop a life-threatening medical problem, you'll probably want to be evacuated to a country with state-of-the-art medical care. As this may cost tens of thousands of dollars, be sure you have insurance to cover this before you depart. A list of medical evacuation and travel insurance companies is on the website of the **US State Department** (www.travel.state.gov/medical.html).

If your health insurance does not cover you for medical expenses abroad, consider supplemental insurance. (Check the Subway section of the Lonely Planet website at www.lonelyplanet.com/subwwway for more information.) Find out in advance if your insurance plan will make payments directly to providers or reimburse you later for overseas health expenditures.

MEDICAL CHECKLIST

- Acetaminophen (Tylenol) or aspirin
- Adhesive or paper tape
- Anti-inflammatory drugs (eg ibuprofen)
- Antibacterial ointment (eg Bactroban) for cuts and abrasions
- Antibiotics
- Antidiarrheal drugs (eg loperamide)
- Antihistamines (for hay fever and allergic reactions)
- Bandages, gauze, gauze rolls
- DEET-containing insect repellent for the skin
- Iodine tablets (for water purification)
- Oral rehydration salts
- Permethrin-containing insect spray for clothing, tents, and bed nets
- Pocket knife
- Scissors, safety pins, tweezers
- Steroid cream or cortisone (for poison ivy and other allergic rashes)
- Sun block
- Syringes and sterile needles
- Thermometer

INTERNET RESOURCES

There is a wealth of travel health advice on the Internet. For further information, the website of **Lonely Planet** (www.lonelyplanet.com) is

RECOMMENDED VACCINATIONS

There are no required vaccinations for entering Costa Rica. However, a number of vaccines are recommended:

Vaccine	Recommended for	Dosage	Side effects
hepatitis A	all travelers	1 dose before trip; booster 6-12 months later	soreness at injection site; headaches; body aches
typhoid	all travelers	4 capsules by mouth, 1 taken every other day	abdominal pain; nausea; rash
hepatitis B	long-term travelers in close contact with the local population	3 doses over 6-month period	soreness at injection site; low-grade fever
tetanus-diphtheria	all travelers who haven't had booster within 10 yrs	1 dose lasts 10 years	soreness at injection site
measles	travelers born after 1956 who've had only 1 measles vaccination	1 dose	fever; rash; joint pains; allergic reactions
chickenpox	travelers who've never had chickenpox	2 doses 1 month apart	fever; mild case of chickenpox

a good place to start. A superb book called *International Travel and Health*, which is revised annually and is available online at no cost, is by the **World Health Organization** (www.who.int/ith/). Another website of general interest is **MD Travel Health** (www.mdtravelhealth.com), which provides complete travel health recommendations for every country, updated daily, also at no cost.

It's usually a good idea to consult your government's travel health website before departure, if one is available:

Australia (www.dfat.gov.au/travel/)
Canada (www.hc-sc.gc.ca/pphb-dgspsp/tmp-pmv/pub_e.html)
UK (www.doh.gov.uk/traveladvice/index.htm)
USA (www.cdc.gov/travel/)

FURTHER READING

For further information, see *Healthy Travel Central & South America*, also from Lonely Planet. If you're traveling with children, Lonely Planet's *Travel with Children* may be useful. The *ABC of Healthy Travel*, by E Walker et al, is another valuable resource.

IN TRANSIT

DEEP VEIN THROMBOSIS (DVT)

Blood clots (deep vein thrombosis) may form in the legs during plane flights, chiefly because of prolonged immobility. The longer the flight, the greater the risk. Though most blood clots are reabsorbed uneventfully, some may break off and travel through the blood vessels to the lungs, where they could cause life-threatening complications.

The chief symptom of DVT is swelling or pain of the foot, ankle or calf, usually but not always on just one side. When a blood clot travels to the lungs, it may cause chest pain and difficulty breathing. Travelers with any of these symptoms should immediately seek medical attention.

To prevent the development of DVT on long flights you should walk about the cabin, perform isometric compressions of the leg muscles (ie contract the leg muscles while sitting), drink plenty of fluids, and avoid alcohol and tobacco.

JET LAG & MOTION SICKNESS

Jet lag is common when crossing more than five time zones, resulting in insomnia, fatigue, malaise or nausea. To avoid jet lag try drinking plenty of fluids (nonalcoholic) and eating light meals. Upon arrival, get exposure to natural sunlight and readjust your schedule (for meals, sleep etc) as soon as possible.

Antihistamines such as dimenhydrinate (Dramamine) and meclizine (Antivert, Bonine) are usually the first choice for treating motion sickness. Their main side effect is drowsiness. An herbal alternative is ginger, which works like a charm for some people.

FOLK REMEDIES

The following are some traditional remedies for common travel-related conditions.

Problem	Treatment
jet lag	melatonin
motion sickness	ginger
mosquito bite prevention	oil of eucalyptus; soybean oil

IN COSTA RICA

AVAILABILITY & COST OF HEALTH CARE

Good medical care is available in most major cities, but may be limited in rural areas. For a medical emergency, you should call one of the following numbers:

CIMA San José (☎ 208 1000; Próspero Fernández Freeway, San José) 500m west of tollbooths on highway to Santa Ana.
Clínica Bíblica (☎ 257 0466, 257 5252; cnr Calle 1 & Av 14, San José)
Hospital Nacional de Niños (☎ 222 0122; Calle 14, Av Central, San José) Only for children under 12.
Poison Center (☎ 223 1028)
Red Cross Ambulance (☎ 911, in San José 221 5818)
San Juan de Dios Hospital (☎ 257 6282; cnr Calle 14 & Av Central, San José)

For an extensive list of physicians, dentists and hospitals go to the US Embassy website (usembassy.or.cr). If you're pregnant, be sure to check this site before departure to find the name of one or two obstetricians, just in case. For some useful words and phrases in Spanish, see p487.

Most pharmacies are well supplied and the pharmacists are licensed to prescribe medication. If you're taking any medication on a regular basis, be sure you know its generic (scientific) name, since many pharmaceuticals go under different names in Costa Rica. Pharmacies that are open 24 hours include the following:

Farmacia Clínica Bíblica (☎ 257 5252; cnr Calle 1 & Av 14, San José)
Farmacia Clínica Católica (☎ 283 6616; Guadalupe, San José)
Farmacia el Hospital (☎ 222 0985)

INFECTIOUS DISEASES

Chagas' Disease

Chagas' disease is a parasitic infection that is transmitted by triatomine insects (reduviid bugs), which inhabit crevices in the walls and roofs of substandard housing in South and Central America. In Costa Rica most cases occur in Alajuela, Liberia and Puntarenas. The triatomine insect lays its feces on human skin as it bites, usually at night. A person becomes infected when he or she unknowingly rubs the feces into the bite wound or any other open sore. Chagas' disease is extremely rare in travelers. However, if you sleep in a poorly constructed house, especially one made of mud, adobe or thatch, you should be sure to protect yourself with a bed net and a good insecticide.

Dengue Fever (Breakbone Fever)

Dengue fever is a viral infection found throughout Central America. In Costa Rica outbreaks involving thousands of people occur every year. Dengue is transmitted by Aedes mosquitoes, which bite preferentially during the daytime and are usually found close to human habitations, often indoors. They breed primarily in artificial water containers such as jars, barrels, cans, cisterns, metal drums, plastic containers and discarded tires. As a result, dengue is especially common in densely populated, urban environments.

Dengue usually causes flu-like symptoms including fever, muscle aches, joint pains, headaches, nausea and vomiting, often followed by a rash. The body aches may be quite uncomfortable, but most cases resolve uneventfully in a few days. Severe cases usually occur in children under age 15 who are experiencing their second dengue infection.

There is no treatment for dengue fever except to take analgesics such as acetaminophen/paracetamol (Tylenol) and drink plenty of fluids. Severe cases may require hospitalization for intravenous fluids and supportive care. There is no vaccine. The cornerstone of prevention is insect protection measures (see p481).

Hepatitis A

Hepatitis A is the second most common travel-related infection (after traveler's diarrhea). It's a viral infection of the liver that is usually acquired by ingestion of contaminated water, food or ice, though it may also be acquired by direct contact with infected persons. The illness occurs throughout the world, but the incidence is higher in developing nations. Symptoms may include fever, malaise, jaundice, nausea, vomiting and abdominal pain. Most cases resolve without complications, though hepatitis A occasionally causes severe liver damage. There is no treatment.

The vaccine for hepatitis A is extremely safe and highly effective. If you get a booster six to 12 months later, it lasts for at least 10 years. You really should get it before you go to Costa Rica or any other developing nation. Because the safety of hepatitis A vaccine has not been established for pregnant women or children under age 2, they should instead be given a gammaglobulin injection.

Hepatitis B

Like hepatitis A, hepatitis B is a liver infection that occurs worldwide but is more common in developing nations. Unlike hepatitis A, the disease is usually acquired by sexual contact or by exposure to infected blood, generally through blood transfusions or contaminated needles. The vaccine is recommended only for long-term travelers (on the road more than six months) who expect to live in rural areas or have close physical contact with the local population. Additionally, the vaccine is recommended for anyone who anticipates sexual contact with the local inhabitants or a possible need for medical, dental or other treatments while abroad, especially if a need for transfusions or injections is expected.

Hepatitis B vaccine is safe and highly effective. However, a total of three injections are necessary to establish full immunity. Several countries added hepatitis B vaccine to the list of routine childhood immunizations in the 1980s, so many young adults are already protected.

HIV/AIDS

This has been reported from all Central American countries. Be sure to use condoms for all sexual encounters.

Leishmaniasis

Leishmaniasis occurs in the mountains and jungles of all Central American countries. The infection is transmitted by sandflies, which are about one-third the size of mosquitoes. Most cases occur in newly cleared forest or areas of secondary growth. The highest incidence is in Talamanca. In Costa Rica the disease is generally limited to the skin, causing slowly-growing ulcers over exposed parts of the body, but more severe infections may occur in those with HIV. There is no vaccine for leishmaniasis. To protect yourself from sandflies, follow the same precautions as for mosquitoes (p481), except that netting must be finer mesh (at least 18 holes to the linear inch).

Leptospirosis

Leptospirosis is acquired by exposure to water contaminated by the urine of infected animals. Whitewater rafters are at particularly high risk. In Costa Rica most cases occur in Limón, Turrialba, San Carlos and Golfito. Cases have been reported among residents of Puerto Limón who have bathed in local streams. Outbreaks may occur at times of flooding, when sewage overflow may contaminate water sources. The initial symptoms, which resemble a mild flu, usually subside uneventfully in a few days, with or without treatment, but a minority of cases are complicated by jaundice or meningitis. There is no vaccine. You can minimize your risk by staying out of bodies of fresh water that may be contaminated by animal urine. If you're engaging in high-risk activities, such as river running, in an area where an outbreak is in progress, you can take 200mg of doxycycline once weekly as a preventative measure. If you actually develop leptospirosis, the treatment is 100mg of doxycycline twice daily.

Malaria

Malaria occurs in every country in Central America. It's transmitted by mosquito bites, usually between dusk and dawn. The main symptom is high spiking fevers, which may be accompanied by chills, sweats, headache, body aches, weakness, vomiting or diarrhea. Severe cases may involve the central nervous system and lead to seizures, confusion, coma and death.

Taking malaria pills is recommended for the provinces of Alajuela, Limón (except for Limón City), Guanacaste and Heredia. The risk is greatest in the cantons of Los Chiles

(Alajuela Province) and Matina and Talamanca (Limón Province).

For Costa Rica the first-choice malaria pill is chloroquine, taken once weekly in a dosage of 500mg, starting one to two weeks before arrival and continuing through the trip and for four weeks after departure. Chloroquine is safe, inexpensive and highly effective. Side-effects are typically mild and may include nausea, abdominal discomfort, headache, dizziness, blurred vision or itching. Severe reactions are uncommon.

Protecting yourself against mosquito bites is just as important as taking malaria pills (see later), since no pills are 100% effective.

If you may not have access to medical care while traveling, you should bring along additional pills for emergency self-treatment, which you should take if you can't reach a doctor and you develop symptoms that suggest malaria, such as high spiking fevers. One option is to take four tablets of Malarone once daily for three days. If you start self-medication, you should try to see a doctor at the earliest possible opportunity.

If you develop a fever after returning home, see a physician as malaria symptoms may not occur for months.

Rabies

Rabies is a viral infection of the brain and spinal cord that is almost always fatal. The rabies virus is carried in the saliva of infected animals and is typically transmitted through an animal bite, though contamination of any break in the skin with infected saliva may result in rabies.

Rabies occurs in all Central American countries. However, in Costa Rica only two cases have been reported over the last 30 years. Rabies vaccine is therefore recommended only for those at particularly high risk, such as spelunkers (cave explorers) and animal handlers.

All animal bites and scratches must be promptly and thoroughly cleansed with large amounts of soap and water, and local health authorities contacted to determine whether or not further treatment is necessary (see Animal Bites later).

Typhoid

Typhoid fever is caused by ingestion of food or water contaminated by a species of *Salmonella* known as *Salmonella typhi*. Fever occurs in virtually all cases. Other symptoms may include headache, malaise, muscle aches, dizziness, loss of appetite, nausea and abdominal pain. Either diarrhea or constipation may occur. Possible complications include intestinal perforation, intestinal bleeding, confusion, delirium or (rarely) coma.

Unless you expect to take all your meals in major hotels and restaurants, typhoid vaccine is a good idea. It's usually given orally, but is also available as an injection. Neither vaccine is approved for use in children under the age of two.

The drug of choice for typhoid fever is usually a quinolone antibiotic such as ciprofloxacin (Cipro) or levofloxacin (Levaquin), which many travelers carry for treatment of traveler's diarrhea. However, if you self-treat for typhoid fever, you may also need to self-treat for malaria, since the symptoms of the two diseases may be indistinguishable.

TRAVELER'S DIARRHEA

To prevent diarrhea, avoid tap water unless it has been boiled, filtered or chemically disinfected (iodine tablets); only eat fresh fruits or vegetables if cooked or peeled; be wary of dairy products that might contain unpasteurized milk; and be highly selective when eating food from street vendors.

If you develop diarrhea, be sure to drink plenty of fluids, preferably an oral rehydration solution containing lots of salt and sugar. A few loose stools don't require treatment, but if you start having more than four or five stools a day you should start taking an antibiotic (usually a quinolone drug) and an antidiarrheal agent (such as loperamide). If diarrhea is bloody or persists for more than 72 hours or is accompanied by fever, shaking chills or severe abdominal pain you should seek medical attention.

ENVIRONMENTAL HAZARDS

Animal Bites

Do not attempt to pet, handle or feed any animal, with the exception of domestic animals known to be free of any infectious disease. Most animal injuries are directly related to a person's attempt to touch or feed the animal.

Any bite or scratch by a mammal, including bats, should be promptly and thoroughly cleansed with large amounts of soap and water, followed by application of an antiseptic such as iodine or alcohol. The local health authorities should be contacted immediately for possible post-exposure rabies treatment, whether or not you've been immunized against rabies. It may also be advisable to start an antibiotic, since wounds caused by animal bites and scratches frequently become infected. One of the newer quinolones, such as levofloxacin (Levaquin), which many travelers carry in case of diarrhea, would be an appropriate choice.

Insect Bites

No matter how much you safeguard, getting bitten by mosquitoes is part of every traveler's experience in the country. While there are occasional outbreaks of dengue (see p478) in Costa Rica, for the most part the greatest worry you will have with bites is the general discomfort that comes with them, namely itching.

The best prevention is to stay covered up – wearing long pants, long sleeves and a hat, and shoes (rather than sandals). Unfortunately, Costa Rica's sweltering temperatures might make this a bit difficult. Therefore the best measure you can take is to invest in a good insect repellent, preferably one containing DEET. (These repellents can also be found in Costa Rica.) This should be applied to exposed skin and clothing (but not to eyes, mouth, cuts, wounds, or irritated skin).

In general, adults and children over 12 can use preparations containing 25% to 35% DEET, which usually lasts about six hours. Children between two and 12 years of age should use preparations containing no more than 10% DEET, applied sparingly, which will usually last about three hours. Neurologic toxicity has been reported from DEET, especially in children, but appears to be extremely uncommon and generally related to overuse. DEET-containing compounds should not be used on children under age two.

Insect repellents containing certain botanical products, including oil of eucalyptus and soybean oil, are effective but last only 1½ to two hours.

A particularly good item for every traveler to take is a bug net to hang over beds (along with a few thumbtacks or nails with which to hang it). Many hotels in Costa Rica don't have windows (or screens) and a cheap little net will save you plenty of night-time aggravation. The mesh size should be less than 1.5mm.

Dusk is the worst time for mosquitoes, so take extra precautions once the sun starts to set.

Snake Bites

Costa Rica is home to all manner of venomous snakes and any foray into forested areas will put you at (a very slight) risk for snake bite.

The best prevention is to wear closed, heavy shoes or boots and to keep a watchful eye on the trail. Snakes like to come out to cleared paths for a nap, so watch where you step. (For more on Costa Rica's fer-de-lance and bushmaster, see p41).

In the event of a bite from a venomous snake, place the victim at rest, keep the bitten area immobilized and move the victim immediately to the nearest medical facility. Avoid tourniquets, which are no longer recommended.

Sun

To protect yourself from excessive sun exposure you should stay out of the midday sun, wear sunglasses and a wide-brimmed sun hat, and apply sunscreen with SPF 15 or higher, with both UVA and UVB protection. Sunscreen should be generously applied to all exposed parts of the body approximately 30 minutes before sun exposure and should be reapplied after swimming or vigorous activity. Travelers should also drink plenty of fluids and avoid strenuous exercise when the temperature is high.

Water

Tap water in Costa Rica is not safe to drink – buying bottled water is your best bet. If you have the means, vigorous boiling for one minute is the most effective means of water purification. At altitudes greater than 2000m (6500 feet), boil for three minutes. Another option is to disinfect water with iodine pills: add 2% tincture of iodine to one quart or liter of water (five drops to clear water, 10 drops to cloudy water) and let stand for 30 minutes. If the water is cold, longer times may be required.

TRAVELING WITH CHILDREN

In general, it's safe for children and pregnant women to go to Costa Rica. However, because some of the vaccines listed above are not approved for use by children or during pregnancy, these travelers should be particularly careful not to drink tap water or consume any questionable food or beverage. Also, when traveling with children, make sure they're up-to-date on all routine immunizations. It's sometimes appropriate to give children some of their vaccines a little early before visiting a developing nation. You should discuss this with your pediatrician.

Lastly, if pregnant, you should bear in mind that should a complication such as premature labor develop while abroad, the quality of medical care may not be comparable to that in your home country.

See p452 for some general information on traveling with children. Some useful Latin American Spanish words and phrases appear on p491.

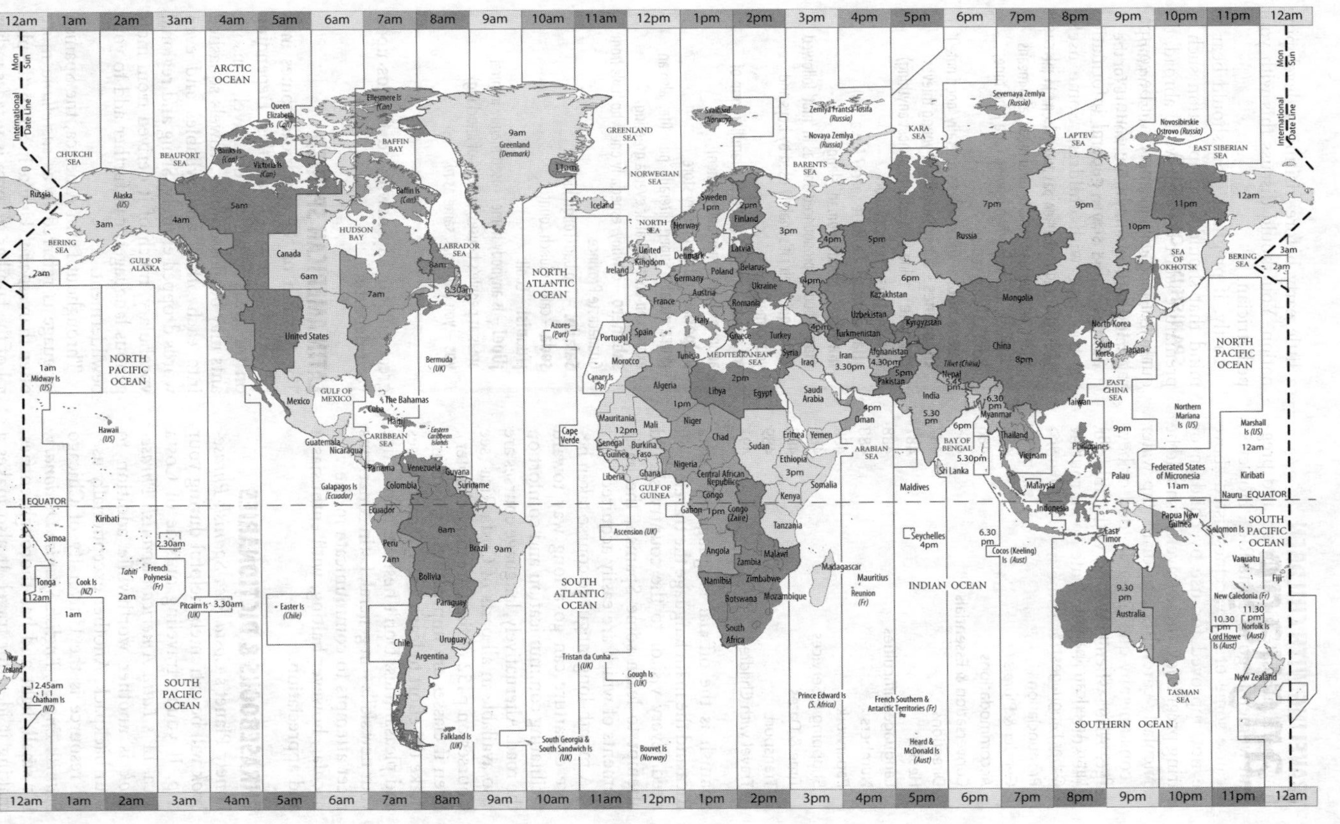
12am
1am
2am
3am
4am
5am
6am
7am
8am
9am
10am
11am
12pm
1pm
2pm
3pm
4pm
5pm
6pm
7pm
8pm
9pm
10pm
11pm
12am
International Date Line
Mon
Sun
ARCTIC OCEAN
CHUKCHI SEA
BEAUFORT SEA
BERING SEA
GULF OF ALASKA
NORTH PACIFIC OCEAN
SOUTH PACIFIC OCEAN
HUDSON BAY
BAFFIN BAY
LABRADOR SEA
GREENLAND SEA
NORWEGIAN SEA
NORTH SEA
BARENTS SEA
KARA SEA
LAPTEV SEA
EAST SIBERIAN SEA
SEA OF OKHOTSK
EAST CHINA SEA
NORTH ATLANTIC OCEAN
SOUTH ATLANTIC OCEAN
GULF OF MEXICO
CARIBBEAN SEA
GULF OF GUINEA
MEDITERRANEAN SEA
ARABIAN SEA
BAY OF BENGAL
INDIAN OCEAN
TASMAN SEA
SOUTHERN OCEAN
EQUATOR
Russia
Alaska (US)
Canada
United States
Mexico
Greenland (Denmark)
Iceland
Queen Elizabeth Is (Can)
Ellesmere Is (Can)
Banks Is (Can)
Victoria Is (Can)
Baffin Is (Can)
Bermuda (UK)
The Bahamas
Cuba
Haiti
Eastern Caribbean Islands
Guatemala
Nicaragua
Panama
Venezuela
Guyana
Suriname
Colombia
Ecuador
Galapagos Is (Ecuador)
Peru
Brazil
Bolivia
Paraguay
Chile
Uruguay
Argentina
Falkland Is (UK)
South Georgia & South Sandwich Is (UK)
Easter Is (Chile)
Pitcairn Is (UK)
French Polynesia (Fr)
Tahiti
Cook Is (NZ)
Samoa
Tonga
Kiribati
Hawaii (US)
Midway Is (US)
Chatham Is (NZ)
New Zealand
Azores (Port)
Canary Is (Sp)
Cape Verde
Ascension (UK)
Tristan da Cunha (UK)
Gough Is (UK)
Bouvet Is (Norway)
Ireland
United Kingdom
Portugal
Spain
France
Morocco
Norway
Sweden
Finland
Denmark
Germany
Poland
Austria
Italy
Latvia
Belarus
Ukraine
Romania
Greece
Turkey
Syria
Tunisia
Algeria
Libya
Egypt
Mauritania
Mali
Niger
Chad
Sudan
Senegal
Guinea
Burkina Faso
Liberia
Ghana
Nigeria
Central African Republic
Gabon
Congo
Congo (Zaire)
Angola
Namibia
Botswana
South Africa
Zambia
Malawi
Zimbabwe
Mozambique
Tanzania
Kenya
Ethiopia
Eritrea
Yemen
Somalia
Madagascar
Mauritius
Reunion (Fr)
Seychelles
Prince Edward Is (S. Africa)
French Southern & Antarctic Territories (Fr)
Heard & McDonald Is (Aust)
Iraq
Saudi Arabia
Iran
Oman
Afghanistan
Pakistan
Turkmenistan
Uzbekistan
Kazakhstan
Kyrgyzstan
India
Nepal
Tibet (China)
Sri Lanka
Maldives
Myanmar
Thailand
Vietnam
Malaysia
Indonesia
Cocos (Keeling) Is (Aust)
Svalbard (Norway)
Zemlya Frantsa-Iosifa (Russia)
Novaya Zemlya (Russia)
Severnaya Zemlya (Russia)
Novosibirskie Ostrova (Russia)
Mongolia
China
North Korea
South Korea
Japan
Taiwan
Philippines
Palau
East Timor
Papua New Guinea
Australia
Northern Mariana Is (US)
Federated States of Micronesia
Marshall Is (US)
Nauru
Solomon Is
Vanuatu
Fiji
New Caledonia (Fr)
Norfolk Is (Aust)
Lord Howe Is (Aust)
3.30pm
4.30pm
5.30 pm
5.45 pm
5.30pm
6.30 pm
9.30 pm
10.30 pm
11.30 pm
2.30am
3.30am
8.30am
12.45am

Language

CONTENTS

Spanish is the official language of Costa Rica and the main language the traveler will need. Every visitor to the country should attempt to learn some Spanish, the basic elements of which are easily acquired.

A month-long language course taken before departure can go a long way toward facilitating communication and comfort on the road. Alternatively, language courses are also available in all parts of Costa Rica (see Courses on p452 of the Directory chapter). Even if classes are impractical, you should make the effort to learn a few basic phrases and pleasantries. Don't hesitate to practice your new skills – in general, Latin Americans meet attempts to communicate in the vernacular, however halting, with enthusiasm and appreciation.

PHRASEBOOKS & DICTIONARIES

Lonely Planet's *Costa Rica Spanish Phrasebook* will be extremely helpful during your trip. If you're traveling outside of Costa Rica, LP's *Latin American Spanish Phrasebook* is another worthwhile addition to your backpack. Another exceptionally useful resource is the University of Chicago *Spanish-English, English-Spanish Dictionary.* It's small, light and has thorough entries, making it ideal for travel. It also makes a great gift for any newfound friends upon your departure.

SPANISH IN COSTA RICA

The following colloquialisms and slang *(tiquismos)* are frequently heard, and are for the most part used only in Costa Rica.

¡Adiós! – Hi! (used when passing a friend in the street, or anyone in remote rural areas; also means 'farewell,' but only when leaving for a long time)
bomba – gas station
Buena nota. – OK/Excellent. (literally 'good note')
chapulines – a gang, usually of young thieves
chunche – thing (can refer to almost anything)
cien metros – one city block
¿Hay campo? – Is there space? (on a bus)
machita – blonde woman (slang)
mae – buddy (pronounced 'ma' as in 'mat' followed with a quick 'eh'; it's mainly used by boys and young men)
mi amor – my love (used as a familiar form of address by both men and women)
pulpería – corner grocery store
¡Pura vida! – Super! (literally 'pure life,' also an expression of approval or even a greeting)
sabanero – cowboy, especially one who hails from Guanacaste Province
Salado. – Too bad/Tough luck.
soda – café or lunch counter
¡Tuanis! – Cool!
¡Upe! – Is anybody home? (used mainly in rural areas at people's houses, instead of knocking)
vos – you (informal, same as *tú*)

LATIN AMERICAN SPANISH

The Spanish of the Americas comes in a bewildering array of varieties. Depending on the areas in which you travel, consonants may be glossed over, vowels squashed into each other, and syllables and even words dropped entirely. Slang and regional vocabulary, much of it derived from indigenous languages, can further add to your bewilderment.

Throughout Latin America, the Spanish language is referred to as *castellano* more often than *español.* Unlike in Spain, the plural of the familiar *tú* form is *ustedes* rather than *vosotros;* the latter term will sound quaint and archaic in the Americas. Another notable difference is that the letters **c** and **z** are never lisped in Latin America; attempts to do so could well provoke amusement.

OTHER LANGUAGES

Travelers will find English is often spoken in the upmarket hotels, airline offices and tourist agencies, and some other European languages are encountered in hotels run by Europeans. On the Caribbean coast, many of the locals speak some English, albeit with a local Creole dialect.

Indigenous languages are spoken in isolated areas, but unless travelers are getting off the beaten track they'll rarely encounter them. The indigenous languages Bribri and Cabécar are understood by an estimated 18,000 people living on both sides of the Cordillera de Talamanca.

PRONUNCIATION

Spanish spelling is phonetically consistent, meaning that there's a clear and consistent relationship between what you see in writing and how it's pronounced. Also, most Spanish sounds have English equivalents, so English speakers shouldn't have too much trouble being understood.

Vowels

- **a** as in 'father'
- **e** as in 'met'
- **i** as in 'marine'
- **o** as in 'or' (without the 'r' sound)
- **u** as in 'rule'; the 'u' is not pronounced after **q** and in the letter combinations **gue** and **gui**, unless it's marked with a diaeresis (eg *argüir*), in which case it's pronounced as English 'w'
- **y** at the end of a word or when it stands alone, it's pronounced as the Spanish **i** (eg *ley*); between vowels within a word it's as the 'y' in 'yonder'

Consonants

As a rule, Spanish consonants resemble their English counterparts. The exceptions are listed below.

While the consonants **ch**, **ll** and **ñ** are generally considered distinct letters, **ch** and **ll** are now often listed alphabetically under **c** and **l** respectively. The letter **ñ** is still treated as a separate letter and comes after **n** in dictionaries.

- **b** similar to English 'b,' but softer; referred to as 'b larga'
- **c** as in 'celery' before **e** and **i**; otherwise as English 'k'
- **ch** as in 'church'
- **d** as in 'dog,' but between vowels and after **l** or **n**, the sound is closer to the 'th' in 'this'
- **g** as the 'ch' in the Scottish *loch* before **e** and **i** ('kh' in our guides to pronunciation); elsewhere, as in 'go'
- **h** invariably silent. If your name begins with this letter, listen carefully if you're waiting for public officials to call you.
- **j** as the 'ch' in the Scottish *loch* (written as 'kh' in our guides to pronunciation)
- **ll** as the 'y' in 'yellow'
- **ñ** as the 'ni' in 'onion'
- **r** a short **r** except at the beginning of a word, and after **l**, **n** or **s**, when it's often rolled
- **rr** very strongly rolled
- **v** similar to English 'b,' but softer; referred to as 'b corta'
- **x** usually pronounced as **j** above; in some indigenous place names **x** is pronounced as the 's' in 'sit'; in other instances, it's as in 'taxi'
- **z** as the 's' in 'sun'

Word Stress

In general, words ending in vowels or the letters **n** or **s** have stress on the next-to-last syllable, while those with other endings have stress on the last syllable. Thus *vaca* (cow) and *caballos* (horses) both carry stress on the next-to-last syllable, while *ciudad* (city) and *infeliz* (unhappy) are both stressed on the last syllable.

Written accents will almost always appear in words that don't follow the rules above, eg *sótano* (basement), *América* and *porción* (portion).

GENDER & PLURALS

In Spanish, nouns are either masculine or feminine, and there are rules to help determine gender (there are of course some exceptions). Feminine nouns generally end with **-a** or with the groups **-ción**, **-sión** or

-dad. Other endings typically signify a masculine noun. Endings for adjectives also change to agree with the gender of the noun they modify (masculine/feminine **-o/-a**). Where both masculine and feminine forms are included in this language guide, they are separated by a slash, with the masculine form first, eg *perdido/a*.

If a noun or adjective ends in a vowel, the plural is formed by adding **s** to the end. If it ends in a consonant, the plural is formed by adding **es** to the end.

ACCOMMODATIONS

I'm looking for ...	*Estoy buscando ...*	e·*stoy* boos·*kan*·do ...
Where is ...?	*¿Dónde hay ...?*	*don*·de ai ...
a cabin	*una cabina*	*oo*·na ca·*bee*·na
a camping ground	*un camping/ campamento*	oon *kam*·ping/ kam·pa·*men*·to
a guesthouse	*una casa de huespedes*	*oo*·na *ka*·sa de *wes*·pe·des
a hostel	*un hospedaje/ una residencia*	oon os·pe·*da*·khe/ oon·a re·see·*den*·sya
a hotel	*un hotel*	oon o·*tel*
a youth hostel	*un albergue juvenil*	oon al·*ber*·ge khoo·ve·*neel*

Are there any rooms available?
¿Hay habitaciones libres? — ay a·bee·ta·*syon*·es *lee*·bres

I'd like a ... room.	*Quisiera una habitación ...*	kee·*sye*·ra oo·na a·bee·ta·*syon* ...
double	*doble*	*do*·ble
single	*individual*	een·dee·vee·*dwal*
twin	*con dos camas*	kon dos *ka*·mas

How much is it per ...?	*¿Cuánto cuesta por ...?*	*kwan*·to *kwes*·ta por ...
night	*noche*	*no*·che
person	*persona*	per·*so*·na
week	*semana*	se·*ma*·na

full board	*pensión completa*	pen·*syon* kom·*ple*·ta
private/shared bathroom	*baño privado/ compartido*	*ba*·nyo pree·*va*·do/ kom·par·*tee*·do
too expensive	*demasiado caro*	de·ma·*sya*·do *ka*·ro
cheaper	*más económico*	mas e·ko·*no*·mee·ko
discount	*descuento*	des·*kwen*·to

Does it include breakfast?
¿Incluye el desayuno? — een·*kloo*·ye el de·sa·*yoo*·no

MAKING A RESERVATION
(for phone or written requests)

To ...	*A ...*
From ...	*De ...*
Date	*Fecha*
I'd like to book ...	*Quisiera reservar ...* (see the list under 'Accommodations' for bed and room options)
in the name of ...	*en nombre de ...*
for the nights of ...	*para las noches del ...*
credit card ...	*tarjeta de crédito ...*
number	*número*
expiry date	*fecha de vencimiento*
Please confirm ...	*Puede confirmar ...*
availability	*la disponibilidad*
price	*el precio*

May I see the room?
¿Puedo ver la habitación? — *pwe*·do ver la a·bee·ta·*syon*

I don't like it.
No me gusta. — no me *goos*·ta

It's fine. I'll take it.
Está bien. La tomo. — es·*ta* byen la *to*·mo

I'm leaving now.
Me voy ahora. — me *voy* a·o·ra

CONVERSATION & ESSENTIALS

In their public behavior, Latin Americans are very conscious of civilities. You should never approach a stranger for information without extending a greeting, such as *buenos días* or *buenas tardes*, and you should use only the polite form of address, especially with the police and public officials.

Central America is generally more formal than many of the South American countries. The polite form *usted* (you) is used in all cases in this guide; where options are given, the form is indicated by the abbreviations 'pol' and 'inf.'

Hi.	*Hola.*	o·la (inf)
Good morning.	*Buenos días.*	*bwe*·nos *dee*·as
Good afternoon.	*Buenas tardes.*	*bwe*·nas *tar*·des
Good evening/ night.	*Buenas noches.*	*bwe*·nas *no*·ches

The three most common greetings are often abbreviated to simply *buenos* (for *buenos días*) and *buenas* (for *buenas tardes* and *buenas noches*).

LANGUAGE

Bye/See you soon. *Hasta luego.* as·ta *lwe*·go
Goodbye. *Adiós.* a·*dyos* (see also the boxed text Spanish in Costa Rica on p484)
Yes. *Sí.* see
No. *No.* no
Please. *Por favor.* por fa·*vor*
Thank you. *Gracias.* *gra*·syas
Many thanks. *Muchas gracias.* *moo*·chas *gra*·syas
You're welcome. *De nada.* de *na*·da
Apologies. *Perdón.* per·*don*
May I? *Permiso.* per·*mee*·so (when asking permission)
Excuse me. *Disculpe.* dees·*kool*·pe (used before a request or when apologizing)

How are things?
¿Qué tal? ke tal
What's your name?
¿Cómo se llama usted? *ko*·mo se *ya*·ma oo·*sted* (pol)
¿Cómo te llamas? *ko*·mo te *ya*·mas (inf)
My name is ...
Me llamo ... me *ya*·mo ...
It's a pleasure to meet you.
Mucho gusto. *moo*·cho *goos*·to
The pleasure is mine.
El gusto es mío. el *goos*·to es *mee*·o
Where are you from?
¿De dónde es/eres? de *don*·de es/*er*·es (pol/inf)
I'm from ...
Soy de ... soy de ...
Where are you staying?
¿Dónde está alojado? *don*·de es·*ta* a·lo·*kha*·do (pol)
¿Dónde estás alojado? *don*·de es·*tas* a·lo·*kha*·do (inf)
May I take a photo?
¿Puedo sacar una foto? *pwe*·do sa·*kar* *oo*·na *fo*·to

DIRECTIONS

How do I get to ...?
¿Cómo llego a ...? *ko*·mo *ye*·go a ...
Is it far?
¿Está lejos? es·*ta le*·khos

SIGNS

Entrada	Entrance
Salida	Exit
Información	Information
Abierto	Open
Cerrado	Closed
Prohibido	Prohibited
Comisaria	Police Station
Servicios/Baños	Toilets
Hombres/Varones	Men
Mujeres/Damas	Women

EMERGENCIES

Help!	*¡Socorro!*	so·*ko*·ro
Fire!	*¡Fuego!*	*fwe*·go
I've been robbed.	*Me han robado.*	me an ro·*ba*·do
Go away!	*¡Déjeme!*	*de*·khe·me
Get lost!	*¡Váyase!*	*va*·ya·se
Call ...!	*¡Llame a ...!*	*ya*·me a
the police	*la policía*	la po·lee·*see*·a
a doctor	*un médico*	oon *me*·dee·ko
an ambulance	*una ambulancia*	oo·na am·boo·*lan*·sya

It's an emergency.
Es una emergencia. es *oo*·na e·mer·*khen*·sya
Could you help me, please?
¿Me puede ayudar, por favor? me *pwe*·de a·yoo·*dar* por fa·*vor*
I'm lost.
Estoy perdido/a. es·*toy* per·*dee*·do/a
Where are the toilets?
¿Dónde están los baños? *don*·de es·*tan* los *ba*·nyos

Go straight ahead.
Siga/Vaya derecho. *see*·ga/*va*·ya de·*re*·cho
Turn left.
Voltée a la izquierda. vol·*te*·e a la ees·*kyer*·da
Turn right.
Voltée a la derecha. vol·*te*·e a la de·*re*·cha
Can you show me (on the map)?
¿Me lo podría señalar (en el mapa)? me lo po·*dree*·a se·nya·*lar* (en el *ma*·pa)

north	*norte*	*nor*·te
south	*sur*	soor
east	*este*	*es*·te
west	*oeste*	o·*es*·te
here	*aquí*	a·*kee*
there	*ahí*	a·*ee*
avenue	*avenida*	a·ve·*nee*·da
block	*cuadra*	*kwa*·dra
street	*calle/paseo*	*ka*·lye/pa·*se*·o

HEALTH

I'm sick.
Estoy enfermo/a. es·*toy* en·*fer*·mo/a
I need a doctor.
Necesito un médico. ne·se·*see*·to oon *me*·dee·ko
Where's the hospital?
¿Dónde está el hospital? *don*·de es·*ta* el os·pee·*tal*
I'm pregnant.
Estoy embarazada. es·*toy* em·ba·ra·*sa*·da
I've been vaccinated.
Estoy vacunado/a. es·*toy* va·koo·*na*·do/a

I'm allergic to ...	*Soy alérgico/a a ...*	soy a·*ler*·khee·ko/a a ...
antibiotics	*los antibióticos*	los an·tee·*byo*·tee·kos
nuts	*las fruta secas*	las *froo*·tas *se*·kas
penicillin	*la penicilina*	la pe·nee·see·*lee*·na

I'm ...	*Soy ...*	soy ...
asthmatic	*asmático/a*	as·*ma*·tee·ko/a
diabetic	*diabético/a*	dya·*be*·tee·ko/a
epileptic	*epiléptico/a*	e·pee·*lep*·tee·ko/a

I have ...	*Tengo ...*	*ten*·go ...
a cough	*tos*	tos
diarrhea	*diarrea*	dya·*re*·a
a headache	*un dolor de cabeza*	oon do·*lor* de ka·*be*·sa
nausea	*náusea*	*now*·se·a

LANGUAGE DIFFICULTIES

Do you speak English?
¿Habla/Hablas inglés? a·bla/*a*·blas een·*gles* (pol/inf)

Does anyone here speak English?
¿Hay alguien que hable inglés? ai al·*gyen* ke *a*·ble een·*gles*

I (don't) understand.
(No) Entiendo. (no) en·*tyen*·do

How do you say ...?
¿Cómo se dice ...? *ko*·mo se *dee*·se ...

What does ...mean?
¿Qué significa ...? ke seeg·*nee*·fee·ka ...

Could you please ...?	*¿Puede ..., por favor?*	*pwe*·de ... por *fa*·vor
repeat that	*repetirlo*	re·pe·*teer*·lo
speak more slowly	*hablar más despacio*	a·*blar* mas des·*pa*·syo
write it down	*escribirlo*	es·kree·*beer*·lo

NUMBERS

1	*uno*	*oo*·no
2	*dos*	dos
3	*tres*	tres
4	*cuatro*	*kwa*·tro
5	*cinco*	*seen*·ko
6	*seis*	says
7	*siete*	*sye*·te
8	*ocho*	*o*·cho
9	*nueve*	*nwe*·ve
10	*diez*	dyes
11	*once*	*on*·se
12	*doce*	*do*·se
13	*trece*	*tre*·se
14	*catorce*	ka·*tor*·se
15	*quince*	*keen*·se
16	*dieciséis*	dye·see·*says*
17	*diecisiete*	dye·see·*sye*·te
18	*dieciocho*	dye·see·*o*·cho
19	*diecinueve*	dye·see·*nwe*·ve
20	*veinte*	*vayn*·te
21	*veintiuno*	vayn·tee·*oo*·no
30	*treinta*	*trayn*·ta
31	*treinta y uno*	trayn·ta ee *oo*·no
40	*cuarenta*	kwa·*ren*·ta
50	*cincuenta*	seen·*kwen*·ta
60	*sesenta*	se·*sen*·ta
70	*setenta*	se·*ten*·ta
80	*ochenta*	o·*chen*·ta
90	*noventa*	no·*ven*·ta
100	*cien*	syen
101	*ciento uno*	syen·to *oo*·no
200	*doscientos*	do·*syen*·tos
1000	*mil*	meel
5000	*cinco mil*	*seen*·ko meel

PAPERWORK

birth certificate	*certificado de nacimiento*
border (frontier)	*la frontera*
car-owner's title	*título de propiedad*
car registration	*registración*
customs	*aduana*
driver's license	*licencia de manejar*
identification	*identificación*
immigration	*migración*
insurance	*seguro*
passport	*pasaporte*
temporary vehicle import permit	*permiso de importación temporal de vehículo*
tourist card	*tarjeta de turista*
visa	*visado*

SHOPPING & SERVICES

I'd like to buy ...
Quisiera comprar ... kee·*sye*·ra kom·*prar* ...

I'm just looking.
Sólo estoy mirando. so·lo es·*toy* mee·*ran*·do

May I look at it?
¿Puedo verlo/a? *pwe*·do *ver*·lo/a

How much is it?
¿Cuánto cuesta? *kwan*·to *kwes*·ta

That's too expensive for me.
Es demasiado caro para mí. es de·ma·*sya*·do *ka*·ro *pa*·ra mee

Could you lower the price?
¿Podría bajar un poco el precio? po·*dree*·a ba·*khar* oon *po*·ko el *pre*·syo

I don't like it.
No me gusta. no me *goos*·ta

I'll take it.
Lo llevo. lo *ye*·vo

Do you accept ...?	*¿Aceptan ...?*	a·sep·*tan* ...
American dollars	*dólares americanos*	*do*·la·res a·me·ree·*ka*·nos
credit cards	*tarjetas de crédito*	tar·*khe*·tas de *kre*·dee·to
traveler's checks	*cheques de viajero*	*che*·kes de vya·*khe*·ro

less	*menos*	*me*·nos
more	*más*	mas
large	*grande*	*gran*·de
small	*pequeño/a*	pe·*ke*·nyo/a

I'm looking for the ...	*Estoy buscando ...*	es·*toy* boos·*kan*·do
ATM	*el cajero automático*	el ka·*khe*·ro ow·to·*ma*·tee·ko
bank	*el banco*	el *ban*·ko
bookstore	*la librería*	la lee·bre·*ree*·a
exchange house	*la casa de cambio*	la *ka*·sa de *kam*·byo
general store	*la tienda*	la *tyen*·da
laundry	*la lavandería*	la la·van·de·*ree*·a
market	*el mercado*	el mer·*ka*·do
pharmacy/chemist	*la farmacia*	la far·*ma*·sya
post office	*la officina de correos*	la o·fee·*see*·na de ko·*re*·os
supermarket	*el supermercado*	el soo·per·mer·*ka*·do
tourist office	*la oficina de turismo*	la o·fee·*see*·na de too·*rees*·mo

What time does it open/close?
¿A qué hora abre/cierra?
a ke *o*·ra *a*·bre/*sye*·ra

I want to change some money/traveler's checks.
Quisiera cambiar dinero/cheques de viajero.
kee·*sye*·ra kam·*byar* dee·*ne*·ro/*che*·kes de vya·*khe*·ro

What is the exchange rate?
¿Cuál es el tipo de cambio?
kwal es el *tee*·po de *kam*·byo

I want to call ...
Quisiera llamar a ...
kee·*sye*·ra lya·*mar* a ...

airmail	*correo aéreo*	ko·*re*·o a·e·re·o
letter	*carta*	*kar*·ta
registered (mail)	*certificado*	ser·tee·fee·*ka*·do
stamps	*timbres*	*teem*·bres

TIME & DATES

What time is it?	*¿Qué hora es?*	ke *o*·ra es
It's one o'clock.	*Es la una.*	es la *oo*·na
It's seven o'clock.	*Son las siete.*	son las *sye*·te
Half past two.	*Dos y media.*	dos ee *me*·dya
midnight	*medianoche*	me·dya·*no*·che
noon	*mediodía*	me·dyo·*dee*·a

now	*ahora*	a·*o*·ra
today	*hoy*	oy
tonight	*esta noche*	es·ta *no*·che
tomorrow	*mañana*	ma·*nya*·na
yesterday	*ayer*	a·*yer*

Monday	*lunes*	*loo*·nes
Tuesday	*martes*	*mar*·tes
Wednesday	*miércoles*	*myer*·ko·les
Thursday	*jueves*	*khwe*·ves
Friday	*viernes*	*vyer*·nes
Saturday	*sábado*	*sa*·ba·do
Sunday	*domingo*	do·*meen*·go

January	*enero*	e·*ne*·ro
February	*febrero*	fe·*bre*·ro
March	*marzo*	*mar*·so
April	*abril*	a·*breel*
May	*mayo*	*ma*·yo
June	*junio*	*khoo*·nyo
July	*julio*	*khoo*·lyo
August	*agosto*	a·*gos*·to
September	*septiembre*	sep·*tyem*·bre
October	*octubre*	ok·*too*·bre
November	*noviembre*	no·*vyem*·bre
December	*diciembre*	dee·*syem*·bre

TRANSPORT
Public Transport

What time does ... leave/arrive?	*¿A qué hora ... sale/llega?*	a ke *o*·ra ... *sa*·le/*ye*·ga
the bus	*el bus/autobús*	el bus/ow·to·*boos*
the ferry	*el barco*	el *bar*·ko
the minibus	*el colectivo/ la buseta/ el microbus*	el ko·lek·*tee*·vo/ la boo·*se*·ta/ el *mee*·kro·boos
the plane	*el avión*	el a·*vyon*
the train	*el tren*	el tren

the airport	*el aeropuerto*	el a·e·ro·*pwer*·to
the bus station	*la estación de autobuses*	la es·ta·*syon* de ow·to·*boo*·ses
the bus stop	*la parada de autobuses*	la pa·*ra*·da de ow·to·*boo*·ses
the train station	*la estación de ferrocarril*	la es·ta·*syon* de fe·ro·ka·*reel*
the luggage locker	*la consigna para el equipaje*	la kon·*see*·nya para el e·kee·*pa*·khe
the ticket office	*la boletería/ ticketería*	la bo·le·te·*ree*·ya/ tee·ke·te·*ree*·ya

A ticket to ..., please.
Un boleto a ..., por favor.
oon bo·*le*·to a ... por fa·*vor*

What's the fare to ...?
¿Cuánto cuesta hasta ...?
kwan·to *kwes*·ta *a*·sta ...

student's	*de estudiante*	de es·too·*dyan*·te
1st class	*primera clase*	*pree*·me·ra *kla*·se
2nd class	*segunda clase*	se·*goon*·da *kla*·se
single/one-way	*de ida*	de *ee*·da
return/round trip	*de ida y vuelta*	de *ee*·da e *vwel*·ta
taxi	*taxi*	*tak*·see

Private Transport

I'd like to hire a ...	*Quisiera alquilar ...*	kee·*sye*·ra al·kee·*lar* ...
4WD	*un todo terreno*	oon *to*·do te·*re*·no
car	*un auto/carro*	oon *ow*·to/*ka*·ro
motorcycle	*una motocicleta*	*oo*·na *mo*·to·see·*kle*·ta
bicycle	*una bicicleta*	*oo*·na bee·see·*kle*·ta

pickup (truck)	*camioneta*	ka·myo·*ne*·ta
truck	*camión*	*ka*·myon
hitchhike	*hacer dedo*	*a*·ser *de*·do

Where's a petrol station?
¿Dónde hay una gasolinera/bomba?
don·de ai oo·na *ga*·so·lee·*ne*·ra/*bom*·ba

How much is a liter of gasoline?
¿Cuánto cuesta el litro de gasolina?
kwan·to *kwes*·ta el *lee*·tro de ga·so·*lee*·na

Please fill it up.
Lleno, por favor.
ye·no por fa·*vor*

I'd like (2000 colones) worth.
Quiero (dos mil colones) en gasolina.
kye·ro (dos meel ko·*lo*·nes) en ga·so·*lee*·na

diesel	*diesel*	*dee*·sel
leaded (regular)	*gasolina con plomo*	ga·so·*lee*·na kon *plo*·mo
petrol (gas)	*gasolina*	ga·so·*lee*·na
unleaded	*gasolina sin plomo*	ga·so·*lee*·na seen *plo*·mo
oil	*aceite*	a·*say*·te
tire	*llanta*	*yan*·ta
puncture	*agujero*	a·goo·*khe*·ro

Is this the road to ...?
¿Por acquí se va a ...?
por a·*kee* se va a ...

ROAD SIGNS

Though Costa Rica mostly uses the familiar international road signs, you should be prepared to encounter these other signs as well:

Acceso	Entrance
Acceso Prohibido	No Entry
Acceso Permanente	24-Hour Access
Construcción de Carreteras	Roadworks
Ceda el Paso	Give Way
Curva Peligrosa	Dangerous Curve
Derrumbes	Landslides
Despacio	Slow
Desvío/Desviación	Detour
Mantenga Su Derecha	Keep to the Right
No Adelantar	No Passing
No Hay Paso	Road Closed
No Pase	No Overtaking
Pare/Stop	Stop
Peligro	Danger
Prohibido Estacionar	No Parking
Prohibido el Paso	No Entry
Puente Angosto	Narrow Bridge
Salida (de Autopista)	Exit (Freeway)
Una Via	One Way

(How long) Can I park here?
¿(Por cuánto tiempo) Puedo estacionar aquí?
(por *kwan*·to *tyem*·po) *pwe*·do ess·ta·syo·*nar* a·*kee*

Where do I pay?
¿Dónde se paga?
don·de se *pa*·ga

I need a mechanic/tow truck.
Necesito un mecánico/remolque.
ne·se·*see*·to oon me·*ka*·nee·ko/re·*mol*·ke

Is there a garage near here?
¿Hay un garaje cerca de aquí?
ai oon ga·*ra*·khe ser·ka de a·*kee*

The car has broken down in ...
El carro se ha averiado en ...
el *ka*·ro se a a·ve·*rya*·do en ...

The motorbike won't start.
La moto no arranca.
la *mo*·to no a·*ran*·ka

I have a flat tire.
Tengo una llanta desinflada.
ten·go *oo*·na *yan*·ta des·een·*fla*·da

I've run out of petrol.
Me quedé sin gasolina.
me ke·*de* seen ga·so·*lee*·na

I've had an accident.
Tuve un accidente.
too·ve oon ak·see·*den*·te

LANGUAGE

TRAVEL WITH CHILDREN

I need ...
Necesito ...
ne·se·*see*·to ...

Do you have ...?
¿Hay ...?
ai ...

a car baby seat
un asiento de seguridad para bebés
oon a·*syen*·to de se·goo·ree·*da* pa·ra be·*bes*

a child-minding service
oon club para niños
oon kloob pa·*ra nee*·nyos

a children's menu
un menú infantil
oon me·*noo* een·fan·*teel*

a creche
una guardería
oo·na gwar·de·*ree*·a

(disposable) diapers/nappies
pañales (de usar y tirar)
pa·*nya*·les (de oo·*sar* ee tee·*rar*)

an (English-speaking) babysitter
una niñera (que habla inglesa)
oo·na nee·*nye*·ra (ke *a*·bla een·*gle*·sa)

formula (milk)
leche en polvo
le·che en *pol*·vo

a highchair
una silla para bebé
oo·na *see*·ya *pa*·ra be·*be*

a potty
una bacinica
oo·na ba·see·*nee*·ka

a stroller
una carreola
oona ka·re·*o*·la

Do you mind if I breast-feed here?
¿Le molesta que dé el pecho aquí?
le mo·*les*·ta ke de el *pe*·cho a·*kee*

Are children allowed?
¿Se admiten niños?
se ad·*mee*·ten *nee*·nyos

Also available from Lonely Planet:
Costa Rica Spanish and *Latin American Spanish Phrasebook*

Glossary

See p62 in the Food & Drink chapter for useful words and phrases dealing with food and dining. See the Language chapter (p484) for other useful words and phrases.

abrazo – hug
adiós – means 'goodbye' universally, but used in rural Costa Rica as a greeting
aguas negras – sewage
aguila – eagle
aldea – hamlet
alquiler de automóviles – car rental
apartado – post-office box
árbol – tree
ardilla – squirrel
aspirina – aspirin
ATH – A Toda Hora (open all hours); used to denote ATM machines
automóvil (auto) – car
ave – bird; see also *pájaro*
avión – airplane

baño – bathroom; see also *servicio*
barrio – district, neighborhood
barro – mud
beso – kiss
bicicleta – bicycle
billete – bank note, bill
boleto – ticket (bus, train, museum etc)
bomba – gas station; short funny verse; bomb
borracho/a – drunk male/female
bosque – forest
bosque nuboso – cloud forest
bote – boat
buena nota – excellent, right on; literally 'good grade'

caballeros – gentlemen; the usual sign on male-toilet doors
caballo – horse
cabinas – cheap hotel
cafetalero – coffee baron
cafetera – coffee-making machine
cajero automático – ATM
cama – bed
cama matrimonial – double bed
caminata – walk; hike
caminata pajarera – birding walk
camión – truck
camioneta – pick-up truck
camiseta – T-shirt
campesino – peasant; person who works in agriculture
carretas – colorfully painted wooden ox carts; form of folk art
carretera – road
casado – married; set meal
cascada – waterfall
catedral – cathedral
caverna – cave
cerro – mountain
Chepe – affectionate nickname for José; also used in reference to San José
chicle – chewing gum
chinga – small boat; see also *panga* and *lancha*; in other parts of Latin America, it's a description of the sexual act along the lines of 'to screw'
chorizo – mess; spicy sausage (*chorizear* or *dejar un chorizo* means to 'make a mess of things' or to do something illegitimate
chunche – literally, a 'thing'
cigarrillo – cigarette
cochino – pig; also means 'filthy'
cocina – kitchen; cooking
colectivo – buses, minivans, or cars operating as shared taxis; see also *normal* and *directo*
colibrí – hummingbird
colina – hill
colón – Costa Rican unit of currency (plural colones)
condón – condom
cordillera – mountain range
correo – mail service
correo electrónico – email
costarricense – Costa Rican
cruce – crossing
cruda – often used to describe a hangover: '*tengo una cruda*', literally 'raw'
cuadraciclo – all-terrain vehicle (ATV)
cuchara – spoon
cuchillo – knife
cueva – cave
culebra – snake; see also *serpiente*

damas – ladies; the usual sign found on female-toilet doors
derecha – right
dios – god
directo – direct; long-distance bus that has only a few stops
doble – double (as in double room)
doble tracción – 4WD

emergencia – emergency
encomienda – sending packages, usually via bus
estación – station (as in ranger station or bus station); season
estero – estuary
estudiante – student

farmacia – pharmacy
fauna silvestre – wildlife
fiesta – party or festival
finca – farm or plantation
flor – flower
frontera – border
fuego – flame
futból – soccer

galón – US gallon (not commonly used)
garza – cattle egret
gasolina – gas, petrol
gracias – thanks
gringo/a – male/female North American or European visitor (can be affectionate or insulting, depending on the tone used)
guapote – large fish caught for sport, equivalent to rainbow bass

hacienda – a rural estate
hay – pronounced 'eye,' meaning 'there is' or 'there are;' *no hay* means 'there is none'
hielo – ice
Holdridge Life Zones – classification system developed in the 1960s by US botanist LR Holdridge, whereby climate, latitude, and altitude are used to define 116 distinct natural environmental zones, each with a particular type of vegetation
hombre – man

ICE – Instituto Costarricense de Electricidad (Costa Rican phone and electricity company)
ICT – Instituto Costarricense de Turismo (Costa Rican tourism institute), which provides tourist information
iglesia – church
IGN – Instituto Geográfico Nacional (National Geographic Institute), which publishes topographic maps of Costa Rica
incendio – fire
indígena – indigenous
Interamericana – Pan-American Highway
invierno – winter; the rainy season in Costa Rica
isla – island
izquierda – left

jardín – garden
josefino – resident of San José

kilometraje – distance in kilometers; mileage
lancha – boat (usually small); see also *chinga* and *panga*
lapa – parrot
lavabó – hand sink
lavandería – laundry facility, usually offering dry-cleaning services
lentes – eyeglasses
liciado – hurt
llanuras – tropical plains

machismo – an exaggerated sense of masculine pride
macho – a virile figure, typically a man
maje – slang that means 'dude,' used among men
malecón – pier; sea wall; waterfront promenade
manglar – mangrove
marías – local name for taxi meters
marimba – word xylophone
menso – dumb
mercado – market
mesa – table
meseta central – central plateau; Central Valley
mestizo – person of mixed descent, usually Spanish and Indian
migración – immigration
Minae – Ministerio de Ambiente y Energía (Ministry of Environment and Energy), which is in charge of the national-park system
minisuper – small convenience store
mirador – lookout point
mochilero – backpacker (though the English word is being used more and more)
mono – monkey
mono cara blanca – capuchin monkey
mono colorado – spider monkey
mono congo – howler monkey
mono tití – squirrel monkey
motocicleta (moto) – motorcycle
muelle – dock
mujer – woman
murciélago – bat
museo – museum

niñera – nanny or babysitter
niño – child
normal – long-distance bus with many stops

Oficina de Migración – Immigration Office
ojalá – hopefully; literally, 'if God wills it'
OTS – Organization for Tropical Studies

página web – website
pájaro – bird; a birding walk is referred to as *caminata pajarera;* see also *ave*
palacio municipal – city hall
palma africana – African palm
paloma – pigeon, dove
pañales – diapers, nappies

panga – light boat; see also *chinga* and *lancha*
paños – towel or rag
pántano – swamp or wetland
papel higiénico – toilet paper
parada – bus stop
páramo – habitat characterized by highland shrub and tussock grass, common to the Andes of Colombia, Ecuador and Peru, as well as parts of Costa Rica
parche curita – band-aid
parque – park
parque central – central town square or plaza
parque nacional – national park
peón – someone who does heavy unskilled labor
perezoso – sloth
perico – mealy parrot
periódico – newspaper
piso – floor (as in 2nd floor)
pista de aterrizaje – landing strip, tarmac
pista de baile – dance floor
plato – plate
playa – beach
PLN – Partido de Liberación Nacional (National Liberation Party)
posada – guesthouse
propina – tip for service
prostituta – prostitute (also shortened to the more vulgar *puta*)
puerto – port
pulpería – corner grocery store
puro – cigar (as in *un puro)*
PUSC – Partido Unidad Social Cristiana (Social Christian Unity Party)

rana – frog or toad
refresco – soda or bottled refreshment
refugio nacional de vida silvestre – national wildlife refuge
repelente – bug repellent
río – river
roja – used to refer to the 1000 colón note, which is red (*dos rojas* is 2000 colones)

sabanero – cowboy from Guanacaste
sacerdote – priest
saco de dormir – sleeping bag
salado – frequently meant as 'tough luck;' literally 'salty'
sencilla – single room
sencillo – simple; monetary change (small bills or coinage)
sendero – trail; path
serpiente – snake; see also *culebra*
servicio – toilet; see also *baño*
servicio a domicilio – home delivery
servilleta – napkin
soda – lunch counter; inexpensive eatery
sucio – dirty
supermercado – supermarket

taller mecánico – mechanic's shop
taza – cup
tenedor – fork
tepezcuinte – jungle rodent that is a relative of the guinea pig, often eaten by locals
Tico – Costa Rican (inhabitant of Costa Rica)
tienda – store
tienda de campaña – camping tent
típica/o – typical; particularly used to describe food (*comida típica* means 'typical cooking')
toallas higienicas – sanitary napkins
tortuga – turtle
trago – cocktail
tuanis – cool, excellent
tucán – toucan

Unesco – United Nations Educational, Scientific, and Cultural Organization
upe – expression used in the countryside when arriving at a home, which lets everyone know you're there
USGS – US Geological Survey

vaso – glass
vecino – neighbor
venenoso – poisonous
verano – summer; the dry season in Costa Rica
viajero – traveler
vino – wine
vivero – plant nursery

zancudo – mosquito
zapato – shoe
zonas – zone
zoológico – zoo

Behind the Scenes

THIS BOOK

This 6th edition of *Costa Rica* was written by Carolina A Miranda, who also coordinated the book, and Paige R Penland, with assistance from David Lukas who wrote the Environment chapter and Wildlife Guide, Bridget Crocker who wrote the Water Sports boxed text and Dr David Goldberg who prepared the Health chapter. The previous five editions were penned by Rob Rachowiecki.

THANKS from the Authors

Carolina A Miranda *Pura vida* to my peeps in Costa Rica: Andrés and Adrián of Hostel Pangea in Chepe; Lance and Chris at Rainbow Adventures in the Golfo Dulce; Rick and Lori (and Morgan!) at Sol y Mar in Zancudo; fellow traveler Misha Shulman (I owe you); 'Jungle' Jerry and Walter at Río Nuevo Lodge; Herb, Marleny and Co at Drake Bay Wilderness Resort; the Lipworths at the Lookout in Playa Tortuga and Anja at Villas Macondo in Tamarindo. A shout out to LP (in SF and Oz) and to EB and Big Chile in NYC for unobstructed printer abuse, as well as Joey B for chapter proofing. *Muchas gracias* to Los Mirandas in the OC and to Ed Tahaney, my husband/editor/therapist, who kept me going on long days (and nights) during this project.

Paige R Penland First, hats off to Rob Rachowiecki, author of the first five editions! Thanks also to David Zingarelli, for yet another gig of a lifetime, and both Carolina Miranda and Alex Hershey for their patience and guidance, as well as the diligent production team who mashed the raw materials into this fine final product. Thanks to everyone who lent a hand along the way, especially Andres Poveda, for getting me off to a good start, Frederico Castro, for getting my computer out of customs, and Walter and Sonny, for your gracious hospitality. I couldn't have done this without my mom, Wanda Olson, or sister, Beth Penland, who authored a couple of potassium-rich boxed texts. And an extra special *gracias*, *danke*, thank you and *dziekuje barolzo* to the crew at Agua Buena: Richard, Milka, Julian, Joana, Cathi and especially Colin – I would have succumbed to zip-line fatigue early on without you.

CREDITS

This 6th edition of *Costa Rica* was commissioned and assessed by Alex Hershey in Lonely Planet's Oakland office. Coordinating production in the Melbourne office were Evan Jones (editorial), Herman So (cartography) and Katherine Marsh (layout). Overseeing production were Charles Rawlings-Way and Andrew Weatherill (who shared the project-manager duties), Jennifer Garrett and Melanie Dankel (who shared the managing editor's role), and Alison Lyall (managing cartographer).

Assisting Evan with the editing were Andrea Dobbin, Miriam Cannell, Jocelyn Harewood, Brigitte Barta, Carolyn Boicos, Craig Kilburn and Adam Bextream. Anthony Phelan assisted Herman with the cartography. Herman also prepared the color map. Katherine prepared the rest of the color pages and also laid out the book. The Language chapter was compiled by Quentin Frayne. The cover was designed by Sophie Rivoire and

THE LONELY PLANET STORY

The story begins with a classic travel adventure: Tony and Maureen Wheeler's 1972 journey across Europe and Asia to Australia. There was no useful information about the overland trail then, so Tony and Maureen published the first Lonely Planet guidebook to meet a growing need.

From a kitchen table, Lonely Planet has grown to become the largest independent travel publisher in the world, with offices in Melbourne (Australia), Oakland (USA), London (UK) and Paris (France).

Today Lonely Planet guidebooks cover the globe. There is an ever-growing list of books and information in a variety of media. Some things haven't changed. The main aim is still to make it possible for adventurous travelers to get out there – to explore and better understand the world.

At Lonely Planet we believe travelers can make a positive contribution to the countries they visit – if they respect their host communities and spend their money wisely.

Brendan Dempsey. Layout checks were done by Adriana Mammarella and Kate McDonald.

THANKS from Lonely Planet

Many thanks to the following travelers who used the last edition and wrote to us with helpful hints, useful advice and interesting anecdotes.

A Ida Aasterud, Avishai Abrahami, Paula Adam, Rich Adam, Justin Adame, Christa Adams, Chris Addy, Phyllis Adkinson, Petra Aepli, Margaret Ambrose, Paula Anderson, Barney Andrews, Sue & Scott Applin, FR Arnold, Sylvia Atsalis, Brooke Azie **B** Juan Carlos Badilla Rojas, Liz & Harry Baerlocher, Kate Bailey, Radim Bajgar, Rini Bakx, C Banares, Joy Banares, Itai Bar, Shifi Bar, Adrian Bardon, Doug Barnet, Julie Baron, Ingeborg Bassant, Ursina Baumann, Susan Baus, David Beach, Sylvie Bechard, Earl Bellamy, Davide & Romina Bennici, Jairo Bermudez, Paula Bermudez, Marna Berry, Jenny Berzai, Buzz Betny, Andy Bily, Clint & Carly Blackbourn, Carol Blackburn, Lisa Blaire, Victoria Blake, Lien Blanken, Pat Bliss, David Blum, Marcel Bokhorst, Matthieu Bonnard, Laetitia Bonnet, David Boren, Jen Bouchet, Tom Boyd, Elizabeth Branstetter, Karin Branzell, Lilian Bravo, Ainsley Bristowe, Gage Brogan, Eric Brouwer, Ryan & Mandi Brown, Corina Browne, Tom Bruininkx, Dani Brunner, Andrea Bryson, David Buck, Maggie Buck, Peter Burghouts, Scott Burner, Colleen Byers **C** Hernan Cornejo Caballero, Arlene Calandria, Alana Callagy, Justin Callison, Emel Cambel, Tamara Cameron, Olegario Cantos, Doug Capelin, Silvia Carballo, Jenny Carson, Lee Carter, Franco Caruso, Israel Castanedo Oporta, Omar Castro, Ashlee Caswell, Kate Chang, Chris Chapman, Jill Chatanow, Derek Cheesebrough, Rob Chisholm, David Clayton, Matthew Clements, Ben Cohen, Shirley Cohn, Joy Coker, Konrad Collao, Christine Cooper, Leonardo Cordero, Paola Cordero Salazar, Barb Crane, Nicolas Cremers, Mathieu Crevier, Karina Csolty **D** Hila Dagan, Zoe Dagan, Robarn Danzman, Chandra Davda, Stuart Davis, Hannah Dawson, Luc De Clerck, Albert de Haas, Paula de Man, Maribel de Maya, Wouter de Ridder, Pierre de Somer, Katherine Degenaar, Louis Dell, Sevda Demirci, Axelle d'Epenoux, Keith Derman, Elaine Desorcy, Eve Diamond, Chris Diaz, Julie DiBiase, John Dillard, Gina DiMaggio, Sylvia Disco, Emma Ditrinco, Katharina Dlhos, Scott Dobson, Eva Domínguez, Seema Dosaj, Ian & Lita Drever, Jane Drewry, Jean Duggleby, Kate Dunnells, Laura Dzubin **E** Todd Edgar, Nils Elvemo, Margaret Epler, Renate Erlacher, Scott Espie, Malcolm Etherington, Caroline Evans, Katie Eyer **F** Nichole Fane, Tim Ferguson, Francesca Ferrari, Heather Finlay, Nick Fisher, William Fisher, Steve Fisk, Dan Fitzgerald, Jan Fitzgerald, Rick Fleischman, Robert Forbes, Gabi Ford, Jed Fowler, Zachary Fox, Shannon Freix, Carol Froese, Laura Fuller, Liz Fuller **G** Regan Gage, Clara Gallego, Angie Gammage, Tawnya Ganfield, Sandra Garin, Susan Garvey, Guro Gasmann Rogstad, Markus Gasplmayr, Diane Gedye, Elaina Gentilini, Isabelle George, Vanessa Gérard-Lemieux, Rainer Germann, Jolanda van Gerwen, Larry Gillispie, Lee Gimpel, Tim Gittins, Pete Goldie, Angela Gonzalez, Maria Gonzalez-Beato, Wessel Gossink, Judith Gottesman, Celine Goyette, Lisa Graham, Scott Graham, Oliver Grandin, Ross Greek, Tamara Griffioen, Dawn Grillo, Jasper Groos, Stephen Gross, Amit Gruber, Collard Gruene, Linda Gubler, Jan Gudell, Arantxa Guereña, Sabine Günther, Svent Gustav, Pamela Gutierrez, Karin Gygax, Roger Gygli **H** Marita Hagen, Bernard Hager, Adam Hall, Jim Hamilton, Marisa Haralson, Yair Harel, Sandy Hart, Toryalai Hart, Arno Harteveld, Kati Hays, Paul Head, Karin Heemskerk, Michael Heffernan, David Hellmer, Laurie Henry, Melissa Herbert, Iván Hervoso Candia, Erik Hink, Skye Hitt, Camilla Hjorne, Laura Hodge, Jessica Hodgkins, Kristel Hoebers, Axel Hofer, Allison Hoffman, Terese Holm, Chris Holmes, Bryan Huang, Jamie Hubble, Ton-Tijn Hulleman, Rommie Huntington, Marissa Hutter, John & Ae Hyland **I** Sarah Ice, Natalie Ihr, Elaine Illoso, Margret van Irsel, Bovey Isabelle, Janice Israel **J** Jeremy Jaeger, Abby James, Marianne Jaschke, Jan Jasiewicz, Susie Jefferis, Angelica Jekel, Jeffrey G Jensen, Christopher Johnson, Laura Johnson, Jordan Jones, Lyndsey Jordan, Harriet Joslin, Frank J Joyce **K** Nadine Kaschak, Shlomit Yust Katz, Yariv Kav, Lorraine Kaye, Dorien Kelly, Justin Kelly, Karen Kelly, Amanda Kennedy, Kyle Kepner, Deb Klipper, Kirjten Kluivers, Frank Knab, Shelley Knakoske, Michael Knox, Florence Koenderink, Olivier Koenig, Mart Kok, Sanne Kok, Sandra Kolodziej, Roberto Kopper, Phillip Koza, Paul Krause, Vladimir Krull **L** Tom & Beverly Lachenman, David Lacy, David Laderman, Lorri Lamb, Ad Landheer, Jacqueline Lans, Keri LaRocque, David Lawrence, Mike Lawson, Michele Lebascle, Cis Lebour, Carole Lee, Gloria Lee, Hans Leenen, Vanessa & Lucas Leonardi, Chris Leurs, JJ Levesque, Curt Lewis, Mervyn Lewis, Ruth & Neil Libby, Christian Liechti, Lauren Liesman, Jolande Lindenberg, Devora M Liss, Stu Lloyd, Terrie Lootens, Katherine Love, Laird Lucas, Stuart Lustig **M** Sherry MacDonald, Penny MacInnes, John Mackenzie,

SEND US YOUR FEEDBACK

We love to hear from travelers – your comments keep us on our toes and help make our books better. Our well-traveled team reads every word on what you loved or loathed about this book. Although we cannot reply individually to postal submissions, we always guarantee that your feedback goes straight to the appropriate authors, in time for the next edition. Each person who sends us information is thanked in the next edition – and the most useful submissions are rewarded with a free book.

To send us your updates – and find out about LP events, newsletters and travel news – visit our award-winning website: **www.lonelyplanet.com**.

Note: We may edit, reproduce and incorporate your comments in Lonely Planet products such as guidebooks, websites and digital products, so let us know if you don't want your comments reproduced or your name acknowledged. For a copy of our privacy policy visit www.lonelyplanet.com/privacy.

Brenda Madunic, François Malaise, David Maldin, Charles Maliszewski, Laura Manganotti, Ashley Mangham, Pat Manion, Paul Mantia, George Margellos, Barbara Marrero, Jost Maurin, Alain Mauris, Esteban Mazzoncini, Kristine McCaffrey, Ralph B McCuen, Peta McDougall, Sandra McGirr, Steve Mckay, Hanita Mekuz, Martin Mels, Miriam Merino, Michael Mesiano, Ingrid Metselaar, Colleen Meyer, Kristen Meyer, Sarah Meyer, John Michelotti, Jonny Millar, Jacob Miller, Michell Miscisin, Anna Mitchell, Carolyn Mo, Diego Molina, Nate Monnig, Roberto Montero Z, Tom Moore, Alison Moran, Melinda Moreaux, Sonja Morf, N Morris, Craig Morrison, Michele Morrissey, Anne Moses, Steve Mosseau, Isabelle Mouret, Andrew Mulder, Bryan M Muntzer, Shannon Murphy, Erika Murray, Kate Murray, Anita Mutis Arcila **N** Margreet Nagel, Gregg Nakano, Maite Navarrete, Sharon Nelmes, Menkin Nelson, Isabel Neto, Merete Nielsen, Shanti Nijhowne, Tracy Nishida, Sharon Noach, William Nuñez **O** Maya Offemberg, Rowan Ogden, Jessica Olesh, Meghan OMalley, Krysti Orella, Pablo Ortiz, Karina Osgood, Eline Otto, David Oudermans **P** Paul Pagani, Luis Carlos Palazuelos, Mary Palisoul, Jessie Passa, Dylan Passmore, Liz Paton, Scott Pearson, Frank Pellegrom, Mindi Pelletier, Lissette Penny, Sabina Pensek, Amanda Perez, Georgio Perversi, Peter Petras, Sonja Pfefferkorn, John Phippen, Cuong Pho, Armand Piette, Arani Pillai, Keri Pink, Simone Pizzi, Don L Platt, Nitzan Pollak, Krystina Poludnikiewicz, Tina Poppy, Gladys Portela, Scott Porter, Jocelyn Potter, Aaron Powell, A Praet-Havshush, Michel Prevo, Christoph Prinz, Paul Proulx, Ellen Psychas, Sara Pugach, Lander Purvis, Trey Pyfer **Q** Brian Quinn, Cate Quinn **R** Michael Radtke, Heather Rafferty, Jurgen Rahmer, Gregg Ramshaw, Marisa Raphael, Mauricio Rascon, Rebecca Raworth, Ine Reijnen, Markus Reischl, Richard Remsberg, Rick Reno, Meloney Retallack, Cory Reynolds, Harmony Reynolds, Jamie Rezmovits, Lisa Reznik, Angela Ribbon, Steve Richardson, Steve Rickard, Chris Ridley, Steve Rock, Hilda & Erika Rodgveller, Betty Rodriguez, Dennis Rogers, Luis Roges, Janie Rommel-Eichorn, Ylona Rood, Joelle Roos, Jocelyn Roper, Eva-Johanna Rosa, Jennifer Rose, Jeffrey Rosebaum, Alessandro Rossi, Yuval Roth, Dan Ruff, Claudia Russell, Cathy Russo, Rob Rustenburg **S** Aaron Sagers, Malin Sahlen, Lucy Sanderson, Annette van Sant, Rupesh Santoshi, Theresia Sauter-Bailliet, Peter A Sawtell, Laura Sawyer, Peter Schaefer, Paul Schippers, Allan Schlittler, Georgia Schneider, Alexandra Schoolmeesters, Rob Schroeder, Thijs Schwartz, Rick Schwolsky, Jared Scott, Molly Seaverns, Alice Segal, Anastasia Selby, Claudia Senecal, Scott Serfas, Wendy Serrano-Matte, Audra Sexton, Gavin Sexton, Mansi Shah, Larry Shamash, Erek Sherwood, Zac & Wendy Shinar, Stanley Sie, Veronika Siebenkotten, Tomas Simons, Rebecca Singer, Karen Skibo, Colin Smith, Giles Smith, Lance Smith, Nuyens Sofie, Holger Sørensen, Colin Sorenson, Bernardo Sottomayor, Emily Spencer, Toby Sprunk, Jakke St Clair, Maaike Staal, Jennifer Steinberg, Gabriel Steinhardt, Ed Steinschneider, Anouhk Sterken, Richard Stewart, Brook Stone, Anne Marit Storodegard, Heather Story, Ian C Story, Wolfram Strempfer, Ron Strikker, Jeff Stuart, Carey Suckow, Judith Sullivan, Gerwin Sweep, Michael Swisher, Chris Sylvia **T** Leah Tai, Neta Talmor, Marcela Tamayo, Texas Tea, Alexander Teal, Marcel & Mara ten Cate, Ellen ter Braak, Marc Tétreau, Lucy Thackery, Janice Theriault, Anahid Thomas, Michael Thomas, Heather Thoreau, Peter Thornley, Craig Tompkins, Frank Tool, Sarah Topp, Lindsay Tossberg, Christopher Trench, Gerhild Trübswasser, Lukas Tschupp **U** Gabriel Umana **V** Ricardo Valdes, Roderick van de Weg, Mike van de Wouw, FJ van der Ploeg, Tanja van Dijk, Ludo van Hijfte, Ayca van Ingen Schenau, Wouter van Lonkhuyzen, Elise van Vliet, Rose Van Winkle, Viola van Wonderen, Liselotte van Wunnik, Gualtiero Vietti, Peter Villain, Manuel Villanueva, Céline Villeneuve, Rolf Von Behrens **W** Roberto WaChong, Claudia Waibel, Victoria Waimey, Rob Walker, Emma Louise Walmsley, Katrin Wanner, Peter Ward, Maika Watanabe, Eleanor Watkin Jones, Matthew Watson, Sandra Waumans, Keith Webb, Jenny Webster, Sybille Wegler, Janet & Mike Weidinger, Vanessa Weigall, Robin Weiss, Kimberly Welch, Jonas Wernli, Greg Wesson, Jeanne Wheeler, Isabel White, Juday White, Sherri Wierzba, Rolf Wietlisbach, Denise Wilder, Justin Wilkinson, Ron Wille, James J Williams, Merlin Williams, Karin Wipraechtiger, Alec Wohlgroth, Susanne Wolf, Wayne Woo, John Wood, Joanna Woolf, Bernie Wright, Charlotte Wright, Marie Wright, Margery Wurster, Irene Wyndham **Y** Jim Yaeger, Udi Yanku, Stephanie Young, John Yu **Z** Lynn Zamora, Melissa Zanetich, Sara Zdeb, Jacek Zielinski, Jacques Zimmerman, Titia Zuidersma

ACKNOWLEDGMENTS

Many thanks to the following for the use of their content:

Globe on back cover © Mountain High Maps 1993 Digital Wisdom, Inc.

Beth Penland and Ileana Castro.

Index

ABBREVIATIONS

PN	Parque Nacional
RB	Reserva Biológica
RN	Refugio Nacional

INDEX

C

000 Map pages
000 Location of colour photographs

D

INDEX

000 Map pages
000 Location of colour photographs

000 Map pages
000 Location of colour photographs

INDEX

V

W

Y

Z

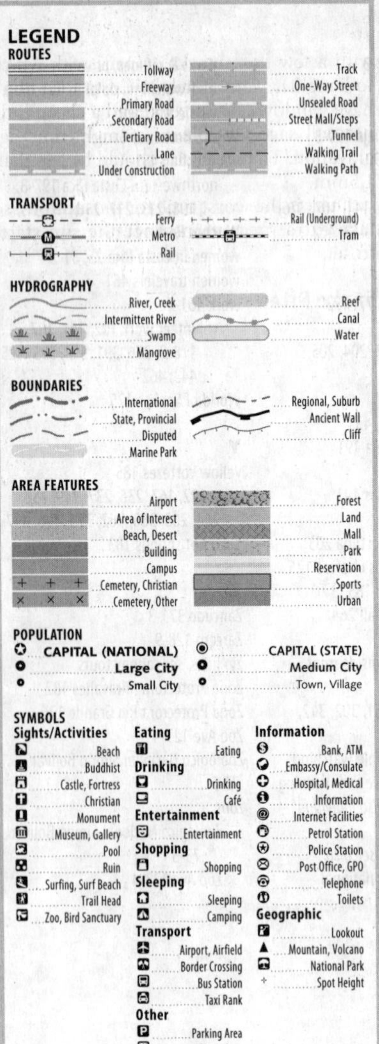

LONELY PLANET OFFICES

Australia
Head Office
Locked Bag 1, Footscray, Victoria 3011
☎ 03-8379 8000, fax 03-8379 8111
talk2us@lonelyplanet.com.au

USA
150 Linden St, Oakland, CA 94607
☎ 510-893 8555, toll free 800 275 8555
fax 510-893 8572, info@lonelyplanet.com

UK
72–82 Rosebery Ave,
Clerkenwell, London EC1R 4RW
☎ 020-7841 9000, fax 020-7841 9001
go@lonelyplanet.co.uk

France
1 rue du Dahomey, 75011 Paris
☎ 01 55 25 33 00, fax 01 55 25 33 01
bip@lonelyplanet.fr, www.lonelyplanet.fr

Published by Lonely Planet Publications Pty Ltd
ABN 36 005 607 983

Cover photographs by Lonely Planet Images: A Heliconiid Butterfly *(Philaethria dido)* at Parque Nacional Corcovado, Costa Rica, Tom Boyden (front); A farmer and his ox and cart toil the fields in Playa Camaronal, Soncin Gerometta (back). Many of the images in this guide are available for licensing from Lonely Planet Images: www.lonelyplanetimages.com.

Printed through Colorcraft Ltd, Hong Kong
Printed in China